Your Companion Site —
Even more help for studying!

bedfordstmartins.com/mckaywest

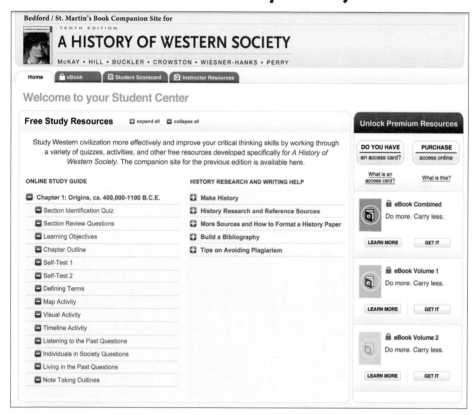

FREE Online Study Guide — Improve your performance!
Get immediate feedback on your progress with

- Quizzing
- Key terms review
- Map and visual activities
- Timeline activities
- Note-taking outlines

FREE History Research and Writing Help
Refine your research skills, evaluate sources, and organize your findings with

- *Make History* maps, documents, images, and Web sites
- History Research and Reference Sources
- More Sources and How to Format a History Paper
- Build a Bibliography
- Tips on Avoiding Plagiarism

A History of Western Society

■ Vasili Andreevich Tropinin, *The Lacemaker*, 1823.

A History of Western Society

SINCE 1300 FOR ADVANCED PLACEMENT*

Tenth Edition

John P. McKay
University of Illinois at Urbana-Champaign

Bennett D. Hill
Late of Georgetown University

John Buckler
University of Illinois at Urbana-Champaign

Clare Haru Crowston
University of Illinois at Urbana-Champaign

Merry E. Wiesner-Hanks
University of Wisconsin–Milwaukee

Joe Perry
Georgia State University

BEDFORD/ST. MARTIN'S

Boston • New York

FOR BEDFORD/ST. MARTIN'S

Publisher for History: Mary Dougherty
Director of Development for History: Jane Knetzger
Executive Editor for History: Traci Mueller Crowell
Senior Developmental Editor for History: Laura Arcari
Senior Production Editor: Christina Horn
Senior Production Supervisor: Nancy Myers
Executive Marketing Manager: Jenna Bookin Barry
Associate Editor: Lynn Sternberger
Production Assistant: Alexis Biasell
Senior Art Director: Anna Palchik
Text Design: Brian Salisbury
Copyeditor: Sybil Sosin
Map Editor: Charlotte Miller
Indexer: Leoni Z. McVey
Page Layout: Boynton Hue Studio
Photo Research: Carole Frohlich and Elisa Gallagher, The Visual
    Connection Image Research, Inc.

Cover Design: Billy Boardman
Cover Art: Vasili Andreevich Tropinin (Russian, 1776–1857), *The
    Lacemaker*, 1823. Oil on canvas. Photo: Tretyakov Gallery, Moscow,
    Russia, Bridgeman Art Library.
Cartography: Mapping Specialists, Ltd.
Composition: NK Graphics
Printing and Binding: RR Donnelley and Sons

President: Joan E. Feinberg
Editorial Director: Denise B. Wydra
Director of Marketing: Karen R. Soeltz
Director of Editing, Design, and Production: Susan W. Brown
Assistant Director of Editing, Design, and Production: Elise S. Kaiser
Managing Editor: Elizabeth M. Schaaf

Library of Congress Control Number: 2010920486

Copyright © 2011, 2008, 2006, 2003 by Bedford/St. Martin's

Manufactured in the United States of America.

5 6   14 13

For information, write: Bedford/St. Martin's, 75 Arlington Street, Boston, MA 02116 (617-399-4000)

ISBN-10: 0-312-68773-7   ISBN-13: 978-0-312-68773-1 (combined edition)
ISBN-10: 0-312-64059-5   ISBN-13: 978-0-312-64059-0 (Vol. 1)
ISBN-10: 0-312-64060-9   ISBN-13: 978-0-312-64060-6 (Vol. 2)
ISBN-10: 0-312-64061-7   ISBN-13: 978-0-312-64061-3 (Vol. A)
ISBN-10: 0-312-64062-5   ISBN-13: 978-0-312-64062-0 (Vol. B)
ISBN-10: 0-312-64063-3   ISBN-13: 978-0-312-64063-7 (Vol. C)
ISBN-10: 0-312-63827-2   ISBN-13: 978-0-312-63827-6 (Since 1300)
ISBN-10: 0-312-64058-7   ISBN-13: 978-0-312-64058-3 (Since 1300 for Advanced Placement)

*AP and the Advanced Placement Program are registered trademarks of the College Board, which was not involved in
the production of, and does not endorse, this product.

▪ Brief Contents

▪ Contents

12 The Crisis of the Later Middle Ages

1300–1450   338

15 European Exploration and Conquest
1450–1650   442

16 Absolutism and Constitutionalism
ca. 1589–1725   478

17 Toward a New Worldview
1540–1789   518

18 The Expansion of Europe
1650–1800   552

19 The Changing Life of the People
1700–1800 584

20 The Revolution in Politics
1775–1815 618

21 The Revolution in Energy and Industry
ca. 1780–1850   654

22 Ideologies and Upheavals
1815–1850   684

23 Life in the Emerging Urban Society
1840–1900   716

24 The Age of Nationalism
1850–1914   748

27 The Age of Anxiety
ca. 1900–1940   852

28 Dictatorships and the Second World War
1919–1945   886

29 Cold War Conflict and Consensus
1945–1965   922

30 Challenging the Postwar Order
1960–1991   958

31 Europe in an Age of Globalization
1990 to the Present   994

Maps, Figures, and Tables

Maps

Figures and Tables

▪ Special Features

Living in the Past

Listening to the Past

Individuals in Society

▪ Preface

With this, the tenth edition of *A History of Western Society*, we invite our colleagues and current and past adopters to join us in seeing the book as if for the first time. For us, this edition—undertaken at a new publishing house—has been an opportunity to revisit our original vision and to thereby realize the most thorough reconsideration of our text since we first began. *A History of Western Society* grew out of the initial three authors' desire to infuse new life into the study of Western Civilization. We knew that historians were using imaginative questions and innovative research to open up vast new areas of historical interest and knowledge. At that point, social history was dramatically changing the ways we understood the past, and we decided to create a book that would re-create the lives of ordinary people in appealing human terms, while also giving major economic, political, cultural, and intellectual developments the attention they unquestionably deserve. The three new authors who have joined the original author team—and who first used the book as students or teachers—remain committed to advancing this vision for today's classroom. With its new look, line-by-line edits aimed at increasing the book's readability and accessibility, reinvigorated scholarship, and broader definition of social history that reflects where instructors and students are now, we've rethought every element of the book to bring the original vision into the twenty-first century and make the past memorable for a new generation of students and instructors.

History as a discipline never stands still, and over the last several decades cultural history has joined social history as a source of dynamism. Because of its emphasis on the ways people made sense of their lives, *A History of Western Society* has always included a large amount of cultural history, ranging from foundational works of philosophy and literature to popular songs and stories. The focus on cultural history has been heightened in this tenth edition in a way that highlights the interplay between men's and women's lived experiences and the ways men and women reflect on these experiences to create meaning. The joint social and cultural perspective requires—fortunately, in our opinion—the inclusion of objects as well as texts as important sources for studying history, which has allowed us to incorporate the growing emphasis on material culture in the work of many historians.

These new directions have not changed the central mission of the book, which is to introduce students to the broad sweep of Western Civilization in a fresh yet balanced manner. Every edition has incorporated new research to keep the book up-to-date and respond to the changing needs of readers and instructors, and we have continued to do this in the tenth edition. As we have made these changes, large and small,

we have sought to give students and teachers an integrated perspective so that they could pursue—on their own or in the classroom—the historical questions that they find particularly exciting and significant.

Textual Changes

For the tenth edition we took the time to revisit, reconsider, and revise every paragraph of the book. We paid painstaking attention to the writing, and we're proud of the results. Informed by recent scholarship, every chapter was revised with an aim toward readability and accessibility. Several main lines of revision have guided our many changes. In particular, as noted above, we have broadened the book's focus on social history to include a greater emphasis on cultural history. This increased emphasis is supported in every chapter by the use of artifacts that make history tangible and by the new Living in the Past visual feature, described below, that demonstrates the intersection between society and culture. In addition, the social and cultural context of Western Civilization has been integrated throughout the narrative, including expanded and new sections on artistic patronage during the Renaissance, identities and communities of the Atlantic world, eighteenth-century education, nineteenth-century family life, consumer society between the two world wars, life under Nazi occupation, and state and society in the East Bloc, among others.

The tenth edition continues to reflect Europe's interactions with the rest of the world and the role of gender in shaping human experience. The global context of European history is reflected in new scholarship on the steppe peoples of Central Asia, Muslim views of the Crusades, the Atlantic world, decolonization, and globalization. New scholarship on gender is woven throughout the book and is included in sections on Frankish queens, medieval prostitution, female humanists, politics and gender during the French Revolution, and gender roles during industrialization.

These major aspects of revision are accompanied by the incorporation of a wealth of new scholarship and subject areas. Additions, among others, include material on the bubonic plague in eastern Europe (Chapter 12); the Jesuits (Chapter 14); the limits of enlightened absolutism (Chapter 17); eighteenth-century beliefs and practices (Chapter 19); expanded coverage of the peasant revolt (Chapter 20); sections on the Battle of the Somme, waging total war, and the human costs of World War I (Chapter 26); popular support for National Socialism (Chapter 27); the affluent society (Chapter 30); and up-to-date coverage of the economic downturn in Europe, the Iraq War, and the global recession (Chapter 31).

Organizational Changes

To meet the demands of the evolving course, we took a close and critical look at the book's organization, and have made several major changes in the organization of chapters to reflect the way the course is taught today. To increase clarity, we've combined the separate chapters on absolutism in western and eastern Europe into a single chapter on absolutism and constitutionalism. The text also features a completely revised and updated post-1945 section featuring a third, new, postwar chapter, "Europe in an Age of Globalization, 1990 to the Present." In response to the growth in new and exciting scholarship for this period, the postwar chapters have been completely rewritten by new author Joe Perry with new scholarship on decolonization, consumerism as an aspect of the Cold War, new patterns of immigration and guest worker programs, the growth and decline of the welfare state in eastern and western Europe, and Europe's place in an era of increasing globalization, including the challenges to liberalism mounted by new social movements.

Features

Document-Based Questions (DBQs) tied to each chapter appear in a special section at the back of the book, giving students experience in critically reading and interpreting primary sources. The DBQs are in the same format as those found on the AP exam. This edition features five new DBQs, so that each chapter in the book now includes a DBQ that relates to it. New topics include long-distance trade in medieval Europe, the romantic movement, science and philosophy in the nineteenth century, the growth of nationalism, and western Europeans' relations with Muslims and the Islamic world.

We are proud of the diverse special features that expand upon the narrative and offer opportunities for classroom discussion and assignments, and in the new edition we have expanded our offerings to include a brand new feature created in response to current research trends that is sure to get students and instructors talking. This **NEW** visual feature, **Living in the Past**, uses social and cultural history to show how life in the past was both similar to and different from our lives today. Focusing on relatively narrow aspects of social and cultural history to write compelling stories that would encourage students to think about the way the past informs the present was both a challenge and a pleasure. The resulting thirty-one essays—one in each chapter—introduce students to the study of material culture, encourage critical analysis, and engage and inform with fascinating details about life in the past. Richly illustrated with images and artifacts, each feature includes a short essay and questions for analysis.

We use these features to explore the deeper ramifications of things students might otherwise take for granted, such as consumer goods, factories, and even currency. Students connect to the people of the past through a diverse range of topics such as "Foods of the Columbian Exchange," "Coffeehouse Culture," "The Immigrant Experience," "A Model Socialist Steel Town," and "The Supermarket Revolution."

In our years of teaching Western Civilization, we have often noted that students come alive when they encounter stories about real people in the past. To give students a chance to see the past through ordinary people's lives, each chapter includes one of the popular **Individuals in Society** biographical essays that offer brief studies of individuals or groups, informing students about the societies in which they lived. This feature grew out of our long-standing focus on people's lives and the varieties of historical experience, and we believe that readers will empathize with these human beings as they themselves seek to define their own identities. The spotlighting of individuals, both famous and obscure, perpetuates the book's continued attention to cultural and intellectual developments, highlights human agency, and reflects changing interests within the historical profession as well as the development of "micro-history." **NEW** features include essays on Meister Eckhart; Rose Bertin, "Minister of Fashion"; Josiah Wedgwood; Germaine de Staël; and Armando Rodrigues, West Germany's "One-Millionth Guest Worker."

Each chapter also continues to include a primary source feature titled **Listening to the Past**, chosen to extend and illuminate a major historical issue through the presentation of a single original source or several voices. Each opens with an introduction and closes with questions for analysis that invite students to evaluate the evidence as historians would. Selected for their interest and importance and carefully fitted into their historical context, these sources allow students to hear the past and to observe how history has been shaped by individuals. **NEW** topics include "Perspectives on Humanist Learning and Women," "Denis Diderot's 'Supplement to Bougainville's Voyage,'" "Contrasting Views on the Effects of Rural Industry," "Abbé de Sieyès, 'What Is the Third Estate?,'" "Von Herder and Mazzini on the Development of Nationalism," "Lin Zexu and Yamagata Aritomo, Confronting Western Imperialism," and "The Nixon-Khrushchev 'Kitchen Debate.'" In addition to using documents as part of our special feature program, we have quoted extensively from a wide variety of primary sources in the narrative, demonstrating that such quotations are the "stuff" of history. We believe that our extensive program of using primary sources as an integral part of the narrative as well as in extended form in the "Listening to the Past" chapter feature will help readers learn to interpret and think critically.

With the goal of making this the most student-centered edition yet, we paid renewed attention to the book's pedagogy. To help guide students, each chapter opens with a **chapter preview with focus questions** keyed to the main chapter headings. These questions are repeated within the chapter and again in **NEW chapter reviews**. Many of the questions have been reframed for this edition, and new summary answers have been added to the chapter review. Each chapter review concludes with a carefully selected list of annotated suggestions for further reading, revised and updated to keep them current with the vast amount of new work being done in many fields.

To help students understand the material and prepare for exams, each chapter includes NEW Looking Back, Looking Ahead conclusions. Replacing the former chapter summaries, each conclusion provides an insightful synthesis of the chapter's main developments, while connecting to events that students will encounter in the chapters to come. In this way students are introduced to history as an ongoing process of interrelated events.

To promote clarity and comprehension, boldface key terms in the text are defined in the margins and listed in the chapter review. NEW phonetic spellings are located directly after terms that readers are likely to find hard to pronounce. The chapter chronologies, which review major developments discussed in each chapter, have been improved to more closely mirror the key events of the chapter, and the number of topic-specific thematic chronologies has been expanded, with a new chronology on "Major Figures of the Enlightenment," among others. Once again we also provide a unified timeline at the end of the text. Comprehensive and easy to locate, this useful timeline allows students to compare developments over the centuries.

The high-quality art and map program has been thoroughly revised and expanded. The new edition features more than 400 contemporaneous illustrations. To make the past tangible, and as an extension of our enhanced attention to cultural history, we include over 75 artifacts—from swords and fans to playing cards and record players. As in earlier editions, all illustrations have been carefully selected to complement the text, and all include captions that inform students while encouraging them to read the text more deeply. Completely redesigned and reconceptualized for the new edition, 52 full-size maps illustrate major developments in the narrative. In addition, 42 NEW spot maps are embedded in the narrative to show areas under discussion. NEW maps in the tenth edition highlight such topics as the Russian civil war, the Holocaust, Cold War Europe, pollution in Europe, and the Soviet war in Afghanistan, among others.

We recognize students' difficulties with geography and visual analysis, and the new edition includes the popular Mapping the Past map activities and NEW Picturing the Past visual activities. Included in each chapter, these activities give students valuable skills in reading and interpreting maps and images by asking them to analyze the maps or visuals and make connections to the larger processes discussed in the narrative. All these activities can be completed online and submitted directly to instructors at the free online study guide.

To showcase the book's rich art program and to signal our commitment to this thorough and deep revision, the book has been completely redesigned. The dynamic new contemporary design engages and assists students with its clear, easy-to-use pedagogy.

Acknowledgments

It is a pleasure to thank the many instructors who read and critiqued the manuscript through its development:

High School Instructors:

Shane Caldwell, Zionsville Community High School
Scott Carter, St. Pius X High School
Elisa Case, Lake High School
Robert Cavender, Chesapeake High School
Paul Diamond, Clarkstown High School
Clayton Duba, Adlai Stevenson High School
Paul Fitzgerald, Miramonte High School
Tom Funk, Satellite Beach High School
Alicia Hale, Ballard High School
Kent Holubar, Crystal Springs Upland School
Kimberly Hughes, Pembroke Pines Charter High School
Lynn Khadija, Lansing Eastern High School
Ronald Lee, Keith Country Day School
Robert McCraw, McKinney High School
Jeff Meyers, Pleasant Valley High School
Robert Peck, Douglas S. Freeman High School
Carol Pixton, Polytechnic School
Gloria Sesso, Patchogue-Medford Schools
Tammie Spencer, Fishers High School
S. Elizabeth ter Haseborg, Morgantown High School
Gary D. Tillery, Jackson County High School
Eric VandeBerg, Eastview High School

College Instructors:

Georgia Bonny Bazemore, Eastern Washington University
John Beeler, University of Alabama
Dudley R. Belcher, Tri-County Technical College
Stephen A. Beluris, Moorpark College
Nancy B. Bjorklund, Fullerton College
Paul Bookbinder, University of Massachusetts, Boston
Edward A. Boyden, Nassau Community College
Harry T. Burgess, St. Clair County Community College
Daniel Finn, Valencia Community College
Jennifer Foray, Purdue University
Gary Forsythe, Texas Tech University
Lucille M. Fortunato, Bridgewater State College
Robert Genter, Nassau Community College
Stephen Gibson, Allegany College of Maryland
Andrew L. Goldman, Gonzaga University
Anthony Heideman, Front Range Community College
Jennifer Hevelone-Harper, Gordon College
Allen E. Jones, Troy University
Jason M. Kelly, Indiana University
Keith Knutson, Viterbo University
Lynn Lubamersky, Boise State University
Susan A. Maurer, Nassau Community College
Greg Mauriocourt, Technical College of the Lowcountry

Jennifer McNabb, Western Illinois University

James M. Mini, Montgomery County Community College

Mary Lou Mosley, Paradise Valley Community College

Lisa Ossian, Des Moines Area Community College

Scott W. Palmer, Western Illinois University

Dennis Ricci, Community College of Rhode Island and Quinsigamond Community College

James Robertson, Montgomery County Community College

Daniel Robison, Troy University

Jahan Salehi, Guilford Tech Community College

Carol Longenecker Schmidt, Tri-County Technical College

Robert Shipley, Widener University

Karen Sonnelitter, Purdue University

Donathan Taylor, Hardin-Simmons University

Patricia Turning, Arizona State University

Norman R. West, SUNY at Suffolk

Shelley Wolbrink, Drury University

Robert Zajkowski, Hudson Valley Community College

Special thanks also go to Ane Lintvedt, AP History teacher at the McDonogh School, and David Gould, AP History teacher at Durham Academy, for their work writing and revising the DBQ appendix of the Advanced Placement edition of this text. We are thankful too for Louise Forsyth, AP History teacher at Poly Prep Country Day School, for preparing the new edition of *Strive for a 5: Preparing for the AP* European History Examination.*

It is also a pleasure to thank the many editors who have assisted us over the years, first at Houghton Mifflin and now at Bedford/St. Martin's. At Bedford/St. Martin's, these include senior development editor Laura Arcari, with assistance from Beth Welch, for developing the new "Living in the Past" features; freelance development editor Michelle McSweeney; associate editors Lynn Sternberger and Jack Cashman; executive editor Traci Mueller Crowell; director of development

Jane Knetzger; publisher for history Mary Dougherty; map editor Charlotte Miller; photo researcher Carole Frohlich; text permissions editor Sandy Schechter; and Christina Horn, senior production editor, with the assistance of Alexis Biasell and the guidance of managing editor Elizabeth Schaaf and assistant managing editor John Amburg. Other key contributors were designer Brian Salisbury, page makeup artist Cia Boynton, copyeditor Sybil Sosin, proofreaders Andrea Martin and Angela Hoover Morrison, indexer Leoni McVey, and cover designer Billy Boardman. We would also like to thank editorial director Denise Wydra and president Joan E. Feinberg.

Many of our colleagues at the University of Illinois, the University of Wisconsin–Milwaukee, and Georgia State University continue to provide information and stimulation, often without even knowing it. We thank them for it. We also thank the many students over the years with whom we have used earlier editions of this book. Their reactions and opinions helped shape the revisions to this edition, and we hope it remains worthy of the ultimate praise that they bestowed on it, that it's "not boring like most textbooks." Merry Wiesner-Hanks would, as always, also like to thank her husband Neil, without whom work on this project would not be possible. Clare Haru Crowston thanks her husband Ali and her children Lili, Reza, and Kian, who are a joyous reminder of the vitality of life that we try to showcase in this book. John McKay expresses his deep appreciation to JoAnn McKay for her keen insights and unfailing encouragement. Joe Perry thanks Andrzej S. Kaminski and the expert team assembled at Lazarski University for their insightful comments and is most grateful to Joyce de Vries for her unstinting support and encouragement.

Each of us has benefited from the criticism of our coauthors, although each of us assumes responsibility for what he or she has written. John Buckler has written the first six chapters; building on text originally written by Bennett Hill, Merry Wiesner-Hanks has assumed primary responsibility for Chapters 7 through 14; building on text originally written by Bennett Hill and John McKay, Clare Crowston has assumed primary responsibility for Chapters 15 through 20; John McKay has written and revised Chapters 21 through 25; and Joe Perry has written and revised Chapters 26 through 31, building on text originally written by John McKay.

---

*AP and the Advanced Placement Program are registered trademarks of the College Board, which was not involved in the production of, and does not endorse, this product.

▪ Versions and Supplements

A History of Western Society is supported by numerous resources—study tools for students, materials for teachers, and many options for packaging the book with documents readers, trade books, atlases, and other guides—that are free or available at a substantial discount. Descriptions follow; for more information, visit the book's catalog site at **bfwpub .com/highschool/mckaywest**, or contact your local Bedford, Freeman & Worth sales representative.

Available Versions of This Book

To accommodate different course lengths and course budgets, *A History of Western Society* is available in several different formats, including three-hole punched loose-leaf Budget Books versions and e-books, which are available at a substantial discount.

- Combined edition (Chapters 1–31): available in hardcover, loose-leaf, and e-book formats
- Volume 1, From Antiquity to the Enlightenment (Chapters 1–17): available in paperback, loose-leaf, and e-book formats
- Volume 2, From the Age of Exploration to the Present (Chapters 15–31): available in paperback, loose-leaf, and e-book formats
- Volume A, From Antiquity to 1500 (Chapters 1–13): available in paperback
- Volume B, From the Later Middle Ages to 1815 (Chapters 12–20): available in paperback
- Volume C, From the Revolutionary Era to the Present (Chapters 20–31): available in paperback
- Since 1300 (Chapters 12–31): available in paperback and e-book formats
- Since 1300 for Advanced Placement (Chapters 12–31): available in hardcover and e-book formats

Our innovative e-books give your students the content you want in a convenient format at about half the cost of a print book. **Bedford/St. Martin's e-Books** have been optimized for reading and studying online. **CourseSmart e-Books** can be purchased directly by students and downloaded or used online, whichever is more convenient.

Companion Site

Our new companion site at **bedfordstmartins.com/ mckaywest** gathers free and premium resources, giving students a way to extend *A History of Western Society* online. This book-specific site provides a single destination that students can use to practice, read, write, and study, and to find and access quizzes and activities, study aids, and history research and writing help.

FREE Online Study Guide. Available at the companion site, this popular resource provides students with self-review quizzes and activities for each chapter, including a multiple-choice self-test that focuses on important concepts; an identification quiz that helps students remember key people, places, and events; a flash-card activity that tests students' knowledge of key terms; and map activities to strengthen students' geography skills. Instructors can monitor students' progress through an online Quiz Gradebook or receive e-mail updates.

FREE History Research and Writing Help. Also available at the companion site, this resource includes **History Research and Reference Sources**, with links to history-related databases, indexes, and journals; **More Sources and How to Format a History Paper**, with clear advice on how to integrate primary and secondary sources into research papers and how to cite and format sources correctly; **Build a Bibliography**, a simple Web-based tool that generates bibliographies in four commonly used documentation styles; and **Tips on Avoiding Plagiarism**, an online tutorial that reviews the consequences of plagiarism and features exercises to help students practice integrating sources and recognize acceptable summaries.

Strive for a 5: Preparing for the AP* European History Examination. This guide provides students with narrative overviews of each historical period, thematically organized chapter reviews, and four complete AP-style practice exams. Special AP Tips present chapter material in the context of test-taking strategies.

Instructor Resources

Bedford/St. Martin's has developed a wide range of teaching resources for this book and for this course. They range from assessment tools and lecture and presentation materials to course management options.

Teacher's Resource Guide. The instructor's manual offers both experienced and first-time instructors tools for presenting textbook material in engaging ways. It includes chapter outlines, lesson plans, activities, and special consideration of AP topics.

Guide to Changing Editions. Designed to facilitate an instructor's transition from the previous edition of *A History of Western Society* to the current edition, this guide presents an overview of major changes as well as of changes in each chapter.

Computerized Test Bank. The test bank includes a mix of fresh, carefully crafted multiple-choice, definition, short-answer, and essay questions for each chapter. The questions appear in Microsoft Word format and in easy-to-use test bank software that allows instructors to easily add, edit, resequence, and print questions and answers. Instructors can also export questions into a variety of formats, including WebCT and Blackboard.

PowerPoint Maps, Images, Lecture Outlines, and i>clicker Content. These presentation materials are available on *The Bedford Lecture Kit* Instructor's Resource CD-ROM. They include ready-made and fully customizable PowerPoint multimedia presentations built around lecture outlines with embedded maps, figures, and selected images from the textbook and with detailed instructor notes on key points. Also available are maps and selected images in JPEG and PowerPoint formats; content for i>clicker, a classroom response system, in Microsoft Word and PowerPoint formats; and outline maps in PDF format for quizzing or handing out. All files are suitable for copying onto transparency acetates.

Overhead Map Transparencies. This set of full-color acetate transparencies includes 130 maps for the European history course.

Make History: Free Documents, Maps, Images, and Web Sites. Finding the source material you need is simple with Make History. Here the best Web resources are combined with hundreds of carefully chosen maps and images and helpfully annotated. Browse the collection of thousands of resources by course or by topic, date, and type.

Videos and Multimedia. A wide assortment of videos and multimedia CD-ROMs on various topics in European history is available to qualified adopters through your Bedford, Freeman & Worth sales representative.

HistoryClass for *A History of Western Society*. HistoryClass, a Bedford/St. Martin's Online Course Space, puts the online resources available with this textbook in one convenient and completely customizable place. There you can access an interactive e-book and primary sources reader; maps, images, documents, and links; chapter review quizzes; interactive multimedia exercises; and research and writing help. In HistoryClass you can get all our premium content and tools and assign, rearrange, and mix them with your own resources. For more information visit **yourhistoryclass.com**.

Bedford/St. Martin's Course Cartridges. Whether you use Blackboard, WebCT, Desire2Learn, Angel, Sakai, or Moodle, we have free content and support available to help you plug our content into your course management system. Registered instructors can download cartridges with no hassle and no strings attached. Content includes our most popular free resources and book-specific content for *A History of Western Society*. Visit **bedfordstmartins.com/cms** to get a demo, find your version, or download your cartridge.

Packaging Opportunities

Stretch your budget and package your favorite text with more! For information on free packages and discounts up to 50 percent, visit **bfwpub.com/highschool/history**, or contact your local Bedford, Freeman & Worth sales representative.

e-Book. One year of the e-book of this title can be packaged with the print text at no additional cost. For six years of access, the cost is just $15.00.

***Sources of Western Society*, Second Edition**. This primary source collection provides a revised and expanded selection of sources to accompany *A History of Western Society: Since 1300*, Tenth Edition. Each chapter features five or six written and visual sources by well-known figures and ordinary individuals alike. Now including nineteen visual sources and 30 percent more documents, this edition offers both breadth and depth. A new Viewpoints feature highlights two or three sources that address the same topic from different perspectives. Document headnotes and reading and discussion questions promote student understanding. Available for just $5.00 when packaged with the text.

***Sources of Western Society* e-Book**. The reader is also available as an e-book. When packaged with the print or electronic version of the textbook, it is free.

Rand McNally Atlas of Western Civilization. This collection of over fifty full-color maps highlights social, political, and cross-cultural change and interaction from classical Greece and Rome to the postindustrial Western world. Each map is thoroughly indexed for fast reference. Available for $3.00 when packaged with the text.

The Bedford Glossary for European History. This handy supplement for the survey course gives students historically contextualized definitions for hundreds of terms—from *Abbasids* to *Zionism*—that they will encounter in lectures, reading, and exams. Available for $2.00 when packaged with the text.

The Bedford Series in History and Culture. More than one hundred titles in this highly praised series combine first-rate scholarship, historical narrative, and important primary documents for undergraduate courses. Each book is brief, inexpensive, and focused on a specific topic or period. For a complete list of titles, visit **bedfordstmartins.com/history/series**. Package discounts are available.

Trade Books. Titles published by sister companies Hill and Wang; Farrar, Straus and Giroux; Henry Holt and Company; St. Martin's Press; Picador; and Palgrave Macmillan are available at a 50 percent discount when packaged with Bedford/St. Martin's textbooks. For more information, visit **bedfordstmartins.com/tradeup**.

The Social Dimension of Western Civilization. Combining current scholarship with classic pieces, this reader's forty-eight secondary sources, compiled by Richard M. Golden, hook students with the fascinating and often surprising details of how everyday European people worked, ate, played, celebrated, worshiped, married, procreated, fought, persecuted, and died. Package discounts are available.

The West in the Wider World: Sources and Perspectives. Edited by Richard Lim and David Kammerling Smith, the first college reader to focus on the central historical question "How did the West become the West?" offers a wealth of written and visual source materials that reveal the influence of non-European regions on the origins and development of Western Civilization. Package discounts are available.

A Pocket Guide to Writing in History. This portable and affordable reference tool by Mary Lynn Rampolla provides reading, writing, and research advice useful to students in all history courses. Concise yet comprehensive advice on approaching typical history assignments, developing critical reading skills, writing effective history papers, conducting research, using and documenting sources, and avoiding plagiarism—enhanced by practical tips and examples throughout—have made this slim reference a bestseller. Package discounts are available.

A Student's Guide to History. This complete guide provides the practical help students need to be successful in any history course. In addition to introducing students to the nature of the discipline, author Jules Benjamin teaches a wide range of skills from preparing for exams to approaching common writing assignments, and explains the research and documentation process with plentiful examples. Package discounts are available.

12
The Crisis of the Later Middle Ages

1300–1450

During the later Middle Ages the last book of the New Testament, the Book of Revelation, inspired thousands of sermons and hundreds of religious tracts. The Book of Revelation deals with visions of the end of the world, with disease, war, famine, and death — often called the "Four Horsemen of the Apocalypse" — triumphing everywhere. It is no wonder this part of the Bible was so popular, for between 1300 and 1450 Europeans experienced a frightful series of shocks. The climate turned colder, leading to poor harvests and famine. People weakened by hunger were more susceptible to disease, and in the middle of the fourteenth century a new disease, probably the bubonic plague, spread throughout Europe. Over several years the plague killed millions of people, and there was no effective treatment. War devastated the countryside, especially in France, leading to widespread discontent and peasant revolts. Workers in cities also revolted against dismal working conditions, and violent crime and ethnic tensions increased. Death and preoccupation with death make the fourteenth century one of the most wrenching periods of Western civilization. Yet, in spite of the pessimism and crises, important institutions and cultural forms, including representative assemblies and national literatures, emerged. Even institutions that experienced severe crisis, such as the Christian church, saw new types of vitality. ■

Bibliothèque nationale de France

Life in the Later Middle Ages. Peasants and urban workers rose up in revolt across Europe in the fourteenth century. In this French illustration, Wat Tyler, the leader of the English Peasants' Revolt, is stabbed during a meeting with the king. Tyler died soon afterward, and the revolt was ruthlessly crushed.

CHAPTER PREVIEW

Prelude to Disaster
■ What were the demographic, economic, and social consequences of climate change?

The Black Death
■ How did the spread of the plague shape European society?

The Hundred Years' War
■ What were the causes of the Hundred Years' War, and how did the war affect European politics, economics, and cultural life?

Challenges to the Church
■ What challenges faced the Christian church in the fourteenth century, and how did church leaders, intellectuals, and ordinary people respond?

Social Unrest in a Changing Society
■ How did economic and social tensions contribute to revolts, crime, violence, and a growing sense of ethnic and national distinctions?

Prelude to Disaster

What were the demographic, economic, and social consequences of climate change? ■

In the first half of the fourteenth century, Europe experienced a series of climate changes that led to lower levels of food production, which had dramatic and disastrous ripple effects. Political leaders attempted to find solutions but were unable to deal with the economic and social problems that resulted.

Climate Change and Famine

The period from about 1000 to about 1300 saw a warmer than usual climate in Europe, which underlay all the changes and vitality of the High Middle Ages. About 1300 the climate changed, becoming colder and wetter. Historical geographers refer to the period from 1300 to 1450 as a "little ice age," which they can trace through both natural and human records.

Evidence from nature emerges through the study of Alpine and po-

Great Famine A terrible famine in 1315–1322 that hit much of Europe after a period of climate change.

lar glaciers, tree rings, and pollen left in bogs. Human-produced sources include written reports of rivers freezing and crops never ripening, as well as archaeological evidence such as the abandoned villages of Greenland, where ice floes cut off contact with the rest of the world and the harshening climate meant that the few hardy crops grown earlier could no longer survive. The Viking colony on Greenland died out completely, though Inuit people who relied on hunting sea mammals continued to live in the far north, as they had before the arrival of Viking colonists.

An unusual number of storms brought torrential rains, ruining the wheat, oat, and hay crops on which people and animals almost everywhere depended. Since long-distance transportation of food was expensive and difficult, most urban areas depended for bread and meat on areas no more than a day's journey away. Poor harvests—and one in four was likely to be poor—led to scarcity and starvation. Almost all of northern Europe suffered a **Great Famine** in the years 1315 to 1322, which contemporaries interpreted as a recurrence of the biblical "seven lean years" (Genesis 42).

Even in non-famine years, the cost of grain, livestock, and dairy products rose sharply, in part because diseases hit cattle and sheep. Increasing prices meant that

Death from Famine In this fifteenth-century painting, dead bodies lie in the middle of a path, while a funeral procession at the right includes a man with an adult's coffin and a woman with the coffin of an infant under her arm. People did not simply allow the dead to lie in the street in medieval Europe, though during famines and epidemics it was sometimes difficult to maintain normal burial procedures. (Erich Lessing/Art Resource, NY)

fewer people could afford to buy food. Reduced caloric intake meant increased susceptibility to disease, especially for infants, children, and the elderly. Epidemics of typhoid fever carried away thousands. Workers on reduced diets had less energy, which in turn meant lower productivity, lower output, and higher grain prices.

Social Consequences

The changing climate and resulting agrarian crisis of the fourteenth century had grave social consequences. Poor harvests and famine led to the abandonment of homesteads. In parts of the Low Countries and in the Scottish-English borderlands, entire villages were abandoned, and many people became vagabonds, wandering in search of food and work. In Flanders and East Anglia (eastern England), some peasants were forced to mortgage, sublease, or sell their holdings to richer farmers in order to buy food. Throughout the affected areas, young men and women sought work in the towns, postponing marriage. Overall, the population declined because of the deaths caused by famine and disease, though the postponement of marriages and the resulting decline in offspring may have also played a part.

As the subsistence crisis deepened, starving people focused their anger on the rich, speculators, and the Jews, who were often targeted as creditors fleecing the poor through pawnbroking. (As seen in recent chapters, Jews often became moneylenders because Christian authorities restricted their ownership of land and opportunities to engage in other trades.) Rumors spread of a plot by Jews and their agents, the lepers, to kill Christians by poisoning the wells. Based on "evidence" collected by torture, many lepers and Jews were killed, beaten, or heavily fined.

Meanwhile, the international character of trade and commerce meant that a disaster in one country had serious implications elsewhere. For example, the infection that attacked English sheep in 1318 caused a sharp decline in wool exports in the following years. Without wool, Flemish weavers could not work, and thousands were laid off. Without woolen cloth, the businesses of Flemish, Hanseatic, and Italian merchants suffered. Unemployment encouraged people to turn to crime.

Government responses to these crises were ineffectual. The three sons of Philip the Fair who sat on the French throne between 1314 and 1328 condemned speculators who held stocks of grain back until conditions were desperate and prices high; forbade the sale of grain abroad; and published legislation prohibiting fishing with traps

Chronology

that took large catches. These measures remained largely a wish list and had few actual results.

In England, Edward I's incompetent son, Edward II (r. 1307–1327), also condemned speculators after his attempts to set price controls on livestock and ale proved futile. He did try to buy grain abroad, but little was available: yields in the Baltic were low; the French crown, as we have seen, forbade exports; and the grain shipped from northern Spain was grabbed by pirates. Such grain as reached southern English ports was stolen by looters and sold on the black market. The Crown's efforts at famine relief failed.

The Black Death

How did the spread of the plague shape European society? ∎

Around 1300 improvements in ship design allowed year-round shipping for the first time. European merchants took advantage of these advances, and ships continually at sea carried all types of cargo. They also carried vermin of all types, especially insects and rats, which often harbored disease pathogens. Rats, fleas, and cockroaches could live for months on the cargo carried along the coasts, disembarking at ports with the grain, cloth, or other merchandise. Just as modern air travel has allowed diseases such as AIDS and the H1N1 virus to spread quickly over very long distances, medieval shipping did the same. The most frightful of these diseases, carried on Genoese ships, first emerged in western Europe in 1347, a disease that was later called the **Black Death**.

Black Death Plague that first struck Europe in 1347 and killed perhaps one-third of the population.

Pathology

Most historians and microbiologists identify the disease that spread in the fourteenth century as the bubonic plague caused by the bacillus *Yersinia pestis*. The disease normally afflicts rats. Fleas living on the infected rats drink their blood and then pass the bacteria that cause the plague on to the next rat they bite. Usually the disease is limited to rats and other rodents, but at certain points in history—perhaps when most rats have been killed off—the fleas have jumped from their rodent hosts to humans and other animals. One of these times appears to have occurred in the Eastern Roman Empire in the sixth century, when a plague killed millions of people. Another was in China and India in the 1890s, when millions died. Doctors and epidemiologists closely studied this outbreak, identified the bacillus as bubonic plague, and learned about the exact cycle of infection for the first time.

The fourteenth-century outbreak showed many similarities to the nineteenth-century outbreak, but also some differences. There are no reports of massive rat die-offs in fourteenth-century records. The plague was often transmitted directly from one person to another through coughing and sneezing (what epidemiologists term *pneumonic* transmission) as well as through flea bites. The fourteenth-century outbreak spread much faster than the nineteenth-century outbreak and was much more deadly, killing as much as one-third of the population when it first spread to an area. These differences have led some historians to question whether the fourteenth-century outbreak was actually not the bubonic plague, but a different disease, perhaps something like the Ebola virus. Other scholars counter that the differences could be explained by variant strains of the disease or improvements in sanitation and public health that would have limited the mortality rate of later outbreaks significantly, even in poor countries such as India. These debates fuel continued study of medical aspects of the plague, with scientists using innovative techniques such as studying the tooth pulp of bodies in medieval cemeteries to see if it contains DNA from plague-causing agents.

Though there is some disagreement about exactly what kind of disease the plague was, there is no dispute about its dreadful effects on the body. The classic symptom of the bubonic plague was a growth the size of a nut or an apple in the armpit, in the groin, or on the neck. This was the boil, or *bubo*, that gave the disease its name and caused agonizing pain. If the bubo was lanced and the pus thoroughly drained, the victim had a chance of recovery. The next stage was the appearance of black spots or blotches caused by bleeding under the skin. (This syndrome did not give the disease its common name; contemporaries did not call the plague the Black Death. Sometime in the fifteenth century the Latin phrase *atra mors*, meaning "dreadful death," was translated as "black death," and the phrase stuck.) Finally, the victim began to cough violently and spit blood. This stage, indicating the presence of millions of bacilli in the bloodstream, signaled the end, and death followed in two or three days.

Spread of the Disease

Plague symptoms were first described in 1331 in southwestern China, part of the Mongol Empire. Plague-infested rats accompanied Mongol armies and merchant caravans carrying silk, spices, and gold across Central Asia in the 1330s. The rats then stowed away on ships, carrying the disease to the ports of the Black Sea by the 1340s. Later stories told of more dramatic means of spreading the disease as well, reporting that Mongol armies besieging the city of Kaffa on the shores of the Black Sea catapulted plague-infected corpses over the walls to infect those inside. The city's residents dumped the corpses into the sea as fast as they could, but they were already infected.

In October 1347 Genoese ships brought the plague from Kaffa to Messina, from which it spread across Sicily. Venice and Genoa were hit in January 1348, and from the port of Pisa the disease spread south to Rome and east to Florence and all of Tuscany. By late spring southern Germany was attacked. Frightened French authorities chased a galley bearing the disease away from the port of Marseilles, but not before plague had infected the city, from which it spread to southern France and Spain. In June 1348 two ships entered the Bristol Channel and introduced it into England, and from there it traveled north into Scandinavia. The plague seems to have entered Poland through the Baltic seaports and spread eastward from there (Map 12.1).

Although urban authorities from London to Paris to Rome had begun to try to achieve a primitive level of sanitation by the fourteenth century, urban conditions remained ideal for the spread of disease. Narrow streets filled with refuse and human excrement were as much cesspools as thoroughfares. Dead animals and sore-covered beggars greeted the traveler. Houses whose upper stories projected over the lower ones blocked light and air, and extreme overcrowding was commonplace. When all members of an aristocratic family lived and slept in one room, it should not be surprising that six or eight persons in a middle-class or poor household slept in one bed—if they had one. Closeness, after all, provided warmth. Houses were beginning to be constructed of brick, but many wood, clay, and mud houses remained. A determined rat had little trouble entering such a house.

People were already weakened by famine, and standards of personal hygiene remained frightfully low. Fleas and body lice were universal afflictions: everyone from peasants to archbishops had them. One more bite

Mapping the Past

Map 12.1 **The Course of the Black Death in Fourteenth-Century Europe** The bubonic plague spread northward across Europe, beginning in the late 1340s with the first cases of disease reported in the ports of the Black Sea.

ANALYZING THE MAP When did the plague reach Paris? How much time passed before it spread to the rest of northern France and southern Germany? Which cities and regions were spared?

CONNECTIONS How did the expansion of trade that resulted from the commercial revolution contribute to the spread of the Black Death?

To complete this activity online, go to the Online Study Guide at bedfordstmartins.com/mckaywest.

did not cause much alarm, and the association among rats, fleas, and the plague was as yet unknown. If that nibble came from a bacillus-bearing flea, an entire household or area was doomed.

Mortality rates can be only educated guesses because population figures for the period before the arrival of the plague do not exist for most countries and cities. Of a total English population of perhaps 4.2 million, probably 1.4 million died of the Black Death. Densely populated Italian cities endured incredible losses. Florence lost between one-half and two-thirds of its population when the plague visited in 1348. Islamic parts of Europe were not spared, nor was the rest of the Muslim world. The most widely accepted estimate for western Europe and the Mediterranean is that the plague killed about one-third of the population in the first wave of infection.

Nor did central and eastern Europe escape the ravages of the disease. One chronicler records that, in the summer and autumn of 1349, between five hundred and six hundred died every day in Vienna. As the Black Death took its toll on the Holy Roman Empire, waves of emigrants fled to Poland, Bohemia, and Hungary, sometimes taking plague with them. In the Byzantine Empire the plague ravaged the population. The youngest son of Emperor John VI Kantakouzenos died just as his father took over the throne in 1347. "So incurable was the evil," wrote John later in his history of the Byzantine Empire, "that neither any regularity of life, nor any bodily strength could resist it. Strong and weak

Treating the Plague

LIVING IN THE PAST

MEDIEVAL PHYSICIANS BASED TREATMENTS FOR THE PLAGUE on their understanding of how the body worked, as do doctors in any era. Fourteenth-century people — lay, scholarly, and medical — attributed the disease to "poisons" in the air that caused the fluids in the body to become unbalanced. The imbalance in fluids led to illness, an idea that had been the core of Western ideas about the primary cause of disease since the ancient Greeks. Certain symptoms of the plague, such as boils that oozed and blood-filled coughing, were believed to be the body's natural reaction to too much fluid.

Doctors thus recommended preventive measures that would block the poisoned air from entering the body, such as holding strong-smelling herbs or other substances, like rosemary, juniper, or sulfur, in front of the nose or burning incense. Treatment concentrated on ridding the body of poisons and bringing the fluids into balance. As one fifteenth-century treatise put it, "everyone over seven should be made to vomit daily" and twice a week wrap up in sheets to "sweat copiously." The best way to regain health, however, was to let blood: "as soon as [the patient] feels an itch or pricking in his flesh [the physician] must use a goblet or cupping horn to let blood and draw down the blood from his heart, and this should be done two or three times at intervals of one or two days at the most." Letting blood was considered the most effective way to rebalance the fluids and also to flush the body of poisons.

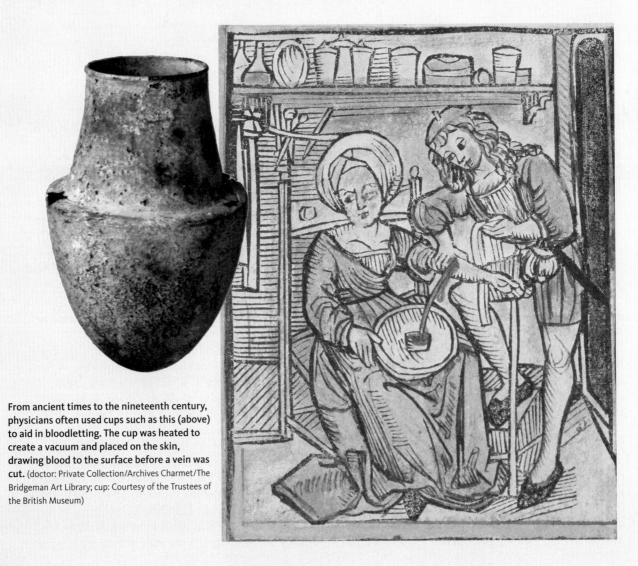

From ancient times to the nineteenth century, physicians often used cups such as this (above) to aid in bloodletting. The cup was heated to create a vacuum and placed on the skin, drawing blood to the surface before a vein was cut. (doctor: Private Collection/Archives Charmet/The Bridgeman Art Library; cup: Courtesy of the Trustees of the British Museum)

A plague doctor in a seventeenth-century German engraving published during a later outbreak of the dreaded disease. The doctor is fully covered, with a coat waxed smooth so that poisons just slide off. The beaked mask contains strong-smelling herbs, and the stick, beaten on the ground as he walks along, warns people away. (akg-images)

QUESTIONS FOR ANALYSIS

1. In the background of the plague doctor engraving, the artist shows a group of children running away as the plague doctor approaches. What aspects of his appearance or treatment methods contributed to this reaction?

2. Many people who lived through the plague reported that it created a sense of hopeless despair. Do these sources support this idea? Why?

Quotations from Rosemary Horrox, *The Black Death* (Manchester: Manchester University Press, 1994), p. 194.

bodies were all similarly carried away, and those best cared for died in the same manner as the poor."[1]

Across Europe the Black Death recurred intermittently from the 1360s to 1400. It reappeared from time to time over the following centuries, though never with the same virulence because Europeans now had some resistance. Improved standards of hygiene and strictly enforced quarantine measures also lessened the plague's toll, but only in 1721 did it make its last appearance in Europe, in the French port city of Marseilles. And only in 1947, six centuries after the arrival of the plague in Europe, did the American microbiologist Selman Waksman discover an effective treatment, streptomycin. Plague continues to infect rodent and human populations sporadically today.

> **❝ So incurable was the evil that neither any regularity of life, nor any bodily strength could resist it. Strong and weak bodies were all similarly carried away. ❞**
>
> —**EMPEROR JOHN VI KANTAKOUZENOS**

Care of the Sick

Fourteenth-century medical literature indicates that physicians tried many different things to prevent and treat the plague. They observed that crowded cities had high death rates, especially when the weather was warm and moist. We understand that warm, moist conditions make it easier for germs, viruses, and bacteria to grow and spread, but fourteenth-century people thought in terms of "poisons" in the air or "corrupted air" coming from swamps, unburied animals, or the positions of the stars, rather than germs. Their treatments thus focused on ridding the air and the body of these poisons, and on rebalancing bodily fluids to bring people back to health. (See "Living in the Past: Treating the Plague," at left.)

People tried anything they thought might help. Perhaps loud sounds like ringing church bells or firing the newly invented cannon would clean poisoned air. Medicines made from plants that were bumpy or that oozed liquid might work, keeping the more dangerous swelling and oozing of the plague away. Magical letter and number combinations, called cryptograms, were especially popular in Muslim areas. They were often the first letters of words in prayers or religious sayings, and they gave people a sense of order when faced with the randomness with which the plague seemed to strike.

❝ Almost no one cared for his neighbor . . . brother abandoned brother . . . and—even worse, almost unbelievable—fathers and mothers neglected to tend and care for their children. **❞**

—Giovanni Boccaccio

It is noteworthy that, in an age of mounting criticism of clerical wealth (see page 356), the behavior of the clergy during the plague was often exemplary. Priests, monks, and nuns cared for the sick and buried the dead. In places like Venice, from which even physicians fled, priests remained to give what ministrations they could. Consequently, their mortality rate was phenomenally high. The German clergy especially suffered a severe decline in personnel in the years after 1350.

There were limits to care, however. The Italian writer Giovanni Boccaccio (1313–1375), describing the course of the disease in Florence in the preface to his book of

Picturing the Past

Patients in a Hospital Most victims of the plague died at home, but some went to special plague hospitals. This fifteenth-century painting shows what would have been a common scene, with female members of a religious order or Beguines caring for patients in a hospital. Here the women are also allegorical figures, judging the patients' worth as they take their pulse. At the right stands Justice holding scales, and at the left Prudence holding a rod. (Giraudon/The Bridgeman Art Library)

ANALYZING THE IMAGE What does this image suggest about the care for plague victims? Do the conditions shown at this hospital suggest that there is hope for these patients?

CONNECTIONS How does the allegorical depiction of the nuns shown here explain how medieval people understood the plague?

To complete this activity online, go to the Online Study Guide at bedfordstmartins.com/mckaywest.

tales, *The Decameron*, identified what many knew — that the disease passed from person to person:

> *This pestilence was so powerful that it was transmitted to the healthy by contact with the sick, the way a fire close to dry or oily things will set them aflame. And the evil of the plague went even further: not only did talking to or being around the sick bring infection and a common death, but also touching the clothes of the sick or anything touched or used by them seemed to communicate this very disease to the person involved.[2]*

To avoid contagion, wealthier people often fled cities for the countryside, though sometimes this simply spread the plague faster. Some cities tried shutting their gates to prevent infected people and animals from coming in, which worked in a few cities. They also walled up houses in which there was plague, trying to isolate those who were sick from those who were still healthy. In Boccaccio's words, "almost no one cared for his neighbor . . . brother abandoned brother . . . and — even worse, almost unbelievable — fathers and mothers neglected to tend and care for their children."[3]

Economic, Religious, and Cultural Effects

Economic historians and demographers sharply dispute the impact of the plague on the economy in the late fourteenth century. The traditional view that the plague had a disastrous effect has been greatly modified. The clearest evidence comes from England, where by the early fifteenth century most landlords enjoyed the highest revenues of the medieval period. Why? The answer appears to lie in the fact that England and many parts of Europe suffered from overpopulation in the early fourteenth century. Population losses caused by famines and the Black Death led to increased productivity by restoring a more efficient balance between labor, land, and capital.

What impact did visits of the plague have on urban populations? The rich evidence from a census of the city of Florence and its surrounding territory taken between 1427 and 1430 is fascinating. The region had suffered repeated epidemics since 1347. The census showed a high proportion of people who were age sixty or older, suggesting that the plague took the young rather than the mature. The high mortality rate of craftsmen between the ages of twenty and fifty-nine led Florentine guilds to recruit many new members, and also to develop new ways to organize production on a larger scale. Thus the post-plague years represent an age of "new men."

The Black Death brought on a general European inflation. High mortality produced a fall in production, shortages of goods, and a general rise in prices. The price of wheat in most of Europe increased, as did the costs of meat, sausage, and cheese. This inflation continued to the end of the fourteenth century. But labor shortages meant that workers could demand better wages, and the broad mass of people enjoyed a higher standard of living. The greater demand for labor also meant greater mobility for peasants in rural areas and for industrial workers in the towns and cities. Labor shortages caused by the Black Death throughout the Mediterranean region, from Constantinople to Spain, presented aggressive businessmen with a golden opportunity, and the price of slaves rose sharply.

The plague also had effects on religious practices. Despite Boccaccio's comments about family members' coldness, people were saddened by the loss of their loved ones, especially their children. It is not surprising that some people sought release from the devastating affliction in wild living, but more became more deeply pious. Rather than seeing the plague as a medical issue, they instead interpreted it as the result of an evil within themselves. God must be punishing them for terrible sins, they thought, so the best remedies were religious ones: asking for forgiveness, prayer, trust in God, making donations to churches, and trying to live better lives. John VI Kantakouzenos reported that in Constantinople, "many of the sick turned to better things in their minds . . . they abstained from all vice during that time and they lived virtuously; many divided their property among the poor, even before they were attacked by the disease."[4] In Muslim areas, religious leaders urged virtuous living in the face of death: give to the poor, reconcile with your enemies, free your slaves, and say a proper goodbye to your friends and family.

> **flagellants** People who believed that the plague was God's punishment for sin and sought to do penance by flagellating (whipping) themselves.

Some Christians turned to the severest forms of asceticism and frenzied religious fervor, joining groups of **flagellants** (FLA-juh-lunts), who whipped and scourged themselves as penance for their and society's sins in the belief that the Black Death was God's punishment for humanity's wickedness. Groups of flagellants traveled from town to town, often growing into unruly mobs. Officials worried that they would provoke violence and riots, and ordered groups to disband or forbade them to enter cities.

Along with seeing the plague as a call to reform their own behavior, however, people also searched for scapegoats, and savage cruelty sometimes resulted. Just as in the decades before the plague, many people believed that the Jews had poisoned the wells of Christian communities and thereby infected the drinking water. This charge led to the murder of thousands of Jews across Europe.

The literature and art of the late Middle Ages reveal a terribly morbid concern with death. One highly popular literary and artistic motif, the Dance of Death,

Flagellants In this manuscript illumination from 1349, shirtless flagellants scourge themselves with whips as they walk through the streets of the Flemish city of Tournai. The text notes that they are asking for God's grace to return to the city after it had been struck with the "most grave" illness. (HIP/Art Resource, NY)

depicted a dancing skeleton leading away living people, often in order of their rank. In the words of one early fifteenth-century English poem:

> *Death spareth not low nor high degree*
> *Popes, Kings, nor worthy Emperors*
> *When they shine most in felicity*
> *He can abate the freshness of their flowers*
> *Eclipse their bright suns with his showers . . .*
> *Sir Emperor, lord of all the ground,*
> *Sovereign Prince, and highest of nobles*
> *You must forsake your round apples of gold*
> *Leave behind your treasure and riches*
> *And with others to my dance obey.*[5]

Popular endowments of educational institutions multiplied. The years of the Black Death witnessed the foundation of new colleges at old universities and of entirely new universities. The foundation charters specifically mention the shortage of priests and the decay of learning. Whereas universities such as those at Bologna and Paris had international student bodies, new institutions established in the wake of the Black Death had more national or local constituencies. Thus the international character of medieval culture weakened, paving the way for schism (SKIH-zuhm) in the Catholic Church even before the Reformation.

As is often true with devastating events, the plague highlighted central qualities of medieval society: deep religious feeling, suspicion of those who were different, and a view of the world shaped largely by oral tradition, with a bit of classical knowledge mixed in among the educated elite.

The Hundred Years' War

What were the causes of the Hundred Years' War, and how did the war affect European politics, economics, and cultural life? ∎

The plague ravaged populations in Asia, North Africa, and Europe; in western Europe a long international war added further misery to the frightful disasters of the plague. England and France had engaged in sporadic military hostilities from the time of the Norman Conquest in 1066, and in the middle of the fourteenth century these became more intense. From 1337 to 1453, the two countries intermittently fought one another in what was the longest war in European history, ultimately dubbed the Hundred Years' War, though it actually lasted 116 years.

Causes

The Hundred Years' War had both distant and immediate causes, including disagreements over rights to land, a dispute over the succession to the French throne, and economic conflicts. A distant cause was the duchy of

Dance of Death In this fifteenth-century fresco from a tiny church in Croatia, skeletons lead people from all social classes to their death. No one is spared, for the procession includes a king and queen, a pope, a bishop, and a little child. (Vladimir Bugarin, photographer)

Aquitaine, which became part of the holdings of the English crown when Eleanor of Aquitaine married King Henry II of England in 1152 (see Chapter 9; a duchy is a territory ruled by a duke). In 1259 Henry III of England had signed the Treaty of Paris with Louis IX of France, affirming English claims to Aquitaine in return for becoming a vassal of the French crown. French policy in the fourteenth century was strongly expansionist, however, and the French kings resolved to absorb the duchy into the kingdom of France. Aquitaine therefore became a disputed territory.

The immediate political cause of the war was a dispute over who would inherit the French throne after Charles IV of France, the last surviving son of Philip the Fair, died childless in 1328. With him ended the Capetian dynasty of France. Charles IV did have a sister—Isabella—and her son was Edward III, king of England. An assembly of French high nobles, meaning to exclude Isabella and Edward from the French throne, proclaimed that "no woman nor her son could succeed to the [French] monarchy." French lawyers defended the position with the claim that the exclusion of women from ruling or passing down the right to rule was part of Salic Law, a sixth-century law code of the Franks (see Chapter 7), and that Salic Law itself was part of the fundamental law of France. They used this invented tradi-

tion to argue that Edward should be barred from the French throne. (This notion became part of French legal tradition until the end of the monarchy in 1789.) The nobles passed the crown to Philip VI of Valois (r. 1328–1350), a nephew of Philip the Fair.

In 1329 Edward III paid homage to Philip VI for Aquitaine. In 1337 Philip, eager to exercise full French jurisdiction in Aquitaine, confiscated the duchy. Edward III interpreted this action as a gross violation of the treaty of 1259 and as a cause for war. Moreover, Edward argued, as the eldest directly surviving male descendant of Philip the Fair, he deserved the title of king of France. Edward III's dynastic argument upset the feudal order in France: to increase their independent power, French vassals of Philip VI used the excuse that they had to transfer their loyalty to a different overlord, Edward III. One reason the war lasted so long was that it became a French civil war, with some French nobles, most important the dukes of Burgundy, supporting English monarchs in order to thwart the centralizing goals of the French crown. On the other side, Scotland often allied with France; the French supported Scottish raids in northern England, and Scottish troops joined with French armies on the continent.

The governments of both England and France manipulated public opinion to support the war. The

English public was convinced that the war was waged for one reason: to secure for King Edward the French crown he had been unjustly denied. Edward III issued letters to the sheriffs describing the evil deeds of the French in graphic terms and listing royal needs. Kings in both countries instructed the clergy to deliver sermons filled with patriotic sentiment. Philip VI sent agents to warn communities about the dangers of invasion and to stress the French crown's revenue needs to meet the attack. The English were led to believe that King Philip intended to seize and slaughter all of England. Royal propaganda on both sides fostered a kind of early nationalism, and both sides developed a deep hatred of the other.

Economic factors involving the wool trade and the control of Flemish towns were linked to these long-term and immediate political issues. The wool trade between England and Flanders served as the cornerstone of both countries' economies; they were closely interdependent. Flanders was a fief of the French crown, and the Flemish aristocracy was highly sympathetic to the monarchy in Paris. But the wealth of Flemish merchants and cloth manufacturers depended on English wool, and Flemish burghers strongly supported the claims of Edward III. The disruption of commerce with England threatened their prosperity.

The war also presented opportunities for wealth and advancement. Poor knights and knights who were unemployed were promised regular wages. Criminals who enlisted were granted pardons. The great nobles expected to be rewarded with estates. Royal exhortations to the troops before battles repeatedly stressed that, if victorious, the men might keep whatever they seized. The French chronicler Jean Froissart (FROI-sahrt) wrote of one English invasion that some of the men of all ranks who flocked to the English king's banner came to acquire honor, but many came "to loot and pillage the fair and plenteous land of France."[6]

English Successes

The war began with a series of French sea raids on English coastal towns in 1337, but the French fleet was almost completely destroyed when it attempted to land soldiers on English soil, and from that point on the war was fought almost entirely in France and the Low Countries (Map 12.2). It consisted mainly of a series of random sieges and cavalry raids, fought in fits and starts, with treaties along the way to halt hostilities.

During the war's early stages, England was highly successful. At Crécy in northern France in 1346, English longbowmen scored a great victory over French knights and crossbowmen. Although the aim of the longbow was not very accu-

Agincourt The location near Arras in Flanders where an English victory in 1415 led to the reconquest of Normandy.

The Hundred Years' War

1337	Philip VI of France confiscates Aquitaine
1346	English longbowmen defeat French knights at Crécy
1356	English defeat French at Poitiers
1370s–1380s	French recover some territory
1415	English defeat the French at Agincourt
1429	French victory at Orléans; Charles VII crowned king
1431	Joan of Arc declared a heretic and burned at the stake
1440s	French reconquer Normandy and Aquitaine
1453	War ends
1456	Joan cleared of charges of heresy and declared a martyr

rate, it allowed for rapid reloading, and an English archer could send off three arrows to the French crossbowman's one. The result was a blinding shower of arrows that unhorsed the French knights and caused mass confusion. The ring of cannon—probably the first use of artillery in the West—created further panic. Thereupon the English horsemen charged and butchered the French. This was not war according to the chivalric rules that Edward III would have preferred. Nevertheless, his son, Edward the Black Prince, used the same tactics ten years later to smash the French at Poitiers, where he captured the French king and held him for ransom. Edward was not able to take all of France, but the English held Aquitaine and other provinces, and allied themselves with many of France's feudal vassals. After a brief peace, the French fought back and recovered some territory, and a treaty again halted hostilities as both sides concentrated on conflicts over power at home.

War began again in 1415 when the able English soldier-king Henry V (r. 1413–1422) invaded. At **Agincourt** (AH-jihn-kort), Henry's army defeated a much larger French force, again primarily through the skill of English longbowmen. Henry followed up his triumph at Agincourt with the reconquest of Normandy, and by 1419 the English had advanced to the walls of Paris (see Map 12.2). Henry married the daughter of the French king, and a treaty made Henry and any sons the couple would have heir to the French throne. It appeared as if Henry would indeed rule both England and France, but he died unexpectedly in 1422, leaving an infant son as

Map 12.2 The Hundred Years' War, 1337–1453 These maps show the change in English and French landholdings over the course of the Hundred Years' War. Which year marked the greatest extent of English holdings in France?

Suit of Armor This fifteenth-century suit of Italian armor protected its wearer, but its weight made movement difficult. Both English and French mounted knights wore full armor at the beginning of the Hundred Years' War, but by the end they wore only breastplates and helmets, which protected their vital organs but allowed greater mobility. This particular suit has been so well preserved that it was most likely never used in battle; it may have been made for ceremonial purposes. (Image copyright © The Metropolitan Museum of Art/Art Resource, NY)

heir. The English continued their military victories, however, and besieged the city of Orléans (or-lay-AHN), the only major city in northern France not under their control. But the French cause was not lost.

Joan of Arc and France's Victory

The ultimate French success rests heavily on the actions of Joan, an obscure French peasant girl whose vision and military leadership revived French fortunes and led to victory. (Over the centuries, she acquired the name "of Arc"—*d'Arc* in French—based on her father's name; she never used this name for herself, but called herself "the maiden"—*la Pucelle* in French.) Born in 1412 to well-to-do peasants in the village of Domrémy in Champagne, Joan grew up in a religious household. During adolescence she began to hear voices, which she later said belonged to Saint Michael, Saint Catherine, and Saint Margaret. In 1428 these voices spoke to her with great urgency, telling her that the dauphin (DOH-fuhn), the uncrowned King Charles VII, had to be crowned and the English expelled from France. Joan traveled to the French court wearing a male disguise for safety. She had an audience with Charles, who had her questioned about her angelic visions and examined to make sure she was the virgin she said she was. She secured his support to travel with the French army to Orléans dressed as a knight—with armor and sword loaned to her by the French troops—and dictated a letter to the English ordering them to surrender:

> *King of England . . . , do right in the King of Heaven's sight. Surrender to The Maid sent hither by God the King of Heaven, the keys of all the good towns you have taken and laid waste in France. She comes in God's name to establish the Blood Royal, ready to make peace if you agree to abandon France and repay what you have taken. And you, archers, comrades in arms, gentles and others, who are before the town of Orléans, retire in God's name to your own country.*[7]

Such words coming from a teenage girl—even one inspired by God—were laughable given the recent course of the conflict, but Joan was amazingly successful. She inspired and led French attacks, and the English retreated from Orléans. The king made Joan co-commander of the entire army, and she led it to a string of military victories; other cities simply surrendered without a fight and returned their allegiance to France. In July 1429, two months after Orléans, Charles VII was crowned king at Reims.

Joan and the French army continued their fight against the English and their Burgundian allies. In 1430 the Burgundians captured Joan. Charles refused to ransom her, and she was sold to the English. The English wanted Joan eliminated for obvious political reasons, but the primary charge against her was heresy, and the trial was conducted by church authorities. She was interrogated about the angelic voices and about why she wore men's clothing. The extensive trial transcript reveals that she apparently answered skillfully, but in 1431 the court condemned her as a heretic and burned her at the stake in the marketplace at Rouen.

The French army continued its victories without her. The Burgundians switched their allegiance to the French, who reconquered Normandy and, finally, ejected the English from Aquitaine. As the war dragged on, loss of life mounted, and money appeared to be flowing into a bot-tomless pit, demands for an end increased in England. Parliamentary opposition to additional war grants stiffened, fewer soldiers were sent, and more territory passed into French hands. At the war's end in 1453, only the town of Calais (KA-lay) remained in English hands.

What of Joan? A new trial in 1456 — requested by Charles VII, who either had second thoughts about his abandonment of Joan or did not wish to be associated with a condemned heretic — was held by the pope. This cleared her of all charges and declared her a martyr. She became a political symbol of France from that point on, and sometimes also a symbol of the Catholic Church in opposition to the government of France. In 1920, for example, she was canonized as a saint shortly after the French government declared separation of church and state in France. Similarly, Joan has been (and continues to be) a symbol of deep religious piety to some, of conservative nationalism to others, and of gender-bending cross-dressing to others. Beneath the pious and popular legends is a teenage girl who saved the French monarchy, which was the embodiment of France.

Siege of the Castle of Mortagne Medieval warfare usually consisted of small skirmishes and attacks on castles. This miniature shows the French besieging an English-held castle near Bordeaux in 1377 that held out for six months. Most of the soldiers use longbows, although at the left two men shoot primitive muskets above a pair of cannon. Painted in the late fifteenth century, the scene reflects military technology available at the time it was painted, not at the time of the actual siege. (© British Library Board, MS Royal 14 e. IV f. 23)

Aftermath

In France thousands of soldiers and civilians had been slaughtered and hundreds of thousands of acres of rich farmland were ruined, leaving the rural economy of many parts of France a shambles. The war had disrupted trade and the great fairs, resulting in the drastic reduction of French participation in international commerce. Defeat in battle and heavy taxation contributed to widespread dissatisfaction and aggravated peasant grievances.

The war had wreaked havoc in England as well, even though only the southern coastal ports saw battle. England spent the huge sum of over £5 million on the war effort, and despite the money raised by some victories, the net result was an enormous financial loss. The government attempted to finance the war by raising taxes on the wool crop, which priced wool out of the export market.

In both England and France, men of all social classes had volunteered to serve in the war in the hope of acquiring booty and becoming rich. Some were successful in the early years of the war, as one chronicler reported: "For the woman was of no account who did not possess something from the spoils of . . . cities overseas in clothing, furs, quilts, and utensils . . . tablecloths and jewels, bowls of murra [semiprecious stone] and silver, linen and linen cloths."[8] As time went on, however, most fortunes seem to have been squandered as fast as they were made. In addition, the social order was disrupted as the knights who ordinarily served as sheriffs, coroners, jurymen, and justices of the peace were abroad.

The war stimulated technological experimentation, especially with artillery. Cannon revolutionized warfare, making the stone castle no longer impregnable. Because only central governments, not private nobles, could afford cannon, they strengthened the military power of national states.

The long war also had a profound impact on the political and cultural lives of the two countries. Most notably, it stimulated the development of the English Parliament. Between 1250 and 1450, **representative assemblies** flourished in many European countries. In the English Parliament, German diets, and Spanish cortes, deliberative practices developed that laid the foundations for the representative institutions of modern democratic nations. While representative assemblies declined in most countries after the fifteenth century, the English Parliament endured. Edward III's constant need for money to pay for the war compelled him to summon not only the great barons and bishops, but knights of the shires and burgesses from the towns as well. Parliament met in thirty-seven of the fifty years of Edward's reign.

representative assemblies Deliberative meetings of lords and wealthy urban residents that flourished in many European countries between 1250 and 1450 and were the precursors to the English Parliament, German diets, and Spanish cortes.

The frequency of the meetings is significant. Representative assemblies were becoming a habit. Knights and wealthy urban residents—or the "Commons," as they came to be called—recognized their mutual interests and began to meet apart from the great lords. The Commons gradually realized that they held the country's purse strings, and a parliamentary statute of 1341 required parliamentary approval of all nonfeudal levies. By signing the law, Edward III acknowledged that the king of England could not tax without Parliament's consent. During the course of the war, money grants were increasingly tied to royal redress of grievances: to raise money, the government had to correct the wrongs its subjects protested.

In England, theoretical consent to taxation and legislation was given in one assembly for the entire country. France had no such single assembly; instead, there were many regional or provincial assemblies. Why did a national representative assembly fail to develop in France? Linguistic, geographical, economic, legal, and political differences were very strong. People tended to think of themselves as Breton, Norman, Burgundian, and so on, rather than French. Provincial assemblies, highly jealous of their independence, did not want a national assembly. The costs of sending delegates to it would be high, and the result was likely to be increased taxation. In addition, the initiative for convening assemblies rested with the king. But some monarchs lacked the power to call such assemblies, and others, including Charles VI, found the idea of representative assemblies thoroughly distasteful.

In both countries, however, the war did promote the growth of nationalism—the feeling of unity and identity that binds together a people. After victories, each country experienced a surge of pride in its military strength. Just as English patriotism ran strong after Crécy and Poitiers, so French national confidence rose after Orléans. French national feeling demanded the expulsion of the enemy not merely from Normandy and Aquitaine but from all French soil. Perhaps no one expressed this national consciousness better than Joan when she exulted that the enemy had been "driven out of *France*."

Challenges to the Church

What challenges faced the Christian church in the fourteenth century, and how did church leaders, intellectuals, and ordinary people respond? ■

In times of crisis or disaster, people of all faiths have sought the consolation of religion. In the fourteenth century, however, the official Christian church offered little solace. In fact, although many monks, nuns, and friars had committed their lives to helping the sick and the hungry, the leaders of the church added to the sorrow and misery of the times. In response to this lack of leadership, members of the clergy challenged the power of the pope, and laypeople challenged the authority of the church itself. Women and men increasingly relied on direct approaches to God, often through mystical encounters, rather than on the institutional church.

The Babylonian Captivity and Great Schism

Conflicts between the secular rulers of Europe and the popes were common throughout the High Middle Ages, and in the early fourteenth century the dispute between King Philip the Fair of France and Pope Boniface VIII became particularly bitter (see Chapter 11). With Boniface's death, in order to control the church and its policies, Philip pressured the new pope, Clement V, to settle permanently in Avignon in southeastern France, where the popes already had their summer residence. Clement, critically ill with cancer, lacked the will to resist Philip. The popes lived in Avignon from 1309 to 1376, a period in church history often called the **Babylonian Captivity** (referring to the seventy years the ancient Hebrews were held captive in Mesopotamian Babylon; see Chapter 3).

The Babylonian Captivity badly damaged papal prestige. The Avignon papacy reformed its financial administration and centralized its government. But the seven popes at Avignon concentrated on bureaucratic matters to the exclusion of spiritual objectives. Though some of the popes led austere lives, the general atmosphere was one of luxury and extravagance. The leadership of the church was cut off from its historic roots and the source of its ancient authority, the city of Rome. In 1377 Pope Gregory XI brought the papal court back to Rome. Unfortunately, he died shortly after the return. Between the time of Gregory's death and the opening of the conclave, Roman citizens put great pressure on the cardinals to elect an Italian. At the time, none of the cardinals protested this pressure, and they chose a distinguished administrator, the archbishop of Bari, Bartolomeo Prignano, who took the name Urban VI.

Urban VI (pontificate 1378–1389) had excellent intentions for church reform, but he went about it in a tactless and bullheaded manner. He attacked clerical luxury, denouncing individual cardinals by name, and even threatened to excommunicate certain of them. The cardinals slipped away from Rome and met at Anagni. They declared Urban's election invalid because it had come about under threats from the Roman mob, and they asserted that Urban himself was excommunicated. The cardinals then elected Cardinal Robert of Geneva, the cousin of King Charles V of France, as pope. Cardinal Robert took the name Clement VII. There were thus two popes in 1378 — Urban at Rome and Clement VII

(pontificate 1378–1394), who set himself up at Avignon in opposition to Urban. So began the **Great Schism**, which divided Western Christendom until 1417.

The powers of Europe aligned themselves with Urban or Clement along strictly political lines. France naturally recognized the French pope, Clement. England, France's long-time enemy, recognized the Italian pope, Urban. Scotland, whose attacks on England were subsidized by France, followed the French and supported Clement. Aragon, Castile, and Portugal hesitated before deciding for Clement at Avignon. The German emperor, who bore ancient hostility to France, recognized Urban. At first the Italian city-states recognized Urban; when he alienated them with his attacks on luxury, they opted for Clement.

John of Spoleto, a professor at the law school at Bologna, eloquently summed up intellectual opinion of the schism: "The longer this schism lasts, the more it appears to be costing, and the more harm it does; scandal, massacres, ruination, agitations, troubles and disturbances."[9] The common people, wracked by inflation, wars, and plague, were thoroughly confused about which pope was legitimate. The schism weakened the religious faith of many Christians and brought church leadership into serious disrepute.

Allegiance to Rome
Allegiance to Avignon
Official allegiance to Rome but with shifting local allegiances

The Great Schism, 1378–1417

Critiques, Divisions, and Councils

Criticism of the church during the Avignon papacy and the Great Schism often came from the ranks of highly learned clergy and lay professionals. One of these was William of Occam (1289?–1347?), a Franciscan friar and philosopher. Occam saw the papal court at Avignon firsthand and became convinced that the Avignon popes were heretics. He argued vigorously against the papacy and also wrote philosophical works in which he questioned the connection between reason and faith that had been developed by Thomas Aquinas (see Chapter 11). All governments should have limited powers and be accountable to those they govern, according to Occam, and church and state should be separate.

The Italian lawyer and university official Marsiglio of Padua (ca. 1275–1342)

Babylonian Captivity The period from 1309 to 1376 when the popes resided in Avignon rather than in Rome. The phrase refers to the seventy years when the Hebrews were held captive in Babylon.

Great Schism The division, or split, in church leadership from 1378 to 1417 when there were two, then three, popes.

Decorative Spoon Taking as his text a contemporary proverb, "When the fox preaches, beware your geese," the artist shows, in the bowl of this spoon from the southern Netherlands, a fox dressed as a monk or friar, preaching with three dead geese in his hood, while another fox grabs one of the congregation. The preaching fox reads from a scroll bearing the word *pax* (peace), implying the perceived hypocrisy of the clergy. The object from about 1430 suggests the widespread criticism of churchmen in the later Middle Ages. (Painted enamel and gilding on silver; 17.6 cm [6-⅞ in]. Museum of Fine Arts, Boston, Helen and Alice Coburn Fund, 51.2472)

agreed with Occam. In his *Defensor Pacis* (The Defender of the Peace), Marsiglio argued against the medieval idea of a society governed by both church and state, with church supreme. Instead, Marsiglio claimed, the state was the great unifying power in society, and the church should be subordinate to it. Church leadership should rest in a general council made up of laymen as well as priests, and superior to the pope. Marsiglio was excommunicated for these radical ideas, and his work was condemned as heresy—as was Occam's—but in the later fourteenth century many thinkers agreed with these two critics of the papacy. They believed that reform of the church could best be achieved through periodic assemblies, or councils, representing all the Christian people. Those who argued this position were called **conciliarists**. Some believed a council of clergy should share power with the papacy, while others be-

conciliarists People who believed that the authority in the Roman church should rest in a general council composed of clergy, theologians, and laypeople, rather than in the pope alone.

lieved that an elected council should be supreme and should even have the power to depose popes.

The English scholar and theologian John Wyclif (WIH-klihf) (ca. 1330–1384) went further than the conciliarists in his argument against medieval church structure. Wyclif wrote that Scripture alone should be the standard of Christian belief and practice, and papal claims of secular power had no foundation in the Scriptures. He urged that the church be stripped of its property. He wanted Christians to read the Bible for themselves and produced the first complete translation of the Bible into English. Although his ideas were condemned by church leaders, they were spread by humble clerics and enjoyed great popularity in the early fifteenth century.

Wyclif's followers, called Lollards by those who ridiculed them, from a Dutch word for "mumble," spread his ideas and made many copies of his Bible. Lollard teaching allowed women to preach, and women played a significant role in the movement. Lollards were persecuted in the fifteenth century; some were executed, some recanted, and others continued to meet secretly in houses, barns, and fields to read and discuss the Bible and other religious texts in English. Historians differ in their views on how widespread their beliefs were by the time Protestant ideas came into England in the sixteenth century, for Lollard records were intentionally hidden and thus are difficult to trace; however, the Lollard emphasis on biblical literacy certainly created groups of individuals who were open to Protestant views and practices.

Students returning from study at the University of Oxford around 1400 brought Wyclif's ideas with them to Prague, the capital of what was then Bohemia and is now the Czech Republic. There another university theologian, Jan Hus (ca. 1372–1415), built on them; he also denied papal authority, called for translations of the Bible into the local Czech language, and declared indulgences—papal offers of remission of penance—useless. Hus preached in Czech, first in Prague and, when he was forced to leave the city, throughout the countryside. He gained many followers, who linked his theological ideas with their opposition to the church's wealth and power and with a growing sense of Czech nationalism in opposition to the international power of the pope. Hus's followers were successful at defeating the combined armies of the pope and the emperor many times. In the 1430s the emperor finally agreed to recognize the Hussite church in Bohemia, which later merged with other Protestant churches.

Division of any type threatened the church, and in response to continued calls throughout Europe for a council, the cardinals of Rome and Avignon summoned a council at Pisa in 1409. That gathering of prelates and theologians deposed both popes and selected another. Neither the Avignon pope nor the Roman pope would resign, however, and the appalling result was the creation of a threefold schism.

Finally, under pressure from the German emperor Sigismund (SIH-guhs-muhnd), a great council met at the imperial city of Constance (1414–1418). It had three objectives: to end the schism, to reform the church "in head and members" (from top to bottom), and to wipe out heresy. The council moved first on the last point: despite being granted a safe-conduct to go to Constance by the emperor, Jan Hus was tried, condemned, and burned at the stake as a heretic in 1415. The council also eventually healed the schism. It deposed both the Roman pope and the successor of the pope chosen at Pisa, and it isolated the Avignon antipope. A conclave elected a new leader, the Roman cardinal Colonna, who took the name Martin V (pontificate 1417–1431).

Martin proceeded to dissolve the council. Nothing was done about reform, the third objective of the council. In the later fifteenth century the papacy concentrated on Italian problems to the exclusion of universal Christian interests. But the schism and the conciliar movement had exposed the crying need for ecclesiastical reform, thus laying the foundation for the great reform efforts of the sixteenth century.

The Hussite Revolution, 1415–1436

■ Area under Hussite control

Lay Piety and Mysticism

The moral failings of the monks and parish clergy and the scandal of the Great Schism did much to weaken the spiritual mystique of the clergy in the popular mind. Thus during the fourteenth and fifteenth centuries laypeople began to develop their own forms of piety. They also exercised increasing control over parish affairs, taking responsibility for the management of parish lands and securing jurisdiction over the structure of the church building and its vestments, books, and furnishings.

Lay Christian men and women often formed **confraternities**, voluntary lay groups organized by occupation, devotional preference, neighborhood, or charitable activity. Confraternities expanded rapidly in larger cities and many villages with the growth of the mendicant orders in the thirteenth century. Some confraternities specialized in praying for souls in purgatory, either for specific individuals or for the anonymous mass of all souls. In England confraternities were generally associated with a parish and are called parish guilds, parish fraternities, or lights; by the late Middle Ages they held dances, church

> **confraternities** Voluntary lay groups organized by occupation, devotional preference, neighborhood, or charitable activity.

The Execution of Jan Hus This fifteenth-century manuscript illustration shows workers placing logs on Hus's funeral pyre at the Council of Constance, while soldiers, officials, a priest, and a cardinal look on. Hus became an important symbol of Czech independence, and in 1990 the Czech Republic declared July 6, the date of his execution in 1415, a national holiday. (University Library, Prague/Gianni Dagli Orti/The Art Archive)

festivals, and collections to raise money to clean and repair church buildings and to supply churches with candles and other liturgical objects. Like craft guilds, most confraternities were groups of men, but separate women's confraternities were formed in some towns, often to oversee the production of vestments, altar cloths, and other items made of fabric. All confraternities carried out special devotional practices such as prayers or processions, often without the leadership of a priest.

In Holland beginning in the late fourteenth century, a group of pious laypeople called the Brethren and Sisters of the Common Life lived in stark simplicity while daily carrying out the Gospel teaching of feeding the hungry, clothing the naked, and visiting the sick. The Brethren also taught in local schools with the goal of preparing devout candidates for the priesthood. They sought to make religion a personal inner experience. The spirituality of the Brethren and Sisters of the Common Life found its finest expression in the classic *The Imitation of Christ* by the Dutch monk Thomas à Kempis (1380?–1471), which gained wide appeal among laypeople. It urges Christians to take Christ as their model, seek perfection in a simple way of life, and look to the Scriptures for guidance in living a spiritual life. In the mid-fifteenth century the movement had founded houses in the Netherlands, in central Germany, and in the Rhineland.

Most of this piety centered on prayer, pious actions, and charitable giving, but for some individuals, both laypeople and clerics, religious devotion included mystical experiences. (See "Individuals in Society: Meister Eckhart," at right.) Bridget of Sweden (1303–1373) was a noblewoman who journeyed to Rome after her husband's death. She began to see visions and gave advice based on these visions to both laypeople and church officials. Because she could not speak Latin, she dictated her visions in Swedish; these were later translated and eventually published in Latin. At the end of her life Bridget made a pilgrimage to Jerusalem, where she saw visions of the Virgin Mary, who described to her exactly how she was standing "with my knees bent" when she gave birth to Jesus, and how she "showed to the shepherds the nature and male sex of the child."[10] Bridget's visions convey her deep familiarity with biblical texts taught to her through sermons or stories, as there was no Bible available in Swedish. They also provide evidence of the ways in which laypeople used their own experiences to enhance their religious understanding; Bridget's own experiences of childbirth shaped the way she viewed the birth of Jesus, and she related to the Virgin Mary in part as one mother to another.

The confraternities and mystics were generally not considered heretical unless they began to challenge the authority of the papacy the way some conciliarists and

Jacquerie A massive uprising by French peasants in 1358 protesting heavy taxation.

Wyclif and Hus did. However, the movement of lay piety did alter many people's perceptions of their own spiritual power.

Social Unrest in a Changing Society

How did economic and social tensions contribute to revolts, crime, violence, and a growing sense of ethnic and national distinctions? ■

At the beginning of the fourteenth century famine and disease profoundly affected the lives of European peoples. As the century wore on, decades of slaughter and destruction, punctuated by the decimating visits of the Black Death, added further woes. In many parts of France and the Low Countries, fields lay in ruin or untilled for lack of labor power. In England, as taxes increased, criticisms of government policy and mismanagement multiplied. Crime and new forms of business organization aggravated economic troubles, and throughout Europe the frustrations of the common people erupted into widespread revolts.

Peasant Revolts

Nobles and clergy lived on the produce of peasant labor, thinking little of adding taxes to the burden of peasant life. While peasants had endured centuries of exploitation, the difficult conditions of the fourteenth and fifteenth centuries spurred a wave of peasant revolts across Europe. Peasants were sometimes joined by their urban counterparts on the social ladder, resulting in a wider revolution of poor against rich.

The first large-scale rebellion was in Flanders in the 1320s (Map 12.3). In order to satisfy peace agreements, Flemish peasants were forced to pay taxes to the French, who claimed fiscal rights over the county of Flanders. Monasteries also pressed peasants for additional money above their customary tithes. In retaliation, peasants burned and pillaged castles and aristocratic country houses. A French army crushed peasant forces, and savage repression and the confiscation of peasant property followed in the 1330s.

In 1358, when French taxation for the Hundred Years' War fell heavily on the poor, the frustrations of the French peasantry exploded in a massive uprising called the **Jacquerie** (zhah-kuh-REE), after a mythical agricultural laborer, Jacques Bonhomme (Good Fellow). Peasants blamed the nobility for oppressive taxes, for the criminal banditry of the countryside, for losses on the battlefield, and for the general misery. Crowds swept through the countryside, slashing the throats of nobles,

INDIVIDUALS IN SOCIETY

MYSTICISM — THE DIRECT EXPERIENCE OF THE DIVINE through sudden insight or intuition — is an aspect of many world religions and has been part of Christianity throughout its history. During the late Middle Ages, however, mysticism became an important part of the piety of many laypeople, especially in the Rhineland area of Germany, rather than a rare experience of only a few. In this they were guided by the sermons of the churchman generally known as Meister Eckhart. Born into a German noble family, Eckhart (1260–1329?) joined the Dominican order and studied theology at Paris and Cologne, attaining the academic title of "master" (*Meister* in German). The leaders of the Dominican order appointed him to a series of administrative and teaching positions, and he wrote learned treatises in Latin that reflected his scholastic training and deep understanding of classical philosophy.

He also began to preach in German, attracting many listeners through his beautiful language and mystical insights. God, he said, was "an oversoaring being and an overbeing nothingness," whose essence was beyond the ability of humans to express: "if the soul is to know God, it must know Him outside time and place, since God is neither in this or that, but One and above them." Only through "unknowing," emptying oneself, could one come to experience the divine. Yet God was also present in individual human souls, and to a degree in every creature, all of which God called into being before the beginning of time. Within each soul there was what Eckhart called a "little spark," an innermost essence that allows the soul — with God's grace and Christ's redemptive action — to come to God. "Our salvation depends upon our knowing and recognizing the Chief Good which is God Himself," preached Eckhart; "the Eye with which I see God is the same Eye with which God sees me." "I have a capacity in my soul for taking in God entirely," he went on, a capacity that was shared by all humans, not simply members of the clergy or those with special spiritual gifts. Although Eckhart did not reject church sacraments or the hierarchy, he frequently stressed that union with God was best accomplished through quiet detachment and simple prayer rather than pilgrimages, extensive fasts, or other activities: "If the only prayer you said in your whole life was 'thank you,' that would suffice."*

Eckhart's unusual teachings led to charges of heresy in 1327, which Eckhart denied. The pope — who was at this point in Avignon — presided over a trial condemning him, but Eckhart appears to have died during the course of the proceedings or shortly thereafter. His writings were ordered destroyed, but many survived, and his teachings continued to be spread by his followers.

In the last few decades, Meister Eckhart's ideas have been explored and utilized by philosophers and mystics in other religious traditions, including Buddhism, Hinduism, and neo-paganism, as well as by Christians. Books of his sermons sell widely for their spiritual insights, and quotations from them — including the one above about thank-you prayers — can be found on coffee mugs, tote bags, and T-shirts.

A sixteenth-century woodcut of Meister Eckhart teaching. (Visual Connection Archive)

QUESTIONS FOR ANALYSIS

1. Why might Meister Eckhart's preaching have been viewed as threatening by the leaders of the church?
2. Given the situation of the church in the late Middle Ages, why might mysticism have been attractive to pious Christians?

Meister Eckhart's Sermons, trans. Claud Field (London: n.p., 1909).

burning their castles, raping their wives and daughters, and killing or maiming their horses and cattle. Artisans, small merchants, and parish priests joined the peasants. Urban and rural groups committed terrible destruction, and for several weeks the nobles were on the defensive. Then the upper class united to repress the revolt with merciless ferocity. Thousands of the "Jacques," innocent as well as guilty, were cut down. That forcible suppression of social rebellion, without any effort to alleviate its underlying causes, served to drive protest underground.

The 1381 **English Peasants' Revolt** involved thousands of people. Its causes were complex and varied from place to place. In general, though, the thirteenth century had witnessed the steady replacement of labor services by cash rents, and the Black Death had drastically cut the labor supply. As a result, peasants demanded higher wages and fewer manorial obligations. Their lords countered

English Peasants' Revolt
Revolt by English peasants in 1381 in response to changing economic conditions.

in 1351 with the Statute of Laborers, a law freezing wages and binding workers to their manors:

> *Whereas to curb the malice of servants who after the pestilence were idle and unwilling to serve without securing excessive wages, it was recently ordained . . . that such servants, both men and women, shall be bound to serve in return for salaries and wages that were customary . . . five or six years earlier.*[11]

This attempt to freeze wages and social mobility could not be enforced, but a huge gap remained between peasants and their lords, and the peasants sought release for their economic frustrations in revolt. Economic grievances combined with other factors. The south of England, where the revolt broke out, had been subjected to destructive French raids during the Hundred Years' War. The English government did little to protect the south, and villagers grew increasingly frightened and insecure. Moreover, decades of aristocratic violence against the

Map 12.3 Fourteenth-Century Revolts In the later Middle Ages, peasant and urban uprisings were endemic, as common as factory strikes in the industrial world. The threat of insurrection served to check unlimited exploitation.

weak peasantry had bred hostility and bitterness. Social and religious agitation by the popular preacher John Ball fanned the embers of discontent. Ball's famous couplet calling for a return to the social equality that had existed in the Garden of Eden — "When Adam delved and Eve span; / Who was then the gentleman?" — reflected real revolutionary sentiment.

The English revolt was ignited by the reimposition of a tax on all adult males. Despite widespread opposition to the tax in 1380, the royal council ordered the sheriffs to collect it again in 1381 on penalty of a huge fine. Beginning with assaults on the tax collectors, the uprising in England followed a course similar to that of the Jacquerie in France. Castles and manors were sacked. Manorial records were destroyed. Many nobles, including the archbishop of Canterbury who had ordered the collection of the tax, were murdered. The center of the revolt lay in the highly populated and economically advanced south and east, but sections of the north also witnessed rebellions (see Map 12.3).

The boy-king Richard II (r. 1377–1399) met the leaders of the revolt, agreed to charters ensuring peasants' freedom, tricked them with false promises, and then crushed the uprising with terrible ferocity. In the aftermath of the revolt, the nobility tried to restore the labor obligations of serfdom, but they were not successful, and the conversion to money rents continued. The English Peasants' Revolt did not bring social equality to England, but rural serfdom continued to decline, and it disappeared in England by 1550.

Urban Conflicts

In Flanders, France, and England, peasant revolts often blended with conflicts involving workers in cities. Unrest also occurred in Italian, Spanish, and German cities. The revolts typically flared in urban centers, where the conditions of work were changing for many people. In the thirteenth century craft guilds had organized the production of most goods, with masters, journeymen, and apprentices working side by side. In the fourteenth century a new system evolved to make products on a larger scale. Capitalist investors hired many households, with each household performing only one step of the process. Initially these investors were wealthy bankers and merchants, but eventually shop masters themselves embraced the system. This promoted a greater division within guilds between wealthier masters and the poorer masters and journeymen they hired. Some masters became so wealthy from the profits of their workers that they no longer had to work in a shop themselves, nor did their wives and family members, though they still generally belonged to the craft guild.

While capitalism provided opportunities for some artisans to become investors and entrepreneurs, especially in cloth production, for many it led to a decrease in income and status. Guilds sometimes responded to crises by opening up membership, as they did in some places immediately after the Black Death, but they more often responded to competition by limiting membership to existing guild families, which meant that journeymen who were not master's sons or who could not find a master's widow or daughter to marry could never become masters themselves. They remained journeymen their entire lives, losing their sense of solidarity with the masters of their craft. Resentment led to rebellion over economic issues.

Urban uprisings were also sparked by issues involving honor, such as employers' requiring workers to do tasks they regarded as beneath them. As their actual status and economic prospects declined and their work became basically wage labor, journeymen and poorer masters emphasized skill and honor as qualities that set them apart from less-skilled workers.

Guilds increasingly came to view the honor of their work as tied to an all-male workplace. When urban economies were expanding in the High Middle Ages, the master's wife and daughters worked alongside him, and female domestic servants also carried out productive tasks. (See "Listening to the Past: Christine de Pizan, Advice to the Wives of Artisans," page 362.) Masters' widows ran shops after the death of their husbands. But in the fourteenth century a woman's right to work slowly eroded. First, masters' widows were limited in the amount of time they could keep operating a shop or were prohibited from hiring journeymen; then female domestic servants were excluded from any productive tasks; then the number of daughters a master craftsman could employ was limited. When women were allowed to work, it was viewed as a substitute for charity.

Sex in the City

Peasant and urban revolts and riots had clear economic bases, but some historians have suggested that late medieval marital patterns may have also played a role in unrest. In northwestern Europe, people believed that couples should be economically independent before they married, so both spouses spent long periods as servants or workers in other households, saving money and learning skills, or they waited until their own parents had died and the family property was distributed.

The most unusual feature of this pattern was the late age of marriage for women. Unlike in earlier time periods and in most other parts of the world, a woman in late medieval northern and western Europe entered marriage as an adult and took charge of running a household immediately. She was thus not as dependent on her husband or mother-in-law as was a woman who married at a younger age. She had fewer pregnancies than

Christine de Pizan, Advice to the Wives of Artisans

LISTENING TO THE PAST

Christine de Pizan (1364?–1430) was the daughter and wife of highly educated men who held positions at the court of the king of France. She was widowed at twenty-five with young children and an elderly mother to support. Christine, who herself had received an excellent education, decided to support her family through writing, an unusual choice for anyone in this era and unheard of for a woman. She began to write prose works and poetry, sending them to wealthy individuals in the hope of receiving their support. Her works were well received, and Christine gained commissions to write specific works, including a biography of the French king Charles V, several histories, a long poem celebrating Joan of Arc's victory, and a book of military tactics. She became the first woman in Europe to make her living as a writer.

Among Christine's many works were several in which she considered women's nature and proper role in society, which had been a topic of debate since ancient times. The best known of these was The City of Ladies *(1404), in which she ponders why so many men have a negative view of women and provides examples of virtuous women to counter this view. A second book,* The Treasure of the City of Ladies *(1405, also called* The Book of Three Virtues*), provides moral suggestions and practical advice on behavior and household management for women of all social classes. Most of the book is directed toward princesses and court ladies (who would have been able to read it), but she also includes shorter sections for the wives of merchants and artisans, serving-women, female peasants, and even prostitutes. This is her advice to the wives of artisans, whose husbands were generally members of urban craft guilds, such as blacksmiths, bakers, or shoemakers.*

❝ All wives of artisans should be very painstaking and diligent if they wish to have the necessities of life. They should encourage their husbands or their workmen to get to work early in the morning and work until late, for mark our words, there is no trade so good that if you neglect your work you will not have difficulty putting bread on the table. And besides encouraging the others, the wife herself should be involved in the work to the extent that she knows all about it, so that she may know how to oversee his workers if her husband is ab-

sent, and to reprove them if they do not do well. She ought to oversee them to keep them from idleness, for through careless workers the master is sometimes ruined. And when customers come to her husband and try to drive a hard bargain, she ought to warn him solicitously to take care that he does not make a bad deal. She should advise him to be chary of giving too much credit if he does not know precisely where and to whom it is going, for in this way many come to poverty, although sometimes the greed to

Several manuscripts of Christine's works, such as this one, included illustrations showing her writing, which would have increased their appeal to the wealthy individuals who purchased them.

(© British Library Board, Harl. 79487, fol. 3r Det.)

earn more or to accept a tempting proposition makes them do it.

In addition, she ought to keep her husband's love as much as she can, to this end: that he will stay at home more willingly and that he may not have any reason to join the foolish crowds of other young men in taverns and indulge in unnecessary and extravagant expense, as many tradesmen do, especially in Paris. By treating him kindly she should protect him as well as she can from this. It is said that three things drive a man from his home: a quarrelsome wife, a smoking fireplace and a leaking roof. She too ought to stay at home gladly and not go every day traipsing hither and yon gossiping with the neighbours and visiting her chums to find out what everyone is doing. That is done by slovenly housewives roaming about the town in groups. Nor should she go off on these pilgrimages got up for no good reason and involving a lot of needless expense. Furthermore, she ought to remind her husband that they should live so frugally that their expenditure does not exceed their income, so that at the end of the year they do not find themselves in debt.

If she has children, she should have them instructed and taught first at school by educated people so that they may know how better to serve God. Afterwards they may be put to some trade by which they may earn a living, for whoever gives a trade or business training to her child gives a great possession. The children should be kept from wantonness and from voluptuousness above all else, for truly it is something that most shames the children of good towns and is a great sin of mothers and fathers, who ought to be the cause of the virtue and good behavior of their children, but they are sometimes the reason (because of bringing them up to be finicky and indulging them too much) for their wickedness and ruin. **〉〉**

Source: Christine de Pisan, *The Treasure of the City of Ladies*, translated with an Introduction by Sarah Lawson (Penguin Classics, 1985), pp. 167–168. This translation copyright © 1985 by Sarah Lawson. Used with permission of Penguin Group (UK). For more on Christine, see C. C. Willard, *Christine de Pisan: Her Life and Works* (1984), and S. Bell, *The Lost Tapestries of the City of Ladies: Christine de Pizan's Renaissance Legacy* (2004).

QUESTIONS FOR ANALYSIS

1. How would you describe Christine's view of the ideal artisan's wife?

2. The regulations of craft guilds often required that masters who ran workshops be married. What evidence does Christine's advice provide for why guilds would have stipulated this?

3. How are economic and moral virtues linked for Christine?

a woman who married earlier, though not necessarily fewer surviving children.

Men of all social groups were older when they married. In general, men were in their middle or late twenties at first marriage, with wealthier urban merchants often much older. Journeymen and apprentices were often explicitly prohibited from marrying, as were the students at universities, who were understood to be in "minor orders" and thus like clergy, even if they were not intending to have careers in the church.

The prohibitions on marriage for certain groups of men and the late age of marriage for most men meant that cities and villages were filled with large numbers of young adult men with no family responsibilities who often formed the core of riots and unrest. Not surprisingly, this situation also contributed to a steady market for sexual services outside of marriage, what in later centuries was termed prostitution. Research on the southern French province of Languedoc in the fourteenth and fifteenth centuries has revealed the establishment of legal houses of prostitution in many cities. Municipal authorities set up houses or red-light districts either outside the city walls or away from respectable neighborhoods. For example, authorities in Montpellier set aside Hot Street for prostitution, required public women to live there, and forbade anyone to molest them. Prostitution thus passed from being a private concern to a social matter requiring public supervision. The towns of Languedoc were not unique. Public authorities in Amiens, Dijon, Paris, Venice, Genoa, London, Florence, Rome, most of the larger German towns, and the English port of Sandwich set up brothels.

Young men associated visiting brothels with achieving manhood, though for the women themselves their activities were work. Some women had no choice, for they had been traded to the brothel manager by their parents or other people as payment for debt, or had quickly become indebted to the manager (most of whom were men) for the clothes and other finery regarded as essential to their occupation. The small amount they received from their customers did not equal what they had to pay for their upkeep in a brothel. Poor women — and men — also sold sex illegally outside of city brothels, combining this with other sorts of part-time work such as laundering or sewing. Prostitution was an urban phenomenon because only populous towns had large numbers of unmarried young men, communities of transient merchants, and a culture accustomed to a cash exchange.

Though selling sex for money was legal in the Middle Ages, the position of women who did so was always marginal. In the late fifteenth century cities began to limit brothel residents' freedom of movement and choice of clothing, requiring them to wear distinctive head coverings or bands on their clothing so that they would not be mistaken for "honorable" women. The cities also began to impose harsher penalties on women who did not

City Brothel In this rather fanciful scene of a medieval brothel, two couples share baths and wine, while a third is in bed in the back, and two nobles peer in from a window across the street. Most brothels were not this elaborate, although some did have baths. Many cities also had commercial bath houses where people paid a small fee to take a hot bath, a luxury otherwise unavailable. Bath houses did sometimes offer sex, but their main attraction was hot water. (Bibliothèque nationale de France)

live in the designated house or section of town. A few prostitutes did earn enough to donate money to charity or buy property, but most were very poor.

Along with buying sex, young men also took it by force. Unmarried women often found it difficult to avoid sexual contact. Many of them worked as domestic servants, where their employers or employers' sons or male relatives could easily coerce them, or they worked in proximity to men. Notions of female honor kept upper-class women secluded in their homes, particularly in southern and eastern Europe, but there was little attempt anywhere to protect female servants or day laborers from the risk of seduction or rape. Rape was a capital crime in many parts of Europe, but the actual sentences handed out were more likely to be fines and brief imprisonment,

with the severity of the sentence dependent on the social status of the victim and the perpetrator.

According to laws regarding rape in most parts of Europe, the victim had to prove that she had cried out and had attempted to repel the attacker, and she had to bring the charge within a short period of time after the attack had happened. Women bringing rape charges were often more interested in getting their own honorable reputations back than in punishing the perpetrators, and for this reason they sometimes asked the judge to force their rapists to marry them.

Same-sex relations—what in the late nineteenth century would be termed "homosexuality"—were another feature of medieval urban life (and of village life, though there are very few sources relating to sexual relations of any type in the rural context). Same-sex relations were of relatively little concern to church or state authorities in the early Middle Ages, but this attitude changed beginning in the late twelfth century. By 1300 most areas had defined such actions as "crimes against nature," with authorities seeing them as particularly reprehensible because they thought they did not occur anywhere else in creation. Same-sex relations, usually termed "sodomy," became a capital crime in most of Europe, with adult offenders threatened with execution by fire. The Italian cities of Venice, Florence, and Lucca created special courts to deal with sodomy, which saw thousands of investigations.

How prevalent were same-sex relations? This is difficult to answer, even in modern society, but the city of Florence provides a provocative case study. In 1432 Florence set up a special board of adult men, the Office of the Night, to "root out . . . the abominable vice of sodomy."[12] Between 1432 and the abolition of the board in 1502, about seventeen thousand men came to its attention, which, even over a seventy-year period, represents a great number in a population of about forty thousand. The men came from all classes of society, but almost all cases involved an adult man and an adolescent boy; they ranged from sex exchanged for money or gifts to long-term affectionate relationships. Florentines believed in a generational model in which

different roles were appropriate to different stages in life. In a socially and sexually hierarchical world, the boy in the passive role was identified as subordinate, dependent, and mercenary, words usually applied to women. Florentines, however, never described the dominant partner in feminine terms, for he had not compromised his masculine identity or violated a gender ideal; in fact, the adult partner might be married or have female sexual partners as well as male. Only if an adult male assumed the passive role was his masculinity jeopardized.

Thus in Florence, and no doubt elsewhere in Europe, sodomy was not a marginal practice, which may account for the fact that, despite harsh laws and special courts, actual executions for sodomy were rare. Same-sex relations often developed within the context of all-male environments, such as the army, the craft shop, and the artistic workshop, and were part of the collective male experience. Homoerotic relationships played important roles in defining stages of life, expressing distinctions of status, and shaping masculine gender identity. Same-sex relations involving women almost never came to the attention of legal authorities, so it is difficult to find out how common they were. However, female-female desire was expressed in songs, plays, and stories, as was male-male desire, offering evidence of the way people understood same-sex relations.

Same-Sex Relations This illustration, from a thirteenth-century French book of morals, interprets female and male same-sex relations as the work of devils. The illustration was painted at the time that religious and political authorities were increasingly criminalizing same-sex relations. (ONB/Vienna, Picture Archives, Cod. 2554, fol. 2r)

> **❝ Men who come there . . . should be judged on account of any crime . . . according to Polish custom if they are Poles and according to German custom if they are Germans. ❞**
>
> —**LAW ON THE POLISH FRONTIER**

Fur-Collar Crime

The Hundred Years' War had provided employment and opportunity for thousands of idle and fortune-seeking knights. But during periods of truce and after the war finally ended, many nobles once again had little to do. Inflation hurt them. Although many were living on fixed incomes, their chivalric code demanded lavish generosity and an aristocratic lifestyle. Many nobles turned to crime as a way of raising money. The fourteenth and fifteenth centuries witnessed a great deal of "fur-collar crime," so called for the miniver fur nobles alone were allowed to wear on their collars.

Groups of noble bandits roamed the English countryside, stealing from both rich and poor. Operating like modern urban racketeers, knightly gangs demanded that peasants pay "protection money" or else have their hovels burned and their fields destroyed. They seized wealthy travelers and held them for ransom. When accused of wrongdoing, fur-collar criminals intimidated witnesses, threatened jurors, and used "pull" or cash to bribe judges. As a fourteenth-century English judge wrote to a young nobleman, "For the love of your father I have hindered charges being brought against you and have prevented execution of indictment actually made."[13] Criminal activity by nobles continued decade after decade because governments were too weak to stop it.

The ballads of Robin Hood, a collection of folk legends from late medieval England, describe the adventures of the outlaw hero and his merry men as they avenge the common people against fur-collar criminals—grasping landlords, wicked sheriffs, and mercenary churchmen. Robin Hood was a popular figure because he symbolized the deep resentment of aristocratic corruption and abuse; he represented the struggle against tyranny and oppression.

Ethnic Tensions and Restrictions

Large numbers of people in the twelfth and thirteenth centuries migrated from one part of Europe to another in search of food, work, and peace: the English into Scotland and Ireland; Germans, French, and Flemings into Poland, Bohemia, and Hungary; the French into Spain. The colonization of frontier regions meant that peoples of different ethnic backgrounds lived side by side. Everywhere in Europe, towns recruited people from the countryside (see Chapter 11). In frontier regions, townspeople were usually long-distance immigrants and, in eastern Europe, Ireland, and Scotland, ethnically different from the surrounding rural population. In eastern Europe, German was the language of the towns; in Irish towns, French, the tongue of Norman or English settlers, predominated.

In the early periods of conquest and colonization, and in all regions with extensive migrations, a legal dualism existed: native peoples remained subject to their traditional laws; newcomers brought and were subject to the laws of the countries from which they came. On the Prussian and Polish frontier, for example, the law was that "men who come there . . . should be judged on account of any crime or contract engaged in there according to Polish custom if they are Poles and according to German custom if they are Germans."[14] Likewise, the conquered Muslim subjects of Christian kings in Spain had the right to be judged under Muslim law by Muslim judges.

The great exception to this broad pattern of legal pluralism was Ireland. From the start, the English practiced an extreme form of discrimination toward the native Irish. The English distinguished between the free and the unfree, and the entire Irish population, simply by the fact of Irish birth, was unfree. When English legal structures were established beginning in 1210, the Irish were denied access to the common-law courts. In civil (property) disputes, an English defendant need not respond to his Irish plaintiff; no Irish person could make a will. In criminal procedures, the murder of an Irishman was not considered a felony. This emphasis on blood descent provoked bitterness.

Other than in Ireland, although native peoples commonly held humbler positions, both immigrant and native townspeople prospered during the expanding economy of the thirteenth century. But with the economic turmoil of the fourteenth century, ethnic tensions multiplied.

The later Middle Ages witnessed a movement away from legal pluralism or dualism and toward legal homogeneity and an emphasis on blood descent. The dominant ethnic group in an area tried to bar others from positions of church leadership and guild membership. Marriage laws were instituted that attempted to maintain ethnic purity by prohibiting intermarriage, and some church leaders actively promoted ethnic discrimination. As Germans moved eastward, for example, German bishops refused to appoint non-Germans to any church office, while Czech bishops closed monasteries to Germans.

The most extensive attempt to prevent intermarriage and protect ethnic purity is embodied in Ireland's **Statute of Kilkenny** (1366), which states that "there were to be no marriages between those of immigrant and native stock; that the English inhabitants of Ireland must employ the English language and bear English names; that they must ride in the English way [that is, with saddles] and have English apparel; that no Irishmen were to be granted ecclesiastical benefices or admitted to monasteries in the English parts of Ireland."[15]

Late medieval chroniclers used words such as *gens* (race or clan) and *natio* (NAH-tee-oh; species, stock, or kind) to refer to different groups. They held that peoples differed according to language, traditions, customs, and laws. None of these were unchangeable, however, and commentators increasingly also described ethnic differences in terms of "blood" — "German blood," "English blood," and so on — which made ethnicity heritable. Religious beliefs also came to be conceptualized as blood, with people regarded as having Jewish blood, Muslim blood, or Christian blood. The most dramatic expression of this was in Spain, where "purity of blood" — having no Muslim or Jewish ancestors — became an obsession. Blood was also used as a way to talk about social differences, especially for nobles. Just as Irish and English were prohibited from marrying each other, those of "noble blood" were prohibited from marrying

commoners in many parts of Europe. As Europeans increasingly came into contact with people from Africa and Asia, and particularly as they developed colonial empires, these notions of blood also became a way of conceptualizing racial categories.

Literacy and Vernacular Literature

The development of ethnic identities had many negative consequences, but a more positive effect was the increasing use of the vernacular, that is, the local language that people actually spoke, rather than Latin. Two masterpieces of European culture, Dante's *Divine Comedy* (1310–1320) and Chaucer's *Canterbury Tales* (1387–1400), illustrate a sophisticated use of the rhythms and rhymes of the vernacular.

Statute of Kilkenny
Laws issued in 1366 that discriminated against the Irish, forbidding marriage between the English and the Irish, requiring the use of the English language, and denying the Irish access to ecclesiastical offices.

Chaucer's Wife of Bath Chaucer's *Canterbury Tales* were filled with memorable characters, including the often-married Wife of Bath, shown here in a fifteenth-century manuscript. In the prologue that details her life, she denies the value of virginity and criticizes her young and handsome fifth husband for reading a book about "wicked wives." "By God, if women had but written stories . . . ," she comments, "They would have written of men more wickedness, Than all the race of Adam could redress." (British Library/HIP/ Art Resource, NY)

und meidin noch den fronuaften wie gewonheit ift · 1 5 1 6 ·

School Signboard Ambrosius Holbein, elder brother of the artist Hans Holbein, produced this signboard for the Swiss educator Myconius. It is an excellent example of what we would call commercial art — art used to advertise, in this case Myconius's profession. The German script above promised that all who enrolled, girls and boys, would learn to read and write. Most schools were for boys only, but a few offered instruction for girls as well. (Kunstmuseum Basel/Martin Buhler, photographer)

Dante Alighieri (DAHN-tay ah-luh-GYER-ee) (1265–1321) called his work a "comedy" because he wrote it in Italian and in a different style from the "tragic" Latin; a later generation added the adjective *divine*, referring both to its sacred subject and to Dante's artistry. The *Divine Comedy* is an epic poem of one hundred cantos (verses), each of whose three equal parts (1 + 33 + 33 + 33) describes one of the realms of the next world: Hell, Purgatory, and Paradise. The Roman poet Virgil, representing reason, leads Dante through Hell, where Dante observes the torments of the damned and denounces the disorders of his own time, especially ecclesiastical ambition and corruption. Passing up into Purgatory, Virgil shows the poet how souls are purified of their disordered inclinations. From Purgatory, Beatrice, a woman Dante once loved and the symbol of divine revelation in the poem, leads him to Paradise. In Paradise, home of the angels and saints, Saint Bernard — representing mystic contemplation — leads Dante to the Virgin Mary. Through her intercession, he at last attains a vision of God.

The *Divine Comedy* portrays contemporary and historical figures, comments on secular and ecclesiastical affairs, and draws on the Scholastic philosophy of uniting faith and reason. Within the framework of a symbolic pilgrimage to the City of God, the *Divine*

Comedy embodies the psychological tensions of the age. A profoundly Christian poem, it also contains bitter criticism of some church authorities. In its symmetrical structure and use of figures from the ancient world such as Virgil, the poem perpetuates the classical tradition, but as the first major work of literature in the Italian vernacular, it is distinctly modern.

Geoffrey Chaucer (CHAW-suhr) (1342–1400) was an official in the administrations of the English kings Edward III and Richard II and wrote poetry as an avocation. Chaucer's *Canterbury Tales* is a collection of stories in lengthy rhymed narrative. On a pilgrimage to the shrine of Saint Thomas Becket at Canterbury (see Chapter 9), thirty people of various social backgrounds tell tales. For example, the gross Miller tells a vulgar story about a deceived husband; the earthy Wife of Bath, who has buried five husbands, sketches a fable about the selection of a spouse; and the elegant Prioress, who violates her vows by wearing jewelry, delivers a homily on the Virgin. In depicting the interests and behavior of all types of people, Chaucer presents a rich panorama of English social life in the fourteenth century. Like the *Divine Comedy*, the *Canterbury Tales* reflects the cultural tensions of the times. Ostensibly Christian, many of the pilgrims are also materialistic, sensual, and worldly, suggesting the ambivalence of the broader society's concern for the next world and frank enjoyment of this one.

Beginning in the fourteenth century, a variety of evidence attests to the increasing literacy of laypeople. Wills and inventories reveal that many people, not just nobles, possessed books—mainly devotional, but also romances, manuals on manners and etiquette, histories, and sometimes legal and philosophical texts. In England the number of schools in the diocese of York quadrupled between 1350 and 1500. Information from Flemish and German towns is similar: children were sent to schools and were taught the fundamentals of reading, writing, and arithmetic. Laymen increasingly served as managers or stewards of estates and as clerks to guilds and town governments; such positions obviously required the ability to keep administrative and financial records.

The penetration of laymen into the higher positions of governmental administration, long the preserve of clerics, also illustrates rising lay literacy. With growing frequency, the upper classes sent their daughters to convent schools, where, in addition to instruction in singing, religion, needlework, deportment, and household management, girls gained the rudiments of reading and sometimes writing.

The spread of literacy represents a response to the needs of an increasingly complex society. Trade, commerce, and expanding government bureaucracies required more and more literate people. Late medieval culture remained an oral culture in which most people received information by word of mouth. But by the fifteenth century the evolution toward a more literate culture was already perceptible, and craftsmen would develop the new technology of the printing press in response to the increased demand for reading materials.

LOOKING BACK LOOKING AHEAD

THE FOURTEENTH AND EARLY fifteenth centuries were certainly times of crisis in western Europe, meriting the label "calamitous" given to them by one prominent historian. Famine, disease, and war decimated the European population, and traditional institutions, including secular governments and the church, did little or nothing or, in some cases, made things worse. Trading connections that had been reinvigorated in the High Middle Ages spread the most deadly epidemic ever experienced through western Asia, North Africa, and almost all of Europe. No wonder survivors experienced a sort of shell shock and a fascination with death.

The plague did not destroy the prosperity of the medieval population, however, and it may in fact have indirectly improved the European economy. Wealthy merchants had plenty of money to spend on luxuries and talent. In the century after the plague, Italian artists began to create new styles of painting, writers new literary forms, educators new types of schools, and philosophers new ideas about the purpose of human life. These cultural changes eventually spread to the rest of Europe, following the same paths that the plague had traveled.

CHAPTER REVIEW

■ **What were the demographic, economic, and social, consequences of climate change? (p. 340)**

Colder climate and bad weather brought poor harvests, which contributed to widespread famine and disease. People abandoned homesteads, and the number of vagabonds and criminals increased. Political leaders attempted to find solutions but were unable to deal with the economic and social problems that resulted.

■ **How did the spread of the plague shape European society? (p. 341)**

In 1348 a new disease, most likely the bubonic plague, came to mainland Europe, carried from the Black Sea by ships. It spread quickly by land and sea and within two years may have killed as much as one-third of the European population. Medical explanations at the time linked the plague to poisoned air or water, and treatments were ineffective. Many people regarded the plague as a divine punishment and sought remedies in religious practices such as prayer, pilgrimages, or donations to churches. Art and literature showed an obsession with death. Population losses caused by the Black Death led to inflation but in the long run may have contributed to more opportunities for the peasants and urban workers who survived the disease.

■ **What were the causes of the Hundred Years' War, and how did the war affect European politics, economics, and cultural life? (p. 348)**

The Hundred Years' War, which was fought intermittently in France from 1337 to 1453, began as a dispute over the succession to the French crown, though economic factors also helped justify the war. Royal propaganda on both sides fostered a kind of early nationalism, and Joan of Arc became a powerful symbol in France. The war also served as a catalyst for the development of Parliament in England. While many people made fortunes during the war, most of this wealth was squandered. Both the French and English economies were devastated by the war, and the resulting taxation led to widespread discontent and peasant revolts.

■ **What challenges faced the Christian church in the fourteenth century, and how did church leaders, intellectuals, and ordinary people respond? (p. 354)**

Religious beliefs offered people solace through the difficult times of the later Middle Ages, but the Western Christian church was going through a particularly difficult period in the fourteenth and early fifteenth centuries. The papacy was pressured to move to Avignon in France, where it was dominated by the French monarchy. This eventually led some cardinals to elect a second, Roman, pope, a division in the church called the Great Schism. The Avignon papacy and the Great Schism weakened the prestige of the church and people's faith in papal authority. The conciliar movement, by denying the church's universal sovereignty, strengthened the claims of secular governments to jurisdiction over all their peoples. As members of the clergy challenged the power of the pope, laypeople challenged the authority of the church itself. Women and men increasingly relied on direct approaches to God, often through mystical encounters, rather than on the institutional church. Some, including John Wyclif and Jan Hus, questioned basic church doctrines.

■ **How did economic and social tensions contribute to revolts, crime, violence, and a growing sense of ethnic and national distinctions? (p. 358)**

The plague and the war both led to higher taxes and economic dislocations, which sparked peasant revolts in Flanders, France, and England. Peasant revolts often blended with conflicts involving workers in cities, where working conditions were changing, widening the gap between wealthy merchant-producers and poor workers. Unrest in the countryside and cities may have been further exacerbated by marriage patterns that left large numbers of young men unmarried and rootless. The pattern of late marriage for men contributed to a growth in prostitution. Along with peasant revolts and urban crime and unrest, violence perpetrated by nobles was a common part of late medieval life. The economic and demographic crises of the fourteenth century also contributed to increasing ethnic tensions in the many parts of Europe where migration had brought different population groups together. A growing sense of ethnic and national identity led to restrictions and occasionally to violence, but also to the increasing use of vernacular languages for works of literature. The increasing number of schools that led to the growth of lay literacy represents another positive achievement of the later Middle Ages.

Suggested Reading

Allmand, Christopher. *The Hundred Years War: England and France at War, ca 1300–1450*, rev. ed. 2005. Designed for students; examines the war from political, military, social, and economic perspectives and compares the way England and France reacted to the conflict.

Boswell, John. *Christianity, Social Tolerance, and Homosexuality: Gay People in Western Europe from the Beginning of the Christian Era to the Fourteenth Century*. 1981. Remains an important broad analysis of attitudes toward same-sex relations throughout the Middle Ages.

Dunn, Alastair. *The Peasants' Revolt: England's Failed Revolution of 1381*. 2004. Offers new interpretations of the causes and consequences of the English Peasants' Revolt.

Dyer, Christopher. *Standards of Living in the Later Middle Ages*. 1989. Examines economic realities and social conditions more generally.

Herlihy, David. *The Black Death and the Transformation of the West*, 2d ed. 1997. A fine treatment of the causes and cultural consequences of the disease that remains the best starting point for study of the great epidemic.

Holt, James Clarke. *Robin Hood*. 1982. A soundly researched and highly readable study of the famous outlaw.

Jordan, William Chester. *The Great Famine: Northern Europe in the Early Fourteenth Century*. 1996. Discusses catastrophic weather, soil exhaustion, and other factors that led to the Great Famine and the impact of the famine on community life.

Karras, Ruth M. *Sexuality in Medieval Europe: Doing unto Others*. 2005. A brief overview designed for undergraduates that incorporates the newest scholarship.

Kieckhefer, Richard. *Unquiet Souls: Fourteenth-Century Saints and Their Religious Milieu*. 1984. Sets the ideas of the mystics in their social and intellectual contexts.

Koch, H. W. *Medieval Warfare*. 1978. A beautifully illustrated book covering strategy, tactics, armaments, and costumes of war.

Lehfeldt, Elizabeth, ed. *The Black Death*. 2005. Includes excerpts from debates about many aspects of the Black Death.

Oakley, Frances. *The Western Church in the Later Middle Ages*. 1979. An excellent broad survey.

Robertson, D. W., Jr. *Chaucer's London*. 1968. Evokes the social setting of *Canterbury Tales* brilliantly.

Swanson, R. N. *Religion and Devotion in Europe, c. 1215–c. 1515*. 2004. Explores many aspects of spirituality.

Tuchman, Barbara. *A Distant Mirror: The Calamitous Fourteenth Century*. 1978. Written for a general audience, it remains a vivid description of this tumultuous time.

Notes

1. Christos S. Bartsocas, "Two Fourteenth Century Descriptions of the 'Black Death,'" *Journal of the History of Medicine*, October 1966, p. 395.
2. Giovanni Boccaccio, *The Decameron*, trans. Mark Musa and Peter Bondanella (New York: W.W. Norton, 1982), p. 7.
3. Ibid., p. 9.
4. Bartsocas, "Two Fourteenth Century Descriptions," p. 397.
5. Florence Warren, ed., *The Dance of Death* (Oxford: Early English Text Society, 1931), p. 8. Spelling modernized.
6. Quoted in J. Barnie, *War in Medieval English Society: Social Values and the Hundred Years' War* (Ithaca, N.Y.: Cornell University Press, 1974), p. 34.
7. W. P. Barrett, trans., *The Trial of Jeanne d'Arc* (London: George Routledge, 1931), pp. 165–166.
8. Quoted in Barnie, *War in Medieval English Society*, pp. 36–37.
9. Quoted in J. H. Smith, *The Great Schism, 1378: The Disintegration of the Medieval Papacy* (New York: Weybright & Talley, 1970), p. 15.
10. Quoted in Katharina M. Wilson, ed., *Medieval Women Writers* (Athens: University of Georgia Press, 1984), p. 245.
11. C. Stephenson and G. Marcham, eds., *Sources of English Constitutional History*, rev. ed. (New York: Harper & Row, 1972), p. 225.
12. Michael Rocke, *Forbidden Friendships: Homosexuality and Male Culture in Renaissance Florence* (New York: Oxford University Press, 1996), p. 45.
13. Quoted in Barbara A. Hanawalt, "Fur Collar Crime: The Pattern of Crime Among the Fourteenth-Century English Nobility," *Journal of Social History* 8 (Spring 1975): 7.
14. Quoted in R. Bartlett, *The Making of Europe: Conquest, Colonization and Cultural Change, 950–1350* (Princeton, N.J.: Princeton University Press, 1993), p. 205.
15. Quoted ibid., p. 239.

Key Terms

Great Famine (p. 340)
Black Death (p. 341)
flagellants (p. 347)
Agincourt (p. 350)
representative assemblies (p. 354)
Babylonian Captivity (p. 355)
Great Schism (p. 355)
conciliarists (p. 356)
confraternities (p. 357)
Jacquerie (p. 358)
English Peasants' Revolt (p. 360)
Statute of Kilkenny (p. 367)

For practice quizzes and other study tools, visit the Online Study Guide at **bedfordstmartins.com/mckaywest**.

For primary sources from this period, see **Sources of Western Society, Second Edition**.

For Web sites, images, and documents related to topics in this chapter, visit Make History at **bedfordstmartins.com/mckaywest**.

13
European Society in the Age of the Renaissance

1350–1550

While war gripped northern Europe, a new culture emerged in southern Europe. The fourteenth century witnessed remarkable changes in Italian intellectual, artistic, and cultural life. Artists and writers thought that they were living in a new golden age, but not until the sixteenth century was this change given the label we use today — the *Renaissance*, derived from the French word for "rebirth." That word was first used by art historian Giorgio Vasari (1511–1574) to describe the art of "rare men of genius" such as his contemporary Michelangelo. Through their works, Vasari judged, the glory of the classical past had been reborn after centuries of darkness. Over time, the word's meaning was broadened to include many aspects of life during that period. The new attitude had a slow diffusion out of Italy, so that the Renaissance "happened" at different times in different parts of Europe.

Later scholars increasingly saw the cultural and political changes of the Renaissance, along with the religious changes of the Reformation (see Chapter 14) and the European voyages of exploration (see Chapter 15), as ushering in the "modern" world. Some historians view the Renaissance as a bridge between the medieval and modern eras because it corresponded chronologically with the late medieval period and because there were many continuities along with the changes. Others have questioned whether the word *Renaissance* should be used at all to describe an era in which many social groups saw decline rather than advance. The debates remind us that these labels — medieval, Renaissance, modern — are intellectual constructs devised after the fact, and all contain value judgments. ∎

Life in the Renaissance. In this detail from a fresco, Italian painter Lorenzo Lotto captures the mixing of social groups in a Renaissance Italian city. Wealthy merchants, soldiers, and boys intermingle, while at the right women sell vegetables and bread, a common sight at any city marketplace.

CHAPTER PREVIEW

Wealth and Power in Renaissance Italy
■ What economic and political developments in Italy provided the setting for the Renaissance?

Intellectual Change
■ What were the key ideas of the Renaissance, and how were they different for men and women and for southern and northern Europeans?

Art and the Artist
■ How did changes in art reflect new Renaissance ideals?

Social Hierarchies
■ What were the key social hierarchies in Renaissance Europe, and how did ideas about hierarchy shape people's lives?

Politics and the State in Western Europe, ca. 1450–1521
■ How did the nation-states of western Europe evolve in this period?

Wealth and Power in Renaissance Italy

What economic and political developments in Italy provided the setting for the Renaissance? ▪

The magnificent art and new ways of thinking in the **Renaissance** rest on economic and political developments in the city-states of northern Italy. Economic growth laid the material basis for the Italian Renaissance, and ambitious merchants gained political power to match their economic power. They then used their money and power to buy luxuries and hire talent in a system of **patronage**, through which cities, groups, and individuals commissioned writers and artists to produce specific works. Political leaders in Italian cities admired the traditions and power of ancient Rome, and this esteem shaped their commissions. Thus, economics, politics, and culture were interconnected.

Renaissance A French word meaning "rebirth," first used by art historian and critic Giorgio Vasari to refer to the rebirth of the culture of classical antiquity.

patronage Financial support of writers and artists by cities, groups, and individuals, often to produce specific works or works in specific styles.

Trade and Prosperity

Northern Italian cities led the way in the great commercial revival of the eleventh century. By the middle of the twelfth century Venice, supported by a huge merchant marine, had grown enormously rich through overseas trade, as had Genoa and Milan. These cities made important strides in shipbuilding that allowed their ships to sail all year long at accelerated speeds and carrying ever more merchandise.

Another commercial leader, and the city where the Renaissance began, was Florence, situated on the fertile soil along the Arno River. Julius Caesar founded the city in the first century B.C.E. as a home for army veterans, rewarding them with land after their long years of service in the Roman army. The veterans worked hard, as did the settlers who came after them, and the city flourished. Its favorable location on the main road northward from Rome made Florence a commercial hub, and the city grew wealthy buying and selling all types of goods throughout Europe and the Mediterranean — grain, cloth, wool, weapons, armor, spices, glass, and wine.

Florentine merchants also loaned and invested money, and they acquired control of papal banking toward the end of the thirteenth century. Florentine mercantile

A Florentine Bank Scene Originally a "bank" was just a counter; moneychangers who sat behind the counter became "bankers," exchanging different currencies and holding deposits for merchants and business people. In this scene from fifteenth-century Florence, the bank is covered with an imported Ottoman geometric rug, one of many imported luxury items handled by Florentine merchants. Most cities issued their own coins, but the gold coins of Florence, known as "florins" (left), were accepted throughout Europe as a standard currency. (bank scene: Prato, San Francesco/Scala/Art Resource, NY; coins: Scala/Art Resource, NY)

families began to dominate European banking on both sides of the Alps, setting up offices in major European and North African cities. The profits from loans, investments, and money exchanges that poured back to Florence were pumped into urban industries, and by the early fourteenth century the city had about eighty thousand people, about twice the population of London at that time. Profits contributed to the city's economic vitality and allowed banking families to control the city's politics and culture.

By the first quarter of the fourteenth century, the economic foundations of Florence were so strong that even severe crises could not destroy the city. In 1344 King Edward III of England repudiated his huge debts to Florentine bankers, forcing some of them into bankruptcy. Florence suffered frightfully from the Black Death, losing at least half its population, and serious labor unrest shook the political establishment (see Chapter 12). Nevertheless, the basic Florentine economic structure remained stable. The Florentine merchant and historian Benedetto Dei (DAY-ee) boasted proudly of his city in a letter to an acquaintance from Venice:

> *Our beautiful Florence contains within the city in this present year two hundred seventy shops belonging to the wool merchants' guild . . . eighty-three rich and splendid warehouses of the silk merchants' guild. . . . The number of banks amounts to thirty-three; the shops of the cabinet-makers, whose business is carving and inlaid work, to eighty-four . . . there are forty-four goldsmiths' and jewelers shops.*[1]

In Florence and other cities, wealth allowed many people greater material pleasures, a more comfortable life, and leisure time to appreciate and patronize the arts. Merchants and bankers commissioned public and private buildings from architects, and hired sculptors and painters to decorate their homes and churches. The rich, social-climbing residents of Venice, Florence, Genoa, and Rome came to see life more as an opportunity to be enjoyed than as a painful pilgrimage to the City of God.

Communes and Republics of Northern Italy

The northern Italian cities were **communes**, sworn associations of free men who, like other town residents, began in the twelfth century to seek political and economic independence from local nobles. The merchant guilds that formed the communes built and maintained

Chronology

ca. 1350	Petrarch develops ideas of humanism
1434–1737	Medici family in power in Florence
1440s	Invention of movable metal type
1447–1514	Sforza family in power in Milan
1455–1471	Wars of the Roses in England
1469	Marriage of Isabella of Castile and Ferdinand of Aragon
1477	Louis XI conquers Burgundy
1478	Establishment of the Inquisition in Spain
1492	Spain conquers Granada, ending reconquista; practicing Jews expelled from Spain
1494	Invasion of Italy by Charles VIII of France
1508–1512	Michelangelo paints ceiling of Sistine Chapel
1513	Machiavelli, *The Prince*
1563	Establishment of first formal academy for artistic training in Florence

the city walls, regulated trade, collected taxes, and kept civil order. The local nobles frequently moved into the cities, marrying into rich commercial families and starting their own businesses. This merger of the northern Italian feudal nobility and the commercial elite created a powerful oligarchy, a small group that ruled the city and surrounding countryside. Yet because of rivalries among different powerful families within the ruling oligarchy, Italian communes were often politically unstable.

Unrest coming from below exacerbated the instability. Merchant elites made citizenship in the communes dependent on a property qualification, years of residence within the city, and social connections. Only a tiny percentage of the male population possessed these qualifications and thus could hold office in a commune's political councils. The common people, called the **popolo**, were disenfranchised and heavily taxed, and they bitterly resented their exclusion from power. Throughout most of the thirteenth century, in city after city, the popolo used armed force and violence to take over the city governments. Republican governments—in which political power theoretically resides in the people and is exercised by their chosen representatives—were established in Bologna, Siena, Parma, Florence, Genoa, and other cities. The victory of the popolo proved temporary, however, because they could not establish civil order within their cities. Merchant oligarchies reasserted their power and

communes Sworn associations of free men in Italian cities led by merchant guilds that sought political and economic independence from local nobles.

popolo Disenfranchised common people in Italian cities who resented their exclusion from power.

Battle of San Romano Fascinated by perspective—the representation of spatial depth or distance on a flat surface—the Florentine artist Paolo Uccello (1397–1475) celebrated the 1432 Florentine victory over Siena in this painting. Though a minor battle, it started Florence on the road to domination over smaller nearby states. The painting hung in Lorenzo de' Medici's bedroom. (National Gallery, London/Erich Lessing/Art Resource, NY)

sometimes brought in powerful military leaders to establish order. These military leaders, called *condottieri* (kahn-duh-TYER-ee) (singular, *condottiero*), had their own mercenary armies, and in many cities they took over political power as well.

Many cities in Italy became **signori** (seen-YOHR-ee), in which one man ruled and handed down the right to rule to his son. Some signori (the word is plural in Italian and is used for both persons and forms of government) kept the institutions of communal government in place, but these had no actual power. Oligarchic regimes possessed constitutions and often boasted about how much more democratic their form of government was than the government in neighboring signori. In actuality, there wasn't much difference. Oligarchies maintained a façade of republican government, but the judicial, executive, and legislative functions of government were restricted to a small class of wealthy merchants.

In the fifteenth and sixteenth centuries the signori in many cities and the most powerful merchant oligarchs in others transformed their households into **courts**. Courtly culture afforded signori and oligarchs the opportunity to display and assert their wealth and power. They built magnificent palaces in the centers of cities and required all political business to be done there. The rulers of Florence, Milan, and other northern Italian cities became patrons of the arts, hiring architects to design and build private palaces and public city halls, artists to fill them with paintings and sculptures, and musicians and composers to fill them with music. They supported writers and philosophers, flaunting their patronage of learning and the arts. Ceremonies connected with family births, baptisms, marriages, and funerals offered occasions for magnificent pageantry and elaborate ritual. Cities welcomed rulers who were visiting with magnificent entrance parades that often included fireworks, colorful banners, mock naval battles, decorated wagons filled with people in costume, and temporary triumphal arches modeled on those of ancient Rome. Rulers of nation-states later copied and adapted all these aspects of Italian courts.

City-States and the Balance of Power

Renaissance Italians had a passionate attachment to their individual city-states: political loyalty and feeling centered on the local city. This intensity of local feeling perpetuated the dozens of small states and hindered the development of one unified state.

In the fifteenth century five powers dominated the Italian peninsula: Venice, Milan, Florence, the Papal States, and the kingdom of Naples (Map 13.1). Venice,

signori Government by one-man rule in Italian cities such as Milan.

courts Magnificent households and palaces where signori and other rulers lived, conducted business, and supported the arts.

with its enormous trade empire, ranked as an international power. Though Venice was a republic in name, an oligarchy of merchant-aristocrats actually ran the city. Milan was also called a republic, but the condottieri-turned-signori of the Sforza (SFORT-sah) family ruled harshly and dominated Milan and several smaller cities in the north from 1447 to 1535. Likewise, in Florence the form of government was republican, with authority vested in several councils of state. In reality, starting in 1434 the great Medici (MEH-duh-chee) banking family held power almost continually for centuries. Though not public officials, Cosimo (1434–1464) and Lorenzo (1469–1492) ruled from behind the scenes, and in the sixteenth century their descendants became the hereditary rulers of Florence and the surrounding area as the Grand Dukes of Tuscany, ruling until 1737. The Medici family produced three popes, and most other Renaissance popes were also members of powerful Italian families, selected for their political skills, not their piety. Pope Alexander VI (pontificate 1492–1503) was the

most ruthless; aided militarily and politically by his illegitimate son Cesare Borgia, he reasserted papal authority in the papal lands. South of the Papal States, the kingdom of Naples was under the control of the king of Aragon.

The major Italian city-states controlled the smaller ones, such as Siena, Mantua, Ferrara, and Modena, and competed furiously among themselves for territory. The large cities used diplomacy, spies, paid informers, and any other available means to get information that could be used to advance their ambitions. While the states of northern Europe were moving toward centralization and consolidation, the world of Italian politics resembled a jungle where the powerful dominated the weak.

In one significant respect, however, the Italian city-states anticipated future relations among competing European states after 1500. Whenever one Italian state appeared to gain a predominant position within the peninsula, other states combined to establish a balance of power against the major threat. In the formation of these

Map 13.1 The Italian City-States, ca. 1494 In the fifteenth century the Italian city-states represented great wealth and cultural sophistication, though their many political divisions throughout the peninsula invited foreign intervention.

alliances, Renaissance Italians invented the machinery of modern diplomacy: permanent embassies with resident ambassadors in capitals where political relations and commercial ties needed continual monitoring. The resident ambassador was one of the great political achievements of the Italian Renaissance.

At the end of the fifteenth century Venice, Florence, Milan, and the papacy possessed great wealth and represented high cultural achievement. Wealthy and divided, however, they were also an inviting target for invasion. When Florence and Naples entered into an agreement to acquire Milanese territories, Milan called on France for support, and the French king Charles VIII (r. 1483–1498) invaded Italy in 1494.

In Florence, the French invasion was interpreted as the fulfillment of a prophecy by the Dominican friar Girolamo Savonarola (1452–1498). In a number of fiery sermons attended by large crowds, Savonarola had predicted that God would punish Italy for its moral vice and corrupt leadership. The Medici dynasty that ruled Florence fell after the French invasion, and Savonarola became the political and religious leader of the city. He reorganized the government and called on people to destroy anything that might lead them to sin: fancy clothing, cosmetics, pagan books, musical instruments, paintings, or poetry that celebrated human beauty. These were gathered together and burned on the main square of Florence in what became known as "bonfires of the vanities."

For a time Savonarola was wildly popular, but eventually people tired of his moral denunciations, and he was excommunicated by the pope, tortured, and burned at the very spot where he had overseen the bonfires. The Medici returned as the rulers of Florence. Savonarola's story has fascinated novelists and playwrights, but in the political history of Renaissance Italy he best serves as a reminder of the internal instability of Italian cities, an instability that invited foreign invasion.

The French invasion inaugurated a new period in Italian and European power politics. Italy became the focus of international ambitions and the battleground of foreign armies, particularly those of France and the Holy Roman Empire in a series of conflicts called the Habsburg-Valois wars (named for the German and French dynasties). The Italian cities suffered severely from continual warfare, especially in the frightful sack of Rome in 1527 by imperial forces under the emperor Charles V. Thus the failure of the city-states to form a federal system, to consolidate, or at least to establish a common foreign policy led to centuries of subjection by outside invaders. Italy was not to achieve unification until 1870.

humanism A program of study designed by Italians that emphasized the critical study of Latin and Greek literature with the goal of understanding human nature.

Intellectual Change

What were the key ideas of the Renaissance, and how were they different for men and women and for southern and northern Europeans? ■

The Renaissance was characterized by self-conscious awareness among educated Italians that they were living in a new era. Somewhat ironically, this idea rested on a deep interest in ancient Latin and Greek literature and philosophy. Through reflecting on the classics, Renaissance thinkers developed new notions of human nature, new plans for education, and new concepts of political rule. The advent of the printing press with movable type would greatly accelerate the spread of their ideas throughout Europe.

Humanism

Giorgio Vasari was the first to use the word *Renaissance* in print, but he was not the first to feel that something was being reborn. Two centuries earlier the Florentine poet and scholar Francesco Petrarch (1304–1374) spent long hours searching for classical Latin manuscripts in dusty monastery libraries and wandering around the many ruins of the Roman Empire remaining in Italy. He became obsessed with the classical past and felt that the writers and artists of ancient Rome had reached a level of perfection in their work that had never since been duplicated. Writers of his own day should follow these ancient models, thought Petrarch, and should ignore the thousand-year period between his own time and that of Rome, which he called the "dark ages" ushered in by the barbarian invasions. Petrarch believed that the recovery of classical texts would bring about a new golden age of intellectual achievement, an idea that many others came to share.

Petrarch clearly thought he was witnessing the dawning of a new era in which writers and artists would recapture the glory of the Roman republic. Around 1350 he proposed a new kind of education to help them do this, in which young men would study the works of ancient Latin and Greek authors, using them as models of how to write clearly, argue effectively, and speak persuasively. The study of Latin classics became known as the *studia humanitates* (STOO-dee-uh oo-mahn-ee-TAH-tayz), usually translated as "liberal studies" or the "liberal arts." People who advocated it were known as *humanists* and their program as **humanism**. Like all programs of study, humanism contained an implicit philosophy: that human nature and achievements, evident in the classics, were worthy of contemplation.

The glory of Rome had been brightest, in the opinion of the humanists, in the works of the Roman author and statesman Cicero (106 B.C.E.–43 B.C.E.). Cicero had lived during the turbulent era when Julius Caesar and other powerful generals transformed the Roman republic into an empire (see Chapter 5). In forceful and elegantly worded speeches, letters, and treatises, Cicero supported a return to republican government. Petrarch and other humanists admired Cicero's use of language, literary style, and political ideas. Many humanists saw Caesar's transformation of Rome as a betrayal of the great society, marking the beginning of a long period of decay that the barbarian migrations had simply sped up. In his history of Florence written in 1436, the humanist historian and Florentine city official Leonardo Bruni (1374–1444) closely linked the decline of the Latin language after the death of Cicero and the decline of the Roman republic: "After the liberty of the Roman people had been lost through the rule of the emperors . . . the flourishing condition of studies and of letters perished, together with the welfare of the city of Rome."[2] In this same book, Bruni was also very clear that by the time of his writing, the period of decay had ended and a new era had begun. He was the first to divide history into three eras—ancient, medieval, and modern—though another humanist historian actually invented the term "Middle Ages."

In the fifteenth century Florentine humanists became increasingly interested in Greek philosophy as well as Roman literature, especially in the ideas of Plato. Under the patronage of Cosimo de' Medici (1389–1464), the most powerful man in Florence, the scholar Marsilio Ficino (1433–1499), who would eventually become an ordained priest, began to lecture to an informal group of Florence's cultural elite; his lectures became known as the Platonic Academy, but they were not really a school. Ficino regarded Plato as a divinely inspired precursor to Christ, and he translated Plato's dialogues into Latin, attempting to synthesize Christian and Platonic teachings. Plato's emphasis on the spiritual and eternal over the material and transient fit well with Christian teachings about the immortality of the soul. Platonic ideas about love, that the highest form of love was spiritual desire for pure, perfect beauty uncorrupted by bodily desires, could easily be interpreted as Christian desire for the perfection of God.

For Ficino and his most brilliant student, Giovanni Pico della Mirandola (1463–1494), both Christian and classical texts taught that the universe was a hierarchy of beings from God down through spiritual beings to material beings, with humanity the crucial link right in the middle, both material and spiritual. In a remarkable essay, *On the Dignity of Man* (1486), Pico stressed that man possesses great dignity because he was made as Adam in the image of God before the Fall and as Christ after the Resurrection. According to Pico, man is the one part of the created world that has no fixed place, but can freely choose whether to rise to the realm of the angels or descend to the realm of the animals; because of

Saltcellar of Francis I In gold and enamel, Benvenuto Cellini depicts on this precursor of the saltshaker from about 1540 the Roman sea god, Neptune, sitting beside a small boat-shaped container holding salt from the sea. Opposite him, a female figure personifying Earth guards the pepper. Portrayed on the base are the four seasons and the times of day, symbolizing seasonal festivities and daily meal schedules. Classical figures were common subjects in Renaissance art. (Kunsthistorisches Museum, Vienna/The Bridgeman Art Library)

the divine image planted in him, he is truly a "miraculous creature."

Man's miraculous nature meant there are no limits to what he can accomplish. Families, religious brotherhoods, neighborhoods, workers' organizations, and other groups continued to have meaning in peoples' lives, but Renaissance thinkers increasingly viewed these groups as springboards to far greater individual achievement. They were especially interested in individuals who had risen above their background to become brilliant, powerful, or unique. (See "Individuals in Society: Leonardo da Vinci," page 391.) Such individuals had the admirable quality of **virtù** (ver-TOO), which is not virtue in the sense of moral goodness, but the ability to shape the world around them according to their will. Bruni and other historians included biographies of individuals with virtù in their histories of cities and nations, describing ways in which they had affected the course of history. Through the quality of their works and their influence on others, artists could also exhibit virtù, an idea that Vasari captures in the title of his major work, "The Lives of the Most Excellent Painters, Sculptors and Architects." His subjects were not simply excellent, but had achieved the pinnacle of excellence.

> **virtù** The quality of being able to shape the world according to one's own will.

❝ It is much safer for the prince to be feared than loved, but he ought to avoid making himself hated. ❞

—Niccolò Machiavelli

The last artist included in Vasari's book is Vasari himself, for Renaissance thinkers did not exclude themselves when they searched for models of talent and achievement. Vasari begins his discussion of his own works with a bit of modesty, saying that these might "not lay claim to excellence and perfection" when compared with those of other artists, but he then goes on for more than thirty pages, clearly feeling he has achieved some level of excellence.

Leon Battista Alberti (1404–1472) had similar views of his own achievements. He had much to be proud of: he wrote novels, plays, legal treatises, a study of the family, and the first scientific analysis of perspective; he designed churches, palaces, and fortifications effective against cannon; he invented codes for sending messages secretly and a machine that could cipher and decipher them. In his autobiography—written late in his life, and in the third person, so that he calls himself "he" instead of "I"—Alberti described his personal qualities and accomplishments:

> *Assiduous in the science and skill of dealing with arms and horses and musical instruments, as well as in the pursuit of letters and the fine arts, he was devoted to the knowledge of the most strange and difficult things. . . . He played ball, hurled the javelin, ran, leaped, wrestled. . . . He learned music without teachers . . . and then turned to physics and the mathematical arts. . . . Ambition was alien to him. . . . When his favorite dog died he wrote a funeral oration for him.*[3]

His achievements in many fields did make Alberti a "Renaissance man," as we use the term, though it may be hard to believe his assertion that "ambition was alien to him."

Biographies and autobiographies presented individuals their humanist authors thought were worthy models, but sometimes people needed more direct instruction. The ancient Greek philosopher Plato, whom humanists greatly admired, taught that the best way to learn something was to think about its perfect, ideal form. If you wanted to learn about justice, for example, you should imagine what ideal justice would be, rather than look at actual examples of justice in the world around you, for these would never be perfect. Following Plato's ideas, Renaissance authors speculated about perfect examples of many things. Alberti wrote about the ideal country house, which was to be useful, convenient, and elegant, and the English humanist Thomas More described a perfect society, which he called Utopia (see page 385).

Education

Humanists thought that their recommended course of study in the classics would provide essential skills for future diplomats, lawyers, military leaders, businessmen, and politicians, as well as writers and artists. It would provide a much broader and more practical type of training than that offered at universities, which at the time focused on theology and philosophy or on theoretical training for lawyers and physicians. Humanists poured out treatises, often in the form of letters, on the structure and goals of education and the training of rulers and leaders. They taught that a life active in the world should be the aim of all educated individuals and that education was not simply for private or religious purposes, but benefited the public good.

Humanists put their ideas into practice. Beginning in the early fifteenth century, they opened schools and academies in Italian cities and courts in which pupils began with Latin grammar and rhetoric, went on to study Roman history and political philosophy, and then learned Greek in order to study Greek literature and philosophy. Gradually, humanist education became the basis for intermediate and advanced education for well-to-do urban boys and men. Humanist schools were established in Florence, Venice, and other Italian cities, and by the early sixteenth century across the Alps in Germany, France, and England.

Humanists disagreed about education for women. Many saw the value of exposing women to classical models of moral behavior and reasoning, but they also wondered whether a program of study that emphasized eloquence and action was proper for women, whose sphere was generally understood to be private and domestic. In his book on the family, Alberti stressed that a wife's role should be restricted to the orderliness of the household, food and the serving of meals, the education of children, and the supervision of servants. (Alberti never married, so he never put his ideas into practice in his own household.) Women themselves were more bold in their claims about the value of the new learning. Although humanist academies were not open to women, through tutors or programs of self-study a few women did become educated in the classics. They argued in letters and published writings that reason was not limited to men and that learning was compatible with virtue for women as well as men. (See "Listening to the Past: Perspectives on Humanist Learning and Women," page 382.)

No book on education had broader influence than Baldassare Castiglione's *The Courtier* (1528). This treatise sought to train, discipline, and fashion the young man into the courtly ideal, the gentleman. According to

Portrait of Baldassare Castiglione In this portrait by Raphael, the most sought-after portrait painter of the Renaissance, Castiglione is shown dressed exactly as he advised courtiers to dress, in elegant but subdued clothing that would enhance the splendor of the court, but never outshine the ruler. (Scala/Art Resource, NY)

ceived positions at court, or at least substantial payments. Particularly in Italian cities, however, which often were divided by political factions, taken over by homegrown or regional despots, and attacked by foreign armies, such ideal rulers were hard to find. Humanists thus looked to the classical past for their models. Some, such as Bruni, argued that republicanism was the best form of government. Others used the model of Plato's philosopher-king in the *Republic* to argue that rule by an enlightened single individual might be best. Both sides agreed that educated men should be active in the political affairs of their city, a position historians have since termed "civic humanism."

The most famous (or infamous) civic humanist, and ultimately the best-known political theorist of this era, was Niccolò Machiavelli (1469–1527). After the ouster of the Medici with the French invasion of 1494, Machiavelli was secretary to one of the governing bodies in the city of Florence, responsible for diplomatic missions and organizing a citizen army. Power struggles in Florence between rival factions brought the Medici family back to power, and Machiavelli was arrested, tortured, and imprisoned on suspicion of plotting against them. He was released but had no government position, and he spent the rest of his life writing — political theory, poetry, prose works, plays, and a multivolume history of Florence — and making fruitless attempts to regain employment.

The first work Machiavelli finished — though not the first to be published — is his most famous, *The Prince* (1513), which uses the examples of classical and contemporary rulers to argue that the function of a ruler (or any government) is to preserve order and security. Weakness would only lead to disorder, which might end in civil war or conquest by an outsider, clearly situations that were not conducive to any people's well-being. To preserve the state a ruler should use whatever means he needs — brutality, lying, manipulation — but should not do anything that would make the populace turn against him; stealing or cruel actions done for a ruler's own pleasure would lead to resentment and destroy the popular support needed for a strong, stable realm. "It is much safer

Castiglione (kahs-teel-YOH-nay), who himself was a courtier serving several different rulers, the educated man should have a broad background in many academic subjects, and his spiritual and physical as well as intellectual capabilities should be trained. Castiglione envisioned a man who could compose a sonnet, wrestle, sing a song and accompany himself on an instrument, ride expertly, solve difficult mathematical problems, and, above all, speak and write eloquently. Castiglione also included discussion of the perfect court lady, who, like the courtier, was to be well educated and able to play a musical instrument, to paint, and to dance. Physical beauty, delicacy, affability, and modesty were also important qualities for court ladies.

In the sixteenth and seventeenth centuries, *The Courtier* was translated into every European language and widely read. It influenced the social mores and patterns of conduct of elite groups in Renaissance and early modern Europe and became a how-to manual for people seeking to improve themselves and rise in the social hierarchy as well. Echoes of its ideal for women have perhaps had an even longer life.

Political Thought

Ideal courtiers should preferably serve an ideal ruler, and biographies written by humanists often described rulers who were just, wise, pious, dignified, learned, brave, kind, and distinguished. For such flattering portraits of living rulers or their ancestors, authors sometimes re-

LISTENING TO THE PAST

Italian humanists set out the type of education that they regarded as ideal and promoted its value to society and the individual. Several women from the bustling cities of northern Italy became excited by the new style of learning, and through tutors or programs of self-study became extremely well educated. Like male humanists, they wrote letters, orations, lectures, and dialogues demonstrating their learning on such topics as

truth, virtue, knowledge, fame, and friendship, and circulated these to acquaintances and people whose good opinion they valued. Occasionally they presented orations and lectures orally in public settings or noble courts.

Some male humanists, including the influential Florentine official Leonardo Bruni, suggested that no woman who shared her ideas in public could possibly be virtuous, but by the middle of the fifteenth century other humanists celebrated the entrance of at least a few women into the largely male world of learning. The Venetian humanist nobleman Lauro Quirini (ca. 1420–ca. 1475), for example, had heard about the learned Isotta Nogarola (1418–1466) from her brother and from reading a collection of her letters. In this letter he praises her accomplishments and advises her on a plan of study.

Letter from Lauro Quirini to Isotta Nogarola, ca. 1450

❝ This letter asks of you nothing else than that you pursue in the most splendid way, until death, that same course of right living that you have followed since childhood. . . . Rightful therefore, should you also, famous Isotta, receive the highest praises, since you have, if I may so speak, overcome your own nature. For that true virtue that is proper to men you have pursued with remarkable zeal — not the mediocre virtue that many men seek, but that which would befit a man of the most flawless and perfect wisdom. . . . Therefore dissatisfied with the lesser studies, you have applied your noble mind to those highest disciplines, in which there is need for keenness of intelligence and mind. For you are engaged in the art of dialectic, which shows the way to learning the truth. Having mastered it, you may become engaged in a still more splendid and fertile field of philosophy [metaphysics]. . . .

Read studiously, then, the glorious works of Boethius Severnius, unquestionably a most intelligent and abundantly learned man.* Read all the treatises he learnedly composed on the dialectic art. . . . After you have mastered dialectic, which is the method of knowing, you should read diligently and carefully the moral books of Aristotle, which he writes divinely, in which you may unfailingly recognize the essence of true and solid virtue. . . . Then, after you have also digested this part of phi-

losophy, which is concerned with human matters, equipped with your nobility of the soul you should also set out for that ample and vast other part [divine matters]. . . . Here you should begin especially with those disciplines that we call by the Greek term mathematics. . . .

Diligently and carefully follow the Arabs, who very nearly approach the Greeks. You should constantly and assiduously read Averroes, admittedly a barbarous and uncultivated man, but otherwise an exceptional philosopher and rare judge of things.† . . . Read Thomas Aquinas often, who provides as it were an entryway to the understanding of Aristotle and Averroes.‡ . . .

You should also make use of those studies, moreover, that you have splendidly embraced from your youth, and especially history, for history is as it were the teacher of life, which somehow makes the wisdom of the ancients ours and inflames us to imitate great men. . . .

Take care of yourself so that you may be well, and study so that you may be wise. . . . For nothing is more lovely than philosophy, nothing more beautiful, nothing more lovable, as our Cicero said, to which I add, perhaps more truly, that there is nothing among human things more divine than philosophy. ❞

The Venetian Cassandra Fedele (1465–1558) applied advice such as Quirini's to her own studies and became the best-known female scholar in her time, corresponding with humanist writers, church officials, university professors, nobles, and even the rulers of Europe, including Isabella and Ferdinand of Spain, and becoming a positive example in the debate about women. She gave this oration in Latin at the University of Padua in honor of her (male) cousin's graduation.

for the prince to be feared than loved," Machiavelli advised, "but he ought to avoid making himself hated."[4]

Like the good humanist he was, Machiavelli knew that effective rulers exhibited the quality of virtù. He presented examples from the classical past of just the type of ruler he was describing, but also wrote about

contemporary leaders. Cesare Borgia (1475?–1507), Machiavelli's primary example, was the son of Rodrigo Borgia, a Spanish nobleman who later became Pope Alexander VI. Cesare Borgia combined his father's power and his own ruthlessness to build up a city-state in central Italy. He made good use of new military equip-

In Praise of Letters

❝ I shall speak very briefly on the study of the liberal arts, which for humans is useful and honorable, pleasurable and enlightening since everyone, not only philosophers but also the most ignorant man, knows and admits that it is by reason that man is separated from beasts. For what is it that so greatly helps both the learned and the ignorant? What so enlarges and enlightens men's minds the way that an education in and knowledge of literature and the liberal arts do? . . . But erudite men who are filled with the knowledge of divine and human things turn all their thoughts and considerations toward reason as though toward a target, and free their minds from all pain, though plagued by many anxieties. These men are scarcely subjected to fortune's innumerable arrows and they prepare themselves to live well and in happiness. They follow reason as their leader in all things; nor do they consider themselves only, but they are also accustomed to assisting others with their energy and advice in matters public and private.

And so Plato, a man almost divine, wrote that those states would be fortunate in which the men who were heads of state were philosophers or in which philosophers took on the duty of administration. . . . The study of literature refines men's minds, forms and makes bright the power of reason, and washes away all stains from the mind, or at any rate, greatly cleanses it. It perfects the gifts and adds much beauty and elegance to the physical and material advantages that one has received by nature. States, however, and their princes who foster and cultivate these studies become more humane, more gracious, and more noble. For this reason, these studies have won for themselves the sweet appellation, "humanities." . . . Just as places that lie unused and uncultivated become fertile and rich in fruits and vegetables with men's labor and hard work and are always made beautiful, so are our natures cultivated, enhanced, and enlightened by the liberal arts. . . .

But enough on the utility of literature since it produces not only an outcome that is rich, precious, and sublime, but also provides one with advantages that are extremely pleasurable, fruitful, and lasting — benefits that I myself have enjoyed. And when I meditate on the idea of marching forth in life with the lowly and execrable weapons of the little woman — the needle and the distaff [the rod onto which yarn is wound after spinning] — even if the study of literature offers women no rewards or honors, I believe women must nonetheless pursue and embrace such studies alone for the pleasure and enjoyment they contain. ❞

Sources: Excerpt from *Nogarola, Complete Writings*, ed. and trans. Margaret L. King and Diana Robin, in *The Other Voices in Early Modern Europe*, pp. 108–113. Copyright © 2004 University of Chicago Press; excerpt from Cassandra Fedele, *Letters and Orations*, pp. 159–162, ed. and trans. Diana Robin. Copyright © 2000 University of Chicago Press. Used with permission of the publisher.

QUESTIONS FOR ANALYSIS

1. What do Quirini and Fedele view as the best course of study?

2. What do they see as the purposes of such study? Are these purposes different for men and women?

3. Quirini is male and Fedele female. Does the gender of the authors shape their ideas about humanist learning in general, or about its appropriateness for women?

*Boethius (ca. 480–524) was a philosopher and adviser to King Theoderic (see page 191); he translated Aristotle's works on logic from Greek into Latin.

†Averroes (1126–1198) was an Islamic philosopher from Spain who wrote commentaries on Aristotle.

‡Thomas Aquinas (1225–1274) was a scholastic theologian and philosopher who brought together Aristotelian philosophy and Christian teachings (see page 322).

Woodcut showing Isotta Nogarola with her books, from Jacopo Bergamo's *Of Many Renowned and Wicked Women* (1497), a listing of good and evil women. ([Ferrara: Laurentius de Rubeis de Valentia, 1497]. Photo: Visual Connection Archive)

ment and tactics, hiring Leonardo da Vinci (1452–1519) as a military engineer, and murdered his political enemies, including one of the husbands of his sister, Lucrezia. Despite Borgia's efforts, his state fell apart after his father's death, which Machiavelli ascribed not to weakness, but to the operations of fate (*fortuna*, for-TOO-nah, in Italian), whose power even the best-prepared and most merciless ruler could not fully escape, though he should try. Fortuna was personified and portrayed as a goddess in ancient Rome and Renaissance Italy, and Machiavelli's last words about fortune are expressed in gendered terms: "It is better to be impetuous than cautious, for fortune is a woman, and if one wishes to keep her down, it is necessary to beat her and knock her down."[5]

The Prince is often seen as the first modern guide to politics, though Machiavelli was denounced for writing it, and people later came to use the word *Machiavellian* to mean cunning and ruthless. Medieval political philosophers had debated the proper relation between church and state, but they regarded the standards by which all governments were to be judged as emanating from moral principles established by God. Machiavelli argued that governments should instead be judged by how well they provided security, order, and safety to their populace. A ruler's moral code in maintaining these was not the same as a private individual's, for a leader could—indeed, should—use any means necessary. Machiavelli put a new spin on the Renaissance search for perfection, arguing that ideals needed to be measured in the cold light of the real world. This more pragmatic view of the purposes of government, and Machiavelli's discussion of the role of force and cruelty, was unacceptable to many.

Even today, when Machiavelli's more secular view of the purposes of government is widely shared, scholars debate whether Machiavelli actually meant what he wrote. Most regard him as realistic or even cynical, but some suggest that he was being ironic or satirical, showing princely government in the worst possible light to contrast it with republicanism. He dedicated *The Prince* to the new Medici ruler of Florence, however, so any criticism was deeply buried within what was, in that era of patronage, essentially a job application.

Christian humanists
Northern humanists who interpreted Italian ideas about and attitudes toward classical antiquity and humanism in terms of their own religious traditions.

Christian Humanism

In the last quarter of the fifteenth century, students from the Low Countries, France, Germany, and England flocked to Italy, absorbed the "new learning," and carried it back to their own countries. Northern humanists shared the ideas of Ficino and Pico about the wisdom of ancient texts, but they went beyond Italian efforts to synthesize the Christian and classical traditions to see humanist learning as a way to bring about reform of the church and deepen people's spiritual lives. These **Christian humanists**, as they were later called, thought that the best elements of classical and Christian cultures should be combined. For example, the classical ideals of calmness, stoical patience, and broad-mindedness should be joined in human conduct with the Christian virtues of love, faith, and hope.

The English humanist Thomas More (1478–1535) began life as a lawyer, studied the classics, and entered government service. This left him time to write, and he became most famous for his controversial dialogue

Procession of the Magi This segment of a huge fresco covering three walls of a chapel in the Medici Palace in Florence shows members of the Medici family and other contemporary individuals in a procession accompanying the biblical three wise men (*magi* in Italian) as they brought gifts to the infant Jesus. The painting was ordered in 1459 by Cosimo and Piero de' Medici, who had just finished building the family palace in the center of the city. Reflecting the self-confidence of his patrons, artist Bennozzo Gozzoli places the elderly Cosimo and Piero at the head of the procession, accompanied by their grooms. The group behind them includes Pope Pius II (in the last row in a red hat that ties under the chin) and the artist (in the second to the last row in a red hat with gold lettering). (Scala/Art Resource, NY)

Utopia (1516), a word More invented from the Greek words for "nowhere." *Utopia* describes a community on an island somewhere beyond Europe where all children receive a good education, primarily in the Greco-Roman classics, and adults divide their days between manual labor or business pursuits and intellectual activities. The problems that plagued More's fellow citizens, such as poverty and hunger, have been solved by a beneficent government. Because private property promoted inequality and greed, profits from business and property are held in common. There is religious toleration, and order and reason prevail. Because Utopian institutions are perfect, however, dissent and disagreement are not acceptable.

More's purposes in writing *Utopia* have been just as debated as have Machiavelli's in *The Prince*. Some view it as a revolutionary critique of More's own hierarchical and violent society, some as a call for an even firmer hierarchy, and others as part of the humanist tradition of satire. It was widely read by learned Europeans in the Latin in which More wrote it, and later in vernacular translations, and its title quickly became the standard word for any imaginary society.

Better known by contemporaries than Thomas More was the Dutch humanist Desiderius Erasmus (dez-ih-DARE-ee-us ih-RAZ-muhs) (1466?–1536) of Rotterdam. His fame rested largely on his exceptional knowledge of Greek and the Bible. Erasmus's long list of publications includes *The Education of a Christian Prince* (1504), a book combining idealistic and practical suggestions for the formation of a ruler's character through the careful study of Plutarch, Aristotle, Cicero, and Plato; *The Praise of Folly* (1509), a satire of worldly wisdom and a plea for the simple and spontaneous Christian faith of children; and, most important, a critical edition of the Greek New Testament (1516). In the preface to the New Testament, Erasmus explained the purpose of his great work: "I wish that even the weakest woman should read the Gospel—should read the epistles of Paul. And I wish these were translated into all languages, so that they might be read and understood, not only by Scots and Irishmen, but also by Turks and Saracens."[6]

Two fundamental themes run through all of Erasmus's work. First, education is the means to reform, the key to moral and intellectual improvement. The core of education ought to be study of the Bible and the classics. Second, the essence of Erasmus's thought is, in his own phrase, "the philosophy of Christ." By this Erasmus meant that Christianity is an inner attitude of the heart or spirit. Christianity is not formalism, special ceremonies, or law; Christianity is Christ—his life and what he said and did, not what theologians have written.

The Printed Word

The fourteenth-century humanist Petrarch and the sixteenth-century humanist Erasmus had similar ideas about many things, but the immediate impact of their ideas was very different because of one thing: the printing press with movable metal type. The ideas of Petrarch were spread slowly from person to person by hand copying. The ideas of Erasmus were spread quickly through print, in which hundreds or thousands of identical copies could be made in a short time.

Printing with movable metal type developed in Germany in the 1440s as a combination of existing technologies. Several metal-smiths, most prominently Johann Gutenberg, recognized that the metal stamps used to mark signs on jewelry could be covered with ink and used to mark symbols onto a surface, in the same way that other craftsmen were using carved wood stamps to print books. (This woodblock printing technique originated in China and Korea centuries earlier.) Gutenberg and his assistants made stamps—later called *type*—for every letter of the alphabet and built racks that held the type in rows. This type could be rearranged for every page and so used over and over.

Printing Press In this reproduction of Gutenberg's printing press, metal type sits in a frame ready to be placed in the bottom part of the press, with a leather-covered ink ball nearby for spreading ink on the type. Paper was then placed over the type, and a heavy metal plate brought down onto the paper with a firm pull of the large wooden handle, a technology adapted from wine presses. (Erich Lessing/Art Resource, NY)

Printing centers with date of establishment
◆ 15th century
▲ 16th century
— Political boundaries in 1490

SCOTLAND
Edinburgh *1507*
IRELAND
Dublin *1551*
ENGLAND
Oxford *1478*
London *1480*
NORWAY SWEDEN
Stockholm *1483*
DENMARK
Copenhagen *1493*
North Sea
Baltic Sea
Amsterdam *1523*
Emden *1554*
Lübeck *1475*
Hamburg *1491*
Deventer *1477*
Utrecht *1472*
HOLY ROMAN EMPIRE
Berlin *1540*
Bruges *1474*
Antwerp *1470*
Brussels *1474*
Cologne *1466*
Bonn *1543*
Leipzig *1481*
POLAND
ATLANTIC OCEAN
Gutenberg establishes first printing press, 1448
Paris *1470*
Frankfurt *1478*
Mainz
Bamberg *1460*
Nuremberg *1470*
Wrocław *1475*
Prague *1478*
Kraków *1474*
Strasbourg *1460*
FRANCE
Basel *1462*
Bern *1525*
Zürich *1508*
Augsburg *1468*
Munich *1482*
Vienna *1482*
Buda *1473*
Cluny *1483*
Lyons *1473*
Geneva *1478*
HUNGARY
MOLDAVIA
PORTUGAL
NAVARRE
Milan *1470*
VENICE
Venice *1469*
Belgrade *1552*
Danube R.
Madrid *1499*
ARAGON
Florence *1471*
PAPAL STATES
Rhône R.
Lisbon *1489*
CASTILE
Barcelona *1475*
Rome *1467*
Subiaco *1465*
OTTOMAN EMPIRE
Thessalonica *1515*
Constantinople *1488*
Valencia *1473*
Naples *1471*
NAPLES
GRANADA
Mediterranean Sea
Reggio di Calabria *1480*
AFRICA

Mapping the Past

Map 13.2 **The Growth of Printing in Europe, 1448–1551** The speed with which artisans spread printing technology across Europe provides strong evidence for the growing demand for reading material. Presses in the Ottoman Empire were first established by Jewish immigrants who printed works in Hebrew, Greek, and Spanish.

ANALYZING THE MAP What part of Europe had the greatest number of printing presses by 1550? What explains this?

CONNECTIONS Printing was developed in response to a market for reading materials. Use Maps 11.2 and 11.3 (pages 309 and 318) to help explain why printing spread the way it did.

To complete this activity online, go to the Online Study Guide at bedfordstmartins.com/mckaywest.

The printing revolution was also enabled by the ready availability of paper, which was also made using techniques that had originated in China and were brought into Europe through Muslim Spain. (See "Living in the Past: Muslim Technology: Advances in Papermaking," page 214.)

By the fifteenth century the increase in urban literacy, the development of primary schools, and the opening of more universities had created an expanding market for reading materials (see Chapter 12). When Gutenberg developed what he saw at first as a faster way to copy, professional copyists writing by hand and block-book makers, along with monks and nuns, were already churn-

ing out reading materials on paper as fast as they could for the growing number of people who could read.

Gutenberg's invention involved no special secret technology or materials, and he was not the only one to recognize the huge market for books. Other craftsmen made their own type, built their own presses, and bought their own paper, setting themselves up in business (Map 13.2). Historians estimate that, within a half century of the publication of Gutenberg's Bible in 1456, somewhere between 8 million and 20 million books were printed in Europe. Whatever the actual figure, the number is far greater than the number of books produced in all of Western history up to that point.

The effects of the invention of movable-type printing were not felt overnight. Nevertheless, movable type brought about radical changes, transforming both the private and the public lives of Europeans by the dawn of the sixteenth century. Print shops were gathering places for people interested in new ideas. Though printers were trained through apprenticeships just like blacksmiths or butchers, they had connections to the world of politics, art, and scholarship that other craftsmen did not.

Printing gave hundreds or even thousands of people identical books, so that they could more easily discuss the ideas that the books contained with one another in person or through letters. Printed materials reached an invisible public, allowing silent individuals to join causes and groups of individuals widely separated by geography to form a common identity; this new group consciousness could compete with older, localized loyalties.

Government and church leaders both used and worried about printing. They printed laws, declarations of war, battle accounts, and propaganda, and they also attempted to censor books and authors whose ideas they thought were wrong. Officials developed lists of prohibited books and authors, enforcing their prohibitions by confiscating books, arresting printers and booksellers, or destroying the presses of printers who disobeyed. None of this was very effective, and books were printed secretly, with fake title pages, authors, and places of publication, and smuggled all over Europe.

Printing also stimulated the literacy of laypeople and eventually came to have a deep effect on their private lives. Although most of the earliest books and pamphlets dealt with religious subjects, printers produced anything that would sell. They printed professional reference sets for lawyers, doctors, and students, and historical romances, biographies, and how-to manuals for the general public. They discovered that illustrations increased a book's sales, so they published books on a wide range of topics — from history to pornography — full of woodcuts and engravings. Single-page broadsides and flysheets allowed great public events and "wonders" such as comets and two-headed calves to be experienced vicariously by a stay-at-home readership. Since books and other printed materials were read aloud to illiterate listeners, print bridged the gap between the written and oral cultures.

Art and the Artist

How did changes in art reflect new Renaissance ideals? ◼

No feature of the Renaissance evokes greater admiration than its artistic masterpieces. The 1400s (*quattrocento*) and 1500s (*cinquecento*) bore witness to dazzling creativity in painting, architecture, and sculpture. In all the arts, the city of Florence led the way. But Florence was not the only artistic center, for Rome and Venice also became important, and northern Europeans perfected their own styles.

Patronage and Power

As we saw earlier in this chapter, powerful urban groups often flaunted their wealth by commissioning works of art in early Renaissance Italy. The Florentine cloth merchants, for example, delegated Filippo Brunelleschi (fihl-EEP-oh broo-nayl-LAYS-kee) to build the magnificent dome on the cathedral of Florence and selected Lorenzo Ghiberti (law-REHN-tsoh gee-BEHR-tee) to design the bronze doors of the adjacent Baptistery, a separate building in which baptisms were performed. These works represented the merchants' dominant influence in the community.

Increasingly in the later fifteenth century, wealthy individuals and rulers, rather than corporate groups, sponsored works of art. Patrician merchants and bankers, popes, and princes spent vast sums on the arts as a means of glorifying themselves and their families. Writing in about 1470, Florentine ruler Lorenzo de' Medici declared that his family had spent hundreds of thousands of gold florins for artistic and architectural commissions, but commented, "I think it casts a brilliant light on our estate [public reputation] and it seems to me that the monies were well spent and I am very pleased with this."[7]

Patrons varied in their level of involvement as a work progressed; some simply ordered a specific subject or scene, while others oversaw the work of the artist or architect very closely, suggesting themes and styles and demanding changes while the work was in progress. For example, Pope Julius II (pontificate 1503–1513), who commissioned Michelangelo to paint the ceiling of the Vatican's Sistine Chapel in Rome in 1508, demanded that the artist work as fast as he could and frequently visited him at his work with suggestions and criticisms. Michelangelo, a Florentine who had spent his young adulthood at the court of Lorenzo de' Medici, complained in person and by letter about the pope's meddling, but his reputation did not match the power of the pope, and he kept working until the chapel was finished in 1512.

In addition to power, art reveals changing patterns of consumption among the nobility and wealthy merchants in Renaissance Italy. In the rural world of the Middle Ages, society had been organized for war, and men of wealth spent their money on military gear. As Italian nobles settled in towns (see Chapter 11), they adjusted to an urban culture. Rather than employing knights for warfare, cities hired mercenaries. Expenditures on military hardware declined. For the rich merchant or the noble recently arrived from the countryside, a grand urban palace represented the greatest outlay of cash. Wealthy individuals and families ordered gold

Michelangelo's David (1501–1504) and the Last Judgment (detail, 1537–1541)
Like all Renaissance artists, Michelangelo worked largely on commissions from
patrons. Officials of the city of Florence contracted the young sculptor to produce a
statue of the Old Testament hero David (left) to be displayed on the city's main
square. Michelangelo portrayed David anticipating his fight against the giant Goliath,
and the statue came to symbolize the republic of Florence standing up to its larger
and more powerful enemies. More than thirty years later, Michelangelo was commissioned by the pope to paint a scene of the Last Judgment on the altar wall of the
Sistine Chapel, where he had earlier spent four years covering the ceiling with
magnificent frescoes. The massive work shows a powerful Christ standing in judgment, with souls ascending into Heaven while others are dragged by demons into
Hell (above). The *David* captures ideals of human perfection and has come to be an
iconic symbol of Renaissance artistic brilliance, while the dramatic and violent Last
Judgment conveys both terror and divine power. (sculpture: Scala/Ministero per i Beni e le
Attività Culturali/Art Resource, NY; painting: Alinari/The Bridgeman Art Library)

dishes, embroidered tablecloths, wall tapestries, paintings on canvas (an innovation), and sculptural decorations to adorn their homes. By the late sixteenth century
the Strozzi banking family of Florence spent even more
on household goods than they did on clothing, jewelry, or food, though these were increasingly elaborate
as well.

After the palace itself, the private chapel within the
palace symbolized the largest expenditure for the wealthy
of the sixteenth century. Decorated with religious scenes
and equipped with ecclesiastical furniture, the chapel
served as the center of the household's religious life and
its cult of remembrance of the dead.

Changing Artistic Styles

The content and style of Renaissance art were often different from those of the Middle Ages. Religious topics, such as the Annunciation of the Virgin and the Nativity, remained popular among both patrons and artists, but frequently the patron had himself and his family portrayed in the scene. As the fifteenth century advanced and humanist ideas spread more widely, classical themes and motifs, such as the lives and loves of pagan gods and goddesses, figured increasingly in painting and sculpture, with the facial features of the gods sometimes modeled on living people.

The individual portrait emerged as a distinct artistic genre. Rather than reflecting a spiritual ideal, as medieval painting and sculpture tended to do, Renaissance portraits showed human ideals, often portrayed in a more realistic style. The Florentine painter Giotto (JAH-toh) (1276–1337) led the way in the use of realism; his treatment of the human body and face replaced the formal stiffness and artificiality that had long characterized representation of the human body. Piero della Francesca (frahn-CHAY-skah) (1420–1492) and Andrea Mantegna (mahn-TEN-yuh) (1430/31–1506) seem to have pioneered perspective in painting, the linear representation of distance and space on a flat surface. The

sculptor Donatello (1386–1466) revived the classical figure, with its balance and self-awareness. In architecture, Filippo Brunelleschi (1377–1446) looked to the classical past for inspiration, designing a hospital for orphans and foundlings in which all proportions—of the windows, height, floor plan, and covered walkway with a series of rounded arches—were carefully thought out to achieve a sense of balance and harmony.

Art produced in northern Europe in the fourteenth and fifteenth centuries tended to be more religious in orientation than that produced in Italy. Some Flemish painters, notably Rogier van der Weyden (1399/1400–1464) and Jan van Eyck (1366–1441), were considered the artistic equals of Italian painters and were much admired in Italy. Van Eyck was one of the earliest artists to use oil-based paints successfully, and his religious scenes and portraits all show great realism and remarkable attention to human personality. Northern architecture was little influenced by the classical revival so obvious in Renaissance Italy.

In the early sixteenth century the center of the new art shifted from Florence to Rome, where wealthy cardinals and popes wanted visual expression of the church's and their own families' power and piety. Renaissance popes expended enormous enthusiasm and huge sums of money to beautify the city. Pope Julius II tore down the

***Descent from the Cross**, ca. 1435* Taking as his subject the suffering and death of Jesus, a popular theme of Netherlandish piety, Rogier van der Weyden shows Christ's descent from the cross, surrounded by nine sorrowing figures. An appreciation of human anatomy, the rich fabrics of the clothes, and the pierced and bloody hands of Jesus were all intended to touch the viewers' emotions. (Museo del Prado/Scala/Art Resource, NY)

old Saint Peter's Basilica and began work on the present structure in 1506. Michelangelo went to Rome from Florence in about 1500 and began the series of statues, paintings, and architectural projects from which he gained an international reputation: the Pieta, Moses, the redesigning of the Capitoline Hill in central Rome, and, most famously, the dome for Saint Peter's and the ceiling and altar wall of the nearby Sistine Chapel.

Raphael Sanzio (1483–1520), another Florentine, got the commission for frescoes in the papal apartments, and in his relatively short life he painted hundreds of portraits and devotional images, becoming the most sought after artist in Europe. Raphael also oversaw a large workshop with many collaborators and apprentices—who assisted on the less difficult sections of some paintings—and wrote treatises on his philosophy of art in which he emphasized the importance of imitating nature and developing an orderly sequence of design and proportion.

Venice became another artistic center in the sixteenth century. Titian (TIH-shuhn) (1490–1576) produced portraits, religious subjects, and mythological scenes, developing techniques of painting in oil without doing elaborate drawings first, which speeded up the process and pleased patrons eager to display their acquisitions. Titian and other sixteenth-century painters developed an artistic style known in English as "mannerism" (from *maniera* or "style" in Italian) in which artists sometimes distorted figures, exaggerated musculature, and heightened color to express emotion and drama more intently. (A painting by Titian can be found on page 394; this is also the style in which Michelangelo painted the Last Judgment in the Sistine Chapel, shown on page 388.)

The Renaissance Artist

Some patrons rewarded certain artists very well, and some artists gained great public acclaim as, in Vasari's words, "rare men of genius." This adulation of the artist has led many historians to view the Renaissance as the beginning of the concept of the artist as having a special talent. In the Middle Ages people believed that only God created, albeit through individuals; the medieval conception recognized no particular value in artistic originality. Renaissance artists and humanists came to think that a work of art was the deliberate creation of a unique personality who transcended traditions, rules, and theories. A genius had a peculiar gift, which ordinary laws should not inhibit. Michelangelo and Leonardo da Vinci perhaps best embody the new concept of the Renaissance artist as genius. (See "Individuals in Society: Leonardo da Vinci," at right.)

It is important not to overemphasize the Renaissance notion of genius. As certain artists became popular and well known, they could assert their own artistic styles and pay less attention to the wishes of patrons, but even major artists like Raphael generally worked according to the patron's specific guidelines. Whether in Italy or northern Europe, most Renaissance artists trained in the workshops of older artists; Botticelli, Raphael, Titian, and at times even Michelangelo were known for their large, well-run, and prolific workshops. Though they might be men of genius, artists were still expected to be well trained in proper artistic techniques and stylistic conventions, for the notion that artistic genius could show up in the work of an untrained artist did not emerge until the twentieth century. Beginning artists spent years copying drawings and paintings, learning

Villa Capra Architecture as well as literature and art aimed to recreate classical styles. The Venetian architect Andrea Palladio modeled this country villa, constructed for a papal official in 1566, on the Pantheon of ancient Rome (see page 157). Surrounded by statues of classical deities, it is completely symmetrical, capturing humanist ideals of perfection and balance. This villa and others of Palladio's designs influenced later buildings all over the world, including the U.S. Capitol in Washington, D.C., and countless state capitol buildings.

(age fotostock/Superstock)

Leonardo da Vinci

INDIVIDUALS IN SOCIETY

WHAT MAKES A GENIUS? A deep curiosity about an extensive variety of subjects? A divine spark that emerges in talents that far exceed the norm? Or is it just "one percent inspiration and ninety-nine percent perspiration," as Thomas Edison said? However it is defined, Leonardo da Vinci counts as a genius. In fact, Leonardo was one of the individuals whom the Renaissance label "genius" was designed to describe: a special kind of human

being with exceptional creative powers. Leonardo (who, despite the title of a recent bestseller, is always called by his first name) was born in Vinci, near Florence, the illegitimate son of Caterina, a local peasant girl, and Ser Piero da Vinci, a notary public. Caterina later married another native of Vinci. When Ser Piero's marriage to Donna Albrussia produced no children, he and his wife took in Leonardo. Ser Piero secured Leonardo's apprenticeship with the painter and sculptor Andrea del Verrocchio in Florence. In 1472, when Leonardo was just twenty years old, he was listed as a master in Florence's "Company of Artists."

Leonardo's most famous portrait, *Mona Lisa*, shows a woman with an enigmatic smile that Giorgio Vasari described as "so pleasing that it seemed divine rather than human." The portrait, probably of the young wife of a rich Florentine merchant (her exact identity is hotly debated), may actually be the best known painting in the history of art. One of its competitors in that designation would be another work of Leonardo, *The Last Supper*, which has been called "the most revered painting in the world."

Leonardo's reputation as a genius does not rest simply on his paintings, however, which are actually few in number, but rather on the breadth of his abilities and interests. He is often understood to be the first "Renaissance man," a phrase we still use for a multitalented individual. He wanted to reproduce what the eye can see, and he drew everything he saw around him, including executed criminals hanging on gallows as well as the beauties of nature. Trying to understand how the human body worked, Leonardo studied live and dead bodies, doing autopsies and dissections to investigate muscles and circulation. He carefully analyzed the effects of light, and he experimented with perspective.

Leonardo used his drawings as the basis for his paintings and as a tool of scientific investigation. He drew plans for hundreds of inventions, many of which would become reality centuries later, such as the helicopter, tank, machine gun, and parachute. He was hired by one of the powerful new rulers in Italy, Duke Ludovico Sforza of Milan, to design weapons, fortresses, and water systems, as well as to produce works of art. Leonardo left Milan when Sforza was overthrown in war and spent the last years of his life painting, drawing, and designing for the pope and the French king.

Leonardo experimented with new materials for painting and sculpture, some of which worked and some of which did not. The experimental method he used to paint *The Last Supper* caused the picture to deteriorate rapidly, and it began to flake off the wall as soon as it was finished. Leonardo regarded it as never quite completed, for he could not find a model for the face of Christ who would evoke the spiritual depth he felt the figure deserved. His gigantic equestrian statue in honor of Ludovico's father, Duke Francesco Sforza, was never made, and the clay model collapsed. He planned to write books on many subjects but

Lady with an Ermine: **The enigmatic smile and smoky quality of this portrait can be found in many of Leonardo's works.**
(Czartoryski Museum, Krakow/The Bridgeman Art Library)

never finished any of them, leaving only notebooks. Leonardo once said that "a painter is not admirable unless he is universal." The patrons who supported him — and he was supported very well — perhaps wished that his inspirations would have been a bit less universal in scope, or at least accompanied by more perspiration.

Sources: Giorgio Vasari, *Lives of the Artists*, vol. 1, trans. G. Bull (London: Penguin Books, 1965); S. B. Nuland, *Leonardo da Vinci* (New York: Lipper/Viking, 2000).

QUESTIONS FOR ANALYSIS

1. In what ways do the notion of a "genius" and of a "Renaissance man" both support and contradict one another? Which better fits Leonardo?
2. Has the idea of artistic genius changed since the Renaissance? How?

Botticelli, *Primavera* (Spring), ca. 1482 Framed by a grove of orange trees, Venus, goddess of love, is flanked on the right by Flora, goddess of flowers and fertility, and on the left by the Three Graces, goddesses of banquets, dance, and social occasions. Above, Venus's son Cupid, the god of love, shoots darts of desire, while at the far right the wind god Zephyrus chases the nymph Chloris. The entire scene rests on classical mythology, though some art historians claim that Venus is an allegory for the Virgin Mary. Botticelli captured the ideal for female beauty in the Renaissance: slender, with pale skin, a high forehead, red-blond hair, and sloping shoulders. (Digital image © The Museum of Modern Art/Licensed by Scala/Art Resource, NY)

how to prepare paint and other artistic materials, and, by the sixteenth century, reading books about design and composition. Younger artists gathered together in the evenings for further drawing practice; by the later sixteenth century some of these informal groups had turned into more formal artistic "academies," the first of which was begun in 1563 in Florence by Vasari under the patronage of the Medicis.

As Vasari's phrase indicates, the notion of artistic genius that developed in the Renaissance was gendered. All the most famous and most prolific Renaissance artists were male; there are no female architects whose names are known and only one female sculptor. The types of art in which more women were active, such as textiles, needlework, and painting on porcelain, were not regarded as "major arts," but only as "minor" or "decorative" arts. (The division between "major" and "minor" arts begun in the Renaissance continues to influence the way museums and collections are organized today.) Like painting, embroidery changed in the Renaissance to become more classical in its subject matter, naturalistic, and visually complex. Embroiderers

were not trained to view their work as products of individual genius, however, so they rarely included their names on the works, and there is no way to discover who they were.

Several women did become well known as painters in their day. Stylistically, their works are different from one another, but their careers show many similarities. The majority of female painters were the daughters of painters or of minor noblemen with ties to artistic circles. Many were eldest daughters or came from families in which there were no sons, so their fathers took unusual interest in their careers. Many women began their careers before they were twenty and produced far fewer paintings after they married, or stopped painting entirely. Women were not allowed to study the male nude, which was viewed as essential if one wanted to paint large history or biblical paintings with many figures. Women could also not learn the technique of fresco, in which colors are applied directly to wet plaster walls, because such works had to be done in public, which was judged inappropriate for women. Joining a group of male artists for informal practice was also seen as improper, and the artistic academies that were established were for men only. Like universities, humanist academies, and most craft guild shops, artistic workshops were male-only settings in which men of different ages came together for training and created bonds of friendship, influence, patronage, and sometimes intimacy.

Women were not alone in being excluded from the institutions of Renaissance culture. Though a few rare men of genius such as Leonardo and Michelangelo emerged from artisanal backgrounds, most scholars and artists came from families with at least some money. Renaissance culture did not influence the lives of most people in cities and did not affect life in the villages at all. A small, highly educated minority of literary humanists and artists created the culture of and for an exclusive elite. The Renaissance maintained, or indeed enhanced, a gulf between the learned minority and the uneducated multitude that has survived for many centuries.

Social Hierarchies

What were the key social hierarchies in Renaissance Europe, and how did ideas about hierarchy shape people's lives? ▨

The division between educated and uneducated people was only one of many social hierarchies evident in the Renaissance. Every society has social hierarchies; in ancient Rome, for example, there were patricians and plebeians (see Chapter 5). Such hierarchies are to some degree descriptions of social reality, but they are also idealizations—that is, they describe how people imagined their society to be, without all the messy reality of social-climbing plebeians or groups that did not fit the standard categories. Social hierarchies in the Renaissance were built on the orders of the Middle Ages—those

Esther Before Ahasuerus, ca. 1630 In this oil painting, Artemisia Gentileschi (jehn-tuh-LEHS-kee) shows an Old Testament scene of the Jewish woman Esther who saved her people from being killed by her husband, King Ahasuerus. This deliverance is celebrated in the Jewish holiday of Purim. The elaborate clothes shown are of the type worn in Renaissance courts. Typical of a female painter, Artemisia Gentileschi was trained by her father. She mastered the dramatic style favored in the early seventeenth century and became known especially for her portraits of strong biblical and mythological heroines. (Image copyright © The Metropolitan Museum of Art/Art Resource, NY)

who fight, pray, and work—but they also developed new features that contributed to modern social hierarchies, such as those of race, class, and gender.

Race and Slavery

Renaissance people did not use the word *race* the way we do, but often used "race," "people," and "nation" interchangeably for ethnic, national, religious, or other groups—the French race, the Jewish nation, the Irish people, "the race of learned gentlemen," and so on. They did make distinctions based on skin color that provide some of the background for later conceptualizations of race, but these distinctions were interwoven with other characteristics when people thought about human differences.

Ever since the time of the Roman republic, a small number of black Africans had lived in western Europe. They had come, along with white slaves, as the spoils of war. Even after the collapse of the Roman Empire, Muslim and Christian merchants continued to import them. Unstable political conditions in many parts of Africa enabled enterprising merchants to seize people and sell them into slavery. Local authorities afforded them no protection. Long tradition, moreover, sanctioned the practice of slavery. The evidence of medieval art attests to the continued presence of Africans in Europe throughout the Middle Ages and to Europeans' awareness of them.

Beginning in the fifteenth century sizable numbers of black slaves entered Europe. Portuguese sailors brought perhaps a thousand Africans a year to the markets of Seville, Barcelona, Marseilles, and Genoa. In the late fifteenth century this flow increased, with thousands of people leaving the west coast of Africa. By 1530 between four thousand and five thousand were being sold to the Portuguese each year. By the mid-sixteenth century blacks, slave and free, constituted about 10 percent of the population of the Portuguese cities of Lisbon and Évora and roughly 3 percent of the Portuguese population overall. In the Iberian Peninsula African slaves intermingled with the people they lived among and sometimes intermarried. Cities such as Lisbon had significant numbers of people of mixed African and European descent.

Although blacks were concentrated in the Iberian Peninsula, there must have been some Africans in northern Europe as well. In the 1580s, for example, Queen Elizabeth I of England complained that there were too many "blackamoores" competing with needy English people for places as domestic servants. Black servants were much sought after; the medieval interest in curiosities, the exotic, and the marvelous continued in the Renaissance. Italian aristocrats had their portraits painted with their black page-boys to indicate their wealth (as in the painting on this page). Blacks were so greatly in demand at the Renaissance courts of northern Italy, in fact, that the Venetians defied papal threats of excommunication to secure them. In 1491 Isabella of Este, duchess of Mantua, instructed her agent to secure a black girl between four and eight years old, "shapely and as black as possible." She hoped the girl would become "the best buffoon in the world," noting that "we shall make her very happy and shall have great fun with her."[8] The girl would join musicians, acrobats, and

Laura de Dianti, 1523 The Venetian artist Titian shows a young Italian woman with a gorgeous blue dress and an elaborate pearl and feather headdress, accompanied by a young black page with a gold earring. Both the African page and the headdress connect the portrait's subject with the exotic, though slaves from Africa and the Ottoman Empire were actually common in wealthy Venetian households. (Courtesy, Heinz Kisters Collection)

Renaissance Fireplace, ca. 1458 This marble fireplace, carved for the palace of the Boni family in Florence, shows the family coat of arms in the center, with two heads on either side, possibly of ancestors. Wealthy people often had busts or painted portraits of their ancestors above the fireplaces around which they gathered in the evening for warmth and conversation. (V&A Images/Victoria and Albert Museum)

dancers as a source of entertainment, her status similar to that of the dwarves who could be found at many Renaissance courts.

Africans were not simply amusements at court. In Portugal, Spain, and Italy slaves supplemented the labor force in virtually all occupations — as servants, agricultural laborers, craftsmen, and seamen on ships going to Lisbon and Africa. Agriculture in Europe did not involve large plantations, so large-scale agricultural slavery did not develop there as it would in the late fifteenth century in the New World.

Until the voyages down the African coast in the late fifteenth century, Europeans had little concrete knowledge of Africans and their cultures. They perceived Africa as a remote place, the home of strange people isolated by heresy and Islam from superior European civilization. Africans' contact, even as slaves, with Christian Europeans could only "improve" the blacks, they thought. The expanding slave trade reinforced negative preconceptions about the inferiority of black Africans.

Wealth and the Nobility

The word *class* — working class, middle class, upper class — was not used in the Renaissance to describe social divisions, but by the thirteenth century, and even more so by the fifteenth, the idea of a hierarchy based on wealth was emerging alongside the medieval concept of orders (see Chapter 10). This was particularly true in towns. Most residents of towns were technically members of the "third order" — that is, "those who work" rather than "those who fight" and "those who pray." However, this group now included wealthy merchants who oversaw vast trading empires and lived in splendor that rivaled the richest nobles. As we saw earlier, in many cities these merchants had gained political power to match their economic might, becoming merchant oligarchs who ruled through city councils. This hierarchy of wealth was more changeable than the hierarchy of orders, allowing individuals and families to rise — and fall — within one generation.

The development of a hierarchy of wealth did not mean an end to the hierarchy of orders, however, and even poorer nobility still had higher status than wealthy commoners. If this had not been the case, wealthy Italian merchants would not have bothered to buy noble titles and country villas as they began doing in the fifteenth century, nor would wealthy English or Spanish merchants have been so eager to marry their daughters and sons into often-impoverished noble families. The nobility maintained its status in most parts of Europe not by maintaining rigid boundaries, but by taking in and integrating the new social elite of wealth.

Along with being tied to hierarchies of wealth and orders, social status was linked with considerations of honor. Among the nobility, for example, certain weapons and battle tactics were favored because they were viewed as more honorable. Among urban dwellers, certain occupations, such as city executioner or manager of the municipal brothel, might be well paid but were understood to be "dishonorable" and so of low status. In cities, sumptuary laws reflected both wealth and honor (see Chapter 11); merchants were specifically allowed fur and jewels, while prostitutes were ordered to wear yellow bands that would remind potential customers of the flames of Hell.

Gender Roles

Renaissance people would not have understood the word *gender* to refer to categories of people, but they would have easily grasped the concept. Toward the end of the fourteenth century, learned men (and a few women) began what was termed the **debate about women** (*querelle des femmes*), a debate about women's character and nature that would last for centuries. Misogynist (muh-SAH-juh-nihst) critiques of women from both clerical and secular authors denounced females as devious, domineering, and demanding. In answer, several authors compiled long lists of famous and praiseworthy women exemplary for their loyalty, bravery, and morality. Christine de Pizan was among the writers who were not only interested in defending women, but also in exploring the reasons behind women's secondary status — that is, why the great philosophers, statesmen, and poets had generally been men. In this they were anticipating discussions about the "social construction of gender" by six hundred years. (See "Listening to the Past: Christine de Pizan, Advice to the Wives of Artisans," page 362, and "Listening to the Past: Perspectives on Humanist Learning and Women," page 382.)

With the development of the printing press, popular interest in the debate about women grew, and works were translated, reprinted, and shared around Europe. Prints that juxtaposed female virtues and vices were also very popular, with the virtuous women depicted as those of the classical or biblical past and the vice-ridden dressed in contemporary clothes. The favorite metaphor for the virtuous wife was either the snail or the tortoise, both animals that never leave their "houses" and are totally silent, although such images were never as widespread as those depicting wives beating their husbands or hiding their lovers from them.

Beginning in the sixteenth century, the debate about women also became a debate about female rulers, sparked primarily by dynastic accidents in many countries, including Spain, England, France, and Scotland, which led to women serving as advisers to child kings or ruling in their own right. The questions were vigorously and at times viciously disputed. They directly concerned the social construction of gender: could a woman's being born into a royal family and educated to rule allow

debate about women
Debate among writers and thinkers in the Renaissance about women's qualities and proper role in society.

Phyllis Riding Aristotle Among the many scenes that expressed the debate about women visually were woodcuts, engravings, paintings, and even cups and plates that showed the classical philosopher Aristotle as an old man being ridden by the young, beautiful Phyllis (shown here in a German woodcut). The origins of the story are uncertain, but in the Renaissance everyone knew the tale of how Aristotle's infatuation with Phyllis led to his ridicule. Male moralists used it as a warning about the power of women's sexual allure, though women may have interpreted it differently. (Réunion des Musées Nationaux/Art Resource, NY)

« The employer . . . may also give them soup and vegetables to eat in the morning—but no wine—milk and bread at midday, but nothing in the evening. »

—SIXTEENTH-CENTURY WORKERS' REGULATION

her to overcome the limitations of her sex? Should it? Or stated another way: which was (or should be) the stronger determinant of character and social role, gender or rank? Despite a prevailing sentiment that women were not as fit to rule as men, there were no successful rebellions against female rulers simply because they were women, but in part this was because female rulers, especially Queen Elizabeth I of England, emphasized qualities regarded as masculine—physical bravery, stamina, wisdom, duty—whenever they appeared in public.

Ideas about women's and men's proper roles determined the actions of ordinary men and women even more forcefully. The dominant notion of the "true" man was that of the married head of household, so men whose social status and age would have normally conferred political power but who remained unmarried did not participate to the same level as their married brothers. Unmarried men in Venice, for example, could not be part of the ruling council. (See "Living in the Past: Male Clothing and Masculinity," page 398.)

Women were also understood as either "married or to be married," even if the actual marriage patterns in Europe left many women (and men) unmarried until quite late in life (see Chapter 12). This meant that women's work was not viewed as supporting a family—even if it did—and was valued less than men's. If they worked for wages, and many women did, women earned about half to two-thirds of what men did even for the same work. Regulations for vineyard workers in the early sixteenth century, for example, specified that

> Men who work in the vineyards, doing work that is skilled, are to be paid 16 pence per day; in addition, they are to receive soup and wine in the morning, at midday beer, vegetables and meat, and in the evening soup, vegetables and wine. Young boys are to be paid 10 pence per day. Women who work as haymakers are to be given 6 pence a day. If the employer wants to have them doing other work, he may make an agreement with them to pay them 7 or 8 pence. He may also give them soup and vegetables to eat in the morning—but no wine—milk and bread at midday, but nothing in the evening.[9]

The maintenance of appropriate power relationships between men and women, with men dominant and women subordinate, served as a symbol of the proper functioning of society as a whole. Disorder in the proper gender hierarchy was linked with social upheaval and was viewed as threatening. Of all the ways in which Renaissance society was hierarchically arranged—social rank, age, level of education, race, occupation—gender was regarded as the most "natural" and therefore the most important to defend.

Politics and the State in Western Europe, ca. 1450–1521

How did the nation-states of western Europe evolve in this period? ▪

The High Middle Ages had witnessed the origins of many of the basic institutions of the modern state. Sheriffs, inquests, juries, circuit judges, professional bureaucracies, and representative assemblies all trace their origins to the twelfth and thirteenth centuries. The linchpin for the development of states, however, was strong monarchy, and during the period of the Hundred Years' War, no ruler in western Europe was able to provide effective leadership. The resurgent power of feudal nobilities weakened the centralizing work begun earlier.

Beginning in the fifteenth century rulers utilized aggressive methods to rebuild their governments. First in the regional states of Italy, then in the expanding monarchies of France, England, and Spain, rulers began the work of reducing violence, curbing unruly nobles, and establishing domestic order. They attempted to secure their borders and enhanced methods of raising revenue. The monarchs of western Europe emphasized royal majesty and royal sovereignty and insisted on the respect and loyalty of all subjects, including the nobility. In central Europe the Holy Roman emperors attempted to do the same, but they were not able to overcome the power of local interests to create a unified state (see Chapter 14).

France

The Black Death and the Hundred Years' War left France drastically depopulated, commercially ruined, and agriculturally weak. Nonetheless, the ruler whom Joan of Arc had seen crowned at Reims, Charles VII (r. 1422–1461), revived the monarchy and France. He seemed

Male Clothing and Masculinity

LIVING IN THE PAST

WEALTHY RENAISSANCE PEOPLE DISPLAYED THEIR POWER AND PROSPERITY on their bodies as well as in their houses and household furnishings. Expanded trade brought in silks, pearls, gemstones, feathers, dyestuffs, and furs, which tailors, goldsmiths, seamstresses, furriers, and hatmakers turned into magnificent clothing and jewelry. Nowhere was fashion more evident than on the men in Renaissance cities and courts. Young men favored multicolored garments that fit tightly, often topping the ensemble with a matching hat on carefully combed long hair. The close-cut garments emphasized the male form, which was further accentuated by tight hose stylishly split to reveal a brightly colored codpiece. Older men favored more subdued colors but with multiple padded shirts, vests, and coats that emphasized real or pretended upper-body strength and that allowed the display of many layers of expensive fabrics. Golden rings, earrings, pins, and necklaces provided additional glamour.

Padded leather jerkin embroidered with silk and metal thread from the late sixteenth century. There are eyelets for tying up hose inside. (Museo Stibbert, Florence)

Two young men, who are side figures in *The Adoration of the Magi*, by Luca Signorelli (1445–1523). (Scala/Art Resource, NY)

The Venetian painter Titian's portrait of Emperor Charles V with one of his hunting dogs. (Scala/Art Resource, NY)

QUESTIONS FOR ANALYSIS

1. Male clothing in any era communicates social values and ideas about masculinity. What does Renaissance fashion suggest about notions of manhood in this era?

2. In *The Prince*, Machiavelli used the word *effeminate* to describe the worst kind of ruler, though the word carried different connotations from what it does today. Strong heterosexual passion was not a sign of manliness but could make one "effeminate"— that is, dominated by as well as similar to a woman. Look at the portrait of Charles V here and at the other portraits in this chapter. How did male rulers visually symbolize their masculinity?

an unlikely person to do so. Frail, indecisive, and burdened with questions about his paternity (his father had been deranged; his mother, notoriously promiscuous), Charles VII nevertheless began France's long recovery.

Charles reconciled the Burgundians and Armagnacs (ahr-muhn-YAKZ), who had been waging civil war for thirty years. By 1453 French armies had expelled the English from French soil except in Calais. Charles reorganized the royal council, giving increased influence to lawyers and bankers, and strengthened royal finances through such taxes as the *gabelle* (guh-BEL) on salt and the *taille* (TA-yuh), a land tax. These taxes remained the Crown's chief sources of income until the Revolution of 1789.

By establishing regular companies of cavalry and archers—recruited, paid, and inspected by the state—Charles created the first permanent royal army. His son Louis XI (r. 1461–1483), called the "Spider King" because of his treacherous character, improved upon Charles's army and used it to control the nobles' separate militias and to curb urban independence. The army was also employed in 1477 when Louis conquered Burgundy upon the death of its ruler Charles the Bold. Three years later, the extinction of the house of Anjou (AN-joo) with the death of its last legitimate male heir brought Louis the counties of Anjou, Bar, Maine, and Provence.

Two further developments strengthened the French monarchy. The marriage of Louis XII (r. 1498–1515) and Anne of Brittany added the large western duchy of Brittany to the state. Then the French king Francis I and Pope Leo X reached a mutually satisfactory agreement about church and state powers in 1516. The new treaty, the Concordat of Bologna, approved the pope's right to receive the first year's income of new bishops and abbots. In return, Leo X recognized the French ruler's right to select French bishops and abbots. French kings thereafter effectively controlled the appointment and thus the policies of church officials in the kingdom.

The Expansion of France, 1475–1500

England

English society also suffered severely from the disorders of the fifteenth century. The aristocracy dominated the government of Henry IV (r. 1399–1413) and indulged in disruptive violence at the local level. Population continued to decline. Between 1455 and 1471 adherents of the ducal houses of York and Lancaster waged civil war, commonly called the Wars of the Roses because the symbol of the Yorkists was a white rose and that of the Lancastrians a red one. The chronic disorder hurt trade, agriculture, and domestic industry. Under the pious but mentally disturbed Henry VI (r. 1422–1461), the authority of the monarchy sank lower than it had been in centuries.

The Yorkist Edward IV (r. 1461–1483) began establishing domestic tranquility. He succeeded in defeating the Lancastrian forces and after 1471 began to reconstruct the monarchy. Edward, his brother Richard III (r. 1483–1485), and Henry VII (r. 1485–1509) of the Welsh house of Tudor worked to restore royal prestige, to crush the power of the nobility, and to establish order and law at the local level. All three rulers used methods that Machiavelli himself would have praised—ruthlessness, efficiency, and secrecy.

Edward IV and subsequently the Tudors, excepting Henry VIII, conducted foreign policy on the basis of diplomacy, avoiding expensive wars. Thus the English monarchy did not depend on Parliament for money, and the Crown undercut that source of aristocratic influence.

Henry VII did summon several meetings of Parliament in the early years of his reign, primarily to confirm laws, but the center of royal authority was the royal council, which governed at the national level. There Henry VII revealed his distrust of the nobility: though not completely excluded, very few great lords were among the king's closest advisers. Instead he chose men from among the smaller landowners and urban residents trained in law. The council conducted negotiations with foreign governments and secured international recognition of the Tudor dynasty through the marriage in 1501 of Henry VII's eldest son Arthur to Catherine of Aragon, the daughter of Ferdinand and Isabella of Spain. The council dealt with real or potential aristocratic threats through a judicial offshoot, the Court of Star Chamber, so called because of the stars painted on the ceiling of the room. The court applied methods that were sometimes terrifying: accused persons were not entitled to see evidence against them; sessions were secret; torture could be applied to extract confessions; and juries were not called. These procedures ran directly counter to English common-law precedents, but they effectively reduced aristocratic troublemaking.

When Henry VII died in 1509, he left a country at peace both domestically and internationally, a substantially augmented treasury, an expanding wool trade, and the dignity and role of the royal majesty much enhanced. He was greatly missed after he died "by all his subjects," wrote the historian Polydore Vergil, "who had been able to conduct their lives peaceably, far removed from the assaults and evildoings of scoundrels."[10]

Spain

While England and France laid the foundations of unified nation-states during the Middle Ages, Spain remained a conglomerate of independent kingdoms. By the middle of the fifteenth century, the kingdoms of Castile and Aragon dominated the weaker Navarre, Portugal, and Granada; and the Iberian Peninsula, with the exception of Granada, had been won for Christianity. But even the wedding in 1469 of the dynamic and aggressive Isabella of Castile and the crafty and persistent Ferdinand of Aragon did not bring about administrative unity. Rather, their marriage constituted a dynastic union of two royal houses, not the political union of two peoples. Although Ferdinand and Isabella (r. 1474–1516) pursued a common foreign policy, until about 1700 Spain existed as a loose confederation of separate kingdoms, each maintaining its own *cortes* (parliament), laws, courts, and systems of coinage and taxation (Map 13.3).

Ferdinand and Isabella were able to exert their authority in ways similar to the rulers of France and England, however. They curbed aristocratic power by excluding high nobles from the royal council, which had full executive, judicial, and legislative powers under the monarchy, instead appointing lesser landowners. The council and various government boards recruited men trained in Roman law, which exalted the power of the Crown. They also secured from the Spanish Borgia pope Alexander VI—Cesare Borgia's father—the right to appoint bishops in Spain and in the Hispanic territories in America, enabling them to establish the equivalent of a national church. With the revenues from ecclesiastical estates, they were able to expand their territories to include the remaining land held by Arabs in southern Spain. The victorious entry of Ferdinand and Isabella into Granada on January 6, 1492, signaled the conclusion of the reconquista (see Map 9.3 on page 248). Granada in the south was incorporated into the Spanish kingdom, and in 1512 Ferdinand conquered Navarre in the north.

There still remained a sizable and, in the view of the majority of the Spanish people, potentially dangerous minority, the Jews. When the kings of France and England had expelled the Jews from their kingdoms (see Chapter 9), many had sought refuge in Spain. During the long centuries of the reconquista, Christian kings had renewed Jewish rights and privileges; in fact, Jewish industry, intelligence, and money had supported royal power. While Christians borrowed from Jewish moneylenders and while all who could afford them sought Jewish physicians, a strong undercurrent of resentment of Jewish influence and wealth festered.

In the fourteenth century anti-Semitism in Spain was aggravated by fiery anti-Jewish preaching, by economic

Map 13.3 The Unification of Spain and the Expulsion of the Jews, Fifteenth Century The marriage of Ferdinand of Aragon and Isabella of Castile in 1469 brought most of the Iberian Peninsula under one monarchy, although different parts of Spain retained distinct cultures, languages, and legal systems. In 1492 Ferdinand and Isabella conquered Granada, where most people were Muslim, and expelled the Jews from all of Spain. Spanish Jews resettled in cities of Europe and the Mediterranean that allowed them in, including many in Muslim states such as the Ottoman Empire. Muslims were also expelled from Spain over the course of the sixteenth and early seventeenth centuries.

dislocation, and by the search for a scapegoat during the Black Death. Anti-Semitic pogroms swept the towns of Spain, and perhaps 40 percent of the Jewish population was killed or forced to convert. Those converted were called *conversos* or **New Christians**. Conversos were often well educated and held prominent positions in government, the church, medicine, law, and business. Numbering perhaps two hundred thousand in a total Spanish population of about 7.5 million, New Christians and Jews in fifteenth-century Spain exercised influence disproportionate to their numbers.

Such successes bred resentment. Aristocratic grandees resented their financial dependence; the poor hated the converso tax collectors; and churchmen doubted the sincerity of their conversions. Queen Isabella shared these suspicions, and she and Ferdinand had received permission from Pope Sixtus IV in 1478 to establish their own Inquisition to "search out and punish converts from Judaism who had transgressed against Christianity by

New Christians A fourteenth-century term for Jews and Muslims who accepted Christianity; in many cases they included Christians whose families had converted centuries earlier.

Picturing the Past

Tax Collectors New types of taxes, and more effective methods of tax collection, were essential to the growth of Renaissance states, but were often highly unpopular. In this painting from about 1540 the Dutch artist Marinus van Reymerswaele depicts two tax collectors as they count their take and record it in a ledger. Tax collectors were men of middling status, but here they are wearing clothing more appropriate for nobles. (Erich Lessing/Art Resource, NY)

ANALYZING THE IMAGE What elements of the men's clothing suggest wealth? How would you describe the expressions on their faces? What does the painting suggest about the artist's opinion of tax collectors?

CONNECTIONS In Spain converso tax collectors were widely resented. What were some of the reasons behind this resentment? What public event was an outgrowth of this hatred, and what were its aims?

To complete this activity online, go to the Online Study Guide at bedfordstmartins.com/mckaywest.

secretly adhering to Jewish beliefs and performing rites of the Jews."[11] Investigations and trials began immediately, as officials of the Inquisition looked for conversos who showed any sign of incomplete conversion, such as not eating pork.

Recent scholarship has carefully analyzed documents of the Inquisition. Most conversos identified themselves as sincere Christians; many came from families that had received baptism generations before. In response, officials of the Inquisition developed a new type of anti-Semitism. A person's status as a Jew, they argued, could not be changed by religious conversion, but was in the person's blood and was heritable, so Jews could never be true Christians. In what were known as "purity of blood" laws, having pure Christian blood became a requirement for noble status. Ideas about Jews developed in Spain were important components in European concepts of race, and discussions of "Jewish blood" later expanded into notions of the "Jewish race."

In 1492, shortly after the conquest of Granada, Isabella and Ferdinand issued an edict expelling all practicing Jews from Spain. Of the community of perhaps 200,000 Jews, 150,000 fled. Many Muslims in Granada were forcibly baptized and became another type of New Christian investigated by the Inquisition. Absolute religious orthodoxy and purity of blood served as the theoretical foundation of the Spanish national state.

The Spanish national state rested on marital politics as well as military victories and religious courts. In 1496 Ferdinand and Isabella married their second daughter Joanna, heiress to Castile, to the archduke Philip, heir to the Burgundian Netherlands and the Holy Roman Empire. Philip and Joanna's son, Charles V (r. 1519–1556), thus succeeded to a vast inheritance. When Charles's son Philip II joined Portugal to the Spanish crown in 1580, the Iberian Peninsula was at last politically united.

Saint Dominic Presiding over an Auto-da-Fe
In this 1495 painting the Spanish artist Pedro Berruguete shows an auto-da-fe, a public ritual of penance for those found guilty of religious crimes. In the foreground, the guilty wear tall hats with their crimes described on them, while above them two men are about to be burned at the stake. Technically execution did not happen at the auto-da-fe, but rather at a later secular execution, although the two events sometimes blended into one another. Berruguete portrays Saint Dominic, the founder of the Dominican order, as presiding over this trial, although autos-da-fe were not common until centuries after Dominic's death in 1221. (Museo del Prado, Madrid/Institut Amatller d'Art Hispànic)

 LOOKING BACK LOOKING AHEAD THE ART HISTORIAN Giorgio Vasari, who first called this era the Renaissance, thought that his contemporaries had both revived the classical past and gone beyond it. Vasari's judgment was echoed for centuries, as the art, architecture, educational ideas, social structures, and attitude toward life of the Renaissance were set in sharp contrast with those of the Middle Ages: whereas the Middle Ages were corporate and religious, the Renaissance was individualistic and secular. More recently, historians and other scholars have stressed continuity as well as change. Families, kin networks, guilds, and other corporate groups remained important in the Renaissance, and religious belief remained firm. This re-evaluation changes our view of the relationship between the Middle Ages and the Renaissance. It may also change our view of the relationship between the Renaissance and the dramatic changes in religion that occurred in Europe in the sixteenth century. Those religious changes, the Reformation, used to be viewed as a rejection of the values of the Renaissance and a return to the intense concern with religion of the Middle Ages. This idea of the Reformation as a sort of counter-Renaissance may be true to some degree, but there are powerful continuities as well. Both movements looked back to a time they regarded as purer and better than their own, and both offered opportunities for strong individuals to shape their world in unexpected ways.

CHAPTER REVIEW

■ **What economic and political developments in Italy provided the setting for the Renaissance? (p. 374)**

In the commercial revival of the Middle Ages, ambitious merchants amassed great wealth, especially in the city-states of northern Italy. These city-states were communes in which all citizens shared power, but political instability led to their transformation into signori or oligarchies. As their riches and power grew, signori and oligarchs displayed their wealth in great public buildings as well as magnificent courts — palaces where they lived and conducted business. Political rulers, popes, and powerful families hired writers, artists, musicians, and architects through the system of patronage, which allowed for a great outpouring of culture.

■ **What were the key ideas of the Renaissance, and how were they different for men and women and for southern and northern Europeans? (p. 378)**

The Renaissance was characterized by self-conscious awareness among fourteenth- and fifteenth-century Italians, particularly scholars and writers known as humanists, that they were living in a new era. Key to this attitude was a serious interest in the Latin, and later the Greek, classics, especially the works of Cicero and Plato. Humanists also believed in striving for perfection, and they greatly admired individuals who exhibited the quality of virtù, the ability to shape the world around them to their will. These qualities are evident in political theory developed during the Renaissance, particularly that of Machiavelli. Humanists opened schools for boys and young men to train them for active lives of public service, but they had doubts about whether humanist education was appropriate for women. Some self-taught women did argue that study of the classics should not be limited to men. In northern Europe, religious concerns among humanists were more pronounced, and adherents came to be known as Christian humanists. Well-known writers such as Thomas More of England and Desiderius Erasmus of Rotterdam set out plans for the reform of church and society. Their ideas reached a much wider audience than those of early humanists because of the development of the printing press with movable metal type, which revolutionized communication.

■ **How did changes in art reflect new Renaissance ideals? (p. 387)**

Artistic patronage in the early Renaissance was primarily provided by groups such as guilds, but in the later Renaissance individuals increasingly supported the arts as a way of glorifying themselves and their families. At the same time, humanist interest in the classical past and in the individual shaped Renaissance art in terms of style and subject matter. Painting became more naturalistic, and the individual portrait emerged as a distinct artistic genre. Perspective was pioneered in painting, and balance and harmony became hallmarks of Italian architecture. Art in Italy became more secular and classical, with more works focused on pagan gods and goddesses. In northern Europe, where humanist thinking was more connected to Christian ideals, art retained a more religious tone. The style of mannerism evolved, which exaggerated the color and musculature of painted figures in order to provide more drama and emotion. Artists began to understand themselves as having a special creative genius, though they were still expected to undergo extensive technical training, and they continued to produce works on order for patrons, who often determined the content and form. Women were largely excluded from the major arts, as were most people from working families, and art itself was created for consumption mainly by an elite minority.

■ **What were the key social hierarchies in Renaissance Europe, and how did ideas about hierarchy shape people's lives? (p. 393)**

Social hierarchies in the Renaissance built on those of the Middle Ages, with the addition of new features that evolved into the modern social hierarchies of race, class, and gender. In the fifteenth century black slaves entered Europe in sizable numbers for the first time since the collapse of the Roman Empire. Europeans saw Africans as inferior, and they felt that contact with Christians would serve to improve the lives of blacks, even as slaves. The medieval hierarchy of orders based on function in society intermingled with a new hierarchy based on wealth, with new types of elites becoming more powerful through political and marital alliances. Noble families that were experiencing declining wealth could rebuild their fortunes by integrating with the newly rich. The Renaissance debate about women led to discussions of women's character and questioning of whether women could serve effectively as rulers. There was little debate, however, that among the nonruling classes, both men and women were expected to fit neatly into "natural" roles, with men as heads of households and women as subordinate; any deviation from this pattern was seen as a threat to societal order.

■ **How did the nation-states of western Europe evolve in this period? (p. 397)**

With taxes provided by business people, kings in western Europe established armies to maintain greater peace and order, both essential for trade, and feudal monarchies gradually evolved in the direction of nation-states. French kings benefited from opportunistic marriages and an alliance with the pope, and English kings used Machiavellian methods to crush the nobility. Spain used similar practices, though unification came more slowly, and Spanish rulers focused intently on expelling practicing Jews from their country.

Suggested Reading

Clark, Samuel. *State and Status: The Rise of the State and Aristocratic Power*. 1995. Discusses the relationship between centralizing states and the nobility.

Earle, T. F., and K. J. P. Lowe, eds. *Black Africans in Renaissance Europe*. 2005. Includes essays discussing many aspects of ideas about race and the experience of Africans in Europe.

Eisenstein, Elizabeth. *The Printing Press as an Agent of Change: Communications and Cultural Transformations in Early Modern Europe*. 1979. The definitive study of the impact of printing.

Ertman, Thomas. *The Birth of Leviathan: Building States and Regimes in Medieval and Early Modern Europe*. 1997. A good introduction to the creation of nation-states.

Grafton, Anthony, and Lisa Jardine. *From Humanism to the Humanities: Education and the Liberal Arts in Fifteenth and Sixteenth Century Europe*. 1986. Discusses humanist education and other developments in Renaissance learning.

Hale, J. R. *The Civilization of Europe in the Renaissance*. 1994. A comprehensive treatment of the period, arranged thematically.

Harbison, Craig. *The Mirror of the Artist: Northern Renaissance Art in Its Historical Context*. 1995. The best introduction to the art of northern Europe.

Hartt, Frederick, and David Wilkins. *History of Italian Renaissance Art*, 6th ed. 2008. Comprehensive survey of painting, sculpture, and architecture in Italy.

Holmes, George, ed. *Art and Politics in Renaissance Italy*. 1993. Treats the art of Florence and Rome against a political background.

Jardine, Lisa. *Worldly Goods: A New History of the Renaissance*. 1998. Discusses changing notions of social status, artistic patronage, and consumer goods.

Johnson, Geraldine. *Renaissance Art: A Very Short Introduction*. 2005. Excellent brief survey that includes male and female artists, and sets the art in its cultural and historical context.

King, Ross. *Machiavelli: Philosopher of Power*. 2006. Brief biography that explores Machiavelli's thought in its social and political context.

Lubkin, Gregory. *A Renaissance Court: Milan Under Galeazzo Maria Sforza*. 1994. A wonderful study of one of the most important Renaissance courts.

Man, John. *Gutenberg Revolution: The Story of a Genius and an Invention That Changed the World*. 2002. Presents a rather idealized view of Gutenberg, but has good discussions of his milieu and excellent illustrations.

McConica, James. *Erasmus*. 1991. A sensitive treatment of the leading northern humanist.

Nauert, Charles. *Humanism and the Culture of Renaissance Europe*, 2d ed. 2006. A thorough introduction to humanism throughout Europe.

Netanyahu, Benzion. *The Origins of the Inquisition in Fifteenth Century Spain*. 1995. An analysis of issues relating to the expulsion of the Jews.

Wiesner-Hanks, Merry E. *Women and Gender in Early Modern Europe*, 3d ed. 2008. Discusses all aspects of women's lives and ideas about gender.

Key Terms

Renaissance (p. 374)
patronage (p. 374)
communes (p. 375)
popolo (p. 375)
signori (p. 376)
courts (p. 376)
humanism (p. 378)
virtù (p. 379)
Christian humanists (p. 384)
debate about women (p. 396)
New Christians (p. 401)

Notes

1. In Gertrude R. B. Richards, *Florentine Merchants in the Age of the Medici* (Cambridge: Harvard University Press, 1932).
2. In James Bruce Ross and Mary Martin McLaughlin, *The Portable Renaissance Reader* (New York: Penguin, 1953), p. 27.
3. Ibid., pp. 480–481, 482, 492.
4. Niccolò Machiavelli, *The Prince*, trans. Leo Paul S. de Alvarez (Prospect Heights, Ill.: Waveland Press, 1980), p. 101.
5. Ibid., p. 149.
6. Quoted in F. Seebohm, *The Oxford Reformers* (London: J. M. Dent & Sons, 1867), p. 256.
7. Quoted in Lauro Martines, *Power and Imagination: City-States in Renaissance Italy* (New York: Vintage Books, 1980), p. 253.
8. Quoted in J. Devisse and M. Mollat, *The Image of the Black in Western Art*, vol. 2, trans. W. G. Ryan (New York: William Morrow, 1979), pt. 2, pp. 187–188.
9. Stuttgart, Württembergische Hauptstaatsarchiv, Generalreskripta, A38, Bü. 2, 1550; trans. Merry Wiesner-Hanks.
10. Denys Hay, ed. and trans., *The Anglia Historia of Polydore Vergil, AD 1485–1537*, book 74 (London: Camden Society, 1950), p. 147.
11. Quoted in Benzion Netanyahu, *The Origins of the Inquisition in Fifteenth Century Spain* (New York: Random House, 1995), p. 921.

For practice quizzes and other study tools, visit the Online Study Guide at **bedfordstmartins.com/mckaywest**.

For primary sources from this period, see **Sources of Western Society**, **Second Edition**.

For Web sites, images, and documents related to topics in this chapter, visit Make History at **bedfordstmartins.com/mckaywest**.

14 Reformations and Religious Wars

1500–1600

Erich Lessing/Art Resource, NY

Calls for reform of the Christian church began very early in its history. Throughout the centuries, men and women believed that the early Christian church represented a golden age, akin to the golden age of the classical past celebrated by Renaissance humanists. When Christianity became the official religion of the Roman Empire in the fourth century, many believers thought that the church had abandoned its original mission, and they called for a return to a church that was not linked to the state. Throughout the Middle Ages individuals and groups argued that the church had become too wealthy and powerful and urged monasteries, convents, bishoprics, and the papacy to give up their property and focus on service to the poor. Some asserted that basic teachings of the church were not truly Christian and that changes were needed in theology as well as in institutional structures and practices. The Christian humanists of the late fifteenth and early sixteenth centuries urged reform, primarily through educational and social change. What was new in the sixteenth century was the breadth of acceptance and the ultimate impact of the calls for reform. This acceptance was due not only to religious issues and problems within the church, but also to political and social factors. In 1500 there was one Christian church in western Europe to which all Christians at least nominally belonged. One hundred years later there were many, a situation that continues today. ■

Religious Violence in Urban Life. This 1590 painting shows Catholic military forces, including friars in their robes, processing through one of the many towns affected by the French religious wars that followed the Reformation.

CHAPTER PREVIEW

The Early Reformation
■ What were the central ideas of the reformers, and why were they appealing to different social groups?

The Reformation and German Politics
■ How did the political situation in Germany shape the course of the Reformation?

The Spread of Protestant Ideas
■ How did Protestant ideas and institutions spread beyond German-speaking lands?

The Catholic Reformation
■ How did the Catholic Church respond to the new religious situation?

Religious Violence
■ What were the causes and consequences of religious violence, including riots, wars, and witch-hunts?

The Early Reformation

What were the central ideas of the reformers, and why were they appealing to different social groups? ■

In early sixteenth-century Europe a wide range of people had grievances with the church. Educated laypeople such as Christian humanists and urban residents, villagers and artisans, and church officials themselves called for reform. This widespread dissatisfaction helps explain why the ideas of an obscure professor from a new and not very prestigious German university found a ready audience. Within a decade of his first publishing his ideas (using the new technology of the printing press), much of central Europe and Scandinavia had broken with the Catholic Church, and even more radical concepts of the Christian message were being developed and linked to calls for social change.

anticlericalism
Opposition to the clergy.

pluralism The clerical practice of holding more than one church benefice (or office) at the same time and enjoying the income from each.

The Christian Church in the Early Sixteenth Century

If external religious observances are an indication of conviction, Europeans in the early sixteenth century were deeply pious. Villagers participated in processions honoring the local saints. Merchants and guild members made pilgrimages to the great shrines, such as Saint Peter's in Rome, and paid for altars in local churches. Men and women continued to remember the church in their wills. People of all social groups devoted an enormous amount of their time and income to religious causes and foundations.

Despite — or perhaps because of — the depth of their piety, many people were also highly critical of the Roman Catholic Church and its clergy. The papal conflict with the German emperor Frederick II in the thirteenth century, followed by the Babylonian Captivity and the Great Schism, badly damaged the prestige of church leaders, and the fifteenth-century popes' concentration on artistic patronage and building up family power did not help matters. Papal tax collection methods were attacked orally and in print. Some criticized the papacy itself as an institution, and even the great wealth and powerful courts of the entire church hierarchy. Some groups and individuals argued that certain doctrines taught by the church, such as the veneration of saints and the centrality of the sacraments, were incorrect. They suggested measures to reform institutions, improve clerical education and behavior, and alter basic doctrines.

Occasionally these reform efforts had some success, and in at least one area, Bohemia (the modern-day Czech Republic), they led to the formation of a church independent of Rome a century before Luther (see Chapter 12).

In the early sixteenth century court records, bishops' visitations of parishes, and popular songs and printed images show widespread **anticlericalism**, or opposition to the clergy. The critics concentrated primarily on three problems: clerical immorality, clerical ignorance, and clerical **pluralism** (the practice of holding more than one church office at a time), with the related problem of absenteeism. Charges of clerical immorality were aimed at a number of priests who were drunkards, neglected the rule of celibacy, gambled, or indulged in fancy dress. Charges of clerical ignorance were motivated by barely literate priests who simply mumbled the Latin words of the Mass by rote without understanding their meaning. Many priests, monks, and nuns lived pious lives of devotion, learning, and service and had strong support from the laypeople in their areas, but everyone also knew (and repeated) stories about lecherous monks, lustful nuns, and greedy priests.

In regard to absenteeism and pluralism, many clerics held several benefices, or offices, simultaneously, but they seldom visited the benefices, let alone performed the spiritual responsibilities those offices entailed. Instead, they collected revenues from all of them and hired a poor priest, paying him just a fraction of the income to fulfill the spiritual duties of a particular local church. Many Italian officials in the papal curia, the pope's court in Rome, held benefices in England, Spain, and Germany. Revenues from those countries paid the Italian clerics' salaries, provoking not only charges of absenteeism but also nationalistic resentment aimed at the upper levels of the church hierarchy, which was increasingly viewed as foreign. This was particularly the case in Germany, where the lack of a strong central government to negotiate with the papacy meant that demands for revenue were especially high.

There was also local resentment of clerical privileges and immunities. Priests, monks, and nuns were exempt from civic responsibilities, such as defending the city and paying taxes. Yet religious orders frequently held large amounts of urban property, in some cities as much as one-third. City governments were increasingly determined to integrate the clergy into civic life by reducing their privileges and giving them public responsibilities. Urban leaders wanted some say in who would be appointed to high church offices, rather than having this decided far away in Rome. This brought city leaders into opposition with bishops and the papacy, which for centuries had stressed the independence of the church from lay control and the distinction between members of the clergy and laypeople.

Martin Luther

By itself, widespread criticism of the church did not lead to the dramatic changes of the sixteenth century. Those resulted from the personal religious struggle of a German university professor and priest, Martin Luther (1483–1546). Luther was born at Eisleben in Saxony. At considerable sacrifice, his father sent him to school and then to the University of Erfurt, where he earned a master's degree with distinction. Luther was to proceed to the study of law and a legal career, which for centuries had been the stepping-stone to public office and material success. Instead, however, a sense of religious calling led him to join the Augustinian friars, a religious order whose members often preached to, taught, and assisted the poor. (Religious orders were groups whose members took vows and followed a particular set of rules.) Luther was ordained a priest in 1507 and after additional study earned a doctorate of theology. From 1512 until his death in 1546, he served as professor of the Scriptures at the new University of Wittenberg. Throughout his life, he frequently cited his professorship as justification for his reforming work.

Martin Luther was a very conscientious friar, but his scrupulous observance of religious routine, frequent confessions, and fasting gave him only temporary relief from anxieties about sin and his ability to meet God's demands. Through his study of Saint Paul's letters in the New Testament, he gradually arrived at a new understanding of Christian doctrine. His understanding is often summarized as "faith alone, grace alone, Scripture alone." He believed that salvation and justification come through faith. Faith is a free gift of God's grace, not the result of human effort. God's word is revealed only in Scripture, not in the traditions of the church.

At the same time that Luther was engaged in scholarly reflections and professorial lecturing, Pope Leo X authorized the sale of a special Saint Peter's indulgence to finance his building plans in Rome. The archbishop who controlled the area in which Wittenberg was located, Albert of Mainz, was an enthusiastic promoter of this indulgence sale. For his efforts, he received a share of the profits in order to pay off a debt he had incurred in order to purchase a papal dispensation allowing him to become the bishop of several other territories as well.

Chronology

What exactly was an **indulgence**? According to Catholic theology, individuals who sin could be reconciled to God by confessing their sins to a priest and by doing an assigned penance, such as praying or fasting. But beginning in the twelfth century learned theologians increasingly emphasized the idea of purgatory, a place where souls on their way to Heaven went to make further amends for their earthly sins. Both earthly penance and time in purgatory could be shortened by drawing on what was termed the "treasury of merits." This was a collection of all the virtuous acts that Christ, the apostles, and the saints had done during their lives. People thought of it as a sort of strongbox, like those in which merchants carried coins. An indulgence was a piece of parchment (later, paper), signed by the pope or another church official, that substituted a virtuous act from the treasury of merits for penance or time in purgatory. The papacy and bishops had given Crusaders such

> **indulgence** A document issued by the Catholic Church lessening penance or time in purgatory, widely believed to bring forgiveness of all sins.

409

Selling Indulgences A woodcut advertising Johann Tetzel's sale of indulgences in 1517, which shows him blessed by the Holy Spirit in the form of a dove, while people run to buy, as the rhyme here puts it, "grace and forgiveness for your sins, for you, your parents, wife, and child." Indulgences were often printed fill-in-the-blank forms. This indulgence (upper left), purchased in 1521, has space for the indulgence seller's name at the top, the buyer's name in the middle, and the date at the bottom. (woodcut: akg-images; indulgence: Visual Connection Archive)

indulgences, and by the later Middle Ages they were offered for making pilgrimages or other pious activities and also sold outright (see Chapter 10).

Albert's indulgence sale, run by a Dominican friar named Johann Tetzel who mounted an advertising blitz, promised that the purchase of indulgences would bring full forgiveness for one's own sins or release from purgatory for a loved one. One of the slogans—"As soon as coin in coffer rings, the soul from purgatory springs"—brought phenomenal success, and people traveled from miles around to buy indulgences.

Luther was severely troubled that many people believed they had no further need for repentance once they had purchased indulgences. In 1517 he wrote a letter to Archbishop Albert on the subject and enclosed in Latin his "Ninety-five Theses on the Power of Indulgences." His argument was that indulgences undermined the seriousness of the sacrament of penance, competed with the preaching of the Gospel, and downplayed the importance of charity in Christian life. After Luther's death, biographies reported that the theses were also nailed to the door of the church at Wittenberg Castle on October 31, 1517. Such an act would have been very strange—they were in Latin and written for those learned in theology, not for normal churchgoers—but it has become a standard part of Luther lore.

Whether the theses were posted or not, they were quickly printed, first in Latin and then in German translation. Luther was ordered to come to Rome, although because of the political situation in the empire, he was able instead to engage in formal scholarly debate with a representative of the church, Johann Eck, at Leipzig in 1519. He refused to take back his ideas and continued to develop his calls for reform, publicizing them in a series of pamphlets in which he moved further and further away from Catholic theology. Both popes and church councils could err, he wrote, and secular leaders should reform the church if the pope and clerical hierarchy did not. There was no distinction between clergy and laypeople, and requiring clergy to be celibate was a fruitless attempt to control a natural human drive. Luther clearly understood the power of the new medium of print, and so authorized the publication of his works.

The papacy responded with a letter condemning some of Luther's propositions, ordering that his books be burned, and giving him two months to recant or be excommunicated. Luther retaliated by publicly burning the letter. By 1521, when the excommunication was supposed to become final, Luther's theological issues had become interwoven with public controversies about the church's wealth, power, and basic structure. The papal legate wrote of the growing furor, "All Germany is in revolution. Nine-tenths shout 'Luther' as their war cry; and the other tenth cares nothing about Luther, and cries 'Death to the court of Rome.'"[1] In this highly charged atmosphere, the twenty-one-year-old emperor Charles V held his first diet (assembly of the nobility, clergy, and cities of the Holy Roman Empire) in the German city of Worms, and summoned Luther to appear. Luther refused to give in to demands that he take back his ideas. "Unless I am convinced by the evidence of Scripture or by plain reason," he said, "I cannot and will not recant anything, for it is neither safe nor right to go against conscience."[2] His appearance at the Diet of Worms in 1521 created an even broader audience for reform ideas, and throughout central Europe other individuals began to preach and publish against the existing doctrines and practices of the church, drawing on the long tradition of calls for change as well as on Luther.

Protestant Thought

The most important early reformer other than Luther was the Swiss humanist, priest, and admirer of Erasmus, Ulrich Zwingli (ZWIHN-glee) (1484–1531). Zwingli announced in 1519 that he would preach not from the church's prescribed readings but, relying on Erasmus's New Testament, go right through the New Testament "from A to Z," that is, from Matthew to Revelation. Zwingli was convinced that Christian life rested on the Scriptures, which were the pure words of God and the sole basis of religious truth. He went on

The Ten Commandments Lucas Cranach the Elder, the court painter for the elector of Saxony, painted this giant illustration of the Ten Commandments (more than 5 feet by 11 feet) for the city hall in Wittenberg in 1516, just at the point that Luther was beginning to question Catholic doctrine. Cranach was an early supporter of Luther, and many of his later works depict the reformer and his ideas. Paintings were used by both Protestants and Catholics to teach religious ideas. (Lutherhalle, Wittenberg/The Bridgeman Art Library)

to attack indulgences, the Mass, the institution of monasticism, and clerical celibacy. In his gradual reform of the church in Zurich, he had the strong support of the city authorities, who had long resented the privileges of the clergy.

The followers of Luther, Zwingli, and others who called for a break with Rome came to be called Protestants. The word **Protestant** derives from the protest drawn up by a small group of reforming German princes at the Diet of Speyer in 1529. The princes "protested" the decisions of the Catholic majority, and the word gradually became a general term applied to all non-Catholic western European Christians.

Protestant The name originally given to Lutherans, which came to mean all non-Catholic Western Christian groups.

Luther, Zwingli, and other early Protestants agreed on many things. First, how is a person to be saved? Traditional Catholic teaching held that salvation is achieved by both faith and good works. Protestants held that salvation comes by faith alone, irrespective of good works or the sacraments. God, not people, initiates salvation. (See "Listening to the Past: Martin Luther, *On Christian Liberty*," page 414.) Second, where does religious authority reside? Christian doctrine had long maintained that authority rests both in the Bible and in the traditional teaching of the church. For Protestants, authority rested in the Bible alone. For a doctrine or issue to be valid, it had to have a scriptural basis. Because of this, most Protestants rejected Catholic teachings about the sacraments—the rituals that the church had defined as imparting God's benefits on the believer (see Chapter 10)—holding that only baptism and the Eucharist have scriptural support.

Third, what is the church? Protestants held that the church is a spiritual priesthood of all believers, an invisible fellowship not fixed in any place or person, which differed markedly from the Roman Catholic practice of a hierarchical clerical institution headed by the pope in Rome. Fourth, what is the highest form of Christian life? The medieval church had stressed the superiority of the monastic and religious life over the secular. Protestants disagreed and argued that every person should serve God in his or her individual calling.

Protestants did not agree on everything, and one important area of dispute was the ritual of the Eucharist (also called communion, the Lord's Supper, and, in Catholicism, the Mass). Catholicism holds the dogma of transubstantiation: by the consecrating words of the priest during the Mass, the bread and wine become the actual body and blood of Christ. In opposition, Luther believed that Christ is really present in the consecrated bread and wine, but this is the result of God's mystery, not the actions of a priest. Zwingli understood the Eucharist as a memorial in which Christ was present in spirit among the faithful, but not in the bread and wine. The Colloquy of Marburg, summoned in 1529 to unite Protestants, failed to resolve these differences, though Protestants reached agreement on almost everything else.

The Appeal of Protestant Ideas

Pulpits and printing presses spread the Protestant message all over Germany, and by the middle of the sixteenth century people of all social classes had rejected Catholic teachings and had become Protestant. What was the immense appeal of Luther's religious ideas and those of other Protestants?

Educated people and many humanists were much attracted by Luther's ideas. He advocated a simpler personal religion based on faith, a return to the spirit of the early church, the centrality of the Scriptures in the liturgy and in Christian life, and the abolition of elaborate ceremonies—precisely the reforms the Christian humanists had been calling for. The Protestant insistence that everyone should read and reflect on the Scriptures attracted literate and thoughtful city residents. This included many priests and monks who left the Catholic Church to become clergy in the new Protestant churches. In addition, townspeople who envied the church's wealth and resented paying for it were attracted by the notion that the clergy should also pay taxes and should not have special legal privileges. After Zurich became Protestant, the city council taxed the clergy and placed them under the jurisdiction of civil courts.

Scholars in many disciplines have attributed Luther's fame and success to the invention of the printing press, which rapidly reproduced and made known his ideas. Many printed works included woodcuts and other illustrations, so that even those who could not read could grasp the main ideas. (See "Living in the Past: Uses of Art in the Reformation," page 418.) Equally important was Luther's incredible skill with language, as seen in his two catechisms (compendiums of basic religious knowledge) and in hymns that he wrote for congregations to sing. Luther's linguistic skill, together with his translation of the New Testament into German in 1523, led to the acceptance of his dialect of German as the standard written version of the German language.

Both Luther and Zwingli recognized that for reforms to be permanent, political authorities as well as concerned individuals and religious leaders would have to accept them. Zwingli worked closely with the city council of Zurich, and city councils themselves took the lead in other cities and towns of Switzerland and south Germany. They appointed pastors whom they knew had accepted Protestant ideas, required them to swear an oath of loyalty to the council, and oversaw their preaching and teaching.

Luther lived in a territory ruled by a noble—the elector of Saxony—and he also worked closely with political authorities, viewing them as fully justified in as-

Picturing the Past

Domestic Scene The Protestant notion that the best form of Christian life was marriage and a family helps explain its appeal to middle-class urban men and women, such as those shown in this domestic scene. The engraving, titled "Concordia" (harmony), includes the biblical inscription of what Jesus called the greatest commandment — "You shall love the Lord your God with all your heart and all your soul and your neighbor as yourself" (Deuteronomy 6; Matthew 22) — on tablets at the back. The large covered bed at the back was both a standard piece of furniture in urban homes and a symbol of proper marital sexual relations. (Mary Evans Picture Library)

ANALYZING THE IMAGE What are the different family members doing? What elements of this image suggest that this is a pious, Christian family?

CONNECTIONS How do the various family roles shown here support the Protestant ideal of marriage and family?

To complete this activity online, go to the Online Study Guide at bedfordstmartins.com/mckaywest.

serting control over the church in their territories. Indeed, he demanded that German rulers reform the papacy and its institutions, and he instructed all Christians to obey their secular rulers, whom he saw as divinely ordained to maintain order. Individuals may have been convinced of the truth of Protestant teachings by hearing sermons, listening to hymns, or reading pamphlets, but a territory became Protestant when its ruler, whether a noble or a city council, brought in a reformer or two to reeducate the territory's clergy, sponsored public sermons, and con-

fiscated church property. This happened in many of the states of the Holy Roman Empire during the 1520s.

The Radical Reformation and the German Peasants' War

While Luther and Zwingli worked with political authorities, some individuals and groups rejected the idea that church and state needed to be united. Beginning in the 1520s, they sought instead to create a voluntary

Martin Luther, *On Christian Liberty*

LISTENING TO THE PAST

The idea of liberty has played a powerful role in the history of Western society and culture, but the meaning and understanding of liberty has undergone continual change and interpretation. In the Roman world, where slavery was a basic institution, liberty meant the condition of being a free man, independent of obligations to a master. In the Middle Ages possessing liberty meant having special privileges or rights that other persons or

institutions did not have. A lord or a monastery, for example, might speak of his or its liberties, and citizens in London were said to possess the "freedom of the city," which allowed them to practice trades and own property without interference.

The idea of liberty also has a religious dimension, and the reformer Martin Luther formulated a classic interpretation of liberty in his treatise On Christian Liberty *(sometimes translated as* On the Freedom of a Christian*), arguably his finest piece. Written in Latin for the pope but translated immediately into German and published widely, it contains the main themes of Luther's theology: the importance of faith, the relationship of Christian faith and good works, the dual nature of human beings, and the fundamental importance of Scripture. Luther writes that Christians were freed from sin and death through Christ, not through their own actions.*

❝ A Christian man is the most free lord of all, and subject to none; a Christian man is the most dutiful servant of all, and subject to everyone. Although these statements appear contradictory, yet, when they are found to agree together, they will do excellently for my purpose. They are both the statements of Paul himself, who says, "Though I be free from all men, yet have I made myself a servant unto all" (I Corinthians 9:19) and "Owe no man anything but to love one another" (Romans 13:8). Now love is by its own nature dutiful and obedient to the beloved object. Thus even Christ, though Lord of all things, was yet made of a woman; made under the law; at once free and a servant; at once in the form of God and in the form of a servant.

Let us examine the subject on a deeper and less simple principle. Man is composed of a twofold nature, a spiritual and a bodily. As regards the spiritual nature, which they name the soul, he is called the spiritual, inward, new man; as regards the bodily nature, which they name the flesh, he is called the fleshly, outward, old man. The Apostle speaks of this: "Though our outward man perish, yet the inward man is renewed day by day" (II Corinthians 4:16). The result of this diversity is that in the Scriptures opposing statements are made concerning the same man, the fact being that in the same man these two men are opposed to one another; the flesh lusting against the spirit, and the spirit against the flesh (Galatians 5:17).

We first approach the subject of the inward man, that we may see by what means a man becomes justified, free, and a true Christian; that is, a spiritual, new, and inward man. It is certain that absolutely none among outward things, under whatever name they may be reckoned, has any influence in producing Christian righteousness or liberty, nor, on the other hand, unrighteousness or slavery. This can be shown by an easy argument. What can it profit to the soul that the body should be in good condition, free, and full of life, that it should eat, drink, and act according to its pleasure, when even the most impious slaves of every kind of vice are prosperous in these matters? Again, what harm can ill health, bondage, hunger, thirst, or any other outward evil, do to the soul, when even the most pious of men, and the freest in the purity of their conscience, are harassed by these things? Neither of these states of things has to do with the liberty or the slavery of the soul.

And so it will profit nothing that the body should be adorned with sacred vestment, or dwell in holy places, or be occupied in sacred offices, or pray, fast, and abstain from certain meats, or do whatever works can be done through the body and in the body. Something widely different will be necessary for the justification and liberty of the soul, since the things I have spoken of can be done by an impious person, and only hypocrites are produced by devotion to these things. On the other hand, it will not at all injure the soul that the body should be clothed in profane raiment, should dwell in profane places, should eat and drink in the ordinary fashion, should not pray aloud, and should leave undone all the things above mentioned, which may be done by hypocrites.

. . . One thing, and one alone, is necessary for life, justification, and Christian liberty; and that is the most Holy Word of God, the Gospel of Christ, as He says, "I am the resurrection and the life; he that believeth in me shall not die eternally" (John 9:25), and also, "If the Son shall make you free, ye shall be free indeed" (John 8:36), and "Man shall not live by bread alone, but by every word that proceedeth out of the mouth of God" (Matthew 4:4).

Let us therefore hold it for certain and firmly established that the soul can do without everything except the Word of God, without which none at all of its wants is provided for. But, having the Word, it is rich and wants for nothing, since that is the Word of life, of truth, of light, of peace, of justification, of salvation,

On effective preaching, especially to the uneducated, Luther urged the minister "to keep it simple for the simple."
(Church of St. Marien, Wittenberg/The Bridgeman Art Library)

of joy, of liberty, of wisdom, of virtue, of grace, of glory, and of every good thing. . . .

But you will ask, "What is this Word, and by what means is it to be used, since there are so many words of God?" I answer, "The Apostle Paul (Romans 1) explains what it is, namely the Gospel of God, concerning His Son, incarnate, suffering, risen, and glorified through the Spirit, the Sanctifier." To preach Christ is to feed the soul, to justify it, to set it free, and to save it, if it believes the preaching. For faith alone, and the efficacious use of the Word of God, bring salvation. "If thou shalt confess with thy mouth the Lord Jesus, and shalt believe in thine heart that God hath raised Him from the dead, thou shalt be saved" (Romans 9:9); . . . and "The just shall live by faith" (Romans 1:17). . . .

But this faith cannot consist of all with works; that is, if you imagine that you can be justified by those works, whatever they are, along with it. . . . Therefore, when you begin to believe, you learn at the same time that all that is in you is utterly guilty, sinful, and damnable, according to that saying, "All have sinned, and come short of the glory of God"

(Romans 3:23). . . . When you have learned this, you will know that Christ is necessary for you, since He has suffered and risen again for you, that, believing on Him, you might by this faith become another man, all your sins being remitted, and you being justified by the merits of another, namely Christ alone.

. . . [A]nd since it [faith] alone justifies, it is evident that by no outward work or labour can the inward man be at all justified, made free, and saved; and that no works whatever have any relation to him. . . . Therefore the first care of every Christian ought to be to lay aside all reliance on works, and strengthen his faith alone more and more, and by it grow in knowledge, not of works, but of Christ Jesus, who has suffered and risen again for him, as Peter teaches (I Peter 5). 🢥

QUESTIONS FOR ANALYSIS

1. What did Luther mean by liberty?
2. Why, for Luther, was Scripture basic to Christian life?

Source: *Luther's Primary Works*, ed. H. Wace and C. A. Buchheim (London: Holder and Stoughton, 1896). Reprinted in *The Portable Renaissance Reader*, ed. James Bruce Ross and Mary Martin McLaughlin (New York: Penguin Books, 1981), pp. 721–726.

❝ Let everyone who can smite, slay, and stab [the peasants], secretly and openly, remembering that nothing can be more poisonous, hurtful or devilish than a rebel. **❞**

—MARTIN LUTHER

community of believers separate from the state, as they understood it to have existed in New Testament times. In terms of theology and spiritual practices, these individuals and groups varied widely, though they are generally termed "radicals" for their insistence on a more extensive break with prevailing ideas. Some adopted the baptism of believers—for which they were given the title of "Anabaptists" or rebaptizers by their enemies—while others saw all outward sacraments or rituals as misguided. Some groups attempted communal ownership of property, living very simply and rejecting anything they thought unbiblical. Some reacted harshly to members who deviated, but others argued for complete religious toleration and individualism.

Religious radicals were often pacifists and refused to hold office or swear oaths, which marked them as societal outcasts and invited fanatical hatred and bitter persecution. Both Protestant and Catholic authorities felt threatened by the social, political, and economic implications of their religious ideas, and by their rejection of a state church, which the authorities saw as key to maintaining order. In Saxony, in Strasbourg, and in the Swiss cities, radicals were either banished or cruelly executed by burning, beating, or drowning. Their community spirit and heroism in the face of martyrdom, however, contributed to the survival of radical ideas. Later, the Quakers, with their pacifism; the Baptists, with their emphasis on inner spiritual light; the Congregationalists, with their democratic church organization; and in 1787 the authors of the U.S. Constitution, with their opposition to the "establishment of religion" (state churches), would all trace their origins, in part, to the radicals of the sixteenth century.

Radical reformers sometimes called for social as well as religious change, a message that German peasants heard. In the early sixteenth century the economic condition of the peasantry varied from place to place but was generally worse than it had been in the fifteenth century and was deteriorating. Crop failures in 1523 and 1524 aggravated an explosive situation. Nobles had aggrieved peasants by seizing village common lands, by imposing new rents and requiring additional services, and by taking the peasants' best horses or cows whenever a head of household died. The peasants made demands that they believed conformed to the Scriptures, and they cited radical thinkers as well as Luther as proof that they did.

Luther wanted to prevent rebellion. Initially he sided with the peasants, blasting the lords for robbing their subjects. But when rebellion broke out, peasants who expected Luther's support were soon disillusioned. Freedom for Luther meant independence from the authority of the Roman church; it did not mean opposition to legally established secular powers.

As for biblical support for the peasants' demands, he maintained that Scripture had nothing to do with earthly justice or material gain, a position that Zwingli supported. Firmly convinced that rebellion would hasten the end of civilized society, Luther wrote the tract *Against the Murderous, Thieving Hordes of the Peasants*: "Let everyone who can smite, slay, and stab [the peasants], secretly and openly, remembering that nothing can be more poisonous, hurtful or devilish than a rebel."[3] The nobility ferociously crushed the revolt. Historians estimate that more than seventy-five thousand peasants were killed in 1525.

The German Peasants' War of 1525 greatly strengthened the authority of lay rulers. Not surprisingly, the Reformation lost much of its popular appeal after 1525, though peasants and urban rebels sometimes found a place for their social and religious ideas in radical groups. Peasants' economic conditions did moderately improve, however. For example, in many parts of Germany, enclosed fields, meadows, and forests were returned to common use.

Marriage and Sexuality

Luther and Zwingli both believed that a priest's or nun's vows of celibacy went against human nature and God's commandments, and that marriage brought spiritual advantages and so was the ideal state for nearly all human beings. Luther married a former nun, Katharina von Bora (1499–1532), and Zwingli married a Zurich widow, Anna Reinhart (1491–1538). Both women quickly had several children. Most other Protestant reformers also married, and their wives had to create a new and respectable role for themselves—pastor's wife—to overcome being viewed as simply a new type of priest's concubine. They were living demonstrations of their husband's convictions about the superiority of marriage to celibacy, and they were expected to be models of wifely obedience and Christian charity.

Though they denied that marriage was a sacrament, Protestant reformers stressed that it had been ordained by God when he presented Eve to Adam, served as a "remedy" for the unavoidable sin of lust, provided a site for the pious rearing of the next generation of God-fearing Christians, and offered husbands and wives companionship and consolation. A proper marriage was one that reflected both the spiritual equality of men and

Martin Luther and Katharina von Bora Lucas Cranach the Elder painted this double marriage portrait to celebrate Luther's wedding in 1525 to Katharina von Bora, a former nun. The artist was one of the witnesses at the wedding and, in fact, had presented Luther's marriage proposal to Katharina. Using a go-between for proposals was very common, as was having a double wedding portrait painted. This particular couple quickly became a model of the ideal marriage, and many churches wanted their portraits. More than sixty similar paintings, with slight variations, were produced by Cranach's workshop and hung in churches and wealthy homes. (Uffizi, Florence/Scala/Art Resource, NY)

women and the proper social hierarchy of husbandly authority and wifely obedience.

Protestants did not break with medieval scholastic theologians in their idea that women were to be subject to men. Women were advised to be cheerful rather than grudging in their obedience, for in doing so they demonstrated their willingness to follow God's plan. Men were urged to treat their wives kindly and considerately, but also to enforce their authority, through physical coercion if necessary. European marriage manuals used the metaphor of breaking a horse for teaching a wife obedience, though laws did set limits on the husband's power to do so. A few women took Luther's idea about the priesthood of all believers to heart. Argula von Grumbach, a German noblewoman, wrote religious pamphlets supporting Protestant ideas, asserting, "I am not unfamiliar with Paul's words that women should be silent in church but when I see that no man will or can speak, I am driven by the word of God when he said, he who confesses me on earth, him will I confess, and he who denies me, him will I deny."[4] No sixteenth-

century Protestants officially allowed women to be members of the clergy, however, though monarchs such as Elizabeth I of England and female territorial rulers of the states of the Holy Roman Empire did determine religious policies just as male rulers did.

Protestants saw marriage as a contract in which each partner promised the other support, companionship, and the sharing of mutual goods. Because, in Protestant eyes, marriage was created by God as a remedy for human weakness, marriages in which spouses did not comfort or support one another physically, materially, or emotionally endangered their own souls and the surrounding community. The only solution might be divorce and remarriage, which most Protestants came to allow. Protestant allowance of divorce differed markedly from Catholic doctrine, which viewed marriage as a sacramental union that, if validly entered into, could not be dissolved (Catholic canon law allowed only separation with no remarriage). Although it was a dramatic legal change, divorce did not have a dramatic impact on newly Protestant areas. Because marriage was the cornerstone

LIVING IN THE PAST

IN THE REFORMATION ERA, CONTROVERSY RAGED over the purpose and function of art. Protestants and Catholics disagreed, and Protestant groups disagreed with one another. Some Protestant leaders, including Ulrich Zwingli and John Calvin, stressed that "the Word of God" should be the only instrument used in the work of evangelization. Swiss Protestants and Calvinists in many parts of Europe stripped

statues, images, and decoration out of many formerly Catholic churches or redesigned them with a stark, bare simplicity. Martin Luther, by contrast, believed that painting and sculpture had value in spreading the Gospel message because "children and simple folk are more apt to retain the divine stories when taught by pictures and parables than merely by words or instruction." He collaborated with artists such as Lucas Cranach the Elder (1472–1553), who conveyed Protestant ideas in woodcuts and paintings. (See Cranach's *The Ten Commandments*, page 411.)

Both Protestants and Catholics used pictures for propaganda purposes. In *The True and False Churches*, Lucas Cranach the Younger (1515–1586) shows Luther standing in a pulpit, preaching the word of God from an open Bible. At the right, a flaming open mouth symbolizing the jaws of Hell engulfs the pope, cardinals, and friars, one kind of "false church." At the left, Cranach shows a crucified Christ emerging out of

the "lamb of God" on the altar as people are receiving communion. This image of the "true church" represents the Lutheran understanding of the Lord's Supper, in which Christ is really present in the bread and wine, in contrast to other Protestants such as Zwingli who saw the ceremony as a symbol or memorial.

The Catholic Church officially addressed the subject of art at the Council of Trent in 1563. The church declared that honor and veneration should be given to likenesses of Christ, the Virgin Mary, and the saints; that images should remind people of the saints' virtues in order to encourage imitation; and that pictorial art should promote piety and the love of God. Consider the anonymous painting *Jesuit Priest Distributing Holy Pictures*. Parish priests and Jesuits often distributed such pictures to laypeople, including children, to help educate them in matters of doc-

Lucas Cranach the Younger, *The True and False Churches*.
(Staatliche Kunstsammlungen Dresden)

Jesuit Priest Distributing Holy Pictures. (From Pierre Chenu, *The Reformation* [New York: St. Martin's Press, 1986])

trine. Church leaders also sponsored the building of lavishly decorated churches that appealed to the senses and proclaimed the power of the reformed Catholic Church. (See Jesuit Church of the Gesù on page 430.)

QUESTIONS FOR ANALYSIS

1. What does Cranach's woodcut suggest about Protestants who had a different interpretation than Luther's about the Lord's Supper?

2. Cranach's woodcut could be easily reproduced through the technology of the printing press. How would this have enhanced its impact?

3. In what way does the artist of the Jesuit image suggest that people are eager for the Catholic message? How might this painting itself have aroused piety?

of society socially and economically, divorce was a desperate last resort. In many Protestant jurisdictions the annual divorce rate hovered around 0.02 to 0.06 per thousand people. (By contrast, in 2007 the U.S. divorce rate was 3.6 per thousand people.)

As Protestants believed marriage was the only proper remedy for lust, they uniformly condemned prostitution. The licensed brothels that were a common feature of late medieval urban life (see Chapter 12) were closed in Protestant cities, and harsh punishments were set for prostitution. Many Catholic cities soon closed their brothels as well, although Italian cities favored stricter regulations rather than closure. Selling sex was couched in moral rather than economic terms, as simply one type of "whoredom," a term that also included premarital sex, adultery, and other unacceptable sexual activities. "Whore" was also a term that reformers used for their theological opponents; Protestants compared the pope to the biblical whore of Babylon, a symbol of the end of the world, while Catholics called Luther's wife a whore because she had first been married to Christ as a nun before her marriage to Luther. Closing brothels did not end the exchange of sex for money, of course, but simply reshaped it. Smaller illegal brothels were established, or women moved to areas right outside city walls.

The Protestant Reformation clearly had a positive impact on marriage, but its impact on women was more mixed. Many nuns were in convents because their parents placed them there and did not have a strong sense of religious calling, but convents nevertheless provided women of the upper classes with scope for their literary, artistic, medical, or administrative talents if they could not or would not marry. The Reformation generally brought the closing of monasteries and convents, and marriage became virtually the only occupation for upper-class Protestant women. Women in some convents recognized this and fought the Reformation, or argued that they could still be pious Protestants within convent walls. Most nuns left, however, and we do not know what happened to them. The Protestant emphasis on marriage made unmarried women (and men) suspect, for they did not belong to the type of household regarded as the cornerstone of a proper, godly society.

The Reformation and German Politics

How did the political situation in Germany shape the course of the Reformation? ◼

Although criticism of the church was widespread in Europe in the early sixteenth century, reform movements could be more easily squelched by the strong central governments that had evolved in Spain and France.

England, too, had a strong monarchy, but the king broke from the Catholic Church for other reasons (see page 423). The Holy Roman Empire, in contrast, included hundreds of largely independent states. Against this background of decentralization and strong local power, Martin Luther had launched a movement to reform the church. Two years after he published the "Ninety-five Theses," the electors of the Holy Roman Empire chose as emperor a nineteen-year-old Habsburg prince who ruled as Charles V (r. 1519–1556). The course of the Reformation was shaped by this election and by the political relationships surrounding it.

The Rise of the Habsburg Dynasty

War and diplomacy were important ways that states increased their power in sixteenth-century Europe, but so was marriage. Royal and noble sons and daughters were important tools of state policy. The benefits of an advantageous marriage stretched across generations, a process that can be seen most dramatically with the Habsburgs. The Holy Roman emperor Frederick III, a Habsburg who was the ruler of most of Austria, acquired only a small amount of territory—but a great deal of money—with his marriage to Princess Eleonore

of Portugal in 1452. He arranged for his son Maximilian to marry Europe's most prominent heiress, Mary of Burgundy, in 1477; she inherited the Netherlands, Luxembourg, and the County of Burgundy in what is now eastern France. Through this union with the rich and powerful duchy of Burgundy, the Austrian house of Habsburg, already the strongest ruling family in the empire, became an international power. The marriage of Maximilian and Mary angered the French, however, who considered Burgundy French territory, and inaugurated centuries of conflict between the Austrian house of Habsburg and the kings of France.

Maximilian learned the lesson of marital politics well, marrying his son and daughter to the children of Ferdinand and Isabella, the rulers of Spain, much of southern Italy, and eventually the Spanish New World empire. His grandson Charles V (1500–1558) fell heir to a vast and incredibly diverse collection of states and peoples, each governed in a different manner and held together only by the person of the emperor (Map 14.1). Charles's Italian adviser, the grand chancellor Gattinara, told the young ruler, "God has set you on the path toward world monarchy." Charles not only believed this but also was convinced that it was his duty to maintain the political and religious unity of Western Christendom.

Fresco of Pope Clement VII and the Emperor Charles V In this double portrait, artist Giorgio Vasari uses matching hand gestures to indicate agreement between the pope and the emperor, though the pope's red hat and cape make him the dominant figure. Charles V remained loyal to Catholicism, though the political situation and religious wars in Germany eventually required him to compromise with Protestants. (Palazzo Vecchio, Florence/Scala/Art Resource, NY)

Religious Wars in Switzerland and Germany

In the sixteenth century the practice of religion remained a public matter. The ruler determined the official form of religious practice in his (or occasionally her) jurisdiction. Almost everyone believed that the presence of a faith different from that of the majority represented a political threat to the security of the state, and few believed in religious liberty.

Luther's ideas appealed to German rulers for a variety of reasons. Though Germany was not a nation, people did have an understanding of being German because of their language and traditions. Luther frequently used the phrase "we Germans" in his attacks on the papacy. Luther's appeal to national feeling influenced many rulers otherwise confused by or indifferent to the complexities of the religious matters. Some German rulers were sincerely attracted to Lutheran ideas, but material considerations swayed many others to embrace the new faith. The rejection of Roman Catholicism and adoption of Protestantism would mean the legal confiscation of lush farmlands, rich monasteries, and wealthy shrines. Thus many political authorities in the empire used the religious issue to extend their financial and political power and to enhance their independence from the emperor.

Charles V was a vigorous defender of Catholicism, so it is not surprising that the Reformation led to religious wars. The first battleground was Switzerland, which was officially part of the Holy Roman Empire, though it was really a loose confederation of thirteen largely autonomous territories called "cantons." Some cantons remained Catholic, and some became Protestant, and in the late 1520s the two sides went to war. Zwingli was killed on the battlefield in 1531, and both sides quickly decided

Map 14.1 **The Global Empire of Charles V, ca. 1556** Charles V exercised theoretical jurisdiction over more European territory than anyone since Charlemagne. He also claimed authority over large parts of North and South America (see Map 15.2 on page 452), though actual Spanish control was weak in much of the area.

that a treaty was preferable to further fighting. The treaty basically allowed each canton to determine its own religion and ordered each side to give up its foreign alliances, a policy of neutrality that has been characteristic of modern Switzerland.

Trying to halt the spread of religious division, Charles V called an Imperial Diet in 1530, to meet at Augsburg. The Lutherans developed a statement of faith, later called the Augsburg Confession, and the Protestant princes presented this to the emperor. (The Augsburg Confession remains an authoritative statement of belief for many Lutheran churches.) Charles refused to accept it and ordered all Protestants to return to the Catholic Church and give up any confiscated church property. This demand backfired, and Protestant territories in the empire—mostly northern German principalities and southern German cities—formed a military alliance. The emperor could not respond militarily, as he was in the midst of a series of wars with the French: the Habsburg-Valois wars (1521–1559), fought in Italy along the eastern and southern borders of France and eventually in Germany. The Ottoman Turks had also taken much of Hungary and in 1529 were besieging Vienna.

The 1530s and early 1540s saw complicated political maneuvering among many of the powers of Europe. Various attempts were made to heal the religious split with a church council, but stubbornness on both sides made it increasingly clear that this would not be possible and that war was inevitable. Charles V realized that he was fighting not only for religious unity, but also for a more unified state, against territorial rulers who wanted to maintain their independence. He was thus defending both church and empire.

Fighting began in 1546, and initially the emperor was very successful. This success alarmed both France and the pope, however, who did not want Charles to become even more powerful. The pope withdrew papal troops, and the Catholic king of France sent money and troops to the Lutheran princes. Finally, in 1555 Charles agreed to the Peace of Augsburg, which, "in order to bring peace into the holy empire," officially recognized Lutheranism. The political authority in each territory was permitted to decide whether the territory would be Catholic or Lutheran and was ordered to let other territories "enjoy their religious beliefs, liturgy, and ceremonies as well as their estates in peace." Most of northern and central Germany became Lutheran, while the south remained Roman Catholic. There was no freedom of religion within the territories, however. Princes or town councils established state churches to which all subjects of the area had to belong. Dissidents had to convert or leave, although the treaty did order that "they shall neither be hindered in the sale of their estates after due payment of the local taxes nor injured in their honor."[5] Religious refugees became a common feature on the roads of the empire, though rulers did not always let their subjects leave as easily as the treaty stipulated.

The Peace of Augsburg ended religious war in Germany for many decades. His hope of uniting his empire under a single church dashed, Charles V abdicated in 1556 and moved to a monastery, transferring power over his holdings in Spain and the Netherlands to his son Philip and his imperial power to his brother Ferdinand.

The Spread of Protestant Ideas

How did Protestant ideas and institutions spread beyond German-speaking lands? ▪

States within the Holy Roman Empire were the earliest territories to accept the Protestant Reformation, but by the later 1520s and 1530s religious change came to Denmark-Norway, Sweden, England, France, and eastern Europe. In most of these areas, a second generation of reformers built on Lutheran and Zwinglian ideas to develop their own theology and plans for institutional change. The most important of the second-generation reformers was John Calvin, whose ideas would profoundly influence the social thought and attitudes of European peoples and their descendants all over the world.

Scandinavia

The first area outside the empire to officially accept the Reformation was the kingdom of Denmark-Norway under King Christian III (r. 1536–1559). Danish scholars studied at the University of Wittenberg, and Lutheran ideas spread into Denmark very quickly. In the 1530s the king officially broke with the Catholic Church, and most clergy followed. The process went smoothly in Denmark, but in northern Norway and Iceland (which Christian also ruled) there were violent reactions, and Lutheranism was only gradually imposed on a largely unwilling populace.

In Sweden, Gustavus Vasa (r. 1523–1560), who came to the throne during a civil war with Denmark, also took over control of church personnel and income. Protestant ideas spread, though the Swedish church did not officially accept Lutheran theology until later in the century.

Henry VIII and the Reformation in England

As on the continent, the Reformation in England had economic and political as well as religious causes. The

Allegory of the Tudor Dynasty The unknown creator of this work intended to glorify the virtues of the Protestant succession; the painting has no historical reality. Henry VIII (seated) hands the sword of justice to his Protestant son Edward VI. The Catholic Queen Mary and her husband Philip of Spain (left) are followed by Mars, god of war, signifying violence and civil disorder. At right the figures of Peace and Plenty accompany the Protestant Elizabeth I, symbolizing England's happy fate under her rule. (Yale Center for British Art, Paul Mellon Collection/The Bridgeman Art Library)

impetus for England's break with Rome was the desire of King Henry VIII (r. 1509–1547) for a new wife, though ultimately his own motives also combined personal, political, social, and economic elements.

Henry VIII was married to Catherine of Aragon, the daughter of Ferdinand and Isabella and widow of Henry's older brother Arthur. Marriage to a brother's widow went against canon law, and Henry had been required to obtain a special papal dispensation to marry Catherine. The marriage had produced only one living heir, a daughter, Mary. By 1527 Henry decided that God was showing his displeasure with the marriage by denying him a son, and he appealed to the pope to have the marriage annulled. He was also in love with a court lady-in-waiting, Anne Boleyn, and assumed that she would give him the son he wanted. Normally an annulment would not have been a problem, but the troops of Emperor Charles V were in Rome at that point, and Pope Clement VII was essentially their prisoner. Charles V was the nephew of Catherine of Aragon and thus was

vigorously opposed to an annulment, which would have declared his aunt a fornicator and his cousin Mary a bastard. The pope stalled.

With Rome thwarting his matrimonial plans, Henry decided to remove the English church from papal jurisdiction. In a series of measures during the 1530s, Henry used Parliament to end the authority of the pope and make himself the supreme head of the church in England. Some opposed the king and were beheaded, among them Thomas More, the king's chancellor and author of *Utopia* (see Chapter 13). When Anne Boleyn failed twice to produce a male child, Henry VIII charged her with adulterous incest and in 1536 had her beheaded. His third wife, Jane Seymour, gave Henry the desired son, Edward, but she died in childbirth. Henry went on to three more wives.

Theologically, Henry was conservative, and the English church retained such traditional Catholic practices and doctrines as confession, clerical celibacy, and transubstantiation. Between 1535 and 1539, however, under the influence of his chief minister, Thomas Cromwell, Henry decided to dissolve the English monasteries because he wanted their wealth. Working through Parliament, the king ended nine hundred years of English monastic life, dispersing the monks and nuns and confiscating their lands. Their proceeds enriched the royal treasury, and hundreds of properties were sold to the middle and upper classes, the very groups represented in Parliament. The dissolution of the monasteries did not achieve a more equitable distribution of land and wealth; rather, the redistribution of land strengthened the upper classes and tied them to both the Tudor dynasty and the new Protestant church.

The nationalization of the church and the dissolution of the monasteries led to important changes in government administration. Vast tracts of formerly monastic land came temporarily under the Crown's jurisdiction, and new bureaucratic machinery had to be developed to manage those properties. Cromwell reformed and centralized the king's household, the council, the secretariats, and the Exchequer. New departments of state were set up. Surplus funds from all departments went into a liquid fund to be applied to areas where there were deficits. This balancing resulted in greater efficiency and economy, and Henry VIII's reign saw the growth of the modern centralized bureaucratic state.

Did the religious changes under Henry VIII have broad popular support? Some English people had been dissatisfied with the existing Christian church before Henry's measures, and Protestant literature circulated. Traditional Catholicism exerted an enormously strong and vigorous hold over the imagination and loyalty of the people, however. Most clergy and officials accepted Henry's moves, but all did not quietly acquiesce. In 1536 popular opposition in the north to the religious changes led to the Pilgrimage of Grace, a massive rebellion that proved the largest in English history. The "pilgrims" accepted a truce, but their leaders were arrested, tried, and executed. Recent scholarship points out that people rarely "converted" from Catholicism to Protestantism overnight. People responded to an action of the Crown that was played out in their own neighborhood—the closing of a monastery, the ending of Masses for the dead—with a combination of resistance, acceptance, and collaboration. Some enthusiastically changed to Protestant forms of prayer, for example, while others recited Protestant prayers in church while keeping pictures of the Catholic saints at home.

Loyalty to the Catholic Church was particularly strong in Ireland. Ireland had been claimed by English kings since the twelfth century, but in reality the English had firm control of only the area around Dublin, known as the Pale. In 1536, on orders from London, the Irish parliament, which represented only the English landlords and the people of the Pale, approved the English laws severing the church from Rome. The Church of Ireland was established on the English pattern, and the (English) ruling class adopted the new reformed faith. Most of the Irish people remained Roman Catholic, thus adding religious antagonism to the ethnic hostility that had been a feature of English policy toward Ireland for centuries (see Chapter 12). Irish armed opposition to the Reformation led to harsh repression by the English. Catholic property was confiscated and sold, and the profits were shipped to England. The Roman church was essentially driven underground, and the Catholic clergy acted as national as well as religious leaders.

Upholding Protestantism in England

In the short reign of Henry's sickly son, Edward VI (r. 1547–1553), Protestant ideas exerted a significant influence on the religious life of the country. Archbishop Thomas Cranmer simplified the liturgy, invited Protestant theologians to England, and prepared the first *Book of Common Prayer* (1549), which was later approved by Parliament. In stately and dignified English, the *Book of Common Prayer* included the order for all services and prayers of the Church of England.

The equally brief reign of Mary Tudor (r. 1553–1558) witnessed a sharp move back to Catholicism. The devoutly Catholic daughter of Catherine of Aragon, Mary rescinded the Reformation legislation of her father's reign and restored Roman Catholicism. Mary's marriage to her cousin Philip II of Spain, son of the emperor Charles V, proved highly unpopular in England, and her execution of several hundred Protestants further alienated her subjects. During her reign, about a thousand Protestants fled to the continent. Mary's death raised to the throne her sister Elizabeth, Henry's daughter with Anne Boleyn, who had been raised a Protestant. Her reign from 1558 to 1603 inaugurated the beginnings of religious stability.

At the start of Elizabeth's reign sharp differences existed in England. On the one hand, Catholics wanted a Roman Catholic ruler. On the other hand, a vocal number of returning exiles wanted all Catholic elements in the Church of England eliminated. The latter, because they wanted to "purify" the church, were called "Puritans."

Shrewdly, Elizabeth chose a middle course between Catholic and Puritan extremes. She referred to herself as the "supreme governor of the Church of England," using the term *governor* instead of the traditional *head* because this allowed Catholics to remain loyal to her without denying the pope. She required her subjects to attend services in the Church of England or risk a fine, but she did not interfere with their privately held beliefs. As she put it, she did not "want to make windows into men's souls." The Anglican Church, as the Church of England was called, moved in a moderately Protestant direction. Services were conducted in English, monasteries were not re-established, and clergymen were (grudgingly) allowed to marry. But the church remained hierarchical, with archbishops and bishops, and services continued to be elaborate, with the clergy in distinctive robes, in contrast to the simpler services favored by many continental Protestants.

Toward the end of the sixteenth century Elizabeth's reign was threatened by European powers attempting to re-establish Catholicism. Philip II of Spain had hoped that his marriage to Mary Tudor would reunite England with Catholic Europe, but Mary's death ended those plans. Another Mary—Mary, Queen of Scots—provided a new opportunity. Mary was Elizabeth's cousin, but she was Catholic. Mary was next in line to the English throne, and Elizabeth imprisoned her because she worried—quite rightly—that Mary would become the center of Catholic plots to overthrow her. In 1587 Mary became implicated in a plot to assassinate Elizabeth, a conspiracy that had Philip II's full backing. When the English executed Mary, the Catholic pope urged Philip to retaliate.

Philip prepared a vast fleet to sail from Lisbon to Flanders, where a large army of Spanish troops was stationed because of religious wars in the Netherlands (see page 435). The Spanish ships were to escort barges carrying some of the troops across the English Channel to attack England. On May 9, 1588, *la felícissima armada*—"the most fortunate fleet," as it was ironically called in official documents—composed of more than 130 vessels, sailed from Lisbon harbor. The **Spanish Armada** met an English fleet in the channel before it reached Flanders. The English ships were smaller, faster, and more maneuverable, and many of them had greater firing power than their Spanish counterparts. A combination of storms and squalls, spoiled food and rank water, inadequate Spanish ammunition, and, to a lesser extent, English fire ships that caused the Spanish to scatter gave England the victory. On the journey home many Spanish ships went down in the rough seas around Ireland; perhaps 65 ships managed to reach home ports.

The battle in the English Channel has frequently been described as

one of the decisive battles in world history. In fact, it had mixed consequences. Spain soon rebuilt its navy, and after 1588 the quality of the Spanish fleet improved. The war between England and Spain dragged on for years. Yet the defeat of the Spanish Armada prevented Philip II from reimposing Catholicism on England by force. In England the victory contributed to a David and Goliath legend that enhanced English national sentiment.

Spanish Armada The fleet sent by Philip II of Spain in 1588 against England as a religious crusade against Protestantism. Weather and the English fleet defeated it.

The Institutes of the Christian Religion Calvin's formulation of Christian doctrine, which became a systematic theology for Protestantism.

Calvinism

In 1509, while Luther was preparing for a doctorate at Wittenberg, John Calvin (1509–1564) was born in Noyon in northwestern France. As a young man he studied law, which had a decisive impact on his mind and later his thought. In 1533 he experienced a religious crisis, as a result of which he converted to Protestantism.

Calvin believed that God had specifically selected him to reform the church. Accordingly, he accepted an invitation to assist in the reformation of the city of Geneva. There, beginning in 1541, Calvin worked assiduously to establish a Christian society ruled by God through civil magistrates and reformed ministers. Geneva became the model of a Christian community for Protestant reformers.

To understand Calvin's Geneva, it is necessary to understand Calvin's ideas. These he embodied in ***The Institutes of the Christian Religion***, published first in 1536 and in its final form in 1559. The cornerstone of Calvin's theology was his belief in the absolute sovereignty and omnipotence of God and the total weakness of humanity. Before the infinite power of God, he asserted, men and women are as insignificant as grains of sand.

Calvin did not ascribe free will to human beings because that would detract from the sovereignty of God. Men and women cannot actively work to achieve salvation; rather, God in his infinite wisdom decided at the beginning of time who would be saved and who damned. This viewpoint constitutes the theological

The Route of the Spanish Armada, 1588

→ Advance of the Armada
- → Retreat of the Armada
✳ Major battle
▼ Shipwreck

principle called **predestination**. Calvin explained his view:

> *Predestination we call the eternal decree of God, by which he has determined in himself, what he would have become of every individual. . . . For they are not all created with a similar destiny; but eternal life is foreordained for some, and eternal damnation for others. . . . To those whom he devotes to condemnation, the gate of life is closed by a just and irreprehensible, but incomprehensible, judgment. How exceedingly presumptuous it is only to inquire into the causes of the Divine will; which is in fact, and is justly entitled to be, the cause of everything that exists. . . . For the will of God is the highest justice; so that what he wills must be considered just, for this very reason, because he wills it.*[6]

Many people consider the doctrine of predestination, which dates back to Saint Augustine and Saint Paul, to be a pessimistic view of the nature of God. But "this terrible decree," as even Calvin called it, did not lead to pessimism or fatalism. Rather, the Calvinist believed in the redemptive work of Christ and was confident that God had elected (saved) him or her. Predestination served as an energizing dynamic, giving a person the strength to undergo hardships in the constant struggle against evil.

predestination The teaching that God has determined the salvation or damnation of individuals based on his will and purpose, not on their merit or works.

In his reform of Geneva, Calvin had several remarkable assets, including complete mastery of the Scriptures and exceptional eloquence. He also understood the importance of institutions and established the Genevan Consistory, a body of laymen and pastors, "to keep watch over every man's life [and] to admonish amiably those whom they see leading a disorderly life" and provide "medicine to turn sinners to the Lord."[7]

Although all municipal governments in early modern Europe regulated citizens' conduct, none did so with the severity of Geneva's Consistory under Calvin's leadership. Absence from sermons, criticism of ministers, dancing, card playing, family quarrels, and heavy drinking were all investigated and punished by the Consistory.

Serious crimes and heresy were handled by the civil authorities, which, with the Consistory's approval, sometimes used torture to extract confessions. Between 1542 and 1546 alone seventy-six persons were banished from Geneva, and fifty-eight were executed for heresy, adultery, blasphemy, and witchcraft (see page 435). Among them was the Spanish humanist and refugee Michael Servetus, who was burned at the stake for denying the scriptural basis for the Trinity, rejecting child baptism, and insisting that a person under twenty cannot commit a mortal sin, all of which were viewed as threats to society.

Religious refugees from France, England, Spain, Scotland, and Italy visited Calvin's Geneva, and many of the most prominent exiles from Mary Tudor's England stayed. Subsequently, the church of Calvin—often termed "Reformed"—served as the model for the Presbyterian church in Scotland, the Huguenot church in France (see page 433), and the Puritan churches in England and New England.

Calvinism became the compelling force in international Protestantism. The Calvinist ethic of the "calling" dignified all work with a religious aspect. Hard work, well done, was pleasing to God. This doctrine encouraged an aggressive, vigorous activism, and Calvinism became the most dynamic force in sixteenth- and seventeenth-century Protestantism.

Calvinism spread on the continent of Europe, and also found a ready audience in Scotland. There as elsewhere,

Young John Calvin This oil painting of the reformer as a young man captures his spiritual intensity and determination, qualities that the artist clearly viewed as positive. (Bibliothèque de Genève, Département iconographique)

❝ Predestination we call the eternal decree of God, by which he has determined in himself, what he would have become of every individual. ❞

—JOHN CALVIN

political authority was the decisive influence in reform. The monarchy was weak, and factions of virtually independent nobles competed for power. King James V and his daughter Mary, Queen of Scots (r. 1560–1567), staunch Catholics and close allies of Catholic France, opposed reform, but the Scottish nobles supported it. One man, John Knox (1505?–1572), dominated the reform movement, which led to the establishment of a state church.

Knox was determined to structure the Scottish church after the model of Geneva, where he had studied and worked with Calvin. In 1560 Knox persuaded the Scottish parliament, which was dominated by reform-minded barons, to end papal authority and rule by bishops, substituting governance by presbyters, or councils of ministers. The Presbyterian Church of Scotland was strictly Calvinist in doctrine, adopted a simple and dignified service of worship, and laid great emphasis on preaching.

The Reformation in Eastern Europe

While political and economic issues determined the course of the Reformation in western and northern Europe, ethnic factors often proved decisive in eastern Europe, where people of diverse backgrounds had settled in the later Middle Ages. In Bohemia in the fifteenth century, a Czech majority was ruled by Germans. Most Czechs had adopted the ideas of Jan Hus, and the emperor had been forced to recognize a separate Hussite church (see Chapter 12). Yet Lutheranism appealed to Germans in Bohemia in the 1520s and 1530s, and the nobility embraced Lutheranism in opposition to the Catholic Habsburgs. The forces of the Catholic Reformation (see page 428) promoted a Catholic spiritual revival in Bohemia, and some areas reconverted. This complicated situation would be one of the causes of the Thirty Years' War in the early seventeenth century.

By 1500 Poland and the Grand Duchy of Lithuania were jointly governed by king, senate, and diet (parliament), but the two territories retained separate officials, judicial systems, armies, and forms of citizenship. The combined realms covered almost 500,000 square miles, making Poland-Lithuania the largest European polity. A population of only about 7.5 million people was very thinly scattered over that land.

The population of Poland-Lithuania was also very diverse; Germans, Italians, Tartars, and Jews lived with Poles and Lithuanians. Such peoples had come as merchants, invited by medieval rulers because of their wealth or to make agricultural improvements. Each group spoke its native language, though all educated people spoke Latin. Luther's ideas took root in Germanized towns but were opposed by King Sigismund I (r. 1506–1548) as well as by ordinary Poles, who held strong anti-German feeling. The Reformed tradition of John Calvin, with its stress on the power of church elders, appealed to the Polish nobility, however. The fact that Calvinism originated in France, not in Germany, also made it more attractive than Lutheranism. But doctrinal differences among Calvinists, Lutherans, and other groups prevented united opposition to Catholicism, and a Counter-Reformation gained momentum. By 1650, due to the efforts of Stanislaus Hosius (1505–1579) and those of the Jesuits (see page 431), Poland was again staunchly Roman Catholic.

Hungary's experience with the Reformation was even more complex. Lutheranism was spread by Hungarian students who had studied at Wittenberg, and sympathy for it developed at the royal court of King Louis II in Buda. But concern about "the German heresy" by the Catholic hierarchy and among the high nobles found expression in a decree of the Hungarian diet in 1523 that "all Lutherans and those favoring them . . . should have their property confiscated and themselves punished with death as heretics."[8]

Before such measures could be acted on, a military event on August 26, 1526, had profound consequences for both the Hungarian state and the Protestant Reformation there. On the plain of Mohács in southern Hungary, the Ottoman sultan Suleiman the Magnificent inflicted a crushing defeat on the Hungarians, killing King Louis II, many of the nobles, and more than sixteen thousand ordinary soldiers. The Hungarian kingdom was then divided into three parts: the Ottoman Turks absorbed the great plains, including the capital, Buda; the Habsburgs ruled the north and west; and Ottoman-supported Janos Zapolya held eastern Hungary and Transylvania.

The Turks were indifferent to the religious conflicts of Christians, whom they regarded as infidels. Christians of all types paid extra taxes to the sultan, but kept their faith. Many Magyar (Hungarian) nobles accepted Lutheranism; Lutheran schools and parishes headed by men educated at Wittenberg multiplied; and peasants

The Battle of Mohács Massed armies on both sides confront each other in this Turkish illustration of the Battle of Mohács. In the right panel, Suleiman in a white turban sits on a black horse surrounded by his personal guard, while his soldiers fire muskets and large cannon at the enemy. In the left panel the Europeans are in disarray, and their weapons are clearly inferior. (Topkapi Saray Museum)

welcomed the new faith. The majority of people were Protestant until the late seventeenth century, when Hungarian nobles recognized Habsburg (Catholic) rule and Ottoman Turkish withdrawal in 1699 led to Catholic restoration.

The Catholic Reformation

How did the Catholic Church respond to the new religious situation? ■

Between 1517 and 1547 Protestantism made remarkable advances. Nevertheless, the Roman Catholic Church made a significant comeback. After about 1540 no new large areas of Europe, other than the Netherlands, accepted Protestant beliefs (Map 14.2). Many historians see the developments within the Catholic Church after the Protestant Reformation as two interrelated move-

ments, one a drive for internal reform linked to earlier reform efforts, and the other a Counter-Reformation that opposed Protestants intellectually, politically, militarily, and institutionally. In both movements, the papacy, new religious orders, and the Council of Trent that met from 1545 to 1563 were important agents.

Papal Reform and the Council of Trent

Renaissance popes and their advisers were not blind to the need for church reforms, but they resisted calls for a general council representing the entire church, and feared that any transformation would mean a loss of power, revenue, and prestige. This changed beginning with Pope Paul III (pontificate 1534–1549), when the papal court became the center of the reform movement rather than its chief opponent. The lives of the pope and his reform-minded cardinals, abbots, and bishops were models of

Predominant religion in 1555

- Lutheran
- Calvinist (Reformed)
- Church of England
- Roman Catholic
- Eastern Orthodox
- Muslim
- → Spread of Calvinism, from 1541
- ▲ Huguenot center
- — Ottoman Empire, 1566

Penetration of Calvinism to England after 1558

Wittenburg
Martin Luther writes Ninety-five Theses 1517

Worms
Edict of Worms 1521

Nantes
Edict of Nantes 1598

Trent
Council of Trent 1545–1563

Augsburg
Peace of Augsburg 1555

Geneva
Calvin assists in Reformation beginning in 1541

Mapping the Past

Map 14.2 Religious Divisions in Europe, ca. 1555

The Reformations shattered the religious unity of Western Christendom. The situation was even more complicated than a map of this scale can show. Many cities within the Holy Roman Empire, for example, accepted a different faith than the surrounding countryside; Augsburg, Basel, and Strasbourg were all Protestant, though surrounded by territory ruled by Catholic nobles.

ANALYZING THE MAP Which countries were the most religiously diverse in Europe? Which were the least diverse?

CONNECTIONS Where was the first arena of religious conflict in sixteenth-century Europe, and why did it develop there and not elsewhere? To what degree can nonreligious factors be used as an explanation for the religious divisions in sixteenth-century Europe?

To complete this activity online, go to the Online Study Guide at bedfordstmartins.com/mckaywest.

decorum and piety, in contrast to Renaissance popes who concentrated on building churches and enhancing the power of their own families. Paul III and his successors supported improvements in education for the clergy, the end of simony (the selling of church offices), and stricter control of clerical life.

In 1542 Pope Paul III established the Supreme Sacred Congregation of the Roman and Universal Inquisition, often called the **Holy Office**, with jurisdiction over the Roman Inquisition, a powerful instrument of the Catholic Reformation. The Roman Inquisition was a committee of six cardinals with judicial authority over all Catholics and the power to arrest, imprison, and execute suspected heretics. The Holy Office published the *Index of Prohibited Books*, a catalogue of forbidden reading that included works by Christian humanists such as Erasmus as well as by Protestants. Within the Papal States, the Inquisition effectively destroyed heresy, but outside the papal territories, its influence was slight.

> **Holy Office** The official Roman Catholic agency founded in 1542 to combat international doctrinal heresy.

Pope Paul III also called a general council, which met intermittently from 1545 to 1563 at Trent, an imperial city close to Italy. It was called not only to reform the Catholic Church but also to secure reconciliation with the Protestants. Lutherans and Calvinists were invited to participate, but their insistence that the Scriptures be the sole basis for discussion made reconciliation impossible. In addition, the political objectives of Charles V and France both worked against reconciliation: Charles wanted to avoid alienating the Lutheran nobility in the empire, and France wanted the Catholics and Lutherans to remain divided in order to keep Germany decentralized and weak.

Nonetheless, the decrees of the Council of Trent laid a solid basis for the spiritual renewal of the Catholic Church. It gave equal validity to the Scriptures and to tradition as sources of religious truth and authority. It reaffirmed the seven sacraments and the traditional Catholic teaching on transubstantiation. It tackled the disciplinary matters that had disillusioned the faithful, requiring bishops to reside in their own dioceses, suppressing pluralism and simony, and forbidding the sale of indulgences. Clerics who kept concubines were to give them up, and bishops were given greater authority. In a highly original decree, the council required every diocese to establish a seminary for the education and training of the clergy. Seminary professors were to determine whether candidates for ordination had vocations,

Church of the Gesù   Begun in 1568 as the mother church for the Jesuit order, the Church of the Gesù conveyed a sense of drama, motion, and power through its lavish decorations and shimmering frescoes. Gesù served as a model for Catholic churches elsewhere in Europe and the New World, their triumphant and elaborate style reflecting the dynamic and proselytizing spirit of the Catholic Reformation. (The Art Archive/Corbis)

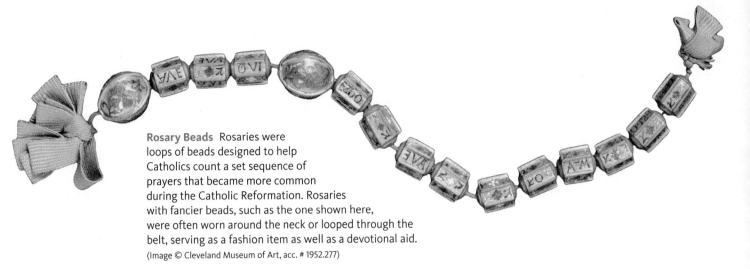

Rosary Beads Rosaries were loops of beads designed to help Catholics count a set sequence of prayers that became more common during the Catholic Reformation. Rosaries with fancier beads, such as the one shown here, were often worn around the neck or looped through the belt, serving as a fashion item as well as a devotional aid. (Image © Cleveland Museum of Art, acc. # 1952.277)

genuine callings to the priesthood. This was a novel idea, since from the time of the early church, parents had determined their sons' (and daughters') religious careers. For the first time, great emphasis was laid on preaching and instructing the laity, especially the uneducated.

One decision had especially important social consequences for laypeople. The Council of Trent stipulated that for a marriage to be valid, the marriage vows had to be made publicly before a priest and witnesses. Trent thereby ended the widespread practice of private marriages in Catholic countries, curtailing the number of denials and conflicts that inevitably resulted from marriages that took place in secret.

Although it did not achieve all of its goals, the Council of Trent composed decrees that laid a solid basis for the spiritual renewal of the church. The doctrinal and disciplinary legislation of Trent served as the basis for Roman Catholic faith, organization, and practice through the middle of the twentieth century.

New Religious Orders

The establishment of new religious orders within the church reveals a central feature of the Catholic Reformation. Most of these new orders developed in response to one crying need: to raise the moral and intellectual level of the clergy and people. (See "Individuals in Society: Teresa of Ávila," page 432.) Education was a major goal of the two most famous orders.

The Ursuline order of nuns, founded by Angela Merici (1474–1540), attained enormous prestige for the education of women. The daughter of a country gentleman, Angela Merici worked for many years among the poor, sick, and uneducated around her native Brescia in northern Italy. In 1535 she established the first women's religious order concentrating exclusively on teaching young girls, with the goal of re-Christianizing society by training future wives and mothers. After receiving papal approval in 1565, the Ursulines rapidly spread to France and the New World.

The Society of Jesus, or **Jesuits**, founded by Ignatius Loyola (1491–1556) played a powerful international role in strengthening Catholicism in Europe and spreading the faith around the world. While recuperating from a severe battle wound in his legs, Loyola studied books about Christ and the saints and decided to give up his military career and become a soldier of Christ. During a year spent in seclusion, prayer, and asceticism, he gained insights that went into his great classic, *Spiritual Exercises* (1548). This work, intended for study during a four-week period of retreat, set out a training program of structured meditation designed to develop spiritual discipline and allow one to meld one's will with that of God. Loyola introduces his program by noting:

> **Jesuits** Members of the Society of Jesus, founded by Ignatius Loyola, whose goal was the spread of the Roman Catholic faith.

> *By the term "Spiritual Exercises" is meant every method of examination of conscience, of meditation, of contemplation, of vocal and mental prayer, and of other spiritual activities. For just as taking a walk, journeying on foot, and running are bodily exercises, so we call Spiritual Exercises every way of preparing and disposing the soul to rid itself of all inordinate attachments, and, after their removal, of seeking and finding the will of God in the disposition of our life for the salvation of our soul.[9]*

Just as do today's physical trainers, Loyola provides daily exercises that build in intensity over the four weeks of the program, and charts on which the exerciser can track his progress.

Loyola was a man of considerable personal magnetism. After study at universities in Salamanca and Paris, he gathered a group of six companions and in 1540 secured papal approval of the new Society of Jesus. The first Jesuits, recruited primarily from wealthy merchant

Teresa of Ávila

HER FAMILY DERIVED FROM TOLEDO, center of the Moorish, Jewish, and Christian cultures in medieval Spain. Her grandfather, Juan Sanchez, made a fortune in the cloth trade. A New Christian (a convert from Judaism or Islam), he was accused of secretly practicing Judaism. He endured the humiliation of a public repentance and moved his family south to Ávila. Beginning again, he recouped his wealth and, perhaps hoping to hide his status as a convert, bought noble status. Juan's son Alzonzo Sanchez de Cepeda married a woman of thoroughly Christian background, giving his family an aura of impeccable orthodoxy. The third of their nine children, Teresa, became a saint and in 1970 was the first woman declared a Doctor of the Church, a title given to a theologian of outstanding merit.

At age twenty, inspired more by the fear of Hell than the love of God, Teresa (1515–1582) entered the Carmelite Convent of the Incarnation in Ávila. Most of the nuns were daughters of Ávila's leading citizens; they had entered the convent because of family decisions about which daughters would marry and which would become nuns. Their lives were much like those of female family members outside the convent walls, with good food, comfortable surroundings, and frequent visits from family and friends. Teresa was frequently ill, but she lived quietly in the convent for many years. In her late thirties, she began to read devotional literature intensely and had profound mystical experiences — visions and voices in which Christ chastised her for her frivolous life and friends. She described one such experience in 1560:

> It pleased the Lord that I should see an angel. . . . Short, and very beautiful, his face was so aflame that he appeared to be one of the highest types of angels. . . . In his hands I saw a long golden spear and at the end of an iron tip I seemed to see a point of fire. With this he seemed to pierce my heart several times so that it penetrated to my entrails. When he drew it out . . . he left me completely afire with the great love of God.*

Teresa responded with a new sense of purpose and resolved to found a reformed house. Four basic principles guided the new convent. First, poverty was to be fully observed, symbolized by the nuns' being barefoot, with charity and the nuns' own work supporting the community. Second, the convent must keep strict enclosure, with no visitors allowed, even if they were the convent's wealthy supporters. Third, the convent was to have an egalitarian atmosphere in which class distinctions were forbidden and all sisters, including those of aristocratic background, shared the manual chores. The discriminatory measures common in Spanish society that applied to New Christians were also not to be prac-

ticed. Fourth, like Ignatius Loyola and the Jesuits, Teresa placed great emphasis on obedience, especially to one's confessor.

Between 1562 and Teresa's death in 1582, she founded or reformed fourteen other houses of nuns, traveling widely to do so. Teresa thought of the new religious houses she founded as answers to the Protestant takeover of Catholic churches elsewhere in Europe. From her brother, who had obtained wealth in the Spanish colonies, she learned about conditions in Peru and instructed her nuns "to pray unceasingly for the missionaries working among the heathens." Through prayer, Teresa wrote, her nuns could share in the exciting tasks of evangelization and missionary work otherwise closed to women. Her books, along with her five hundred surviving letters, show her as a practical and down-to-earth woman as well as a mystic and a creative theologian.

Seventeenth-century cloisonné enamelwork illustrating Teresa of Ávila's famous vision of an angel piercing her heart. (By gracious permission of Catherine Hamilton Kappauf)

QUESTIONS FOR ANALYSIS

1. How did convent life in Ávila reflect the values of sixteenth-century society, and how did Teresa's reforms challenge these?

2. How is the life of Teresa of Ávila typical of developments in the Catholic Reformation? How is her life unusual?

*The Autobiography of St. Teresa of Ávila, trans. and ed. E. A. Peers (New York: Doubleday, 1960), pp. 273–274.

and professional families, saw the Reformation as a pastoral problem, its causes and cures related not to doctrinal issues but to people's spiritual condition. Reform of the church, as Luther and Calvin understood that term, played no role in the future the Jesuits planned for themselves. Their goal was "to help souls."

The Society of Jesus developed into a highly centralized, tightly knit organization. In addition to the traditional vows of poverty, chastity, and obedience, professed members vowed special obedience to the pope. Flexibility and the willingness to respond to the needs of time and circumstance formed the Jesuit tradition, which proved attractive to many young men. The Jesuits achieved phenomenal success for the papacy and the reformed Catholic Church, carrying Christianity to India and Japan before 1550 and to Brazil, North America, and the Congo in the seventeenth century. Within Europe the Jesuits brought southern Germany and much of eastern Europe back to Catholicism. Jesuit schools adopted the modern humanist curricula and methods, educating the sons of the nobility as well as the poor. As confessors and spiritual directors to kings, Jesuits exerted great political influence.

Religious Violence

What were the causes and consequences of religious violence, including riots, wars, and witch-hunts? ■

In 1559 France and Spain signed the Treaty of Cateau-Cambrésis (CAH-toh kam-BRAY-sees), which ended the long conflict known as the Habsburg-Valois wars. Spain was the victor. France, exhausted by the struggle, had to acknowledge Spanish dominance in Italy, where much of the fighting had taken place. However, true peace was elusive, and over the next century religious differences led to riots, civil wars, and international conflicts. Especially in France and the Netherlands, Protestants and Catholics used violent actions as well as preaching and teaching against each other, for each side regarded the other as a poison in the community that would provoke the wrath of God. Catholics continued to believe that Calvinists and Lutherans could be reconverted; Protestants persisted in thinking that the Roman church should be destroyed. Catholics and Protestants alike feared people of other faiths, whom they often saw as agents of Satan. Even more, they feared those who were explicitly identified with Satan: witches living in their midst. This era was the time of the most virulent witch persecutions in European history, as both Protestants and Catholics tried to make their cities and states more godly.

French Religious Wars

The costs of the Habsburg-Valois wars, waged intermittently through the first half of the sixteenth century, forced the French to increase taxes and borrow heavily. King Francis I (r. 1515–1547) also tried two new devices to raise revenue: the sale of public offices and a treaty with the papacy. The former proved to be only a temporary source of money: once a man bought an office he and his heirs were exempt from taxation. But the latter, known as the Concordat of Bologna (see page 399), gave the French crown the right to appoint all French bishops and abbots, ensuring a rich supplement of money and offices. Because French rulers possessed control over appointments and had a vested financial interest in Catholicism, they had no need to revolt against Rome.

Significant numbers of those ruled, however, were attracted to the Reformed religion of Calvinism. Initially, Calvinism drew converts from among reform-minded members of the Catholic clergy, industrious city dwellers, and artisan groups. Most French Calvinists (called **Huguenots**) lived in major cities, such as Paris, Lyons, and Rouen. When King Henry II (r. 1547–1559) died in 1559 — accidentally shot in the face at a tournament celebrating the Treaty of Cateau-Cambrésis — perhaps one-tenth of the population had become Calvinist.

Huguenots French Calvinists.

The feebleness of the French monarchy was the seed from which the weeds of civil violence sprang. The three weak sons of Henry II who occupied the throne could not provide the necessary leadership, and they were often dominated by their mother, Catherine de' Medici. The French nobility took advantage of this monarchical weakness. Just as German princes in the Holy Roman Empire had adopted Lutheranism as a means of opposition to Emperor Charles V, so French nobles frequently adopted Protestantism as a religious cloak for their independence. Armed clashes between Catholic royalist lords and Calvinist antimonarchical lords occurred in many parts of France. Both Calvinists and Catholics believed that the others' books, services, and ministers polluted the community. Preachers incited violence, and religious ceremonies such as baptisms, marriages, and funerals triggered it.

Calvinist teachings called the power of sacred images into question, and mobs in many cities took down and smashed statues, stained-glass windows, and paintings, viewing this as a way to purify the church. Though it was often inspired by fiery Protestant sermons, this iconoclasm, or destruction of religious images, is an example of ordinary men and women carrying out the Reformation themselves. Catholic mobs responded by defending images, and crowds on both sides killed their opponents, often in gruesome ways.

A savage Catholic attack on Calvinists in Paris on Saint Bartholomew's Day, August 24, 1572, followed the usual pattern. The occasion was the marriage ceremony of the king's sister Margaret of Valois to the Protestant Henry of Navarre, which was intended to help reconcile Catholics and Huguenots. Instead, Huguenot wedding guests in Paris were massacred, and other Protestants were slaughtered by mobs. Religious violence spread to the provinces, where thousands were killed. This Saint Bartholomew's Day massacre led to a civil war that dragged on for fifteen years. Agriculture in many areas was destroyed; commercial life declined severely; and starvation and death haunted the land.

What ultimately saved France was a small group of moderates of both faiths, called **politiques**, who believed that only the restoration of strong monarchy could reverse the trend toward collapse. The politiques also favored accepting the Huguenots as an officially recognized and organized group. The death of Catherine de' Medici, followed by the assassination of King Henry III, paved the way for the accession of Henry of Navarre (the unfortunate bridegroom of the Saint Bartholomew's Day massacre), a politique who became Henry IV (r. 1589–1610).

Henry's willingness to sacrifice religious principles to political necessity saved France. He converted to Catholicism but also issued the **Edict of Nantes** in 1598, which granted liberty of conscience and liberty of public worship to Huguenots in 150 fortified towns. The reign of Henry IV and the Edict of Nantes prepared the way for French absolutism in the seventeenth century by helping restore internal peace in France.

politiques Catholic and Protestant moderates who held that only a strong monarchy could save France from total collapse.

Edict of Nantes A document issued by Henry IV of France in 1598, granting liberty of conscience and of public worship to Calvinists, which helped restore peace in France.

The Netherlands Under Charles V

In the Netherlands, what began as a movement for the reformation of the church developed into a struggle for Dutch independence. Emperor Charles V had inherited the seventeen provinces that compose present-day Belgium and the Netherlands (see page 420). Each was self-governing and enjoyed the right to make its own laws and collect its own taxes. The provinces were united politically only in recognition of a common ruler, the emperor. The cities of the Netherlands made their living by trade and industry.

In the Low Countries as elsewhere, corruption in the Roman church and the critical spirit of the Renaissance provoked pressure for reform, and Lutheran ideas took root. Charles V had grown up in the Netherlands, however, and he was able to limit their impact. But Charles V abdicated in 1556 and transferred power over the Netherlands to his son Philip II, who had grown up in Spain. Protestant ideas spread.

By the 1560s Protestants in the Netherlands were primarily Calvinists. Calvinism's intellectual seriousness, moral gravity, and emphasis on any form of labor well done appealed to urban merchants, financiers, and artisans. Whereas Lutherans taught respect for the powers that be, Calvinism tended to encourage opposition to political authorities who were judged to be ungodly.

Iconoclasm in the Netherlands Calvinist men and women break stained-glass windows, remove statues, and carry off devotional altarpieces. Iconoclasm, or the destruction of religious images, is often described as a "riot," but here the participants seem very purposeful. Calvinist Protestants regarded pictures and statues as sacrilegious and saw removing them as a way to purify the church. (The Fotomas Index/The Bridgeman Art Library)

When Spanish authorities attempted to suppress Calvinist worship and raised taxes in the 1560s, rioting ensued. Calvinists sacked thirty Catholic churches in Antwerp, destroying the religious images in them in a wave of iconoclasm. From Antwerp the destruction spread. Philip II sent twenty thousand Spanish troops under the duke of Alva to pacify the Low Countries. Alva interpreted "pacification" to mean ruthless extermination of religious and political dissidents. On top of the Inquisition, he opened his own tribunal, soon called the "Council of Blood." On March 3, 1568, fifteen hundred men were executed. To Calvinists, all this was clear indication that Spanish rule was ungodly and should be overthrown.

Between 1568 and 1578 civil war raged in the Netherlands between Catholics and Protestants and between the seventeen provinces and Spain. Eventually the ten southern provinces, the Spanish Netherlands (the future Belgium), came under the control of the Spanish Habsburg forces. The seven northern provinces, led by Holland, formed the **Union of Utrecht** and in 1581 declared their independence from Spain. The north was Protestant; the south remained Catholic. Philip did not accept this, and war continued. England was even drawn into the conflict, supplying money and troops to the northern United Provinces. (Spain launched an unsuccessful invasion of England in response; see page 425.) Hostilities ended in 1609 when Spain agreed to a truce that recognized the independence of the United Provinces.

The Great European Witch-Hunt

The relationship between the Reformation and the upsurge in trials for witchcraft that occurred at roughly the same time is complex. Increasing persecution for witchcraft actually began before the Reformation in the 1480s, but it became especially common about 1560, and the mania continued until roughly 1660. Religious reformers' extreme notions of the Devil's powers and the insecurity created by the religious wars contributed to this increase. Both Protestants and Catholics tried and executed witches, with church officials and secular authorities acting together.

The heightened sense of God's power and divine wrath in the Reformation era was an important factor in the witch-hunts, but so was a change in the idea of what a witch was. Nearly all premodern societies believe in witchcraft and make some attempts to control witches,

□ United Provinces
■ Spanish Netherlands
— Treaty line, 1609

North Sea

Amsterdam
Utrecht
Bruges
Ghent
Antwerp
Brussels
HOLY ROMAN EMPIRE
FRANCE

The Netherlands, 1609

who are understood to be people who use magical forces. In the later Middle Ages, however, many educated Christian theologians, canon lawyers, and officials added a demonological component to this notion of what a witch was. For them, the essence of witchcraft was making a pact with the Devil. Witches were no longer simply people who used magical power to get what they wanted, but rather people used by the Devil to do what he wanted. Witches were thought to engage in wild sexual orgies with the Devil, fly through the night to meetings called sabbats that parodied Christian services, and steal communion wafers and unbaptized babies to use in their rituals. Some demonological theorists also claimed that witches were organized in an international conspiracy to overthrow Christianity. Witchcraft was thus spiritualized, and witches became the ultimate heretics, enemies of God.

Trials involving this new notion of witchcraft as diabolical heresy began in Switzerland and southern Germany in the late fifteenth century, became less numerous in the early decades of the Reformation when Protestants and Catholics were busy fighting each other, and then picked up again in about 1560. Scholars estimate that during the sixteenth and seventeenth centuries between 100,000 and 200,000 people were officially tried for witchcraft and between 40,000 and 60,000 were executed.

> **Union of Utrecht**
> The alliance of seven northern provinces (led by Holland) that declared its independence from Spain and formed the United Provinces of the Netherlands.

Though the gender balance varied widely in different parts of Europe, between 75 and 85 percent of those tried and executed were women. Ideas about women and the roles women actually played in society were thus important factors shaping the witch-hunts. Some demonologists expressed virulent misogyny, or hatred of women, and particularly emphasized women's powerful sexual desire, which could be satisfied only by a demonic lover. Most people viewed women as weaker and so more likely to give in to an offer by the Devil. In both classical and Christian traditions, women were associated with nature, disorder, and the body, all of which were linked with the demonic. Women's actual lack of power in society and gender norms about the use of violence meant that they were more likely to use scolding and cursing to get what they wanted instead of taking people to court or beating them up. Curses were generally expressed (as they often are today) in religious terms; "go to Hell" was calling on the powers of Satan. Women also had more contact with areas of life in which bad things happened unexpectedly, such as preparing food or caring for new mothers, children, and animals.

Legal changes also played a role in causing, or at least allowing for, massive witch trials. One of these was a change from an accusatorial legal procedure to an inquisitorial procedure. In the former, a suspect knew the accusers and the charges they had brought, and an accuser could in turn be liable for trial if the charges were not proven. In the latter, legal authorities themselves brought the case. This change made people much more willing to accuse others, for they never had to take personal responsibility for the accusation or face the accused person's relatives. Areas in Europe that did not make this legal change saw very few trials. Inquisitorial procedure involved intense questioning of the suspect, often with torture. Torture was also used to get the names of addi-

tional suspects, as most lawyers firmly believed that no witch could act alone.

The use of inquisitorial procedure did not always lead to witch-hunts. The most famous inquisitions in early modern Europe, those in Spain, Portugal, and Italy, were in fact very lenient in their treatment of people accused of witchcraft. The Inquisition in Spain executed only a handful of witches, the Portuguese Inquisition only one, and the Roman Inquisition none, though in each of these there were hundreds of cases. Inquisitors believed in the power of the Devil and were no less misogynist than other judges, but they doubted very much whether the people accused of witchcraft had actually made pacts with the Devil that gave them special powers. They viewed such people not as diabolical Devil-worshipers but as superstitious and ignorant peasants who should be educated

Witch Pamphlet This printed pamphlet presents the confession of "Mother Waterhouse," a woman convicted of witchcraft in England in 1566, who describes her "many abominable deeds" and "execrable sorcery" committed over fifteen years, and asks for forgiveness right before her execution. Enterprising printers often produced cheap, short pamphlets during witch trials, knowing they would sell, sometimes based on the actual trial proceedings and sometimes just made up. They both reflected and helped create stereotypes about what witches were and did. (The Granger Collection, New York)

rather than executed. Thus most people brought up before the Inquisition for witchcraft were sent home with a warning and a penance.

Most witch trials began with a single accusation in a village or town. Individuals accused someone they knew of using magic to spoil food, make children ill, kill animals, raise a hailstorm, or do other types of harm. Tensions within families, households, and neighborhoods often played a role in these accusations. Women number very prominently among accusers and witnesses as well as among those accused of witchcraft because the actions witches were initially charged with, such as harming children or curdling milk, were generally part of women's sphere. A woman also gained economic and social security by conforming to the standard of the good wife and mother and by confronting women who deviated from it.

Once a charge was made, the suspect was brought in for questioning. One German witch pamphlet from 1587 described a typical case:

> *Walpurga Hausmännin . . . upon kindly questioning and also torture . . . confessed . . . that the Evil One indulged in fornication with her . . . and made her many promises to help her in her poverty and need. . . . She promised herself body and soul to him and disowned God in heaven. . . . She destroyed a number of cattle, pigs, and geese . . . and dug up [the bodies] of one or two innocent children. With her devil-paramour and other playfellows she has eaten these and used their hair and their little bones for witchcraft.*

Confession was generally followed by execution. In this case, Hausmännin was "dispatched from life to death by burning at the stake . . . her body first to be torn five times with red-hot irons."[10]

Detailed records of witch trials survive for many parts of Europe. They have been used by historians to study many aspects of witchcraft, but they cannot directly answer what seems to us an important question: did people really practice witchcraft and think they were witches? They certainly confessed to evil deeds and demonic practices, sometimes without torture, but where would we draw the line between reality and fantasy? Clearly people were not riding through the air on pitchforks, but did they think they did? Did they actually invoke the Devil when they were angry at a neighbor, or was this simply in the minds of their accusers? Trial records cannot tell us, and historians have answered these questions very differently, often using insights from

> ❝ Walpurga Hausmännin . . . dug up [the bodies] of one or two innocent children. With her devil-paramour and other playfellows she has eaten these and used their hair and their little bones for witchcraft. ❞
>
> —GERMAN WITCH PAMPHLET

psychoanalysis or the study of more recent victims of torture in their explanations.

After the initial suspect had been questioned, and particularly if he or she had been tortured, the people who had been implicated were brought in for questioning. This might lead to a small hunt, involving from five to ten suspects, and it sometimes grew into a much larger hunt, what historians have called a "witch panic." Panics were most common in the part of Europe that saw the most witch accusations in general: the Holy Roman Empire, Switzerland, and parts of France. Most of this area consisted of very small governmental units that were jealous of each other and, after the Reformation, were divided by religion. The rulers of these small territories often felt more threatened than did the monarchs of western Europe, and they saw persecuting witches as a way to demonstrate their piety and concern for order. Moreover, witch panics often occurred after some type of climatic disaster, such as an unusually cold and wet summer, and they came in waves.

In large-scale panics a wider variety of suspects were taken in — wealthier people, children, a greater proportion of men. Mass panics tended to end when it became clear to legal authorities, or to the community itself, that the people being questioned or executed were not what they understood witches to be, or that the scope of accusations was beyond belief. Some from their community might be in league with Satan, they thought, but not this type of person and not as many people as this.

As the seventeenth century ushered in new ideas about science and reason, many began to question whether witches could make pacts with the Devil or engage in the wild activities attributed to them. Doubts about whether secret denunciations were valid or torture would ever yield truthful confessions gradually spread among the same type of religious and legal authorities who had so vigorously persecuted witches. Prosecutions for witchcraft became less common and were gradually outlawed. The last official execution for witchcraft in England was in 1682, though the last one in the Holy Roman Empire was not until 1775.

LOOKING BACK LOOKING AHEAD

ALONG WITH THE RENAISSANCE, the Reformation is often seen as a key element in the creation of the "modern" world. This radical change contained many elements of continuity, however. Sixteenth-century reformers looked back to the early Christian church for their inspiration, and many of their reforming ideas had been advocated for centuries. Most Protestant reformers worked with political leaders to make religious changes, just as early church officials had worked with Emperor Constantine and his successors as Christianity became the official religion of the Roman Empire in the fourth century. The spread of Christianity and the spread of Protestantism were accomplished not only by preaching, persuasion, and teaching, but also by force and violence. The Catholic Reformation was carried out by activist popes, a church council, and new religious orders, just as earlier reforms of the church had been.

Just as they linked with earlier developments, the events of the Reformation were also closely connected with what is often seen as the third element in the "modern" world: European exploration and colonization. Only a week after Martin Luther stood in front of Charles V at the Diet of Worms declaring his independence in matters of religion, Ferdinand Magellan, a Portuguese sea captain with Spanish ships, was killed in a group of islands off the coast of Southeast Asia. Charles V had provided the backing for Magellan's voyage, the first to circumnavigate the globe. Magellan viewed the spread of Christianity as one of the purposes of his trip, and later in the sixteenth century institutions created as part of the Catholic Reformation, including the Jesuit order and the Inquisition, would operate in European colonies overseas as well as in Europe itself. The islands where Magellan was killed were later named the Philippines, in honor of Charles's son Philip, who sent the ill-fated Spanish Armada against England. Philip's opponent Queen Elizabeth was similarly honored when English explorers named a huge chunk of territory in North America "Virginia" as a tribute to their "Virgin Queen." The desire for wealth and power was an important motivation in the European voyages and colonial ventures, but so was religious zeal.

CHAPTER REVIEW

■ **What were the central ideas of the reformers, and why were they appealing to different social groups? (p. 408)**

By the early sixteenth century many lay Christians and members of the clergy had grown disillusioned with the church's wealth and certain practices, particularly its sale of indulgences and church offices. People were also critical of the immorality, ignorance, and absenteeism that they perceived among the clergy, and for centuries many individuals and groups had called for reform. Amid this background Luther and other Protestants developed a new understanding of Christian doctrine that emphasized faith, the power of God's grace, and the centrality of the Bible. Protestant ideas were attractive to educated people and urban residents, among whom anticlericalism had become widespread, and the new concepts spread rapidly among many groups through preaching, hymns, and the printing press. Most Protestant reformers worked with rulers to bring about religious change, but more radical thinkers and

the German peasants wanted political and social, as well as religious, changes. Both radicals and the peasants were put down harshly. The Protestant reformers did not break with medieval ideas about the proper gender hierarchy, though they did elevate the status of marriage and viewed orderly households as the key building blocks of society.

■ **How did the political situation in Germany shape the course of the Reformation? (p. 419)**

Beginning in 1519 the Habsburg emperor Charles V ruled almost half of Europe along with Spain's overseas colonies. Within the empire his authority was limited, however, and local princes, nobles, and cities actually held most power. This decentralization allowed the Reformation to spread as local rulers assumed religious authority. Charles remained firmly Catholic, and in the late 1520s religious wars began in central Europe. The papacy and Catholic kings of France initially supported Charles V's cause, but they withdrew support when he began gaining too much ground. The wars were brought to an end with the Peace of Augsburg in 1555, which officially recognized Lutheranism and allowed rulers in each territory to choose whether their territory would be Catholic or Lutheran.

■ How did Protestant ideas and institutions spread beyond German-speaking lands? (p. 422)

Outside of Germany, Protestantism spread first to Scandinavia and then elsewhere in northern Europe. In England, Henry VIII's desire for an annulment triggered the split with Rome, and a Protestant church was established, first differing little from Catholicism in terms of theology and later, under Queen Elizabeth, breaking more firmly with Catholic practice. The printing press and increased literacy of European society, as well as the growing number of universities, allowed Protestant ideas to spread rapidly into France and eastern Europe. In all these areas, a second generation of reformers built on Lutheran and Zwinglian ideas to develop their own theology and plans for institutional change. The most important of the second-generation reformers was John Calvin, whose ideas would come to shape Christianity over a much wider area than did Luther's.

■ How did the Catholic Church respond to the new religious situation? (p. 428)

By the 1530s the papacy was leading a movement for reform within the church and countering Protestant challenges. Catholic doctrine was reaffirmed at the Council of Trent, and reform measures such as the opening of seminaries for priests, the insistence on morality for the clergy, and a ban on holding multiple church offices were introduced. New religious orders such as the Jesuits and the Ursulines spread Catholic ideas through teaching, and in the case of the Jesuits through missionary work.

■ What were the causes and consequences of religious violence, including riots, wars, and witch-hunts? (p. 433)

Religious differences led to riots, civil wars, and international conflicts in the later sixteenth century. In France and the Netherlands, Calvinist Protestants and Catholics used violent actions against one another, and religious differences mixed with political and economic grievances. Long civil wars resulted, with that in the Netherlands becoming an international conflict. War ended in France with the Edict of Nantes in which Protestants were given some civil rights, and in the Netherlands with a division of the country into a Protestant north and Catholic south. The era of religious wars was also a time of the most extensive witch persecutions in European history, as both Protestants and Catholics tried to rid their cities and states of people they regarded as linked to the Devil.

Suggested Reading

Bossy, John. *Christianity in the West, 1500–1700.* 1985. A lively brief overview.

Gordon, Bruce. *John Calvin.* 2009. Situates Calvin's theology and life within the context of his relationships and the historical events of his time.

Haigh, Christopher. *English Reformations: Religion, Politics, and Society under the Tudors.* 1998. Explores the religious views and practices of ordinary English people as well as of the political elite.

Hendrix, Scott. *Luther.* 2009. A brief introduction to his thought, in the Abingdon Pillars of Theology series.

Holt, Mack P. *The French Wars of Religion, 1562–1629.* 1995. A thorough survey designed for students.

Hsia, R. Po-Chia. *The World of Catholic Renewal, 1540–1770.* 1998. Situates the Catholic Reformation in a global context and provides coverage of colonial Catholicism.

Karant-Nunn, Susan C., and Merry E. Wiesner-Hanks, eds. and trans. *Luther on Women: A Sourcebook.* 2003. An extensive collection of Luther's writings on marriage, women, and sexuality.

Levack, Brian. *The Witchhunt in Early Modern Europe,* 3d ed. 2007. A good introduction to the witch-hunts, with helpful bibliographies of the vast literature on witchcraft.

Levi, Anthony. *Renaissance and Reformation: The Intellectual Genesis.* 2002. Surveys the ideas of major Reformation figures against the background of important political issues.

Lindbergh, Carter. *The European Reformations.* 1996. A thorough discussion of the Protestant Reformation and some discussion of Catholic issues.

Monter, William E. *Calvin's Geneva.* 1967. Shows the effect of Calvin's reforms on the social life of the Swiss city.

O'Malley, John W. *Trent and All That: Renaming Catholicism in the Early Modern Era.* 2000. Provides an excellent historiographical review of the literature, and explains why and how early modern Catholicism influenced early modern European history.

Roper, Lyndal. *The Holy Household: Women and Morals in Reformation Augsburg.* 1991. An important study in local religious history as well as the history of gender and the family.

Shagan, Ethan. *Popular Politics and the English Reformation.* 2003. Analyzes the process of the Reformation in local areas.

Wheatcroft, Andrew. *The Habsburgs: Embodying Empire.* 1995. A solid study of political developments surrounding the Reformation.

Key Terms

anticlericalism (p. 408)

pluralism (p. 408)

indulgence (p. 409)

Protestant (p. 412)

Spanish Armada (p. 425)

The Institutes of the Christian Religion (p. 425)

predestination (p. 426)

Holy Office (p. 430)

Jesuits (p. 431)

Huguenots (p. 433)

politiques (p. 434)

Edict of Nantes (p. 434)

Union of Utrecht (p. 435)

Notes

1. Quoted in Owen Chadwick, *The Reformation* (Baltimore: Penguin Books, 1976), p. 55.
2. Quoted in E. H. Harbison, *The Age of Reformation* (Ithaca, N.Y.: Cornell University Press, 1963), p. 52.
3. Quoted in S. E. Ozment, *The Age of Reform, 1250–1550: An Intellectual and Religious History of Late Medieval and Reformation Europe* (New Haven, Conn.: Yale University Press, 1980), p. 284.
4. Ludwig Rabus, *Historien der heyligen Außerwolten Gottes Zeugen, Bekennern und Martyrern* (n.p., 1557), fol. 41. Trans. Merry Wiesner-Hanks.
5. From Henry Bettenson, ed., *Documents of the Christian Church*, 2d ed. (London: Oxford University Press, 1963), pp. 301–302.
6. J. Allen, trans., *John Calvin: The Institutes of the Christian Religion* (Philadelphia: Westminster Press, 1930), bk. 3, chap. 21, para. 5, 7.
7. Quoted in E. William Monter, *Calvin's Geneva* (New York: John Wiley & Sons, 1967), p. 137.
8. Quoted in David P. Daniel, "Hungary," in *The Oxford Encyclopedia of the Reformation*, vol. 2, ed. H. J. Hillerbrand (New York: Oxford University Press, 1996), p. 273.
9. *The Spiritual Exercise of St. Ignatius of Loyola*, trans. Louis J. Puhl, S.J. (Chicago: Loyola University, 1951), p. 1.
10. From *the Fugger News-Letters*, ed. Victor von Klarwell, trans. P. de Chary (London: John Lane, The Boley Head Ltd., 1924), quoted in James Bruce Ross and Mary Martin McLaughlin, *The Portable Renaissance Reader* (New York: Penguin, 1968), pp. 258, 260, 262.

For practice quizzes and other study tools, visit the Online Study Guide at **bedfordstmartins.com/mckaywest**.

For primary sources from this period, see ***Sources of Western Society*, Second Edition**.

For Web sites, images, and documents related to topics in this chapter, visit Make History at **bedfordstmartins.com/mckaywest**.

15

European Exploration and Conquest

1450–1650

Before 1450 Europeans were relatively marginal players in a centuries-old trading system that linked Africa, Asia, and Europe. Elites everywhere prized Chinese porcelains and silks, while wealthy members of the Celestial Kingdom, as China called itself, wanted ivory and black slaves from Africa, and exotic goods and peacocks from India. African people wanted textiles from India and cowrie shells from the Maldives in the Indian Ocean. Europeans craved Asian silks and spices but they had few desirable goods to offer their trading partners.

The European search for better access to Asian trade led to a new overseas empire in the Indian Ocean and the accidental discovery of the Western Hemisphere. Within a few decades European colonies in South and North America would join this worldwide web. Europeans came to dominate trading networks and political empires of truly global proportions. The era of globalization had begun.

Global contacts created new forms of cultural exchange, assimilation, conversion, and resistance. Europeans struggled to comprehend the peoples and societies they found and sought to impose European cultural values on them. New forms of racial prejudice emerged, but so did new openness and curiosity about different ways of life. Together with the developments of the Renaissance and the Reformation, the Age of Discovery — as the period of European exploration and conquest from 1450 to 1650 is known — laid the foundations for the modern world. ■

Life in the Age of Discovery. A detail from an early-seventeenth-century Flemish painting depicting maps, illustrated travel books, a globe, a compass, and an astrolabe. The voyages of discovery revolutionized Europeans' sense of space and inspired a passion among the wealthy for collecting objects related to navigation and travel.

CHAPTER PREVIEW

World Contacts Before Columbus
■ What was the Afro-Eurasian trading world before Columbus?

The European Voyages of Discovery
■ How and why did Europeans undertake ambitious voyages of expansion?

The Impact of Conquest
■ What was the impact of European conquest on the peoples and ecologies of the New World?

Europe and the World After Columbus
■ How was the era of global contact shaped by new commodities, commercial empires, and forced migrations?

Changing Attitudes and Beliefs
■ How did new ideas about race and the works of Montaigne and Shakespeare reflect the encounter with new peoples and places?

World Contacts Before Columbus

What was the Afro-Eurasian trading world before Columbus? ■

Columbus did not sail west on a whim. To understand his and other Europeans' explorations, we must first understand late medieval trade networks. Historians now recognize that a type of world economy, known as the Afro-Eurasian trade world, linked the products and people of Europe, Asia, and Africa in the fifteenth century. The West was not the dominant player before Columbus, and the European voyages derived from a desire to share in and control the wealth coming from the Indian Ocean.

The Trade World of the Indian Ocean

The Indian Ocean was the center of the Afro-Eurasian trade world. Its location made it a crossroads for commercial and cultural exchange between China, India, the Middle East, Africa, and Europe (Map 15.1). From

Map 15.1 The Fifteenth-Century Afro-Eurasian Trading World After a period of decline following the Black Death and the Mongol invasions, trade revived in the fifteenth century. Muslim merchants dominated trade, linking ports in East Africa and the Red Sea with those in India and the Malay Archipelago. Chinese Admiral Zheng He's voyages (1405–1433) followed the most important Indian Ocean trade routes, in the hope of imposing Ming dominance of trade and tribute.

the seventh through the fourteenth centuries, the volume of this trade steadily increased, declining only during the years of the Black Death.

Merchants congregated in a series of multicultural, cosmopolitan port cities strung around the Indian Ocean. Most of these cities had some form of autonomous self-government. Mutual self-interest had largely limited violence and attempts to monopolize trade. The most developed area of this commercial web was in the South China Sea. In the fifteenth century the port of Malacca (muh-LAH-kuh) became a great commercial entrepôt (AHN-truh-poh), a trading post to which goods were shipped for storage while awaiting redistribution to other places. To Malacca came Chinese porcelains, silks, and camphor (used in the manufacture of many medications); pepper, cloves, nutmeg, and raw materials such as sandalwood from the Moluccas; sugar from the Philippines; and Indian textiles, copper weapons, incense, dyes, and opium.

The Mongol emperors opened the doors of China to the West, encouraging Europeans like the Venetian trader and explorer Marco Polo to do business there. Marco Polo's tales of his travels from 1271 to 1295 and his encounter with the Great Khan fueled Western fantasies about the exotic Orient. After the Mongols fell to the Ming Dynasty in 1368, China entered a period of agricultural and commercial expansion, population growth, and urbanization. By the end of the dynasty in 1644, the Chinese population had tripled to between 150 million and 200 million. The city of Nanjing had one million inhabitants, making it the largest city in the world, while the new capital, Beijing, had more than six hundred thousand inhabitants, larger than any European city. Historians agree that China had the most advanced economy in the world until at least the start of the eighteenth century.

China also took the lead in exploration, sending Admiral Zheng He's fleet along the trade web as far west as Egypt. From 1405 to 1433, each of his seven expeditions involved hundreds of ships and tens of thousands of men. In one voyage alone, Zheng He sailed more than 12,000 miles, compared to Columbus's 2,400 miles on his first voyage some sixty years later.[1] Court conflicts and the need to defend against renewed Mongol encroachment led to the abandonment of the expeditions after the deaths of Zheng He and the emperor. China's turning away from external trade opened new opportunities for European states to claim a decisive role in world trade.

Another center of trade in the Indian Ocean was India, the crucial link between the Persian Gulf and the Southeast Asian and East Asian trade networks. The subcontinent had ancient links with its neighbors to the northwest: trade between South Asia and Mesopotamia dates back to the origins of human civilization. Romans had acquired cotton textiles, exotic animals, and other luxury goods from India. Arab merchants who circumnavigated India on their way to trade in the South China Sea established trading posts along the southern coast of India, where the cities of Calicut and Quilon became thriving commercial centers. India was an important contributor of goods to the world trading system; much of the world's pepper was grown there, and Indian cotton textiles were highly prized.

The Trading States of Africa

Africa also played an important role in the world trade system before Columbus. By 1450 Africa had a few large and developed empires along with hundreds of smaller states. From 1250 until its defeat by the Ottomans in 1517, the Mamluk Egyptian empire was one of the most powerful on the continent. Its capital, Cairo, was a center of Islamic learning and religious authority as well as a hub for Indian Ocean trade goods. Sharing in Cairo's prosperity was the African highland state of Ethiopia, a Christian kingdom with scattered contacts with European rulers. On the east coast of Africa Swahili-speaking city-states engaged in the Indian Ocean trade, exchanging ivory, rhinoceros horn, tortoise shells, and slaves for textiles, spices, cowrie shells, porcelain, and other goods. Peopled by confident and urbane merchants, cities like Mogadishu and Mombasa were known for their prosperity and culture.

Another important African contribution to world trade was gold. In the fifteenth century most of the gold that reached Europe came from Sudan in West Africa and from the Akan (AH-kahn) peoples living near present-day Ghana (GAH-nuh). Transported across the Sahara by Arab and African traders on camels, the gold was sold in the ports of North Africa. Other trading routes led to the Egyptian cities of Alexandria and Cairo, where the Venetians held commercial privileges.

1443	Portuguese establish first African trading post at Arguin
1492	Columbus lands in the Americas
1511	Portuguese capture Malacca from Muslims
1518	Spanish king authorizes slave trade to New World colonies
1519–1522	Magellan's expedition circumnavigates the world
1521	Cortés conquers the Mexica Empire
1533	Pizarro conquers the Inca Empire
1602	Dutch East India Company established

The Port of Banten in Western Java Influenced by Muslim traders and emerging in the early sixteenth century as a Muslim kingdom, Banten evolved into a thriving entrepôt. The city stood on the trade route to China and, as this Dutch engraving suggests, in the seventeenth century the Dutch East India Company used Banten as an important collection point for spices purchased for sale in Europe. (Archives Charmet/The Bridgeman Art Library)

Nations inland that sat astride the north-south caravan routes grew wealthy from this trade. In the mid-thirteenth century the kingdom of Mali emerged as an important player on the overland trade route. Malian ruler Mansa Musa reportedly discussed sending vessels to explore the Atlantic Ocean, which suggests that not only the Europeans envisaged westward naval exploration. In later centuries the diversion of gold away from the trans-Sahara routes would weaken the inland states of Africa politically and economically.

Gold was one important object of trade; slaves were another. Slavery was practiced in Africa, as virtually everywhere else in the world, before the arrival of Europeans. Arabic and African merchants took West African slaves to the Mediterranean to be sold in European, Egyptian, and Middle Eastern markets and also brought eastern Europeans—a major element of European slavery—to West Africa as slaves. In addition, Indian and Arabic merchants traded slaves in the coastal regions of East Africa.

Legends about Africa also played an important role

in Europeans' imagination of the outside world. They long cherished the belief in a Christian nation in Africa ruled by a mythical king, Prester John, who was believed to be a descendant of one of the three kings who visited Jesus after his birth.

The Ottoman and Persian Empires

The Middle East served as an intermediary for trade between Europe, Africa, and Asia and was also an important supplier of goods for foreign exchange, especially silk and cotton. Two great rival empires, the Persian Safavids (sah-FAH-vidz) and the Turkish Ottomans, dominated the region. Persian merchants could be found in trading communities as far away as the Indian Ocean. Persia was also a major producer and exporter of silk.

The Persians' Shi'ite Muslim faith clashed with the Ottomans' adherence to Sunnism. Economically, the two competed for control over western trade routes to the East. Under Sultan Mohammed II (r. 1451–1481), the Ottomans captured Europe's largest city, Constantinople, in May 1453. Renamed Istanbul, the city became the capital of the Ottoman Empire. By the mid-sixteenth century the Ottomans controlled the sea trade in the eastern Mediterranean, Syria, Palestine, Egypt, and the rest of North Africa, and their power extended into Europe as far west as Vienna.

Ottoman expansion frightened Europeans. The Ottoman armies seemed nearly invincible and the empire's desire for expansion limitless. In France in the sixteenth century, twice as many books were printed about the Turkish threat as about the American discoveries. The strength of the Ottomans helps explain some of the missionary fervor Christians brought to new territories. It also raised economic concerns. With trade routes to the east in the hands of the Ottomans, Europeans needed to find new trade routes.

Genoese and Venetian Middlemen

Compared to the riches and vibrancy of the East, Europe constituted a minor outpost in the world trading system. European craftsmen produced few products to rival the fine wares and expensive spices of Asia. In the late Middle Ages, the Italian city-states of Venice and Genoa controlled the European luxury trade with the East.

In 1304 Venice established formal relations with the sultan of Mamluk Egypt, opening operations in Cairo, the gateway to Asian trade. Venetian merchants specialized in expensive luxury goods like spices, silks, and carpets, which they obtained from middlemen in the eastern Mediterranean and Asia Minor. A little went a long way. Venetians purchased no more than five hundred tons of spices a year around 1400, but with a profit of about 40 percent. The most important spice was pepper, grown in India and Indonesia, which composed 60 percent of the spices they purchased in 1400.[2]

The Venetians exchanged Eastern luxury goods for European products they could trade abroad, including Spanish and English wool, German metal goods, Flemish textiles, and silk cloth made in their own manufactures with imported raw materials. Eastern demand for such goods was low. To make up the difference, the Venetians earned currency in the shipping industry and through trade in firearms and slaves. At least half of what they traded with the East took the form of precious metal, much of it acquired in Egypt and North Africa. When the Portuguese arrived in Asia in the late fifteenth century, they found Venetian coins everywhere.

Venice's ancient rival was Genoa. In the wake of the Crusades, Genoa dominated the northern route to Asia through the Black Sea. Expansion in the thirteenth and fourteenth centuries took the Genoese as far as Persia and the Far East. In 1291 they sponsored an expedition into the Atlantic in search of India. The ships were lost,

The Taking of Constantinople by the Turks, April 22, 1453 The Ottoman conquest of the capital of the Byzantine Empire in 1453 sent shock and despair through Europe. Capitalizing on the city's strategic and commercial importance, the Ottomans made it the center of their empire. (Bibliothèque nationale de France)

and their exact destination and motivations remain unknown. This voyage reveals the long roots of Genoese interest in Atlantic exploration.

In the fifteenth century, with Venice claiming victory in the spice trade, the Genoese shifted focus from trade to finance and from the Black Sea to the western Mediterranean. Located on the northwestern coast of Italy, Genoa had always been active in the western Mediterranean, trading with North African ports, southern France, Spain, and even England and Flanders through the Strait of Gibraltar. When Spanish and Portuguese voyages began to expore the western Atlantic (see pages 451–456), Genoese merchants, navigators, and financiers provided their skills to the Iberian monarchs, whose own subjects had much less commercial experience. The Genoese, for example, ran many of the sugar plantations established on the Atlantic islands colonized by the Portuguese. Genoese merchants would eventually help finance Spanish colonization of the New World in return for a share in the profits.

A major element of both Venetian and Genoese trade was slavery. Merchants purchased slaves, many of whom were fellow Christians, in the Balkans. The men were sold to Egypt for the sultan's army or sent to work as agricultural laborers in the Mediterranean. Young girls, who made up the majority of the trade, were sold in western Mediterranean ports as servants or concubines. After the loss of the Black Sea—and thus the source of slaves—to the Ottomans, the Genoese sought new supplies of slaves in the West, taking the Guanches (indigenous peoples from the Canary Islands), Muslim prisoners and Jewish refugees from Spain, and by the early 1500s both black and Berber Africans. With the growth of Spanish colonies in the New World, Genoese and Venetian merchants would become important players in the Atlantic slave trade.

Italian experience in colonial administration, slaving, and international trade and finance served as a model for the Iberian states as they pushed European expansion to new heights. Mariners, merchants, and financiers from Venice and Genoa—most notably Christopher Columbus—played a crucial role in bringing the fruits of this experience to the Iberian Peninsula and to the New World.

The European Voyages of Discovery

How and why did Europeans undertake ambitious voyages of expansion? ■

As we have seen, Europe was by no means isolated before the voyages of exploration and its "discovery" of the New World. But because they did not produce many products desired by Eastern elites, Europeans were modest players in the Indian Ocean trading world. As Europe recovered after the Black Death, new European players entered the scene with new technology, eager to spread Christianity and to undo Italian and Ottoman domination of trade with the East. A century after the plague, Iberian explorers began the overseas voyages that helped create the modern world, with staggering consequences for their own continent and the rest of the planet.

Causes of European Expansion

European expansion had multiple causes. By the middle of the fifteenth century, Europe was experiencing a revival of population and economic activity after the lows of the Black Death. This revival created demands for luxury goods, especially spices, from the East. The fall of Constantinople and subsequent Ottoman control of trade routes created obstacles to fulfilling these demands. Europeans needed to find new sources of precious metal to trade with the Ottomans or trade routes that bypassed the Ottomans.

Why were spices so desirable? Introduced into western Europe by the Crusaders in the twelfth century, pepper, nutmeg, ginger, mace, cinnamon, and cloves added flavor and variety to the monotonous European diet. Spices evoked the scent of the Garden of Eden and of divinity itself; they seemed a marvel and a mystery. They were used not only as flavorings for food, but also for anointing oil and incense in religious rituals and as perfumes, medicines, and dyes in daily life. Take, for example, cloves, for which Europeans found many uses. If picked green and sugared, the buds could be transformed into jam; if salted and pickled, cloves became a flavoring for vinegar. Cloves sweetened the breath. When added to food or drink, they were thought to stimulate the appetite and clear the intestines and bladder. When crushed and powdered, they were a medicine rubbed on the forehead to relieve head colds and applied to the eyes to strengthen vision. Taken with milk, they were believed to enhance sexual pleasure.

Religious fervor was another important catalyst for expansion. The passion and energy ignited by the Christian reconquista (reconquest) of the Iberian Peninsula encouraged the Portuguese and Spanish to continue the Christian crusade. Just seven months separated the Spanish conquest of Granada, the last remaining Muslim state on the Iberian Peninsula, and Columbus's departure across the Atlantic. Overseas exploration was in some ways a transfer of religious zeal, enthusiasm for conquest, and certainty of God's blessing to new non-Christian territories. Since the remaining Muslim states, such as the mighty Ottoman Empire, were too strong to defeat, Iberians turned their attention elsewhere.

Combined with eagerness for profits and to spread Christianity was the desire for glory and the urge to chart new waters. Scholars have frequently described the European discoveries as a manifestation of Renaissance curiosity about the physical universe—the desire to know more about the geography and peoples of the world. The detailed journals kept by such voyagers as Christopher Columbus and Antonio Pigafetta (a survivor of Magellan's world circumnavigation) attest to their wonder and fascination with the new peoples and places they visited.

" I have come to win gold, not to plow the fields like a peasant. "

—HERNANDO CORTÉS

Individual explorers combined these motivations in unique ways. Christopher Columbus was a devout Christian who was increasingly haunted by messianic obsessions in the last years of his life. As Portuguese explorer Bartholomew Diaz put it, his own motives were "to serve God and His Majesty, to give light to those who were in darkness and to grow rich as all men desire to do." When the Portuguese explorer Vasco da Gama reached the port of Calicut, India, in 1498 and a native asked what he wanted, he replied, "Christians and spices."[3] The bluntest of the Spanish **conquistadors** (kahn-KEES-tuh-dorz), Hernando Cortés, announced as he prepared to conquer Mexico, "I have come to win gold, not to plow the fields like a peasant."[4]

Eagerness for exploration was heightened by a lack of opportunity at home. After the reconquista, young men of the Spanish upper classes found their economic and political opportunities greatly limited. The ambitious turned to the sea to seek their fortunes.

Whatever the reasons, the voyages were made possible by the growth of government power. The Spanish monarchy was stronger than before and in a position to support foreign ventures. In Portugal explorers also looked to the monarchy, to Prince Henry the Navigator in particular (page 451), for financial support and encouragement. Like voyagers, monarchs shared a mix of motivations, from the desire to please God to the desire to win glory and profit from trade. Competition among European monarchs was an important factor in encouraging the steady stream of expeditions that began in the late fifteenth century.

Ordinary sailors were ill paid, and life at sea meant danger, overcrowding, unbearable stench, and hunger. For months at a time, 100 to 120 people lived and worked in a space of 1,600 to 2,000 square feet. A lucky sailor would find enough space on deck to unroll his sleeping mat. Horses, cows, pigs, chickens, rats, and lice accompanied them on the voyages. As one scholar concluded, "traveling on a ship must have been one of the most uncomfortable and oppressive experiences in the world."[5]

conquistador Spanish for "conqueror"; Spanish soldier-explorers, such as Hernando Cortés and Francisco Pizarro, who sought to conquer the New World for the Spanish crown.

Men choose to join these miserable crews to escape poverty at home, to continue a family trade, to win a few crumbs of the great riches of empire, or to find better lives as illegal immigrants in the colonies. Many orphans and poor boys were placed on board as young pages and had little say in the decision. Women also paid a price for the voyages of exploration. Left alone for months or years at a time, and frequently widowed, sailors' wives struggled to feed their families. The widow of a sailor lost on Magellan's 1519 voyage had to wait until 1547 to collect her husband's salary from the Spanish crown.[6]

The people who stayed at home had a powerful impact on the process. Royal ministers and factions at court influenced monarchs to provide or deny support for exploration. The small number of people who could read served as a rapt audience for tales

The Travels of Sir John Mandeville The author of this tale claimed to be an English knight who traveled extensively in the Middle East and Asia from the 1320s to the 1350s. Although historians now consider the work a skillful fiction, it had a great influence on how Europeans understood the world at the time. This illustration, from an edition published around 1410, depicts Mandeville approaching a walled city on the first stage of his voyage to Constantinople. (© British Library Board)

caravel A small, maneuverable, three-mast sailing ship developed by the Portuguese in the fifteenth century that gave the Portuguese a distinct advantage in exploration and trade.

Ptolemy's *Geography*
A second-century-C.E. work that synthesized the classical knowledge of geography and introduced the concepts of longitude and latitude. Reintroduced to Europeans in 1410 by Arab scholars, its ideas allowed cartographers to create more accurate maps.

of fantastic places and unknown peoples. Cosmography, natural history, and geography aroused enormous interest among educated people in the fifteenth and sixteenth centuries. One of the most popular books of the time was the fourteenth-century text *The Travels of Sir John Mandeville*, which purported to be a firsthand account of the author's travels in the Holy Land, Egypt, Ethiopia, the Middle East, and India and his service to the Mamluk sultan of Egypt and the Mongol Great Khan of China. Although we now know the stories were fictional, these fantastic tales of cannibals, one-eyed giants, men with the heads of dogs, and other marvels were believed for centuries and constituted the core of many Europeans' knowledge of such places. Christopher Columbus took a copy of Mandeville and the equally popular and more reliable *The Travels of Marco Polo* on his voyage in 1492.

Technology and the Rise of Exploration

Technological developments in shipbuilding, weaponry, and navigation provided another impetus for European expansion. Since ancient times, most seagoing vessels had been narrow, open boats called galleys, propelled largely by slaves or convicts manning the oars. Though well suited to the placid waters of the Mediterranean, galleys could not withstand the rough winds and uncharted shoals of the Atlantic. The need for sturdier craft, as well as population losses caused by the Black Death, forced the development of a new style of ship that would not require much manpower to sail. In the course of the fifteenth century, the Portuguese developed the **caravel**, a small, light, three-mast sailing ship. Though somewhat slower than the galley, the caravel held more cargo. Its triangular lateen sails and sternpost rudder also made the caravel a much more maneuverable vessel. When fitted with cannon, it could dominate larger vessels.

Great strides in cartography and navigational aids were also made during this period. Around 1410 Arab scholars reintroduced Europeans to **Ptolemy's *Geography***. Written in the second century C.E. by a Helle-

Ptolemy's *Geography* The recovery of Ptolemy's *Geography* in the early fifteenth century gave Europeans new access to ancient geographical knowledge. This 1486 world map, based on Ptolemy, is a great advance over medieval maps but contains errors with significant consequences for future exploration. It shows a single continent watered by a single ocean, with land covering three-quarters of the world's surface. Africa and Asia are joined with Europe, making the Indian Ocean a landlocked sea and rendering the circumnavigation of Africa impossible. The continent of Asia is stretched far to the east, greatly shortening the distance from Europe to Asia via the Atlantic. (Giraudon/Art Resource, NY)

nized Egyptian, the work synthesized the geographical knowledge of the classical world. Ptolemy's work provided significant improvements over medieval cartography, showing the world as round and introducing the idea of latitude and longitude to plot position accurately. It also contained crucial errors. Unaware of the Americas, Ptolemy showed the world as much smaller than it is, so that Asia appeared not very distant from Europe to the west. Based on this work, cartographers fashioned new maps that combined classical knowledge with the latest information from mariners. First the Genoese and Venetians, and then the Portuguese and Spanish, took the lead in these advances.

The magnetic compass enabled sailors to determine their direction and position at sea. The astrolabe, an instrument invented by the ancient Greeks and perfected by Muslim navigators, was used to determine the altitude of the sun and other celestial bodies. It permitted mariners to plot their latitude, that is, their precise position north or south of the equator.

Like the astrolabe, much of the new technology that Europeans used on their voyages was borrowed from the East. Gunpowder, the compass, and the sternpost rudder were Chinese inventions. The lateen sail, which allowed European ships to tack against the wind, was a product of the Indian Ocean trade world and was brought to the Mediterranean on Arab ships. Advances in cartography also drew on the rich tradition of Judeo-Arabic mathematical and astronomical learning in Iberia. Sometimes assistance to Europeans came from humans rather than instruments. The famed explorer Vasco da Gama employed a local Indian pilot to guide his expedition from the East African coast to India. In exploring new territories, European sailors thus called on techniques and knowledge developed over centuries in China, the Muslim world, and the Indian Ocean.

The Portuguese Overseas Empire

For centuries Portugal was a small and poor nation on the margins of European life whose principal activities were fishing and subsistence farming. It would have been hard for a European to predict Portugal's phenomenal success overseas after 1450. Yet Portugal had a long history of seafaring and navigation. Blocked from access to western Europe by Spain, the Portuguese turned to the Atlantic and North Africa, whose waters they knew better than did other Europeans. Nature favored the Portuguese: winds blowing along their coast offered passage to Africa, its Atlantic islands, and, ultimately, Brazil.

In the early phases of Portuguese exploration, Prince Henry (1394–1460), a younger son of the king, played a

leading role. A nineteenth-century scholar dubbed Henry "the Navigator" because of his support for the study of geography and navigation and for the annual expeditions he sponsored down the western coast of Africa. Although he never personally participated in voyages of exploration, Henry's involvement ensured that Portugal did not abandon the effort despite early disappointments.

The Portuguese Fleet Embarked for the Indies The image below shows a Portuguese trading fleet in the late fifteenth century bound for the riches of the Indies. Between 1500 and 1635 over nine hundred ships sailed from Portugal to ports on the Indian Ocean, in annual fleets composed of five to ten ships. Portuguese sailors used astrolabes, such as the one pictured at left, to accurately plot their position. (fleet: British Museum/HarperCollins Publishers/The Art Archive; astrolabe: Courtesy of the Trustees of the British Museum)

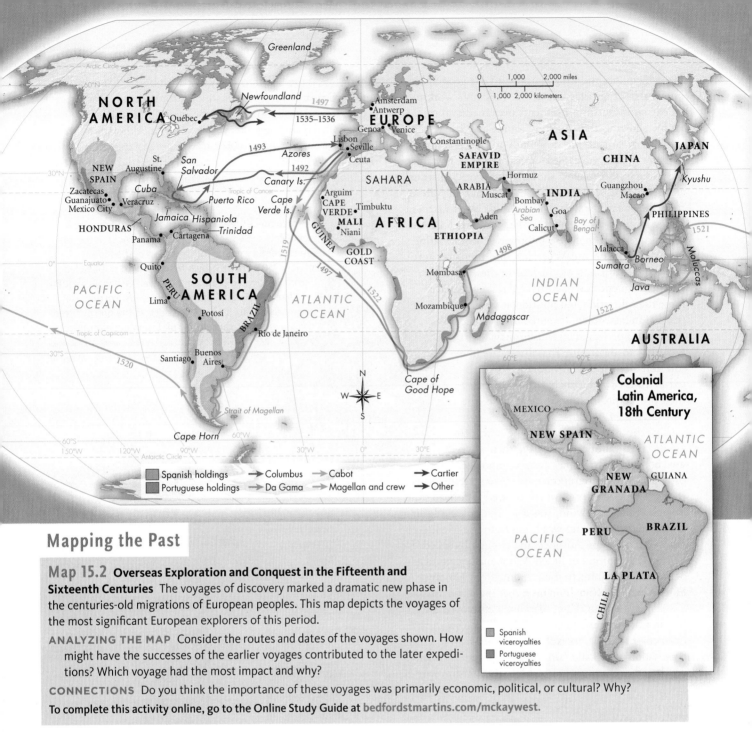

Mapping the Past

Map 15.2 Overseas Exploration and Conquest in the Fifteenth and Sixteenth Centuries The voyages of discovery marked a dramatic new phase in the centuries-old migrations of European peoples. This map depicts the voyages of the most significant European explorers of this period.

ANALYZING THE MAP Consider the routes and dates of the voyages shown. How might have the successes of the earlier voyages contributed to the later expeditions? Which voyage had the most impact and why?

CONNECTIONS Do you think the importance of these voyages was primarily economic, political, or cultural? Why?

To complete this activity online, go to the Online Study Guide at bedfordstmartins.com/mckaywest.

The objectives of Portuguese exploration policy included desires for military glory; crusades to Christianize Muslims and to locate a mythical Christian king of Africa, Prester John; and the quest to find gold, slaves, and an overseas route to the spice markets of India. Portugal's conquest of Ceuta, an Arab city in northern Morocco, in 1415 marked the beginning of European overseas expansion. In the 1420s, under Henry's direction, the Portuguese began to settle the Atlantic islands of Madeira (ca. 1420) and the Azores (1427). In 1443 they founded their first African commercial settlement at Arguin in North Africa. By the time of Henry's death in 1460, his support for exploration was vindicated by thriving sugar

plantations on the Atlantic islands, the first arrival of enslaved Africans in Portugal (see page 465), and new access to African gold.

The Portuguese next established trading posts and forts on the gold-rich Guinea coast and penetrated into the African continent all the way to Timbuktu (Map 15.2). By 1500 Portugal controlled the flow of African gold to Europe. The golden century of Portuguese prosperity had begun.

The Portuguese then pushed farther south down the west coast of Africa. In 1487 Bartholomew Diaz rounded the Cape of Good Hope at the southern tip, but storms and a threatened mutiny forced him to turn back. A decade later Vasco da Gama succeeded in rounding the Cape while commanding a fleet of four ships in search of a sea route to India. With the help of an Indian guide, da Gama reached the port of Calicut in India. Overcoming local hostility, he returned to Lisbon loaded with spices and samples of Indian cloth. He had failed to forge any trading alliances with local powers, and Portuguese arrogance ensured the future hostility of Muslim merchants who dominated the trading system. Nonetheless, de Gama proved the possibility of lucrative trade with the East via the Cape route. Thereafter, a Portuguese convoy set out for passage around the Cape every March.

Lisbon became the entrance port for Asian goods into Europe, but this was not accomplished without a fight. Muslim-controlled port city-states had long controlled the rich spice trade of the Indian Ocean, and they did not surrender it willingly. Portuguese cannon blasted open the port of Malacca in 1511, followed by Calicut, Ormuz, and Goa. The bombardment of these cities laid the foundation for Portuguese imperialism in the sixteenth and seventeenth centuries.

In March 1493, between the voyages of Diaz and da Gama, Spanish ships under a triumphant Genoese mariner named Christopher Columbus (1451–1506), in the service of the Spanish crown, entered Lisbon harbor. Spain also had begun the quest for an empire.

The Problem of Christopher Columbus

Christopher Columbus is a controversial figure in history—glorified by some as the brave discoverer of America, vilified by others as a cruel exploiter of Native Americans. Rather than judging Columbus by debates and standards of our time, it is more important to understand him in the context of his own time. First, what kind of man was Columbus, and what forces or influences shaped him? Second, in sailing westward from Europe, what were his goals? Third, did he achieve his goals, and what did he make of his discoveries?

In his dream of a westward passage to the Indies, Columbus embodied a long-standing Genoese ambition to circumvent Venetian domination of eastward trade, which was now being claimed by the Portuguese. Columbus was very knowledgeable about the sea. He had worked as a mapmaker, and he was familiar with such fifteenth-century Portuguese navigational developments as *portolans*—written descriptions of the courses along which ships sailed—and the use of the compass as a nautical instrument. As he implied in his *Journal*, he had acquired not only theoretical but also practical experience: "I have spent twenty-three years at sea and have not left it for any length of time worth mentioning, and I have seen every thing from east to west [meaning he had been to England] and I have been to Guinea [North and West Africa]."[7] His successful thirty-three-day voyage to the Caribbean owed a great deal to his seamanship.

Columbus was also a deeply religious man. He began the *Journal* of his voyage to the Americas in the form of a letter to Ferdinand and Isabella of Spain:

> On 2 January in the year 1492, when your Highnesses had concluded their war with the Moors who reigned in Europe, I saw your Highnesses' banners victoriously raised on the towers of the Alhambra, the citadel of the city, and the Moorish king come out of the city gates and kiss the hands of your Highnesses and the prince, My Lord. And later in that same month, on the grounds of information I had given your Highnesses concerning the lands of India . . . your Highnesses decided to send me, Christopher Columbus, to see these parts of India and the princes and peoples of those lands and consider the best means for their conversion.

Columbus had witnessed the Spanish conquest of Granada and shared fully in the religious and nationalistic fervor surrounding that event. Like the Spanish rulers and most Europeans of his age, he understood Christianity as a missionary religion that should be carried to places where it did not exist. He viewed himself as a divine agent: "God made me the messenger of the new heaven and the new earth of which he spoke in the Apocalypse of St. John . . . and he showed me the post where to find it."[8]

What was the object of this first voyage? Columbus gave the answer in the very title of the expedition, "The Enterprise of the Indies." He wanted to find a direct ocean trading route to Asia. Rejected for funding by the Portuguese in 1483 and by Ferdinand and Isabella in 1486, the project finally won the backing of the Spanish monarchy in 1492. The Spanish crown named Columbus viceroy over any territory he might discover and gave him one-tenth of the material rewards of the journey. Inspired by the stories of Mandeville and Marco Polo, Columbus dreamed of reaching the court of the Mongol emperor, the Great Khan (not realizing that the Ming Dynasty had overthrown the Mongols in 1368). Based on Ptolemy's *Geography* and other texts, he expected to pass the islands of Japan and then land on the east coast of China.

How did Columbus interpret what he had found, and in his mind did he achieve what he had set out to do? Columbus's small fleet left Spain on August 3, 1492. He landed in the Bahamas, which he christened San Salvador, on October 12, 1492. Columbus believed he had found some small islands off the east coast of Japan. On encountering natives of the islands, he gave them some beads and "many other trifles of small value," pronouncing them delighted with these gifts and eager to trade. In a letter he wrote to Ferdinand and Isabella on his return to Spain, Columbus described the natives as handsome, peaceful, and primitive people whose body painting reminded him of the Canary Islands natives.

Columbus Describes His First Voyage

LISTENING TO THE PAST

On his return voyage to Spain in February 1493, Christopher Columbus composed a letter intended for wide circulation and had copies of it sent ahead to Isabella and Ferdinand. Because the letter sums up Columbus's understanding of his achievements, it is considered the most important document of his first voyage. Remember that his knowledge of Asia rested heavily on Marco Polo's Travels, published around 1298.

❝ Since I know that you will be pleased at the great success with which the Lord has crowned my voyage, I write to inform you how in thirty-three days I crossed from the Canary Islands to the Indies, with the fleet which our most illustrious sovereigns gave me. I found very many islands with large populations and took possession of them all for their Highnesses; this I did by proclamation and unfurled the royal standard. No opposition was offered.

I named the first island that I found "San Salvador," in honour of our Lord and Saviour who has granted me this miracle. . . . When I reached Cuba, I followed its north coast westwards, and found it so extensive that I thought this must be the mainland, the province of Cathay.* . . . From there I saw another island eighteen leagues eastwards which I then named "Hispaniola.". . .†

Hispaniola is a wonder. The mountains and hills, the plains and meadow lands are both fertile and beautiful. They are most suitable for planting crops and for raising cattle of all kinds, and there are good sites for building towns and villages. The harbours are incredibly fine and there are many great rivers with broad channels and the majority contain gold.‡ The trees, fruits and plants are very different from those of Cuba. In Hispaniola there are many spices and large mines of gold and other metals.§ . . .

The inhabitants of this island, and all the rest that I discovered or heard of, go naked, as their mothers bore them, men and women alike. A few of the women, however, cover a single place with a leaf of a plant or piece of cotton which they weave for the purpose. They have no iron or steel or arms and are not capable of using them, not because they are not strong and well built but because they are amazingly timid. All the weapons they have are canes cut at seeding time, at the end of which they fix a sharpened stick, but they have not the courage to make use of these, for very often when I have sent two or three men to a village to have conversation with them a great number of them have come out. But as soon as they saw my men all fled immediately, a father not even waiting for his son. And this is not because we have harmed any of them; on the contrary, wherever I have gone and been able to have conversation with them, I have given them some of the various things I had, a cloth and other articles, and received nothing in exchange. But they have still remained incurably timid.

*Cathay is the old name for China. In the logbook and later in this letter, Columbus accepts the native story that Cuba is an island that can be circumnavigated in something more than twenty-one days, yet he insists here and during the second voyage that it is part of the Asiatic mainland.

†Hispaniola is the second largest island of the West Indies. Haiti occupies the western third of the island, the Dominican Republic the rest.

‡This did not prove to be true.

§These statements are also inaccurate.

True, when they have been reassured and lost their fear, they are so ingenuous and so liberal with all their possessions that no one who has not seen them would believe it. If one asks for anything they have they never say no. On the contrary, they offer a share to anyone with demonstrations of heartfelt affection, and they are immediately content with any small thing, valuable or valueless, that is given them. I forbade the men to give them bits of broken crockery, fragments of glass or tags of laces, though if they could get them they fancied them the finest jewels in the world. . . .

I hoped to win them to the love and service of their Highnesses and of the whole Spanish nation and to persuade them to collect and give us of the things which they possessed in abundance and which we needed. They have no religion and are not idolaters; but all believe that power and goodness dwell in the sky and they are firmly convinced that I have come from the sky with these ships and people. In this belief they gave me a good reception everywhere, once they had overcome their fear; and this is not because they are stupid—far from it, they are men of great intelligence, for they navigate all those seas, and give a marvellously good account of every thing—but because they have never before seen men clothed or ships like these. . . .

In all these islands the men are seemingly content with one woman, but their chief or king is allowed more than twenty. The women appear to work more than the men and I have not been able to find out if they have private property. As far as I could see whatever a man had was shared among all the rest and this particularly applies to food. . . . In another island, which I am told is larger than Hispaniola, the people have no hair. Here there is a vast quantity of gold, and from here and the other islands I bring Indians as evidence.

In conclusion, to speak only of the results of this very hasty voyage, their Highnesses can see that I will give them as much gold as they require, if they will render me some very slight assistance; also I will give them all the spices and cotton they want. . . . I will also bring them as much aloes as they ask and as many slaves, who will be taken from the idolaters. I believe

Christopher Columbus, by Ridolpho Ghirlandio. Friend of Raphael and teacher of Michelangelo, Ghirlandio (1483–1561) enjoyed distinction as a portrait painter, and so we can assume that this is a good likeness of the older Columbus. (Scala/Art Resource, NY)

also that I have found rhubarb and cinnamon and there will be countless other things in addition. . . .

So all Christendom will be delighted that our Redeemer has given victory to our most illustrious King and Queen and their renowned kingdoms, in this great matter. They should hold great celebrations and render solemn thanks to the Holy Trinity with many solemn prayers, for the great triumph which they will have, by the conversion of so many peoples to our holy faith and for the temporal benefits which will follow, for not only Spain, but all Christendom will receive encouragement and profit.

This is a brief account of the facts. Written in the caravel off the Canary Islands.**

15 February 1493

At your orders   THE ADMIRAL **99**

QUESTIONS FOR ANALYSIS

1. How did Columbus explain the success of his voyage?

2. What was Columbus's view of the Native Americans he met?

3. Does he exaggerate about the Caribbean islands possessing gold, cotton, and spices?

Source: From *The Four Voyages of Christopher Columbus*, pp. 115–123, ed. and trans. J. M. Cohen (Penguin Classics, 1969). Copyright © J. M. Cohen, 1969. Used with permission of Penguin Group (UK).

**Actually, Columbus was off Santa Maria in the Azores.

Believing he was in the Indies, he called them "Indians," a name that was later applied to all inhabitants of the Americas. Columbus concluded that they would make good slaves and could quickly be converted to Christianity. (See "Listening to the Past: Columbus Describes His First Voyage," at left.)

Scholars have identified the inhabitants of the islands as the Taino people, speakers of the Arawak language, who inhabited Hispaniola (modern-day Haiti and Dominican Republic) and other islands in the Caribbean. Columbus received reassuring reports from Taino villagers—via hand gestures and mime—of the presence of gold and of a great king in the vicinity. From San Salvador, Columbus sailed southwest, believing that this course would take him to Japan or the coast of China. He landed instead on Cuba on October 28. Deciding that he must be on the mainland near the coastal city of Quinsay (now Hangzhou), he sent a small embassy inland with letters from Ferdinand and Isabella and instructions to locate the grand city.

The landing party found only small villages. Confronted with this disappointment, Columbus apparently gave up on his aim to meet the Great Khan. Instead, he focused on trying to find gold or other valuables among the peoples he had discovered. The sight of Taino people wearing gold ornaments on Hispaniola seemed to prove that gold was available in the region. In January, confident that its source would soon be found, he headed back to Spain to report on his discovery. News of his voyage spread rapidly across Europe.[9]

Columbus's First Voyage to the New World, 1492–1493

Over the next decades, the Spanish would follow a policy of conquest and colonization in the New World, rather than one of exchange with equals (as envisaged for the Mongol khan). On his second voyage, Columbus forcibly subjugated the island of Hispaniola and enslaved its indigenous peoples. On this and subsequent voyages, Columbus brought with him settlers for the new Spanish territories, along with agricultural seed and livestock. Columbus himself, however, had little interest in or capacity for governing. Revolt soon broke out against him and his brother on Hispaniola. A royal expedition sent to investigate returned the brothers to Spain in chains. Columbus was quickly cleared of wrongdoing, but he did not recover his authority over the territories. Instead, they came under royal control.

Columbus was very much a man of his times. To the end of his life in 1506, he believed that he had found small islands off the coast of Asia. He never realized the scope of his achievement: to have found a vast continent unknown to Europeans, except for a fleeting Viking presence centuries earlier. He could not know that the scale of his discoveries would revolutionize world power, raising issues of trade, settlement, government bureaucracy, and the rights of native and African peoples.

Later Explorers

The Florentine navigator Amerigo Vespucci (veh-SPOO-chee) (1454–1512) realized what Columbus had not. Writing about his discoveries on the coast of modern-day Venezuela, Vespucci stated: "Those new regions which we found and explored with the fleet . . . we may rightly call a New World." This letter, titled *Mundus Novus* (The New World), was the first document to describe America as a continent separate from Asia. In recognition of Amerigo's bold claim, the continent was named for him. (When later cartographers realized that Columbus had made the discovery first, it was too late to change the maps.)

To settle competing claims to the Atlantic discoveries, Spain and Portugal turned to Pope Alexander VI. The resulting **Treaty of Tordesillas** (tor-duh-SEE-yuhs) in 1494 gave Spain everything to the west of an imaginary line drawn down the Atlantic and Portugal everything to the east. This arbitrary division worked in Portugal's favor when in 1500 an expedition led by Pedro Alvares Cabral, en route to India, landed on the coast of Brazil, which Cabral claimed as Portuguese territory.

The search for profits determined the direction of Spanish exploration and expansion into South America. With insignificant profits from the Caribbean compared to the enormous riches that the Portuguese were reaping in Asia, Spain renewed the search for a western passage to Asia. In 1519 Charles V of Spain (and the Holy Roman Empire) sent the Portuguese mariner Ferdinand Magellan (1480–1521) to find a sea route to the spices of the Moluccas off the southeast coast of Asia. Magellan sailed southwest across the Atlantic to Brazil, and after a long search along the coast he located the treacherous straits that now bear his name (see Map 15.1). The new ocean he sailed into after a rough passage through the straits seemed so peaceful that Magellan dubbed it the Pacific, from the Latin word for peaceful. He was soon to realize his mistake. His fleet sailed north up the west coast of South America and then headed west into the immense expanse of the Pacific toward the Malay Archipelago.

Treaty of Tordesillas The 1494 agreement giving Spain everything to the west of an imaginary line drawn down the Atlantic and giving Portugal everything to the east.

World Map of Diogo Ribeiro, 1529 This map integrates the wealth of new information provided by European explorers in the decades after Columbus's 1492 voyage. Working on commission for the Spanish king Charles V, mapmaker Diogo Ribeiro incorporated new details on Africa, South America, India, the Malay Archipelago, and China. Note the inaccuracy in his placement of the Moluccas, or Spice Islands, which are much too far east. This "mistake" was intended to serve Spain's interests in trade negotiations with the Portuguese. (Biblioteca Apostolica Vaticana)

❝ Those new regions which we found and explored with the fleet . . . we may rightly call a New World. **❞**

—**AMERIGO VESPUCCI**

Some of these islands were conquered in the 1560s and named the "Philippines" for Philip II of Spain.

Terrible storms, disease, starvation, and violence haunted the expedition. Magellan had set out with a fleet of five ships and around 270 men. Sailors on two of the ships attempted mutiny on the South American coast; one ship was lost, and another ship deserted and returned to Spain before even traversing the straits. The trip across the Pacific took ninety-eight days, and the men survived on rats and sawdust. Magellan himself was killed in a skirmish in the Philippines. The expedition had enough survivors to man only two ships, and one of them was captured by the Portuguese. One ship with only eighteen men returned to Spain from the east by way of the Indian Ocean, the Cape of Good Hope, and the Atlantic in 1522. The voyage—the first to circumnavigate the globe—had taken close to three years.

Despite the losses, this voyage revolutionized Europeans' understanding of the world by demonstrating the vastness of the Pacific. The earth was clearly much larger than Columbus had believed. Although the voyage made a small profit in spices, the westward passage to the Indies was too long and dangerous for commercial purposes. Spain soon abandoned the attempt to oust Portugal from the Eastern spice trade and concentrated on exploiting her New World territories.

The English and French also set sail across the Atlantic during the early days of exploration in search of a northwest passage to the Indies. In 1497 John Cabot, a Genoese merchant living in London, aimed for Brazil but discovered Newfoundland. The next year he returned and explored the New England coast. These forays proved futile, and the English established no permanent colonies in the territories they explored. One hundred years later, English efforts to find a passage to Asia focused on the extreme north. Between 1576 and 1578, Martin Frobisher made three voyages in and around the Canadian bay that now bears his name. Frobisher hopefully brought a quantity of ore back to England with him, but it proved to be worthless.

Early French exploration of the Atlantic was equally frustrating. Between 1534 and 1541 Frenchman Jacques Cartier made several voyages and explored the St. Lawrence region of Canada, searching for a passage to the wealth of Asia. His exploration of the St. Lawrence was halted at the great rapids west of the present-day island of Montreal; he named the rapids "La Chine" in the optimistic belief that China lay just beyond. When this hope proved vain, the French turned to a new source of profit within Canada itself: trade in beavers and other furs. As had the Portuguese in Asia, French traders bartered with local peoples, who maintained control over their trade goods. French fishermen also competed with Spanish and English for the teeming schools of cod they found in the Atlantic waters around Newfoundland. Fishing vessels salted the catch on board and brought it back to Europe, where a thriving market for fish was created by the Catholic prohibition of eating meat on Fridays and during Lent.

Spanish Conquest in the New World

In 1519, the year Magellan departed on his worldwide expedition, the Spanish sent an exploratory expedition from their post in Cuba to the mainland under the command of the brash and determined conquistador Hernando Cortés (1485–1547). Accompanied by six hundred men, sixteen horses, and ten cannon, Cortés was to launch the conquest of the **Mexica Empire**. Its people were later called the Aztecs, but now most scholars prefer to use the term *Mexica* to refer to them and their empire.

The Mexica Empire was ruled by Montezuma II (r. 1502–1520) from his capital at Tenochtitlán (tay-noch-teet-LAHN), now Mexico City. Larger than any European city of the time, it was the heart of a sophisticated civilization with advanced mathematics, astronomy, and engineering, with a complex social system, and with oral poetry and historical traditions.

Cortés landed on the coast of the Gulf of Mexico on April 21, 1519. The Spanish camp was soon visited by delegations of unarmed Mexica leaders bearing gifts and news of their great emperor. Impressed by the wealth of the local people, Cortés decided to cut his ties with Spain. He founded the settlement of Vera Cruz and burned his ships to prevent any disloyal followers from returning to Cuba. Cortés soon began to realize that he could exploit internal dissension within the empire to his own advantage. The Mexica state religion necessitated constant warfare against neighboring peoples to secure captives for religious sacrifices and laborers for agricultural and building projects. Conquered peoples were required to pay products of their agriculture and craftsmanship as tribute to the Mexica state through their local chiefs.

> **Mexica Empire** Also known as the Aztec Empire, a large and complex Native American civilization in modern Mexico and Central America that possessed advanced mathematical, astronomical, and engineering technology.

The Aztec Capital of Tenochtitlán Occupying a large island, Tenochtitlán was laid out in concentric circles. The administrative and religious buildings were at the heart of the city, which was surrounded by residential quarters. Cortés himself marveled at the city in his letters: "The city is as large as Seville or Cordoba. . . . There are bridges, very large, strong, and well constructed, so that, over many, ten horsemen can ride abreast. . . . The city has many squares where markets are held. . . . There is one square . . . where there are daily more than sixty thousand souls, buying and selling. In the service and manners of its people, their fashion of living was almost the same as in Spain, with just as much harmony and order." (The Newberry Library)

Cortés quickly forged an alliance with the Tlaxcalas and other subject kingdoms, which chafed under the tribute demanded by the Mexica. In October a combined Spanish-Tlaxcalan force occupied the city of Cholula, second largest in the empire and its religious capital, and massacred many thousands of inhabitants. Strengthened by this display of power, Cortés made alliances with other native kingdoms. In November 1519, with a few hundred Spanish men and some six thousand indigenous warriors, Cortés marched on Tenochtitlán.

Montezuma refrained from attacking the Spaniards as they advanced toward his capital and welcomed Cortés and his men into Tenochtitlán. Historians have often condemned the Mexica ruler for vacillation and weakness. Certainly other native leaders did attack the Spanish. But Montezuma relied on the advice of his state council, itself divided, and on the dubious loyalty of tributary communities. Historians have largely discredited one long-standing explanation, that he feared the Spaniards as living gods. This idea seems to have been a myth spread by Spanish missionaries and their converts after the fact, as a way of justifying and explaining the conquest. Montezuma's long hesitation proved disastrous. When Cortés—with incredible boldness—took Montezuma hostage, the emperor's influence over his people crumbled.

During the ensuing attacks and counterattacks, Montezuma was killed. The Spaniards and their allies escaped from the city and began gathering forces and making new alliances against the Mexica. In May 1520 Cortés led a second assault on

Invasion of Tenochtitlán, 1519–1521

Gulf of Mexico

Texcoco
Otumba
Zautla
Jalapa
Veracruz
Tlaxcala
Cholula
Tenochtitlán

→ Cortés's original route, 1519
→ Cortés's retreat, 1520
→ Cortés's return route, 1520–1521

Picturing the Past

Doña Marina Translating for Hernando Cortés During His Meeting with Montezuma In April 1519 Doña Marina (or La Malinche as she is known in Mexico) was among twenty women given to the Spanish as slaves. Fluent in Nahuatl (NAH-wha-tuhl) and Yucatec Mayan (spoken by a Spanish priest accompanying Cortés), she acted as an interpreter and diplomatic guide for the Spanish. She had a close relationship with Cortés and bore his son, Don Martín Cortés, in 1522. This image was created by Tlaxcalan artists shortly after the conquest of Mexico and represents one indigenous perspective on the events. (The Granger Collection, New York)

ANALYZING THE IMAGE What role does Doña Marina (far right) appear to be playing in this image? Does she appear to be subservient or equal to Cortés (right, seated)? How did the painter indicate her identity as non-Spanish?

CONNECTIONS How do you think the native rulers negotiating with Cortés might have viewed her? What about a Spanish viewer of this image? What does the absence of other women here suggest about the role of women in these societies?

To complete this activity online, go to the Online Study Guide at bedfordstmartins.com/mckaywest.

Tenochtitlán at the head of an army of approximately 1,000 Spanish and 75,000 native warriors.[10] Spanish victory in late summer 1521 was hard-won and greatly aided by the effects of smallpox, which had weakened and reduced the Mexica population. After the defeat of Tenochtitlán, Cortés and other conquistadors began the systematic conquest of Mexico. Over time, a series of indigenous kingdoms gradually fell under Spanish domination, although not without decades of resistance.

More surprising than the defeat of the Mexicas was the fall of the remote **Inca Empire**. Perched more than 9,800 feet above sea level, the Incas were isolated from other indigenous cultures and knew nothing of the Mexica civilization or its

Inca Empire The vast and sophisticated Peruvian empire centered at the capital city of Cuzco that was at its peak from 1438 until 1532.

collapse. Like the Mexica, the Incas had created a civilization that rivaled the Europeans in population and complexity. To unite their vast and well-fortified empire, the Incas built an extensive network of roads, along which traveled a highly efficient postal service. The imperial government taxed, fed, and protected its subjects.

At the time of the Spanish invasion the Inca Empire had been weakened by disease and warfare. An epidemic of disease, possibly smallpox, had begun spreading among the people. Even worse, the empire had been embroiled in a civil war over succession. Francisco Pizarro (ca. 1475–1541), a conquistador of modest Spanish origins, landed on the northern coast of Peru on May 13, 1532, the very day Atahualpa (ah-tuh-WAHL-puh) won control of the empire after five years of fighting. As Pizarro advanced across the steep Andes toward Cuzco, Atahualpa was proceeding to the capital for his coronation.

Like Montezuma in Mexico, Atahualpa was aware of the Spaniards' movements. He sent envoys to greet the Spanish and invite them to meet him in the provincial town of Cajamarca. His plan was to lure the Spaniards into a trap, seize their horses and ablest men for his army, and execute the rest. With a loyal army of some forty thousand men stationed nearby, Atahualpa felt he had little to fear. Instead, the Spaniards ambushed and captured him, collected an enormous ransom in gold, and then executed him in 1533 on trumped-up charges. The Spanish now marched on the capital of the empire itself, profiting once again from internal conflicts to form alliances with local peoples. When Cuzco fell in 1533, the Spanish plundered immense riches in gold and silver.

As with the Mexica, decades of violence and resistance followed the defeat of the Incan capital. Struggles also broke out among the Spanish for the spoils of empire. Nevertheless, Spanish conquest opened a new chapter in European relations with the New World. It was not long before rival European nations attempted to forge their own overseas empires.

Early French and English Settlement in the New World

For over a hundred years, the Spanish and the Portuguese dominated settlement in the New World. The first English colony was founded at Roanoke (in what is now North Carolina) in 1585. After a three-year loss of contact with England, the settlers were found to have disappeared; their fate remains a mystery. The colony of Virginia, founded at Jamestown in 1607, had better luck and gained a steady hold producing tobacco for a growing European market. While these colonies originated as bases for harassing Spanish shipping, settlement on the coast of New England was undertaken for different reasons. There, radical Protestants sought to escape Anglican repression in England and begin new lives. The small and struggling outpost of Plymouth (1620) was followed by Massachusetts (1630), which grew into a prosperous settlement. Religious disputes in Massachusetts itself led to the dispersion of settlers into the new communities of Providence, Connecticut, Rhode Island, and New Haven. Catholics acquired their own settlement in Maryland (1632) and Quakers in Pennsylvania (1681).

Where the Spanish conquered indigenous empires and established whole-scale dominance over Mexico and Peru, English settlements hugged the Atlantic coastline. This did not prevent conflict with the indigenous inhabitants over land and resources. The haphazard nature of English colonization also led to conflicts of authority within the colonies. As the English crown grew more interested in colonial expansion, efforts were made to acquire the territory between New England in the north and Virginia in the south. This would allow the English to unify their holdings and overcome French and Dutch competition on the North American mainland.

French navigator and explorer Samuel de Champlain founded the first permanent French settlement, at Quebec, in 1608, a year after the English founding of Jamestown. Ville-Marie, latter-day Montreal, was founded in 1642. Although the French population in New France was small compared to the English and Spanish colonies, the French were energetic and industrious traders and explorers. Following the waterways of the St. Lawrence, the Great Lakes, and the Mississippi, they ventured into much of modern-day Canada and at least thirty-five of the fifty states of the United States. In 1682 French explorer LaSalle descended the Mississippi to the Gulf of Mexico, opening the way for French occupation of Louisiana.

While establishing their foothold in the north, the French slowly acquired new territories in the West Indies. These included Cayenne (1604), St. Christophe (1625), Martinique, Guadeloupe, and Saint-Domingue (1697) on the western side of the island of Hispaniola. Originally used as bases for plundering Spanish shipping, these islands became centers of tobacco and then sugar production. French ambitions on the mainland and in the Caribbean sparked a century-long competition with the English that culminated in the Seven Years' War from 1756 to 1763. France lost Canada and Louisiana, but retained profitable colonies in the West Indies. France regained part of Louisiana by treaty in 1800 and sold it to the United States in 1803.

European involvement in the Americas led to profound transformation of pre-existing indigenous societies and the rise of a transatlantic slave trade. It also led to an acceleration of global trade and cultural exchange.

Over time, the combination of indigenous, European, and African cultures gave birth to new societies in the New World. In turn, the profits of trade and the impact of cultural exchange greatly influenced European society.

The Impact of Conquest

What was the impact of European conquest on the peoples and ecologies of the New World?

The growing European presence in the New World transformed its land and its peoples forever. Violence and disease wrought devastating losses, while surviving peoples encountered new political, social, and economic organizations imposed by Europeans. The Columbian exchange brought infectious diseases to the Americas, but also gave new crops to the Old World that altered consumption patterns in Europe and across the globe (see page 463).

Colonial Administration

Columbus, Cortés, and Pizarro had claimed the lands they had "discovered" for the Spanish crown. How were these lands governed? In the sixteenth century the Crown divided its New World territories into four **viceroyalties** or administrative divisions: New Spain, with the capital at Mexico City; Peru, with the capital at Lima; New Granada, with Bogotá as its administrative center; and La Plata, with Buenos Aires as the capital (see Map 15.2).

Within each territory, the viceroy, or imperial governor, exercised broad military and civil authority as the direct representative of Spain. The viceroy presided over the *audiencia* (ow-dee-EHN-see-ah), a board of twelve to fifteen judges that served as his advisory council and the highest judicial body. Later, the reform-minded Spanish king Charles III (r. 1759–1788) introduced the system of intendants to the New World territories. These royal officials possessed broad military, administrative, and financial authority within their intendancies and were responsible not to the viceroy but to the monarchy in Madrid. The intendant system was pioneered by the Bourbon kings of France and was used by the French in their overseas colonies.

The Portuguese governed their colony of Brazil in a similar manner. After the union of the crowns of Portugal and Spain in 1580, Spanish administrative forms were introduced. Local officials called *corregidores* (kuh-REH-gih-dawr-eez) held judicial and military powers. Royal policies placed severe restrictions on Brazilian industries that might compete with those of Portugal and Spain.

Impact of European Settlement on the Lives of Indigenous Peoples

Before Columbus's arrival, the Americas were inhabited by thousands of groups of indigenous peoples with different languages and cultures. Their patterns of life varied widely, from hunter-gatherer tribes organized into tribal confederations on the North American plains to large-scale agriculture-based empires connecting bustling cities and towns in modern-day Mexico and South America. Although historians continue to debate the numbers, the best estimate is that the peoples of the Americas numbered around 50 million in 1492.

Their lives were radically transformed by the arrival of Europeans. In the sixteenth century perhaps two hundred thousand Spaniards immigrated to the New World. After assisting in the conquest of the Mexica and the Incas, these men carved out vast estates called haciendas in temperate grazing areas and imported Spanish livestock for the kinds of ranching with which they were familiar. In coastal tropical areas, the Spanish erected huge plantations to supply sugar to the European market. Around 1550 silver was discovered in present-day Bolivia and Mexico. To work the cattle ranches, sugar plantations, and silver mines, the conquistadors first turned to the indigenous peoples.

The Spanish quickly established the **encomienda system**, in which the Crown granted the conquerors the right to employ groups of Native Americans as laborers or to demand tribute from them in exchange for providing food and shelter. Theoretically, the Spanish were forbidden to enslave the natives; in actuality, the encomiendas were a legalized form of slavery.

The new conditions and hardships imposed by conquest and colonization resulted in enormous native population losses. The major cause of death was disease. Having little or no resistance to diseases brought from the Old World, the inhabitants of the New World fell victim to smallpox, typhus, influenza, and other illnesses. Another factor was overwork. Unaccustomed to forced labor, especially in the blistering heat of tropical cane fields or in dank and dangerous mines, native workers died in staggering numbers. Moreover, forced labor diverted local people from agricultural work, leading to malnutrition, reduced fertility rates, and starvation. Women forced to work were separated from their infants, leading to high infant morality rates in a population with no livestock to supply alternatives to breast milk. Malnutrition and hunger in turn lowered resistance to disease. Finally,

viceroyalties The name for the four administrative units of Spanish possessions in the Americas: New Spain, Peru, New Granada, and La Plata.

encomienda system A system whereby the Spanish crown granted the conquerors the right to forcibly employ groups of Indians; it was a disguised form of slavery.

spañol con India, Mestizo.

Mestizo con Españolo Castizo.

5

6

Mulato con Española, Morisco.

Morisco con Española Chino.

9

10

Lobo con China Cribaro.

Gibaro con Mulata Albarazado

13

14

Sanbaigo con Loba Calpamulata

Calpamulato con Canbuja Tentzen al Aire

many indigenous peoples also died through outright violence in warfare.[11]

The Franciscan Bartolomé de Las Casas (1474–1566) was one of the most outspoken critics of Spanish brutality against indigenous peoples. Las Casas documented their treatment at the hands of the Spanish:

> To these quiet Lambs . . . came the Spaniards like most c(r)uel Tygres, Wolves and Lions, enrag'd with a sharp and tedious hunger; for these forty years past, minding nothing else but the slaughter of these unfortunate wretches, whom with divers kinds of torments neither seen nor heard of before, they have so cruelly and inhumanely butchered, that of three millions of people which Hispaniola itself did contain, there are left remaining alive scarce three hundred persons.[12]

Las Casas and other missionaries asserted that the Indians had human rights, and through their persistent pressure the Spanish emperor Charles V abolished the worst abuses of the encomienda system in 1531.

Franciscan, Dominican, and Jesuit missionaries who accompanied the conquistadors and other European settlers played an important role in converting indigenous peoples to Christianity, teaching them European methods of agriculture, and instilling loyalty to their colonial masters. In terms of numbers of people baptized, missionaries enjoyed phenomenal success, though the depth of the native peoples' adherence to Christianity remains debatable.

The pattern of devastating disease and population loss established in the Spanish colonies was repeated everywhere Europeans settled. Although precise figures are impossible to establish, the best estimate is that the native population declined from roughly 50 million in 1492 to around 9 million by 1700. It is important to note, however, that native populations and cultures did survive the conquest period, sometimes by blending with European incomers and sometimes by maintaining cultural autonomy.

For colonial administrators the main problem posed by the astronomically high death rate was the loss of a subjugated labor force to work the mines and sugar plantations. As early as 1511 King Ferdinand of Spain observed that the Indians seemed to be "very frail" and that

Mixed Races The unprecedented mixing of peoples in the Spanish New World colonies inspired great fascination. An elaborate terminology emerged to describe the many possible combinations of indigenous, African, and European blood, which were known collectively as *castas*. This painting belongs to a popular genre of the eighteenth century depicting couples composed of individuals of different ethnic origin and the children produced of their unions. (Schalkwijk/Art Resource, NY) "one black could do the work of four Indians."[13] Thus was born an absurd myth and the new tragedy of the Atlantic slave trade (see page 468).

Life in the Colonies

Many factors helped to shape life in European colonies, including geographical location, religion, indigenous cultures and practices, patterns of European settlement, and the cultural attitudes and official policies of the European nations that claimed them as empire. Throughout the New World, Europeanized settlements were hedged by immense borderlands of European and non-European contact.

Women played a crucial role in the creation of new identities and the continuation of old ones. The first explorers formed unions with native women, through coercion or choice, and relied on them as translators and guides and to form alliances with indigenous powers. As settlement developed, the character of each colony was influenced by the presence or absence of European women. Where women and children accompanied men, as in the British colonies and the Spanish mainland colonies, new settlements took on European languages, religion, and ways of life that have endured, with input from local cultures, to this day. Where European women did not, as on the west coast of Africa and most European outposts in Asia, local populations largely retained their own cultures, to which male Europeans acclimatized themselves. The scarcity of women in all colonies, at least initially, opened up opportunities for those who did arrive, leading one cynic to comment that even "a whore, if handsome, makes a wife for some rich planter."[14]

It was not just the availability of Englishwomen that prevented Englishmen from forming unions with indigenous women. English cultural attitudes drew strict boundaries between civilized and savage, and even settlements of Christianized native peoples were segregated physically and socially from the English. This was in strong contrast with the situation in New France, where royal officials initially encouraged French traders to form ties with native peoples, including marrying local women. Assimilation of the native population was seen as one solution to the low levels of immigration from France.

Most women who crossed the Atlantic were Africans, constituting four-fifths of the female newcomers before 1800.[15] Wherever slavery existed, masters profited from their power to engage in sexual relations with enslaved women. One important difference among European colonies was in the status of children born from such unions. In some colonies, mostly those dominated by the Portuguese, Spanish, or French, substantial populations of free blacks descended from the freed children of such unions. In English colonies, masters were less likely to free children they fathered with female slaves.

The mixing of indigenous peoples with Europeans and Africans created whole new populations and ethnicities and complex self-identities. In Spanish America the word *mestizo*—*métis* in French—described people of mixed Native American and European descent. The blanket terms "mulatto" and "people of color" were used for those of mixed African and European origin. With its immense slave-based plantation agriculture system, large indigenous population, and relatively low Portuguese immigration, Brazil developed a particularly complex racial and ethnic mosaic.

The Columbian Exchange

The migration of peoples to the New World led to an exchange of animals, plants, and disease, a complex process known as the **Columbian exchange**. European immigrants to the Americas wanted the diet with which they were familiar, so they searched for climatic zones favorable to those crops.

> **Columbian exchange** The exchange of animals, plants, and diseases between the Old and the New Worlds.

Columbus had brought sugar plants on his second voyage; Spaniards also introduced rice and bananas from the Canary Islands, and the Portuguese carried these items to Brazil. Everywhere they settled, the Spanish and Portuguese brought and raised wheat with labor provided by the encomienda system. By 1535 Mexico was exporting wheat. Grapes and olives brought over from Spain did well in parts of Peru and Chile. Not all plants arrived intentionally. In clumps of mud on shoes and in the folds of textiles came the seeds of immigrant grasses, including the common dandelion.

Apart from wild turkeys and game, Native Americans had no animals for food. Moreover, they did not domesticate animals for travel or use as beasts of burden,

> ❝ To these quiet Lambs . . . came the Spaniards like most cruel Tygres, Wolves and Lions, enrag'd with a sharp and tedious hunger; for these forty years past, minding nothing else but the slaughter of these unfortunate wretches. ❞
>
> —**BARTOLOMÉ DE LAS CASAS**

except for alpacas and llamas in the Inca Empire. On his second voyage in 1493 Columbus introduced horses, cattle, sheep, dogs, pigs, chickens, and goats. The multiplication of these animals proved spectacular. The horse enabled the Spanish conquerors and native populations to travel faster and farther and to transport heavy loads. In turn, Europeans returned home with many food crops that became central elements of their diet. (See "Living in the Past: Foods of the Columbian Exchange," page 466.)

Disease was perhaps the most important form of exchange. The wave of catastrophic epidemic disease that swept the Western Hemisphere after 1492 can be seen as an extension of the swath of devastation wreaked by the Black Death in the 1300s, first on Asia and then on Europe. The world after Columbus was thus unified by disease as well as by trade and colonization. The old belief that syphilis originated in the New World and was brought to Europe by Columbus's sailors, however, has been challenged by the discovery of pre-Columbian skeletons in Europe that seem to bear signs of the disease.

Europe and the World After Columbus

How was the era of global contact shaped by new commodities, commercial empires, and forced migrations? ∎

The centuries-old Afro-Eurasian trade world was forever changed by the European voyages of discovery and their aftermath. For the first time, a truly global economy emerged in the sixteenth and seventeenth centuries, and it forged new links among far-flung peoples, cultures, and societies. The ancient civilizations of Europe, Africa, the Americas, and Asia confronted one another in new and rapidly evolving ways. Those confrontations often led to conquest and exploitation, but they also contributed to cultural exchange and renewal.

Sugar and Slavery

Throughout the Middle Ages slavery was deeply entrenched in the Mediterranean, but it was not based on race; many slaves were white. How, then, did black African slavery enter the European picture and take root in South and then North America? In 1453 the Ottoman capture of Constantinople halted the flow of white slaves from the eastern Mediterranean. The successes of the

A New World Sugar Refinery, Brazil Sugar was the most important and most profitable plantation crop in the New World. This image shows the processing and refinement of sugar on a Brazilian plantation. Sugar cane was grown, harvested, and processed by African slaves who labored under brutal and ruthless conditions to generate enormous profits for plantation owners. (The Bridgeman Art Library/Getty Images)

Map 15.3 Seaborne Trading Empires in the Sixteenth and Seventeenth Centuries By the mid-seventeenth century, trade linked all parts of the world except for Australia. Notice that trade in slaves was not confined to the Atlantic but involved almost all parts of the world.

Iberian reconquista also meant that the supply of Muslim captives had drastically diminished. Cut off from its traditional sources of slaves, Mediterranean Europe then turned to sub-Saharan Africa, which had a long history of slave trading. (See "Individuals in Society: Juan de Pareja," page 469.) As Portuguese explorers began their voyages along the western coast of Africa, one of the first commodities they sought was slaves. In 1444 the first ship returned to Lisbon with a cargo of enslaved Africans; the Crown was delighted, and more shipments followed.

While the first slaves were simply seized by small raiding parties, Portuguese merchants soon found that it was easier to trade with local leaders, who were accustomed to dealing in slaves captured through warfare with

neighboring powers. From 1490 to 1530 Portuguese traders brought between three hundred and two thousand enslaved Africans to Lisbon each year (Map 15.3), where they performed most of the manual labor and constituted 10 percent of the city's population.

In this stage of European expansion, the history of slavery became intertwined with the history of sugar. Originally sugar was an expensive luxury that only the very affluent could afford, but population increases and monetary expansion in the fifteenth century led to increasing demand. Native to the South Pacific, sugar was taken in ancient times to India, where farmers learned to preserve cane juice as granules that could be stored and shipped. From there, sugar traveled to China and the Mediterranean, where islands like

LIVING IN THE PAST

MANY STUDENTS ARE AWARE of the devastating effects of European diseases on peoples of the New World and of the role of gunpowder and horses in the conquest of native civilizations. They may be less aware of how New World foodstuffs transformed Europeans' daily life.

Prior to Christopher Columbus's voyages, many common elements of today's European diet were unknown in Europe. It's hard to imagine Italian pizza without tomato sauce or Irish stew without potatoes, yet tomatoes and potatoes were both unknown in Europe before 1492. Additional crops originating in the Americas included many varieties of beans, squash, pumpkins, avocados, and peppers.

One of the most important of such crops was maize (corn), first introduced to Europe by Columbus in 1493. Because maize gives a high yield per unit of land, has a short growing season, and thrives in climates too dry for rice and too wet for wheat, it proved an especially important crop for Europeans. By the late seventeenth century the crop had become a staple in Spain, Portugal, southern France, and Italy, and in the eighteenth century it became one of the chief foods of southeastern Europe. Even more valuable was the nutritious white potato, which slowly spread from west to east — to Ireland, England, and France in the seventeenth century, and to Germany, Poland, Hungary, and Russia in the eighteenth, contributing everywhere to a rise in population. Ironically, the white potato reached New England from old England in the early eighteenth century.

Europeans' initial reaction to these crops was often fear or hostility. Adoption of the tomato and the potato was long hampered by belief that they were unfit for human consumption and potentially poisonous. Both plants belong to the deadly nightshade family, and both contain poison in their leaves and stems. It took time and persuasion for these plants to win over tradition-minded European peasants, who

Saint Diego of Alcala Feeding the Poor (1645–1646), by Bartolome Esteban Murillo, the first dated European depiction of the potato in art. (Joseph Martin/akg-images)

Incan women milking goats, from a collection of illustrations by a Spanish bishop that offers a valuable view of life in Peru in the 1780s. (Oronoz)

The first European scientific illustration of maize appeared in 1542, a half century after it was introduced to the continent. (The LuEsther T. Mertz Library, NYBG/Art Resource, NY)

used potatoes mostly as livestock feed. During the eighteenth-century Enlightenment, scientists and doctors played an important role in popularizing the nutritive benefits of the potato.

Columbus himself contributed to misconceptions about New World foods when he mistook the chili pepper for black pepper, one of the spices he had hoped to find in the Indies. The Portuguese quickly began exporting chili peppers from Brazil to Africa, India, and Southeast Asia along the trade routes they dominated. The chili pepper arrived in North America through its place in the diet of enslaved Africans.

European settlers introduced various foods to the native peoples of the New World, including rice, wheat, lettuce, and onions. Perhaps the most significant introduction to the diet of Native Americans came via the meat and milk of the livestock that the early conquistadors brought with them, including cattle, sheep, and goats.

The foods of the Columbian exchange traveled a truly global path. They provided important new sources of nutrition to people all over the world, as well as creating new and beloved culinary traditions. French fries with ketchup, anyone?

QUESTIONS FOR ANALYSIS

1. Why do you think it was so difficult for Europeans to accept new types of food, even when they were high in nutritional quality?

2. What do these illustrations suggest about the importance of the Columbian exchange?

3. List the foods you typically eat in a day. How many of them originated in the New World, and how many in the Old World? How does your own life exemplify the outcome of the Columbian exchange?

Crete, Sicily, and Cyprus had the warm and wet climate needed for growing sugar cane. When Genoese and other Italians colonized the Canary Islands and the Portuguese settled on the Madeira Islands, sugar plantations came to the Atlantic.

Sugar was a particularly difficult and demanding crop to produce for profit. Seed-stems were planted by hand, thousands to the acre. When mature, the cane had to be harvested and processed rapidly to avoid spoiling, forcing days and nights of work with little rest. Moreover, its growing season is virtually constant, meaning that there is no fallow period when workers could recuperate from the arduous labor. The demands of sugar production were only increased with the invention of roller mills to crush the cane more efficiently. Yields could be augmented, but only if a sufficient labor force was found to supply the mills. Europeans solved the labor problem by forcing first native islanders and then enslaved Africans to provide the backbreaking work.

Sugar gave New World slavery its distinctive shape. Columbus himself, who spent a decade in Madeira, brought sugar plants on his voyages to "the Indies." The transatlantic slave trade began in 1518 when Spanish king Charles I authorized traders to bring African slaves to New World colonies. The Portuguese brought the first slaves to Brazil around 1550; by 1600 four thousand were being imported annually. After its founding in 1621, the Dutch West India Company, with the full support of the United Provinces, transported thousands of Africans to Brazil and the Caribbean, mostly to work on sugar plantations. In the late seventeenth century, with the chartering of the Royal African Company, the English got involved.

European sailors found the Atlantic passage cramped and uncomfortable, but conditions for African slaves were lethal. Before 1700, when slavers decided it was better business to improve conditions, some 20 percent of slaves died on the voyage.[16] The most common cause of death was from dysentery induced by poor quality food and water, intense crowding, and lack of sanitation. Men were often kept in irons during the passage, while women and girls were considered fair game for sailors. To increase profits, slave traders packed several hundred captives on each ship. One slaver explained that he removed his boots before entering the slave hold because he had to crawl over the slaves' packed bodies.[17] On sugar plantations, death rates among slaves from illness and exhaustion were extremely high, leading to a constant stream of new shipments of slaves from Africa.

In total, scholars estimate that European traders embarked over 10 million African slaves across the Atlantic from 1518 to 1800 (of whom roughly 8.5 million disembarked), with the peak of the trade occurring in the eighteenth century.[18] By comparison, only 2 to 2.5 million Europeans migrated to the New World during the same period. Enslaved Africans worked in an infinite variety of occupations: as miners, soldiers, sailors, servants, and artisans and in the production of cotton, rum, indigo, tobacco, wheat, corn, and, most predominantly, sugar.

Spanish Silver and Its Economic Effects

The sixteenth century has often been called Spain's golden century, but silver mined in the Americas was the true source of Spain's incredible wealth. In 1545, at an altitude of fifteen thousand feet, the Spanish discovered an extraordinary source of silver at Potosí (poh-toh-SEE) (in present-day Bolivia) in territory conquered from the Inca Empire. The frigid place where nothing grew had been unsettled. A half century later 160,000 people lived there, making it about the size of the city of London. By 1550 Potosí yielded perhaps 60 percent of all the silver mined in the world. From Potosí and the mines at Zacatecas (za-kuh-TAY-kuhhs) and Guanajuato (gwah-nah-HWAH-toh) in Mexico, huge quantities of precious metals poured forth. To protect this treasure from French and English pirates, armed convoys transported it to Spain each year. Between 1503 and 1650, 35 million pounds of silver and over 600,000 pounds of gold entered Seville's port. Spanish predominance, however, proved temporary.

In the sixteenth century Spain experienced a steady population increase, creating a sharp rise in the demand for food and goods. Spanish colonies in the Americas also demanded consumer goods that were not produced in the colonies, such as cloth and luxury goods. Since Spain had expelled some of its best farmers and businessmen—the Muslims and Jews—in the fifteenth century, the Spanish economy was suffering and could not meet the new demands. The excess of demand over supply led to widespread inflation. The result was a rise in production costs and a further decline in Spain's productive capacity.

Did the flood of silver bullion from America cause the inflation? Prices rose most steeply before 1565, but bullion imports reached their peak between 1580 and 1620. Thus silver did not cause the initial inflation. It did, however, exacerbate the situation, and, along with the ensuing rise in population, the influx of silver significantly contributed to the upward spiral of prices. Inflation severely strained government budgets. Several times between 1557 and 1647, Spain's King Philip II and his successors wrote off the state debt, thereby undermining confidence in the government and leaving the economy in shambles. After 1600, when the population declined, prices gradually stabilized.

As Philip II paid his armies and foreign debts with silver bullion, Spanish inflation was transmitted to the rest of Europe. Between 1560 and 1600 much of Europe

INDIVIDUALS IN SOCIETY

DURING THE LONG WARS OF THE RECONQUISTA, Muslims and Christians captured each other in battle and used the defeated as slaves. As the Muslims were gradually eliminated from Iberia in the fifteenth and sixteenth centuries, the Spanish and Portuguese turned to the west coast of Africa for a new supply of slaves. Most slaves worked as domestic servants, rather than in the fields. Some received specialized training as artisans.

Not all people of African descent were slaves, and some experienced both freedom and slavery in a single lifetime. The life and career of Juan de Pareja (pah-REH-huh) illustrates the complexities of the Iberian slave system and the heights of achievement possible for those who achieved freedom.

Pareja was born in Antequera, an agricultural region and the old center of Muslim culture near Seville in southern Spain. Of his parents we know nothing. Because a rare surviving document calls him a "mulatto," one of his parents must have been white and the other must have had some African blood. In 1630 Pareja applied to the mayor of Seville for permission to travel to Madrid to visit his brother and "to perfect his art." The document lists his occupation as "a painter in Seville." Since it

Velázquez, *Juan de Pareja*, 1650. (The Metropolitan Museum of Art, Fletcher Fund, Rogers Fund, and Bequest of Miss Adelaide Milton de Groot (1876–1967), by exchange, supplemented by gifts from friends of the Museum, 1971. [1971.86]. Image copyright © The Metropolitan Museum of Art)

mentions no other name, it is reasonable to assume that Pareja arrived in Madrid a free man. Sometime between 1630 and 1648, however, he came into the possession of the artist Diego Velázquez (1599–1660); Pareja became a slave.

How did Velázquez acquire Pareja? By purchase? As a gift? Had Pareja fallen into debt or committed some crime and thereby lost his freedom? We do not know. Velázquez, the greatest Spanish painter of the seventeenth century, had a large studio with many assistants. Pareja was set to grinding powders to make colors and to preparing canvases. He must have demonstrated ability because when Velázquez went to Rome in 1648, he chose Pareja to accompany him.

In 1650, as practice for a portrait of Pope Innocent X, Velázquez painted Pareja. The portrait shows Pareja dressed in fine clothing and gazing self-confidently at the viewer. Displayed in Rome in a public exhibition of Velázquez's work, the painting won acclaim from his contemporaries. That same year, Velázquez signed the document that gave Pareja his freedom, to become effective in 1654. Pareja lived out the rest of his life as an independent painter.

What does the public career of Pareja tell us about the man and his world? Pareja's career suggests that a person of African descent might fall into slavery and yet still acquire professional training and work alongside his master in a position of confidence. Moreover, if lucky enough to be freed, a former slave could exercise a profession and live his own life in Madrid. Pareja's experience was far from typical for a slave in the 1600s, but it reminds us of the myriad forms that slavery took in this period.

QUESTIONS FOR ANALYSIS

1. Since slavery was an established institution in Spain, speculate on Velázquez's possible reasons for giving Pareja his freedom.

2. To what extent was Pareja a marginal person in Spanish society? Was he an insider or an outsider to Spanish society?

Sources: Jonathan Brown, *Velázquez: Painter and Courtier* (New Haven, Conn.: Yale University Press, 1986); *Grove Dictionary of Art* (New York: Macmillan, 2000); Sister Wendy Beckett, *Sister Wendy's American Collection* (New York: Harper Collins Publishers, 2000), p. 15.

Philip II, ca. 1533 This portrait of Philip II as a young man and crown prince of Spain is by the celebrated artist Titian, court painter to Philip's father, Charles V. After taking the throne, Philip became another great patron of the artist. (Museo Nacional del Prado, Madrid)

experienced large price increases. Prices doubled and in some cases quadrupled. Spain suffered most severely, but all European countries were affected. Because money bought less, people who lived on fixed incomes, such as nobles, were badly hurt. Those who owed fixed sums of money, such as the middle class, prospered because in a time of rising prices, debts lessened in value each year. Food costs rose most sharply, and the poor fared worst of all.

In many ways, though, it was not Spain but China that controlled the world trade in silver. The Chinese demanded silver for their products and for the payment of imperial taxes. China was thus the main buyer of world silver, absorbing half the world's production. The silver market drove world trade, with New Spain and Japan being mainstays on the supply side and China dominating the demand side. The world trade in silver is one of the best examples of the new global economy that emerged in this period.

The Birth of the Global Economy

With the Europeans' discovery of the Americas and their exploration of the Pacific, the entire world was linked for the first time in history by seaborne trade. The opening of that trade brought into being three successive commercial empires: the Portuguese, the Spanish, and the Dutch.

The Portuguese were the first worldwide traders. In the sixteenth century they controlled the sea route to India (see Map 15.3). From their fortified bases at Goa on the Arabian Sea and at Malacca on the Malay Peninsula, ships carried goods to the Portuguese settlement at Macao in the South China Sea. From Macao Portuguese ships loaded with Chinese silks and porcelains sailed to the Japanese port of Nagasaki and to the Philippine port of Manila, where Chinese goods were exchanged for Spanish silver from New Spain. Throughout Asia the Portuguese traded in slaves—sub-Saharan Africans, Chinese, and Japanese. The Portuguese exported horses from Mesopotamia and copper from Arabia to India; from India they exported hawks and peacocks for the Chinese and Japanese markets. Back to Portugal they brought Asian spices that had been purchased with textiles produced in India and with gold and ivory from East Africa. They also shipped back sugar from their colony in Brazil, produced by enslaved Africans whom they had transported across the Atlantic.

Coming to empire a few decades later than the Portuguese, the Spanish were determined to claim their place in world trade. The Spanish Empire in the New World was basically a land empire, but across the Pacific the Spaniards built a seaborne empire centered at Manila in the Philippines. The city of Manila served as the transpacific bridge between Spanish America and China. In Manila, Spanish traders used silver from American mines to purchase Chinese silk for European markets. The European demand for silk was so huge that in 1597, for example, 12 million pesos of silver, almost the total value of the transatlantic trade, moved from Acapulco in New Spain to Manila (see Map 15.3). After 1640 the Spanish silk trade declined in the face of stiff competition from Dutch imports.

In the seventeenth century the Dutch challenged the Spanish and Portuguese Empires. Drawing on their commercial wealth and long experience in European trade, the Dutch emerged by the end of the century as the most powerful worldwide seaborne trading power. The Dutch Empire was built on spices. In 1599 a Dutch fleet returned to Amsterdam carrying 600,000 pounds of pepper and 250,000 pounds of cloves and nutmeg. Those who had invested in the expedition received a 100 percent profit. The voyage led to the establishment in 1602 of the Dutch East India Company, founded with the stated intention of capturing the spice trade from the Portuguese.

The Dutch set their sights on gaining direct access to and control of the Indonesian sources of spices. The Dutch fleet, sailing from the Cape of Good Hope in

Goods from the Global Economy Spices from Southeast Asia were a driving force behind the new global economy, and among the most treasured European luxury goods. They were used not only for cooking but also as medicines and health tonics. This fresco (center) shows a fifteenth-century Italian pharmacist measuring out spices for a customer. After the discovery of the Americas, a wave of new items entered European markets, silver foremost among them. The incredibly rich silver mines at Potosí (modern-day Bolivia) were the source of this eight-reale coin (left) struck at the mine during the reign of Charles II. Such coins were the original "pieces of eight" prized by pirates and adventurers. Soon Asian and American goods were mixed together by enterprising tradesmen. The mid-seventeenth-century Chinese teapot (right) was made of porcelain with the traditional Chinese design prized in the West, but with a silver handle added to suit European tastes. (teapot: Private Collection/Paul Freeman/The Bridgeman Art Library; coin: Hoberman Collection/SuperStock; spice shop: Alfredo Dagli Orti/The Art Archive)

Africa and avoiding the Portuguese forts in India, steered directly for the Sunda Strait in Indonesia (see Map 15.3). In return for assisting Indonesian princes in local squabbles and disputes with the Portuguese, the Dutch won broad commercial concessions. Through agreements, seizures, and outright war, they gained control of the western access to the Indonesian archipelago in the first half of the seventeenth century. Gradually, they acquired political domination over the archipelago itself. By the 1660s the Dutch had managed to expel the Portuguese from Ceylon and other East Indian islands, thereby establishing control of the lucrative spice trade.

Not content with challenging the Portuguese in the Indian Ocean, the Dutch also aspired to a role in the Americas. Founded in 1621 in a period of war with Spain, the Dutch West India Company aggressively sought to open trade with North and South America and capture Spanish territories there. The company captured or destroyed hundreds of Spanish ships, seized the Spanish silver fleet in 1628, and captured portions of Brazil and the Caribbean. The Dutch also successfully interceded in the transatlantic slave trade, bringing much of the west coast of Africa under Dutch control. Ironically, the nation that was known throughout Europe as a bastion of tolerance and freedom came to be one of the principal operators of the slave trade starting in the 1640s.

Dutch efforts to colonize North America were less successful. The colony of New Netherland, governed from New Amsterdam (modern-day New York City), was hampered by lack of settlement and weak governance and was easily captured by the British in 1664.

Changing Attitudes and Beliefs

How did new ideas about race and the works of Montaigne and Shakespeare reflect the encounter with new peoples and places? ▬

The age of overseas expansion heightened Europeans' contacts with the rest of the world. These contacts gave birth to new ideas about the inherent superiority or inferiority of different races, in part to justify European participation in the slave trade. Cultural encounters also inspired more positive views. The essays of Michel de Montaigne epitomized a new spirit of skepticism and cultural relativism, while the plays of William Shakespeare reflected the efforts of one great writer to come to terms with the cultural complexity of his day.

New Ideas About Race

At the beginning of the transatlantic slave trade, most Europeans would have thought of Africans, if they thought of them at all, as savages because of their eating habits, morals, clothing, and social customs and as barbarians because of their language and methods of war. Despite lingering belief in a Christian Ethiopia under the legendary Prester John, they grouped Africans into the despised categories of pagan heathens and Muslim infidels. Africans were certainly not the only peoples subject to such dehumanizing attitudes. Jews were also viewed as an alien group that was, like Africans, naturally given to sin and depravity. More generally, elite people across Europe were accustomed to viewing the peasant masses as a lower form of humanity. They scornfully compared rustic peasants to dogs, pigs, and donkeys and even reviled the dark skin color peasants acquired while laboring in the sun.[19]

As Europeans turned to Africa for new sources of slaves, they drew on and developed ideas about Africans' primitiveness and barbarity to defend slavery and even argue that enslavement benefited Africans by bringing the light of Christianity to heathen peoples. In 1444 an observer defended the enslavement of the first Africans by Portuguese explorers as necessary for their salvation "because they lived like beasts, without any of the customs of rational creatures, since they did not even know what were bread and wine, nor garments of cloth, nor life in the shelter of a house; and worse still was their ignorance, which deprived them of knowledge of good, and permitted them only a life of brutish idleness."[20] Compare this with an early seventeenth-century Englishman's complaint that the Irish "be so beastly that they are better like beasts than Christians."[21]

Over time, the institution of slavery fostered a new level of racial inequality. In contrast to peasants, Jews, and the Irish, Africans gradually became seen as utterly distinct from and wholly inferior to Europeans. From rather vague assumptions about non-Christian religious beliefs and a general lack of civilization, Europeans developed increasingly rigid ideas of racial superiority and inferiority to safeguard the growing profits gained from plantation slavery. Black skin became equated with slavery itself as Europeans at home and in the colonies convinced themselves that blacks were destined by God to serve them as slaves in perpetuity.

Support for this belief went back to the Greek philosopher Aristotle's argument that some people are naturally destined for slavery and to biblical associations between darkness and sin. A more explicit justification was found in the story of Noah's curse upon Canaan. According to the Bible, Ham defied his father's ban on sexual relations on the ark and further

❝ They lived like beasts, without any of the customs
of rational creatures, since they did not even know
what were bread and wine, nor garments of cloth,
nor life in the shelter of a house. **❞**

—**EUROPEAN OBSERVER**

enraged Noah by entering his tent and viewing his father unclothed. To punish Ham, Noah cursed Ham's son Canaan and all his descendants to be the "servant of servants." Biblical genealogies listing Ham's sons as those who peopled North Africa and Cush were read to mean that all inhabitants of those regions bore Noah's curse. From the sixteenth century onward, this story was often cited as justification for the enslavement of an entire race.

After 1700 the emergence of new methods of observing and describing nature led to the use of science to define race. From referring to a nation or an ethnic group, henceforth "race" would mean biologically distinct groups of people, whose physical differences produced differences in culture, character, and intelligence. Biblical justifications for inequality thereby gave way to supposedly scientific ones.

Michel de Montaigne and Cultural Curiosity

Racism was not the only possible reaction to the new worlds emerging in the sixteenth century. Decades of religious fanaticism, bringing civil anarchy and war, led both Catholics and Protestants to doubt that any one faith contained absolute truth. Added to these doubts was the discovery of peoples in the New World who had radically different ways of life. These shocks helped produce ideas of skepticism and cultural relativism in the sixteenth and seventeenth centuries. Skepticism is a school of thought founded on doubt that total certainty or definitive knowledge is ever attainable. The skeptic is cautious and critical and suspends judgment. Cultural relativism suggests that one culture is not necessarily superior to another, just different. Both notions found expression in the work of Frenchman Michel de Montaigne (duh mahn-TAYN) (1533–1592).

Montaigne developed a new literary genre, the essay—from the French *essayer*, meaning "to test or try"—to express his thoughts and ideas. Published in 1580, Montaigne's *Essays* consisted of short personal reflections drawing on his extensive reading in ancient texts, his experience as a government official, and his own moral judgment. Intended to be accessible to ordinary

people, Montaigne wrote in French rather than Latin and in an engaging conversational style.

Montaigne's essay "Of Cannibals" reveals the impact of overseas discoveries on one thoughtful European's consciousness. In contrast to the prevailing views of the time, he rejected the notion that one culture is superior to another. Speaking of native Brazilians, he wrote:

> I find that there is nothing barbarous and savage in this nation [Brazil], . . . except, that everyone gives the title of barbarism to everything that is not according to his usage; as, indeed, we have no other criterion of truth and reason, than the example and pattern of the opinions and customs of the place wherein we live. . . . They are savages in the same way that we say fruits are wild, which nature produces of herself and by her ordinary course; whereas, in truth, we ought rather to call those wild whose natures we have changed by our artifice and diverted from the common order.[22]

In his own time and throughout the seventeenth century, few would have agreed with Montaigne's challenge to ideas of European superiority or his even more radical questioning of the superiority of humans over animals. The publication of his ideas, however, contributed to a basic shift in attitudes. Montaigne inaugurated an era of doubt. "Wonder," he said, "is the foundation of all philosophy, research is the means of all learning, and ignorance is the end."[23]

William Shakespeare and His Influence

In addition to the essay as a literary genre, the period fostered remarkable creativity in other branches of literature. England—especially in the latter part of Queen Elizabeth I's reign and in the first years of her successor, James I (r. 1603–1625)—witnessed remarkable literary expression. The terms *Elizabethan* and *Jacobean* (referring to the reign of James) are used to designate the English music, poetry, prose, and drama of this period.

The undisputed master of the period was the dramatist William Shakespeare, whose genius lay in the originality of his characterizations, the diversity of his plots,

Titus Andronicus With classical allusions, fifteen murders and executions, a Gothic queen who takes a black lover, and incredible violence, this early Shakespearean tragedy (1594) was a melodramatic thriller that enjoyed enormous popularity with the London audience. The shock value of a dark-skinned character on the English stage is clearly shown in this illustration. (Reproduced by permission of the Marquess of Bath, Longleat House, Warminster, Wilts)

his understanding of human psychology, and his unsurpassed gift for language. Born in 1564 to a successful glove manufacturer in Stratford-on-Avon, Shakespeare grew into a Renaissance man with a deep appreciation of classical culture, individualism, and humanism. Such plays as *Julius Caesar* and *Antony and Cleopatra* deal with classical subjects and figures. Several of his comedies have Italian Renaissance settings. His history plays, including *Richard III* and *Henry IV*, express English national consciousness. Shakespeare's later tragedies, including *Hamlet*, *Othello*, and *Macbeth*, explore an enormous range of human problems and are open to an almost infinite variety of interpretations.

Like Montaigne, Shakespeare's work reveals the impact of the new discoveries and contacts of his day. The title character of *Othello* is described as a "Moor of Venice." In Shakespeare's day, the term "moor" referred to Muslims of Moroccan or North African origin, including those who had migrated to the Iberian Peninsula. It could also be applied, though, to natives of the Iberian Peninsula who converted to Islam or to non-Muslim Berbers in North Africa. To complicate things even more, references in the play to Othello as "black" in skin color have led many to believe that Shakespeare intended him

to be a sub-Saharan African, and he is usually depicted as such in modern performances. This confusion in the play reflects the uncertainty in Shakespeare's own day about racial and religious classifications.

The character of Othello is both vilified in racist terms by his enemies and depicted as a brave warrior, a key member of the city's military leadership, and a man capable of winning the heart of an aristocratic white woman. In contrast to the prevailing view of Moors as inferior, Shakespeare presents Othello as a complex human figure, whose only crime is to have "loved [his wife] not wisely, but too well." Shakespeare's play thus demonstrates both the intolerance of contemporary society and the possibility for some individuals to look beyond racial stereotypes.

Shakespeare's last play, *The Tempest*, displays a similar interest in race and race relations. The plot involves the stranding on an island of sorcerer Prospero and his daughter Miranda. There Prospero finds and raises Caliban, a native of the island, whom he instructs in his own language and religion. After Caliban's attempted rape of Miranda, Prospero enslaves him, earning the rage and resentment of his erstwhile pupil. Modern scholars often note the echoes between this play and the realities of imperial conquest and settlement in Shakespeare's day. It is no accident, they argue, that the poet portrayed Caliban as a monstrous dark-skinned island native who was best-suited for slavery. Shakespeare himself borrows words from Montaigne's essay "Of Cannibals," suggesting that he may have intended to criticize, rather than endorse, racial intolerance. Shakespeare's work shows us one of the finest minds of the age grasping to come to terms with the racial and religious complexities around him.

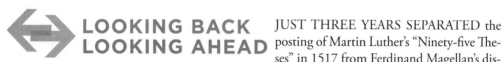

LOOKING BACK LOOKING AHEAD

JUST THREE YEARS SEPARATED the posting of Martin Luther's "Ninety-five Theses" in 1517 from Ferdinand Magellan's discovery of the Pacific Ocean in 1520. Within a few short years, the religious unity of western Europe and its notions of terrestrial geography were shattered. Old medieval certainties about Heaven and earth collapsed. In the ensuing decades, Europeans struggled to come to terms with religious difference at home and the multitudes of new peoples and places they encountered abroad. These processes were intertwined, as Puritans and Quakers fled religious persecution at home to colonize the New World and the new Jesuit order proved its devotion to the pope by seeking Catholic converts across the globe. While some Europeans were fascinated and inspired by this new diversity, too often the result was violence. Europeans endured decades of civil war between Protestants and Catholics, and indigenous peoples suffered massive population losses as a result of European warfare, disease, and exploitation. Tragically, both Catholic and Protestant religious leaders condoned the African slave trade that was to bring suffering and death to millions of Africans.

Even as the voyages of discovery contributed to the fragmentation of European culture, they also belonged to longer-term processes of state centralization and consolidation. The new monarchies of the Renaissance produced stronger and wealthier governments capable of financing the huge expenses of exploration and colonization. Competition to gain overseas colonies became an integral part of European politics. Spain's investment in conquest proved spectacularly profitable and yet, as we will see in Chapter 16, the ultimate result was a weakening of its power. Other European nations took longer to realize financial gain, yet over time the Netherlands, England, and France reaped tremendous profits from colonial trade, which helped them build modernized, centralized states. The path from medieval Christendom to modern nation-states led through religious warfare and global encounter.

CHAPTER REVIEW

■ What was the Afro-Eurasian trading world before Columbus? (p. 444)

Prior to Columbus's voyages, well-developed trade routes linked the peoples and products of Africa, Asia, and Europe. The Indian Ocean was the center of the Afro-Eurasian trade world, ringed by cosmopolitan commercial cities such as Mombasa in Africa, Calicut in India, and Malacca in Southeast Asia. Chinese silk and porcelain were desired by elites throughout the trading system. The Ottoman and Persian Empires produced textiles and other goods for the world market, while also serving as intermediaries for trade between East and West. Venetian and Genoese merchants brought spices, silks, and other luxury goods into western Europe from the East. Overall, Europeans played a minor role in the Afro-Eurasian trading world because they did not produce many products desired by Eastern elites.

■ How and why did Europeans undertake ambitious voyages of expansion? (p. 448)

In the sixteenth and seventeenth centuries Europeans gained access to large parts of the globe for the first time. A revival of populations and economies after the time of the Black Death created markets for spices and other goods from the East. In addition to searching for routes that would undo the Italian and Ottoman dominance of trade in the East, Europeans were motivated by intellectual curiosity, driving ambition, religious zeal, and a lack of opportunities at home. The revived monarchies of the sixteenth century now possessed sufficient resources to back ambitious seafarers like Christopher Columbus and Vasco da Gama. Technological developments such as the invention of the caravel and magnetic compass enabled Europeans to undertake ever more ambitious voyages.

■ What was the impact of European conquest on the peoples and ecologies of the New World? (p. 461)

In the aftermath of conquest, the Spanish established new forms of governance to dominate native peoples and exploit their labor. The arrival of Europeans also brought enormous population losses to native communities, primarily through the spread of infectious diseases. Women played an important role in creating new colonial societies, both through the union of native and African women with European men and through the migration of European women to the colonies. The Age of Discovery sparked a complex exchange of germs, flora, and fauna between the Old and New Worlds, which is known as the "Columbian exchange." Europeans brought familiar crops and livestock to the Americas, and brought home new ones, some of which became staples of the European diet.

■ How was the era of global contact shaped by new commodities, commercial empires, and forced migrations? (p. 464)

One of the most important consequences of the Age of Discovery was the creation of the first truly global economy in the sixteenth and seventeenth centuries. Tragically, a major component of global trade was the transatlantic slave trade, in which Europeans transported many millions of Africans to labor in horrific conditions in the mines and sugar plantations of the New World. The discovery of extraordinarily rich silver mines in New Spain brought enormous wealth to the Spanish crown, but little economic development. European nations vied for supremacy in global trade, with early Portuguese success in India and Asia being challenged first by the Spanish and then by the Dutch, who successfully imposed control of trade with the East in the mid-seventeenth century.

■ How did new ideas about race and the works of Montaigne and Shakespeare reflect the encounter with new peoples and places? (p. 472)

Increased contact with the outside world led Europeans to develop new ideas about cultural and racial difference. Europeans had long held negative attitudes toward Africans; as the slave trade grew, they began to express more rigid notions of racial inequality and to claim that Africans were inherently suited for slavery. Most Europeans shared such views, with some important exceptions. In his essays, Michel de Montaigne challenged the idea that natives of the Americas were inferior barbarians, while William Shakespeare's plays contain ambivalent attitudes toward complex non-European characters.

Suggested Reading

Crosby, Alfred W. *The Columbian Exchange: Biological and Cultural Consequences of 1492.* 30th anniversary ed. 2003. An innovative and highly influential account of the environmental impact of Columbus's voyages.

Elliot, J. H. *Empires of the Atlantic World: Britain and Spain in America, 1492–1830.* 2006. A masterful account of the differences and similarities between the British and Spanish Empires in the Americas.

Fernández-Armesto, Felip. *Columbus.* 1992. An excellent biography of Christopher Columbus.

Greenblatt, Stephen. *Marvelous Possessions: The Wonder of the New World.* 1991. Describes the cultural impact of New World discoveries on Europeans.

Menard, Russell. *Sweet Negotiations: Sugar, Slavery and Plantation Agriculture in Early Barbados.* 2006. Explores the intertwined history of sugar plantations and slavery in seventeenth-century Barbados.

Northrup, David, ed. *The Atlantic Slave Trade*. 1994. Collected essays by leading scholars on many different aspects of the slave trade.

Pérez-Mallaína, Pablo E. *Spain's Men of the Sea: Daily Life on the Indies Fleet in the Sixteenth Century*. 1998. A description of recruitment, daily life, and career paths of ordinary sailors and officers in the Spanish fleet.

Pomeranz, Kenneth, and Steven Topik. *The World That Trade Created: Society, Culture and the World Economy, 1400 to the Present*. 1999. The creation of a world market presented through rich and vivid stories of merchants, miners, slaves, and farmers.

Restall, Matthew. *Seven Myths of Spanish Conquest*. 2003. A re-examination of common ideas about why and how the Spanish conquered native civilizations in the New World.

Scammell, Geoffrey V. *The World Encompassed: The First European Maritime Empires, c. 800–1650*. 1981. A detailed overview of the first European empires, including the Italian city-states, Portugal, and Spain.

Schmidt, Benjamin. *Innocence Abroad: The Dutch Imagination and the New World, 1570–1670*. 2001. Examines changing Dutch attitudes toward the New World, from criticism of the cruelty of the Spanish conquest to eagerness for their own overseas empire.

Subrahamanyam, Sanjay. *The Career and Legend of Vasco da Gama*. 1998. A probing biography that places Vasco da Gama in the context of Portuguese politics and society.

Notes

1. Thomas Benjamin, *The Atlantic World: Europeans, Africans, Indians and Their Shared History, 1400–1900* (Cambridge, U.K.: Cambridge University Press, 2009), p. 56.
2. G. V. Scammell, *The World Encompassed: The First European Maritime Empires, c. 800–1650* (Berkeley: University of California Press, 1981), pp. 101, 104.
3. Quoted in C. M. Cipolla, *Guns, Sails, and Empires: Technological Innovation and the Early Phases of European Expansion, 1400–1700* (New York: Minerva Press, 1965), p. 132.
4. Quoted in F. H. Littell, *The Macmillan Atlas: History of Christianity* (New York: Macmillan, 1976), p. 75.
5. Pablo E. Pérez-Mallaína, *Spain's Men of the Sea: Daily Life on the Indies Fleet in the Sixteenth Century* (Baltimore: Johns Hopkins University Press, 1998), p. 133.
6. Ibid., p. 19.
7. Quoted in F. Maddison, "Tradition and Innovation: Columbus' First Voyage and Portuguese Navigation in the Fifteenth Century," in *Circa 1492: Art in the Age of Exploration*, ed. J. A. Levenson (Washington, D.C.: National Gallery of Art, 1991), p. 69.
8. Quoted in R. L. Kagan, "The Spain of Ferdinand and Isabella," in *Circa 1492: Art in the Age of Exploration*, ed. J. A. Levenson (Washington, D.C.: National Gallery of Art, 1991), p. 60.
9. Peter Hulme, *Colonial Encounters: Europe and the Native Caribbean, 1492–1797* (London and New York: Methuan, 1986), pp. 22–31.
10. Benjamin, *The Atlantic World*, p. 141.
11. Ibid., pp. 35–59.
12. Quoted in C. Gibson, ed., *The Black Legend: Anti-Spanish Attitudes in the Old World and the New* (New York: Knopf, 1971), pp. 74–75.
13. Quoted in L. B. Rout, Jr., *The African Experience in Spanish America* (New York: Cambridge University Press, 1976), p. 23.
14. Cited in Geoffrey Vaughn Scammell, *The First Imperial Age: European Overseas Expansion, c. 1400–1715* (London and New York: Routledge, 2002), p. 62.
15. Ibid., p. 432.
16. Herbert S. Klein, "Profits and the Causes of Mortality," in David Northrup, ed., *The Atlantic Slave Trade* (Lexington, Mass.: D. C. Heath and Co., 1994), p. 116.
17. Malcolm Cowley and Daniel P. Mannix, "The Middle Passage," in David Northrup, ed., *The Atlantic Slave Trade* (Lexington, Mass.: D. C. Heath and Co., 1994), p. 101.
18. Voyages: The Trans-Atlantic Slave Trade Database, http://www.slavevoyages.org/tast/assessment/estimates.faces (accessed May 9, 2009).
19. Paul Freedman, *Images of the Medieval Peasant* (Stanford, Calif.: Stanford University Press, 1999).
20. Quoted in James H. Sweet, "The Iberian Roots of American Racist Thought," *The William and Mary Quarterly*, Third Series, Vol. 54, No. 1 (Jan. 1997), p. 155.
21. Quoted in Sean J. Connolly, *Contested Island: Ireland, 1460–1630* (Oxford: Oxford University Press, 2007), p. 397.
22. C. Cotton, trans., *The Essays of Michel de Montaigne* (New York: A. L. Burt, 1893), pp. 207, 210.
23. Ibid., p. 523.

Key Terms

conquistador (p. 449)
caravel (p. 450)
Ptolemy's *Geography* (p. 450)
Treaty of Tordesillas (p. 456)
Mexica Empire (p. 457)
Inca Empire (p. 459)
viceroyalties (p. 461)
encomienda system (p. 461)
Columbian exchange (p. 463)

For practice quizzes and other study tools, visit the Online Study Guide at **bedfordstmartins.com/mckaywest**.

For primary sources from this period, see *Sources of Western Society*, **Second Edition**.

For Web sites, images, and documents related to topics in this chapter, visit Make History at **bedfordstmartins.com/mckaywest**.

16

Absolutism and Constitutionalism

ca. 1589–1725

The seventeenth century was a period of crisis and transformation in Europe. Agricultural and manufacturing slumps led to food shortages and shrinking population rates. Religious and dynastic conflicts led to almost constant war, visiting violence and destruction on ordinary people and reshaping European states. Armies grew larger than they had been since the time of the Roman Empire, resulting in new government bureaucracies and higher taxes. Despite these obstacles, European states succeeded in gathering more power, and by 1680 much of the unrest that originated with the Reformation was resolved.

These crises were not limited to western Europe. Central and eastern Europe experienced even more catastrophic dislocation, with German lands serving as the battleground of the Thirty Years' War and borders constantly vulnerable to attack from the east. In Prussia and in Habsburg Austria absolutist states emerged in the aftermath of this conflict. Russia and the Ottoman Turks also developed absolutist governments. The Russian and Ottoman Empires seemed foreign and exotic to western Europeans, who saw them as the antithesis of their political, religious, and cultural values. While absolutism emerged as the solution to crisis in many European states, a small minority adopted a different path, placing sovereignty in the hands of privileged groups rather than the Crown. Historians refer to states where power was limited by law as "constitutional." The two most important seventeenth-century constitutionalist states were England and the Dutch Republic. Constitutionalism should not be confused with democracy. The elite rulers of England and the Dutch Republic pursued familiar policies of increased taxation, government authority, and social control. Nonetheless, they served as influential models to onlookers across Europe as a form of government that checked the power of a single ruler. ■

Life in Absolutist France. King Louis XIV receives foreign ambassadors to celebrate a peace treaty. The king grandly occupied the center of his court, which in turn served as the pinnacle for the French people and, at the height of his glory, for all of Europe.

CHAPTER PREVIEW

Seventeenth-Century Crisis and Rebuilding
■ What were the common crises and achievements of seventeenth-century European states?

Absolutism in France and Spain
■ What factors led to the rise of the French absolutist state under Louis XIV, and why did absolutist Spain experience decline in the same period?

Absolutism in Austria and Prussia
■ How did the rulers of Austria and Prussia transform their nations into powerful absolutist monarchies?

The Development of Russia and the Ottoman Empire
■ What were the distinctive features of Russian and Ottoman absolutism?

Alternatives to Absolutism in England and the Dutch Republic
■ How and why did the constitutional state triumph in the Dutch Republic and England?

Baroque Art and Music
■ What was the baroque style in art and music, and where was it popular?

What were the common crises and achievements of seventeenth-century European states? ▪

Historians often refer to the seventeenth century as an "age of crisis." After the economic and demographic growth of the sixteenth century, Europe faltered into stagnation and retrenchment. This was partially due to climate changes beyond anyone's control, but it also resulted from bitter religious divides, increased governmental pressures, and war. Overburdened peasants and city-dwellers took action to defend themselves, sometimes profiting from conflicts to obtain relief. In the long run, however, governments proved increasingly able to impose their will on the populace. The period witnessed spectacular growth in army size as well as new forms of taxation, government bureaucracies, and increased state sovereignty.

Peasant Life in the Midst of Economic Crisis

In the seventeenth century most Europeans lived in the countryside. The hub of the rural world was the small peasant village centered on a church and a manor. Life was in many ways circumscribed by the village, although we should not underestimate the mobility induced by war, food shortage, fortune-seeking, and religious pilgrimage.

In western Europe, a small number of peasants in each village owned enough land to feed themselves and had the livestock and ploughs necessary to work their land. These independent farmers were leaders of the peasant village. They employed the landless poor, rented out livestock and tools, and served as agents for the noble lord. Below them were small landowners and tenant farmers who did not have enough land to be self-sufficient. These families sold their best produce on the market to earn cash for taxes, rent, and food. At the bottom were the rural workers who worked as dependent

An English Food Riot Nothing infuriated ordinary women and men more than the idea that merchants and landowners were withholding grain from the market in order to push high prices even higher. In this cartoon an angry crowd hands out rough justice to a rich farmer accused of hoarding. (Courtesy of the Trustees of the British Museum)

laborers and servants. In eastern Europe, the vast majority of peasants toiled as serfs for noble landowners and did not own land in their own right (see page 482).

Rich or poor, east or west, bread was the primary element of the diet. The richest ate a white loaf, leaving brown bread to those who could not afford better. Peasants paid stiff fees to the local miller for grinding grain into flour and sometimes to the lord for the right to bake bread in his oven. Bread was most often accompanied by a soup made of roots, herbs, beans, and perhaps a small piece of salt pork. An important annual festival in many villages was the killing of the family pig. The whole family gathered to help, sharing a rare abundance of meat with neighbors and carefully salting the extra and putting down the lard. In some areas, menstruating women were careful to stay away from the kitchen for fear they might cause the lard to spoil.

European rural society lived on the edge of subsistence. Because of the crude technology and low crop yield, peasants were constantly threatened by scarcity and famine. In the seventeenth century a period of colder and wetter climate throughout Europe, dubbed the "little ice age" by historians, meant a shorter farming season with lower yields. A bad harvest created food shortages; a series of bad harvests could lead to famine. Recurrent famines significantly reduced the population of early modern Europe. Most people did not die of outright starvation, but rather of diseases brought on by malnutrition and exhaustion. Facilitated by the weakened population, outbreaks of bubonic plague continued in Europe until the 1720s.

The Estates of Normandy, a provincial assembly, reported on the dire conditions in northern France during an outbreak of plague in which disease was compounded by the disruption of agriculture and a lack of food:

Of the 450 sick persons whom the inhabitants were unable to relieve, 200 were turned out, and these we saw die one by one as they lay on the roadside. A large number still remain, and to each of them it is only possible to dole out the least scrap of bread. We only give bread to those who would otherwise die. The staple dish here consists of mice, which the inhabitants hunt, so desperate are they from hunger. They devour roots which the animals cannot eat; one can, in fact, not put into words the things one sees. . . . We certify to having ourselves seen herds, not of cattle, but of men and women, wandering about the fields between Rheims and Rhétel, turning up the earth like pigs

Chronology

ca. 1500–1650	Consolidation of serfdom in eastern Europe
1533–1584	Reign of Ivan the Terrible in Russia
1589–1610	Reign of Henry IV in France
1598–1613	Time of Troubles in Russia
1620–1740	Growth of absolutism in Austria and Prussia
1642–1649	English civil war, which ends with execution of Charles I
1643–1715	Reign of Louis XIV in France
1653–1658	Military rule in England under Oliver Cromwell (the Protectorate)
1660	Restoration of English monarchy under Charles II
1665–1683	Jean-Baptiste Colbert applies mercantilism to France
1670	Charles II agrees to re-Catholicize England in secret agreement with Louis XIV
1670–1671	Cossack revolt led by Stenka Razin
ca. 1680–1750	Construction of baroque palaces
1682	Louis XIV moves court to Versailles
1682–1725	Reign of Peter the Great in Russia
1683–1718	Habsburgs push the Ottoman Turks from Hungary
1685	Edict of Nantes revoked
1688–1689	Glorious Revolution in England
1701–1713	War of the Spanish Succession

to find a few roots; and as they can only find rotten ones, and not half enough of them, they become so weak that they have not strength left to seek food.[1]

Given the harsh conditions of life, industry also suffered. The output of woolen textiles, one of the most important European manufactures, declined sharply in the first half of the seventeenth century. Food prices were high, wages stagnated, and unemployment soared. This economic crisis was not universal: it struck various regions at different times and to different degrees. In the middle decades of the century, Spain, France, Germany, and England all experienced great economic difficulties; but these years were the golden age of the Netherlands.

The urban poor and peasants were the hardest hit. When the price of bread rose beyond their capacity to pay, they frequently expressed their anger by rioting. In towns they invaded bakers' shops to seize bread and resell it at a "just price." In rural areas they attacked convoys taking grain to the cities. Women often led these actions, since their role as mothers gave them some impunity in authorities' eyes. Historians have labeled this vision of a world in which community needs predominate over competition and profit a moral economy.

The Return of Serfdom in the East

While economic and social hardship was common across Europe, important differences existed between east and west. In the west the demographic losses of the Black Death allowed peasants to escape from serfdom as they acquired enough land to feed themselves and the livestock and ploughs necessary to work their land. In eastern Europe seventeenth-century peasants had largely lost their ability to own land independently. Eastern lords dealt with the labor shortages caused by the Black Death by restricting the right of their peasants to move to take advantage of better opportunities elsewhere. In Prussian territories by 1500 the law required that runaway peasants be hunted down and returned to their lords. Moreover, lords steadily took more and more of their peasants' land and arbitrarily imposed heavier and heavier labor obligations. By the early 1500s lords in many eastern territories could command their peasants to work for them without pay for as many as six days a week.

The gradual erosion of the peasantry's economic position was bound up with manipulation of the legal system. The local lord was also the local prosecutor, judge, and jailer. There were no independent royal officials to provide justice or uphold the common law. The power of the lord reached far into serfs' everyday lives. Not only was their freedom of movement restricted, but they required permission to marry or could be forced to marry. Lords could reallocate the lands worked by their serfs at will or sell serfs apart from their families. These conditions applied even on lands owned by the church.

Between 1500 and 1650 the consolidation of serfdom in eastern Europe was accompanied by the growth of commercial agriculture, particularly in Poland and eastern Germany. As economic expansion and population growth resumed after 1500, eastern lords increased the production of their estates by squeezing sizable surpluses out of the impoverished peasants. They then sold these surpluses to foreign merchants, who exported them to the growing cities of wealthier western Europe. The Netherlands and England benefited the most from inexpensive grain from the east.

It was not only the peasants who suffered in eastern Europe. With the approval of kings, landlords systematically undermined the medieval privileges of the towns and the power of the urban classes. Instead of selling products to local merchants, landlords sold directly to foreigners, bypassing local towns. Eastern towns also lost their medieval right of refuge and were compelled to return runaways to their lords. The population of the towns and the urban middle classes declined greatly. This development both reflected and promoted the supremacy of noble landlords in most of eastern Europe in the sixteenth century.

The Thirty Years' War

In the first half of the seventeenth century, the fragile balance of life was violently upturned by the ravages of the Thirty Years' War (1618–1648). The Holy Roman Empire was a confederation of hundreds of principalities, in-

Estonian Serfs in the 1660s The Estonians were conquered by German military nobility in the Middle Ages and reduced to serfdom. The German-speaking nobles ruled the Estonian peasants with an iron hand, and Peter the Great reaffirmed their domination when Russia annexed Estonia. (Mansell Collection/Time Life Pictures/Getty Images)

Soldiers Pillage a Farmhouse
Billeting troops among civilian populations during the Thirty Years' War caused untold hardships. In this late-seventeenth-century Dutch illustration, brawling soldiers take over a peasant's home, eat his food, steal his possessions, and insult his family. Peasant retaliation sometimes proved swift and bloody. (Rijksmuseum-Stichting Amsterdam)

dependent cities, duchies, and other polities loosely united under an elected emperor. The uneasy truce between Catholics and Protestants created by the Peace of Augsburg in 1555 deteriorated as the faiths of various areas shifted. Lutheran princes felt compelled to form the Protestant Union (1608), and Catholics retaliated with the Catholic League (1609). Each alliance was determined that the other should make no religious or territorial advance. Dynastic interests were also involved; the Spanish Habsburgs strongly supported the goals of their Austrian relatives: the unity of the empire and the preservation of Catholicism within it.

The war is traditionally divided into four phases. The first, or Bohemian, phase (1618–1625) was characterized by civil war in Bohemia between the Catholic League and the Protestant Union. In 1620 Catholic forces defeated Protestants at the Battle of the White Mountain. The second, or Danish, phase of the war (1625–1629) — so called because of the leadership of the Protestant king Christian IV of Denmark (r. 1588–1648) — witnessed additional Catholic victories. The Catholic imperial army led by Albert of Wallenstein swept through Silesia, north to the Baltic, and east into Pomerania, scoring smashing victories. Habsburg power peaked in 1629. The emperor issued the Edict of Restitution, whereby all Catholic properties lost to Protestantism since 1552 were restored, and only Catholics and Lutherans were allowed to practice their faiths.

The third, or Swedish, phase of the war (1630–1635) began with the arrival in Germany of the Swedish king Gustavus Adolphus (r. 1594–1632) and his army. The ablest administrator of his day and a devout Lutheran, he intervened to support the empire's Protestants. The French chief minister, Cardinal Richelieu, subsidized the Swedes, hoping to weaken Habsburg power in Europe. Gustavus Adolphus won two important battles but was fatally wounded in combat. The final, or French, phase of the war (1635–1648) was prompted by Richelieu's concern that the Habsburgs would rebound after the death of Gustavus Adolphus. Richelieu declared war on Spain and sent military as well as financial assistance. Finally, in October 1648 peace was achieved.

The 1648 **Peace of Westphalia** that ended the Thirty Years' War marked a turning point in European history. For the most part, conflicts fought over religious faith receded. The treaties recognized the independent authority of more than three hundred German princes (Map 16.1), reconfirming the emperor's severely limited authority. The Augsburg agreement of 1555 became permanent, adding Calvinism to Catholicism and Lutheranism as legally permissible creeds. The north German states remained Protestant; the south German states, Catholic.

The Thirty Years' War was probably the most destructive event for the central European economy and society prior to the world wars of the twentieth century. Perhaps one-third of urban residents and two-fifths of

Peace of Westphalia The name of a series of treaties that concluded the Thirty Years' War in 1648 and marked the end of large-scale religious violence in Europe.

Map 16.1 Europe After the Thirty Years' War This map shows the political division of Europe after the Treaty of Westphalia (1648) ended the war. Which country emerged from the Thirty Years' War as the strongest European power? What dynastic house was that country's major rival in the early modern period?

the rural population died, leaving entire areas depopulated. Trade in southern German cities, such as Augsburg, was virtually destroyed. Agricultural areas suffered catastrophically. Many small farmers lost their land, allowing nobles to enlarge their estates and consolidate their control.[2]

Achievements in State-Building

In this context of economic and demographic depression, monarchs began to make new demands on their people. Traditionally, historians have distinguished between the "absolutist" governments of France, Spain, central Europe, and Russia and the constitutionalist governments of England and the Dutch Republic.

Whereas absolutist monarchs gathered all power under their personal control, English and Dutch rulers were obliged to respect laws passed by representative institutions. More recently, historians have emphasized commonalities among these powers. Despite their political differences, all these states shared common projects of protecting and expanding their frontiers, raising new taxes, consolidating central control, and competing for the new colonies opening up in the New and Old Worlds.

Rulers who wished to increase their authority encountered formidable obstacles. Some were purely material. Without paved roads, telephones, or other modern technology, it took weeks to convey orders from the central government to the provinces. Rulers also suffered from lack of information about their realms, making it impossible to police and tax the population effectively. Local power structures presented another serious obstacle. Nobles, the church, provincial and national assemblies, town councils, guilds, and other bodies held legal privileges, which could not easily be rescinded. In some kingdoms many people spoke a language different from the Crown's, further diminishing their willingness to obey its commands.

Nonetheless, over the course of the seventeenth century both absolutist and constitutional governments achieved new levels of central control. This increased authority focused in four areas in particular: greater taxation, growth in armed forces, larger and more efficient bureaucracies, and the increased ability to compel obedience from their subjects. Over time, centralized power added up to something close to sovereignty. A state may be termed sovereign when it possesses a monopoly over the instruments of justice and the use of force within clearly defined boundaries. In a sovereign state, no system of courts, such as ecclesiastical tribunals, competes with state courts in the dispensation of justice; and private armies, such as those of feudal lords, present no threat to central authority. While seventeenth-century states did not acquire total sovereignty, they made important strides toward that goal.

Warfare and the Growth of Army Size

The driving force of seventeenth-century state-building was warfare, characterized by dramatic changes in the size and style of armies. Medieval armies had been raised by feudal lords for particular wars or campaigns, after which the troops were disbanded. In the seventeenth century monarchs took command of recruiting and maintaining armies—in peacetime as well as wartime. Kings deployed their troops both inside and outside the country in the interests of the monarchy. Instead of serving their own interests, army officers were required to be loyal and obedient to the monarchs who commanded them. New techniques for training and deploying soldiers meant a rise in the professional standards of the army.

Along with professionalization came an explosive growth in army size. The French took the lead, with the army growing from roughly 125,000 men in the Thirty Years' War to 340,000 at the end of the seventeenth century.[3] This growth was caused in part by changes in the style of armies. Mustering a royal army took longer than simply hiring a mercenary band, giving enemies time to form coalitions. For example, the large coalitions Louis XIV confronted (see page 492) required him to fight on multiple fronts with huge armies. In turn, the relative size and wealth of France among European nations allowed Louis to field enormous armies and thereby to pursue the ambitious foreign policies

The Professionalization of the Swedish Army Swedish king Gustavus Adolphus, surrounded by his generals, gives thanks to God for the safe arrival of his troops in Germany during the Thirty Years' War. A renowned military leader, the king imposed constant training drills and rigorous discipline on his troops, which contributed to their remarkable success in the war. (Photo courtesy of The Army Museum, Stockholm)

that caused his alarmed neighbors to form coalitions against him.

The death toll during war for noble officers, who personally led their men in battle, was startlingly high. The paramount noble value of honor outshone concerns for safety or material benefit. Nobles had to purchase their positions in the army and supply horses, food, uniforms, and weapons for themselves and their troops. Royal stipends did not begin to cover these expenses. The only legacy an officer's widow received was the debt incurred to fund her husband's military career. It was not until the 1760s that the French government assumed the costs of equipping troops.

Other European powers were quick to follow the French example. The rise of absolutism in central and eastern Europe led to a vast expansion in the size of armies. Great Britain followed a similar, albeit distinctive pattern. Instead of building a land army, the British focused on naval forces and eventually built the largest navy in the world.

Popular Political Action

In the seventeenth century increased pressures of taxation and warfare turned neighborhood riots over the cost of bread into armed uprisings. Popular revolts were extremely common in England, France, Spain, Portugal, and Italy in the mid-seventeenth century. In 1640 Philip IV of Spain faced revolt in Catalonia, the economic center of his realm. At the same time he struggled to put down uprisings in Portugal and in the northern provinces of the Netherlands. In 1647 the city of Palermo, in Spanish-occupied Sicily, exploded in protest over food shortages caused by a series of bad harvests. Fearing public unrest, the city government subsidized the price of bread, attracting even more starving peasants from the countryside. When Madrid ordered an end to subsidies, municipal leaders decided to lighten the loaf rather than raise prices. Not fooled by this change, local women led a bread riot, shouting "Long live the king and down with the taxes and the bad government!" As riot transformed to armed revolt, insurgency spread to the rest of the island and eventually to Naples on the mainland. Apart from affordable food, rebels demanded the suppression of extraordinary taxes and participation in municipal government. Some dreamed of a republic in which noble tax exemptions would be abolished. Despite initial successes, the revolt lacked unity and strong leadership and could not withstand the forces of the state.

In France urban uprisings became a frequent aspect of the social and political landscape. Beginning in 1630 and continuing on and off through the early 1700s, major insurrections occurred at Dijon, Bordeaux (bor-DOH), Montpellier, Lyons, and Amiens. All were characterized by deep popular anger and violence directed at outside officials sent to collect taxes. These officials were sometimes seized, beaten, and hacked to death. For example, in 1673 Louis XIV's imposition of new taxes on legal transactions, tobacco, and pewter ware provoked an uprising in Bordeaux.

Municipal and royal authorities often struggled to overcome popular revolt. They feared that stern repressive measures, such as sending in troops to fire on crowds, would create martyrs and further inflame the situation, while forcible full-scale military occupation of a city would be very expensive. The limitations of royal authority gave some leverage to rebels. To quell riots, royal edicts were sometimes suspended, prisoners released, and discussions initiated.

By the beginning of the eighteenth century, this leverage had largely disappeared. Municipal governments were better integrated into the national structure, and local authorities had prompt military support from the central government. People who publicly opposed royal policies and taxes received swift and severe punishment.

Absolutism in France and Spain

What factors led to the rise of the French absolutist state under Louis XIV, and why did absolutist Spain experience decline in the same period? ■

In the Middle Ages jurists held that as a consequence of monarchs' coronation and anointment with sacred oil, they ruled "by the grace of God." Law was given by God; kings "found" the law and acknowledged that they must respect and obey it. Kings in absolutist states amplified these claims, asserting that, as they were chosen by God, they were responsible to God alone. They claimed exclusive power to make and enforce laws, denying any other institution or group the authority to check their power. In France the founder of the Bourbon monarchy, Henry IV, established foundations upon which his successors Louis XIII and Louis XIV built a stronger, more centralized French state. Louis XIV is often seen as the epitome of an "absolute" monarch, with his endless wars, increased taxes and economic regulation, and glorious palace at Versailles. In truth, his success relied on collaboration with nobles, and thus his example illustrates both the achievements and the compromises of absolutist rule.

As French power rose in the seventeenth century, the glory of Spain faded. Once the fabulous revenue from American silver declined, Spain's economic stagnation could no longer be disguised, and the country faltered under weak leadership.

The Foundations of Absolutism

Louis XIV's absolutism had long roots. In 1589 his grandfather Henry IV (r. 1589–1610), the founder of the Bourbon dynasty, acquired a devastated country. Civil wars between Protestants and Catholics had wracked France since 1561. Poor harvests had reduced peasants to starvation, and commercial activity had declined drastically. "Henri le Grand" (Henry the Great), as the king was called, promised "a chicken in every pot" and inaugurated a remarkable recovery.

He did so by keeping France at peace during most of his reign. Although he had converted to Catholicism, he issued the Edict of Nantes, allowing Protestants the right to worship in 150 traditionally Protestant towns throughout France. He sharply lowered taxes and instead charged royal officials an annual fee to guarantee the right to pass their positions down to their heirs. He also improved the infrastructure of the country, building new roads and canals and repairing the ravages of years of civil war. Despite his efforts at peace, Henry was murdered in 1610 by a Catholic zealot, setting off a national crisis.

After the death of Henry IV his wife, the queen-regent Marie de' Medici, headed the government for the nine-year-old Louis XIII (r. 1610–1643). In 1628 Armand Jean du Plessis — Cardinal Richelieu (1585–1642) — became first minister of the French crown. Richelieu's maneuvers allowed the monarchy to maintain power within Europe and within its own borders despite the turmoil of the Thirty Years' War.

Cardinal Richelieu's political genius is best reflected in the administrative system he established to strengthen royal control. He extended the use of intendants, commissioners for each of France's thirty-two districts who were appointed directly by the monarch, to whom they were solely responsible. They recruited men for the army, supervised the collection of taxes, presided over the administration of local law, checked up on the local nobility, and regulated economic activities in their districts. As the intendants' power increased under Richelieu, so did the power of the centralized French state.

Under Richelieu, the French monarchy also acted to repress Protestantism. Louis personally supervised the siege of La Rochelle, an important port city and a major commercial center with strong ties to Protestant Holland and England. After the city fell in October 1628, its municipal government was suppressed. Protestants retained the right of public worship, but the Catholic liturgy was restored. The fall of La Rochelle was one step in the removal of Protestantism as a strong force in French life.

Richelieu did not aim to wipe out Protestantism in the rest of Europe, however. His main foreign policy goal was to destroy the Catholic Habsburgs' grip on territories that surrounded France. Consequently, Richelieu supported Habsburg enemies, including Protestants. In 1631 he signed a treaty with the Lutheran king Gustavus Adolphus promising French support against the Habsburgs in the Thirty Years' War. For the French cardinal, interests of state outweighed religious considerations.

Richelieu's successor as chief minister for the next child-king, the four-year-old Louis XIV, was Cardinal Jules Mazarin (1602–1661). Along with the regent, Queen Mother Anne of Austria, Mazarin continued Richelieu's centralizing policies. His struggle to increase royal revenues to meet the costs of war led to the uprisings of 1648–1653 known as the **Fronde**. A *frondeur* was originally a street urchin who threw mud at the passing carriages of the rich, but the word came to be applied to the many individuals and groups who opposed the policies of the government. In Paris, magistrates of the Parlement of Paris, the nation's most important court, were outraged by the Crown's autocratic measures. These so-called robe nobles (named for the robes they wore in court) encouraged violent protest by the common people. During the first of several riots, the queen mother fled Paris with Louis XIV. As rebellion spread outside Paris and to the sword nobles (the traditional warrior nobility), civil order broke down completely. In 1651 Anne's regency ended with the declaration of Louis as king in his own right. Much of the rebellion died away, and its leaders came to terms with the government.

The violence of the Fronde had significant results for the future. The twin evils of noble rebellion and popular riots left the French wishing for peace and for a strong monarch to reimpose order. This was the legacy that Louis XIV inherited in 1661 when he assumed personal rule of the largest and most populous country in western Europe at the age of twenty-three. Humiliated by his flight from Paris, he was determined to avoid any recurrence of rebellion.

Louis XIV and Absolutism

In the reign of Louis XIV (r. 1643–1715), the longest in European history, the French monarchy reached the peak of absolutist development. In the magnificence of his court and the brilliance of the culture that he presided over, Louis dominated his age. Religion, Anne, and Mazarin all taught Louis the doctrine of the divine right of kings: God had established kings as his rulers on earth, and they were answerable ultimately to him alone. Kings were divinely anointed and shared in the sacred nature of divinity, but they could not simply do as they pleased. They had to obey God's laws and rule for the good of the people. To symbolize his central role in the divine order, when he was fifteen years old Louis danced at a court ballet dressed as the sun, thereby acquiring the title of the "Sun King."

In addition to parading his power before the court, Louis worked very hard at the business of governing. He ruled his realm through several councils of state and insisted on taking a personal role in many of the councils' decisions. He selected councilors from the recently ennobled or the upper middle class because he believed "that the public should know, from the rank of those whom I chose to serve me, that I had no intention of sharing power with them."[4] Despite increasing financial problems, Louis never called a meeting of the Estates General. The nobility, therefore, had no means of united expression or action. Nor did Louis have a

Fronde A series of violent uprisings during the early reign of Louis XIV triggered by growing royal control and oppressive taxation.

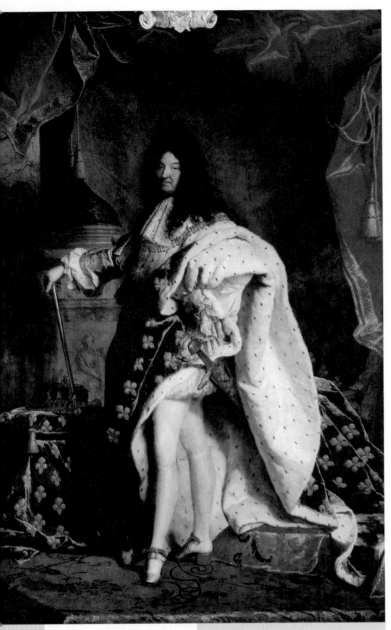

Picturing the Past

Hyacinthe Rigaud, *Louis XIV, King of France and Navarre*, 1701 This was one of Louis XIV's favorite portraits of himself. He liked it so much that he had many copies of the portrait made, in full and half-size format. (Scala/Art Resource, NY)

ANALYZING THE IMAGE Why do you think the king liked the portrait so much? What image of the king does it present to the viewer? What details does the painter include, and what impression do they convey?

CONNECTIONS How does this representation of royal power compare with the images of Peter the Great (page 503) and Charles I (page 506)? Which do you find the most impressive, and why?

To complete this activity online, go to the Online Study Guide at bedfordstmartins.com/mckaywest.

first minister. In this way he kept himself free from worry about the inordinate power of a Richelieu.

Although personally tolerant, Louis hated division within the realm and insisted that religious unity was essential to his royal dignity and to the security of the state. He thus pursued the policy of Protestant repression launched by Richelieu. In 1685 Louis revoked the Edict of Nantes. The new law ordered the destruction of Huguenot churches, the closing of schools, the Catholic baptism of Huguenots, and the exile of Huguenot pastors who refused to renounce their faith. The result was the departure of some of his most loyal and industrially skilled subjects.

Despite his claims to absolute authority, there were multiple constraints on Louis's power. As a representative of divine power, he was obliged to rule in a way that seemed consistent with virtue and benevolent authority. He had to uphold the laws issued by his royal predecessors. Moreover, he also relied on the collaboration of nobles, who maintained tremendous prestige and authority in their ancestral lands. Without their cooperation, it would have been impossible to extend his power throughout France or wage his many foreign wars. Louis's need to elicit noble cooperation led him to revolutionize court life at his spectacular palace at Versailles.

Life at Versailles

Through most of the seventeenth century, the French court had no fixed home, following the monarch to his numerous palaces and country residences. In 1682 Louis moved his court and government to the newly renovated palace at Versailles, a former hunting lodge. The palace quickly became the center of political, social, and cultural life. The king required all great nobles to spend at least part of the year in attendance on him there, so he could keep an eye on their activities. Since he controlled the distribution of state power and wealth, nobles had no choice but to obey and compete with each other for his favor at Versailles.

The glorious palace, with its sumptuous interiors and extensive formal gardens, was a mirror to the world of French glory, soon copied by would-be absolutist monarchs across Europe. (See "Living in the Past: The Absolutist Palace," page 490.) The reality of daily life in the palace was less glamorous. Versailles served as government offices for royal bureaucrats, as living quarters for the royal family and nobles, and as a place of work for hundreds of domestic servants. It was also open to the public at certain hours of the day. As a result, it was crowded with three thousand to ten thousand people every day. Even high nobles had to put up with cramped living space, and many visitors complained of the noise, smell, and crowds.

Louis further revolutionized court life by establishing an elaborate set of etiquette rituals to mark every moment of his day, from waking up and dressing in the morning to removing his clothing and retiring at night. He required nobles to serve him in these rituals, and they vied for the honor of doing so, with the highest in rank claiming the privilege of handing the king his shirt. Endless squabbles broke out over what type of chair one could sit on at court and the order in which great nobles entered and were seated in the chapel for Mass.

These rituals may seem absurd, but they were far from meaningless or trivial. The king controlled immense resources and privileges; access to him meant favored treatment for government offices, military and religious posts, state pensions, honorary titles, and a host of other benefits. The Duke of Saint-Simon wrote of the king's power at court in his memoirs:

> *No one understood better than Louis XIV the art of enhancing the value of a favour by his manner of bestowing it; he knew how to make the most of a word, a smile, even of a glance. If he addressed any one, were it but to ask a trifling question or make some commonplace remark, all eyes were turned on the person so honored; it was a mark of favour which always gave rise to comment.*[5]

Courtiers sought these rewards for themselves and their family members and followers. A system of patronage—in which a higher-ranked individual protected a lower-ranked one in return for loyalty and services—flowed from the court to the provinces. Through this mechanism Louis gained cooperation from powerful nobles.

Although they were denied public offices and posts, women played a central role in the patronage system. At court the king's wife, mistresses, and other female relatives recommended individuals for honors, advocated policy decisions, and brokered alliances between noble factions. Noblewomen played a similar role among courtiers, bringing their family connections to marriage to form powerful social networks. Onlookers sometimes resented the influence of powerful women at court. The Duke of Saint-Simon said of Madame de Maintenon, Louis XIV's mistress and secret second wife, "Many people have been ruined by her, without having been able to discover the author of the ruin, search as they might."

Louis XIV was also an enthusiastic patron of the arts, having danced gracefully in court ballets in his youth. He commissioned many sculptures and paintings for Versailles as well as performances of dance and music. Scholars characterize the art and literature of the age of Louis XIV as French classicism. By this they mean that the artists and writers of the late seventeenth century imitated the subject matter and style of classical antiquity, that their work resembled that of Renaissance Italy, and that French art possessed the classical qualities of discipline, balance, and restraint. Louis XIV also loved the stage, and in the plays of Molière and Racine his court witnessed the finest achievements in the history of the French theater.

With Versailles as the center of European politics, French culture grew in international prestige. French became the language of polite society and international diplomacy, gradually replacing Latin as the language of scholarship and learning. The royal courts of Sweden, Russia, Poland, and Germany all spoke French. In the eighteenth century the great Russian aristocrats were more fluent in French than in Russian. In England George I spoke fluent French and only halting English. France inspired a cosmopolitan European culture in the late seventeenth century that looked to Versailles as its center.

French Financial Management Under Colbert

France's ability to build armies and fight wars depended on a strong economy. Fortunately for Louis, his controller general, Jean-Baptiste Colbert (1619–1683), proved to be a financial genius. Colbert's central principle was that the wealth and the economy of France should serve the state. To this end, from 1665 to his death in 1683, Colbert rigorously applied mercantilist policies to France.

Mercantilism is a collection of governmental policies for the regulation of economic activities by and for the state. It derives from the idea that a nation's international power is based on its wealth, specifically its supply of gold and silver. To accumulate wealth, a country always had to sell more goods abroad than it bought. To decrease the purchase of goods outside France, Colbert insisted that French industry should produce everything needed by the French people.

> **mercantilism** A system of economic regulations aimed at increasing the power of the state based on the belief that a nation's international power was based on its wealth, specifically its supply of gold and silver.

To increase exports, Colbert supported old industries and created new ones, focusing especially on textiles, which were the most important sector of the economy. Colbert enacted new production regulations, created guilds to boost quality standards, and encouraged foreign craftsmen to immigrate to France. To encourage the purchase of French goods, he abolished many domestic tariffs and raised tariffs on foreign products. In 1664 Colbert founded the Company of the East Indies with (unfulfilled) hopes of competing with the Dutch for Asian trade.

Colbert also hoped to make Canada—rich in untapped minerals and some of the best agricultural land in the world—part of a vast French empire. He sent four thousand colonists to Quebec, whose capital was founded in 1608 under Henry IV. Subsequently, the Jesuit Jacques Marquette and the merchant Louis Joliet

The Absolutist Palace

LIVING IN THE PAST

BY 1700 PALACE BUILDING HAD BECOME a veritable obsession for European rulers. Their dramatic palaces symbolized the age of absolutist power, just as soaring Gothic cathedrals had expressed the idealized spirit of the High Middle Ages. With its classically harmonious, symmetrical, and geometric design, Versailles served as the model for the wave of palace building that began in the last decade of the seventeenth century. Royal palaces like Versailles were intended to overawe the people and proclaim their owners' authority and power.

Located ten miles southwest of Paris, Versailles began as a modest hunting lodge built by Louis XIII in 1623. His son, Louis XIV, spent decades enlarging and decorating the original structure. Between 1668 and 1670, architect Louis Le Vau (luh VOH) enveloped the old building within a much larger one that still exists today. In 1682 the new palace became the official residence of the Sun King and his court, although construction continued until 1710, when the royal chapel was completed. At any one time, several thousand people occupied the bustling and crowded palace. The awesome splendor of the eighty-yard Hall of Mirrors, replete with floor-to-ceiling mirrors and ceiling murals illustrating the king's triumphs, contrasted with the strong odors from the courtiers who commonly relieved themselves in discreet corners.

In 1693 Charles XI of Sweden, having reduced the power of the aristocracy, ordered the construction of his Royal Palace, which domi-

View of the Chateau de Versailles, 1722. Right: Louis XIV leading a tour of the extensive grounds at Versailles. (below: Châteaux de Versailles et de Trianon, Versailles/Réunion des Musées Nationaux/Art Resource, NY; right: Erich Lessing/Art Resource)

Prince Eugene's Summer Palace in Vienna. (Erich Lessing/Art Resource, NY)

nates the center of Stockholm to this day. Another such palace was Schönbrunn, an enormous Viennese Versailles begun in 1695 by Emperor Leopold to celebrate Austrian military victories and Habsburg might. Shown at right is architect Joseph Bernhard Fischer von Erlach's ambitious plan for Schönbrunn palace. Fischer's plan emphasizes the palace's vast size and its role as a site for military demonstrations. Ultimately, financial constraints resulted in a more modest building.

In central and eastern Europe, the favorite noble servants of royalty became extremely rich and powerful, and they too built grandiose palaces in the capital cities. These palaces were in part an extension of the monarch, for they surpassed the buildings of less-favored nobles and showed all the high road to fame and fortune. Take, for example, the palaces of Prince Eugene of Savoy, a French nobleman who became Austria's most famous military hero. It was Eugene who led the Austrian army, smashed the Turks, fought Louis XIV to a standstill, and generally guided the triumph of absolutism in Austria. Rewarded with great wealth by his grateful king, Eugene called on the leading architects of the day, Fischer von Erlach and Johann Lukas von Hildebrandt, to consecrate his glory in stone and fresco. Fischer built Eugene's Winter (or Town) Palace in Vienna, and he and Hildebrandt collaborated on the prince's Summer Palace on the city's outskirts. The prince's summer residence featured two baroque gems, the Lower Belvedere and the Upper Belvedere, completed in 1722 and shown above. The building's interior is equally stunning, with crouching giants serving as pillars and a magnificent great staircase.

Plans for the Palace at Schönbrunn, ca. 1700. (ONB/Vienna, Picture Archive, L 8001-D)

QUESTIONS FOR ANALYSIS

1. Compare these images. What did concrete objects and the manipulation of space accomplish for these rulers that mere words could not?

2. What disadvantages might stem from using architecture in this way?

3. Is the use of space and monumental architecture still a political tool in today's world?

491

sailed down the Mississippi River, which they named Colbert in honor of their sponsor (the name soon reverted to the original Native American one). Marquette and Joliet claimed possession of the land on both sides of the river as far south as present-day Arkansas. In 1684 French explorers continued down the Mississippi to its mouth and claimed vast territories for Louis XIV. The area was called, naturally, "Louisiana."

During Colbert's tenure as controller general, Louis was able to pursue his goals without massive tax increases and without creating a stream of new offices. The constant pressure of warfare after Colbert's death, however, undid many of his economic achievements.

Louis XIV's Wars

Louis XIV wrote that "the character of a conqueror is regarded as the noblest and highest of titles." In pursuit of the title of conqueror, he kept France at war for thirty-three of the fifty-four years of his personal rule.

Peace of Utrecht A series of treaties, from 1713 to 1715, that ended the War of the Spanish Succession, ended French expansion in Europe, and marked the rise of the British Empire.

François le Tellier, Marquis de Louvois, Louis's secretary of state for war, equaled Colbert's achievements in the economic realm. Louvois created a professional army in which the French state, rather than private nobles, employed the sol-

diers. Uniforms and weapons were standardized, and a rational system of training and promotion was devised. Many historians believe that the new loyalty, professionalism, and growth of the French army represented the peak of Louis's success in reforming government. As in so many other matters, his model was followed across Europe.

Louis's goal was to expand France to what he considered its natural borders. His armies managed to extend French borders to include important commercial centers in the Spanish Netherlands and Flanders as well as the entire province of Franche-Comté between 1667 and 1678. In 1681 Louis seized the city of Strasbourg, and three years later he sent his armies into the province of Lorraine. At that moment the king seemed invincible. In fact, Louis had reached the limit of his expansion. The wars of the 1680s and 1690s brought no additional territories but placed unbearable strains on French resources. Colbert's successors resorted to desperate measures to finance these wars, including devaluation of the currency and new taxes.

The Acquisitions of Louis XIV, 1668–1713

Territory gained
1668
1678
1713

Louis's last war was endured by a French people suffering high taxes, crop failure, and widespread malnutrition and death. In 1700 the childless Spanish king Charles II (r. 1665–1700) died, opening a struggle for control of Spain and its colonies. His will bequeathed the Spanish crown and its empire to Philip of Anjou, Louis XIV's grandson (Louis's wife, Maria-Theresa, had been Charles's sister). The will violated a prior treaty by which the European powers had agreed to divide the Spanish possessions between the king of France and the Holy Roman emperor, both brothers-in-law of Charles II. Claiming that he was following both Spanish and French interests, Louis broke with the treaty and accepted the will, thereby triggering the War of the Spanish Succession (1701–1713).

In 1701 the English, Dutch, Austrians, and Prussians formed the Grand Alliance against Louis XIV. War dragged on until 1713. The **Peace of Utrecht**, which ended the war, allowed Louis's grandson Philip to remain king of Spain on the understanding that the French and Spanish crowns would never be united. France surrendered Newfoundland, Nova Scotia, and the Hudson Bay territory to England, which also acquired Gibraltar, Minorca, and control of the African slave trade from Spain (Map 16.2).

The Peace of Utrecht represented the balance-of-power principle in operation, setting limits on the extent to which any one power—in this case, France—could expand. It also marked the end of French expansion. Thirty-five years of war had given France the rights to all of Alsace and some commercial centers in the north. But at what price? In 1714 an exhausted France hovered on the brink of bankruptcy. It is no wonder that when Louis XIV died on September 1, 1715, many subjects felt as much relief as they did sorrow.

The Decline of Absolutist Spain in the Seventeenth Century

At the beginning of the seventeenth century, France's position appeared extremely weak. Struggling to recover from decades of religious civil war that had destroyed its infrastructure and economy, France could not dare to compete with Spain's European and overseas empire or its mighty military. Yet by the end of the century their positions were reversed, and France had surpassed all expectations to attain European dominance.

By the early seventeenth century the seeds of Spanish disaster were sprouting. Between 1610 and 1650

Map 16.2 Europe After the Peace of Utrecht, 1715 The series of treaties commonly called the Peace of Utrecht ended the War of the Spanish Succession and redrew the map of Europe. A French Bourbon king succeeded to the Spanish throne. France surrendered the Spanish Netherlands (later Belgium), then in French hands, to Austria, and recognized the Hohenzollern rulers of Prussia. Spain ceded Gibraltar to Great Britain, for which it has been a strategic naval station ever since. Spain also granted Britain the *asiento*, the contract for supplying African slaves to the Americas.

ANALYZING THE MAP Identify the areas on the map that changed hands as a result of the Peace of Utrecht. How did these changes affect the balance of power in Europe?

CONNECTIONS How and why did so many European countries possess scattered or discontiguous territories? What does this suggest about European politics in this period? Does this map suggest potential for future conflict?

To complete this activity online, go to the Online Study Guide at bedfordstmartins.com/mckaywest.

Spanish trade with the colonies in the New World fell 60 percent due to competition from local industries in the colonies and from Dutch and English traders. At the same time, the native Indian and African slaves who toiled in the South American silver mines suffered frightful epidemics of disease. Ultimately, the mines that filled the empire's treasury started to run dry, and the quantity of metal produced steadily declined after 1620.

In Madrid, however, royal expenditures constantly exceeded income. To meet mountainous state debt, the Crown repeatedly devalued the coinage and declared bankruptcy, which resulted in the collapse of national credit. Meanwhile, manufacturing and commerce shrank. In contrast to the other countries of western Europe, Spain had a tiny middle class. The elite condemned moneymaking as vulgar and undignified. Thousands entered economically unproductive professions: there were said to be nine thousand monasteries in the province of Castile alone. To make matters worse, the Crown expelled some three hundred thousand *Moriscos*, or former Muslims, in 1609, significantly reducing the pool of skilled workers and merchants. Those working in the

Spanish Troops The long wars that Spain fought over Dutch independence, in support of Habsburg interests in Germany, and against France left the country militarily exhausted and financially drained by the mid-1600s. In this detail from a painting by Peeter Snayers, Spanish troops — thin, emaciated, and probably unpaid — straggle away from battle. (Museo Nacional del Prado, Madrid. Photo: José Baztan y Alberto Otero)

textile industry were forced out of business by steep inflation that pushed their production costs to the point where they could not compete in colonial and international markets.[6]

Spanish aristocrats, attempting to maintain an extravagant lifestyle they could no longer afford, increased the rents on their estates. High rents and heavy taxes in turn drove the peasants from the land, leading to a decline in agricultural productivity. In cities wages and production stagnated. Spain also ignored new scientific methods that might have improved agricultural or manufacturing techniques because they came from the heretical nations of Holland and England.

The Spanish crown had no solutions to these dire problems. Philip III, a melancholy and deeply pious man, handed the running of the government over to the duke of Lerma, who used it to advance his personal and familial wealth. Philip IV left the management of his several kingdoms to Gaspar de Guzmán, Count-Duke of Olivares. Olivares was an able administrator who has often been compared to Richelieu. He did not lack energy and ideas, and he succeeded in devising new sources of revenue. But he clung to the grandiose belief that the solution to Spain's difficulties rested in a return to the imperial tradition of the sixteenth century. Unfortunately, the imperial tradition demanded the revival of war with the Dutch at the expiration of a twelve-year truce in 1622 and a long war with France over Mantua (1628–1659). Spain thus became embroiled in the Thirty Years' War. These conflicts, on top of an empty treasury, brought disaster.

Spain's situation worsened with internal conflicts and fresh military defeats through the remainder of the seventeenth century. In 1640 Spain faced serious revolts in Catalonia and Portugal. In 1643 the French inflicted a crushing defeat on a Spanish army at Rocroi in what is now Belgium. By the Treaty of the Pyrenees of 1659, which ended the French-Spanish conflict, Spain was compelled to surrender extensive territories to France. In 1688 the Spanish crown reluctantly recognized the independence of Portugal, almost a century after the two crowns were joined. The era of Spanish dominance in Europe had ended.

Absolutism in Austria and Prussia

How did the rulers of Austria and Prussia transform their nations into powerful absolutist monarchies? ■

The rulers of eastern Europe also labored to build strong absolutist states in the seventeenth century. But they built on social and economic foundations far different from those in western Europe, namely serfdom and the strong nobility who benefited from it. The endless wars of the seventeenth century allowed monarchs to increase their power by building large armies, increasing taxation, and suppressing representative institutions. In exchange for their growing political authority, monarchs allowed nobles to remain as unchallenged masters of their peasants, a deal that appeased both king and nobility, but left serfs at the mercy of the lords. The most successful states were Austria and Prussia, which witnessed the rise of absolutism between 1620 and 1740.

The Austrian Habsburgs

Like all of central Europe, the Habsburgs emerged from the Thirty Years' War impoverished and exhausted. Their efforts to destroy Protestantism in the German lands and to turn the weak Holy Roman Empire into a real state had failed. Although the Habsburgs remained the hereditary emperors, real power lay in the hands of a bewildering variety of separate political jurisdictions. Defeat in central Europe encouraged the Habsburgs to turn away from a quest for imperial dominance and to focus inward and eastward in an attempt to unify their diverse holdings. If they could not impose Catholicism in the empire, at least they could do so in their own domains.

Habsburg victory over Bohemia during the Thirty Years' War was an important step in this direction. Ferdinand II (r. 1619–1637) drastically reduced the power of the Bohemian Estates, the largely Protestant representative assembly. He also confiscated the landholdings of Protestant nobles and gave them to loyal Catholic nobles and to the foreign aristocratic mercenaries who led his armies. After 1650 a large portion of the Bohemian nobility was of recent origin and owed its success to the Habsburgs.

With the support of this new nobility, the Habsburgs established direct rule over Bohemia. Under their rule the condition of the enserfed peasantry worsened substantially: three days per week of unpaid labor became the norm. Protestantism was also stamped out. These changes were important steps in creating absolutist rule in Bohemia.

Ferdinand III (r. 1637–1657) continued to build state power. He centralized the government in the empire's German-speaking provinces, which formed the core Habsburg holdings. For the first time, a permanent standing army was ready to put down any internal opposition.

The Habsburg monarchy then turned east toward the plains of Hungary, which had been divided between the Ottomans and the Habsburgs in the early sixteenth century. Between 1683 and 1699 the Habsburgs pushed the Ottomans from most of Hungary and Transylvania. The recovery of all the former kingdom of Hungary was completed in 1718.

The Hungarian nobility, despite its reduced strength, effectively thwarted the full development of Habsburg absolutism. Throughout the seventeenth century Hungarian nobles rose in revolt against attempts to impose absolute rule. They never triumphed decisively, but neither were they crushed the way the nobility in Bohemia had been in 1620. In 1703, with the Habsburgs bogged down in the War of the Spanish Succession, the Hungarians rose in one last patriotic rebellion under Prince Francis Rákóczy.

Rákóczy and his forces were eventually defeated, but the Habsburgs agreed to restore many of the traditional privileges of the aristocracy in return for Hungarian acceptance of hereditary Habsburg rule. Thus Hungary, unlike Austria and Bohemia, was never fully integrated into a centralized, absolute Habsburg state.

Despite checks on their ambitions in Hungary, the Habsburgs made significant achievements in state-building elsewhere by forging consensus with the church and the nobility. A sense of common identity and loyalty to the monarchy grew among elites in Habsburg lands, even to a certain extent in Hungary. German became the language of the state, and zealous Catholicism helped fuse a collective identity. Vienna became the political and cultural center of the empire. By 1700 it was a thriving city with a population of one hundred thousand and its own version of Versailles, the royal palace of Schönbrunn.

Prussia in the Seventeenth Century

In the fifteenth and sixteenth centuries, the Hohenzollern family had ruled parts of eastern Germany as the imperial electors of Brandenburg and the dukes of Prussia. The title of "elector" gave its holder the privilege of being one of only seven princes or archbishops entitled to elect the Holy Roman emperor, but the electors had little real power. When he came to power in 1640, the twenty-year-old Frederick William, later known as the "Great Elector," was determined to unify his three provinces and enlarge them by diplomacy and war. These provinces were Brandenburg; Prussia, inherited in 1618; and scattered holdings along the Rhine inherited in 1614 (Map 16.3). Each was inhabited by German-speakers, but each had its own estates. Although the estates had not met regularly during the chaotic Thirty Years' War, taxes could not be levied without their consent. The estates of Brandenburg and Prussia were dominated by the nobility and the landowning classes, known as the **Junkers**.

Frederick William profited from ongoing European war and the threat of invasion from Russia when he argued for the need for a permanent standing army. In 1660 he persuaded Junkers in the estates to accept taxation without consent in order to fund an army. They agreed to do so in exchange for reconfirmation of their own privileges, including authority over the serfs. Having won over

Junkers The nobility of Brandenburg and Prussia, they were reluctant allies of Frederick William in his consolidation of the Prussian state.

Map 16.3 The Growth of Austria and Brandenburg-Prussia to 1748 Austria expanded to the southwest into Hungary and Transylvania at the expense of the Ottoman Empire. It was unable to hold the rich German province of Silesia, however, which was conquered by Brandenburg-Prussia.

the Junkers, the king crushed potential opposition to his power from the towns. One by one, Prussian cities were eliminated from the estates and subjected to new taxes on goods and services.

Thereafter, the estates' power declined rapidly, for the Great Elector had both financial independence and superior force. State revenue tripled during his reign, and the army expanded drastically. In 1688 a population of one million supported a peacetime standing army of thirty thousand. In 1701 the elector's son, Frederick I, received the elevated title of king of Prussia (instead of elector) as a reward for aiding the Holy Roman emperor in the War of the Spanish Succession.

The Consolidation of Prussian Absolutism

Frederick William I, "the Soldiers' King" (r. 1713–1740), completed his grandfather's work, eliminating the last traces of parliamentary estates and local self-government. It was he who truly established Prussian absolutism and transformed Prussia into a military state. Frederick

William was intensely attached to military life. He always wore an army uniform, and he lived the highly disciplined life of the professional soldier. Years later he summed up his life's philosophy in his instructions to his son: "A formidable army and a war chest large enough to make this army mobile in times of need can create great respect for you in the world, so that you can speak a word like the other powers."[7]

Penny-pinching and hard-working, Frederick William achieved results. The king and his ministers built an exceptionally honest and conscientious bureaucracy to administer the country and foster economic development. Twelfth in Europe in population, Prussia had the fourth largest army by 1740. The Prussian army was the best in Europe, astonishing foreign observers with its precision, skill, and discipline. As one Western traveler put it: "There is no theatre in Berlin whatsoever, diversion is understood to be the handsome troops who parade daily. A special attraction is the great Potsdam Grenadier Regiment . . . when they practice drill, when they fire and when they parade up and down, it is as if they form a single body."[8]

A Prussian Giant Grenadier Frederick William I wanted tall, handsome soldiers. He dressed them in tight bright uniforms to distinguish them from the peasant population from which most soldiers came. He also ordered several portraits of his favorites, such as this one, from his court painter, J. C. Merk. Grenadiers (greh-nuh-DEERZ) wore the miter cap instead of an ordinary hat so that they could hurl their heavy grenades unimpeded by a broad brim. (The Royal Collection © 2010, Her Majesty Queen Elizabeth II)

> **❝** A formidable army and a war chest large enough to make this army mobile in times of need can create great respect for you in the world, so that you can speak a word like the other powers. **❞**
>
> —KING FREDERICK WILLIAM I

The Development of Russia and the Ottoman Empire

What were the distinctive features of Russian and Ottoman absolutism? ▪

A favorite parlor game of nineteenth-century intellectuals was debating whether Russia was a Western (European) or non-Western (Asian) society. This question was particularly fascinating because it was unanswerable. To this day, Russia differs from the West in some fundamental ways, though its history has paralleled that of the West in other aspects.

There was no question in the mind of Europeans, however, that the Ottomans were outsiders. Even absolutist rulers disdained Ottoman sultans as cruel and tyrannical despots. Despite stereotypes, the Ottoman Empire was in many ways more tolerant than its Western counterparts, providing protection and security to other religions while steadfastly maintaining the Muslim faith. The Ottoman state combined the Byzantine heritage of the territory it had conquered with Persian and Arab traditions. Flexibility and openness to other ideas and practices were sources of strength for the empire.

The Mongol Yoke and the Rise of Moscow

The two-hundred-year period of rule by the Mongol khan (king) set the stage for the rise of absolutist Russia. The Mongols, a group of nomadic tribes from present-day Mongolia, established an empire that, at its height, stretched from Korea to eastern Europe. In the thirteenth century, the Mongols forced the Slavic princes

Nevertheless, Prussians paid a heavy and lasting price for the obsessions of their royal drillmaster. Army expansion was achieved in part through forced conscription, which was declared lifelong in 1713. Desperate draftees fled the country or injured themselves to avoid service. Finally, in 1733 Frederick William I ordered that all Prussian men would undergo military training and serve as reservists in the army, allowing him to preserve both agricultural production and army size. To appease the Junkers, the king enlisted them to lead his growing army. The proud nobility thus commanded the peasantry in the army as well as on the estates.

With all men harnessed to the war machine, Prussian civil society became rigid and highly disciplined. As a Prussian minister later summed up, "To keep quiet is the first civic duty."[9] Thus the policies of Frederick William I, combined with harsh peasant bondage and Junker tyranny, laid the foundations for a highly militaristic country.

Legend:
- Moscow, ca. 1300
- Gains by 1505
- Gains by 1584
- Gains by 1725
- Major battle

The Expansion of Russia to 1725

boyars The highest-ranking members of the Russian nobility.

Cossacks Free groups and outlaw armies originally comprising runaway peasants living on the borders of Russian territory from the fourteenth century onward. By the end of the sixteenth century they had formed an alliance with the Russian state.

to submit to their rule and to render payments of goods, money, and slaves. The princes of Moscow became particularly adept at serving the Mongols and were awarded the title of "great prince." Ivan III (r. 1462–1505), known as Ivan the Great, successfully expanded the principality of Moscow toward the Baltic Sea.

By 1480 Ivan III felt strong enough to stop acknowledging the khan as his supreme ruler and to cease paying tribute to the Mongols. To legitimize their new autonomy, the princes of Moscow modeled themselves on the Mongol khans. Like the khans, they declared themselves to be autocrats, meaning that they were the sole source of power. The Muscovite state also forced weaker Slavic principalities to render tribute previously paid to Mongols and borrowed Mongol institutions such as the tax system, postal routes, and census. Loyalty from the highest-ranking nobles, or **boyars**, helped the Muscovite princes consolidate their power.

Another source of legitimacy lay in Moscow's claim to the political and religious inheritance of the Byzantine Empire. After the fall of Constantinople to the Turks in 1453, the princes of Moscow saw themselves as the heirs of both the caesars (or emperors) and Orthodox Christianity. The title "tsar," first taken by Ivan IV in 1547, is in fact a contraction of *caesar*. The tsars considered themselves rightful and holy rulers, an idea promoted by Orthodox churchmen who spoke of "holy Russia" as the "Third Rome." The marriage of Ivan III to the daughter of the last Byzantine emperor further enhanced Moscow's claim to inherit imperial authority.

The Tsar and His People

Developments in Russia took a chaotic turn with the reign of Ivan IV (r. 1533–1584), the famous "Ivan the Terrible," who ascended to the throne at age three. His mother died, possibly poisoned, when he was eight,

leaving Ivan to suffer insults and neglect from the boyars at court. At age sixteen he suddenly pushed aside his hated advisers, and in an awe-inspiring ceremony, complete with gold coins pouring down on his head, Ivan majestically crowned himself tsar.

Ivan's reign was successful in defeating the remnants of Mongol power, adding vast new territories to the realm, and laying the foundations for the huge, multiethnic Russian empire. After the sudden death of his beloved wife Anastasia Romanov, however, Ivan began a campaign of persecution against those he suspected of opposing him. Many were intimates of the court from leading boyar families, whom he had killed along with their families, friends, servants, and peasants. To further crush the power of the boyars, Ivan created a new service nobility, whose loyalty was guaranteed by their dependence on the state for noble titles and estates. Ivan portioned out the large estates seized from boyars to this new nobility, taking some of the land for his own personal domain.

Ivan also moved toward making all commoners servants of the tsar. As landlords demanded more from the serfs who survived the wars and persecutions, growing numbers of peasants fled toward wild, recently conquered territories to the east and south. There they joined free groups and warrior bands known as **Cossacks**. The solution to the problem of peasant flight was to tie peasants ever more firmly to the land and to the noble landholders, who in turn served the tsar.

Simultaneously, Ivan bound urban traders and artisans to their towns and jobs so that he could tax them more heavily. The urban classes had no security in their work or property, and even the wealthiest merchants were dependent agents of the tsar. These restrictions checked the growth of the Russian middle classes and stood in sharp contrast to developments in western Europe, where the middle classes were gaining security in their private property. From nobles down to merchants and peasants, all of the Russian people were thus brought into the tsar's service. Ivan even made use of Cossack armies in forays to the southeast, forging a new alliance between Moscow and the Cossacks.

After the death of Ivan and his successor, Russia entered a chaotic period known as the "Time of Troubles" (1598–1613). While Ivan's relatives struggled for power, ordinary people suffered drought, crop failure, and plague, leading to much suffering and death. The Cossacks and peasants rebelled against nobles and officials, demanding fairer treatment. This social explosion from below brought the nobles, big and small, together. They crushed the Cossack rebellion and elected Ivan's sixteen-year-old grandnephew, Michael Romanov, the new hereditary tsar (r. 1613–1645). Michael's election was represented as a restoration of tsarist autocracy. (See "Listening to the Past: A German Account of Russian Life," page 500.)

Russian Peasant An eighteenth-century French artist visiting Russia recorded his impressions of the daily life of the Russian people in this etching of a fish merchant pulling his wares through a snowy village on a sleigh. Two caviar vendors behind him make a sale to a young mother standing at her doorstep with her baby in her arms. (From Jean-Baptiste Le Prince's second set of Russian etchings, 1765. Private Collection/www.amis-paris-petersbourg.org)

Although the new tsar successfully reconsolidated central authority, he and his successors did not improve the lot of the common people. In 1649 a law extended serfdom to all peasants in the realm, giving lords unrestricted rights over their serfs and establishing penalties for harboring runaways. Social and religious uprisings among the poor and oppressed continued through the seventeenth century. One of the largest rebellions was led by the Cossack Stenka Razin, who in 1670 attracted a great army of urban poor and peasants, killing landlords and government officials and proclaiming freedom from oppression. In 1671 this rebellion was defeated.

Despite the turbulence of the period, the Romanov tsars, like their Western counterparts, made several important achievements during the second half of the seventeenth century. After a long war, Russia gained land in Ukraine from Poland in 1667 and completed the conquest of Siberia by the end of the century. Territorial expansion was accompanied by growth of the bureaucracy and the army. Foreign experts were employed to help build and reform the Russian army, and Cossack warriors were enlisted to fight Siberian campaigns. The great profits from Siberia's natural re-

sources, especially furs, funded the Romanovs' bid for Great Power status. Thus, Russian imperialist expansion to the east paralleled the Western powers' exploration and conquest of the Atlantic world in the same period.

The Reforms of Peter the Great

Heir to Romanov efforts at state-building, Peter the Great (r. 1682–1725) embarked on a tremendous campaign to accelerate and complete these processes. A giant for his time at six feet seven inches, and possessing enormous energy and willpower, Peter was determined to build and improve the army and to continue the tsarist tradition of territorial expansion. After ruling as co-tsar with his half-brother and sister from 1682 to 1696, Peter reigned independently for thirty-six years. Only one of those years was peaceful.

Fascinated by weapons and foreign technology, the tsar led a group of 250 Russian officials and young nobles on an eighteen-month tour of western European capitals. Traveling unofficially to avoid lengthy diplomatic ceremonies, Peter worked with his hands at various crafts and met with foreign kings and experts. He

A German Account of Russian Life

LISTENING TO THE PAST

Seventeenth-century Russia remained a remote and mysterious land for western and even central Europeans, who had few direct contacts with the tsar's dominion. Westerners portrayed eastern Europe as more "barbaric" and less "civilized" than their homelands. Thus they expanded eastern Europe's undeniably harsher social and economic conditions to encompass a very debatable cultural and moral inferiority.

Knowledge of Russia came mainly from occasional travelers who had visited Muscovy and sometimes wrote accounts of what they saw. The most famous of these accounts was by the German Adam Olearius (ca. 1599–1671), who was sent to Moscow on three diplomatic missions in the 1630s. These missions ultimately proved unsuccessful, but they provided Olearius with a rich store of information for his Travels in Muscovy, *from which the following excerpts are taken. Published in German in 1647 and soon translated into several languages (but not Russian), Olearius's unflattering but well-informed study played a major role in shaping European ideas about Russia.*

❝ The government of the Russians is what political theorists call a "dominating and despotic monarchy," where the sovereign, that is, the tsar or the grand prince who has obtained the crown by right of succession, rules the entire land alone, and all the people are his subjects, and where the nobles and princes no less than the common folk — townspeople and peasants — are his serfs and slaves, whom he rules and treats as a master treats his servants. . . .

If the Russians be considered in respect to their character, customs, and way of life, they are justly to be counted among the barbarians. . . . The vice of drunkenness is so common in this nation, among people of every station, clergy and laity, high and low, men and women, old and young, that when they are seen now and then lying about in the streets, wallowing in the mud, no attention is paid to it, as something habitual. If a cart driver comes upon such a drunken pig whom he happens to know, he shoves him onto his cart and drives him home, where he is paid his fare. No one ever refuses an opportunity to drink and to get drunk, at any time and in any place, and usually it is done with vodka. . . .

The Russians being naturally tough and born, as it were, for slavery, they must be kept under a harsh and strict yoke and must be driven to do their work with clubs and whips, which they suffer without impatience, because such is their station, and they are accustomed to it. Young and

The brutality of serfdom is shown in this illustration from Olearius's *Travels in Muscovy*.
(University of Illinois Library, Champaign)

was particularly impressed with the growing power of the Dutch and the English, and he considered how Russia could profit from their example.

Returning to Russia, Peter entered into a secret alliance with Denmark and Poland to wage a sudden war of aggression against Sweden with the goal of securing access to the Baltic Sea and opportunities for westward expansion. Peter and his allies believed that their com-

bined forces could win easy victories because Sweden was in the hands of a new and inexperienced king.

Eighteen-year-old Charles XII of Sweden (1697–1718) surprised Peter. He defeated Denmark quickly in 1700, then turned on Russia. In a blinding snowstorm, his well-trained professional army attacked and routed unsuspecting Russians besieging the Swedish fortress of Narva on the Baltic coast. Peter and the survihalf-grown fellows sometimes come together on certain days and train themselves in fisticuffs, to accustom themselves to receiving blows, and, since habit is second nature, this makes blows given as punishment easier to bear. Each and all, they are slaves and serfs. . . .

Because of slavery and their rough and hard life, the Russians accept war readily and are well suited to it. On certain occasions, if need be, they reveal themselves as courageous and daring soldiers. . . .

Although the Russians, especially the common populace, living as slaves under a harsh yoke, can bear and endure a great deal out of love for their masters, yet if the pressure is beyond measure, then it can be said of them: "Patience, often wounded, finally turned into fury." A dangerous indignation results, turned not so much against their sovereign as against the lower authorities, especially if the people have been much oppressed by them and by their supporters and have not been protected by the higher authorities. And once they are aroused and enraged, it is not easy to appease them. Then, disregarding all dangers that may ensue, they resort to every kind of violence and behave like madmen. . . . They own little; most of them have no feather beds; they lie on cushions, straw, mats, or their clothes; they sleep on benches and, in winter, like the non-Germans [natives] in Livonia, upon the oven, which serves them for cooking and is flat on the top; here husband, wife, children, servants, and maids huddle together. In some houses in the countryside we saw chickens and pigs under the benches and the ovens. . . . Russians are not used to delicate food and dainties; their daily food consists of porridge, turnips, cabbage, and cucumbers, fresh and pickled, and in Moscow mostly of big salt fish which stink badly, because of the thrifty use of salt, yet are eaten with relish. . . .

The Russians can endure extreme heat. In the bathhouse they stretch out on benches and let themselves be beaten and rubbed with bunches of birch twigs and wisps of bast (which I could not stand); and when they are hot and red all over and so exhausted that they can bear it no longer in the bathhouse, men and women rush outdoors naked and pour cold water over their bodies; in winter they even wallow in the snow and rub their skin with it as if it were soap; then they go back into the hot bathhouse. And since bathhouses are usually near rivers and brooks, they can throw themselves straight from the hot into the cold bath. . . .

Generally noble families, even the small nobility, rear their daughters in secluded chambers, keeping them hidden from outsiders; and a bridegroom is not allowed to have a look at his bride until he receives her in the bridal chamber. Therefore some happen to be deceived, being given a misshapen and sickly one instead of a fair one, and sometimes a kinswoman or even a maidservant instead of a daughter; of which there have been examples even among the highborn. No wonder therefore that often they live together like cats and dogs and that wife-beating is so common among Russians. . . .

In the Kremlin and in the city there are a great many churches, chapels, and monasteries, both within and without the city walls, over two thousand in all. This is so because every nobleman who has some fortune has a chapel built for himself, and most of them are of stone. The stone churches are round and vaulted inside. . . . They allow neither organs nor any other musical instruments in their churches, saying: Instruments that have neither souls nor life cannot praise God. . . .

In their churches there hang many bells, sometimes five or six, the largest not over two hundredweights. They ring these bells to summon people to church, and also when the priest during mass raises the chalice. In Moscow, because of the multitude of churches and chapels, there are several thousand bells, which during the divine service create such a clang and din that one unaccustomed to it listens in amazement. �"

Source: "A Foreign Traveler in Russia" excerpt from pp. 249–251 in *A Source Book for Russian History from Early Times to 1917*, volume 1, *Early Times to the Late Seventeenth Century*, edited by George Vernadsky, Ralph T. Fisher, Jr., Alan D. Ferguson, Andrew Lossky, and Sergei Pushkarev, compiler. Copyright © 1972 by Yale University Press. Used with permission of the publisher.

QUESTIONS FOR ANALYSIS

1. How did Olearius characterize the Russians in general? What supporting evidence did he offer for his judgment?

2. How might Olearius's account help explain Stenka Razin's rebellion (page 499)?

3. On the basis of these representative passages, why do you think Olearius's book was so popular and influential in central and western Europe?

vors fled in panic to Moscow. It was, for the Russians, a grim beginning to the long and brutal Great Northern War, which lasted from 1700 to 1721.

Peter responded to this defeat with measures designed to increase state power, strengthen his armies, and gain victory. He required all nobles to serve in the army or in the civil administration—for life. Since a more modern army and government required skilled technicians and experts, Peter created schools and universities to produce them. One of his most hated reforms was requiring a five-year education away from home for every young nobleman. Peter established an interlocking military-civilian bureaucracy with fourteen ranks, and he decreed that all had to start at the bottom and work toward the top. The system allowed some people of non-noble origins to rise to high posi-

Saint Basil's Cathedral, Moscow With its sloping roofs and colorful onion-shaped domes, Saint Basil's is a striking example of powerful Byzantine influences on Russian culture. According to tradition, an enchanted Ivan the Terrible blinded the cathedral's architects to ensure that they would never duplicate their fantastic achievement, which still dazzles the beholder in today's Red Square. (George Holton/Photo Researchers)

tions, a rarity in Europe at the time. Drawing on his experience abroad, Peter sought talented foreigners and placed them in his service. These measures gradually combined to make the army and government more powerful and efficient.

Peter also greatly increased the service requirements of commoners. In the wake of the Narva disaster, he established a regular standing army of more than two hundred thousand peasant-soldiers commanded by officers from the nobility. In addition, one hundred thousand men were brought into the Russian army in special regiments of Cossacks and foreign mercenaries. The departure of a drafted peasant boy was celebrated by his family almost like a funeral, since the recruit was drafted for life. To fund the army, taxes on peasants increased threefold during Peter's reign. Serfs were also arbitrarily assigned to work in the growing number of factories and mines that supplied the military.

Peter's new war machine was able to crush the small army of Sweden in Ukraine at Poltava in 1709, one of the most significant battles in Russian history. Russia's victory against Sweden was conclusive in 1721, and Estonia and present-day Latvia came under Russian rule for the first time. The cost was high—warfare consumed 80 to 85 percent of all revenues. But Russia became the dominant power in the Baltic and very much a European Great Power.

After his victory at Poltava, Peter channeled enormous resources into building a new Western-style capital on the Baltic to rival the great cities of Europe. Originally a desolate and swampy Swedish outpost, the magnificent city of St. Petersburg was designed to reflect modern urban planning, with wide, straight avenues, buildings set in a uniform line, and large parks.

Peter the Great dictated that all in society realize his vision. Just as the government drafted the peasants for the armies, so it drafted twenty-five thousand to forty thousand men each summer to labor in St. Petersburg without pay. Many peasant construction workers died from hunger, sickness, and accidents. Nobles were ordered to build costly stone houses and palaces in St. Petersburg and to live in them most of the year. Merchants and artisans were also commanded to settle and build in the new capital. These nobles and merchants were then required to pay for the city's infrastructure. The building of St. Petersburg was, in truth, an enormous direct tax levied on the wealthy, with the peasantry forced to do the manual labor.

There were other important consequences of Peter's reign. For Peter, modernization meant westernization,

Peter the Great This compelling portrait by Grigory Musikiysky captures the strength and determination of the warrior-tsar in 1723, after more than three decades of personal rule. In his hand Peter holds the scepter, symbol of royal sovereignty, and across his breastplate is draped an ermine fur, a mark of honor. In the background are the battleships of Russia's new Baltic fleet and the famous St. Peter and St. Paul Fortress that Peter built in St. Petersburg. Peter the Great commissioned this magnificent new crown (left) for himself for his joint coronation in 1682 with his half-brother Ivan. (portrait: Kremlin Museums, Moscow/The Bridgeman Art Library; crown: Bildarchiv Preussischer Kulturbesitz/Art Resource, NY)

and both Westerners and Western ideas flowed into Russia for the first time. He required nobles to shave their heavy beards and wear Western clothing, previously banned in Russia. He required them to attend parties where young men and women would mix together and freely choose their own spouses. He forced a warrior elite to accept administrative service as an honorable occupation. From these efforts a new elite class of Western-oriented Russians began to emerge.

Peter's reforms were unpopular with many Russians. For nobles, one of Peter's most detested reforms was the imposition of unigeniture—inheritance of land by one son alone—cutting daughters and other sons from family property. For peasants, the reign of the tsar saw a significant increase in the bonds of serfdom, and the gulf between the enserfed peasantry and the educated nobility increased.

Peter's reforms were in some ways a continuation of Russia's distinctive history. He built on the service obligations of Ivan the Terrible and his successors, and his monarchical absolutism can be seen as the culmination of the long development of a unique Russian civilization.

Yet the creation of a more modern army and state introduced much that was new and Western to Russia. This development paved the way for Russia to move somewhat closer to the European mainstream in its thought and institutions during the Enlightenment, especially under Catherine the Great.

The Growth of the Ottoman Empire

Most Christian Europeans perceived the Ottomans as the antithesis of their own values and traditions and viewed the empire as driven by an insatiable lust for warfare and conquest. In their view the fall of Constantinople was a historic catastrophe and the taking of the Balkans a form of despotic imprisonment. To Ottoman eyes, the world looked very different. The siege of Constantinople liberated a glorious city from its long decline under the Byzantines. Rather than being a despoiled captive, the Balkans became a haven for refugees fleeing the growing intolerance of Western Christian powers. The Ottoman Empire provided Jews, Muslims,

Map 16.4 The Ottoman Empire at Its Height, 1566 The Ottomans, like their great rivals the Hapsburgs, rose to rule a vast dynastic empire encompassing many different peoples and ethnic groups. The army and the bureaucracy served to unite the disparate territories into a single state under an absolutist ruler.

and even some Christians safety from the Inquisition and religious war.

The Ottomans came out of Central Asia as conquering warriors, settled in Anatolia (present-day Turkey), and, at their peak in the mid-sixteenth century, ruled one of the most powerful empires in the world (see Chapter 15). Their possessions stretched from western Persia across North Africa and into the heart of central Europe (Map 16.4).

The Ottoman Empire was originally built on a unique model of state and society. There was an almost complete absence of private landed property. Agricultural land was the personal hereditary property of the **sultan**, and peasants paid taxes to use the land. There was therefore no security of landholding and no hereditary nobility.

The Ottomans also employed a distinctive form of government administration. The top ranks of the bureaucracy were staffed by the sultan's slave corps. Because Muslim law prohibited enslaving other Muslims, the sultan's agents purchased slaves along the borders of the empire. Within the realm, the sultan levied a "tax" of one thousand to three thousand male children on the conquered Christian populations in the Balkans every year. These young slaves were raised in Turkey as Muslims and were trained to fight and to administer. Unlike the dire fate reserved for enslaved Africans in European colonies, the most talented Ottoman slaves rose to the top of the bureaucracy, where they might acquire wealth and power. The less fortunate formed the core of the sultan's army, the **janissary corps**. These highly organized and efficient troops gave the Ottomans a formidable advantage in war with western Europeans. By 1683 service in the janissary corps had become so prestigious that the sultan ceased recruitment by force, and it became a volunteer army open to Christians and Muslims.

sultan The ruler of the Ottoman Empire; he owned all the agricultural land of the empire and was served by an army and bureaucracy composed of highly trained slaves.

janissary corps The core of the sultan's army, composed of slave conscripts from non-Muslim parts of the empire; after 1683 it became a volunteer force.

The Ottomans divided their subjects into religious communities, and each *millet* (MIH-luht), or "nation," enjoyed autonomous self-government under its religious leaders. The Ottoman Empire recognized Orthodox Christians, Jews, Armenian Christians, and Muslims as distinct millets, but despite its tolerance, the empire was an explicitly Islamic state. The **millet system** created a powerful bond between the Ottoman ruling class and religious leaders, who supported the sultan's rule in return for extensive authority over their own communities. Each millet collected taxes for the state, regulated group behavior, and maintained law courts, schools, houses of worship, and hospitals for its people.

Istanbul (known outside the empire by its original name, Constantinople) was the capital of the empire. The "old palace" was for the sultan's female family members, who lived in isolation under the care of eunuchs, men who were castrated to prevent sexual relations with women. The newer Topkapi palace was where officials worked and young slaves trained for future administrative or military careers. Sultans married women of the highest social standing, while keeping many concubines of low rank. To prevent the elite families into which they married from acquiring influence over the government, sultans procreated only with their concubines and not with official wives. They also adopted a policy of allowing each concubine to produce only one male heir. At a young age, each son went to govern a province of the empire accompanied by his mother. These practices were intended to stabilize power and prevent a recurrence of the civil wars of the late fourteenth and early fifteenth centuries.

Sultan Suleiman undid these policies when he boldly married his concubine, a former slave of Polish origin named Hürrem, and had several children with her. He established a wing in the Topkapi palace for Hürrem, his other female family members, and his brothers' families. Starting with Suleiman, imperial wives began to take on more power. Marriages were arranged between sultans' daughters and high-ranking servants, creating powerful new members of the imperial household. Over time, the sultan's exclusive authority waned in favor of a more bureaucratic administration.

> **millet system** A system used by the Ottomans whereby subjects were divided into religious communities with each millet (nation) enjoying autonomous self-government under its religious leaders.

Hürrem and Her Ladies in the Harem In Muslim culture *harem* means a sacred place or a sanctuary. The term was applied to the part of the household occupied by women and children and forbidden to men outside the family. The most famous member of the Ottoman sultan's harem was Hürrem (1505–1585), wife of Suleiman the Magnificent. Captured, according to tradition, in modern-day Ukraine in a Tartar raid and brought to the harem as a slave-concubine, she quickly won the sultan's trust and affection. Suleiman's love for Hürrem led him to break all precedents and marry his concubine, a decision that shocked some courtiers. (Bibliothèque nationale de France)

Alternatives to Absolutism in England and the Dutch Republic

How and why did the constitutional state triumph in the Dutch Republic and England?

While France, Prussia, Russia, and Austria developed the absolutist state, England and Holland evolved toward **constitutionalism**, which is the limitation of government by law. Constitutionalism also implies a balance between the authority and power of the government, on the one hand, and the rights and liberties of the subjects, on the other. By definition, all constitutionalist governments have a constitution, be it written or unwritten. A nation's constitution may be embodied in one basic document and occasionally revised by amendment, like the Constitution of the United States. Or it may be only partly formalized and include parliamentary statutes, judicial decisions, and a body of traditional procedures and practices, like the English and Dutch constitutions.

Despite their common commitment to constitutional government, England and the Dutch Republic represented significantly different alternatives to absolute rule. After decades of civil war and an experiment with **republicanism**, the English opted for a constitutional monarchy in 1688. This settlement, which has endured to this day, retained a monarch as the titular head of government but vested sovereignty in an elected parliament. Upon gaining independence from Spain in 1648, the Dutch rejected monarchical rule, adopting a republican form of government in which elected estates held supreme power. Neither was democratic by any standard, but to other Europeans they were shining examples of the restraint of arbitrary power and the rule of law.

constitutionalism A form of government in which power is limited by law and balanced between the authority and power of the government on the one hand, and the rights and liberties of the subjects or citizens on the other hand; could include constitutional monarchies or republics.

republicanism A form of government in which there is no monarch and power rests in the hands of the people as exercised through elected representatives.

Absolutist Claims in England

In 1588 Queen Elizabeth I of England exercised very great personal power; by 1689 the English monarchy was severely circumscribed. A rare female monarch, Elizabeth was able to maintain control over her realm in part by refusing to marry and submit to a husband. She was immensely popular with her people, but left no immediate heir to continue her legacy.

In 1603 Elizabeth's Scottish cousin James Stuart succeeded her as James I (r. 1603–1625). King James was well educated and had thirty-five years' experience as king of Scotland. But he was not as interested in displaying the majesty of monarchy as Elizabeth had been. Urged to wave at the crowds who waited to greet their new ruler, James complained that he was tired and threatened to drop his breeches "so they can cheer at my arse."[10]

James's greatest problem, however, stemmed from his absolutist belief that a monarch has a divine right to his authority and is responsible only to God. James went so far as to lecture the House of Commons: "There

Van Dyck, *Charles I at the Hunt*, ca. 1635 Anthony Van Dyck was the greatest of Rubens's many students. In 1633 he became court painter to Charles I. This portrait of Charles just dismounted from a horse emphasizes the aristocratic bearing, elegance, and innate authority of the king. Van Dyck's success led to innumerable commissions by members of the court and aristocratic society. He had a profound influence on portraiture in England and beyond; some scholars believe that this portrait influenced Rigaud's 1701 portrayal of Louis XIV (see page 488). (Scala/Art Resource, NY)

are no privileges and immunities which can stand against a divinely appointed King." Such a view ran directly counter to the long-standing English idea that a person's property could not be taken away without due process of law. James I and his son Charles I considered such constraints intolerable and a threat to their divine-right prerogative. Consequently, at every Parliament between 1603 and 1640, bitter squabbles erupted between the Crown and the articulate and legally minded Commons. Charles I's attempt to govern without Parliament (1629–1640) and to finance his government by emergency taxes brought the country to a crisis.

Religious Divides and the English Civil War

Religious issues also embittered relations between the king and the House of Commons. In the early seventeenth century increasing numbers of English people felt dissatisfied with the Church of England established by Henry VIII and reformed by Elizabeth. Many **Puritans** believed that the Reformation had not gone far enough. They wanted to "purify" the Anglican Church of Roman Catholic elements—elaborate vestments and ceremonials, bishops, and even the giving and wearing of wedding rings.

James I responded to such ideas by declaring, "No bishop, no king." For James, bishops were among the chief supporters of the throne. His son and successor, Charles I, further antagonized religious sentiments. Not only did he marry a Catholic princess, but he also supported the heavy-handed policies of the Archbishop of Canterbury William Laud (1573–1645). In 1637

> **Puritans** Members of a sixteenth- and seventeenth-century reform movement within the Church of England that advocated purifying it of Roman Catholic elements, such as bishops, elaborate ceremonials, and wedding rings.

Puritan Occupations These twelve engravings depict typical Puritan occupations and show that the Puritans came primarily from the artisan and lower middle classes. The governing classes and peasants made up a much smaller percentage of the Puritans and generally adhered to the traditions of the Church of England. (Visual Connection Archive)

Laud attempted to impose two new elements on church organization in Scotland: a new prayer book, modeled on the Anglican *Book of Common Prayer*, and bishoprics. The Presbyterian Scots rejected these elements and revolted. To finance an army to put down the Scots, King Charles was compelled to summon Parliament in November 1640.

Charles had ruled from 1629 to 1640 without Parliament, financing his government through extraordinary stopgap levies considered illegal by most English people. For example, the king revived a medieval law requiring coastal districts to help pay the cost of ships for defense, but he levied the tax, called "ship money," on inland as well as coastal counties. Most members of Parliament believed that such taxation without consent amounted to despotism. Consequently, they were not willing to trust the king with an army. Moreover, many supported the Scots' resistance to Charles's religious innovations. Accordingly, this Parliament, called the "Long Parliament" because it sat from 1640 to 1660, enacted legislation that limited the power of the monarch and made government without Parliament impossible.

In 1641 the Commons passed the Triennial Act, which compelled the king to summon Parliament every three years. The Commons impeached Archbishop Laud and then threatened to abolish bishops. King Charles, fearful of a Scottish invasion—the original reason for summoning Parliament—reluctantly accepted these measures.

The next act in the conflict was precipitated by the outbreak of rebellion in Ireland, where English governors and landlords had long exploited the people. In 1641 the Catholic gentry of Ireland led an uprising in response to a feared invasion by anti-Catholic forces of the British Long Parliament.

Without an army, Charles I could neither come to terms with the Scots nor respond to the Irish rebellion. After a failed attempt to arrest parliamentary leaders, Charles left London for the north of England. There, he recruited an army drawn from the nobility and its cavalry staff, the rural gentry, and mercenaries. In response, Parliament formed its own army, the New Model Army, composed of the militia of the city of London and country squires with business connections. During the spring of 1642 both sides prepared for war. In July a linen weaver became the first casualty of the

Protectorate The English military dictatorship (1653–1658) established by Oliver Cromwell following the execution of Charles I.

The English Civil War, 1642–1649

□ Parliamentarians
□ Royalists
✳ Major battle

civil war during a skirmish between royal and parliamentary forces in Manchester.

The English civil war (1642–1649) pitted the power of the king against that of the Parliament. After three years of fighting, Parliament's New Model Army defeated the king's armies at the Battles of Naseby and Langport in the summer of 1645. Charles, though, refused to concede defeat. Both sides jockeyed for position, waiting for a decisive event. This arrived in the form of the army under the leadership of Oliver Cromwell, a member of the House of Commons and a devout Puritan. In 1647 Cromwell's forces captured the king and dismissed members of the Parliament who opposed his actions. In 1649 the remaining representatives, known as the "Rump Parliament," put Charles on trial for high treason. Charles was found guilty and beheaded on January 30, 1649, an act that sent shock waves around Europe.

Cromwell and Puritanical Absolutism in England

With the execution of Charles, kingship was abolished. The question remained of how the country would be governed. One answer was provided by philosopher Thomas Hobbes (1588–1679). Hobbes held a pessimistic view of human nature and believed that, left to themselves, humans would compete violently for power and wealth. The only solution, as he outlined in his 1651 treatise *Leviathan*, was a social contract in which all members of society placed themselves under the absolute rule of a monarch, who would maintain peace and order. Hobbes imagined society as a human body in which the monarch served as head and individual subjects together made up the body. Just as the body cannot sever its own head, so Hobbes believed that society could not, having accepted the contract, rise up against its king. Deeply shocked by Charles's execution, he utterly denied the right of subjects to rebellion.

Hobbes's longing for a benevolent absolute monarch was not widely shared in England. Instead, a commonwealth, or republican government, was proclaimed. Theoretically, legislative power rested in the surviving members of Parliament, and executive power was lodged in a council of state. In fact, the army that had defeated the king controlled the government, and Oliver Cromwell controlled the army. Though called the **Protectorate**, the rule of Cromwell (1653–1658) constituted military dictatorship.

"The Royall Oake of Brittayne" The chopping down of this tree, as shown in this cartoon from 1649, signifies the end of royal authority, stability, and the rule of law. As pigs graze (representing the unconcerned common people), being fattened for slaughter, Oliver Cromwell, with his feet in Hell, quotes Scripture. This is a royalist view of the collapse of Charles I's government and the rule of Cromwell. (Courtesy of the Trustees of the British Museum)

The army prepared a constitution, the Instrument of Government (1653), that invested executive power in a lord protector (Cromwell) and a council of state. It provided for triennial parliaments and gave Parliament the sole power to raise taxes. But after repeated disputes, Cromwell dismissed Parliament in 1655, and the instrument was never formally endorsed. Cromwell continued the standing army and proclaimed quasi-martial law. He divided England into twelve military districts, each governed by a major general. Reflecting Puritan ideas of morality, Cromwell's state forbade sports, kept the theaters closed, and rigorously censored the press.

On the issue of religion, Cromwell favored some degree of toleration, and the Instrument of Government gave all Christians except Roman Catholics the right to practice their faith. Cromwell had long associated Catholicism in Ireland with sedition and heresy, and led an army there to reconquer the country in August 1649. One month later, his forces crushed a rebellion at Drogheda and massacred the garrison. After Cromwell's departure for England, atrocities worsened. The English banned Catholicism in Ireland, executed priests, and confiscated land from Catholics for English and Scottish settlers. These brutal acts left a legacy of Irish hatred for England.

Cromwell adopted mercantilist policies similar to those of absolutist France. He enforced a Navigation Act (1651) requiring that English goods be transported on English ships. The act was a great boost to the development of an English merchant marine and brought about a short but successful war with the commercially threatened Dutch. Cromwell also welcomed the immigration of Jews because of their skills, and they began to return to England after four centuries of absence.

The Protectorate collapsed when Cromwell died in 1658 and his ineffectual son succeeded him. Fed up with military rule, the English longed for a return to civilian government and, with it, common law and social stability. By 1660 they were ready to restore the monarchy.

The Restoration of the English Monarchy

The Restoration of 1660 brought to the throne Charles II (r. 1660–1685), eldest son of Charles I, who had been living on the continent. Both houses of Parliament were also restored, together with the established Anglican Church. The Restoration failed to resolve two serious problems, however. What was to be the attitude of the state toward Puritans, Catholics, and dissenters from the established church? And what was to be the relationship between the king and Parliament?

Test Act Legislation, passed by the English parliament in 1673, to secure the position of the Anglican Church by stripping Puritans, Catholics, and other dissenters of the right to vote, preach, assemble, hold public office, and attend or teach at the universities.

To answer the first question, Parliament enacted the **Test Act** of 1673 against those outside the Church of England, denying them the right to vote, hold public office, preach, teach, attend the universities, or even assemble for meetings. But these restrictions could not be enforced. When the Quaker William Penn held a meeting of his Friends and was arrested, the jury refused to convict him.

In politics Charles II was determined to avoid exile by working well with Parliament. This intention did not last, however. Finding that Parliament did not grant him an adequate income, in 1670 Charles entered into a secret agreement with his cousin Louis XIV. The French king would give Charles two hundred thousand pounds annually, and in return Charles would relax the laws against Catholics, gradually re-Catholicize England, and convert to Catholicism himself. When the details of this treaty leaked out, a great wave of anti-Catholic sentiment swept England.

When James II (r. 1685–1688) succeeded his brother, the worst English anti-Catholic fears were realized. In violation of the Test Act, James appointed Roman Catholics to positions in the army, the universities, and local government. When these actions were challenged in the courts, the judges, whom James had appointed, decided in favor of the king. The king was suspending the law at will and appeared to be reviving the absolutism of his father and grandfather. He went further. Attempting to broaden his base of support with Protestant dissenters and nonconformists, James granted religious freedom to all.

Seeking to prevent the return of Catholic absolutism, a group of eminent persons in Parliament and the Church of England offered the English throne to James's Protestant daughter Mary and her Dutch husband, Prince William of Orange. In December 1688 James II, his queen, and their infant son fled to France and became pensioners of Louis XIV. Early in 1689 William and Mary were crowned king and queen of England.

Constitutional Monarchy and Cabinet Government

The English call the events of 1688 and 1689 the "Glorious Revolution" because it replaced one king with another with a minimum of bloodshed. It also represented the destruction, once and for all, of the idea of divine-right monarchy. William and Mary accepted the English throne from Parliament and in so doing explicitly recognized the supremacy of Parliament. The revolution of 1688 established the principle that sovereignty, the ultimate power in the state, was divided between king and Parliament and that the king ruled with the consent of the governed.

The men who brought about the revolution framed their intentions in the Bill of Rights (1689), which was formulated in direct response to Stuart absolutism. Law was to be made in Parliament; once made, it could not be suspended by the Crown. Parliament had to be called at least once every three years. The independence of the judiciary was established, and there was to be no standing army in peacetime. Protestants could possess arms, but the Catholic minority could not. No Catholic could ever inherit the throne. Additional legislation granted freedom of worship to Protestant dissenters, but not to Catholics.

The Glorious Revolution and the concept of representative government found its best defense in political philosopher John Locke's *Second Treatise of Civil Government* (1690). Locke (1632–1704) maintained that a government that oversteps its proper function — protecting the natural rights of life, liberty, and property — becomes a tyranny. By "natural" rights Locke meant rights basic to all men because all have the ability to reason. (His idea that there are natural or universal rights equally valid for all peoples and societies was especially popular in colonial America.) Under a tyrannical government, the people have the natural right to rebellion. On the basis of this link, he justified limiting the vote to property owners. (American colonists also appreciated his arguments that Native Americans had no property rights since they did not cultivate the land and, by extension, no political rights because they possessed no property.)

The events of 1688 and 1689 did not constitute a democratic revolution. The revolution placed sovereignty in Parliament, and Parliament represented the upper classes. The age of aristocratic government lasted at least until 1832 and in many ways until 1928, when women received full voting rights.

In the course of the eighteenth century, the cabinet

system of government evolved. The term *cabinet* derives from the small private room in which English rulers consulted their chief ministers. In a cabinet system, the leading ministers, who must have seats in and the support of a majority of the House of Commons, formulate common policy and conduct the business of the country. During the administration of one royal minister, Sir Robert Walpole, who led the cabinet from 1721 to 1742, the idea developed that the cabinet was responsible to the House of Commons. The Hanoverian king George I (r. 1714–1727) normally presided at cabinet meetings throughout his reign, but his son and heir, George II (r. 1727–1760), discontinued the practice. The influence of the Crown in decision making accordingly declined. Walpole enjoyed the favor of the monarchy and of the House of Commons and came to be called the king's first, or "prime," minister. In the English cabinet system, both legislative power and executive power are held by the leading ministers, who form the government.

England's brief and chaotic experiment with republicanism under Oliver Cromwell convinced its people of the advantages of a monarchy, albeit with strong checks on royal authority. The eighteenth-century philosopher David Hume went so far as to declare that he would prefer England to be peaceful under an absolute monarch than in constant civil war as a republic. These sentiments would have found little sympathy among the proud burghers of the Dutch Republic.

The Dutch Republic in the Seventeenth Century

In the late sixteenth century the seven northern provinces of the Netherlands fought for and won their independence from Spain. The independence of the Republic of the United Provinces of the Netherlands was recognized in 1648 in the treaty that ended the Thirty Years' War. In this period, often called the "golden age of the Netherlands," Dutch ideas and attitudes played a profound role in shaping a new and modern worldview. At the same time, the United Provinces developed its own distinctive model of a constitutional state.

Jan Steen, *The Merry Family*, 1668 In this painting from the Dutch golden age, a happy family enjoys a boisterous song while seated around the dining table. Despite its carefree appearance, the painting was intended to teach a moral lesson. The children are shown drinking wine and smoking, bad habits they have learned from their parents. The inscription hanging over the mantelpiece (upper right) spells out the message clearly: "As the Old Sing, so Pipe the Young." (Gianni Dagli Orti/The Art Archive)

Glückel of Hameln

INDIVIDUALS IN SOCIETY

IN 1690 A JEWISH WIDOW IN THE SMALL GERMAN TOWN OF HAMELN in Lower Saxony sat down to write her autobiography. She wanted to distract her mind from the terrible grief she felt over the death of her husband and to provide her twelve children with a record "so you will know from what sort of people you have sprung, lest today or to-morrow your beloved children or grandchildren came and know naught of their family." Out of her pain and heightened consciousness, Glückel (1646–1724) produced an invaluable source for scholars.

She was born in Hamburg two years before the end of the Thirty Years' War. In 1649 the merchants of Hamburg expelled the Jews, who moved to nearby Altona, then under Danish rule. When the Swedes overran Altona in 1657–1658, the Jews returned to Hamburg "purely at the mercy of the Town Council." Glückel's narrative proceeds against a background of the constant harassment to which Jews were subjected — special papers, permits, bribes — and in Hameln she wrote, "And so it has been to this day and, I fear, will continue in like fashion."

When Glückel was "barely twelve," her father betrothed her to Chayim Hameln. She married at age fourteen. She describes him as "the perfect pattern of the pious Jew," a man who stopped his work every day for study and prayer, fasted, and was scrupulously honest in his business dealings. Only a few years older than Glückel, Chayim earned his living dealing in precious metals and in making small loans on pledges (pawned goods). This work re-quired his constant travel to larger cities, markets, and fairs, often in bad weather, always over danger-ous roads. Chayim consulted his wife about all his business dealings. As he lay dying, a friend asked if he had any last wishes. "None," he replied. "My wife knows everything. She shall do as she has always done." For thirty years Glückel had been his friend, full business partner, and wife. They had thirteen children, twelve of whom survived their father, eight then unmarried. As Chayim had foretold, Glückel succeeded in launching the boys in careers and in providing dowries for the girls.

Although no images of Glückel exist, Rembrandt's *The Jewish Bride* suggests the mutual devotion that Glückel and her husband felt for each other. (Rijksmuseum-Stichting Amsterdam)

Glückel's world was her family, the Jewish community of Hameln, and the Jewish communities into which her children married. Her social and business activities took her across Europe, from Amsterdam to Berlin, from Danzig to Vienna, so her world was not narrow or provincial. She took great pride that Prince Frederick of Cleves, later king of Prussia, danced at the wedding of her eldest daughter. The rising prosperity of Chayim's businesses allowed the couple to maintain up to six servants.

Glückel was deeply religious, and her culture was steeped in Jewish literature, legends, and mystical and secular works. Above all, she relied on the Bible. Her language, heavily sprinkled with scriptural references, testifies to a rare familiarity with the Scriptures.

Students who would learn about seventeenth-century business practices, the importance of the dowry in marriage, childbirth, Jewish life, birthrates, family celebrations, and even the meaning of life can gain a good deal from the memoirs of this extraordinary woman who was, in the words of one of her descendants, the poet Heinrich Heine, "the gift of a world to me."

Source: *The Memoirs of Glückel of Hameln* (New York: Schocken Books, 1977).

QUESTIONS FOR ANALYSIS

1. Consider the ways in which Glückel of Hameln was both an ordinary and an extraordinary woman of her times. Would you call her a marginal or a central person in her society?

2. How might Glückel's successes be attributed to the stabilizing force of absolutism in the seventeenth century?

Rejecting the rule of a monarch, the Dutch established a republic, a state in which power rested in the hands of the people and was exercised through elected representatives. Other examples of republics in early modern Europe included the Swiss Confederation and several autonomous city-states of Italy and the Holy Roman Empire. Among the Dutch, an oligarchy of wealthy businessmen called "regents" handled domestic affairs in each province's Estates (assemblies). The provincial Estates held virtually all the power. A federal assembly, or States General, handled foreign affairs and war, but it did not possess sovereign authority. All issues had to be referred back to the local Estates for approval, and each of the seven provinces could veto any proposed legislation. Holland, the province with the largest navy and the most wealth, usually dominated the republic and the States General.

In each province, the Estates appointed an executive officer, known as the **stadholder**, who carried out ceremonial functions and was responsible for military defense. Although in theory freely chosen by the Estates and answerable to them, in practice the reigning prince of Orange usually held the office of stadholder in several of the seven provinces of the Republic. This meant that tensions always lingered between supporters of the House of Orange and those of the staunchly republican Estates, who suspected the princes of harboring monarchical ambitions. When one of them, William III, took the English throne in 1688 with his wife, Mary, the republic simply continued without stadholders for several decades.

> **stadholder** The executive officer in each of the United Provinces of the Netherlands, a position often held by the princes of Orange.

The political success of the Dutch rested on their phenomenal commercial prosperity. The moral and ethical bases of that commercial wealth were thrift, frugality, and religious toleration. Although there is scattered evidence of anti-Semitism, Jews enjoyed a level of acceptance and assimilation in Dutch business and general culture unique in early modern Europe. (See "Individuals in Society: Glückel of Hameln," at left.) In the Dutch Republic, toleration paid off: it attracted a great deal of foreign capital and investment.

The Dutch came to dominate the shipping business by putting profits from their original industry—herring fishing—into shipbuilding. They boasted the lowest shipping rates and largest merchant marine in Europe, allowing them to undersell foreign competitors (see Chapter 15). Trade and commerce brought the Dutch the highest standard of living in Europe, perhaps in the world. Salaries were high, and all classes of society ate well. A scholar has described the Netherlands as "an island of plenty in a sea of want." Consequently, the Netherlands experienced very few of the food riots that characterized the rest of Europe.[11]

Baroque Art and Music

What was the baroque style in art and music, and where was it popular? ■

Throughout European history, the cultural tastes of one age have often seemed unsatisfactory to the next. So it was with the baroque. The term *baroque* may have come from the Portuguese word for an "odd-shaped, imperfect pearl" and was commonly used by late-eighteenth-century art critics as an expression of scorn for what they considered an overblown, unbalanced style. Specialists now agree that the baroque style marked one of the high points in the history of Western culture.

Rome and the revitalized Catholic Church of the later sixteenth century played an important role in the early development of the baroque. The papacy and the Jesuits encouraged the growth of an intensely emotional, exuberant art. These patrons wanted artists to go beyond the Renaissance focus on pleasing a small, wealthy cultural elite. They wanted artists to appeal to the senses and thereby touch the souls and kindle the faith of ordinary churchgoers while proclaiming the power and confidence of the reformed Catholic Church. In addition to this underlying religious emotionalism, the baroque drew its sense of drama, motion, and ceaseless striving from the Catholic Reformation. The interior of the famous Jesuit Church of Jesus in Rome—the Gesù—combined all these characteristics in its lavish, wildly active decorations and frescoes.

Taking definite shape in Italy after 1600, the baroque style in the visual arts developed with exceptional vigor in Catholic countries—in Spain and Latin America, Austria, southern Germany, and Poland. Yet baroque art was more than just "Catholic art" in the

Rubens, *Garden of Love*, 1633–1634 This painting is an outstanding example of the lavishness and richness of baroque art. Born and raised in northern Europe, Peter Paul Rubens trained as a painter in Italy. Upon his return to the Spanish Netherlands, he became a renowned and amazingly prolific artist, patronized by rulers across Europe. Rubens was a devout Catholic, and his work conveys the emotional fervor of the Catholic Reformation. (Scala/Art Resource, NY)

seventeenth century and the first half of the eighteenth. True, neither Protestant England nor the Netherlands ever came fully under the spell of the baroque, but neither did Catholic France. And Protestants accounted for some of the finest examples of baroque style, especially in music. The baroque style spread partly because its tension and bombast spoke to an agitated age that was experiencing great violence and controversy in politics and religion.

In painting, the baroque reached maturity early with Peter Paul Rubens (1577–1640), the most outstanding and most representative of baroque painters. Studying in his native Flanders and in Italy, where he was influenced by masters of the High Renaissance such as Michelangelo, Rubens developed his own rich, sensuous, colorful style, which was characterized by animated figures, melodramatic contrasts, and monumental size. Rubens excelled in glorifying monarchs such as Queen

Mother Marie de' Medici of France. He was also a devout Catholic; nearly half of his pictures treat Christian subjects. Yet one of Rubens's trademarks was fleshy, sensual nudes who populate his canvases as Roman goddesses, water nymphs, and remarkably voluptuous saints and angels.

In music, the baroque style reached its culmination almost a century later in the dynamic, soaring lines of the endlessly inventive Johann Sebastian Bach (1685–1750). Organist and choirmaster of several Lutheran churches across Germany, Bach was equally at home writing secular concertos and sublime religious cantatas. Bach's organ music combined the baroque spirit of invention, tension, and emotion in an unforgettable striving toward the infinite. Unlike Rubens, Bach was not fully appreciated in his lifetime, but since the early nineteenth century his reputation has grown steadily.

 LOOKING BACK LOOKING AHEAD THE SEVENTEENTH CENTURY represented a difficult passage between two centuries of dynamism and growth. On one side lay the sixteenth century of religious enthusiasm and strife, overseas expansion, rising population, and vigorous commerce. On the other side stretched the eighteenth-century era of renewed population growth, economic development, and cultural flourishing. The first half of the seventeenth century was marked by the spread of religious and dynastic warfare across Europe, resulting in the death and dislocation of many millions. This catastrophe was compounded by recurrent episodes of crop failure, famine, and epidemic disease, all of which contributed to a stagnant economy and population loss. In the middle decades of the seventeenth century, the very survival of the European monarchies established in the Renaissance appeared in doubt.

With the re-establishment of order in the second half of the century, maintaining political and social stability appeared of paramount importance to European rulers and elites. In western and eastern Europe, a host of monarchs proclaimed their God-given and "absolute" authority to rule in the name of peace, unity, and good order. Rulers' ability to impose such claims in reality depended a great deal on compromise with local elites, who acquiesced to state power in exchange for privileges and payoffs. In this way, absolutism and constitutionalism did not always differ as much as they claimed. Both systems relied on political compromises forged from decades of strife.

The eighteenth century was to see this status quo thrown into question by new Enlightenment aspirations for human society, which themselves derived from the inquisitive and self-confident spirit of the scientific revolution. By the end of the century, demands for real popular sovereignty challenged the very bases of political order so painfully achieved in the seventeenth century.

CHAPTER REVIEW

■ What were the common crises and achievements of seventeenth-century European states? (p. 480)

Most parts of Europe experienced the seventeenth century as a period of severe economic, social, and military crisis. Across the continent, rulers faced popular rebellions from their desperate subjects, who were pushed to the brink by poor harvests, high taxes, and decades of war. Many forces, including powerful noblemen, the church, and regional and local loyalties, constrained the state's authority. Despite these obstacles, most European states emerged from the seventeenth century with increased powers and more centralized control. Whether they ruled through monarchical fiat or parliamentary negotiation, European governments strengthened their bureaucracies, raised more taxes, and significantly expanded their armies.

■ What factors led to the rise of the French absolutist state under Louis XIV, and why did absolutist Spain experience decline in the same period? (p. 486)

Under Louis XIV France witnessed the high point of monarchical ambitions in western Europe. Louis used the doctrine of the divine right of kings to justify his hold on power. Under his rule, France developed a centralized bureaucracy, a professional army, and a state-directed economy, all of which he personally supervised. Despite his claims to absolute power, Louis XIV ruled by securing the collaboration of high nobles. In exchange for confirmation of their ancient privileges, the nobles were willing to cooperate with the expansion of state power. In Spain, where monarchs made similar claims to absolute power, the seventeenth century witnessed economic catastrophe and a decline in royal capacities. This decline was due to a fall in colonial trade revenue, massive state debt, and a decline in manufacturing and agricultural productivity.

■ How did the rulers of Austria and Prussia transform their nations into powerful absolutist monarchies? (p. 494)

Within a framework of resurgent serfdom and entrenched nobility, Austrian and Prussian monarchs fashioned strong absolutist states in the seventeenth and early eighteenth centuries. These monarchs won absolutist control over standing armies, taxation, and representative bodies, but left intact the underlying social and economic relationships between the nobles and their peasants. In exchange for entrenched privileges over their peasants, nobles thus cooperated with the growth of state power.

■ What were the distinctive features of Russian and Ottoman absolutism? (p. 497)

In Russia, Mongol conquest and rule set the stage for absolutism, and a harsh tsarist autocracy was firmly in place by the reign of Ivan the Terrible in the sixteenth century. Ivan's brutal rule brought all segments of Russian society into state service, sparking resentment and revolt. The reign of Ivan and his successors saw a great expansion of Russian territory, laying the foundations for a huge, multiethnic empire. More than a century later Peter the Great succeeded in modernizing Russia's traditional absolutism by reforming the army and the bureaucracy. Farther to the east, the Ottoman sultans developed a distinctive political and economic system in which all land theoretically belonged to the sultan, who was served by a slave corps of administrators and soldiers. The Ottoman Empire was relatively tolerant on religious matters and served as a haven for Jews and other marginalized religious groups.

■ How and why did the constitutional state triumph in the Dutch Republic and England? (p. 506)

Holland and England defied the general trend toward absolute monarchy. Violently resisting Stuart kings' claims to absolute power, England descended into civil war and finally emerged with a constitutional monarchy. After the Glorious Revolution in 1688, English power was divided between king and Parliament, with Parliament enjoying the greater share. The Bill of Rights established parliamentary control of the legal system and dictated that Parliament had to be called at least once every three years. By contrast, the Dutch rejected monarchical rule after winning independence from Spain. Instead, the United Provinces of the Netherlands adopted a decentralized republican system in which local affairs were run by provincial Estates and the national States General handled foreign affairs and war.

■ What was the baroque style in art and music, and where was it popular? (p. 514)

The baroque style, practiced by artists such as Rubens and Bach, was intensely emotional and exuberant. It was inspired by the religious enthusiasm of the late-sixteenth-century Catholic Reformation, but appeared in both religious and secular themes. The baroque style in art and music thrived during the seventeenth century and was most popular in Catholic countries—Spain and Latin America, Austria, southern Germany, and Poland—though it never gained popularity in Catholic France and was practiced by Protestant artists.

Suggested Reading

Benedict, Philip, and Myron P. Gutmann, eds. *Early Modern Europe: From Crisis to Stability.* 2005. A helpful introduction to the many facets of the seventeenth-century crisis.

Burke, Peter. *The Fabrication of Louis XIV.* 1992. Explains the use of architecture, art, medals, and other symbols to promote the king's image.

Clark, Christopher. *Iron Kingdom: The Rise and Downfall of Prussia, 1600–1947.* 2006. A fascinating long-term account tracing Prussia's emergence as an international power and the impact of Prussian history on later political developments in Germany.

Collins, James B. *The State in Early Modern France.* 1995. A detailed and well-argued survey of French administration from Louis XIII to Louis XVI.

Elliott, John H. *Imperial Spain, 1469–1716,* 2d ed. 2002. An authoritative account of Spain's rise to imperial greatness and its slow decline.

Gaunt, Peter, ed. *The English Civil War: The Essential Readings.* 2000. A collection showcasing leading historians' interpretations of the civil war.

Hagen, William W. *Ordinary Prussians: Brandenburg Junkers and Villagers, 1500–1840.* 2002. Provides a fascinating encounter with the people of a Prussian estate.

Hughes, Lindsey, ed. *Peter the Great and the West: New Perspectives.* 2001. Essays by leading scholars on the reign of Peter the Great and his opening of Russia to the West.

Ingrao, Charles W. *The Habsburg Monarchy, 1618–1815.* 2d ed. 2000. An excellent synthesis of the political and social development of the Habsburg empire in the early modern period.

Parker, Geoffrey. *The Thirty Years War,* 2d ed. 1997. The standard account of the Thirty Years' War.

Roman, Rolf, ed. *Baroque: Architecture, Sculpture, Painting.* 2007. A beautifully illustrated presentation of multiple facets of the baroque across Europe.

Schama, Simon. *The Embarrassment of Riches: An Interpretation of Dutch Culture in the Golden Age.* 1987. A lengthy but vivid and highly readable account of Dutch culture in the seventeenth century, including a chapter on the mania for speculation on the tulip market.

Notes

1. Quoted in Cecile Hugon, *Social France in the XVIIe Century* (London: McMilland, 1911), p. 189.
2. H. Kamen, "The Economic and Social Consequences of the Thirty Years' War," *Past and Present* 39 (April 1968): 44–61.
3. John A. Lynn, "Recalculating French Army Growth," in *The Military Revolution Debate: Readings on the Military Transformation of Early Modern Europe,* ed. Clifford J. Rogers (Boulder, Colo.: Westview Press, 1995), p. 125.
4. Quoted in John A. Lynn, *Giant of the Grand Siècle: The French Army, 1610–1715* (Cambridge, U.K.: Cambridge University Press, 1997), p. 74.
5. F. Arkwright, ed., *The Memoirs of the Duke de Saint-Simon,* vol. 5 (New York: Brentano's, n.d.), p. 276.
6. J. H. Elliott, *Imperial Spain, 1469–1716* (New York: Mentor Books, 1963), pp. 306–308.
7. H. Rosenberg, *Bureaucracy, Aristocracy, and Autocracy: The Prussian Experience, 1660–1815* (Boston: Beacon Press, 1966), p. 43.
8. Cited in Giles MacDonogh, *Frederick the Great: A Life in Deed and Letters* (New York: St. Martin's, 2001), p. 23.
9. Rosenberg, *Bureaucracy, Aristocracy, and Autocracy,* p. 40.
10. For a revisionist interpretation, see J. Wormald, "James VI and I: Two Kings or One?" *History* 62 (June 1983): 187–209.
11. S. Schama, *The Embarrassment of Riches: An Interpretation of Dutch Culture in the Golden Age* (New York: Alfred A. Knopf, 1987), pp. 165–170; quotation is on p. 167.

Key Terms

Peace of Westphalia (p. 483)
Fronde (p. 487)
mercantilism (p. 489)
Peace of Utrecht (p. 492)
Junkers (p. 495)
boyars (p. 498)
Cossacks (p. 498)
sultan (p. 504)
janissary corps (p. 504)
millet system (p. 505)
constitutionalism (p. 506)
republicanism (p. 506)
Puritans (p. 507)
Protectorate (p. 508)
Test Act (p. 510)
stadholder (p. 513)

For practice quizzes and other study tools, visit the Online Study Guide at **bedfordstmartins.com/mckaywest**.

For primary sources from this period, see ***Sources of Western Society*, Second Edition**.

For Web sites, images, and documents related to topics in this chapter, visit Make History at **bedfordstmartins.com/mckaywest**.

17

Toward a New Worldview

1540–1789

The intellectual developments of the seventeenth and eighteenth centuries created the modern worldview that the West continues to hold — and debate — to this day. In the seventeenth century fundamentally new ways of understanding the natural world emerged. Those leading the changes saw themselves as philosophers and referred to their field of study as "natural philosophy." In the nineteenth century scholars hailed these achievements as a "scientific revolution" that produced modern science as we know it. The new science created in the seventeenth century entailed the search for precise knowledge of the physical world based on the union of experimental observations with sophisticated mathematics. Whereas medieval scholars looked to authoritative texts like the Bible or the classics, seventeenth-century natural philosophers performed experiments and relied on increasingly complex mathematical calculations. The resulting conception of the universe and its laws remained in force until Einstein's discoveries in the first half of the twentieth century.

In the eighteenth century philosophers extended the use of reason from the study of nature to the study of human society. They sought to bring the light of reason to bear on the darkness of prejudice, outmoded traditions, and ignorance. Self-proclaimed members of an "Enlightenment" movement, they wished to bring the same progress to human affairs as their predecessors had brought to the understanding of the natural world. While the scientific revolution ushered in modern science, the Enlightenment created concepts of human rights, equality, progress, universalism, and tolerance that still guide Western societies today. At the same time, some people used their new understanding of reason to explain their own superiority, thus rationalizing such attitudes as racism and male chauvinism. ■

Life During the Scientific Revolution. This 1768 painting by Joseph Wright captures the popularization of science and experimentation during the Enlightenment. Here, a scientist demonstrates the creation of a vacuum by withdrawing air from a flask, with the suffocating cockatoo serving as shocking proof of the experiment.

CHAPTER PREVIEW

The Scientific Revolution
■ What was revolutionary in the new attitudes toward the natural world?

The Enlightenment
■ How did the new worldview affect the way people thought about society and human relations?

Enlightened Absolutism
■ What impact did new ways of thinking have on political developments and monarchical absolutism?

What was revolutionary in the new attitudes toward the natural world? ▪

The emergence of modern science was a development of tremendous long-term significance. A noted historian has said that the scientific revolution was "the real origin both of the modern world and the modern mentality."[1] With the scientific revolution, which lasted roughly from 1540 to 1690, Western society began to acquire its most distinctive traits.

Scientific Thought in 1500

The term "science" as we use it today only came into use in the nineteenth century. Prior to the scientific revolution, many different scholars and practitioners were involved in aspects of what came together to form science. One of the most important disciplines was **natural philosophy**, which focused on fundamental questions about the nature of the universe, its purpose,

natural philosophy An early modern term for the study of the nature of the universe, its purpose, and how it functioned; it encompassed what we would call "science" today.

and how it functioned. In the early 1500s natural philosophy was still based primarily on the ideas of Aristotle, the great Greek philosopher of the fourth century B.C.E. Medieval theologians such as Thomas Aquinas brought Aristotelian philosophy into harmony with Christian doctrines. According to the revised Aristotelian view, a motionless earth was fixed at the center of the universe and was encompassed by ten separate concentric crystal spheres that revolved around it. In the first eight spheres were embedded, in turn, the moon, the sun, the five known planets, and the fixed stars. Then followed two spheres added during the Middle Ages to account for slight changes in the positions of the stars over the centuries. Beyond the tenth sphere was Heaven, with the throne of God and the souls of the saved. Angels kept the spheres moving in perfect circles.

Aristotle's cosmology made intellectual sense, but it could not account for the observed motions of the stars and planets and, in particular, provided no explanation for the apparent backward motion of the planets (which we now know occurs as planets closer to the sun periodically overtake the earth on their faster orbits). The great second-century Greek scholar Ptolemy (see Chapter 15) offered a cunning solution to this dilemma. According to Ptolemy, the planets moved in small circles,

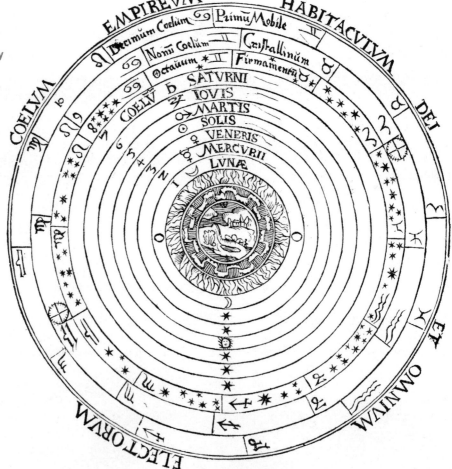

The Aristotelian Universe as Imagined in the Sixteenth Century A round earth is at the center, surrounded by spheres of water, air, and fire. Beyond this small nucleus, the moon, the sun, and the five planets were embedded in their own rotating crystal spheres, with the stars sharing the surface of one enormous sphere. Beyond, the heavens were composed of unchanging ether. (Image Select/Art Resource, NY)

called epicycles, each of which moved in turn along a larger circle or deferent. Ptolemaic astronomy was less elegant than Aristotle's neat nested circles and required complex calculations, but it provided a surprisingly accurate model for predicting planetary motion.

Aristotle's views, revised by medieval philosophers, also dominated thinking about physics and motion on earth. Aristotle had distinguished sharply between the world of the celestial spheres and that of the earth—the sublunar world. The spheres consisted of a perfect, incorruptible "quintessence," or fifth essence. The sublunar world, however, was made up of four imperfect, changeable elements. The "light" elements (air and fire) naturally moved upward, while the "heavy" elements (water and earth) naturally moved downward. These natural directions of motion did not always prevail, however, for elements were often mixed together and could be affected by an outside force such as a human being. Aristotle and his followers also believed that a uniform force moved an object at a constant speed and that the object would stop as soon as that force was removed.

Aristotle's ideas about astronomy and physics were accepted, with revisions, for two thousand years, and with good reason. First, they offered an understandable, commonsense explanation for what the eye actually saw. Second, Aristotle's science as interpreted by Christian theologians fit neatly with Christian doctrines. It established a home for God and a place for Christian souls. It put human beings at the center of the universe and made them the critical link in a "great chain of being" that stretched from the throne of God to the lowliest insect on earth. This approach to the natural world was thus a branch of theology, and it reinforced religious thought.

Origins of the Scientific Revolution

Why did Aristotelian teachings give way to new views about the universe? The scientific revolution drew on long-term developments in European culture, as well as borrowings from Arabic scholars. The first important development was the medieval university. By the thirteenth century permanent universities with professors and large student bodies had been established in western Europe to train the lawyers, doctors, and church leaders society required. By 1300 philosophy had taken its place alongside law, medicine, and theology. Medieval philosophers developed a limited but real independence from theologians and a sense of free inquiry. They nobly pursued a body of knowledge and tried to arrange it meaningfully with abstract theories.

In the fourteenth and fifteenth centuries leading universities established new professorships of mathematics, astronomy, and physics (natural philosophy) within their faculties of philosophy. Although the prestige of the new fields was low, critical thinking was now applied to scientific problems by a permanent community of scholars.

The Renaissance also stimulated scientific progress. Many ancient works were recovered, often through Arabic translations of the original Greek and Latin that were then translated into European vernacular languages. In fields such as mathematics, the translations were accompanied by learned Arabic commentaries that went beyond ancient learning. Renaissance patrons played a role in funding scientific investigations, as they did for art and literature. In addition, Renaissance artists' turn toward realism and their use of geometry to convey three-dimensional perspective encouraged scholars to practice close observation and to use mathematics to describe the natural world. The rise of printing provided a faster and less expensive way to circulate knowledge across Europe.

The navigational problems of long sea voyages in the age of overseas expansion were another factor in the scientific revolution. As early as 1484 the king of Portugal appointed a commission of mathematicians to perfect tables to help seamen find their latitude. Navigational problems were also critical in the development of many new scientific instruments, such as the telescope, barometer, thermometer, pendulum clock, microscope, and air pump. Better instruments, which permitted more accurate observations, often led to important new knowledge.

Recent historical research has also focused on the contribution to the scientific revolution of practices now relegated far beyond the realm of science. For most of human history, interest in astronomy was inspired by belief that the changing relationships between planets and stars influenced events on earth. This was true in Europe up to and during the scientific revolution (and continues today). Many of the most celebrated astronomers were also astrologers and spent much time devising horoscopes for their patrons. Used as a diagnostic tool in medicine, astrology formed a regular part of the curriculum of medical schools.

Copernican hypothesis
The idea that the sun, not the earth, was the center of the universe.

Centuries-old practices of magic and alchemy also remained important traditions for participants in the scientific revolution. For many observers there was little to distinguish the conjuring tricks of magicians from the experiments and instruments of the emerging scientists, and, in fact, there was a great deal of crossover between the two. The idea that objects possessed hidden or "occult" qualities that allowed them to affect other objects was a particularly important legacy of the magical tradition. Belief in occult qualities — or numerology or cosmic harmony — was not antithetical to belief in God. On the contrary, adherents believed that only a divine creator could infuse the universe with such meaningful mystery.

The Copernican Hypothesis

The desire to explain and thereby glorify God's handiwork led to the first great departure from the medieval system. This departure was the work of the Polish cleric Nicolaus Copernicus (1473–1543). As a young man Copernicus was drawn to the intellectual and cultural vitality of the Italian Renaissance. After studies at the university of Kraków, he departed for Italy, where he studied astronomy, medicine, and church law at the famed universities of Bologna, Padua, and Ferrara. Copernicus noted how professional astronomers still depended for their most accurate calculations on the work of Ptolemy. Copernicus felt that Ptolemy's cumbersome and occasionally inaccurate rules detracted from the majesty of a perfect creator. He preferred an ancient Greek idea: that the sun, rather than the earth, was at the center of the universe.

Finishing his university studies and returning to a church position in East Prussia, Copernicus worked on his hypothesis from 1506 to 1530. Unlike other leaders of the scientific revolution, Copernicus was not a professional astronomer or a university professor and had limited instruments and free time for research. With-

out questioning the Aristotelian belief in crystal spheres or the idea that circular motion was divine, Copernicus theorized that the stars and planets, including the earth, revolved around a fixed sun. Fearing the ridicule of other astronomers, Copernicus did not publish his *On the Revolutions of the Heavenly Spheres* until 1543, the year of his death.

The **Copernican hypothesis** had enormous scientific and religious implications, many of which the conservative Copernicus did not anticipate. First, it put the stars at rest, their apparent nightly movement simply a result of the earth's rotation. Thus it destroyed the main reason for believing in crystal spheres capable of moving the stars around the earth. Second, Copernicus's theory suggested a universe of staggering size. If in the course of a year the earth moved around the sun and yet the stars appeared to remain in the same place, then the universe was unthinkably large. Finally, by characterizing the earth as just another planet, Copernicus destroyed the basic idea of Aristotelian physics — that the earthly world was quite different from the heavenly one. Where then were Heaven and the throne of God?

The Copernican hypothesis brought sharp attacks from religious leaders, especially Protestants, who objected to the idea that the earth moved but the sun did not. Protestant leaders John Calvin and Martin Luther condemned Copernicus. Luther noted that the theory was counter to the Bible: "as the Holy Scripture tells us, so did Joshua bid the sun stand still and not the earth."[2] Catholic reaction was milder at first. The Catholic Church had never held to literal interpretations of the Bible, and not until 1616 did it officially declare the Copernican hypothesis false.

Other events were almost as influential in creating doubts about traditional astronomical ideas. In 1572 a new star appeared and shone very brightly for almost two years. The new star, which was actually a distant exploding star, made an enormous impression on people. It seemed to contradict the idea that the heavenly spheres were unchanging and therefore perfect. In 1577 a new comet suddenly moved through the sky, cutting a straight path across the supposedly impenetrable crystal spheres. It was time, as a sixteenth-century scientific writer put it, for "the radical renovation of astronomy."[3]

Brahe, Kepler, and Galileo: Proving Copernicus Right

One astronomer who agreed with Copernicus was Tycho Brahe (TEE-koh BRAH-hee) (1546–1601). Born into a prominent Danish noble family, Brahe became passionately interested in astronomy as a young boy and spent many nights gazing at the skies. Completing his studies abroad and returning to Denmark, he established himself as Europe's leading astronomer with his de-

Hevelius and His Wife Portable sextants were used to chart a ship's position at sea by measuring the altitude of celestial bodies above the horizon. Astronomers used much larger sextants to measure the angular distances between two bodies. Here, Johannes Hevelius makes use of the great brass sextant at the Danzig observatory, with the help of his wife, Elisabetha. Six feet in radius, this instrument was closely modeled on the one used by Tycho Brahe. (Houghton Library, Harvard College Library)

tailed observations of the new star of 1572. Aided by generous grants from the king of Denmark, Brahe built the most sophisticated observatory of his day.

Upon the king's death, Brahe acquired a new patron in the Holy Roman emperor Rudolph II and built a new observatory in Prague. In return for the emperor's support, he pledged to create new and improved tables of planetary motions, dubbed the *Rudolfine Tables*. For twenty years Brahe meticulously observed the stars and planets with the naked eye, compiling much more complete and accurate data than ever before. His limited understanding of mathematics and his sudden death in 1601, however, prevented him from making much sense out of his mass of data. Part Ptolemaic, part Copernican, he believed that all the planets except the earth revolved around the sun and that the entire group of sun and planets revolved in turn around the earth-moon system.

It was left to Brahe's young assistant, Johannes Kepler (1571–1630), to rework Brahe's mountain of observations. From a minor German noble family, Kepler suffered a bout of smallpox as a small child, leaving him with permanently damaged hands and eyesight. A brilliant mathematician, Kepler was inspired by belief that the universe was built on mystical mathematical relationships and a musical harmony of the heavenly bodies.

Kepler's examination of his predecessor's meticulously recorded findings convinced him that they could not be explained by Ptolemy's astronomy. Abandoning the notion of epicycles and deferents—which even Copernicus had retained in part—Kepler developed three new and revolutionary laws of planetary motion. First, largely through observations of the planet Mars, he demonstrated that the orbits of the planets around the sun are elliptical rather than circular. Second, he demonstrated that the planets do not move at a uniform speed in their orbits. When a planet is close to the sun it moves more rapidly, and it slows as it moves farther away from the sun. Kepler published the first two laws in his 1609 book, *The New Astronomy*, which heralded the arrival of an entirely new theory of the cosmos. In 1619 Kepler put forth his third law: the time a planet takes to make its complete orbit is precisely related to its distance from the sun.

Kepler's contribution was monumental. Whereas Copernicus had speculated, Kepler proved mathematically the precise relations of a sun-centered (solar) system. He thus united for the first time the theoretical cosmology of natural philosophy with mathematics. His work demolished the old system of Aristotle and Ptolemy, and in his third law he came close to formulating the idea of universal gravitation (see page 526). In 1627 he also fulfilled Brahe's pledge by completing the Rudolfine Tables begun so many years earlier. These tables were used by astronomers for many years.

Kepler was a genius with many talents. Beyond his great contribution to astronomy, he pioneered the field of optics. He was the first to explain the role of refraction within the eye in creating vision, and he invented an improved telescope. He was also a great mathematician whose work furnished the basis for integral calculus and advances in geometry.

Kepler was not, however, the consummate modern scientist that these achievements suggest. His duties as court mathematician included casting horoscopes, and his own diary was based on astrological principles. He also wrote at length on cosmic harmonies and explained, for example, elliptical motion through ideas about the beautiful music created by the combined motion of the planets. Kepler's fictional account of travel to the moon, written partly to illustrate the idea of a non-earth-centered universe, caused controversy and may have contributed to the arrest and trial of his mother as a witch in 1620. Kepler also suffered deeply as a result of his unorthodox brand of Lutheranism, which led to his rejection by both Lutherans and Catholics. His career exemplifies the complex interweaving of ideas and beliefs in the emerging science of his day.

While Kepler was unraveling planetary motion, a young Florentine named Galileo Galilei (ga-luh-LEE-oh ga-luh-LAY) (1564–1642) was challenging all the old ideas about motion. Like Kepler and so many early scientists, Galileo was a poor nobleman first marked for a religious career. Instead, his fascination with mathematics led to a professorship in which he examined motion and mechanics in a new way. His great achievement was the elaboration and consolidation of the **experimental method**. That is, rather than speculate about what might or should happen, Galileo conducted controlled experiments to find out what actually did happen.

In some of his experiments Galileo measured the movement of a rolling ball across a surface that he constructed, repeating the action again and again to verify his results. In his famous acceleration experiment, he showed that a uniform force—in this case, gravity—produced a uniform acceleration. Through another experiment, he formulated the **law of inertia**. He found

experimental method
The approach, pioneered by Galileo, that the proper way to explore the workings of the universe was through repeatable experiments rather than speculation.

law of inertia A law formulated by Galileo that states that motion, not rest, is the natural state of an object, that an object continues in motion forever unless stopped by some external force.

Galileo's Telescopic Observations of the Moon Among the many mechanical devices Galileo invented was a telescope that could magnify objects twenty times (other contemporary telescopes could magnify objects only three times). Using this telescope, he obtained the empirical evidence that proved the Copernican system. He sketched many illustrations of his observations, including the six phases of the moon shown here. (moons: Scala/Art Resource, NY; telescope: Museum of Science, Florence/Art Resource, NY)

that rest was not the natural state of objects. Rather, an object continues in motion forever unless stopped by some external force. His discoveries proved Aristotelian physics wrong.

Galileo also applied the experimental method to astronomy. On hearing details about the invention of the telescope in Holland, Galileo made one for himself and trained it on the heavens. He quickly discovered the first four moons of Jupiter, which clearly suggested that Jupiter could not possibly be embedded in any impenetrable crystal sphere as Aristotle and Ptolemy maintained. This discovery provided new evidence for the Copernican theory, in which Galileo already believed. Galileo then pointed his telescope at the moon. He wrote in 1610 in *Siderus Nuncius*:

> By the aid of a telescope anyone may behold [the Milky Way] in a manner which so distinctly appeals to the senses that all the disputes which have tormented philosophers through so many ages are exploded by the irrefutable evidence of our eyes, and we are freed from wordy disputes upon the subject. For the galaxy is nothing else but a mass of innumerable stars planted together in clusters.[4]

Reading these famous lines, one feels a crucial corner in Western civilization being turned. No longer should one rely on established authority. A new method of learning and investigating was being developed, one that proved useful in any field of inquiry. A historian investigating documents of the past, for example, is not so different from a Galileo studying stars and rolling balls.

As early as 1597, when Johannes Kepler sent Galileo an early publication defending Copernicus, Galileo wrote back agreeing with his position and confessing he lacked the courage to follow Kepler's example. Within the Catholic world, expressing public support for Copernicus was increasingly dangerous. In 1616 the Holy Office placed the works of Copernicus and his supporters, including Kepler, on a list of books Catholics were forbidden to read. The accompanying decree declared that belief in a heliocentric world was "foolish and absurd, philosophically false and formally heretical."[5]

Galileo was a devout Catholic who sincerely believed that his theories did not detract from the perfection of God. Out of caution he silenced his beliefs for several years, until in 1623 he saw new hope with the ascension of Pope Urban VIII, a man sympathetic to developments in the new science. However, Galileo's 1632 *Dialogue on the Two Chief Systems of the World* went too far. Published in Italian and widely read, this work openly lampooned the traditional views of Aristotle and Ptolemy and defended those of Copernicus. Galileo was tried for heresy by the papal Inquisition. Imprisoned and threatened with torture, the aging Galileo recanted, "renouncing and cursing" his Copernican errors. Like Kepler, his correspondent and fellow pioneer, Galileo suffered personal hardship through religious persecution.

Newton's Synthesis

Despite the efforts of the church, by about 1640 the work of Brahe, Kepler, and Galileo had been largely accepted by the scientific community. The old Aristotelian astronomy and physics were in ruins, and several fundamental breakthroughs had been made. But the new findings failed to explain what forces controlled the movement of the planets and objects on earth. That challenge was taken up by English scientist Isaac Newton (1642–1727).

Newton was born into the lower English gentry in 1642, the year of Galileo's death, and he enrolled at Cambridge University in 1661. A genius who spectacularly united the experimental and theoretical-mathematical sides of modern science, Newton was also fascinated by alchemy. He left behind thirty years' worth of encoded journals recording experiments to discover the elixir of life and a way to change base metals into gold and silver. Newton was also intensely religious. Like Kepler and other practitioners of the scientific revolution, he was far from being the perfect rationalist so glorified by writers in the eighteenth and nineteenth centuries.

Isaac Newton This portrait suggests the depth and complexity of Isaac Newton. Is the powerful mind behind those piercing eyes thinking of science or of religion, or perhaps of both? (Scala/Art Resource, NY)

> ❝ I seem to have been only like a boy, playing on the seashore, and diverting myself, in now and then finding a smoother pebble or a prettier shell than ordinary, whilst the great ocean of truth lay all undiscovered before me. ❞
>
> —ISAAC NEWTON

Newton arrived at some of his most basic ideas about physics between 1664 and 1666, during a break from studies at Cambridge caused by an outbreak of plague. During this period, he later claimed to have discovered his law of universal gravitation as well as the concepts of centripetal force and acceleration. Not realizing the significance of his findings, the young Newton did not publish them, and upon his return to Cambridge he took up the study of optics. It was in reference to his experiments in optics that Newton outlined his method of scientific inquiry most clearly, explaining the need for scientists "first to enquire diligently into the properties of things, and to establish these properties by experiment, and then to proceed more slowly to hypotheses for the explanation of them."[6]

In 1684 Newton returned to physics and the preparation of his ideas for publication. The result appeared three years later in *Philosophicae Naturalis Principia Mathematica* (Mathematical Principles of Natural Philosophy). Newton's towering accomplishment was a single explanatory system that could integrate the astronomy of Copernicus, as corrected by Kepler's laws, with the physics of Galileo and his predecessors. *Principia Mathematica* laid down Newton's three laws of motion, using a set of mathematical laws that explain motion and mechanics. These laws of dynamics are complex, and it took scientists and engineers two hundred years to work out all their implications.

The key feature of the Newtonian synthesis was the **law of universal gravitation**. According to this law, every body in the universe attracts every other body in the universe in a precise mathematical relationship, whereby the force of attraction is proportional to the quantity of matter of the objects and inversely proportional to the square of the distance between them. The whole universe—from Kepler's elliptical orbits to Galileo's rolling balls—was unified in one coherent system. The German mathematician Gottfried von Leibniz, with whom Newton

law of universal gravitation Newton's law that all objects are attracted to one another and that the force of attraction is proportional to the object's quantity of matter and inversely proportional to the square of the distance between them.

empiricism A theory of inductive reasoning that calls for acquiring evidence through observation and experimentation rather than reason and speculation.

contested the invention of calculus, was outraged by Newton's claim that the "occult" force of gravity could allow bodies to affect one another at great distances. Newton's religious faith, as well as his alchemical belief in the innate powers of certain objects, allowed him to dismiss such criticism.

Newton's synthesis of mathematics with physics and astronomy prevailed until the twentieth century and established him as one of the most important figures in the history of science. Yet, near the end of his life, this acclaimed figure declared: "I do not know what I may appear to the world; but to myself I seem to have been only like a boy, playing on the seashore, and diverting myself, in now and then finding a smoother pebble or a prettier shell than ordinary, whilst the great ocean of truth lay all undiscovered before me."[7]

Bacon, Descartes, and the Scientific Method

The creation of a new science was not accomplished by a handful of brilliant astronomers working alone. Scholars in many fields sought answers to long-standing problems, sharing their results in a community that spanned Europe. One of the keys to the achievement of a new worldview in the seventeenth century was the development of better ways of obtaining knowledge about the world. Two important thinkers, Francis Bacon (1561–1626) and René Descartes (day-KAHRT) (1596–1650), were influential in describing and advocating for improved scientific methods based, respectively, on experimentation and mathematical reasoning.

The English politician and writer Francis Bacon was the greatest early propagandist for the new experimental method. Rejecting the Aristotelian and medieval method of using speculative reasoning to build general theories, Bacon argued that new knowledge had to be pursued through empirical research. The researcher who wants to learn more about leaves or rocks, for example, should not speculate about the subject but should rather collect a multitude of specimens and then compare and analyze them to derive general principles. Bacon's contribution was to formalize the empirical method, which had already been used by Brahe and Galileo, into the general theory of inductive reasoning known as **empiricism**. Bacon's work, and his prestige as lord chancellor under James I, led to the widespread adoption of what was called the "experimental philosophy" in England after his death.

On the continent, more speculative methods retained support. The French philosopher René Descartes was a multitalented genius who made his first great discovery in mathematics. As a twenty-three-year-old soldier serving in the Thirty Years' War, he experienced a life-changing intellectual vision one night in 1619. Descartes saw that there was a perfect correspondence between geometry and algebra and that geometrical spatial figures could be expressed as algebraic equations and vice versa. A major step forward in the history of mathematics, Descartes's discovery of analytic geometry provided scientists with an important new tool.

Descartes used mathematics to elaborate a highly influential vision of the workings of the cosmos. Accepting Galileo's claim that all elements of the universe are composed of the same matter, Descartes began to investigate the basic nature of matter. Drawing on ancient Greek atomist philosophies, Descartes developed the idea that matter was made up of identical "corpuscules" that collided together in an endless series of motions. All occurrences in nature could be analyzed as matter in motion and, according to Descartes, the total "quantity of motion" in the universe was constant. Descartes's mechanistic view of the universe depended on the idea that a vacuum was impossible, so that every action had an equal reaction, continuing in an eternal chain reaction.

Although Descartes's hypothesis about the vacuum was proved wrong, his notion of a mechanistic universe intelligible through the physics of motion proved highly influential. Decades later, Newton rejected Descartes's idea of a full universe and several of his other ideas, but retained the notion of a mechanistic universe as a key element of his own system.

Descartes's greatest achievement was to develop his initial vision into a whole philosophy of knowledge and science. The Aristotelian cosmos was appealing in part because it corresponded with the evidence of the human senses. When the senses were proven to be wrong, Descartes decided it was necessary to doubt them and everything that could reasonably be doubted, and then, as in geometry, to use deductive reasoning from self-evident principles to ascertain scientific laws. Descartes's reasoning ultimately reduced all substances to "matter" and "mind" — that is, to the physical and the spiritual. The devout Descartes believed that God had endowed man with reason for a purpose and that rational speculation could provide a path to the truths of creation. His view of the world as consisting of two fundamental entities is known as **Cartesian dualism**. Descartes's thought was highly influential in France and the Netherlands, but less so in England, where experimental philosophy won the day.

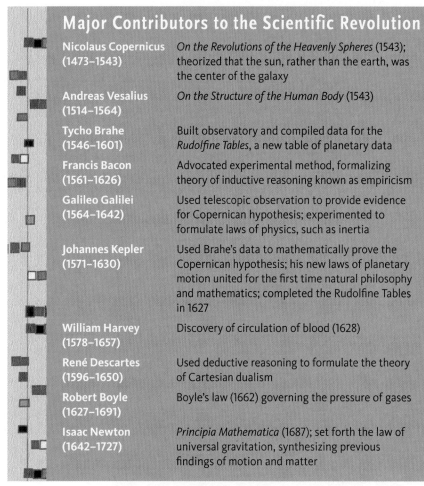

Major Contributors to the Scientific Revolution

Nicolaus Copernicus (1473–1543)	*On the Revolutions of the Heavenly Spheres* (1543); theorized that the sun, rather than the earth, was the center of the galaxy
Andreas Vesalius (1514–1564)	*On the Structure of the Human Body* (1543)
Tycho Brahe (1546–1601)	Built observatory and compiled data for the *Rudolfine Tables*, a new table of planetary data
Francis Bacon (1561–1626)	Advocated experimental method, formalizing theory of inductive reasoning known as empiricism
Galileo Galilei (1564–1642)	Used telescopic observation to provide evidence for Copernican hypothesis; experimented to formulate laws of physics, such as inertia
Johannes Kepler (1571–1630)	Used Brahe's data to mathematically prove the Copernican hypothesis; his new laws of planetary motion united for the first time natural philosophy and mathematics; completed the Rudolfine Tables in 1627
William Harvey (1578–1657)	Discovery of circulation of blood (1628)
René Descartes (1596–1650)	Used deductive reasoning to formulate the theory of Cartesian dualism
Robert Boyle (1627–1691)	Boyle's law (1662) governing the pressure of gases
Isaac Newton (1642–1727)	*Principia Mathematica* (1687); set forth the law of universal gravitation, synthesizing previous findings of motion and matter

Both Bacon's inductive experimentalism and Descartes's deductive mathematical reasoning had their faults. Bacon's inability to appreciate the importance of mathematics and his obsession with practical results clearly showed the limitations of antitheoretical empiricism. Likewise, some of Descartes's positions — he believed, for example, that it was possible to deduce the whole science of medicine from first principles — demonstrated the inadequacy of rigid, dogmatic rationalism. Although insufficient on their own, Bacon's and Descartes's extreme approaches are combined in the modern scientific method, which began to crystallize in the late seventeenth century.

Cartesian dualism
Descartes's view that all of reality could ultimately be reduced to mind and matter.

Science and Society

The rise of modern science had many consequences, some of which are still unfolding. First, it went hand in hand with the rise of a new and expanding social group — the international scientific community. Members of this community were linked together by common interests and shared values as well as by journals and the learned scientific societies founded in many countries in the later seventeenth and the eighteenth centuries. The personal success of scientists and scholars depended on making new discoveries, and science became competitive. Second, as governments intervened to support and sometimes direct research, the new scientific community became closely tied to the state and its agendas. National academies of science were created under state sponsorship in London in 1662, Paris in 1666, Berlin in 1700, and later across Europe. At the same time, scientists developed a critical attitude toward established authority that would inspire thinkers to question traditions in other domains as well.

Metamorphoses of the Caterpillar and Moth Maria Sibylla Merian (1647–1717), the stepdaughter of a Dutch painter, became a celebrated scientific illustrator in her own right. Her finely observed pictures of insects in the South American colony of Surinam introduced many new species. For Merian, science was intimately tied with art: she not only painted but also bred caterpillars and performed experiments on them. Her two-year stay in Surinam, accompanied by a teenage daughter, was a daring feat for a seventeenth-century woman. (Bildarchiv Preussischer Kulturbesitz/Art Resource, NY)

Some things did not change in the scientific revolution. Scholars have recently analyzed representations of femininity and masculinity in the scientific revolution and have noted that nature was often depicted as a female, whose veil of secrecy needed to be stripped away and penetrated by male experts. New "rational" methods for approaching nature did not question traditional inequalities between the sexes—and may have worsened them in some ways. When Renaissance courts served as centers of learning, talented noblewomen could find niches in study and research. The rise of a professional scientific community raised barriers for women because the new academies that furnished professional credentials did not accept female members. (This continued for a long time. Marie Curie, the first person to win two Nobel prizes, was rejected by the French Academy of Science in 1911 because she was a woman.[8])

There were, however, a number of noteworthy exceptions. In Italy, universities and academies did offer posts to women, attracting some foreigners spurned by their own countries. Women across Europe were allowed to work as makers of wax anatomical models and as botanical and zoological illustrators. Women were also very much involved in informal scientific communities, attending salons, participating in scientific experiments, and writing learned treatises. Some female intellectuals were recognized as full-fledged members of the philosophical dialogue. In England, Margaret Cavendish, Anne Conway, and Mary Astell all contributed to debates about Descartes's mind-body dualism, among other issues. Descartes himself conducted an intellectual correspondence with the princess Elizabeth of Bohemia, of whom he stated: "I attach more weight to her judgment than to those messieurs the Doctors, who take for a rule of truth the opinions of Aristotle rather than the evidence of reason."[9]

The scientific revolution had few consequences for economic life and the living standards of the masses until the late eighteenth century. True, improvements in the techniques of navigation facilitated overseas trade and helped enrich states and merchant companies. But science had relatively few practical economic applications. Thus the scientific revolution of the seventeenth century was first and foremost an intellectual revolution. For more than a hundred years its greatest impact was on how people thought and believed.

Finally, there is the question of the role of religion in the development of science. Just as some historians have argued that Protestantism led to the rise of capitalism, others have concluded that Protestantism was a fundamental factor in the rise of modern science. According to this view, Protestantism, particularly in its Calvinist varieties, made scientific inquiry a question of individual conscience, not of religious doctrine. The Catholic Church, in contrast, supposedly suppressed scientific theories that conflicted with its teachings and thus discouraged scientific progress. The truth is more complicated. All Western religious authorities—Catholic, Protestant, and Jewish—opposed the Copernican system to a greater or lesser extent until about 1630, by which time the scientific revolution was definitely in progress. The Catholic Church was initially less hostile than Protestant and Jewish religious leaders, and Italian scientists played a crucial role in scientific progress right up to the trial of Galileo in 1633. Thereafter, the Counter-Reformation church became more hostile to science, a change that helped account for the decline of science in Italy (but not in Catholic France) after 1640. At the same time, Protestant countries such as the Netherlands and Denmark became quite "pro-science," especially countries that lacked a strong religious authority capable of imposing religious orthodoxy on scientific questions.

This was certainly the case with Protestant England after 1630. English religious conflicts became so intense that the authorities could not impose religious unity on anything, including science. The work of Bacon's many followers during Oliver Cromwell's commonwealth (see Chapter 16) helped solidify the independence of science. Bacon advocated the experimental approach precisely because it was open-minded and independent of preconceived religious and philosophical ideas. Neutral and useful, science became an accepted part of life and developed rapidly in England after about 1640.

Medicine, the Body, and Chemistry

The scientific revolution, which began with the study of the cosmos, soon inspired renewed study of the microcosm of the human body. For many centuries the ancient Greek physician Galen's explanation of the body carried the same authority as Aristotle's account of the universe. According to Galen, the body contained four humors: blood, phlegm, black bile, and yellow bile. Illness was believed to result from an imbalance of humors, which is why doctors frequently prescribed bloodletting to expel excess blood.

Swiss physician and alchemist Paracelsus (1493–1541) was an early proponent of the experimental method in medicine and pioneered the use of chemicals and drugs to address what he saw as chemical, rather than humoral, imbalances. Another experimentalist, Flemish physician Andreas Vesalius (1516–1564) studied anatomy by dissecting human bodies, often those of executed criminals. In 1543, the same year Copernicus published *On the Revolutions*, Vesalius issued his masterpiece, *On the Structure of the Human Body*. Its two hundred precise drawings revolutionized the understanding of human anatomy. The experimental approach also led English royal physician William Harvey (1578–1657) to discover the circulation of blood through the veins and arteries in 1628. Harvey was the first to explain that the heart worked like a pump and to explain the function of its muscles and valves.

Irishman Robert Boyle (1627–1691) founded the modern science of chemistry. Following Paracelsus's lead, he undertook experiments to discover the basic

ANDREÆ VESALII.

Frontispiece to *De Humani Corporis Fabrica* (On the Structure of the Human Body) The frontispiece to Vesalius's pioneering work, published in 1543, shows him dissecting a corpse before a crowd of students. This was a revolutionary new hands-on approach for physicians, who usually worked from a theoretical, rather than a practical, understanding of the body. Based on direct observation, Vesalius replaced ancient ideas drawn from Greek philosophy with a much more accurate account of the structure and function of the body. (© SSPL/Science Museum/The Image Works) elements of nature, which he believed was composed of infinitely small atoms. Boyle was the first to create a vacuum, thus disproving Descartes's belief that a vacuum could not exist in nature, and he discovered Boyle's law (1662), which states that the pressure of a gas varies inversely with volume.

The Enlightenment

How did the new worldview affect the way people thought about society and human relations? ◼

The scientific revolution was the single most important factor in the creation of the new worldview of the eighteenth-century **Enlightenment**. This worldview, which has played a large role in shaping the modern mind, grew out of a rich mix of diverse and often conflicting ideas. For the writers who espoused them, these ideas competed vigorously for the attention of a growing public of well-educated but fickle readers, who remained a minority of the population.

Despite the diversity, three central concepts stand at the core of Enlightenment thinking. The most important and original idea was that the methods of natural science could and should be used to examine and understand all aspects of life. This was what intellectuals meant by *reason*, a favorite word of Enlightenment thinkers. Nothing was to be accepted on faith; everything was to be submitted to **rationalism**, a secular, critical way of thinking. A second important Enlightenment concept was that the scientific method was capable of discovering the laws of human society as well as those of nature. Thus was social science born. Its birth led to the third key idea, that of progress. Armed with the proper method of discovering the laws of human existence, Enlightenment thinkers believed, it was at least possible for human beings to create better societies and better people.

Enlightenment The influential intellectual and cultural movement of the late seventeenth and eighteenth centuries that introduced a new worldview based on the use of reason, the scientific method, and progress.

rationalism A secular, critical way of thinking in which nothing was to be accepted on faith, and everything was to be submitted to reason.

The Emergence of the Enlightenment

Loosely united by certain key ideas, the European Enlightenment (ca. 1690–1789) was a broad intellectual and cultural movement that gained strength gradually and did not reach its maturity until about 1750. Yet it was the generation that came of age between the publication of Newton's *Principia* in 1687 and the death of Louis XIV in 1715 that tied the crucial knot between the scientific revolution and a new outlook on life. Talented writers of that generation popularized hard-to-understand scientific achievements for the educated elite.

A new generation came to believe that the human mind itself is capable of making great progress. Medieval and Reformation thinkers had been concerned primarily with the abstract concepts of sin and salvation. The humanists of the Renaissance had emphasized worldly matters (especially art and literature), but their inspiration came from the classical past. Enlightenment thinkers came to believe that their era had gone far beyond antiquity and that intellectual progress was very possible.

The excitement of the scientific revolution also generated doubt and uncertainty, contributing to a widespread crisis in late-seventeenth-century European thought. In the wake of the devastation wrought by the Thirty Years' War, some people asked whether ideological conformity in religious matters was really necessary. Others skeptically asked if religious truth could ever be known with absolute certainty and concluded that it could not. This was a new development because many seventeenth-century scientists, Catholic and Protestant, believed that their work exalted God and helped explain his creation to fellow believers.

The most famous of these skeptics was Pierre Bayle (1647–1706), a French Huguenot who despised Louis XIV and found refuge in the Netherlands. Bayle critically examined the religious beliefs and persecutions of the past in his *Historical and Critical Dictionary* (1697). Demonstrating that human beliefs had been extremely varied and very often mistaken, he concluded that nothing can ever be known beyond all doubt, a view known as skepticism. His very influential *Dictionary* was reprinted frequently in the Netherlands and in England and was found in more private libraries of eighteenth-century France than any other book.

As they questioned religious teachings and traditions, some early Enlightenment philosophers became interested in Judaism. They read Jewish scripture mostly in the abstract to help define what true religion should be like. Some Jewish scholars participated in the early Enlightenment movement. The philosopher Baruch Spinoza (1632–1677) was excommunicated by the relatively large Jewish community of Amsterdam for his controversial religious ideas. Rejecting his youthful support for Descartes, Spinoza came to believe that mind and body are united in one substance and that God and nature were two names for the same thing. He envisioned a deterministic universe in which good and evil were merely relative values. Few of Spinoza's radical writings were published during his lifetime, but he is now recognized as among the most original thinkers of the early Enlightenment.

The rapidly growing travel literature on non-European lands and cultures was another cause of

ENTRETIENS.
SUR LA PLURALITÉ DES MONDES.

Popularizing Science The frontispiece illustration of Fontenelle's *Conversations on the Plurality of Worlds* (1686) invites the reader to share the pleasures of astronomy with an elegant lady and an entertaining teacher. The drawing shows the planets revolving around the sun. (By permission of the Syndics of Cambridge University Library)

their ideas. Whereas Descartes based his deductive logic on the conviction that certain first premises, or innate ideas, are imbued in all humans by God, Locke insisted that all ideas are derived from experience. The human mind at birth is like a blank tablet, or tabula rasa on which the environment writes the individual's understanding and beliefs. Human development is therefore determined by education and social institutions, for good or for evil. Locke's essay contributed to the theory of sensationalism, the idea that all human ideas and thoughts are produced as a result of sensory impressions. With his emphasis on the role of perception in the acquisition of knowledge, Locke provided a systematic justification of Bacon's emphasis on the importance of observation and experimentation. The *Essay Concerning Human Understanding* passed through many editions and translations and, along with Newton's *Principia*, was one of the dominant intellectual inspirations of the Enlightenment.

The Influence of the Philosophes

By the time Louis XIV died in 1715, many of the ideas that would soon coalesce into the new worldview had been assembled. Yet Christian Europe was still strongly attached to its established political and social structures and its traditional spiritual beliefs. By 1775, however, a large portion of western Europe's educated elite had embraced many of the new ideas. This acceptance was the work of the **philosophes** (fee-luh-zawfz), a group of influential intellectuals who proudly proclaimed that they, at long last, were bringing the light of knowledge to their ignorant fellow creatures.

> **philosophes** A group of French intellectuals who proclaimed that they were bringing the light of knowledge to their fellow creatures in the Age of Enlightenment.

Philosophe is the French word for "philosopher," and it was in France that the Enlightenment reached its highest development. There were at least three reasons for this. First, French was the international language of the educated classes in the eighteenth century, and France was still the wealthiest and most populous country in Europe. Second, although French intellectuals were not free to openly criticize either church or state, they were not as strongly restrained as intellectuals in eastern and east-central Europe. Third, the French philosophes made it their goal to reach a larger audience of elites, many of whom were joined together in the eighteenth-century concept of the "republic of letters"—an imaginary transnational realm of the well-educated.

Knowing that published attacks on society and the church would probably be banned or burned, the philosophes circulated their most radical works in manuscript form. To appeal to the public and get around the censors, they wrote novels and plays, histories and philosophies, dictionaries and encyclopedias, all filled with

questioning among thinkers. In the wake of the great discoveries, Europeans were learning that the peoples of China, India, Africa, and the Americas all had their own very different beliefs and customs. Europeans shaved their faces and let their hair grow. Turks shaved their heads and let their beards grow. In Europe a man bowed before a woman to show respect. In Siam a man turned his back on a woman when he met her because it was disrespectful to look directly at her. Countless similar examples discussed in travel accounts helped change the perspective of educated Europeans. They began to look at truth and morality in relative, rather than absolute, terms. If anything was possible, who could say what was right or wrong?

Out of this period of intellectual turmoil came John Locke's *Essay Concerning Human Understanding* (1690), often viewed as the first major text of the Enlightenment. In this work Locke (1632–1704) brilliantly set forth a new theory about how human beings learn and form

Voltaire and Philosophes This painting belongs to a series commissioned by Catherine the Great to depict daily life at the philosopher's retreat at Ferney in Switzerland. It shows Voltaire seated at the dinner table surrounded by his followers, including *Encyclopedia* editors Diderot and d'Alembert. The scene is imaginary, for Diderot never visited Ferney. (Photo by permission of the Voltaire Foundation, University of Oxford)

satire and double meanings to spread their message to an eager audience.

One of the greatest philosophes, the baron de Montesquieu (mahn-tuhs-KYOO) (1689–1755), brilliantly pioneered this approach in *The Persian Letters*, an extremely influential social satire published in 1721. This work consisted of amusing letters supposedly written by two Persian travelers, Usbek and Rica, who as outsiders see European customs in unique ways and thereby allow Montesquieu a vantage point for criticizing existing practices and beliefs.

Like many Enlightenment philosophes, Montesquieu saw relations between men and women as highly representative of the overall social and political system. He used the oppression of women in the Persian harem, described in letters from Usbek's wives, to symbolize Eastern political tyranny. At the end of the book, the rebellion of Usbek's harem against the cruel eunuchs he left in charge demonstrates that despotism must ultimately fail. Montesquieu also used the Persians' observations of habitual infidelity among French wives and the strength of female power behind the throne to poke fun at European social and political customs. As Rica remarks:

The thing is that, for every man who has any post at court, in Paris, or in the country, there is a woman through whose hands pass all the favours and sometimes the injustices that he does. These women are all in touch with one another, and compose a sort of commonwealth whose members are always busy giving each other mutual help and support.[10]

Montesquieu was exaggerating, but he echoed other critics of the informal power women gained in an absolutist system, where royal mistresses and female courtiers could have more access to the king than government ministers (see Chapter 16). Having gained fame by using wit as a weapon against cruelty and superstition, Montesquieu settled down on his family estate to study history and politics. His interest was partly personal, for, like many members of the French robe nobility, he was disturbed by the growth in royal absolutism under Louis XIV. But Montesquieu was also inspired by the example of the physical sciences, and he set out to apply the critical method to the problem of government in *The Spirit of Laws* (1748). The result was a complex comparative study of republics, monarchies, and despotisms — a great pioneering inquiry in the emerging social sciences.

❝ The thing is that, for every man who has any post at court, in Paris, or in the country, there is a woman through whose hands pass all the favours and sometimes the injustices that he does. **❞**

—MONTESQUIEU

Showing that forms of government were shaped by history, geography, and customs, Montesquieu focused on the conditions that would promote liberty and prevent tyranny. He argued for a separation of powers, with political power divided and shared by a variety of classes and legal estates holding unequal rights and privileges. Admiring greatly the English balance of power among the king, the houses of Parliament, and the independent courts, Montesquieu believed that in France the thirteen high courts—the *parlements*—were frontline defenders of liberty against royal despotism. Apprehensive about the uneducated poor, Montesquieu was clearly no democrat, but his theory of separation of powers had a great impact on the constitutions of the young United States in 1789 and of France in 1791.

The most famous and in many ways most representative philosophe was François Marie Arouet, who was known by the pen name Voltaire (vohl-TAIR) (1694–1778). In his long career, this son of a comfortable middle-class family wrote more than seventy witty volumes, hobnobbed with kings and queens, and died a millionaire because of shrewd business speculations. His early career, however, was turbulent, and he was arrested on two occasions for insulting noblemen. Voltaire moved to England for three years in order to avoid a longer prison term in France, and there he came to share Montesquieu's enthusiasm for English liberties and institutions.

Returning to France and soon threatened again with prison in Paris, Voltaire had the great fortune of meeting Gabrielle-Emilie Le Tonnelier de Breteuil, marquise du Châtelet (SHAH-tuh-lay) (1706–1749), a gifted woman from the high aristocracy with a passion for science. Inviting Voltaire to live in her country house at Cirey in Lorraine and becoming his long-time companion (under the eyes of her tolerant husband), Madame du Châtelet studied physics and mathematics and published scientific articles and translations, including the first—and only—translation of Newton's *Principia* into French. Excluded from the Royal Academy of Sciences because she was a woman, Madame du Châtelet had no doubt that women's limited role in science was due to their unequal education. She once wrote that if she were a ruler, "I would reform an abuse which cuts off, so to speak, half the human race. I would make women participate in all the rights of humankind, and above all in those of the intellect."[11]

While living at Cirey, Voltaire wrote various works praising England and popularizing English scientific progress. Newton, he wrote, was history's greatest man, for he had used his genius for the benefit of humanity. "It is," wrote Voltaire, "the man who sways our minds by the prevalence of reason and the native force of truth, not they who reduce mankind to a state of slavery by force and downright violence . . . that claims our reverence and admiration."[12] In the true style of the Enlightenment, Voltaire mixed the glorification of science and reason with an appeal for better individuals and institutions.

Yet, like almost all of the philosophes, Voltaire was a reformer, not a revolutionary, in social and political matters. He pessimistically concluded that the best one could hope for in the way of government was a good monarch, since human beings "are very rarely worthy to govern themselves." He lavishly praised Louis XIV

Madame du Châtelet The marquise du Châtelet was fascinated by the new world system of Isaac Newton. She helped spread Newton's ideas in France by translating his *Principia* and by influencing Voltaire, her companion for fifteen years until her death. (Giraudon/Art Resource, NY)

in a biography and conducted an enthusiastic correspondence with Prussian King Frederick the Great, whom he admired as an enlightened monarch. Nor did Voltaire believe in social and economic equality in human affairs. The idea of making servants equal to their masters was "absurd and impossible." The only realizable equality, Voltaire thought, was that "by which the citizen only depends on the laws which protect the freedom of the feeble against the ambitions of the strong."[13]

Voltaire's philosophical and religious positions were much more radical than his social and political beliefs. In the tradition of Bayle, his voluminous writings challenged, often indirectly, the Catholic Church and Christian theology at almost every point. Voltaire clearly believed in God, but his was a distant, deistic God. Drawing on Newton, he envisioned a mechanistic universe in which God acted like a great clockmaker who built an orderly system and then stepped aside and let it run. Above all, Voltaire and most of the philosophes hated all forms of religious intolerance, which they believed often led to fanaticism and savage, inhuman action. Simple piety and human kindness—as embodied in Christ's great commandments to "love God and your neighbor as yourself"—were religion enough, he believed.

The ultimate strength of the philosophes lay in their number, dedication, and organization. The philosophes felt keenly that they were engaged in a common undertaking that transcended individuals. Their greatest and most representative intellectual achievement was, quite fittingly, a group effort—the seventeen-volume *Encyclopedia: The Rational Dictionary of the Sciences, the Arts, and the Crafts*, edited by Denis Diderot (deh-nee DEE-duh-roh) (1713–1784) and Jean le Rond d'Alembert (dah-lum-BEHR) (1717–1783). From different circles and with different interests, the two men set out in 1751 to find coauthors who would examine the rapidly expanding whole of human knowledge. Even more fundamentally, they set out to teach people how to think critically and objectively about all matters. As Diderot said, he wanted the *Encyclopedia* to "change the general way of thinking."[14]

The *Encyclopedia* survived initial resistance from the French government and the Catholic Church. Completed in 1765, it contained seventy-two thousand articles by leading scientists, writers, skilled workers, and progressive priests, and it treated every aspect of

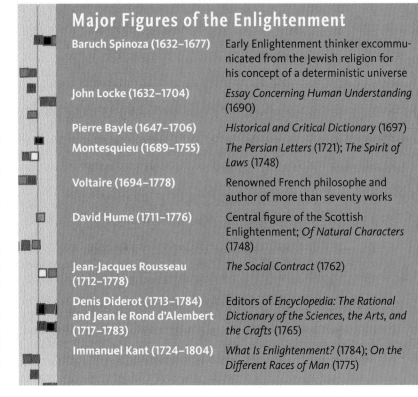

Major Figures of the Enlightenment

Baruch Spinoza (1632–1677)	Early Enlightenment thinker excommunicated from the Jewish religion for his concept of a deterministic universe
John Locke (1632–1704)	*Essay Concerning Human Understanding* (1690)
Pierre Bayle (1647–1706)	*Historical and Critical Dictionary* (1697)
Montesquieu (1689–1755)	*The Persian Letters* (1721); *The Spirit of Laws* (1748)
Voltaire (1694–1778)	Renowned French philosophe and author of more than seventy works
David Hume (1711–1776)	Central figure of the Scottish Enlightenment; *Of Natural Characters* (1748)
Jean-Jacques Rousseau (1712–1778)	*The Social Contract* (1762)
Denis Diderot (1713–1784) and Jean le Rond d'Alembert (1717–1783)	Editors of *Encyclopedia: The Rational Dictionary of the Sciences, the Arts, and the Crafts* (1765)
Immanuel Kant (1724–1804)	*What Is Enlightenment?* (1784); *On the Different Races of Man* (1775)

life and knowledge. Not every article was daring or original, but the overall effect was little short of revolutionary. Science and the industrial arts were exalted, religion and immortality questioned. Intolerance, legal injustice, and out-of-date social institutions were openly criticized. The encyclopedists were convinced that greater knowledge would result in greater human happiness, for knowledge was useful and made possible economic, social, and political progress. Summing up the new worldview of the Enlightenment, the *Encyclopedia* was widely read, especially in less-expensive reprint editions, and it was extremely influential.

The Enlightenment Outside of France

Historians now recognize the existence of important strands of Enlightenment thought outside of France. They have identified distinctive Enlightenment movements in eighteenth-century Italy, Spain, Greece, the Balkans, Poland, Hungary, and Russia. Different areas developed different forms of Enlightenment thinking. In England and Germany, scholars have described a more conservative Enlightenment that tried to integrate the findings of the scientific revolution with religious faith. After the Act of Union with England and Ireland in 1707, Scotland was freed from political crisis to experience a vigorous period of intellectual growth. The Scottish Enlightenment, centered in Edinburgh, was marked by an emphasis on pragmatic and scientific reasoning. Intellectual revival there was stimulated by the creation of the first public educational system in Europe.

The most important figure in Edinburgh was David Hume (1711–1776), whose carefully argued religious skepticism had a powerful impact at home and abroad. Building on Locke's teachings on learning, Hume argued that the human mind is really nothing but a bundle of impressions. These impressions originate only in sense experiences and our habits of joining these experiences together. Since our ideas ultimately reflect only our sense experiences, our reason cannot tell us anything about questions that cannot be verified by sense experience (in the form of controlled experiments or mathematics), such as the origin of the universe or the existence of God. Paradoxically, Hume's rationalistic inquiry ended up undermining the Enlightenment's faith in the power of reason.

Urban Culture and Life in the Public Sphere

A series of new institutions and practices encouraged the spread of Enlightenment ideas in the late seventeenth and the eighteenth centuries. First, the European production and consumption of books grew significantly. In Germany, for example, the number of new titles appearing annually rose from roughly six hundred in 1700 to twenty-six hundred in 1780. Moreover, the types of books people read changed dramatically. The proportion of religious and devotional books published in Paris declined after 1750; history and law held constant; the arts and sciences surged.

Reading more books on many more subjects, the educated public in France and throughout Europe increasingly approached reading in a new way. The result was what some scholars have called a **reading revolution**. The old style of reading in Europe had been centered on a core of sacred texts that inspired reverence and taught earthly duty and obedience to God. Reading had been patriarchal and communal, with the father of the family slowly reading the text aloud and the audience savoring each word. Now reading involved a broader field of books that constantly changed. Reading became individual and silent, and texts could be questioned. Subtle but profound, the reading revolution ushered in new ways of relating to the written word.

> **reading revolution** The transition in Europe from a society where literacy consisted of patriarchal and communal reading of religious texts to a society where literacy was commonplace and reading material was broad and diverse.

Conversation, discussion, and debate also played a critical role in the Enlightenment. Paris set the example, and other French and European cities followed. In Paris from about 1740 to 1789, a number of talented, wealthy women presided over regular social gatherings

The French Book Trade Book consumption surged in the eighteenth century and, along with it, new bookstores. This appealing bookshop in France with its intriguing ads for the latest works offers to put customers "Under the Protection of Minerva," the Roman goddess of wisdom. Large packets of books sit ready for shipment to foreign countries. (Musée des Beaux-Arts, Dijon/Art Resource, NY)

salons Regular social gatherings held by talented and rich Parisian women in their homes, where philosophes and their followers met to discuss literature, science, and philosophy.

named after their elegant private drawing rooms, or **salons**. There they encouraged the exchange of witty, uncensored observations on literature, science, and philosophy with great aristocrats, wealthy middle-class financiers, high-ranking officials, and noteworthy foreigners. Talented hostesses, or *salonnières* (sah-lahn-ee-EHRZ), mediated the public's freewheeling examination of Enlightenment thought. As one philosophe described his Enlightenment hostess and her salon:

> She could unite the different types, even the most antagonistic, sustaining the conversation by a well-aimed phrase,

animating and guiding it at will. . . . Politics, religion, philosophy, news: nothing was excluded. Her circle met daily from five to nine. There one found men of all ranks in the State, the Church, and the Court, soldiers and foreigners, and the leading writers of the day.[15]

As this passage suggests, the salons created a cultural realm free from religious dogma and political censorship. There a diverse but educated public could debate issues and form its own ideas. Through their invitation lists, salon hostesses brought together members of the intellectual, economic, and social elites. In such an atmosphere, the philosophes, the French nobility, and the prosperous middle classes intermingled and influenced one another. Thinking critically about almost any ques-

Picturing the Past

Enlightenment Culture An actor performs the first reading of a new play by Voltaire at the salon of Madame Geoffrin in this painting from 1755. Voltaire, then in exile, is represented by a bust statue. (Réunion des Musées Nationaux/Art Resource, NY)

ANALYZING THE IMAGE Which of these people do you think is the hostess, Madame Geoffrin, and why? Using details from the painting to support your answer, how would you describe the status of the people shown?

CONNECTIONS What does this image suggest about the reach of Enlightenment ideas to common people? To women? Does the painting of the bookstore on page 535 suggest a broader reach? Why?

To complete this activity online, go to the Online Study Guide at **bedfordstmartins.com/mckaywest**.

tion became fashionable and flourished alongside hopes for human progress through greater knowledge and enlightened public opinion.

Elite women also exercised great influence on artistic taste. Soft pastels, ornate interiors, sentimental portraits, and starry-eyed lovers protected by hovering cupids were all hallmarks of the style they favored. This style, known as **rococo** (ruh-KOH-koh), was popular throughout Europe in the period from 1720 to 1780. It has been argued that feminine influence in the drawing room went hand in hand with the emergence of polite society and the general attempt to civilize a rough military nobility. Similarly, some philosophes championed greater rights and expanded education for women, claiming that the position and treatment of women were the best indicators of a society's level of civilization and decency.[16] For these male philosophes, greater rights for women did not mean equal rights, and the philosophes were not particularly disturbed by the fact that elite women remained legally subordinate to men in economic and political affairs. Elite women lacked many rights, but so did the majority of European men, who were poor.

While membership at the salons was restricted to the well-born, the well-connected, and the exceptionally talented, a number of institutions emerged for the rest of society. Lending libraries served an important function for people who could not afford their own books. The coffeehouses that first appeared in the late seventeenth century became meccas of philosophical discussion. (See "Living in the Past: Coffeehouse Culture," page 538.) In addition to these institutions, book clubs, Masonic lodges (groups of Freemasons, a secret egalitarian society that existed across Europe), and journals all played roles in the creation of a new **public sphere** that celebrated open debate informed by critical reason. The public sphere was an idealized space where members of society came together as individuals to discuss issues relevant to the society, economics, and politics of the day.

What of the common people? Did they participate in the Enlightenment? Enlightenment philosophes did not direct their message to peasants or urban laborers. They believed that the masses had no time or talent for philosophical speculation and that elevating them would be a long, slow, potentially dangerous process. Deluded by superstitions and driven by violent passions, they thought, the people were like little children in need of firm parental guidance. D'Alembert characteristically made a sharp distinction between "the truly enlightened public" and "the blind and noisy multitude."[17]

There is some evidence, however, that the people were not immune to the words of the philosophes. At a time of rising literacy, book prices were dropping in cities and towns, and many philosophical ideas were popularized in cheap pamphlets. Moreover, even illiterate people had access to written material through the practice of public reading. Although they were barred from salons and academies, ordinary people were not immune to the new ideas in circulation.

Race and the Enlightenment

If philosophers did not believe the lower classes qualified for enlightenment, how did they regard individuals of different races? In recent years, historians have found in the scientific revolution and the Enlightenment a crucial turning point in European ideas about race. A primary catalyst for new ideas about race was the urge to classify nature unleashed by the scientific revolution's insistence on careful empirical observation. In *The System of Nature* (1735) Swedish botanist Carl von Linné argued that nature was organized into a God-given hierarchy. As scientists developed more elaborate taxonomies of plant and animal species, they also began to classify humans into hierarchically ordered "races" and to investigate the origins of race. The Comte de Buffon (komt duh buh-FOHN) argued that humans originated with one species that then developed into distinct races due largely to climatic conditions.

Enlightenment thinkers such as David Hume and Immanuel Kant (see page 541) helped popularize these ideas. In *Of Natural Characters* (1748), Hume wrote:

> I am apt to suspect the negroes and in general all other species of men (for there are four or five different kinds) to be naturally inferior to the whites. There never was a civilized nation of any other complexion than white, nor even any individual eminent amongst them, no arts, no sciences. . . . Such a uniform and constant difference could not happen, in so many countries and ages if nature had not made an original distinction between these breeds of men.[18]

Kant taught and wrote as much about "anthropology" and "geography" as he did about standard philosophical themes such as logic, metaphysics, and moral philosophy. He shared and elaborated Hume's views about race in *On the Different Races of Man* (1775), claiming that there were four human races, each of which had derived from a supposedly original race of "white brunette" people. According to Kant, the closest descendants of the original race were the white inhabitants of northern Germany. In deriving new physical characteristics, the other races had degenerated both physically and culturally from this origin. (Scientists now believe humans originated in Africa.)

rococo A popular style in Europe in the eighteenth century, known for its soft pastels, ornate interiors, sentimental portraits, and starry-eyed lovers protected by hovering cupids.

public sphere An idealized intellectual space that emerged in Europe during the Enlightenment, where the public came together to discuss important issues relating to society, economics, and politics.

Coffeehouse Culture

LIVING IN THE PAST

CUSTOMERS IN TODAY'S COFFEE SHOPS may be surprised to learn that they are participating in a centuries-old institution that has contributed a great deal to the idea of "modernity." Tradition has it that an Ethiopian goatherd first discovered coffee when he noticed that his goats became frisky and danced after consuming the berries. Botanists agree that coffee probably originated in Ethiopia and then spread to Yemen and across the Arabian peninsula by around 1000 C.E. In 1457, the first public coffeehouse opened in Istanbul, and from there coffeehouses became a popular institution throughout the Muslim world.

European travelers in Istanbul were astonished at its inhabitants' passion for coffee, which one described as "blacke as soote, and tasting not much unlike it."* However, Italian merchants introduced coffee to Europe around 1600, and the first European coffee shop opened in Venice in 1645, soon followed by shops in Oxford, England, in 1650, London in 1652, and Paris in 1672. By the 1730s, coffee shops had become so popular in London that one observer noted, "There are some people of moderate Fortunes, that lead their Lives mostly in Coffee-Houses, they eat, drink and sleep (in the Day-time) in them."†

Coffeehouses helped spread the ideas and values of the scientific revolution and the Enlightenment. They provided a new public space where urban Europeans could learn about and debate the issues of the day. Open to all social classes, they were a rare equalizing force in highly unequal societies. Within a few years, each political party, philosophical sect, scientific society, and literary circle had its own coffeehouse, which served as a central gathering point for

Seventeenth-century English coffeehouse. (The Granger Collection, NY)

*Quoted in Markman Ellis, *The Coffee-House: A Cultural History* (London: Phoenix, 2004), p. 8.

†Quoted ibid, p. 198.

its members and an informal recruiting site for new ones.

European coffeehouses also played a key role in the development of modern business, as their proprietors began to provide specialized business news to attract customers. Lloyd's of London, the famous insurance house, got its start in the shipping lists published by coffeehouse owner Edward Lloyd in the 1690s. The streets around London's stock exchange were crowded with coffeehouses where merchants and traders congregated to strike deals and hear the latest news.

Coffeehouses succeeded in Europe because they met a need common to politics, business, and intellectual life: the spread and sharing of information. In the late seventeenth century, newspapers were rare and expensive; there were no banks to guarantee credit; and politics was limited to a tiny elite. To break through these constraints, people needed reliable information. The coffeehouse was an ideal place to acquire it, along with a new kind of stimulant that provided the energy and attention to fuel a lively discussion.

QUESTIONS FOR ANALYSIS

1. What do these images suggest about the customers of eighteenth-century coffeehouses? Who frequented these establishments? Who was excluded?

2. What limitations on the exchange of information existed in early modern Europe? Why were coffeehouses so useful as sites for exchanging information?

3. What social role do coffeehouses play where you live? Do you see any continuities with the eighteenth-century coffeehouse?

Eighteenth-century Viennese coffeehouse. (Erich Lessing/Art Resource, NY)

Using the word *race* to designate biologically distinct groups of humans, akin to distinct animal species, was new. Previously, Europeans grouped other peoples into "nations" based on their historical, political, and cultural affiliations, rather than on supposedly innate physical differences. Unsurprisingly, when European thinkers drew up a hierarchical classification of human species, their own "race" was placed at the top. Europeans had long believed they were culturally superior to "barbaric" peoples in Africa and, since 1492, the New World. Now emerging ideas about racial difference taught them they were biologically superior as well. In turn, scientific racism helped legitimate and justify the tremendous growth of slavery that occurred during the eighteenth century. If one "race" of humans was fundamentally different and inferior, its members could be seen as particularly fit for enslavement and liable to benefit from tutelage by the superior race.

Racist ideas did not go unchallenged. *Encyclopedia* editor Denis Diderot penned a scathing critique of Euro-pean arrogance and exploitation in the voice of Tahitian villagers. (See "Listening to the Past: Denis Diderot's 'Supplement to Bougainville's Voyage,'" page 542.) Scottish philosopher James Beattie (1735–1803) responded directly to claims of white superiority by pointing out that Europeans had started out as savage as nonwhites and that many non-European peoples in the Americas, Asia, and Africa had achieved high levels of civilization. German thinker Johann Gottfried von Herder (1744–1803) criticized Kant, arguing that humans could not be classified into races based on skin color and that each culture was as intrinsically worthy as any other. These challenges to ideas of racial inequality, however, were in the minority. Many other Enlightenment voices agreeing with Kant and Hume — Thomas Jefferson among them — may be found.

Scholars are only at the beginning of efforts to understand links between Enlightenment ideas about race and its notions of equality, progress, and reason. There are clear parallels, though, between the use of science to

Encyclopedia **Image of the Cotton Industry** This romanticized image of slavery in the West Indies cotton industry was published in Diderot and d'Alembert's *Encyclopedia*. It shows enslaved men, at right, gathering and picking over cotton bolls, while the woman at left mills the bolls to remove their seeds. The *Encyclopedia* presented mixed views on slavery; one article described it as "indispensable" to economic development, while others argued passionately for the natural right to freedom of all mankind. (Courtesy, Dover Publications)

propagate racial hierarchies and its use to defend social inequalities between men and women. French philosopher Jean-Jacques Rousseau used women's "natural" passivity to argue for their passive role in society, just as other thinkers used non-Europeans' "natural" inferiority to defend slavery and colonial domination. The new powers of science and reason were thus marshaled to imbue traditional stereotypes with the force of natural law.

Late Enlightenment

After about 1770 a number of thinkers and writers began to attack the Enlightenment's faith in reason, progress, and moderation. The most famous of these was the Swiss Jean-Jacques Rousseau (1712–1778), the son of a poor watchmaker who made his way into the world of Paris salons through his brilliant intellect. Appealing but neurotic, Rousseau came to believe that his philosophe friends and the women of the Parisian salons were plotting against him. In the mid-1750s he broke with them, living thereafter as a lonely outsider with his uneducated common-law wife and going in his own highly original direction.

Like other Enlightenment thinkers, Rousseau was passionately committed to individual freedom. Unlike them, however, he attacked rationalism and civilization as destroying, rather than liberating, the individual. Warm, spontaneous feeling had to complement and correct cold intellect. Moreover, the basic goodness of the individual and the unspoiled child had to be protected from the cruel refinements of civilization. Rousseau's ideals greatly influenced the early romantic movement, which rebelled against the culture of the Enlightenment in the late eighteenth century.

Echoing Montesquieu's critique of women's influence in public affairs, Rousseau called for a rigid division of gender roles. According to Rousseau, women and men were radically different beings. Destined by nature to assume a passive role in sexual relations, women should also be passive in social life. Women's love for displaying themselves in public, attending salons, and pulling the strings of power was unnatural and had a corrupting effect on both politics and society. Rousseau thus rejected the sophisticated way of life of Parisian elite women. His criticism led to broader calls for privileged women to renounce their frivolous ways and stay at home to care for their children.

Rousseau's contribution to political theory in *The Social Contract* (1762) drew less attention at first but proved to be highly significant. His contribution was based on two fundamental concepts: the general will and popular sovereignty. According to Rousseau, the general will is sacred and absolute, reflecting the common interests of all the people, who have displaced the monarch as the holder of sovereign power. The general will is not necessarily the will of the majority, however. At times the general will may be the authentic, long-term needs of the people as correctly interpreted by a farseeing minority. Little noticed before the French Revolution, Rousseau's concept of the general will appealed greatly to democrats and nationalists after 1789. (The concept has since been abused by dictators who have claimed that they, rather than some momentary majority of voters, represent the general will.) Rousseau was both one of the most influential voices of the Enlightenment and, in his rejection of rationalism and social discourse, a harbinger of reaction against Enlightenment ideas.

As the reading public developed, it joined forces with the philosophes to call for the autonomy of the printed word. Immanuel Kant (1724–1804), a professor in East Prussia and the greatest German philosopher of his day, posed the question of the age when he published a pamphlet in 1784 entitled *What Is Enlightenment?* Kant answered, "*Sapere Aude* (dare to know)! 'Have the courage to use your own understanding' is therefore the motto of enlightenment." He argued that if serious thinkers were granted the freedom to exercise their reason publicly in print, enlightenment would almost surely follow. Kant was no revolutionary; he also insisted that in their private lives, individuals must obey all laws, no matter how unreasonable, and should be punished for "impertinent" criticism. Kant thus tried to reconcile absolute monarchical authority with a critical public sphere. This balancing act characterized experiments with "enlightened absolutism" in the eighteenth century.

Enlightened Absolutism

What impact did new ways of thinking have on political developments and monarchical absolutism?

How did the Enlightenment influence political developments? To this important question there is no easy answer. Most Enlightenment thinkers outside of England and the Netherlands, especially in central and eastern Europe, believed that political change could best come from above—from the ruler—rather than from below. Royal absolutism was a fact of life, and the kings and queens of Europe's leading states clearly had no intention of giving up their great power. Therefore, the philosophes and their sympathizers realistically concluded that a benevolent absolutism offered the best opportunities for improving society.

Many government officials were interested in philosophical ideas. They were among the best-educated members of society, and their daily involvement in complex affairs of state made them naturally attracted to ideas for improving human society. Encouraged and instructed

LISTENING TO THE PAST

Denis Diderot (1713–1784) was born in a provincial town in eastern France and educated in Paris. Rejecting careers in the church and the law, he devoted himself to literature and philosophy. In 1749, sixty years before Charles Darwin's birth, Diderot was jailed by Parisian authorities for publishing an essay questioning God's role in the creation and suggesting the autonomous evolution of species. Following these difficult beginnings,

Diderot's editorial work and writing on the Encyclopedia *were the crowning intellectual achievements of his life and, according to some, of the Enlightenment itself.*

Like other philosophes, Diderot employed numerous genres to disseminate Enlightenment thought, ranging from scholarly articles in the Encyclopedia *to philosophical treatises, novels, plays, book reviews, and erotic stories. His "Supplement to Bougainville's Voyage" (1772) was a fictional account of a European voyage to Tahiti inspired by the writings of traveler Louis-Antoine de Bougainville. In this passage, Diderot expresses his own loathing of colonial conquest and exploitation through the voice of an elderly Tahitian man. The character's praise for his own culture allows Diderot to express his Enlightenment idealization of "natural man," free from the vices of civilized societies.*

❝ He was the father of a numerous family. At the time of the Europeans' arrival, he cast upon them a look that was filled with scorn, though it revealed no surprise, no alarm and no curiosity. They approached him; he turned his back on them and retired into his hut. His thoughts were only too well revealed by his silence and his air of concern, for in the privacy of his thoughts he groaned inwardly over the happy days of his people, now gone forever. At the moment of Bougainville's departure, when all the natives ran swarming onto the beach, tugging at his clothing and throwing their arms around his companions and weeping, the old man stepped forward and solemnly spoke:

"Weep, wretched Tahitians, weep — but rather for the arrival than for the departure of these wicked and grasping men! The day will come when you will know them for what they are. Someday they will return, bearing in one hand that piece of wood you see suspended from this one's belt and in the other the

piece of steel that hangs at the side of his companions. They will load you with chains, slit your throats and enslave you to their follies and vices. Someday you will be slaves to them, you will be as corrupt, as vile, as wretched as they are. . . ."

Then, turning to Bougainville, he went on: "And you, leader of these brigands who obey you, take your vessel swiftly from our shores. We are innocent and happy, and you can only spoil our happiness. We follow the pure instinct of nature, and you have tried to efface her imprint from our hearts. Here all things

This image depicts the meeting of French explorer Louis-Antoine de Bougainville with Tahitians in April 1768. Of his stay on the island, Bougainville wrote: "I felt as though I had been transported to the Garden of Eden. . . . Everywhere reigned hospitality, peace, joy, and every appearance of happiness." Diderot's philosophical tract was a fictional sequel to Bougainville's account.

(Unknown artist, Tahitians presenting fruit to Bougainville attended by his officers. PIC T2996 NK5066 LOC7321, National Library of Australia)

are for all, and you have preached to us I know not what distinctions between mine and thine. . . .

". . . You are not slaves; you would suffer death rather than be enslaved, yet you want to make slaves of us! Do you believe, then, that the Tahitian does not know how to die in defense of his liberty? This Tahitian, whom you want to treat as a chattel, as a dumb animal—this Tahitian is your brother. You are both children of Nature—what right do you have over him that he does not have over you?

"You came; did we attack you? Did we plunder your vessel? Did we seize you and expose you to the arrows of our enemies? Did we force you to work in the fields alongside our beasts of burden? We respected our own image in you. Leave us our own customs, which are wiser and more decent than yours. We have no wish to barter what you call our ignorance for your useless knowledge. We possess already all that is good or necessary for our existence. Do we merit your scorn because we have not been able to create superfluous wants for ourselves? When we are hungry, we have something to eat; when we are cold, we have clothing to put on. You have been in our huts—what is lacking there, in your opinion? You are welcome to drive yourselves as hard as you please in pursuit of what you call the comforts of life, but allow sensible people to stop when they see they have nothing to gain but imaginary benefits from the continuation of their painful labors. If you persuade us to go beyond the bounds of strict necessity, when shall we come to the end of our labor? When shall we have time for enjoyment? We have reduced our daily and yearly labors to the least possible amount, because to us nothing seemed more desirable than leisure. Go and bestir yourselves in your own country; there you may torment yourselves as much as you like; but leave us in peace, and do not fill our heads with a hankering after your false needs and imaginary virtues." »

Source: From Denis Diderot, *Supplement to Bougainville's Voyage*, edited by Jacques Barzun (Upper Saddle River, N.J.: Prentice-Hall, 1965. © 2010 by Jacques Barzun. All rights reserved, c/o Writers Representatives LLC, New York, NY, 10011, permissions@writersrep.com.

QUESTIONS FOR ANALYSIS

1. On what grounds does the speaker argue for the Tahitians' basic equality with the Europeans?

2. What is the good life according to the speaker, and how does it contrast with the European way of life? Which do you think is the better path?

3. In what ways could Diderot's thoughts here be seen as representative of Enlightenment ideas? Are there ways in which they are not?

4. How realistic do you think this account is? How might defenders of expansion respond?

by these officials, some absolutist rulers tried to reform their governments in accordance with Enlightenment ideals—what historians have often called the **enlightened absolutism** of the later eighteenth century. The most influential of the new-style monarchs were in Prussia, Russia, and Austria. Their example illustrates both the achievements and the great limitations of enlightened absolutism.

> **enlightened absolutism** Term coined by historians to describe the rule of eighteenth-century monarchs who, without renouncing their own absolute authority, adopted Enlightenment ideals of rationalism, progress, and tolerance.

Frederick the Great of Prussia

Frederick II (r. 1740–1786), commonly known as Frederick the Great, built masterfully on the work of his father, Frederick William I (see Chapter 16). Although in his youth he embraced culture and literature rather than the crude life of the barracks championed by his father, by the time he came to the throne Frederick was determined to use the splendid army that his father had left him.

Therefore, when the young Maria Theresa of Austria inherited the Habsburg dominions upon the death of her father Charles VI, Frederick pounced. He invaded her rich, mainly German province of Silesia (sigh-LEE-zhuh), defying solemn Prussian promises to respect the Pragmatic Sanction, a diplomatic agreement that had guaranteed Maria Theresa's succession. In 1742, as other greedy powers vied for her lands in the European War of the Austrian Succession (1740–1748), Maria Theresa was forced to cede almost all of Silesia to Prussia. In one stroke Prussia had doubled its population to 6 million people. Now Prussia unquestionably towered above all the other German states and stood as a European Great Power.

Though successful in 1742, Frederick had to fight against great odds to save Prussia from total destruction after the ongoing competition between Britain and France for colonial empire brought another great conflict in 1756. Maria Theresa, seeking to regain Silesia, formed an alliance with the leaders of France and Russia. The aim of the alliance during the resulting Seven Years' War (1756–1763) was to conquer Prussia and divide

The War of the Austrian Succession, 1740–1748

Prussia, 1740
Prussian gains, 1742
Austria, 1740
Boundary of the Holy Roman Empire

Königsberg
Berlin
POLAND
SILESIA
Prague
Vienna
AUSTRIA
HUNGARY

❝ I must enlighten my people, cultivate their manners and morals, and make them as happy as human beings can be, or as happy as the means at my disposal permit. **❞**

—FREDERICK THE GREAT

up its territory. Despite invasions from all sides, Frederick fought on with stoic courage. In the end he was miraculously saved: Peter III came to the Russian throne in 1762 and called off the attack against Frederick, whom he greatly admired.

The terrible struggle of the Seven Years' War tempered Frederick's interest in territorial expansion and brought him to consider how more humane policies for his subjects might also strengthen the state. Thus Frederick went beyond a superficial commitment to Enlightenment culture for himself and his circle. He tolerantly allowed his subjects to believe as they wished in religious and philosophical matters. He promoted the advancement of knowledge, improving his country's schools and permitting scholars to publish their findings. Moreover, Frederick tried to improve the lives of his subjects more directly. As he wrote his friend Voltaire, "I must enlighten my people, cultivate their manners and morals, and make them as happy as human beings can be, or as happy as the means at my disposal permit."

The legal system and the bureaucracy were Frederick's primary tools. Prussia's laws were simplified, torture of prisoners was abolished, and judges decided cases quickly and impartially. Prussian officials became famous for their hard work and honesty. After the Seven Years' War ended in 1763, Frederick's government energetically promoted the reconstruction of agriculture and industry in his war-torn country. Frederick himself set a good example. He worked hard and lived modestly, claiming that he was "only the first servant of the state." Thus Frederick justified monarchy in terms of practical results and said nothing of the divine right of kings.

Frederick's dedication to high-minded government went only so far, however. While he condemned serfdom in the abstract, he accepted it in practice and did not free the serfs on his own estates. He accepted and extended the privileges of the nobility, who remained the backbone of the army and the entire Prussian state.

In reforming Prussia's bureaucracy, Frederick drew on the principles of **cameralism**, the German science of public administration

cameralism View that monarchy was the best form of government, that all elements of society should serve the monarch, and that, in turn, the state should use its resources and authority to increase the public good.

that emerged in the decades following the Thirty Years' War. Influential throughout the German lands, cameralism held that monarchy was the best of all forms of government, that all elements of society should be placed at the service of the state, and that, in turn, the state should make use of its resources and authority to improve society. Predating the Enlightenment, cameralist interest in the public good was usually inspired by the needs of war. Cameralism shared with the Enlightenment an emphasis on rationality, progress, and utilitarianism; in the eighteenth century, they overlapped a lot.

Catherine the Great of Russia

Catherine the Great of Russia (r. 1762–1796) was one of the most remarkable rulers of her age, and the French philosophes adored her. Catherine was a German princess from Anhalt-Zerbst, an insignificant principality sandwiched between Prussia and Saxony. Her father commanded a regiment of the Prussian army, but her mother was related to the Romanovs of Russia, and that proved to be Catherine's opening to power.

At the age of fifteen Catherine's Romanov connection made her a suitable bride for the heir to the Russian throne. It was a mismatch from the beginning, but her *Memoirs* made her ambitions clear: "I did not care about Peter, but I did care about the crown." When her husband Peter III came to power during the Seven Year's War, his decision to withdraw Russian troops from the coalition against Prussia alienated the army. Catherine profited from his unpopularity to form a conspiracy to depose her husband. In 1762 Catherine's lover Gregory Orlov and his three brothers, all army officers, murdered Peter, and the German princess became empress of Russia.

Catherine had drunk deeply at the Enlightenment well. Never questioning that absolute monarchy was the best form of government, she set out to rule in an enlightened manner. She had three main goals. First, she worked hard to continue Peter the Great's effort to bring the culture of western Europe to Russia (see Chapter 16). To do so, she imported Western architects, sculptors, musicians, and intellectuals. She bought masterpieces of Western art and patronized the philosophes. An enthusiastic letter writer, she corresponded extensively with Voltaire and praised him as the "champion of the human race." When the French government banned the *Encyclopedia*, she offered to publish it in St. Petersburg, and she sent money to Diderot when he needed it. With these actions, Catherine won good press in the West for herself and for her country. Moreover, this intellectual ruler, who wrote plays and loved good talk, set the tone for the entire Russian nobility. Peter the Great westernized Russian armies, but it was Catherine who westernized the imagination of the Russian nobility.

Catherine the Great Strongly influenced by the Enlightenment, Catherine the Great cultivated the French philosophes and instituted moderate reforms, only to reverse them in the aftermath of Pugachev's rebellion. This equestrian portrait now hangs above her throne in the palace throne room in St. Petersburg. (Musée des Beaux-Arts, Chartres/The Bridgeman Art Library)

Catherine's second goal was domestic reform, and she began her reign with sincere and ambitious projects. In 1767 she appointed a special legislative commission to prepare a new law code. This project was never completed, but Catherine did restrict the practice of torture and allowed limited religious toleration. She also tried to improve education and strengthen local government. The philosophes applauded these measures and hoped more would follow.

Such was not the case. In 1773 a common Cossack soldier named Emelian Pugachev sparked a gigantic uprising of serfs, very much as Stenka Razin had done a century earlier (see Chapter 16). Proclaiming himself the true tsar, Pugachev issued orders abolishing serfdom, taxes, and army service. Thousands joined his cause, slaughtering landlords and officials over a vast area of southwestern Russia. Pugachev's untrained forces eventually proved no match for Catherine's noble-led army. Betrayed by his own company, Pugachev was captured and savagely executed.

Pugachev's rebellion put an end to any intentions Catherine might have had about reforming the system. The peasants were clearly dangerous, and her empire rested on the support of the nobility. After 1775 Catherine gave the nobles absolute control of their serfs, and she extended serfdom into new areas, such as Ukraine. In 1785 she formalized the nobility's privileged position, freeing nobles forever from taxes and state service. Under Catherine the Russian nobility attained its most exalted position, and serfdom entered its most oppressive phase.

Catherine's third goal was territorial expansion, and in this respect she was extremely successful. Her armies subjugated the last descendants of the Mongols and the Crimean Tartars, and began the conquest of the Caucasus (KAW-kuh-suhs). Her greatest coup by far was the partition of Poland (Map 17.1). When, between 1768 and 1772, Catherine's armies scored unprecedented victories against the Turks and thereby threatened to disturb the balance of power between Russia and Austria in eastern Europe, Frederick of Prussia obligingly came forward with a deal. He proposed that Turkey be let off easily and that Prussia, Austria, and Russia each compensate itself by taking a gigantic slice of the weakly ruled Polish territory. Catherine jumped at the chance. The first partition of Poland took place in 1772. Subsequent

KINGDOM OF SWEDEN

KINGDOM OF DENMARK AND NORWAY

FINLAND

Gulf of Finland

St. Petersburg

ESTONIA

LIVONIA

RUSSIA

Moscow

Baltic Sea

Riga

Smolensk

Königsberg

Vilna

Danzig

PRUSSIA

BRANDENBURG

Berlin

POLAND

Elbe R.

Oder R.

Warsaw

Lublin

UKRAINE

SAXONY

Dresden

SILESIA

Kraków

Kiev

HOLY ROMAN EMPIRE

BOHEMIA

Danube R.

GALICIA

Vienna

AUSTRIAN EMPIRE

HUNGARY

Sea of Azov

Venice

CROATIA

CRIMEA

OTTOMAN EMPIRE

Danube R.

Black Sea

Poland in 1772

To Austria

| 1772 | 1795 |

To Prussia

| 1772 | 1793 | 1795 |

To Russia

| 1772 | 1793 | 1795 |

0   150   300 miles
0   150   300 kilometers

Mapping the Past

Map 17.1 **The Partition of Poland, 1772–1795** In 1772 war between Russia and Austria threatened over Russian gains from the Ottoman Empire. To satisfy desires for expansion without fighting, Prussia's Frederick the Great proposed that parts of Poland be divided among Austria, Prussia, and Russia. In 1793 and 1795 the three powers partitioned the remainder, and the ancient republic of Poland vanished from the map.

ANALYZING THE MAP Of the three powers that divided the kingdom of Poland, which benefited the most? How did the partition affect the geographical boundaries of each state, and what was the significance? What border with the former Poland remained unchanged? Why do you think this was the case?

CONNECTIONS Why was Poland vulnerable to partition in the latter half of the eighteenth century? What does it say about European politics at the time that a country could simply cease to exist on the map? Could that happen today?

To complete this activity online, go to the Online Study Guide at bedfordstmartins.com/mckaywest.

partitions in 1793 and 1795 gave away the rest of Polish territory, and the ancient republic of Poland vanished from the map.

The Austrian Habsburgs

Another female monarch, Maria Theresa (r. 1740–1780) of Austria, set out to reform her nation, although traditional power politics was a more important motivation for her than were Enlightenment teachings. A devout mother and wife who inherited power from her

father, Charles VI, Maria Theresa was a remarkable but old-fashioned absolutist. Her more radical son, Joseph II (r. 1780–1790), drew on Enlightenment ideals, earning the title of "revolutionary emperor."

Emerging from the long War of the Austrian Succession in 1748 with the serious loss of Silesia, Maria Theresa was determined to introduce reforms that would make the state stronger and more efficient. First, she introduced measures aimed at limiting the papacy's political influence in her realm. Second, a whole series of administrative reforms strengthened the central

Maria Theresa The empress and her husband pose with twelve of their sixteen children at Schönbrunn palace in this family portrait by court painter Martin Meytens (1695–1770). Joseph, the heir to the throne, stands at the center of the star on the floor. Wealthy women often had very large families, in part because they, unlike poor women, seldom nursed their babies. (Réunion des Musées Nationaux/Art Resource, NY)

bureaucracy, smoothed out some provincial differences, and revamped the tax system, taxing even the lands of nobles, previously exempt from taxation. Third, the government sought to improve the lot of the agricultural population, cautiously reducing the power of lords over their hereditary serfs and their partially free peasant tenants.

Coregent with his mother from 1765 onward and a strong supporter of change, Joseph II moved forward rapidly when he came to the throne in 1780. Most notably, Joseph abolished serfdom in 1781, and in 1789 he decreed that peasants could pay landlords in cash rather than through compulsory labor on their land. This measure was violently rejected not only by the nobility but also by the peasants it was intended to help, because they lacked the necessary cash. When a disillusioned

Joseph died prematurely at forty-nine, the entire Habsburg empire was in turmoil. His brother Leopold II (r. 1790–1792) canceled Joseph's radical edicts in order to re-establish order. Peasants once again were required to do forced labor for their lords.

Despite differences, Joseph II and the other eastern European absolutists of the later eighteenth century combined old-fashioned state-building with the culture and critical thinking of the Enlightenment. In doing so, they succeeded in expanding the role of the state in the life of society. They perfected bureaucratic machines that were to prove surprisingly adaptive and capable of enduring into the twentieth century. Their failure to implement policies we would recognize as humane and enlightened—such as abolishing serfdom—may reveal inherent limitations in Enlightenment

Moses Mendelssohn and the Jewish Enlightenment

INDIVIDUALS IN SOCIETY

IN 1743 A SMALL, HUMPBACKED JEWISH BOY with a stammer left his poor parents in Dessau (DE-sow) in central Germany and walked eighty miles to Berlin, the capital of Frederick the Great's Prussia. According to one story, when the boy reached the Rosenthaler (ROH-zuhn-taw-lehr) Gate, the only one through which Jews could pass, he told the inquiring watchman that his name was Moses and that he had come to Berlin "to learn." The watchman laughed and waved him through. "Go Moses, the sea has opened before you."*

In Berlin the young Mendelssohn studied Jewish law and eked out a living copying Hebrew manuscripts in a beautiful hand. But he was soon fascinated by an intellectual world that had been closed to him in the Dessau ghetto. There, like most Jews throughout central Europe, he had spoken Yiddish—a mixture of German, Polish, and Hebrew. Now, working mainly on his own, he mastered German; learned Latin, Greek, French, and English; and studied mathematics and Enlightenment philosophy. Word of his exceptional abilities spread in Berlin's Jewish community (the dwelling of 1,500 of the city's 100,000 inhabitants). He began tutoring the children of a wealthy Jewish silk merchant, and he soon became the merchant's clerk and later his partner. But his great passion remained the life of the mind and the spirit, which he avidly pursued in his off hours.

Gentle and unassuming in his personal life, Mendelssohn was a bold thinker. Reading eagerly in Western philosophy since antiquity, he was, as a pious Jew, soon convinced that Enlightenment teachings need not be opposed to Jewish thought and religion. He concluded that reason could complement and strengthen religion, although each would retain its integrity as a separate sphere.† Developing his idea in his first great work, "On the Immortality of the Soul" (1767), Mendelssohn used the neutral setting of a philosophical dialogue between Socrates and his followers in ancient Greece to argue that the human soul lived forever. In refusing to bring religion and critical thinking into conflict, he was strongly influenced by contemporary German philosophers who argued similarly on behalf of Christianity. He reflected the way the German Enlightenment generally supported established religion, in contrast to the French Enlightenment, which attacked it.

Mendelssohn's treatise on the human soul captivated the educated German public, which marveled that a Jew could have written a philosophical masterpiece. In the excitement, a Christian zealot named Lavater challenged Mendelssohn in a pamphlet to accept Christianity or to demonstrate how the Christian faith was not "reasonable." Replying politely but passionately, the Jewish philosopher affirmed that his studies had only strengthened him in his faith, although he did not seek to convert anyone not born into Judaism. Rather, he urged toleration in religious matters and spoke up courageously against Jewish oppression.

Orthodox Jew and German philosophe, Moses Mendelssohn serenely combined two very different worlds. He built a bridge from the ghetto to the dominant culture over which many Jews would pass, including his novelist daughter Dorothea and his famous grandson, the composer Felix Mendelssohn.

QUESTIONS FOR ANALYSIS

1. How did Mendelssohn seek to influence Jewish religious thought in his time?

2. How do Mendelssohn's ideas compare with those of the French Enlightenment?

Lavater (right) attempts to convert Mendelssohn, in a painting of an imaginary encounter by Moritz Oppenheim. (Collection of the Judah L. Magnes Museum, Berkeley)

*H. Kupferberg, *The Mendelssohns: Three Generations of Genius* (New York: Charles Scribner's Sons, 1972), p. 3.

†D. Sorkin, *Moses Mendelssohn and the Religious Enlightenment* (Berkeley: University of California Press, 1996), pp. 8 ff.

thinking about equality and social justice, rather than in their execution of Enlightenment programs. The fact that leading philosophes supported rather than criticized eastern rulers' policies suggests some of the blinders of the era.

Jewish Life and the Limits of Enlightened Absolutism

Perhaps the best example of the limitations of enlightened absolutism are the debates surrounding the possible emancipation of the Jews. Europe's small Jewish populations lived under highly discriminatory laws. For the most part, Jews were confined to tiny, overcrowded ghettos, were excluded by law from most business and professional activities, and could be ordered out of a kingdom at a moment's notice. Still, a very few did manage to succeed and to obtain the right of permanent settlement, usually by performing some special service for the state. Many rulers relied on Jewish bankers for loans to raise armies and run their kingdoms. Because of their large and closely knit diaspora, Jewish merchants and traders were prominent in international trade.

In the eighteenth century, an Enlightenment movement known as the **Haskalah** emerged from within the European Jewish community, led by the Prussian philosopher Moses Mendelssohn (1729–1786). (See "Individuals in Society: Moses Mendelssohn and the Jewish Enlightenment," at left.) Christian and Jewish Enlightenment philosophers, including Mendelssohn, began to advocate for freedom and civil rights for European Jews. In an era of reason, tolerance, and universality, they argued, restrictions on religious grounds could not stand. The Haskalah accompanied a period of controversial social change within Jewish communities, in which rabbinic controls loosened and heightened interaction with Christians took place.

Arguments for tolerance won some ground. The British Parliament passed a law allowing naturalization of Jews in 1753, but later repealed the law due to public outrage. The most progressive reforms took place under Austrian emperor Joseph II. Among his liberal edicts of the 1780s were measures intended to integrate Jews more fully into society, including eligibility for military service, admission to higher education and artisanal trades, and removal of requirements for special clothing or emblems. Welcomed by many Jews, these reforms raised fears among traditionalists of assimilation into the general population.

Many monarchs refused to entertain the idea of emancipation. Although he permitted freedom of religion to his Christian subjects, Frederick the Great of Prussia firmly opposed any general emancipation for the Jews, as he did for the serfs. Catherine the Great, who acquired most of Poland's large Jewish population when she annexed part of that country in the late eighteenth century, similarly refused. In 1791 she established the Pale of Settlement, a territory including parts of modern-day Poland, Latvia, Lithuania, Ukraine, and Belorussia, in which most Jews were required to live. Jewish habitation was restricted to the Pale until the Russian Revolution in 1917.

The first European state to remove all restrictions on the Jews was France under the French Revolution. Over the next hundred years, Jews gradually won full legal and civil rights throughout the rest of western Europe. Emancipation in eastern Europe took even longer and aroused more conflict and violence.

Haskalah The Jewish Enlightenment of the second half of the eighteenth century, led by the Prussian philosopher Moses Mendelssohn.

The Pale of Settlement, 1791

LOOKING BACK LOOKING AHEAD

HAILED AS THE ORIGIN of modern thought, the scientific revolution must also be seen as a product of its past. Medieval universities gave rise to important new scholarship, and the ambition and wealth of Renaissance patrons nurtured intellectual curiosity. Religious faith also impacted the scientific revolution, inspiring thinkers to understand the glory of God's creation, while bringing censure and personal tragedy to others. Natural philosophers following Copernicus pioneered new methods of observing and explaining nature while drawing on centuries-old traditions of mysticism, astrology, alchemy, and magic.

The Enlightenment ideas of the eighteenth century were a similar blend of past and present; they could serve as much to bolster authoritarian regimes as to inspire revolutionaries to fight for individual rights and liberties. Although the Enlightenment fostered critical thinking about everything from science to religion, the majority of Europeans, including many prominent thinkers, remained devout Christians.

The achievements of the scientific revolution and the Enlightenment are undeniable. Key Western values of rationalism, human rights, and open-mindedness were born from these movements. With their new notions of progress and social improvement, Europeans would embark on important revolutions in industry and politics in the centuries that followed. Nonetheless, others have seen a darker side. For these critics, the mastery over nature permitted by the scientific revolution now threatens to overwhelm the earth's fragile equilibrium, and the Enlightenment belief in the universal application of reason can lead to arrogance and intolerance, particularly intolerance of other people's spiritual, cultural, and political values. Such vivid debate about the legacy of these intellectual and scientific developments testifies to their continuing importance in today's world.

CHAPTER REVIEW

■ What was revolutionary in the new attitudes toward the natural world? (p. 520)

Decisive breakthroughs in astronomy and physics in the seventeenth century demolished the medieval synthesis of Aristotelian philosophy and Christian theology. One of the most notable discoveries was that the sun, not the earth, was the center of the galaxy. Although the early scientists considered their ideas to be in line with religion, their discoveries ran counter to long-held beliefs about the design of the universe by the Creator; therefore, Copernicus, Kepler, Galileo, and others were branded as heretics. Meanwhile, Bacon promoted the experimental method that drew conclusions based on empirical evidence, and Descartes championed deductive reasoning that speculated truths based on known principles. These two important methods eventually combined to form the modern scientific method that relies on both experimentation and reason. Following these early innovators, Newton devised the law of universal gravitation, which for the first time synthesized the orbiting planets of the solar system with the motion of objects on earth. These scientific breakthroughs had only limited practical consequences at the time, but their impact on intellectual life was enormous, nurturing a new critical attitude in many disciplines. In addition, an international scientific community arose, and state-sponsored academies, which were typically closed to women, advanced scientific research.

■ How did the new worldview affect the way people thought about society and human relations? (p. 530)

Interpreting scientific findings and Newtonian laws in a manner that was both antitradition and antireligion, Enlightenment philosophes extolled the superiority of rational, critical thinking. This new method, they believed, promised not just increased knowledge but even the discovery of the fundamental laws of human society. Believing that all aspects of life were open to question and skepticism, Enlightenment thinkers opened the doors to religious tolerance, representative government, and general intellectual debate. One important downside of the new scientific method was that it led to the classification of human races, with white Europeans placing themselves at the top of a new racial hierarchy.

■ **What impact did new ways of thinking have on political developments and monarchical absolutism? (p. 541)**

The ideas of the Enlightenment were an inspiration for monarchs, particularly absolutist rulers in central and eastern Europe who saw in them important tools for reforming and rationalizing their governments. Their primary goal was to strengthen their states and increase the efficiency of their bureaucracies and armies. Enlightened absolutists believed that these reforms would ultimately improve the lot of ordinary people, but this was not their chief concern. With few exceptions, they did not question the institution of serfdom. The fact that leading philosophes supported rather than criticized Eastern rulers' policies suggests some of the limitations of the era. Christian and Jewish Enlightenment thinkers argued in favor of emancipating Europe's small Jewish population. Some reforms took place, but full emancipation did not take place until the nineteenth century in the West and even later in the East.

Suggested Reading

Alexander, John T. *Catherine the Great: Life and Legend*. 1989. The best biography of the famous Russian tsarina.

Beales, Derek. *Joseph II*. 1987. A fine biography of the reforming Habsburg ruler.

Delborgo, James, and Nicholas Dew, eds. *Science and Empire in the Atlantic World*. 2008. A collection of essays examining the relationship between the scientific revolution and the imperial expansion of European powers across the Atlantic.

Ellis, Markman. *The Coffee-House: A Cultural History*. 2004. An engaging study of the rise of the coffeehouse and its impact on European cultural and social life.

Eze, E. Chukwudi, ed. *Race and the Enlightenment: A Reader*. 1997. A pioneering source on the origins of modern racial thinking in the Enlightenment.

Goodman, Dena. *The Republic of Letters: A Cultural History of the Enlightenment*. 1994. An innovative study of the role of salons and salon hostesses in the rise of the Enlightenment.

MacDonogh, Giles. *Frederick the Great*. 2001. An outstanding biography of the Prussian king.

Osler, Margaret J., ed. *Rethinking the Scientific Revolution*. 2000. A collection of essays focusing on new historical approaches to the scientific revolution.

Outram, Dorinda. *The Enlightenment*, 2d ed. 2006. An outstanding and accessible introduction to Enlightenment debates that emphasizes the Enlightenment's social context and global reach.

Shapin, Steven. *The Scientific Revolution*. 2001. A concise and well-informed general introduction to the scientific revolution.

Sorkin, David. *Moses Mendelssohn and the Religious Enlightenment*. 1996. A brilliant study of the Jewish philosopher and of the role of religion in the Enlightenment.

Notes

1. H. Butterfield, *The Origins of Modern Science* (New York: Macmillan, 1951), p. viii.
2. Quoted in A. G. R. Smith, *Science and Society in the Sixteenth and Seventeenth Centuries* (New York: Harcourt Brace Jovanovich, 1972), p. 97.
3. Quoted in Butterfield, *The Origins of Modern Science*, p. 47.
4. Ibid., p. 120.
5. Quoted in John Freely, *Aladdin's Lamp: How Greek Science Came to Europe Through the Islamic World* (New York: Knopf, 2009), p. 206.
6. Ibid., p. 217.
7. Ibid., p. 225.
8. L. Schiebinger, *The Mind Has No Sex? Women in the Origins of Modern Science* (Cambridge, Mass.: Harvard University Press, 1989), p. 2.
9. Jacqueline Broad, *Women Philosophers of the Seventeenth Century* (Cambridge, U.K.: Cambridge University Press, 2003), p. 17.
10. Montesquieu, *Persian Letters*, trans. C. J. Betts (London: Penguin Books), 1993, p. 197.
11. Schiebinger, *The Mind Has No Sex?* p. 64.
12. Quoted in L. M. Marsak, ed., *The Enlightenment* (New York: John Wiley & Sons, 1972), p. 56.
13. Quoted in G. L. Mosse et al., eds., *Europe in Review* (Chicago: Rand McNally, 1964), p. 156.
14. Quoted in P. Gay, "The Unity of the Enlightenment," *History* 3 (1960): 25.
15. Quoted in G. P. Gooch, *Catherine the Great and Other Studies* (Hamden, Conn.: Archon Books, 1966), p. 149.
16. See E. Fox-Genovese, "Women in the Enlightenment," in *Becoming Visible: Women in European History*, 2d ed., ed. R. Bridenthal, C. Koonz, and S. Stuard (Boston: Houghton Mifflin, 1987), esp. pp. 252–259, 263–265.
17. Jean Le Rond d'Alembert, *Eloges lus dans les séances publiques de l'Académie française* (Paris, 1779), p. ix, quoted in Mona Ozouf, "'Public Opinion' at the End of the Old Regime," *The Journal of Modern History* 60, *Supplement: Rethinking French Politics in 1788* (September 1988): S9.
18. Quoted in Emmanuel Chukwudi Ezc, ed., *Race and the Enlightenment: A Reader* (Oxford: Blackwell, 1997), p. 33.

Key Terms

natural philosophy (p. 520)

Copernican hypothesis (p. 522)

experimental method (p. 524)

law of inertia (p. 524)

law of universal gravitation (p. 526)

empiricism (p. 526)

Cartesian dualism (p. 527)

Enlightenment (p. 530)

rationalism (p. 530)

philosophes (p. 531)

reading revolution (p. 535)

salons (p. 536)

rococo (p. 537)

public sphere (p. 537)

enlightened absolutism (p. 543)

cameralism (p. 544)

Haskalah (p. 549)

For practice quizzes and other study tools, visit the Online Study Guide at **bedfordstmartins.com/mckaywest**.

For primary sources from this period, see ***Sources of Western Society*, Second Edition**.

For Web sites, images, and documents related to topics in this chapter, visit Make History at **bedfordstmartins.com/mckaywest**.

18

The Expansion of Europe

1650–1800

Musée de la Marine Paris/Gianni Dagli Orti/The Art Archive

Absolutism and aristocracy, a combination of raw power and elegant refinement, were a world apart from the common people. For most people in the eighteenth century, life remained a struggle with poverty and uncertainty, with the landlord and the tax collector. In 1700 peasants on the land and artisans in their shops lived little better than had their ancestors in the Middle Ages, primarily because European societies still could not produce very much as measured by modern standards. Despite the hard work of ordinary men and women, there was seldom enough good food, warm clothing, and decent housing. The idea of progress, of substantial improvement in the lives of great numbers of people, was still the dream of only a small elite in fashionable salons.

Yet the economic basis of European life was beginning to change. In the course of the eighteenth century, the European economy emerged from the long crisis of the seventeenth century, responded to challenges, and began to expand once again. Population resumed its growth, while colonial empires developed and colonial elites prospered. Some areas were more fortunate than others. The rising Atlantic powers — Holland, France, and above all England — and their colonies led the way. The expansion of agriculture, industry, trade, and population marked the beginning of a surge comparable to that of the eleventh- and twelfth-century springtime of European civilization. But this time, broadly based expansion was not cut short by plague and famine. This time the response to new challenges led toward one of the most influential developments in human history, the Industrial Revolution, considered in Chapter 21. ■

Life in the Expanding Europe of the Eighteenth Century. The activities of the bustling cosmopolitan port of Marseilles were common to ports across Europe in the eighteenth century. Here a wealthy Frenchwoman greets a group of foreign merchants, while dockhands struggle to shift their heavy loads.

CHAPTER PREVIEW

Working the Land
■ What important developments led to the agricultural revolution, and how did these changes affect peasants?

The Beginning of the Population Explosion
■ Why did the European population rise dramatically in the eighteenth century?

The Growth of Rural Industry
■ How and why did rural industry intensify in the eighteenth century?

The Debate over Urban Guilds
■ What were guilds, and why did they become controversial in the eighteenth century?

Building the Global Economy
■ How did colonial markets boost Europe's economic and social development, and what conflicts and adversity did world trade entail?

Working the Land

What important developments led to the agricultural revolution, and how did these changes affect peasants? ▪

At the end of the seventeenth century the economy of Europe was agrarian. With the possible exception of Holland, at least 80 percent of the people of all western European countries drew their livelihoods from agriculture. In eastern Europe the percentage was considerably higher. Men and women were tied to the land, plowing fields and sowing seed, reaping harvests and storing grain. Yet even in a rich agricultural region such as the Po Valley in northern Italy, every bushel of wheat seed sown yielded on average only five or six bushels of grain at harvest. By modern standards, output was distressingly low.

In most regions of Europe in the sixteenth and seventeenth centuries, climatic conditions produced poor or disastrous harvests every eight or nine years. Unbalanced and inadequate food in famine years made people extremely susceptible to illness. Eating material unfit for human consumption during times of crop failure, such as bark or grass, resulted in intestinal ailments of many kinds. Influenza and smallpox preyed on populations weakened by malnourishment. In famine years the number of deaths soared far above normal. A third of a village's population might disappear in a year or two. But new developments in agricultural technology and methods gradually brought an end to the ravages of hunger in western Europe.

The Legacy of the Open-Field System

Why, in the late seventeenth century, did Europeans produce barely enough food to survive? The answer lies in the pattern of farming that had developed in the Middle Ages, which sustained fairly large numbers of people, but did not produce material abundance. From the Middle Ages up to the seventeenth century, much of Europe was farmed through the open-field system. The land to be cultivated was divided into several large fields, which were in turn cut up into long, narrow strips. The fields were open, and the strips were not enclosed into small plots by fences or hedges. The whole peasant village followed the same pattern of plowing, sowing, and

Enclosure Mapmakers in Henlow, England This rare image shows the process of making new maps to document the enclosure of fields in England. Drawn on the enclosure map for Henlow, Bedfordshire, around 1795, the scene shows a surveyor and his assistants at work. (Bedfordshire and Luton Archives Service, Bedfordshire, U.K.)

harvesting in accordance with tradition and the village leaders.

The ever-present problem was soil exhaustion. Wheat planted year after year in a field will deplete nitrogen in the soil. Since the supply of manure for fertilizer was limited, the only way for the land to recover was to lie fallow for a period of time. Clover and other annual grasses that grew in unplanted fields restored nutrients to the soil and also provided food for livestock. In the early Middle Ages a year of fallow was alternated with a year of cropping; then three-year rotations were introduced, especially on more fertile lands. On each strip of land, a year of wheat or rye was followed by a year of oats or beans and only then by a year of fallow. Peasants staggered the rotation of crops, so some wheat, legumes, and pastureland were always available. The three-year system was an important achievement because cash crops could be grown two years out of three, rather than only one year in two.

Traditional village rights reinforced communal patterns of farming. In addition to rotating field crops in a uniform way, villages maintained open meadows for hay and natural pasture. After the harvest villagers also pastured their animals on the wheat or rye stubble. In many places such pasturing followed a brief period, also established by tradition, for the gleaning of grain. In this process, poor women would go through the fields picking up the few single grains that had fallen to the ground in the course of the harvest. Many villages were surrounded by woodlands, also held in common, which provided essential firewood, building materials, and nutritional roots and berries.

In the age of absolutism and nobility, the state and landlords continued to levy heavy taxes and high rents, thereby stripping peasants of much of their meager earnings. The level of exploitation varied. Generally speaking, the peasants of eastern Europe were worst off. As we saw in Chapter 16, they were serfs bound to their lords in hereditary service. In much of eastern Europe, working five or six days per week on the lord's land for no pay was not uncommon. Well into the nineteenth century, individual Russian serfs and serf families were regularly sold with and without land.

Social conditions were better in western Europe, where peasants were generally free from serfdom. In France, western Germany, England, and the Low Countries (modern-day Belgium and the Netherlands), they owned land and could pass it on to their children. Yet life in the village was unquestionably hard, and poverty was the great reality for most people. Owning only a portion of the land that they worked (the village lord typically owned as much as half), poor peasants were forced to seek wages in a variety of jobs in order to eke out a living. The privileges of Europe's ruling elites weighed heavily on the people of the land.

The Agricultural Revolution

One way for European peasants to improve their difficult position was to revolt and take land from those who owned it but did no labor. Yet the social and political conditions that sustained the ruling elites were ancient and deeply rooted, and powerful forces stood ready to crush protest. Only with the coming of the French Revolution in 1789 were European peasants, mainly in France, able to improve their position by means of radical mass action. Technological progress offered another possibility. If peasants (and their noble landlords) could replace the idle fallow with crops, they could greatly increase the land under cultivation. So remarkable were the possibilities and the results that historians have often spoken of the progressive elimination of the fallow, which occurred gradually throughout Europe from about 1650 to 1850, as an **agricultural revolution**, a great milestone in human development.

agricultural revolution
The period in Europe from the mid-seventeenth through the mid-nineteenth centuries during which great agricultural progress was made and the fallow, or idling of a field to replenish nutrients, was gradually eliminated.

Chronology

1650–1850	Agricultural revolution
1651–1663	British Navigation Acts
1652–1674	Anglo-Dutch wars
1700–1790	Height of Atlantic slave trade; expansion of rural industry in Europe
1701–1763	British and French mercantilist wars of empire
1720–1722	Last outbreak of bubonic plague in Europe
1720–1789	Growth of European population
1756–1763	Seven Years' War
1760–1815	Height of parliamentary enclosure in England
1763	Treaty of Paris; France cedes its possessions in India and North America
1770	James Cook claims the east coast of Australia for England
1776	Smith, *Inquiry into the Nature and Causes of the Wealth of Nations*
1805	British takeover of India complete
1807	British slave trade abolished

Because grain crops exhaust the soil and make fallowing necessary, the secret to eliminating the fallow lies in alternating grain with nitrogen-storing crops. The most important of these land-reviving crops are peas and beans, root crops such as turnips and potatoes, and clovers and grasses. As the eighteenth century went on, the number of crops that were systematically rotated grew. New patterns of organization allowed some farmers to develop increasingly sophisticated patterns of crop rotation to suit different kinds of soils. For example, in the late eighteenth century farmers in French Flanders near Lille alternated a number of grain, root, and hay crops in a given field on a ten-year schedule. Continual experimentation, fueled by developments in the scientific revolution (see Chapter 17), led to more methodical farming.

Improvements in farming had multiple effects. The new crops made ideal feed for animals; with more fodder, hay, and root crops for the winter months, peasants and larger farmers could build up their herds of cattle and sheep. More animals meant more meat and better diets. More animals also meant more manure for fertilizer and therefore more grain for bread and porridge.

Advocates of the new crop rotations, who included an emerging group of experimental scientists, some government officials, and a few big landowners, believed that new methods were scarcely possible within the traditional framework of open fields and common rights. A farmer who wanted to experiment with new methods would have to get all the landholders in the village to agree to the plan. Advocates of improvement argued that innovating agriculturalists needed to enclose and consolidate their scattered holdings into compact, fenced-in fields in order to farm more effectively. In doing so, the innovators also needed to enclose their individual shares of a village's natural pastureland, the common.

enclosure The movement to fence in fields in order to farm more effectively, at the expense of poor peasants who relied on common fields for farming and pasture.

According to proponents of this movement, known as **enclosure**, a revolution in village life and organization was the necessary price of technical progress.

That price seemed too high to many poor rural people who had small, inadequate holdings or very little land at all. Traditional rights were precious to these poor peasants, who used commonly held pastureland to graze livestock, and marshlands or forest outside the village as a source for foraged goods that could make the difference between survival and famine in harsh times. Thus, when the small landholders and the village poor could effectively oppose the enclosure of the open fields and the common lands, they did so. In many countries they found allies among the larger, predominately noble landowners who were also wary of enclosure because it required large investments in purchasing and fencing land and thus posed risks for them as well.

The old system of unenclosed open fields and the new system of continuous rotation coexisted in Europe for a long time. Open fields could still be found in much of France and Germany as late as the nineteenth century because peasants there had successfully opposed eighteenth-century efforts to introduce the new techniques. Throughout the end of the eighteenth century, the new system of enclosure was extensively adopted only in the Low Countries and England.

The Leadership of the Low Countries and England

The new methods of the agricultural revolution originated in the Low Countries. Seventeenth-century republican Holland, already the most advanced country in Europe in many areas of human endeavor (see Chapter 16), led the way. By the middle of the seventeenth century intensive farming was well established, and the innovations of enclosed fields, continuous rotation, heavy manuring, and a wide variety of crops were all present. Agriculture was highly specialized and commercialized.

One reason for early Dutch leadership in farming was that the area was one of the most densely populated in Europe. In order to feed themselves and provide employment, the Dutch were forced at an early date to seek maximum yields from their land and to increase the cultivated area through the steady draining of marshes and swamps. The pressure of population was connected with the second cause: the growth of towns and cities. Stimulated by commerce and overseas trade, Amsterdam grew from thirty thousand to two hundred thousand inhabitants in its golden seventeenth century. The growing urban population provided Dutch peasants with markets for all they could produce and allowed each region to specialize in what it did best. Thus the Dutch could develop their potential, and the Low Countries became, as one historian wrote, "the Mecca of foreign agricultural experts who came . . . to see Flemish agriculture with their own eyes, to write about it and to propagate its methods in their home lands."[1]

The English were the best students. Drainage and water control were one subject in which they received instruction. Large parts of seventeenth-century Holland had once been sea and sea marsh, and the efforts of centuries had made the Dutch the world's leaders in drainage. In the first half of the seventeenth century Dutch experts made a great contribution to draining the extensive marshes, or fens, of wet and rainy England. The most famous of these Dutch engineers, Cornelius Vermuyden, directed one large drainage project in Yorkshire and another in Cambridgeshire. In the Cambridge fens, Vermuyden and his Dutch workers eventually reclaimed forty thousand acres, which were then farmed intensively in the Dutch manner. Swampy wilderness was converted into thousands of acres of some of the best land in England.

Jethro Tull (1674–1741), part crank and part genius, was an important English innovator. A true son of the early Enlightenment, Tull adopted a critical attitude toward accepted ideas about farming and tried to develop better methods through empirical research. He was especially enthusiastic about using horses, rather than slower-moving oxen, for plowing. He also advocated sowing seed with drilling equipment rather than scattering it by hand. Drilling distributed seed in an even manner and at the proper depth. There were also improvements in livestock, inspired in part by the earlier successes of English country gentlemen in breeding ever-faster horses for the races and fox hunts that were their passions. Selective breeding of ordinary livestock was a marked improvement over the haphazard breeding of the past.

By the mid-eighteenth century English agriculture was in the process of a long but radical transformation. The eventual result was that by 1870 English farmers were producing 300 percent more food than they had produced in 1700, even though the number of people working the land had increased by only 14 percent. This great surge of agricultural production provided food for England's rapidly growing urban population. Growth in production was achieved in part by land enclosures. About half the farmland in England was enclosed through private initiatives prior to 1700; Parliament completed this work in the eighteenth century. From the 1760s to the end of the Napoleonic era in 1815, a series of acts of Parliament enclosed most of the remaining common land.

By eliminating common rights and greatly reducing the access of poor men and women to the land, the eighteenth-century enclosure movement marked the completion of two major historical developments in England—the rise of market-oriented estate agriculture and the emergence of a landless rural proletariat. By the early nineteenth century a tiny minority of wealthy English and Scottish landowners held most of the land and pursued profits aggressively, leasing their holdings through agents at competitive prices to middle-size farmers, who relied on landless laborers for their workforce.

The Vegetable Market, 1662 The wealth and well-being of the industrious, capitalistic Dutch shine forth in this winsome market scene by Dutch artist Hendrick Sorgh. The market woman's baskets are filled with delicious fresh produce that ordinary citizens can afford—eloquent testimony to the responsive, enterprising character of Dutch agriculture. (Rijksmuseum, Amsterdam)

These landless laborers worked very long hours, usually following a dawn-to-dusk schedule six days a week all year long. Not only was the small landholder deprived of his land, but fewer laborers were needed to work the large farms, and unemployment spread throughout the countryside. As one sympathetic observer commented:

> *It is no uncommon thing for four or five wealthy graziers to engross a large inclosed lordship, which was before in the hands of twenty or thirty farmers, and as many smaller tenants or proprietors. All these are thereby thrown out of their livings, and many other families, who were chiefly employed and supported by them, such as blacksmiths, carpenters, wheelwrights and other artificers and tradesmen, besides their own labourers and servants.[2]*

In no other European country had this **proletarianization** (proh-luh-tair-ee-uh-nuh-ZAY-shun)—this transformation of large numbers of small peasant farmers into landless rural wage earners—gone so far. England's village poor found the cost of change heavy and unjust.

proletarianization The transformation of large numbers of small peasant farmers into landless rural wage earners.

The Beginning of the Population Explosion

Why did the European population rise dramatically in the eighteenth century?

Another factor that affected the existing order of life and forced economic changes in the eighteenth century was the beginning of the population explosion. Explosive growth continued in Europe until the twentieth century, by which time it was affecting nonwestern areas of the globe. In this section we examine the causes of the population growth; the following section considers how the challenge of more mouths to feed and more hands to employ affected the European economy.

Long-standing Obstacles to Population Growth

Until 1700 the total population of Europe grew slowly much of the time, and it followed an irregular cyclical pattern (Figure 18.1). This cyclical pattern had a great influence on many aspects of social and economic life. The terrible ravages of the Black Death caused a sharp drop in population and food prices after 1350 and also created a labor shortage throughout Europe. Some economic historians calculate that for those common people in western Europe who managed to steer clear of warfare and of power struggles within the ruling class, the later Middle Ages was an era of exceptional well-being.

But this well-being eroded in the course of the sixteenth century. The second great surge of population growth outstripped the growth of agricultural production after about 1500. There was less food per person, and food prices rose more rapidly than wages, a development intensified by the inflow of precious metals from the Americas (see Chapter 15) and a general, if uneven, European price revolution. The result was a substantial decline in living standards throughout Europe. By 1600 the pressure of population on resources was severe in much of Europe, and widespread poverty was an undeniable reality.

For this reason, population growth slowed and stopped in seventeenth-century Europe. Births and deaths, fertility and mortality, were in a crude but effective balance. The population grew modestly in normal years at a rate of perhaps 0.5 to 1 percent, or enough to double the population in 70 to 140 years. This is, of course, a generalization encompassing many different patterns. In areas such as Russia and colonial New England, where there was a great deal of frontier to be settled, the annual rate of natural increase, not counting in-migration, might well have exceeded 1 percent. In a country such as France, where the land had long been densely settled, the rate of increase might have been less than 0.5 percent.

Although population growth of even 1 percent per year seems fairly modest, it will produce a very large increase over a long period: in three hundred years it will result in sixteen times as many people. Yet such gigantic increases did not occur in agrarian Europe. In certain abnormal years and tragic periods—the Black Death was only the most extreme example—many more people died than were born, and total population fell sharply, even catastrophically. A number of years of

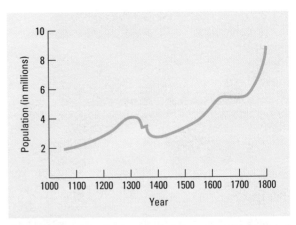

Figure 18.1 The Growth of Population in England, 1000–1800 England is a good example of both the uneven increase of European population before 1700 and the third great surge of growth that began in the eighteenth century.
(Source: Adapted from E. A. Wrigley, *Population and History*. Copyright © 1969 by E. A. Wrigley. Reprinted with permission of Weidenfeld & Nicolson, an imprint of The Orion Publishing Group, London.)

modest growth would then be necessary to make up for those who had died in an abnormal year. Such savage increases in deaths occurred periodically in the seventeenth century on a local and regional scale, and these demographic crises combined to check the growth of population until after 1700.

The grim reapers of demographic crisis were famine, epidemic disease, and war. Famine, the inevitable result of low yields and periodic crop failures, was particularly murderous because it was accompanied by disease. With a brutal one-two punch, famine stunned and weakened a population, and disease finished it off. Disease, as the example of the Black Death illustrates, could also ravage the population independently of famine.

War was another scourge, and its indirect effects were even more harmful than the organized killing. Soldiers and camp followers passed all manner of contagious diseases throughout the countryside. Armies also requisitioned scarce food supplies and disrupted the agricultural cycle while battles destroyed precious crops and farmlands. The Thirty Years' War witnessed all possible combinations of distress. The number of inhabitants in the German states alone declined by more than two-thirds in some large areas and by at least one-third almost everywhere else.

The New Pattern of the Eighteenth Century

In the eighteenth century the population of Europe began to grow markedly. This increase in numbers occurred in all regions of Europe. The size of the European population grew steadily from 1720 to 1789, with especially dramatic increases after about 1750 (Figure 18.2).

What caused this population growth? In some areas women had more babies than before because new opportunities for employment in rural industry (see page 560) allowed them to marry at an earlier age. But the basic cause of European population increase as a whole was a decline in mortality — fewer deaths.

One of the primary reasons behind this decline was the mysterious disappearance of the bubonic plague. Following the Black Death in the fourteenth century, plagues had remained part of the European experience, striking again and again with savage force, particularly in towns. In 1720 a ship from Syria and the Levant brought the disease to Marseilles. As a contemporary account described it, "The Porters employ'd in unloading the Vessel, were immediately seiz'd with violent Pains in the Head . . . soon after they broke out in Blotches and Buboes, and died in three Days."[3] Plague quickly spread within and beyond Marseilles, killing up to one hundred thousand. By 1722 the epidemic had passed, and that was the last time plague fell on western and central Europe. Exactly why plague disappeared is unknown. Stricter measures of quarantine in Mediterra-

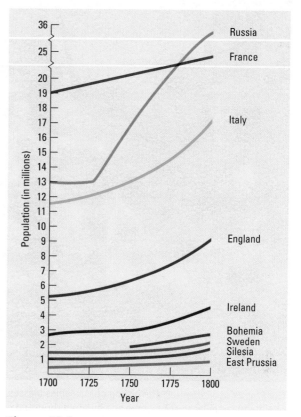

Figure 18.2 **The Increase of Population in Europe in the Eighteenth Century** Population grew across Europe in the eighteenth century, though the most dramatic increases occurred after 1750. Russia experienced the largest increase and emerged as Europe's most populous state as natural increase was complemented by growth from territorial expansion.

nean ports and along the Austrian border with Turkey helped by carefully isolating human carriers of plague. Chance and plain good luck were probably just as important.

Advances in medical knowledge did not contribute much to reducing the death rate in the eighteenth century. The most important advance in preventive medicine in this period was inoculation against smallpox, and this great improvement was long confined mainly to England, probably doing little to reduce deaths throughout Europe until the latter part of the century. However, improvements in the water supply and sewage, which were frequently promoted by strong absolutist monarchies, resulted in somewhat better public health and helped reduce such diseases as typhoid and typhus in some urban areas of western Europe. Improvements in water supply and the drainage of swamps also reduced Europe's large insect population. Flies and mosquitoes played a major role in spreading diseases, especially those striking children and young adults. Thus early public health measures helped the decline in mortality that

The Plague at Marseilles The bishop of Marseilles blesses victims of the plague that over-whelmed Marseilles in 1720. Some one hundred thousand people died in the outbreak, which was the last great episode of plague in western Europe. (Louvre/Réunion des Musée Nationaux/Art Resource, NY)

began with the disappearance of plague and continued into the early nineteenth century.

Human beings also became more successful in their efforts to safeguard the supply of food. The eighteenth century was a time of considerable canal and road building in western Europe. These advances in transportation, which were also among the more positive aspects of strong absolutist states, lessened the impact of local crop failure and famine. Emergency supplies could be brought in, and localized starvation became less frequent. Wars became less destructive than in the seventeenth century and spread fewer epidemics. Nutritious new foods, particularly the potato from South America, were introduced. In short, population grew in the eighteenth century primarily because years of higher than average death rates were less catastrophic. Famines, epidemics, and wars continued to occur and to affect population growth, but their severity moderated.

cottage industry A stage of industrial development in which rural workers used hand tools in their homes to manufacture goods on a large scale for sale in a market.

Renewed population growth in the eighteenth century intensified the imbalance between the number of people and the economic opportunities available to them. At a time of rapidly rising population, improvements in agricultural efficiency lessened the need for rural laborers. The rural poor were forced to look for new ways to make a living.

The Growth of Rural Industry

How and why did rural industry intensify in the eighteenth century? ▪

The growth of population increased the number of rural workers with little or no land, and this in turn contributed to the development of industry in rural areas. The poor in the countryside increasingly needed to supplement their agricultural earnings with other types of work, and urban capitalists were eager to employ them, often at lower wages than urban workers received. **Cottage industry**, which consisted of manufacturing with hand tools in peasant cottages and work sheds, grew markedly in the eighteenth century and became a crucial feature of the European economy.

To be sure, peasant communities had always made clothing, processed food, and constructed housing for their own use. But medieval peasants did not produce manufactured goods on a large scale for sale in a market. By the eighteenth century, however, the pressures of rural poverty led many poor villagers to seek additional work, and far-reaching changes for daily rural life were set in motion.

The Putting-Out System

Cottage industry was often organized through the **putting-out system**. The two main participants in the putting-out system were the merchant capitalist and the rural worker. In this system, the merchant loaned, or "put out," raw materials to cottage workers, who processed the raw materials in their own homes and returned the finished products to the merchant. There were endless variations on this basic relationship. Sometimes rural workers bought their own raw materials and worked as independent producers before they sold to the merchant. Sometimes whole families were involved in domestic industry; at other times the tasks were closely associated with one gender. Sometimes several workers toiled together to perform a complicated process in a workshop outside the home. The relative importance of earnings from the land and from industry varied greatly for handicraft workers, although industrial wages usually became more important for a given family with time.

As industries grew in scale and complexity, production was often broken into many stages. For example, a merchant would provide raw wool to one group of workers for spinning into thread. He would then pass the thread to another group of workers to be bleached, to another for dyeing, and to another for weaving into cloth. The merchant paid outworkers by the piece and proceeded to sell the finished product to regional, national, or international markets.

The putting-out system grew because it had competitive advantages. Underemployed labor was abundant, and poor peasants and landless laborers would work for low wages. Since production in the countryside was unregulated, workers and merchants could change procedures and experiment as they saw fit. Because workers did not need to meet rigid guild standards, cottage industry became capable of producing many kinds of goods. Textiles; all manner of knives, forks, and housewares; buttons and gloves; and clocks could be produced quite satisfactorily in the coun-

tryside. Although luxury goods for the rich, such as exquisite tapestries and fine porcelain, demanded special training, close supervision, and centralized workshops, the limited skills of rural industry were sufficient for everyday articles.

Rural manufacturing did not spread across Europe at an even rate. It developed most successfully in England, particularly for the spinning and weaving of woolen cloth. By 1500 half of England's textiles were being produced in the countryside. By 1700 English industry was generally more rural than urban and heavily reliant on the putting-out system. Most continental countries, with the exception of Flanders and the Netherlands, developed rural industry more slowly. The latter part of the eighteenth century witnessed a remarkable expansion of rural industry in certain densely populated regions of continental Europe (Map 18.1).

> **putting-out system** The eighteenth-century system of rural industry in which a merchant loaned raw materials to cottage workers, who processed them and returned the finished products to the merchant.

The Lives of Rural Textile Workers

Until the nineteenth century, the industry that employed the most people in Europe was textiles. The making of linen, woolen, and eventually cotton cloth was the typical activity of cottage workers engaged in the putting-out system. A look inside the cottage of the English weaver illustrates a way of life as well as an economic system. The rural worker lived in a small cottage with tiny windows and little space. The cottage was often a

The Weaver's Repose This painting by Decker Cornelis Gerritz (1594–1637) captures the pleasure of release from long hours of toil in cottage industry. The loom realistically dominates the cramped living space and the family's modest possessions. (Musées Royaux des Beaux-Arts, Brussels. Copyright A.C.I.)

Mapping the Past

Map 18.1 Industry and Population in Eighteenth-Century Europe The growth of cottage manufacturing in rural areas helped country people increase their income and contributed to population growth. The putting-out system began in England, and much of the work was in the textile industry. Cottage industry was also strong in the Low Countries — modern-day Belgium and Holland.

ANALYZING THE MAP What does this map suggest about the relationship between population density and the growth of textile production? What geographical characteristics seem to have played a role in encouraging this industry?

CONNECTIONS How would you account for the distribution of each type of cloth across Europe? Did metal production draw on different demographic and geographical conditions? Why do you think this was the case?

To complete this activity online, go to the Online Study Guide at bedfordstmartins.com/mckaywest.

single room that served as workshop, kitchen, and bedroom. There were only a few pieces of furniture, of which the weaver's loom was by far the largest and most important. That loom had changed somewhat in the early eighteenth century when John Kay's invention of the flying shuttle enabled the weaver to throw the shuttle back and forth between the threads with one hand. Aside from that improvement, however, the loom was as it had been for much of history and as it would remain until the arrival of mechanized looms in the first decades of the nineteenth century.

Handloom weaving was a family enterprise. All members of the family helped in the work, so that "every person from seven to eighty (who retained their sight and who could move their hands) could earn their bread," as one eighteenth-century English observer put it.[4] Operating the loom was considered a man's job, reserved for the male head of the family. Women and children worked at auxiliary tasks; they prepared the warp (vertical) threads and mounted them on the loom, wound threads on bobbins for the weft (horizontal) threads, and sometimes operated the warp frame while the father passed the shuttle.

The work of four or five spinners was needed to keep one weaver steadily employed. Since the weaver's family usually could not produce enough thread, alternate sources of labor were needed. Merchants turned to the wives and daughters of agricultural workers, who took on spinning work in their spare time. In England, many widows and single women also became "spinsters," so many in fact that the word became a synonym for an unmarried woman. In parts of Germany, spinning employed whole families and was not reserved for women. As the industry expanded and merchants covered ever greater distances in search of workers, they sometimes turned to local shopkeepers to manage the spinners in their villages.

Relations between workers and employers were often marked by sharp conflict. (See "Listening to the Past: Contrasting Views on the Effects of Rural Industry," page 564.) There were constant disputes over the weights of materials and the quality of finished work. Merchants accused workers of stealing raw materials, and weavers complained that merchants delivered underweight bales. Suspicion abounded.

Conditions were particularly hard for female workers. While men could earn decent wages through long hours of arduous labor, women's wages were always terribly low. In England's Yorkshire wool industry, a male wool comber earned a good wage of twelve shillings or more a week, while a spinner could hope for only three-and-a-half shillings.[5] A single or widowed spinner faced a desperate struggle with poverty. Any period of illness or unemployment could spell disaster for her and her children. In 1788 one English writer condemned the low wages of spinners in Norwich: "The suffering of thousands of wretched individuals, willing to work, but starving from their ill requited labour; of whole families of honest industrious children offering their little hands to the wheel, and asking bread of the helpless mother, unable through this well regulated manufacture to give it to them."[6]

From the merchant capitalist's point of view, the problem was not low wages but the control of rural labor. Scattered across the countryside, cottage workers were difficult to supervise and direct. Moreover, the pace of their work depended on the agricultural calendar. In spring and late summer planting and haymaking occupied all hands in the rural village, leading to shortages in the supply of thread. Merchants, whose livelihood depended on their ability to meet orders on time, bitterly resented their lack of control over rural labor. They accused workers—especially female spinners—of laziness, drunkenness, and immorality. If workers failed to produce enough thread, they reasoned, it must be because their wages were too high and they had little incentive to work.

Merchants thus insisted on maintaining the lowest possible wages to force the "idle" poor into productive labor. They also lobbied for, and obtained, new police powers over workers. Imprisonment and public whipping became common punishments for pilfering small amounts of yarn or cloth. For poor workers, their right to hold on to the bits and pieces left over in the production process was akin to the traditional peasant right of gleaning in common lands. With progress came the loss of traditional safeguards for the poor.

The Linen Industry in Ireland Many steps went into making textiles. Here the women are beating away the woody part of the flax plant so that the man can comb out the soft part. The combed fibers will then be spun into thread and woven into cloth by this family enterprise. The increased labor of women and girls from the late seventeenth century helped produce an industrious revolution. (Victoria & Albert Museum, London/Eileen Tweedy/The Art Archive)

Contrasting Views on the Effects of Rural Industry

LISTENING TO THE PAST

English commentators quickly noted the effects of rural industry on families and daily life. Some were greatly impressed by the rise in living standards made possible by the putting-out system, while others noted the rising economic inequality between merchant and workers and the power the former acquired over the latter. In the first excerpt, novelist and economic writer Daniel Defoe enthusiastically praises cottage industry.

He notes that the labor of women and children in spinning and weaving brought in as much as or more income than the man's agricultural work, allowing the family to eat well and be warmly clothed. It is interesting to note that Defoe assumes a rural world in which the process of enclosure is complete; poor men do not own their own land, but toil as wage laborers on the land of others. He also offers one explanation for the increasing use of Africans as slaves in British colonies: reliable wages from cottage industry meant that the English poor did not have to "sell themselves to the Plantations," thus leading plantation owners to seek other sources of labor.

The second source is a popular song written around 1700. Couched in the voice of the ruthless cloth merchant, it expresses the bitterness and resentment textile workers felt against the employers. One can imagine a group of weavers gathered together at the local tavern singing their protest on a rare break from work.

Daniel Defoe, *A Plan of the English Commerce*

❝ *Being a compleat prospect of the trade of this nation, as well the home trade as the foreign*, 1728

[A] poor labouring man that goes abroad to his Day Work, and Husbandry, Hedging, Ditching, Threshing, Carting, &c. and brings home his Week's Wages, suppose at eight Pence to twelve Pence a Day, or in some Counties less; if he has a Wife and three or four Children to feed, and who get little or nothing for themselves, must fare hard, and live poorly; 'tis easy to suppose it must be so.

But if this Man's Wife and Children can at the same Time get Employment, if at next Door, or at the next Village there lives a Clothier, or a Bay Maker, or a stuff or Drugget Weaver;* the Manufacturer sends the poor Woman combed Wool, or carded Wool every Week to spin, and she gets eight Pence or nine Pence a day at home; the Weaver sends for her two little Children, and they work by the Loom, winding, filling quills, &c. and the two bigger Girls spin at home with their Mother, and these earn three Pence or four Pence a Day each: So that put it together, the Family at Home gets as much as the Father gets Abroad, and generally more.

This alters the Case extremely, the Family feels it, they all feed better, are cloth'd warmer, and do not so easily nor so often fall into Misery and Distress; the Father gets them Food, and the Mother gets them Clothes; and as they grow, they do not run away to be Footmen and Soldiers, Thieves and Beggars or sell themselves to the Plantations to

avoid the Goal and the Gallows, but have a Trade at their Hands, and every one can get their Bread.

N.B. I once went through a large populous manufacturing Town in England, and observ'd, that an Officer planted there, with a Serjeant and two Drums, had been beating up a long Time and could get no Recruits, except two or three Sots . . . Enquiring the Reason of it, an honest Clothier of the Town answered me effectually thus, *The Case is plain*, says he, thus there is at this Time a brisk Demand for Goods, we have 1100 Looms, *added he*, in this Town and the Villages about it and not one of them want Work; and there is not a poor Child in the Town of above four Years old, but can earn his Bread; besides, there being so good a Trade at this Time, causes us to advance Wages a little and the Weaver and the Spinner get more than they used to do; and while it is so, they may beat the Heads of their Drums out, if they will, they'll get no Soldiers here. ❞

Anonymous, *The Clothier's Delight*

❝ *Or the rich Men's Joy, and the poor Men's Sorrow, wherein is exprest the Craftiness and Subtility of many Clothiers in England, by beating down their Workmen's Wages*, ca. 1700

Of all sorts of callings that in England be
There is none that liveth so gallant as we;
Our trading maintains us as brave as a knight,
We live at our pleasure and take our delight;
We heapeth up richest treasure great store
Which we get by griping and grinding the poor.
   And this is a way for to fill up our purse
   Although we do get it with many a curse.

Throughout the whole kingdom, in country and town,
There is no danger of our trade going down,
So long as the Comber can work with his comb,
And also the Weaver weave with his lomb;
The Tucker and Spinner that spins all the year,
We will make them to earn their wages full dear.
   And this is a way, etc.

And first for the Combers, we will bring them down,
From eight groats a score until half a crown;

*Bay, stuff, and drugget were types of coarse woolen cloth typical of the inexpensive products of rural weaving.

If at all they murmur and say 'tis too small
We bid them choose whether they will work at all.
We'll make them believe that trading is bad
We care not a pin, though they are n'er so sad.
   And this is a way, etc.

We'll make the poor Weavers work at a low rate,
We'll find fault where there's no fault, and so we
   will bate;
If trading grows dead, we will presently show it,
But if it grows good, they shall never know it;
We'll tell them that cloth beyond sea will not go,
We care not whether we keep clothing or no.
   And this is a way, etc.

Then next for the Spinners we shall ensue;
We'll make them spin three pound instead
   of two;
When they bring home their work unto
   us, they complain
And say that their wages will not them
   maintain;
But that if an ounce of weight they do
   lack,
Then for to bate threepence we will not
   be slack.
   And this is a way, etc.

But if it holds weight, then their wages they
   crave,
We have got no money, and what's that you'd
   have?
We have bread and bacon and butter that's good,
With oatmeal and salt that is wholesome for food;
We have soap and candles whereby to give light,
That you may work by them so long as you have
   sight.
   And this is a way, etc.

. . .

And thus, we do gain our wealth and estate
By many poor men that work early and late;
If it were not for those that labour so hard,
We might go and hang ourselves without regard;
The combers, the weavers, the tuckers also,
With the spinners that work for wages full low,
By these people's labour we fill up our purse,
Although we do get it with many a curse. 〞

Sources: Daniel Defoe, *A Plan of the English Commerce. Being a compleat prospect of the trade of this nation, as well the home trade as the foreign.* London, 1728, pp. 90–91; Paul Mantoux and Marjorie Vernon, eds., *The Industrial Revolution in the Eighteenth Century: An Outline of the Beginnings of the Modern Factory System in England* (1928; Taylor and Francis, 2006), pp. 76–77.

QUESTIONS FOR ANALYSIS

1. What division of labor in the textile industry does Defoe describe? How does this division of labor resemble or differ from the household in which you grew up?

2. On what basis are wages paid, and what strategies do merchants use to keep wages down, according to *The Clothier's Delight*? How are they able to impose such strategies on workers?

3. How do you reconcile the difference of opinion between the two sources? Was one right and the other wrong, or could a more complex analysis be true?

This spinning wheel was powered by the spinner's foot by means of the treadle, which was connected to the wheel by a rod and crankshaft. Purchasing a spinning wheel, which cost a few days of a laborer's wage, allowed rural women and children to generate precious supplemental income in the off-season. The work was relatively slow, however, and thread from four or five wheels was required to supply one weaver.
(Science and Society Picture Library/SuperStock)

The Industrious Revolution

One scholar has used the term **industrious revolution** to summarize the social and economic changes taking place in Europe in the late seventeenth and early eighteenth centuries.[7] This occurred as households in northwestern Europe reduced leisure time, stepped up the pace of work, and, most important, redirected the labor of women and children away from the production of goods for household consumption and toward wage work. In the countryside, the spread of cottage industry can be seen as one manifestation of the industrious revolution, while in the cities there was a rise in female employment outside the home (see page 568). By working harder and increasing the number of wageworkers, rural and urban households could purchase more goods, even in a time of stagnant or falling wages.

The effect of these changes is still debated. While some scholars lament the encroachment of longer work hours and stricter discipline, others insist that poor families made decisions based on their own self-interests. With more finished goods becoming available at lower prices, households sought cash income to participate in an emerging consumer economy.

The role of women and girls in this new economy is particularly controversial. When women entered the labor market, they almost always worked at menial, tedious jobs for very low wages. Yet when women earned their own wages, they also seem to have taken on a proportionately greater role in household decision making. Most of their scant earnings went for household necessities, items they could no longer produce now that they worked full-time, but there were sometimes a few shillings left for a few ribbons or a new pair of stockings. Women's use of their surplus income thus helped spur the rapid growth of the textile industries in which they labored so hard.

These new sources and patterns of labor established important foundations for the Industrial Revolution of the late eighteenth and nineteenth centuries. They created households in which all members worked for wages rather than in a united family business and in which consumption relied on market-produced rather than homemade goods. It was not until the mid-nineteenth century, with rising industrial wages, that a new model emerged in which the male "breadwinner" was expected to earn enough to support the whole family and women and children were relegated back to the domestic sphere. With women estimated to compose 39 percent of the global workforce, today's world is experiencing a second industrious revolution in a similar climate of stagnant wages and increased demand for consumer goods.[8]

industrious revolution The shift that occurred as families in northwestern Europe focused on earning wages instead of producing goods for household consumption; this reduced their economic self-sufficiency but increased their ability to purchase consumer goods.

guild system The organization of artisanal production into trade-based associations, or guilds, each of which received a monopoly over its trade and the right to train apprentices and hire workers.

The Debate over Urban Guilds

What were guilds, and why did they become controversial in the eighteenth century? ■

One consequence of the growth of rural industry was an undermining of the traditional **guild system** that protected urban artisans. Guilds continued to dominate production in towns and cities, providing their masters with economic privileges as well as a proud social identity, but they increasingly struggled against competition from rural workers. Meanwhile, those excluded from guild membership—women, day laborers, Jews, and foreigners—worked on the margins of the urban economy.

In the second half of the eighteenth century, critics attacked the guilds as outmoded institutions that obstructed technical progress and innovation. Until recently, most historians repeated that view. An ongoing reassessment of guilds now emphasizes their ability to adapt to changing economic circumstances.

Urban Guilds

Originating around 1200 during the economic boom of the Middle Ages, the guild system reached its peak in most of Europe in the seventeenth and eighteenth centuries. During this period, urban guilds grew dramatically in number in cities and towns across Europe. In Louis XIV's France, for example, finance minister Jean-Baptiste Colbert revived the urban guilds and used them to encourage high-quality production and to collect taxes (see Chapter 16). In this period, the number of guilds in the city of Paris grew from 60 in 1672 to 129 in 1691.

Guild masters in Paris occupied the summit of the world of work. Each guild received a detailed set of privileges from the French crown, including exclusive rights to produce and sell certain goods, access to restricted markets in raw materials, and the rights to train apprentices, hire workers, and open shops. Any individual who violated these monopolies could be prosecuted. Guilds also served social and religious functions, providing a locus of sociability and group identity to the middling classes of European cities.

Guild Procession in Seventeenth-Century Brussels Guilds played an important role in the civic life of the early modern city. They collected taxes from their members, imposed quality standards and order on the trades, and represented the interests of commerce and industry to the government. In return, they claimed exclusive monopolies over their trades and the right to govern their own affairs. Guilds marched in processions, like the one shown here, at important city events, proudly displaying their corporate insignia. (Victoria & Albert Museum, London/Art Resource, NY)

To ensure there was enough work to go around, guilds jealously restricted their membership to local men who were good Christians, had several years of work experience, paid stiff membership fees, and completed a masterpiece. They also favored family connections. Masters' sons enjoyed automatic access to their fathers' guilds, while outsiders were often barred from entering. In the 1720s Parisian guild masters numbered only about thirty-five thousand in a population of five hundred thousand. Most urban men and women worked in non-guild trades as domestic servants, as manual laborers, and as vendors of food, used clothing, and other goods.

The guilds' ability to enforce their rigid barriers varied a great deal across Europe. In England, national regulations superseded guild regulations, sapping their importance. In France, the Crown developed an ambiguous attitude toward guilds, relying on them for taxes and enforcement of quality standards, yet allowing non-guild production to flourish in the countryside in the 1760s, and even in some urban neighborhoods. The Faubourg Saint-Antoine, an eastern suburb of Paris, maintained freedom from guild privileges through an old legal loophole, acting as a haven for the "false-workers" bitterly denounced by masters. The German guilds were perhaps the most powerful in Europe, and the most conservative. Journeymen in German cities, with their masters'

support, violently protested the encroachment of non-guild workers.

At the same time that cottage industry began to infringe on the livelihoods of urban artisans, new Enlightenment ideals called into question the very existence of the guild system. Eighteenth-century critics of guilds derided them as outmoded and exclusionary institutions that obstructed technical innovation and progress. Reform minister Anne-Robert-Jacques Turgot's 1776 law that abolished French guilds embodied the sentiments of many enlightened government officials.

> *We wish to abolish these arbitrary institutions, which do not allow the poor man to earn his living; which reject a sex whose weakness has given it more needs and fewer resources . . . ; which destroy emulation and industry and nullify the talents of those whose circumstances have excluded them from membership of a corporation; which deprive the state and the arts of all the knowledge brought to them by foreigners; which retard the progress of these arts . . . ; [and which] burden industry with an oppressive tax, which bears heavily on the people.*[9]

Although many historians have repeated Turgot's charges, more recent scholarship has emphasized the flexibility and adaptability of the guild system and its vitality through the eighteenth century. Guild masters

❝ No society can surely be flourishing and happy, of which the far greater part of the members are poor and miserable. ❞

—ADAM SMITH

adopted new technologies and found creative ways to circumvent impractical rules. Instead of reviling non-guild workers, some masters gave them piecework or even formed partnerships with them. For many merchants and artisans, economic regulation did not hinder commerce but instead fostered the confidence necessary to stimulate it. In an economy with few banks or credit institutions, knowing that a guild had examined a master's qualifications and regularly inspected his shop helped potential buyers trust the goods they purchased.

Contrary to Turgot's statement, some guilds were accessible to women in Paris and a handful of other European cities. Most involved needlework and textiles, occupations that were considered appropriate for women.

economic liberalism

A belief in free trade and competition based on Adam Smith's argument that the invisible hand of free competition would benefit all individuals, rich and poor.

In 1675 seamstresses gained a new all-female guild in Paris, and soon seamstresses joined tailors' guilds in parts of France, England, and the Netherlands. In the same period new vocational training programs were established for poor girls in many European cities. By the mid-eighteenth century male masters began to hire more female workers, often in defiance of their own guild statutes. One eighteenth-century observer of this phenomenon blamed the decline of the London button trade on women's involvement in it:

> *[Button-making] requires no great Strength, and is follow'd by Women as well as Men, which has reduced the Trade to small Profits, and a small Share of Reputation; the Women are generally Gin-Drinkers, and consequently bad Wives; this makes them poor, and to get something to keep Soul and Body together, work for a mere Trifle, and hawk their Work about to the Trade at an Under-Price. . . . This has reduced the Craft to a very low Ebb.*[10]

Whatever the complaints, urban women, like their counterparts in the countryside, were entering the paid labor market in greater numbers. Some attempts were made to redress the discrimination they faced. When Turgot's anti-guild law was repealed and French guilds received new statutes in 1777, the government formally opened all of them to women. But the guilds' abolition in the French Revolution in 1791 makes it impossible to know how this experiment in sexual equality would have fared.

Adam Smith and Economic Liberalism

The impact of new patterns of labor inspired comment and controversy. One of the best-known critics of government regulation of trade or industry was Adam Smith (1723–1790), a professor of philosophy and a leading figure of the Scottish Enlightenment. Smith developed the general idea of freedom of enterprise and established the basis for modern economics in his groundbreaking work, *Inquiry into the Nature and Causes of the Wealth of Nations* (1776). Like Turgot, Smith criticized guilds, or corporations, for their stifling and outmoded restrictions, a critique he extended to all state-approved monopolies and privileged companies. Far preferable was free competition, which would best protect consumers from price gouging and give all citizens a fair and equal right to do what they did best.

In keeping with his deep-seated fear of political oppression and with the "system of natural liberty" that he advocated, Smith argued that government should limit itself to "only three duties": it should provide a defense against foreign invasion, maintain civil order with courts and police protection, and sponsor certain indispensable public works and institutions that could never adequately profit private investors. He believed that the pursuit of self-interest in a competitive market would be sufficient to improve the living conditions of citizens, a view that quickly emerged as the classic argument for **economic liberalism**.

Many artisans welcomed the eighteenth-century economic liberalization that came with Smith, the Enlightenment, and the French Revolution, but some continued to uphold the ideals of the guilds. In parts of Germany guilds persisted until the second half of the nineteenth century. Clandestine journeymen's associations in France also survived into the nineteenth century. Skilled artisans across Europe espoused the values of hand craftsmanship and limited competition in contrast to the proletarianization and loss of skills they endured in mechanized production. Nevertheless, by the middle of the nineteenth century economic deregulation was championed by most European governments and elites.

In the nineteenth and twentieth centuries Smith was often seen as an advocate of unbridled capitalism, but his ideas were considerably more complex. In his own mind, Smith spoke for truth, not for special interests. Unlike many disgruntled merchant capitalists, he applauded the modest rise in real wages of British workers in the eighteenth century and went on to say that "No society can surely be flourishing and happy, of which the far greater part of the members are poor and miserable." Quite realistically, Smith concluded that employers were "always and everywhere in a sort of tacit, but constant and uniform combination, not to raise the wages of labour above their actual rate" and sometimes entered "into particular combinations to sink the wages even below this rate." He also deplored the deadening effects of the division of labor and called for government intervention to raise workers' living standards.[11] Smith's provocative work had a great international impact, going through eight editions in English and being translated into several languages within twenty years. His ideas inspired not only domestic reformers, but also independent merchants around the globe who campaigned against the monopolies of colonial empires and called for free trade.

Building the Global Economy

How did colonial markets boost Europe's economic and social development, and what conflicts and adversity did world trade entail? ▪

In addition to agricultural improvement, population pressure, and growing cottage industry, the expansion of Europe in the eighteenth century was characterized by the increase of world trade. Adam Smith himself declared that "the discovery of America and that of a passage to the East Indies by the Cape of Good Hope, are the two greatest and most important events recorded in the history of mankind."[12] In the eighteenth century Spain and Portugal revitalized their empires and began drawing more wealth from renewed colonial development. Yet once again the countries of northwestern Europe—the Netherlands, France, and above all Great Britain—benefited most.

The Atlantic economy that these countries developed from 1650 to 1790 would prove crucial in the building of a global economy. Great Britain, which was formed in 1707 by the union of England and Scotland into a single kingdom, gradually became the leading maritime power. Thus the British played the critical role in building a fairly unified Atlantic economy that provided remarkable opportunities for them and their colonists. They also competed ruthlessly with France and the Netherlands for trade and territory in Asia.

Mercantilism and Colonial Wars

Britain's commercial leadership in the eighteenth century had its origins in the mercantilism of the seventeenth century (see Chapter 16). Eventually eliciting criticism from Enlightenment thinker Adam Smith and other proponents of free trade in the late eighteenth century, European mercantilism was a system of economic regulations aimed at increasing the power of the state. As practiced by a leading advocate such as Colbert under Louis XIV, mercantilism aimed particularly at creating a favorable balance of foreign trade in order to increase a country's stock of gold. A country's gold holdings served as an all-important treasure chest that could be opened periodically to pay for war in a violent age.

In England the desire to increase both military power and private wealth resulted in the mercantile system of the **Navigation Acts**. Oliver Cromwell established the first of these laws in 1651, and the restored monarchy of Charles II extended them in 1660 and 1663. The acts required that most goods imported from Europe into England and Scotland (Great Britain after 1707) be carried on British-owned ships with British crews or on ships of the country producing the article. Moreover, these laws gave British merchants and shipowners a virtual monopoly on trade with British colonies. The colonists were required to ship their products on British (or American) ships and to buy almost all European goods from Britain. It was believed that these economic regulations would eliminate foreign competition, thereby helping British merchants and workers as well as colonial plantation owners and farmers. It was hoped, too, that the emerging British Empire would develop a shipping industry with a large number of experienced seamen who could serve when necessary in the Royal Navy.

> **Navigation Acts** A series of English laws that controlled the import of goods to Britain and British colonies.

The Navigation Acts were a form of economic warfare. Their initial target was the Dutch, who were far ahead of the English in shipping and foreign trade in the mid-seventeenth century (see Chapter 16). In conjunction with three Anglo-Dutch wars between 1652 and 1674, the Navigation Acts seriously damaged Dutch shipping and commerce. The British seized the thriving Dutch colony of New Amsterdam in 1664 and renamed it New York. By the late seventeenth century the Netherlands was falling behind England in shipping, trade, and colonies. Thereafter France stood clearly as England's most serious rival in the competition for overseas empire. Rich in natural resources, with a population three or four times that of England, and allied with Spain, continental Europe's leading military power was already building a powerful fleet and a worldwide system of rigidly monopolized colonial trade. Thus from 1701 to 1763 Britain and France were locked in a series of wars to decide, in part, which nation would become the leading maritime power and claim the profits of Europe's overseas expansion (Map 18.2).

The first round was the War of the Spanish Succession (see Chapter 16), which started in 1701 when Louis XIV accepted the Spanish crown willed to his grandson. Besides upsetting the continental balance of power, a union of France and Spain threatened to encircle and destroy the British colonies in North America (see Map 18.2). Defeated by a great coalition of states

Map 18.2 The Atlantic Economy in 1701 The growth of trade encouraged both economic development and military conflict in the Atlantic basin. Four continents were linked together by the exchange of goods and slaves.

after twelve years of fighting, Louis XIV was forced in the Peace of Utrecht (YOO-trehkt) in 1713 to cede its North American holdings in Newfoundland, Nova Scotia, and the Hudson Bay territory to Britain. Spain was compelled to give Britain control of its West African slave trade — the so-called *asiento* (ah-SYEN-toh) — and

to let Britain send one ship of merchandise into the Spanish colonies annually.

Conflict continued among the European powers over both domestic and colonial affairs. The War of the Austrian Succession (1740–1748), which started when Frederick the Great of Prussia seized Silesia from Austria's Maria Theresa (see Chapter 17), gradually became a world war that included Anglo-French conflicts in India and North America. The war ended with no change in the territorial situation in North America. This inconclusive standoff helped set the stage for the Seven Years' War (1756–1763). In central Europe, Austria's Maria Theresa sought to win back Silesia and crush Prussia, thereby re-establishing the Habsburgs' traditional leadership in German affairs. She almost succeeded in her goals, but Prussia survived with its boundaries intact.

Inconclusive in Europe, the Seven Years' War was the decisive round in the Franco-British competition for colonial empire. The fighting began in North America. The population of New France was centered in Quebec and along the St. Lawrence River, but French soldiers and Canadian fur traders had also built forts and trading posts along the Great Lakes, through the Ohio country, and down the Mississippi to New Orleans (Map 18.3). Allied with many Native American tribes, the French built more forts in 1753 in what is now western Pennsylvania to protect their claims. The following year a Virginia force attacked a small group of French soldiers, and soon the war to conquer Canada was on.

Although the inhabitants of New France were greatly outnumbered—Canada counted fifty-five thousand inhabitants, as opposed to 1.2 million in the thirteen English colonies—French and Canadian forces under the experienced marquis de Montcalm fought well and scored major victories until 1758. Then, led by their new chief minister, William Pitt, whose grandfather had made a fortune in India, the British diverted men and money from the war in Europe, using superior sea power to destroy the French fleet and choke off French commerce around the world. In 1759 a combined British naval and land force laid siege to Quebec for four long months, defeating Montcalm's army in a dramatic battle that sealed the fate of France in North America.

British victory on all colonial fronts was ratified in the 1763 **Treaty of Paris**. France lost its remaining possessions on mainland North America. Canada and all French territory east of the Mississippi River passed to Britain, and France ceded Louisiana to Spain as compensation for Spain's loss of Florida to Britain. France also gave up most of its holdings in India, opening the way to British dominance on the subcontinent. By 1763 British naval power, built in large part on the rapid growth of the British shipping industry after the passage of the Navigation Acts, had triumphed decisively: Britain had realized its goal of monopolizing a vast trading and colonial empire.

Eighteenth-Century Colonial Trade

In the eighteenth century, stimulated by trade and empire building, London grew into the West's largest and richest city. (See "Living in the Past: The Remaking of

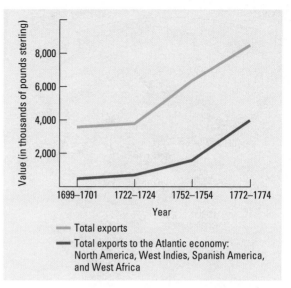

Figure 18.3 Exports of English Manufactured Goods, 1700–1774 While trade between England and Europe stagnated after 1700, English exports to Africa and the Americas boomed and greatly stimulated English economic development.

(Source: Data from R. Davis, "English Foreign Trade, 1700–1774," *Economic History Review*, 2d ser., 15 [1962]: 302–303.)

London," page 574.) Above all, the rapidly growing and increasingly wealthy agricultural populations of the mainland colonies provided an expanding market for English manufactured goods. This situation was extremely fortunate, for England in the eighteenth century was gradually losing, or only slowly expanding, its sales to many of its traditional European markets.

English exports of manufactured goods to the Atlantic economy came to the rescue. Sales to the mainland colonies of North America and the West Indian sugar islands—with an important assist from West Africa and Latin America—soared from £500,000 to £4.0 million (Figure 18.3). Exports to England's other colonies in Ireland and India also rose substantially in the eighteenth century. English exports also became more balanced and diversified. To America and Africa went large quantities of metal items—axes to frontier settlers, firearms and chains to slave owners. There were also clocks and coaches, buttons and saddles, china and furniture, musical instruments and scientific equipment, and a host of other things. Foreign trade became the bread and butter of some industries; for example, by 1750 half the nails made in England were going to the colonies. Thus, the mercantilist system achieved remarkable success for England in the eighteenth century, and by the 1770s England stood on the threshold of the epoch-making

> **Treaty of Paris** The treaty that ended the Seven Years' War in Europe and the colonies in 1763 and ratified British victory on all colonial fronts.

Map 18.3 **European Claims in North America Before and After the Seven Years' War, 1755–1763** As a result of the war, France lost its vast territories. In an effort to avoid costly conflicts with Native Americans living in the newly conquered territory, the British government in 1763 prohibited colonists from settling west of the Appalachian Mountains. One of the few remaining French colonies in the Americas, Saint-Domingue (on the island of Hispaniola) was the most profitable plantation colony in the New World.

industrial changes that would become known as the Industrial Revolution.

Although they lost many possessions to the English, the French still profited enormously from colonial trade. The colonies of Saint-Domingue (modern-day Haiti) and Martinique and Guadeloupe remained in French hands and provided immense fortunes in plantation agriculture and slave trading during the second half of the eighteenth century. By 1789 the population of Saint-Domingue included five hundred thousand slaves whose labor had allowed the colony to become the world's leading producer of coffee and sugar and the most profitable plantation colony in the New World.[13] The wealth generated from colonial trade fostered the confidence of the merchant classes in Paris, Bordeaux, and other large cities, and merchants soon joined other elite groups clamoring for more political power.

The third major player in the Atlantic economy, Spain, also saw its colonial fortunes improve during the eighteenth century. Not only did it gain Louisiana from France in 1763, but its influence expanded westward all the way to northern California through the efforts of Spanish missionaries and ranchers. Its mercantilist goals were boosted by a recovery in silver production, which had dropped significantly in the seventeenth century.

Silver mining also stimulated food production for the mining camps, and wealthy Spanish landowners developed a system of **debt peonage** to keep indigenous workers on their estates. Under this system, which was

debt peonage A form of serfdom that allowed a planter or rancher to keep his workers or slaves in perpetual debt bondage by periodically advancing food, shelter, and a little money.

Atlantic slave trade The forced migration of Africans across the Atlantic for slave labor on plantations and in other industries; the trade reached its peak in the eighteenth century and ultimately involved more than twelve million Africans.

similar to serfdom, a planter or rancher would keep workers in perpetual debt bondage by advancing them food, shelter, and a little money.

The Atlantic Slave Trade

As the volume of transatlantic trade increased, the four continents bordering the ocean were increasingly drawn into an integrated economic system. At the core of this Atlantic world were the misery and profit of the **Atlantic slave trade**. The forced migration of millions of Africans—cruel, unjust, and tragic—was a key element in the Atlantic system and western European economic expansion throughout the eighteenth century. The brutal practice intensified dramatically after 1700 and especially after 1750 with the growth of trade and demand for slave-produced goods like sugar and cotton. According to the most authoritative source, European traders purchased and shipped 6.5 million African slaves across the Atlantic between 1701 and 1800—more than half of the estimated total of 12.5 million Africans

transported between 1450 and 1900, of whom 15 percent died in procurement and transit.[14] By the peak decade of the 1780s, shipments averaged about eighty thousand individuals per year in an attempt to satisfy the constantly rising demand for labor power—and also for slave owners' profits—in the Americas.

The rise of plantation agriculture was responsible for the tremendous growth of the slave trade. Among all European colonies, the plantations of Portuguese Brazil received by far the largest number of enslaved Africans over the entire period of the slave trade—45 percent of the total. Another 45 percent were divided among the many

Plantation Zones, ca. 1700

The Atlantic Slave Trade This engraving from 1814 shows traders leading a group of slaves to the West African coast, where they will board ships to cross the Atlantic. Many slaves died en route or arrived greatly weakened and ill. The newspaper advertisement of the sale of a ship's cargo of slaves in Charleston, South Carolina, promises "fine, healthy negroes," testifying to the dangers of the crossing and to the frequency of epidemic diseases like smallpox. (engraving: Bibliothèque de l'Arsenal, Paris/Archives Charmet/The Bridgeman Art Library; advertisement: The Granger Collection, New York)

The Remaking of London

LIVING IN THE PAST

THE IMPERIAL CAPITAL OF LONDON dominated Britain and astonished the visitor. Equal in population to Paris with four hundred thousand inhabitants in 1650, London grew to nine hundred thousand by 1800, while second-place Paris had six hundred thousand. And as London grew, its citizens created a new urban landscape and style of living.

In 1666 the Great Fire of London destroyed about 80 percent of the old, predominately wooden central city. Reconstruction proceeded quickly, with brick structures made mandatory to prevent fires. As London rebuilt and kept growing, noble landowners sought to increase their incomes by setting up residential developments on their estates west of the city. A landowner would lay out a square with streets and building lots and lease the lots to speculative builders who put up fine houses for sale or rent. Soho Square, first laid out in the 1670s and shown here as it appeared in 1731, was fairly typical. The spacious square with its gated park is surrounded by three-story row houses on deep, narrow lots. Set in the country but close to the city, a square like Soho was a kind of elegant village with restrictive building codes that catered to aristocrats, officials, and successful professionals who were served by the artisans and shopkeepers living in side streets. The classy new area,

known as the West End, contrasted sharply with the shoddy rentals and makeshift shacks of laborers and sailors in the mushrooming East End, which artists rarely painted. Residential segregation by income level increased substantially in eighteenth-century London and became a key feature of the modern city.

As the suburban villages grew and gradually merged, the West End increasingly attracted the well-to-do from all over England. Rural landowners and provincial notables came for the social season from October to May. The picture at right of Bloomsbury Square in 1787 and the original country mansion of the enterprising noble developer provides a glimpse into this well-born culture.

London before the Great Fire. (Hulton Archive/Getty Images)

Caribbean colonies. The colonies of mainland North America took only 3 percent of slaves arriving from Africa, a little under four hundred thousand, relying mostly on natural growth of the enslaved population.

Eighteenth-century intensification of the slave trade resulted in fundamental changes in its organization. After 1700, as Britain became the undisputed leader in shipping slaves across the Atlantic, European governments and ship captains cut back on fighting among themselves and concentrated on commerce. They generally adopted the shore method of trading, which was less expensive than maintaining fortified trading posts. Under this system, European ships sent boats ashore or invited African dealers to bring traders and slaves out to their ships. This method allowed ships to move easily

along the coast from market to market and to depart more quickly for the Americas.

Some African merchants and rulers who controlled exports profited from the greater demand for slaves. With their newfound wealth, some Africans gained access to European and colonial goods, including firearms. But generally such economic returns did not spread very far, and the negative consequences of the expanding slave trade predominated. Wars among African states to obtain salable captives increased, and leaders used slave profits to purchase more arms than textiles and consumer goods. While the populations of Europe and Asia grew substantially in the eighteenth century, the population of Africa stagnated or possibly declined. As one contemporary critic observed:

Soho Square, 1731. (Private Collection/The Stapleton Collection/The Bridgeman Art Library)

Bloomsbury Square, 1787. (HarperCollins Publishers/The Art Archive)

QUESTIONS FOR ANALYSIS

1. Examining the picture shown at left, how would you characterize pre-Fire London?

2. Compare the paintings of Soho and Bloomsbury Squares. How are they complementary? Why did the artist choose to include a milkmaid and her cows in the illustration of Bloomsbury Square?

I do not know if coffee and sugar are essential to the happiness of Europe, but I know that these two products have accounted for the unhappiness of two great regions of the world: America has been depopulated so as to have land on which to plant them; Africa has been depopulated so as to have the people to cultivate them.[15]

Most Europeans did not personally witness the horrors of the slave trade between Africa and the Americas, and until the early part of the eighteenth century, they considered the African slave trade a legitimate business. But as details of the plight of slaves became known, a campaign to abolish slavery developed in Britain. In the late 1780s the abolition campaign grew into a mass movement of public opinion, the first in British history. British women were prominent in this movement, denouncing the immorality of human bondage and stressing the cruel and sadistic treatment of female slaves and slave families. These attacks put the defenders of slavery on the defensive. In 1807 Parliament abolished the British slave trade, although slavery continued in British colonies and the Americas for decades.

Identities and Communities of the Atlantic World

Not only slaves and commodities but also free people and ideas circulated through the eighteenth-century Atlantic world. As contacts among the Atlantic coasts of the Americas, Africa, and Europe became more

Slaves Harvesting Sugar Cane In this 1828 print a long line of hard-working slaves systematically harvests the ripe cane on the island of Antigua, while on the right more slaves load cut cane into wagons for refining at the plantation's central crushing mill. The manager on horseback may be ordering the overseer to quicken the work pace, always brutal and unrelenting at harvest time. Slave labor made high-intensity capitalist production of sugar possible in the Americas. (John Carter Brown Library at Brown University)

> ❝ A turn of mind peculiar to the planter, occasioned by a physical difference of constitution, climate, customs, and education, tends . . . to repress the remains of his former attachment to his native soil. ❞
>
> —**EUROPEAN OBSERVER**

frequent, and as European settlements grew into well-established colonies, new identities and communities emerged.

The term *Creole* referred to people of Spanish ancestry born in the Americas. Wealthy Creoles and their counterparts throughout the Atlantic colonies prided themselves on following European ways of life. In addition to their lavish plantation estates, they maintained townhouses in colonial cities built on the European model, with theaters, central squares, churches, and cof-

feehouses. They purchased luxury goods made in Europe, and their children were often sent to be educated in the home country. Over time, however, the colonial elite came to feel that their circumstances gave them different interests and characteristics from those of their home population. As one observer explained, "a turn of mind peculiar to the planter, occasioned by a physical difference of constitution, climate, customs, and education, tends . . . to repress the remains of his former attachment to his native soil."[16] Creole traders and planters increasingly resented the regulations and taxes imposed by colonial bureaucrats.

Not all Europeans in the colonies were wealthy. Numerous poor or middling whites worked as clerks, shopkeepers, craftsmen, and plantation managers. Whether rich or poor, however, white Europeans usually made up a small proportion of the population. Since most European migrants were men, much of the population of the Atlantic world descended from unions—forced or through choice—of European men and indigenous or African women (see Chapter 15). Colonial attempts to classify and systematize racial categories greatly influenced developing Enlightenment thought on racial difference (see Chapter 16).

Mixed-race populations sometimes rose to the colonial elite. The Spanish conquistadores often consolidated their power through marriage to the daughters of local rulers, and their descendants were among the most powerful inhabitants of Spanish America. In the Spanish and French Caribbean, as in Brazil, many masters acknowledged and freed their mixed-race children, leading to sizable populations of free people of color. Advantaged by their fathers, some became wealthy land and slave owners in their own right. In the second half of the eighteenth century, the prosperity of some free people of color brought a backlash from the white population of Saint-Domingue in the form of new race laws prohibiting nonwhites from marrying whites and forcing them to adopt distinctive attire. In the British colonies of the Caribbean and the southern mainland, by contrast,

Picturing the Past

Mulatto Painting The caption in the upper left-hand corner of this mid-eighteenth-century painting identifies the family as being composed of a Spanish father and a black mother, whose child is described as "mulato." The painting was number six in a series of sixteen images by the painter Jose de Alcibar, each showing a different racial and ethnic combination. The series belonged to a popular genre in the Spanish Americas known as *castas* paintings, which commonly depicted sixteen different forms of racial mixing. (Attrib. Jose de Alcibar, 6, *De Espanol y Negra, Mulato*, ca. 1760–1770. Denver Art Museum: Collection of Frederick and Jan Mayer. Photography provided by the Denver Art Museum)

ANALYZING THE IMAGE How would you characterize the relations among mother, father, and child as shown in this painting? Does the painter suggest power relations within the family? What attitude does the painter seem to have toward the family?

CONNECTIONS Why do you think such paintings were so popular? Who do you think the audience might have been, and why would viewers be fascinated by such images?

To complete this activity online, go to the Online Study Guide at bedfordstmartins.com/mckaywest.

masters tended to leave their mixed-race progeny in slavery, maintaining a stark discrepancy between free whites and enslaved people of color.[17] British colonial law forbade marriage between English men and women and Africans or Native Americans.

The identities inspired by racial and ethnic mixing were equally complex. Colonial elites became "Americanized" by adopting native foods, like chocolate and potatoes, and sought relief from tropical disease in native remedies. Some mixed-race people sought to enter Creole society and obtain its many official and unofficial privileges by passing as white. Where they existed in any number, though, free people of color established their own proud social hierarchies based on wealth, family connections, occupation, and skin color. Olaudah Equiano, who traveled throughout the Atlantic as a slave and later as a free man, was an eloquent spokesman for the mixing of African and European cultures in his own life experience. (See "Individuals in Society: Olaudah Equiano," at right.)

Converting indigenous people to Christianity was a key ambition for all European powers in the New World. Galvanized by the Protestant Reformation and the perceived need to protect and spread Catholicism, Catholic powers actively sponsored missionary efforts. Jesuits, Franciscans, Dominicans, and other religious orders established missions throughout Spanish, Portuguese, and French colonies. Rather than a straightforward imposition of Christianity, conversion entailed a complex process of cultural exchange. Catholic friars were among the first Europeans to seek understanding of native cultures and languages as part of their effort to render Christianity comprehensible to indigenous people. In turn, Christian ideas and practices in the New World took on a distinctive character. For example, a sixteenth-century apparition of the Virgin Mary in Mexico City, known as the Virgin of Guadalupe, became a central icon of Spanish-American Catholicism.

Missionaries' success in the New World varied over time and space. In Central and South America, large-scale conversion forged enduring Catholic cultures in Portuguese and Spanish colonies. For example, it is estimated that missionaries baptized up to 10 million indigenous people in New Spain in the first two decades of Spanish rule.[18] Conversion efforts in North America were less effective due to the scattered nature of settlement and the lesser integration of native people into the colonial community. On the whole, Protestants were less active as missionaries in this period, although some dissenters, like Quakers and Methodists, did seek converts among native people.

The practice of slavery reveals important limitations on efforts to spread Christianity. Slave owners often refused to baptize their slaves in case baptism would confer additional rights upon them. In some areas, particularly among the mostly African-born slaves of the Caribbean, elements of African religious belief and practice endured, often incorporated with Christian traditions.

Restricted from owning land and holding many occupations in Europe, Jews were eager participants in the new Atlantic economy and established a network of mercantile communities along its trade routes. As in the Old World, Jews in European colonies faced discrimination; for example, restrictions existed on the number of slaves they could own in Barbados in the early eighteenth century.[19] Jews were considered to be white Europeans and thus ineligible to be slaves, but they did not enjoy equal status with Christians. The status of Jews adds one more element to the complexity of Atlantic identities.

Trade and Empire in Asia and the Pacific

As the Atlantic economy took shape, Europeans continued to vie for dominance in the Asian trade. Between 1500 and 1600 the Portuguese had become major players in the Indian Ocean trading world, eliminating Venice as Europe's chief supplier of spices and other Asian luxury goods. The Portuguese dominated but did not fundamentally alter the age-old pattern of Indian Ocean trade, which involved merchants from many areas as more or less autonomous players. This situation changed radically with the intervention of the Dutch and then the English (see Chapter 15).

Formed in 1602, the Dutch East India Company had taken control of the Portuguese spice trade in the Indian Ocean, with the port of Batavia (Jakarta) in Java as its center of operations. Within a few decades they had expelled the Portuguese from Ceylon and other East Indian islands. Unlike the Portuguese, the Dutch transformed the Indian Ocean trading world. Whereas East Indian states and peoples maintained independence under the Portuguese, who treated them as autonomous business partners, the Dutch established outright control and reduced them to dependents.

After these successes, the Dutch hold in Asia faltered in the eighteenth century due to the company's failure to diversify to meet changing consumption patterns. Spices continued to compose much of its shipping, despite their declining importance in the European diet, probably due to changing fashions in food and luxury consumption. Fierce competition from its main rival, the English East India Company (established 1600), also severely undercut Dutch trade.

Britain initially struggled for a foothold in Asia. With the Dutch monopolizing the Indian Ocean, the British turned to India, the source of lucrative trade in silks, textiles, and pepper. Throughout the seventeenth century the English East India Company relied on trade concessions from the powerful Mughal emperor, who granted only piecemeal access to the subcontinent. Finally, in

INDIVIDUALS IN SOCIETY

THE SLAVE TRADE WAS A MASS MIGRATION involving millions of human beings. It was also the sum of individual lives spent partly or entirely in slavery. Although most of the individuals remain hidden to us, Olaudah Equiano (1745–1797) is an important exception. According to his autobiography, Equiano was born in Benin (modern Nigeria) of Ibo ethnicity. His father, one of the village elders (or chieftains), presided over a large household that included "many slaves," prisoners captured in local wars. All people, slave and free, shared in the cultivation of family lands. One day when all the adults were in the fields, two strange men and a woman broke into the family compound, kidnapped the eleven-year-old boy and his sister, tied them up, and dragged them into the woods. Brother and sister were separated, and Olaudah was sold several times to various dealers before reaching the coast. As it took six months to walk there, his home must have been far inland.

The slave ship and the strange appearance of the white crew terrified the boy. Much worse was the long voyage from Benin to Barbados in the Caribbean, as Equiano later recounted. "The stench of the [ship's] hold ... became absolutely pestilential ... [and] brought on a sickness among the slaves, of which many died. . . . The shrieks of the women and the groans of the dying rendered the whole a scene of horror almost inconceivable." Placed on deck with the sick and dying, Equiano saw two and then three of his "enchained countrymen" escape somehow through the nettings and jump into the sea, "preferring death to such a life of misery."*

Equiano's new owner, an officer in the Royal Navy, took him to England and saw that the lad received some education. Engaged in bloody action in Europe for almost four years as a captain's boy in the Seven Years' War, Equiano hoped that his loyal service and Christian baptism would help secure his freedom. He also knew that slavery was generally illegal in England. But his master deceived him. Docking in London, the slave owner and his accomplices forced a protesting and heartbroken Equiano onto a ship bound for the Caribbean. There he was sold to Robert King, a Quaker merchant from Philadelphia who dealt in sugar and rum. Equiano developed his mathematical skills, worked hard to please as a clerk in King's warehouse, and became first mate on one of King's ships. Allowed to trade on the side for his own profit, Equiano amassed capital, repaid King his original purchase price, and received his deed of manumission, authorizing his freedom, at the age of twenty-one. King urged his talented former slave to stay on as a business partner, but Equiano hated the limitations and dangers of black freedom in the colonies—he was almost kidnapped back into slavery while loading a ship in Georgia—and could think only of England. Settling in London, Equiano studied, worked as a hairdresser, and went to sea periodically as a merchant seaman. He developed his ardent Christian faith and became a leading member of London's sizable black community.

Olaudah Equiano, in an engraving from his autobiography. (National Portrait Gallery, Smithsonian Institution/Art Resource, NY)

Equiano loathed the brutal slavery and the vicious exploitation that he saw in the West Indies and Britain's mainland colonies. A complex and sophisticated man, he also respected the integrity of Robert King and admired British navigational and industrial technologies. He encountered white oppressors and made white friends. He once described himself as "almost an Englishman." In the 1780s he joined with white and black activists in the antislavery campaign and wrote *The Interesting Narrative of the Life of Olaudah Equiano Written by Himself*, a well-documented autobiographical indictment of slavery. Above all, he urged Christians to live by the principles they professed and to treat Africans equally as free human beings and children of God. With the success of his widely read book, he carried his message to large audiences across Britain and Ireland and inspired the growing movement to abolish slavery.

Recently, scholars have unearthed contemporary documents in which Equiano gave an American, rather than African, birthplace.† This discovery has raised controversy about the authenticity of parts of his autobiography; whatever his place of birth, Equiano's account of the Middle Passage was certainly based on discussions with many fellow slaves even if not on his own experience.

QUESTIONS FOR ANALYSIS

1. What aspects of Olaudah Equiano's life as a slave were typical? What aspects were atypical?

2. Describe Equiano's culture and personality. What aspects are most striking? Why?

*Olaudah Equiano, *The Interesting Narrative of the Life of Olaudah Equiano Written by Himself*, ed. with an introduction by Robert J. Allison (Boston: Bedford Books, 1995), pp. 56–57. Recent scholarship has re-examined Equiano's life and thrown some details of his identity into question.

†Vincent Carretta, "Olaudah Equiano or Gustavus Vassa? New Light on an Eighteenth-Century Question of Identity," *Slavery and Abolition* 20, 3 (December 1999): 96–105.

The British in India, ca. 1785 This Indian miniature shows the wife (center) of a British officer attended by many Indian servants. A British merchant (left) awaits her attention. The picture reflects the luxurious lifestyle of the British elite in India, many members of which returned home with colossal fortunes. (Scala/Art Resource, NY)

1716 the Mughals conceded empire-wide trading privileges. To further their economic interests, British East India Company agents increasingly intervened in local affairs and made alliances or waged war against Indian princes.

Britain's great rival for influence in India was France. During the War of the Austrian Succession, British and French forces in India supported opposing rulers in local power struggles. Their rivalry was finally resolved by the Treaty of Paris, which granted all of France's possessions

in India to the British with the exception of Pondicherry, an Indian Ocean port city. With the elimination of their rival, British ascendancy in India accelerated. In 1764 company forces defeated the Mughal emperor, leaving him on the throne as a ruler in title only. Robert Clive, a company agent who had led its forces in battle, became the first British governor general of Bengal, in northeast India, with direct authority over the province. By about 1805 the British had overcome vigorous Indian resistance to gain economic and political dominance of much of the subcontinent, and India was lauded as the "jewel" in the British Empire in the nineteenth century.

The late eighteenth century also witnessed the beginning of British settlement of the continent of Australia. The continent was first sighted by Europeans in the early seventeenth century, and thereafter parts of the coast were charted by European ships. Captain James Cook claimed the east coast of Australia for England in 1770, naming it New South Wales. The first colony was established there in the late 1780s, relying on the labor of convicted prisoners forcibly transported from Britain. Settlement of the western portion of the continent followed in the 1790s. The first colonies struggled for survival and, after an initial period of friendly relations, soon aroused the hostility and resistance of aboriginal peoples. Cook himself was killed by islanders in Hawaii in 1779, having charted much of the Pacific Ocean for the first time.

The rising economic and political power of Europeans in this period drew on the connections they established between the Asian and Atlantic trade worlds. An outstanding example is the trade in cowry shells. These seashells, originating in the Maldive Islands in the Indian Ocean, were used as a form of currency in West Africa. European traders obtained them in Asia, packing them alongside porcelains, spices, and silks for the journey home. The cowries were then brought from European ports to the West African coast to be traded for slaves. Indian textiles were also prized in Africa and played a similar role in exchange. Thus, the trade of the Atlantic was inseparable from Asian commerce, and Europeans were increasingly found dominating commerce in both worlds.

India, 1805

LOOKING BACK
LOOKING AHEAD

BY THE TURN of the eighteenth century, western Europe had begun to shake off the effects of long decades of famine, disease, warfare, economic depression, and demographic stagnation. The eighteenth century witnessed a breakthrough in agricultural production that, along with improved infrastructure and the retreat of epidemic disease, contributed to a substantial increase in population. One crucial catalyst for agricultural innovation was the scientific revolution, which provided new tools of empirical observation and experimentation. The Enlightenment as well, with its emphasis on progress and public welfare, convinced government officials, scientists, and informed landowners to seek better solutions to old problems. By the end of the century, industry and trade also attracted enlightened commentators who advocated free markets and less government control. Modern political economy is thus one more legacy of the Enlightenment.

As the era of European exploration and conquest gave way to colonial empire-building, the eighteenth century witnessed increased consolidation of global markets and bitter competition among Europeans for the spoils of empire. From its slow inception in the mid-fifteenth century, the African slave trade reached brutal heights in the second half of the eighteenth century. The eighteenth-century Atlantic world thus tied the shores of Europe, the Americas, and Africa in a web of commercial and human exchange that also had strong ties with the Pacific and the Indian Ocean.

The new dynamics of the eighteenth century prepared the way for world-shaking changes. Population growth and rural industry began to undermine long-standing traditions of daily life in western Europe. The transformed families of the industrious revolution developed not only new habits of work, but also a new sense of confidence in their abilities. By the 1770s England was approaching an economic breakthrough as fully significant as the great political upheaval destined to develop shortly in neighboring France. In the same period, the first wave of resistance to European domination rose up in the colonies. The great revolutions of the late eighteenth century would change the world forever.

CHAPTER REVIEW

▪ What important developments led to the agricultural revolution, and how did these changes affect the peasants? (p. 554)

The agricultural revolution consisted of new techniques of working the land and new crops, which together greatly improved agricultural production. It began in the Low Countries and then England, where farmers drained wetlands to create more farmland, introduced new crops, and intensified crop rotation. Better breeding of horses for farm work and improved seed-sowing methods also increased crop yields. These innovations, inspired in part by the experimentation of the scientific revolution and the reform ideals of the Enlightenment, created new food sources for people and livestock. Along with new techniques came the enclosure of the open fields that had characterized much of European agriculture. Enclosure permitted reform-minded landowners to experiment with new techniques, but it also allowed wealthy landowners to enlarge their own holdings. Thus, increased production came at a high cost to poor farmers, who lost access to common village land that had provided pasture and food and were often forced to sell their small holdings to the rich. The landless poor became wage laborers, a transformation known as proletarianization.

▪ Why did the European population rise dramatically in the eighteenth century? (p. 558)

The decrease in mortality from famine, disease, and war all contributed to the eighteenth-century population explosion. The agricultural revolution led to increased food production, and better storage and transportation systems meant that more food reached hungry populations. Also, for reasons historians do not yet understand, the recurring curse of bubonic plague disappeared, and improved public health and sanitation generally cut down on other diseases as well. In addition, wars became more gentlemanly, wreaking less havoc on farmlands and resulting in fewer overall deaths. As a result of all these factors, the European population recovered from the stagnation and losses of the seventeenth century to reach unprecedented new levels in the eighteenth century.

▪ How and why did rural industry intensify in the eighteenth century? (p. 560)

The combination of the enclosure movement and population increases led to growth in the number of people in the countryside with little or no land. Peasant households set up industrial production within their cottages, allocating family members' labor during the slack seasons of agriculture or, in some cases, abandoning farming altogether for a new life of weaving or spinning. Merchant capitalists distributed such work among rural laborers in order to escape the constraints of the urban guilds. Although they profited

from the low wages paid to rural workers, merchants complained about their lack of control over them. The spread of cottage industry was one sign of an industrious revolution that helped pave the path of the Industrial Revolution of the late eighteenth century. The labor of women and children was crucial to the spread of cottage industry.

▪ What were guilds, and why did they become controversial in the eighteenth century? (p. 566)

Guilds were associations of master craftsmen in the towns and cities. Each guild received a monopoly over its trade from the state and was responsible for ensuring high-quality standards among workers. In most cases, guilds were restricted to Christian men, although some female guilds existed, mostly in needlework and textiles. Critics like Adam Smith attacked guilds in the second half of the eighteenth century as part of a larger call for free trade and an end to government economic regulation. With the growth of liberal political and economic views, most of Europe's guilds disappeared by the mid-nineteenth century.

▪ How did colonial markets boost Europe's economic and social development, and what conflicts and adversity did world trade entail? (p. 569)

During the eighteenth century Europeans continued their overseas expansion, fighting for empire and profit and, in particular, consolidating their hold on the Americas. Britain's Navigation Acts imposed a form of economic warfare, which allowed it to profit mightily from overseas trade and expand its global empire. France and Spain continued to profit from their own colonial trade, but England and its empire proved most successful. The Atlantic slave trade grew enormously as colonial plantations used slaves to produce commodities for trade. Although public outcry at slavery's horrors led Britain to abolish slavery in 1807, the practice continued throughout the European colonies. The movement of people and ideas across the Atlantic in the eighteenth century led to new ethnic identities as inhabitants of the colonies developed customs and attitudes apart from those of their homeland.

Suggested Reading

Allen, Robert, et al., eds. *Living Standards in the Past: New Perspectives on Well-Being in Asia and Europe.* 2004. Offers rich comparative perspectives on population growth and living standards among common people.

Bell, Dean Philip. *Jews in the Early Modern World.* 2008. A broad examination of Jewish life and relations with non-Jews in the early modern period.

Carpenter, Roger M. *The Renewed, the Destroyed, and the Remade: The Three Thought Worlds of the Iroquois and the Huron, 1609–1650.* 2004. Explores the culture and beliefs of two Native American peoples in the period of European colonization.

De Vries, Jan, and Ad van der Woude. *The First Modern Economy: Success, Failure, and Perseverance of the Dutch Economy, 1500–1815.* 1997. Examines the early success of the Dutch economy and the challenges it faced in the eighteenth century.

Epstein, S. R., and Maarten Prak, eds. *Guilds, Innovation and the European Economy, 1400–1800.* 2008. A recent contribution to the debate on European guilds that emphasizes their adaptability and responsiveness to economic change.

Farr, James R. *Artisans in Europe, 1300–1914.* 2000. Provides an overview of guilds and artisanal labor in early modern Europe.

Gullickson, Gary L. *Spinners and Weavers of Auffay: Rural Industry and the Sexual Division of Labor in a French Village, 1750–1850.* 1986. Examines women's labor in cottage industry in northern France.

Harms, Robert W. *The Diligent: A Voyage Through the Worlds of the Slave Trade.* 2002. A deeply moving account of a French slave ship and its victims.

Klein, Herbert S. *The Atlantic Slave Trade.* 1999. An excellent short synthesis on slavery in the Atlantic world.

Liebersohn, Harry. *The Traveler's World: Europe to the Pacific.* 2006. Imaginatively recounts European explorations and imaginations of the Pacific.

Morgan, Jennifer Lyle. *Laboring Women: Reproduction and Gender in New World Slavery.* 2004. Focuses on the role of women's labor in the evolution of slavery in Britain's North American colonies.

Ormrod, David. *The Rise of Commercial Empires: England and the Netherlands in the Age of Mercantilism, 1650–1770.* 2003. Examines the battle for commercial and maritime supremacy in the North Sea.

Overton, Mark. *Agricultural Revolution in England.* 1996. Charts the path of agricultural progress in England.

Porter, Roy. *London: A Social History.* 1994. A sparkling combination of fine scholarship and exciting popular history.

Prak, Maarten, ed. *Early Modern Capitalism: Economic and Social Change in Europe, 1400–1800.* 2001. Collected essays on economic and social developments in early modern Europe.

Rothschild, Emma. *Economic Sentiments: Adam Smith, Condorcet, and the Enlightenment.* 2001. A fascinating reconsideration of Smith and the birth of modern economic thought.

Notes

1. B. H. Slicher van Bath, *The Agrarian History of Western Europe, A.D. 500–1850* (New York: St. Martin's Press, 1963), p. 240.
2. Cited in Paul Mantoux, *The Industrial Revolution in the Eighteenth Century: An Outline of the Beginnings of the Modern Factory System* (1961; Abingdon, U.K.: Routledge, 2005), p. 175.
3. Thomas Salmon, *Modern History: Or the Present State of All Nations* (London, 1730), p. 406.
4. Quoted in I. Pinchbeck, *Women Workers and the Industrial Revolution, 1750–1850* (New York: F. S. Crofts, 1930), p. 113.
5. Richard J. Soderlund, "'Intended as a Terror to the Idle and Profligate': Embezzlement and the Origins of Policing in the Yorkshire Worsted Industry, c. 1750–1777," *Journal of Social History* 31 (Spring 1998): 658.
6. Cited in Maxine Berg, *The Age of Manufactures, 1700–1820: Industry, Innovation, and Work in Britain* (London: Routledge, 1994), p. 124.
7. Jan de Vries, *The Industrious Revolution: Consumer Behavior and the Household Economy, 1650 to the Present* (Cambridge, U.K.: Cambridge University Press, 2008).
8. Jan de Vries, "The Industrial Revolution and the Industrious Revolution," *The Journal of Economic History* 54, 2 (June 1994): 249–270, discusses the industrious revolution of the second half of the twentieth century.
9. S. Pollard and C. Holmes, eds., *Documents of European Economic History*, vol. 1: *The Process of Industrialization, 1750–1870* (New York: St. Martin's Press, 1968), p. 53.
10. R. Campbell, *The London Tradesman* (London, 1757), p. 152.
11. R. Heilbroner, *The Essential Adam Smith* (New York: W. W. Norton, 1986), p. 196.
12. Ibid., p. 281.
13. Laurent Dubois and John D. Garrigus, *Slave Revolution in the Caribbean, 1789–1904* (New York: Palgrave, 2006), p. 8.
14. Figures obtained from Voyages: The Trans-Atlantic Slave Trade Database, http://www.slavevoyages.org/tast/assessment/estimates.faces (accessed June 11, 2009).
15. Cited in Thomas Benjamin, *The Atlantic World: Europeans, Africans, Indians and Their Shared History, 1400–1900* (Cambridge, U.K.: Cambridge University Press, 2009), p. 211.
16. Pierre Marie François Paget, *Travels Round the World in the Years 1767, 1768, 1769, 1770, 1771* (London, 1793), vol. 1, p. 262.
17. Orlando Patterson, *Slavery and Social Death* (Cambridge, Mass.: Harvard University Press, 1982), p. 255.
18. Mark A. Noll, *The Old Religion in a New World: The History of North American Christianity* (Grand Rapids, Mich.: Wm. B. Eerdmans, 2002), pp. 28–29.
19. Erik R. Seeman, "Jews in the Early Modern Atlantic: Crossing Boundaries, Keeping Faith," in *The Atlantic in Global History, 1500–2000*, ed. Jorge Cañizares-Esguerra and Erik R. Seeman (Upper Saddle River, N.J.: Pearson Prentice Hall, 2007), p. 43.

Key Terms

agricultural revolution (p. 555)

enclosure (p. 556)

proletarianization (p. 558)

cottage industry (p. 560)

putting-out system (p. 561)

industrious revolution (p. 566)

guild system (p. 566)

economic liberalism (p. 568)

Navigation Acts (p. 569)

Treaty of Paris (p. 571)

debt peonage (p. 572)

Atlantic slave trade (p. 573)

For practice quizzes and other study tools, visit the Online Study Guide at **bedfordstmartins.com/mckaywest**.

For primary sources from this period, see ***Sources of Western Society*, Second Edition**.

For Web sites, images, and documents related to topics in this chapter, visit Make History at **bedfordstmartins.com/mckaywest**.

19

The Changing Life of the People

1700–1800

The discussion of agriculture and industry in the last chapter showed the common people at work, straining to make ends meet within the larger context of population growth, gradual economic expansion, and ferocious political competition at home and overseas. This chapter shows us how that world of work was embedded in a rich complex of family organization, community practices, everyday experiences, and collective attitudes. As with the economy, traditional habits and practices of daily life changed considerably over the eighteenth century. Change was particularly dramatic in the growing cities of north-western Europe, where traditional social controls were undermined by the anonymity and increased social interaction of the urban setting.

Historians have intensively studied many aspects of popular life, including marriage patterns and family size, childhood and education, nutrition, health care, and religious worship. Uncovering the life of the common people has been a formidable challenge because they left few written records and regional variations abounded. Yet imaginative research has resulted in major findings and much greater knowledge. It is now possible to follow the common people into their homes, workshops, churches, and taverns and to ask, "What were the everyday experiences of ordinary people, and how did they change over the eighteenth century?" ■

Life in the Eighteenth Century. The huge fresh-food market known as Les Halles was the pulsing heart of eighteenth-century Paris. Here, peddlers offer food and drink to the men and women of the market, many of whom had arrived in the predawn hours to set up their stalls.

CHAPTER PREVIEW

Marriage and the Family
■ What changes occurred in marriage and the family in the course of the eighteenth century?

Children and Education
■ What was life like for children, and how did attitudes toward childhood evolve?

Popular Culture and Consumerism
■ How did increasing literacy and new patterns of consumption affect people's lives?

Religious Authority and Beliefs
■ What were the patterns of popular religion, and how did they interact with the worldview of the educated public and their Enlightenment ideals?

Medical Practice
■ How did the practice of medicine evolve in the eighteenth century?

Marriage and the Family

What changes occurred in marriage and the family in the course of the eighteenth century? ▪

The basic unit of social organization is the family. Within the structure of the family human beings love, mate, and reproduce. It is primarily the family that teaches the child, imparting values and customs that condition an individual's behavior for a lifetime. The family is also an institution woven into the web of history. It evolves and changes, assuming different forms in different times and places. The eighteenth century witnessed such an evolution, as patterns of marriage shifted and individuals adapted and conformed to the new and changing realities of the family unit.

Late Marriage and Nuclear Families

Because census data before the modern period are rare, historians have turned to parish registers of births, deaths, and marriages to uncover details of European family life before the nineteenth century. These registers reveal that the three-generation extended family was a rarity in western and central Europe by 1700. Indeed, the extended family may never have been common in Europe, although it is hard to know about the early Middle Ages because very few records survive. When young European couples married, they normally established their own households and lived apart from their parents, much like the nuclear families (a family group consisting of parents and their children with no other relatives) common in America today. If a three-generation household came

Young Serving Girl Increased migration to urban areas in the eighteenth century contributed to a loosening of traditional morals and soaring illegitimacy rates. Young women who worked as servants or shopgirls could not be supervised as closely as those who lived at home. The themes of seduction, fallen virtue, and familial conflict were popular in eighteenth-century art, such as in this painting by Pietro Longhi (1702–1785). (Cameraphoto Arte, Venice/Art Resource, NY)

into existence, it was usually because a widowed parent moved into the home of a married child.

Most people did not marry young in the seventeenth and eighteenth centuries. The average person married surprisingly late, many years after reaching adulthood and many more after beginning to work. Studies of England and France in the seventeenth and eighteenth centuries show that both men and women married for the first time at an average age of twenty-five to twenty-seven. Ten to 20 percent of men and women never married at all.

Why was marriage delayed? The main reason was that couples normally did not marry until they could start an independent household and support themselves and their future children. Peasants often needed to wait until the father's death to inherit land and marry. In the towns, men and women worked to accumulate enough savings to start a small business and establish their own home. Laws and tradition also stemmed the tide of early marriage. In some areas couples needed the legal permission or tacit approval of the local lord or landowner in order to marry. Poor couples had particular difficulty securing the approval of local officials, who believed that freedom to marry for the lower classes would result in more landless paupers, more abandoned children, and more money for welfare. Village elders often agreed.

The custom of late marriage combined with the nuclear-family household distinguished European society from other areas of the world. It seems likely that the economic advantage early modern Europe acquired relative to other world regions derived in large part from this marriage pattern. Late marriage joined a mature man and a mature woman — two adults who had already accumulated social and economic capital and could transmit self-reliance and skills to the next generation. This marriage pattern also favored a greater degree of equality between husband and wife.

Work Away from Home

Many young people worked within their families until they could start their own households. Boys plowed and wove; girls spun and tended the cows. Many others left home to work elsewhere. In the trades, a lad would enter apprenticeship around age sixteen and finish in his late teens or early twenties. During that time he would not be permitted to marry. An apprentice from a rural village would typically move to a city or town to learn a trade, earning little and working hard. If he was lucky and had connections, he might eventually be admitted to

Chronology

1717	Elementary school attendance mandatory in Prussia
1750–1790	John Wesley preaches revival in England
1750–1850	Illegitimacy explosion
1757	Madame du Coudray, *Manual on the Art of Childbirth*
1762	Jean-Jacques Rousseau advocates more attentive child care in *Emile*
1763	Louis XV orders Jesuits out of France
1774	Elementary school attendance mandatory in Austria
1776	Thomas Paine, *Common Sense*
1796	Jenner performs first smallpox vaccination

a guild and establish his economic independence. Many poor families could not afford apprenticeships for their sons. Without craft skills, these youths drifted from one tough job to another: hired hand for a small farmer, wage laborer on a new road, carrier of water or domestic servant in a nearby town. They were always subject to economic fluctuations and unemployment.

Many adolescent girls also left their families to work. The range of opportunities open to them was more limited, however. Apprenticeship was sometimes available with mistresses in traditionally female occupations like seamstress, linen draper, or midwife. With the growth in production of finished goods for the emerging consumer economy during the eighteenth century (see Chapter 18), demand rose for skilled female labor and, with it, greater opportunities for women. Even male guildsmen hired girls and women, despite guild restrictions.

Service in another family's household was by far the most common job for girls, and even middle-class families often sent their daughters into service. The legions of young servant girls worked hard but had little independence. Sometimes the employer paid the girl's wages directly to her parents. Constantly under the eye of her mistress, the servant girl had many tasks — cleaning, shopping, cooking, child care. Often the work was endless, for there were few laws to limit exploitation. Court records are full of servant girls' complaints of physical mistreatment by their mistresses. There were many like the fifteen-year-old English girl in the early eighteenth century who told the judge that her mistress had not only called her "very opprobrious names, as Bitch, Whore and the like," but also "beat her without provocation and beyond measure."[1]

Male apprentices told similar tales of abuse, but they were far less vulnerable to the sexual harassment and assault that threatened female servants. In theory, domestic service offered a young girl protection and security in a new family. But in practice she was often the easy prey of a lecherous master or his sons or friends. If the girl became pregnant, she could be fired without notice and thrown out in disgrace. Many families could not or would not accept such a girl back into the home. Forced to make their own way, they had no choice but to turn to a harsh life of prostitution and petty thievery (see page 590). "What are we?" exclaimed a bitter Parisian prostitute. "Most of us are unfortunate women, without origins, without education, servants and maids for the most part."[2]

Premarital Sex and Community Controls

Ten years between puberty and marriage was a long time for sexually mature young people to wait. Many unmarried couples satisfied their sexual desires with fondling and petting. Others went further and engaged in premarital intercourse. Those who did so risked pregnancy and the stigma of illegitimate birth. Birth

community controls A pattern of cooperation and common action in a traditional village that sought to uphold the economic, social, and moral stability of the closely knit community.

control was not unknown in Europe before the nineteenth century, but it was primitive and unreliable. Condoms, made from sheep intestines, became available in the mid-seventeenth century, replacing uncomfortable earlier versions made from cloth. They were expensive and mainly used by aristocratic libertines and by prostitutes. The most common method of contraception was coitus interruptus—withdrawal by the male before ejaculation. The French, who were early leaders in contraception, were using this method extensively by the end of the eighteenth century.

Did the combination of sexual activity and lack of reliable contraception mean that late marriage in preindustrial Europe went hand in hand with many illegitimate children? For most of western and central Europe until at least 1750, the answer is no. English parish registers seldom listed more than one illegitimate child out of every twenty children baptized. Some French parishes in the seventeenth century had extraordinarily low rates of illegitimacy, with less than 1 percent of babies born out of wedlock. Illegitimate babies were apparently a rarity, at least as far as the official church records are concerned.

Where collective control over sexual behavior among youths failed, community pressure to marry often prevailed. A study of seven representative parishes in seventeenth-century England shows that around 20 percent of children were conceived before the couple was married, while only 2 percent were born out of wedlock.[3] Figures for the French village of Auffay in Normandy in the eighteenth century were remarkably similar. No doubt many of these French and English couples were

already engaged, or at least in a committed relationship, before they entered into intimate relations, and pregnancy simply set the marriage date once and for all.

The combination of low rates of illegitimate birth with large numbers of pregnant brides reflects the powerful **community controls** of the traditional village, particularly the open-field village, with its pattern of cooperation and common action. That spirit of common action was rapidly mobilized by the prospect of an unwed mother with an illegitimate child, a condition inevitably viewed as a grave threat to the economic, social, and moral stability of the community. Irate parents, anxious village elders, indignant priests, and stern landlords all combined to pressure young people who wavered about marriage in the face of unexpected pregnancies. In the countryside these controls meant that premarital sex was not entered into lightly and that it was generally limited to those contemplating marriage.

The concerns of the village and the family weighed heavily on couples' lives after marriage as well. Whereas uninvolved individuals today try to stay out of the domestic disputes of their neighbors, the people in peasant communities gave such affairs loud and unfavorable publicity either at the time or during the carnival season (see page 597). Relying on degrading public rituals, the young men of the village would typically gang up on their victim and force him or her to sit astride a donkey facing backward and holding up the donkey's tail. They would parade the overly brutal spouse-beater or the adulterous couple around the village, loudly proclaiming the offenders' misdeeds. The donkey ride and other colorful humiliations ranging from rotten vegetables splattered on the doorstep to obscene and insulting midnight serenades were common punishments throughout much of Europe. They epitomized the community's effort to police personal behavior and maintain moral standards.

New Patterns of Marriage and Illegitimacy

In the second half of the eighteenth century, longstanding patterns of marriage and illegitimacy shifted dramatically. One important change was a rise in young people's ability to choose partners for themselves, rather than following the economic or social interests of their families. This change occurred because social and economic transformations made it harder for families and communities to supervise their behavior. More youths in the countryside worked for their own wages, rather than on a family farm, and their economic autonomy translated into increased freedom of action. Moreover, many youths joined the flood of migrants to the cities, either with their families or in search of work on their own. Urban life provided young people with more social contacts and less social control.

The Village Wedding The spirited merrymaking of a peasant wedding was a popular theme of European artists in the eighteenth century. Given the harsh conditions of life, a wedding provided a treasured moment of feasting, dancing, and revelry. With the future of the village at stake, the celebration of marriage was a public event. (Private Collection/The Bridgeman Art Library)

One less positive outcome of loosening social control was an **illegitimacy explosion**. In Frankfurt, Germany, for example, births out of wedlock rose steadily from about 2 percent of all births in the early 1700s to a peak of about 25 percent around 1850. In Bordeaux, France, 36 percent of all babies were being born out of wedlock by 1840. Small towns and villages experienced less startling climbs, but between 1750 and 1850, increases from a range of 1 to 3 percent initially and then 10 to 20 percent were commonplace. The rise in numbers did not alter social disapproval of single mothers and their offspring, leaving them in desperate circumstances.

Why did the number of illegitimate births skyrocket? One reason was a rise in sexual activity among young people. The loosened social controls that gave young people more choice in marriage also provided them with more opportunities to yield to the attraction of the opposite sex. As in previous generations, many of the young couples who engaged in sexual activity intended to marry. In one medium-size French city in 1787–1788, the great majority of unwed mothers stated that sexual intimacy had followed promises

of marriage. Their sisters in rural Normandy reported again and again that they had been "seduced in anticipation of marriage."[4]

The problem for young women who became pregnant was that fewer men followed through on their promises. The second half of the eighteenth century witnessed sharply rising prices for food, homes, and other necessities of life. Wages rose too, but not enough to offset price increases. Many soldiers, day laborers, and male servants were no doubt sincere in their proposals, but their lives were insecure, and they hesitated to take on the burden of a wife and child.

Other men profited from the eased social controls to make false promises. For seduced women, there was little recourse against a deceitful suitor, especially since recrimination meant revealing their sexual activity. In 1788 a female servant in London pressed charges of rape against a man whom she said had forced her into

> **illegitimacy explosion**
> The sharp increase in out-of-wedlock births that occurred in Europe between 1750 and 1850, caused by low wages and the breakdown of community controls.

> ❝ Most of us are unfortunate women, without origins, without education, servants and maids for the most part. ❞
>
> —**Parisian prostitute**

sexual relations under pretense of courtship. According to her statement in court, after the act:

> *He began talking to me, and said, if I would not say any thing about it, he would marry me, he did not go away out of the room, but he quitted me; he said, if I would not mention it to my master or mistress, or any body, he would be married to me, that was the most of his discourse, and then afterwards he went away.*

The judge did not believe the charge of rape, perhaps because the woman admitted to subsequent sexual relations apparently without physical coercion. Nevertheless, he told the accused: "The seduction of these young women, under pretense of marrying, is not a crime of much less criminality than that which you have been tried for; and you will some time or another get your neck into the halter, if you do not leave off these practices." For the seduced woman who had been forced to recount each detail of the encounters in a public courtroom, this scolding provided little comfort.[5]

Thus, while some happy couples benefited from matches of love rather than convenience, in many cases the intended marriage did not take place. The romantic, yet practical dreams and aspirations of young people were frustrated by low wages, inequality, and changing economic and social conditions. Old patterns of marriage and family were breaking down. Only in the late nineteenth century would more stable patterns reappear.

Sex on the Margins of Society

Not all sex acts took place between men and women hopeful of marriage. Prostitution offered both single and married men an outlet for sexual desire. After a long period of relative tolerance, prostitutes encountered increasingly harsh and repressive laws in the sixteenth and early seventeenth centuries as officials across Europe began to close licensed brothels and declare prostitution illegal.

Despite this repression, prostitution continued to flourish in the eighteenth century. Most prostitutes were working women who turned to the sex trade when confronted with unemployment or seasonal shortages of work. Such women did not become social pariahs, but retained ties with the communities of laboring poor to which they belonged. If caught by the police, however, they were liable to imprisonment or banishment. Venereal disease was also a constant threat. Prostitutes were often subjected to humiliating police examinations for disease, although medical treatments were at best rudimentary. Farther up the social scale were courtesans whose wealthy protectors provided apartments, servants, fashionable clothing, and cash allowances. After a brilliant, but brief, career, an aging courtesan faced with the loss of her wealthy client could descend once more to streetwalking.

Relations between individuals of the same sex attracted even more condemnation than prostitution, since they defied the Bible's limitation of sex to the purposes of procreation. Male same-sex relations, described as "sodomy" or "buggery," were prohibited by law in most European states, under pain of death. Such laws, however, were enforced unevenly, most strictly in Spain and far less so in the Scandinavian countries and Russia.[6]

Protected by their status, nobles and royals sometimes openly indulged their same-sex passions, which were accepted as long as they married and produced legitimate heirs. It was common knowledge that King James I, sponsor of the first translation of the Bible into English, had male lovers, but such relations did not prevent him from having seven children with his wife, Anne of Denmark. The duchess of Orléans, sister-in-law of French king Louis XIV, repeated rumors in her letters about the homosexual inclinations of King William of England, hero of the Glorious Revolution (see Chapter 16). She was hardly shocked by the news, given the fortune and favor her own husband lavished on his many *mignons*, as they were called.

In the late seventeenth century new homosexual subcultures began to emerge in Paris, Amsterdam, and London, with their own slang, meeting places, and styles of dress. Unlike the relations described above, which involved men who took both wives and male lovers, these groups included men exclusively oriented toward other men. In London they called themselves "mollies," a term originally applied to prostitutes, and some began to wear women's clothing and act in effeminate ways. A new self-identity began to form among homosexual men: a belief that their same-sex desire made them fundamentally different from other men. As a character in one late eighteenth-century fiction explained, he was in "a category of men different from the other, a class Nature has created in order to diminish or minimize propagation."[7]

Same-sex relations existed among women as well, but they attracted less anxiety and condemnation than those among men. Some women were prosecuted for "unnatural" relations; others attempted to escape the narrow confines imposed on them by dressing as men.

Cross-dressing women occasionally snuck into the armed forces, such as Ulrika Elenora Stålhammar, who served as a man in the Swedish army for thirteen years and married a woman. After confessing her transgressions, she was sentenced to a lenient one-month imprisonment.[8] The beginnings of a distinctive lesbian subculture appeared in London at the end of the eighteenth century.

Across the early modern period, traditional tolerance for sexual activities outside of heterosexual marriage—be they sex with prostitutes or same-sex relations among male courtiers—began to fade. This process accelerated in the eighteenth century, as Enlightenment critics attacked court immortality and preached virtue and morality for middle-class men, who should prove their worthiness to take over the reins of power.

Children and Education

What was life like for children, and how did attitudes toward childhood evolve?

On the whole, European women married late, but then began bearing children rapidly. If a woman married before she was thirty, and if both she and her husband lived to fifty, she would most likely give birth to six or more children. Infant mortality was extremely high by modern standards, and many women died in childbirth due to limited medical knowledge and techniques.

For those children who did survive, new Enlightenment ideals in the latter half of the century stressed the importance of parental nurturing. New worldviews also led to an increase in elementary schools throughout Europe, but despite the efforts of enlightened absolutists and religious institutions, formal education played only a modest role in the lives of ordinary children.

Child Care and Nursing

Newborns entered a dangerous world. They were vulnerable to infectious diseases, and many babies died of dehydration brought about by bad bouts of ordinary diarrhea. Of those who survived infancy, many more died in childhood. Even in a rich family, little could be done for an ailing child. Childbirth was also dangerous. Women who bore six children faced a cumulative risk of dying in childbirth of 5 to 10 percent, a thousand times as great as the risk in Europe today.[9] They died from blood loss and shock during delivery and from infections caused by unsanitary conditions. The joy of pregnancy was thus shadowed by fear of loss of the mother or her child. The creation of life in early modern families was always accompanied by suffering and death.

In the countryside, women of the lower classes generally breast-fed their infants for two years or more.

Although not a foolproof means of birth control, breast-feeding decreases the likelihood of pregnancy by delaying the resumption of ovulation. By nursing their babies, women limited their fertility and spaced their children two or three years apart. Nursing also saved lives: breast-fed infants received precious immunity-producing substances and were more likely to survive than those who were fed other food.

Women of the aristocracy and upper middle class seldom nursed their own children. The upper-class woman felt that breast-feeding was undignified and interfered with her social responsibilities. Instead, she hired a live-in wet nurse to suckle her child (which usually meant sending the nurse's own infant away to be nursed by someone else). Working women in the cities also relied on wet nurses because they needed to earn a living. Unable to afford live-in wet nurses, they often turned to the cheaper services of women in the countryside. Rural **wet-nursing** was a widespread business in the eighteenth century, conducted within the framework of the putting-out system. The traffic was in babies rather than in yarn or cloth, and two or three years often passed before the wet-nurse worker in the countryside finished her task.

> **wet-nursing** A widespread and flourishing business in the eighteenth century in which women were paid to breast-feed other women's babies.

Wet-nursing was particularly common in northern France. Whereas the trend was toward more maternal nursing in other parts of Europe, wet-nursing grew substantially in Paris and other northern cities over the eighteenth century. Toward the end of the century roughly twenty thousand babies were born in Paris each year. Almost half were placed with rural wet nurses through a government-supervised distribution network; 20 to 25 percent were placed in the homes of Parisian nurses personally selected by their parents; and another 20 to 25 percent were abandoned to foundling hospitals, which would send them to wet nurses in the countryside. The remainder (perhaps 10 percent) were nursed at home by their mothers or live-in nurses.[10]

Reliance on wet nurses contributed to the high levels of infant mortality due to the dangers of travel, the lack of supervision of conditions in wet nurses' homes, and the need to share milk between a wet nurse's own baby and the one or more babies she was hired to feed. A study of parish registers in northern France during the late seventeenth and early eighteenth centuries reveals that 35 percent of babies died before their first birthdays, and another 20 percent before age ten.[11] In England, where more mothers nursed, only some 30 percent of children did not reach their tenth birthdays.

Why did Frenchwomen send their babies to wet-nurses, given these high mortality rates? Historians have offered several explanations, including parental indifference to the babies' survival. The likeliest explanation appears to be a combination of cultural, socioeconomic,

Arrival of the Wet Nurses   Wet-nursing was big business in eighteenth-century France, particularly in Paris and the north. Here, rural wet nurses bring their charges back to the city to be reunited with their families after around two years of care. These children were lucky survivors of a system that produced high mortality rates. (Réunion des Musées Nationaux/Art Resource, NY)

and biological factors. Wet-nursing was a centuries-old tradition in France, so families were merely following well-established patterns. Moreover, in this period migration to the cities, high prices, and stagnant wages pushed more women into the workforce, often into jobs outside the home where it was impossible to nurse their own babies. A third factor was that few alternatives to breast milk existed. In an era before germ theory and sterilization, artificial feeding methods were known to be dangerous to the newborn. By turning to wet nurses, mothers who could not nurse sought the safest affordable alternative.

In the second half of the eighteenth century critics mounted a harsh attack against wet-nursing. Enlightenment thinkers proclaimed that wet-nursing was robbing European society of reaching its full potential. They were convinced, incorrectly, that the population was declining (in fact it was rising, but they lacked accurate population data) and blamed this decline on women's failure to nurture their children properly. Some also railed against practices of contraception and masturbation, which they believed were robbing their nations of potential children. Despite these complaints, many women had no choice but to rely on wet nurses until the late-nineteenth-century introduction of sterilized cows' milk and artificial nipples.

Foundlings and Infanticide

The young woman who could not provide for an unwanted child had few choices, especially if she had no prospect of marriage. Abortions were illegal, dangerous, and apparently rare. In desperation, some women, particularly in the countryside, hid unwanted pregnancies, delivered in secret, and smothered their newborn infants. If discovered, infanticide was punishable by death.

Women in cities had more choices to dispose of babies they could not support. Foundling homes (orphanages) first took hold in Italy, Spain, and Portugal in the sixteenth century, spreading to France in 1670 and the rest of Europe in the following decades. In eighteenth-century England the government acted on a petition calling for a foundling hospital "to prevent the frequent murders of poor, miserable infants at birth" and "to suppress the inhuman custom of exposing newborn children to perish in the streets." As new homes were established and old ones expanded, the number of foundlings being cared for surged. By the end of the century European foundling hospitals were admitting annually about one hundred thousand abandoned children, nearly all of them infants. Across Europe, foundling homes emerged as a favorite charity of the rich and powerful. At their best, eighteenth-century foundling homes were a good example of Christian charity and social concern in an age of great poverty and inequality. Yet the foundling home was no panacea. By the 1770s one-third of all babies born in Paris were being immediately abandoned to foundling homes by their mothers. Many were the offspring of single women, the result of the illegitimacy explosion of the second half of the eighteenth century. But fully one-third of all the foundlings were abandoned by married couples too poor to feed another child.[12]

Great numbers of babies entered foundling homes, but few left. Even in the best of these homes, 50 percent of the babies normally died within a year. In the worst, fully 90 percent did not survive.[13] They succumbed to long journeys over rough roads, neglect by their wet nurses, and customary childhood illnesses. So great were the losses that some contemporaries called the foundling hospitals "legalized infanticide."

Attitudes Toward Children

What were the typical circumstances of children's lives? The topic of parental attitudes toward children in the early modern period remains controversial. Some scholars have claimed that parents did not risk forming emotional attachments to young children because of high mortality rates. With a reasonable expectation that a child might die, some scholars believe, parents maintained an attitude of indifference, if not downright negligence.

Contemporaries were well aware of the dangers of childhood and of the high mortality rates. The great eighteenth-century English historian Edward Gibbon (1737–1794) wrote, with some exaggeration, that "the death of a new born child before that of its parents may seem unnatural but it is a strictly probable event, since of any given number the greater part are extinguished

> ❝ The death of a new born child before that of its parents may seem unnatural but it is a strictly probable event, since of any given number the greater part are extinguished before the ninth year, before they possess the faculties of the mind and the body. ❞
>
> —**Edward Gibbon**

before the ninth year, before they possess the faculties of the mind and the body." Gibbon's father named all his boys Edward after himself, hoping that at least one of them would survive to carry his name. His prudence was not misplaced. Edward the future historian and eldest survived. Five brothers and sisters who followed him all died in infancy.

Emotional prudence could lead to emotional distance. The French essayist Michel de Montaigne, who lost five of his six daughters in infancy, wrote, "I cannot abide that passion for caressing new-born children, which have neither mental activities nor recognisable bodily shape by which to make themselves loveable and I have never willingly suffered them to be fed in my presence."[14] In contrast to this harsh picture, however, historians have drawn ample evidence from diaries, letters, and family portraits that many parents did cherish their children and suffered greatly when they died. The English poet Ben Jonson wrote movingly in "On My First Son" of the death of his six-year-old son Benjamin, which occurred during a London plague outbreak in 1603:

> *Farewell, thou child of my right hand, and joy;*
> *My sin was too much hope of thee, loved boy.*
> *Seven years thou wert lent to me, and I thee pay,*
> *Exacted by thy fate, on the just day.*

In a society characterized by much violence and brutality, discipline of children was often severe. The axiom "Spare the rod and spoil the child" seems to have been coined in the mid-seventeenth century. Susannah Wesley (1669–1742), mother of John Wesley, the founder of Methodism (see page 607), agreed. According to her, the first task of a parent toward her children was "to conquer the will, and bring them to an obedient temper." She reported that her babies were "taught to fear the rod, and to cry softly; by which means they escaped the abundance of correction they might otherwise have had, and that most odious noise of the crying of children was rarely heard in the house."[15]

The Enlightenment produced an enthusiastic new discourse about childhood and child rearing. Starting around 1760 critics called for greater tenderness toward children and proposed imaginative new teaching methods. In addition to supporting foundling

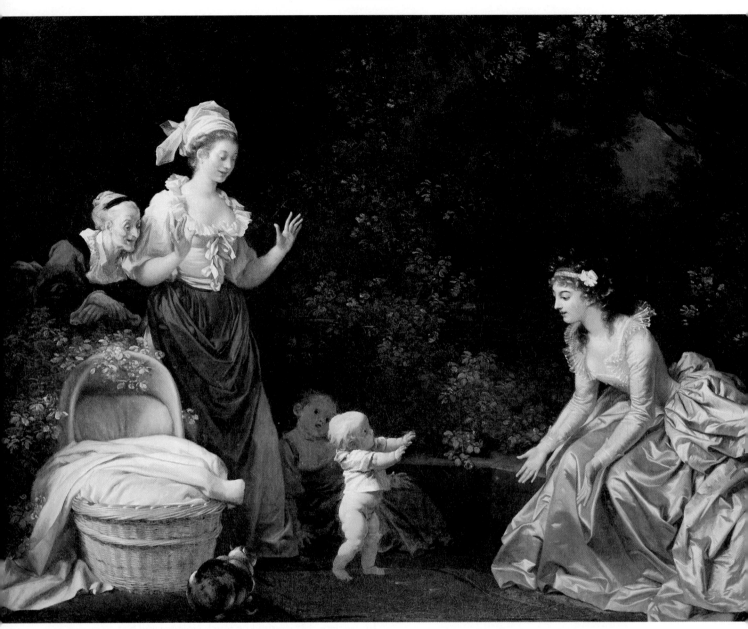

The First Step of Childhood This tender snapshot of a baby's first steps toward an adoring mother exemplifies new attitudes toward children and raising them ushered in by the Enlightenment. Authors like Jean-Jacques Rousseau encouraged elite mothers like the one pictured here to take a more personal interest in raising their children, instead of leaving them in the hands of indifferent wet nurses and nannies. Many women responded eagerly to this call, and the period saw a more sentimentalized view of childhood and family life. (Erich Lessing/Art Resource, NY)

homes and urging women to nurse their babies, these new voices ridiculed the practice of swaddling babies and using rigid whale-boned corsets to mold children's bones. Instead of dressing children in miniature versions of adult clothing, critics called for loose and comfortable clothing to allow freedom of movement. These voices belonged to the overall Enlightenment celebration of nature and the natural laws that should guide human behavior. For Enlightenment thinkers, the best hopes for creating a new society, untrammeled by the prejudices of the past, lay in a radical reform of child-rearing techniques.

One of the century's most influential works on child rearing was Jean-Jacques Rousseau's *Emile or On Education* (1762), which fervently advocated breast-feeding and natural dress. Rousseau argued that boys' education should include plenty of fresh air and exercise and that they should be taught practical craft skills in addition to book learning. Reacting to what he perceived as the vanity and frivolity of upper-class Parisian women,

Rousseau insisted that girls' education focus on their future domestic responsibilities. For Rousseau, women's "nature" destined them solely for a life of marriage and child rearing. The ideas of Rousseau and other reformers were enthusiastically adopted by elite women, who did not adopt universal nursing but did at least begin to supervise their wet nurses more carefully.

For all his influence, Rousseau also reveals the occasional hypocrisy of Enlightenment thinkers. With regard to the child-rearing techniques he believed would create a better society, Rousseau had extremely high expectations; when it came to the five children he fathered with his common-law wife, however, he abandoned them all in foundling hospitals despite their mother's protests. None are known to have survived. For Rousseau, the idea of creating a natural man was more important than raising real children.

The Spread of Elementary Schools

The availability of education outside the home gradually increased over the early modern period. The wealthy led the way in the sixteenth century with special colleges, often run by Jesuits in Catholic areas. Schools charged specifically with educating children of the common people began to appear in the second half of the seventeenth century. Such schools specialized in teaching six- to twelve-year-old children basic literacy, religion, and perhaps some arithmetic for the boys and needlework for the girls. The number of such schools expanded in the eighteenth century, although they were never sufficient to educate the mass of the population.

Religious faith played an important role in the spread of education. From the middle of the seventeenth century, Presbyterian Scotland was convinced that the path to salvation lay in careful study of the Scriptures, and it established an effective network of parish schools for rich and poor alike. The Church of England and the dissenting congregations — Puritans, Presbyterians, Quakers, and so on — established "charity schools" to instruct poor children. The first proponents of universal education, in Prussia, were inspired by the Protestant idea that every believer should be able to read the Bible and by the new idea of a population capable of effectively serving the state. As early as 1717 Prussia made attendance at elementary schools compulsory for boys and girls, albeit only in areas where schools already existed.[16] More Protestant German states, such as Saxony and Württemberg (VUHR-tuhm-burg), followed suit in the eighteenth century.

Catholic states pursued their own programs of popular education. In the 1660s France began setting up charity schools to teach poor children their catechism and prayers as well as reading and writing. These were run by parish priests or by new teaching orders created for this purpose. One of the most famous orders was Jean-Baptiste de la Salle's Brothers of the Christian Schools. Founded in 1684 and still in existence today, the schools had thirty-five thousand students across France by the 1780s. Enthusiasm for popular education was even greater in the Habsburg empire, inspired by the expansion of schools in rival German states. In 1774 Maria Theresa issued her own compulsory education edict, imposing five hours of school, five days a week, for all children aged six to twelve.[17] Across Europe some elementary education was becoming a reality, and schools were of growing significance in the life of the child.

Popular Culture and Consumerism

How did increasing literacy and new patterns of consumption affect people's lives? ■

Because of the new efforts in education, basic literacy was growing among the popular classes, whose reading habits centered primarily on religious material, but who also began to incorporate more practical and entertaining literature. In addition to reading, people of all classes enjoyed a range of leisure activities including storytelling, fairs, festivals, and sports.

One of the most important developments in European society in the eighteenth century was the emergence of a fledgling consumer culture. Much of the expansion took place among the upper and upper-middle classes, but a boom in cheap reproductions of luxury items also permitted people of modest means to participate. From food to ribbons and from coal stoves to umbrellas, the material worlds of city dwellers grew richer and more diverse. This "consumer revolution," as it has been called, created new expectations for comfort, hygiene, and self-expression in daily life, thus dramatically changing European life in the eighteenth century.

Popular Literature

The surge in childhood education in the eighteenth century led to a remarkable growth in basic literacy between 1600 and 1800. Whereas in 1600 only one male in six was barely literate in France and Scotland, and one in four in England, by 1800 almost nine out of ten Scottish males, two out of three French males (Map 19.1), and more than half of English males were literate. In all three countries, the bulk of the jump occurred in the eighteenth century. Women were also increasingly literate, although they lagged behind men.

The growth in literacy promoted growth in reading, and historians have carefully examined what the common people read. While the Bible remained the overwhelming favorite, especially in Protestant countries, short pamphlets known as chapbooks were the staple of popular literature. Printed on the cheapest paper, many chapbooks featured Bible stories, prayers, devotions, and the lives of saints and exemplary Christians. This pious literature gave believers moral teachings and a confidence in God that helped them endure the struggles of daily living.

Entertaining, often humorous stories formed a second element of popular literature. Fairy tales, medieval romances, true crime stories, and fantastic adventures were some of the delights that filled the peddler's pack as he approached a village. These tales presented a world of danger and magic, of supernatural powers, fairy godmothers, and evil trolls, that provided a temporary flight from harsh everyday reality. They also contained nuggets of ancient folk wisdom, counseling prudence in a world full of danger and injustice, where wolves dress like grandmothers and eat Little Red Riding Hoods.

Finally, some popular literature was highly practical, dealing with rural crafts, household repairs, useful plants, and similar matters. Much lore was stored in almanacs, where calendars listing secular, religious, and astrological events were mixed with agricultural schedules, arcane

facts, and jokes. The almanac was universal, was not controversial, and was highly appreciated even by many in the comfortable classes. In this way, elites still shared some elements of a common culture with the masses.

While it is safe to say that the vast majority of ordinary people—particularly peasants in isolated villages—did not read the great works of the Enlightenment, that does not mean they were immune to the ideas. Urban working people were exposed to new ideas through the rumors and gossip that spread across city streets, workshops, markets, cafés, and taverns. They also had access to cheap pamphlets that helped translate Enlightenment critiques into ordinary language. Servants, who usually came from rural areas and traveled home periodically, were well situated to transmit ideas from educated employers to the village.

Certainly some ordinary people did assimilate Enlightenment ideals. Thomas Paine, author of some of the most influential texts of the American Revolution, was an English corset-maker's son who left school at age twelve and carried on his father's trade before emigrating to the colonies. His 1776 pamphlet *Common Sense* attacked the weight of custom and the evils of govern-

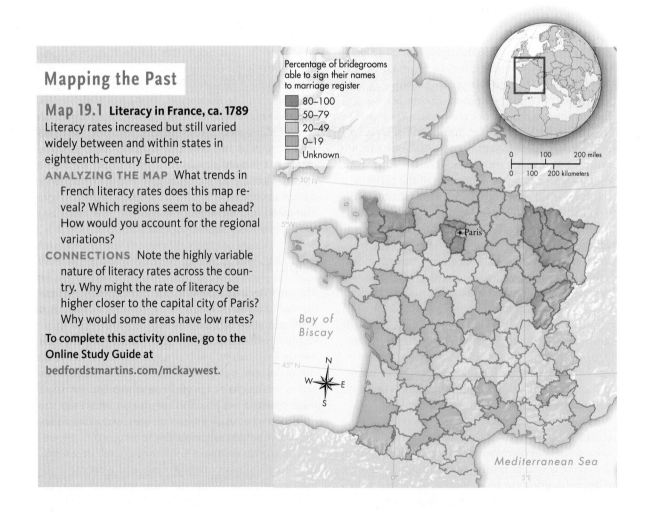

Mapping the Past

Map 19.1 Literacy in France, ca. 1789
Literacy rates increased but still varied widely between and within states in eighteenth-century Europe.

ANALYZING THE MAP What trends in French literacy rates does this map reveal? Which regions seem to be ahead? How would you account for the regional variations?

CONNECTIONS Note the highly variable nature of literacy rates across the country. Why might the rate of literacy be higher closer to the capital city of Paris? Why would some areas have low rates?

To complete this activity online, go to the Online Study Guide at bedfordstmartins.com/mckaywest.

Percentage of bridegrooms able to sign their names to marriage register
- 80–100
- 50–79
- 20–49
- 0–19
- Unknown

Paris

Bay of Biscay

Mediterranean Sea

Young Woman Reading a Letter Literacy rates for men and women rose substantially during the eighteenth century. The novel also emerged as a new literary genre in this period. With its focus on emotions, love, and family melodrama, the novel was seen as a particularly feminine genre, and it allowed women writers more access to publication. Writing and reading letters were also associated with women. Some contemporaries worried that women's growing access to reading and writing would excite their imaginations and desires, leading to moral dissolution. (Réunion des Musées Nationaux/Art Resource, NY)

ment against the natural society of men. This text, which sold 120,000 copies in its first months of publication and was soon translated into French and German, is vivid proof of working people's ability to receive Enlightenment ideas. Paine's stirring mastery of them was perhaps unique, but his access to them was certainly not.

Leisure and Recreation

Despite the spread of literacy, the culture of the village remained largely oral rather than written. In the cold, dark winter months, peasant families gathered around the fireplace to talk, sing, tell stories, do craftwork, and keep warm. In some parts of Europe, women would gather together in someone's cottage to chat, sew, spin, and laugh. Sometimes a few young men would be invited so that the daughters (and mothers) could size up potential suitors in a supervised atmosphere. A favorite recreation of men was drinking and talking with buddies in public places, and it was a sorry village that had no tavern. In addition to old favorites such as beer and wine, the common people turned with gusto to cheap and potent hard liquor, which fell in price because of improved techniques for distilling grain in the eighteenth century.

Towns and cities offered a wider range of amusements, including pleasure gardens, theaters, and lending libraries. Urban fairs featured prepared foods, acrobats, freak shows, and conjuring acts. Leisure activities were another form of consumption marked by growing commercialization. For example, commercial, profit-oriented spectator sports emerged in this period, such as horse races, boxing matches, and bullfights. Modern sports heroes, such as brain-bashing heavyweight champions and haughty bull-fighting matadors, made their appearance on the historical scene.

Blood sports, such as bull-baiting and cockfighting, also remained popular with the masses. In bull-baiting, the bull, usually staked on a chain in the courtyard of an inn, was attacked by ferocious dogs for the amusement of the innkeeper's clients. Eventually the maimed and tortured animal was slaughtered by a butcher and sold as meat. In cockfighting, two roosters, carefully trained

by their owners and armed with razor-sharp steel spurs, slashed and clawed each other in a small ring until the victor won—and the loser died. An added attraction of cockfighting was that the screaming spectators could bet on the lightning-fast combat and its uncertain outcome.

Popular recreation merged with religious celebration in a variety of festivals and processions throughout the year. The most striking display of these religiously inspired events was **carnival**, a time of reveling and excess in Catholic Europe, especially in Mediterranean countries. Carnival preceded Lent—the forty days of fasting and penitence before Easter—and for a few exceptional days in February or March, a wild

blood sports Popular with the eighteenth-century European masses, events such as bull-baiting and cockfighting that involved inflicting violence and bloodshed on animals.

carnival The few days of revelry in Catholic countries that preceded Lent and that included drinking, masquerading, dancing, and rowdy spectacles that turned the established order upside down.

A Boxing Match The eighteenth century witnessed a rise in commercial sporting events and other leisure activities. Here two men spar in a boxing match staged in London for the entertainment of the gathered crowd. The popularity of boxing rose among wealthy spectators in the eighteenth century as bear-baiting and bull-baiting were increasingly condemned as excessively brutal. In the early years, female boxers were as popular as men. (Bildarchiv Preussischer Kulturbesitz/Art Resource, NY)

release of drinking, masquerading, and dancing reigned. Moreover, a combination of plays, processions, and raucous spectacles turned the established order upside down. Peasants dressed as nobles and men as women, and rich masters waited on their servants at the table. This annual holiday gave people a much appreciated chance to release their pent-up frustrations and aggressions before life returned to the usual pattern of hierarchy and hard work.

In trying to place the vibrant popular culture of the common people in broad perspective, historians have stressed the growing criticism levied against it by the educated elites in the second half of the eighteenth century. These elites, which had previously shared the popular enthusiasm for religious festivals, carnival, drinking in taverns, blood sports, and the like, now tended to see superstition, sin, disorder, and vulgarity.[18] The re-

sulting attack on popular culture, which was tied to the clergy's efforts to eliminate paganism and superstition, was intensified as an educated public embraced the critical worldview of the Enlightenment.

New Foods and Appetites

At the beginning of the eighteenth century, ordinary men and women depended on grain as fully as they had in the past. Bread was quite literally the staff of life. Peasants in the Beauvais region of France ate two pounds of bread a day, washing it down with water, wine, or beer. Their dark bread was made from roughly ground wheat and rye—the standard flour of the common people. Even peasants normally needed to buy some grain for food, and, in full accord with landless laborers and urban workers, they believed in the moral economy and the **just price**. That is, they believed that prices should be "fair," protecting both consumers and producers, and that just prices should be imposed by government decree if necessary. When prices rose above this level, they often took action in the form of bread riots (see Chapter 16).

The rural poor also ate a fair quantity of vegetables. Peas and beans were probably the most common. Grown as field crops in much of Europe since the Middle Ages, they were eaten fresh in late spring and summer. Dried, they became the basic ingredients in the soups and stews of the long winter months. In most regions other vegetables appeared on the tables of the poor in season, primarily cabbages, carrots, and wild greens. Fruit was mostly limited to the summer months. Too precious to drink, milk was used to make cheese and butter, which peasants sold in the market to earn cash for taxes and land rents.

The common people of Europe ate less meat in 1700 than in 1500 because their general standard of living had declined and meat was more expensive. Moreover, harsh laws in most European countries reserved the right to hunt and eat game, such as rabbits, deer, and partridges, to nobles and large landowners. Few laws were more bitterly resented—or more frequently broken—by ordinary people than those governing hunting.

The diet of small traders and artisans—the people of the towns and cities—was less monotonous than that of the peasantry. Bustling markets provided a substantial variety of meats, vegetables, and fruits, although bread and beans still formed the bulk of such families' diets. Not surprisingly, the diet of the rich was quite different from that of the poor. The upper classes were rapacious carnivores, and a truly elegant dinner consisted of an abundance of rich meat and fish dishes laced with piquant sauces and complemented with sweets, cheeses, and nuts of all kinds. During such dinners, it was common to spend five or more hours at table, eating and drinking and enjoying the witty banter of polite society.

Patterns of food consumption changed markedly as the century progressed. Because of a growth of market gardening, a greater variety of vegetables appeared in towns and cities. This was particularly the case in the Low Countries and England, which pioneered new methods of farming. Introduced into Europe from the Americas—along with corn, squash, tomatoes, and many other useful plants—the humble potato provided an excellent new food source. Containing a good supply of carbohydrates, calories, and vitamins A and C, the potato offset the lack of vitamins from unavailable green vegetables in the poor person's winter and early-spring diet, and it provided a much higher caloric yield

just price The idea that prices should be fair, protecting both consumers and producers, and that they should be imposed by government decree if necessary.

Chocolate Drinking These Spanish tiles from 1710 illustrates the new practice of preparing and drinking hot chocolate. Originating in the New World, chocolate was one of the many new foods imported to Europe in the wake of the voyages of discovery. The first Spanish chocolate mills opened in the mid-seventeenth century, and consumption of chocolate rapidly increased. The inclusion of this tile in the decoration of a nobleman's house testifies to public interest in the new drink. (Courtesy, Museu de Ceramica. Photo: Guillem Fernandez-Huerta)

Rose Bertin, "Minister of Fashion"

INDIVIDUALS IN SOCIETY

ONE DAY IN 1779, AS THE FRENCH ROYAL FAMILY RODE in a carriage through the streets of Paris, Queen Marie-Antoinette noticed her fashion merchant, Rose Bertin, observing the royal procession. "Ah! there is mademoiselle Bertin," the queen exclaimed, waving her hand. Bertin responded with a curtsey. The king then stood and greeted Bertin, followed by the royal family and their entourage.* The incident shocked the public, for no common merchant had ever received such homage from royalty.

Bertin had come a long way from her humble beginnings. Born in 1747 to a poor family in northern France, she moved to Paris in the 1760s to work as a shop assistant. Bertin eventually opened her own boutique on the fashionable rue Saint-Honoré. In 1775 Bertin received the highest honor of her profession when she was selected by Marie-Antoinette as one of her official purveyors.

Based on the queen's patronage, and riding the wave of the new consumer revolution, Bertin became one of the most successful entrepreneurs in Europe. Bertin established not only a large clientele, but also a reputation for arrogance. She refused to work for non-noble customers, claiming that the orders of the queen and her court claimed all her attention. She astounded courtiers by referring to her "work" with the queen, as though the two were collaborators rather than absolute monarch and lowly subject. Bertin's close relationship with Marie Antoinette and the fortune the queen spent on her wardrobe hurt the royal family's image. One journalist derided Bertin as a "minister of fashion," whose influence outstripped that of all the others in royal government.

In January 1787 rumors spread through Paris that Bertin had filed for bankruptcy with debts of 2 to 3 million livres (a garment worker's annual salary was around 200 livres). Despite her notoriously high prices and rich clients, this news did not shock Parisians, because the nobility's reluctance to pay its debts was equally well-known. Bertin somehow held on to her business. Some said she had spread the bankruptcy rumors herself to shame the court into paying her bills.

Bertin remained loyal to the Crown during the tumult of the French Revolution and sent dresses to the queen even after the arrest of the royal family. Fearing for her life, she left France for Germany in 1792 and continued to ply her profession in exile. She returned to France in 1800 and died in 1813, one year before the restoration of the Bourbon monarchy might have renewed her acclaim.†

Rose Bertin scandalized public opinion with her self-aggrandizement and ambition, yet history was on her side. She was the first celebrity fashion stylist and one of the first self-made career women to rise from obscurity to fame and fortune based on her talent, taste, and hard work. Her legacy remains in the exalted status of today's top fashion designers and in the dreams of small-town girls to make it in the big city.

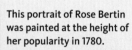

This portrait of Rose Bertin was painted at the height of her popularity in 1780. (Jean-Francois Janinet, French, 1752–1814, *Mademoiselle Bertin*, n.d., engraving on paper, 155 x 135 mm (image/plate); 120 x 105 mm (primary support); 280 x 215 mm (secondary support), Celia Culver Gilbert Memorial Collection, 1924.1309, The Art Institute of Chicago. Photography © The Art Institute of Chicago)

QUESTIONS FOR ANALYSIS

1. Why was the relationship between Queen Marie Antoinette and Rose Bertin so troubling to public opinion? Why would relations between a queen and a fashion merchant have political implications?

2. Why would someone who sold fashionable clothing and accessories rise to such a prominent position in business and society? What makes fashion so important in the social world?

Mémoires secrets pour servir à l'histoire de la république des lettres en France, vol. 13, 299, 5 mars 1779 (London: John Adamson, 1785).

†On Rose Bertin, see Clare Haru Crowston, "The Queen and Her 'Minister of Fashion': Gender, Credit and Politics in Pre-Revolutionary France," *Gender and History* 14, 1 (April 2002): 92–116.

than grain for a given piece of land. After initial resistance, the potato became an important dietary supplement in much of Europe by the end of the century. In the course of the eighteenth century the large towns and cities of maritime Europe also began to receive semitropical fruits, such as oranges and lemons, from Portugal and the West Indies, but they remained expensive.

The most remarkable dietary change in the eighteenth century was in the consumption of sugar and tea. No other commodities grew so quickly in popularity. Previously expensive and rare luxury items, they became dietary staples for people of all social classes. This was possible because of the steady drop in prices created by the expansion of colonial slave labor in the New World. Other colonial goods also became important items of daily consumption in this period, including coffee, tobacco, and chocolate.

Why were colonial products so popular? Part of the motivation for consuming these products was a desire to emulate the luxurious lifestyles of the elite. Having seen pictures of or read about the fine lady's habit of "tea time" or the gentleman's appreciation for a pipe, common Europeans sought to experience these pleasures for themselves. Moreover, the quickened pace of work in the eighteenth century created new needs for stimulants among working people. (See "Listening to the Past: Louis-Sébastien Mercier, a Day in the Life of Paris," page 604.) Whereas the gentry took tea as a leisurely and genteel ritual, the lower classes usually drank tea at work to fight monotony or fatigue. With the widespread adoption of these products (which turned out to be mildly to extremely addictive), working people in Europe became increasingly dependent on faraway colonial economies and slave labor. Their understanding of daily necessities and how to procure those necessities shifted definitively, linking them to global trade networks beyond their ability to shape or control.

Toward a Consumer Society

Along with foodstuffs, all manner of other goods increased in variety and number in the eighteenth century. This proliferation led to a growth in consumption and new attitudes toward consumer goods so wide-ranging that some historians have referred to an eighteenth-century **consumer revolution**.[19] The result of this revolution was the birth of a new type of society in which people derived their self-identity as much from their consuming practices as from their working lives and place in the production process. As people were provided the opportunity to pick and choose among a new variety of consumer goods, new notions of individuality and self-expression developed. A shopgirl could stand out from her peers by her choice of a striped jacket, a colored

parasol, or simply a new ribbon for her hair. The full emergence of a consumer society did not take place until much later, but its roots lie in the eighteenth century.

Increased demand for consumer goods was not merely an innate response to increased supply. Eighteenth-century merchants cleverly pioneered new techniques to incite demand: they initiated marketing campaigns, opened fancy boutiques with large windows, and advertised the patronage of royal princes and princesses. By diversifying their product lines and greatly accelerating the turnover of styles, they seized the reins of fashion from the courtiers who had earlier controlled it. Instead of setting new styles, duchesses and marquises now bowed to the dictates of fashion merchants. (See "Individuals in Society: Rose Bertin, 'Minister of Fashion,'" at left.) Fashion also extended beyond court circles to touch many more items and social groups.

Clothing was one of the chief indicators of the growth of consumerism. Shrewd entrepreneurs made fashionable clothing seem more desirable, while legions of women entering the textile and needle trades made it ever cheaper. As a result, eighteenth-century western Europe witnessed a dramatic rise in the consumption of clothing, particularly in large cities. One historian has documented an enormous growth in the size and value of Parisians' wardrobes from 1700 to 1789, as well as a new level of diversity in garments and accessories, colors, and fabrics.[20] Colonial economies again played an important role lowering the cost of materials, such as cotton and vegetable dyes, largely due to the unpaid toil of enslaved Africans. Cheaper copies of elite styles made it possible for working people to aspire to follow fashion for the first time. Elite onlookers were bemused by the sight of lower-class people in fashionable dress. In 1784 Mrs. Fanny Cradock described encountering her milkman during an evening stroll "dressed in a fashionable suit, with an embroidered waistcoat, silk knee-breeches and lace cuffs."[21]

Mrs. Cradock's milkman notwithstanding, the spread of fashion was primarily a female phenomenon. Parisian women significantly out-consumed men, acquiring larger and more expensive wardrobes than those of their husbands, brothers, and fathers. This was true across the social spectrum; in ribbons, shoes, gloves, and lace, European working women reaped in the consumer revolution what they had sown in the industrious revolution (see Chapter 18). There were also new gender distinctions in dress. Previously, noblemen vied with noblewomen in the magnificence and ostentation of their apparel; by the end of the eighteenth century men had renounced brilliant colors and voluptuous

> **consumer revolution**
> The wide-ranging growth in consumption and new attitudes toward consumer goods that emerged in the cities of northwestern Europe in the second half of the eighteenth century.

fabrics to don early versions of the plain dark suit that remains standard male formal wear in the West. This was one more aspect of the increasingly rigid differences drawn between appropriate male and female behavior.

Changes in outward appearances were reflected in inner spaces as new attitudes about privacy and intimate life also emerged. Historians have used notaries' after-death inventories to peer into ordinary people's homes. In 1700 the cramped home of a modest family consisted of a few rooms, each of which had multiple functions. The same room was used for sleeping, receiving friends, and working. In the eighteenth century rents rose sharply, making it impossible to gain more space, but families began attributing specific functions to specific rooms. They also began to erect inner barriers within the home to provide small niches in which individuals could seek privacy.

New levels of comfort and convenience accompanied this trend toward more individualized ways of life. In 1700 a meal might be served in a common dish, with each person dipping his or her spoon into the pot. By the end of the eighteenth century even humble households contained a much greater variety of cutlery and dishes, making it possible for each person to eat from his or her own plate. More books and prints, which also proliferated at lower prices, decorated the shelves and walls. Improvements in glass-making provided more transparent

The Consumer Revolution From the mid-eighteenth century on, the cities of western Europe witnessed a new proliferation of consumer goods. Items once limited to the wealthy few — such as fans (lower right), watches, snuffboxes, umbrellas, ornamental containers (right), and teapots — were now reproduced in cheaper versions for middling and ordinary people. The fashion for wide hoopskirts was so popular that the armrests on the chairs of the day, known as Louis XV chairs (left), were specially designed to accommodate them. (fan: Scala/White Images/Art Resource, NY; jar: Victoria & Albert Museum, London/The Bridgeman Art Library; chair: Louvre/Réunion des Musées Nationaux/Art Resource, NY)

glass, which allowed daylight to penetrate into gloomy rooms. Cold and smoky hearths were increasingly replaced by more efficient and cleaner coal stoves, which also eliminated the backache of cooking over an open fire. Rooms were warmer, better lit, more comfortable, and more personalized.

The scope of the new consumer economy should not be exaggerated. These developments were concentrated in large cities in northwestern Europe and in the colonial cities of North America. Even in these centers the elite benefited the most from new modes of life. This was not yet the society of mass consumption that emerged toward the end of the nineteenth century with the full expansion of the Industrial Revolution. The eighteenth century did, however, lay the foundations for one of the most distinctive features of modern Western life: societies based on the consumption of goods and services obtained through the market in which individuals form their identities and self-worth through the goods they consume.

Louis-Sébastien Mercier, a Day in the Life of Paris

LISTENING TO THE PAST

Louis-Sébastien Mercier (1740–1814) was the best chronicler of everyday life in eighteenth-century Paris. His masterpiece was the Tableau de Paris *(1781–1788), a multivolume work composed of 1,049 chapters that covered subjects ranging from convents to cafés, bankruptcy to book-sellers, the latest fashions to royal laws. As this excerpt demonstrates, he aimed to convey the infinite diversity of people, places, and things he saw around him, and in so doing he left future generations a pre-cious record of the changing dynamics of Parisian society in the second half of the eighteenth century.*

Mercier's family belonged to the respectable artisan classes. This middling position ideally suited Mercier for observing the extremes of wealth and poverty around him. Although these volumes contain many wonderful glimpses of daily life, they should not be taken for an objec-tive account. Mercier brought his own moral and political sensibilities, influenced by Jean-Jacques Rousseau, to the task.

Chapter 39: How the Day Goes

❝ It is curious to see how, amid what seems perpetual life and move-ment, certain hours keep their own characteristics, whether of bustle or of leisure. Every round of the clock-hand sets another scene in motion, each different from the last, though all about equal in length. Seven o'clock in the morning sees all the gardeners, mounted on their nags and with their baskets empty, heading back out of town again. No carriages are about, and not a presentable soul, except a few neat clerks hurrying to their offices. Nine o'clock sets all the barbers in motion, covered from head to foot with flour — hence their soubriquet of "whitings"* — wig in one hand, tongs in the other. Waiters from the lemonade-shops are busy with trays of coffee and rolls, breakfast for those who live in fur-nished rooms. . . . An hour later the Law comes into action; a black cloud of legal practitioners and hangers-on descend upon the Châtelet,† and the other courts; a procession of wigs and gowns and briefbags, with plaintiffs and defendants at their heels. Midday is the stockbrokers' hour, and the idlers'; the former hurry off to the Exchange, the latter to the Palais-Royal.‡ The Saint-Honoré§ quarter, where all the financiers live, is at its busiest now, its streets are crowded with the customers and clients of the great.

At two o'clock those who have invitations to dine set out, dressed in their best, powdered, adjusted, and walking on tiptoe not to soil their stockings. All the cabs are engaged, not one is to be found on the rank; there is a good deal of competition for these vehicles, and you may see two would-be passengers jumping into a cab together from different sides, and furiously disputing which was first. . . .

Three o'clock and the streets are not so full; everyone is at dinner; there is a momentary calm, soon to be broken, for at five fifteen the din is as though the gates of hell were opened, the streets are impass-able with traffic going all ways at once, towards the playhouses or the public gardens. Cafés are at their busiest.

Towards seven the din dies down, everywhere and all at once. You can hear the cab-horses' hoofs pawing the stones as they wait — in vain. It is as though the whole town were gagged and bound, suddenly, by an invisible hand. This is the most dangerous time of the whole day for thieves and such, especially towards autumn when the days begin to draw in; for the watch is not yet about, and violence takes its opportunity.

Night falls; and, while scene-shifters set to work at the play-houses, swarms of other workmen, carpen-ters, masons and the like, make their way towards the poorer quarters. They leave white footprints from the plaster on their shoes, a trail that any eye can follow. They are off home, and to bed, at the hour which finds elegant ladies sitting down to their dressing-tables to prepare for the business of the night.

At nine this begins; they all set off for the play. Houses tremble as the coaches rattle by, but soon the noise ceases; all the fine ladies are making their eve-ning visits, short ones, before supper. Now the pros-titutes begin their night parade, breasts uncovered, heads tossing, colour high on their cheeks, and eyes as bold as their hands. These creatures, careless of the light from shop-windows and street lamps, follow and accost you, trailing through the mud in their silk stock-ings and low shoes, with words and gestures well matched for obscenity. . . .

By eleven, renewed silence. People are at supper, private people, that is; for the cafés begin at this hour to turn out their patrons, and to send the various idlers and workless and poets back to their garrets for the night. A few prostitutes still linger, but they have to use more circumspection, for the watch is about, patrolling the streets, and this is the hour when they "gather 'em in"; that is the traditional expression.

A quarter after midnight, a few carriages make their way home, taking the non–card players back to bed. These lend the town a sort of transitory life; the trades-man wakes out of his first sleep at the sound of them, and turns to his wife, by no means unwilling. More than one young Parisian must owe his existence to this sudden passing rattle of wheels. . . .

---

* Small fish typically rolled in flour and fried.

† The main criminal court of Paris.

‡ A garden surrounded by arcades with shops and cafés.

§ A fashionable quarter for the wealthy.

In this Parisian street scene, a milk seller doubles as a provider of news, reading a hand-printed news sheet to a small gathering. Gossip, rumor, and formal or informal newspapers, like the one pictured here, ensured that information traversed the city at astonishing speeds. (Musée de la Ville de Paris, Musée Carnavalet, Paris/Lauros/Giraudon/The Bridgeman Art Library)

At one in the morning six thousand peasants arrive, bringing the town's provision of vegetables and fruits and flowers, and make straight for the Halles**; . . . As for the market itself, it never sleeps. . . . Perpetual noise, perpetual motion, the curtain never rings down on the enormous stage; first come the fishmongers, and after these the egg-dealers, and after these the retail buyers; for the Halles keep all the other markets of Paris going; they are the warehouses whence these draw their supplies. The food of the whole city is shifted and sorted in high-piled baskets; you may see eggs, pyramids of eggs, moved here and there, up steps and down, in and out of the throngs, miraculous; not one is ever broken. . . .

This impenetrable din contrasts oddly with the sleeping streets, for at that hour none but thieves and poets are awake.

Twice a week, at six, those distributors of the staff of life, the bakers of Gonesse,†† bring in an enormous quantity of loaves to the town, and may take none back through the barriers. And at this same hour workmen take up their tools, and trudge off to their day's labour. Coffee with milk is, unbelievably, the favoured drink among these stalwarts nowadays. . . .

So coffee-drinking has become a habit, and one so deep-rooted that the working classes will start the day on nothing else. It is not costly, and has more flavour to it, and more nourishment too, than anything else they can afford to drink; so they consume immense quantities, and say that if a man can only have coffee for breakfast it will keep him going till nightfall. »

Source: Excerpt from *Panorama of Paris: Selections from "Le Tableau de Paris,"* by Louis Sébastien Mercier, based on the translation by Helen Simpson, edited with a new preface and translations by Jeremy D. Popkin. Copyright © 1999 The Pennsylvania State University. Reprinted by permission of Penn State Press.

QUESTIONS FOR ANALYSIS

1. What different social groups does Mercier describe? Does he approve or disapprove of Parisian society as he describes it?

2. How do the social classes described by Mercier differ in their use of time, and why? Do you think the same distinctions exist today?

3. What evidence of the consumer revolution can you find in Mercier's account? How do the goods used by eighteenth-century Parisians compare to the ones you use in your life today?

** The city's central wholesale food market.

†† A suburb of Paris, famous for the excellent bread baked there.

Religious Authority and Beliefs

What were the patterns of popular religion, and how did they interact with the worldview of the educated public and their Enlightenment ideals? ■

Though the critical spirit of the Enlightenment made great inroads in the eighteenth century, the majority of ordinary men and women, especially those in rural areas, remained committed Christians. Religious faith promised salvation, and it gave comfort in the face of sorrow and death. Religion also remained strong because it was embedded in local traditions and everyday social experience.

Yet the popular religion of village Europe was also enmeshed in a larger world of church hierarchies and state power. These powerful outside forces sought to regulate religious life at the local level. Their efforts created tensions that helped set the scene for vigorous religious revivals in Protestant Germany and England as well as in Catholic France. Tensions arose between authorities and the people as powerful elites began to criticize many popular religious practices that their increasingly rationalistic minds deemed foolish and superstitious.

Church Hierarchy

As in the Middle Ages, the local parish church remained the focal point of religious devotion and community cohesion. Congregants gossiped and swapped stories after services, and neighbors came together in church for baptisms, marriages, funerals, and special events. Priests and parsons kept the community records of births, deaths, and marriages; distributed charity; looked after orphans; and provided primary education to the common people. Thus the parish church was woven into the very fabric of community life.

While the parish church remained central to the community, it was also subject to greater control from the state. In Protestant areas princes and monarchs headed the official church, and they regulated their "territorial churches" strictly, selecting personnel and imposing detailed rules. By the eighteenth century the radical ideas of the Reformation had resulted in another version of church bureaucracy.

Catholic monarchs in this period also took greater control of religious matters in their kingdoms, weakening papal authority. Spain, a deeply Catholic country with devout rulers, took firm control of ecclesiastical appointments. Papal proclamations could not even be read in Spanish churches without prior approval from the government. Spain also asserted state control over the Spanish Inquisition, which pursued heresy as an independent agency under Rome's direction and went far toward creating a "national" Catholic Church, as France had done earlier.

A more striking indication of state power and papal weakness was the fate of the Society of Jesus, or Jesuits. The well-educated Jesuits were extraordinary teachers, missionaries, and agents of the papacy. In many Catholic countries they exercised tremendous political influence, holding high government positions and educating the nobility in their colleges. Yet by playing politics so effectively, the Jesuits eventually elicited a broad coalition of enemies. Bitter controversies led Louis XV to order the Jesuits out of France in 1763 and to confiscate their property. France and Spain then pressured Rome to dissolve the Jesuits completely. In 1773 a reluctant pope caved in, although the order was revived after the French Revolution.

Some Catholic rulers also believed that the clergy in monasteries and convents should make a more practical contribution to social and religious life. Austria, a leader in controlling the church (see Chapter 17) and promoting primary education, showed how far the process could go. Maria Theresa began by sharply restricting entry into "unproductive" orders. In his Edict on Idle Institutions, her successor, Joseph II, abolished contemplative orders, henceforth permitting only orders that were engaged in teaching, nursing, or other practical work. The state expropriated the dissolved monasteries and used their wealth for charitable purposes and higher salaries for ordinary priests. Joseph II also issued edicts of religious tolerance, including for Jews, making Austria one of the first European states to lift centuries-old restrictions on its Jewish population.

Protestant Revival

By the late seventeenth century the vast reforms of the Protestant Reformation were complete and had been widely adopted in most Protestant churches. Medieval practices of idolatry, saint worship, and pageantry were abolished; stained-glass windows were smashed and murals whitewashed. Yet many official Protestant churches had settled into a smug complacency. This, along with the growth of state power and bureaucracy in local parishes, threatened to eclipse one of the Reformation's main goals—to bring all believers closer to God.

In the Reformation heartland, one concerned German minister wrote that the Lutheran church "had become paralyzed in forms of dead doctrinal conformity" and badly needed a return to its original inspiration.[22] His voice was one of many that prepared and then guided a powerful Protestant revival that succeeded because it answered the intense but increasingly unsatisfied needs of common people.

The Protestant revival began in Germany in the late seventeenth century. It was known as **Pietism** (PIGH-uh-tih-zum), and three aspects helped explain its powerful appeal. First, Pietism called for a warm, emotional religion that everyone could experience. Enthusiasm—in prayer, in worship, in preaching, in life itself—was the key concept. "Just as a drunkard becomes full of wine, so must the congregation become filled with spirit," declared one exuberant writer. Another said simply, "The heart must burn."[23]

Second, Pietism reasserted the earlier radical stress on the priesthood of all believers, thereby reducing the gulf between official clergy and Lutheran laity. Bible reading and study were enthusiastically extended to all classes, and this provided a powerful spur for popular literacy as well as individual religious development (see page 595). Pietists were largely responsible for the educational reforms implemented by Prussia in the early eighteenth century. Finally, Pietists believed in the practical power of Christian rebirth in everyday affairs. Reborn Christians were expected to lead good, moral lives and to come from all social classes.

Pietism soon spread through the German-speaking lands and to Scandinavia. It also had a major impact on John Wesley (1703–1791), who served as the catalyst for popular religious revival in England. Wesley came from a long line of ministers, and when he went to Oxford University to prepare for the clergy, he mapped a fanatically earnest "scheme of religion." After becoming a teaching fellow at Oxford, Wesley organized a Holy Club for similarly minded students, who were soon known contemptuously as **Methodists** because they were so methodical in their devotion. Yet like the young Martin Luther, Wesley remained intensely troubled about his own salvation even after his ordination as an Anglican priest in 1728.

Wesley's anxieties related to grave problems of the faith in England. The government shamelessly used the Church of England to provide favorites with high-paying jobs. Both church and state officials failed to respond to the spiritual needs of the people, abandoning the construction of new churches while the population grew, and in many parishes there was a shortage of pews. Services and sermons had settled into an uninspiring routine. The separation of religion from local customs and social life was symbolized by church doors that were customarily locked on weekdays. Moreover, Enlightenment skepticism was making inroads among the educated classes, and deism—a belief in God but not in organized religion—was becoming popular. Some bishops and church leaders seemed to believe that doctrines such as the virgin birth were little more than elegant superstitions.

Pietism A Protestant revival movement in early-eighteenth-century Germany and Scandinavia that emphasized a warm and emotional religion, the priesthood of all believers, and the power of Christian rebirth in everyday affairs.

Methodists Members of a Protestant revival movement started by John Wesley, so called because they were so methodical in their devotion.

Hogarth's Satirical View of the Church William Hogarth (1697–1764) was one of the foremost satirical artists of his day. This image mocks a London Methodist meeting, where the congregation swoons in enthusiasm over the preacher's sermon. The woman in the foreground giving birth to rabbits refers to a hoax perpetrated in 1726 by a servant named Mary Tofts; the gullibility of those who believed Tofts is likened to that of the Methodist congregation. (HIP/Art Resource, NY)

Spiritual counseling from a sympathetic Pietist minister from Germany prepared Wesley for a mystical, emotional "conversion" in 1738. He described this critical turning point in his *Journal*:

> In the evening I went to a [Christian] society in Aldersgate Street where one was reading Luther's preface to the Epistle to the Romans. About a quarter before nine, while he was describing the change which God works in the heart through faith in Christ, I felt my heart strangely warmed. I felt I did trust in Christ, Christ alone for salvation; and an assurance was given me that he had taken away my sins, even mine, and saved me from the law of sin and death.[24]

Wesley's emotional experience resolved his intellectual doubts. Moreover, he was convinced that any person, no matter how poor or uneducated, might have a similarly heartfelt conversion and gain the same blessed assurance. He took the good news to the people, traveling some 225,000 miles by horseback and preaching more than forty thousand sermons between 1750 and 1790. Since existing churches were often overcrowded and the church-state establishment was hostile, Wesley preached in open fields. People came in large numbers. Of critical importance was Wesley's rejection of Calvinist predestination—the doctrine of salvation granted to only a select few. Instead, he preached that all men and women who earnestly sought salvation might be saved. It was a message of hope and joy, of free will and universal salvation.

Jansenism A sect of Catholicism originating with Cornelius Jansen that emphasized the heavy weight of original sin and accepted the doctrine of predestination; it was outlawed as heresy by the pope.

Wesley's ministry won converts, formed Methodist cells, and eventually resulted in a new denomination. And just as Wesley had been inspired by the Pietist revival in Germany, so evangelicals in the Church of England and the old dissenting groups now followed Wesley's example of preaching to all people, giving impetus to an even broader awakening among the lower classes. Thus, in Protestant countries religion continued to be a vital force in the lives of the people.

Catholic Piety

Religion also flourished in Catholic Europe around 1700, but there were important differences from Protestant practice. First, the visual contrast was striking; baroque art still lavished rich and emotionally exhilarating figures and images on Catholic churches, just as most Protestants had removed theirs during the Reformation. Moreover, people in Catholic Europe on the whole participated more actively in formal worship than did Protestants. More than 95 percent of the population probably attended church for Easter communion, the climax of the religious year.

The tremendous popular strength of religion in Catholic countries can in part be explained by the church's integral role in community life and popular culture. Thus, although Catholics reluctantly confessed their sins to priests, they enthusiastically joined together in religious festivals to celebrate the passage of the liturgical year. In addition to the great processional days—such as Palm Sunday, the joyful reenactment of Jesus' triumphal entry into Jerusalem—each parish had its own saints' days, processions, and pilgrimages. Led by its priest, a congregation might march around the village or across the countryside to a local shrine. Before each procession or feast day, the priest explained its religious significance to kindle group piety. Processions were also folklore and tradition, an escape from work, and a form of recreation. The Reformation had largely eliminated such festivities in Protestant areas.

Catholicism had its own version of the Pietist revivals that shook Protestant Europe. **Jansenism** has been described by one historian as the "illegitimate off-spring of the Protestant Reformation and the Catholic Counter-Reformation."[25] It originated with Cornelius Jansen (1585–1638), bishop of Ypres in the Spanish Netherlands, who called for a return to the austere early Christianity of Saint Augustine. In contrast to the worldly Jesuits, Jansen emphasized the heavy weight of original sin and accepted the doctrine of predestination. Although outlawed by papal and royal edicts as Calvinist heresy, Jansenism attracted Catholic followers eager for religious renewal, particularly among the French. Many members of France's urban elite, especially judicial nobles and some parish priests, became known for their Jansenist piety and spiritual devotion. Such stern religious values encouraged the judiciary's increasing opposition to the French monarchy in the second half of the eighteenth century.

Among the urban poor, a different strain of Jansenism took hold. Prayer meetings brought men and women together in ecstatic worship, and some participants fell into convulsions and spoke in tongues. The police of Paris posted spies to report on such gatherings and conducted mass raids and arrests.

Marginal Beliefs and Practices

In the countryside, many peasants continued to hold religious beliefs that were marginal to the Christian faith altogether, often of obscure or even pagan origin. On the Feast of Saint Anthony, for example, priests were expected to bless salt and bread for farm animals to protect them from disease. Catholics believed that saints' relics could bring fortune or attract lovers, and there were healing springs for many ailments. In 1796 the Lutheran villagers of Beutelsbach incurred the ire of local officials when they buried a live bull at a crossroads to ward off an epidemic of hoof and mouth disease.[26]

Procession of Nuns at Port-Royal des Champs The convent of Port-Royal, located twenty miles southwest of Paris, was a center of Jansenist activity throughout the seventeenth century. Angered by the nuns' defiance, Louis XIV ordered them forcibly relocated in 1709. To generate support, the artist Magdelaine Horthemels painted a series of images depicting the pious and placid religious life at the convent. The convent was nonetheless destroyed by Louis's forces in 1710. This image is one of many copies of Horthemels's work made by Jansenists in the eighteenth century. (Réunion des Musées Nationaux/Art Resource, NY)

The ordinary person combined strong Christian faith with a wealth of time-honored superstitions.

Inspired initially by the fervor of the Reformation era, then by the critical rationalism of the Enlightenment, religious and secular authorities sought increasingly to "purify" popular spirituality. Thus one parish priest in France lashed out at his parishioners, claiming that they were "more superstitious than devout . . . and sometimes appear as baptized idolators."[27] French priests particularly denounced the "various remnants of paganism" found in popular bonfire ceremonies during Lent, in which young men, "yelling and screaming like madmen," tried to jump over the bonfires in order to help the crops grow and protect themselves from illness. One priest saw rational Christians regressing into pagan animals—"the triumph of Hell and the shame of Christianity."[28]

The severity of the attack on popular belief varied widely by country and region. Where authorities pursued purification vigorously, as in Austria under Joseph II, pious peasants saw only an incomprehensible attack on age-old faith and drew back in anger. Their reaction dramatized the growing tension between the attitudes of educated elites and the common people.

It was in this era of growing intellectual disdain for popular beliefs that the persecution of witches slowly came to an end across Europe. Common people in the countryside continued to fear the Devil and his helpers, but the elite increasingly dismissed such fears and refused to prosecute suspected witches. The last witch was executed in England in 1682, the same year France prohibited witchcraft trials. By the late eighteenth century most European states and their colonies had followed suit.

Medical Practice

How did the practice of medicine evolve in the eighteenth century? ■

Although significant breakthroughs in medical science would not come until the middle and late nineteenth century, the Enlightenment's growing focus on discovering the laws of nature and on human problems did give rise to a great deal of research and experimentation in the 1700s. Medical practitioners greatly increased in number, although their techniques did not differ much from those of previous generations. Care of the sick in this era was the domain of several competing groups: faith healers, apothecaries (pharmacists), physicians, surgeons, and midwives. From the Middle Ages through the seventeenth century, both men and women were medical practitioners. However, since women were

An Eighteenth-Century Pharmacy In this lively painting a woman consults an apothecary (in the elegant red suit) while his assistants assemble drugs for new prescriptions. By 1700 apothecaries had emerged as a separate group of state-licensed medical professionals. They drew on published lists and books describing the properties and dosages of their concoctions, but there were many different "recipes" and trade secrets. (Civico Museo Bibliograco Musicale, Bologna, Italy/ The Bridgeman Art Library)

ecaries advertised their wares, their high-class customers, and their miraculous cures in newspapers and commercial circulars. Medicine, like food and fashionable clothing, thus joined the era's new commercial culture.

Physicians, who were invariably men, were apprenticed in their teens to practicing physicians for several years of on-the-job training. This training was then rounded out with hospital work or some university courses. Because such prolonged training was expensive, physicians came mainly from prosperous families, and they usually concentrated on urban patients from similar social backgrounds. They had little contact with urban workers and less with peasants.

generally denied admission to medical colleges and lacked the diplomas necessary to practice, the range of medical activities open to them was restricted. In the eighteenth century women's traditional roles as midwives and healers eroded even further.

Faith Healing and General Practice

In the course of the eighteenth century, faith healers remained active. They and their patients believed that evil spirits caused illness by lodging in people and that the proper treatment was to exorcise, or drive out, the offending devil. This demonic view of disease was strongest in the countryside, where popular belief placed great faith in the healing power of religious relics, prayer, and the laying on of hands.

In the larger towns and cities, apothecaries sold a vast number of herbs, drugs, and patent medicines for every conceivable "temperament and distemper." Some of the drugs and herbs undoubtedly worked. For example, strong laxatives were given to the rich for their constipated bowels, and regular purging of the bowels was considered essential for good health and the treatment of illness. Like all varieties of medical practitioners, apoth-

Physicians in the eighteenth century were increasingly willing to experiment with new methods, but time-honored practices lay heavily on them. Like apothecaries, they laid great stress on purging, and bloodletting was still considered a medical cure-all. It was the way "bad blood," the cause of illness, was removed and the balance of humors necessary for good health was restored.

Hospitals and Surgery

Long considered to be craftsmen comparable to butchers and barbers, surgeons began studying anatomy seriously and improved their art in the eighteenth century. With endless opportunities to practice, army surgeons on gory battlefields led the way. They learned that a soldier with an extensive wound, such as a shattered leg or arm, could perhaps be saved if the surgeon could obtain a flat surface above the wound that could be cauterized with fire. Thus if a soldier (or a civilian) had a broken limb and the bone stuck out, the surgeon amputated so that the remaining stump could be cauterized and the likelihood of death reduced.

The eighteenth-century surgeon (and patient) labored in the face of incredible difficulties. Almost all operations were performed without painkillers, for the anesthesia of the day was hard to control and too dangerous for general use. Many patients died from the agony and shock of such operations. Surgery was also performed in utterly unsanitary conditions, for there was no knowledge of bacteriology and the nature of infection. The simplest wound treated by a surgeon could fester and lead to death.

Midwifery

Midwives continued to deliver the overwhelming majority of babies throughout the eighteenth century. Trained initially by another woman practitioner—and regulated by a guild in many cities—the midwife primarily assisted in labor and delivering babies. She also treated female problems, such as irregular menstrual cycles, breast-feeding difficulties, infertility, and venereal disease, and ministered to small children.

The midwife orchestrated labor and birth in a woman's world, where friends and relatives assisted the pregnant woman in the familiar surroundings of her own home. The male surgeon (and the husband) rarely entered this female world, because most births, then as now, were normal and spontaneous. After the invention of forceps became publicized in 1734, surgeon-physicians used their monopoly over this and other instruments to seek lucrative new business. Attacking midwives as ignorant and dangerous, they sought to undermine faith in midwives and persuaded growing numbers of wealthy women of the superiority of their services.

Research suggests that women practitioners successfully defended much but not all of their practice in the eighteenth century. One enterprising French midwife, Madame du Coudray, wrote a widely used textbook, *Manual on the Art of Childbirth* (1757). She then secured royal financing for her campaign to teach better birthing techniques to village midwives. Du Coudray traveled all over France using a life-size model of the female torso and fetus to help teach illiterate women. (See "Living in the Past: Improvements in Childbirth," page 612.) It appears that midwives generally lost no more babies than did male doctors, who were still summoned to treat nonelite women only when life-threatening situations required surgery.

The Conquest of Smallpox

Experimentation and the intensified search for solutions to human problems led to some real advances in medicine after 1750. The eighteenth century's greatest medical triumph was the eradication of smallpox. With the progressive decline of bubonic plague, smallpox became the most terrible of the infectious diseases, and it is estimated that 60 million Europeans died of it in the eighteenth century. Fully 80 percent of the population was stricken at some point in life.

The first step in the conquest of this killer in Europe came in the early eighteenth century. An English aristocrat whose beauty had been marred by the pox, Lady Mary Wortley Montagu, learned about the

"The Wonderful Effects of the New Inoculation!" The talented caricaturist James Gillray satirized widespread anxieties about the smallpox vaccination in this lively image. The discoveries of Edward Jenner a few years prior to Gillray's caricature had led to the adoption of a safer vaccine derived from cowpox. The artist mocks this breakthrough by showing cows bursting from the boils supposedly brought on by the vaccine. (Private Collection/The Bridgeman Art Library)

LIVING IN THE PAST

MOST WOMEN IN EIGHTEENTH-CENTURY EUROPE gave birth to five or six children over their lifetimes. They were assisted in the arduous, often dangerous process of childbirth by friends, relatives, and, in many cases, professional midwives. Birth took place at home, sometimes with the aid of a birthing chair, such as the folding chair from Sicily shown here.

The training and competency of midwives was often rudimentary, especially in the countryside. Enlightenment interest in education and public health helped inspire a movement across Europe to raise standards. One of its pioneers was Madame Angelique Marguerite Le Boursier du Coudray. Du Coudray herself had undergone a rigorous three-year apprenticeship and was a member of the Parisian surgeons' guild. She set off on a mission to teach rural midwives in the French province of Auvergne.

Du Coudray saw that her unlettered pupils learned through the senses, not through books. Thus she made, possibly for the first time in history, a life-size obstetrical model—a "machine"—out of fabric and stuffing for use in her classes. "I had . . . the students maneuver in front of me on a machine . . . which represented the pelvis of a woman, the womb, its opening, its ligaments, the conduit called the vagina, the bladder, and *rectum intestine*. I added [an artificial] child of natural size, whose joints were flexible enough to be able to be put in different positions."* Now du Coudray could demonstrate the problems of childbirth, and each student could practice on the model in the "lab session."

As her reputation grew, du Coudray sought to reach a national audience. In 1757 she published her *Manual on the Art of Childbirth*. The *Manual* incorporated her hands-on teaching method and served as a reference for students and graduates. In 1759 the government autho-

Eighteenth-century birthing chair from Sicily. (Science & Society Picture Library)

Du Coudray's life-size model for simulating childbirth. (Musée Flaubert d'histoire de la médecine, Rouen)

*Quotes are from Nina Gelbart, *The King's Midwife: A History and Mystery of Madame du Coudray* (Berkeley: University of California Press, 1998), pp. 60–61.

Childbirth was traditionally a woman's world that brought female relatives, friends, and the midwife to the laboring woman's bedside, as shown in this Dutch painting from the late seventeenth century. (Image copyright © The Metropolitan Museum of Art/Art Resource, NY)

rized du Coudray to carry her instruction "throughout the realm" and promised financial support.

Her classes brought women from surrounding villages to meet mornings and afternoons six days a week, with ample time to practice on the mannequin. After two to three months of instruction, Madame du Coudray and her entourage moved on. Teaching thousands of midwives, Madame du Coudray and her model may well have contributed to the decline in infant mortality and to the increase in population occurring in France in the eighteenth century—an increase she and her royal supporters fervently desired. Certainly she spread better knowledge about childbirth from the educated elite to the common people.

QUESTIONS FOR ANALYSIS

1. How do you account for du Coudray's remarkable success? What does her story suggest about women's lives in this period, both within their families and in the economic realm? What kind of opportunities were available to women?

2. What is painted on the Italian birthing chair where a woman's head would rest during labor? What might this suggest about childbirth in this period?

3. How might the Dutch painting of childbirth shown here differ if painted by a Western artist today?

"Incorrect method of delivery" from du Coudray's *Manual.* (Rare Books Division, Countway [Francis A.] Library of Medicine)

long-established practice of smallpox inoculation in the Muslim lands of western Asia while her husband was serving as British ambassador to the Ottoman Empire. She had her own son successfully inoculated with the pus from a smallpox victim and was instrumental in spreading the practice in England after her return in 1722. But inoculation was risky and was widely condemned because about one person in fifty died from it. In addition, people who had been inoculated were infectious and often spread the disease.

While the practice of inoculation with the smallpox virus was refined over the century, the crucial breakthrough was made by Edward Jenner (1749–1823), a talented country doctor. His starting point was the countryside belief that dairy maids who had contracted cowpox did not get smallpox. Cowpox produces sores that resemble those of smallpox, but the disease is mild and is not contagious.

For eighteen years Jenner practiced a kind of Baconian science, carefully collecting data. Finally, in 1796 he performed his first vaccination on a young boy using matter taken from a milkmaid with cowpox. After performing more successful vaccinations, Jenner published his findings in 1798. The new method of treatment spread rapidly, and smallpox soon declined to the point of disappearance in Europe and then throughout the world.

LOOKING BACK LOOKING AHEAD

THE FUNDAMENTAL PATTERNS of life in early modern Europe remained very much the same up to the eighteenth century. The vast majority of people lived in the countryside and followed age-old rhythms of seasonal labor in the fields and farmyard. Community ties were close in small villages, where the struggle to prevail over harsh conditions called on all hands to work together and to pray together. The daily life of a peasant in 1700 would have been familiar to his ancestors in the 1400s. Indeed, the three orders of society enshrined in the medieval social hierarchy were binding legal categories in France up to 1789.

And yet, the economic changes inaugurated in the late seventeenth century — enclosure, cottage industry, industrious revolution, and colonial expansion — contributed to the profound social and cultural transformation of daily life in eighteenth-century Europe. Men and women of the laboring classes, especially in the cities, experienced change in many facets of their daily lives: in loosened community controls over sex and marriage, rising literacy rates, new goods and ways of utilizing space, and a wave of religious piety that challenged traditional orthodoxies. Both their age-old cultural practices and new religious fervor were met with mounting disbelief and ridicule by the educated classes in a period of increased distance between popular and elite culture.

Economic, social, and cultural change would culminate in the late eighteenth century with the outbreak of revolution in the Americas and Europe. Initially led by the elite, political upheavals relied on the enthusiastic participation of the poor and their desire for greater inclusion in the life of the nation. Such movements also encountered resistance from the common people when revolutionaries trampled on their religious sentiments and practices. For many observers, contemporaries and historians alike, the transformations of the eighteenth century constituted a fulcrum between the old world of hierarchy and tradition and the modern world with its claims to equality and freedom.

CHAPTER REVIEW

■ **What changes occurred in marriage and the family in the course of the eighteenth century? (p. 586)**

In the first half of the eighteenth century, tradition, routine, and well-established codes of behavior framed much of the everyday experience. People's primarily rural lives remained oriented toward the local community, with shared values strongly encouraging family guidance in choosing mates and a low rate of illegitimate births. As the century wore on, however, closely knit villages began to lose control over families and marital practices. Young people gained social and economic autonomy through wage work in cottage industry and in urban settings. As a result, they exercised more personal choice in selecting marriage partners. At the same time, loosening social controls also led to a steep increase in the number of illegitimate births.

■ **What was life like for children, and how did attitudes toward childhood evolve? (p. 591)**

Infancy and childhood were highly vulnerable stages of life. In some parts of Europe only half of all children reached the age of ten. Infant mortality was particularly high in France, where wet-nursing was commonly practiced. Treatment of children could be harsh in an early modern society that was characterized by much higher levels of violence and brutality than are Western societies today. The second half of the eighteenth century witnessed a new concern with methods of child rearing inspired by Enlightenment efforts to reform human society, and schools for nonelite children spread across Europe.

■ How did increasing literacy and new patterns of consumption affect people's lives? (p. 595)

Increasing literacy rates allowed many more commoners to read the large numbers of texts that were becoming available: religious pamphlets, how-to manuals, and escapist fantasies. But the oral tradition continued, as did the many fairs, festivals, and sports that had existed for centuries. The urban populace benefited from the surge in agricultural and industrial production. People found a greater variety of food products at the market, including new stimulants produced in the colonies that soon became staples of elite and popular consumption. New foods, especially the potato, provided appealing new flavors and important vitamins. Within homes, standards of comfort and hygiene increased, and the emerging consumer society offered new possibilities for self-expression and individuality.

■ What were the patterns of popular religion, and how did they interact with the worldview of the educated public and their Enlightenment ideals? (p. 606)

As the Enlightenment swept through the circles of the intellectual elite, many long-standing beliefs and practices remained strong forces and sustained continuity in popular life. Protestant religious revival sought to reaffirm Martin Luther's original mission and carried the promise of salvation to the common people. Through Jansenism, which found a particularly willing audience in France, Catholicism also experienced a type of revival that emphasized original sin and predestination. Obscure and pagan beliefs persisted in rural areas, where they were roundly criticized by secular officials and increasingly rational religious authorities.

■ How did the practice of medicine evolve in the eighteenth century? (p. 609)

Although the number of medical practitioners — faith healers, apothecaries, physicians, surgeons, and midwives — grew, methods of healing the sick continued to be crude and primitive. Women began to lose prominence in midwifery beginning with the introduction of forceps in the mid-eighteenth century, and their lack of access to medical schools eroded their ability to compete with male physicians. In 1796 Edward Jenner devised a vaccine for smallpox, the most deadly disease in Europe since the disappearance of the plague earlier in the century.

Suggested Reading

Bongie, Laurence L. *From Rogue to Everyman: A Foundling's Journey to the Bastille.* 2005. The life story of an eighteenth-century foundling and, through his eyes, the Parisian underworld of gamblers, prostitutes, and police spies.

Brewer, John, and Roy Porter, eds. *Consumption and the World of Goods.* 1993. Pioneering essays from leading scholars on the consumer revolution of eighteenth-century Europe.

Burke, Peter. *Popular Culture in Early Modern Europe*, 3d ed. 2009. A thoroughly updated version of a classic introduction to everyday life, mentalities, and leisure pursuits.

Carrell, Jennifer. *The Speckled Monster: A Historical Tale of Battling Smallpox.* 2003. A lively popular account of the spread of inoculation.

Crawford, Katherine. *European Sexualities, 1400–1800.* 2007. A broad survey of cultural and social aspects of sex and sexuality in early modern Europe.

Gawthrop, Richard. *Pietism and the Making of Eighteenth-Century Prussia.* 2006. An examination of the importance of Pietist morality and institutions in the making of the Prussian state.

Gelbart, Nina. *The King's Midwife: A History and Mystery of Madame du Coudray.* 2002. A vivid and accessible biography of the most famous midwife of eighteenth-century France.

Hartman, Mary S. *The Household and the Making of History.* 2004. A bold study of the economic and social ramifications of the European pattern of late marriage.

Immel, Andrea, and Michael Witmore. *Childhood and Children's Books in Early Modern Europe, 1550–1800.* 2005. A collection of essays describing the experience of childhood and the rise of children's literature, mostly in Britain.

Kertzer, David I., and Marzio Barbagli, eds. *Family Life in Early Modern Times, 1500–1789.* 2001. A rich collection of essays on the history of the family, women, and children in early modern Europe.

Lindeman, Mary. *Health and Healing in Eighteenth-Century Germany.* 2001. A study of the day-to-day activities of German medical practitioners — doctors, surgeons, faith healers, quacks — and their patients.

Mintz, Sidney W. *Sweetness and Power: The Place of Sugar in Modern History.* 1985. A fascinating exploration of the shifting cultural significance of sugar and its transformation from elite luxury good to everyday staple.

Sussman, George D. *Selling Mother's Milk: The Wet-Nursing Business in France, 1715–1914.* 1982. An engrossing account of the large-scale organization of wet-nursing in eighteenth-century France.

Key Terms

community controls (p. 588)
illegitimacy explosion (p. 589)
wet-nursing (p. 591)
blood sports (p. 597)
carnival (p. 597)
just price (p. 599)
consumer revolution (p. 601)
Pietism (p. 607)
Methodists (p. 607)
Jansenism (p. 608)

Notes

1. Quoted in J. M. Beattie, "The Criminality of Women in Eighteenth-Century England," *Journal of Social History* 8 (Summer 1975): 86.
2. Quoted in R. Cobb, *The Police and the People: French Popular Protest, 1789–1820* (Oxford, U.K.: Clarendon Press, 1970), p. 238.
3. Peter Laslett, *Family Life and Illicit Love: Essays in Historical Sociology* (Cambridge, U.K.: Cambridge University Press, 1977).
4. G. Gullickson, *Spinners and Weavers of Auffay: Rural Industry and the Sexual Division of Labor in a French Village, 1750–1850* (Cambridge, U.K.: Cambridge University Press, 1986), p. 186.
5. Trial of Barton Dorrington, *Old Bailey Proceedings Online*, September 10, 1788, www.oldbaileyonline.org, October 9, 2009, t17880910-46.
6. Louis Crompton, *Homosexuality and Civilization* (Cambridge, Mass.: Belknap Press, 2003), p. 321.
7. D. S. Neff, "Bitches, Mollies, and Tommies: Byron, Masculinity and the History of Sexualities," in *Journal of the History of Sexuality* 11, 3 (July 2002): 404.
8. George E. Haggerty, ed., *Encyclopedia of Gay Histories and Cultures* (New York: Garland Publishing, 2000), pp. 1311–1312.
9. Pier Paolo Viazzo, "Mortality, Fertility, and Family," in *Family Life in Early Modern Times, 1500–1789*, ed. David I. Kertzer and Marzio Barbagli (New Haven, Conn.: Yale University Press, 2001), p. 180.
10. George Sussman, *Selling Mother's Milk: The Wet-Nursing Business in France, 1715–1914* (Urbana: University of Illinois Press, 1982), p. 22.
11. Robert Woods, "Did Montaigne Love His Children? Demography and the Hypothesis of Parental Indifference," *Journal of Interdisciplinary History* 33, 3 (2003): 426.
12. P. Viazzo, "Mortality, Fertility, and Family," in *The History of the European Family*, vol. 1, ed. D. Kertzer and M. Barbagli (New Haven, Conn.: Yale University Press, 2001), pp. 176–178.
13. Alysa Levene, "The Estimation of Mortality at the London Foundling Hospital, 1741–99," *Population Studies* 59, 1 (2005): 87–97.
14. Cited in Woods, "Did Montaigne Love His Children?" p. 421.
15. Ibid., pp. 13, 16.
16. James Van Horn Melton, *Absolutism and the Eighteenth-Century Origins of Compulsory Schooling in Prussia and Austria* (Cambridge, U.K.: Cambridge University Press, 2003), p. 46.
17. James Van Horn Melton, "The Theresian School Reform of 1774," in *Early Modern Europe*, ed. James B. Collins and Karen L. Taylor (Oxford, U.K.: Blackwell, 2006).
18. I. Woloch, *Eighteenth-Century Europe: Tradition and Progress, 1715–1789* (New York: W. W. Norton, 1982), pp. 220–221.
19. Neil McKendrik, John Brewer, and J. H. Plumb, *The Birth of a Consumer Society: The Commercialization of Eighteenth-Century England* (Bloomington: Indiana University Press, 1982).
20. Daniel Roche, *The Culture of Clothing: Dress and Fashion in the Ancien Regime*, trans. Jean Birrell (Cambridge, U.K.: Cambridge University Press, 1996).
21. Quoted in Cissie Fairchilds, "The Production and Marketing of Populuxe Goods in Eighteenth-Century Paris," in *Consumption and the World of Goods*, ed. John Brewer and Roy Porter (London: Routledge, 1993), p. 228.
22. Quoted in K. Pinson, *Pietism as a Factor in the Rise of German Nationalism* (New York: Columbia University Press, 1934), p. 13.
23. Ibid., pp. 43–44.
24. Quoted in S. Andrews, *Methodism and Society* (London: Longmans, Green, 1970), p. 327.
25. Dale Van Kley, "The Rejuvenation and Rejection of Jansenism in History and Historiography," *French Historical Studies* 29 (Fall 2006): 649–684.
26. David Sabean, *The Power in the Blood: Popular Culture and Village Discourse in Early Modern Germany* (Cambridge, U.K.: Cambridge University Press, 1984), p. 174.
27. Quoted in Woloch, *Eighteenth-Century Europe*, p. 292.
28. Quoted in T. Tackett, *Priest and Parish in Eighteenth-Century France* (Princeton, N.J.: Princeton University Press, 1977), p. 214.

For practice quizzes and other study tools, visit the Online Study Guide at **bedfordstmartins.com/mckaywest.**

For primary sources from this period, see ***Sources of Western Society*, Second Edition.**

For Web sites, images, and documents related to topics in this chapter, visit Make History at **bedfordstmartins.com/mckaywest.**

20
The Revolution in Politics

1775–1815

The last years of the eighteenth century were a time of great upheaval as a series of revolutions and wars challenged the old order of monarchs and aristocrats. The ideas of freedom and equality, ideas that have not stopped shaping the world since that era, flourished and spread. The revolutionary era began in North America in 1775. Then in 1789 France, the most populous country in western Europe and a center of culture and intellectual life, became the leading revolutionary nation. It established first a constitutional monarchy, then a radical republic, and finally a new empire under Napoleon that would last until 1815. During this period of constant domestic turmoil, French armies violently exported revolution beyond the nation's borders, eager to establish new governments throughout much of Europe. Inspired both by the ideals of the Revolution on the continent and by internal colonial conditions, the slaves of Saint-Domingue rose up in 1791. Their rebellion would eventually lead to the creation of the new independent nation of Haiti in 1804. In Europe and its colonies abroad, the world of modern politics was born. ■

Life in Revolutionary France. On the eve of the French Revolution, angry crowds like this one gathered in Paris to protest the high-handed actions of the royal government. Throughout the Revolution, decisive events took place in the street as much as in the chambers of the National Assembly.

CHAPTER PREVIEW

Background to Revolution
■ What social, political, and economic factors formed the background to the French Revolution?

Politics and the People, 1789–1791
■ How did the events of 1789 result in a constitutional monarchy in France, and how did the new constitution affect the various members of French society at home and in the colony of Saint-Domingue?

World War and Republican France, 1791–1799
■ How and why did the Revolution take a radical turn at home and in the colonies?

The Napoleonic Era, 1799–1815
■ Why did Napoleon Bonaparte assume control of France, and what factors led to his downfall? How did the new republic of Haiti gain independence from France?

Background to Revolution

What social, political, and economic factors formed the background to the French Revolution? ▪

The origin of the French Revolution has been one of the most debated topics in history. In order to understand the path to revolution, numerous interrelated factors must be taken into account. These include deep social changes in France, a long-term political crisis that eroded monarchical legitimacy, the practical and ideological effects of the American Revolution, the impact of new political ideas derived from the Enlightenment, and, perhaps most important, a financial crisis created by France's participation in expensive overseas wars.

estates The three legal categories, or orders, of France's inhabitants: the clergy, the nobility, and everyone else.

A FAUT ESPERER Q'EU JEU LA FINIRA BEN TOT

l'auteur en Campagne Ap. 1789.

Legal Orders and Social Reality

As in the Middle Ages, France's 25 million inhabitants were still legally divided into three orders, or **estates**—the clergy, the nobility, and everyone else. As the nation's first estate, the clergy numbered about one hundred thousand and had important privileges. It owned about 10 percent of the land and paid only a "voluntary gift," rather than regular taxes, to the government every five years. Moreover, the church levied a property tax (tithe) on landowners.

The second estate consisted of some four hundred thousand nobles, the descendants of "those who fought" in the Middle Ages. Nobles owned about 25 percent of the land in France outright, and they too were lightly taxed. Moreover, nobles continued to enjoy certain manorial rights, or privileges of lordship, that dated back to medieval times. These included exclusive rights to hunt and fish, village monopolies on baking bread and pressing grapes for wine, fees for justice, and a host of other entitlements. In addition, nobles had "honorific privileges" such as the right to precedence on public occasions and the right to wear swords. These rights conspicuously proclaimed the nobility's legal superiority and exalted social position.

Everyone else—nearly 98 percent of the population—was a commoner, legally a member of the third estate. A few commoners—prosperous merchants, lawyers, and officials—were well educated and rich, and they might have purchased manorial rights as a way of obtaining profit and social honor. Yet the vast majority of the third estate consisted of peasants, rural agricultural workers, urban artisans, and unskilled day laborers. Thus the third estate was a conglomeration of very different social groups united only by their shared legal status.

In discussing the origins of the French Revolution, historians long focused on growing tensions between the nobility and the comfortable members of the third estate, the bourgeoisie (boorzh-wah-ZEE), or upper middle class. Increasing in size, wealth, culture, and self-confidence, this rising bourgeoisie became progressively exasperated by feudal laws restraining the economy and by the pretensions of a nobility that was closing ranks against middle-class aspirations. As a result, the French bourgeoisie eventually rose up to lead the entire third estate in a great social revolution that destroyed feudal privileges and established a capitalist order based on individualism and a market economy.

The Three Estates In this political cartoon from 1789 a peasant of the third estate struggles under the weight of a happy clergyman and a plumed nobleman. The caption—"Let's hope this game ends soon"—sets forth a program of reform that any peasant could understand. (Réunion des Musées Nationaux/Art Resource, NY)

In the last thirty years, the French Revolution's origins have been subject to what historians refer to as revisionism, or new interpretations. A flood of research uncovered in the late twentieth century challenged the long-accepted view and led to revised theories. Above all, revisionist historians have questioned the existence of growing social conflict between a progressive capitalistic bourgeoisie and a reactionary feudal nobility in eighteenth-century France. Instead, they see both bourgeoisie and nobility as highly fragmented, riddled with internal rivalries. The ancient sword nobility, for example, made up of people who descended from the oldest noble families, was separated by differences in wealth, education, and worldview from the newer robe nobility, people who acquired noble titles through service in the royal administration and judiciary. Differences within the bourgeoisie—between wealthy financiers and local lawyers, for example—were no less profound. Rather than standing as unified blocs against each other, nobility and bourgeoisie formed two parallel social ladders increasingly linked together at the top by wealth, marriage, and Enlightenment culture.

Revisionist historians note that the nobility and the bourgeoisie were not really at odds in the economic sphere. Investment in land and government service were the preferred activities of both groups, and the ideal of the merchant capitalist was to gain enough wealth to retire from trade, purchase an estate, and live nobly as a large landowner. Wealthy members of the third estate could even move into the second estate by serving the government and purchasing noble positions. At the same time, wealthy nobles often acted as aggressive capitalists, investing especially in mining, metallurgy, and foreign trade. In addition, until the Revolution actually began, key sections of the nobility were liberal and generally joined the bourgeoisie in opposition to the government.

Revisionists have clearly shaken the belief that the bourgeoisie and the nobility were inevitably locked in growing conflict before the Revolution. Yet they also make clear that the Old Regime had ceased to correspond with social reality by the 1780s. Legally, society was still based on rigid orders inherited from the Middle Ages, but in reality those distinctions were often blurred.

An upper echelon of aristocratic and bourgeois notables saw itself as an educated elite that stood well above the common masses. Although wealthy and influential, society's upper crust was frustrated by a bureaucratic monarchy that continued to claim the right to absolute power. Meanwhile, for France's laboring poor—the vast majority of the population—traditions remained strong and life itself remained a struggle.

Chronology

1773	Boston Tea Party
1775–1783	American Revolution
1786–1789	Height of French monarchy's financial crisis
1789	Feudalism abolished in France; ratification of U.S. Constitution; storming of the Bastille
1789–1799	French Revolution
1790	Burke, *Reflections on the Revolution in France*
1791	Slave insurrection in Saint-Domingue
1792	Wollstonecraft, *A Vindication of the Rights of Woman*
1793	Execution of Louis XVI
1793–1794	Robespierre's Reign of Terror
1794	Robespierre deposed and executed; France abolishes slavery in all territories
1794–1799	Thermidorian reaction
1799–1815	Napoleonic era
1804	Haitian republic declares independence
1812	Napoleon invades Russia
1814–1815	Napoleon defeated and exiled

The Crisis of Political Legitimacy

Overlying these social changes was a structural deadlock in France's tax system and the century-long political and fiscal struggle between the monarchy and its opponents sparked by the expenses of a series of foreign wars. When the Sun King, Louis XIV, finally died in 1715 and was succeeded by his five-year-old great-grandson, Louis XV (r. 1715–1774), the system of absolutist rule was challenged. Under the young monarch's regent, the duke of Orléans (1674–1723), a number of institutions retrieved powers they had lost under the Sun King. Most important, the high courts of France—the parlements—regained their ancient right to evaluate royal decrees publicly in writing before they were registered and given the force of law. The restoration of this right, which had been suspended under Louis XIV, was a fateful step. The magistrates of the parlements were leaders of the robe nobility who passed their judicial offices from father to son. By allowing a well-entrenched and highly articulate branch of the nobility to evaluate the king's decrees before they became law, the duke of Orléans sanctioned a counterweight to absolute power.

These implications became clear when the heavy expenses of war in the eighteenth century proved unbearable for the state treasury. Because many privileged groups escaped direct taxes and indirect taxes were relatively low, revenue from taxation could not meet the costs of war. The War of the Austrian Succession (see Chapter 17) plunged France into financial crisis and pushed the state to attempt a reform of the tax system. In 1748 Louis XV's finance minister decreed a 5 percent income tax on every individual regardless of social status. The result was a vigorous protest from those previously exempt from taxation — the nobility, the clergy, towns, and some wealthy bourgeoisie — led by the influential Parlement of Paris. The monarchy retreated; the new tax was dropped.

Following the disastrously expensive Seven Years' War (see Chapter 18), the conflict re-emerged. The government tried to maintain emergency taxes after the war ended; the Parlement of Paris protested and even challenged the basis of royal authority, claiming that the king's power had to be limited to protect liberty. Once again the government caved in and withdrew the taxes. The judicial opposition then asserted that the king could not levy taxes without the consent of the Parlement of Paris.

After years of attempted compromise, Louis XV finally roused himself to defend his absolutist inheritance. "The magistrates," he angrily told the Parlement of Paris in a famous face-to-face confrontation, "are my officers. . . . In my person only does the sovereign power rest."[1] In 1768 Louis appointed a tough career official named René de Maupeou (moh-POO) as chancellor and ordered him to crush the judicial opposition. Maupeou abolished the existing parlements and exiled the vociferous members of the Parlement of Paris to the provinces. He created new and docile parlements of royal officials, known as the Maupeou parlements, and he began once again to tax the privileged groups. Public opinion as a whole sided with the old parlements, however, and there was widespread criticism of "royal despotism."

Learned dissent was accompanied by scandalous libels. Known as Louis *le bien-aimé* (beloved Louis) in his youth, the king found his people turning against him for moral as well as political reasons. Kings had always maintained mistresses, who were invariably chosen from the court nobility. Louis XV broke that pattern with Madame de Pompadour, daughter of a disgraced bourgeois financier. As the king's favorite mistress from 1745 to 1750, Pompadour exercised tremendous influence over literature, art, and the decorative arts, using her patronage to support Voltaire and promote the rococo style (see Chapter 17). Even after their love affair ended, Pompadour wielded considerable influence over the king, helping bring about the alliance with Austria that resulted in the Seven Years' War. Pompadour's low birth and hidden political influence generated a stream of resentful and illegal pamphleteering.

After Pompadour, the king appeared to sink ever lower in immorality, and the stream of scandalmongering became a torrent. Lurid and pornographic depictions of the court ate away at the foundations of royal authority, especially among the common people. The king was being stripped of the sacred aura of God's anointed on earth (a process called *desacralization*) and was being reinvented in the popular imagination as a degenerate.

Despite the progressive desacralization (dee-SAY-kruh-ligh-ZAY-shun) of the monarchy, its power was still great enough to overcome opposition; Louis XV would probably have prevailed had he lived to a ripe old age, but he died in 1774. The new king, Louis XVI (r. 1774–1792), was a shy twenty-year-old with good intentions. Taking the throne, he is reported to have said, "What I should like most is to be loved."[2] The eager-to-please monarch yielded in the face of vehement opposition from France's educated elite. He dismissed chancellor Maupeou and repudiated the strong-willed minister's work. Louis also waffled on the economy, dismissing controller-general Turgot when his attempts to liberalize the economy drew fire (see Chapter 18). A weakened but unreformed monarchy now faced a judicial opposition that claimed to speak for the entire French nation.

The American Revolution and Its Impact

Coinciding with the first years of Louis XVI's reign, the American Revolution had an enormous impact on France in both practical and ideological terms. French expenses to support the colonists bankrupted the Crown, while the ideals of liberty and equality provided heady inspiration for political reform.

Like the French Revolution, the American Revolution had its immediate origin in struggles over increased taxes. The high cost of the Seven Years' War — fought with little financial contribution from the colonies — doubled the British national debt. When the government tried to recoup some of the losses by increasing taxes in the colonies in 1765, the colonists reacted with anger. The key questions were political rather than economic. To what extent could the home government assert its power while limiting the authority of colonial legislatures and their elected representatives? Accordingly, who should represent the colonies, and who had the right to make laws for Americans? The British government replied that Americans were represented in Parliament, albeit indirectly (like most British people themselves), and that the absolute supremacy of Parliament throughout the empire could not be questioned. Many Americans felt otherwise.

In 1773 the dispute over taxes and representation flared up again after the British government awarded a monopoly on Chinese tea to the East India Company, suddenly excluding colonial merchants from a lucrative business. In response, Boston men disguised as Indians held a rowdy "tea party" and threw the company's tea into the harbor. This led to extreme measures. The so-called Coercive Acts closed the port of Boston, curtailed local elections, and greatly expanded the royal governor's power. County conventions in Massachusetts protested vehemently and urged that the acts be "rejected as the attempts of a wicked administration to enslave America."

Other colonial assemblies joined in the denunciations. In September 1774 the First Continental Congress met in Philadelphia, where the more radical members argued successfully against concessions to the Crown. Compromise was also rejected by the British Parliament, and in April 1775 fighting began at Lexington and Concord. The uncompromising attitude of the British government and its use of German mercenaries dissolved long-standing loyalties to the home country and rivalries among the separate colonies. Some colonists remained loyal to the Crown; large numbers of these Loyalists emigrated to the northern colonies of Canada.

On July 4, 1776, the Second Continental Congress adopted the Declaration of Independence. Written by Thomas Jefferson, it boldly listed the tyrannical acts committed by George III (r. 1760–1820) and confidently proclaimed the natural rights of mankind and the sovereignty of the American states. The Declaration of Independence in effect universalized the traditional rights of English people and made them the rights of all mankind. It stated that "all men are created equal. . . . They are endowed by their Creator with certain unalienable rights. . . . Among these are life, liberty, and the pursuit of happiness."

The European powers closely followed the course of the American Revolution. The French wanted revenge

Toward Revolution in Boston
The Boston Tea Party was only one of many angry confrontations between British officials and Boston patriots. On January 27, 1774, an angry crowd seized a British customs collector and tarred and feathered him. This English cartoon from 1774 satirizes the event. What does the noose in the "liberty tree" suggest about the cartoonist's view of these events? (The Granger Collection, New York)

Commemorative Teapot
Manufacturers were quick to bring products to the market celebrating weighty political events, like this British teapot heralding "Stamp Act Repeal'd." By purchasing such items, ordinary people could champion political causes of the day and bring public affairs into their private lives. (Peabody Essex Museum, Salem, Massachusetts)

for the humiliating defeats of the Seven Years' War. They sympathized with the rebels and supplied guns and gunpowder. By 1777 French volunteers were arriving in Virginia, and a dashing young nobleman, the marquis de Lafayette (1757–1834), quickly became one of George Washington's most trusted generals. In 1778 the French government offered a formal alliance to the American ambassador in Paris, Benjamin Franklin, and in 1779 and 1780 the Spanish and Dutch declared war on Britain, their rival in transatlantic trade. Catherine the Great of Russia helped organize the League of Armed Neutrality in order to protect neutral shipping rights, which Britain refused to recognize.

Thus by 1780 Great Britain was engaged in an imperial war against most of Europe as well as against the thirteen colonies. In these circumstances, and in the face of severe reverses, a new British government decided to cut its losses and offered peace on extremely generous terms. By the Treaty of Paris in 1783, Britain recognized the independence of the thirteen colonies and ceded all its territory between the Allegheny Mountains and the Mississippi River to the Americans. Out of the bitter rivalries of the Old World, the Americans snatched dominion over a vast territory.

Europeans who dreamed of a new era were fascinated by the political lessons of the American Revolution. The Americans had begun with a revolutionary defense against tyrannical oppression, and they had been victorious. They had then shown how rational beings could assemble to exercise sovereignty and write a permanent constitution—a new social contract. All this gave greater reality to the concepts of individual liberty and representative government and reinforced one of the primary ideas of the Enlightenment: that a better world was possible.

No country felt the consequences of the American Revolution more directly than France. Hundreds of French officers served in America and were inspired by the experience, the marquis de Lafayette chief among them. French intellectuals and publicists engaged in passionate analysis of the new federal Constitution—ratified in 1789—as well as the constitutions of the

various states of the new United States.

Perhaps more important, the expenses of supporting America's revolutionary forces provided the last nail in the coffin for the French treasury.

Financial Crisis

The French Revolution thus had its immediate origins in the king's financial difficulties. Thwarted by the Parlement of Paris in its efforts to raise revenues by reforming the tax system, the government was forced to finance all of its enormous expenditures during the American war with borrowed money. As a result, the national debt and the annual budget deficit soared.

By the 1780s fully 50 percent of France's annual budget went for interest payments on the debt. Another 25 percent went to maintain the military, while 6 percent was absorbed by the king and his court at Versailles. Less than 20 percent of the entire national budget was available for the productive functions of the state, such as transportation and general administration. This was an impossible financial situation.

The king was too weak to take the drastic measure of declaring partial bankruptcy and forcing his creditors to accept greatly reduced payments, as previous monarchs had done. Nor could the king and his ministers print money and create inflation to cover their deficits. Unlike England and Holland, which had far larger national debts relative to their populations, France had no central bank, no paper currency, and no means of creating credit. Faced with imminent financial disaster in 1786, the royal government had no alternative but to try to increase taxes. Since France's tax system was unfair and out-of-date, increased revenues were possible only through fundamental reform.

In 1787 Louis XVI's minister of finance revived old proposals to impose a general tax on all landed property as well as to form provincial assemblies to help administer the tax, and he convinced the king to call an Assembly of Notables to gain support for the idea. The notables, who were mainly important noblemen and high-ranking clergy, insisted that such sweeping tax changes required the approval of the **Estates General**, the representative body of all three estates, which had not met since 1614.

In an attempt to reassert his authority, the king dismissed the notables and established new taxes by decree. In stirring language, the judges of the Parlement of Paris promptly declared the royal initiative null and void. When the king tried to exile the judges, a tremendous wave of protest swept the country. Frightened investors also refused to advance more loans to the state. Finally, in July 1788, Louis XVI bowed to public opinion and called for a spring session of the Estates General.

Politics and the People, 1789–1791

How did the events of 1789 result in a constitutional monarchy in France, and how did the new constitution affect the various members of French society at home and in the colony of Saint-Domingue? ▧

The calling of the Estates General opened a Pandora's box of social and political demands across the country. The process of electing delegates and formulating grievances politicized the French as no event in their prior history had done. As delegates at Versailles struggled over who truly represented the nation, the common people of France took matters into their own hands, rising up against noble lords and even reaching out to the royal family in their demands for change. Meanwhile, the complex slave society of colonial Saint-Domingue was rocked by conflicting political aspirations inspired by events in Paris.

The Formation of the National Assembly

Once Louis had agreed to hold the Estates General, the three orders — clergy, nobility, and commoners — separately elected delegates in each electoral district and prepared their own lists of grievances. The process of drafting their complaints unleashed a flood of debate and discussion across France, helping to galvanize public opinion and demands for reform.

Results of the elections reveal the political loyalties and mindsets of each estate on the eve of the Revolution. The local assemblies of the clergy elected mostly parish priests rather than church leaders, demonstrating their dissatisfaction with the church hierarchy. The nobility voted in a majority of conservatives, primarily from the provinces, where nobles were less wealthy and more numerous. Despite this conservative showing, fully one-

third of noble representatives were liberals committed to major changes. The third estate experienced great popular participation in the elections. Almost all male commoners over age twenty-four had the right to vote, and they elected primarily lawyers and government officials to represent them, with few delegates representing business or the poor.

Although the elected representatives displayed a range of differing political viewpoints, the petitions for change coming from the three estates showed a surprising degree of consensus about the issues at stake. There was general agreement that royal absolutism should give way to a constitutional monarchy in which laws and taxes would require the consent of the Estates General in regular meetings. All agreed that individual liberties would have to be guaranteed by law and that economic regulations should be loosened. The striking similarities in the grievance petitions of the clergy, nobility, and third estate reflected a shared commitment to a basic reform platform among the educated elite.

On May 5, 1789, the twelve hundred delegates of the three estates paraded in medieval pageantry through the streets of Versailles to an opening session resplendent with feudal magnificence. Hopes were high throughout France for serious reform of state finance and politics in cooperation with the king. For the moment, there was no talk of revolution, only reform, and cries of "long live the king" interrupted his opening speech to the Estates General.

Despite these high hopes, the Estates General was almost immediately deadlocked due to arguments about voting procedures. Controversy had begun during the electoral process, when the government confirmed that, following precedent, each estate should meet and vote separately. During the lead-up to the Estates General, critics denounced this situation and demanded a single assembly dominated by the third estate to ensure fundamental reforms. In his famous pamphlet "What Is the Third Estate?" the abbé Emmanuel Joseph Sieyès (himself a member of the first estate) argued that the nobility was a tiny overprivileged minority and that the neglected third estate constituted the true strength of the French nation. (See "Listening to the Past: Abbé de Sieyès, 'What Is the Third Estate?'" page 626.) The government conceded that the third estate should have as many delegates as the clergy and the nobility combined, but then rendered this act meaningless by upholding voting by separate order. Reform-minded critics saw fresh evidence of an aristocratic conspiracy.

The issue came to a head in June 1789 when the delegates of the third estate refused to transact any business until the king ordered the clergy and nobility

Estates General
A legislative body in prerevolutionary France made up of representatives of each of the three classes, or estates; it was called into session in 1789 for the first time since 1614.

Abbé de Sieyès, "What Is the Third Estate?"

LISTENING TO THE PAST

In the flood of pamphlets that appeared after Louis XVI's call for a meeting of the Estates General, the most influential was written in 1789 by a Catholic priest named Emmanuel Joseph Sieyès. In "What is the Third Estate?" the abbé Sieyès vigorously condemned the system of privilege that lay at the heart of French society. The term "privilege" combined the Latin words for "private" and "law." In Old Regime France, no one set of laws

applied to all; over time, the monarchy had issued a series of particular laws, or privileges, that enshrined special rights and entitlements for select individuals and groups. Noble privileges were among the weightiest.

Sieyès rejected this entire system of legal and social inequality. Deriding the nobility as a foreign parasite, he argued that the common people of the third estate, who did most of the work and paid most of the taxes, constituted the true nation. His pamphlet galvanized public opinion and played an important role in convincing representatives of the third estate to proclaim themselves a "National Assembly" in June 1789. Sieyès later helped bring Napoleon Bonaparte to power, abandoning the radicalism of 1789 for an authoritarian regime.

66 1. What is the Third Estate? Everything.
2. What has it been until now in the political order? Nothing.
3. What does it want? To become something.

. . . What is a Nation? A body of associates living under a *common* law and represented by the same *legislature*.

Is it not more than certain that the noble order has privileges, exemptions, and even rights that are distinct from the rights of the great body of citizens? Because of this, it [the noble order] does not belong to the common order, it is not covered by the law common to the rest. Thus its civil rights already make it a people apart inside the great Nation. It is truly *imperium in imperio* [a law unto itself].

As for its *political* rights, the nobility also exercises them separately. It has its own representatives who have no mandate from the people. Its deputies sit separately, and even when they assemble in the same room with the deputies of the ordinary citizens, the nobility's representation still remains essentially distinct and separate: it is foreign to the Nation by its very principle, for its mission does not emanate from the people, and by its purpose, since it consists in defending, not the general interest, but the private interests of the nobility.

The Third Estate therefore contains everything that pertains to the Nation and nobody outside of the Third Estate can claim to be part of the Nation. What is the Third Estate? EVERYTHING. . . .

By Third Estate is meant the collectivity of citizens who belong to the common order. Anybody who holds a legal privilege of any kind leaves that common order, stands as an exception to the common law, and in consequence does not belong to the Third Estate. . . . It is certain that the moment a citizen acquires privileges contrary to common law, he no longer belongs to the common order. His new interest is opposed to the general interest; he has no right to vote in the name of the people. . . .

In vain can anyone's eyes be closed to the revolution that time and the force of things have brought to pass; it is none the less real. Once

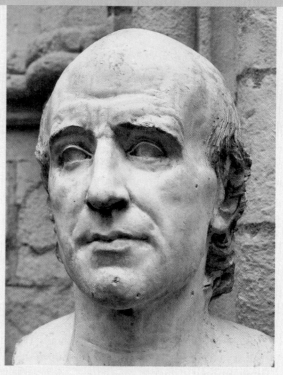

This bust, by the sculptor Pierre Jean David d'Angers, shows an aged and contemplative Sieyès reflecting, perhaps, on his key role in the outbreak and unfolding of the Revolution.
(Erich Lessing/Art Resource, NY)

upon a time the Third Estate was in bondage and the noble order was everything that mattered. Today the Third is everything and nobility but a word. Yet under the cover of this word a new and intolerable aristocracy has slipped in, and the people has every reason to no longer want aristocrats. . . .

What is the will of a Nation? It is the result of individual wills, just as the Nation is the aggregate of the individuals who compose it. It is impossible to conceive of a legitimate association that does not have for its goal the common security, the common liberty, in short, the public good. No doubt each individual also has his own personal aims. He says to himself, "protected by the common security, I will be able to peacefully pursue my own personal projects, I will seek my happiness where I will, assured of encountering only those legal obstacles that society will prescribe for the common interest, in which I have a part, and with which my own personal interest is so usefully allied."...

Advantages which differentiate citizens from one another lie outside the purview of citizenship. Inequalities of wealth or ability are like the inequalities of age, sex, size, etc. In no way do they detract from the *equality* of citizenship. These individual advantages no doubt benefit from the protection of the law; but it is not the legislator's task to create them, to give privileges to some and refuse them to others. The law grants nothing; it protects what already exists until such time that what exists begins to harm the common interest. These are the only limits on individual freedom. I imagine the law as being at the center of a large globe; we the citizens without exception, stand equidistant from it on the surface and occupy equal places; all are equally dependent on the law, all present it with their liberty and their property to be protected; and this is what I call the *common rights* of citizens, by which they are all alike. All these individuals communicate with each other, enter into contracts, negotiate, always under the common guarantee of the law. If in this general activity somebody wishes to get control over the person of his neighbor or usurp his property, the common law goes into action to repress this criminal attempt and puts everyone back in their place at the same distance from the law....

It is impossible to say what place the two privileged orders [the clergy and the nobility] ought to occupy in the social order: this is the equivalent of asking what place one wishes to assign to a malignant tumor that torments and undermines the strength of the body of a sick person. It must be *neutralized*. We must re-establish the health and working of all organs so thoroughly that they are no longer susceptible to these fatal schemes that are capable of sapping the most essential principles of vitality. »

Source: Excerpt from pp. 65–70 in *The French Revolution and Human Rights: A Brief Documentary History*, edited, translated and with an introduction by Lynn Hunt. Copyright © 1996 by Bedford Books of St. Martin's Press. Used by permission of Bedford/St. Martin's.

QUESTIONS FOR ANALYSIS

1. What criticism of noble privileges does Sieyès offer? Why does he believe nobles are "foreign" to the nation?

2. How does Sieyès define the nation, and why does he believe that the third estate constitutes the nation?

3. What relationship between citizens and the law does Sieyès envision? What limitations on the law does he propose?

to sit with them in a single body. Finally, after a six-week war of nerves, a few parish priests began to go over to the third estate, which on June 17 voted to call itself the **National Assembly**. On June 20 the delegates of the third estate, excluded from their hall because of "repairs," moved to a large indoor tennis court where they swore the famous Oath of the Tennis Court, declaring:

> *The National Assembly, considering that it has been called to establish the constitution of the realm, to bring about the regeneration of public order, and to maintain the true principles of the monarchy, nothing may prevent it from continuing its deliberations in any place it is forced to establish itself and, finally, the National Assembly exists wherever its members are gathered.*

Taking the first step toward revolution, the members of the National Assembly pledged not to disband until they had written a new constitution.

The king's response to this crucial challenge to his authority was disastrously ambivalent. On June 23 he made a conciliatory speech to a joint session in which he urged reforms, and four days later he ordered the three estates to meet together. At the same time, the vacillating and indecisive monarch apparently followed the advice of relatives and court nobles who urged him to dissolve the National Assembly by force. Belatedly asserting his divine right to rule, the king called an army of eighteen thousand troops toward the capital, and on July 11 he dismissed his finance minister and other more liberal ministers. It appeared that the monarchy was prepared to renege on its promises for reform and to use violence to restore its control.

National Assembly The first French revolutionary legislature, made up primarily of representatives of the third estate and a few from the nobility and clergy, in session from 1789 to 1791.

The Storming of the Bastille

While delegates at Versailles were pressing for political rights, economic hardship gripped the common people. A poor grain harvest in 1788 had caused the price of bread to soar, unleashing a classic economic depression of the preindustrial age. With food so expensive and with so much uncertainty, the demand for manufactured goods collapsed. Thousands of artisans and small traders were thrown out of work. Bread riots broke out in Paris and the surrounding area in late April and May. In Paris perhaps 150,000 of the city's 600,000 people were without work by July 1789.

Against this background of poverty and ongoing political crisis, the people of Paris entered decisively onto the revolutionary stage. They believed that they should

The Tennis Court Oath, June 20, 1789 Painted two years after the event shown, this dramatic painting by Jacques-Louis David depicts a crucial turning point in the early days of the Revolution. On June 20 delegates of the third estate arrived at their meeting hall in the Versailles palace to find the doors closed and guarded. Fearing the king was about to dissolve their meeting by force, the deputies reassembled at a nearby indoor tennis court and swore a solemn oath not to disperse until they had been recognized as the National Assembly. (Musée de la Ville de Paris, Musée Carnavalet, Paris/Lauros/Giraudon, The Bridgeman Art Library)

have steady work and enough bread at fair prices to survive. They also feared that the dismissal of the king's moderate finance minister would put them at the mercy of aristocratic landowners and grain speculators. At the beginning of July, knowledge spread of the massing of troops near Paris, and it seemed that the royal government was prepared to use violence to impose order. Angry crowds formed, and passionate voices urged action. On July 13, 1789, the people began to seize arms for the defense of the city, and on July 14 several hundred people marched to the Bastille (in English ba-STEEL) to search for weapons and gunpowder.

The Bastille, once a medieval fortress, was a royal prison guarded by eighty retired soldiers and thirty Swiss mercenaries. The governor of the fortress-prison refused to hand over the powder, panicked, and ordered his men to resist; the guards killed ninety-eight people attempting to enter. Cannon were brought to batter the main gate, and fighting continued until the prison surrendered. The

governor of the prison was later hacked to death, and his head was stuck on a pike and paraded through the streets. The next day a committee of citizens appointed the marquis de Lafayette commander of the city's armed forces.

The popular uprising forestalled the king's attempt to reassert his authority. On July 17 Louis announced the reinstatement of his liberal finance minister and the withdrawal of troops from Paris. The National Assembly was now free to continue its work without the threat of royal military intervention.

Peasant Revolt and the Rights of Man

Just as the laboring poor of Paris had been roused to a revolutionary fervor, the struggling French peasantry had also reached its boiling point, and in the summer of 1789 the countryside sent the delegates at

> ❝ Free expression of thoughts and opinions is one of the most precious rights of mankind: every citizen may therefore speak, write, and publish freely. ❞
>
> —DECLARATION OF THE RIGHTS OF MAN AND OF THE CITIZEN

The Figure of Liberty In this painting, the figure of Liberty bears a copy of the Declaration of the Rights of Man and of the Citizen in one hand and a pike to defend them in the other. The painting, by female artist and ardent revolutionary Nanine Vallain, hung in the Jacobin club until its fall from power. (Musée de la Revolution Française, Vizille/The Bridgeman Art Library)

Versailles a radical and unmistakable message. Throughout France peasants began to rise in insurrection against their lords, ransacking manor houses and burning feudal documents that recorded their obligations. In some areas peasants reinstated traditional village practices, undoing recent enclosures and reoccupying old common lands. They seized forests, and taxes went unpaid. Fear of marauders and vagabonds hired by vengeful landlords—called the **Great Fear** by contemporaries—seized the rural poor and fanned the flames of rebellion.

Faced with chaos, yet afraid to call on the king to restore order, some liberal nobles and middle-class delegates at Versailles responded to peasant demands with a surprise maneuver on the night of August 4, 1789. The duke of Aiguillon, a powerful noble landowner, declared that the peasantry was seeking "to throw off at last a yoke that has for many centuries weighted it down."[3] He urged equality in taxation and the elimination of feudal dues. In the end, all the old noble privileges—peasant serfdom where it still existed, exclusive hunting rights, fees for justice, village monopolies, the right to make peasants work on the roads, and a host of other dues—were abolished along with the tithes paid to the church. Thus the French peasantry achieved an unprecedented victory in the early days of revolutionary upheaval. Henceforth, French peasants would seek mainly to protect and consolidate their triumph.

Having granted new rights to the peasantry, the National Assembly moved forward with its mission of reform. On August 27, 1789, it issued the Declaration of the Rights of Man and of the Citizen, which stated, "Men are born and remain free and equal in rights." The declaration also maintained that mankind's natural rights are "liberty, property, security, and resistance to oppression" and that "every man is presumed innocent until he is proven guilty." As for law, "it is an expression of the general will; all citizens have the right to concur personally or through their representatives in its formation. . . . Free expression of thoughts and opinions is one of the most precious rights of mankind: every citizen may therefore speak, write, and publish freely." In short, this call of the liberal revolutionary ideal guaranteed equality before the law, representative government for a sovereign people, and individual freedom. This revolutionary credo, only two pages long, was disseminated throughout France and Europe and around the world.

AUSTRIAN NETHERLANDS
Paris
Versailles
Bay of Biscay
FRANCE
SWISS CONFED.

■ Area of Great Fear revolts
• Revolutionary center

The Great Fear, 1789

Great Fear The fear of noble reprisals against peasant uprisings that seized the French countryside and led to further revolt.

Parisian Women March on Versailles

While high-minded in principle, the National Assembly's declaration had little practical effect for the poor and hungry people of Paris, where a revolutionary spirit continued to smolder. The economic crisis in the city worsened after the fall of the Bastille, as aristocrats fled the country and the luxury market collapsed. Foreign markets also shrank in the aftermath of the crisis, and unemployment among the urban working class grew. In addition, women—the traditional managers of food and resources in poor homes—could no longer look to the church, which had been stripped of its tithes, for aid.

On October 5 some seven thousand desperate women marched the twelve miles from Paris to Versailles to demand action. This great crowd, "armed with scythes, sticks and pikes," invaded the National Assembly. Interrupting a delegate's speech, a tough old woman defiantly shouted into the debate, "Who's that talking down there? Make the chatterbox shut up. That's not the point: the point is that we want bread."[4] Hers was the genuine voice of the people, essential to any understanding of the French Revolution.

constitutional monarchy A form of government in which the king retains his position as head of state, while the authority to tax and make new laws resides in an elected body.

The women invaded the royal apartments, killed some of the royal bodyguards, and furiously searched for the queen, Marie Antoinette, who was widely despised for her frivolous and supposedly immoral behavior. "We are going to cut off her head, tear out her heart, fry her liver, and that won't be the end of it," they shouted, surging through the palace. It seems likely that only the intervention of Lafayette and the National Guard saved the royal family. But the only way to calm the disorder was for the king to live closer to his people in Paris, as the crowd demanded.

A Constitutional Monarchy and Its Challenges

The day after the women's march on Versailles, the National Assembly followed the king to Paris, and the next two years, until September 1791, saw the consolidation of the liberal revolution. Under middle-class leadership, the National Assembly abolished the French nobility as a legal order and pushed forward with the creation of a **constitutional monarchy**, which Louis XVI reluctantly agreed to accept in July 1790. In the final constitution, the king remained the head of state, but all lawmaking power now resided in the National Assembly, elected by the wealthiest half of French males. New laws broadened women's rights to seek divorce, to inherit

The Women of Paris March to Versailles On October 5, 1789, a large group of poor Parisian women marched to Versailles to protest the price of bread. For the people of Paris, the king was the baker of last resort, responsible for feeding his people during times of scarcity. The angry women forced the royal family to return with them and to live in Paris, rather than remain isolated from their subjects at court. (Erich Lessing/Art Resource, NY)

a Versaille a Versaille. du 5 Octobre 1789.

Village Festival in Honor of Old Age, 1795 The French Revolution inaugurated many new civic festivals in an attempt to erase memories of the Catholic holidays and feast days of the prerevolutionary era. As in bygone days, the new festivals, like this one honoring village elders, included dancing, drinking, and courting among the young couples of the village. Many people, however, especially in rural France, missed the religious tenor of prerevolutionary holidays. (Bibliothèque nationale de France/Archives Charmet/The Bridgeman Art Library)

property, and to obtain financial support for illegitimate children from fathers, but women were not allowed to hold political office or even vote.

This decision was attacked by a small number of men and women who believed that the rights of man should be extended to all French citizens. The liberal marquis de Condorcet accused the legislators of having "violated the principle of equality of rights by quietly depriving half of mankind of the right to participate in the formation of the laws."[5] Olympe de Gouges (1748–1793), a self-taught writer and woman of the people, took up her pen to protest the evils of slavery as well as the injustices done to women. In September 1791 she published her "Declaration of the Rights of Woman," a direct challenge to revolutionaries to respect the ideals of the great 1789 declaration. De Gouges's pamphlet echoed its famous predecessor, proclaiming, "Woman is born free and remains equal to man in rights." She further demanded that both sexes be "equally admissible to all public dignities, offices, and employments, according to their ability, and with no other distinction than their virtues and talents."

Such arguments found little sympathy among leaders of the Revolution. The editor of one revolutionary journal offered a public response to complaints he had received from women about their exclusion from politics. He agreed that they should be allowed to speak in assemblies, but not to vote or serve as representatives. As he explained, "a household should never remain deserted for a single instant. When the father of a family leaves to defend or lay claim to the rights of property, security, equality, or liberty in a public assembly, the mother of the family, focused on her domestic duties, must make order and cleanliness, ease and peace reign at home."[6] His sentiments represented the opinions of the vast majority of legislators and ordinary Frenchmen.

In addition to ruling on women's rights, the National Assembly replaced the complicated patchwork of historic provinces with eighty-three departments of approximately equal size. Monopolies, guilds, and workers' associations were prohibited, and barriers to trade within France were abolished in the name of economic liberty.

Thus the National Assembly applied the spirit of the Enlightenment in a thorough reform of France's laws and institutions.

The National Assembly also imposed a radical reorganization on the country's religious life. It granted religious freedom to the small minority of French Jews and Protestants. In November 1789 it nationalized the Catholic Church's property and abolished monasteries as useless relics of a distant past. The government used all former church property as collateral to guarantee a new paper currency, the assignats (A-sihg-nat), and then sold the property in an attempt to put the state's finances on a solid footing. Although the land was sold in large blocks, peasants eventually purchased much when it was subdivided. These purchases strengthened their attachment to the new revolutionary order in the countryside.

Imbued with the rationalism and skepticism of the eighteenth-century philosophes (see Chapter 17), many delegates distrusted popular piety and "superstitious religion." Thus in July 1790, with the Civil Constitution of the Clergy, they established a national church with priests chosen by voters. The National Assembly then forced the Catholic clergy to take a loyalty oath to the new government. The pope formally condemned this attempt to subjugate the church, and only half the priests of France swore the oath. Many sincere Christians, especially those in the countryside, were upset by these changes in the religious order. The attempt to remake the Catholic Church, like the abolition of guilds and workers' associations, sharpened the conflict between the educated classes and the common people that had been emerging in the eighteenth century.

Revolutionary Aspirations in Saint-Domingue

The French Revolution radically transformed not only the territorial nation of France but its overseas colonies as well. On the eve of the Revolution, Saint-Domingue—the most profitable of all Caribbean colonies—was even more rife with social tensions than France itself. The island was inhabited by a variety of social groups who resented and mistrusted one another. The European population included French colonial officials, wealthy plantation owners and merchants, and poor immigrants. Greatly outnumbering the white population were the

Saint-Domingue Slave Life Although the brutal conditions of plantation slavery left little time or energy for leisure, slaves on Saint-Domingue took advantage of their day of rest on Sunday to engage in social and religious activities. The law officially prohibited slaves of different masters from mingling together, but such gatherings were often tolerated if they remained peaceful. This image depicts a fight between two slaves, precisely the type of unrest and violence feared by authorities. (Musée du Nouveau Monde, La Rochelle/Photos12.com — ARJ)

colony's five hundred thousand slaves, along with a sizable population of free people of African and mixed African and European descent. Members of this last group referred to themselves as "free coloreds" or free people of color.

The 1685 *Code Noir* (Black Code) that set the parameters of slavery had granted free people of color the same legal status as whites: they could own property, live where they wished, and pursue any education or career they desired. From the 1760s on, however, colonial administrators began rescinding these rights, and by the time of the Revolution, myriad aspects of free coloreds' lives—from the professions they could practice, to the names they could adopt, to the clothes they could wear—were ruled by discriminatory laws. White planters eagerly welcomed these laws, convinced that the best defense of slavery was a rigid color line.

The political and intellectual turmoil of the 1780s, with its growing rhetoric of liberty, equality, and fraternity, raised new challenges and possibilities for each of these groups. For slaves, news of abolitionist movements in France and the royal government's own attempts to rein in the worst abuses of slavery led to hopes that the mother country might grant them freedom. Free people of color found in such rhetoric the principles on which to shore up their eroded legal and political rights. They looked to reforms in Paris as a means of gaining political enfranchisement and reasserting equal status with whites. The white elite, not surprisingly, saw matters very differently. Infuriated by talk of abolition and determined to protect their way of life, they looked to revolutionary ideals of representative government for the chance to gain control of their own affairs, as had the American colonists before them. The meeting of the Estates General and the Declaration of the Rights of Man and of the Citizen raised these conflicting colonial aspirations to new levels.

The National Assembly frustrated the hopes of all these groups. Cowed by colonial representatives who claimed that support for free people of color would result in slave insurrection and independence, the Assembly refused to extend French constitutional safeguards to the colonies. Instead, it ruled that each colony would draft its own constitution, with free rein over decisions on slavery and the enfranchisement of free people of color. After dealing this blow to the aspirations of slaves and free coloreds, the committee also reaffirmed French monopolies over colonial trade, thereby angering planters as well.

In July 1790 Vincent Ogé (aw-ZHAY), a free man of color, returned to Saint-Domingue from Paris determined to redress these issues. He raised an army of several hundred and sent letters to the new Provincial Assembly of Saint-Domingue demanding political rights for all free citizens, a statute already passed in France. After initial victories, his army was defeated, and Ogé himself was tortured and executed by colonial officials. In May 1791, in an attempt to respond to what it perceived as partly justified grievances, the National Assembly granted political rights to free people of color born to two free parents who possessed sufficient property. When news of this legislation arrived in Saint-Domingue, the white elite was furious, and the colonial governor refused to enact it. Violence now erupted between groups of whites and free coloreds in parts of the colony. The liberal revolution had failed to satisfy the contradictory ambitions in the colonies.

World War and Republican France, 1791–1799

How and why did the Revolution take a radical turn at home and in the colonies? ■

When Louis XVI accepted the final version of the National Assembly's constitution in September 1791, a young and still obscure provincial lawyer and delegate named Maximilien Robespierre (1758–1794) concluded that "The Revolution is over." Robespierre (ROHBZ-pee-air) was right in the sense that the most constructive and lasting reforms were in place; no substantial reforms in the way of liberty would be gained in the next generation. Yet he was wrong in the sense that a much more radical stage lay ahead. New heroes and new ideologies were to emerge in revolutionary wars and international conflict in which Robespierre himself would play a central role.

Foreign Reactions to the Revolution

The outbreak and progress of revolution in France produced great excitement and a sharp division of opinion in Europe and the United States. Liberals and radicals saw a mighty triumph of liberty over despotism. In Great Britain, especially, they hoped that the French example would lead to a fundamental reordering of Parliament, which was in the hands of the aristocracy and a few wealthy merchants. On the other hand, conservative leaders such as British statesman Edmund Burke (1729–1797) were deeply troubled by the aroused spirit of reform. In 1790 Burke published *Reflections on the Revolution in France*, in which he defended inherited privileges in general and those of the English monarchy and aristocracy in particular. He glorified the unrepresentative Parliament and predicted that reform like that occurring in France would lead only to chaos and tyranny. Burke's work sparked much debate.

One passionate rebuttal came from a young writer in London, Mary Wollstonecraft (1759–1797). Determined to be independent in a society that expected women of her class to become obedient wives, Wollstonecraft (WOOL-stuhn-kraft) struggled for years to earn her living as a governess and a teacher—practically the only acceptable careers for single educated women—before attaining success as a translator and author. Incensed by Burke's book, she immediately wrote a blistering, widely read attack, *A Vindication of the Rights of Man* (1790). Two years later, she published her masterpiece, *A Vindication of the Rights of Woman* (1792). Like de Gouges one year before her, Wollstonecraft demanded equal rights for women. She advocated rigorous coeducation, which would make women better wives and mothers, good citizens, and economically independent. Women could manage businesses and enter politics if only men would give them the chance. Wollstonecraft's analysis testifies to the power of the Revolution to excite and inspire outside of France. The controversial book was quickly reissued in French and American editions. It became a classic of the early feminist movement.

Jacobin club A political club in revolutionary France whose members were well-educated radical republicans.

The kings and nobles of continental Europe, who had at first welcomed the revolution in France as weakening a competing power, began to feel as threatened by its message, as did conservatives such as Burke. In June 1791 Louis XVI and Marie Antoinette were arrested and returned to Paris after trying unsuccessfully to slip out of France. For supporters of the Revolution, the attempted flight was proof that the king's professed acceptance of the constitution was a sham and that he was a traitor intent on procuring foreign support for an invasion of France. The shock of the arrest of a crowned head of state led the monarchs of Austria and Prussia to issue the Declaration of Pillnitz two months later. The Declaration professed the rulers' willingness to intervene in France to restore Louis XVI's monarchical rule if necessary. It was expected to have a sobering effect on revolutionary France without causing war.

But the crowned heads of Europe misjudged the revolutionary spirit in France. The new representative body that convened in Paris in October 1791, called the Legislative Assembly, had completely new delegates and a different character. The great majority of the legislators were still prosperous, well-educated middle-class men, but they were younger and less cautious than their predecessors. Many of the deputies belonged to the political **Jacobin club**, named after the former monastery in which they held their meetings. Such clubs had proliferated in Parisian neighborhoods since the beginning of the Revolution, drawing men and women to debate the burning political questions of the day.

The Outbreak of War

The new representatives to the Assembly whipped themselves into a patriotic fury against the Declaration of

The Capture of Louis XVI, June 1791 This painting commemorates the midnight arrest of Louis XVI and the royal family as they tried to flee France in disguise and reach counter-revolutionaries in the Austrian Netherlands. Recognized and stopped at Varennes, just forty miles from the border, the king still nearly succeeded, telling municipal officers that dangerous mobs controlled Paris and securing promises of safe passage. But within hours the local leaders reversed themselves, and by morning Louis XVI was headed back to Paris. (Bibliothèque nationale de France)

Pillnitz. If the kings of Europe were attempting to incite war against France, then "we will incite a war of people against kings. . . . Ten million Frenchmen, kindled by the fire of liberty, armed with the sword, with reason, with eloquence would be able to change the face of the world and make the tyrants tremble on their thrones."[7] Only Robespierre and a very few others argued that people would not welcome liberation at the point of a gun. Such warnings were brushed aside. France would "rise to the full height of her mission," as one deputy urged. In April 1792 France declared war on Francis II, the Habsburg monarch.

France's crusade against tyranny went poorly at first. Prussian forces joined Austria against the French, who broke and fled at their first military encounter with this First Coalition. The road to Paris lay open, and it is possible that only conflict between the Eastern monarchs over the division of Poland (see Chapter 17) saved France from an early and total defeat.

The Assembly declared the country in danger, and volunteers rallied to the capital. In this supercharged wartime atmosphere, rumors of treason by the king and queen spread in Paris. On August 10, 1792, a revolutionary crowd attacked the royal palace at the Tuileries (TWEE-luh-reez), while the king and his family fled for their lives to the nearby Legislative Assembly. Rather than offering refuge, the Assembly suspended the king from all his functions, imprisoned him, and called for a new National Convention to be elected by universal male suffrage. Monarchy in France was on its deathbed, mortally wounded by war and popular upheaval.

The Second Revolution

The fall of the monarchy marked a rapid radicalization of the Revolution, a phase that historians often call the **second revolution**. Louis's imprisonment was followed by the September Massacres. Wild stories that imprisoned counter-revolutionary aristocrats and priests were plotting with the allied invaders seized the city. As a result, angry crowds invaded the prisons of Paris and slaughtered half the men and women they found. In late September 1792 the new, popularly elected National Convention proclaimed France a republic, a nation in which the people, instead of a monarch, held sovereign power.

All the members of the National Convention were republicans, and at the beginning almost all belonged to the Jacobin (JA-kuh-bihn) club of Paris. But the Jacobins themselves were increasingly divided into two bitterly competitive groups—the **Girondists** (juh-RAHN-dihsts), named after a department in southwestern France that was home to several of their leaders, and **the Mountain**, led by Robespierre and another young lawyer, Georges Jacques Danton. The Mountain was so called because its members sat on the uppermost benches on the left side of the assembly hall. A

majority of the indecisive Convention members, seated in the "Plain" below, floated back and forth between the rival factions.

This division emerged clearly after the National Convention overwhelmingly convicted Louis XVI of treason. The Girondists accepted his guilt but did not wish to put the king to death. By a narrow majority, the Mountain carried the day, and Louis was executed on January 21, 1793, on the newly invented guillotine. One of his last statements was "I am innocent and shall die without fear. I would that my death might bring happiness to the French, and ward off the dangers which I foresee."[8] But both the Girondists and the Mountain were determined to continue the "war against tyranny." The Prussians had been stopped at the Battle of Valmy on September 20, 1792, one day before the republic was proclaimed. French armies then invaded Savoy and captured Nice, moved into the German Rhineland, and by November 1792 were occupying the entire Austrian Netherlands (modern Belgium).

Everywhere they went, French armies of occupation chased the princes, abolished feudalism, and found support among some peasants and middle-class people. But the French armies also lived off the land, requisitioning food and supplies and plundering local treasures. The liberators looked increasingly like foreign invaders. International tensions mounted. In February 1793 the National Convention, at war with Austria and Prussia, declared war on Britain, Holland, and Spain as well. Republican France was now at war with almost all of Europe, a great war that would last almost without interruption until 1815.

Groups within France added to the turmoil. Peasants in western France revolted against being drafted into the army, with the Vendée region of Brittany emerging as the epicenter of revolt. Devout Catholics, royalists, and foreign agents encouraged their rebellion, and the counter-revolutionaries recruited veritable armies to fight for their cause.

In March 1793 the National Convention was locked in a life-and-death political

> **second revolution** From 1792 to 1795, the second phase of the French Revolution, during which the fall of the French monarchy introduced a rapid radicalization of politics.
>
> **Girondists** A moderate group that fought for control of the French National Convention in 1793.
>
> **the Mountain** Led by Robespierre, the French National Convention's radical faction, which seized legislative power in 1793.

Areas of Insurrection, 1793

- Vendée Rebellion
- Counter-revolutionary insurrections

struggle between members of the Mountain and the more moderate Girondists, with the radicals accusing the Girondists of inciting sedition in the provinces. With the middle-class delegates so bitterly divided, the laboring poor of Paris once again emerged as the decisive political factor. The laboring poor and the petty traders were often known as the **sans-culottes** (sanz-koo-LAHT, "without breeches") because their men wore trousers instead of the knee breeches of the aristocracy and the solid middle class. They demanded radical political action to guarantee them their daily bread. The Mountain, sensing an opportunity to outma-

sans-culottes The laboring poor of Paris, so called because the men wore trousers instead of the knee breeches of the aristocracy and middle class; the word came to refer to the militant radicals of the city.

neuver the Girondists, joined with sans-culottes activists in the city government to engineer a popular uprising. On June 2, 1793, armed sans-culottes invaded the Convention and forced deputies to arrest twenty-nine Girondist deputies for treason. All power passed to the Mountain.

The Convention also formed the Committee of Public Safety in April 1793 to deal with the threats from within and outside France. The committee, which Robespierre led, was given dictatorial power to deal with the national emergency. Moderates in the leading provincial cities of Caen, Bordeaux, Lyon, and Marseilles revolted against the committee's power and demanded a decentralized government. Counter-revolutionary forces in the Vendée won significant victories, and the repub-

Picturing the Past

Contrasting Visions of the Sans-Culottes These two images offer profoundly different representations of a sans-culotte woman. The image on the left was created by a French artist, while the image on the right is English. The French words above the image on the right read in part, "Heads! Blood! Death! . . . I am the Goddess of Liberty! . . . Long Live the Guillotine!" (Bibliothèque nationale de France)

ANALYZING THE IMAGE   How would you describe the woman on the left? What qualities does the artist seem to ascribe to her, and how do you think these qualities relate to the sans-culottes and the Revolution? How would you characterize the facial expression and attire of the woman on the right? How does the inclusion of the text contribute to your impressions of her?

CONNECTIONS   What does the contrast between these two images suggest about differences between French and English perceptions of the sans-culottes and of the French Revolution? Why do you think the artists have chosen to depict women?

To complete this activity online, go to the Online Study Guide at bedfordstmartins.com/mckaywest.

lic's armies were driven back on all fronts. By July 1793 only the areas around Paris and on the eastern frontier were firmly held by the central government. Defeat seemed imminent.

Total War and the Terror

A year later, in July 1794, the central government had reasserted control over the provinces. In addition, the Austrian Netherlands and the Rhineland were once again in the hands of conquering French armies, and the First Coalition was falling apart. This remarkable change of fortune was due to the revolutionary government's success in harnessing, for perhaps the first time in history, the explosive forces of a planned economy, revolutionary terror, and modern nationalism in a total war effort.

Robespierre and the Committee of Public Safety advanced with implacable resolution on several fronts in 1793 and 1794. Claiming they alone could speak for the "general will" of the French people, they sought to impose republican unity across the nation, on pain of death if necessary. First, they collaborated with the fiercely patriotic and democratic sans-culottes, who retained the common people's faith in fair prices and a moral economic order and who distrusted most wealthy capitalists and all aristocrats. Thus in September 1793 Robespierre and his coworkers established, as best they could, a planned economy with egalitarian social overtones. Rather than let supply and demand determine prices, the government set maximum allowable prices for key products. Though the state was too weak to enforce all its price regulations, it did fix the price of bread in Paris at levels the poor could afford. Rationing was introduced, and bakers were permitted to make only the "bread of equality"—a brown bread made of a mixture of all available flours. White bread and pastries were outlawed as luxuries. The poor of Paris may not have eaten well, but at least they ate.

The people also worked, mainly to produce arms and munitions for the war effort. The government told craftsmen what to produce, nationalized many small workshops, and requisitioned raw materials and grain. The second

revolution and the ascendancy of the sans-culottes had produced an embryonic emergency socialism, which thoroughly frightened Europe's propertied classes and greatly influenced the subsequent development of socialist ideology.

Second, while radical economic measures supplied the poor with bread and the armies with weapons, the **Reign of Terror** (1793–1794) solidified the home front. Special revolutionary courts responsible only to Robespierre's Committee of Public Safety tried "enemies of the nation" for political crimes. Some forty thousand French men and women were executed or died in prison. Another three hundred thousand suspects were arrested. Robespierre's Reign of Terror is one of the most controversial phases of the French Revolution. Presented as a necessary measure to save the republic, the Terror was a political weapon directed against all suspected of opposing the revolutionary government. As Robespierre himself put it, "Terror is nothing more than prompt, severe inflexible justice."[9] For many Europeans of the time, however, the Reign of Terror represented a frightening perversion of the generous ideals of 1789, strengthening the belief that France

Reign of Terror The period from 1793 to 1794 during which Robespierre's Committee of Public Safety tried and executed thousands suspected of treason and a new revolutionary culture was imposed.

❝ **Terror is nothing more than prompt, severe inflexible justice.** ❞

—**ROBESPIERRE**

The Guillotine Prior to the French Revolution, methods of execution included hanging and being broken at the wheel. Only nobles enjoyed the privilege of a relatively swift and painless death by decapitation, delivered by an executioner's ax. The guillotine, a model of which is shown here, was devised by French revolutionaries as a humane and egalitarian form of execution. Ironically, due to the mass executions under the Terror, it is now seen instead as a symbol of revolutionary cruelty. (Musée de la Ville de Paris, Musée Carnavalet, Paris/ Lauros/Giraudon, The Bridgeman Art Library) had foolishly replaced a weak king with a bloody dictatorship.

In their efforts to impose unity, the Jacobins took actions to suppress women's participation in political debate, which they perceived as disorderly and a distraction from women's proper place in the home. On October 30, 1793, the National Convention declared that "The clubs and popular societies of women, under whatever denomination are prohibited." Included in the ban were such groups as the Society of Revolutionary Republican Women, a club of militant women that had called for the creation of female armies to combat counter-revolution.[10] Among those convicted of sedition was writer Olympe de Gouges, who was sent to the guillotine in November 1793.

Beyond imposing political unity by force, the program of the Terror also included efforts to transform French citizens into true republican patriots by bringing the Revolution into all aspects of everyday life. The government sponsored revolutionary art and songs as well as a new series of secular holidays and open-air festivals to celebrate republican virtue and a love of nation. They attempted to rationalize French daily life by adopting the decimal system for weights and measures and a new calendar based on ten-day weeks. (See "Living in the Past: A Revolution of Culture and Daily Life," page 640.) An important element of this cultural revolution was the campaign of **dechristianization**, which aimed to eliminate Catholic symbols and beliefs. Many churches were sold, clerics were humiliated and persecuted, and religious images and statues were destroyed. Fearful of the hostility aroused in rural France, Robespierre called for a halt to dechristianization measures in mid-1794.

The third and perhaps most decisive element in the French republic's victory over the First Coalition was its ability to draw on the explosive power of patriotic dedication to a national state and a national mission. An essential part of modern nationalism, which would fully emerge

dechristianization
Campaign to eliminate Christian faith and practice in France undertaken by the revolutionary government.

The French Revolution

■ National Assembly (1789–1791)

May 5, 1789	Estates General meets at Versailles
June 17, 1789	Third estate declares itself the National Assembly
June 20, 1789	Oath of the Tennis Court
July 14, 1789	Storming of the Bastille
July–August 1789	Great Fear
August 4, 1789	Abolishment of feudal privileges
August 27, 1789	Declaration of the Rights of Man and of the Citizen
October 5, 1789	Women march on Versailles; royal family returns to Paris
November 1789	National Assembly confiscates church land
July 1790	Civil Constitution of the Clergy establishes a national church; Louis XVI agrees to constitutional monarchy
June 1791	Royal family arrested while fleeing France
August 1791	Declaration of Pillnitz; slave insurrections in Saint-Domingue

■ Legislative Assembly (1791–1792)

April 1792	France declares war on Austria; enfranchisement of free people of color
August 1792	Mob attacks the palace, and Legislative Assembly takes Louis XVI prisoner

■ National Convention (1792–1795)

September 1792	September Massacres; National Convention abolishes monarchy and declares France a republic
January 1793	Louis XVI executed
February 1793	France declares war on Britain, Holland, and Spain; revolts take place in some provinces
March 1793	Struggle between Girondists and the Mountain
April 1793	Creation of the Committee of Public Safety
June 1793	Arrest of Girondist leaders
September 1793	Price controls instituted; British troops invade Saint-Domingue
October 1793	National Convention bans women's political societies
1793–1794	Reign of Terror
February 1794	Abolishment of slavery in all French territories
Spring 1794	French armies victorious on all fronts
July 1794	Robespierre executed; Thermidorian reaction begins

■ The Directory (1795–1799)

1795	Economic controls abolished; suppression of the sans-culottes begins
1796	France regains control of Saint-Domingue under Toussaint L'Ouverture
1799	Napoleon seizes power

throughout Europe in the nineteenth century, this commitment was something new in history. With a common language and a common tradition newly reinforced by the ideas of popular sovereignty and democracy, large numbers of French people were stirred by a common loyalty. They developed an intense emotional commitment to the defense of the nation, and they saw the war as a life-and-death struggle between good and evil.

Everyone had to participate in the national effort. According to a famous decree of August 23, 1793:

The young men shall go to battle and the married men shall forge arms. The women shall make tents and clothes, and shall serve in the hospitals; children shall tear rags into lint. The old men will be guided to the public places of the cities to kindle the courage of the young warriors and to preach the unity of the Republic and the hatred of kings.

The all-out mobilization of French resources under the Terror combined with the fervor of modern nationalism to create an awesome fighting machine. After August 1793 all unmarried young men were subject to the draft, and by January 1794 the French had about eight hundred thousand soldiers on active duty in fourteen armies. A force of this size was unprecedented in the history of European warfare; French armed forces outnumbered their enemies almost four to one.[11] The revolutionary government deployed this awesome force to combat internal as well as external enemies. Bitter resistance from the Vendée rebels could not withstand the ruthless forces of the republic, resulting in some one hundred thousand deaths among the opposition forces.

Well-trained, well-equipped, and constantly indoctrinated, the enormous armies of the republic were led by young, impetuous generals. These generals often had risen from the ranks, and they personified the opportunities the Revolution offered gifted sons of the people. Following orders from Paris to attack relentlessly, French generals used mass assaults at bayonet point to overwhelm the enemy. "No maneuvering, nothing elaborate," declared the fearless General Hoche. "Just cold steel, passion and patriotism."[12] By spring 1794 French armies were victorious on all fronts. The republic was saved.

Revolution in Saint-Domingue

Just as the sans-culottes had been instrumental in pushing forward more radical reforms in France, the second stage of revolution in Saint-Domingue also resulted from decisive action from below. In August 1791 slaves, who had been witnesses to the confrontation between whites and free coloreds for over a year, took events into their own hands. Groups of slaves held a series of nighttime meetings to plan a mass insurrection. These meetings reportedly included religious ceremonies in which participants made ritual offerings and swore a sacred oath

Slave Revolt on Saint-Domingue Starting in August 1791 the slaves of Saint-Domingue rose in revolt, an event captured vividly by this engraving. (Giraudon/Art Resource, NY)

LIVING IN THE PAST

THE FRENCH REVOLUTION BROUGHT SWEEPING POLITICAL AND SOCIAL CHANGE to France, removing one of the oldest monarchies in Europe in favor of broad-based representative government and eliminating age-old distinctions between nobles and commoners. Revolutionaries feared, however, that these measures were not enough to transform the nation. They therefore undertook a parallel revolution of culture intended to purify and regenerate the French people and turn former royal subjects into patriotic citizens capable of realizing the dream of liberty, equality, and fraternity.

To bring about cultural revolution, officials of the new republic targeted the most fundamental elements of daily life: the experience of space and time. Prior to the Revolution, regions of France had their own systems of measurement, meaning that the length of an inch or the weight of a pound differed substantially across the realm. Disgusted with the inefficiency of this state of affairs and determined to impose national unity, the government adopted the decimal-based metric system first proposed in 1670. The length of the meter was scientifically set at one ten-millionth of the distance from the pole to the equator. Henceforth, all French citizens would inhabit spaces that were measured and divided in the same way.

The government attempted a similar rationalization of the calendar. Instead of twelve months of varying lengths, each of the twelve months on the new revolutionary calendar was made up of three ten-day weeks, with a five- or six-day interval at the end of each year. To mark the total rebirth of time, the new calendar began at Year 1 on the day of the foundation of the French Republic (September 22, 1792). A series of festivals with patriotic themes replaced the traditional Catholic feast days. There was even a short-lived attempt to put the clock on a decimal system.

Cultural revolution also took on more concrete forms. Every citizen was required to wear a cockade on his or her hat, like the one shown on this plate celebrating the festival of the Supreme Being (a form of deism promoted by Robespierre as the state religion), to symbolize loyalty to the republic. Enterprising merchants sold a plethora of everyday goods with revolutionary themes. One could eat from revolutionary plates, drink from revolutionary mugs, waft revolutionary fans, and even decorate the home with revolutionary wallpaper. Living the French Revolution meant entering a whole new world of sense and experience.

Plate showing a festival of the Cult of the Supreme Being. (Erich Lessing/Art Resource, NY)

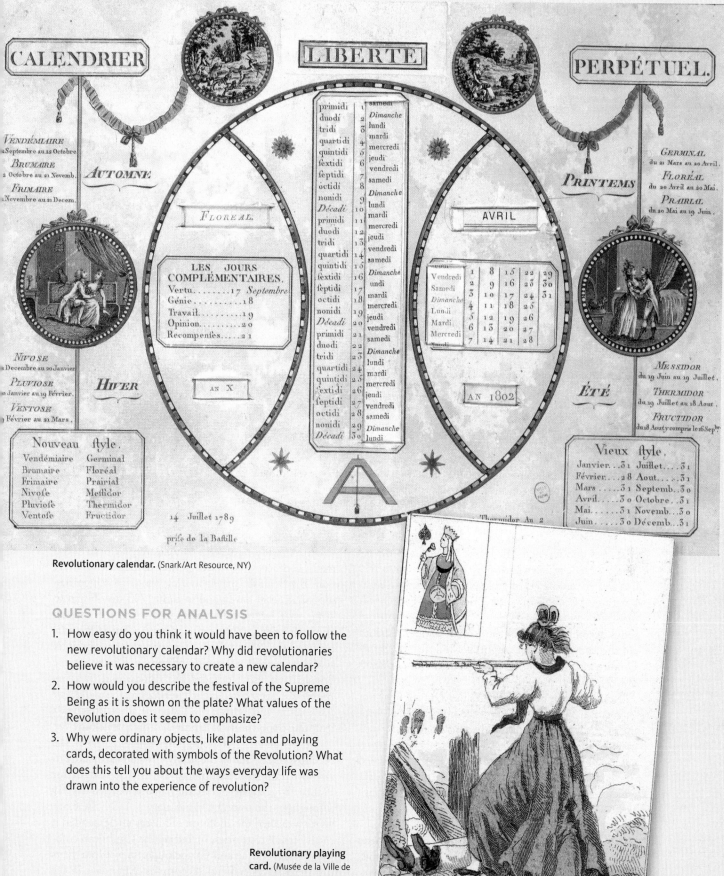

Revolutionary calendar. (Snark/Art Resource, NY)

QUESTIONS FOR ANALYSIS

1. How easy do you think it would have been to follow the new revolutionary calendar? Why did revolutionaries believe it was necessary to create a new calendar?

2. How would you describe the festival of the Supreme Being as it is shown on the plate? What values of the Revolution does it seem to emphasize?

3. Why were ordinary objects, like plates and playing cards, decorated with symbols of the Revolution? What does this tell you about the ways everyday life was drawn into the experience of revolution?

Revolutionary playing card. (Musée de la Ville de Paris, Musée Carnavalet, Paris/Lauros/Giraudon, The Bridgeman Art Library)

Map 20.1 **The War of Haitian Independence, 1791–1804** Neighbored by the Spanish colony of Santo Domingo, Saint-Domingue was the most profitable European colony in the Caribbean. In 1770 the French transferred the capital from Le Cap to Port-au-Prince. Slave revolts erupted in the north near Le Cap in 1791. Port-au-Prince became capital of the newly independent Haiti in 1804.

of secrecy and revenge. The rituals belonged to the religious practices, later known as "voodoo," that slaves had created on Saint-Domingue plantations from a combination of Catholicism and African cults. French soldiers later reported that religious incantations and African songs accompanied rebel slaves into combat. African culture thus played an important role in the Saint-Domingue revolution, alongside Enlightenment ideals of freedom and equality.

Revolts began on a few plantations on the night of August 22. Within a few days the uprising had swept much of the northern plain, creating a slave army estimated at around 2,000 individuals. By August 27 it was described by one observer as "10,000 strong, divided into 3 armies, of whom 700 or 800 are on horseback, and tolerably well-armed."[13] During the next month slaves attacked and destroyed hundreds of sugar and coffee plantations.

On April 4, 1792, as war loomed with the European states, the National Assembly issued a decree enfranchising all free blacks and free people of color. The Assembly hoped this measure would win the loyalty of free blacks and their aid in defeating the slave rebellion.

Warfare in Europe soon spread to Saint-Domingue (Map 20.1), adding another complicating factor to its domestic conflicts. Since the beginning of the slave insurrection, the Spanish in neighboring Santo Domingo had supported rebel slaves, and in early 1793 they began to bring slave leaders and their soldiers into the Spanish army. Toussaint L'Ouverture (TOO-sahn LOO-vair-toor) (1743–1803), a freed slave who had joined the revolt, was named a Spanish officer. In September the British navy also blockaded the colony, and invading British troops captured French territory on the island. For the Spanish and British, revolutionary chaos provided a tempting opportunity to capture a profitable colony.

Desperate for forces to oppose France's enemies, the commissioners sent by the newly elected National Convention promised freedom to slaves who fought for France. By October 1793 they had abolished slavery throughout the colony. On February 4, 1794, the Convention ratified the abolition of slavery and extended it to all French territories, including the Caribbean colonies of Martinique and Guadeloupe. In just four years insurgent slaves had ended centuries of bondage in the French Caribbean and won full political rights.

For the future, the problem loomed of how these rights would be applied. The most immediate question, however, was whether France would be able to retain the colony, which was still under attack by Spanish and British forces. The tide began to turn when Toussaint L'Ouverture switched sides, bringing his military and political skills, along with four thousand well-trained soldiers, to support the French war effort.

By 1796 the French had gradually regained control of the colony, and L'Ouverture had emerged as the key leader of the combined slave and free colored forces. In May 1796 he was named commander of the western province of Saint-Domingue (see Map 20.1). The increasingly conservative nature of the French government during the Thermidorian reaction, however, threatened to undo the gains made by former slaves and free people of color. As exiled planters gained a stronger voice in French policymaking, L'Ouverture and other local leaders grew ever more wary of what the future might hold.

The Thermidorian Reaction and the Directory

The success of the French armies led Robespierre and the Committee of Public Safety to relax the emergency economic controls, but they extended the political Reign of Terror. In March 1794, to the horror of many sans-culottes, Robespierre's Terror wiped out many of his critics. Two weeks later, Robespierre sent long-standing collaborators, including the famous orator Danton, up the steps to the guillotine. A group of radicals and moderates in the Convention, knowing that they might be next, organized a conspiracy. They howled down Robespierre when he tried to speak to the National Convention on July 27, 1794—a date known as "9 Thermidor" according to France's newly adopted republican calendar. The next day it was Robespierre's turn to be shaved by the revolutionary razor.

As Robespierre's closest supporters followed their leader to the guillotine, France unexpectedly experienced a thorough reaction to the despotism of the Reign of Terror. In a general way, this **Thermidorian reaction** recalled the early days of the Revolution. The respectable middle-class lawyers and professionals who had led the liberal Revolution of 1789 reasserted their authority, drawing support from their own class,

the provincial cities, and the better-off peasants. In 1795 the National Convention abolished many economic controls, let prices rise sharply, and severely restricted the local political organizations in which the sans-culottes had their strength.

The collapse of economic controls, coupled with runaway inflation, hit the working poor very hard. After the Convention used the army to suppress the sans-culottes' protests, the urban poor lost their revolutionary fervor. Excluded and disillusioned, they would have little interest in and influence on politics until 1830. The poor of the countryside turned toward religion as a relief from earthly cares. Rural women, especially, brought back the Catholic Church and the open worship of God as the government began to soften its antireligious revolutionary stance.

As for the middle-class members of the National Convention, in 1795 they wrote yet another constitution that they believed would guarantee their economic position and political supremacy. As in previous elections, the mass of the population voted only

> **Thermidorian reaction** A reaction to the violence of the Reign of Terror in 1794, resulting in the execution of Robespierre and the loosening of economic controls.

The Execution of Robespierre Completely wooden except for the heavy iron blade, the guillotine was painted red for Robespierre's execution, a detail not captured in this black-and-white engraving of the 1794 event. Large crowds witnessed the execution in a majestic public square in central Paris, then known as the Place de la Revolution and now called the Place de la Concorde (Harmony Square). (Snark/Art Resource, NY)

for electors, whose number was cut back to men of substantial means. Electors then elected the members of a reorganized legislative assembly as well as key officials throughout France. The new assembly also chose a five-man executive called the Directory.

The Directory continued to support French military expansion abroad. War was no longer so much a crusade as a means to meet ever-present, ever-unsolved economic problems. Large, victorious French armies reduced unemployment at home and were able to live off the territories they conquered and plundered. Yet the French people felt a widespread disgust with war and food rationing, and they quickly grew weary of the unprincipled actions of the Directory. This general dissatisfaction revealed itself clearly in the national elections of 1797, which returned a large number of conservative and even monarchist deputies who favored peace at almost any price. The members of the Directory, fearing for their skins, used the army to nullify the elections and began to govern dictatorially. Two years later Napoleon Bonaparte ended the Directory in a coup d'état (koo day-TAH) and substituted a strong dictatorship for a weak one. The effort to establish stable representative government had failed.

The Napoleonic Era, 1799–1815

Why did Napoleon Bonaparte assume control of France, and what factors led to his downfall? How did the new republic of Haiti gain independence from France? ■

For almost fifteen years, from 1799 to 1814, France was in the hands of a keen-minded military dictator of exceptional ability. One of history's most fascinating leaders, Napoleon Bonaparte (1769–1821) realized the need to put an end to civil strife in France in order to create unity and consolidate his rule. And he did. But Napoleon saw himself as a man of destiny, and the glory of war and the dream of universal empire proved irresistible. For years he spiraled from victory to victory, but in the end he was destroyed by a mighty coalition united in fear of his restless ambition.

Napoleonic Code French civil code promulgated in 1804 that reasserted the 1789 principles of the equality of all male citizens before the law and the absolute security of wealth and private property as well as restricting rights accorded to women by previous revolutionary laws.

Napoleon's Rule of France

Born in Corsica into an impoverished noble family in 1769, Napoleon left home and became a lieutenant in the French artillery in 1785. After a brief and unsuc-

❝ May they learn from you that the God of peace is also the God of armies, and that He fights alongside those who defend the independence and liberty of France. ❞

—NAPOLEON BONAPARTE

cessful adventure fighting for Corsican independence in 1789, he returned to France as a French patriot and a dedicated revolutionary. Rising rapidly in the new army, Napoleon was placed in command of French forces in Italy and won brilliant victories there in 1796 and 1797. His next campaign, in Egypt, was a failure, but Napoleon returned to France before the fiasco was generally known, and his reputation remained intact.

Napoleon soon learned that some prominent members of the legislature were plotting against the Directory. The dissatisfaction of these plotters stemmed not so much from the fact that the Directory was a dictatorship as from the fact that it was a weak dictatorship. Ten years of upheaval and uncertainty had made firm rule much more appealing than liberty and popular politics to these disillusioned revolutionaries. The abbé Sieyès personified this evolution in thinking. In 1789 he had written that the nobility was grossly overprivileged and that the entire people should rule the French nation. Now Sieyès's motto was "Confidence from below, authority from above."

Like the other members of his group, Sieyès wanted a strong military ruler. The flamboyant thirty-year-old Napoleon, nationally revered for his heroism, was ideal. Thus the conspirators and Napoleon organized a takeover. On November 9, 1799, they ousted the Directors, and the following day soldiers disbanded the legislature at bayonet point. Napoleon was named first consul of the republic, and a new constitution consolidating his position was overwhelmingly approved in a plebiscite in December 1799. Republican appearances were maintained, but Napoleon became the real ruler of France.

The essence of Napoleon's domestic policy was to use his popularity and charisma to maintain order and end civil strife. He did so by working out unwritten agreements with powerful groups in France whereby the groups received favors in return for loyal service. Napoleon's bargain with the solid middle class was codified in the famous Civil Code of March 1804, also known as the **Napoleonic Code**, which reasserted two

The Coronation of Napoleon, 1804 In this detail from a grandiose painting by Jacques-Louis David, Napoleon, instead of the pope, prepares to crown his wife, Josephine, in an elaborate ceremony in Notre Dame Cathedral. Napoleon, the ultimate upstart, also crowned himself. Pope Pius VII, seated glumly behind the emperor, is reduced to being a spectator. (Louvre/Réunion des Musées Nationaux/Art Resource, NY)

of the fundamental principles of the Revolution of 1789: equality of all male citizens before the law, and absolute security of wealth and private property. Napoleon and the leading bankers of Paris established the privately owned Bank of France in 1800, which loyally served the interests of both the state and the financial oligarchy. Peasants were appeased when Napoleon defended the gains in land and status they had claimed during the Revolution.

At the same time, Napoleon built on the bureaucracy inherited from the Revolution and the Old Regime to create a thoroughly centralized state. He consolidated his rule by recruiting disillusioned revolutionaries for the network of ministers, prefects, and centrally appointed mayors that depended on him and came to serve him well. Only former revolutionaries who leaned too far to the left or to the right were pushed to the sidelines.[14] Nor were members of the old nobility slighted. In 1800 and again in 1802 Napoleon granted amnesty to one hundred thousand émigrés on the condition that they return to France and take a loyalty oath. Members of this returning elite soon ably occupied many high posts in the expanding centralized state. Napoleon also created a new imperial nobility in order to reward his most talented generals and officials.

Napoleon applied his diplomatic skills to healing the Catholic Church in France so that it could serve as a bulwark of social stability. After arduous negotiations, Napoleon and Pope Pius VII (pontificate 1800–1823) signed the Concordat (kuhn-KOHR-dat) of 1801. The pope gained the precious right for French Catholics to practice their religion freely, but Napoleon gained political power: his government now nominated bishops, paid the clergy, and exerted great influence over the church in France. In an 1802 proclamation, he called on priests to help instill patriotism for the "fatherland":

Exert for it all the force and ascendancy of spirit that your ministry gives you; that your lessons and examples may form in young citizens the love of our institutions, respect for and attachment to the tutelary authorities which have been created to protect them; may they learn from you that the God of peace is also the God of armies, and that He fights alongside those who defend the independence and liberty of France.

The domestic reforms of Napoleon's early years were his greatest achievement. Much of his legal and administrative reorganization has survived in France to this day. More generally, Napoleon's domestic initiatives gave the great majority of French people a welcome sense of stability and national unity.

Order and unity had a price: authoritarian rule. Women, who had often participated in revolutionary politics without having legal equality, lost many of the gains they made in the 1790s. Under the new Napoleonic Code, women were dependents of either their fathers or their husbands, and they could not make contracts or have bank accounts in their own names. Napoleon and his advisers aimed at re-establishing a family monarchy, where the power of the husband and father was as absolute over the wife and the children as that of Napoleon was over his subjects.

Free speech and freedom of the press were continually violated. By 1811 only four newspapers were left, and they were little more than organs of government propaganda. The occasional elections were a farce. Later laws prescribed harsh penalties for political offenses, and people were watched carefully under an efficient spy system. People suspected of subversive activities were arbitrarily detained, placed under house arrest, or consigned to insane asylums. After 1810 political suspects were held in state prisons, as they had been during the Terror. There were about twenty-five hundred such political prisoners in 1814.

Napoleon's Expansion in Europe

Napoleon was above all a great military man. After coming to power in 1799 he sent peace feelers to Austria and Great Britain, the two remaining members of the Second Coalition that had been formed against France in 1798. When these overtures were rejected, French armies led by Napoleon decisively defeated the Austrians. In the Treaty of Lunéville (1801), Austria accepted the loss of almost all its Italian possessions, and German territory on the west bank of the Rhine was incorporated into France. The British agreed to the Treaty of Amiens in 1802, allowing France to remain in control of Holland, the Austrian Netherlands, the west bank of the Rhine, and most of the Italian peninsula. The Treaty of Amiens was clearly a diplomatic triumph for Napoleon, and peace with honor and profit increased his popularity at home.

In 1802 Napoleon was secure but driven to expand his power. Aggressively redrawing the map of Germany so as to weaken Austria and encourage the secondary states of southwestern Germany to side with France, Napoleon tried to restrict British trade with all of Eu-

rope. He then plotted to attack Great Britain, but his Mediterranean fleet was destroyed by Lord Nelson at the Battle of Trafalgar on October 21, 1805. Invasion of England was henceforth impossible. Renewed fighting had its advantages, however, for the first consul used the wartime atmosphere to have himself proclaimed emperor in late 1804.

Austria, Russia, and Sweden joined with Britain to form the Third Coalition against France shortly before the Battle of Trafalgar. Actions such as Napoleon's assumption of the Italian crown had convinced both Alexander I of Russia and Francis II of Austria that Napoleon was a threat to their interests and to the European balance of power. Yet the Austrians and the Russians were no match for Napoleon, who scored a brilliant victory over them at the Battle of Austerlitz in December 1805. Alexander I decided to pull back, and Austria accepted large territorial losses in return for peace as the Third Coalition collapsed.

German Confederation of the Rhine, 1806

Napoleon then proceeded to reorganize the German states to his liking. In 1806 he abolished many of the tiny German states as well as the ancient Holy Roman Empire and established by decree the German Confederation of the Rhine, a union of fifteen German states minus Austria, Prussia, and Saxony. Naming himself "protector" of the confederation, Napoleon firmly controlled western Germany.

Napoleon's intervention in German affairs alarmed the Prussians, who mobilized their armies after more than a decade of peace with France. Napoleon attacked and won two more brilliant victories in October 1806 at Jena and Auerstädt, where the Prussians were outnumbered two to one. The war with Prussia, now joined by Russia, continued into the following spring. After Napoleon's larger armies won another victory, Alexander I of Russia was ready to negotiate the peace. In the subsequent treaties of Tilsit in 1807, Prussia lost half of its population, while Russia accepted Napoleon's reorganization of western and central Europe and promised to enforce Napoleon's economic blockade against British goods.

The War of Haitian Independence

In the midst of these victories, Napoleon was forced to accept defeat overseas. With Toussaint L'Ouverture acting increasingly as an independent ruler of the western province of Saint-Domingue, another general, André

Rigaud, set up his own government in the southern peninsula, which had long been more isolated from France than the rest of the colony. Both leaders maintained policies, initially established by the French, of requiring former slaves to continue to work on their plantations. They believed that reconstructing the plantation economy was crucial to maintaining their military and political victories, and thus harshly suppressed resistance from former slaves.

Tensions mounted, however, between L'Ouverture and Rigaud. While L'Ouverture was a freed slave of African descent, Rigaud belonged to the free colored elite. This elite resented the growing power of former slaves like L'Ouverture, who in turn accused them of adopting the racism of white settlers. Civil war broke out between the two sides in 1799 when L'Ouverture's forces, led by his lieutenant Jean Jacques Dessalines (dehsuh-LEEN), invaded the south. Victory over Rigaud gave L'Ouverture control of the entire colony. (See "Individuals in Society: Toussaint L'Ouverture," page 648.)

This victory was soon challenged by Napoleon, who had his own plans for using profits from Caribbean plantations as a basis for expanding French power. His new constitution of 1799 opened the way for a re-establishment of slavery much feared in the colony. When the colonial assembly of Saint-Domingue, under L'Ouverture's direction, drafted its own constitution — which reaffirmed the abolition of slavery and granted L'Ouverture governorship for life — Napoleon viewed it as a seditious act. He ordered his brother-in-law, General Charles-Victor-Emmanuel Leclerc, to lead an expedition to the island to crush the new regime. Napoleon placed a high premium on bringing the colony to heel, writing to Leclerc: "Once the blacks have been disarmed and the principal generals sent to France, you will have done more for the commerce and civilization of Europe than we have done in our most brilliant campaigns." An officer sent to serve in the colony had a more cynical interpretation, writing that he was being sent to "fight with the Negroes for their own sugar."[15]

In 1802 Leclerc landed in Saint-Domingue. Although Toussaint L'Ouverture cooperated with the French and turned his army over to them, he was arrested and deported to France, along with his family, where he died in 1803. Jean Jacques Dessalines united the resistance under his command and led it to a crushing victory over the French forces. Of the fifty-eight thousand French

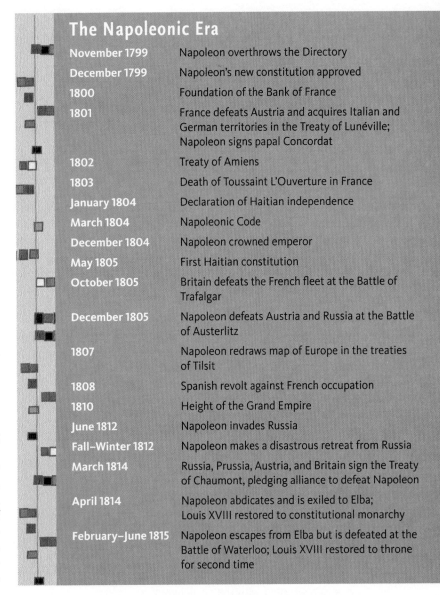

The Napoleonic Era

November 1799	Napoleon overthrows the Directory
December 1799	Napoleon's new constitution approved
1800	Foundation of the Bank of France
1801	France defeats Austria and acquires Italian and German territories in the Treaty of Lunéville; Napoleon signs papal Concordat
1802	Treaty of Amiens
1803	Death of Toussaint L'Ouverture in France
January 1804	Declaration of Haitian independence
March 1804	Napoleonic Code
December 1804	Napoleon crowned emperor
May 1805	First Haitian constitution
October 1805	Britain defeats the French fleet at the Battle of Trafalgar
December 1805	Napoleon defeats Austria and Russia at the Battle of Austerlitz
1807	Napoleon redraws map of Europe in the treaties of Tilsit
1808	Spanish revolt against French occupation
1810	Height of the Grand Empire
June 1812	Napoleon invades Russia
Fall–Winter 1812	Napoleon makes a disastrous retreat from Russia
March 1814	Russia, Prussia, Austria, and Britain sign the Treaty of Chaumont, pledging alliance to defeat Napoleon
April 1814	Napoleon abdicates and is exiled to Elba; Louis XVIII restored to constitutional monarchy
February–June 1815	Napoleon escapes from Elba but is defeated at the Battle of Waterloo; Louis XVIII restored to throne for second time

soldiers, fifty thousand were lost in combat and to disease. On January 1, 1804, Dessalines formally declared the independence of Saint-Domingue and the creation of the new sovereign nation of Haiti, the name used by the pre-Columbian inhabitants of the island. The Haitian constitution was ratified in 1805.

Haiti, the second independent state in the Americas and the first in Latin America, was thus born from the first successful large-scale slave revolt in history. Fearing the spread of slave rebellion to the United States, President Thomas Jefferson refused to recognize Haiti. Both the American and the French Revolutions thus exposed their limits by acting to protect economic interests at the expense of revolutionary ideals of freedom and equality. Yet Haitian independence had fundamental repercussions for world history, helping spread the idea that liberty, equality, and fraternity must apply to all people.

Toussaint L'Ouverture

INDIVIDUALS IN SOCIETY

LITTLE IS KNOWN OF THE EARLY LIFE of Saint-Domingue's brilliant military and political leader Toussaint L'Ouverture. He was born in 1743 on a plantation outside Le Cap owned by the Count de Bréda. According to tradition, L'Ouverture was the eldest son of a captured African prince from modern-day Benin. Toussaint Bréda, as he was then called, occupied a privileged position among slaves. Instead of performing backbreaking labor in the fields, he served his master as a coachman and livestock keeper. He also learned to read and write French and some Latin, but he was always more comfortable with the Creole dialect.

During the 1770s the plantation manager emancipated L'Ouverture, who subsequently leased his own small coffee plantation, worked by slaves. He married Suzanne Simone, who already had one son, and the couple had another son during their marriage. In 1791 he joined the slave uprisings that swept Saint-Domingue, and he took on the *nom de guerre* ("war name") "L'Ouverture," meaning "the opening." L'Ouverture rose to prominence among rebel slaves allied with Spain and by early 1794 controlled his own army. A devout Catholic who led a frugal and ascetic life, L'Ouverture impressed others with his enormous physical energy, intellectual acumen, and air of mystery. In 1794 he defected to the French side and led his troops to a series of victories against the Spanish. In 1795 the National Convention promoted L'Ouverture to brigadier general.

Over the next three years L'Ouverture successively eliminated rivals for authority on the island. First he freed himself of the French commissioners sent to govern the colony. With a firm grip on power in the northern province, L'Ouverture defeated General André Rigaud in 1800 to gain control in the south. His army then marched on the capital of Spanish Santo Domingo on the eastern half of the island, meeting little resistance. The entire island of Hispaniola was now under his command.

With control of Saint-Domingue in his hands, L'Ouverture was confronted with the challenge of building a post-emancipation society, the first of its kind. The task was made even more difficult by the chaos wreaked by war, the destruction of plantations, and bitter social and racial tensions. For L'Ouverture the most pressing concern was to re-establish the plantation economy. Without revenue to pay his army, the gains of the rebellion could be lost. He therefore encouraged white planters to return and reclaim their property. He also adopted harsh policies toward former slaves, forcing them back to their plantations and restricting their ability to acquire land. When they resisted, he sent troops across the island to enforce submission. L'Ouverture's 1801 constitution reaffirmed his draconian labor policies and named L'Ouverture governor for life, leaving Saint-Domingue as a colony in name alone. In June 1802 French forces arrested L'Ouverture and jailed him at Fort de Joux in France's Jura Mountains near the Swiss border. L'Ouverture died of pneumonia on April 7, 1803. It was left to his lieutenant, Jean Jacques Dessalines, to win independence for the new Haitian nation.

QUESTIONS FOR ANALYSIS

1. Toussaint L'Ouverture was both slave and slave owner. How did each experience shape his life and actions?

2. What did Toussaint L'Ouverture and Napoleon Bonaparte have in common? How did they differ?

Equestrian portrait of Toussaint L'Ouverture.
(Réunion des Musées Nationaux/Art Resource, NY)

The Grand Empire and Its End

Napoleon resigned himself to the loss of Saint-Domingue, but he still maintained imperial ambitions in Europe. Increasingly, he saw himself as the emperor of Europe, not just of France. The so-called **Grand Empire** he built had three parts. The core, or first part, was an ever-expanding France, which by 1810 included Belgium, Holland, parts of northern Italy, and much German territory on the east bank of the Rhine. The second part consisted of a number of dependent satellite kingdoms, on the thrones of which Napoleon placed (and replaced) the members of his large family. The third part comprised the independent but allied states of Austria, Prussia, and Russia. After 1806 both satellites and allies were expected to support Napoleon's **Continental System**, a blockade in which no ship coming from Britain or her colonies was allowed to dock at any port controlled by the French. It was intended to halt all trade between Britain and continental Europe, thereby destroying the British economy and its military force.

The impact of the Grand Empire on the peoples of Europe was considerable. In the areas incorporated into France and in the satellites (Map 20.2), Napoleon abolished feudal dues and serfdom. Some of the peasants and middle class benefited from these reforms. Yet Napoleon had to put the prosperity and special interests of France first in order to safeguard his power base. Levying heavy taxes in money and men for his armies, he came to be regarded more as a conquering tyrant than as an enlightened liberator. Thus French rule sparked patriotic upheavals and encouraged the growth of reactive nationalism, for individuals in different lands learned to identify emotionally with their own embattled national families as the French had done earlier.

The first great revolt occurred in Spain. In 1808 a coalition of Catholics, monarchists, and patriots rebelled against Napoleon's attempts to make Spain a French satellite. French armies occupied Madrid, but the foes of Napoleon fled to the hills and waged uncompromising guerrilla warfare. Spain was a clear warning: resistance to French imperialism was growing.

Yet Napoleon pushed on, determined to hold his complex and far-flung empire together. In 1810, when

Grand Empire The empire over which Napoleon and his allies ruled, encompassing virtually all of Europe except Great Britain and Russia.

Continental System A blockade imposed by Napoleon to halt all trade between continental Europe and Britain, thereby weakening the British economy and military.

Francisco Goya, *The Third of May 1808* Spanish master Francisco Goya created a passionate and moving indictment of the brutality of war in this painting from 1814, which depicts the close-range execution of Spanish rebels by Napoleon's forces in May 1808. Goya's painting evoked the bitterness and despair of many Europeans who suffered through Napoleon's invasions. (Erich Lessing/Art Resource, NY)

Legend:
- French empire
- Dependent states
- Allied with Napoleon
- ⚔ French victory
- ⚔ French defeat

KINGDOM OF NORWAY AND DENMARK

KINGDOM OF SWEDEN

• Stockholm

• St. Petersburg

North Sea

Baltic Sea

Napoleon's invasion of Russia, June–Sept. 1812

Borodino 1812

• Moscow

GREAT BRITAIN

• Copenhagen

SWEDISH POMERANIA

Königsberg

Tilsit   Vilna

Smolensk

Maloyaroslavets 1812

• London

Hamburg • Lübeck

Bremen •

• Berlin

Danzig

Friedland 1807

Neman R.

French retreat, Oct.–Dec. 1812

RUSSIAN EMPIRE

PRUSSIA

WESTPHALIA

GRAND DUCHY OF WARSAW

Rhine

Brussels •

Auerstädt 1806

SAXONY

• Kiev

Waterloo 1815

Jena 1806

Amiens •

CONFEDERATION OF THE RHINE

Austerlitz 1805

Paris •

Wagram 1804

Pressburg

Lunéville •

BAVARIA

Vienna •

Buda • Pest

FRANCE

WÜRTTEMBERG

Zurich •

BADEN

AUSTRIAN EMPIRE

ATLANTIC OCEAN

Marengo 1800

Milan •

KINGDOM OF ITALY

ILLYRIAN PROVINCES

Genoa •

Marseilles •

Danube R.

Black Sea

Lisbon •

• Madrid

Elba

PORTUGAL

SPAIN

Corsica

OTTOMAN EMPIRE

Trafalgar 1805

Rome •

Sardinia

• Naples

GIBRALTAR (Gr. Br.)

KINGDOM OF NAPLES

Mediterranean Sea

0   100   200 miles
0   100   200 kilometers

Palermo •

KINGDOM OF SICILY

Ionian Is. (Gr. Br.)

• Athens

Malta (Gr. Br.)

Mapping the Past

Map 20.2 Napoleonic Europe in 1812 Only Great Britain remained at war with Napoleon at the height of the Grand Empire. Many British goods were smuggled through Helgoland, a tiny but strategic British possession off the German coast. Compare this map with Map 16.2 (page 493), which shows the division of Europe in 1715.

ANALYZING THE MAP How had the balance of power shifted in Europe from 1715 to 1812? What changed, and what remained the same? What was the impact of Napoleon's wars on Germany and the Italian peninsula?

CONNECTIONS Why did Napoleon succeed in achieving vast territorial gains where Louis XIV did not?

To complete this activity online, go to the Online Study Guide at bedfordstmartins.com/mckaywest.

the Grand Empire was at its height, Britain still remained at war with France, helping the guerrillas in Spain and Portugal. The Continental System, expected to force the British "nation of shopkeepers" to its knees, was a failure. Instead, it was France that suffered from Britain's counter-blockade, which created hard times for French artisans and the middle class. Perhaps looking for a scapegoat, Napoleon turned on Alexander I of Russia, who in

1811 openly repudiated Napoleon's war of prohibitions against British goods.

Napoleon's invasion of Russia began in June 1812 with a force that eventually numbered 600,000, probably the largest force yet assembled in a single army. Only one-third of this Great Army was French, however; nationals of all the satellites and allies were drafted into the operation. Originally planning to winter in the Russian city of Smolensk if Alexander did not sue for peace, Napoleon reached Smolensk and recklessly pressed on toward Moscow. The great Battle of Borodino that followed was a draw, and the Russians retreated in good order. Alexander ordered the evacuation of Moscow, which the Russians then burned in part, and he refused to negotiate. Finally, after five weeks in the scorched and abandoned city, Napoleon ordered a retreat. That retreat was one of the greatest military disasters in history. The Russian army, the Russian winter, and starvation cut Napoleon's army to pieces. When the frozen remnants staggered into Poland and Prussia in December, 370,000 men had died and another 200,000 had been taken prisoner.[16]

Leaving his troops to their fate, Napoleon raced to Paris to raise yet another army. Possibly he might still have saved his throne if he had been willing to accept a France reduced to its historical size—the proposal offered by Austria's foreign minister, Prince Klemens von Metternich. But Napoleon refused. Austria and Prussia deserted Napoleon and joined Russia and Great Britain in the Treaty of Chaumont in March 1814, by which the four powers pledged allegiance to defeat the French emperor.

All across Europe patriots called for a "war of liberation" against Napoleon's oppression. Less than a month later, on April 4, 1814, a defeated Napoleon abdicated his throne. After this unconditional abdication, the victorious allies granted Napoleon the island of Elba off the coast of Italy as his own tiny state. Napoleon was

allowed to keep his imperial title, and France was required to pay him a yearly income of 2 million francs.

The allies also agreed to the restoration of the Bourbon dynasty under Louis XVIII (r. 1814–1824) and promised to treat France with leniency in a peace settlement. The new monarch tried to consolidate support among the people by issuing the Constitutional Charter, which accepted many of France's revolutionary changes and guaranteed civil liberties.

Yet Louis XVIII—old, ugly, and crippled by gout—lacked the magnetism of Napoleon. Hearing of political unrest in France and diplomatic tensions in Vienna, Napoleon staged a daring escape from Elba in February 1815. Landing in France, he issued appeals for support and marched on Paris with a small band of followers. French officers and soldiers who had fought so long for their emperor responded to the call. Louis XVIII fled, and once more Napoleon took command. But Napoleon's gamble was a desperate long shot, for the allies were united against him. At the end of a frantic period known as the Hundred Days, they crushed his forces at Waterloo on June 18, 1815, and imprisoned him on the rocky island of St. Helena, far off the western coast of Africa. Louis XVIII returned to the throne, and the allies dealt more harshly with the apparently incorrigible French. As for Napoleon, he took revenge by writing his memoirs, nurturing the myth that he had been Europe's revolutionary liberator, a romantic hero whose lofty work had been undone by oppressive reactionaries.

LOOKING BACK LOOKING AHEAD

UNTIL 1789 the medieval ordering of French society into three estates remained in force, and the king, claiming to embody the nation in his person by the grace of God, continued to rule absolutely. Yet monumental changes had occurred over the eighteenth century as population grew, urbanization spread, and literacy increased. Enlightenment ideals influenced members of all three estates, who increasingly questioned the power of the monarchy and the rigid structure of society. As the sacred aura of the monarchy diminished, the royal government became increasingly incapable of resolving the urgent financial and political crises of the Old Regime. Exactly who should have the power, however, and how France should be governed, were questions that had many conflicting answers and resulted in decades of war and instability.

The age of revolution both drew on and affected European colonies in the Americas. The high stakes of colonial empire had heightened competition among European states, leading to a series of wars that generated crushing costs for overburdened treasuries. As was the case for the British in their North American colonies, the desperate need for new taxes weakened the French state and opened the door to revolution. In turn, the ideals of the French Revolution inspired slaves and free people of color in Saint-Domingue, thus opening the promise of liberty, equality, and fraternity to people of all races.

As complex as its origins are the long legacies of this period of revolution. Nineteenth- and early-twentieth-century Europe experienced periodic convulsions of revolution as successive generations struggled over political rights first proclaimed by the generation of 1789. Meanwhile, as dramatic events unfolded in France, a parallel revolution had gathered steam across the Channel. This was the British Industrial Revolution, originating around 1750 and accelerating through the end of the eighteenth century. After 1815 the twin forces of industrialization and democratization would combine to create the modern nation-states of Europe.

CHAPTER REVIEW

◼ What social, political, and economic factors formed the background to the French Revolution? (p. 620)

An earlier generation of historians believed that the origins of the French Revolution lay in a single cause: class struggle between the nobility and the rising bourgeoisie. It is now clear that there were multiple causes of the Revolution. One was the growing ties — rather than conflict — between nobles and the wealthy bourgeoisie, who had grown economically and culturally closer over the course of the eighteenth century. The upper echelon's frustration with absolute rule emerged in political struggles between the monarchy and its officers, particularly in the high law courts. Public opinion turned against the monarchy as a rising torrent of political theory, cheap pamphlets, and gossip offered scathing and even pornographic depictions of the king and his court. With their sacred royal aura severely tarnished, Louis XV and his successor Louis XVI were unable to respond to the financial crises generated by French involvement in the Seven Years' War and the American Revolution. French support of the American colonists' fight for independence from Britain, moreover, inspired many to embrace the real possibility of political freedom. Louis XVI's half-hearted efforts to redress the situation were quickly overwhelmed by elite and popular demands for fundamental reform.

◼ How did the events of 1789 result in a constitutional monarchy in France, and how did the new constitution affect the various members of French society at home and in the colony of Saint-Domingue? (p. 625)

When the Estates General gathered in 1789, delegates from the third estate refused to accept the old system of one vote per estate. Instead, they proclaimed that they alone constituted a "National Assembly" and refused to disband. Popular revolts prevented the king from intervening, and he was forced to accept the situation. Pushed forward by calls for freedom and equality from the streets of Paris to the faraway countryside, the National Assembly established a constitutional monarchy in 1791. The new constitution abolished the second estate and ended feudalism, thereby eliminating Old Regime privileges. Only men were given the right to vote for the new Assembly, however, and even among men, those in the lower economic stratum were disenfranchised. In the spirit of economic freedom, guilds and workers' associations were outlawed, which benefited merchants but threatened the livelihoods of master artisans and prevented workers from defending their rights. To the horror of the pope and devout French Catholics, the government seized church property and imposed an oath of loyalty on priests. The new constitution waffled in regard to the

French colony of Saint-Domingue. By allowing the colonies to make their own laws regarding slavery and voting rights, it disheartened the slaves and free coloreds. And by reaffirming French trade monopolies, it angered the white planters.

◼ How and why did the Revolution take a radical turn at home and in the colonies? (p. 633)

Support for constitutional monarchy ended with the royal family's attempted flight in June 1791. The new Legislative Assembly, comprising younger and more radical delegates led by members of the Jacobin club, declared war on Austria and proclaimed France a republic. With the execution of the royal couple and the declaration of terror as the order of the day, the French Revolution took an increasingly radical turn from the end of 1792.

After initial military defeats, France was largely victorious, mostly because of the total war effort undertaken by the Jacobin leadership. To defend the Revolution against its perceived internal enemies, Jacobins eliminated political opponents and then factions within their own party. They also attempted to bring about a cultural revolution, in part by attacking Christianity and substituting secular republican festivals. The Directory government that took power after the fall of Robespierre restored political equilibrium at the cost of the radical platform of social equality he had pursued. In Saint-Domingue, Spain and England profited from revolutionary conflict to invade the colony. To gain military support, the National Assembly agreed to enfranchise free people of color and to free any slave who fought on their side.

◼ Why did Napoleon Bonaparte assume control of France, and what factors led to his downfall? How did the new republic of Haiti gain independence from France? (p. 644)

Wearied by the weaknesses of the Directory, a group of conspirators gave Napoleon Bonaparte control of France. His reputation as a brilliant military leader and his charisma and determination made him seem ideal to lead France to victory over its enemies. However, Napoleon's relentless ambitions ultimately led to his downfall. Not satisfied with his successes throughout Europe, and struggling to maintain his hold on Spain and Portugal, Napoleon made the fatal mistake of attempting to invade Russia in the summer of 1812. After a disastrous retreat from Moscow, he was eventually forced to abdicate the throne in 1814. His story is paralleled by that of Toussaint L'Ouverture, another soldier who emerged into the political limelight from the chaos of revolution, only to endure exile and defeat. Unlike Napoleon, L'Ouverture's cause ultimately prevailed. After his exile, war between the French forces and the armies he had led and inspired resulted in French defeat and independence for Saint-Domingue.

Suggested Reading

Bell, David A. *The Cult of the Nation in France: Inventing Nationalism, 1680–1800*. 2001. Traces early French nationalism through its revolutionary culmination.

Blanning, T. C. W. *The French Revolutionary Wars (1787–1802)*. 1996. A masterful account of the revolutionary wars that also places the French Revolution in its European context.

Broers, Michael. *Europe Under Napoleon*. 2002. Probes Napoleon's impact on the territories he conquered.

Connelly, Owen. *The French Revolution and Napoleonic Era*. 1991. An excellent introduction to the French Revolution and Napoleon.

Desan, Suzanne. *The Family on Trial in Revolutionary France*. 2004. Studies the effects of revolutionary law on the family, including the legalization of divorce.

Dubois, Laurent. *Avengers of the New World: The Story of the Haitian Revolution*. 2004. An excellent and highly readable account of the revolution that transformed the French colony of Saint-Domingue into the independent state of Haiti.

Englund, Steven. *Napoleon: A Political Life*. 2004. A good biography of the French emperor.

Hunt, Lynn. *Politics, Culture and Class in the French Revolution*, 2d ed. 2004. A pioneering examination of the French Revolution as a cultural phenomenon that generated new festivals, clothing, and songs, and even a new calendar.

Landes, John B. *Visualizing the Nation: Gender, Representation, and Revolution in Eighteenth-Century France*. 2001. Analyzes images of gender and the body in revolutionary politics.

Schechter, Ronald. *Obstinate Hebrews: Representations of Jews in France, 1715–1815*. 2003. An illuminating study of Jews and attitudes toward them in France from Enlightenment to emancipation.

Sutherland, Donald. *France, 1789–1815*. 1986. An overview of the French Revolution that emphasizes its many opponents, as well as its supporters.

Tackett, Timothy. *When the King Took Flight*. 2003. An exciting re-creation of the royal family's doomed effort to escape from Paris.

Notes

1. Quoted in R. R. Palmer, *The Age of Democratic Revolution*, vol. 1 (Princeton, N.J.: Princeton University Press, 1959), pp. 95–96.
2. Quoted in G. Wright, *France in Modern Times*, 4th ed. (New York: W. W. Norton, 1987), p. 34.
3. P. H. Beik, ed., *The French Revolution* (New York: Walker, 1970), p. 89.
4. G. Pernoud and S. Flaisser, eds., *The French Revolution* (Greenwich, Conn.: Fawcett, 1960), p. 61.
5. Quoted in Lynn Hunt, ed., *The French Revolution and Human Rights: A Brief Documentary History* (Boston/New York: Bedford/St. Martin's, 1996), p. 119.
6. Louis-Marie Prudhomme, *Revolutions of Paris*, quoted in Hunt, *The French Revolution and Human Rights*, p. 130.
7. Quoted in L. Gershoy, *The Era of the French Revolution, 1789–1799* (New York: Van Nostrand, 1957), p. 150.
8. Pernoud and Flaisser, *The French Revolution*, pp. 193–194.
9. Cited in Wim Klooster, *Revolutions in the Atlantic World: A Comprehensive History* (New York and London: New York University Press, 2009), p. 74.
10. Quotation from Hunt, *The French Revolution and Human Rights*, p. 138.
11. T. Blanning, *The French Revolutionary Wars, 1787–1802* (London: Arnold, 1996), pp. 116–128.
12. Quoted ibid., p. 123.
13. Quoted in Laurent Dubois, *Avengers of the New World: The Story of the Haitian Revolution* (Cambridge, Mass.: Harvard University Press, 2004), p. 97.
14. I. Woloch, *Napoleon and His Collaborators: The Making of a Dictatorship* (New York: W. W. Norton, 2001), pp. 36–65.
15. Quoted in Dubois, *Avengers of the New World*, pp. 255–256.
16. D. Sutherland, *France, 1789–1815: Revolution and Counterrevolution* (New York: Oxford University Press, 1986), p. 420.

Key Terms

estates (p. 620)

Estates General (p. 625)

National Assembly (p. 627)

Great Fear (p. 629)

constitutional monarchy (p. 630)

Jacobin club (p. 634)

second revolution (p. 635)

Girondists (p. 635)

the Mountain (p. 635)

sans-culottes (p. 636)

Reign of Terror (p. 637)

dechristianization (p. 638)

Thermidorian reaction (p. 643)

Napoleonic Code (p. 644)

Grand Empire (p. 649)

Continental System (p. 649)

For practice quizzes and other study tools, visit the Online Study Guide at **bedfordstmartins.com/mckaywest**.

For primary sources from this period, see ***Sources of Western Society*, Second Edition**.

For Web sites, images, and documents related to topics in this chapter, visit Make History at **bedfordstmartins.com/mckaywest**.

21

The Revolution in Energy and Industry

ca. 1780–1850

While the revolution in France was opening a new political era, another revolution was beginning to transform economic and social life. The Industrial Revolution began in Great Britain around the 1780s and started to influence continental Europe after 1815. Some historians see industrial development as basically moderate and evolutionary, but it was rapid and brought about numerous radical changes. Quite possibly only the development of agriculture during Neolithic times had a comparable impact and significance.

The Industrial Revolution profoundly modified much of human experience. It changed patterns of work, transformed the social class structure and the way people thought about class, and eventually altered the international balance of political power. The Industrial Revolution also helped ordinary people gain a higher standard of living as the widespread poverty of the preindustrial world was gradually reduced.

Unfortunately, the improvement in the European standard of living was limited until about 1850 for at least two reasons. First, even in Britain, only a few key industries experienced a technological revolution. Many more industries continued to use old methods, especially on the continent, and this held down the increase in total production. Second, the increase in total population, which began in the eighteenth century (see Chapter 18), continued across Europe as the era of the Industrial Revolution unfolded. The rapid growth in population threatened to eat up the growth in production and to leave most individuals poorer than ever. As a consequence, rapid population growth provided a somber background for European industrialization and made the wrenching transformation all the more difficult. ■

Life in the Industrial Revolution. This realistic painting from mid-nineteenth-century northern England shows women textile workers as they relax and socialize on their lunch break. Most of the workers are young and probably unmarried.

CHAPTER PREVIEW

The Industrial Revolution in Britain
■ What were the origins of the Industrial Revolution in Britain, and how did it develop between 1780 and 1850?

Industrialization in Continental Europe
■ How after 1815 did continental countries respond to the challenge of industrialization?

Relations Between Capital and Labor
■ How did the Industrial Revolution affect people of all social classes, and what measures were taken to improve the conditions of workers?

The Industrial Revolution in Britain

What were the origins of the Industrial Revolution in Britain, and how did it develop between 1780 and 1850? ■

The Industrial Revolution began in Great Britain, that historic union of Scotland and Wales with England—the wealthiest and the dominant part of the country. The transformation in industry was something new in history, and it was quite unplanned. With no models to copy and no idea of what to expect, Britain had to pioneer not only in industrial technology but also in social relations and urban living. Between 1793 and 1815, these formidable tasks were complicated by almost constant war with France. Just as France was the trailblazer in political change, Britain was the leader in economic development, and it must therefore command special attention.

Eighteenth-Century Origins

Although many aspects of the British Industrial Revolution are still matters for scholarly debate, it is generally agreed that the industrial changes that did occur grew out of a long process of development. Without a doubt, the expanding Atlantic economy of the eighteenth century served mercantilist Britain remarkably well. The colonial empire that Britain aggressively built, augmented by a strong position in Latin America and in the African slave trade, provided a growing market for British manufactured goods.

Agriculture also played a central role in bringing about the Industrial Revolution in Britain. English farmers were second only to the Dutch in productivity in 1700, and they were continually adopting new methods of farming as the century went on. The result, especially before 1760, was a period of bountiful crops and low food prices. The ordinary English family did not have to spend almost everything it earned just to buy bread. Thus the family could spend more on manufactured goods—a razor for the man or a shawl for the woman. Moreover, in the eighteenth century the members

Industrial areas
- ■ Coal deposit
- ○ Metal goods
- ▨ Woolen cloth
- — Canals, 1800
- — Navigable rivers

SCOTLAND

Newcastle

North Sea

Manchester
Sheffield
Iron
Birmingham
WALES
Iron
London
Bath
Iron
Exeter

English Channel

Cottage Industry and Transportation in Eighteenth-Century England

of the average British family were redirecting their labor away from unpaid work for household consumption toward work for wages that they could spend on goods, a trend reflecting the increasing commercialization of the entire European economy (see Chapter 18).

As manufacturing expanded to supply both foreign and British customers, the domestic market for raw materials was well-positioned to meet the growing demands of manufacturers. In an age when it was much cheaper to ship goods by water than by land, no part of England was more than fifty miles from navigable water. Beginning in the 1770s, a canal-building boom greatly enhanced this natural advantage. Rivers and canals provided easy movement of England's and Wales's enormous deposits of iron and coal, resources that would be critical raw materials in Europe's early industrial age. Nor were there any tariffs within the country to hinder trade, as there were in France before 1789 and in politically fragmented Germany.

Britain had a host of other assets that helped give rise to its industrial leadership. Unlike eighteenth-century France, Britain had an effective central bank and well-developed credit markets. The monarchy and the aristocratic oligarchy, which had jointly ruled the country since 1688, spent lavishly on stylish luxuries and provided stable and predictable government. At the same time, the government let the domestic economy operate with few controls, encouraging personal initiative, technical change, and a free market. Finally, Britain had long had a large class of hired agricultural laborers, rural proletarians whose numbers were further increased by the second great round of enclosures (the division of common lands into privately held and managed properties) in the late eighteenth century. These rural wage earners were relatively mobile—compared to village-bound peasants in France and western Germany, for example—and along with cottage workers they formed a potential industrial labor force for capitalist entrepreneurs.

All these factors combined to initiate the **Industrial Revolution**, a term first coined by awed contemporaries in the 1830s to describe the burst of major inventions and technical changes they had witnessed in certain industries. This technical revolution went hand in hand with an impressive quickening in the annual rate of industrial growth in Britain. Whereas industry had grown at only 0.7 percent between 1700 and 1760

Industrial Revolution
A term first coined in the 1830s to describe the burst of major inventions and economic expansion that took place in certain industries, such as cotton textiles and iron.

(before the Industrial Revolution), it grew at the much higher rate of 3 percent between 1801 and 1831 (when industrial transformation was in full swing).[1] The decisive quickening of growth probably came in the 1780s, after the American War of Independence (1775–1783) and just before the French Revolution (1789–1799).

Therefore, the great economic and political revolutions that shaped the modern world occurred almost simultaneously, though they began in different countries. The Industrial Revolution was, however, a longer process than the political upheavals. It was not complete in Britain until 1850 at the earliest, and it had no real impact on continental countries until after the end of the Napoleonic wars in 1815.

The First Factories

The pressure to produce more goods for a growing market was directly related to the first decisive breakthrough of the Industrial Revolution—the creation of the world's first large factories in the British cotton textile industry. Technological innovations in the manufacture of cotton cloth led to a new system of production and social relationships. Since no other industry experienced such a rapid or complete transformation before 1830, these trailblazing developments deserve special consideration. Although the putting-out system of merchant capitalism (see Chapter 18) was expanding all across Europe in the eighteenth century, this pattern of rural industry was most fully developed in Britain. There, under the pressure of growing demand, the system's limitations began to outweigh its advantages for the first time. This was especially true in the British textile industry after about 1760.

A constant shortage of thread in the textile industry focused attention on ways of improving spinning. Many a tinkering worker knew that a better spinning wheel promised rich rewards. It proved hard to spin the traditional raw materials—wool and flax—with improved machines, but cotton was different. Cotton textiles had first been imported into Britain from India by the East India Company as a rare and delicate luxury for the upper classes, and by 1760 a tiny domestic cotton industry had emerged in northern England. After many experiments over a generation, a gifted carpenter and jack-of-all-trades, James Hargreaves, invented his cotton-spinning jenny about 1765. At almost the same moment, a barber-turned-manufacturer named Richard Arkwright invented (or possibly pirated) another kind of spinning machine, the water frame. These breakthroughs produced an explosion in the infant cotton textile industry in the 1780s, when it was increasing the value of its output at an unprecedented rate of about 13 percent each year. By 1790 the new machines were producing ten times as much cotton yarn as had been made in 1770.

Hargreaves's **spinning jenny** was simple, inexpensive, and powered by hand. Arkwright's **water frame**, however, quickly acquired a capacity of several hundred spindles and demanded much more power—waterpower. The water frame thus required large specialized mills, factories that employed as many as one thousand workers from the very beginning. The water frame could spin only a coarse, strong thread, which was then put out for respinning on hand-powered cottage jennies. Around 1790, an alternative technique invented by Samuel Crompton also began to require more power than the human arm could supply. After that time, all cotton spinning was gradually concentrated in factories.

The first consequences of these revolutionary developments in the textile industry were more beneficial than is generally believed. Cotton goods became much cheaper, and they were increasingly bought and treasured by all classes. In the past, only the wealthy could afford the comfort and cleanliness of underwear, which was called body linen because it was made from expensive linen cloth. Now millions of poor people, who had earlier worn nothing underneath their coarse, filthy

spinning jenny A simple, inexpensive, hand-powered spinning machine created by James Hargreaves in 1765.

water frame A spinning machine created by Richard Arkwright that had a capacity of several hundred spindles and used waterpower; it therefore required a larger and more specialized mill—a factory.

Woman Working a Spinning Jenny The loose cotton strands on the slanted bobbins shown in this illustration of Hargreaves's spinning jenny passed up to the sliding carriage and then on to the spindles (inset) in back for fine spinning. The worker, almost always a woman, regulated the sliding carriage with one hand, and with the other she turned the crank on the wheel to supply power. By 1783 one woman could spin by hand a hundred threads at a time. (spinning jenny: Mary Evans Picture Library/The Image Works; spindle: Picture Research Consultants & Archives)

outer garments, could afford to wear cotton slips and underpants as well as cotton dresses and shirts. Families using cotton in cottage industry were freed from their constant search for adequate yarn from scattered part-time spinners, since all the thread needed could be spun in the cottage on the jenny or obtained from a nearby factory. The wages of weavers, now hard-pressed to keep up with the spinners, rose markedly until about 1792. Weavers were among the best-paid workers in England. As a result, large numbers of agricultural laborers became hand-loom weavers, while mechanics and capitalists sought to invent a power loom to save on labor costs. This Edmund Cartwright achieved in 1785. But the power looms of the factories worked poorly at first, and hand-loom weavers continued to receive good wages until at least 1800.

Unfortunately, working conditions in the early cotton factories were less satisfactory than those of cottage weavers and spinners, and adult workers were reluctant to work in them. Therefore, factory owners often turned to young children who had been abandoned by their parents and put in the care of local parishes. Parish officers often "apprenticed" such unfortunate foundlings to factory owners. The parish thus saved money, and the factory owners gained workers over whom they exercised almost the authority of slave owners.

Apprenticed as young as five or six years of age, boy and girl workers were forced by law to labor for their "masters" for as many as fourteen years. Housed, fed, and locked up nightly in factory dormitories, the young workers received little or no pay. Hours were appalling—commonly thirteen or fourteen hours a day, six days a week. Harsh physical punishment maintained brutal discipline. To be sure, poor children typically worked long hours and frequently outside the home for brutal masters, but the wholesale coercion of orphans as factory apprentices constituted exploitation on a truly unprecedented scale. This exploitation ultimately piqued the conscience of reformers, reinforced more humanitarian attitudes toward children and their labor in the early nineteenth century, and resulted in laws to protect young workers (see page 678).

A Pioneering Silk Mill In the 1600s Italians invented a machine to spin the thread for the silk that rich people loved. Their carefully guarded secret was stolen in 1717 by John Lombe, who then built this enormous silk mill in England. But the factory production of textiles only took off when the spinning of cotton — a fabric for all classes — was mechanized in the later eighteenth century. (© The Art Gallery Collection/Alamy)

The creation of the world's first modern factories in the British cotton textile industry in the 1770s and 1780s, which grew out of the putting-out system of cottage production, was a major historical development. Both symbolically and substantially, the big new cotton mills marked the beginning of the Industrial Revolution in Britain. By 1831 the largely mechanized cotton textile industry towered above all others, accounting for fully 22 percent of the country's entire industrial production.

The Problem of Energy

The growth of the cotton textile industry might have been stunted or cut short if water from rivers and streams had remained the primary source of power for the new factories, but this did not occur. Instead, an epoch-making solution was found to the age-old problem of energy and power.

Human beings have long used their toolmaking abilities to construct machines that convert one form of energy into another for their own benefit. In the medi-

eval period, people began to develop water mills to grind their grain and windmills to pump water and drain swamps. More efficient use of water and wind in the sixteenth and seventeenth centuries enabled human beings to accomplish more; intercontinental sailing ships were a prime example. Nevertheless, even into the eighteenth century, society continued to rely mainly on wood for energy, and human beings and animals continued to perform most work. This dependence meant that Western civilization remained poor in energy and power. No matter how hard people worked, they could not produce very much.

The shortage of energy had become particularly severe in Britain by the eighteenth century. Wood was in ever-shorter supply, yet it remained tremendously important. It served as the primary source of heat for all homes and industries and as a basic raw material. Processed wood (charcoal) was the fuel that was mixed with iron ore in the blast furnace to produce pig iron. The iron industry's appetite for wood was enormous, and by 1740 the British iron industry was stagnating.

The Steam Engine Breakthrough

As this early energy crisis grew worse, Britain looked toward its abundant and widely scattered reserves of coal as an alternative to its vanishing wood. Coal was first used in Britain in the late Middle Ages as a source of heat. By 1640 most homes in London were heated with coal, and it was also used in industry to provide heat for making beer, glass, soap, and other products. The breakthrough came when industrialists began to use coal to produce mechanical energy and to power machinery.

As more coal was produced, mines were dug deeper and deeper and were constantly filling with water. Mechanical pumps, usually powered by animals walking in circles at the surface, had to be installed. At one mine, fully five hundred horses were used in pumping. Such power was expensive and bothersome. In an attempt to overcome these disadvantages, Thomas Savery in 1698 and Thomas Newcomen in 1705 invented the first primitive **steam engines**. Both engines burned coal to produce steam, which was then used to operate a pump. Although both models were extremely inefficient, by the early 1770s many of the Savery engines and hundreds of the Newcomen engines were operating successfully in English and Scottish mines.

In the early 1760s, a gifted young Scot named James Watt (1736–1819) was drawn to a critical study of the steam engine. Watt was employed at the time by the University of Glasgow as a skilled craftsman making scientific instruments. The Scottish universities were pioneers in practical technical education, and in 1763 Watt was called on to repair a Newcomen engine being used in a physics course. After a series of observations, Watt saw

steam engines A breakthrough invention by Thomas Savery in 1698 and Thomas Newcomen in 1705 that burned coal to produce steam, which was then used to operate a pump; the early models were superseded by James Watt's more efficient steam engine, patented in 1769.

James Nasmyth's Mighty Steam Hammer Nasmyth's invention was the forerunner of the modern pile driver, and its successful introduction in 1832 epitomized the rapid development of steam power technology in Britain. In this painting by the inventor himself, workers manipulate a massive iron shaft being hammered into shape at Nasmyth's foundry near Manchester. (Science & Society Picture Library, London)

that the Newcomen engine's waste of energy could be reduced by adding a separate condenser. This splendid invention, patented in 1769, greatly increased the efficiency of the steam engine.

To invent something in a laboratory is one thing; to make it a practical success is quite another. Watt needed skilled workers, precision parts, and capital, and the relatively advanced nature of the British economy proved essential. A partnership in 1775 with Matthew Boulton, a wealthy English industrialist, provided Watt with adequate capital and exceptional skills in salesmanship that equaled those of the renowned pottery king, Josiah Wedgwood. (See "Individuals in Society: Josiah Wedgwood," page 662.) In the craft tradition of locksmiths, tinsmiths, and millwrights, Watt found skilled mechanics who could install, regulate, and repair his sophisticated engines. From ingenious manufacturers such as the cannonmaker John Wilkinson, Watt was gradually able to purchase precision parts. This support allowed him to create an effective vacuum and regulate a complex engine. In more than twenty years of constant effort, Watt made many further improvements. By the late 1780s, the firm of Boulton and Watt had made the steam engine a practical and commercial success in Britain.

The steam engine of Watt and his followers was the Industrial Revolution's most fundamental advance in technology. For the first time in history, humanity had, at least for a few generations, almost unlimited power at its disposal. For the first time, inventors and engineers could devise and implement all kinds of power equipment to aid people in their work. For the first time, abundance was at least a possibility for ordinary men and women.

The steam engine was quickly put to use in several industries in Britain. It drained mines and made possible the production of ever more coal to feed steam engines elsewhere. Steam power began to replace waterpower in the cotton-spinning mills during the 1780s, contributing greatly to that industry's phenomenal rise. Steam also took the place of waterpower in flour mills, in the malt mills used in breweries, in the flint mills supplying the pottery industry, and in the

mills exported by Britain to the West Indies to crush sugar cane.

Steam power promoted important breakthroughs in other industries. The British iron industry was radically transformed. The use of powerful steam-driven bellows in blast furnaces helped ironmakers switch over rapidly from limited charcoal to unlimited coke (which is made from coal) in the smelting of pig iron after 1770. In the 1780s, Henry Cort developed the puddling furnace, which allowed pig iron to be refined in turn with coke.

Strong, skilled ironworkers—the puddlers— "cooked" molten pig iron in a great vat, raking off globs of refined iron for further processing. Cort also developed heavy-duty steam-powered rolling mills, which were capable of spewing out finished iron in every shape and form. The economic consequence of these technical innovations was a great boom in the British iron industry. In 1740 annual British iron production was only 17,000 tons. With the spread of coke smelting and the impact of Cort's inventions, production had reached 260,000 tons by 1806. In 1844 Britain produced 3 million tons of iron. This was a truly amazing expansion. Once scarce and expensive, iron became the cheap, basic, indispensable building block of the economy.

The Coming of the Railroads

The second half of the eighteenth century saw extensive construction of hard and relatively smooth roads, particularly in France before the Revolution. Yet it was passenger traffic that benefited most from this construction. Overland shipment of freight, relying solely on horsepower, was still quite limited and frightfully expensive; shippers used rivers and canals for heavy freight

The New World of Speed A colorful timetable poster lists the trains from London to Folkstone, the English Channel's gateway port to the European continent, and proudly proclaims a speedy journey. Tunneling through hills and spanning rivers with bridges, railroad construction presented innumerable challenges and required enormous amounts of capital and labor. (Private Collection/The Bridgeman Art Library)

Josiah Wedgwood

INDIVIDUALS IN SOCIETY

AS THE MAKING OF CLOTH AND IRON WAS REVOLUTIONIZED by technical change and factory organization, so too were the production and consumption of pottery. Acquiring beautiful tableware became a craze for eighteenth-century consumers, and continental monarchs often sought prestige in building royal china works. But the grand prize went to Josiah Wedgwood, who wanted to "astonish the world."

The twelfth child of a poor potter, Josiah Wedgwood (1730–1795) grew up in the pottery district of Staffordshire in the English Midlands, where many tiny potteries made simple earthenware utensils for sale in local markets. Growing up as an apprentice in the family business inherited by his oldest brother, Wedgwood struck off on his own in 1752. Soon manager of a small pottery, Wedgwood learned that new products recharged lagging sales. Studying chemistry and determined to succeed, Wedgwood spent his evenings experimenting with different chemicals and firing conditions.

In 1759, after five years of tireless efforts, Wedgwood perfected a beautiful new green glaze. Now established as a master potter, he opened his own factory and began manufacturing teapots and tableware finished in his green and other unique glazes, or adorned with printed scenes far superior to those being produced by competitors. Wedgwood's products caused a sensation among consumers, and his business quickly earned substantial profits. Subsequent breakthroughs, including ornamental vases imitating classical Greek models and jasperware for jewelry, contributed greatly to Wedgwood's success.

Competitors were quick to copy Wedgwood's new products and sell them at lower prices. Thus Wedgwood and his partner Thomas Bentley sought to cultivate an image of superior fashion, taste, and quality in order to develop and maintain a dominant market position. They did this by first capturing the business of the trend-setting elite. In one brilliant coup the partners first sold a very large cream-colored dinner set to Britain's queen, which they quickly christened "Queen's ware" and sold as a very expensive, must-have luxury to English aristocrats. Equally brilliant was Bentley's suave expertise in the elegant London showroom selling Wedgwood's imitation Greek vases, which became the rage after the rediscovery of the Roman towns Pompeii and Herculaneum in the mid-eighteenth century.

Above all, once Wedgwood had secured his position as the luxury market leader, he was able to successfully extend his famous brand to the growing middle class, capturing an enormous mass market for his "useful ware." Thus when sales of a luxury good grew "stale," Wedgwood made tasteful modifications and sold it to the middling classes for twice the price his competitors could charge. This unbeatable combination of mass appeal and high prices all across Europe brought Wedgwood great fame and enormous wealth.

A workaholic with an authoritarian streak, Wedgwood contributed substantially to the development of the factory system. In 1769, he opened a model factory on a new canal he had promoted. With two hun-

Typical Wedgwood jasperware, this elegant cylindrical vase, decorated in the form of a miniature Roman household altar, was destined for the luxury market. (Image copyright © The Metropolitan Museum of Art/Art Resource, NY)

Josiah Wedgwood perfected jasperware, a fine-grained pottery usually made in "Wedgwood blue" with white decoration. (Down House, Kent, Darwin Heirlooms Trust)

dred workers in several departments, Wedgwood exercised tremendous control over his workforce, imposing fines for many infractions, such as being late, drinking on the job, or wasting material. He wanted, he said, to create men who would be like "machines" that "cannot err." Yet Wedgwood also recognized the value in treating workers well. He championed a division of labor that made most workers specialists who received ongoing training. He also encouraged employment of family groups, who were housed in company row houses with long narrow backyards suitable for raising vegetables and chickens. Paying relatively high wages and providing pensions and some benefits, Wedgwood developed a high-quality labor force that learned to accept his rigorous discipline and carried out his ambitious plans.

QUESTIONS FOR ANALYSIS

1. How and why did Wedgwood succeed?
2. Was Wedgwood a good boss or a bad one? Why?
3. How did Wedgwood exemplify the new class of factory owners?

whenever possible. It was logical, therefore, that inventors would try to use steam power.

As early as 1800, an American drove a "steamer on wheels" through city streets. Other experiments followed. In the 1820s, English engineers created steam cars capable of carrying fourteen passengers at ten miles an hour—as fast as the mail coach. But the noisy, heavy steam automobiles frightened passing horses and damaged themselves as well as the roads with their vibrations. For the rest of the century, horses continued to reign on highways and city streets.

The coal industry had long been using plank roads and rails to move coal wagons within mines and at the surface. Rails reduced friction and allowed a horse or a human being to pull a heavier load. Thus once a rail capable of supporting a heavy locomotive was developed in 1816, all sorts of experiments with steam engines on rails went forward. In 1825 after ten years of work, George Stephenson built an effective locomotive. In 1830 his *Rocket* sped down the track of the just-completed Liverpool and Manchester Railway at sixteen miles per hour. This was the world's first important railroad, fittingly steaming in the heart of industrial England. The line from Liverpool to Manchester was a financial as well as a technical success, and many private companies were quickly organized to build more rail lines. Within twenty years, they had completed the main trunk lines of Great Britain (Map 21.1). Other countries were quick to follow.

Rocket The name given to George Stephenson's effective locomotive that was first tested in 1830 on the Liverpool and Manchester Railway at 16 miles per hour.

The significance of the railroad was tremendous. It dramatically reduced the cost and uncertainty of shipping freight over land. This advance had many economic consequences. Previously, markets had tended to be small and local; as the barrier of high transportation costs was lowered, markets became larger and even nationwide. Larger markets encouraged larger factories with more sophisticated machinery in a growing number of industries. Such factories could make goods more cheaply and gradually subjected most cottage workers and many urban artisans to severe competitive pressures.

In all countries, the construction of railroads created a strong demand for unskilled labor and contributed to the growth of a class of urban workers. Hard work on construction gangs was done in the open air with animals and hand tools. Many landless farm laborers and poor peasants, long accustomed to leaving their villages for temporary employment, went to build railroads. By the time the work was finished, life back home in the village often seemed dull and unappealing, and many men drifted to towns in search of work. By the time they sent for their wives and sweethearts to join them, they had become urban workers.

The railroad changed the outlook and values of the entire society. The last and culminating invention of the Industrial Revolution, the railroad dramatically revealed the power and increased the speed of the new age. Racing down a track at sixteen miles per hour or, by 1850, at a phenomenal fifty miles per hour was a new and awesome experience. As a French economist put it after a ride on the Liverpool and Manchester in 1833, "There are certain impressions that one cannot put into words!" Some great painters, notably Joseph M. W. Turner (1775–1851) and Claude Monet (moh-NAY) (1840–1926), succeeded in expressing this sense of power and awe. So did the massive new train stations, the cathedrals of the industrial age. Leading railway engineers such as Isambard Kingdom Brunel and Thomas Brassey, whose tunnels pierced mountains and whose bridges spanned valleys, became public idols — the astronauts of their day. Everyday speech absorbed the images of railroading. After you got up a "full head of steam," you "highballed" along. And if you didn't "go off the track," you might "toot your own whistle." The railroad fired the imagination.

Crystal Palace The location of the Great Exhibition in 1851 in London, an architectural masterpiece made entirely of glass and iron.

Industry and Population

In 1851 London hosted a famous industrial fair called the Great Exhibition in the newly built **Crystal Palace**, an architectural masterpiece that helped draw millions of visitors. (See "Living in the Past: Visiting the Crystal Palace Exhibition," page 666.) For the visiting multitude, one fact stood out: the little island of Britain was the "workshop of the world." Britain alone produced two-thirds of the world's coal and more than one-half of its iron and cotton cloth. More generally, it has been carefully estimated that in 1860 Britain produced a truly remarkable 20 percent of the entire world's output of industrial goods, whereas it had produced only about 2 percent of the world total in 1750.[2] Experiencing revolutionary industrial change, Britain became the first industrial nation (see Map 21.1).

As the British economy significantly increased its production of manufactured goods, the gross national product (GNP) rose roughly fourfold at constant prices between 1780 and 1851. In other words, the British people as a whole increased their wealth and their national income dramatically. At the same time, the population of Britain boomed, growing from about 9 million in 1780 to almost 21 million in 1851. Thus growing numbers consumed much of the increase in total production. According to one important study, average consumption per person increased by only 75 percent between 1780 and 1851, as the growth in the total population ate up a large part of the fourfold increase in GNP in those years.[3]

Although the question is still debated, many economic historians now believe that rapid population growth in Great Britain was not harmful because it facilitated industrial expansion. More people meant a more mobile labor force, with a wealth of young workers in need of employment and ready to go where the jobs were.

Contemporaries were much less optimistic. In his famous and influential *Essay on the Principle of Population* (1798), Thomas Malthus (1766–1834) examined the dynamics of human populations. He argued that "there are few states in which there is not a constant effort in the population to increase beyond the means of subsistence. This constant effort as constantly tends to subject the lower classes of society to distress, and to prevent any great permanent melioration of these conditions."[4]

Map 21.1 The Industrial Revolution in England, ca. 1850 Industry concentrated in the rapidly growing cities of the north and the center of England, where rich coal and iron deposits were close to one another.

Towns with over 20,000 people are shown

50 400 2.4
Thousand Million
Cities with over 100,000 people are labeled

Exposed coal deposit
Industrial area
Principal railroad

SCOTLAND

North Sea

0 50 100 miles
0 50 100 kilometers

Cotton and woolen textiles
Machinery, Iron
Bradford
Manchester
Liverpool
Leeds
Sheffield
Iron Hardware
54°N

Irish Sea

Norwich

WALES
Birmingham
Iron Machinery Pottery

Iron

Bristol
Bath
London

Tin and copper mining
Exeter
Machinery Consumer goods

English Channel
50°N
4°W 0°

❝ There are few states in which there is not a constant effort in the population to increase beyond the means of subsistence. **❞**

—**Thomas Malthus**

Since, in his opinion, population would always tend to grow faster than the food supply, Malthus concluded that the only hope of warding off such "positive checks" to population growth as war, famine, and disease was "prudential restraint." That is, young men and women had to limit the growth of population by the old tried-and-true means of marrying late in life. But Malthus was not optimistic about this possibility. The powerful attraction of the sexes would cause most people to marry early and have many children.

Wealthy English stockbroker and leading economist David Ricardo (1772–1823) coldly spelled out the pessimistic implications of Malthus's thought. Ricardo's depressing **iron law of wages** posited that because of the pressure of population growth, wages would always sink to subsistence level. That is, wages would be just high enough to keep workers from starving. With Malthus and Ricardo setting the tone, economics was soon dubbed "the dismal science."

Malthus, Ricardo, and their many followers were proved wrong—in the long run. However, until the 1820s, or even the 1840s, contemporary observers might reasonably have concluded that the economy and the total population were racing neck and neck, with the outcome very much in doubt. The closeness of the race added to the difficulties inherent in the journey toward industrial civilization. There was another problem as well. Perhaps workers, farmers, and ordinary people did not get their rightful share of the new wealth. Perhaps only the rich got richer, while the poor got poorer or made no progress. We will turn to this great issue after looking at the process of industrialization in continental countries.

Industrialization in Continental Europe

How after 1815 did continental countries respond to the challenge of industrialization? ■

The new technologies developed in the British Industrial Revolution were adopted rather slowly by businesses in continental Europe. Yet by the end of the nineteenth century, several European countries as well as the United States had also industrialized their economies to a con-

siderable but variable degree. This meant that the process of Western industrialization proceeded gradually, with uneven jerks and national and regional variations. Scholars are still struggling to explain these variations, especially since good answers may offer valuable lessons in our own time for poor countries seeking to improve their material condition through industrialization and economic development. The latest findings on the Western experience are encouraging. They suggest that there were alternative paths to the industrial world in the nineteenth century and that, today as then, there was no need to follow a rigid, predetermined British model.

National Variations

European industrialization, like most economic developments, requires some statistical analysis as part of the effort to understand it. Comparative data on industrial production in different countries over time help give us an overview of what happened. One set of data, the work of a Swiss scholar, compares the level of industrialization on a per capita basis in several countries from 1750 to 1913. These data are far from perfect because there are gaps in the underlying records. But they reflect basic trends and are presented in Table 21.1 for closer study.

iron law of wages
Theory proposed by English economist David Ricardo suggesting that the pressure of population growth prevents wages from rising above the subsistence level.

As the heading of Table 21.1 makes clear, this is a per capita comparison of levels of industrialization—a comparison of how much industrial product was produced, on average, for each person in a given country in a given year. Therefore, all the numbers in Table 21.1 are expressed in terms of a single index number of 100, which equals the per capita level of industrial goods in Great Britain (and Ireland) in 1900. Every number in the table is thus a percentage of the 1900 level in Britain and is directly comparable with other numbers. The countries are listed in roughly the order that they began to use large-scale, power-driven technology.

What does this overview of European industrialization tell us? First, and very significantly, one sees in the first column that in 1750 all countries were fairly close together and that Britain was only slightly ahead of its archenemy, France. Second, the column headed 1800 shows that Britain had opened up a noticeable lead over all continental countries by 1800, and that gap progressively widened as the British Industrial Revolution accelerated to 1830 and reached full maturity by 1860. The British level of per capita industrialization was twice

LIVING IN THE PAST

IN 1851 BRITAIN HOSTED A SPECTACULAR EVENT, the Great Exhibition of the Works of Industry of All the Nations, popularly known as the Crystal Palace Exhibition. The more than 6 million visitors from all over Europe marveled at the gigantic new exhibition hall set in the middle of a large, centrally located park. The building was made entirely of glass and iron, both of which were now cheap and abundant in Great Britain. Little wonder that people bought millions of souvenirs picturing the Crystal Palace. The handsome depiction shown here brightened the lid of a ceramic pot.

Entering the 1,800-foot-long domed hall — five times the length of an American football field — visitors could peruse an astonishing 1,500 exhibits arranged by country of origin. Many other exhibits featured machines and industrial products, for the Crystal Palace was the grandest and most recent staging of the industrial fair, which was designed to promote prosperity and the diffusion of technical knowledge. Half of the exhibits were British, and many proudly demonstrated the country's dominant position in machine tools and factory production.

Other countries' displays showed that industrial progress was spreading. For example, the small American exhibit featured a few sophisticated industrial products, such as Samuel Colt's prizewinning six-shot revolver.

This great industrial fair was also a consumer's paradise. In many ways the exhibits foretold the creation of big department stores in the 1860s and 1870s, and even the coming of mass consumption and enclosed shopping malls. While the British dominated in industrial goods, other countries led in the

Lid to a souvenir pot showing the Crystal Palace.
(Fitzwilliam Museum, Cambridge University, UK/Bridgeman Giraudon/The Bridgeman Art Library)

View of the French furniture exhibit. (Private Collection/The Stapleton Collection/The Bridgeman Art Library)

luxury products that greatly appealed to aspiring members of the middle class. The luxury products of French artisans stood out, and France won more prizes in the furniture category than any other nation. Many other handmade luxuries came from Persia, China, and India. Last but not least, the Crystal Palace was equipped with some of the very first public toilets, where a small fee purchased a clean seat, a towel, a comb, and a shoeshine.

QUESTIONS FOR ANALYSIS

1. Describe the Crystal Palace. In what ways was it a revolutionary building?
2. Compare the products that Britain and France presented. How do you explain the differences?
3. The Crystal Palace Exhibition exceeded all expectations. How do you account for its success?

Samuel Colt's six-shot revolver. (Visual Connection Archive)

Table 21.1
Per Capita Levels of Industrialization, 1750–1913

	1750	1800	1830	1860	1880	1900	1913
Great Britain	10	16	25	64	87	100	115
Belgium	9	10	14	28	43	56	88
United States	4	9	14	21	38	69	126
France	9	9	12	20	28	39	59
Germany	8	8	9	15	25	52	85
Austria-Hungary	7	7	8	11	15	23	32
Italy	8	8	8	10	12	17	26
Russia	6	6	7	8	10	15	20
China	8	6	6	4	4	3	3
India	7	6	6	3	2	1	2

Note: All entries are based on an index value of 100, equal to the per capita level of industrialization in Great Britain in 1900. Data for Great Britain includes Ireland, England, Wales, and Scotland.

Source: P. Bairoch, "International Industrialization Levels from 1750 to 1980," *Journal of European Economic History* 11 (Spring 1982): 294, U.S. Journals at Cambridge University Press.

the French level in 1830, for example, and more than three times the French level in 1860. All other large countries (except the United States) had fallen even further behind Britain than France had at both dates.

Third, variations in the timing and in the extent of industrialization in the continental powers and the United States are also apparent. Belgium, achieving independence from the Netherlands in 1831 and rich in iron and coal, led in adopting Britain's new technology, and it experienced a truly revolutionary surge between 1830 and 1860. France developed factory production more gradually, and most historians now detect no burst in French mechanization and no acceleration in the growth of overall industrial output that may accurately be called revolutionary. They stress instead France's relatively good pattern of early industrial growth, which was unjustly tarnished by the spectacular rise of Germany and the United States after 1860. In general, eastern and southern Europe began the process of modern industrialization later than northwestern and central Europe. Nevertheless, these regions made real progress in the late nineteenth century, as growth after 1880 in Austria-Hungary, Italy, and Russia suggests.

Finally, the late but substantial industrialization in eastern and southern Europe meant that all European states (as well as the United States, Canada, and Japan) managed to raise per capita industrial levels in the nineteenth century. These continent-wide increases stood in stark contrast to the large and tragic decreases that occurred at the same time in many non-Western countries, most notably in China and India, as Table 21.1 clearly shows. European countries industrialized to a greater or lesser extent even as most of the non-Western world

deindustrialized. Thus differential rates of wealth- and power-creating industrial development, which heightened disparities within Europe, also greatly magnified existing inequalities between Europe and the rest of the world. We shall return to this momentous change in world economic relationships in Chapter 25.

The Challenge of Industrialization

The different patterns of industrial development suggest that the process of industrialization was far from automatic. Indeed, building modern industry was an awesome challenge. To be sure, throughout Europe the eighteenth century was an era of agricultural improvement, population increase, expanding foreign trade, and growing cottage industry. Thus when the pace of British industry began to accelerate in the 1780s, continental businesses began to adopt the new methods as they proved their profitability. British industry enjoyed clear superiority, but at first the continent was close behind.

By 1815, however, the situation was quite different. No wars in the early industrial period had been fought on British soil, so Britain did not experience nearly as much physical destruction or economic dislocation as the continent did. Rather, despite the wartime challenges that it did face, British industry maintained the momentum of the 1780s and continued to grow and improve between 1789 and 1815. On the continent, by contrast, the upheavals that began with the French Revolution disrupted trade, created runaway inflation, and fostered social anxiety. War severed normal communications between Britain and the continent, severely handicapping continental efforts to use new British machinery and technology. Moreover, the years from 1789 to 1815 were, even for the privileged French economy receiving special favors from Napoleon, a time of "national catastrophe"—in the graphic words of a famous French scholar.[5] Thus France and the rest of Europe were further behind Britain in 1815 than in 1789.

This widening gap made it more difficult, if not impossible, for other countries to follow the British pattern in energy and industry after peace was restored in 1815. Above all, in the newly mechanized industries, British goods were being produced very economically, and these goods had come to dominate world markets completely while the continental states were absorbed in war between 1792 and 1815. In addition, British technology had become so advanced and complicated that very few engineers or skilled technicians outside England understood it. Moreover, the technology of steam power had grown much more expensive. It involved large investments in the iron and coal industries and, after 1830, required the existence of railroads, which were very costly. Continental business people had great difficulty finding the large sums of money the new methods demanded, and there was a shortage of laborers accus-

Mapping the Past

Map 21.2 Continental Industrialization, ca. 1850 Although continental countries were beginning to make progress by 1850, they still lagged far behind Britain. For example, continental railroad building was still in an early stage, whereas the British rail system was essentially complete (see Map 21.1). Coal played a critical role in nineteenth-century industrialization both as a power source for steam engines and as a raw material for making iron and steel.

ANALYZING THE MAP Locate the major exposed (that is, known) coal deposits in 1850. Which countries and areas appear rich in coal resources, and which appear poor? Is there a difference between northern and southern Europe?

CONNECTIONS What is the relationship between known coal deposits and emerging industrial areas in continental Europe? In England (see Map 21.1)?

To complete this activity online, go to the Online Study Guide at bedfordstmartins.com/mckaywest.

tomed to working in factories. All these disadvantages slowed the spread of modern industry (Map 21.2).

After 1815, however, when continental countries began to face up to the British challenge, they had at least three important advantages. First, most continental countries had a rich tradition of putting-out enterprise, merchant capitalists, and skilled urban artisans (see Chapter 18). Such a tradition gave continental firms the ability to adapt and survive in the face of new market conditions. Second, continental capitalists did not need to develop their own advanced technology. Instead,

they could simply "borrow" the new methods developed in Great Britain, as well as engineers and some of the financial resources these countries lacked. European countries such as France and Russia also had a third asset that many non-Western areas lacked in the nineteenth century. They had strong independent governments that did not fall under foreign political control. These governments could fashion economic policies to serve their own interests, as they proceeded to do. They would eventually use the power of the state to promote industry and catch up with Britain.

Agents of Industrialization

The British realized the great value of their technical discoveries and tried to keep their secrets to themselves. Until 1825 it was illegal for artisans and skilled mechanics to leave Britain; until 1843 the export of textile machinery and other equipment was forbidden. Many talented, ambitious workers, however, slipped out of the country illegally and introduced the new methods abroad.

One such man was William Cockerill, a Lancashire carpenter. He and his sons began building cotton-spinning equipment in French-occupied Belgium in 1799. In 1817 the most famous son, John Cockerill, purchased the old summer palace of the deposed bishops of Liège in southern Belgium. Cockerill converted the palace into a large industrial enterprise, which produced machinery, steam engines, and then railway locomotives. He also established modern ironworks and coal mines.

Cockerill's plants in the Liège area became an industrial nerve center, continually gathering new information and transmitting it across Europe. Many skilled British workers came illegally to work for Cockerill, and some went on to found their own companies throughout Europe. Newcomers brought the latest plans and secrets, so Cockerill could boast that ten days after an industrial advance occurred in Britain, he knew all about it in Belgium.

Thus British technicians and skilled workers were a powerful force in the spread of early industrialization. A second agent of industrialization were talented entrepreneurs such as Fritz Harkort, a business pioneer in the German machinery industry. Serving in England as a Prussian army officer during the Napoleonic wars, Harkort was impressed and enchanted with what he saw. He concluded that Germany had to match all these English achievements as quickly as possible. Setting up shop in an abandoned castle in the still-tranquil Ruhr Valley, Harkort felt an almost religious calling to build steam engines and become the "Watt of Germany."

Harkort's basic idea was simple, but it was enormously difficult to carry out. Lacking skilled laborers to do the job, Harkort turned to England for experienced, though expensive, mechanics. Getting materials also posed a great problem. He had to import the thick iron boilers that he needed from England at great cost. In spite of all these problems, Harkort built and sold engines, winning fame and praise. His ambitious efforts over sixteen years also resulted in large financial losses for himself and his partners, and in 1832 he was forced

tariff protection
A government's way of supporting and aiding its own economy by laying high taxes on imported goods from other countries, as when the French responded to cheaper British goods flooding their country by imposing high tariffs on some imported products.

out of his company by his financial backers, who cut back operations to reduce losses. His career illustrates both the great efforts of a few important business leaders to duplicate the British achievement and the difficulty of the task.

Entrepreneurs like Harkort were obviously exceptional. Most continental businesses adopted factory technology slowly, and handicraft methods lived on. Indeed, continental industrialization usually brought substantial but uneven expansion of handicraft industry in both rural and urban areas for a time. Artisan production of luxury items grew in France as the rising income of the international middle class created foreign demand for silk scarves, embroidered needlework, perfumes, and fine wines.

Government Support and Corporate Banking

Another major force in continental industrialization was government, which often helped business people in continental countries to overcome some of their difficulties. **Tariff protection** was one such support, and it proved quite important. For example, after Napoleon's wars ended in 1815, France was suddenly flooded with cheaper and better British goods. The French government responded by laying high tariffs on many British imports in order to protect the French economy. After 1815 continental governments bore the cost of building roads and canals to improve transportation. They also bore to a significant extent the cost of building railroads. Belgium led the way in the 1830s and 1840s. In an effort to tie the newly independent nation together, the Belgian government decided to construct a state-owned system. Built rapidly as a unified network, Belgium's state-owned railroads stimulated the development of heavy industry and made the country an early industrial leader. Several of the smaller German states also built state systems.

The Prussian government provided another kind of invaluable support. It guaranteed that the state treasury would pay the interest and principal on railroad bonds if the closely regulated private companies in Prussia were unable to do so. Thus railroad investors in Prussia ran little risk, and capital was quickly raised. In France the state shouldered all the expense of acquiring and laying roadbed, including bridges and tunnels. Finished roadbed was leased to a carefully supervised private company, which usually benefited from a state guarantee of its debts. In short, governments helped pay for railroads, the all-important leading sector in continental industrialization.

The career of German journalist and thinker Friedrich List (1789–1846) reflects government's greater role in industrialization on the continent than in England. List considered the growth of modern industry of the utmost importance because manufacturing was a primary means of increasing people's well-being and relieving their poverty. Moreover, List was a dedicated nationalist. He wrote that the "wider the gap between the backward and advanced nations becomes, the more dangerous it is to remain behind." A backward, agricultural nation was not only poor but also weak, increasingly unable to defend itself and maintain its political independence. To promote industry was to defend the nation.

The practical policies that List focused on in articles and in his influential *National System of Political Economy* (1841) were railroad building and the tariff. List supported the formation of a customs union, or *Zollverein* (TSOL-feh-rign), among the separate German states. Such a tariff union came into being in 1834, allowing goods to move between the German member states without tariffs, while erecting a single uniform tariff against other nations. List wanted a high protective tariff, which would encourage infant industries, allowing them to de-

❝ The wider the gap between the backward and advanced nations becomes, the more dangerous it is to remain behind. ❞
—**FRIEDRICH LIST**

velop and eventually hold their own against their more advanced British counterparts. He denounced the British doctrine of free trade as part of Britain's attempt to dominate the entire world.

> *At no other epoch has the world seen a manufacturing and commercial power possessing such immense resources as those in the hands of the power which now holds sway [Britain] pursuing a system that is so consistently selfish. It is absorbing with untiring energy the manufacturing and commercial industries of the world and the important colonies, and it is making the rest of the world, like the Hindus, its serfs in all industrial and commercial relations.*[6]

A German Ironworks, 1845 The Borsig ironworks in Berlin mastered the new British method of smelting iron ore with coke. Germany, and especially the state of Prussia, was well endowed with both iron and coal, and the rapid exploitation of these resources after 1840 transformed a poor agricultural country into an industrial powerhouse. (akg-images)

By the 1840s List's **economic nationalism**, designed to protect and develop the national economy, had become increasingly popular in Germany and elsewhere.

economic nationalism Policies aimed at protecting and developing a country's economy.

class-consciousness An individual's sense of class differentiation.

Finally, banks, like governments, also played a larger and more creative role on the continent than in Britain. Previously, almost all banks in Europe had been private, organized as secretive partnerships. Because of the possibility of unlimited financial loss, the partners of private banks tended to be quite conservative and were content to deal with a few rich clients and a few big merchants. They generally avoided industrial investment as being too risky.

In the 1830s, two important Belgian banks pioneered in a new direction. They received permission from the growth-oriented government to establish themselves as corporations enjoying limited liability. That is, stockholders could now lose only their original investments in the bank's common stock, and they could not be forced by the courts to pay for any additional losses out of other property they owned if the bank went bankrupt. Publicizing the risk-reducing advantage of limited liability for investors, these Belgian banks were able to attract many shareholders, large and small. They mobilized impressive resources for investment in big companies, became industrial banks, and successfully promoted industrial development.

Similar corporate banks became important in France and Germany in the 1850s and 1860s. Usually working in collaboration with governments, corporate banks established and developed many railroads and many companies working in heavy industry, which were also increasingly organized as limited liability corporations. The most famous such bank was the Crédit Mobilier of Paris, founded by Isaac and Emile Pereire, two young Jewish journalists from Bordeaux. The Crédit Mobilier advertised extensively. It used the savings of thousands of small investors as well as the resources of big ones. The activities of the bank were far-reaching; it built railroads all over France and Europe. As Emile Pereire had said in 1835, "It is not enough to outline gigantic programs on paper. I must write my ideas on the earth."

The combined efforts of skilled workers, entrepreneurs, governments, and industrial banks meshed successfully between 1850 and the financial crash of 1873. This was a period of unprecedentedly rapid economic growth on the continent. In Belgium, Germany, and France, key indicators of modern industrial development—such as railway mileage, iron and coal production, and steam-engine capacity—increased at average annual rates of 5 to 10 percent. As a result, rail networks were completed in western and much of central Europe, and the leading continental countries mas-

tered the industrial technologies that had first been developed in Great Britain. In the early 1870s, Britain was still Europe's most industrial nation, but a select handful of countries were closing the gap that had been opened up by the Industrial Revolution.

Relations Between Capital and Labor

How did the Industrial Revolution affect people of all social classes, and what measures were taken to improve the conditions of workers? ■

Industrial development brought new social relations and intensified long-standing problems between capital and labor in both urban workshops and cottage industry (see Chapter 18). A new group of factory owners and industrial capitalists arose. These men and women and their families strengthened the wealth and size of the middle class, which had previously been made up mainly of merchants and professional people. The nineteenth century became the golden age of the middle class. Modern industry also created a much larger group, the factory workers. For the first time, large numbers of men, women, and children came together under one roof to work with complicated machinery for a single owner or a few partners in large companies.

The growth of new occupational groups in industry stimulated new thinking about social relations. Often combined with reflections on the French Revolution, this thinking led to the development of a new overarching interpretation—a new paradigm—regarding social relationships. Briefly, this paradigm argued, with considerable success, that individuals were members of economically determined classes that had conflicting interests. Accordingly, the comfortable, well-educated "public" of the eighteenth century came increasingly to see itself as the backbone of the middle class (or the middle classes), and the "people" gradually transformed themselves into the modern working class (or working classes). And if the new class interpretation was more of a deceptive simplification than a fundamental truth for some critics, it appealed to many because it seemed to explain what was happening. Therefore, conflicting classes existed, in part, because many individuals came to believe they existed and developed an appropriate sense of class feeling—what Marxists call **class-consciousness**.

The New Class of Factory Owners

Early industrialists operated in a highly competitive economic system. As the careers of Watt and Harkort illustrate, there were countless production problems, and

Picturing the Past

Ford Maddox Brown, *Work* This midcentury painting provides a rich and realistic visual representation of the new concepts of social class that became common by 1850. (Birmingham Museums and Art Gallery/The Bridgeman Art Library)

ANALYZING THE IMAGE Describe the different types of work shown. What different social classes are depicted, and what kinds of work (or leisure) are the members of the different social classes engaged in?

CONNECTIONS What does this painting and Ford's title for it (*Work*) suggest about the artist's opinion of the work of common laborers?

To complete this activity online, go to the Online Study Guide at bedfordstmartins.com/mckaywest.

success and large profits were by no means certain. Manufacturers therefore waged a constant battle to cut their production costs and stay afloat. Much of the profit had to go back into the business for new and better machinery. "Dragged on by the frenzy of this terrible life," according to one of the dismayed critics, the struggling manufacturer had "no time for niceties. He must conquer or die, make a fortune or drown himself."[7]

Most early industrialists drew upon their families and friends for labor and capital, but they came from a variety of backgrounds. Many, such as Harkort, were from well-established merchant families with a rich network of contacts and support. Others, such as Watt, Wedgwood, and Cockerill, were of modest means, especially in the early days. Artisans and skilled workers of exceptional ability had unparalleled opportunities.

Members of ethnic and religious groups who had been discriminated against in the traditional occupations controlled by the landed aristocracy jumped at the new chances and often helped one another. Scots, Quakers, and other Protestant dissenters were tremendously important in Britain; Protestants and Jews dominated banking in Catholic France. Many of the industrialists were newly rich, and, not surprisingly, they were very proud and self-satisfied.

As factories and firms grew larger, opportunities declined, at least in well-developed industries. It became considerably harder for a gifted but poor young mechanic to start a small enterprise and end up as a wealthy manufacturer. Formal education (for sons and males) became more important as a means of success and advancement, and formal education at the advanced level was expensive. In Britain by 1830 and in France and Germany by 1860, leading industrialists were more likely to have inherited their well-established enterprises, and they were financially much more secure than their struggling fathers and mothers had been. They also had a greater sense of class-consciousness; they were fully aware that ongoing industrial development had widened the gap between themselves and their workers.

The wives and daughters of successful businessmen also found fewer opportunities for active participation in Europe's increasingly complex business world. Rather than contributing as vital partners in a family-owned enterprise, as so many middle-class women had done, these women were increasingly valued for their ladylike gentility. By 1850 some influential women writers and most businessmen assumed that middle-class wives and daughters should steer clear of undignified work in offices and factories. Rather, a middle-class lady should protect and enhance her femininity. She should concentrate on her proper role as wife and mother, preferably in an elegant residential area far removed from ruthless commerce and the volatile working class.

The New Factory Workers

The social consequences of the Industrial Revolution have long been hotly debated. The condition of British workers during the transformation has always generated the most controversy among historians because Britain was the first country to industrialize and because the social consequences seemed harshest there. Before 1850 other countries had not proceeded very far with industrialization, and almost everyone agrees that the economic conditions of European workers improved after 1850. Thus the experience of British workers to about 1850 deserves special attention. (Industrial growth also promoted rapid urbanization, with its own awesome problems, as will be shown in Chapter 23.)

From the beginning, the Industrial Revolution in Britain had its critics. Among the first were the romantic poets. William Blake (1757–1827) called the early factories "satanic mills" and protested against the hard life of the London poor. William Wordsworth (1770–1850) lamented the destruction of the rural way of life and the pollution of the land and water. Some handicraft workers—notably the **Luddites**, who attacked whole factories in northern England in 1812 and after—smashed the new machines, which they believed were putting them out of work. Doctors and reformers wrote eloquently of problems in the factories and new towns, while Malthus and Ricardo concluded that workers would earn only enough to stay alive.

Luddites Group of handicraft workers who attacked whole factories in northern England in 1812 and after, smashing the new machines that they believed were putting them out of work.

This pessimistic view was accepted and reinforced by Friedrich Engels (1820–1895), the future revolutionary and colleague of Karl Marx. After studying conditions in northern England, this young middle-class German published in 1844 *The Condition of the Working Class in England*, a blistering indictment of the middle classes. "At the bar of world opinion," he wrote, "I charge the English middle classes with mass murder, wholesale robbery, and all the other crimes in the calendar." The new poverty of industrial workers was worse than the old poverty of cottage workers and agricultural laborers, according to Engels. The culprit was industrial capitalism, with its relentless competition and constant technical change. Engels's extremely influential charge of middle-class exploitation and increasing worker poverty was embellished by Marx and later socialists.

Meanwhile, other observers believed that conditions were improving for the working people. Andrew Ure (yoo-RAY) wrote in 1835 in his study of the cotton industry that conditions in most factories were not harsh and were even quite good. Edwin Chadwick, a great and conscientious government official well acquainted with the problems of the working population, concluded that the "whole mass of the laboring community" was increasingly able "to buy more of the necessities and minor luxuries of life."[8] Nevertheless, those who thought conditions were getting worse for working people were probably in the majority.

In an attempt to go beyond the contradictory judgments of contemporaries, some historians have looked at different kinds of sources. Statistical evidence is one such source. If working people suffered a great economic decline, as Engels and later socialists asserted, then the purchasing power of the working person's wages must have declined drastically.

Scholarly statistical studies have weakened the idea that the condition of the working class got much worse with industrialization. But the most recent scholarship also confirms the view that the early years of the Industrial Revolution were hard ones for British workers. There was little or no increase in the purchasing power of the average British worker from about 1780 to about 1820. The years from 1792 to 1815, a period of almost constant warfare with France, were particularly difficult. Food prices rose faster than wages, and the living conditions of the laboring poor declined. Only after 1820, and especially after 1840, did real wages rise substantially, so that the average worker earned and consumed roughly 50 percent more in real terms in 1850 than in 1770.[9] In short, there was considerable economic improvement for workers throughout Great Britain by 1850, but that improvement was hard won and slow in coming.

This important conclusion must be qualified, however. First, the hours in the average workweek increased, as some economic historians now believe it had been increasing in parts of northern Europe since the late seventeenth century. Thus, to a large extent, workers earned more simply because they worked more. Indeed, in England nonagricultural workers labored about 250 days per year in 1760 as compared to 300 days per year in 1830, while the normal workday remained an exhausting eleven hours throughout the entire period. In 1760 nonagricultural workers still observed many religious and public holidays by not working, and Monday was popularly known as "Saint Monday" because so many workers took the day off. These days of leisure and relaxation declined rapidly after 1760, and by 1830 nonagricultural workers had joined landless agricultural laborers in toiling six rather than five days a week.[10]

Second, the wartime decline in the average worker's real wages and standard of living from 1792 to 1815 had a powerful negative impact on workers. These difficult war years, with more unemployment and sharply higher prices for bread, were formative years for the new factory labor force, and they colored the early experience of modern industrial life in somber tones.

Another way to consider the workers' standard of living is to look at the goods that they purchased. Again

the evidence is somewhat contradictory. Speaking generally, workers ate somewhat more food of higher nutritional quality as the Industrial Revolution progressed, except during wartime. Diets became more varied; people ate more potatoes, dairy products, fruits, and vegetables. Clothing improved, but housing for working people probably deteriorated somewhat. In short, per capita use of specific goods supports the position that the standard of living of the working classes rose, at least moderately, after the long wars with France.

Work in Early Factories

What about working conditions? Did workers eventually earn more only at the cost of working longer and harder? Were workers exploited harshly by the new factory owners?

The first factories were cotton mills, which began functioning in the 1770s along fast-running rivers and streams and were often located in sparsely populated areas. Cottage workers in the vicinity, accustomed to the putting-out system, were reluctant to work in the new factories even when they received relatively good wages because factory work was unappealing. In the

Workers at a Large Cotton Mill This 1833 engraving shows adult women operating power looms under the supervision of a male foreman, and it accurately reflects both the decline of family employment and the emergence of a gender-based division of labor in many English factories. The jungle of belts and shafts connecting the noisy looms to the giant steam engine on the ground floor created a constant din. (Time Life Pictures/Getty Images)

LISTENING TO THE PAST

The use of child labor in British industrialization quickly attracted the attention of humanitarians and social reformers. This interest led to investigations by parliamentary commissions, which resulted in laws limiting the hours and the ages of children working in large factories. Designed to build a case for remedial legislation, parliamentary inquiries gave large numbers of workers a rare chance to speak directly to contemporaries and to historians.

The moving passages that follow are taken from testimony gathered in 1841 and 1842 by the Ashley Mines Commission. Interviewing employers and many male and female workers, the commissioners focused on the physical condition of the youth and on the sexual behavior of workers far underground. The subsequent Mines Act of 1842 sought to reduce immoral behavior and sexual bullying by prohibiting underground work for all women and girls (and for boys younger than ten).

Mr. Payne, coal master

❝ That children are employed generally at nine years old in the coal pits and sometimes at eight. In fact, the smaller the vein of coal is in height, the younger and smaller are the children required; the work occupies from six to seven hours per day in the pits; they are not ill-used or worked beyond their strength; a good deal of depravity exists but they are certainly not worse in morals than in other branches of the Sheffield trade, but upon the whole superior; the morals of this district are materially improving; Mr. Bruce, the clergyman, has been zealous and active in endeavoring to ameliorate their moral and religious education. . . . ❞

Ann Eggley, hurrier, 18 years old

❝ I'm sure I don't know how to spell my name. We go at four in the morning, and sometimes at half-past four. We begin to work as soon as we get down. We get out after four, sometimes at five, in the evening. We work the whole time except an hour for dinner, and sometimes we haven't time to eat. I hurry [move coal wagons underground] by myself, and have done so for long. I know the corves [small coal wagons] are very heavy, they are the biggest corves anywhere about. The work is far too hard for me; the sweat runs off me all over sometimes. I am very tired at night. Sometimes when we get home at night we have not power to wash us, and then we go to bed. Sometimes we fall asleep in the chair. Father said last night it was both a shame and a disgrace for girls to work as we do, but there was naught else for us to do. I began to hurry when I was seven and I have been hurrying ever since. I have been 11 years in the pits. The girls are always tired. I was poorly twice this winter; it was with headache. I hurry for Robert Wiggins; he is not akin to me. . . . We don't always get enough to eat and drink, but we get a good supper. I have known my father go at two in the morning to work . . . and he didn't come out till four. I am quite sure that we work constantly 12 hours except on Saturdays. We wear trousers and our shifts in the pit and great big shoes clinkered and nailed. The girls never work naked to the waist in our pit. The men don't insult us in the pit. The conduct of the girls in the pit is good enough sometimes and sometimes bad enough. I never went to a day-school. I went a little to a Sunday-school, but I soon gave it over. I thought it too bad to be confined both Sundays and week-days. I walk about and get the fresh air on Sundays. I have not learnt to read. I don't know my letters. I never learnt naught. I never go to church or chapel; there is no church or chapel at Gawber, there is none nearer than a mile. . . . I have never heard that a good man came into the world who was God's son to save sinners. I never heard of Christ at all. Nobody has ever told me about him, nor have my father and mother ever taught me to pray. I know no prayer; I never pray. ❞

Patience Kershaw, aged 17

❝ My father has been dead about a year; my mother is living and has ten children, five lads and five lasses; the oldest is about thirty, the youngest is four; three lasses go to mill; all the lads are colliers, two getters and three hurriers; one lives at home and does nothing; mother does nought but look after home.

factory, workers had to keep up with the machine and follow its relentless tempo. Moreover, they had to show up every day, on time, and work long, monotonous hours under the constant supervision of demanding overseers, and they were punished systematically if they broke the work rules. For example, if a worker was late to work, or accidentally spoiled material, or nodded off late in the day, the employer imposed fines that were deducted from the weekly pay. Children and adolescents were often beaten for their infractions.

Cottage workers were not used to that kind of life and discipline. All members of the family worked hard and long, but in spurts, setting their own pace. They could interrupt their work when they wanted to. Women

This illustration of a girl dragging a coal wagon was one of several that shocked public opinion and contributed to the Mines Act of 1842. (© British Library Board)

All my sisters have been hurriers, but three went to the mill. Alice went because her legs swelled from hurrying in cold water when she was hot. I never went to day-school; I go to Sunday-school, but I cannot read or write; I go to pit at five o'clock in the morning and come out at five in the evening; I get my breakfast of porridge and milk first; I take my dinner with me, a cake, and eat it as I go; I do not stop or rest any time for the purpose; I get nothing else until I get home, and then have potatoes and meat, not every day meat. I hurry in the clothes I have now got on, trousers and ragged jacket; the bald place upon my head is made by thrusting the corves; my legs have never swelled, but sisters' did when they went to mill; I hurry the corves a mile and more under ground and back; they weigh 300 cwt.;* I hurry 11 a day; I wear a belt and chain at the workings to get the corves out; the putters [miners] that I work for are *naked* except their caps; they pull off all their clothes; I see them at work when I go up; sometimes they beat me, if I am not quick enough, with their hands; they strike me upon my back; the boys take liberties with me, sometimes, they pull me about; I am the only girl in the pit; there are about 20 boys and 15 men; all the men are naked; I would rather work in mill than in coal-pit. 〞

*An old English unit of weight equaling 112 pounds.

Isabel Wilson, 38 years old, coal putter

〝When women have children thick [fast] they are compelled to take them down early. I have been married 19 years and have had 10 bairns [children]; seven are in life. When on Sir John's work was a carrier of coals, which caused me to miscarry five times from the strains, and was gai [very] ill after each. Putting is no so oppressive; last child was born on Saturday morning, and I was at work on the Friday night.

Once met with an accident; a coal brake my cheek-bone, which kept me idle some weeks. I have wrought below 30 years, and so has the guid man; he is getting touched in the breath now.

None of the children read, as the work is no regular. I did read once, but no able to attend to it now; when I go below lassie 10 years of age keeps house and makes the broth or stir-about. 〞

Source: *Voices of the Industrial Revolution: Selected Readings from the Liberal Economists and Their Critics*, pp. 87–90, edited by J. Bowditch and C. Ramsland (Ann Arbor: The University of Michigan Press, 1961). Reprinted by permission of the publisher.

QUESTIONS FOR ANALYSIS

1. How does Payne's testimony compare with that of Ann Eggley and Patience Kershaw?

2. Describe the work of Eggley, Kershaw, and Wilson. What strikes you most about the testimonies of these workers?

3. The witnesses were responding to questions from middle-class commissioners. What did the commissioners seem interested in? Why?

and children could break up their long hours of spinning with other tasks. On Saturday afternoon the head of the family delivered the week's work to the merchant manufacturer and got paid. Saturday night was a time of relaxation and drinking, especially for the men. Recovering from his hangover on Tuesday, the weaver bent to his task on Wednesday and then worked frantically to meet his deadline on Saturday. Like some students today, he might "pull an all-nighter" on Thursday or Friday in order to get his work in.

Also, early factories resembled English poorhouses, where totally destitute people went to live at public expense. Some poorhouses were industrial prisons, where the inmates had to work in order to receive their food and lodging. The similarity between large brick factories and large stone poorhouses increased the cottage workers' fear of factories and their hatred of factory discipline. It was cottage workers' reluctance to work in factories that prompted the early cotton mill owners to turn to abandoned and pauper children for their labor. As we have seen, these owners contracted with local officials to employ large numbers of these children, who had no say in the matter. Pauper children were often badly treated and terribly overworked in the mills, as they were when they were apprenticed as chimney sweeps, market girls, shoemakers, and so forth. In the eighteenth century, semi-forced child labor seemed necessary and was socially accepted. From our modern point of view, it was cruel exploitation and a blot on the record of the new industrial system.

Working Families and Children

By the 1790s the early pattern was rapidly changing. The use of pauper apprentices was in decline, and in 1802 it was forbidden by Parliament. Many more textile factories were being built, mainly in urban areas, where they could use steam power rather than water-power and attract a workforce more easily than in the countryside. The need for workers was great. As a result, people came from near and far to work in the cities, both as factory workers and as laborers, builders, and domestic servants. Yet as they took these new jobs, working people did not simply give in and accept the highly disciplined system of labor that had formerly repelled them. Rather, they helped modify the system by carrying over old, familiar working traditions.

For one thing, workers often came to the mills and the mines as family units. This was how they had worked on farms and in the putting-out system. The mill or mine owner bargained with the head of the family and paid him or her for the work of the whole family. In the cotton mills, children worked for their mothers or fathers, collecting scraps and "piecing" broken threads together. In the mines, children sorted coal and worked the ventilation equipment. Their mothers hauled coal in the tunnels below the surface, while their fathers hewed with pick and shovel at the face of the seam.

The preservation of the family as an economic unit in the factories from the 1790s on made the new surroundings more tolerable, both in Great Britain and in other countries, during the early stages of industrialization. Parents disciplined their children, making firm measures socially acceptable, and directed their upbringing. The presence of the whole family meant that children and adults worked the same long hours (twelve-hour shifts were normal in cotton mills in 1800). In the early years, some very young children were employed solely to keep the family together. For example, the early industrialist Jedediah Strutt believed that children should be at least ten years old to work in his textile mills, but he reluctantly employed seven-year-olds to satisfy their parents. Adult workers were not particularly interested in limiting the minimum working age or hours of their children as long as family members worked side by side. Only when technical changes threatened to place control and discipline in the hands of impersonal managers and overseers did adult workers protest against inhuman conditions in the name of their children.

Some enlightened employers and social reformers in Parliament definitely felt otherwise. They argued that more humane standards were necessary, and they used widely circulated parliamentary reports to influence public opinion. For example, Robert Owen (1771–1858), a very successful manufacturer in Scotland, testified in 1816 before an investigating committee on the basis of his experience. He stated that "very strong facts" demonstrated that employing children under ten years of age as factory workers was "injurious to the children, and not beneficial to the proprietors."[11] Workers also provided graphic testimony at such hearings as the reformers pressed Parliament to pass corrective laws. They scored some important successes.

Their most significant early accomplishment was the **Factory Act of 1833**. It limited the factory workday for children between nine and thirteen to eight hours and that of adolescents between fourteen and eighteen to twelve hours, although the act made no effort to regulate the hours of work for children at home or in small businesses. Children under nine were to be enrolled in the elementary schools that factory owners were required to establish. The employment of children declined rapidly. Thus the Factory Act broke the pattern of whole families working together in the factory because efficiency required standardized shifts for all workers.

Ties of blood and kinship were important in other ways in Great Britain in the formative years between about 1790 and 1840. Many manufacturers and builders hired workers through subcontractors. They paid the subcontractors on the basis of what the subcontractors and their crews produced—for smelting so many tons of pig iron or moving so much dirt or gravel for a canal or roadbed. Subcontractors in turn hired and fired their own workers, many of whom were friends and relations. The subcontractor might be as harsh as the greediest capitalist, but the relationship between subcontractor and work crew was close and personal. This kind of personal relationship had traditionally existed in cottage industry and in urban crafts, and it was more acceptable to many workers than impersonal factory discipline. This system also provided people with an easy way to find a job. Even today, a friend or relative who is

Factory Act of 1833 English law that led to a sharp decline in the employment of children by limiting the hours that children over age nine could work and requiring younger children to attend factory-run elementary schools.

a supervisor is frequently worth a host of formal application forms.

Ties of kinship were particularly important for newcomers, who often traveled great distances to find work. Many urban workers in Great Britain were from Ireland. Forced out of rural Ireland by population growth and deteriorating economic conditions from 1817 on, Irish in search of jobs took what they could get. As early as 1824, most of the workers in the Glasgow cotton mills were Irish; in 1851 one-sixth of the population of Liverpool was Irish. Like many other immigrant groups held together by ethnic and religious ties, the Irish worked together, formed their own neighborhoods, and not only survived but also thrived.

The Sexual Division of Labor

The era of the Industrial Revolution witnessed major changes in the sexual division of labor. In preindustrial Europe most people generally worked in family units. By tradition, certain jobs were defined by gender—women and girls for milking and spinning, men and boys for plowing and weaving—but many tasks might go to either sex. Family employment carried over into early factories and subcontracting, but by the 1830s it was collapsing as child labor was restricted and new attitudes emerged. A different sexual division of labor gradually arose to take its place. By 1850 the man was emerging as the family's primary wage earner, while the married woman found only limited job opportunities. Generally denied good jobs at good wages in the growing urban economy, women were expected to concentrate on housework, raising the children, and some craftwork at home.

This new pattern of **separate spheres**, which will be considered further in Chapter 23, had several aspects. First, all studies agree that married women from the working classes were much less likely to work full-time for wages outside the house after the first child arrived, although they often earned small amounts doing putting-out handicrafts at home and taking in boarders. Second, when married women did work for wages outside the house, they usually came from the poorest families, where the husbands were poorly paid, sick, unemployed, or missing. Third, these poor married or widowed women were joined by legions of young unmarried women, who worked full-time but only in certain jobs, of which textile factory work, laundering, and domestic service were particularly important. Fourth, all women were generally confined to low-paying, dead-end jobs. Virtually no occupation open to women paid a wage sufficient for a person to live independently. Men predominated in the better-paying, more promising employments. Evolving gradually, but largely in place by 1850, the new sexual division of labor in Britain constituted a major development in the history of women and of the family.

If the reorganization of paid work along gender lines is widely recognized, there is no agreement on its causes. One school of scholars sees little connection with industrialization and finds the answer in the deeply ingrained sexist attitudes of a "patriarchal tradition," which predated the economic transformation. These scholars stress the role of male-dominated craft unions in denying working women access to good jobs and relegating them to unpaid housework. Other scholars, stressing that the gender roles of women and men can vary enormously with time and culture, look more to a combination of economic and biological factors in order to explain the emergence of a sex-segregated division of labor.

Three ideas stand out in this more recent interpretation. First, the new and unfamiliar discipline of the clock and the machine was especially hard on married women of the laboring classes. Above all, relentless factory discipline conflicted with child care in a way that labor on the farm or in the cottage had not. A woman operating earsplitting spinning machinery could mind a child of seven or eight working beside her (until such work was outlawed), but she could no longer pace herself through pregnancy or breast-feed her baby on the job. Thus a working-class woman had strong incentives to concentrate on child care within her home if her family could afford it.

Second, running a household in conditions of primitive urban poverty was an extremely demanding job in its own right. There were no supermarkets or public transportation. Everything had to be done on foot. Shopping and feeding the family constituted a never-ending challenge. The wife marched from one tiny shop to another, dragging her tired children (for who was to watch them?) and struggling valiantly with heavy sacks and tricky shopkeepers. Yet another brutal job outside the house—a "second shift"—had limited appeal for the average married woman from the working class. Thus many women might well have accepted the emerging division of labor as the best available strategy for family survival in the industrializing society.[12]

> **separate spheres** A gender division of labor with the wife at home as mother and homemaker and the husband as wage earner.

Third, why were the young, generally unmarried women who did work for wages outside the home segregated and confined to certain "women's jobs"? No doubt the desire of males to monopolize the best opportunities and hold women down provides part of the answer. Yet as some feminist scholars have argued, sex-segregated employment was also a collective response to the new industrial system. Previously, at least in theory, young people worked under a watchful parental eye. The growth of factories and mines brought unheard-of opportunities for girls and boys to mix on the job, free of familial supervision. Continuing to mix after work, they were "more likely to form liaisons, initiate courtships, and respond to advances."[13] Such intimacy also led to more unplanned pregnancies and fueled the illegitimacy explosion that had begun in the late eighteenth century and that gathered force until at least 1850 (see Chapter 19). Thus segregation of jobs by gender was partly an effort by older people to help control the sexuality of working-class youths.

Investigations into the British coal industry before 1842 provide a graphic example of this concern. (See "Listening to the Past: The Testimony of Young Mine Workers," page 676.) The middle-class men leading the inquiry, who expected their daughters and wives to pursue ladylike activities, often failed to appreciate the physical effort of the girls and women who dragged with belt and chain the heavy carts of coal along narrow underground passages. But they professed horror at the sight of girls and women working without shirts, which was a common practice because of the heat, and they quickly assumed the prevalence of licentious sex with the male miners, who also wore very little clothing. In fact, most girls and married women worked for related males in a family unit that provided considerable protection and restraint. Yet many witnesses from the working class also believed that "blackguardism and debauchery" were common and that "they are best out of the pits, the lasses." Some miners stressed particularly the danger of sexual aggression for girls working past puberty. As one explained: "I consider it a scandal for girls to work in the pits. Till they are 12 or 14 they may work very well but after that it's an abomination. . . . The work of the pit does not hurt them, it is the effect on their morals that I complain of."[14]

Mines Act of 1842 English law prohibiting underground work for all women and girls as well as for boys under ten.

The **Mines Act of 1842** prohibited underground work for all women and girls as well as for boys under ten.

Some women who had to support themselves protested against being excluded from coal mining, which paid higher wages than most other jobs open to working-class women. But provided they were part of families that could manage economically, the girls and the women who had worked underground were generally pleased with the law. In explaining her satisfaction in 1844, one mother of four provided real insight into why many married working women accepted the emerging sexual division of labor:

While working in the pit I was worth to my [miner] husband seven shillings a week, out of which we had to pay 2½ shillings to a woman for looking after the younger children. I used to take them to her house at 4 o'clock in the morning, out of their own beds, to put them into hers. Then there was one shilling a week for washing; besides, there was mending to pay for, and other things. The house was not guided. The other children broke things; they did not go to school when they were sent; they would be playing about, and get ill-used by other children, and their clothes torn. Then when I came home in the evening, everything was to do after the day's labor, and I was so tired I had no heart for it; no fire lit, nothing cooked, no water fetched, the house dirty, and nothing comfortable for my husband. It is all far better now, and I wouldn't go down again.[15]

The Early Labor Movement in Britain

Many kinds of employment changed slowly during and after the Industrial Revolution in Great Britain. In 1850 more British people still worked on farms than in any other occupation. The second-largest occupation was domestic service, with more than one million household servants, 90 percent of whom were women. Thus many old, familiar jobs outside industry lived on and provided alternatives for individual workers. This helped ease the transition to industrial civilization.

Within industry itself, the pattern of artisans working with hand tools in small shops remained unchanged in many trades, even as others were revolutionized by technological change. For example, as in the case of cotton and coal, the British iron industry was completely dominated by large-scale capitalist firms by 1850. Many large ironworks had more than one thousand people on their payrolls. Yet the firms that fashioned iron into small metal goods, such as tools, tableware, and toys, employed on average fewer than ten wage workers who used time-honored handicraft skills. Only gradually after 1850 did some owners find ways to reorganize some handicraft industries with new machines and new patterns of work. The survival of small workshops gave many workers an alternative to factory employment.

Working-class solidarity and class-consciousness developed in small workshops as well as in large factories. In the northern factory districts, where thousands of "hired hands" looked across at a tiny minority of managers and owners, anticapitalist sentiments were frequent by the 1820s. Commenting in 1825 on a strike in the woolen center of Bradford and the support it had gathered from other regions, one paper claimed with pride that "it is all the workers of England against a few masters of Bradford."[16] Modern technology and factory organization had created a few versus the many.

The transformation of some traditional trades by organizational changes, rather than technological innovations, could by themselves also create ill will and class feeling. The classical liberal concept of economic freedom and laissez faire emerged in the late eighteenth century, and it continued to gather strength in the early nineteenth century (see Chapter 22). As in France during the French Revolution, the British government attacked monopolies, guilds, and workers combinations in the name of individual liberty. In 1799 Parliament passed the **Combination Acts**, which outlawed unions and strikes. In 1813 and 1814, Parliament repealed the old and often disregarded law of 1563 regulating the wages of artisans and the conditions of apprenticeship. As a result of these and other measures, certain skilled artisan workers, such as bootmakers and high-quality tailors, found aggressive capitalists ignoring traditional work rules and trying to flood their trades with unorganized women workers and children to beat down wages.

The capitalist attack on artisan guilds and work rules was bitterly resented by many craftworkers, who subsequently played an important part in Great Britain and in other countries in gradually building a modern labor movement to improve working conditions and to serve worker needs. The Combination Acts were widely disregarded by workers. Printers, papermakers, carpenters, tailors, and other such craftsmen continued to take collective action, and societies of skilled factory workers also organized unions. Unions sought to control the number of skilled workers, limit apprenticeship to members' own children, and bargain with owners over wages.

They were not afraid to strike; there was, for example, a general strike of adult cotton spinners in Manchester in 1810. In the face of widespread union activity, Parliament repealed the Combination Acts in 1824, and unions were tolerated, though not fully accepted, after 1825. The next stage in the development of the British trade-union movement was the attempt to create a single large national union. This effort was led not so much by working people as by social reformers such as Robert Owen. Owen, a self-made cotton manufacturer (see page 678), had pioneered in industrial relations by combining firm discipline with concern for the health, safety, and hours of his workers. After 1815 he experimented with cooperative and socialist communities, including one at New Harmony, Indiana. Then in 1834 Owen organized one of the largest and most visionary of the early national unions, the Grand National Consolidated Trades Union.

When Owen's and other grandiose schemes collapsed, the British labor movement moved once again after 1851 in the direction of craft unions. The most famous of these "new model unions" was the Amalgamated Society of Engineers, which represented skilled machinists. These unions won real benefits for members by

fairly conservative means and thus became an accepted part of the industrial scene.

British workers also engaged in direct political activity in defense of their own interests. After the collapse of Owen's national trade union, many working people went into the Chartist movement, which sought political democracy. The key Chartist demand—that all men be given the right to vote—became the great hope of millions of aroused people. Workers were also active in campaigns to limit the workday in factories to ten hours and to permit duty-free importation of wheat into Great Britain to secure cheap bread. Thus working people developed a sense of their own identity and played an active role in shaping the new industrial system. They were neither helpless victims nor passive beneficiaries.

Combination Acts English laws passed in 1799 that outlawed unions and strikes, favoring capitalist business people over skilled artisans. Bitterly resented and widely disregarded by many craft guilds, the acts were repealed by Parliament in 1824.

Union Membership Certificate This handsome membership certificate belonged to Arthur Watton, a properly trained and certified papermaker of Kings Norton in Birmingham, England. Members of such unions proudly framed their certificates and displayed them in their homes, showing that they were skilled workers. (Courtesy, Sylvia Waddell)

LOOKING BACK LOOKING AHEAD

ONE POPULAR IDEA in the 1830s, first developed by a French economist, was that Britain had experienced an "industrial revolution" at the same time that France had experienced the French Revolution. One revolution was economic, while the other was political; one was ongoing and successful, while the other had failed and come to a definite end in 1815, when Europe's conservative monarchs defeated Napoleon and restored the French kings of the Old Regime.

In fact, in 1815 the French Revolution, like the Industrial Revolution, was an unfinished revolution. Just as Britain was in the midst of its economic transformation and the states of northwestern Europe would begin rapid industrialization only in the 1850s, so too after 1815 were the political conflicts and ideologies of revolutionary France still very much alive. The French Revolution had opened the era of modern political life in Europe. It had brought into existence many of the political forces and ideologies that would interact with industrialization to refashion Europe and create a new urban society. Moreover, in 1815 the unfinished French Revolution carried the very real possibility of renewed political upheaval. This possibility, which conservatives feared and radicals longed for, would become dramatic reality in 1848, when political revolutions swept across Europe like a whirlwind.

CHAPTER REVIEW

■ **What were the origins of the Industrial Revolution in Britain, and how did it develop between 1780 and 1850? (p. 656)**

As markets for manufactured goods increased both domestically and overseas, Britain was able to respond with increased production, largely because of its stable government, abundant natural resources, and flexible labor force. The first factories arose as a result of technical innovations in spinning cotton, thereby revolutionizing the textile industry. The widespread availability and affordability of cotton provided benefits for many, but also resulted in the brutal forced labor of orphaned children on a large scale. The demand for improvements in energy led to innovations and improvements in the steam engine, which transformed the iron industry among others. In the early nineteenth century, transportation of goods was greatly enhanced when railroads were built, largely by unskilled farm workers who subsequently often left their villages for a more exciting life in towns.

■ **How after 1815 did continental countries respond to the challenge of industrialization? (p. 665)**

For reasons including warfare on home soil and barriers to trade, continental Europe lagged behind England in industrialization in 1815. But after 1815, some continental countries, especially France, Belgium, and Germany, gradually built on England's technical breakthroughs, such as textile machinery and steam engines. Entrepreneurs set up their own factories and hired skilled urban workers from the area along with English immigrants experienced in the new technologies.

England tried to limit the spread of trade secrets, and financing was difficult for early continental capitalists, but government intervention, such as tariff protection and infrastructure, was a great boon to industrialization on the continent. In addition, newly established corporate banks worked in conjunction with governments to invest heavily in railroads and other industries.

■ **How did the Industrial Revolution affect people of all social classes, and what measures were taken to improve the conditions of workers? (p. 672)**

The rise of modern industry had a profound impact on people and their lives, beginning in Britain in the late eighteenth century. Industrialization led to the growing size and wealth of the middle class, as factory owners took their place beside successful merchants and professional people. These early entrepreneurs at first came from diverse backgrounds, providing economic opportunities for religious and ethnic minorities, but by the middle of the nineteenth century, wealthy industrial families controlled large enterprises, and it was difficult for the poor but talented person to break in. The modern industrial working class also developed during this time, filling the need for vast quantities of labor power. Rigid rules, stern discipline, and long hours weighed heavily on factory workers, and improvements in the standard of living came slowly, but they were substantial by 1850. Family members often worked together in early factories, but as restrictions were placed on child labor, married women withdrew increasingly from wage work and concentrated on child care and household responsibilities.

At the same time many young women worked before they were married, and jobs for young workers were often separated by gender in an attempt to control sexual behavior. The era of industrialization also fostered new attitudes toward child labor, encouraged protective factory legislation, and called forth a new sense of class feeling and an assertive labor movement.

Suggested Reading

Cameron, Rondo, and Larry Neal. *A Concise Economic History of the World*, 4th ed. 2003. Provides an introduction to key issues related to the Industrial Revolution and has a carefully annotated bibliography.

Davidoff, Leonore, and Catherine Hall. *Family Fortunes: Men and Women of the English Middle Class, 1750–1850*, rev. ed. 2003. Examines both economic activities and cultural beliefs with great skill.

Dolan, Brian. *Wedgwood: The First Tycoon*. 2004. A comprehensive study of the famous entrepreneur.

Fuchs, Rachel G. *Gender and Poverty in Nineteenth-Century Europe*. 2005. Provides a broad comparative perspective.

Gaskell, Elizabeth. *Mary Barton*. 1848. Gaskell's famous novel offers a realistic portrayal of the new industrial society.

Goodman, Jordan, and Katrina Honeyman. *Gainful Pursuits: The Making of Industrial Europe, 1600–1914*. 1988. An excellent general treatment of European industrial growth.

Horn, Jeff. *Understanding the Industrial Revolution: Milestones in Business History*. 2007. Clear, concise, and engaging, this is an excellent work for students.

Kemp, Tom. *Industrialization in Europe*, 2d ed. 1985. A useful overview.

Landes, David. *Dynasties: Fortunes and Misfortunes of the World's Great Family Businesses*. 2006. A collection offering fascinating and insightful histories of famous enterprises and leading capitalists.

Pomeranz, Kenneth. *The Great Divergence: China, Europe, and the Making of the Modern World Economy*. 2000. A sophisticated reconsideration of why western Europe underwent industrialization and China did not.

Stearns, Peter N. *The Industrial Revolution in World History*, 3d ed. 2007. A useful brief survey.

Thompson, E. P. *The Making of the English Working Class*. 1963. A fascinating book in the Marxian tradition that is rich in detail and early working-class lore.

Valenze, Deborah. *The First Industrial Woman*. 1995. A gender study that reinvigorates the debate between optimists and pessimists about the consequences of industrialization in Britain.

Walton, Whitney. *France and the Crystal Palace: Bourgeois Taste and Artisan Manufacture in the 19th Century*. 1992. Examines the gradual transformation of handicraft techniques and their persistent importance in the international economy.

Notes

1. N. F. R. Crafts, *British Economic Growth During the Industrial Revolution* (Oxford: Oxford University Press, 1985), p. 32.
2. P. Bairoch, "International Industrialization Levels from 1750 to 1980," *Journal of European Economic History* 11 (Spring 1982): 269–333.
3. Crafts, *British Economic Growth*, pp. 45, 95–102.
4. Quoted by J. Bowditch and C. Ramsland, eds., *Voices of the Industrial Revolution* (Ann Arbor: University of Michigan Press, 1961), p. 55, from the fourth edition of Thomas Malthus, *Essay on the Principle of Population* (1807).
5. M. Lévy-Leboyer, *Les banques européennes et l'industrialisation dans la première moitié du XIXe siècle* (Paris: Presses Universitaires de France, 1964), p. 29.
6. Friedrich List, *The National System of Political Economy*, trans. G. A. Matile (Philadelphia: J. B. Lippincott, 1856), p. 61; edited slightly.
7. J. Michelet, *The People*, trans. with an introduction by J. P. McKay (Urbana: University of Illinois Press, 1973; original publication, 1846), p. 64.
8. Quoted in W. A. Hayek, ed., *Capitalism and the Historians* (Chicago: University of Chicago Press, 1954), p. 126.
9. Crafts, *British Economic Growth*, p. 95.
10. H-J. Voth, *Time and Work in England, 1750–1830* (Oxford: Oxford University Press, 2000), pp. 268–270; also pp. 118–133.
11. Quoted in E. R. Pike, *"Hard Times": Human Documents of the Industrial Revolution* (New York: Praeger, 1966), p. 109.
12. See especially J. Brenner and M. Rama, "Rethinking Women's Oppression," *New Left Review* 144 (March–April 1984): 33–71, and sources cited there.
13. J. Humphries, "... 'The Most Free from Objection'...: The Sexual Division of Labor and Women's Work in Nineteenth-Century England," *Journal of Economic History* 47 (December 1987): 948.
14. Ibid., p. 941; Pike, *"Hard Times,"* p. 266.
15. Pike, *"Hard Times,"* p. 208.
16. Quoted in D. Geary, ed., *Labour and Socialist Movements in Europe Before 1914* (Oxford: Berg, 1989), p. 29.

Key Terms

Industrial Revolution (p. 656)
spinning jenny (p. 657)
water frame (p. 657)
steam engines (p. 660)
***Rocket* (p. 663)**
Crystal Palace (p. 664)
iron law of wages (p. 665)
tariff protection (p. 670)
economic nationalism (p. 672)
class-consciousness (p. 672)
Luddites (p. 674)
Factory Act of 1833 (p. 678)
separate spheres (p. 679)
Mines Act of 1842 (p. 680)
Combination Acts (p. 680)

For practice quizzes and other study tools, visit the Online Study Guide at **bedfordstmartins.com/mckaywest**.

For primary sources from this period, see ***Sources of Western Society*, Second Edition**.

For Web sites, images, and documents related to topics in this chapter, visit Make History at **bedfordstmartins.com/mckaywest**.

22

Ideologies and Upheavals

1815–1850

The momentous economic and political transformation of modern times began in the late eighteenth century with the Industrial Revolution in England and then the French Revolution. Until about 1815, these economic and political revolutions were separate, involving different countries and activities and proceeding at very different paces. After peace returned in 1815, economic and political changes tended to fuse, reinforcing each other and bringing about what historian Eric Hobsbawm has incisively called the dual revolution. For instance, the growth of the industrial middle class encouraged the drive for representative government, and the demands of the French sans-culottes (laboring poor) in 1793 and 1794 inspired many socialist thinkers. Radical change was eventually a constant, but the particular results varied enormously. In central and eastern Europe especially, the traditional elites — the monarchs, noble landowners, and bureaucrats — proved capable of defending their privileges and eventually used nationalism to respond to the dual revolution and to serve their interests, as we shall see in Chapter 24.

The dual revolution also posed a tremendous intellectual challenge. The meanings of the economic, political, and social changes that were occurring, as well as the ways they would be shaped by human action, were anything but clear. In literature, art, and music, the uncertainty of the era was reflected in the exuberance of the romantic movement. In politics, powerful new ideological forces emerged: a revitalized conservatism and three ideologies of change — liberalism, nationalism, and socialism. All played critical roles in the political and social battles of the era and the great popular upheaval that eventually swept across Europe in the revolutions of 1848. ■

Erich Lessing/Art Resource, NY

Life in the Revolutionary Era. The sight of revolutionaries storming public areas was widespread in many parts of Europe between 1830 and 1848. Here Louis Philippe, the new French king, leaves in 1830 for the Paris city hall to greet the people. The three-colored Republican flag he has just accepted goes before him.

CHAPTER PREVIEW

The Aftermath of the Napoleonic Wars
■ How did the victorious allies fashion a general peace settlement, and how did Metternich uphold a conservative European order?

The Spread of Radical Ideas
■ What were the basic tenets of liberalism, nationalism, and socialism, and what groups were most attracted to these ideologies?

The Romantic Movement
■ What were the characteristics of the romantic movement, and who were some of the great romantic artists?

Reforms and Revolutions Before 1848
■ How after 1815 did liberal, national, and socialist forces challenge conservatism in Greece, Great Britain, and France?

The Revolutions of 1848
■ Why in 1848 did revolution triumph briefly throughout most of Europe, and why did it fail almost completely?

The Aftermath of the Napoleonic Wars

How did the victorious allies fashion a general peace settlement, and how did Metternich uphold a conservative European order? ■

The eventual triumph of revolutionary economic and political forces was by no means certain as the Napoleonic era ended. Quite the contrary. The conservative, aristocratic monarchies of Russia, Prussia, Austria, and Great Britain — known as the Quadruple Alliance — had finally defeated France and reaffirmed their determination to hold France in line. But many other international questions were outstanding, and the allies agreed to meet at the **Congress of Vienna** to fashion a general peace settlement.

Most people felt a profound longing for peace. The great challenge for political leaders in 1814 was to construct a settlement that would last and not sow the seeds of another war. Their efforts were largely successful and contributed to a century unmarred by destructive generalized war (Map 22.1).

Congress of Vienna A meeting of the Quadruple Alliance — Russia, Prussia, Austria, and Great Britain — and restoration France to fashion a general peace settlement that began after the defeat of Napoleon's France in 1814.

The European Balance of Power

The allied powers were concerned first and foremost with the defeated enemy, France. Agreeing to the restoration of the Bourbon dynasty (see Chapter 20), the allies were lenient toward France after Napoleon's abdication. The first Peace of Paris gave France the boundaries it possessed in 1792, which were larger than those of 1789, and France did not have to pay any war repa-

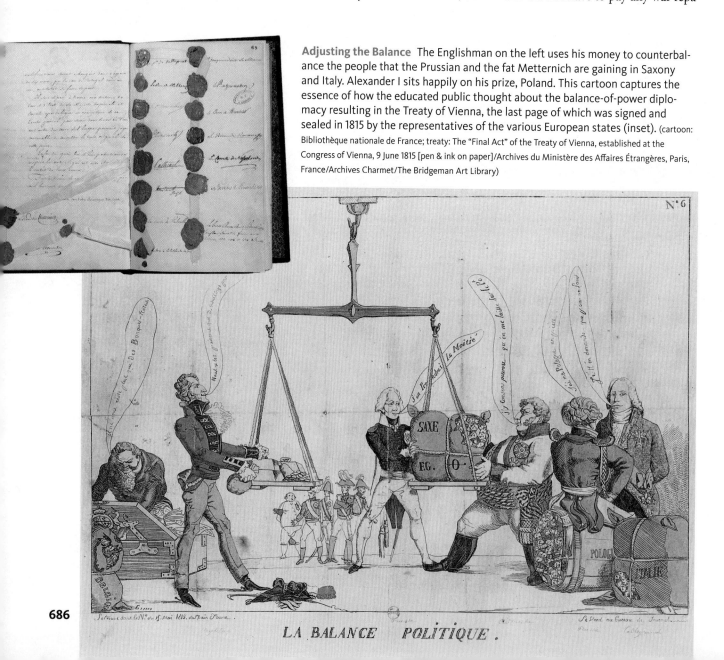

Adjusting the Balance The Englishman on the left uses his money to counterbalance the people that the Prussian and the fat Metternich are gaining in Saxony and Italy. Alexander I sits happily on his prize, Poland. This cartoon captures the essence of how the educated public thought about the balance-of-power diplomacy resulting in the Treaty of Vienna, the last page of which was signed and sealed in 1815 by the representatives of the various European states (inset). (cartoon: Bibliothèque nationale de France; treaty: The "Final Act" of the Treaty of Vienna, established at the Congress of Vienna, 9 June 1815 [pen & ink on paper]/Archives du Ministère des Affaires Étrangères, Paris, France/Archives Charmet/The Bridgeman Art Library)

LA BALANCE POLITIQUE.

rations. Thus the victorious powers did not foment a spirit of injustice and revenge in the defeated country.

When the four allies of the Quadruple Alliance (plus a representative of the restored Bourbon monarch in France) met together at the Congress of Vienna, assisted in a minor way by a host of delegates from the smaller European states, they also agreed to raise a number of formidable barriers against renewed French aggression. The Low Countries—Belgium and Holland—were united under an enlarged Dutch monarchy capable of opposing France more effectively. Above all, Prussia received considerably more territory on France's eastern border so as to stand as the "sentinel on the Rhine" against France. In these ways, the Quadruple Alliance combined leniency toward France with strong defensive measures.

In their moderation toward France, the allies were motivated by self-interest and traditional ideas about the balance of power. To Klemens von Metternich (MEH-tuhr-nihk) and Robert Castlereagh (KA-suhl-ray), the foreign ministers of Austria and Great Britain, respectively, as well as their French counterpart, Charles Talleyrand, the balance of power meant an international equilibrium of political and military forces that would discourage aggression by any combination of states or, worse, the domination of Europe by any single state.

The Great Powers—Austria, Britain, Prussia, Russia, and France—used the balance of power to settle their own dangerous disputes at the Congress of Vienna. There was general agreement among the victors that each of them should receive compensation in the form of territory for their successful struggle against the French. Great Britain had already won colonies and strategic outposts during the long wars. Metternich's Austria gave up territories in Belgium and southern Germany but expanded greatly elsewhere, taking the rich provinces of Venetia and Lombardy in northern Italy as well as former Polish possessions and new lands on the eastern coast of the Adriatic. More contentious was the push for greater territory by Russia and Prussia. When France, Austria, and Great Britain allied against these powers, Russia accepted a small Polish kingdom and Prussia took only part of Saxony (see Map 22.1). This compromise was very much within the framework of balance-of-power ideology.

Unfortunately for France, Napoleon suddenly escaped from his "comic kingdom" on the island of Elba and reignited his wars of expansion for a brief time (see Chapter 20). Yet the second Peace of Paris, concluded after Napoleon's final defeat at Waterloo in 1815, was still relatively moderate toward France. Fat old Louis XVIII was restored to his throne for a second time. France lost only a little territory, had to pay an indemnity of 700 million francs, and had to support a large army of occupation for five years. The rest of the settlement already concluded at the Congress of Vienna was left intact. The members of the Quadruple Alliance, however, did agree to meet periodically to discuss their common interests and to consider appropriate measures for the maintenance of peace in Europe. This agreement marked the beginning of the European "congress system," which lasted long into the nineteenth century and settled many international crises through international conferences and balance-of-power diplomacy.

Repressing the Revolutionary Spirit

There was also a domestic political side to the reestablishment of peace. Within their own countries, the leaders of the victorious states were much less flexible. In 1815 under Metternich's leadership, Austria, Prussia, and Russia embarked on a crusade against the ideas and politics of the **dual revolution**. This crusade lasted until 1848. The first step was the **Holy Alliance**, formed by Austria, Prussia, and Russia in September 1815. First proposed by Russia's Alexander I, the alliance soon became a symbol of the repression of liberal and revolutionary movements all over Europe.

In 1820 revolutionaries succeeded in forcing the monarchs of Spain and the southern Italian kingdom of the Two Sicilies to grant liberal constitutions against their wills. Metternich was horrified: revolution was rising once

dual revolution A term that historian Eric Hobsbawm used for the economic and political changes that tended to fuse and reinforce each other after 1815.

Holy Alliance An alliance formed by the conservative rulers of Austria, Russia, and Prussia in September 1815 that became a symbol of the repression of liberal and revolutionary movements all over Europe.

Mapping the Past

Map 22.1 Europe in 1815 In 1815 Europe contained many different states, but after the defeat of Napoleon international politics was dominated by the five Great Powers: Russia, Prussia, Austria, Great Britain, and France. (The number rises to six if one includes the Ottoman Empire.)

ANALYZING THE MAP Trace the political boundaries of each Great Power, and compare their geographical strengths and weaknesses. What territories did Prussia and Austria gain as a result of the war with Napoleon?

CONNECTIONS How did Prussia's and Austria's territorial gains contribute to the balance of power established at the Congress of Vienna? What other factors enabled the Great Powers to achieve such a long-lasting peace?

To complete this activity online, go to the Online Study Guide at bedfordstmartins.com/mckaywest.

again. Calling a conference at Troppau in Austria under the provisions of the Quadruple Alliance, he and Alexander I proclaimed the principle of active intervention to maintain all autocratic regimes whenever they were threatened. Austrian forces then marched into Naples in 1821 and restored Ferdinand I to the throne of the Two Sicilies, while French armies in 1823 likewise restored the Spanish regime.

In the following years, Metternich continued to battle against liberal political change. Sometimes he could do

little, as in the case of the new Latin American republics that broke away from Spain. Nor could he undo the dynastic change of 1830 in France or Belgium's achieving independence from the Netherlands in 1831. Nonetheless, until 1848 Metternich's system proved quite effective in central Europe, where his power was the greatest.

Metternich's policies dominated not only Austria and the Italian peninsula but also the entire German Confederation, which the peace settlement of Vienna

1820 Revolts in Spain and Italy

had called into being. The confederation comprised thirty-eight independent German states, including Prussia and Austria (see Map 22.1). These states met in complicated assemblies dominated by Austria, with Prussia a willing junior partner in the execution of repressive measures. It was through the German Confederation that Metternich had the infamous **Carlsbad Decrees** issued in 1819. These decrees required the thirty-eight German member states to root out subversive ideas in their universities and newspapers. The decrees also established a permanent committee with spies and informers to investigate and punish any liberal or radical organizations.

Metternich and Conservatism

Metternich's determined defense of the status quo made him a villain in the eyes of most progressive, optimistic historians of the nineteenth century. Yet rather than denounce the man, we can try to understand him and the general conservatism he represented. Born into the middle ranks of the landed nobility of the Rhineland, Prince Klemens von Metternich (1773–1859) was an internationally oriented aristocrat who made a brilliant diplomatic career in Austria. Austrian foreign minister from 1809 to 1848, the cosmopolitan and conservative Metternich had a pessimistic view of human nature, which he believed was ever prone to error, excess, and self-serving behavior. Thus Metternich concluded that strong governments were necessary as a bulwark to protect society from the baser elements of human behavior. Metternich also defended his class and its rights and privileges with a clear conscience. The nobility was

one of Europe's most ancient institutions, and conservatives regarded tradition as the basic source of human institutions.

Metternich firmly believed that liberalism, as embodied in revolutionary America and France, had been responsible for a generation of war with untold bloodshed and suffering. Like many other conservatives then and since, Metternich blamed liberal middle-class revolutionaries for stirring up the lower classes, which he believed desired nothing more than peace and quiet.

The threat of liberalism appeared doubly dangerous to Metternich because it generally went with national aspirations. Liberals believed that each people, each national group, had a right to establish its own independent government and seek to fulfill its own destiny. The idea of national self-determination was repellent to Metternich because it threatened to destroy the Austrian Empire and revolutionize central Europe.

The vast Austrian Empire of the Habsburgs was a great dynastic state. Formed over centuries by war, marriage, and luck, it was made up of many peoples (Map 22.2). The Germans had long

Carlsbad Decrees Issued in 1819, these decrees were designed to uphold Metternich's conservatism, requiring the German states to root out subversive ideas and squelch any liberal organizations.

Prince Klemens von Metternich This portrait by Sir Thomas Lawrence reveals much about Metternich the man. Handsome, refined, and intelligent, Metternich was a great aristocrat who was passionately devoted to the defense of his class and its interests. (The Royal Collection © 2010 Her Majesty Queen Elizabeth II)

Map 22.2 Peoples of the Habsburg Monarchy, 1815 The old dynastic state was a patchwork of nationalities. Note the widely scattered pockets of Germans and Hungarians.

Map legend:
- Germans
- Magyars (Hungarians)
- Italians
- Romanians
- Poles
- Czechs
- Carpatho-Ukrainians (Ruthians)
- Croats and Serbs
- Slovaks
- Slovenes
- Boundary of the Austrian Empire

dominated the empire, yet they accounted for only one-fourth of the population. The Magyars (Hungarians), a substantially smaller group, dominated the kingdom of Hungary, though they did not account for a majority of the population in that part of the Austrian Empire.

The Czechs, the third major group, were concentrated in Bohemia and Moravia. There were also large numbers of Italians, Poles, and Ukrainians as well as smaller groups of Slovenes, Croats, Serbs, and Romanians. The various Slavic peoples, together with the Italians and the Romanians, represented a widely scattered and completely divided majority in an empire politically dominated by Germans and Hungarians. Different ethnic groups often lived in the same provinces and even in the same villages. Thus the different parts and provinces of the empire differed in languages, customs, and institutions.

The multiethnic state Metternich served was both strong and weak. It was strong because of its large population and vast territories; it was weak because of its

many and potentially dissatisfied nationalities. In these circumstances, Metternich virtually had to oppose liberalism and nationalism, for Austria was simply unable to accommodate these ideologies of the dual revolution.

In his efforts to hold back liberalism and nationalism Metternich was supported by Russia and, to a lesser extent, by the Ottoman Empire. Bitter enemies, these far-flung empires were both absolutist states with powerful armies and long traditions of expansion and conquest. Both were multinational empires made up of many peoples, languages, and religions, but in each case most of the ruling elite came from the dominant ethnic group—the Orthodox Christian Russians centered in central and northern Russia, and the Muslim Ottoman Turks of Anatolia (much of modern Turkey). After 1815, both of these multinational absolutist states worked to preserve their respective traditional conservative orders. Only after 1850 did each in turn experience a profound crisis and embark on a program of fundamental reform and modernization, as we shall see in Chapter 24.

The Spread of Radical Ideas

What were the basic tenets of liberalism, nationalism, and socialism, and what groups were most attracted to these ideologies? ■

In the years following the peace settlement of 1815 intellectuals and social observers sought to understand the revolutionary changes that had occurred and were still taking place. Almost all of these basic ideas were radical. In one way or another, the new ideas rejected conservatism, with its stress on tradition, a hereditary monarchy, a strong and privileged landowning aristocracy, and an official church. Radical thinkers developed and refined alternative visions—alternative ideologies—and tried to convince society to act on them. In contrast to Metternich and conservatism, these new philosophies of liberalism, nationalism, and socialism started with an optimistic premise about human nature. Although they reached very different conclusions about how best to achieve progress, or how far progress should extend, with time, each of the new movements was very successful.

Liberalism and the Middle Class

The principal ideas of **liberalism**—liberty and equality—were by no means defeated in 1815. First realized successfully in the American Revolution and then achieved in part in the French Revolution, liberalism demanded representative government as opposed to autocratic monarchy, and equality before the law as opposed to legally separate classes. The idea of liberty also meant specific individual freedoms: freedom of the press, freedom of speech, freedom of assembly, and freedom from arbitrary arrest. In Europe only France with Louis XVIII's Constitutional Charter and Great Britain with its Parliament and historic rights of English men and women had realized much of the liberal program in 1815. Even in those countries, liberalism had not fully succeeded.

Although liberalism retained its cutting edge, it was seen by many as being a somewhat duller tool than it had been. The reasons for this were that liberalism faced more radical ideological competitors in the early nineteenth century. Opponents of liberalism especially criticized its economic principles, which called for unrestricted private enterprise and no government interference in the economy. This philosophy was popularly known as the doctrine of **laissez faire** (lay-say FEHR). (This form of liberalism is often called "classical" liberalism in the United States in order to distinguish it sharply from modern American liberalism, which usually favors more government programs to meet social needs and to regulate the economy.)

As we saw in Chapter 18 Adam Smith posited the idea of a free economy in 1776 in opposition to mercantilism and its attempt to regulate trade. Smith argued that freely competitive private enterprise would give all citizens a fair and equal opportunity to do what they did best and would result in greater income for everyone, not just the rich. In early-nineteenth-century Britain this economic liberalism was embraced most enthusiastically by business groups and thus became a doctrine associated with business interests. Businessmen used the doctrine to defend their right to do as they wished in their factories. Labor unions were outlawed because they supposedly restricted free competition and the individual's "right to work."

In the early nineteenth century liberal political ideals also became more closely associated with narrow class interests. Early-nineteenth-century liberals favored representative government, but they generally wanted property qualifications attached to the right to vote. In practice, this meant limiting the vote to the well-to-do. Workers and peasants, as well as the lower middle class of shopkeepers, clerks, and artisans, did not own the necessary property and thus could not vote.

As liberalism became increasingly identified with the middle class after 1815, some intellectuals and foes of conservatism felt that liberalism did not go nearly far enough. Inspired by memories of the French Revolution and the example of Jacksonian democracy in the young American republic, they called for universal voting rights, at least for males, and for democracy. These democrats and republicans were more radical than the liberals, and they were more willing than most liberals to endorse violent upheaval to achieve goals. All of this meant that liberals and radical democratic republicans could join forces against conservatives only up to a point.

liberalism The principal ideas of this movement were equality and liberty; liberals demanded representative government and equality before the law as well as individual freedoms such as freedom of the press, freedom of speech, freedom of assembly, and freedom from arbitrary arrest.

laissez faire A doctrine of economic liberalism that believes in unrestricted private enterprise and no government interference in the economy.

nationalism The idea that each people had its own genius and its own specific unity, which manifested itself especially in a common language and history, and often led to the desire for an independent political state.

The Growing Appeal of Nationalism

Nationalism was a second radical idea in the years after 1815—an idea destined to have an enormous influence in the modern world. Nationalism had its immediate origins in the French Revolution and the Napoleonic wars, and there were already hints of its remarkable ability to spread and develop.

Early advocates of the "national idea," or nationalism, were strongly influenced by Johann Gottfried von Herder, an eighteenth-century philosopher and historian who argued that each people had its own genius and its own cultural unity. (See "Listening to the Past: Herder and Mazzini on the Development of Nationalism," page 694.) For nationalists coming after Herder this cultural unity was basically self-evident, manifesting itself especially in a common language, history, and territory. In fact, in the early nineteenth century such cultural unity was more a dream than a reality as far as most nationalities were concerned. Local dialects abounded, and peasants from nearby villages often failed to understand each other. As for historical memory, it divided the inhabitants of the different German or Italian states as much as it unified them. Moreover, a variety of ethnic groups shared the territory of most states.

Despite these basic realities, sooner or later European nationalists usually sought to turn the cultural unity that they perceived into political reality. They sought to make the territory of each people coincide with well-defined boundaries in an independent nation-state. It was this political goal that made nationalism so explosive in central and eastern Europe after 1815, when there were either too few states (Austria, Russia, and the Otto-

man Empire) or too many (the Italian peninsula and the German Confederation), and when different peoples overlapped and intermingled.

In recent years scholars have been trying to understand how the nationalist vision, often fitting so poorly with existing conditions and promising so much upheaval, was so successful in the long run. Of fundamental importance in the rise of nationalism was the development of complex industrial and urban society, which required much better communication between individuals and groups.[1] These communication needs promoted the use of a standardized national language within many countries, creating at least a superficial cultural unity as a standard tongue spread through mass education. When a minority population was large and concentrated, the nationalist campaign for a standardized language often led the minority group to push for a separate nation-state.

Many scholars also argue that nations are recent creations, the product of the new, self-conscious nationalist ideology. Thus nation-states emerged in the nineteenth century as "imagined communities" that sought to bind millions of strangers together around the abstract concept of an all-embracing national identity. This meant bringing citizens together with emotionally charged symbols and ceremonies, such as independence holidays and patriotic parades. On these occasions the imagined nation of spiritual equals might celebrate its most hallowed traditions, which were often recent inventions.[2]

Historians also stress the dynamic, ever-changing character of nationalism. Industrialism and mass education, so important in the later nineteenth century, played only a minor role before 1850. In those years the faith in nationhood was fresh, idealistic, and progressive.

Between 1815 and 1850 most people who believed in nationalism also believed in either liberalism or radical democratic republicanism. A common faith in the creativity and nobility of the people was perhaps the single most important reason for the linking of these two concepts. Liberals and especially democrats saw the people as the ultimate source of all government. Yet liberals and nationalists agreed that the benefits of self-government would be possible only if the people were united by common traditions that transcended local interests and even class differences.

Building German Nationalism As popular upheaval in France spread to central Europe in March 1848, Germans from the solid middle classes came together in Frankfurt to draft a constitution for a new united Germany. This woodcut commemorates the solemn procession of delegates entering Saint Paul's Cathedral in Frankfurt, where the delegates would hold their deliberations. Festivals, celebrations, and parades helped create a feeling of belonging to a large unseen community, a nation binding millions of strangers together. (akg-images)

In laboring according to the true principles of our country we are laboring for Humanity.

— GIUSEPPE MAZZINI

Early nationalists usually believed that every nation, like every citizen, had the right to exist in freedom and to develop its character and spirit. They were confident that a symphony of nations would promote the harmony and ultimate unity of all peoples. As the French historian Jules Michelet (zhool meesh-LAY) put it in *The People* in 1846, each citizen "learns to recognize his country . . . as a note in the grand concert; through it he himself participates and loves the world." Similarly, the great Italian patriot Guiseppe Mazzini (1805–1872) believed that "in laboring according to the true principles of our country we are laboring for Humanity." (See "Listening to the Past: Herder and Mazzini on the Development of Nationalism," page 694.) Thus the liberty of the individual and the love of a free nation overlapped greatly in the early nineteenth century.

Yet early nationalists also stressed the differences among peoples. Even early nationalism developed a strong sense of "we" and "they." To this "we-they" outlook, it was all too easy for nationalists to add two highly volatile ingredients: a sense of national mission and a sense of national superiority. Even Michelet, so alive to the national aspirations of other peoples, could not help speaking in 1846 of the "superiority of France"; the principles espoused in the French Revolution had made France the "salvation of mankind."

Russian and German nationalists had a very different opinion of France. In the narratives they constructed, the French often seemed oppressive, as the Russians did to the Poles and as the Germans did to the Czechs. Thus "they" often emerged as the enemy, and underlying ideas of national superiority and national mission would eventually lead to aggression and conflict.

French Utopian Socialism

Socialism, the new radical doctrine after 1815, began in France, although France lagged far behind Great Britain in developing modern industry and experiencing the industrial conflicts that arose between a few factory owners and a multitude of factory workers. Early French socialist thinkers were acutely aware that the political revolution in France, the rise of laissez faire, and the emergence of modern industry in Britain were transforming society. They were disturbed because they saw these developments as fomenting selfish individualism and splitting the community into isolated fragments.

There was, they believed, an urgent need for a further reorganization of society to establish cooperation and a new sense of community.

Early French socialists believed in economic planning. Inspired by the emergency measures of 1793 and 1794 in France, they argued that the government should rationally organize the economy and not depend on destructive competition to do the job. Early socialists also shared an intense desire to help the poor, and they preached that the rich and the poor should be more nearly equal economically. Finally, socialists believed that private property should be strictly regulated by the government or that it should be abolished and replaced by state or community ownership. Planning, greater economic equality, and state regulation of property—these were the key ideas of early French socialism and of all socialism since.

One of the most influential early socialist thinkers was a nobleman, Count Henri de Saint-Simon (awn-REE duh san-see-MOHN) (1760–1825). Saint-Simon optimistically proclaimed the tremendous possibilities of industrial development: "The age of gold is before us!" The key to progress was proper social organization that required the "parasites"—the court, the aristocracy, lawyers, and churchmen—to give way, once and for all, to the "doers"—the leading scientists, engineers, and industrialists. The doers would carefully plan the economy and guide it forward by undertaking vast public works projects and establishing investment banks. Saint-Simon also stressed in highly moralistic terms that every social institution ought to have as its main goal improved conditions for the poor.

After 1830 the socialist critique of capitalism became sharper. Charles Fourier (sharl FOR-ee-ay) (1772–1837), a lonely, saintly man, envisaged a socialist utopia of mathematically precise, self-sufficient communities, each made up of 1,620 people. Fourier was also an early proponent of the total emancipation of women. According to Fourier, young single women were shamelessly "sold" to their future husbands for dowries and other financial considerations. Therefore, Fourier called for the abolition of marriage, free unions based only on love, and sexual freedom. Many middle-class men and women found these ideas, which were shared and even practiced by some followers of Saint-Simon, shocking and immoral.

Louis Blanc (1811–1882), a sharp-eyed, intelligent journalist, focused on practical improvements. In his *Organization of Work* (1839), he urged workers to agitate for universal voting rights and to take control of the state peacefully. Blanc believed that the state should set up

socialism A backlash against the emergence of individualism and the fragmentation of society, and a move toward cooperation and a sense of community; the key ideas were economic planning, greater economic equality, and state regulation of property.

Herder and Mazzini on the Development of Nationalism

LISTENING TO THE PAST

The German historian and philosopher Johann Gottfried von Herder (1744–1803) established the foundations of cultural nationalism. Writing shortly before the French Revolution, Herder's multivolume Ideas for the Philosophy of History of Humanity *(1784–1791) focused on the long, unconscious evolution of human communities. This process had produced national communities, each of which was joined together by a common language and by popular traditions, such as legends, proverbs, and folk songs. Herder believed that each language and each people was equally valid and equally worthy of respect.*

A German born in Prussia, Herder hated Prussian militarism and was in no way partial to the Germans in his study. For example, he lauded the peaceful character of the Slavs and often decried the barbaric behavior of the warrior Germans. Stressing the cultural genius of each nationality, Herder advocated the preservation of traditions but not the creation of political entities or nation-states. The following passage is taken from Herder's concluding section on the different peoples of northern Europe.

Johann Gottfried von Herder, "Ideas for the Philosophy of History of Humanity"

❝ This is more or less a picture of the peoples of Europe. What a multicolored and composite picture! . . . Sea voyages and long migrations of people finally produced on the small continent of Europe the conditions for a great league of nations. Unwittingly the Romans had prepared it by their conquests. Such a league of nations was unthinkable outside of Europe. Nowhere else have people intermingled so much, nowhere else have they changed so often and so much their habitats and thereby their customs and ways of life. In many European countries it would be difficult today for the inhabitants, especially for single families and individuals, to say, from which people they descend, whether from Goths, Moors, Jews, Carthaginians or Romans, whether from Gauls, Burgundians, Franks, Normans, Saxons, Slavs, Finns or Illyrians, or how in the long line of their ancestors their blood had been mixed. Hundreds of causes have tempered and changed the old tribal composition of the European nations in the course of the centuries; without such an intermingling the common spirit of Europe could hardly have been awakened.

. . . Like the geological layers of our soil, the European peoples have been superimposed on each other and intermingled with each other, and yet can still be discerned in their original character. The scholars who study their customs and languages must hurry and do

so while these peoples are still distinguishable: for everything in Europe tends towards the slow extinction of national character. But the historian of mankind should beware lest he exclusively favors one nationality and thereby slights others who were deprived by circumstances of chance and glory. . . .

No European people has become cultured and educated by itself. Each one has tended to keep its old barbarian customs as long as it could, supported therein by the roughness of the climate and the need of primitive warfare. No European people for instance has invented its own alphabet; the whole civilization of northern, eastern and western Europe has grown out of seeds sown by Romans, Greeks and Arabs. It took a long time before this could grow in the hard soil and could produce its own fruit, which at first lacked sweetness and ripeness. A strange vehicle, an

Johann Gottfried von Herder, renowned eighteenth-century philosopher and historian (left), and Giuseppe Mazzini, Italian patriot in later life after years in exile (far right). (Herder: akg-images; Mazzini: Hulton Archive/Getty Images)

alien religion [Christianity], was necessary to accomplish by spiritual means that which the Romans had not been able to do through conquest. Thus we must consider above all this new means of human education, which had no lesser aim than to educate all peoples to become one people, in this world and for a future world, and which was nowhere more effective than in Europe. 🙭

Like Herder, Giuseppe Mazzini (1805–1872) believed that language determined nationality and that each people had its particular genius. But unlike Herder, Mazzini and many other nationalists of the pre-1848 era also believed that each nationality required a politically independent nation-state. Only a Europe of nation-states would provide the proper framework for securing freedom, democracy, social justice, and even international peace.

The leading prophet of Italian nationalism and unification before 1848, Mazzini founded a secret society called Young Italy to fight for the unification of the Italian states in a democratic republic. Mazzini's group inspired numerous local insurrections and led Italy's radicals in the unsuccessful revolutions of 1848. Mazzini's best-known work was The Duties of Man, *a collection of essays. The following selection from this work was written in 1858 and addressed to Italian workingmen.*

Giuseppe Mazzini, "Duties Towards Your Country"

🙭 Your first Duties . . . are to Humanity. . . . But what can each of you, with his isolated powers, do for the moral improvement, for the progress of Humanity? . . .

God gave you the means of multiplying your forces and your powers of action indefinitely when he gave you a Country, when, like a wise overseer of labor, who distributes the different parts of the work according to the capacity of the workmen, he divided Humanity into distinct groups upon the face of our globe, and thus planted the seeds of nations. Evil governments have disfigured the design of God, which you may see clearly marked out, as far, at least, as regards Europe, by the courses of the great rivers, by the lines of the lofty mountains, and by other geographical conditions; they have disfigured it by conquest, by greed, by jealousy of the just sovereignty of others; disfigured it so much that today there is perhaps no nation except England and France whose confines correspond to this design.

[These evil governments] did not, and they do not, recognize any country except their own families and dynasties, the egoism of caste. But the divine design will infallibly be fulfilled. Natural divisions, the innate spontaneous tendencies of the peoples will replace the arbitrary divisions sanctioned by evil governments. The map of Europe will be remade. The Countries of the People will rise, defined by the voice of the free, upon the ruins of the Countries of Kings and privileged castes. Between these Countries there will be harmony and brotherhood. And then the work of Humanity for the general amelioration, for the discovery and application of the real law of life, carried on in association and distributed according to local capacities, will be accomplished by peaceful and progressive development.

Then each of you, strong in the affections and in the aid of many millions of men speaking the same language, endowed with the same tendencies, and educated by the same historic tradition, may hope by your personal effort to benefit the whole of Humanity.

Without Country you have neither name, voice, nor rights, no admission as brothers into the fellowship of the Peoples. You are the bastards of Humanity. Soldiers without a banner, . . . you will find neither faith nor protection. . . . Do not beguile yourselves with the hope of emancipation from unjust social conditions if you do not first conquer a Country for yourselves; where there is no Country there is no common agreement to which you can appeal; the egoism of self-interest rules alone, and he who has the upper hand keeps it, since there is no common safeguard for the interests of all. 🙭

Sources: Hans Kohn, *Nationalism: Its Idea and History* (Princeton, N.J.: D. Van Nostrand Company Inc., 1955), pp. 108–110; G. Mazzini, *The Duties of Man and Other Essays* (London: J. M. Dent and Sons, 1907), pp. 51–54.

QUESTIONS FOR ANALYSIS

1. How, according to Herder, did European nationalities evolve to create "the common spirit of Europe"?

2. Why, according to Mazzini, should Italian workers support Italian unification?

3. How are Herder's and Mazzini's views similar? How do they differ?

government-backed workshops and factories to guarantee full employment. The right to work had to become as sacred as any other right.

Finally, there was Pierre Joseph Proudhon (1809–1865), a self-educated printer who wrote a pamphlet *What Is Property?* in 1840. His answer was that it was nothing but theft. Property was profit that was stolen from the worker, who was the source of all wealth.

Of great importance, the message of French utopian socialists interacted with the experiences of French urban workers. Workers cherished the memory of the radical phase of the French Revolution, and they became violently opposed to laissez-faire laws that denied workers the right to organize in guilds and unions. Developing a sense of class in the process, workers favored collective action and government intervention in economic life. Thus the aspirations of workers and utopian theorists reinforced each other, and a genuine socialist movement emerged in Paris in the 1830s and 1840s. To Karl Marx was left the task of establishing firm foundations for modern socialism.

The Birth of Marxian Socialism

In 1848 Karl Marx (1818–1883) and Friedrich Engels (see Chapter 21) published *The Communist Manifesto*, which became the bible of socialism. The son of a Jewish lawyer who had converted to Christianity, the atheistic young Marx had studied philosophy at the University of Berlin before turning to journalism and economics. He read widely in French socialist thought, and like Fourier he looked forward to the emancipation of women and the abolition of the family. By the time Marx was twenty-five, he was developing his own socialist ideas.

Early French socialists often appealed to the middle class and the state to help the poor. Marx ridiculed such appeals as naive. He argued that the interests of the middle class and those of the industrial working class were inevitably opposed to each other. Indeed, according to the *Manifesto*, the "history of all previously existing society is the history of class struggles." In Marx's view, one class had always exploited the other, and with the advent of modern industry, society was split more clearly than ever before: between the middle class — the **bourgeoisie** (boor-ZHWAH-zee) — and the modern working class — the **proletariat**.

Just as the bourgeoisie had triumphed over the feudal aristocracy, Marx predicted that the proletariat would conquer the bourgeoisie in a violent revolution. While a tiny minority owned the means of production and grew richer, the ever-poorer proletariat was constantly growing in size and in class-consciousness.

bourgeoisie The middle-class minority who owned the means of production and, according to Marx, exploited the working-class proletariat.

proletariat The industrial working class who, according to Marx, were unfairly exploited by the profit-seeking bourgeoisie.

The history of all previously existing society is the history of class struggles.

—KARL MARX

In this process, the proletariat was aided, according to Marx, by a portion of the bourgeoisie who had gone over to the proletariat and who (like Marx and Engels) "had raised themselves to the level of comprehending theoretically the historical moment." The critical moment, Marx thought, was very near, as the last lines of *The Communist Manifesto* make very clear.

> *Germany . . . is on the eve of a bourgeois revolution, that is bound to be . . . the prelude to an immediately following proletarian revolution. . . .*
>
> *The Communists disdain to conceal their views and aims. They openly declare that their ends can be attained only by the forcible overthrow of all existing social conditions. Let the ruling classes tremble at a Communist revolution. The proletarians have nothing to lose but their chains. They have a world to win. WORKING MEN OF ALL COUNTRIES, UNITE!*

Marx's ideas united sociology, economics, and all human history in a vast and imposing edifice. He synthesized in his socialism not only French utopian schemes but also English classical economics and German philosophy — the major intellectual currents of his day. Following David Ricardo, who had taught that labor was the source of all value, Marx went on to argue Proudhon's case that profits were really wages stolen from the workers. Moreover, Marx incorporated Engels's charges of terrible oppression of the new class of factory workers in England. Thus Marx's doctrines seemed to be based on hard facts.

Marx's theory of historical evolution was built on the philosophy of the German Georg Hegel (1770–1831). Hegel believed that each age is characterized by dominant ideas that produce opposing ideas and eventually a new synthesis. The idea of being had been dominant initially, for example, and it had produced its antithesis, the idea of nonbeing. This idea in turn had resulted in the synthesis of becoming. Thus history has pattern and purpose.

Marx retained Hegel's view of history as a dialectic process of change but made economic relationships between classes the driving force. This dialectic explained the decline of agrarian feudalism and the rise of industrial capitalism. Marx stressed repeatedly that the "bourgeoisie, historically, has played a most revolutionary

Mr. and Mrs. Karl Marx Active in the revolution of 1848, Marx fled from Germany in 1849 and settled in London. There Marx and his young wife lived a respectable middle-class life while he wrote *Capital*, the weighty exposition of his socialist theories. Marx also worked to organize the working class, and he earned a modest income as a journalist and received financial support from his coauthor, Friedrich Engels. (Time Life Pictures/Mansell/Getty Images)

part. . . . During its rule of scarcely one hundred years the bourgeoisie has created more massive and more colossal productive forces than have all preceding generations together."

Marx's next idea, that it was now the bourgeoisie's turn to give way to the socialism of revolutionary workers, appeared to many the irrefutable capstone of a brilliant interpretation of humanity's long development. Thus Marx pulled together powerful ideas and insights to create one of the great secular religions out of the intellectual ferment of the early nineteenth century.

The Romantic Movement

What were the characteristics of the romantic movement, and who were some of the great romantic artists? ■

The early nineteenth century was a time of change in literature and the other arts as well as politics. Known as the romantic movement, this artistic change was in part a revolt against the emphasis on rationality, order, and restraint that characterized the Enlightenment and the controlled style of classicism.

Forerunners of the romantic movement appeared from about 1750 on. Of these, Rousseau (see Chapter 17)—the passionate advocate of feeling, freedom, and natural goodness—was the most influential. Romanticism then crystallized fully in the 1790s, primarily in England and Germany. The French Revolution kindled the belief that radical reconstruction was also possible in cultural and artistic life (even though many early English and German romantics became disillusioned with events in France and turned from liberalism to conservatism in politics). Romanticism gained strength until the 1840s, when it gradually gave way to realism (see Chapter 23).

Romanticism's Tenets

Romanticism was characterized by a belief in emotional exuberance, unrestrained imagination, and spontaneity in both art and personal life. In Germany early romantics of the 1770s and 1780s called themselves the Sturm und Drang (storm and stress), and many romantic artists of the early nineteenth century lived lives of tremendous emotional intensity. Suicide, duels to the death, madness, and strange illnesses were not uncommon among leading romantics. Romantic artists typically led bohemian lives, wearing their hair long and uncombed in preference to powdered wigs, and rejecting the materialism of refined society. Great individualists, the romantics believed the full development of one's unique human potential to be the supreme purpose in life.

Nowhere was the break with classicism more apparent than in romanticism's general conception of nature. Classicism was not particularly interested in nature. In the words of the eighteenth-century English author Samuel Johnson, "A blade of grass is always a blade of grass; men and women are my subjects of inquiry." The romantics, in contrast, were enchanted by nature. For some it was awesome and tempestuous, while others saw nature as a source of spiritual inspiration. As the great

romanticism A movement at its height from about 1790 to the 1840s that was in part a revolt against classicism and the Enlightenment, characterized by a belief in emotional exuberance, unrestrained imagination, and spontaneity in both art and personal life.

English landscape artist John Constable declared, "Nature is Spirit visible."

Most romantics saw the growth of modern industry as an ugly, brutal attack on their beloved nature and on the human personality. They sought escape—in the unspoiled Lake District of northern England, in exotic North Africa, in an imaginary idealized Middle Ages.

Diverse, exciting, and important, the study of history became a romantic passion. History was the key to a universe that was now perceived to be organic and dynamic, not mechanical and static as the Enlightenment thinkers had believed. Nor was it restricted to the biographies of great men or the work of divine providence. Historians such as Jules Michelet, who focused on the development of societies and human institutions, promoted the growth of national aspirations, fanning the embers of memory and encouraging entire peoples to seek in the past their special destinies.

Literature

Romanticism found its distinctive voice in poetry, as the Enlightenment had in prose. Its first great poets were British: Wordsworth, Coleridge, and Scott were all active by 1800, to be followed shortly by Byron, Shelley, and Keats.

A towering leader of English romanticism, William Wordsworth (1770–1850) was deeply influenced by Rousseau and the spirit of the early French Revolution. Wordsworth settled in the rural Lake District of England with his sister, Dorothy, and Samuel Taylor Coleridge (1772–1834). In 1798 Wordsworth and Coleridge published their *Lyrical Ballads*, which abandoned flowery classical conventions for the language of ordinary speech and endowed simple subjects with the loftiest majesty. One of the best examples of Wordsworth's romantic credo and genius is "Daffodils." After describing the joyful experience of wandering into a field of flowers, the writer reflects on the power of that single experience in the last stanza of the poem:

> *For oft, when on my couch I lie*
> *In vacant or in pensive mood,*
> *They flash upon that inward eye*
> *Which is the bliss of solitude;*
> *And then my heart with pleasure fills,*
> *And dances with the daffodils.*

Here indeed are simplicity and love of nature in commonplace forms that could be appreciated by everyone. Wordsworth's conception of poetry as the "spontaneous overflow of powerful feeling recollected in tranquility" is well illustrated by this stanza.

Classicism remained strong in France under Napoleon and inhibited the growth of romanticism there. In 1813 Germaine de Staël (duh STAHL) (1766–1817), a Franco-Swiss writer living in exile, urged the French to throw away their worn-out classical models. Her study *On Germany* (1810) extolled the spontaneity and enthusiasm of German writers and thinkers, and it had a powerful impact on the post-1815 generation in France. (See "Individuals in Society: Germaine de Staël," at right.) Between 1820 and 1850, the romantic impulse broke through in the poetry and prose of Lamartine, de Vigny, Hugo, Dumas, and Sand. Of these, Victor Hugo (1802–1885) became the most well known in both poetry and prose.

Son of a Napoleonic general, Hugo achieved an amazing range of rhythm, language, and image in his lyric poetry. His powerful novels exemplified the romantic fascination with fantastic characters, exotic historical settings, and human emotions. The hero of Hugo's famous *The Hunchback of Notre Dame* (1831) is the great cathedral's deformed bell-ringer, a "human gargoyle" overlooking the teeming life of fifteenth-century Paris. Renouncing his early conservatism, Hugo equated freedom in literature with liberty in politics and society. Hugo's political evolution was thus exactly the opposite of Wordsworth's, in whom youthful radicalism gave way to middle-aged caution. As the contrast between the two artists suggests, romanticism was a cultural movement compatible with many political beliefs.

Amandine Aurore Lucie Dupin (1804–1876), generally known by her pen name, George Sand, defied the narrow conventions of her time in an unending search for self-fulfillment. After eight years of unhappy marriage she abandoned her husband and took her two children to Paris to pursue a career as a writer. There Sand soon achieved fame and wealth, eventually writing over eighty novels on a variety of romantic and social themes. George Sand's striking individualism went far beyond her flamboyant preference for men's clothing and her notorious affairs. Her semi-autobiographical novel *Lélia* was shockingly modern, delving deeply into her tortuous quest for sexual and personal freedom.

In central and eastern Europe, literary romanticism and early nationalism often reinforced each other. Seeking a unique greatness in every people, well-educated romantics plumbed their own histories and cultures. Like modern anthropologists, they turned their attention to peasant life and transcribed the folk songs, tales, and proverbs that the cosmopolitan Enlightenment had disdained. The brothers Jacob and Wilhelm Grimm were particularly successful at rescuing German fairy tales from oblivion. In the Slavic lands, romantics played a decisive role in converting spoken peasant languages into modern written languages. The most influential of all Russian poets, Aleksander Pushkin (1799–1837), rejecting eighteenth-century attempts to force Russian poetry into a classical straitjacket, used his lyric genius to mold the modern literary language.

INDIVIDUALS IN SOCIETY

Germaine de Staël

RICH, INTELLECTUAL, PASSIONATE, AND ASSERTIVE, Germaine Necker de Staël (1766–1817) astonished contemporaries and still fascinates historians. She was strongly influenced by her parents, poor Swiss Protestants who soared to the top of prerevolutionary Parisian society. Her brilliant but rigid mother filled Germaine's head with knowledge, and each week the precocious child listened, wide-eyed and attentive, to illustrious writers and philosophers performing at her mother's salon. At age twelve, she suffered a physical and mental breakdown. Only then was she allowed to have a playmate and romp and run on the family estate. Her adoring father was Jacques Necker, a banker who made an enormous fortune and became France's reform-minded minister of finance before the Revolution. Worshiping her father in adolescence, Germaine also came to love politics.

Accepting at nineteen an arranged marriage with Baron de Staël-Holstein, a womanizing Swedish diplomat bewitched by her dowry, Germaine began her life's work. She opened an intellectual salon and began to write and publish. Her wit and exuberance attracted foreigners and liberal French aristocrats, one of whom became the first of many lovers as her marriage soured and she searched unsuccessfully for the happiness of her parents' union. Fleeing Paris in 1792 and returning after the Thermidorian reaction (see page 643), she subsequently angered Napoleon by criticizing his dictatorial rule. In 1803 he permanently banished her from Paris.

Retiring again to her isolated estate in Switzerland and skillfully managing her inherited wealth, Staël fought insomnia with opium and boredom with parties that attracted luminaries from all over Europe. Always seeking stimulation for her restless mind, she traveled widely in Italy and Germany and drew upon these experiences in her novel *Corinne* (1807) and her study *On Germany* (1810). Both works summed up her romantic faith and enjoyed enormous success.

Staël urged creative individuals to abandon traditional rules and classical models. She encouraged them to embrace experimentation, emotion, and enthusiasm. Enthusiasm, which she had in abundance, was the key, the royal road to creativity, personal fulfillment, and human improvement. Thrilling to music, for example, she felt that only an enthusiastic person could really appreciate this gift of God, this wordless message that "unifies our dual nature and blends senses and spirit in a common rapture."*

Yet a profound sadness runs through her writing. This sadness, so characteristic of the romantic temperament, grew in part out of disappointments in love and prolonged exile. But it also grew out of the insoluble predicament of being an enormously gifted woman in an age of intense male chauvinism. Little wonder that uneasy male competitors and literary critics took delight in ridiculing and defaming her as a neurotic and masculine woman, a mediocre and unnatural talent who had foolishly dared to enter the male world of serious thought and action. Even her supporters could not accept her for what she was. The admiring poet Lord Byron recognized her genius and called her "the most eminent woman author of this, or perhaps of any century." But he quickly added that "she should have been born a man."†

*Quoted in G. R. Besser, *Germaine de Staël Revisited* (New York: Twayne Publishers, 1994), p. 106. Enhanced by a feminist perspective, this fine study is highly recommended.

†Quoted ibid., p. 139.

Germaine de Staël. (Erich Lessing/Art Resource, NY)

Buffeted and saddened by scorn and condescension because of her gender, Staël advocated equal rights for women throughout her life. Only with equal rights and duties — in education and careers, in love and marital relations — could an exceptional woman like herself, or indeed any woman, ever hope to realize her intellectual and emotional potential. Practicing what she preached as best she could, Germaine de Staël was a trailblazer in the struggle for women's rights.

QUESTIONS FOR ANALYSIS

1. In what ways did Germaine de Staël's life and thought reflect basic elements of the romantic movement?
2. Why did male critics often attack Staël? What do these criticisms tell us about gender relations in the early nineteenth century?

699

John Constable, *The Hay Wain* Constable's love of a spiritualized and poetic nature radiates from this masterpiece of romantic art. Exhibited in Paris in 1829, *The Hay Wain* created a sensation and made a profound impression on the young Delacroix. The cottage on the left still stands, open to the public as a small museum devoted to Constable and his paintings. (National Gallery, London, U.K./The Bridgeman Art Library)

Art and Music

One of the greatest and most moving romantic painters in France was Eugène Delacroix (oe-ZHEHN deh-luh-KWAH) (1798–1863), probably the illegitimate son of French foreign minister Talleyrand (see page 687). Delacroix was a master of dramatic, colorful scenes that stirred the emotions. He was fascinated with remote and exotic subjects, whether lion hunts in Morocco or dreams of languishing, sensuous women in a sultan's harem. Yet he was also a passionate spokesman for freedom.

In England the most notable romantic painters were Joseph M. W. Turner (1775–1851) and John Constable (1776–1837). Both were fascinated by nature, but their interpretations of it contrasted sharply, aptly symbolizing the tremendous emotional range of the romantic movement. Turner depicted nature's power and terror; wild storms and sinking ships were favorite subjects. Constable painted gentle Wordsworthian landscapes in which human beings were at one with their environment, the comforting countryside of unspoiled rural England.

It was in music that romanticism realized most fully and permanently its goals of free expression and emotional intensity. Abandoning well-defined structures, the great romantic composers used a wide range of forms to create a thousand musical landscapes and evoke a host of powerful emotions. Romantic composers also transformed the small classical orchestra, tripling its size by adding wind instruments, percussion, and more brass and strings. The crashing chords evoking the surge of the masses in Chopin's Revolutionary Etude, and the bottomless despair of the funeral march in Beethoven's Third Symphony—such were the modern orchestra's musical paintings that plumbed the depths of human feeling.

This range and intensity gave music and musicians much greater prestige than in the past. Music no longer simply complemented a church service or helped a nobleman digest his dinner. It became a sublime end in itself, most perfectly realizing the endless yearning of the soul. The unbelievable one-in-a-million performer—the great virtuoso who could transport the listener to ecstasy and hysteria—became a cultural hero. People swooned for Franz Liszt (1811–1886), the greatest pianist of his age, as they scream for rock stars today.

The first great romantic composer is also the most famous today. Ludwig van Beethoven (BAY-toh-vuhn)

(1770–1827) used contrasting themes and tones to produce dramatic conflict and inspiring resolutions. As one contemporary admirer wrote, "Beethoven's music sets in motion the lever of fear, of awe, of horror, of suffering, and awakens just that infinite longing which is the essence of Romanticism." Beethoven's range and output were tremendous. At the peak of his fame, he began to lose his hearing. He considered suicide but eventually overcame despair: "I will take fate by the throat; it will not bend me completely to its will."[3] Beethoven continued to pour out immortal music, although his last years were silent, spent in total deafness.

Reforms and Revolutions Before 1848

How after 1815 did liberal, national, and socialist forces challenge conservatism in Greece, Great Britain, and France? ■

While the romantic movement was developing, liberal, national, and socialist forces battered against the conservatism of 1815. In some countries, change occurred gradually and peacefully. Elsewhere, pressure built up like steam in a pressure cooker without a safety valve and eventually caused an explosion in 1848. Three important countries—Greece, Great Britain, and France—experienced variations on this basic theme between 1815 and 1848.

National Liberation in Greece

National, liberal revolution, frustrated in Italy and Spain by conservative statesmen, succeeded first after 1815 in Greece. Since the fifteenth century, the Greeks had been living under the domination of the Ottoman Turks. In spite of centuries of foreign rule, the Greeks had survived as a people, united by their language and the Greek Orthodox religion. It was natural that the general growth of national aspirations and a desire for independence would inspire some Greeks in the early nineteenth century. This rising national movement led to the formation of secret societies and then to revolt in 1821, led by Alexander Ypsilanti (ip-suh-LAN-tee), a Greek patriot and a general in the Russian army.

At first, the Great Powers, particularly Metternich, were opposed to all revolution, even revolution against the Islamic Turks. They refused to back Ypsilanti and supported the Ottoman Empire. Yet for many Europeans, the Greek cause became a holy one. Educated Americans and Europeans were in love with the culture of classical Greece; Russians were stirred by the piety of their Orthodox brethren. Writers and artists, moved by the romantic impulse, responded enthusiastically to the Greek national struggle. The famous English romantic poet Lord Byron even joined the Greeks to fight "that Greece may yet be free."

The Greeks, though often quarreling among themselves, battled on against the Turks and hoped for the eventual support of European governments. In 1827 Great Britain, France, and Russia yielded to popular demands at home and directed Turkey to accept an

Delacroix, *Massacre at Chios*
The Greek struggle for freedom and independence won the enthusiastic support of liberals, nationalists, and romantics. The Ottoman Turks were portrayed as cruel oppressors who were holding back the course of history, as in this moving masterpiece by Delacroix. (Réunion des Musées Nationaux/Art Resource, NY)

Greek Independence, 1830

armistice. When the Turks refused, the navies of these three powers trapped the Turkish fleet at Navarino and destroyed it. Russia then declared another of its periodic wars of expansion against the Turks. This led to the establishment of a Russian protectorate over much of present-day Romania, which had also been under Turkish rule. Great Britain, France, and Russia finally declared Greece independent in 1830 and installed a German prince as king of the new country in 1832. In the end, the Greeks had won: a small nation had gained its independence in a heroic war of liberation against a foreign empire.

Liberal Reform in Great Britain

Eighteenth-century British society had been both flexible and remarkably stable. It was dominated by the landowning aristocracy, but that class was neither closed nor rigidly defined. Successful business and professional people could buy land and become gentlefolk, while the common people had more than the usual opportunities of the preindustrial world. Basic civil rights for all were balanced by a tradition of deference to one's social superiors. Parliament was manipulated by the king and was thoroughly undemocratic, with only about 8 percent of the population allowed to vote for representatives.

By the 1780s there was growing interest in some kind of political reform, but the French Revolution threw the British aristocracy into a panic for a generation, making it extremely hostile to any attempts to change the status quo. Conflicts between the ruling class and laborers were sparked in 1815 with revision of the **Corn Laws**. Britain had been unable to import cheap grain from eastern Europe during the war years, leading to high prices and large profits for the landed aristocracy. With the war over, grain could be imported again, allowing the price of wheat and bread to go down and benefiting almost everyone except the aristocracy. The aristocracy, however, rammed far-reaching changes in the Corn Laws

through Parliament. The new regulation prohibited the importation of foreign grain unless the price at home rose to improbable levels. Seldom has a class legislated more selfishly for its own narrow economic advantage or done more to promote a class-based view of political action.

The change in the Corn Laws, coming as it did at a time of widespread unemployment and postwar economic distress, triggered protests and demonstrations by urban laborers, who were supported by radical intellectuals. In 1817 the Tory government, which was completely controlled by the landed aristocracy, responded by temporarily suspending the traditional rights of peaceable assembly and habeas corpus. Two years later, Parliament passed the infamous Six Acts, which, among other things, placed controls on a heavily taxed press and practically eliminated all mass meetings. These acts followed an enormous but orderly protest, at Saint Peter's Fields in Manchester, that had been savagely broken up by armed cavalry. Nicknamed the **Battle of Peterloo**, in scornful reference to the British victory at Waterloo, this incident demonstrated the government's determination to repress dissenters.

Strengthened by ongoing industrial development, the new manufacturing and commercial groups insisted on a place for their new wealth alongside the landed wealth of the aristocracy in the framework of political power and social prestige. They called for many kinds of liberal reform: reform of town government, organization of a new police force, more rights for Catholics and dissenters, and reform of the Poor Laws that provided aid to some low-paid workers. In the 1820s, a less frightened Tory government moved in the direction of better urban administration, greater economic liberalism, civil equality for Catholics, and limited imports of foreign grain. These actions encouraged the middle classes to press on for reform of Parliament so they could have a larger say in government.

The Whig Party, though led like the Tories by great aristocrats, had by tradition been more responsive to middle-class commercial and manufacturing interests. In 1830 a Whig ministry introduced "an act to amend the representation of the people of England and Wales." After a series of setbacks, the Whigs' **Reform Bill of 1832** was propelled into law by a mighty surge of popular support. Significantly, the bill moved British politics in a democratic direction and allowed the House of Commons to emerge as the all-important legislative body. The new industrial areas of the country gained representation in the Commons, and many old "rotten boroughs"—electoral districts that had very few voters and that the landed aristocracy had bought and sold— were eliminated. The number of voters increased by about 50 percent, giving about 12 percent of adult men in Britain and Ireland the right to vote. Comfortable middle-class groups in the urban population, as well as

---

Corn Laws British laws, revised in 1815, that prohibited the importation of foreign grain unless the price at home rose to improbable levels, thus benefiting the aristocracy but making food prices high for working people.

Battle of Peterloo A protest that took place at Saint Peter's Fields in Manchester in reaction to the revision of the Corn Laws; it was broken up by armed cavalry.

Reform Bill of 1832 A major British political reform that increased the number of male voters by about 50 percent and gave political representation to new industrial areas.

The Anti–Corn Law Movement in Action This contemporary illustration focuses on the Anti–Corn Law League's remarkable ability to mobilize a broad urban coalition that was dedicated to free trade and the end of tariffs on imported grain (or "corn"). Each League supporter was encouraged to join the national organization and receive a membership card like the one shown here, attend meetings and lectures, and demonstrate in the streets. (cartoon: The Granger Collection, New York; card: © Museum of London, U.K./The Bridgeman Art Library)

some substantial farmers who leased their land, received the vote. Thus the pressures building in Great Britain were successfully—though only temporarily—released. A major reform had been achieved peacefully. Continued fundamental reform within the system appeared difficult but not impossible.

The principal radical program for continued reform was embodied in the "People's Charter" of 1838 and the Chartist movement (see Chapter 21). Partly inspired by the economic distress of the working class in the 1830s and 1840s, the Chartists' core demand was universal male (but not female) suffrage. They saw complete political democracy and rule by the common people—the great majority of the population—as the means to a good and just society. Hundreds of thousands of people signed gigantic petitions calling on Parliament to grant all men the right to vote, first and most seriously in 1839, again in 1842, and yet again in 1848. Parliament rejected all three petitions. In the short run, the working poor failed with their Chartist demands, but they learned a valuable lesson in mass politics.

While calling for universal male suffrage, many working-class people joined with middle-class manufac-

turers in the Anti–Corn Law League, founded in Manchester in 1839. Mass participation made possible a popular crusade led by fighting liberals, who argued that lower food prices and more jobs in industry depended on repeal of the Corn Laws. Much of the working class agreed. When Ireland's potato crop failed in 1845 (see page 705) and famine prices for food seemed likely in England, Tory prime minister Robert Peel joined with the Whigs and a minority of his own party to repeal the Corn Laws in 1846 and allow free imports of grain. England escaped famine. Thereafter the liberal doctrine of free trade became almost sacred dogma in Great Britain.

The following year, the Tories passed a bill designed to help the working classes, but in a different way. The Ten Hours Act of 1847 limited the workday for women and young people in factories to ten hours. Tory aristocrats continued to champion legislation regulating factory conditions. They were competing vigorously with the middle class for the support of the working class. This healthy competition between a still-vigorous aristocracy and a strong middle class was a crucial factor in Great Britain's peaceful evolution. The working classes could make temporary alliances with either competitor to better their own conditions.

Ireland and the Great Famine

The people of Ireland did not benefit from the political competition in Britain. The great mass of the population (outside of the northern counties of Ulster, which were partly Presbyterian) were Irish Catholics, who rented their land from a tiny minority of Church of England Protestants. These landlords were content to use their power to grab as much as possible.

The result was that the condition of the Irish peasantry around 1800 was abominable. The typical peasant lived in a wretched cottage and could afford neither shoes nor stockings. Hundreds of shocking accounts describe hopeless poverty. The novelist Sir Walter Scott wrote:

> The poverty of the Irish peasantry is on the extreme verge of human misery; their cottages would scarce serve for pig styes even in Scotland; and their rags seem the very refuse of a sheep, and are spread over their bodies with such an ingenious variety of wretchedness that you would think nothing but some sort of perverted taste could have assembled so many shreds together.[4]

A compassionate French traveler agreed, writing that Ireland was "pure misery, naked and hungry. . . . I saw the American Indian in his forests and the black slave in his chains, and I believed that I was seeing the most extreme form of human misery; but that was before I knew the lot of poor Ireland."[5]

Yet in spite of terrible conditions, population growth sped onward. The 3 million of 1725 reached 4 million in 1780 and doubled to 8 million by 1840. In addition, between 1780 and 1840, another 1.75 million people left Ireland for Britain and America in search of better living conditions.

Ireland's population explosion, part of Europe's general population growth since the early eighteenth century (see Chapter 18), was caused in part by the extensive cultivation of the potato. A single acre of land spaded and planted with potatoes could feed an Irish family of six for a year, and the potato also could thrive on boggy wastelands. Needing only a big potato patch to survive, Irish men and women married early. To be sure, the young couple was embracing a life of extreme poverty. They would literally live on potatoes—ten pounds a day for an average male—moistened at best with a cup of milk.

Yet the decision to marry and have large families made sense. Landlords leased land for short periods only.

The Discovery of the Potato Blight Although the leaves usually shriveled and died, they could also look deceptively healthy. In this painting by Daniel McDonald an Irish family has dug up its potato harvest and just discovered to its horror that the blight has rotted the crop. Like thousands of Irish families, the family now faces the starvation and mass epidemics of the Great Famine. (Department of Irish Folklore, University College, Dublin)

Peasants had no incentive to make permanent improvements because anything beyond what was needed for survival would quickly be taken by higher rent. Rural poverty was inescapable and better shared with a spouse, while a dutiful son or a loving daughter was an old person's best hope of escaping destitution.

As population and potato dependency grew, conditions became more precarious. From 1820 onward deficiencies and diseases in the potato crop became more common. In 1845 and 1846, and again in 1848 and 1851, the potato crop failed in Ireland. The result was unmitigated disaster — the **Great Famine**. Blight attacked the young plants, and the tubers rotted. Widespread starvation and mass fever epidemics followed. Yet the British government, committed to rigid laissez-faire ideology, was slow to act. When it did, its relief efforts were tragically inadequate. Moreover, the government continued to collect taxes, landlords demanded their rents, and tenants who could not pay were evicted and their homes destroyed. Famine or no, Ireland remained the conquered jewel of foreign landowners.

The Great Famine shattered the pattern of Irish population growth. Fully 1 million emigrants fled the famine between 1845 and 1851, and at least 1.5 million died or went unborn because of the disaster. Alone among the countries of Europe, Ireland experienced a declining population in the second half of the nineteenth century, as it became a land of continuous out-migration, late marriage, early death, and widespread celibacy.

The Great Famine also intensified anti-British feeling and promoted Irish nationalism, for the bitter memory of starvation, exile, and British inaction was burned deeply into the popular consciousness. Patriots could call on powerful collective emotions in their campaigns for land reform, home rule, and, eventually, Irish independence.

The Revolution of 1830 in France

Louis XVIII's Constitutional Charter of 1814— theoretically a gift from the king but actually a response to political pressures—was basically a liberal constitution (see Chapter 20). The economic and social gains made by sections of the middle class and the peasantry in the French Revolution were fully protected, great

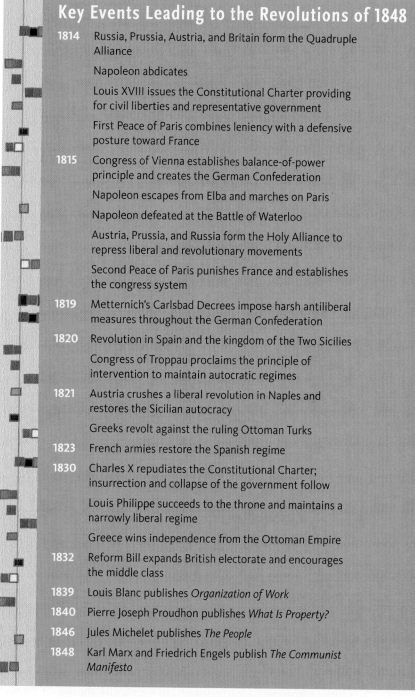

Key Events Leading to the Revolutions of 1848

1814	Russia, Prussia, Austria, and Britain form the Quadruple Alliance
	Napoleon abdicates
	Louis XVIII issues the Constitutional Charter providing for civil liberties and representative government
	First Peace of Paris combines leniency with a defensive posture toward France
1815	Congress of Vienna establishes balance-of-power principle and creates the German Confederation
	Napoleon escapes from Elba and marches on Paris
	Napoleon defeated at the Battle of Waterloo
	Austria, Prussia, and Russia form the Holy Alliance to repress liberal and revolutionary movements
	Second Peace of Paris punishes France and establishes the congress system
1819	Metternich's Carlsbad Decrees impose harsh antiliberal measures throughout the German Confederation
1820	Revolution in Spain and the kingdom of the Two Sicilies
	Congress of Troppau proclaims the principle of intervention to maintain autocratic regimes
1821	Austria crushes a liberal revolution in Naples and restores the Sicilian autocracy
	Greeks revolt against the ruling Ottoman Turks
1823	French armies restore the Spanish regime
1830	Charles X repudiates the Constitutional Charter; insurrection and collapse of the government follow
	Louis Philippe succeeds to the throne and maintains a narrowly liberal regime
	Greece wins independence from the Ottoman Empire
1832	Reform Bill expands British electorate and encourages the middle class
1839	Louis Blanc publishes *Organization of Work*
1840	Pierre Joseph Proudhon publishes *What Is Property?*
1846	Jules Michelet publishes *The People*
1848	Karl Marx and Friedrich Engels publish *The Communist Manifesto*

intellectual and artistic freedom was permitted, and a parliament with upper and lower houses was created. Immediately after Napoleon's abortive Hundred Days, the moderate, worldly king refused to bow to the wishes of die-hard aristocrats who wanted to sweep away all the revolutionary changes. Instead, Louis appointed as his ministers moderate royalists, who sought and obtained the support of a majority of the representatives elected to the lower Chamber of Deputies between 1816 and Louis's death in 1824.

Great Famine The result of four years of potato crop failure in Ireland, a country that had grown dependent on potatoes as a dietary staple.

The Fall of Algiers In July 1830 France assembled more than six hundred ships and attacked the Ottoman dependency of Algeria. The ferocious naval bombardment shown in this engraving destroyed the capital's fortifications. After the surrender French soldiers rampaged through the city, and news of this brutal behavior encouraged Muslims in the interior to revolt and fight on until 1847. (Musée de la Ville de Paris, Musée Carnavalet, Paris, France/Lauros/Giraudon/The Bridgeman Art Library)

Louis XVIII's charter was anything but democratic. Only about 100,000 of the wealthiest males out of a total population of 30 million had the right to vote for the deputies who, with the king and his ministers, made the laws of the nation. Nonetheless, the "notable people" who did vote came from very different backgrounds. There were wealthy businessmen, war profiteers, successful professionals, ex-revolutionaries, large landowners from the old aristocracy and the middle class, Bourbons, and Bonapartists. The old aristocracy, with its pre-1789 mentality, was a minority within the voting population. It was this situation that Louis's successor, Charles X (r. 1824–1830), could not abide. A true reactionary, Charles wanted to re-establish the old order in France. Increasingly blocked by the opposition of the deputies, Charles's government turned in 1830 to military adventure in an effort to rally French nationalism and gain popular support. A long-standing economic and diplomatic dispute with Muslim Algeria, a vassal state of the Ottoman Empire, provided the opportunity.

In June 1830, a French force of thirty-seven thousand crossed the Mediterranean, landed to the west of Algiers, and took the capital city in three short weeks. Victory seemed complete, but in 1831 tribes in the in-terior revolted and waged a fearsome war until 1847, when French armies finally subdued the country. Bringing French, Spanish, and Italian settlers to Algeria and leading to the expropriation of large tracts of Muslim land, the conquest of Algeria marked the rebirth of French colonial expansion.

Emboldened by the good news from Algeria, Charles repudiated the Constitutional Charter in an attempted coup in July 1830. He issued decrees stripping much of the wealthy middle class of its voting rights, and he censored the press. The immediate reaction, encouraged by journalists and lawyers, was an insurrection in the capital by printers, other artisans, and small traders. In "three glorious days," the government collapsed. Paris boiled with revolutionary excitement, and Charles fled. Then the upper middle class, which had fomented the revolt, skillfully seated Charles's cousin, Louis Philippe, duke of Orléans, on the vacant throne.

Louis Philippe (r. 1830–1848) accepted the Constitutional Charter of 1814; adopted the red, white, and blue flag of the French Revolution; and admitted that he was merely the "king of the French people." In spite of such symbolic actions, the situation in France remained fundamentally unchanged. The vote was extended only from 100,000 to 170,000 citizens. For the upper middle class, there had been a change in dynasty in order to protect the status quo and the narrowly liberal institutions of 1815. Republicans, democrats, social reformers, and the poor of Paris were bitterly disappointed. They had made a revolution, but it seemed for naught.

The Revolutions of 1848

Why in 1848 did revolution triumph briefly throughout most of Europe, and why did it fail almost completely? ▪

The late 1840s in Europe were hard economically and tense politically. The potato famine in Ireland in 1845 and 1846 had many echoes on the continent. Bad harvests jacked up food prices and caused misery and unemployment in the cities and in the countryside. A profound economic crisis, caused in the final analysis by a combination of rapid population growth and industrialization efforts that were only beginning to provide more jobs and income, gripped continental Europe.

The political and social response to the economic crisis was unrest and protest. (See "Living in the Past: Revolutionary Experiences in 1848," page 710.) "Prerevolutionary" outbreaks occurred all across Europe: in the northern part of Austria in 1846, a civil war in Switzerland in 1847, and an uprising in Naples, Italy, in January 1848. Only the most advanced and the most backward major countries — reforming Great Britain and immobile Russia — escaped untouched. Governments toppled; monarchs and ministers bowed or fled. National independence, liberal democratic constitutions, and social reform: the lofty aspirations of a generation seemed at hand. Yet in the end, the revolutions failed.

A Democratic Republic in France

By the late 1840s, revolution in Europe was almost universally expected, but it took revolution in Paris — once again — to turn expectations into realities. For eighteen years Louis Philippe's "bourgeois monarchy" had been characterized by stubborn inaction and complacency. There was a glaring lack of social legislation, and politics was dominated by corruption and selfish special interests. With only the rich voting for deputies, many of the deputies were docile government bureaucrats.

The government's stubborn refusal to consider electoral reform heightened a sense of class injustice among middle-class shopkeepers, skilled artisans, and unskilled working people, and it eventually touched off a popular revolt in Paris. Workers joined by some students began tearing up the cobblestones and building barricades in the narrow streets of Paris on the night of February 22, 1848. Armed with guns and dug in behind their makeshift fortresses, the workers and students demanded a new government. By February 24, as the National Guard broke ranks and joined the revolutionaries, Louis Philippe had refused to order a full-scale attack by the regular army and had abdicated in favor of his grandson. But the common people in arms would tolerate no more monarchy. This refusal led to the proclamation of a provisional republic, headed by a ten-man executive committee and certified by cries of approval from the revolutionary crowd.

The revolutionaries immediately set about drafting a constitution for France's Second Republic. Moreover, they wanted a truly popular and democratic republic so that the common people — the peasants, the artisans, and the unskilled workers — could participate in reforming society. In practice, building such a republic meant giving the right to vote to every adult male, and this was quickly done. Revolutionary compassion and sympathy for freedom were expressed in the freeing of all slaves in French colonies, the abolition of the death penalty, and the establishment of a ten-hour workday for Paris.

Yet there were profound differences within the revolutionary coalition in Paris. On the one hand, there were the moderate liberal republicans of the middle class. They viewed universal male suffrage as the ultimate concession to be made to popular forces, and they strongly opposed any further radical social measures. On the other hand, there were radical republicans and hard-pressed artisans. Influenced by a generation of utopian socialists, and appalled by the poverty and misery of the urban poor, the radical republicans were committed to some kind of socialism. So were many artisans, who hated the unrestrained competition of cutthroat capitalism and advocated a combination of strong craft unions and worker-owned businesses.

Worsening depression and rising unemployment brought these conflicting goals to the fore in 1848. Louis Blanc (see page 693), who along with a worker named Albert represented the republican socialists in the provisional government, pressed for recognition of a socialist right to work. Blanc asserted that permanent government-sponsored cooperative workshops should be established for workers. Such workshops would be an alternative to capitalist employment and a decisive step toward a new, noncompetitive social order.

The moderate republicans wanted no such thing. They were willing to provide only temporary relief. The resulting compromise set up national workshops — soon to become little more than a vast program of pick-and-shovel public works — and established a special commission under Blanc to "study the question." This satisfied no one. The national workshops were, however,

Picturing the Past

The Triumph of Democratic Republics This French illustration offers an opinion of the initial revolutionary breakthrough in 1848. The peoples of Europe, joined together around their respective national banners, are achieving republican freedom, which is symbolized by the Statue of Liberty and the discarded crowns. The woman wearing pants at the base of the statue — very radical attire — represents feminist hopes for liberation.

(Musée de la Ville, Paris/Giraudon/The Bridgeman Art Library)

ANALYZING THE IMAGE How many different flags can you count and/or identify? How would you characterize the types of people marching and the mood of the crowd?

CONNECTIONS What do the angels, Statue of Liberty, and discarded crowns suggest about the artist's view of the events of 1848? Do you think this illustration was created before or after the collapse of the revolution in France? Why?

To complete this activity online, go to the Online Study Guide at bedfordstmartins.com/mckaywest.

better than nothing. An army of desperate poor from the French provinces and even from foreign countries streamed into Paris to sign up. As the economic crisis worsened, the number enrolled in the workshops soared from 10,000 in March to 120,000 by June, and another 80,000 were trying unsuccessfully to join.

While the workshops in Paris grew, the French masses went to the election polls in late April. Voting in most cases for the first time, the people of France elected to the new Constituent Assembly about five hundred moderate republicans, three hundred monarchists, and one hundred radicals who professed various brands of social-

ism. One of the moderate republicans was the author of *Democracy in America*, Alexis de Tocqueville (TOHK-vihl) (1805–1859), who had predicted the overthrow of Louis Philippe's government.

Tocqueville observed that the socialist movement in Paris aroused the fierce hostility of France's peasants as well as the middle and upper classes. The French peasants owned land, and according to Tocqueville, "private property had become with all those who owned it a sort of bond of fraternity."[6] Returning from Normandy to take his seat in the new Constituent Assembly, Tocqueville saw that a majority of the members were firmly committed to the republic and strongly opposed to the socialists and their artisan allies, and he shared their sentiments.

This clash of ideologies—of liberal capitalism and socialism—became a clash of classes and arms after the elections. The new government's executive committee dropped Blanc and thereafter included no representative of the Parisian working class. Fearing that their socialist hopes were about to be dashed, artisans and unskilled workers invaded the Constituent Assembly on May 15 and tried to proclaim a new revolutionary state. But the government was ready and used the middle-class National Guard to squelch this uprising. As the workshops continued to fill and grow more radical, the fearful but powerful propertied classes in the Assembly took the offensive. On June 22, the government dissolved the national workshops in Paris, giving the workers the choice of joining the army or going to workshops in the provinces.

The result was a spontaneous and violent uprising. Frustrated in attempts to create a socialist society, masses of desperate people were now losing even their life-sustaining relief. A voice from the crowd cried out when the famous astronomer François Arago counseled patience, "Ah, Monsieur Arago, you have never been hungry!"[7] Barricades sprang up again in the narrow streets of Paris, and a terrible class war began. Working people fought with the courage of utter desperation, but this time the government had the army and the support of peasant France. After three terrible "June Days" of street fighting and the death or injury of more than ten thousand people, the republican army under General Louis Cavaignac stood triumphant in a sea of working-class blood and hatred.

The revolution in France thus ended in spectacular failure. The February coalition of the middle and working classes had in four short months become locked in mortal combat. In place of a generous democratic republic, the Constituent Assembly completed a constitution featuring a strong executive. This allowed Louis Napoleon, nephew of Napoleon Bonaparte, to win a landslide victory in the election of December 1848. The appeal of his great name as well as the desire of the propertied classes for order at any cost had produced a semi-authoritarian regime.

The Austrian Empire in 1848

Throughout central Europe, the first news of the upheaval in France evoked feverish excitement and eventually revolution. Liberals demanded written constitutions, representative government, and greater civil liberties from authoritarian regimes. When governments hesitated, popular revolts followed. Urban workers and students served as the shock troops, but they were allied with middle-class liberals and peasants. In the face of this united front, monarchs collapsed and granted almost everything. The popular revolutionary coalition, having secured great and easy victories, then broke down as it had in France. The traditional forces—the monarchy, the aristocracy, the regular army—recovered their nerve, reasserted their authority, and took back many, though not all, of the concessions. Reaction was everywhere victorious.

The revolution in the Austrian Empire began in Hungary in 1848, where nationalistic Hungarians demanded national autonomy, full civil liberties, and universal suffrage. When the monarchy in Vienna hesitated, Viennese students and workers took to the streets and raised the barricades in defiance of the government, while peasant disorders broke out in parts of the empire. The Habsburg emperor Ferdinand I (r. 1835–1848) capitulated and promised reforms and a liberal constitution. Metternich fled in disguise toward London. The old absolutist order seemed to be collapsing with unbelievable rapidity.

The coalition of revolutionaries was not stable, however. When the monarchy abolished serfdom, with its degrading forced labor and feudal services, the newly free peasants lost interest in the political and social questions agitating the cities. Meanwhile, the coalition of urban revolutionaries also broke down along class lines over the issue of socialist workshops and universal voting rights for men.

The revolutionary coalition was also weakened, and ultimately destroyed, by conflicting national aspirations. In March the Hungarian revolutionary leaders pushed through an extremely liberal, almost democratic, constitution. But the Hungarian revolutionaries also sought to transform the mosaic of provinces and peoples that was the kingdom of Hungary into a unified, centralized, Hungarian nation. To the minority groups that formed half of the population—the Croats, Serbs, and Romanians—such unification was completely unacceptable. Each felt entitled to political autonomy and cultural independence. In a somewhat similar way, Czech nationalists based in Bohemia and the city of Prague came into conflict with German nationalists. Thus conflicting national aspirations within the Austrian Empire enabled the monarchy to play off one ethnic group against the other.

Finally, the conservative aristocratic forces regained their nerve under the rallying call of the archduchess Sophia, a Bavarian princess married to the emperor's brother. Deeply ashamed of the emperor's collapse before a "mess of students," she insisted that Ferdinand, who had no heir, abdicate in favor of her son, Francis Joseph.[8] Powerful nobles organized around Sophia in a secret conspiracy to reverse and crush the revolution.

Their first breakthrough came when the army bombarded Prague and savagely crushed a working-class revolt there on June 17. Other Austrian officials and

Revolutionary Experiences in 1848

LIVING IN THE PAST

THE STRIKING SIMILARITIES between the different national revolutions in 1848 suggest that Europeans lived through common revolutionary experiences that shaped a generation, and this was indeed true. The first such experience was raising the barricades, fighting in the streets, and overthrowing rulers or forcing major concessions. The result of this astonishing triumph was a tremendous surge in political participation and civic activity throughout most of Europe. This unprecedented "mass politics" took many forms. Politics in the streets—demonstrations, protests, open-air meetings—played an ongoing role as large crowds pressured kings and legislatures. Newspaper publishing exploded as censorship ended and interest in public affairs soared. In Paris, where many new papers like *Le Salut Public* (The Public Safety) appeared, daily newspaper production increased eightfold in three months. In the Austrian Empire peasants freed from serfdom listened to newspapers read aloud in taverns and followed developments. Intense political activity led to a multitude of political clubs and associations based on occupation. Women also formed organizations for the welfare of children and families, although few women as yet pushed for equal rights.

Newly politicized and increasingly divided into competing groups, the peoples of Europe then shared the onslaught of reaction and the trauma of defeat and civil war. In Prague and in Paris, almost simultaneously, army commanders found a deadly response to urban uprisings. First they used cannon and field artillery to bombard and destroy the fighters behind their makeshift fortifications. Only then did obedient infantrymen attack and take the barricades in hand-to-hand combat, as Prussian soldiers did later in Frankfurt. Fleeing insurgents were hunted down and often shot. Thus the remembered experiences of 1848 included a tragic finale of grief and mourning. This is captured in the painting *Memory of the Civil War* by Ernest Meissonier, an artillery captain in the French National Guard who viewed at close range the carnage of the June Days in Paris.

Front page of *Le Salut Public* (akg-images)

LE SALUT PUBLIC.

2ᵉ NUMÉRO.

VIVE LA REPUBLIQUE!

Les rédacteurs - propriétaires du Salut pu-

cule dans l'air, et enivre les poumons, comme un parfum.

Où reposer cette tête maudite?

QUESTIONS FOR ANALYSIS

1. Examine the French newspaper. What does it reveal about the rise of mass politics in 1848?

2. The 1848 revolutions increased political activity, yet they were crushed. How does the scene of fighting in Frankfurt help to explain this outcome?

3. Consider Meissonier's *Memory of the Civil War*. In what ways do societies transmit and revise their historical memories?

Ernest Meissonier, *Memory of the
Civil War* (Louvre/Lauros/Giraudon/
The Bridgeman Art Library)

Guarding the Barricades in Vienna Workers and students took full control of Vienna in May 1848, when they raised the barricades and dug in. In this painting a number of men and women eat, relax, and discuss the situation. Women were active in supportive roles during the revolution. (Wien Museum Karlsplatz, Vienna/The Bridgeman Art Library)

nobles began to lead the minority nationalities of Hungary against the revolutionary government. At the end of October, the well-equipped, predominately peasant troops of the regular Austrian army used heavy cannon to attack the student and working-class radicals dug in behind barricades in Vienna and retook the city at the cost of more than four thousand casualties. Thus the determination of the Austrian aristocracy and the loyalty of its army were the final ingredients in the triumph of reaction and the defeat of revolution.

When Francis Joseph (r. 1848–1916) was crowned emperor of Austria immediately after his eighteenth birthday in December 1848, only Hungary had yet to be brought under control. Another determined conservative, Nicholas I of Russia (r. 1825–1855), obligingly lent his iron hand. On June 6, 1849, 130,000 Russian troops poured into Hungary and subdued the country after bitter fighting. For a number of years, the Habsburgs ruled Hungary as a conquered territory.

Prussia and the Frankfurt Assembly

After Austria, Prussia was the largest and most influential German kingdom. Prior to 1848, the goal of middle-class Prussian liberals had been to transform absolutist Prussia into a liberal constitutional monarchy, which would lead the thirty-eight states of the German Confederation into the liberal, unified nation desired by liberals throughout the German states. The agitation following the fall of Louis Philippe encouraged Prussian liberals to press their demands. When the artisans and factory workers in Berlin exploded in March 1848 and joined temporarily with the middle-class liberals in the struggle against the monarchy, the autocratic yet compassionate Frederick William IV (r. 1840–1861) vacillated and finally caved in. On March 21, he promised to grant Prussia a liberal constitution and to merge Prussia into a new national German state that was to be created.

But urban workers wanted much more and the Prussian aristocracy wanted much less than the moderate constitutional liberalism the king conceded. The workers issued a series of democratic and vaguely socialist demands that troubled their middle-class allies, and the conservative clique gathered around the king to urge counter-revolution.

As an elected Prussian Constituent Assembly met in Berlin to write a constitution for the Prussian state, a self-appointed committee of liberals from various German states began organizing for the creation of a unified German state. Meeting in Frankfurt in May, a National Assembly composed of lawyers, professors, doctors, officials, and businessmen convened to write a German federal constitution. However, their attention shifted from drafting a constitution to deciding how to respond to Denmark's claims on the provinces of Schleswig (SHLEHS-wihg) and Holstein, which were inhabited primarily by Germans. Debating ponderously, the National Assembly at Frankfurt finally called on the Prussian army to oppose Denmark in the name of the German nation. Prussia responded and began war with Denmark. As the Schleswig-Holstein issue demonstrated, the national ideal was a crucial factor motivating the German middle classes in 1848.

In March 1849, the National Assembly finally completed its drafting of a liberal constitution and elected King Frederick William of Prussia emperor of the new German national state (minus Austria and Schleswig-Holstein). By early 1849, however, reaction had been successful almost everywhere. Frederick William had reasserted his royal authority, disbanded the Prussian Constituent Assembly, and granted his subjects a limited, essentially conservative constitution. Reasserting that he ruled by divine right, Frederick William contemptuously refused to accept the "crown from the gutter." Bogged down by their preoccupation with nationalist issues, the reluctant revolutionaries in Frankfurt had waited too long and acted too timidly.

When Frederick William, who really wanted to be emperor but only on his own authoritarian terms, tried to get the small monarchs of Germany to elect him emperor, Austria balked. Supported by Russia, Austria forced Prussia to renounce all its schemes of unification in late 1850. The German Confederation was re-established. Attempts to unite the Germans — first in a liberal national state and then in a conservative Prussian empire — had failed completely.

LOOKING BACK LOOKING AHEAD

VIEWED FROM A BROAD historical perspective, Europe's economic and social foundations in 1750 remained agricultural and rural. Peasants living in villages tilled the land, while landlords and the ruling classes collected rents and taxes. Political life was dominated by the authoritarian styles associated with absolutism, although the critical thinking of the Enlightenment was beginning to affect the intellectual and cultural elites, who began to challenge and question the status quo. By the 1790s, the British Industrial Revolution and the French Revolution were bringing fundamental changes to economic and political life in parts of Europe. In Great Britain new technologies and factory organization turned the focus away from agriculture and the land and toward industry and cities. In revolutionary France liberal ideals of representative government and legal equality were being realized, if only briefly. After 1815, the dual revolution provided Europe with new visions of political and social life. Liberalism intermingled with nationalism and socialism to challenge the restoration of the conservative order.

Much of world history in the past two centuries can be seen as the progressive unfolding of the dual revolution. In Europe in the nineteenth century, as in Asia and Africa in more recent times, the interrelated economic and political transformation was built on complicated histories, strong traditions, and highly diverse cultures. Although defeated in 1848, the new political ideologies associated with the French Revolution were destined to triumph after 1850. Above all, nationalism, with its commitment to the nation-state and the imagined community of a great national family, would become the dominant political force, responding to national problems and guiding European imperial expansion after 1875. At the same time, industrialization and new relationships between classes would privilege cities and promote a new urban society, as agriculture and rural life gradually declined. Diverse, complicated, and fascinating, this new urban society was emerging by 1850. By 1900, it dominated northwestern Europe and was making steady inroads to the east and south.

CHAPTER REVIEW

■ **How did the victorious allies fashion a general peace settlement, and how did Metternich uphold a conservative European order? (p. 686)**

In 1814 the victorious allied powers sought to restore peace and stability in Europe. The Quadruple Alliance — Russia, Prussia, Austria, and Great Britain — dealt moderately with France by giving it the boundaries it had possessed in 1792 and by not assigning war reparations. The peace settlement also included strong defensive measures, resolved the various disputes among the Great Powers, and laid the foundations for beneficial international cooperation throughout much of the nineteenth century. Led by Metternich, the conservative powers used intervention and repression as they sought to prevent the spread of subversive ideas and radical changes in domestic politics. The formation of the Holy Alliance was the first step in this crusade against the ideas and politics of the dual revolution.

■ **What were the basic tenets of liberalism, nationalism, and socialism, and what groups were most attracted to these ideologies? (p. 691)**

After 1815 the ideologies of liberalism, nationalism, and socialism all developed to challenge the existing order in this period of early industrialization and rapid population growth. The principal ideas of the liberalism movement were equality and liberty, which were expressed in representative government, civil rights, and limited government regulation of the economy. Nationalism was based on the notion that each people had its own genius and cultural unity; to this was then added the idea that each people also deserved its own political entity and its own government. The key ideas of socialism were economic planning, greater economic equality, and the state regulation of property. All of these basic tenets in one way or another rejected conservatism, with its stress on tradition, hereditary monarchy and aristocracy, and an official church. Business groups and the middle class were attracted to liberalism; liberals and democrats were attracted to nationalism; and workers and utopian theorists were drawn to socialism.

■ **What were the characteristics of the romantic movement, and who were some of the great romantic artists? (p. 697)**

The romantic movement, breaking decisively with the dictates of classicism, reinforced the spirit of change and revolutionary anticipation. The movement was characterized by a belief in self-expression, imagination, and spontaneity in art as well as in personal life. Among the most notable poets and writers, Wordsworth, Hugo, and Pushkin stand out. So do two brilliant Frenchwomen, Germaine de Staël and Amandine Dupin, known by her pen name of George Sand. Famous romantic artists included Turner with his turbulent seascapes, Constable with his peaceful English countryside, and Delacroix with his exotic scenes. In music romantic composers, led by Beethoven, Liszt, and Chopin, plumbed the depths of human emotions, and virtuoso performers became cultural heroes.

■ **How after 1815 did liberal, national, and socialist forces challenge conservatism in Greece, Great Britain, and France? (p. 701)**

Inspired by modern nationalism, Greek patriots rebelled against their Turkish rulers, and with the help of the European powers they won their national independence after a long struggle. In Great Britain the liberal challenge to the conservative order eventually led to fundamental reforms, as high tariffs on imported grain were reduced and then abolished, more men gained the right to vote with the Reform Act of 1832, and the factory workday for women and children was reduced to ten hours in 1847. In France, a three-day revolution in 1832 replaced the reactionary Charles X with the more moderate Louis Philippe, but little else changed.

■ **Why in 1848 did revolution triumph briefly throughout most of Europe, and why did it fail almost completely? (p. 707)**

In 1848 the increasing pressures of bad harvests, unemployment, rapid population growth, and a severe economic crisis exploded dramatically across Europe as they culminated in liberal and nationalistic revolutions. Monarchies panicked and crumbled in the face of popular uprisings and widespread opposition that cut across class lines, and the revolutionaries triumphed, first in France and then all across the continent. Yet very few revolutionary goals were realized. The moderate, nationalistic middle classes were unable to consolidate their initial victories. Instead, they drew back when artisans, factory workers, and radical socialists rose up to present their own much more revolutionary demands. This retreat facilitated the efforts of dedicated aristocrats in central Europe to reassert their power. And it made possible the crushing of Parisian workers by a coalition of solid bourgeoisie and landowning peasantry in France. Thus the lofty ideals of a generation drowned in a sea of blood and disillusion.

Suggested Reading

Berger, Stefan, ed. *A Companion to Nineteenth-Century Europe, 1789–1914*. 2006. A useful study with an up-to-date bibliography.

Chadwick, Owen. *The Secularization of the European Mind in the Nineteenth Century*. 1976. Considers the important place of religion in nineteenth-century thought.

Gildea, Robert. *Barricades and Borders: Europe, 1800–1914*, 2d ed. 1996. A recommended general study.

Greene, Abigail. *Fatherlands: State-Building and Nationhood in Nineteenth-Century Germany*. 2001. A brilliant discussion of the smaller German states.

Lindemann, Albert S. *A History of European Socialism*. 1983. A stimulating survey of early socialism and Marxism.

Malia, Martin, and Terence Emmons. *History's Locomotives: Revolutions and the Making of the Modern World*. 2006. An ambitious comparative work of high quality.

Mann, Thomas. *Buddenbrooks*. 1901. A wonderful historical novel that traces the rise and fall of a prosperous German family over three generations.

Merriman, John. *Police Stories: Building the French State, 1815–1851*. 2006. An outstanding and innovative compendium.

Pilbeam, Pamela. *French Socialists Before Marx: Workers, Women, and the Social Question*. 2000. Shows the significant role of women in utopian socialism.

Rapport, Mike. *1848: Year of Revolution*. 2008. A stimulating, well-written account that examines all of Europe.

Rubinstein, W. D. *Britain's Century: A Political and Social History, 1815–1905*. 1998. An excellent English history.

Sheehan, James J. *German History, 1770–1866*. 1993. A stimulating general history.

Shelley, Mary. *Frankenstein*. 1818. A great nineteenth-century romantic novel that draws an almost lovable picture of the famous monster and is highly recommended.

Sperber, Jonathan. *The European Revolutions, 1848–1851*. 1993. A solid synthesis of the great revolutionary upheaval.

Notes

1. E. Gellner, *Nations and Nationalism* (Oxford: Basil Blackwell, 1983), especially pp. 19–39.
2. This paragraph draws on the influential views of B. Anderson, *Imagined Communities: Reflections on the Origins and Spread of Nationalism*, rev. ed. (London/New York: Verso, 1991), and E. J. Hobsbawm and T. Ranger, eds., *The Invention of Tradition* (Cambridge, U.K.: Cambridge University Press, 1983).
3. Quoted in F. B. Artz, *From the Renaissance to Romanticism: Trends in Style in Art, Literature, and Music, 1300–1830* (Chicago: University of Chicago Press, 1962), pp. 276, 278.
4. Quoted by G. O'Brien, *The Economic History of Ireland from the Union to the Famine* (London: Longmans, Green, 1921), p. 21.
5. Ibid., pp. 23–24.
6. A. de Tocqueville, *Recollections* (New York: Columbia University Press, 1949), p. 94.
7. M. Agulhon, *1848* (Paris: Éditions du Seuil, 1973), pp. 68–69.
8. W. L. Langer, *Political and Social Upheaval, 1832–1852* (New York: Harper & Row, 1969), p. 361.

Key Terms

Congress of Vienna (p. 686)
dual revolution (p. 687)
Holy Alliance (p. 687)
Carlsbad Decrees (p. 689)
liberalism (p. 691)
laissez faire (p. 691)
nationalism (p. 691)
socialism (p. 693)
bourgeoisie (p. 696)
proletariat (p. 696)
romanticism (p. 697)
Corn Laws (p. 702)
Battle of Peterloo (p. 702)
Reform Bill of 1832 (p. 702)
Great Famine (p. 705)

For practice quizzes and other study tools, visit the Online Study Guide at **bedfordstmartins.com/mckaywest**.

For primary sources from this period, see ***Sources of Western Society*, Second Edition**.

For Web sites, images, and documents related to topics in this chapter, visit Make History at **bedfordstmartins.com/mckaywest**.

23
Life in the Emerging Urban Society

1840–1900

The era of intellectual and political upheaval that culminated in the revolutions of 1848 was also an era of rapid industrialization and urbanization. Industrial growth posed enormous challenges for all elements of Western society, from young factory workers confronting relentless discipline to aristocratic elites maneuvering to retain political power. After 1848, as Western political development veered off in an uncharted direction, the growth of towns and cities rushed forward with undiminished force. Thus Western society was urban and industrial in 1900 as surely as it had been rural and agrarian in 1800. Progress, in the form of new industries and big businesses, better living conditions for the masses, growing secularism, and a budding feminist movement, was the order of the day.

This emerging urban society benefited city dwellers, through improvements in health and the urban environment, but living conditions varied greatly according to one's status. While average people experienced wage increases, poverty was not eliminated and the gap between rich and poor remained as great as ever. The size of the middle classes grew in this period, and as middle-class people reaped the benefits of industrialization and scientific progress, they fragmented into an upper middle class that often mimicked the lives of the aristocracy, a solid "middle middle" class defined by the professions and business owners, and a lower middle class made up of shopkeepers and officeworkers. Despite this growing middle class, most urban dwellers continued to belong to the working classes. ■

Urban Life in the Nineteenth Century. The excitement and variety of urban life sparkle in this detail from a depiction of an entertainment gala given for the public by London's Royal Dramatic College.

CHAPTER PREVIEW

Taming the City
■ What was life like in the cities, and how did urban life change in the nineteenth century?

Rich and Poor and Those in Between
■ What did the emergence of urban industrial society mean for rich and poor and those in between?

The Changing Family
■ How did working-class and middle-class families change as they coped with the challenges and the opportunities of the developing urban civilization?

Science and Thought
■ What major changes in science and thought reflected and influenced the new urban society?

Taming the City

What was life like in the cities, and how did urban life change in the nineteenth century? ▪

Since the Middle Ages, European cities had been centers of government, culture, and large-scale commerce. They had also been congested, dirty, and unhealthy. Beginning in the early nineteenth century, the Industrial Revolution took these unfortunate realities of urban life to unprecedented levels. While historians may debate whether the over-

all societal impact of industrialization was generally positive or negative, there is little doubt that rapid urban growth worsened long-standing overcrowding and unhealthy living conditions and posed a frightening challenge for society. It would require the full-scale efforts of government leaders, city planners, reformers, scientists, and reform-minded citizens to tame the ferocious savagery of the traditional city.

Industry and the Growth of Cities

The main causes of such a poor quality of urban life—pervasive poverty, lack of medical knowledge, and deadly overcrowding—had existed for centuries. Because the typical city had always been a "walking city" with no public transportation, masses of people needed to live in close proximity to the shops and markets, resulting in dreadfully dense housing conditions. Packed together almost as tightly as possible, people in cities were always more likely to die from the spread of infectious disease than were their rural counterparts. In the larger towns, more people died each year than were born, on average, and urban populations were able to maintain their numbers only because newcomers were continually arriving from rural areas. Transplanted farm workers fatalistically viewed the grim realities of city life, and death, as the urban equivalents of bad weather and poor crops.

Deplorable urban conditions did not originate with the Industrial Revolution, but the Industrial Revolution did reveal those conditions more nakedly than ever before. The steam engine freed industrialists from dependence on the energy of fast-flowing streams and rivers so that by 1800 there was every incentive to build new factories in urban areas. Cities had better shipping facilities than the countryside and thus better supplies of coal and raw materials. There were also many hands wanting work in the cities, for

Mapping the Past

Map 23.1 European Cities of 100,000 or More, 1800–1900 There were more large cities in Great Britain in 1900 than in all of Europe in 1800.

ANALYZING THE MAP Compare the spatial distribution of cities in 1800 with the distribution in 1900. Where in 1900 are large cities concentrated in clusters?

CONNECTIONS In 1800, what common characteristics were shared by many large European cities? (For example, how many big cities were capitals and/or leading ports?) Were any common characteristics shared by the large cities in 1900? What does this suggest about the reasons behind this dramatic growth?

To complete this activity online, go to the Online Study Guide at bedfordstmartins.com/mckaywest.

cities drew people like a magnet. And it was a great advantage for a manufacturer to have other factories nearby to supply the business's needs and buy its products. Therefore, as industry grew, there was also a rapid expansion of already overcrowded and unhealthy cities.

The challenge of the urban environment was felt first and most acutely in Great Britain. In the 1820s and 1830s, the populations of a number of British cities were increasing by 40 to 70 percent each decade. The number of people living in cities of 20,000 or more in England and Wales jumped from 1.5 million in 1801 to 6.3 million in 1851 and reached 15.6 million in 1891. Such cities accounted for 17 percent of the total English population in 1801, 35 percent as early as 1851, and fully 54 percent in 1891. Other countries duplicated the English pattern as they industrialized (Map 23.1).

Except on the outskirts, early-nineteenth-century cities in Britain were using every scrap of land to the fullest extent. Parks and open areas were almost nonexistent. Buildings were erected on the smallest possible lots in order to pack the maximum number of people into a given space. Narrow houses were built wall to wall in long rows. These row houses had neither front nor back yards, and only a narrow alley in back separated one row from the next. Other buildings were built around tiny courtyards completely enclosed on all four sides. Many people lived in extremely small, often overcrowded cellars or attics. "Six, eight, and even ten occupying one room is anything but uncommon," wrote a Scottish doctor for a government investigation in 1842.

These highly concentrated urban populations lived in extremely unsanitary and unhealthy conditions. Open drains and sewers flowed alongside or down the middle of unpaved streets. Toilet facilities were primitive in the extreme. In parts of Manchester, as many as two hundred people shared a single outhouse. Such privies filled up rapidly, and since they were infrequently emptied, sewage often overflowed and seeped into cellar dwellings. Moreover, some courtyards in poorer neighborhoods became dunghills, collecting excrement that was sometimes sold as fertilizer. By the 1840s there was among the better-off classes a growing, shocking "realization that," as one scholar put it, "millions of English men, women, and children were living in shit."[1]

Who or what was responsible for these awful conditions? The crucial factors were the tremendous pressure of more people and the total absence of public transportation. People simply had to jam themselves together if they were to be able to walk to shops and factories. Another factor was that government in Great Britain,

ca. 1840s–1890s	Realism dominant in Western literature
1848	First public health law in Britain
ca. 1850–1870	Modernization of Paris
1850–1914	Condition of working classes improves
1854	Pasteur studies fermentation and develops pasteurization
1854–1870	Development of germ theory
1859	Darwin, *On the Origin of Species by the Means of Natural Selection*
1869	Mendeleev creates periodic table
1880–1913	Second industrial revolution; birthrate steadily declines in Europe
1890s	Electric streetcars introduced in Europe

both local and national, was slow to provide sanitary facilities and establish adequate building codes. This slow pace was probably attributable more to a need to explore and identify what precisely should be done than to rigid middle-class opposition to government action. Certainly, Great Britain had no monopoly on overcrowded and unhealthy urban conditions; many continental cities were every bit as bad.

Most responsible of all was the sad legacy of rural housing conditions in preindustrial society combined with appalling ignorance. Housing was far down on the newcomer's list of priorities, and many people carried the filth of the mud floor and the dung of the barnyard with them to the city. Moreover, ordinary people generally took dirt for granted. One English miner told an investigator, "I do not think it usual for the lasses [in the coal mines] to wash their bodies; my sisters never wash themselves." As for the men, "their legs and bodies are as black as your hat."[2]

The Advent of the Public Health Movement

Toward the middle of the nineteenth century, people's fatalistic acceptance of their overcrowded, unsanitary surroundings began to give way to a growing interest in reform and improvement. The most famous early reformer was Edwin Chadwick, one of the commissioners charged with the administration of relief to paupers under Britain's revised Poor Law of 1834. Chadwick was a follower of radical philosopher Jeremy Bentham (1748–1832), whose approach to social issues, called **utilitarianism**, had taught that public problems ought to be dealt with on a rational, scientific

utilitarianism The idea of Jeremy Bentham that social policies should promote the "greatest good for the greatest number."

basis and according to the "greatest good for the greatest number." Applying these principles, Chadwick soon became convinced that disease and death actually caused poverty, because a sick worker was an unemployed worker and orphaned children were poor children. Most important, Chadwick believed that disease could be prevented by cleaning up the urban environment. That was his "sanitary idea."

Chadwick collected detailed reports from local Poor Law officials on the "sanitary conditions of the laboring population" and published his hard-hitting findings in 1842. This mass of widely publicized evidence proved that disease was related to filthy environmental conditions, which were in turn caused largely by lack of drainage, sewers, and garbage collection.

Chadwick correctly believed that the stinking excrement of communal outhouses could be dependably carried off by water through sewers at less than one-twentieth the cost of removing it by hand. The cheap iron pipes and tile drains of the industrial age would provide running water and sewerage for all sections of town, not just the wealthy ones. In 1848, with the

cause strengthened by the cholera epidemic of 1846, Chadwick's report became the basis of Great Britain's first public health law, which created a national health board and gave cities broad authority to build modern sanitary systems.

The public health movement won dedicated supporters in the United States, France, and Germany from the 1840s on. Governments accepted at least limited responsibility for the health of all citizens, and their programs broke decisively with the age-old fatalism of urban populations. By the 1860s and 1870s, European cities were making real progress toward adequate water supplies and sewerage systems, city dwellers were beginning to reap the reward of better health, and death rates began to decline (Figure 23.1).

The Bacterial Revolution

Although improved sanitation in cities promoted a better quality of life and some improvements in health care, effective control of communicable disease required a great leap forward in medical knowledge and biological

King Cholera This 1852 drawing from *Punch* tells volumes about the unhealthy living conditions of the urban poor. In the foreground children play with a dead rat and a woman scavenges a dung heap. Cheap rooming houses provide shelter for the frightfully overcrowded population. Such conditions and contaminated water spread deadly cholera epidemics from India throughout Europe in the 1800s. The doctor's medicine chest seen here could only provide patients with opium mixtures to relieve pain and reduce intestinal swelling. (drawing: The British Library; chest: Science & Society Picture Library)

theory. Early reformers such as Chadwick were seriously handicapped by the prevailing miasmatic theory of disease—the belief that people contract disease when they breathe the bad odors of decay and putrefying excrement. In the 1840s and 1850s keen observation by doctors and public health officials pinpointed the role of bad drinking water in the transmission of disease and suggested that contagion was spread through filth and not caused by it, thus weakening the miasmatic idea.

The breakthrough was the development of the **germ theory** of disease by Louis Pasteur (pas-TUHR) (1822–1895), a French chemist who began studying fermentation for brewers in 1854. Using his microscope to develop a simple test that brewers could use to monitor the fermentation process and avoid spoilage, Pasteur found that fermentation depended on the growth of living organisms and that the activity of these organisms could be suppressed by heating the beverage—by pasteurization. The breathtaking implication was that specific diseases were caused by specific living organisms—germs—and that those organisms could be controlled in people as well as in beer, wine, and milk.

By 1870 the work of Pasteur and others had demonstrated the general connection between germs and disease. When, in the middle of the 1870s, German country doctor Robert Koch (kawkh) and his coworkers developed pure cultures of harmful bacteria and described their life cycles, the dam broke. Over the next twenty years, researchers—mainly Germans—identified the organisms responsible for disease after disease. These discoveries led to the development of a number of effective vaccines.

Acceptance of the germ theory brought about dramatic improvements in the deadly environment of hospitals and surgery (see Chapter 19). In 1865, when Pasteur showed that the air was full of bacteria, English surgeon Joseph Lister (1827–1912) immediately grasped the connection between aerial bacteria and the problem of wound infection. He reasoned that a chemical disinfectant applied to a wound dressing would "destroy the life of the floating particles." Lister's antiseptic principle worked wonders. In the 1880s, German surgeons developed the more sophisticated practice of sterilizing not only the wound but also everything—hands, instruments, clothing—that entered the operating room.

The achievements of the bacterial revolution coupled with the public health movement saved millions of lives, particularly after about 1880. Mortality rates began to decline dramatically in European countries (see Figure 23.1) as the awful death sentences of the past—diphtheria, typhoid, typhus, cholera, yellow fever—became vanishing diseases. City dwellers benefited especially from these developments. By 1910 a great silent revolution had occurred: the death rates for people of all ages in urban areas were generally no greater than those for people in rural areas, and sometimes they were lower.

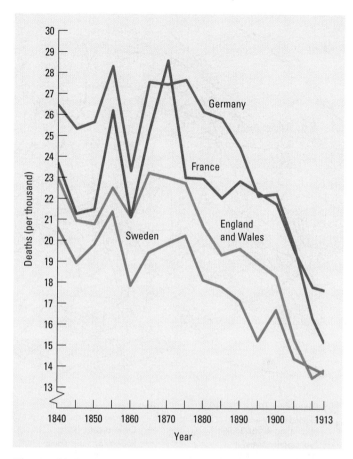

Figure 23.1 The Decline of Death Rates in England and Wales, Germany, France, and Sweden, 1840–1913 A rising standard of living, improvements in public health, and better medical knowledge all contributed to the dramatic decline of death rates in the nineteenth century.

Improvements in Urban Planning

In addition to public health improvements in nineteenth-century cities, more effective urban planning was a major key to a better quality of urban life. France took the lead during the rule of Napoleon III (r. 1848–1870), who sought to promote the welfare of all his subjects through government action. He believed that rebuilding much of Paris would provide employment, improve living conditions, and testify to the power and glory of his empire. In the baron Georges Haussmann (HOWS-muhn) (1809–1884), an aggressive, impatient Alsatian whom he placed in charge of Paris, Napoleon III found an authoritarian planner capable of bulldozing both buildings and opposition. In twenty years, Paris was completely transformed (Map 23.2).

The Paris of 1850 was a labyrinth of narrow, dark streets, the results of desperate overcrowding and a lack of effective planning. In a central city not twice the size

> **germ theory** The idea that disease was caused by the spread of living organisms that could be controlled.

Map 23.2 The Modernization of Paris, ca. 1850–1870 The addition of broad boulevards, large parks, and grandiose train stations transformed Paris. The cutting of the new north-south axis — known as the Boulevard Saint-Michel — was one of Haussmann's most controversial projects. It razed much of Paris's medieval core and filled the Île de la Cité with massive government buildings.

tion of better housing, especially for the middle classes. Small neighborhood parks and open spaces were created throughout the city, and two very large parks suitable for all kinds of holiday activities were developed — one on the affluent west side and one on the poor east side of the city. The city also improved its sewers, and a system of aqueducts more than doubled the city's supply of clean, fresh water.

Rebuilding Paris provided a new model for urban planning and stimulated modern urbanism throughout Europe, particularly after 1870. In city after city, public authorities mounted a coordinated attack on many of the interrelated problems of the urban environment. As in Paris, improvements in public health through better water supply and waste disposal often went hand in hand with new boulevard construction. Cities such as Vienna and Cologne followed the Parisian example of tearing down old walled fortifications and replacing them with broad, circular boulevards on which office buildings, town halls, theaters, opera houses, and museums were erected. These ring roads and the new boulevards that radiated outward eased movement and encouraged urban expansion (see Map 23.2). Zoning expropriation laws, which allowed a majority of the owners of land in a given quarter of the city to impose major street or sanitation improvements on a reluctant minority, were an important mechanism of the new urbanism.

of New York's Central Park lived more than one-third of the city's 1 million inhabitants. Terrible slum conditions and extremely high death rates were facts of life. There were few open spaces and only two public parks for the entire metropolis.

For two decades Haussmann and his fellow planners proceeded on many interrelated fronts. With a bold energy that often shocked their contemporaries, they razed old buildings in order to cut broad, straight, tree-lined boulevards through the center of the city as well as in new quarters on the outskirts (see Map 23.2). These boulevards, designed in part to prevent the easy construction and defense of barricades by revolutionary crowds, permitted traffic to flow freely and afforded impressive vistas. Their creation also demolished some of the worst slums. New streets stimulated the construc-

Public Transportation

The development of mass public transportation often accompanied urban planning, greatly enhancing urban living conditions toward the end of the nineteenth century. In the 1870s, many European cities authorized private companies to operate horse-drawn streetcars, which had been developed in the United States, to carry riders along the growing number of major thoroughfares. Then in the 1890s, the real revolution occurred: European countries adopted another American transit innovation, a streetcar that ran on the newly harnessed power of electricity (see page 741).

Electric streetcars were cheaper, faster, more dependable, cleaner, and more comfortable than their horse-drawn counterparts. Millions of Europeans—workers, shoppers, schoolchildren—hopped on board during the workweek. On weekends and holidays, streetcars carried millions on happy outings to parks and the countryside, to racetracks and music halls. In 1886 the horse-drawn streetcars of Austria-Hungary, France, Germany, and Great Britain were carrying about 900 million riders. By 1910 electric streetcar systems in the four countries were carrying 6.7 billion riders.[3] Each man, woman, and child was using public transportation four times as often in 1910 as in 1886.

Good mass transit helped greatly in the struggle for decent housing. The new boulevards and horse-drawn streetcars had facilitated a middle-class move to better and more spacious housing in the 1860s and 1870s; after 1890 electric streetcars meant people of even modest means could access new, improved housing. Though still crowded, the city was able to expand and become less congested. In England in 1901, only 9 percent of the urban population was "overcrowded" in terms of the official definition of more than two persons per room. On the continent, many city governments in the early twentieth century were building electric streetcar systems that provided transportation to new public and private housing developments for the working classes beyond the city limits. Suburban commuting was born.

Rich and Poor and Those in Between

What did the emergence of urban industrial society mean for rich and poor and those in between? ▨

As the quality of urban life was improving across Europe, the class structure was becoming more complex and diverse. Urban society featured many distinct social groups, all of which existed in a state of constant flux and competition. The gap between rich and poor remained enormous and quite traditional, but there were countless gradations between the extremes.

The Distribution of Income

By 1850 at the latest, working conditions were improving. Moreover, real wages—that is, wages received by workers adjusted for changes in the prices they paid—were rising for the mass of the population, and they continued to do so until 1914. The real wages of British workers, for example, almost doubled between 1850 and 1906. Similar increases occurred in continental countries as industrial development quickened after 1850. Ordinary people took a major step forward in the centuries-old battle against poverty, reinforcing efforts to improve many aspects of human existence.

There is another side to the income coin, however. Greater economic rewards for the average person did not eliminate hardship and poverty, nor did they make the wealth and income of the rich and the poor significantly more equal, as economic historians have clearly demonstrated. In almost every advanced country around 1900, the richest 5 percent of all households in the population received about a third of all national income, and the richest 20 percent of households received from 50 to 60 percent of all national income. At the other end, the entire bottom 80 percent received only 40 to 50 percent of all income. Moreover, the bottom 30 percent of all households received 10 percent or less of all income.

To understand the full significance of these statistics, one must realize that the middle classes were smaller than they are today. In the nineteenth century, they accounted for less than 20 percent of the population. In short, this meant that the upper and middle classes alone received more than half of all income, while the poorest 80 percent—the working classes, including peasants and agricultural laborers—received less altogether than the two richest classes. Moreover, in the nineteenth century income taxes on the wealthy were light or nonexistent. Thus the gap between rich and poor remained enormous at the beginning of the twentieth century. Indeed, it was probably almost as great as it had been in the late eighteenth century, in the age of agriculture and aristocracy.

The great gap between rich and poor endured, in part, because industrial and urban development made society more diverse and less unified. Society had not split into two sharply defined opposing classes, as Karl Marx had predicted (see Chapter 22). Instead, economic specialization enabled society to produce more effectively and in the process created more new social groups than it destroyed. There developed an almost unlimited range of jobs, skills, and earnings; one group or subclass blended into another in a complex, confusing hierarchy. Thus the tiny elite of the very rich and the sizable mass of the dreadfully poor were separated by a range of subclasses, each filled with individuals struggling to rise or at least to hold their own in the social order. In this atmosphere of competition and hierarchy, neither the middle classes nor the working classes acted as a unified force. This social and occupational hierarchy developed enormous

Picturing the Past

Apartment Living in Paris This drawing shows a typical layout for a European city apartment building in about 1850. (Bibliothèque nationale de France)

ANALYZING THE IMAGE Describe the inhabitants of each floor. How does the economic condition of the tenants differ from the 1st Étage (American second floor) to the garret apartments on the top floor?

CONNECTIONS What does this drawing suggest about urban life in the nineteenth century? How might a sketch of a modern, urban American apartment building differ in terms of the types of people who reside in a single building?

To complete this activity online, go to the Online Study Guide at bedfordstmartins.com/mckaywest.

variations, but the age-old pattern of great economic inequality remained firmly intact.

The People and Occupations of the Middle Classes

By the beginning of the twentieth century, the diversity and range within the urban middle class were striking. Indeed, it is more meaningful to think not of a single middle class but of a confederation of middle classes whose members engaged in occupations requiring mental, rather than physical, skill.

At the top of the middle class stood the upper middle class, composed mainly of the most successful business families from banking, industry, and large-scale commerce. As people in the upper middle class gained in income and progressively lost all traces of radicalism after the trauma of 1848, they were almost irresistibly drawn toward the aristocratic lifestyle. And although the genuine hereditary aristocracy constituted only a tiny minority in every European country, it retained imposing wealth, unrivaled social prestige, and substantial political influence. This was especially true in central and eastern Europe, where the monarch — the highest-ranking noble of them all — continued to hold great political power.

The topmost reaches of the upper middle class tended to merge with the old aristocracy to form a new upper class of at most 5 percent of the population. Much of the aristocracy welcomed this development. Having experienced a sharp decline in its relative income in the course of industrialization, the landed aristocracy had met big business coming up the staircase and was often delighted to trade titles, country homes, and snobbish elegance for good hard cash. Some of the best bargains were made through marriages to American heiresses. Correspondingly, wealthy aristocrats tended increasingly to exploit their agricultural and mineral resources as if they were business people.

Below the wealthy upper middle class were much larger, much less wealthy, and increasingly diversified middle-class groups. Here were the moderately successful industrialists and merchants as well as professionals in law and medicine. This was the middle middle class, solid and quite comfortable but lacking great wealth. Below it were independent shopkeepers, small traders, and tiny manufacturers — the lower middle class. Both of these traditional elements of the middle class grew modestly with economic development.

As industry and technology expanded in the nineteenth century, a growing demand developed for experts with specialized knowledge, and advanced education soared in importance among the middle classes. Engineering, for example, emerged from the world of skilled labor as a full-fledged profession with considerable prestige and many branches. Architects, chemists, accoun-

tants, and surveyors, to name only a few, first achieved professional standing in this period. They established criteria for advanced training and certification and banded together in organizations to promote and defend their interests.

Management of large public and private institutions also emerged as a kind of profession as governments provided more services and as very large corporations such as railroads came into being. Government officials and many private executives were not capitalists in the sense that they owned business enterprises, but public and private managers did have specialized knowledge and the capacity to earn a good living. And they shared most of the values of the business-owning entrepreneurs and the older professionals.

Industrialization also expanded and diversified the lower middle class. The number of independent, property-owning shopkeepers and small business people grew, and so did the number of white-collar employees — a mixed group of traveling salesmen, bookkeepers, store managers, and clerks who staffed the offices and branch stores of large corporations. White-collar employees were propertyless and often earned no more than the better-paid skilled or semiskilled workers did. Yet white-collar workers were fiercely committed to the middle class and to the ideal of upward mobility. In the Balkans, for example, clerks let their fingernails grow very long to distinguish themselves from people who worked with their hands. The tie, the suit, and soft, clean hands were no less subtle marks of class distinction than were wages.

Relatively well educated but without complex technical skills, many white-collar groups aimed at achieving professional standing and the accompanying middle-class status. Elementary school teachers largely succeeded in this effort. From being miserably paid part-time workers in the early nineteenth century, teachers rode the wave of mass education to respectable middle-class status and income. Nurses also rose from the lower ranks of unskilled labor to precarious middle-class standing. Dentistry was taken out of the hands of working-class barbers and placed in the hands of highly trained (and middle-class) professionals.

Middle-Class Culture and Values

In spite of growing occupational diversity and conflicting interests, the middle classes were loosely united by a certain style of life and culture. Food was the largest item in the household budget, for middle-class people liked to eat very well. The European middle classes consumed meat in abundance, and a well-off family might spend 10 percent of its substantial earnings on meat and fully 25 percent of its income on food and drink. Spending on food was also great because the dinner party was this class's favored social occasion. A wealthy family might give a lavish party for eight to twelve almost every

A Corner of the Table With photographic precision, the French artist Paul-Émile Chabas (1869–1937) captures the elegance and intimacy of a sumptuous dinner party. Throughout Europe, members of the upper middle class and aristocracy enjoyed dinners like this with eight or nine separate courses, beginning with appetizers and ending with coffee and liqueurs. (Archives Charmet/The Bridgeman Art Library)

week, whereas more modest households would settle for once a month.

The middle-class wife could cope with this endless procession of meals, courses, and dishes because she had both servants and money at her disposal. Indeed, the employment of at least one full-time maid to cook and clean was the clearest sign that a family had crossed the cultural divide separating the working classes from what some contemporary observers called the "servant-keeping classes." The greater a family's income, the greater the number of servants it employed. Food and servants together absorbed about 50 percent of income at all levels of the middle class.

Well fed and well served, the middle classes were also well housed by 1900. Many prosperous families rented, rather than owned, their homes. Apartment living, complete with tiny rooms for servants under the eaves of the top floor, was commonplace. And, just as the aristocracy had long divided the year between palatial country estates and lavish townhouses during "the season," so the upper middle class purchased country places or built beach houses for weekend and summer use.

By 1900 the middle classes were also quite clothes-conscious. The factory, the sewing machine, and the department store had all helped reduce the cost and expand the variety of clothing. Middle-class women were particularly attentive to the dictates of fashion. (See "Living in the Past: Nineteenth-Century Women's Fashion," page 728.) Private coaches and car-

riages, ever-expensive items in the city, were additional signs of rising social status.

Rich businessmen devoted less time to business and more time to "culture" and easy living than was the case in less wealthy or well-established families. The keystones of culture and leisure were books, music, and travel. The long realistic novel, the heroics of composers Wagner and Verdi, the diligent striving of the dutiful daughter at the piano, and the packaged tour to a foreign country were all sources of middle-class pleasure.

In addition to their material tastes, the middle classes generally agreed upon a strict code of behavior and morality. This code laid great stress on hard work, self-discipline, and personal achievement. Men and women who fell into crime or poverty were generally assumed to be responsible for their own circumstances. Christian morality was reaffirmed by this code and was preached tirelessly by middle-class people. Drunkenness and gambling were denounced as vices; sexual purity and fidelity were celebrated as virtues. In short, the middle-class person was supposed to know right from wrong and was expected to act accordingly.

The People and Occupations of the Working Classes

About four out of five people belonged to the working classes at the beginning of the twentieth century. Many members of the working classes — that is, people whose livelihoods depended primarily on physical labor and who did not employ domestic servants — were still small landowning peasants and hired farm hands. This was especially true in eastern Europe. In western and central Europe, however, the typical worker had left the land. In Great Britain, less than 8 percent of the people worked in agriculture, and in rapidly industrializing Germany only 25 percent were employed in agriculture and forestry. Even in less industrialized France, less than 50 percent of the people depended on the land in 1900.

The urban working classes were even less unified and homogeneous than the middle classes. In the first place, economic development and increased specialization expanded the traditional range of working-class skills, earnings, and experiences. Meanwhile, the old sharp distinction between highly skilled artisans and unskilled manual workers gradually broke down. To be sure, highly skilled printers and masons as well as unskilled dockworkers and common laborers continued to exist. But between these extremes there appeared ever more semi-skilled groups, many of which were composed of factory workers and machine tenders (Figure 23.2). In the second place, skilled, semiskilled, and unskilled workers developed widely divergent lifestyles and cultural values, and their differences contributed to a keen sense of social status and hierarchy within the working classes. The result was great variety and limited class unity.

Highly skilled workers, who made up about 15 percent of the working classes, became known as the **labor aristocracy**. These workers earned only about two-thirds of the income of the bottom ranks of the servant-keeping classes, but that was fully twice as much as the earnings of unskilled workers. The most "aristocratic" of the highly skilled workers were construction bosses and factory foremen, men who had risen from the ranks and were fiercely proud of their achievement. The labor aristocracy also included members of the traditional highly skilled handicraft trades that had not been mechanized or placed in factories, like cabinetmakers, jewelers, and printers.

The labor aristocracy as a whole was under constant long-term pressure. Gradually, factory methods were being extended to more crafts, and many skilled artisans were replaced by lower-paid semiskilled factory workers. Traditional wood-carvers and watchmakers virtually disappeared, for example, as the making of furniture and timepieces now took place in factories. At the same time, the labor aristocracy was consistently being enlarged by new kinds of skilled workers such as shipbuilders and railway locomotive engineers. Thus the labor elite remained in a state of flux as individuals and whole crafts moved in and out of it.

To maintain this precarious standing, the upper working class adopted distinctive values and strait-laced, almost puritanical behavior. Like the middle classes, the labor aristocracy was strongly committed to the family and to economic improvement. Families in the upper working class saved money regularly, worried about their children's education, and valued good housing. Wives seldom sought employment outside the home. Despite these similarities, skilled workers viewed themselves

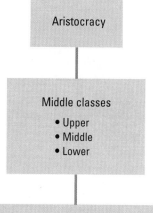

Figure 23.2 **The Urban Social Hierarchy**

- Aristocracy
- Middle classes
  - Upper
  - Middle
  - Lower
- Working classes
  - Highly skilled: the "labor aristocracy"
  - Semiskilled
  - Unskilled

labor aristocracy The highly skilled workers, such as factory foremen and construction bosses, who made up about 15 percent of the working classes from about 1850 to 1914.

The Labor Aristocracy This group of British foremen is attending the International Exhibition in Paris in 1862. Their "Sunday best" includes the silk top hats and long morning coats of the propertied classes, but they definitely remain workers, the proud leaders of laboring people. (© The Board of Trustees of the Victoria & Albert Museum)

LIVING IN THE PAST

IN THE LATER NINETEENTH CENTURY fashionable clothing, especially for middle-class women, became the first modern consumer industry as buyers snapped up the constantly changing ready-to-wear goods sold by large department stores. Before the twentieth century, when society fragmented into many different groups expressing themselves in many dress styles, clothing patterns focused mainly on perceived

differences in class and gender. Most changes in women's fashion originated in Paris in the nineteenth century. The crinoline dresses shown here were worn exclusively by aristocratic and wealthy middle-class Frenchwomen in the 1850s and 1860s. These expensive dresses, flawlessly tailored by skilled seamstresses, abounded in elaborate embroidery, rich velvety materials, and fancy accessories. The circular spread of the gowns was created by the crinoline, a slip with a metal hoop that held the skirt out on all sides. Underneath women wore the corset, the century's most characteristic women's undergarment, which was laced up tightly in back and which pressed unmercifully from the breasts to the hips.

By 1875, as shown in this painting of a middle-class interior (opposite, top), the corset still binds, but the crinoline hoop was replaced by the bustle, a cotton fan with steel reinforcement that pushed the dress out in back to exaggerate gender differences. Worn initially by the wealthy elite, a cheaper ready-to-wear bustle could be purchased throughout Europe from a department store or mail-order catalogue, and it soon became the standard for middle-class women. Emulating the elite in style, conventional middle-class women shopped carefully, scouting for sales,

and drew a boundary separating themselves from working-class women, who wore simple cotton clothes, just as the wealthy had tried to differentiate themselves from the middle class earlier in the century.

By century's end alternative styles of dress began to emerge. The young middle-class Englishwoman in this 1893 photo has chosen a woman's tailored suit, the only major English innovation in nineteenth-century women's fashion. This "alternative dress" combined the tie, suit jacket, vest, and straw hat — all initially items of male attire — with typical feminine elements, such as the skirt and gloves. The practical, socially accepted dress appealed to the growing number of women in paid employment in the 1890s. By the early part of the twentieth century the corset had given way entirely to the more flexible brassiere and the mainstream embrace of loose-fitting garments, as illustrated by this 1910 French advertisement.

Crinoline dresses, Paris, 1859.
(Mary Evans Picture Library/The Image Works)

PARIS FASHIONS FOR SEPTEMBER.

Summer dress with bustle, England, 1875.
(Roy Miles, Esq./The Bridgeman Art Library)

Alternative dress, England, 1893.
(Manchester City Art Galleries)

QUESTIONS FOR ANALYSIS

1. What does the image from 1859 tell you about the life of these women (their work, leisure activities, and so on)? What implications, if any, do you think the later styles shown here had on women's lives? On class distinctions?

2. What does the impractical, restrictive clothing in these images reveal about society's view of women during this period? What is the significance of the emergence of alternative styles of dress?

3. Historian Diana Crane has argued that women's departure from a dominant style can be seen as a symbolic, nonverbal assertion of independence and equality with men. Do you agree? Did the greater freedom of movement in clothing in the twentieth century reflect the emerging emancipation of Western women? Or was the coquettish femininity of loose, flowing dresses only a repackaging of the dominant culture's sharply defined gender boundaries?

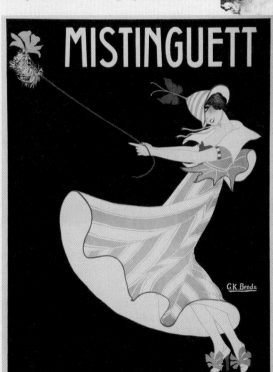

Loose-fitting dress, France, 1910. (© Corbis)

❝ Drunkenness was by far the commonest cause of dispute and misery in working class homes. On account of it one saw many a decent family drift down through poverty into total want. ❞

—ENGLISH SLUM DWELLER

not as aspirants to the middle class but as the pacesetters and natural leaders of all the working classes. Well aware of the degradation not so far below them, they practiced self-discipline and stern morality. They generally frowned on heavy drinking and sexual permissiveness. As one German skilled worker somberly warned, "The path to the brothel leads through the tavern" and from there quite possibly to drastic decline or total ruin for person and family.[4]

Below the labor aristocracy stood an enormously complex sector of the labor world, comprising both semiskilled and unskilled urban workers. Workers in the established crafts—carpenters, bricklayers, pipe fitters—stood near the top of the semiskilled hierarchy, often flirting with (or sliding back from) the labor elite. A large number of the semiskilled were factory workers, including substantial numbers of unmarried women, who earned highly variable but relatively good wages and whose relative importance in the labor force was increasing.

sweated industries Poorly paid handicraft production, often by married women paid by the piece and working at home.

Below the semiskilled workers was a larger group of unskilled workers that included day laborers such as longshoremen, wagon-driving teamsters, teenagers, and every kind of "helper." Many of these people had real skills and performed valuable services, but they were unorganized and divided, united only by the common fate of meager earnings. The same lack of unity characterized street vendors and market people—self-employed workers who competed savagely with each other and with the established shopkeepers of the lower middle class.

One of the largest components of the unskilled group was domestic servants, whose numbers grew steadily in the nineteenth century. In Great Britain, for example, one out of every seven employed persons in 1911 was a domestic servant. The great majority were women; indeed, one out of every three girls in Britain between the ages of fifteen and twenty was a domestic servant. Throughout Europe and America, a great many female domestics in the cities were recent migrants from rural areas. As in earlier times, domestic service was hard work at low pay with limited personal independence and the danger of sexual exploitation. For the full-time general

maid in a lower-middle-class family, there was an unending routine of babysitting, shopping, cooking, and cleaning. In the great households, the girl was at the bottom of a rigid hierarchy of status-conscious butlers and housekeepers.

Nonetheless, domestic service had real attractions for "rough country girls" with strong hands and few specialized skills. Marriage prospects were better, or at least more varied, in the city. And though wages were low, they were higher and more regular than in hard agricultural work. Finally, as one London observer noted, young girls and other migrants were drawn to the city by "the contagion of numbers, the sense of something going on, the theaters and the music halls, the brightly lighted streets and busy crowds—all, in short, that makes the difference between the Mile End fair on a Saturday night, and a dark and muddy country lane, with no glimmer of gas and with nothing to do."[5]

Many young domestics from the countryside made successful transitions to working-class wife and mother. Yet with an unskilled or unemployed husband, a growing family, and limited household income, many working-class wives had to join the broad ranks of working women in the **sweated industries**. These industries flowered after 1850 and resembled the old putting-out and cottage industries of earlier times (see Chapter 18). The women normally worked at home and were paid by the piece, not by the hour. They and their young children earned pitiful wages and lacked any job security. Some women decorated dishes or embroidered linens, or took in laundry for washing and ironing. The majority made clothing, especially after the advent of the sewing machine. An army of poor women, usually working at home, accounted for much of the inexpensive ready-made clothes displayed on department store racks and in tiny shops.

Working-Class Leisure and Religion

Notwithstanding the hard physical labor and their lack of wealth, the urban working classes sought fun and recreation, and they found both. Across the face of Europe, drinking remained unquestionably the favorite leisure-time activity of working people. For many middle-class moralists as well as moralizing historians since, love of drink has been a curse of the modern age—a sign of social dislocation and popular suffering. Certainly, drinking was deadly serious business. One English slum dweller recalled that "drunkenness was by far the commonest cause of dispute and misery in working class homes. On account of it one saw many a decent family drift down through poverty into total want."[6]

Generally, however, heavy problem drinking declined in the late nineteenth century as it became less socially acceptable. This decline reflected in part the moral leadership of the upper working class. At the same time, drinking became more publicly acceptable. Cafés and pubs became increasingly bright, friendly places. Working-class political activities, both moderate and radical, were also concentrated in taverns and pubs. Moreover, social drinking in public places by married couples and sweethearts became an accepted and widespread practice for the first time. This greater participation by women undoubtedly helped civilize the world of drink and hard liquor.

The two other leisure-time passions of working-class culture were sports and music halls. A great decline in "cruel sports," such as bullbaiting and cockfighting, had occurred throughout Europe by the late nineteenth century. Their place was filled by modern, commercialized spectator sports, of which racing and soccer were the most popular. There was a great deal of gambling on sports events, and for many a working person a desire to decipher racing forms provided a powerful incentive toward literacy. Music halls and vaudeville theaters, the working-class counterparts of middle-class opera and classical theater, were enormously popular throughout Europe. In 1900 there were more than fifty such halls and theaters in London alone. Music hall audiences were thoroughly mixed, which may account for the fact that drunkenness, premarital sex, marital difficulties, and mothers-in-law were all favorite themes of broad jokes and bittersweet songs.

In more serious moments, religion continued to provide working people with solace and meaning. The eighteenth-century vitality of popular religion in Catholic countries and the Protestant rejuvenation exemplified by German Pietism and English Methodism (see Chapter 19) carried over into the nineteenth century. Indeed, many historians see the early nineteenth century as an age of religious revival. Yet historians also recognize that by the last few decades of the nineteenth century, a considerable decline in both church attendance and church donations was occurring in most European countries. And it seems clear that this decline was greater for the urban working classes than for their rural counterparts or for the middle classes.

Why did working-class church attendance decline? Part of the reason was that the construction of churches failed to keep up with the rapid growth of urban population, especially in new working-class neighborhoods. Equally important, however, was the fact that throughout the nineteenth century both Catholic and Protestant churches were normally seen as they saw themselves — as conservative institutions defending social order and custom. Therefore, as the European working classes became more politically conscious, they tended to see the established (or quasi-established) "territorial church" as

Big City Nightlife   The most famous dance hall and cabaret in Paris was the Moulin Rouge. There La Goulue ("the Glutton"), who is featured on this poster, performed her provocative version of the cancan and reigned as the queen of Parisian sensuality. This is one of many colorful posters done by Henri de Toulouse-Lautrec (1864–1901), who combined stupendous creativity and dedicated debauchery in his short life. (Bridgeman-Giraudon/Art Resource, NY)

allied with their political opponents. Especially the men of the urban working classes developed vaguely anti-church attitudes, even though they remained neutral or positive toward religion. They tended to regard regular church attendance as "not our kind of thing" — not part of urban working-class culture.

The pattern was different in the United States. There, most churches also preached social conservatism in the nineteenth century. But because church and state had always been separate and because there was always a host of competing denominations and even different religions, working people identified churches much less with the political and social status quo. Instead, individual churches in the United States were often closely identified with an ethnic group rather than with a social class, and churches thrived, in part, as a means of asserting ethnic identity. This same process did occur in Europe if the church or synagogue had never been linked to the state and served as a focus for ethnic cohesion. Irish Catholic churches in Protestant Britain and Jewish synagogues in Russia were outstanding examples.

The Changing Family

How did working-class and middle-class families change as they coped with the challenges and the opportunities of the developing urban civilization? ■

Urban life wrought many fundamental changes in the family. By the second half of the nineteenth century the family had stabilized considerably after the disruption of the late eighteenth and early nineteenth centuries. The home became more important for both men and women. The role of women and attitudes toward children underwent substantial change, and adolescence emerged as a distinct stage of life. These are but a few of the transformations that affected all social classes in varying degrees.

Premarital Sex and Marriage

By 1850 the preindustrial pattern of lengthy courtship and mercenary marriage for financial gain was pretty well dead among the working classes. In its place, the ideal of romantic love had triumphed. Couples were ever more likely to come from different, even distant, towns and to be more nearly the same age, further indicating that romantic sentiment was replacing tradition and financial considerations.

Economic considerations in marriage began to decline among the middle classes after 1850, but by no means did they disappear entirely. In France dowries and elaborate legal marriage contracts were common practice among the middle classes in the later nineteenth century, and marriage remained for many families one of life's most crucial financial transactions. A popular author advised young Frenchmen that "marriage is in general a means of increasing one's credit and one's fortune and of insuring one's success in the world."[7] This preoccupation with money led many middle-class men in France and elsewhere to marry late, after they had been established economically, and to choose women considerably younger than themselves. Age differences

between husband and wife became a source of tension in many middle-class marriages.

A young woman of the middle class found her romantic life carefully supervised by her well-meaning mother, who schemed for a proper marriage and guarded her daughter's virginity like the family's credit. (See "Listening to the Past: Stephan Zweig on Middle-Class Youth and Sexuality," page 734.) After marriage, middle-class morality sternly demanded fidelity.

Middle-class boys were watched, too, but not as vigilantly. By the time they reached late adolescence, they had usually attained considerable sexual experience with maids or prostitutes.

In the early nineteenth century, sexual experimentation before marriage also triumphed for society as a whole, as did illegitimacy. The illegitimacy explosion that had begun in 1750 continued through the 1840s, at which point one-third of the births in many large European cities was occurring outside of wedlock (see Chapter 19). The rising rate of illegitimacy was reversed in the second half of the nineteenth century: in western, northern, and central Europe, more babies were born to married mothers.

Some observers have argued that this shift reflected the growth of puritanism and a lessening of sexual permissiveness among the unmarried. This explanation, however, is unconvincing because the percentage of working-class brides who were pregnant continued to be high and showed little or no tendency to decline after 1850. In many parts of urban Europe around 1900, as many as one woman in three was going to the altar an expectant mother. Moreover, unmarried people almost certainly used the affordable condoms and diaphragms the industrial age had made available to prevent pregnancy, at least in predominately Protestant countries.

Thus unmarried young people were probably engaging in just as much sexual activity as their parents and grandparents who had created the illegitimacy explosion of 1750 to 1850. But in the later nineteenth century, pregnancy for a young single woman, which a couple might see as the natural consequence of a serious relationship, led increasingly to marriage and the establishment of a two-parent household. This important development reflected the growing respectability of the working classes as well as their gradual economic improvement. Skipping out was less acceptable, and marriage was less of an economic challenge. The urban working-class couple of the late nineteenth century thus became more stable, and that stability strengthened the family as an institution.

Prostitution

Sexual activity certainly existed outside of committed relationships in the nineteenth century, as it undoubtedly always had. In Paris alone, 155,000 women were registered as prostitutes between 1871 and 1903, and 750,000 others were suspected of prostitution in the same years. Men of all classes visited prostitutes, but the middle and upper classes supplied much of the motivating cash. Thus, though many middle-class men abided by the publicly professed code of stern puritanical morality, others indulged their appetites for prostitutes and sexual promiscuity.

My Secret Life, the anonymous eleven-volume autobiography of an English sexual adventurer from the servant-keeping classes, provides a remarkable picture of such a man.[8] Beginning at an early age with a maid, the author becomes progressively obsessed with sex and devotes his life to living his sexual fantasies. In almost every one of his innumerable encounters all across Europe, this man of wealth simply buys his pleasure. Usually meetings are arranged in a businesslike manner: regular and part-time prostitutes quote their prices; working-class girls are corrupted by hot meals and baths.

Obviously atypical in its excesses, *My Secret Life* does reveal the dark side of sex and class in urban society. Frequently thinking of their wives largely in terms of money, family, and social position, the men of the comfortable classes often purchased sex and even affection from poor girls both before and after marriage. Moreover, the great continuing differences between rich and poor made for every kind of debauchery and sexual exploitation. The sternly moral women (and men) of the upper working class detested this sad reality and tried to shield their daughters from it. For many poor young women, however, prostitution, like domestic service, was a stage of life and not a permanent employment. Having done it for a while in their twenties, they went on to marry (or live with) men of their own class and establish homes and families.

Kinship Ties

Within working-class homes, ties to relatives after marriage—kinship ties—were generally very strong. Most newlyweds tried to live near their parents, though not in the same house. Indeed, for many married couples in later-nineteenth-century cities, ties to mothers and fathers, uncles and aunts, were more important than ties to unrelated acquaintances.

People turned to their families for help in coping with sickness, unemployment, death, and old age. Although governments typically provided more welfare services by 1900, the average couple and their children inevitably faced crises. Funerals, for example, brought sudden demands, requiring a large outlay for special clothes, carriages, and burial services. Unexpected death

> ❝ Marriage is in general a means of increasing one's credit and one's fortune and of insuring one's success in the world. ❞
>
> —**POPULAR FRENCH AUTHOR**

or desertion could leave the bereaved or abandoned, especially widows and orphans, in need of financial aid or perhaps a foster home. Relatives responded hastily to such cries, knowing full well that their own time of need and repayment would undoubtedly come.

Relatives were also valuable at less tragic moments. If a couple was quite poor, an aged relation often moved in to cook and mind the children so that the wife could earn badly needed income outside the home. Members of a large family group often lived in the same neighborhood, and they frequently shared Sunday dinners, outgrown clothing, and useful information.

Gender Roles and Early Feminism

Industrialization and the growth of modern cities brought great changes to the lives of European women of all classes. These changes were particularly consequential for married women, and most women did marry in the nineteenth century.

After 1850 the work of most wives became increasingly distinct and separate from that of their husbands. Husbands became wage earners in factories and offices, while wives tended to stay home and manage households and care for children. The preindustrial pattern among both peasants and cottage workers, in which husbands and wives worked together and divided up household duties and child rearing, declined. Instead, as economic conditions improved, most men expected only married women in poor families to work outside the home. Thus many historians have stressed that the societal ideal in nineteenth-century Europe became a strict division of labor by gender and rigidly constructed separate spheres: the wife as mother and homemaker, the husband as wage earner and breadwinner.

This rigid gender division of labor meant that married women faced great obstacles when they needed—or wanted—to move into the man's world of paid employment outside the home. Husbands were unsympathetic or hostile. Well-paying jobs were off-limits to women, and a woman's wage was almost always less than a man's, even for the same work.

Moreover, married women were subordinated to their husbands by law and lacked many basic legal rights. In England a wife had no legal identity and hence no right

Stephan Zweig on Middle-Class Youth and Sexuality

LISTENING TO THE PAST

Growing up in Vienna in a prosperous Jewish family, Stephan Zweig (zwighg) (1881–1942) became an influential voice calling for humanitarian values and international culture in early-twentieth-century Europe. Passionately opposed to the First World War, Zweig wrote poetry, plays, and novels. But he was most famous for his biographies: shrewd psychological portraits of historical figures such as Magellan and Marie Antoinette.

After Hitler came to power in 1933, Zweig lived in exile until his death in 1942. Zweig's last work was The World of Yesterday *(1943), one of the truly fascinating autobiographies of the twentieth century. In the following passage, Zweig recalls the romantic experiences and the sexual separation of middle-class youth before the First World War.*

❝ During the eight years of our higher schooling [beyond grade school], something had occurred which was of great importance to each one of us: we ten-year-olds had grown into virile young men of sixteen, seventeen, and eighteen, and Nature began to assert its rights. . . . It did not take us long to discover that those authorities in whom we had previously confided — school, family, and public morals — manifested an astonishing insincerity in this matter of sex. But what is more, they also demanded secrecy and reserve from us in this connection. . . .

This "social morality," which on the one hand privately presupposed the existence of sexuality and its natural course, but on the other would not recognize it openly at any price, was doubly deceitful. While it winked one eye at a young man and even encouraged him with the other "to sow his wild oats," as the kindly language of the home put it, in the case of a woman it studiously shut both eyes and acted as if it were blind. That a man could experience desires, and was permitted to experience them, was silently admitted by custom. But to admit frankly that a woman could be subject to similar desires, or that creation for its eternal purposes also required a female polarity, would have transgressed the conception of the "sanctity of womanhood." In the pre-Freudian era, therefore, the axiom was agreed upon that a female person could have no physical desires as long as they had not been awakened by man, and that, obviously, was officially permitted only in marriage. But even in those moral times, in Vienna in particular, the air was full of dangerous erotic infection, and a girl of good family had to live in a completely sterilized atmosphere, from the day of her birth until the day when she left the altar on her husband's arm. In order to protect young girls, they were not left alone for a single moment. . . . Every book which they read was inspected, and above all else, young girls were constantly kept busy to divert their attention from any possible dangerous thoughts. They had to practise the piano, learn singing and drawing, foreign languages, and the history of literature and art. They were educated and overeducated. But while the aim was to make them as educated and as socially correct as possible, at the same time society anxiously took great pains that they should remain innocent of all natural things to a degree unthinkable today. A young girl of good family was not allowed to have any idea of how the male body was formed, or to know how children came into the world, for the angel was to enter into matrimony not only physically untouched, but completely "pure" spiritually as well. "Good breeding," for a young

An elegant ball for upper-class youth, with debutantes, junior officers, and vigilant chaperons watching in the background. (State Russian Museum, St. Petersburg, Russia/The Bridgeman Art Library)

girl of that time, was identical with ignorance of life; and this ignorance ofttimes lasted for the rest of their lives. . . .

What possibilities actually existed for a young man of the middle-class world? In all the others, in the so-called lower classes, the problem was no problem at all. . . . In most of our Alpine villages the number of natural children greatly exceeded the legitimate ones. Among the proletariat, the worker, before he could get married, lived with another worker in free love. . . . It was only in our middle-class society that such a remedy as an early marriage was scorned. . . . And so there was an artificial interval of six, eight, or ten years between actual manhood and manhood as society accepted it; and in this interval the young man had to take care of his own "affairs" or adventures.

Those days did not give him too many opportunities. Only a very few particularly rich young men could afford the luxury of keeping a mistress, that is, taking an apartment and paying her expenses. And only a very few fortunate young men achieved the literary ideal of love of the times — the only one which it was permitted to describe in novels — an affair with a married woman. The others helped themselves for the most part with shopgirls and waitresses, and this offered little inner satisfaction. . . . But, generally speaking, prostitution was still the foundation of the erotic life outside of marriage; in a certain sense it constituted a dark underground vault over which rose the gorgeous structure of middle-class society with its faultless, radiant façade.

The present generation has hardly any idea of the gigantic extent of prostitution in Europe before the [First] World War. Whereas today it is as rare to meet a prostitute on the streets of a big city as it is to meet a wagon in the road, then the sidewalks were so sprinkled with women for sale that it was more difficult to avoid than to find them. To this was added the countless number of "closed houses," the night clubs, the cabarets, the dance parlours with their dancers and singers, and the bars with their "come-on" girls. At that time female wares were offered for sale at every hour and at every price. . . . And this was the same city, the same society, the same morality, that was indignant when young girls rode bicycles, and declared it a disgrace to the dignity of science when Freud in his calm, clear, and penetrating manner established truths that they did not wish to be true. The same world that so pathetically defended the purity of womanhood allowed this cruel sale of women, organized it, and even profited thereby.

We should not permit ourselves to be misled by sentimental novels or stories of that epoch. It was a bad time for youth. The young girls were hermetically locked up under the control of the family, hindered in their free bodily as well as intellectual development. The young men were forced to secrecy and reticence by a morality which fundamentally no one believed or obeyed. Unhampered, honest relationships — in other words, all that could have made youth happy and joyous according to the laws of Nature — were permitted only to the very few. 》

QUESTIONS FOR ANALYSIS

1. According to Zweig, how did the sex lives of young middle-class women and young middle-class men differ? What accounted for these differences?

2. What were the differences between the sex lives of the middle class and those of the "so-called lower classes"? What was Zweig's opinion of these differences?

3. Zweig ends with a value judgment: "It was a bad time for youth." Do you agree or disagree? Why?

to own property in her own name. Even the wages she might earn belonged to her husband. In France the Napoleonic Code (see Chapter 20) also enshrined the principle of female subordination and gave the wife few legal rights regarding property, divorce, and custody of the children.

With all women facing discrimination in education and employment and with middle-class women suffering especially from a lack of legal rights, there is little wonder that some women rebelled and began the long-continuing fight for equality of the sexes and the rights of women. Their struggle proceeded on two main fronts. First, following in the steps of women such as Mary Wollstonecraft (see Chapter 20), organizations founded by middle-class feminists campaigned for equal legal rights for women as well as access to higher education and professional employment. These middle-class feminists argued that unmarried women and middle-class widows with inadequate incomes simply had to have more opportunities to support themselves. Middle-class feminists also recognized that paid (as opposed to unpaid) work could relieve the monotony that some women found in their sheltered middle-class existence and put greater meaning into their lives.

In the later nineteenth century, these organizations scored some significant victories, such as the 1882 law giving English married women full property rights. More women gradually found professional and white-collar employment, especially after about 1880. But progress was slow and hard won. For example, in Germany before 1900, women were not admitted as fully registered students at a single university. Determined pioneers had to fight with tremendous fortitude to break through sexist barriers to advanced education and subsequent professional employment. (See "Individuals in Society: Franziska Tiburtius," page 737.) In the years before 1914, middle-class feminists increasingly focused their attention on political action and fought for the right for women to vote.

Women inspired by utopian and especially Marxian socialism (see Chapter 22) blazed a second path. Often scorning the programs of middle-class feminists, socialist women leaders argued that the liberation of working-class women would come only with the liberation of the entire working class through revolution. In the meantime, they championed the cause of working women and won some practical improvements, especially in Germany, where the socialist movement was most effectively organized. In a general way, these different approaches to women's issues reflected the diversity of classes in urban society.

The Importance of Homemaking

In recent years some scholars have been rethinking gender roles within the long-term development of consumer behavior and household economies. First, they identified an eighteenth-century "industrious revolu-

The Well-Managed Home This painting humanizes the concept of separate spheres and suggests how many homemakers with modest resources made their dwellings happy and appealing with hard work and housekeeping skills. With her clean laundry folded and fresh vegetables carried home beside her market baskets, this woman may soon be thinking of preparing dinner for her returning breadwinner. (V&A Images, London, Art Resource, NY)

tion" that saw many wives turning from work for household consumption—making the family's clothes, for example—to working for cash income to buy finished manufactured goods (see Chapter 19). In the industrial era, these scholars have reinterpreted the gender roles associated with separate spheres as rational consumer behavior. They argue that the "breadwinner-homemaker" household developed from about 1850 onward in order to improve the lives of all family members, especially in the working classes.[9] Thus husbands specialized in earning an adequate cash income—the "family wage" that labor unions demanded—and wives specialized in managing the home.

In doing so, the wife was able to produce desirable goods that simply could not be bought in a market, such as improved health, better eating habits, and better behavior. For example, higher wages from the breadwinner could buy more raw food, but only the homemaker's careful selection, processing, and cooking would allow the family to benefit from increased spending on food.

The homemaker's managerial skills thus enabled the couple to maximize household well-being.

Although the reinterpretation of late-nineteenth-century gender roles in terms of a breadwinner-homemaker partnership is a matter of debate, it fits rather well with some key aspects of family life after 1850. As women's horizons narrowed, and as home and children became the typical wife's main concerns, her control and influence there apparently became increasingly strong throughout Europe. Among the English working classes, it was the wife who generally determined how the family's money was spent. In many families, the husband gave all his earnings to his wife to manage, and he received only a small allowance in return. All the major domestic decisions, from the children's schooling and religious instruction to the selection of new furniture or a new apartment, were hers. In France women had even greater power in their assigned domain. One English feminist noted in 1908 that "though legally women occupy a much inferior status

INDIVIDUALS IN SOCIETY

WHY DID A SMALL NUMBER OF WOMEN in the late nineteenth century brave great odds and embark on professional careers? And how did a few of them manage to reach their objectives? The career and personal reflections of Franziska Tiburtius (tigh-bur-TEE-uhs), a pioneer in German medicine, suggest that talent, determination, and economic necessity were critical ingredients.*

Like many women of her time who would study and pursue professional careers, Franziska Tiburtius (1843–1927) was born into a property-owning family of modest means. The youngest of nine children on a small estate in northeastern Germany, the sensitive child wilted under a harsh governess but flowered with a caring teacher and became an excellent student. Graduating at sixteen and needing to support herself, Tiburtius had few opportunities. A young woman from a "proper" background could work as a governess or a teacher without losing her respectability and spoiling her matrimonial prospects, but that was about it. She tried both avenues. Working for six years as a governess in a noble family and no doubt learning that poverty was often one's fate in this genteel profession, she then turned to teaching. Called home from her studies in Britain in 1871 to care for her brother, who had contracted typhus as a field doctor in the Franco-Prussian War, she found her calling. She decided to become a medical doctor.

Supported by her family, Tiburtius's decision was truly audacious. In all Europe, only the University of Zurich in republican Switzerland accepted female students. Moreover, if it became known that she had studied medicine and failed, she would never get a job as a teacher. No parent would entrust a daughter to an "emancipated" radical who had carved up dead bodies! Although the male students at the university sometimes harassed the women with crude pranks, Tiburtius thrived. The revolution of the microscope and the discovery of microorganisms

Franziska Tiburtius, pioneering woman physician in Berlin. (Ullstein Bilderdienst/ The Granger Collection, New York)

was rocking Zurich, and she was fascinated by her studies. She became close friends with a fellow female medical student from Germany, Emilie Lehmus, with whom she would form a lifelong partnership in medicine. She did her internship with families of cottage workers around Zurich and loved her work.

Graduating at age thirty-three in 1876, Tiburtius went to stay with her brother — the doctor in Berlin. Though well qualified to practice, she ran into pervasive discrimination. She was not even permitted to take the state medical exams and could practice only as an unregulated (and unprofessional) "natural healer." But after persistent fighting with the bureaucrats, she was able to display her diploma and practice as "Franziska Tiburtius, M.D. University of Zurich." She and Lehmus were in business.

Soon the two women realized their dream and opened a clinic, subsidized by a wealthy industrialist, for women factory workers. The clinic filled a great need and was soon treating many patients. A room with beds for extremely sick women was later expanded into a second clinic.

Tiburtius and Lehmus became famous. For fifteen years, they were the only women doctors in all Berlin. An inspiration for a new generation of women, they added the wealthy to their thriving practice. But Tiburtius's clinics always concentrated on the poor, providing them with subsidized and up-to-date treatment. Talented, determined, and working with her partner, Tiburtius experienced fully the joys of personal achievement and useful service. Above all, Tiburtius overcame the tremendous barriers raised up against women seeking higher education and professional careers, and this provided an inspiring model for those who dared to follow.

QUESTIONS FOR ANALYSIS

1. Analyze Franziska Tiburtius's life. What lessons do you draw from it? How do you account for her bold action and success?
2. In what ways was Tiburtius's career related to improvements in health in urban society and to the expansion of the professions?

*This portrait draws on Conradine Lück, *Frauen: Neun Lebensschicksale* (Reutlingen: Ensslin & Laiblin, n.d.), pp. 153–185.

than men [in France], in practice they constitute the superior sex. They are the power behind the throne."[10]

Women ruled at home partly because running the urban household was a complicated, demanding, and valuable task. Twice-a-day food shopping, penny-pinching, economizing, and the growing crusade against dirt—not to mention child rearing—constituted a full-time occupation. Working yet another job for wages outside the home had limited appeal for most married women unless the earnings were essential for family survival. Still, many married women in the working classes did make a monetary contribution to family income by taking in a boarder or doing piecework at home in the sweated industries (see page 730). The wife also guided the home because a good deal of her effort was directed toward pampering her husband as he expected. In countless humble households, she saw that he had meat while she ate bread, that he relaxed by the fire while she did the dishes.

The woman's guidance of the household went hand in hand with the increased pride and emotional importance of home and family. The home she ran was idealized as a warm shelter in a hard and impersonal urban world. According to one historian, "'Home, sweet home,' first heard in the 1870s, had become 'almost a second national anthem.'"[11] By 1900 home and family were what life was all about for millions of people of all classes.

Married couples also developed stronger emotional ties to each other. Even in the comfortable classes, marriages in the late nineteenth century were based more on sentiment and sexual attraction than they had been earlier in the century, as money and financial calculation declined in importance. Affection and eroticism became more central to the couple after marriage. Gustave Droz (droh), whose bestselling *Mr., Mrs., and Baby* went through 121 editions between 1866 and 1884, saw love within marriage as the key to human happiness. He condemned men who made marriage sound dull and practical, men who were exhausted by prostitutes and rheumatism and who wanted their young wives to be little angels. He urged women to follow their hearts and marry men more nearly their own age:

> A husband who is stately and a little bald is all right, but a young husband who loves you and who drinks out of your glass without ceremony, is better. Let him, if he ruffles your dress a little and places a kiss on your neck as he passes. Let him, if he undresses you after the ball, laughing like a fool. You have fine spiritual qualities, it is true, but your little body is not bad either and when one loves, one loves completely. Behind these follies lies happiness.[12]

Many French marriage manuals of the late 1800s stressed that women had legitimate sexual needs, such as the "right to orgasm." Perhaps the French were a bit more enlightened in these matters than other nation-

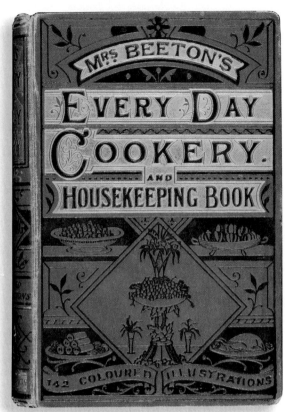

Every Day Cookery and Housekeeping Book The publication of cookbooks and household guides proliferated in the nineteenth century. Mrs. Beeton's bestselling guide offered women housekeeping tips and a wealth of recipes for the homemaker to share with her family. (Graphic Arts Division, Princeton University Library)

alities. But the rise of public socializing by couples in cafés and music halls as well as franker affection within the family suggests a more erotic, pleasurable intimate life for women throughout Western society. This, too, helped make the woman's role as mother and homemaker acceptable and even satisfying.

Child Rearing

Another striking sign of deepening emotional ties within the family was the growing love and concern that mothers gave their tiny infants. Because so many babies in preindustrial Western society died so early in life, mothers of that era often avoided making strong emotional commitments to newborns in order to shield themselves from recurrent heartbreak. Early emotional bonding and a willingness to make real sacrifices for the welfare of the infant were beginning to spread among the comfortable classes by the end of the eighteenth century, but the ordinary mother of modest means adopted new attitudes only as the nineteenth century progressed. The baby became more important, and women became better mothers.

> **" We want to get ahead, and our daughter should have things better than my wife and sisters did. "**

—GERMAN SKILLED WORKER

Mothers increasingly breast-fed their infants, for example, rather than paying wet nurses to do so. Breast-feeding involved sacrifice—a temporary loss of freedom, if nothing else. Yet in an age when there was no good alternative to mother's milk, it saved lives. This surge of maternal feeling also gave rise to a wave of specialized books on child rearing and infant hygiene, such as Droz's phenomenally successful book. Droz urged fathers to get into the act and pitied those "who do not know how to roll around on the carpet, play at being a horse and a great wolf, and undress their baby."[13] Another sign, from France, of increased affection is that fewer illegitimate babies were abandoned as foundlings after about 1850. Moreover, the practice of swaddling disappeared completely. Instead, ordinary mothers allowed their babies freedom of movement and delighted in their spontaneity.

The loving care lavished on infants was matched by greater concern for older children and adolescents. They, too, were wrapped in the strong emotional ties of a more intimate and protective family. For one thing, European women began to limit the number of children they bore in order to care adequately for those they had. It was evident by the end of the nineteenth century that the birthrate was declining across Europe (Figure 23.3), and it continued to do so until after World War II. The Englishwoman who married in the 1860s, for example, had an average of about six children; her daughter marrying in the 1890s had only four; and her granddaughter marrying in the 1920s had only two or possibly three.

The most important reason for this revolutionary reduction in family size, in which the comfortable and well-educated classes took the lead, was parents' desire to improve their economic and social position and that of their children. Children were no longer an economic asset in the later nineteenth century. By having fewer youngsters, parents could give those they had valuable advantages, from music lessons and summer vacations to long, expensive university educations and suitable dowries. A young German skilled worker with only one child spoke for many in his class when he said, "We want to get ahead, and our daughter should have things better than my wife and sisters did."[14]

Thus the growing tendency of couples in the late nineteenth century to use a variety of contraceptive

Life Is Everywhere Emotional ties within ordinary families grew stronger in the nineteenth century, and parents gave their children more love and better care. Painted in 1888 by N. A. Yaroshenko, this outstanding example of Russia's realist tradition of a loving mother and child looking out the window of a railway car while a group of men look on approvingly reflects these new attitudes toward children. The emotional beauty of this painting is darkened, however, by the destination of these passengers: exile in Siberia. (Sovfoto)

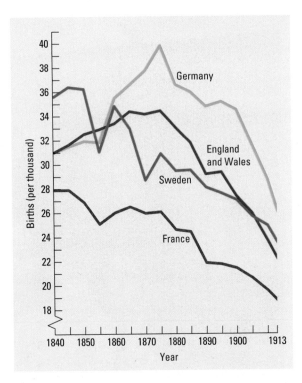

Figure 23.3 **The Decline of Birthrates in England and Wales, France, Germany, and Sweden, 1840–1913**
Women had fewer babies for a variety of reasons, including the fact that their children were increasingly less likely to die before reaching adulthood. How does this compare with Figure 23.1 on page 721?

methods—rhythm method, withdrawal method, and mechanical devices—certainly reflected increased concern for children. Indeed, many parents, especially in the middle classes, probably became too concerned about their children, unwittingly subjecting them to an emotional pressure cooker of almost unbearable intensity. The result was that many children, especially adolescents, came to feel trapped and in need of greater independence.

Prevailing biological and medical theories led parents to believe in the possibility that their own emotional characteristics were passed on to their offspring and that they were thus directly responsible for any abnormality in a child. The moment the child was conceived was thought to be of enormous importance for its future health and vitality, and thus women were warned against getting pregnant during a time of illness or unhappiness. The youthful "sexual excess" of the father might also curse future generations. Although this was true in the case of syphilis, which could be transmitted to unborn children, the rigid determinism of such views left little scope for the child's individual development.

Another area of excessive parental concern was the sexual behavior of their children. Masturbation was viewed with horror, for it represented an act of independence and even defiance. Diet, clothing, games, and sleeping were carefully regulated. Girls were discouraged from riding horses and bicycling because rhythmic friction simulated masturbation. Boys were dressed in trousers with shallow and widely separated pockets.

Attempts to repress the child's sexuality were a source of unhealthy tension, often made worse by the rigid division of gender roles within the family. It was widely believed that mother and child loved each other easily but that relations between father and child were necessarily difficult and often tragic. The father was a stranger; his world of business was far removed from the maternal world of spontaneous affection. Moreover, the father was demanding, often expecting the child to succeed where he himself had failed and making his love conditional on achievement.

Sigmund Freud (1856–1939), the Viennese founder of psychoanalysis, formulated the most striking analysis of the explosive dynamics of the family, particularly the middle-class family in the late nineteenth century. A physician by training, Freud began his career treating mentally ill patients. He noted that the hysteria of his patients appeared to originate in bitter early childhood experiences wherein the child had been obliged to repress strong feelings. When these painful experiences were recalled and reproduced under hypnosis or through the patient's free association of ideas, the patient could be brought to understand the basis of his or her unhappiness and eventually deal with it.

One of Freud's most influential ideas concerned the tensions resulting from the son's instinctive competition with the father for the mother's love and affection. More generally, Freud postulated that much of human behavior is motivated by unconscious emotional needs whose nature and origins are kept from conscious awareness by various mental devices he called defense mechanisms. Freud concluded that much unconscious psychological energy is sexual energy, which is repressed and precariously controlled by rational thinking and moral rules. If Freud exaggerated the sexual and familial roots of adult behavior, that exaggeration was itself a reflection of the tremendous emotional intensity of family life in the late nineteenth century.

The working classes probably had more avenues of escape from such tensions than did the middle classes. Unlike their middle-class counterparts, who remained economically dependent on their families until a long education was finished or a proper marriage secured, working-class boys and girls went to work when they reached adolescence. Earning wages on their own, they could bargain with their parents for greater independence within the household by the time they were sixteen or seventeen. If they were unsuccessful, they could and did leave home to live cheaply as paying lodgers in other working-class homes. Thus the young person from the working classes broke away from the family more easily when emotional ties became oppressive. In the twentieth century, middle-class youths would follow this lead.

Science and Thought

What major changes in science and thought reflected and influenced the new urban society? ■

Major changes in Western science and thought accompanied the emergence of urban society. Several aspects of these complex intellectual developments stand out as especially significant. First, scientific knowledge in many areas expanded rapidly. Breakthroughs in chemistry, physics, and electricity profoundly influenced the Western worldview and spurred the creation of new products and whole industries. The natural and social sciences were also established as highly respected fields of study. In addition, between about the 1840s and the 1890s, European literature underwent a shift from soaring romanticism to tough-minded realism.

The Triumph of Science in Industry

As the pace of scientific advancements quickened and resulted in greater practical benefits, science exercised growing influence on human thought. The intellectual achievements of the scientific revolution (see Chapter 17) had resulted in few such benefits, and theoretical knowledge had also played a relatively small role in the Industrial Revolution in England (see Chapter 21). But breakthroughs in industrial technology in the late eighteenth century enormously stimulated basic scientific inquiry as researchers sought to explain theoretically how such things as steam engines and blast furnaces actually worked. The result was an explosive growth of fundamental scientific discoveries from the 1830s onward. And in contrast to earlier periods, these theoretical discoveries were increasingly transformed into material improvements for the general population.

A perfect example of the translation of better scientific knowledge into practical human benefits was the work of Louis Pasteur and his followers in biology and the medical sciences (see page 721). Another was the development of the branch of physics known as **thermodynamics**. Building on Isaac Newton's laws of mechanics and on studies of steam engines, thermodynamics investigated the relationship between heat and mechanical energy. By midcentury, physicists had formulated the fundamental laws of thermodynamics, which were then applied to mechanical engineering, chemical processes,

and many other fields. The law of conservation of energy held that different forms of energy — such as heat, electricity, and magnetism — could be converted but neither created nor destroyed. Nineteenth-century thermodynamics demonstrated that the physical world was governed by firm, unchanging laws.

Chemistry and electricity were two other fields characterized by extremely rapid scientific progress. And in both fields, "science was put in the service of industry," as the influential economist Alfred Marshall (1842–1924) argued at the time. Chemists devised ways of measuring the atomic weight of different elements, and in 1869 the Russian chemist Dmitri Mendeleev (men-duh-LAY-uhf) (1834–1907) codified the rules of chemistry in the periodic law and the periodic table. Chemistry was subdivided into many specialized branches, such as organic chemistry — the study of the compounds of carbon. Applying theoretical insights gleaned from this new field, researchers in large German chemical companies discovered ways of transforming the dirty, useless coal tar that accumulated in coke ovens into beautiful, expensive synthetic dyes for the world of fashion. German production of synthetic dyes soared, and by 1900 German chemical companies controlled 90 percent of world production.

Electricity, a scientific curiosity in 1800, was totally transformed by a century of tremendous technological advancement. It became a commercial form of energy, first used in communications (the telegraph and underwater cables), then in electro-chemistry (refining aluminum, for example), and finally in central power generation (for lighting, transportation, and industrial motors). By 1890, the internal combustion engine fueled by petroleum was an emerging competitor.

The successful application of scientific research in the fast-growing electrical and organic chemical industries between 1880 and 1913 provided a model for other industries. Systematic "R & D"—research and development—was born in the late nineteenth century. Above all, the burst of industrial creativity and technological innovation, which is often called the **second industrial revolution**, promoted strong economic growth in the later nineteenth century. This ongoing economic development was a leading force driving the urban improvement and the rising standard of living considered in this chapter.

> **thermodynamics** A branch of physics built on Newton's laws of mechanics that investigated the relationship between heat and mechanical energy.
>
> **second industrial revolution** The burst of industrial creativity and technological innovation that promoted strong economic growth toward the end of the nineteenth century.

The triumph of science and technology had three other significant consequences. First, though ordinary citizens continued to lack detailed scientific knowledge, everyday experience and innumerable articles in

Madrid in 1900 This wistful painting of a Spanish square on a rainy day, by Enrique Martinez Cubells y Ruiz (1874–1917), includes a revealing commentary on how scientific discoveries transformed urban life. Coachmen wait atop their expensive hackney cabs for a wealthy clientele, while modern electric streetcars that carry the masses converge on the square from all directions. In this way the development of electricity brought improved urban transportation and enabled the city to expand to the suburbs. (Museo Municipal, Madrid/The Bridgeman Art Library)

newspapers and magazines impressed the importance of science on the popular mind. Second, as science became more prominent in popular thinking, the philosophical implications of science formulated in the Enlightenment spread to broad sections of the population. Natural processes appeared to be determined by rigid laws, leaving little room for either divine intervention or human will. Yet scientific and technical advances had also fed the Enlightenment's optimistic faith in human progress, which now appeared endless and automatic to many middle-class minds. Third, the methods of science acquired unrivaled prestige after 1850. For many, the union of careful experiment and abstract theory was the only reliable route to truth and objective reality. The "unscientific" intuitions of poets and the revelations of saints seemed hopelessly inferior.

Darwin and Natural Selection

Scientific research also progressed rapidly outside of the world of industry and technology, sometimes putting forth direct challenges to traditional beliefs. In geology, for example, Charles Lyell (1797–1875) effectively discredited the long-standing view that the earth's surface had been formed by short-lived cataclysms, such as biblical floods and earthquakes. Instead, according to Lyell's principle of uniformitarianism, the same geological processes that are at work today slowly formed the earth's surface over an immensely long time. Similarly, the evolutionary view of biological development, first proposed by the Greek Anaximander in the sixth century B.C.E., re-emerged in a more modern form in the work of French naturalist Jean Baptiste Lamarck (1744–1829). Lamarck asserted that all forms of life had arisen through a long process of continuous adjustment to the environment.

Lamarck's work was flawed—he believed that the characteristics parents acquired in the course of their lives could be inherited by their children—and was not accepted, but it helped prepare the way for Charles Darwin (1809–1882), the most influential of all nineteenth-century evolutionary thinkers. As the official naturalist on a five-year scientific cruise to Latin America and the South Pacific beginning in 1831, Darwin carefully collected specimens of the different animal species he encountered on the voyage. Back in England, convinced by fossil evidence and by his friend Lyell that the earth and life on it were immensely ancient, Darwin came to doubt the general belief in a special divine creation of each species of animal. Instead, he concluded, all life had gradually evolved from a common ancestral origin in an unending "struggle for survival." After long hesitation, Darwin published his research, which immediately attracted wide attention.

Darwin's great originality lay in suggesting precisely how biological evolution might have occurred. His theory is summarized in the title of his work *On the Origin of Species by the Means of Natural Selection* (1859). Decisively influenced by the gloomy theory of Thomas Malthus (MAL-thuhs) that populations naturally grow faster than their food supplies (see Chapter 21), Darwin argued that chance differences among the members of a given species help some survive while others die. Thus the variations that prove useful in the struggle for survival are selected naturally, and they gradually spread to the entire species through reproduction. Darwin did not explain why such variations occurred in the first place, and not until the early twentieth century did the study of genetics and the concept of mutation provide some answers.

Darwin's theory had a powerful and many-sided influence on European thought and the European middle classes. He was hailed as the great scientist par excellence, the "Newton of biology," who had revealed once again the powers of objective science, and his findings had a significant impact on the young discipline of social science.

Social Science

From the 1830s onward, many thinkers tried to apply the objective methods of science to the study of society. Using the critical thinking methods of the eighteenth-

DARWIN! — PAR GILL

Satirizing Darwin's Ideas
The heated controversies over Darwin's theory of evolution also spawned innumerable jokes and cartoons. This cartoon depicts a bearded Charles Darwin and the French philosopher and atheistic materialist Emile Littré performing as monkeys in a circus as they supposedly break through ignorance and superstition. (Musée de la Ville de Paris, Musée Carnavalet/Archives Charmet/The Bridgeman Art Library)

century philosophes (see Chapter 17), the new "social scientists" studied massive sets of numerical data that governments had begun to collect on everything from children to crime and from population to prostitution. Social scientists developed new statistical methods to analyze these facts "scientifically" and supposedly to test their theories. As a result, the systems of the leading nineteenth-century social scientists were typically more unified, all-encompassing, and dogmatic than those of the philosophes. Karl Marx was a prime example (see Chapter 22).

Another extremely influential system builder was French philosopher Auguste Comte (kont) (1798–1857). Initially a disciple of the utopian socialist Saint-Simon (see Chapter 22), Comte wrote the six-volume *System of Positive Philosophy* (1830–1842), which was largely overlooked during the romantic era. But when the political failures of 1848 completed the swing to realism, Comte's philosophy came into its own. Its influence has remained great to this day.

Comte postulated that all intellectual activity progresses through predictable stages:

> *The great fundamental law . . . is this:— that each of our leading conceptions— each branch of our knowledge— passes successively through three different theoretical conditions: the Theological, or fictitious; the Metaphysical, or abstract; and the Scientific, or positive. . . . The first is the necessary point of departure of human understanding, and the third is the fixed and definitive state. The second is merely a transition.*[15]

By way of example, Comte noted that the prevailing explanation of cosmic patterns had shifted, as knowledge of astronomy developed, from the will of God (the theological) to the will of an orderly nature (the metaphysical) to the rule of unchanging laws (the scientific). Later, this same intellectual progression took place in increasingly complex fields—physics, chemistry, and, finally, the study of society. Comte believed that by applying the scientific method, also called the positivist method, his new discipline of sociology would soon discover the eternal laws of human relations. This colossal achievement would in turn enable expert social scientists to impose a disciplined harmony and well-being on less enlightened citizens. Dismissing the "fictions" of traditional religions, Comte became the chief priest of the religion of science and rule by experts.

Comte's stages of knowledge exemplify the nineteenth-century fascination with the idea of **evolution** and dynamic development so prominent in Darwin's theory of natural selection. Thinkers in many fields, such as the romantic historians and "scientific" Marxists, shared and applied this basic concept. Reinforced by Darwin's findings, the teachings of secularists such as Comte and Marx scornfully dismissed religious belief in favor of agnostic or atheistic materialism. In the great cities, especially, religion was on the defensive.

Many thinkers went a step further and applied Darwin's theory of biological evolution to human affairs. English philosopher Herbert Spencer (1820–1903) saw the human race as driven forward to ever-greater specialization and progress by a brutal economic struggle that determined the "survival of the fittest." The poor were the ill-fated weak; the prosperous were the chosen strong. Not surprisingly, Spencer and other **Social Darwinists** were especially popular with the upper middle class.

Realism in Literature

In literature, the key themes of **realism** emerged in the 1840s and continued to dominate Western culture and style until the 1890s. Realist writers believed that literature should depict life exactly as it was. Forsaking poetry for prose and the personal, emotional viewpoint of the romantics for strict, scientific objectivity, the realists simply observed and recorded—content to let the facts speak for themselves.

The major realist writers focused their extraordinary powers of observation to create fiction based on contemporary everyday life. Emphatically rejecting the romantic search for the exotic and the sublime, they energetically pursued the typical and the commonplace. Beginning with a dissection of the middle classes, from which most of them sprang, many realists eventually focused on the working classes, especially the urban working classes, which had been neglected in imaginative literature before this time. The realists put a microscope to many unexplored and taboo subjects—sex, strikes, violence, alcoholism—and hastened to report that slums and factories teemed with savage behavior. Many shocked middle-class critics denounced realism as ugly sensationalism wrapped provocatively in pseudo-scientific declarations and crude language.

Unlike the romantics, who had gloried in individual freedom and an unlimited universe, realists were strict determinists. Human beings, like atoms, were components of the physical world, and all human actions were caused by unalterable natural laws. Heredity and environment determined human behavior; good and evil were merely social conventions.

The realist movement began in France, where romanticism had never been completely dominant, and three of its greatest practitioners—Balzac, Flaubert, and Zola—were French. Honoré de Balzac (1799–1850)

evolution The idea, applied by thinkers in many fields, that stresses gradual change and continuous adjustment.

Social Darwinists A group of thinkers who applied the theory of biological evolution to human affairs and saw the human race as driven by an unending economic struggle that would determine the survival of the fittest.

realism A literary movement that stressed the depiction of life as it actually was.

spent thirty years writing a vastly ambitious panorama of postrevolutionary French life. Known collectively as *The Human Comedy*, this series of nearly one hundred books vividly portrays more than two thousand characters from virtually all sectors of French society. Balzac pictures urban society as grasping, amoral, and brutal. In *Le Père Goriot* (1835), the hero, a poor student from the provinces, eventually surrenders his idealistic integrity to feverish ambition and society's pervasive greed.

Madame Bovary (1857), the masterpiece of Gustave Flaubert (floh-BEHR) (1821–1880), is far narrower in scope than Balzac's work, but unparalleled in its depth and accuracy of psychological insight. Unsuccessfully prosecuted as an outrage against public morality and religion, Flaubert's carefully crafted novel tells the ordinary, even banal, story of a frustrated middle-class housewife who has an adulterous love affair and is betrayed by her lover. Without moralizing, Flaubert portrays the provincial middle class as petty, smug, and hypocritical.

Émile Zola (1840–1902) was most famous for his seamy, animalistic view of working-class life. But he also wrote gripping, carefully researched stories featuring the stock exchange, the big department store, and the army, as well as urban slums and bloody coal strikes. Like many later realists, Zola sympathized with socialism, a sympathy evident in his overpowering novel *Germinal* (1885).

Realism quickly spread beyond France. In England, Mary Ann Evans (1819–1880), who wrote under the pen name George Eliot, brilliantly achieved a more deeply felt, less sensational kind of realism. Her great novel *Middlemarch: A Study of Provincial Life* (1871–1872) examines masterfully the ways in which people are shaped by their social medium as well as their own inner strivings, conflicts, and moral choices. Thomas Hardy (1840–1928) was more in the Zola tradition. His novels, such as *Tess of the D'Urbervilles* (1891) and *The Return of the Native* (1878), depict men and women frustrated and crushed by fate and bad luck.

The greatest Russian realist Count Leo Tolstoy (1828–1910) combined realism in description and character development with an atypical moralizing, which came to dominate his later work. Tolstoy's greatest work is *War and Peace* (1864–1869), a monumental novel set against the historical background of Napoleon's invasion of Russia in 1812. Tolstoy probed deeply into the lives of a multitude of unforgettable characters, such as the ill-fated Prince Andrei; the shy, fumbling Pierre; and the enchanting Natasha. Tolstoy went to great pains to develop his fatalistic theory of history, which regards free will as an illusion and the achievements of even the greatest leaders as only the channeling of historical necessity. Yet Tolstoy's central message is one that most of the people discussed in this chapter would have readily

Edouard Manet, *Émile Zola* The young novelist's sensitivity and strength of character permeate this famous portrait by the great French painter Edouard Manet. Focusing on nuances and subtle variations, Manet was at first denounced by the critics, and after Zola lost a newspaper job defending Manet they became close friends. Manet was strongly influenced by Japanese prints, seen in the background. (Erich Lessing/Art Resource, NY)

accepted: human love, trust, and everyday family ties are life's enduring values.

Thoroughgoing realism (or "naturalism," as it was often called) arrived late in the United States, most arrestingly in the work of Theodore Dreiser (1871–1945). His first novel, *Sister Carrie* (1900), a story of an ordinary farm girl who does well by going wrong in Chicago, so outraged conventional morality that the publisher withdrew the book. The United States subsequently became a bastion of literary realism in the twentieth century after the movement had faded away in Europe.

LOOKING BACK LOOKING AHEAD WHEN EUROPEANS in northwestern Europe looked back at the economic and social landscape in the early twentieth century, they had good reason to feel that the promise of the Industrial Revolution was being realized. The dark days of urban squalor and brutal working hours had given way after 1850 to a gradual rise in the standard of living for all classes. Scientific discoveries were combining with the applied technology of public health and industrial production to save lives and drive continued economic growth.

Moreover, social and economic advance seemed to be matched by progress in the political sphere. The years following the dramatic failure of the revolutions of 1848 saw the creation of unified nation-states in Italy and Germany, and after 1870 nationalism and the nation-state reigned in Europe. Although the rise of nationalism created tensions among the European countries, these tensions would not explode until 1914 and the outbreak of the First World War. Instead, the most aggressive and destructive aspects of European nationalism found their initial outlet in the final and most powerful surge of Western overseas expansion. Thus Europe, transformed by industrialization and nationalism, rushed after 1875 to seize territory and build new or greatly expanded authoritarian empires in Asia and Africa.

CHAPTER REVIEW

■ What was life like in the cities, and how did urban life change in the nineteenth century? (p. 718)

The revolution in industry had a drastic impact on the urban environment. Because it was economically advantageous to locate new industrial factories and offices in urban areas, urban populations grew at unprecedented rates. Living conditions sharply declined, largely because governments were slow to react and the people, ignorant of the connection between cleanliness and good health, were content to live in squalor. When governments finally took the initiative in the mid-nineteenth century to clean up the cities, general public health improved greatly. Society also benefited from scientific advancements. A new understanding of germ control, improved medical techniques, and new vaccines all led to lower mortality rates in urban areas. Finally, better urban planning and new public transportation systems relieved overcrowding.

■ What did the emergence of urban industrial society mean for rich and poor and those in between? (p. 723)

At the top levels of society, the upper middle class expanded its wealth and power as it emulated the aristocracy in material acquisitions and leisure pursuits. The middle and lower middle classes also expanded and gained income, and their occupations became much more diverse with the Industrial Revolution. The working classes saw an overall improvement in their economic condition, but they still struggled, especially the lower working classes. Large numbers of poor women in particular continued to labor as workers in sweated industries and as domestic servants in order to satisfy the demands of their masters in the servant-keeping classes. The nineteenth century also witnessed a decline in church attendance among urban workers, who may have equated organized religion with the old conservative regimes in an era of progress.

■ How did working-class and middle-class families change as they coped with the challenges and the opportunities of the developing urban civilization? (p. 732)

Major changes in family life accompanied the more complex and diversified class system. Especially among the working classes, family life became more stable, more loving, and less mercenary as society generally improved its standard of living. Among the middle classes, marrying continued to serve as a means for economic gain, and emotional benefits were slower to come. At the same time gender roles for men and women of all classes became sharply defined and rigidly separate. The working class increasingly adopted a breadwinner-homemaker division of labor, while middle-class women lacked important legal rights and were frozen out of professional employment. The number of children per family dropped steadily in the second half of the eighteenth century, as parental love and concern for their offspring tended to strengthen.

What major changes in science and thought reflected and influenced the new urban society? (p. 741)

The scientific discoveries of the nineteenth century had many practical benefits for the general population. New vaccines, synthetic fabric dyes, and the myriad applications of electricity all contributed to economic growth and a better quality of life for urban society. In turn, ordinary people gained a new awareness and appreciation of science, which began to chip away at their traditional religious understanding of the world. Darwin's widely hailed theory of natural selection, for example, challenged the general belief in divine creation. New social scientists such as Marx and Comte rejected religion and sought to analyze human behavior based on objective statistics. In the realm of literature, novelists such as Balzac and Zola abandoned romantic idealism and wrote about the harsh realities of life's struggles. More generally, literary realism reflected Western society's growing faith in science, material progress, and evolutionary thinking.

Suggested Reading

Anderson, Bonnie S., and Judith P. Zinsser. *A History of Their Own: Women in Europe from Prehistory to the Present*, vol. 2, rev. ed. 2000. An excellent wide-ranging survey.

Barnes, David S. *The Great Stink of Paris and the Nineteenth-Century Struggle Against Filth and Germs*. 2006. An outstanding introduction to sanitary developments and attitudes toward public health.

Coontz, Stephanie. *Marriage, a History: From Obedience to Intimacy, or How Love Conquered Marriage*. 2005. A lively investigation of the historical background to current practice.

De Vries, Jan. *The Industrious Revolution: Consumer Behavior and the Household Economy, 1850 to the Present*. 2008. A major interpretative analysis focusing on married couples and their strategies.

Gottlieb, Beatrice. *The Family in the Western World*. 1993. A wide-ranging synthesis.

Hunt, Tristram. *Building Jerusalem: The Rise and Fall of the Victorian City*. 2006. Considers British urban life and civic pride.

Maynes, Mary Jo. *Taking the Hard Road: Life Course in French and German Workers' Biographies in the Era of Industrialization*. 1995. Includes fascinating stories that provide insight into how workers saw themselves.

Olsen, Donald J. *The City as a Work of Art: London, Paris, and Vienna*. 1988. An architectural feast.

Perrot, Michelle, ed. *A History of Private Life*. 1990. A fascinating multivolume work.

Pilbeam, Pamela. *The Middle Classes in Europe, 1789–1914: France, Germany, Italy, and Russia*. 1990. A stimulating introduction to middle-class life.

Schmiechen, James, and Kenneth Carls. *The British Market Hall: A Social and Architectural History*. 1999. A pathbreaking and beautiful study of Britain's enclosed markets and how they revolutionized the sale of food.

Thompson, F. M. L. *The Rise of Respectable Society: A Social History of Victorian Britain, 1830–1900*. 1986. A laudable survey.

Weiner, Jonathan. *The Beak of the Finch: The Story of Evolution in Our Time*. 1994. A prize-winning, highly readable account of Darwin and evolution.

Notes

1. S. Marcus, "Reading the Illegible," in *The Victorian City: Images and Realities*, ed. H. J. Dyos and Michael Wolff, vol. 1 (London: Routledge & Kegan Paul, 1973), p. 266.
2. Quoted in E. Chadwick, *Report on the Sanitary Condition of the Labouring Population of Great Britain*, ed. M. W. Flinn (Edinburgh: University of Edinburgh Press, 1965; original publication, 1842), pp. 315–316.
3. J. McKay, *Tramways and Trolleys: The Rise of Urban Mass Transport in Europe* (Princeton, N.J.: Princeton University Press, 1976), p. 81.
4. Quoted in R. P. Neuman, "The Sexual Question and Social Democracy in Imperial Germany," *Journal of Social History* 7 (Winter 1974): 276.
5. Quoted in J. A. Banks, "The Contagion of Numbers," in *The Victorian City: Images and Realities*, ed. H. J. Dyos and Michael Wolff, vol. 1 (London: Routledge & Kegan Paul, 1973), p. 112.
6. Quoted in R. Roberts, *The Classic Slum: Salford Life in the First Quarter of the Century* (Manchester, U.K.: University of Manchester Press, 1971), p. 95.
7. Quoted in T. Zeldin, *France, 1848–1945*, vol. 1 (Oxford, U.K.: Clarendon Press, 1973), p. 288.
8. For a thorough discussion see S. Marcus, *The Other Victorians: A Study of Sexuality and Pornography in Mid-Nineteenth-Century England* (New York: Basic Books, 1966).
9. See the pioneering work of J. de Vries, *The Industrious Revolution: Consumer Behavior and the Household Economy* (Cambridge, U.K.: Cambridge University Press, 2008), especially pp. 186–237.
10. Quoted in Zeldin, *France*, p. 346.
11. Roberts, *The Classic Slum*, p. 35.
12. Quoted in Zeldin, *France*, p. 295.
13. Quoted ibid., p. 328.
14. Quoted in Neuman, "The Sexual Question," p. 281.
15. A. Comte, *The Positive Philosophy of Auguste Comte*, trans. H. Martineau, vol. 1 (London: J. Chapman, 1853), pp. 1–2.

Key Terms

utilitarianism (p. 719)
germ theory (p. 721)
labor aristocracy (p. 727)
sweated industries (p. 730)
thermodynamics (p. 741)
second industrial revolution (p. 741)
evolution (p. 744)
Social Darwinists (p. 744)
realism (p. 744)

For practice quizzes and other study tools, visit the Online Study Guide at **bedfordstmartins.com/mckaywest**.

For primary sources from this period, see **Sources of Western Society, Second Edition**.

For Web sites, images, and documents related to topics in this chapter, visit Make History at **bedfordstmartins.com/mckaywest**.

24

The Age of Nationalism

1850–1914

The revolutions of 1848 closed one era and opened another. Urban industrial society began to take a strong hold on the continent and in the young United States, as it already had in Great Britain. Internationally, the repressive peace and diplomatic stability of Metternich's time were replaced by a period of war and rapid change. In thought and culture, exuberant romanticism gave way to hardheaded realism. In the Atlantic economy, the hard years of the 1840s were followed by good times and prosperity throughout most of the 1850s and 1860s. Perhaps most important of all, Western society progressively developed, for better or worse, a new and effective organizing principle capable of coping with the many-sided challenge of the dual revolution and the emerging urban civilization. That principle was nationalism — dedication to an identification with the nation-state.

The triumph of nationalism is an enormously significant historical development that was by no means completely predictable. After all, nationalism had been a powerful force since at least 1789, but it had repeatedly failed to realize its goals, most spectacularly in 1848. Yet by 1914 nationalism had become in one way or another an almost universal faith in Europe and in the United States, a faith that had evolved to appeal not only to predominately middle-class liberals but also to the broad masses of society. ■

Life in the Age of Nationalism. Committed to Italian unity, the people of Venice cheer their uplifted nationalist leader, Daniel Manin, during the unsuccessful revolution of 1848. Scenes like this would be validated in the decades to come as nationalism came to predominate in all levels of society across Europe.

CHAPTER PREVIEW

Napoleon III in France
■ How did Napoleon III seek to reconcile popular and conservative forces in an authoritarian nation-state?

Nation Building in Italy and Germany
■ How did the process of unification in Italy and Germany create conservative nation-states?

Nation Building in the United States
■ In what ways did the United States experience nation building?

The Modernization of Russia and the Ottoman Empire
■ What steps did Russia and the Ottoman Turks take toward modernization, and how successful were they?

The Responsive National State, 1871–1914
■ Why after 1871 did ordinary citizens feel a growing loyalty to their governments?

Marxism and the Socialist Movement
■ Why did the socialist movement grow, and how revolutionary was it?

Napoleon III in France

How did Napoleon III seek to reconcile popular and conservative forces in an authoritarian nation-state? ▪

Early nationalism was generally liberal and idealistic and often democratic and radical as well. In the nineteenth century the ideas of nationhood and popular sovereignty posed a fearful revolutionary threat to conservatives like Metternich. Yet from the vantage point of the twenty-first century, it is clear that nationalism wears many masks: it may be narrowly liberal or democratic and radical, as it was for Giuseppe Mazzini and Jules Michelet (see Chapter 22). Yet nationalism can also flourish in dictatorial states, which may be conservative, fascist, or communist, and which may impose social and economic changes from above. Napoleon I's France had already combined national feeling with authoritarian rule. Significantly, it was Napoleon's nephew, Louis Napoleon, who revived and extended this merger.

France's Second Republic

Although Louis Napoleon Bonaparte had played no part in French politics before 1848, universal male suffrage and widespread popular support gave him three times as many votes as the four other presidential candidates combined in the French presidential election of December 1848. This outcome occurred for several reasons. First, Louis Napoleon had the great name of his uncle, whom romantics had transformed from a dictator into a demigod as they created a Napoleonic legend after 1820. Second, as Karl Marx stressed at the time, middle-class and peasant property owners feared the socialist challenge of urban workers, and they wanted a tough ruler to provide protection. Third, in late 1848 Louis Napoleon had a positive "program" for France, which had been elaborated in widely circulated pamphlets before the election and which guided him through his long reign.

Above all, Louis Napoleon believed that the government should represent the people and that it should try hard to help them economically. But how were these tasks to be done? Parliaments and political parties were not the answer, according to Louis Napoleon. French politicians represented special-interest groups, particularly middle-class ones. The answer was a strong, even authoritarian, national leader, like the first Napoleon, a reformer who would serve all the people, rich and poor. This leader would be linked to each citizen by direct democracy, his sovereignty uncorrupted by politicians and legislative bodies. These political ideas meshed well with Louis Napoleon's vision of national unity and social progress. The state and its leader had a sacred duty to

Paris in the Second Empire The flash and glitter of unprecedented prosperity in the Second Empire come alive in this vibrant contemporary painting. Writers and intellectuals chat with elegant women and trade witticisms with financiers and government officials at the Café Tortoni, a favorite rendezvous for fashionable society. Horse-drawn omnibuses with open top decks mingle with cabs and private carriages on the broad new boulevard. (Lauros/Giraudon/The Bridgeman Art Library)

provide jobs and stimulate the economy, which would benefit all classes. Louis Napoleon's political and social ideas were at least vaguely understood by large numbers of French peasants and workers in December 1848. To the many common people who voted for him, he appeared to be a strong man and a forward-looking champion of their interests.

Elected to a four-year term by an overwhelming majority, President Louis Napoleon had to share power with a conservative National Assembly, according to the constitution. With some misgivings, he signed a bill to increase greatly the role of the Catholic Church in primary and secondary education, and he approved a law depriving many poor people of the right to vote. He took these conservative measures for two main reasons: he wanted the Assembly to vote funds to pay his personal debts, and he wanted to change the constitution so he could run for a second term.

But in 1851, after the Assembly failed to cooperate, Louis Napoleon began to conspire with key army officers. On December 2, 1851, he illegally dismissed the Assembly and seized power in a coup d'état. There was some armed resistance in Paris and widespread insurrection in the countryside in southern France, but these protests were crushed by the army. Restoring universal male suffrage and claiming to stand above the bickering and divisive politicians, Louis Napoleon called on the French people, as the first Napoleon had done, to legalize his actions. They did: 92 percent voted to make him president for ten years. A year later, 97 percent in a plebiscite made him hereditary emperor.

Napoleon III's Second Empire

Louis Napoleon—who was now proclaimed Emperor Napoleon III—experienced both success and failure between 1852 and 1870. His greatest success was with the economy, particularly in the 1850s. His government encouraged the new investment banks and massive railroad construction that were at the heart of the Industrial Revolution on the continent (see Chapter 21). The government also fostered general economic expansion through an ambitious program of public works, which included rebuilding Paris to improve the urban environment (see Chapter 23). The profits of business people soared with prosperity, the wages of workers more than kept up with inflation, and unemployment declined greatly.

Chronology

1839–1876	Western-style reforms in Ottoman Empire
1852–1870	Reign of Napoleon III in France
1859–1870	Unification of Italy
1861	Freeing of Russian serfs
1861–1865	U.S. Civil War
1866	Austro-Prussian War
1870–1871	Franco-Prussian War
1870–1878	Kulturkampf, Bismarck's attack on Catholic Church
1873	Stock market crash spurs renewed anti-Semitism in central and eastern Europe
1880s	Educational reforms in France create more secular public schools
1880s–1890s	Widespread return to protectionism among European states
1883	First social security laws to help workers in Germany
1890–1900	Massive industrialization surge in Russia
1905	Revolution in Russia
1906–1914	Social reform in Great Britain
1908	Young Turks in power in Ottoman Empire

Louis Napoleon always hoped that economic progress would reduce social and political tensions. This hope was at least partially realized. Until the mid-1860s there was considerable support from France's most dissatisfied group, the urban workers. Napoleon III's regulation of pawnshops and his support of credit unions and better housing for the working classes were evidence of helpful reform and positive concern in the 1850s. In the 1860s, he granted workers the right to form unions and the right to strike—important economic rights denied by earlier governments.

At first, political power remained in the hands of the emperor. He alone chose his ministers, and they had great freedom of action. At the same time, Napoleon III restricted but did not abolish the Assembly. Members were elected by universal male suffrage every six years, and Louis Napoleon and his government took the parliamentary elections very seriously. They tried to entice notable people, even those who had opposed the regime, to stand as government candidates in order to expand the base of support. Moreover, the government used its officials and appointed mayors to spread the word that the election of the government's candidates—and the defeat of the opposition—was the key to roads, tax rebates, and a thousand other local concerns.

In 1857 and again in 1863, Louis Napoleon's system worked brilliantly and produced overwhelming electoral victories. Yet in the 1860s, Napoleon III's electoral system gradually disintegrated. A sincere nationalist, Napoleon had wanted to reorganize Europe on the principle of nationality and gain influence and territory for France and himself in the process. Instead, problems in Italy and the rising power of Prussia led to increasing criticism at home from his Catholic and nationalist supporters. With increasing effectiveness, the middle-class liberals who had always wanted a less authoritarian regime continued to denounce his rule.

Napoleon was always sensitive to the public mood. Public opinion, he once said, always wins the last victory. Thus in the 1860s, he responded to critics by progressively liberalizing his empire. He gave the Assembly greater powers and the opposition candidates greater freedom, which they used to good advantage. In 1869 the opposition, consisting of republicans, monarchists, and liberals, polled almost 45 percent of the vote.

The next year, a sick and weary Louis Napoleon again granted France a new constitution, which combined a basically parliamentary regime with a hereditary emperor as chief of state. In a final great plebiscite on the eve of the disastrous war with Prussia, 7.5 million Frenchmen voted in favor of the new constitution, and only 1.5 million opposed it. Napoleon III's attempt to reconcile a strong national state with universal male suffrage was still evolving and was doing so in a democratic direction.

Nation Building in Italy and Germany

How did the process of unification in Italy and Germany create conservative nation-states? ■

Louis Napoleon's triumph in 1848 and his authoritarian rule in the 1850s provided the old ruling classes of Europe with a new model in politics. To what extent might the expanding urban middle classes and even portions of the growing working classes rally to a strong and essentially conservative national state that also promised change? This was one of the great political questions in the 1850s and 1860s. In central Europe, a resounding answer came with the national unification of Italy and Germany.

Italy to 1850

Italy had never been united prior to 1850. Part of Rome's great empire in ancient times, the Italian peninsula was divided in the Middle Ages into competing city-states that led the commercial and cultural revival of the West with amazing creativity. A battleground for the Great Powers after 1494, Italy was reorganized in 1815 at the Congress of Vienna. The rich northern provinces of Lombardy and Venetia were taken by Metternich's Austria. Sardinia and Piedmont were under the rule of an Italian monarch, and Tuscany, with its famous capital Florence, shared north-central Italy with several smaller states. Central Italy and Rome were ruled by the papacy, which had always considered an independent political existence necessary to fulfill its spiritual mission. Naples and Sicily were ruled, as they had been for almost a hundred years, by a branch of the Bourbons. Metternich was not wrong in dismissing Italy as "a geographical expression" (Map 24.1).

Between 1815 and 1848, the goal of a unified Italian nation captured the imaginations of many Italians. There were three basic approaches. The first was the radical program of the idealistic patriot Giuseppe Mazzini, who preached a centralized democratic republic based on universal male suffrage and the will of the people. (See "Listening to the Past: Herder and Mazzini on the Development of Nationalism," page 694.) The second was that of Vincenzo Gioberti, a Catholic priest who called for a federation of existing states under the presidency of a progressive pope. The third was the program of those who looked for leadership to the autocratic kingdom of Sardinia-Piedmont, much as many Germans looked to Prussia.

The third alternative was strengthened by the failures of 1848, when Austria smashed Mazzini's republicanism. Sardinia's new monarch, Victor Emmanuel, retained the liberal constitution granted by his father under duress in March 1848. This constitution combined a strong monarchy with a fair degree of civil liberties and parliamentary government, with deputies elected by a limited franchise based on income. To some of the Italian middle classes, Sardinia appeared to be a liberal, progressive state ideally suited to drive Austria out of northern Italy and lead a free Italy of independent states. By contrast, Mazzini's brand of democratic republicanism seemed quixotic and too radical.

As for the papacy, the initial cautious support for unification by Pius IX (pontificate 1846–1878) had given way to fear and hostility after he was temporarily driven from Rome during the upheavals of 1848. For a long generation, the papacy would stand resolutely opposed not only to national unification but also to most modern trends. In 1864 in the *Syllabus of Errors*, Pius IX strongly denounced rationalism, socialism, separation of church and state, and religious liberty, denying that "the Roman pontiff can and ought to reconcile and align himself with progress, liberalism, and modern civilization."

Cavour and Garibaldi in Italy

Sardinia had the good fortune of being led by a brilliant statesman, Count Camillo Benso di Cavour (kuh-VOOR), the dominant figure in the Sardinian govern-

Map 24.1 The Unification of Italy, 1859–1870 The leadership of Sardinia-Piedmont, nationalist fervor, and Garibaldi's attack on the kingdom of the Two Sicilies were decisive factors in the unification of Italy.

ment from 1850 until his death in 1861. Cavour came from a noble family, and he made a substantial fortune in business before entering politics. Cavour's national goals were limited and realistic. Until 1859 he sought unity only for the states of northern and perhaps central Italy in a greatly expanded kingdom of Sardinia.

In the 1850s, Cavour worked to consolidate Sardinia as a liberal constitutional state capable of leading northern Italy. His program of highways and railroads, of civil liberties and opposition to clerical privilege, increased support for Sardinia throughout northern Italy. Yet Cavour realized that Sardinia could not drive Austria out of northern Italy without the help of a powerful ally. Accordingly, he worked for a secret diplomatic alliance with Napoleon III against Austria.

Finally, in July 1858 Cavour succeeded and goaded Austria into attacking Sardinia in 1859. Napoleon III came to Sardinia's defense. Then after the victory of the combined Franco-Sardinian forces, Napoleon III did a sudden about-face. Worried by criticism from French Catholics for supporting the pope's declared enemy, Napoleon III abandoned Cavour. He made a compromise peace with the Austrians at Villafranca in July 1859.

Sardinia would receive only Lombardy, the area around Milan, from Austria. The rest of the map of Italy would remain essentially unchanged. Cavour resigned in a rage.

Yet Cavour's plans were salvaged by the skillful maneuvers of his allies in the moderate nationalist movement. While the war against Austria had raged in the north, pro-Sardinian nationalists in Tuscany and the other small states of central Italy had fanned popular revolts and easily toppled their ruling princes. Using and controlling the popular enthusiasm, the middle-class nationalist leaders in central Italy called for fusion with Sardinia. This was not at all what France and the other Great Powers wanted, but the nationalists held firm. Cavour returned to power in early 1860 and gained Napoleon III's support by ceding Savoy and Nice to France. The people of central Italy then voted overwhelmingly to join a greatly enlarged kingdom of Sardinia under Victor Emmanuel. Cavour had achieved his original goal of a northern Italian state (see Map 24.1).

For superpatriots such as Giuseppe Garibaldi (1807–1882), the job of unification was still only half done. The son of a poor sailor, Garibaldi personified the romantic, revolutionary nationalism and republicanism

Garibaldi and Victor Emmanuel The historic meeting in Naples between the leader of Italy's revolutionary nationalists and the king of Sardinia sealed the unification of northern and southern Italy. With the sleeve of his red shirt showing, Garibaldi offers his hand — and his conquests — to the uniformed king and his moderate monarchical government. (Scala/Art Resource, NY)

of Mazzini and 1848. Leading a corps of volunteers against Austria in 1859, Garibaldi emerged in 1860 as an independent force in Italian politics.

Partly to use him and partly to get rid of him, Cavour secretly supported Garibaldi's bold plan to "liberate" the kingdom of the Two Sicilies. Landing on the shores of Sicily in May 1860, Garibaldi's guerrilla band of a thousand **Red Shirts** captured the imagination of the Sicilian peasantry, which rose in bloody rebellion against their landlords. Outwitting the twenty-thousand-man royal army, the guerrilla leader won battles, gained volunteers, and took Palermo. Then Garibaldi and his men crossed to the mainland, marched triumphantly toward Naples, and prepared to attack Rome and the pope. But the wily Cavour quickly sent Sardinian forces to occupy most of the Papal States (but not Rome) and to intercept Garibaldi.

Red Shirts The guerrilla army of Giuseppe Garibaldi, who invaded Sicily in 1860 in an attempt to liberate it, winning the hearts of the Sicilian peasantry.

Cavour realized that an attack on Rome would bring about war with France, and he also feared Garibaldi's radicalism and popular appeal. Thus he immediately organized a plebiscite in the conquered territories. Despite the urging of some radical supporters, the patriotic Garibaldi did not oppose Cavour, and the people of the south voted to join the kingdom of Sardinia. When Garibaldi and Victor Emmanuel rode together through Naples to cheering crowds, they symbolically sealed the union of north and south, of monarch and nation-state.

Cavour had succeeded. He had controlled Garibaldi and had turned popular nationalism in a conservative direction. The new kingdom of Italy, which expanded to include Venice in 1866 and Rome in 1870, was a parliamentary monarchy under Victor Emmanuel, neither radical nor democratic. It was politically unified, but only a half million out of 22 million Italians had the right to vote. The propertied classes and the common people remained divided. A great and growing social and cultural gap also separated the progressive, industrializing north from the stagnant, agrarian south. The new Italy was united on paper, but profound divisions remained.

The Growing Austro-Prussian Rivalry

In the aftermath of 1848, the German states were locked in a political stalemate. After Austria and Russia blocked Frederick William's attempt in 1850 to unify Germany "from above," tension grew between Austria and Prussia as each power sought to block the other within the German Confederation (see Chapter 22).

At the same time, powerful economic forces were contributing to the Austro-Prussian rivalry. Austria had not been included initially in the German customs union, or Zollverein, which had been founded in 1834 to stimulate trade and increase the revenue of member states. By the end of 1853 Austria was the only state in the German Confederation that had not joined. Middle-class and business groups in the Zollverein were enriching themselves and finding solid economic reasons to bolster their idealistic support of national unification. Prussia's leading role within the Zollverein gave it a valuable advantage in its struggle against Austria's supremacy in German political affairs.

Prussia had emerged from the upheavals of 1848 with a parliament of sorts, which was in the hands of the wealthy liberal middle class by 1859. Patriotic and longing for national unification, these middle-class representatives also wanted to establish once and for all that the parliament, not the king, had the ultimate political power and that the army was responsible to Prussia's elected representatives. The national uprising in Italy in 1859, however, made a profound impression on Prussia's tough-minded William I (r. 1861–1888). Convinced that great political change and war—perhaps with Austria, perhaps with France—were quite possible, William I and his top military advisers pushed to raise taxes and increase the defense budget in order to double the size of the army. The Prussian parliament, reflecting the middle class's desire for a less militaristic society, rejected the military budget in 1862, and the liberals triumphed completely in new elections. King William then called on Count Otto von Bismarck to head a new ministry and defy the parliament. This was a momentous choice.

Bismarck and the Austro-Prussian War

The most important figure in German history between Martin Luther and Adolf Hitler, Otto von Bismarck (1815–1898) has been the object of enormous interest and debate. A great hero to some, a great villain to others,

Bismarck was above all a master of politics. Born into the Prussian landowning aristocracy and always devoted to his Prussian sovereign, Bismarck had a strong personality and an unbounded desire for power. Yet in his drive to secure power for himself and for Prussia, Bismarck was extraordinarily flexible and pragmatic. "One must always have two irons in the fire," he once said. He kept his options open, pursuing one policy and then another as he moved with skill and cunning toward his goal.

Bismarck first honed his political skills as a high-ranking diplomat for the Prussian government. When he took office as chief minister in 1862, he made a strong but unfavorable impression. His speeches were a sensation and a scandal. Declaring that the government would rule without parliamentary consent, Bismarck lashed out at the middle-class opposition: "The great questions of the day will not be decided by speeches and resolutions—that was the blunder of 1848 and 1849—but by blood and iron."

❝ The great questions of the day will not be decided by speeches and resolutions . . . but by blood and iron. ❞

—Otto von Bismarck

Denounced for this view that "might makes right," Bismarck had the Prussian bureaucracy go right on collecting taxes, even though the parliament refused to approve the budget. Bismarck reorganized the army. And for four years, from 1862 to 1866, the voters of Prussia continued to express their opposition by sending large liberal majorities to the parliament.

Opposition at home spurred the search for success abroad. The extremely complicated question of Schleswig-Holstein—two provinces that belonged to Denmark but were members of the German Confederation (Map 24.2)—provided a welcome opportunity. In 1864, when the Danish king tried again, as in 1848, to bring these two provinces into a more centralized Danish state against the will of the German Confederation, Prussia joined Austria in a short and successful war against Denmark. However, Bismarck was convinced that Prussia had to control completely the northern, predominantly Protestant part of the German Confederation, which meant expelling Austria from German affairs. After the victory over Denmark, Bismarck's skillful maneuvering had Prussia in a position to force Austria out by war, if necessary. Bismarck knew that a war with Austria would have to be a localized one that would not provoke a mighty alliance against Prussia. By skillfully neutralizing Russia and France, he was in a position to engage in a war of his own making.

Mapping the Past

Map 24.2 The Unification of Germany, 1866–1871 This map shows how Prussia expanded and a new German Empire was created through two wars, the Austro-Prussian War of 1866 and the Franco-Prussian War of 1870–1871.

ANALYZING THE MAP What losses did Austria experience in 1866? What territories did France lose as a result of the Franco-Prussian War? Which of the predominately Catholic states of southern Germany joined with Prussia to form the German Empire in 1871?

CONNECTIONS How was central Europe remade and the power of Prussia-Germany greatly increased as a result of the Austro-Prussian War and the Franco-Prussian War?

To complete this activity online, go to the Online Study Guide at bedfordstmartins.com/mckaywest.

The Austro-Prussian War of 1866 lasted only seven weeks. Utilizing railroads to mass troops and the new breech-loading needle gun to achieve maximum fire-power, the reorganized Prussian army proved its mettle. It overran northern Germany and defeated Austria decisively at the Battle of Sadowa (SAH-daw-vah) in Bohemia. Anticipating Prussia's future needs, Bismarck offered Austria realistic, even generous, peace terms. Austria paid no reparations and lost no territory to Prussia, although Venetia was ceded to Italy.

But the existing German Confederation was dissolved, and Austria agreed to withdraw from German affairs. Prussia also conquered and annexed several small states north of the Main River and completely dominated the remaining principalities in the newly formed North German Confederation. The mainly Catholic states of the south remained independent while forming alliances with Prussia. Bismarck's fundamental goal of Prussian expansion was being realized (see Map 24.2).

The Taming of the Parliament

Bismarck had long been convinced that the old order he so ardently defended should make peace, on its own terms, with the liberal middle class and the nationalist movement. He realized that nationalism was not necessarily hostile to conservative, authoritarian government. Moreover, Bismarck believed that because of the events of 1848, the German middle class could be led to prefer a national unity under conservative leadership rather than a long, uncertain battle for truly liberal institutions. Thus during the attack on Austria in 1866, he increasingly identified Prussia's fate with the "national development of Germany."

In the aftermath of victory, Bismarck fashioned a federal constitution for the new North German Confederation. Each state retained its own local government, but the king of Prussia became president of the confederation, and the chancellor—Bismarck—was responsible only to the president. The federal government—William I and Bismarck—controlled the army and foreign affairs. There was also a legislature with members of the lower house elected by universal, single-class male suffrage. With this radical innovation, Bismarck opened the door to popular participation and the possibility of going over the head of the middle class directly to the people, much as Napoleon III had done in France. All the while, however, ultimate power rested in the hands of the dominant state of Prussia and its king and army.

In Prussia itself, Bismarck held out an olive branch to the parliamentary opposition. Marshaling all his diplomatic skill, Bismarck asked the parliament to pass a special indemnity bill to approve after the fact all the government's spending between 1862 and 1866. Most of the liberals jumped at the chance to cooperate. With German unity in sight, they repented their "sins." The constitu-

tional struggle in Prussia was over, and the German middle class was accepting respectfully the monarchical authority and the aristocratic superiority that Bismarck represented. In the years before 1914, the values of the aristocratic Prussian army officer increasingly replaced those of the middle-class liberal in public esteem and set the social standard.[1]

The Franco-Prussian War

The final act in the drama of German unification followed quickly. Bismarck realized that a patriotic war with France would drive the south German states into his arms. The French obligingly played their part. The apparent issue—whether a distant relative of Prussia's William I might become king of Spain—was only a diplomatic pretext. By 1870 the French leaders of the Second Empire, goaded by Bismarck and alarmed by their powerful new neighbor on the Rhine, had decided on a war to teach Prussia a lesson.

As soon as war against France began in 1870, Bismarck had the wholehearted support of the south German states. With other governments maintaining their neutrality—Bismarck's generosity to Austria in 1866 was paying big dividends—German forces under Prussian leadership decisively defeated the main French army at Sedan on September 1, 1870. Louis Napoleon himself was captured and humiliated. Three days later, French patriots in Paris proclaimed yet another French republic and vowed to continue fighting. But after five months, in January 1871, a starving Paris surrendered,

Proclaiming the German Empire, January 1871 This commemorative painting by Anton von Werner testifies to the nationalistic intoxication in Germany after the victory over France. William I of Prussia stands on a platform surrounded by princes and generals in the famous Hall of Mirrors in the palace of Versailles, while officers from all the units around a besieged Paris cheer and salute him with uplifted swords as emperor of a unified Germany. Bismarck, in white (center), stands between king and army. (akg-images)

and France went on to accept Bismarck's harsh peace terms. By this time, the south German states had agreed to join a new German Empire. The victorious William I was proclaimed emperor of Germany in the Hall of Mirrors in the palace of Versailles. Europe had a nineteenth-century German "sun king" (see Chapter 16). As in the 1866 constitution, the king of Prussia and his ministers had ultimate power in the new German Empire, and the lower house of the legislature was elected by universal male suffrage.

Bismarck and the German Empire imposed a severe penalty on France. France was forced to pay a colossal indemnity of 5 billion francs and to cede the rich eastern province of Alsace and part of Lorraine to Germany. French men and women of all classes viewed the seizure of Alsace and Lorraine as a terrible crime. They could never forget and never forgive, and thus relations between France and Germany after 1871 were tragically poisoned.

The Franco-Prussian War, which Europeans generally saw as a test of nations in a pitiless Darwinian struggle for existence, released an enormous surge of patriotic feeling in Germany. Bismarck's genius, the invincible Prussian army, the solidarity of king and people in a unified nation — these and similar themes were trumpeted endlessly during and after the war. The weakest of the Great Powers in 1862 (after Austria, Britain, France, and Russia), Prussia had become, with fortification by the other German states, the most powerful state in Europe in less than a decade. Most Germans were enormously proud, blissfully imagining themselves the fittest and best of the European species. Semi-authoritarian nationalism and a "new conservatism," which was based on an alliance of the propertied classes and sought the active support of the working classes, had triumphed in Germany.

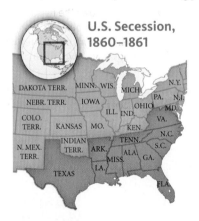

U.S. Secession, 1860–1861

slaveholding states in very different directions. Northerners extended family farms westward and began building English-model factories in the northeast. By 1850 an industrializing, urbanizing North was also building a system of canals and railroads and attracting most of the European immigrants.

In sharp contrast, industry and cities did not develop in the South, and European immigrants largely avoided the region. Even though three-quarters of all Southern white families were small farmers and owned no slaves in 1850, plantation owners holding twenty or more slaves dominated the economy and society. These profit-minded slave owners used gangs of black slaves to claim a vast new kingdom across the Deep South where cotton was king (Map 24.3). By 1850, this kingdom produced 5 million bales a year and satisfied an apparently insatiable demand from textile mills in Europe and New England.

The rise of the cotton empire greatly expanded slave-based agriculture in the South, spurred exports, and played a key role in igniting rapid U.S. economic growth. The large profits flowing from cotton also led influential Southerners to defend slavery. In doing so, Southern whites developed a strong cultural identity and came to see themselves as a closely knit "we" distinct from the Northern "they." Northern whites viewed their free-labor system as being just and economical and morally superior to slavery. Thus regional antagonisms intensified.

These antagonisms came to a climax after 1848 when a defeated Mexico ceded to the United States a vast area stretching from west Texas to the Pacific Ocean. Debate over the extension of slavery in this new territory caused attitudes to harden on both sides. In Abraham Lincoln's famous words, the United States was a "house divided." Lincoln's election as president in 1860 gave Southern secessionists the chance they had been waiting for. Eventually eleven states left the Union, determined to win their own independence, and formed the Confederate States of America. When Southern troops fired on a Union fort in South Carolina's Charleston harbor, war began.

The long Civil War (1861–1865) was the bloodiest conflict in all of American history, but in the end the South was decisively defeated and the Union preserved. In the aftermath of the war, certain dominant characteristics of American life and national culture took shape. Powerful business corporations emerged, steadfastly supported by the Republican Party during and after the war. The **Homestead Act** of 1862, which gave western land to settlers, and the Thirteenth Amendment

Nation Building in the United States

In what ways did the United States experience nation building? ◾

Closely linked to European developments in the nineteenth century, the United States also experienced the full drama of bloody nation building. The "United" States was divided by slavery from its birth, as economic development in the young republic carried free and

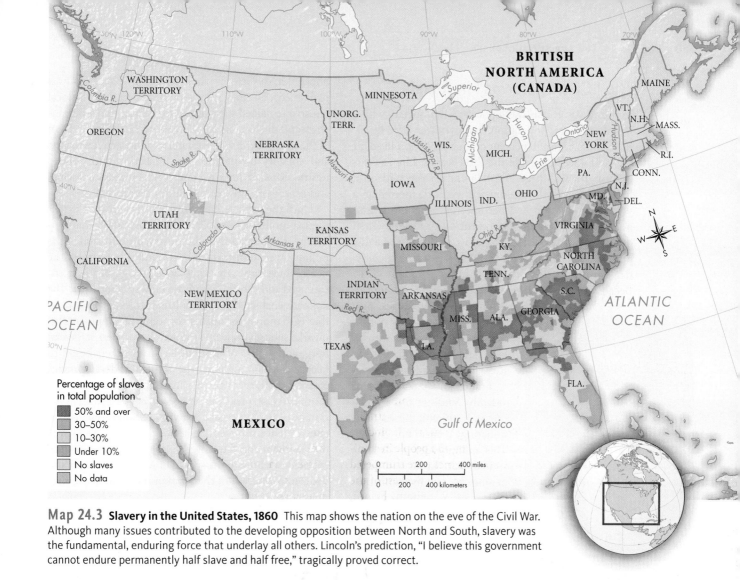

Map 24.3 Slavery in the United States, 1860 This map shows the nation on the eve of the Civil War. Although many issues contributed to the developing opposition between North and South, slavery was the fundamental, enduring force that underlay all others. Lincoln's prediction, "I believe this government cannot endure permanently half slave and half free," tragically proved correct.

Percentage of slaves in total population

- 50% and over
- 30–50%
- 10–30%
- Under 10%
- No slaves
- No data

of 1865, which ended slavery, reinforced the concept of free labor taking its chances in a market economy. Finally, the success of Lincoln and the North in holding the Union together seemed to confirm that the "manifest destiny" of the United States was indeed to straddle a continent as a great world power. Thus a new American nationalism grew out of a civil war.

The Modernization of Russia and the Ottoman Empire

What steps did Russia and the Ottoman Turks take toward modernization, and how successful were they? ▪

The Russian and the Ottoman Empires also experienced profound political crises in the mid-nineteenth century. These crises were unlike those occurring in Italy and Germany, for neither Russia nor the Ottoman Empire aspired to build a single powerful state out of a jumble of principalities. Both empires were already vast multinational states built on long traditions of military conquest and absolutist rule by elites from the dominant ethnic groups—the Russians and the Ottoman Turks. In the early nineteenth century the governing elites in both states were strongly opposed to representative government and national self-determination, and they continued to concentrate on absolutist rule and competition with other Great Powers.

For both states relentless power politics led to serious trouble. It became clear to the leaders of both empires that they had to embrace the process of **modernization**, defined narrowly as the changes that enable a country to compete effectively with the leading countries at a given time. This limited conception of modernization fits Russia after the Crimean War particularly well, and it helps explain developments in the Ottoman Empire.

Homestead Act A result of the American Civil War that gave western land to settlers, reinforcing the concept of free labor in a market economy.

modernization The changes that enable a country to compete effectively with the leading countries at a given time.

759

The "Great Reforms" in Russia

In the 1850s, Russia was a poor agrarian society with a rapidly growing population. Industry was little developed, and almost 90 percent of the population lived off the land. (See "Living in the Past: Peasant Life in Post-Reform Russia," page 762.) Bound to the lord on a hereditary basis, the peasant serf was little more than a slave, and serfdom had become the great moral and political issue for the government by the 1840s. Then the Crimean War of 1853 to 1856, arising out of a dispute with France over who should protect certain Christian shrines in the Ottoman Empire, brought crisis. Because the fighting was concentrated in the Crimean peninsula on the Black Sea, Russia's weak transportation network of rivers and wagons failed to supply the distant Russian armies adequately.

France and Great Britain, aided by Sardinia and the Ottoman Empire, inflicted a humiliating defeat on Russia. This military defeat demonstrated that Russia had fallen behind the rapidly industrializing nations of western Europe in many areas. At the very least, Russia needed railroads, better armaments, and reorganization of the army if it was to maintain its international position. Moreover, the disastrous war had caused hardship and raised the specter of massive peasant rebellion. Reform of serfdom was imperative. Military disaster thus forced Tsar Alexander II (r. 1855–1881) and his ministers along the path of rapid social change and general modernization.

The Crimean War, 1853–1856

The first and greatest of the reforms was the freeing of the serfs in 1861. Human bondage was abolished forever, and the emancipated peasants received, on average, about half of the land. Yet they had to pay fairly high prices for their land, and because the land was owned collectively, each peasant village was jointly responsible for the payments of all the families in the village. Collective ownership and responsibility made it very difficult for individual peasants to improve agricultural methods or leave their villages. Thus old patterns of behavior predominated, and the effects of reform were limited.

Most of the later reforms were also halfway measures. In 1864 the government established a new institution of local government, the zemstvo. Members of this local assembly were elected by a three-class system of towns, peasant villages, and noble landowners. A zemstvo executive council dealt with local problems. Russian liberals hoped that this reform would lead to an elected national parliament, but they were soon disappointed. The local zemstvo remained subordinate to the traditional bureaucracy and the local nobility. More successful was reform of the legal system, which established independent courts and equality before the law. Education and policies toward Russian Jews were also liberalized somewhat, and censorship was relaxed but not removed.

Until the twentieth century, Russia's greatest strides toward modernization were economic rather than political. Transportation and industry, both so vital to the military, were transformed in two industrial surges. The first of these came after 1860, when the government encouraged and subsidized private railway companies. The railroads enabled agricultural Russia to export grain and thus earn money for further economic development. Industrial suburbs grew up around Moscow and St. Petersburg, and a class of modern factory workers began to take shape. Strengthened by industrial development, Russia's military forces began seizing territory to the south and east, greatly exciting many ardent Russian nationalists and superpatriots, who became some of the government's most enthusiastic supporters. Industrial development and the growing proletariat class also contributed mightily to the spread of Marxian thought and the transformation of the Russian revolutionary movement after 1890.

In 1881 Alexander II was assassinated by a small group of anarchist terrorists. The era of reform came to an abrupt end, for the new tsar, Alexander III (r. 1881–1894), was a determined reactionary. Nevertheless, economic modernization sped forward for the second time, as Russia achieved a massive industrialization surge from 1890 to 1900. The key leader was Sergei Witte (suhr-GAY VIH-tuh), the tough, competent minister of finance from 1892 to 1903. Inspired by the writings of Friedrich List (see Chapter 21), Witte believed that the harsh reality of industrial backwardness was threatening Russia's power and greatness. Under Witte's leadership the government built state-owned railroads rapidly, doubling the network to thirty-five thousand miles by the end of the century. Witte established high protective tariffs to build Russian industry, and he put the country on the gold standard of the "civilized world" in order to strengthen Russian finances.

Witte's greatest innovation was to use Westerners to catch up with the West. He encouraged foreigners to build factories in Russia, believing that "the inflow of foreign capital is . . . the only way by which our industry will be able to supply our country quickly with abundant and cheap products."[2] His efforts to entice Westerners to locate their factories in Russia were especially successful in southern Russia. There, in eastern Ukraine, foreign capitalists and their engineers built an enormous and very modern steel and coal industry. In

1900 peasants still constituted the great majority of the population, but Russia was industrializing and catching up with the advanced nations of the West.

The Russian Revolution of 1905

Catching up partly meant vigorous territorial expansion, for this was the age of Western imperialism. By 1903 Russia had established a sphere of influence in Chinese Manchuria and was eyeing northern Korea. When the diplomatic protests of equally imperialistic Japan were ignored, the Japanese launched a surprise attack in February 1904. After Japan scored repeated victories, Russia was forced in September 1905 to accept a humiliating defeat.

As is often the case, military disaster abroad brought political upheaval at home. The business and professional classes had long wanted a liberal, representative government. Urban factory workers had all the grievances of early industrialization and were organized in a radical and still illegal labor movement. Peasants had gained little from the era of reforms and were suffering from poverty and overpopulation. At the same time, nationalist sentiment was emerging among the empire's minorities, and subject nationalities, such as the Poles, the Ukrainians, and the Latvians, were calling for self-rule. With the army pinned down in Manchuria, all these currents of discontent converged in the revolution of 1905.

On a Sunday in January 1905, a massive crowd of workers and their families converged peacefully on the Winter Palace in St. Petersburg to present a petition to the tsar. Suddenly troops opened fire, killing and wounding hundreds. The **Bloody Sunday** massacre turned ordinary workers against the tsar and produced a wave of general indignation.

Outlawed political parties came out into the open, and by the summer of 1905 strikes, peasant uprisings, revolts among minority nationalities,

Bloody Sunday A massacre of peaceful protesters at the Winter Palace in St. Petersburg in 1905 that triggered a revolution that overturned absolute tsarist rule and made Russia into a conservative constitutional monarchy.

The October Manifesto of 1905 This painting by the famous realist Ilya Repin captures the riotous joy that seized most moderate, well-educated Russians after Tsar Nicholas II issued the October Manifesto. At long last, they thought, Russia would become a liberal constitutional state, with guaranteed liberties and representative assemblies. (akg-images)

LIVING IN THE PAST

THE CAUTIOUS EMANCIPATION OF 1861, which freed Russian peasants from their noble lords but tied them to their villages, preserved traditional peasant life until the massive industrial surge of the 1890s. Most peasant families continued to live in one- or two-story log cabins strung out along the village's wide dirt road. A cabin typically had a single living room, a storage room (sometimes shared with animals), and a shallow cellar. Simple furniture—a table, benches, storage shelves—was complemented by a large, flat brick oven that was used for both cooking and sleeping. On Saturdays villagers stoked up the communal bathhouse. On Sundays they attended a long Orthodox service in their wooden church, often followed in summer by socializing with family and friends, drinking tea and mild home-made ale, telling stories, and playing the traditional stringed instrument, the balalaika.

In contrast to western Europe, where women had almost never done heavy field work, Russian peasant women always provided much of the hard labor required for plowing, planting, and harvesting. Infertile soil, sparse population, simple hand tools, and short growing seasons demanded intense physical effort from all family members to get the crops planted and harvested before the first hard freeze and the long brutal winter. Since peasant land in Russia followed a common crop rotation and was owned by the entire peasant community, with each family allotted its share of the long strips of crop land according to the family's size, there were no fences to mark off private property rights that did not exist.

Russian peasants always needed additional, nonagricultural, income. Thus both men and women engaged in many crafts and trades, of which weaving, pottery, embroidering, hauling, logging, and carpen-

In this photograph (ca. 1875), members of a Russian family gather outside a typical peasant cabin to enjoy a Sunday break from their labors. (family: The Granger Collection, New York; balalaika: Museum of Fine Arts, Boston/Lebrecht)

Russian agriculture depended on the contribution of women and girls, as this photograph attests. (The Granger Collection, New York)

try were particularly important. Woodworkers, like this peasant barrel maker with his birch-bark shoes and homemade leggings, used an abundant raw material to fashion elaborate dolls and attractive wooden tableware as well as workaday items. Peasants also went to towns and cities for temporary work, and many settled there permanently as industrial workers in the 1890s.

QUESTIONS FOR ANALYSIS

1. How did the abolition of serfdom affect peasant life in Russia?

2. What role did peasant women play in Russian agriculture? Why?

3. How did Russian peasants interact with their environment? In what ways did their environment influence peasants' lives?

This 1895 photo and the wooden nesting dolls highlight the importance of woodworking as a source of secondary income for Russian peasants. (barrel maker: akg-images; nesting dolls: Sergiev Posad Toy Museum, Sergiev Posad, Russia, Photo RK812)

October Manifesto The result of a great general strike in October 1905, it granted full civil rights and promised a popularly elected Duma (parliament) with real legislative power.

Duma The Russian parliament that opened in 1906, elected indirectly by universal male suffrage but controlled after 1907 by the tsar and the conservative classes.

and troop mutinies were sweeping the country. The revolutionary surge culminated in October 1905 in a great paralyzing general strike that forced the government to capitulate. The tsar issued the **October Manifesto**, which granted full civil rights and promised a popularly elected **Duma** (DOO-muh; parliament) with real legislative power. The manifesto split the opposition. Frightened middle-class leaders helped the government repress the uprising and survive as a constitutional monarchy.

On the eve of the opening of the first Duma in May 1906, the government issued the new constitution, the Fundamental Laws. The tsar retained great powers. The Duma, elected indirectly by universal male suffrage, and a largely appointive upper house could debate and pass laws, but the tsar had an absolute veto. As in Bismarck's Germany, the tsar appointed his ministers, who did not need to command a majority in the Duma.

The disappointed, predominately middle-class liberals, the largest group in the newly elected Duma, saw the Fundamental Laws as a step backward. Efforts to cooperate with the tsar's ministers soon broke down, and after months of deadlock, the tsar dismissed the Duma. Thereupon he and his reactionary advisers unilaterally rewrote the electoral law so as to increase greatly the weight of the propertied classes. When elections were held, the tsar could count on a loyal majority in the Duma. His chief minister then pushed through important agrarian reforms designed to break down collective village ownership of land and encourage the more enterprising peasants—his "wager on the strong." In 1914, Russia was partially modernized, a conservative constitutional monarchy with a peasant-based but industrializing economy.

☐ Area of peasant unrest
• Major strikes and mutinies

St. Petersburg
Moscow
RUSSIA
Warsaw

Black Sea

The Russian Revolution of 1905

Tanzimat A set of reforms designed to remake the Ottoman Empire on a western European model.

Decline and Reform in the Ottoman Empire

The Ottoman Empire had reached its high point of development under Suleiman the Magnificent in the sixteenth century. By the eighteenth century it was falling rapidly behind western Europe in science, industrial skill,

and military technology. Also during the eighteenth century, Russia's powerful westernized army was able to occupy Ottoman provinces on the Danube River. The danger that the Great Powers of Europe would gradually conquer the Ottoman Empire and divide up its vast territories was real.

Caught up in the Napoleonic wars and losing more territory to Russia, the Ottomans were forced in 1816 to grant Serbia local autonomy. In 1830, the Greeks won their national independence, while French armies began their long and bloody conquest of the Arabic-speaking province of Algeria. The Ottoman Empire was losing territory and power. Another threat to the empire came from within: the rise of Muhammad Ali, the Ottoman governor in Egypt. In 1831, and again in 1839, his French-trained forces occupied the Ottoman provinces of Syria and then Iraq and appeared ready to depose the Ottoman sultan (emperor) Mahmud II (r. 1808–1839). The sultan survived, but only because the European powers forced Muhammad Ali to withdraw. The European powers, minus France, preferred a weak and dependent Ottoman state to a strong and revitalized Muslim entity under a dynamic leader such as Muhammad Ali.

Realizing their precarious position, liberal Ottoman statesmen launched in 1839 an era of radical reforms, which lasted with fits and starts until 1876 and culminated in a constitution and a short-lived parliament. Known as the **Tanzimat** (literally, regulations or orders), these reforms were designed to remake the empire on a western European model. The high point of reform came with Sultan Abdul Mejid's Imperial Rescript of 1857. Articles in the decree called for equality before the law, a modernized administration and military, and religious freedom for Muslims, Christians, and Jews.

> *Every distinction or designation tending to make any class whatsoever of the subjects of my Empire inferior to another class, on account of their religion, language, or race, shall be forever effaced from the Administrative Protocol. . . .*
>
> *As all forms of religion are and shall be freely professed in my domains, no subject shall be hindered in the exercise of the religion he professes.*[3]

As part of its new policy of tolerance, new commercial laws allowed free importation of foreign goods and permitted foreign merchants to operate freely throughout the empire. Of great importance for later developments, growing numbers among the elite and the upwardly mobile embraced Western education and accepted secular values to some extent.

Pasha Hilim Receiving Archduke Maximilian of Austria As this painting suggests, Ottoman leaders became well versed in European languages and culture. They also mastered the game of power politics, playing one European state off against another and securing the Ottoman Empire's survival. The black servants on the right may be slaves from Sudan. (Miramare Palace Trieste/Dagli Orti/The Art Archive)

Intended to bring revolutionary modernization, the Tanzimat permitted partial recovery but fell short of its goals for several reasons. First, the liberal reforms failed to halt the growth of nationalism among Christian subjects in the Balkans, which resulted in crises and defeats that undermined all reform efforts. Second, the Ottoman initiatives did not curtail the appetite of Western imperialism, which secured a stranglehold on the Ottoman economy.

Finally, equality before the law for all citizens and religious communities actually increased religious disputes, which were in turn exacerbated by the relentless interference of the European powers. This development embittered relations between the religious communities, distracted the government from its reform mission, and split Muslims into secularists and religious conservatives. Many conservative Muslims detested the religious reforms, which they viewed as an impious departure from Islamic tradition and holy law. These Islamic conserva-

tives became the most dependable support of Sultan Abdülhamid (ahb-dool-hah-MEED) (r. 1876–1909), who abandoned the model of European liberalism in his long and repressive reign.

The combination of declining international power and conservative tyranny eventually led to a powerful resurgence of the modernizing impulse among idealistic Turkish exiles in Europe and young army officers in Istanbul. These fervent patriots, the so-called **Young Turks**, seized power in the revolution of 1908, and they forced the sultan to implement reforms. Although they failed to stop the rising tide of anti-Ottoman nationalism in the Balkans, the Young Turks helped prepare the way for the birth of modern secular Turkey after the defeat and collapse of the Ottoman Empire in World War I.

Young Turks Fervent patriots who seized power in the revolution of 1908 in the Ottoman Empire, forcing the conservative sultan to implement reforms.

The Responsive National State, 1871–1914

Why after 1871 did ordinary citizens feel a growing loyalty to their governments?   ■

For central and western Europe, the unification of Italy and Germany by "blood and iron" marked the end of a dramatic period of nation building. After 1871 the heartland of Europe was organized into strong national states. Only on the borders of Europe—in Ireland and Russia, in Austria-Hungary and the Ottoman Empire— did subject peoples still strive for national unity and political independence.

General Trends

Despite some major differences between countries, European domestic politics after 1871 had a common framework, the firmly established national state. The common themes within that framework were the emergence of mass politics and growing mass loyalty toward the national state.

For good reason, ordinary people—the masses of an industrializing, urbanizing society—felt increasing loyalty to their governments. More people could vote. By 1914 universal male suffrage had become the rule rather than the exception. This development had as much psychological as political significance. Ordinary men were no longer denied the right to vote because they lacked wealth or education. They felt that they counted; they could influence the government to some extent. They were becoming "part of the system."

The women's suffrage movement also made some gains. By 1913 women could vote in twelve of the western United States. Europe, too, moved slowly in this direction. In 1914 Norway gave the vote to most women. Elsewhere, women such as the English Emmeline Pankhurst were very militant in their demands. They heckled politicians and held public demonstrations. These efforts generally failed before 1914, but they prepared the way for the triumph of the women's suffrage movement immediately after World War I.

As the right to vote spread, politicians and parties in national parliaments represented the people more responsively. The multiparty system prevailing in most countries meant that parliamentary majorities were built

"Votes for Women!" The long-simmering campaign for women's suffrage in England came to a boil after 1903, as militants took to the streets, disrupted political meetings, and tried to storm Parliament. This 1908 illustration shows demonstrators giving a hero's welcome to Mary Leigh, the first suffragette imprisoned for property damage after she threw rocks through the windows of the prime minister's house. Emmeline Pankhurst was also imprisoned after refusing to pay a fine for purportedly kicking and spitting at policemen. Militant suffragettes shared their leader's well-known dedication to "deeds, not words." They proudly wore her portrait badge, a symbol of the lengths they would go for the right to vote. (illustration: The Art Archive; badge: © Museum of London Picture Library)

on shifting coalitions of different parties, and this gave individual parties leverage to obtain benefits for their supporters. Governments also passed laws to alleviate general problems, thereby acquiring greater legitimacy and appearing more worthy of support.

There was a less positive side to building popular support for strong nation-states after 1871. Governments found that they could manipulate national feeling to create a sense of unity and to divert attention away from underlying class conflicts. Conservative and moderate leaders found that workers who voted socialist would rally around the flag in a diplomatic crisis or cheer when distant territory of doubtful value was seized in Africa or Asia. Therefore, after 1871 governing elites frequently used antiliberal and militaristic policies to help manage domestic conflicts, but at the expense of increasing the international tensions that erupted in 1914 in the cataclysm of World War I and the Russian Revolution.

In these same years some fanatics and demagogic political leaders also sought to build extreme nationalist movements by whipping up popular animosity toward imaginary enemies, especially the Jews. The growth of modern anti-Semitism after 1880 epitomized the most negative aspects of European nationalism before the First World War.

The German Empire

Politics in Germany after 1871 reflected many of the general European developments. The new German Empire was a federal union of Prussia and twenty-four smaller states. Much of the everyday business of government was conducted by the separate states, but there was a strong national government with a chancellor—until 1890, Bismarck—and a popularly elected lower house called the **Reichstag** (RIGHKHS-tahg). Although Bismarck refused to be bound by a parliamentary majority, he tried nonetheless to maintain one. This situation gave the political parties opportunities. Until 1878 Bismarck relied mainly on the National Liberals, who had rallied to him after 1866. They supported legislation useful for further economic and legal unification of the country.

Less wisely, they backed Bismarck's attack on the Catholic Church, the so-called **Kulturkampf** (kool-TOOR-kahmpf), or "struggle for civilization." Like Bismarck, the middle-class National Liberals were particularly alarmed by Pius IX and his declaration of papal infallibility in 1870. That dogma seemed to ask German Catholics to put loyalty to their church, a foreign power, above their loyalty to their newly unified nation. Kulturkampf initiatives generally aimed at making the Catholic Church subject to government control. However, only in Protestant Prussia did the Kulturkampf have even limited success, because Catholics throughout the country generally voted for the Center Party, which blocked passage of national laws hostile to the church.

In 1878 Bismarck abandoned his attack on the church and instead courted the Catholic Center Party, whose supporters included many Catholic small farmers in western and southern Germany. By enacting high tariffs on cheap grain from the United States, Canada, and Russia, he won over both the Catholic Center and the Protestant Junkers, who had large landholdings in the east. With the tariffs, then, Bismarck won Catholic and conservative support.

Many other governments followed Bismarck's lead, and the 1880s and 1890s saw a widespread return to protectionism in Europe. France, in particular, established very high tariffs to protect agriculture and industry, peasants and manufacturers, from foreign competition. Thus the European governments were responding effectively to a major economic problem and winning greater loyalty. The general rise of protectionism in this period was also an outstanding example of the dangers of self-centered nationalism: new tariffs led to international name-calling and nasty trade wars.

As for socialism, Bismarck tried to stop its growth in Germany because he genuinely feared its revolutionary language and allegiance to a movement transcending the nation-state. In 1878, after two attempts on the life of William I by radicals (though not socialists), Bismarck used a carefully orchestrated national outcry to ram through the Reichstag a law that strictly controlled socialist meetings and publications and outlawed the Social Democratic Party, which was thereby driven underground. German socialists, however, continued to hold influence, and Bismarck decided to try another tack.

In an attempt to win the support of working-class people, Bismarck urged the Reichstag to take bold action and enact a variety of state-supported social measures. Big business and some conservatives accused Bismarck of creating "state socialism," but Bismarck ably pressed his program in many lively speeches to the nation's representatives and its citizens, as the following excerpt suggests.

Reichstag The popularly elected lower house of government of the new German Empire after 1871.

Kulturkampf Bismarck's attack on the Catholic Church within Germany from 1870 to 1878, resulting from Pius IX's declaration of papal infallibility.

> Give the working-man the right to work as long as he is healthy; assure him care when he is sick; assure him maintenance when he is old. If you do that, and do not fear the (financial) sacrifice, or cry out at State Socialism as soon as the words "provision for old age" are uttered, . . . then I believe the gentlemen of the Wyden (Social-Democratic) program will sound their bird-call in vain, and that the thronging toward them will cease as soon as working-men see that the Government and legislative bodies are earnestly concerned with their welfare.[4]

Bismarck and his supporters carried the day and his essentially conservative nation-state pioneered in the provision of social welfare programs. In 1883 he pushed through the Reichstag the first of several modern social security laws to help wage earners. The laws of 1883 and 1884 established national sickness and accident insurance; the law of 1889 established old-age pensions and retirement benefits. Henceforth sick, injured, and retired workers could look forward to some regular benefits from the state. This national social security system, paid for through compulsory contributions by wage earners and employers as well as grants from the state, was the first of its kind anywhere. Bismarck's social security system did not wean workers from voting socialist, but it did give them a small stake in the system and protect them from some of the uncertainties of the complex urban industrial world. This enormously significant development was a product of political competition and government efforts to win popular support.

Increasingly, the great issues in German domestic politics were socialism and the Marxian Social Democratic Party. In 1890 the new emperor, the young, idealistic, and unstable William II (r. 1888–1918), opposed Bismarck's attempt to renew the law outlawing the Social Democratic Party. Eager to rule in his own right and to earn the support of the workers, William II forced Bismarck to resign. After the "dropping of the pilot," German foreign policy changed profoundly and mostly for the worse, but the government did pass new laws to aid workers and to legalize socialist political activity.

Yet William II was no more successful than Bismarck in getting workers to renounce socialism. Indeed, Social Democrats won more and more seats in the Reichstag, becoming Germany's largest single party in 1912. This great electoral victory shocked aristocrats and their wealthy, conservative middle-class allies, heightening the fears of an impending socialist upheaval. Yet the "revolutionary" socialists were actually becoming less radical in Germany. In the years before World War I, the German Social Democratic Party broadened its base by adopting a more patriotic tone, allowing for greater military spending and imperialist expansion. German socialists concentrated instead on gradual social and political reform.

Republican France

Although Napoleon III's reign made some progress in reducing antagonisms between classes, the war with Prussia undid these efforts, and in 1871 France seemed hopelessly divided once again. The patriotic republicans who proclaimed the Third Republic in Paris after the military disaster at Sedan refused to admit defeat. They defended Paris with great heroism for weeks, living off rats and zoo animals until they were starved into submission by German armies in January 1871. When national elections then sent a large majority of conservatives and monarchists to the National Assembly and France's new leaders decided they had no choice but to surrender Alsace (al-SAS) and Lorraine to Germany, the traumatized Parisians exploded in patriotic frustration and proclaimed the Paris Commune in March 1871. Vaguely radical, the leaders of the Commune wanted to govern Paris without interference from the conservative French countryside. The National Assembly, led by aging politician Adolphe Thiers (TEE-ehr), would hear none of it. The Assembly ordered the French army into Paris and brutally crushed the Commune. Twenty thousand people died in the fighting. As in June 1848, it was Paris against the provinces, French against French.

Out of this tragedy, France slowly formed a new national unity, achieving considerable stability before 1914. How is one to account for this? Luck played a part. Until 1875 the monarchists in the "republican" National Assembly had a majority but could not agree who should be king. The compromise Bourbon candidate refused to rule except under the white flag of his absolutist ancestors—a completely unacceptable condition for many supporters of moderate, constitutional monarchy. In the meantime, Thiers's destruction of the radical Commune and his other firm measures showed the fearful provinces and the middle class that the Third Republic might be moderate and socially conservative. France therefore retained the republic, though reluctantly. As President Thiers cautiously said, this was "the government which divides us least."

Another stabilizing factor was the skill and determination of the moderate republican leaders in the early years. The most famous of these was Léon Gambetta (gam-BEH-tuh), the son of an Italian grocer, a warm, easygoing, unsuccessful lawyer who had turned professional politician. By 1879 the great majority of members of both the upper and the lower houses of the National Assembly were republicans, and the Third Republic had firm foundations after almost a decade.

The moderate republicans sought to preserve their creation by winning the hearts and minds of the next generation. Trade unions were fully legalized, and France acquired a colonial empire. More important, a series of laws between 1879 and 1886 established free compulsory elementary education for both girls and boys. At the same time, they greatly expanded the state system of public tax-supported schools. In France and throughout the Western world, the general expansion of public education served as a critical nation-building tool in the late nineteenth century. In France most elementary and much secondary education had traditionally been in the parochial schools of the Catholic Church, which had long been hostile to republics and to much of secular life. Free compulsory elementary education in France became secular republican education.

Although the educational reforms of the 1880s disturbed French Catholics, many of them rallied to the republic in the 1890s. The limited acceptance of the

Captain Alfred Dreyfus Leaving an 1899 reconsideration of his original court martial, Dreyfus receives an insulting "guard of dishonor" from soldiers whose backs are turned. (Roger-Viollet/Getty Images)

modern world by the more liberal Pope Leo XIII (pontificate 1878–1903) eased tensions between church and state. Unfortunately, the **Dreyfus affair** changed all that.

In 1894 Alfred Dreyfus, a Jewish captain in the French army, was falsely accused and convicted of treason. His family never doubted his innocence and fought to reopen the case, enlisting the support of prominent republicans and intellectuals such as novelist Émile Zola. In 1898 and 1899, the case split France apart. On one side was the army, which had manufactured evidence against Dreyfus, joined by anti-Semites and most of the Catholic establishment. On the other side stood the civil libertarians and most of the more radical republicans.

This battle, which eventually led to Dreyfus's being declared innocent, revived republican feeling against the church. Between 1901 and 1905, the government severed all ties between the state and the Catholic Church after centuries of close relations. The salaries of priests and bishops were no longer paid by the government, and all churches were given to local committees of lay Catholics. Catholic schools were put on their own financially and soon lost a third of their students. The state school system's power of indoctrination was greatly strength-

ened. In France only the growing socialist movement, with its very different and thoroughly secular ideology, stood in opposition to patriotic, republican nationalism.

Great Britain and Ireland

Britain in the late nineteenth century has often been seen as a shining example of peaceful and successful political evolution, where an effective two-party parliament skillfully guided the country from classical liberalism to full-fledged democracy with hardly a misstep. This view of Great Britain is not so much wrong as it is incomplete. After the right to vote was granted to males of the solid middle class in 1832, opinion leaders and politicians wrestled with the uncertainties of a further expansion of the franchise. In 1867 the Second Reform Bill of Benjamin Disraeli and the Conservatives extended the vote to all middle-class males and the best-paid workers in order to broaden the Conservative Party's traditional base of aristocratic and landed support. After 1867 English political parties and electoral campaigns became more modern, and the "lower orders" appeared to vote as responsibly as their "betters." Hence the Third Reform Bill of 1884 gave the vote to almost every adult male.

While the House of Commons was drifting toward democracy, the House of Lords was content to slumber nobly. Between 1901 and 1910, however, the House of Lords tried to reassert itself. Acting as supreme court of the land, it ruled against labor unions in two important decisions. And after the Liberal Party came to power in 1906, the Lords vetoed several measures passed by the Commons, including the so-called **People's Budget**, which was designed to increase spending on social welfare services. The Lords finally capitulated, as they had with the Reform Bill of 1832 (see Chapter 22), when the king threatened to create enough new peers to pass the bill, and aristocratic conservatism yielded to popular democracy once and for all.

The result was that extensive social welfare measures, slow to come to Great Britain, were passed in a spectacular rush between 1906 and 1914. During those years, the Liberal Party, inspired by the fiery Welshman David Lloyd George (1863–1945), substantially raised taxes on the rich as part of the People's Budget. This income helped the government pay for national health insurance, unemployment benefits, old-age pensions, and a host of other social measures. The state was integrating the urban masses socially as well as politically.

Dreyfus affair A divisive case in which Alfred Dreyfus, a Jewish captain in the French army, was falsely accused and convicted of treason. The Catholic Church sided with the anti-Semites against Dreyfus; after Dreyfus was declared innocent, the French government severed all ties between the state and the church.

People's Budget A bill proposed after the Liberal Party came to power in England in 1906, it was designed to increase spending on social welfare services, but was initially vetoed in the House of Lords.

This record of accomplishment was only part of the story, however. On the eve of World War I, the unanswered question of Ireland brought Great Britain to the brink of civil war. The terrible Irish famine fueled an Irish revolutionary movement. Thereafter, the English slowly granted concessions, such as the abolition of the privileges of the Anglican Church and rights for Irish peasants. Liberal prime minister William Gladstone (1809–1898), who had proclaimed twenty years earlier that "my mission is to pacify Ireland," introduced bills to give Ireland self-government in 1886 and in 1893. They failed to pass, but in 1913 Irish nationalists in the British Parliament finally gained a home-rule bill for Ireland.

Thus Ireland, the emerald isle, was on the brink of achieving self-government. Yet Ireland was composed of two peoples. As much as the Irish Catholic majority in the southern counties wanted home rule, precisely that much did the Irish Protestants of the northern counties of Ulster come to oppose it. Motivated by the accumulated fears and hostilities of generations, the Protestants of Ulster refused to submerge themselves in a Catholic Ireland, just as Irish Catholics had refused to submit to a Protestant Britain.

The Ulsterites vowed to resist home rule in northern Ireland. By December 1913 they had raised one hundred thousand armed volunteers, and they were supported by much of English public opinion. Thus in 1914 the Liberals in the House of Lords introduced a compromise home-rule bill that did not apply to the northern counties. This bill, which openly betrayed promises made to Irish nationalists, was rejected, and in September the original home-rule bill was passed but simultaneously suspended for the duration of the hostilities — the momentous Irish question had been overtaken by an earth-shattering world war in August 1914.

Irish developments illustrated once again the power of national feeling and national movements in the nineteenth century. Moreover, they were proof that governments could not elicit greater loyalty unless they could capture and control that elemental current of national feeling. Though Great Britain had much going for it — power, Parliament, prosperity — none of these availed in the face of the conflicting nationalisms created by Catholics and Protestants in northern Ireland. Similarly, progressive Sweden was powerless to stop the growth of the Norwegian national movement, which culminated in Norway's breaking away from Sweden and becoming a fully independent nation in 1905. In this light, one can also see how hopeless was the case of the Ottoman Empire in Europe in the later nineteenth century. It was only a matter of time before the Serbs, Bulgarians, and Romanians would break away.

The Austro-Hungarian Empire

The dilemma of conflicting nationalisms in Ireland helps one appreciate how desperate the situation in the Austro-Hungarian Empire had become by the early twentieth century. In 1849 Magyar nationalism had driven Hungarian patriots to declare an independent Hungarian republic, which was savagely crushed by Russian and Austrian armies (see Chapter 22). Throughout the 1850s, Hungary was ruled as a conquered territory, and Emperor Francis Joseph and his bureaucracy tried hard to centralize the state and Germanize the language and culture of the different nationalities.

Then in the wake of defeat by Prussia in 1866, a weakened Austria was forced to strike a compromise and establish the so-called dual monarchy. The empire

"No Home Rule" Posters like this one helped to incite pro-British, anti-Catholic sentiment in the northern Irish counties of Ulster before the First World War. The rifle raised defiantly and the accompanying rhyme are a thinly veiled threat of armed rebellion and civil war. (Reproduced with the kind permission of the Trustees of the National Museums & Galleries of Northern Ireland. Photograph © Ulster Museum, Belfast) was divided in two, and the nationalistic Magyars gained virtual independence for Hungary. Henceforth, each half of the empire agreed to deal with its own ethnic minorities. The two states were joined only by a shared monarch and common ministries for finance, defense, and foreign affairs.

In Austria ethnic Germans were only one-third of the population, and in 1895 many Germans saw their traditional dominance threatened by Czechs, Poles, and other Slavs. A particularly emotional issue in the Austrian parliament was the language used in government and elementary education at the local level. From 1900 to 1914 the parliament was so divided that ministries generally could not obtain a majority and ruled instead by decree. Efforts by both conservatives and socialists to defuse national antagonisms by stressing economic issues that cut across ethnic lines were largely unsuccessful.

In Hungary the Magyar nobility in 1867 restored the constitution of 1848 and used it to dominate both the Magyar peasantry and the minority populations until 1914. Only the wealthiest one-fourth of adult males had the right to vote, making the parliament the creature of the Magyar elite. Laws promoting the use of the Magyar (Hungarian) language in schools and government were rammed through and bitterly resented, especially by the Croatians and Romanians. While Magyar extremists campaigned loudly for total separation from Austria, the radical leaders of the subject nationalities dreamed in turn of independence from Hungary. Unlike most major countries, which harnessed nationalism to strengthen the state after 1871, the Austro-Hungarian Empire was progressively weakened and destroyed by it.

Jewish Emancipation and Modern Anti-Semitism

Revolutionary changes in political principles and the triumph of the nation-state brought equally revolutionary changes in Jewish life in western and central Europe. The decisive turning point came in 1848, when Jews formed part of the revolutionary vanguard in Vienna and Berlin and the Frankfurt Assembly endorsed full rights for German Jews. In 1871 the constitution of the new German Empire consolidated the process of Jewish emancipation in central Europe. It abolished all restrictions on Jewish marriage, choice of occupation, place of residence, and property ownership. Exclusion from government employment and discrimination in social relations remained. However, according to one leading historian, by 1871 "it was widely accepted in Central Europe that the gradual disappearance of anti-Jewish prejudice was inevitable."[5] The process of emancipation presented Jews with challenges and opportunities. Traditional Jewish occupations, such as court financial agent, village moneylender, and peddler, were undermined by free-market reforms, but careers in business, the professions, and the arts were opening to Jewish talent. Many Jews responded energetically and successfully. Active in finance and railroad building, European Jews excelled in wholesale and retail trade, consumer industries, journalism, medicine, and law. By 1871 a majority of Jewish people in western and central Europe had improved their economic situation and entered the middle classes. Most Jewish people also identified strongly with their respective nation-states and with good reason saw themselves as patriotic citizens.

Vicious anti-Semitism reappeared after the stock market crash of 1873, beginning in central Europe. Drawing on long traditions of religious intolerance, ghetto exclusion, and periodic anti-Jewish riots and expulsions, this anti-Semitism was also a modern development, building on the general reaction against liberalism. Modern anti-Semitism whipped up resentment against Jewish achievement and Jewish "financial control," while fanatics claimed that the Jewish race (rather than the Jewish religion) posed a biological threat to the German people. Anti-Semitic beliefs were particularly popular among conservatives, extremist nationalists, and people who felt threatened by Jewish competition, such as small shopkeepers, officeworkers, and professionals.

Anti-Semites also created modern political parties to attack and degrade Jews. In Austrian Vienna in the early 1890s, Karl Lueger (LOO-guhr) and his "Christian socialists" won striking electoral victories, spurring Theodor Herzl to turn from German nationalism and advocate political **Zionism** and the creation of a Jewish state. (See "Individuals in Society: Theodor Herzl," page 772.) Lueger, the popular mayor of Vienna from 1897 to 1910, combined fierce anti-Semitic rhetoric with municipal ownership of basic services, and he appealed especially to the German-speaking lower middle class—and an unsuccessful young artist named Adolf Hitler.

> **Zionism** A movement toward Jewish political nationhood started by Theodor Herzl.

Before 1914 anti-Semitism was most oppressive in eastern Europe, where Jews also suffered from terrible poverty. In the Russian empire, where there was no Jewish emancipation and 4 million of Europe's 7 million Jewish people lived in 1880, officials used anti-Semitism to channel popular discontent away from the government and onto the Jewish minority. Russian Jews were denounced as foreign exploiters who corrupted national traditions, and in 1881–1882 a wave of violent pogroms commenced in southern Russia. The police and the army stood aside for days while peasants looted and destroyed Jewish property. Official harassment continued in the following decades, and some Russian Jews turned toward self-emancipation and the vision of a Zionist settlement in Palestine. Large numbers also emigrated to western Europe and the United States. About 2.75 million Jews left eastern Europe between 1881 and 1914.

Theodor Herzl

INDIVIDUALS IN SOCIETY

IN SEPTEMBER 1897, ONLY DAYS AFTER HIS VISION AND ENERGY had called into being the First Zionist Congress in Basel, Switzerland, Theodor Herzl (1860–1904) assessed the results in his diary: "If I were to sum up the Congress in a word — which I shall take care not to publish — it would be this: At Basel I founded the Jewish state. If I said this out loud today I would be greeted by universal laughter. In five years perhaps, and

certainly in fifty years, everyone will perceive it."*

Herzl's buoyant optimism, which so often carried him forward, was prophetic. Leading the Zionist movement until his death at age forty-four in 1904, Herzl guided the first historic steps toward modern Jewish political nationhood and the creation of Israel in 1948. Theodor Herzl was born in Budapest, Hungary, into an upper-middle-class, German-speaking Jewish family. When Herzl was eighteen, his family moved to Vienna, where he studied law. As a university student, he soaked up the liberal beliefs of most well-to-do Viennese Jews, who also championed the assimilation of German culture. Wrestling with his nonreligious Jewishness and his strong pro-German feeling, Herzl embraced German nationalism and joined a German dueling fraternity.

There he discovered that full acceptance required openly anti-Semitic attitudes and a repudiation of all things Jewish. This Herzl could not tolerate, and he resigned. After receiving his law degree, he embarked on a literary career. In 1889 Herzl married into a wealthy Viennese Jewish family, but he and his socialite wife were mismatched and never happy together.

Herzl achieved considerable success as both a journalist and a playwright. His witty comedies focused on the bourgeoisie, including Jewish millionaires trying to live like aristocrats. Accepting many German stereotypes, Herzl sometimes depicted eastern Jews as uneducated and grasping. But as a dedicated, highly educated liberal, he mainly believed that the Jewish shortcomings he perceived were the results of age-old persecution and would disappear through education and assimilation. Herzl also took a growing pride in Jewish steadfastness in the face of victimization and suffering. He savored memories of his early Jewish education and going with his father to the synagogue.

The emergence of modern anti-Semitism (see page 771) shocked Herzl, as it did many acculturated Jewish Germans. Moving to Paris in 1891 as the correspondent for Vienna's leading liberal newspaper, Herzl studied politics and pondered recent historical developments. He then came to a bold conclusion, published in 1896 as *The Jewish State: An Attempt at a Modern Solution to the Jewish Question.* According to Herzl, Jewish assimilation had failed, and attempts to combat anti-Semitism would never succeed. Only by building an independent Jewish state could the Jewish people achieve dignity and renewal.

Theodor Herzl. (Library of Congress)

Herzl developed his political nationalism, or Zionism, before the anti-Jewish agitation accompanying the Dreyfus affair, which only served to strengthen his faith in his analysis. Generally rebuffed by skeptical Jewish elites in western and central Europe, Herzl turned for support to youthful idealists and the poor Jewish masses. He became an inspiring man of action, rallying the delegates to the annual Zionist congresses, directing the growth of the worldwide Zionist organization, and working himself to death. Herzl also understood that national consciousness required powerful emotions and symbols, such as a Jewish flag. Flags build nations, he said, because people "live and die for a flag."

Putting the Zionist vision before non-Jews and world public opinion, Herzl believed in international diplomacy and political agreements. He traveled constantly to negotiate with European rulers and top officials, seeking their support in securing territory for a Jewish state, usually in the Ottoman Empire. Aptly described by an admiring contemporary as "the first Jewish statesman since the destruction of Jerusalem," Herzl proved most successful in Britain. He paved the way for the 1917 Balfour Declaration, which solemnly pledged British support for a "Jewish homeland" in Palestine.

QUESTIONS FOR ANALYSIS

1. Describe Theodor Herzl's background and early beliefs. Do you see a link between Herzl's early German nationalism and his later Zionism?

2. Why did Herzl believe an independent Jewish state with its own national flag was necessary?

3. How did Herzl work as a leader to turn his Zionist vision into a reality?

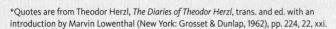

*Quotes are from Theodor Herzl, *The Diaries of Theodor Herzl*, trans. and ed. with an introduction by Marvin Lowenthal (New York: Grosset & Dunlap, 1962), pp. 224, 22, xxi.

GRUSS AUS *Leipzig, d. 15. Aug. 99.* [handwritten postcard message]

Picturing the Past

"The Expulsion of the Jews from Russia" So reads this postcard, correctly suggesting that Russian government officials often encouraged popular anti-Semitism and helped drive many Jews out of Russia in the late nineteenth century. The road signs indicate that these poor Jews are crossing into Germany, where they will find a grudging welcome and a meager meal at the Jolly Onion Inn. Other Jews from eastern Europe settled in France and Britain, thereby creating small but significant Jewish populations in both of these countries for the first time since they had expelled most of their Jews in the Middle Ages. (Alliance Israelite Universelle, Paris/Archives Charmet/The Bridgeman Art Library)

ANALYZING THE IMAGE The inset image in the upper-right corner shows an armed German soldier at the table, carefully watching the Jewish refugees. What similarity do you see between this and the larger image on the postcard to suggest how Jewish refugees were treated in Germany as compared to Russia? The postcard was sent on August 15, 1899, from Leipzig, Germany, and the message is in German. To whom might this card have been sent and what message might the postcard convey to the recipient?

CONNECTIONS What famous event marked the rise of vicious anti-Semitism in the late nineteenth century, and what characterized the modern anti-Semitism of this period? Did the Jews like the ones shown on this postcard find an acceptable haven in Germany in the period before World War I?

To complete this activity online, go to the Online Study Guide at **bedfordstmartins.com/mckaywest.**

Marxism and the Socialist Movement

Why did the socialist movement grow, and how revolutionary was it? ■

Nationalism served, for better or worse, as a new unifying principle. But what about socialism? Socialist parties, which were generally Marxian parties dedicated to an international proletarian revolution, grew rapidly in these years. Did this mean that national states had failed to gain the support of workers? Certainly, many pros-perous and conservative citizens were greatly troubled by the socialist movement. And numerous historians have portrayed the years before 1914 as a time of increasing conflict between revolutionary socialism, on the one hand, and a nationalist alliance of the conservative aristocracy and the prosperous middle class, on the other.

The Socialist International

The growth of socialist parties after 1871 was phenomenal. (See "Listening to the Past: Adelheid Popp, the Making of a Socialist," page 776.) Neither Bismarck's antisocialist laws nor his extensive social security system checked the growth of the German Social Democratic Party, which espoused the Marxian ideology. By 1912 it had millions of followers—mostly people from the working classes—and was the largest party in the Reichstag. Socialist parties also grew in other countries, though nowhere else with such success. In 1883 Russian exiles in Switzerland founded the Russian Social Democratic Party, and various socialist parties were unified in 1905 in the French Section of the Workers International. Belgium and Austria-Hungary also had strong socialist parties.

As the name of the French party suggests, Marxian socialist parties were eventually linked together in an international organization. Marx believed that "the working men have no country," and he had urged proletarians of all nations to unite. Marx himself played an important role in founding the First International of socialists—the International Working Men's Association. In the following years, he battled successfully to control the organization and used its annual meetings as a means of spreading his realistic, "scientific" doctrines of inevitable socialist revolution. Then Marx enthusiastically embraced the passionate, radical patriotism of the Paris Commune and its terrible conflict with the French National Assembly as a giant step toward socialist revolution. This impetuous action frightened many of his early supporters, especially the more moderate British labor leaders. The First International collapsed.

Yet international proletarian solidarity remained an important objective for Marxists. In 1889, as the individual parties in different countries grew stronger, socialist leaders came together to form the Second International, which lasted until 1914. The International was only a federation of national socialist parties, but it had a great psychological impact. Every three years, delegates from the different parties met to interpret Marxian doctrines and plan coordinated action. May 1 (May Day) was declared an annual international one-day strike, a day of marches and demonstrations. A permanent executive for the International was established. Many feared and many others rejoiced in the growing power of socialism and the Second International.

Unions and Revisionism

Was socialism really radical and revolutionary in these years? On the whole, it was not. As socialist parties grew and attracted large numbers of members, they looked more and more toward gradual change and steady improvement for the working class and less and less toward revolution. The mainstream of European socialism became militantly moderate; that is, socialists increasingly combined radical rhetoric with sober action.

"Greetings from the May Day Festival" Workers participated enthusiastically in the annual one-day strike on May 1 in Stuttgart, Germany, to honor internationalist socialist solidarity, as this postcard suggests. Speeches, picnics, and parades were the order of the day, and workers celebrated their respectability and independent culture. Picture postcards like this one and the one on page 773 developed with railroads, mass travel, and high-speed printing. (akg-images)

Workers themselves were progressively less inclined to follow radical programs. There were several reasons for this. As workers gained the right to vote and to participate politically in the nation-state, they focused their attention more on elections than on revolutions. And as workers won real, tangible benefits, this furthered the process. Workers were also not immune to patriotic education and indoctrination during military service, and many responded positively to drum-beating parades and aggressive foreign policy as they loyally voted for socialists. Nor were workers a unified social group.

Perhaps most important of all, workers' standard of living rose gradually but substantially after 1850 as the promise of the Industrial Revolution was at least partially realized. In Great Britain, for example, workers could buy almost twice as much with their wages in 1906 as in 1850, and most of the increase came after 1870. Workers experienced similar gradual increases in most continental countries after 1850, though much less strikingly in late-developing Russia. The quality of life in urban areas improved dramatically as well. For all these reasons, workers tended more and more to become militantly moderate: they demanded gains, but they were less likely to take to the barricades in pursuit of them.

The growth of labor unions reinforced this trend toward moderation. In the early stages of industrialization, modern unions were generally prohibited by law. A famous law of the French Revolution had declared all guilds and unions illegal in the name of "liberty" in 1791. In Great Britain, attempts by workers to unite were considered criminal conspiracies after 1799. Other countries had similar laws that obviously hampered union development. Unions were considered subversive bodies to be hounded and crushed.

From this sad position workers struggled to escape. Great Britain led the way in 1824 and 1825 when unions won the right to exist but (generally) not the right to strike. After the collapse of Robert Owen's attempt to form one big union in the 1830s (see Chapter 21), new and more practical kinds of unions appeared. Limited primarily to highly skilled workers such as machinists and carpenters, these "new model unions" concentrated on winning better wages and hours through collective bargaining and compromise. This approach helped pave the way to full acceptance in Britain in the 1870s, and after 1890 unions for unskilled workers developed.

Developments in Germany, the most industrialized, socialized, and unionized continental country by 1914, were particularly instructive. German unions were not granted important rights until 1869, and until the anti-socialist law was repealed in 1890, they were frequently harassed by the government as socialist fronts. The result was that as late as 1895, there were only about 270,000 union members in a male industrial workforce of nearly 8 million. Then, with German industrialization still

> **“ Driven by the movement of the working classes which is daily becoming stronger, a social reaction has set in against the exploiting tendencies of capital. ”**
>
> —**Eduard Bernstein**

storming ahead and almost all legal harassment eliminated, union membership skyrocketed, reaching roughly 3 million in 1912.

This great expansion both reflected and influenced the changing character of German unions. Increasingly, unions in Germany focused on bread-and-butter issues—wages, hours, working conditions—rather than on the dissemination of pure socialist doctrine. Genuine collective bargaining, long opposed by socialist intellectuals as a "sellout," was officially recognized as desirable by the German Trade Union Congress in 1899. When employers proved unwilling to bargain, a series of strikes forced them to change their minds. In 1913 alone, over ten thousand collective bargaining agreements benefiting 1.25 million workers were signed.

The German trade unions and their leaders were in fact, if not in name, thoroughgoing revisionists. **Revisionism**—that most awful of sins in the eyes of militant Marxists in the twentieth century—was an effort by various socialists to update Marxian doctrines to reflect the realities of the time. Thus the socialist Eduard Bernstein (1850–1932) argued in 1899 in his *Evolutionary Socialism* that many of Marx's predictions had been proved false.

> **revisionism** An effort by moderate socialists to update Marxian doctrines to reflect the realities of the time.

> *Social conditions have not developed to such an acute opposition of things and classes as is depicted in the Communist Manifesto. . . . The number of members of the possessing classes to-day is not smaller but larger. . . .*
>
> *In all advanced countries we see the privileges of the capitalist bourgeoisie yielding step by step to democratic organizations. Under the influence of this, and driven by the movement of the working classes which is daily becoming stronger, a social reaction has set in against the exploiting tendencies of capital.[6]*

Therefore, Bernstein argued, socialists should reform their doctrines and tactics. They should combine with other progressive forces to win continued evolutionary gains for workers through legislation, unions, and further economic development. These views were denounced as heresy by the German Social Democratic

Adelheid Popp, the Making of a Socialist

LISTENING TO THE PAST

Nationalism and socialism appeared locked in bitter competition in Europe before 1914, but they actually complemented each other in many ways. Both faiths were secular as opposed to religious, and both fostered political awareness. A working person who became interested in politics and developed nationalist beliefs might well convert to socialism at a later date.

This was the case for Adelheid Popp (1869–1939), a self-taught working woman who became an influential socialist leader. Born into a desperately poor working-class family in Vienna and remembering only a "hard and gloomy childhood," she was forced by her parents to quit school at age ten to begin full-time work. She struggled with low-paying piecework for years before she landed a solid factory job, as she recounts in the following selection from her widely read autobiography. Always an avid reader, Popp became the editor of a major socialist newspaper for German working women. She then told her life story so that all working women might share her truth: "Socialism could change and strengthen others, as it did me."

[Finally] I found work again; I took everything that was offered me in order to show my willingness to work, and I passed through much. But at last things became better. [At age fifteen] I was recommended to a great factory which stood in the best repute. Three hundred girls and about fifty men were employed. I was put in a big room where sixty women and girls were at work.

Against the windows stood twelve tables, and at each sat four girls. We had to sort the goods which had been manufactured, others had to count them, and a third set had to brand on them the mark of the firm. We worked from 7 A.M. to 7 P.M. We had an hour's rest at noon, half-an-hour in the afternoon. . . . I had never yet been paid so much. . . .

I seemed to myself to be almost rich. . . . [Yet] from the women of this factory one can judge how sad and full of deprivation is the lot of a factory worker. In none of the neighbouring factories were the wages so high; we were envied everywhere. Parents considered themselves fortunate if they could get their daughters of fourteen in there on leaving school. . . . And even here, in this paradise, all were badly nourished. Those who stayed at the factory for the dinner hour would buy themselves for a few pennies a sausage or the leavings of a cheese shop. . . . In spite of all the diligence and economy, every one was poor, and trembled at the thought of losing her work. All humbled themselves, and suffered the worst injustice from the foremen, not to risk losing this good work, not to be without food. . . .

I did not only read novels and tales; I had begun . . . to read the classics and other good books. I also began to take an interest in public events. . . . I was not democratically inclined. I was full of enthusiasm then for emperors, and kings and highly placed personages played no small part in my fancies. . . . I bought myself a strict Catholic paper, that criticised very adversely the workers' movement, which was attracting notice. Its aim was to educate in a patriotic and religious direction. . . . I took the warmest interest in the events that occurred in the royal families, and I took the death of the Crown Prince of Austria so much to heart that I wept a whole day. . . . Political events [also] held me in suspense. The possibility of a war with Russia roused my patriotic enthusiasm. I saw my brother already returning from the battlefield covered with glory. . . .

When a particularly strong anti-Semitic feeling was noticeable in political life, I sympathised with it for a time. A broad sheet, "How Israel Attained Power and Sovereignty over all the Nations of the Earth," fascinated me. . . .

About this time an Anarchist group was active. Some mysterious murders which had taken place were ascribed to the Anarchists, and the police made use of them to oppress the rising workmen's movement. . . . I followed the trial of the Anarchists with passionate sympathy. I read all the speeches, and because, as always happens, Social Democrats, whom the authorities really wanted to attack, were among the accused,

Party and later by the entire Second International. Yet the revisionist, gradualist approach continued to gain the tacit acceptance of many German socialists, particularly in the trade unions.

Moderation found followers elsewhere. In France the great socialist leader Jean Jaurès (1859–1914) formally repudiated revisionist doctrines in order to establish a unified socialist party, but he remained at heart a gradualist and optimistic secular humanist. Questions of revolution also split Russian Marxists.

Socialist parties before 1914 had clear-cut national characteristics. Russians and socialists in the Austro-Hungarian Empire tended to be the most radical. The German party talked revolution and practiced reformism, greatly influenced by its enormous trade-union movement. The French party talked revolution and tried

1890 engraving of a meeting of workers in Berlin.
(Bildarchiv Preussischer Kulturbesitz/Art Resource, NY)

I learned their views. I became full of enthusiasm. Every single Social Democrat . . . seemed to me a hero. . . . There was unrest among the workers . . . and demonstrations of protest followed. When these were repeated the military entered the "threatened" streets. . . . In the evenings I rushed in the greatest excitement from the factory to the scene of the disturbance. The military did not frighten me; I only left the place when it was "cleared."

Later on my mother and I lived with one of my brothers who had married. Friends came to him, among them some intelligent workmen. One of these workmen was particularly intelligent, and . . . could talk on many subjects. He was the first Social Democrat I knew. He brought me many books, and explained to me the difference between Anarchism and Socialism. I heard from him, also for the first time, what a republic was, and in spite of my former enthusiasm for royal dynasties, I also declared myself in favour of a republican form of government. I saw everything so near and so clearly, that I actually counted the weeks which must still elapse before the revolution of state and society would take place. From this workman I received the first Social Democratic party organ. . . . I first learned from it to understand and judge of my own lot. I learned to see that all I had suffered was the result not of a divine ordinance, but of an unjust organization of society. . . .

In the factory I became another woman. . . . I told my [female] comrades all that I had read of the workers' movement. Formerly I had often told stories when they had begged me for them. But instead of narrating . . . the fate of some queen, I now held forth on oppression and exploitation. I told of accumulated wealth in the hands of a few, and introduced as a contrast the shoemakers who had no shoes and the tailors who had no clothes. On breaks I read aloud the articles in the Social Democratic paper and explained what Socialism was as far as I understood it. . . . [While I was reading] it often happened that one of the clerks passing by shook his head and said to another clerk: "The girl speaks like a man." 》

Source: Slightly adapted from A. Popp, *The Autobiography of a Working Woman*, trans. E. C. Harvey (Chicago: F. G. Browne, 1913), pp. 29, 34–35, 39, 66–69, 71, 74, 82–90.

QUESTIONS FOR ANALYSIS

1. How did Popp describe and interpret work in the factory?

2. According to her autobiography, what accounts for Popp's nationalist sentiments early on? How and why did she become a Social Democrat?

3. Was Popp likely to lead other working women to socialism by reading them articles from socialist newspapers? Why or why not?

to practice it, unrestrained by a trade-union movement that was both very weak and very radical. In England the socialist but non-Marxian Labour Party, reflecting the well-established union movement, was formally committed to gradual reform. In Spain and Italy, Marxian socialism was very weak. There anarchism, seeking to smash the state rather than the bourgeoisie, dominated radical thought and action.

In short, socialist policies and doctrines varied from country to country. Socialism itself was to a large extent "nationalized" behind the imposing façade of international unity. This helps explain why when war came in 1914, almost all socialist leaders and most workers supported their governments.

LOOKING BACK LOOKING AHEAD

IN 1900, THE TRIUMPH of nationalism in Europe seemed almost complete. Only in eastern Europe, in the three aging multinational empires of Austria-Hungary, Russia, and the Ottomans, did several nationalities still struggle to form their own states. Elsewhere the ethnically unified nation-state, resting solidly upon the continent's ongoing industrialization and its emerging urban society, governed with the consent and even the devotion of its citizens. Responsive and capable of tackling many practical problems, the European nation-state of 1900 was in part the realization of ideologues and patriots like Mazzini and the middle-class liberals active in the unsuccessful revolutions of 1848. Yet whereas early nationalists had envisioned a Europe of free peoples and international peace, the nationalists of 1900 had been nurtured in the traditional competition between European states and the wars of unification in the 1850s and 1860s. This generation of nationalists reveled in the strength of their unity, and the nation-state became a system of power.

Thus after 1870, at the same time the responsive nation-state improved city life and brought social benefits to ordinary people, Europe's leading countries also projected raw power throughout the world. In the expanding colonies of Asia and Africa, the nations of Britain, France, Germany, and Russia seized territory, fought brutal colonial wars, and built authoritarian empires. Moreover, in Europe itself the universal faith in nationalism, which usually reduced social tensions within states, promoted a bitter, almost Darwinian, competition between states. Thus European nationalism threatened the very progress and unity it had helped to build. In 1914, the power of unified nation-states would turn on itself, unleashing the First World War and doling out self-inflicted wounds of enormous proportions to all of Europe's peoples.

CHAPTER REVIEW

■ How did Napoleon III seek to reconcile popular and conservative forces in an authoritarian nation-state? (p. 750)

Elected president of France in 1848 and then named emperor in 1852, Napoleon III combined authoritarian rule with economic growth and positive measures for the poor. Believing that representative government got in the way of reform and progress, Napoleon III aimed to serve the people directly. He also maintained widespread support by allowing his regime to evolve in a democratic direction, staying in power until France was defeated by Prussia in 1870.

■ How did the process of unification in Italy and Germany create conservative nation-states? (p. 752)

In Italy, Cavour joined traditional diplomacy and war against Austria with nationalist uprisings in central Italy to expand the constitutional monarchy of Sardinia-Piedmont. Cavour then called on Garibaldi's revolutionary patriotism to kindle peasant revolt in southern Italy and succeeded in merging the south and the north together in a conservative nation-state under Victor Emmanuel. In Prussia Bismarck also combined traditional statecraft with national feeling. Ruling without the consent of parliament and reorganizing the army, Bismarck succeeded in making Prussia the dominant

German state and in driving Austria out of German affairs in 1866. War with France completed the unification process, expanding the power of Prussia and its king in a new German Empire, and instilling in all Germans a strong sense of national pride.

■ In what ways did the United States experience nation building? (p. 758)

The question of slavery divided the early Northern and Southern U.S. states for both economic and political reasons. With westward expansion in the mid-nineteenth century, debates over slavery came to the fore, causing the Southern states to secede and leading to a civil war. The Northern states prevailed, and the Union was preserved. The postwar years saw unique national characteristics arise and seemed to confirm America's destiny as a great world power.

■ What steps did Russia and the Ottoman Turks take toward modernization, and how successful were they? (p. 759)

In autocratic Russia, defeat in the Crimean War posed a regime-threatening crisis, which led to the emancipation of the serfs and economic modernization that featured railroad building, military improvements, and industrialization. Political reform was limited, however, and even after the revolution of 1905 led to a popularly elected Duma, the tsar retained very great power. The Ottoman Empire also sought to modernize to protect the state, but it was considerably less successful. Faced with resistance by Christian nationalists and conservative Muslims, and economically hindered by Western imperialism, the modernization efforts failed to salvage the Ottoman sultan's progressive regime.

Why after 1871 did ordinary citizens feel a growing loyalty to their governments? (p. 766)

After 1871 nationalism — the commitment to the nation-state — became the general European creed, nurtured in large part by patriotic education and fueled by foreign wars and increasingly advanced militaries. In addition, most states enacted universal male suffrage and electoral politics, providing citizens with a greater sense of belonging. Representative governments also produced specific social and economic improvements, such as state-sponsored pensions, protective tariffs, and a rising standard of living, that benefited ordinary citizens.

Why did the socialist movement grow, and how revolutionary was it? (p. 773)

The socialist movement grew because it became the champion of working-class interests in the emerging urban society and in domestic politics. Socialist leaders in many countries also supported international revolutionary Marxism in theory, but in practice they usually concentrated on bread-and-butter gains for union members. Thus pre-1914 socialism was militantly moderate and not very revolutionary.

Suggested Reading

Berend, Ivan T. *History Derailed: Central and Eastern Europe in the Long Nineteenth Century.* 2003. Focuses on industrialization and its consequences.

Clyman, Toby W., and Judith Vowles, eds. *Russia Through Women's Eyes: Autobiographies from Tsarist Russia.* 1999. An eye-opening collection detailing women's experiences in Russia.

Fink, Carole. *Defending the Rights of Others: The Great Powers, the Jews, and the International Protection, 1878–1938.* 2004. Skilled consideration of the cruelty and tragedy of ethnic conflict and minority oppression.

Finley, C. *The Turks in World History.* 2005. An exciting reconsideration of the Turks in long-term perspective.

Geary, Dick, ed. *Labour and Socialist Movements in Europe Before 1914.* 1989. An excellent collection that examines labor movements in several different countries.

Grenville, J. A. S. *Europe Reshaped, 1850–1978,* 2d ed. 2000. A careful analysis of political developments in the leading states.

Hennock, E. P. *The Origins of the Welfare State in England and Germany, 1850–1914.* 2007. Compares Germany's statist approach with England's response to demands from below.

Hobsbawm, Eric. *The Age of Empire, 1875–1914.* 1987. A classic interpretive work.

Kitchen, Martin. *The Cambridge Illustrated History of Germany.* 1996. Features handsome pictures and a readable text.

Ridley, Jasper. *Phoenix: Garibaldi.* 2001. A thorough study of the world-renowned revolutionary nationalist.

Schulze, Hagen, and William E. Yuill. *States, Nations and Nationalism: From the Middle Ages to the Present.* 1996. An important study that explores the resurgence of European nationalism since the fall of communism.

Slezkine, Yuri. *The Jewish Century.* 2004. A brilliant interpretation of Jewish achievement in the modern era.

Tombs, Robert. *France, 1814–1914.* 1996. An impressive survey with a useful bibliography.

Vital, David. *A People Apart: The Jews in Europe, 1789–1939.* 1999. An engaging and judicious survey.

Key Terms

Red Shirts (p. 754)
Homestead Act (p. 758)
modernization (p. 759)
Bloody Sunday (p. 761)
October Manifesto (p. 764)
Duma (p. 764)
Tanzimat (p. 764)
Young Turks (p.765)
Reichstag (p. 767)
Kulturkampf (p. 767)
Dreyfus affair (p. 769)
People's Budget (p. 769)
Zionism (p. 771)
revisionism (p. 775)

Notes

1. H. Schulze, *States, Nations and Nationalism: From the Middle Ages to the Present* (Oxford, U.K.: Blackwell, 1994), pp. 222–223, 246–247.
2. Quoted by J. McKay, *Pioneers for Profit: Foreign Entrepreneurship and Russian Industrialization, 1885–1913* (Chicago: University of Chicago Press, 1970), p. 11.
3. E. Van Dyck, *Report upon the Capitulations of the Ottoman Empire Since the Year 1150* (Washington, DC: United States Printing Office, 1881, 1882), part 1, pp. 106–107.
4. W. Dawson, *Bismarck and State Socialism* (London: Swan Sonnenschen & Co., 1890), pp. 63–64.
5. R. Seltzer, *Jewish People, Jewish Thought: The Jewish Experience in History* (New York: Macmillan, 1980), p. 533.
6. Eduard Bernstein, *Evolutionary Socialism: A Criticism and Affirmation*, trans. Edith Harvey (New York: B. W. Huebsch, 1909), pp. x–xvi, quoted in J. H. Hexter et al., *The Traditions of the Western World* (Chicago: Rand McNally, 1967), pp. 797–798.

For practice quizzes and other study tools, visit the Online Study Guide at **bedfordstmartins.com/mckaywest**.

For primary sources from this period, see ***Sources of Western Society*, Second Edition**.

For Web sites, images, and documents related to topics in this chapter, visit Make History at **bedfordstmartins.com/mckaywest**.

25

The West and the World

1815–1914

While industrialization and nationalism were transforming urban and agricultural life throughout Europe, Western society itself was reshaping the world. At the peak of its power and pride, the West entered the third and most dynamic phase of the aggressive expansion that had begun with the Crusades and continued with the great discoveries and the rise of seaborne colonial empires. An ever-growing stream of products and ideas flowed out of Europe in the nineteenth century. Hardly any corner of the globe was left untouched. At the same time millions of Europeans picked up stakes and emigrated abroad, primarily to North and South America but also to Australia, North and South Africa, and Asiatic Russia.

The most spectacular manifestations of Western expansion came in the late nineteenth century when the leading European nations established or enlarged their far-flung political empires. This political annexation of territory in the 1880s — the "new imperialism," as it is often called by historians — was the capstone of Europe's underlying economic and technological transformation. More directly, Europe's new imperialism rested on a formidable combination of superior military might and strong authoritarian rule, and it posed a brutal challenge to African and Asian peoples. Different societies met this Western challenge in different ways and with changing tactics, as we shall see. Nevertheless, by 1914 non-Western elites in many lands were rallying their peoples and leading an anti-imperialist struggle for dignity and genuine independence that would eventually triumph after 1945. ■

Living in the Age of New Imperialism. The late nineteenth century witnessed the spread of European empires abroad and the intertwining of the lives of Europeans and native populations. Here European tourists look on at the well-tended trees and handsome buildings of Cairo's new quarter, a result of European involvement in modernizing the city.

CHAPTER PREVIEW

Industrialization and the World Economy
■ What were some of the global consequences of European industrialization between 1815 and 1914?

The Great Migration
■ How was massive migration an integral part of Western expansion?

Western Imperialism, 1880–1914
■ How and why after 1875 did European nations rush to build political empires in Africa and Asia?

Responding to Western Imperialism
■ What was the general pattern of non-Western responses to Western expansion, and how did India, Japan, and China meet the imperialist challenge?

Industrialization and the World Economy

What were some of the global consequences of European industrialization between 1815 and 1914? ■

The Industrial Revolution created, first in Great Britain and then in continental Europe and North America, a tremendously dynamic economic system. In the course of the nineteenth century, that system was extended across the face of the earth. Some of this extension into non-Western areas was peaceful and beneficial for all concerned, for the West had many products and techniques the rest of the world desired. If peaceful methods failed, however, Europeans used their superior military power to force non-Western nations to open their doors to Western economic interests. In general, Westerners fashioned the global economic system so that the largest share of the ever-increasing gains from trade, technology, and migration flowed to the West and its propertied classes.

The Rise of Global Inequality

The Industrial Revolution in Europe marked a momentous turning point in human history. Those regions of the world that industrialized in the nineteenth century (mainly Europe and North America) increased their wealth and power enormously in comparison to those that did not. A gap between the industrializing regions and the nonindustrializing or **Third World** regions (mainly Africa, Asia, and Latin America) opened up and grew steadily throughout the nineteenth century. Moreover, this pattern of uneven global development became institutionalized, or built into the structure of the world economy. Thus we evolved a "lopsided world," a world of rich lands and poor.

Third World A term that refers to the non-industrialized nations of Africa, Asia, and Latin America as a single unit.

In recent years historical economists have been charting the long-term evolution of this gap, and Figure 25.1 summarizes the findings of one important study. Three main points stand out. First, in 1750 the average standard of living was no higher in Europe as a whole than in the rest of the world. Second, it was industrialization that opened the gaps in average wealth and well-being among countries and regions. Third, income per person stagnated in the Third World before 1913, in striking contrast to the industrializing regions. Only after 1945, in the era of political independence and decolonization, did Third World countries finally make some real economic progress, beginning in their turn the critical process of industrialization.

The rise of these enormous income disparities, which are poignant indicators of equal disparities in food and

British Ships and Shipbuilders The British continued to dominate international trade before the First World War. This handsome membership certificate of the British shipbuilders union features the vessels that tied the world together economically. Britain's thriving shipbuilding industry was concentrated in southern Scotland. (Trade Union Congress, London/ The Bridgeman Art Library)

clothing, health and education, life expectancy and general material well-being, has generated a great deal of debate. One school of interpretation stresses that the West used science, technology, capitalist organization, and even its critical worldview to create its wealth and greater physical well-being. Another school argues that the West used its political and economic power to steal much of its riches, continuing in the nineteenth and twentieth centuries the rapacious colonialism born of the era of expansion. Because these issues are complex and there are few simple answers, it is helpful to consider them in the context of world trade in the nineteenth century.

The World Market

Commerce between nations has always stimulated economic development. In the nineteenth century, Europe directed an enormous increase in international commerce. Great Britain took the lead in cultivating export markets for its booming industrial output, as British manufacturers looked first to Europe and then around the world.

Take the case of cotton textiles. By 1820 Britain was exporting 50 percent of its production. Europe bought 50 percent of these cotton textile exports, while India bought only 6 percent. Then as European nations and the United States erected protective tariff barriers and promoted domestic industry, British cotton textile manufacturers aggressively sought and found other foreign markets in non-Western areas. By 1850 India was buying 25 percent and Europe only 16 percent of a much larger total. As a British colony, India could not raise tariffs to protect its ancient cotton textile industry, and thousands of Indian weavers lost their livelihoods.

In addition to its dominance in the export market, Britain was also the world's largest importer of goods. From the repeal of the Corn Laws in 1846 (see Chapter 22) to the outbreak of World War I in 1914, Britain remained the world's emporium, where not only agricultural products and raw materials but also manufactured goods entered freely. Free access to Britain's market stimulated the development of mines and plantations in many non-Western areas.

International trade also grew as transportation systems improved. Wherever railroads were built, they drastically reduced transportation costs, opened new economic opportunities, and called forth new skills and attitudes. Much of the railroad construction undertaken in Latin America, Asia, and Africa connected seaports with inland cities and regions, as opposed to linking and

developing cities and regions within a given country. Thus railroads dovetailed admirably with Western economic interests, facilitating the inflow and sale of Western manufactured goods and the export and the development of local raw materials.

The power of steam revolutionized transportation by sea as well as by land. Steam power began to supplant sails on the oceans of the world in the late 1860s. Passenger and freight rates tumbled as ship design

Chronology

Figure 25.1 The Growth of Average Income per Person in the Third World, Developed Countries, and Great Britain, 1750–1970 Growth is given in 1960 U.S. dollars and prices.

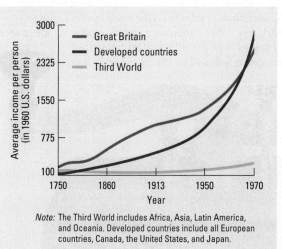

Note: The Third World includes Africa, Asia, Latin America, and Oceania. Developed countries include all European countries, Canada, the United States, and Japan.

became more sophisticated, and the intercontinental shipment of low-priced raw materials became feasible. The opening of the Suez and Panama Canals shortened global transport time considerably. In addition, port facilities were modernized to make loading and unloading cheaper, faster, and more dependable.

The revolution in land and sea transportation encouraged European entrepreneurs to open up vast new territories around the world and develop agricultural products and raw materials there for sale in Europe. Improved transportation enabled Asia, Africa, and Latin America to ship not only the traditional tropical products — spices, tea, sugar, coffee — but also new raw materials for industry, such as jute, rubber, cotton, and coconut oil.

New communications systems directed the flow of goods across global networks. Transoceanic telegraph cables inaugurated rapid communications among the financial centers of the world. While a British tramp freighter steamed from Calcutta to New York, a broker in London was arranging by telegram for it to carry an American cargo to Australia. The same communications network conveyed world commodity prices instantaneously.

As their economies grew, Europeans began to make massive foreign investments beginning about 1840. By the outbreak of World War I in 1914, Europeans had invested more than $40 billion abroad. Great Britain, France, and Germany were the principal investing countries (Map 25.1). The great gap between rich and poor within Europe meant that the wealthy and moderately well-to-do could and did send great sums abroad in search of interest and dividends.

A Revolution in Communications The development of the electromagnetic telegraph in the 1840s permitted rapid long-distance communications for the first time in history. Governments quickly saw the telegraph's revolutionary implications for waging war and invested in the building of telegraph systems. Business people then used the telegraph and underwater cables to tie the world market together. The "Camelback" key shown here was commonly used in Europe to send the "dots and dashes" that trained operators transcribed into messages. (John D. Jenkins, www.sparksmuseum.com)

Most of the capital exported did not go to European colonies or protectorates in Asia and Africa. About three-quarters of total European investment went to other European countries, the United States and Canada, Australia and New Zealand, and Latin America. Europe found its most profitable opportunities for investment in construction of the railroads, ports, and utilities that were necessary to settle and develop the lands in such places as Australia and the Americas. By lending money for a foreign railroad, Europeans also enabled white settlers to buy European rails and locomotives and to develop sources of cheap food and raw materials. Much of this investment was peaceful and mutually beneficial for lenders and borrowers. The victims were Native American Indians and Australian aborigines, who were decimated by the diseases, liquor, and weapons of an aggressively expanding Western society.

The Opening of China

Europe's relatively peaceful development of robust offshoots in sparsely populated North America, Australia, and much of Latin America absorbed huge quantities of goods, investments, and migrants. Yet Europe's economic and cultural penetration of old, densely populated civilizations was also profoundly significant. With such civilizations Europeans also increased their trade and profit, and they were prepared to use force, if necessary, to attain their desires. This was what happened in China, a striking example of the pattern of intrusion into non-Western lands.

Traditional Chinese civilization was self-sufficient. For centuries China had sent more goods and inventions to Europe than it had received, and this was still the case in the early nineteenth century. Trade with Europe was carefully regulated by the Chinese imperial government — the Qing (ching), or Manchu, Dynasty — which required all foreign merchants to live in the southern port of Guangzhou (Canton) and to buy and sell only to licensed Chinese merchants. Practices considered harmful to Chinese interests were strictly forbidden.

For years the little community of foreign merchants in Canton had to accept the Chinese system. By the 1820s, however, the dominant group, the British, were flexing their muscles. Moreover, in the smoking of opium — that "destructive and ensnaring vice" denounced by Chinese decrees — British merchants had found something that the Chinese really wanted. Grown legally in British-occupied India, opium was smuggled into China, where its use and sale were illegal. Huge profits and growing addiction led to a rapid increase in sales. By 1836 the aggressive goal of the British merchants in Canton was an independent British colony in China and "safe and unrestricted liberty" in their Chinese trade. Spurred on by economic motives, they pres-

Map 25.1 European Investment to 1914 Foreign investment grew rapidly after 1850, and Britain, France, and Germany were the major investing nations. As this map suggests, most European investment was not directed to the African and Asian areas seized by the new imperialism after 1880.

sured the British government to take decisive action and enlisted the support of other British manufacturers with visions of vast Chinese markets to be opened.

At the same time, the Qing government decided that the **opium trade** had to be stamped out. It was ruining the people and stripping the empire of its silver, which was going to British merchants to pay for the opium. The government began to prosecute Chinese drug dealers vigorously, and in 1839 it sent special envoy Lin Zexu to Canton to deal with the crisis. Lin Zexu dealt harshly with Chinese who purchased opium, and he seized the opium stores of the British merchants, who then withdrew to the barren island of Hong Kong. He sent a famous letter justifying his policy to Queen Victoria in London. (See "Listening to the Past: Lin Zexu and Yamagata Aritomo, Confronting Western Imperialism," page 808.) Explaining the government's determination to stop the opium trade, Lin Zexu also wrote: "Our great unified Qing Empire regards itself as responsible for the habits and morals of its subjects and cannot rest content to see any of them become victims of a deadly poison."[1]

The wealthy, well-connected British merchants appealed to their allies in London for support, and the British government responded. It also wanted free, unregulated trade with China, as well as the establishment of diplomatic relations on the European model, complete with ambassadors, embassies, and published treaties. Using troops from India and being in control of the seas, Britain occupied several coastal cities and forced China to give in to British demands. In the Treaty of Nanking in 1842, the imperial government was required to cede the island of Hong Kong to Britain forever, pay an indemnity of $100 million, and open up four large cities to unlimited foreign trade with low tariffs.

> **opium trade** The sale of opium — grown legally in British-occupied India — by British merchants in China, where the drug was illegal; it became a destructive and ensnaring vice of the Chinese.

With Britain's new power over Chinese commerce, the opium trade flourished, and Hong Kong developed rapidly as an Anglo-Chinese enclave. China continued to accept foreign diplomats in Beijing (Peking), the imperial capital, but disputes over trade between China and the Western powers continued. Finally, there was a second round of foreign attack between 1856 and 1860, culminating in the occupation of Beijing by seventeen thousand British and French troops and the intentional

Britain and China at War Britain capitalized on its overwhelming naval superiority in its war against China, as shown in this British painting celebrating a dramatic moment in a crucial 1841 battle near Guangzhou. Having received a direct hit from a steam-powered British ironclad, a Chinese sailing ship explodes into a wall of flame. The Chinese lost eleven ships and five hundred men in the two-hour engagement; the British suffered only minor damage. (National Maritime Museum, London)

burning of the emperor's summer palace. Another round of harsh treaties gave European merchants and missionaries greater privileges and protection and forced the Chinese to accept trade and investment on unfavorable terms for several more cities. Thus did Europeans use military aggression to blow a hole in the wall of Chinese seclusion and open the country to foreign trade and foreign ideas.

Japan and the United States

China's neighbor Japan had its own highly distinctive civilization and even less use for Westerners. European traders and missionaries first arrived in Japan in the sixteenth century. By 1640 Japan had reacted quite negatively to their presence. The government decided to seal off the country from all European influences in order to preserve traditional Japanese culture and society. When American and British whaling ships began to appear off Japanese coasts almost two hundred years later, the policy of exclusion was still in effect. An order of 1825 commanded Japanese officials to "drive away foreign vessels without second thought."[2]

Japan's unbending isolation seemed hostile and barbaric to the West, particularly to the United States. It complicated the practical problems of shipwrecked American sailors and the provisioning of whaling ships and China traders sailing in the eastern Pacific. It also thwarted the hope of trade and profit. Moreover, Americans shared the self-confidence and dynamism of expanding Western society, and they felt destined to play a great role in the Pacific. To Americans it seemed the duty of the United States to force the Japanese to share their ports and behave as a "civilized" nation.

After several unsuccessful American attempts to establish commercial relations with Japan, Commodore Matthew Perry steamed into Edo (now Tokyo) Bay in 1853. Relying on **gunboat diplomacy** and threatening to attack, Perry demanded diplomatic negotiations with the emperor. Japan entered a grave crisis. Some Japanese warriors urged resistance, but senior officials realized how defenseless their cities were against naval bombardment. Shocked and humiliated, they reluctantly signed a treaty with the United States that opened two ports and permitted trade. Over the next five years, more treaties spelled

gunboat diplomacy The use or threat of military force to coerce a government into economic or political agreements.

out the rights and privileges of the Western nations and their merchants in Japan. Japan was "opened." What the British had done in China with war, the Americans had done in Japan with the threat of war.

Western Penetration of Egypt

Egypt's experience illustrates not only the explosive power of the expanding European economy and society but also their seductive appeal. European involvement in Egypt also led to a new model of formal political control, which European powers applied widely in Africa and Asia after 1882.

Of great importance in African and Middle Eastern history, the ancient land of the pharaohs had since 525 B.C.E. been ruled by a succession of foreigners, most recently by the Ottoman Turks. In 1798 French armies under young General Napoleon Bonaparte invaded the Egyptian part of the Ottoman Empire and occupied the territory for three years. Into the power vacuum left by the French withdrawal stepped an extraordinary Albanian-born Turkish general, Muhammad Ali (1769–1849).

First appointed governor of Egypt in 1805 by the Turkish sultan, Muhammad Ali set out to build his own state on the strength of a large, powerful army organized along European lines. He drafted for the first time the illiterate, despised peasant masses of Egypt, and he hired French and Italian army officers to train these raw recruits and their Turkish officers. The government was also reformed, new lands were cultivated, and communications were improved. By the end of his reign in 1848, Muhammad Ali had established a strong and virtually independent Egyptian state, to be ruled by his family on a hereditary basis within the Turkish empire.

Muhammad Ali's policies of modernization attracted large numbers of Europeans to the banks of the Nile. The port city of Alexandria had more than fifty thousand Europeans by 1864. Europeans served not only as army officers but also as engineers, doctors, government officials, and police officers. Others turned to trade, finance, and shipping.

To pay for his ambitious plans, Muhammad Ali encouraged the development of commercial agriculture. This development had profound implications. Egyptian peasants were poor but largely self-sufficient, growing food for their own consumption on state-owned lands allotted to them by tradition. Faced with the possibility of export agriculture, high-ranking officials and members of Muhammad Ali's family began carving large private landholdings out of the state domain. The new landlords made the peasants their tenants and forced them to grow cash crops such as cotton and rice geared to European markets. Thus Egyptian landowners "modernized" agriculture, but to the detriment of peasant well-being.

These trends continued under Muhammad Ali's grandson Ismail (ihs-MAH-eel), who in 1863 began his sixteen-year rule as Egypt's khedive (kuh-DEEV), or prince. Educated at France's leading military academy, Ismail was a westernizing autocrat. The large irrigation networks he promoted caused cotton production and exports to Europe to boom, and with his support the

Egyptian Travel Guide Ismail's efforts to transform Cairo were fairly successful. As a result European tourists could more easily visit the country that their governments dominated. Ordinary Europeans were lured to exotic lands by travel books like this colorful "Official Guide" to an exhibition on Cairo held in Berlin. (Private Collection/Archives Charmet/The Bridgeman Art Library)

" My country is no longer in Africa, we now form part of Europe. "

—ISMAIL

Suez Canal was completed by a French company in 1869. The Arabic of the Egyptian masses replaced the Turkish of the foreign conquerors as the official language; young Egyptians educated in Europe spread new skills; and Cairo acquired modern boulevards and Western hotels. As Ismail proudly declared, "My country is no longer in Africa, we now form part of Europe."[3]

The Suez Canal, 1869

Yet Ismail was too impatient and reckless. His projects were enormously expensive, and by 1876 Egypt owed foreign bondholders a colossal debt that it could not pay. France and Great Britain intervened and forced Ismail to appoint French and British commissioners to oversee Egyptian finances so that the Egyptian debt would be paid in full. This momentous decision marked a sharp break with the past. Throughout most of the nineteenth century, Europeans had used military might and political force primarily to make sure that non-Western lands would accept European trade and investment. Now Europeans were going to determine the state budget and effectively rule Egypt.

Foreign financial control evoked a violent nationalistic reaction among Egyptian religious leaders, young intellectuals, and army officers. In 1879, under the leadership of Colonel Ahmed Arabi, they formed the Egyptian Nationalist Party. Continuing diplomatic pressure, which forced Ismail to abdicate in favor of his weak son, Tewfiq (r. 1879–1892), resulted in bloody anti-European riots in Alexandria in 1882. A number of Europeans were killed, and Tewfiq and his court had to flee to British ships for safety. When the British fleet bombarded Alexandria, more riots swept the country, and Colonel Arabi led a revolt. But a British expeditionary force put down the rebellion and occupied all of Egypt.

The British said their occupation was temporary, but British armies remained in Egypt until 1956. They maintained the façade of the khedive's government as

great migration The mass movement of people from Europe in the nineteenth century; one reason that the West's impact on the world was so powerful and many-sided.

an autonomous province of the Ottoman Empire, but the khedive was a mere puppet. British rule did result in tax reforms and somewhat better conditions for peasants, while foreign bondholders received their interest and Egyptian nationalists nursed their injured pride.

British rule in Egypt also provided a new model for European expansion in densely populated lands. Such expansion was based on military force, political domination, and a self-justifying ideology of beneficial reform. This model was to predominate until 1914. Thus did Europe's Industrial Revolution lead to tremendous political as well as economic expansion throughout the world after 1880.

The Great Migration

How was massive migration an integral part of Western expansion? ■

A poignant human drama was interwoven with economic expansion: millions of people pulled up stakes and left their ancestral lands in the course of history's greatest migration. To millions of ordinary people for whom the opening of China and the interest on the Egyptian debt had not the slightest significance, this great movement was the central experience in the saga of Western expansion. It was, in part, because of this **great migration** that the West's impact on the world in the nineteenth century was so powerful and many-sided.

The Pressure of Population

In the early eighteenth century, the growth of European population entered its third and decisive stage, which continued unabated until the early twentieth century (Figure 25.2). Birthrates eventually declined in the nineteenth century, but so did death rates, mainly because of the rising standard of living and secondarily because of the revolution in medicine (see Chapter 23). Thus the population of Europe (including Asiatic Russia) more than doubled, from approximately 188 million in 1800 to roughly 432 million in 1900.

These figures actually understate Europe's population explosion, for between 1815 and 1932 more than 60 million people left Europe. The migrants went primarily to the "areas of European settlement"—North and South America, Australia, New Zealand, and Siberia—where they contributed to a rapid growth in numbers. Since population grew more slowly in Africa and Asia than in Europe and the Americas, as Figure 25.2 shows, Europeans and people of predominately European origin jumped from about 24 percent of the world's total in 1800 to about 38 percent on the eve of World War I.

The growing number of Europeans provided further impetus for Western expansion, and it was a driving

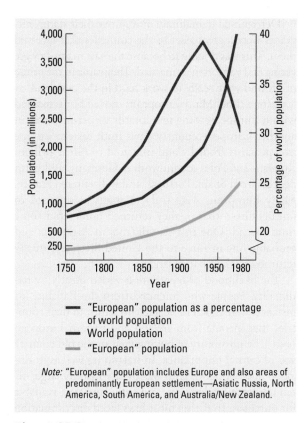

Figure 25.2 The Increase of European and World Populations, 1750–1980 Europeans and peoples of predominantly European origin became a growing percentage of total world population between roughly 1750 and 1914.

force behind emigration. As in the eighteenth century, the rapid increase in numbers put pressure on the land and led to land hunger and relative overpopulation in area after area. In most countries, migration increased twenty years after a rapid growth in population, as many children of the baby boom grew up, saw little available land and few opportunities, and migrated. This pattern was especially prevalent when rapid population increase predated extensive industrial development, which offered the best long-term hope of creating jobs within the country and reducing poverty. Thus millions of country folk went abroad as well as to nearby cities in search of work and economic opportunity.

Before looking at the people who migrated, let us consider three facts. First, the number of men and women who left Europe increased rapidly at the end of the nineteenth century and leading up to World War I. As Figure 25.3 shows, more than 11 million left in the first decade of the twentieth century, over five times the number departing in the 1850s. The outflow of migrants was clearly a defining characteristic of European society for the entire period.

Second, different countries had very different patterns of movement. As Figure 25.3 also shows, people left Britain and Ireland (which are not distinguished in the British figures) in large numbers from the 1840s on. This emigration reflected not only rural poverty but also the movement of skilled industrial technicians and the preferences shown to British migrants in the British Empire. Ultimately, about one-third of all European

Figure 25.3 Emigration from Europe by Decades, 1851–1940 Emigration from Europe grew greatly until the outbreak of World War I in 1914, and it declined rapidly thereafter.

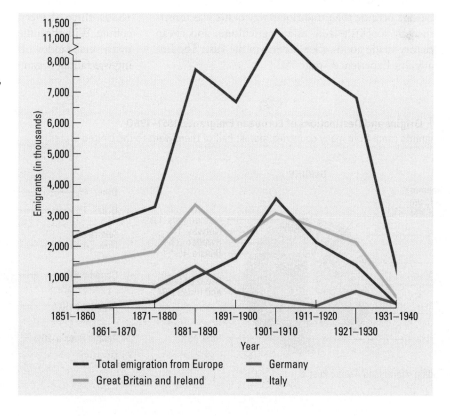

migrants between 1840 and 1920 came from the British Isles. German migration was quite different. It grew irregularly after about 1830, reaching a first peak in the early 1850s and another in the early 1880s. Thereafter it declined rapidly, for Germany's rapid industrialization was providing adequate jobs at home. This pattern contrasted sharply with that of Italy. More and more Italians left the country right up to 1914, reflecting severe problems in Italian villages and relatively slow industrial growth. Thus migration patterns mirrored social and economic conditions in the various European countries and provinces.

Third, although the United States did absorb the largest overall number of European migrants, fewer than half of all migrants went to the United States. Asiatic Russia, Canada, Argentina, Brazil, Australia, and New Zealand also attracted large numbers, as Figure 25.4 shows. Moreover, migrants accounted for a larger proportion of the total population in Argentina, Brazil, and Canada than it did in the United States. The common American assumption that European migration meant migration to the United States is quite inaccurate.

European Migrants

What kind of people left Europe, and what were their reasons for doing so? The European migrant was generally an energetic small farmer or skilled artisan trying hard to stay ahead of poverty, not a desperately impoverished landless peasant or urban proletarian. These small peasant landowners and village craftsmen typically left Europe because their traditional way of life was threatened by too little land, estate agriculture, and cheap factory-made goods. (See "Living in the Past: The Immigrant Experience," page 792.)

Determined to maintain or improve their status, migrants were a great asset to the countries that received them. This was doubly so because the vast majority were young and very often unmarried. They came in the prime of life and were ready to work hard in the new land, at least for a time. Many Europeans moved but remained within Europe, settling temporarily or permanently in another European country. Jews from eastern Europe and peasants from Ireland migrated to Great Britain, Russians and Poles sought work in Germany, and Latin peoples from Spain, Portugal, and Italy entered France. Many Europeans were truly migrants as opposed to immigrants—that is, they returned home after some time abroad. One in two migrants to Argentina and probably one in three to the United States eventually returned to their native land.

The likelihood of repatriation varied greatly by nationality. People who migrated from the Balkans, for instance, were much more likely to return to their countries than people from Ireland and eastern European Jews. The possibility of buying land in the old country was of central importance. In Ireland (as well as in England and Scotland) land was tightly held by large, often absentee landowners, and little land was available for purchase. In Russia most Jews faced discrimination and were forced to live in the Pale of Settlement (see Chapter 17), and most Russian land was held by non-Jews. Therefore, when Irish farmers and Russian Jewish artisans migrated in search of opportunity, it was basically a once-and-for-all departure.

The mass movement of Italians illustrates many of the characteristics of European migration. As late as the 1880s, three of every four Italians depended on agriculture. With the influx of cheap North American wheat, many small landowning peasants whose standard of living was falling began to leave their country. Many Ital-

Figure 25.4 Origins and Destinations of European Emigrants, 1851–1960
European emigrants came from many countries; almost half of them went to the United States.

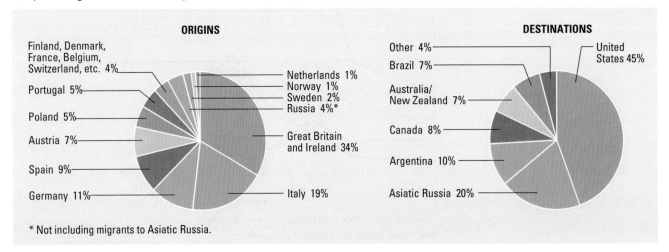

ORIGINS

Finland, Denmark, France, Belgium, Switzerland, etc. 4%
Portugal 5%
Poland 5%
Austria 7%
Spain 9%
Germany 11%

Netherlands 1%
Norway 1%
Sweden 2%
Russia 4%*
Great Britain and Ireland 34%
Italy 19%

DESTINATIONS

Other 4%
Brazil 7%
Australia/New Zealand 7%
Canada 8%
Argentina 10%
Asiatic Russia 20%

United States 45%

* Not including migrants to Asiatic Russia.

An Italian Custom in Argentina   Italian immigrants introduced the game of bocce to Argentina, where it took hold and became a popular recreation for men. Dressed up in their Sunday best, these Argentinean laborers are totally focused on the game, which is somewhat like horseshoes or shuffleboard. (Hulton Archive/Getty Images)

ians went to the United States, but before 1900 more went to Argentina and Brazil.

Many Italians had no intention of settling abroad permanently. Some called themselves "swallows." After harvesting their own wheat and flax in Italy, they "flew" to Argentina to harvest wheat between December and April. Returning to Italy for the spring planting, they repeated this exhausting process. This was a very hard life, but a frugal worker could save $250 to $300 in the course of a season, at a time when an Italian agricultural worker earned less than $1 a day in Italy.

Ties of family and friendship played a crucial role in the movement of peoples. Many people from a given province or village settled together in rural enclaves or tightly knit urban neighborhoods thousands of miles away. Very often a strong individual—a businessman, a religious leader—would blaze the way, and others would follow, forming a "migration chain."

Many landless young European men and women were spurred to leave by a spirit of revolt and independence. In Sweden and in Norway, in Jewish Russia and in Italy, these young people felt frustrated by the small privileged classes, which often controlled both church and government and resisted demands for change and greater opportunity. Many a young Norwegian seconded the passionate cry of Norway's national poet, Martinius

Bjørnson (BYURN-sawn): "Forth will I! Forth! I will be crushed and consumed if I stay."[4] Many young Jews wholeheartedly agreed with a spokesman of Kiev's Jewish community in 1882, who summed up his congregation's growing defiance in the face of brutal discrimination: "Our human dignity is being trampled upon, our wives and daughters are being dishonored, we are looted and pillaged; either we get decent human rights or else let us go wherever our eyes may lead us."[5]

Thus for many, migration was a radical way to "get out from under." Migration slowed down when the people won basic political and social reforms, such as the right to vote, equality before the law, and social security.

Asian Migrants

Not all migration was from Europe. A substantial number of Chinese, Japanese, Indians, and Filipinos—to name only four key groups—responded to rural hardship with temporary or permanent migration. At least 3 million Asians (as opposed to more than 60 million Europeans) moved abroad before 1920. Most went as indentured laborers to work under incredibly difficult conditions on the plantations or in the gold mines of Latin America, southern Asia, Africa, California, Hawaii,

LIVING IN THE PAST

BETWEEN 1800 AND 1930, 60 MILLION EUROPEANS left their homelands in search of better lives. About half moved to the United States; between 1890 and 1925 over 20 million men, women, and children passed through the Ellis Island Immigration Station in New York City harbor. During these years, southern and eastern Europeans, such as Italians, Poles, and Russian Jews, far outnumbered the northern Euro-

peans who had predominated in the mid-nineteenth-century wave of migration to the United States. Today over 40 percent of Americans are descendants of people who went through immigration control on Ellis Island. These figures give some idea of the immense number of people involved in this great migration, but statistics hardly capture what it was like to pull up stakes and move to America.

Transporting migrants across the North Atlantic was big business. Well-established steamship companies such as Cunard, White Star, and Hamburg-America advertised inexpensive fares and good accommodations. The reality was usually different. For the vast majority who could afford only third-class passage in the steerage compartment (so called because it was located near the ship's rudder), the eight- to fourteen-day journey overseas from Naples, Hamburg, or Liverpool was cramped, cold, and unsanitary. Yet poor job prospects and religious or political persecution at home—and the lure of America's booming economy—led many to take the journey.

Once they arrived at Ellis Island, steerage passengers were subjected to a four- to five-hour examination in the Great Hall. Physicians checked their health. Customs officers inspected legal documents. Bureaucrats administered intelligence tests and evaluated the migrants' financial and moral status. The exams worried and sometimes insulted the new arrivals. As one Polish-Jewish immigrant remembered, "They asked us questions. 'How much is two and one? How much is two and two?' But the next young girl, also from our city, went and they asked her, 'How do you wash stairs, from the top or from the bottom?' She says, 'I don't come to America to wash stairs.'"*

Migrants with obvious illnesses were required to stay in the island's hospital for several weeks to see if they improved. Sick passengers whom officials judged either a threat to public health or a likely drain on public finances were sent home. Suspected anarchists and, later, Bolsheviks were also deported.

*"Immigration: Ellis Island," http://library.thinkquest.org/20619/Eivirt .html (16 February 2010).

Italian poster advertising sailings to the United States, Brazil, Uruguay, Argentina, and Central America, 1906. (National Archives, RG85: 51411/53)

By today's standards, it was remarkably easy for those seeking to establish permanent residency to enter the United States: only about 2 percent of all migrants were denied entry. After they cleared processing, the new arrivals were ferried to New York City, where they either stayed or moved to other industrialized cities of the northeast and Midwest. The migrants typically took unskilled jobs for low wages, but by keeping labor costs down, they fueled the rapid industrialization of late-nineteenth-century America. They furthermore transformed the United States from a land of predominately British and northern European settlers into the multicultural melting pot of myth and fame.

QUESTIONS FOR ANALYSIS

1. Why did so many Europeans make the difficult and sometimes dangerous transatlantic trip to the United States?

2. What were the main concerns of U.S. immigration officials as they evaluated the new arrivals? Did U.S. officials treat immigrants fairly?

Conditions for steerage passengers were cramped, as evidenced by this photo from 1902. Passengers were limited to bringing only their most cherished possessions, such as the teddy bear from Switzerland and the Hebrew prayer book from Poland, both of which made the crossing with their owners in 1921. (steerage: The Granger Collection, New York; prayer book: Karen Yamauchi, photographer/NPS, lent by Florence Ercolano; teddy bear: Karen Yamauchi, photographer/NPS, gift of Gertrude Schneider)

and Australia. White estate owners very often used Asians to replace or supplement blacks after the suppression of the slave trade.

In the 1840s, for example, there was a strong demand for field hands in Cuba, and the Spanish government actively recruited Chinese laborers. Between 1853 and 1873, when such migration was stopped, more than 130,000 Chinese laborers went to Cuba. The majority spent their lives as virtual slaves. The great landlords of Peru also brought in more than 100,000 workers from China in the nineteenth century, and there were similar movements of Asians elsewhere.

Such migration from Asia would undoubtedly have grown to much greater proportions if planters and mine owners in search of cheap labor had been able to hire as many Asian workers as they wished. But they could not. Asians fled the plantations and gold mines as soon as possible, seeking greater opportunities in trade and towns. There they came into conflict with local populations, whether in Malaya, East Africa, or areas settled by Europeans. These European settlers demanded a halt to Asian migration. By the 1880s, Americans and Australians were building **great white walls**—discriminatory laws designed to keep Asians out.

great white walls Laws designed by Americans and Australians to keep Asians from settling in their countries in the 1880s.

new imperialism The late-nineteenth-century drive by European countries to create vast political empires abroad.

A crucial factor in the migrations before 1914 was, therefore, the general policy of "whites only" in the open lands of possible permanent settlement. This, too, was part of Western dominance in the increasingly lopsided world. Largely successful in monopolizing the best overseas opportunities, Europeans and people of European ancestry reaped the main benefits from the great migration. By 1913 people in Australia, Canada, and the United States all had higher average incomes than people in Great Britain, still Europe's wealthiest nation.

Western Imperialism, 1880–1914

How and why after 1875 did European nations rush to build political empires in Africa and Asia? ■

The expansion of Western society reached its apex between about 1880 and 1914. In those years, the leading European nations not only continued to send massive streams of migrants, money, and manufactured goods around the world, but also rushed to create or enlarge vast political empires abroad. This political empire building contrasted sharply with the economic penetration of non-Western territories between 1816 and 1880, which had left a China or a Japan "opened" but politically independent. By contrast, the empires of the late nineteenth century recalled the old European colonial empires of the seventeenth and eighteenth centuries and led contemporaries to speak of the **new imperialism**.

Characterized by a frantic rush to plant the flag over as many people and as much territory as possible, the new imperialism had momentous consequences. It resulted in new tensions among competing European states, and it led to wars and threats of war with non-European powers. The new imperialism was aimed primarily at Africa and Asia. It put millions of black, brown, and yellow peoples directly under the rule of whites.

Vaccinating Migrants Bound for Hawaii, 1904
First Chinese, then Japanese, and finally Koreans and Filipinos went across the Pacific in large numbers to labor in Hawaii on American-owned sugar plantations in the late nineteenth century. The native Hawaiians had been decimated by disease, creating a severe labor shortage for Hawaii's plantation economy. (Corbis)

The European Presence in Africa Before 1880

Prior to 1880, European nations controlled only 10 percent of the African continent, and their possessions were hardly increasing. The French had begun conquering Algeria in 1830, and by 1880 substantial numbers of French, Italian, and Spanish colonists had settled among the overwhelming Arab majority there. Yet the overall effect on Africa was minor.

At the southern tip of the continent, Britain had taken possession of the Dutch settlements at Cape Town during the wars with Napoleon I. This British takeover of the Cape Colony had led disgruntled Dutch cattle ranchers and farmers in 1835 to make their so-called Great Trek into the interior, where they fought the Zulu and Xhosa peoples for land. After 1853, while British colonies such as Canada and Australia were beginning to evolve toward self-government, the Boers or **Afrikaners** (a-frih-KAH-nuhrz), as the descendants of the Dutch in the Cape Colony were beginning to call themselves, proclaimed their political independence and defended it against British armies. By 1880 Afrikaner and British settlers, who detested each other, had wrested control of much of South Africa from the Zulu, Xhosa, and other African peoples.

Other than the French presence in the north and the British and Afrikaners in the south, Africa was largely free of Westerners. European trading posts and forts dating back to the Age of Discovery and the slave trade sparsely dotted the coast of West Africa. The Portuguese maintained a loose hold on their old possessions in Angola and Mozambique. Elsewhere over the great mass of the continent, Europeans did not rule.

After 1880, the situation changed drastically. In a spectacular manifestation of the new imperialism, European countries jockeyed for territory in Africa, breaking sharply with previous patterns of colonization and diplomacy.

The Scramble for Africa After 1880

Between 1880 and 1900, Britain, France, Germany, and Italy scrambled for African possessions as if their national livelihoods depended on it (Map 25.2). By 1900 nearly the whole continent had been carved up and placed under European rule: only Ethiopia in northeast Africa, which was able to fight off Italian invaders, and Liberia on the West African coast, which had been settled by freed slaves from the United States, remained independent. In all other African territories, the European powers tightened their control and established colonial governments in the years before 1914.

The Dutch settler republics also succumbed to imperialism, but the final outcome was different. The British, led by Cecil Rhodes (1853–1902) in the Cape Colony, leapfrogged over the two Afrikaner states—Orange Free State and the Transvaal—in the early 1890s and established protectorates over Bechuanaland (bech-WAH-nuh-land) (now Botswana) and Rhodesia (now Zimbabwe and Zambia), named in honor of its founder. Although unable to undermine the stubborn Afrikaners in the Transvaal, English-speaking capitalists like Rhodes developed fabulously rich gold mines there, and the British eventually conquered their white rivals in the bloody South African War (1899–1902). In 1910 the old Afrikaner territories were united with the old Cape Colony and the eastern province of Natal in a new Union of South Africa, established—unlike any other territory in Africa—as a largely "self-governing" colony. This enabled the defeated Afrikaners to use their numerical superiority over the British settlers to gradually take political power, as even the most educated nonwhites lost the right to vote outside the Cape Colony. (See "Individuals in Society: Cecil Rhodes," page 798.)

> **Afrikaners** Descendants of the Dutch settlers in the Cape Colony in southern Africa.

In the complexity of the European seizure of Africa, certain events and individuals stand out. Of enormous importance was the British occupation of Egypt in 1882, which established the new model of formal political control (see pages 787–788). There was also the role of Leopold II of Belgium (r. 1865–1909), an energetic, strong-willed monarch of a tiny country with a lust for distant territory. As early as 1861, he had laid out his vision of expansion: "The sea bathes our coast, the world lies before us. Steam and electricity have annihilated distance, and all the nonappropriated lands on the surface of the globe can become the field of our operations and of our success."[6]

By 1876 Leopold was focusing on central Africa. Subsequently, he formed a financial syndicate under his personal control to send Henry M. Stanley, a sensation-seeking journalist and part-time explorer, to the Congo basin. Stanley was able to establish trading stations, sign "treaties" with African chiefs, and plant Leopold's flag. Leopold's actions alarmed the French, who quickly sent out an expedition under Pierre de Brazza. In 1880 de Brazza signed a treaty of protection with the chief of the large Teke tribe and began to establish a French protectorate on the north bank of the Congo River.

The Struggle for South Africa, 1878

British territory
Boer republics
Battle

KALAHARI DESERT

ATLANTIC OCEAN

TRANSVAAL

ZULULAND

ORANGE FREE STATE

CAPE COLONY

Cape Town

INDIAN OCEAN

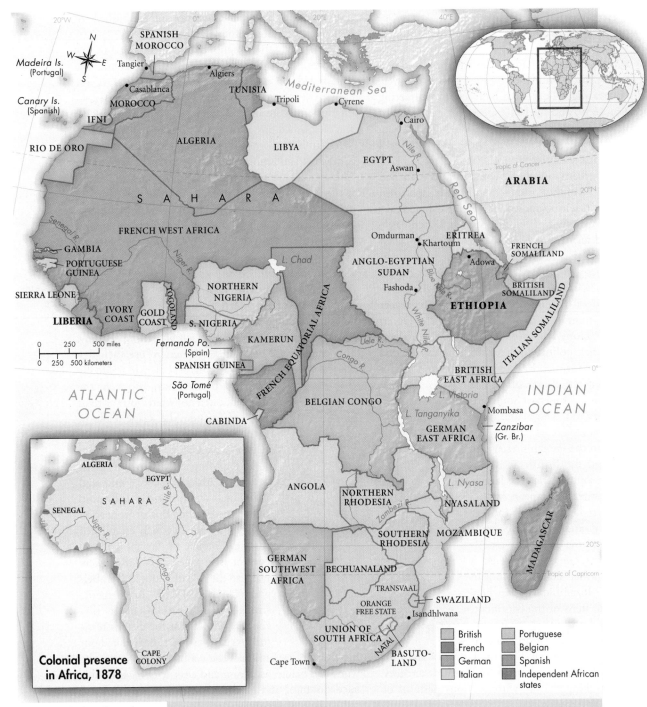

Colonial presence
in Africa, 1878

	British		Portuguese
	French		Belgian
	German		Spanish
	Italian		Independent African states

Mapping the Past

Map 25.2 The Partition of Africa The European powers carved up Africa after 1880 and built vast political empires. European states also seized territory in Asia in the nineteenth century, although some Asian states and peoples managed to maintain their political independence (see Map 25.3, page 800). Compare the patterns of European imperialism in Africa and Asia, using this map and Map 25.3.

ANALYZING THE MAP What European countries were leading imperialist states in both Africa and Asia, and what lands did they hold? What countries in Africa and Asia maintained their political independence? What did the United States and Japan have in common in Africa and Asia?

CONNECTIONS The late nineteenth century was the high point of European imperialism. What were the motives behind the rush for land and empire in Africa and Asia?

To complete this activity online, go to the Online Study Guide at bedfordstmartins.com/mckaywest.

H.M. Leopold, King of the Congo, in his national dress.

European Imperialism at Its Worst This 1908 English cartoon, "Leopold, King of the Congo, in his national dress," focuses on the barbaric practice of cutting off the hands and feet of Africans who refused to gather as much rubber as Leopold's company demanded. In 1908 an international human rights campaign forced the Belgian king to cede his personal fief to the Belgian state. (The Granger Collection, New York)

1880, Bismarck, like many other European leaders at the time, had seen little value in colonies. Then in 1884 and 1885, as political agitation for expansion increased, Bismarck did an abrupt about-face, and Germany established protectorates over a number of small African kingdoms and tribes in Togo, the Cameroons region, southwest Africa, and, later, East Africa. In acquiring colonies, Bismarck cooperated against the British with France's Jules Ferry, an ardent republican who also embraced imperialism. With Bismarck's tacit approval, the French pressed southward from Algeria, eastward from their old forts on the Senegal coast, and northward from their protectorate on the Congo River.

Meanwhile, the British began enlarging their West African enclaves and impatiently pushed northward from the Cape Colony and westward from Zanzibar. Their thrust southward from Egypt was blocked in Sudan by fiercely independent Muslims who massacred a British force at Khartoum in 1885.

A decade later, another British force, under General Horatio H. Kitchener, moved cautiously and more successfully up the Nile River, building a railroad to supply arms and reinforcements as it went. Finally, in 1898 these British troops met their foe at Omdurman (ahm-duhr-MAHN) (see Map 25.2), where Muslim tribesmen armed with spears charged time and time again, only to be cut down by the recently invented Maxim machine gun. In the somber words of one English observer, "It was not a battle but an execution. The bodies were not in heaps . . . but they spread evenly over acres and acres."[7] In the end, eleven thousand brave Muslim tribesmen lay dead, while only twenty-eight Britons had been killed.

Continuing up the Nile after the Battle of Omdurman, Kitchener's armies found that a small French force had already occupied the village of Fashoda (fuh-SHOH-duh). Locked in imperial competition with Britain ever since the British occupation of Egypt, France had tried to beat the British to one of Africa's last unclaimed areas—the upper reaches of the Nile. The result was a serious diplomatic crisis and the threat of war. Eventually, wracked by the Dreyfus affair (see Chapter 24) and unwilling to fight, France backed down and withdrew its forces, allowing the British to take over.

Berlin conference

A meeting of European leaders held in 1884 and 1885 in order to lay down some basic rules for imperialist competition in sub-Saharan Africa.

Leopold's buccaneering intrusion into the Congo area raised the question of the political fate of Africa. By 1882 Europe had caught "African fever." There was a gold rush mentality, and the race for territory was on. To lay down some basic rules for this new and dangerous game of imperialist competition in sub-Saharan Africa, Jules Ferry of France and Otto von Bismarck (see Chapter 24) of Germany arranged an international conference on Africa in Berlin in 1884 and 1885. The **Berlin conference** established the principle that European claims to African territory had to rest on "effective occupation" in order to be recognized by other states. This meant that Europeans would push relentlessly into interior regions from all sides and that no single European power would be able to claim the entire continent. The conference recognized Leopold's personal rule over a neutral Congo free state and agreed to work to stop slavery and the slave trade in Africa.

The Berlin conference coincided with Germany's sudden emergence as an imperial power. Prior to about

Cecil Rhodes

CECIL RHODES (1853-1902) EPITOMIZED THE DYNAMISM and the ruthlessness of the new imperialism. He built a corporate monopoly, claimed vast tracts in Africa, and established the famous Rhodes scholarships to develop colonial (and American) leaders who would love and strengthen the British Empire. But to Africans, he left a bitter legacy.

Rhodes came from a large middle-class family and at seventeen went to southern Africa to seek his fortune. He soon turned to diamonds, newly discovered at Kimberley, picked good partners, and was wealthy by 1876. But Rhodes, often called a dreamer, wanted more. He entered Oxford University, while returning periodically to Africa, and his musings crystallized in a belief in progress through racial competition and territorial expansion. "I contend," he wrote, "that we [English] are the finest race in the world and the more of the world we inhabit the better it is for the human race."*

Rhodes's belief in British expansion never wavered. In 1880 he formed the De Beers Mining Company, and by 1888 his firm monopolized southern Africa's diamond production and earned fabulous profits. Rhodes also entered the Cape Colony's legislature and became the all-powerful prime minister from 1890 to 1896.

His main objective was to dominate the Afrikaner republics and to impose British rule on as much land as possible beyond their northern borders. Working through a state-approved private company financed in part by De Beers, Rhodes's agents forced and cajoled African kings to accept British "protection," then put down rebellions with Maxim machine guns. Britain thus obtained a great swath of empire on the cheap.

But Rhodes, like many high achievers obsessed with power and personal aggrandizement, went too far. He backed, and then in 1896 declined to call back, a failed invasion of the Transvaal, which was designed to topple the Dutch-speaking republic. Repudiated by top British leaders who had encouraged his plan, Rhodes had to resign as prime minister. In declining health, he continued to agitate against the Afrikaner republics. He died at age forty-nine as the South African War (1899–1902) ended.

In accounting for Rhodes's remarkable but flawed achievements, both sympathetic and critical biographers stress his imposing size, enormous energy, and powerful personality. His ideas were commonplace, but he believed in them passionately, and he could persuade and inspire others to follow his lead. Rhodes the idealist was nonetheless a born negotiator, a crafty deal maker who believed that everyone could be had for a price. According to his most insightful biographer, Rhodes's homosexuality—discreet, partially repressed, and undeniable—was also "a major component of his magnetism and his success."†

Never comfortable with women, he loved male companionship. He drew together a "band of brothers," both gay and straight, to share in the pursuit of power.

Rhodes cared nothing for the rights of blacks. Ever a combination of visionary and opportunist, he looked forward to an eventual reconciliation of Afrikaners and British in a united white front. Therefore, as prime minister of the Cape Colony, he broke with the colony's liberal tradition and supported Afrikaner demands to reduce drastically the number of black voters and limit black freedoms. This helped lay the foundation for the Union of South Africa's brutal policy of racial segregation known as *apartheid* after 1948.

QUESTIONS FOR ANALYSIS

1. In what ways does Rhodes's career epitomize the new imperialism in Africa?

2. How did Rhodes relate to Afrikaners and to black Africans? How do you account for the differences and the similarities?

Cecil Rhodes, after crushing the last African revolt in Rhodesia in 1896. (Brown Brothers)

*Robert Rotberg, *The Founder: Cecil Rhodes and the Pursuit of Power* (New York: Oxford University Press, 1988), p. 150.

†Ibid., p. 408.

The British conquest of Sudan exemplifies the general process of empire building in Africa. The fate of the Muslim force at Omdurman was eventually inflicted on all native peoples who resisted European rule: they were blown away by vastly superior military force. But however much the European powers squabbled for territory and privilege around the world, they always had the sense to stop short of actually fighting each other. Imperial ambitions were not worth a great European war.

Imperialism in Asia

Although the sudden division of Africa was more spectacular, Europeans also extended their political control in Asia. In 1815 the Dutch ruled little more than the island of Java in the East Indies. Thereafter they gradually brought almost all of the three-thousand-mile archipelago under their political authority, though—in good imperialist fashion—they had to share some of the spoils with Britain and Germany. In the critical decade of the 1880s, the French under the leadership of Ferry took Indochina. India, Japan, and China also experienced a profound imperialist impact (Map 25.3).

Two other great imperialist powers, Russia and the United States, also acquired rich territories in Asia. Russia moved steadily forward on two fronts throughout the nineteenth century. Russians conquered Muslim areas to the south in the Caucasus and in Central Asia, reaching the border of Afghanistan in 1885. Russia also proceeded to nibble greedily on China's outlying provinces in the Far East, especially in the 1890s.

The great conquest by the United States was the Philippines, taken from Spain in 1898 after the Spanish-American War. When it quickly became clear that the United States had no intention of granting independence, Philippine patriots rose in revolt and were suppressed only after long, bitter fighting. Some Americans protested the taking of the Philippines, but to no avail. Thus another great Western power joined the imperialist ranks in Asia.

Causes of the New Imperialism

Many factors contributed to the late-nineteenth-century rush for territory and empire, which was in turn one aspect of Western society's generalized expansion in the age of industry and nationalism. It is little wonder that controversies have raged over interpretation of the new imperialism, especially since authors of every persuasion have often exaggerated particular aspects in an attempt to prove their own theories. Yet despite complexity and controversy, basic causes are clearly identifiable.

Economic motives played an important role in the extension of political empires, especially in the British Empire. By the late 1870s, France, Germany, and the United States were industrializing rapidly behind ris-

French Seizure of Madagascar Africans in Madagascar transport a French diplomat in 1894, shortly before France annexed the island. (Snark/Art Resource, NY)

ing tariff barriers. Great Britain was losing its early lead and facing increasingly tough competition in foreign markets. In this new economic climate, Britain came to value old possessions, especially its vast colony of India, which it had exploited most profitably for more than a century. When continental powers began to grab Asian and African territory in the 1880s, the British followed suit immediately. They feared that France and Germany would seal off their empires with high tariffs and that future economic opportunities would be lost forever.

Actually, the overall economic gains of the new imperialism proved quite limited before 1914. The new colonies were simply too poor to buy much, and they offered few immediately profitable investments. Nonetheless, even the poorest, most barren desert was jealously prized, and no territory was ever abandoned. This was because colonies became important for political and diplomatic reasons. Each leading country saw colonies as crucial to national security and military power. For instance, safeguarding the Suez Canal played a key

Map 25.3 Asia in 1914 India remained under British rule, while China precariously preserved its political independence. The Dutch empire in modern-day Indonesia was old, but French control of Indochina was a product of the new imperialism.

role in the British occupation of Egypt, and protecting Egypt in turn led to the bloody conquest of Sudan. Far-flung possessions guaranteed ever-growing navies the safe havens and the dependable coaling stations they needed in time of crisis or war.

Many people were convinced that colonies were essential to great nations. "There has never been a great power without great colonies," wrote one French publicist. The famous and influential nationalist historian of Germany, Heinrich von Treitschke (HAHYN-rihkh fuhn TRIGHCH-kuh), spoke for many when he wrote: "Every virile people has established colonial power. . . . All great nations in the fullness of their strength have desired to set their mark upon barbarian lands and those who fail to participate in this great rivalry will play a pitiable role in time to come."[8]

Treitschke's harsh statement reflects not only the increasing aggressiveness of European nationalism after Bismarck's wars of German unification, but also Social

Darwinian theories of brutal competition among races. As one prominent English economist argued, the "strongest nation has always been conquering the weaker . . . and the strongest tend to be best." Thus European nations, which were seen as racially distinct parts of the dominant white race, had to seize colonies to show they were strong and virile. Moreover, since racial struggle was nature's inescapable law, the conquest of "inferior" peoples was just. "The path of progress is strewn with the wreck . . . of inferior races," wrote one professor in 1900. "Yet these dead peoples are, in very truth, the stepping stones on which mankind has risen to the higher intellectual and deeper emotional life of today."[9] Social Darwinism and harsh racial doctrines fostered imperialist expansion.

So did the industrial world's unprecedented technological and military superiority. Three aspects were particularly important. First, the rapidly firing Maxim machine gun, so lethal at Omdurman in Sudan, was an

Tools for Empire Building Western technological advances aided Western political ambitions in Africa and Asia. The Maxim machine gun shown at far right was highly mobile and could lay down a continuous barrage that would decimate charging enemies, as in the slaughter of Muslim tribesmen at the Battle of Omdurman in the Sudan. Quinine was also very important to empire building. First taken around 1850 in order to prevent the contraction of the deadly malaria disease, quinine enabled European soldiers and officials to move safely into the African interior and overwhelm native peoples. (gun: Lordprice Collection/Alamy; quinine: Wellcome Library, London)

ultimate weapon in many another unequal battle. Second, newly discovered quinine proved no less effective in controlling attacks of malaria, which had previously decimated whites in the tropics whenever they left breezy coastal enclaves and dared to venture into mosquito-infested interiors. Third, the combination of the steamship and the international telegraph permitted Western powers to quickly concentrate their firepower in a given area when it was needed. Never before—and never again after 1914—would the technological gap between the West and non-Western regions of the world be so great.

Social tensions and domestic political conflicts also contributed mightily to overseas expansion. In Germany, in Russia, and in other countries to a lesser extent, contemporary critics of imperialism charged conservative political leaders with manipulating colonial issues in order to divert popular attention from the class struggle at home and to create a false sense of national unity. Thus imperial propagandists relentlessly stressed that colonies benefited workers as well as capitalists, providing jobs and cheap raw materials that raised workers' standard of living. Government leaders and their allies in the tabloid press successfully encouraged the masses to savor foreign triumphs and glory in the supposed increase in national prestige. In short, conservative leaders defined imperialist development as a national necessity, which they used to justify the status quo and their hold on power.

Finally, certain special-interest groups in each country were powerful agents of expansion. Shipping companies wanted lucrative subsidies. White settlers demanded more land and greater protection. Missionaries and humanitarians wanted to spread religion and stop the slave trade within Africa. Military men and colonial officials, whose role has often been overlooked, foresaw rapid advancement and highly paid positions in growing empires. The actions of such groups pushed the course of empire forward.

A "Civilizing Mission"

Western society did not rest the case for empire solely on naked conquest and a Darwinian racial struggle or on power politics and the need for naval bases on every ocean. Imperialists developed additional arguments in order to satisfy their consciences and answer their critics.

A favorite idea was that Europeans could and should "civilize" more primitive nonwhite peoples. According to this view, nonwhites would eventually receive the benefits of modern economies, cities, advanced medicine, and higher standards of living. In time, they might be ready for self-government and Western democracy. Thus the French spoke of their sacred "civilizing mission." In 1899 Rudyard Kipling (1865–1936), who wrote masterfully of Anglo-Indian life and was perhaps the most influential British writer of the 1890s, exhorted Europeans (and Americans in the United States) to unselfish service in distant lands in his poem "The White Man's Burden":

> *Take up the White Man's Burden—*
> *Send forth the best ye breed—*
> *Go bind your sons to exile*
> *To serve your captives' need,*
> *To wait in heavy harness,*
> *On fluttered folk and wild—*
> *Your new-caught, sullen peoples*
> *Half-devil and half-child.*[10]

A Missionary School A Swahili schoolboy leads his classmates in a reading lesson in Dar es Salaam in German East Africa before 1914, as portraits of Emperor William II and his wife look down on the classroom. Europeans argued that they were spreading the benefits of a superior civilization with schools like this one, which is unusually well-built and furnished because of its strategic location in the capital city. (Ullstein Bilderdienst/The Granger Collection, New York)

Many Americans accepted the ideology of the **white man's burden**. It was an important factor in the decision to rule, rather than liberate, the Philippines after the Spanish-American War. Like their European counterparts, these Americans believed that their civilization had reached unprecedented heights and that they had unique benefits to bestow on all "less advanced" peoples. Another argument was that imperial government protected natives from tribal warfare as well as from cruder forms of exploitation by white settlers and business people.

white man's burden The idea that Europeans could and should civilize more primitive nonwhite peoples and that imperialism would eventually provide nonwhites with modern achievements and higher standards of living.

Peace and stability under European control also facilitated the spread of Christianity. In Africa Catholic and Protestant missionaries competed with Islam south of the Sahara, seeking converts and building schools to spread the Gospel. Many Africans' first real contact with whites was in mission schools. Some peoples, such as the Ibo in Nigeria, became highly Christianized.

Such occasional successes in black Africa contrasted with the general failure of missionary efforts in India, China, and the Islamic world. There Christians often preached in vain to peoples with ancient, complex religious beliefs. Yet the number of Christian believers around the world did increase substantially in the nineteenth century, and missionary groups kept trying.

Critics of Imperialism

The expansion of empire aroused sharp, even bitter, critics. A forceful attack was delivered in 1902, after the unpopular South African War, by radical English economist J. A. Hobson (1858–1940) in his *Imperialism*, a work that influenced Lenin and others. Hobson contended that the rush to acquire colonies was due to the economic needs of unregulated capitalism, particularly the need of the rich to find outlets for their surplus capital. Yet, Hobson argued, imperial possessions did not pay off economically for the country as a whole. Only unscrupulous special-interest groups profited from them, at the expense of both the European taxpayer and the natives. Moreover, Hobson argued that the quest for empire diverted popular attention away from domestic reform and the need to reduce the great gap between rich and poor. These and similar arguments were not very persuasive, however. Most people then (and now) were sold on the idea that imperialism was economically profitable for the homeland, and a broad and genuine enthusiasm for empire developed among the masses.

Hobson and many other critics struck home, however, with their moral condemnation of whites imperiously ruling nonwhites. They rebelled against crude Social Darwinian thought. "O Evolution, what crimes are committed in thy name!" cried one foe. Another sardonically coined a new beatitude: "Blessed are the strong, for they shall prey on the weak."[11] Kipling and his kind were lampooned as racist bullies whose rule rested on brutality, racial contempt, and the Maxim machine gun. Henry Labouchère, a member of Parliament and prominent spokesman for this position, mocked Kipling's famous poem:

Pile on the Brown Man's burden!
And if ye rouse his hate,
Meet his old-fashioned reasons
With Maxims up to date,
With shells and Dum-Dum bullets
A hundred times plain
The Brown Man's loss must never
Imply the White Man's gain.[12]

Similarly, in 1902 in *Heart of Darkness* Polish-born novelist Joseph Conrad (1857–1924) castigated the "pure selfishness" of Europeans in "civilizing" Africa; the main character, once a liberal scholar, turns into a savage brute.

Critics charged Europeans with applying a degrading double standard and failing to live up to their own noble ideals. At home Europeans had won or were winning representative government, individual liberties, and a certain equality of opportunity. In their empires, Europeans imposed military dictatorships on Africans and Asians; forced them to work involuntarily, almost like slaves; and discriminated against them shamelessly. Only by renouncing imperialism, its critics insisted, and giving captive peoples the freedoms Western society had struggled for since the French Revolution would Europeans be worthy of their traditions. Europeans who denounced the imperialist tide provided colonial peoples with a Western ideology of liberation.

Responding to Western Imperialism

What was the general pattern of non-Western responses to Western expansion, and how did India, Japan, and China meet the imperialist challenge? ■

To peoples in Africa and Asia, Western expansion represented a profoundly disruptive assault. Everywhere it threatened traditional ruling classes, local economies, and existing ways of life. Christian missionaries and European secular ideologies challenged established beliefs and values. Non-Western peoples experienced a crisis of identity, one made all the more painful by the power and arrogance of the white intruders.

The Pattern of Response

Generally, the initial response of African and Asian rulers to aggressive Western expansion was to try to drive the unwelcome foreigners away. This was the case in China, Japan, and upper Sudan, as we have seen. Violent antiforeign reactions exploded elsewhere again and again, but the superior military technology of the industrialized West almost invariably prevailed. Beaten in battle, many Africans and Asians concentrated on preserving their cultural traditions at all costs. Others found themselves forced to reconsider their initial hostility. Some (such as Ismail of Egypt) concluded that the West was indeed superior in some ways and that it was therefore necessary to reform their societies and copy some European achievements, especially if they wished to escape full-blown Western political rule. Thus it is possible to think of responses to the Western impact as a spectrum, with "traditionalists" at one end, "westernizers" or "modernizers" at the other, and many shades of opinion in between. Both before and after European domination, the struggle among these groups was often intense. With time, however, the modernizers tended to gain the upper hand.

When the power of both the traditionalists and the modernizers was thoroughly shattered by superior force, the great majority of Asians and Africans accepted imperial rule. Political participation in non-Western lands was historically limited to small elites, and the masses were used to doing what their rulers told them to do. In these circumstances Europeans, clothed in power and convinced of their righteousness, governed smoothly and effectively. They received considerable support from both traditionalists (local chiefs, landowners, religious leaders) and modernizers (Western-educated professional classes and civil servants).

Nevertheless, imperial rule was in many ways an imposing edifice built on sand. Support for European rule among the conquered masses was shallow and weak. Thus the native people followed with greater or lesser enthusiasm a few determined personalities who came to oppose the Europeans. Such leaders always arose, both when Europeans ruled directly and when they manipulated native governments, for at least two basic reasons.

First, the nonconformists—the eventual anti-imperialist leaders—developed a burning desire for human dignity. They came to feel that such dignity was incompatible with foreign rule. Second, and somewhat ironically, potential leaders found in the Western world the ideologies and justification for their protest. They discovered liberalism, with its credo of civil liberty and political self-determination. They echoed the demands of anti-imperialists in Europe and America that the West live up to its own ideals. Above all, they found themselves attracted to modern nationalism, which asserted that every people had the right to control its own destiny. After 1917 anti-imperialist revolt would find another weapon in Lenin's version of Marxian socialism. Thus the anti-imperialist search for dignity drew strength from Western thought and culture, as is particularly apparent in the development of three major Asian countries—India, Japan, and China.

Empire in India

India was the jewel of the British Empire, and no colonial area experienced a more profound British impact. Unlike Japan and China, which maintained a real or precarious independence, and unlike African territories, which were annexed by Europeans only at the end of the nineteenth century, India was ruled more or less absolutely by Britain for a very long time.

Arriving in India on the heels of the Portuguese in the seventeenth century, the British East India Company had conquered the last independent native state by 1848. The last "traditional" response to European rule—the attempt by the established ruling classes to drive the white man out by military force—was broken in India in 1857 and 1858. Those were the years of the **Great Rebellion** (which the British called a "mutiny"), when an insurrection by Muslim and Hindu mercenaries in the British army spread throughout northern and central India before it was finally crushed, primarily by loyal native troops from southern India. Britain then ruled India directly until Indian independence was gained in 1947.

After 1858 India was ruled by the British Parliament in London and administered by a tiny, all-white civil service in India. In 1900 this elite consisted of fewer than 3,500 top officials, for a population of 300 million. The British white elite, backed by white officers and native troops, was competent and generally well-disposed toward the welfare of the Indian peasant masses. Yet it practiced strict job discrimination and social segregation, and most of its members quite frankly considered the jumble of Indian peoples and castes to

The Great Rebellion, 1857–1858

CHINA
TIBET
NEPAL
Delhi
INDIA
GOA (Port.)
Arabian Sea
Bay of Bengal
Ceylon

☐ Under British control
☐ Area of rebellion

Great Rebellion The 1857 and 1858 insurrection by Muslim and Hindu mercenaries in the British army that spread throughout northern and central India before finally being crushed.

be racially inferior. As Lord Kitchener, one of the most distinguished top military commanders in India, stated:

It is this consciousness of the inherent superiority of the European which has won for us India. However well educated and clever a native may be, and however brave he may prove himself, I believe that no rank we can bestow on him would cause him to be considered an equal of the British officer.[13]

British women played an important part in the imperial enterprise, especially after the opening of the Suez Canal in 1869 made it much easier for civil servants and businessmen to bring their wives and children with them to India. These British families tended to live in their own separate communities, where they occupied large houses with well-shaded porches, handsome lawns, and a multitude of servants. It was the wife's responsibility to manage this complex household. Many officials' wives learned to relish their duties, and they directed their households and servants with the same self-confident authoritarianism that characterized British political rule in India.

A small minority of British women—many of them feminists, social reformers, or missionaries, both married and single—sought to go further and shoulder the "white women's burden" in India, as one historian has described it.[14] These women tried especially to improve the lives of Indian women, both Hindu and Muslim, and to move them closer through education and legislation to the better conditions that they believed Western women had attained. Their greatest success was educating some elite Hindu women who took up the cause of reform.

With British men and women sharing a sense of mission as well as strong feelings of racial and cultural superiority, the British acted energetically and introduced many desirable changes to India. Realizing that they needed well-educated Indians to serve as skilled subordinates in the government and army, the British established a modern system of progressive secondary education in which all instruction was in English. Thus through education and government service, the British offered some Indians excellent opportunities for both economic and social advancement. High-caste Hindus, particularly quick to respond, emerged as skillful intermediaries between the British rulers and the Indian people, and soon they formed a new elite profoundly influenced by Western thought and culture.

This new bureaucratic elite played a crucial role in modern economic development, which was a second result of British rule. Irrigation projects for agriculture, the world's third-largest railroad network for good communications, and large tea and jute plantations geared to the world economy were all developed. Unfortunately, the lot of the Indian masses improved little, for

> **❝** However well educated and clever a native may be, . . . I believe that no rank we can bestow on him would cause him to be considered an equal of the British officer. **❞**

— **LORD KITCHENER**

the increase in production was eaten up by population increase.

Finally, with a well-educated, English-speaking Indian bureaucracy and modern communications, the British created a unified, powerful state. They placed under the same general system of law and administration the different Hindu and Muslim peoples and the vanquished kingdoms of the entire subcontinent — groups that had fought each other for centuries and had been repeatedly conquered by Muslim and Mongol invaders. It was as if Europe, with its many states and varieties of Christianity, had been conquered and united in a single great empire.

In spite of these achievements, the decisive reaction to European rule was the rise of nationalism among the Indian elite. No matter how anglicized and necessary a member of the educated classes became, he or she could never become the white ruler's equal. The top jobs, the best clubs, the modern hotels, and even certain railroad compartments were sealed off to brown-skinned Indians. The peasant masses might accept such inequality as the latest version of age-old oppression, but the well-educated, English-speaking elite eventually could not. For the elite, racial discrimination meant injured pride and bitter injustice. It flagrantly contradicted those cherished Western concepts of human rights and equality. Moreover, it was based on dictatorship, no matter how benign.

By 1885, when educated Indians came together to found the predominately Hindu Indian National Congress, demands were increasing for the equality and self-government that Britain had already granted white-settler colonies, such as Canada and Australia. By 1907, emboldened in part by Japan's success (see the next section), the radicals in the Indian National Congress were calling for complete independence. Although there were sharp divisions between Hindus and Muslims, Indians were finding an answer to the foreign challenge. The common heritage of British rule and Western ideals, along with the reform and revitalization of the Hindu religion, had created a genuine movement for national independence.

Imperial Complexities in India Britain permitted many native princes to continue their rule, if they accepted British domination. This photo shows a road-building project designed to facilitate famine relief in a southern native state. Officials of the local Muslim prince and their British "advisers" watch over workers drawn from the Hindu majority. (Nizam's Good Works Project — Famine Relief: Road Building, Aurangabad 1895–1902, from Judith Mara Gutman, *Through Indian Eyes.* Courtesy, Private Collection)

The Example of Japan

When Commodore Matthew Perry arrived in Japan in 1853 with his crude but effective gunboat diplomacy, Japan was a complex feudal society. At the top stood a figurehead emperor, but real power was in the hands of a hereditary military governor, the shogun. With the help of a warrior nobility known as samurai, the shogun governed a country of hardworking, productive peasants and city dwellers. Often poor and restless, the intensely proud samurai were humiliated by the sudden American intrusion and the unequal treaties with Western countries.

Meiji Restoration The restoration of the Japanese emperor to power in 1867, leading to the subsequent modernization of Japan.

When foreign diplomats and merchants began to settle in Yokohama, radical samurai reacted with a wave of antiforeign terrorism and antigovernment assassinations between 1858 and 1863. The imperialist response was swift and unambiguous. An allied fleet of American, British, Dutch, and French warships demolished key forts, further weakening the power and prestige of the shogun's government. Then in 1867, a coalition led by patriotic samurai seized control of the government with hardly any bloodshed and restored the political power of the emperor. This was the **Meiji Restoration**, a great turning point in Japanese development.

The immediate, all-important goal of the new government was to meet the foreign threat. The battle cry of the Meiji (MAY-jee) reformers was "Enrich the state and strengthen the armed forces." Yet how were these tasks to be done? In an about-face that was one of history's most remarkable chapters, the young but well-trained, idealistic but flexible leaders of Meiji Japan dropped their antiforeign attacks. Convinced that Western civilization was indeed superior in its military and industrial aspects, they initiated from above a series of measures to reform Japan along modern lines. In the broadest sense, the Meiji leaders tried to harness the power inherent in Europe's dual revolution in order to protect their country and catch up with the West.

In 1871 the new leaders abolished the old feudal structure of aristocratic, decentralized government and formed a strong unified state. Following the example of the French Revolution, they dismantled the four-class legal system and declared social equality. They decreed

A Busy Store in Meiji Japan Commercial life was extremely vigorous in Japan before it was opened to Western influence, and Tokyo was already one of the world's largest cities. This colorful print from the Meiji era shows how sophisticated Japanese consumers have adopted various aspects of Western dress. This reflects Japan's willingness to borrow from the West to maintain its independence and meet the Western challenge. (Arthur Sackler Gallery, Smithsonian Institution, Washington, D.C.: Gift of Ambassador and Mrs. William Leonhart, S1998.44a–c)

freedom of movement in a country where traveling abroad had been a most serious crime. They created a free, competitive, government-stimulated economy. Japan began to build railroads and modern factories. Thus the new generation adopted many principles of a free, liberal society, and, as in Europe, such freedom resulted in a tremendously creative release of human energy.

Yet the overriding concern of Japan's political leadership was always a powerful state and a strong military. (See "Listening to the Past: Lin Zexu and Yamagata Aritomo, Confronting Western Imperialism," page 808.) A powerful modern navy was created, and the army was completely reorganized along European lines, with three-year military service required for all males and a professional officer corps. This army of draftees effectively put down disturbances in the countryside, and in 1877 it was used to crush a major rebellion by feudal elements protesting the loss of their privileges. Japan also borrowed rapidly and adapted skillfully the West's science and modern technology, particularly in industry, medicine, and education. Many Japanese were encouraged to study abroad, and the government paid large salaries to attract foreign experts. These experts were replaced by trained Japanese as soon as possible.

By 1890, when the new state was firmly established, the wholesale borrowing of the early restoration had given way to more selective emphasis on those things foreign that were in keeping with Japanese tradition. Following the model of the German Empire, Japan established an authoritarian constitution and rejected democracy. The power of the emperor and his ministers was vast, that of the legislature limited.

Japan successfully copied the imperialism of Western society. Expansion not only proved that Japan was strong; it also cemented the nation together in a great mission. Having "opened" Korea with the gunboat diplomacy of imperialism in 1876, Japan decisively defeated China in a war over Korea in 1894 and 1895 and took Formosa (modern-day Taiwan). In the next years, Japan competed aggressively with the leading European powers for influence and territory in China, particularly in Manchuria. There Japanese and Russian imperialism met and collided. In 1904 Japan attacked Russia without warning, and after a bloody war, Japan emerged with a valuable foothold in China, Russia's former protectorate over Port Arthur (see Map 25.3). By 1910, with the annexation of Korea, Japan had become a major imperialist power.

Japan became the first non-Western country to use an ancient love of country to transform itself and thereby meet the many-sided challenge of Western expansion. Moreover, Japan demonstrated convincingly that a modern Asian nation could defeat and humble a great Western power. Many Chinese and Vietnamese nationalists were fascinated by Japan's achievement. Japan provided patriots throughout Asia and Africa with an inspiring example of national recovery and liberation.

Toward Revolution in China

In 1860 the two-hundred-year-old Qing Dynasty in China appeared on the verge of collapse. Efforts to repel foreigners had failed, and rebellion and chaos wracked the country. Yet the government drew on its traditional strengths and made a surprising comeback that lasted more than thirty years.

Two factors were crucial in this reversal. First, the traditional ruling groups temporarily produced new and effective leadership. Loyal scholar-statesmen and generals quelled disturbances such as the great Tai Ping (tigh-PIHNG) rebellion. The remarkable empress dowager Tzu Hsi (tsoo shee) governed in the name of her young son, combining shrewd insight with vigorous action to revitalize the bureaucracy.

Second, destructive foreign aggression lessened, for the Europeans had obtained their primary goal of commercial and diplomatic relations. Indeed, some Europeans contributed to the dynasty's recovery. A talented Irishman effectively reorganized China's customs office, increasing government tax receipts, and a sympathetic American diplomat represented China in foreign lands, helping to strengthen the central government. Such efforts dovetailed with the dynasty's efforts to adopt some aspects of Western government and technology while maintaining traditional Chinese values and beliefs.

The parallel movement toward domestic reform and limited cooperation with the West collapsed under the blows of Japanese imperialism. The Sino-Japanese War of 1894 to 1895 and the subsequent harsh peace treaty revealed China's helplessness in the face of aggression, triggering a rush for foreign concessions and protectorates in China. At the high point of this rush in 1898, it appeared that the European powers might actually divide China among themselves, as they had recently divided Africa. Probably only the jealousy each nation felt toward its imperialist competitors saved China from partition. In any event, the tempo of foreign encroachment greatly accelerated after 1894.

China's precarious position after the war with Japan led to a renewed drive for fundamental reforms. Like the leaders of the Meiji Restoration, some modernizers saw salvation in Western institutions. In 1898 they convinced the young emperor to launch a desperate **hundred days of reform** in an attempt to meet the foreign challenge. More radical reformers, such as the revolutionary Sun Yatsen (soun yaht-SEN) (1866–1925), who came from the peasantry and was educated

hundred days of reform
A series of Western-style reforms launched in 1898 by the Chinese government in an attempt to meet the foreign challenge.

Lin Zexu and Yamagata Aritomo, Confronting Western Imperialism

LISTENING TO THE PAST

For centuries China was the world's largest and most self-sufficient state, and in 1800 the Qing (Manchu) Dynasty was still upholding China's traditional sovereignty and majesty. Foreign merchants could only trade with licensed Chinese merchants through the port of Guangzhou (Canton) on the south China coast. By 1830, however, British merchants were also smuggling highly addictive opium into China and earning colossal illegal profits.

In 1838 the Chinese government moved aggressively to deal with the crisis. It dispatched Lin Zexu, an energetic top official, to Guangzhou to stamp out the opium trade. Lin dealt harshly with Chinese buyers and then confiscated the opium stores of the British merchants. He also wrote a famous letter to Queen Victoria, calling on her to help end the drug trade and explaining why the Chinese government had acted. Neither Lin's action nor his eloquent letter, a portion of which follows, was successful. British armies attacked, China was "opened," and the opium trade continued.

Lin Zexu, Letter to Queen Victoria

❝ His Majesty the Emperor comforts and cherishes foreigners as well as Chinese: he loves all the people of the world without discrimination. Whenever profit is found, he wishes to share it with all men; whenever harm appears, he likewise will eliminate it on behalf of all mankind. His heart is in fact the heart of the universe.

Generally speaking, the succeeding rulers of your honorable country have been respectful and obedient. Time and again they have sent petitions to China, saying: "We are grateful to His Majesty the Emperor for the impartial and favorable treatment he has granted to the citizens of my country who have come to China to trade. . . ."

As this trade has lasted for a long time, there are bound to be unscrupulous as well as honest traders. Among the unscrupulous are those who bring opium to China to harm the Chinese; they succeed so well that this poison has spread far and wide in all the provinces. You, I hope, will certainly agree that people who pursue material gains to the great detriment of the welfare of others can be neither tolerated by Heaven nor endured by men. . . .

I have heard that the areas under your direct jurisdiction such as London, Scotland, and Ireland do not produce opium; it is produced instead in your Indian possessions. . . . In these possessions the English people . . . also open factories to manufacture this terrible drug. As months accumulate and years pass by, the poison they have produced increases in its wicked intensity, and its repugnant odor reaches as high as the sky. Heaven is furious with anger, and all the gods are moaning with pain. It is hereby suggested that you destroy and plow under all of these opium plants and grow food crops instead, while issuing an order to punish severely anyone who dares to plant opium poppies again. . . .

Since a foreigner who goes to England to trade has to obey the English law, how can an Englishman not obey the Chinese law when he is physically within China? The present law calls for the imposition of the death sentence on any Chinese who has peddled or smoked opium. Since a Chinese could not peddle or smoke opium if foreigners had

not brought it to China, it is clear that the true culprits are the opium traders from foreign countries. Being the cause of other people's death, why should they be spared from capital punishment? A murderer of one person is subject to the death sentence; just imagine how many people opium has killed! This is the rationale behind the new law which says that any foreigner who brings opium to China will be sentenced to death by hanging or beheading. Our purpose is to eliminate this poison once and for all and to the benefit of all mankind. ❞

European traders and missionaries arrived in Japan in the sixteenth century, but in 1640 the government expelled the Europeans in order to preserve the existing Japanese culture and society. Three centuries later, Japan met the challenge of the West by adopting many of the methods and technologies of the West. Yamagata Aritomo (1838–1922) contributed significantly to this effort and its success.

Born into the military nobility known as the samurai, Yamagata Aritomo joined in the Meiji Restoration (see page 806), and to him fell the task of strengthening the armed forces, which the Meiji reformers had separated from the civilian officials. Traveling to Europe and carefully studying European armies and navies, he returned home in 1872 and wrote the memorandum reprinted here, "Opinion on Military Affairs and Conscription." The next year, he helped reorganize Japanese society by writing a new law calling for a Japanese army drafted from the whole male population, on the Western pattern. No longer would fighting be the province of samurai alone.

Yamagata Aritomo, "Opinion on Military Affairs and Conscription"

❝ A military force is required to defend the country and protect its people. Previous laws of this country inculcated in the minds of the samurai those basic functions, and there was no separation between the civilian and military affairs. Nowadays civilian officials and military officials have separate functions, and the

The new Japanese army in about 1870, wearing Western uniforms and marching in formation. (Laurie Platt Winfrey, Inc./The Granger Collection, New York)

practice of having the samurai serve both functions has been abandoned. It is now necessary to select and train those who can serve the military functions, and herein lies the change in our military system. . . .

The creation of a standing army for our country is a task which cannot be delayed. . . .

The so-called reservists do not normally remain within military barracks. During peacetime they remain in their homes, and in an emergency they are called to service. All of the countries in Europe have reservists, and amongst them Prussia has most of them. There is not a single able-bodied man in Prussia who is not trained in military affairs. Recently Prussia and France fought each other and the former won handily. . . .

It is recommended that our country adopt a system under which any able-bodied man twenty years of age be drafted into military service, . . . and after completion of a period of service, they shall be returned to their homes. In this way every man will become a soldier, and not a single region in the country will be without defense. Thus our defense will become complete.

The second concern of the Ministry is coastal defense. This includes building of warships and constructing coastal batteries. Actually, battleships are moveable batteries. Our country has thousands of miles of coastline, and any remote corner of our country can become the advance post of our enemy. . . .

At a time like this it is very clear where the priority of this country must lie. We must now have a well-trained standing army supplemented by a large number of reservists. We must build warships and construct batteries. We must train officers and soldiers. We must manufacture and store weapons and ammunitions. The nation may consider that it cannot bear the expenses . . . [but] we cannot do without our defense for a single day. »

Sources: Excerpt from "A Letter to Queen Victoria" by Lin Tse-hsu (Zexu) in *China in Transition: 1517–1911*, edited and translated by Dun Jen Li, pp 64–66. Copyright © 1967 by D. Van Nostrand Company, Inc. "Opinion on Military Affairs and Conscription" from *Japan: A Documentary History*, ed. David J. Lu. (Armonk, N.Y.: M. E. Sharpe, 1997), pp. 315–318. Translation © 1997 by David J. Lu. Reprinted by permission of M. E. Sharpe, Inc. All rights reserved. Not for reproduction.

QUESTIONS FOR ANALYSIS

1. According to Lin, why did China move against the drug trade, and why should Queen Victoria help?

2. What measures does Yamagata advocate? Why? What lessons does he draw from Europe?

3. What similarities and differences do you see in the situations and the thinking of Lin and Yamagata?

Le Petit Parisien

SUPPLÉMENT LITTÉRAIRE ILLUSTRÉ

TOUS LES JOURS
Le Petit Parisien
5 CENTIMES.

DIRECTION: 18, rue d'Enghien, PARIS

TOUS LES JEUDIS
SUPPLÉMENT LITTÉRAIRE
5 CENTIMES.

Picturing the Past

Demonizing the Boxer Rebellion For months this Sunday supplement to a very popular French newspaper ran gruesome front page pictures of ferocious Boxers burning buildings, murdering priests, and slaughtering Chinese Christians. Whipping up European outrage about native atrocities was a prelude to harsh reprisals by the Western Powers. (Mary Evans Picture Library/The Image Works)

ANALYZING THE IMAGE What is happening in this picture? How would you characterize the mood of the crowd?

CONNECTIONS The images of Africans in Madagascar (page 799), Egyptians (painting and exhibition guide, pages 781 and 787), and the Chinese shown here were all drawn by European artists for Europeans. What, if any, similarities do these images share? What do they suggest to Europeans at home about colonial empires abroad and the native peoples who lived there? How does the perspective in the prints by Japanese artists for a Japanese audience (pages 806 and 809) differ?

To complete this activity online, go to the Online Study Guide at bedfordstmartins.com/mckaywest.

in Hawaii by Christian missionaries, sought to overthrow the dynasty altogether and establish a republic.

The efforts at radical reform by the young emperor and his allies threatened the Qing establishment and the empress dowager Tzu Hsi, who had dominated the court for the past quarter of a century. Pulling a palace coup, she and her supporters imprisoned the emperor, rejected the reform movement, and put reactionary officials in charge. Hope for reform from above was crushed.

A violent reaction swept the country, encouraged by the Qing court and led by a secret society that foreigners called the Boxers. These Boxers blamed China's ills on foreigners, especially the foreign missionaries whom they accused of traveling through China and telling the Chinese that their customs were primitive and their beliefs were wrong. Above all, the conservative, patriotic, antiforeign Boxers charged the foreign missionaries with undermining the Chinese reverence for their ancestors and thereby threatening the Chinese family and the entire society. In the agony of defeat and unwanted reforms, the Boxers and other secret societies struck out at their enemies. In northeastern China, more than two hundred foreign missionaries and several thousand Chinese Christians were killed, prompting threats and demands from Western governments. The empress dowager answered by declaring war, hoping that the Boxers might relieve the foreign pressure on the Qing Dynasty.

The imperialist response was swift and harsh. After the Boxers besieged the embassy quarter in Beijing, foreign governments organized an international force of twenty thousand soldiers to rescue their diplomats and punish China. Beijing was occupied and plundered by Western armies. In 1901 China was forced to accept a long list of penalties, including a heavy financial indemnity payable over forty years.

The years after this heavy defeat were ever more troubled. Anarchy and foreign influence spread as the power and prestige of the Qing Dynasty declined still further. Antiforeign, antigovernment revolutionary groups agitated and plotted. Finally in 1912, a spontaneous uprising toppled the Qing Dynasty. After thousands of years of emperors and empires, a loose coalition of revolutionaries proclaimed a Western-style republic and called for an elected parliament. The transformation of China under the impact of expanding Western society entered a new phase, and the end was not in sight.

LOOKING BACK LOOKING AHEAD

IN THE EARLY TWENTIETH century, educated Europeans had good reason to believe that they were living in an age of progress. The ongoing triumphs of industry and science and the steady improvements in the standard of living from about 1850 were undeniable, and it was generally assumed that these favorable trends would continue. There had also been progress in the political realm. The bitter class conflicts that culminated in the bloody civil strife of 1848 had given way in most European countries to stable nation-states with elected legislative bodies that reflected the general population, responded to real problems, and enjoyed popular support. Moreover, there had been no general European war since Napoleon I had been defeated in 1815. Only the brief, limited wars connected with German and Italian unification at mid-century had broken the peace in the European heartland.

In the global arena, peace was much more elusive. In the name of imperialism, Europeans (and North Americans) used war and the threat of war to open markets and punish foreign governments around the world. Although criticized by some intellectuals and leftists such as J. A. Hobson, these foreign campaigns in the late nineteenth century resonated with European citizens and stimulated popular nationalism. Like fans in a sports bar, the peoples of Europe followed their teams and cheered them on to victories that were almost certain. Thus imperialism and nationalism reinforced and strengthened each other in Europe, especially after 1875.

This was a dangerous development. Easy imperialist victories over weak states and poorly armed non-Western peoples encouraged excessive pride and led Europeans to underestimate the fragility of their accomplishments. Imperialism also made nationalism more aggressive and militaristic. And as European imperialism was dividing the world after 1875, the leading European states were also dividing themselves into two opposing military alliances. Thus when the two armed camps stumbled into war in 1914, there would be a superabundance of nationalistic fervor, patriotic sacrifice, and military destruction.

CHAPTER REVIEW

■ **What were some of the global consequences of European industrialization between 1815 and 1914? (p. 782)**

In the nineteenth century, global inequality in income and well-being increased markedly as a growing gap opened up between the industrializing West and the regions of Africa, Asia, and Latin America. Drawing on the advantages of this growing gap in industry and technology, the West entered the third and most dynamic phase of its centuries-old expansion into non-Western lands. In so doing, Western nations promoted a prodigious growth of world trade and investment, forced reluctant countries such as China and Japan into the globalizing economy, and profitably subordinated many lands to their own economic interests.

■ **How was massive migration an integral part of Western expansion? (p. 788)**

In response to population pressures at home and economic opportunities abroad, Western nations also sent forth millions of emigrants to the sparsely populated areas of European settlement in North and South America, Australia, and Asiatic Russia. As industrialization took hold and provided more decent jobs at home, migration from countries like Germany slowed. But Europeans continued to migrate in large numbers until war came in 1914. Migration from Asia was much more limited, mainly because European settlers raised high barriers to prevent the settlement of Asian immigrants.

■ **How and why after 1875 did European nations rush to build political empires in Africa and Asia? (p. 794)**

After 1875, Western countries used a combination of brute force and the self-justifying ideology of a "civilizing mission" to carve out vast political empires in Africa and rushed to establish political influence in Asia. There were many reasons for this empire building, but economic motives, political competition, and superior military technology were particularly important. In addition, many Europeans justified imperialist expansion on the basis of civilizing and Christianizing primitive peoples, whom they believed they were racially superior to.

■ **What was the general pattern of non-Western responses to Western expansion, and how did India, Japan, and China meet the imperialist challenge? (p. 803)**

African and Asian peoples attempted to defend themselves against the armies and navies of Western imperialism, but they were generally defeated in battle. They then had to develop different strategies. Traditionalists concentrated on preserving their culture, while modernists sought to introduce reforms capable of revitalizing their societies, often turning to Western concepts such as liberalism and, above all, nationalism. In India, an English-speaking elite developed after the failure of the Great Rebellion of 1857, and by 1885 a new Indian National Congress was calling for complete independence. In Japan, the remarkable leaders of the Meiji Restoration turned to Western models to escape Western domination, proclaiming legal equality, modernizing the military, and embracing modern industry and science. The reform movement in China was weaker and less successful, contributing to the fall of the Qing Dynasty in 1912 and the proclamation of a Western-style republic. By 1914 non-Western elites in all three countries were engaged in a national anti-imperialist struggle for dignity, genuine independence, and modernization.

Suggested Reading

Bagchi, Amiya Kumar. *Perilous Passage: Mankind and the Ascendancy of Capital.* 2005. A spirited radical critique of the "rise of the West."

Conklin, Alice. *A Mission to Civilize: The French Republican Ideal and West Africa, 1895–1930.* 1997. An outstanding examination of French imperialism.

Conrad, Joseph. *Heart of Darkness.* 1902. A novel that unforgettably probes European imperial motives.

Cook, Scott B. *Colonial Encounters in the Age of High Imperialism.* 1996. A stimulating overview with a very readable account of the explorer Stanley and central Africa.

Crews, Robert. *For Prophet and Tsar: Islam and Empire in Russia and Central Asia.* 2006. Considers neglected aspects of Russian imperialism.

Curtin, P., et al. *African History: From Earliest Times to Independence,* 2d ed. 1995. An excellent brief introduction to Africa in the age of imperialism.

Ebrey, Patricia Buckley. *The Cambridge Illustrated History of China.* 1999. A lively and beautiful work by a leading specialist.

Fage, J. D. *A History of Africa,* 3d ed. 1995. A highly recommended account.

Goodlad, Graham. *British Foreign and Imperial Policy, 1865–1919.* 2000. A lively examination of Britain's leading position in European imperialism.

Hochschild, Adam. *King Leopold's Ghost: A Story of Greed, Terror, and Heroism in Colonial Africa, 1895–1930.* 1997. A chilling account of Belgian imperialism in the Congo.

Mahfouz, H. *Palace of Desire.* 1991. A great novelist's compelling portrait of an Egyptian family and its social setting before 1914.

Maier, Charles S. *Among Empires: American Ascendancy and Its Predecessors.* 2006. Examines imperial power in history and how well America measures up.

Marshall, P. J., ed. *Cambridge Illustrated History of the British Empire.* 1996. A stunning pictorial history.

Midgley, Clare, ed. *Gender and Imperialism.* 1998. Examines the complex questions related to European women and imperialism.

Rotberg, Robert I. *The Founder: Cecil Rhodes and the Pursuit of Power.* 1988. Examines the imperialist's mind and times with great acuity.

Walthall, Anne. *Japan: A Cultural, Social, and Political History.* 2006. A concise, up-to-date overview covering a broad range of developments.

Notes

1. Quoted in A. Waley, *The Opium War Through Chinese Eyes* (New York: Macmillan, 1958), p. 29.
2. Quoted in J. W. Hall, *Japan, from Prehistory to Modern Times* (New York: Delacorte Press, 1970), p. 250.
3. Quoted in Earl of Cromer, *Modern Egypt* (London, 1911), p. 48.
4. Quoted in T. Blegen, *Norwegian Migration to America*, vol. 2 (Northfield, MN: Norwegian-American Historical Association, 1940), p. 468.
5. Quoted in I. Howe, *World of Our Fathers* (New York: Harcourt Brace Jovanovich, 1975), p. 290.
6. Quoted in W. L. Langer, *European Alliances and Alignments, 1871–1890* (New York: Vintage Books, 1931), p. 290.
7. Quoted in J. Ellis, *The Social History of the Machine Gun* (New York: Pantheon Books, 1975), pp. 86, 101.
8. Quoted in G. H. Nadel and P. Curtis, eds., *Imperialism and Colonialism* (New York: Macmillan, 1964), p. 94.
9. Quoted in W. L. Langer, *The Diplomacy of Imperialism*, 2d ed. (New York: Alfred A. Knopf, 1951), pp. 86, 88.
10. Rudyard Kipling, *The Five Nations* (London, 1903).
11. Quoted in Langer, *The Diplomacy of Imperialism*, p. 88.
12. Quoted in Ellis, *The Social History of the Machine Gun*, pp. 99–100.
13. Quoted in K. M. Panikkar, *Asia and Western Dominance: A Survey of the Vasco da Gama Epoch of Asian History* (London: George Allen & Unwin, 1959), p. 116.
14. A. Burton, "The White Women's Burden: British Feminists and 'The Indian Women,' 1865–1915," in *Western Women and Imperialism: Complicity and Resistance*, ed. N. Chauduri and M. Strobel (Bloomington: Indiana University Press, 1992), pp. 137–157.

Key Terms

Third World (p. 782)
opium trade (p. 785)
gunboat diplomacy (p. 786)
great migration (p. 788)
great white walls (p. 794)
new imperialism (p. 794)
Afrikaners (p. 795)
Berlin conference (p. 797)
white man's burden (p. 802)
Great Rebellion (p. 804)
Meiji Restoration (p. 806)
hundred days of reform (p. 807)

For practice quizzes and other study tools, visit the Online Study Guide at **bedfordstmartins.com/mckaywest**.

For primary sources from this period, see *Sources of Western Society*, **Second Edition**.

For Web sites, images, and documents related to topics in this chapter, visit Make History at **bedfordstmartins.com/mckaywest**.

26
War and Revolution

1914–1919

In the summer of 1914, the nations of Europe went willingly to war. They believed they had no other choice. Both peoples and governments confidently expected a short war leading to a decisive victory and thought that European society would be able to go on as before. These expectations were almost totally mistaken. The First World War was long, indecisive, and tremendously destructive. To the shell-shocked generation of survivors, it was known simply as the Great War because of its unprecedented scope and intensity.

From today's perspective, it is clear that the First World War was closely connected to the ideals and developments of the previous century. Industrialization, which promised a rising standard of living for the people, now produced horrendous weapons that killed and maimed millions. Imperialism, which promised to "civilize" those the Europeans considered savages, now led to intractable international conflicts. Nationalism, which promised to bring compatriots together in a harmonious nation-state, now encouraged hateful prejudice and chauvinism. The extraordinary violence of world war shook confidence in such nineteenth-century certainties to its core.

The war would also have an enormous impact on the century that followed. The need to provide extensive supplies and countless soldiers for the war effort created mass suffering, encouraged the rise of the bureaucratic state, and brought women in increasing numbers into the workplace. Millions were killed or wounded at the front and millions more grieved these losses. Grand states collapsed: the Russian, Austro-Hungarian, and Ottoman Empires passed into history. The trauma of war contributed to the rise of extremist politics—in the Russian Revolution of 1917 the Bolsheviks established a radical communist regime, and totalitarian fascist movements gained popularity across Europe in the postwar decades. Explaining the war's causes and consequences remains one of the great challenges for historians of modern Europe. ■

Life in World War I. This painting by British artist Paul Nash portrays a supply road on the western front. Nash's somber palate, tiny figures, and Cubist-influenced landscape capture the devastation and anonymous violence of total war.

CHAPTER PREVIEW

The Road to War
■ What caused the First World War, and why did it have significant popular support?

Waging Total War
■ How did the First World War change the nature of modern warfare?

The Home Front
■ What was the impact of total war on civilian populations?

The Russian Revolution
■ What led to the Russian Revolution, and what was its outcome?

The Peace Settlement
■ How did the Allies fashion a peace settlement, and why was it unsuccessful?

The Road to War

What caused the First World War, and why did it have significant popular support? ■

Historians have long debated why Europeans so readily pursued a war that was long and costly and failed to resolve the problems faced by the combatant nations. There was no single most important cause. Growing competition over colonies and world markets, a belligerent arms race, and a series of diplomatic crises sharpened international tensions. On the home front, new forms of populist nationalism strengthened people's unquestioning belief in "my country right or wrong." At the same time, ongoing domestic conflicts encouraged governments to pursue aggressive foreign policies in attempts to bolster national unity. All helped pave the road to war.

Growing International Conflict

The First World War began, in part, because European statesmen failed to resolve the diplomatic problems created by Germany's rise to Great Power status. The Franco-Prussian War and the unification of Germany opened a new era in international relations. By war's end in 1871, France was defeated, and Bismarck had made Prussia-Germany the most powerful nation in Europe (see Chapter 24). Yet, as Bismarck never tired of repeating after 1871, Germany was a "satisfied" power. Within Europe, he claimed, Germany had no territorial ambitions and wanted only peace.

But how was peace to be preserved? Bismarck's first concern was to keep an embittered France diplomatically isolated and without military allies. His second concern was the threat to peace posed by the enormous multinational empires of Austria-Hungary and Russia. Those two had many conflicting interests, particularly in southeastern Europe, where the waning strength of the Ottoman Empire had created a threatening power vacuum in the disputed border territories of the Balkans.

Bismarck's accomplishments in foreign policy were great, but only temporary. From 1871 to the late 1880s, he maintained German leadership in international affairs, and he signed a series of defensive alliances with Austria-Hungary and Russia designed to isolate a hostile France, which was still smarting over the loss of Alsace-Lorraine. Yet in 1890 the new emperor William II incautiously dismissed Bismarck, in part because he disagreed with the chancellor's friendly policy toward Russia. Under William II, Bismarck's carefully planned alliance system began to unravel. Germany refused to renew a non-aggression pact with Russia, the centerpiece of Bismarck's system, in spite of Russian willingness to do so. This fateful departure in foreign affairs prompted long-isolated republican France to court absolutist Russia, offering loans, arms, and support. In early 1894 France and Russia became military allies. As a result, continental Europe was divided into

Map 26.1 European Alliances at the Outbreak of World War I, 1914 At the start of World War I, Europe was divided into two hostile alliances: the Triple Entente of Britain, France, and Russia, and the Triple Alliance of Germany, Austria-Hungary, and Italy. Italy joined the Entente in 1915.

Triple Alliance, 1882–1915

Triple Entente, 1907–1917

Sarajevo
June 28, 1914
Assassination of Archduke Ferdinand triggers WWI

two rival blocs. The **Triple Alliance** of Austria, Germany, and Italy faced an increasingly hostile Dual Alliance of Russia and France, and the German general staff began secret preparations for a war on two fronts (Map 26.1).

As rivalries deepened on the continent, Great Britain's foreign policy became increasingly crucial. Long content with its "splendid [geographical] isolation" and without permanent alliances, Britain after 1891 was the only uncommitted Great Power. Many Germans and some Britons felt that the advanced, racially related Germanic and Anglo-Saxon peoples were natural allies. However, the good relations that had prevailed between Prussia and Great Britain since the mid-eighteenth century gave way to a bitter Anglo-German rivalry.

There were several reasons for this ill-fated development. Commercial rivalry in world markets between Germany and Great Britain increased sharply in the 1890s, as Germany became a great industrial power. Germany's ambitious pursuit of colonies further threatened British interests. Above all, Germany's decision in 1900 to expand greatly its battle fleet posed a challenge to Britain's long-standing naval supremacy.

Increased Anglo-German tensions coincided with the South African War between the British and the Dutch in South Africa, which encouraged worldwide opposition to British imperialism (see Chapter 25). In response, British leaders prudently set about shoring up their exposed position with alliances and agreements. Britain improved its often-strained relations with the United States, concluded an alliance with Japan in 1902, and allied with France in the Anglo-French Entente of 1904, which settled all outstanding colonial disputes between Britain and France.

Alarmed by Britain's ever-closer ties to France, Germany's leaders decided to test the strength of their alliance. In 1905 William II declared that Morocco was an independent, sovereign state and demanded that Germany receive the same trading rights as France. This aggressive saber rattling, termed the First Moroccan Crisis, clearly violated long-standing French colonial interests in the region. William II insisted on an international conference in hopes of settling the Moroccan question to Germany's benefit. But William II's crude bullying only brought France and Britain closer together, and Germany left the conference empty-handed.

Chronology

1914–1918	World War I
June 28, 1914	Serbian nationalist assassinates Archduke Francis Ferdinand
August 1914	War begins; Ottoman Empire joins the Central Powers
September 1914	Battle of the Marne; German victories on the eastern front
1915	Italy joins the Triple Entente; German submarine sinks the *Lusitania*; Germany halts unrestricted submarine warfare
1915–1918	Armenian genocide; German armies occupy large parts of east-central Europe
1916	Battles of Verdun and the Somme
1916–1918	Antiwar movement spreads throughout Europe; Arab rebellion against Ottoman Empire
1917	Germany resumes unrestricted submarine warfare
March 1917	February Revolution in Russia
April 1917	United States enters the war
October–November 1917	Battle of Caporetto
November 1917	Bolshevik Revolution in Russia; Balfour Declaration on Jewish Homeland in Palestine
1918	Treaty of Brest-Litovsk; revolution in Germany
1918–1920	Civil war in Russia
1919	Treaty of Versailles; Allies invade Turkey
1923	Treaty of Lausanne recognizes Turkish independence

The result of the First Moroccan Crisis in 1905 was something of a diplomatic revolution. Britain, France, Russia, and even the United States began to see Germany as a potential threat that might seek to dominate all Europe. At the same time, German leaders began to see sinister plots to encircle Germany and block its development as a world power. In 1907 Russia, battered by its disastrous war with Japan and the revolution of 1905, agreed to settle its quarrels with Great Britain in Persia and Central Asia and signed the Anglo-Russian Agreement. This agreement laid the foundation of the **Triple Entente** (ahn-TAHNT), an alliance between Britain, Russia, and France.

Germany's decision to add a large, enormously expensive fleet of big-gun battleships to its already expanding navy also heightened tensions. German patriots saw a large navy as the legitimate right of a great world

Triple Alliance The alliance of Austria, Germany, and Italy. Italy left the alliance when war broke out in 1914 on the grounds that Austria had launched a war of aggression.

Triple Entente The alliance of Great Britain, France, and Russia in the First World War.

power and as a source of national pride. But British leaders saw the German buildup as a military challenge that forced them to spend the "People's Budget" (see Chapter 24) on battleships rather than on social welfare. In 1909 the London *Daily Mail* hysterically informed its readers that "Germany is deliberately preparing to destroy the British Empire."[1] By then Britain had sided psychologically, if not officially, with France and Russia.

The leading nations of Europe were divided into two hostile camps, both ill-prepared to deal with the worsening situation in the Balkans. Britain, France, and Russia — the members of the Triple Entente — were allied in direct opposition to the German-led Triple Alliance. This unfortunate treaty system only confirmed the failure of all European leaders to incorporate Bismarck's mighty empire permanently and peacefully into the international system. By 1914, many believed that war was inevitable (see Map 26.1).

The Mood of 1914

Diplomatic rivalries and international crises played key roles in the rush to war, but a complete understanding of the war's origins requires an account of the "mood of 1914" — the attitudes and convictions of Europeans around 1914.[2] Widespread militarism (the popular approval of military institutions and their values) and nationalism encouraged leaders and citizens alike to see international relations as an arena for the testing of national power, with war if necessary.

Germany was especially famous for its powerful and aggressive army, but military institutions played a prominent role in affairs of state and in the lives of ordinary people across Europe. In a period marked by diplomatic tensions, politicians relied on generals and military experts to help shape public policy. All the Great Powers built up their armed forces and designed mobilization plans to rush men and weapons to the field of battle. Universal conscription in Germany, France, Italy, Austria-Hungary, and Russia — only Britain still relied on a volunteer army — exposed hundreds of thousands of young men each year to military culture and discipline.

The continent had not experienced a major conflict since the Franco-Prussian War (1870–1871), and Europeans vastly underestimated the destructive potential of modern weapons. Encouraged by the patriotic national press, many believed that war was glorious, manly, and heroic. If they expected another conflict, they thought it would be over quickly. Leading politicians and intellectuals likewise portrayed war as a test of strength that would lead to national unity and renewal. Such ideas

German Militarism The German emperor William II reviews his troops with the Italian king Victor Emmanuel in front of the royal palace in Potsdam in 1902. Aggressive militarism and popular nationalism helped pave the road to war. (© Scherl/SV-Bilderdienst/The Image Works)

permeated European society. As one German volunteer wrote in his diary as he left for the front in 1914, "I believe that this war is a challenge for our time and for each individual, a test by fire, that we may ripen into manhood, become men able to cope with the coming stupendous years and events."[3]

Support for military values was closely linked to a growing sense of popular nationalism. Since the 1850s, the spread of the idea that members of an ethnic group should live together in a homogeneous, united national state had provoked all kinds of international conflicts over borders and citizenship rights. Nationalism also drove the spiraling arms race and the struggle over colonies. Broad popular commitment to national interests above all else weakened groups that thought in terms of international communities and consequences. Expressions of antiwar sentiment by socialists or women's groups were seen as a betrayal of country in time of need. Inspired by nationalist beliefs, much of the population was ready for war.

Leading statesmen had practical reasons for promoting militarism and nationalism. Political leaders had long used foreign adventurism and diplomatic posturing to distract the people from domestic conflicts. In Great Britain, leaders faced civil war in Northern Ireland and a vocal and increasingly radical women's movement. In Russia, the revolution of 1905 and defeat in the Russo-Japanese War (1904–1905) had greatly weakened support for the tsarist regime. In Germany, the victory of the Marxist Social Democratic Party in the parliamentary elections of 1912 led government authorities to believe the country was falling apart. The French likewise faced difficult labor and budget problems.

Determined to hold onto power and frightened by rising popular movements, ruling classes across Europe were willing to gamble on diplomatic brinksmanship and even war to postpone dealing with intractable social problems. Victory promised to preserve the privileged positions of elites and rally the masses behind the national cause. Patriotic nationalism did bring unity in the

❝ I am a Yugoslav nationalist, aiming for the unification of all Yugoslavs, and I do not care what form of state, but it must be free from Austria. ❞

—GAVRILO PRINCIP

short run, but the wealthy governing classes underestimated the risk of war to themselves. They had forgotten that great wars and great social revolutions very often go hand in hand.

The Outbreak of War

On June 28, 1914, Archduke Francis Ferdinand, heir to the Austro-Hungarian throne, was assassinated by Serbian revolutionaries during a state visit to the Bosnian capital of Sarajevo (sar-uh-YAY-voh). After a series of failed attempts to bomb the archduke's motorcade, Gavrilo Princip, a fanatical member of the radical group Young Bosnia, shot the archduke and his wife Sophie as they passed by in their automobile. Princip was captured and put on trial, but he remained unrepentant. In court, he proudly asserted, "I am a Yugoslav nationalist, aiming for the unification of all Yugoslavs, and I do not care what form of state, but it must be free from Austria."[4]

Princip's deed, in the crisis-ridden territories of the Balkans on the border between the weakened Ottoman

Nationalist Opposition in the Balkans
This band of well-armed and determined guerrillas from northern Albania was typical of groups fighting against Ottoman rule in the Balkans. Balkan nationalists succeeded in driving the Ottoman Turks out of most of Europe and established an independent Albania in 1912, but their victory increased tensions with Austria-Hungary and among the Great Powers. (Roger-Viollet/Getty Images)

Map 26.2 The Balkans, 1878–1914 After the Congress of Berlin in 1878, the Ottoman Empire suffered large territorial losses but remained a power in the Balkans. By 1914 Ottoman control had given way to ethnic boundaries that did not follow political boundaries, and Serbian national aspirations threatened Austria-Hungary.

and Austro-Hungarian Empires, led Europe into world war. In the early years of the twentieth century, war in the Balkans—"the tinderbox of Europe"—seemed inevitable. The reason was simple: between 1900 and 1914, the Western powers had successfully forced the Ottoman rulers to give up their European territories (Map 26.2). The ethnic nationalism inspired by these changing state boundaries was destroying the Ottoman Empire and threatening Austria-Hungary. The only questions were what kinds of wars would result and where they would lead.

By the early twentieth century, nationalism in southeastern Europe was on the rise. Independent Serbia in particular was eager to build a state that would include all ethnic Serbs. Serbia was thus openly hostile to Austria-Hungary and the Ottoman Empire, since both states included substantial Serbian minorities within their borders. To block Serbian expansion, Austria in 1908 formally annexed the territories of Bosnia and Herzegovina (hert-suh-goh-VEE-nuh). The southern part of the Austro-Hungarian Empire now included an even larger Serbian population, as well as Croats and Muslims.

Serbians expressed rage but could do nothing without support from Russia, their traditional ally.

The tensions in the Balkans soon erupted into a regional war. In the First Balkan War (1912), Serbia joined Greece and Bulgaria to attack the Ottoman Empire and then quarreled with Bulgaria over the spoils of victory. In the Second Balkan War (1913), Bulgaria attacked its former allies. Austria intervened and forced Serbia to give up Albania. After centuries, nationalism had finally destroyed the Ottoman Empire in Europe. Encouraged by their success against the Ottoman Empire, Balkan nationalists increased their demands for freedom from Austrian control, dismaying the leaders of the multinational Austro-Hungarian Empire. The former hoped and the latter feared that Austria might next be broken apart.

Within this complex context, the assassination of Archduke Francis Ferdinand instigated a five-week period of intense diplomatic activity that culminated in world war. The leaders of Austria-Hungary concluded that Serbia was implicated in the assassination and deserved severe punishment. On July 23 Austria-Hungary presented Serbia with an unconditional ultimatum, including demands that would violate Serbian sovereignty. When Serbia replied moderately but evasively, Austria mobilized its armies and declared war on Serbia on July 28. Thus a desperate multinational Austria-Hungary deliberately chose war to stem the rising tide of hostile nationalism within its borders in a last-ditch attempt to save its existing empire.

From the beginning of the crisis, Germany pushed Austria-Hungary to confront Serbia and thus bore much responsibility for turning a little war into a world war. Emperor William II and his chancellor Theobald von Bethmann-Hollweg realized that war between Austria and Russia was likely, for a resurgent Russia would not stand by, as it had in the Balkan wars, and watch the Austrians crush the Serbs. Yet Bethmann-Hollweg hoped that, although Russia (and its ally France) would go to war, Great Britain would remain neutral, unwilling to fight a war for Russia in the distant Balkans. To take advantage of these conditions, the German chancellor sent a telegram to Austria-Hungary that promised Germany's unconditional support in case of war. Germany's actions encouraged the prowar faction in Vienna to take a hard line against the Serbs at a time when moderation might still have limited the crisis.

In fact, the diplomatic situation quickly spiraled out of control as military plans and timetables began to dictate policy. Russia, a vast country, required much more time to mobilize its armies than did Germany and Austria-Hungary. And since the complicated mobilization plans of the Russian general staff assumed a two-front war with both Austria and Germany, Russia could not mobilize against one without mobilizing against the other. Therefore, on July 29 Tsar Nicholas II ordered full mobilization and in effect declared war. The German general staff also thought in terms of a two-front war. Their misguided **Schlieffen Plan** called for a quick victory over France after a lightning attack through neutral Belgium—the quickest way to reach Paris—before turning on Russia. On August 3 German armies invaded Belgium. Great Britain declared war on Germany the following day.

The speed of the so-called July Crisis created shock, panic, and excitement. In the final days of July and the first few days of August, massive crowds thronged the streets of Paris, London, St. Petersburg, Berlin, and Vienna. Shouting enthusiastic prowar slogans, the excited crowds pushed politicians and military leaders toward the increasingly inevitable confrontation. Events proceeded rapidly, and those who might have opposed the war could do little to prevent its arrival. In a little over a month, a limited Austrian-Serbian war had become a European-wide conflict, and the First World War had begun.

Waging Total War

How did the First World War change the nature of modern warfare? ■

When the Germans invaded Belgium in August 1914, they and everyone else thought that the war would be short and relatively painless. Many sincerely believed that "the boys will be home by Christmas." They were wrong. On the western front in France and the eastern front in Russia, the belligerent armies bogged down in a new and extremely costly kind of war, termed **total war** by German general Erich Ludendorff. Total war meant new roles for soldiers and civilians alike. At the front, total war meant lengthy, violent, and deadly battles fought with all the weapons a highly industrialized society could produce. At home, national economies were geared toward the war effort. Governments revoked civil liberties, and many civilians lost lives or livelihoods as occupying armies moved through their towns and cities. The struggle expanded to include nations and peoples outside Europe. The Middle East, Africa, East Asia, and the United States were all brought into the maelstrom of total war.

Schlieffen Plan Failed German plan calling for a lightning attack through neutral Belgium and a quick defeat of France before turning on Russia.

total war A war in which distinctions between the soldiers on the battlefield and civilians at home are blurred, and where the government plans and controls economic social life in order to supply the armies at the front with supplies and weapons.

Stalemate and Slaughter on the Western Front

In the face of the German invasion, the Belgian army heroically defended its homeland and fell back in good order to join a rapidly landed British army corps near the Franco-Belgian border. With the outbreak of the war, Russian armies immediately attacked eastern Germany, forcing the Germans to transfer much-needed troops to the east. Instead of quickly capturing Paris per the Schlieffen Plan, by the end of August dead-tired German soldiers were advancing slowly along an enormous front in the scorching summer heat.

The Schlieffen Plan

← Planned German offensive

☐ Neutral nations

NETHERLANDS

GERMANY

Brussels

BELGIUM

Rhine R.

LUX.

Reims

•Metz

Paris

Seine R.

Marne R.

FRANCE

0   100   200 mi.

0   100   200 km.

SWITZ.

Legend:
- Triple Entente and allies
- Central Powers and allies
- Greatest extent of territory gained by Germany-Austria
- German submarine war zone
- Neutral nations
- Farthest advance by Central Powers on date marked
- Farthest advance by Entente Powers on date marked
- British naval blockade
- Major battle

**Map labels (main map):**

NORWAY, SWEDEN, FINLAND, Helsinki, Petrograd (St. Petersburg), ESTONIA, LATVIA, Riga, COURLAND, LITHUANIA, Vilnius, Masurian Lakes 1914, RUSSIA, Moscow, North Sea, Jutland 1916, DENMARK, Kiel, E. PRUSSIA, Tannenberg 1914, Warsaw, BELARUS, Armistice line, December 1917, March 1918, Treaty of Brest-Litovsk, March 1918, GREAT BRITAIN, Lusitania 1915, London, NETHERLANDS, GERMANY, Berlin, Elbe R., KINGDOM OF POLAND (Russia), Brest-Litovsk, Farthest Russian advance, 1914, Aug. 1914, Vistula R., Rhine R., BELGIUM, Armistice line, November 1918, LUXEMBOURG, ALSACE-LORRAINE, GALICIA, May 1915, Kiev, Dnieper R., Paris, See inset map, 1914, Western front, SWITZERLAND, FRANCE, Bordeaux, Seine R., Loire R., Vienna, AUSTRIA-HUNGARY, Budapest, Farthest German military advance, Aug. 1917, Mar. 1918, Caporetto 1917, Italian front, Po R., Rhône R., Ebro R., SPAIN, Corsica, Elba, ITALY, Rome, Adriatic Sea, Sarajevo, TRANSYLVANIA, ROMANIA, Bucharest, Danube R., Black Sea, March 1918, Caspian Sea, Balearic Is., Sardinia, MONTENEGRO, SERBIA, BULGARIA, Constantinople, Nov. 1917, PERSIA, Mar. 1918, ALBANIA, 1917–1918, 1916, 1915, Dardanelles, Gallipoli 1915, OTTOMAN EMPIRE, Middle Eastern front, IRAQ, Al Kut 1915 1916 1917, Baghdad, Basra, Balkan front, GREECE, Oct. 1918, SYRIA, Damascus, ALGERIA (Fr.), Tunis, TUNISIA (Fr.), Sicily, Malta, Crete, Cyprus, Mediterranean Sea, LIBYA (It.), EGYPT (Gr. Br.), Red Sea, Al Aqabah 1917

Scale: 200 / 400 miles; 200 / 400 kilometers

Compass: N, E, S, W

The Western Front (inset)

Dover, Ostend, FLANDERS, Ghent, Antwerp, NETHERLANDS, Ruhr R., Cologne, Ypres, Calais, Schelde R., Brussels, Louvain, Liège, BELGIUM, Rhine R., English Channel, Arras, Somme R., St. Quentin, Meuse R., Armistice line, November 1918, Coblenz, ARDENNES, Amiens, Somme, Sedan, LUX., Moselle R., GERMANY, Compiègne, Aisne R., ARGONNE FOREST, Saar R., Belleau Wood, Reims, Marne R., Verdun, St. Mihiel, LORRAINE, Marne I, Chateau-Thierry, Châlons-sur-Marne, Paris, Marne II, Seine R., Nancy, Strasbourg, ALSACE, FRANCE, Epinal, Mulhouse, Basel, SWITZ.

Inset scale: 25 / 50 miles; 25 / 50 kilometers

Inset legend:
- Germany, 1914
- Greatest extent of territory gained by Germany, Sept. 1914
- Front at beginning of 1915
- German offensive, Summer 1918
- Major battle

Map 26.3 World War I in Europe and the Middle East, 1914–1918 Trench warfare on the western front was concentrated in Belgium and northern France (inset), while the war in the east encompassed an enormous territory.

On September 6 the French attacked a gap in the German line at the Battle of the Marne. For three days, France threw everything into the attack. At one point, the French government desperately requisitioned all the taxis of Paris to rush reserves to the troops at the front. Finally, the Germans fell back. France had been miraculously saved (Map 26.3).

With the armies stalled, both sides began to dig trenches to protect themselves from machine-gun fire. By November 1914, an unbroken line of four hundred miles of defensive trenches extended from the Belgian coast through northern France and on to the Swiss frontier. Armies on both sides dug in behind rows of trenches, mines, and barbed wire defenses, and slaughter on the western front began in earnest. The cost in lives of **trench warfare** was staggering, the gains in territory minuscule. For ordinary soldiers, conditions in the trenches were atrocious. (See "Living in the Past: Life and Death on the Western Front," page 824.) Recently invented weapons, the products of an industrial age, made battle impersonal, traumatic, and extremely deadly. The machine gun, hand grenades, poison gas, flame-throwers, long-range artillery, the airplane, and the tank were all used to maximum effect, some for the first time. All favored the defense, increased casualty rates, and revolutionized the practice of war.

The high commands of the combatant nations, who had learned military tactics and strategy in the nineteenth century, hardly understood trench warfare. For four years the generals repeated the same mistakes, mounting massive offensives designed to achieve decisive breakthroughs. Brutal frontal assaults against highly fortified trenches might overrun the enemy's front line, but attacking soldiers rarely captured any substantial territory. A French soldier described the bloody reality of high-tech warfare and the anonymous, almost unreal qualities of hand-to-hand combat between the trenches:

> I went over the top, I ran, I shouted, I hit, I can't remember where or who. I crossed the wire, jumped over holes, crawled through shell craters still stinking of explosives, men were falling, shot in two as they ran; shouts and gasps were half muffled by the sweeping surge of gunfire. But it was like a nightmare mist all around me. . . . Now my part in it is over for a few minutes. . . . Something is red over there; something is burning. Something is red at my feet: blood.[5]

The French and British offensives of 1915 never gained more than three miles of territory from the enemy. In 1916 the unsuccessful German campaign against Verdun cost some 700,000 lives on both sides and ended in a draw, the opposing trenches still in place. The results in 1917 were little better. In hard-fought battles on all fronts, millions of young men were wounded or lost their lives for no real gain.

The Battle of the Somme, a great British offensive undertaken in the summer of 1916 in northern France, exemplified the horrors of trench warfare. The battle began with a weeklong heavy artillery bombardment on the German line, intended to cut the barbed wire fortifications, decimate the enemy trenches, and prevent the Germans from making an effective defense. For seven days and nights the British artillery fired nonstop on the German lines, expending 3 million shells. On July 1 the British went "over the top." Fortified by a double shot of harsh navy rum, the troops gathered in their trenches that morning. At precisely 7:30 A.M., line officers ordered the attack. The troops climbed out of the trenches and moved into no-man's land in the direction of the German lines, dug into a series of ridges about half a mile away.

At the beginning of the bombardment, the Germans fled into their dugouts — underground shelters dug deep into the trenches — where they suffered with little water, food, or sleep. But they survived. As the British soldiers neared the German lines and the shelling stopped, the Germans emerged from their bunkers, set up their machine guns, and mowed down the approaching troops. In many places, the wire had not been cut by the bombardment, so the struggling attackers, slowed down by heavy packs weighing over fifty-five pounds, made especially easy targets. About 20,000 British men were killed and 40,000 wounded on the first day of the attack, a crushing defeat that shook troop morale and public opinion. The battle dragged on until November, and in the end the British did push the Germans back — a whole seven miles. Some 420,000 British, 200,000 French, and 600,000 Germans were killed or wounded defending an insignificant piece of land. The war ground on.

trench warfare A type of fighting used in World War I behind rows of trenches, mines, and barbed wire; the cost in lives was staggering and the gains in territory minimal.

The Battle of the Somme, 1916

The Widening War

On the eastern front, the slaughter did not immediately degenerate into trench warfare, and the fighting was dominated by Germany. Repulsing the initial Russian attacks, the Germans won major victories at the Battles of Tannenberg and the Masurian Lakes in August

LIVING IN THE PAST

HARDSHIP AND TEDIUM ALTERNATED with spasms of indescribable violence on the western front. Enlisted men rotated in and out of position, at best spending two weeks at base, two weeks in reserve positions, and two weeks in the trenches on the front lines. They had little leave time to visit loved ones at home, though they exchanged literally billions of letters and postcards with friends and family. At the front, mud and vermin, bad food, damp and cold, and wretched living quarters were the norm. Soldiers spent most of their time repairing rough trenches and dugouts and standing watch for an enemy they rarely saw.

During periods of combat, modern weapons like mustard gas, the machine gun, and long-range artillery resulted in horrific violence. Units were often decimated in poorly planned frontal assaults, and comrades could rarely retrieve the wounded and dead from no-man's land between the lines. Bodies, mangled by high explosives, were ground into the mud and disappeared, or became part of the earthworks themselves. A British soldier described the appalling effects: "the last I saw of him was two arms straining madly at the ground, blood pouring from his mouth while legs and body sank into a shellhole filled with water."*

The statistics tell a no less staggering story. Between 10 and 13 million combatants on all sides died during the war, and some 21 million were wounded. One historian estimates that fully half of all dead soldiers went either missing or unidentified; the tidy rows of crosses in military cemeteries mask a horrible reality. The maimed veteran—traumatized by shell shock or missing limbs or facial features—became an inescapable element of postwar life and culture.

For the dead and wounded, American president Woodrow Wilson's words rang true: World War I was indeed "the war to end all wars." Things were less clear for the survivors. The Peace Treaty of Versailles offered relief from the fighting, but hardly resolved the underlying issues. After 1918 anxious Europeans had to come to terms with numbing losses and the harsh realities of the postwar world.

*Quoted in Denis Winter, *Death's Men: Soldiers of the Great War* (London: Penguin, 1979), p. 180.

This French postcard celebrates victory over the Germans in the 1914 campaign and idealizes the harsh reality of trench warfare. (akg-images)

and September 1914. Russia had also put real pressure on the relatively weak Austro-Hungarian army, but by 1915 the eastern front had stabilized in Germany's favor. A staggering 2.5 million Russian soldiers had been killed, wounded, or captured. German armies occupied huge swaths of the Russian empire in central Europe, including ethnic Polish, Belorussian, and Baltic territories. Yet Russia was not knocked out of the war, marking another failure of the Schlieffen Plan.

To govern the occupied territories in central Europe, the Germans installed a vast military bureaucracy, with some 15,000 army administrators and professional specialists. Anti-Slavic prejudice dominated the mindset of the occupiers. The local Slavs were seen as savages and ethnic "mongrels" who were unable to work like "other, more joyously productive races," as one administrator reported. The military administration used prisoners of war and refugees as forced labor and stole animals and crops from local farmers: 90,000 horses, 140,000 heads of cattle, and 767,000 pigs were used to supply the occupying army or sent home to Germany. About one-third of the civilian population was killed or became

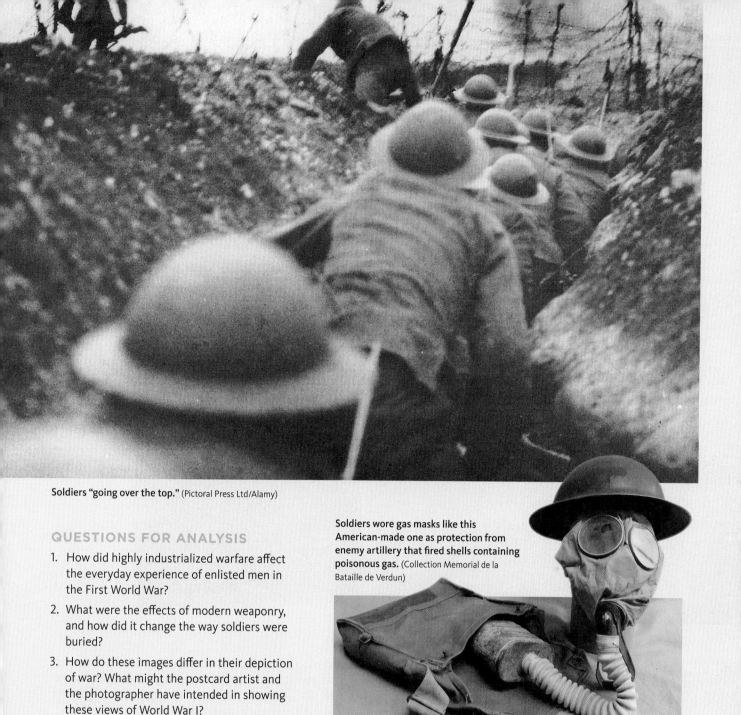

Soldiers "going over the top." (Pictoral Press Ltd/Alamy)

Soldiers wore gas masks like this American-made one as protection from enemy artillery that fired shells containing poisonous gas. (Collection Memorial de la Bataille de Verdun)

QUESTIONS FOR ANALYSIS

1. How did highly industrialized warfare affect the everyday experience of enlisted men in the First World War?

2. What were the effects of modern weaponry, and how did it change the way soldiers were buried?

3. How do these images differ in their depiction of war? What might the postcard artist and the photographer have intended in showing these views of World War I?

refugees under this brutal occupation. In the long run, the German state hoped to turn these territories into German possessions, a chilling forerunner of Nazi policies in World War II.[6]

The changing tides of victory and hopes for territorial gains brought neutral countries into the war (see Map 26.3). Italy, a member of the Triple Alliance since 1882, had declared its neutrality in 1914 on the grounds that Austria had launched a war of aggression. Then in May 1915 Italy joined the Triple Entente of Great Britain, France, and Russia in return for prom-

ises of Austrian territory. The war along the Italian-Austrian front was bitter and deadly and cost some 600,000 Italian lives.

In October 1914 the Ottoman Empire joined Austria and Germany, by then known as the Central Powers. The following September Bulgaria decided to follow the Ottoman Empire's lead in order to settle old scores with Serbia. The Balkans, with the exception of Greece, were occupied by the Central Powers.

The entry of the Ottoman Turks carried the war into the Middle East. Heavy fighting between the

Writing Home from the Front Cramped within the tight network of trenches on the western front, a British soldier writes a letter home while his compatriots rest before the next engagement. The post was typically the only connection between soldiers and their relatives, and over 28 billion pieces of mail passed between home and front on all sides during the war. Mass-produced postcards such as this one often displayed fantasies about loved ones at home. (photo: Courtesy of the Trustees of the Imperial War Museum; postcard: Imperial War Museum/The Art Archive)

For country and You

La Pensée

504

Ottomans and the Russians enveloped the Armenians, who lived on both sides of the border and had experienced brutal repression by the Turks in 1909. When in 1915 some Armenians welcomed Russian armies as liberators, the Ottoman government, with German support, ordered a mass deportation of its Armenian citizens from their homeland. In this murderous example of modern ethnic cleansing, now termed the Armenian genocide, a million innocent civilians died from murder, starvation, and disease.

In 1915, at the Battle of Gallipoli, British forces tried and failed to take the Dardanelles and Constantinople from the Ottoman Turks. The invasion force was pinned down on the beaches, and the ten-month-long battle cost the Turks 300,000 and the British 265,000 men killed, wounded, or missing.

The British were more successful at inciting the Arabs to revolt against their Turkish rulers. They bargained with the foremost Arab leader, Hussein ibn-Ali (1856–1931), who was a direct descendant of the prophet Muhammad and the chief magistrate (*sharif*) of Mecca, the holiest city in the Muslim world. Controlling much of the Ottoman Empire's territory along the Red Sea, an area known as the Hejaz (see Map 26.5, on page 844), Hussein managed in 1915 to win vague British commitments for an independent Arab kingdom. Thus in

The Armenian Genocide, 1915–1918

Black Sea

RUSSIAN EMPIRE

Caspian Sea

Constantinople

GREECE

O T T O M A N   E M P I R E

PERSIA (IRAN)

☐ Armenian ethnic area

● Massacre and deportation site (size indicates relative death toll)

☐ Modern Armenia

1916 Hussein revolted against the Turks, proclaiming himself king of the Arabs. He joined forces with the British under T. E. Lawrence, who in 1917 helped lead Arab soldiers in a successful guerrilla war against the Turks on the Arabian peninsula.

Similar victories were eventually scored in the Ottoman province of Iraq. Britain occupied the southern Iraqi city of Basra in 1914 and captured Baghdad in 1917. In September 1918 British armies and their Arab allies rolled into Syria. This offensive culminated in the triumphal entry of Hussein's son Faisal (FIGH-suhl) into Damascus. Arab patriots in Syria and Iraq now expected a large, unified Arab nation-state to rise from the dust of the Ottoman collapse—though in the event they were disappointed by the Western Powers (see page 843).

The war spread to colonial Africa and East Asia as well. Instead of revolting as the Germans hoped, the colonial subjects of the British and French generally supported the Allied powers. Colonized peoples helped local British and French commanders seize Germany's colonies around the globe. More than a million Africans and Asians served in the various armies of the warring powers; more than double that number served as porters to carry equipment. The French, facing a shortage of young men, made especially heavy use of colonial troops.

In April 1917 the United States declared war on Germany, another crucial development in the expanding conflict. American intervention grew out of the war at sea and general sympathy for the Triple Entente. At the beginning of the war, Britain and France established a naval blockade to strangle the Central Powers. No neutral cargo ship was permitted to sail to Germany. In early 1915 Germany retaliated with the murderously effective submarine, a new weapon that violated traditional niceties of fair warning under international law.

In May 1915 a German submarine sank the British passenger liner *Lusitania*, claiming more than 1,000 lives, among them 139 U.S. citizens. President Woodrow Wilson protested vigorously, using the tragedy to incite American public opinion against the Germans. As a result, Germany halted its submarine warfare for almost two years; the alternative was almost certain war with the United States.

Early in 1917 the German military command—confident that improved submarines could starve Britain into submission before the United States could come to its rescue—resumed unrestricted submarine warfare. This was a reckless gamble, and the United States declared war on Germany. Eventually the United States tipped the balance in favor of the Triple Entente and its allies.

Armenian Deportation In 1915 when some Armenians welcomed Russian armies as liberators after years of persecution, the Ottoman government ordered a genocidal mass deportation of its Armenian citizens from their homeland in the empire's eastern provinces. This photo, taken from a hotel window in Kharpert by a German businessman in 1915, shows Turkish guards marching Armenian men off to prison, where they were tortured to death. A million Armenians died from murder, starvation, and disease during World War I. (Courtesy of the Armenian Library, Watertown, Mass.)

The Home Front

What was the impact of total war on civilian populations? ∎

The war's impact on civilians was no less massive than it was on the men crouched in the trenches. Total war encouraged the growth of state bureaucracies, changed the lives of ordinary women and men, and by the end inspired mass antiwar protest movements.

Mobilizing for Total War

In August 1914 many people greeted the outbreak of hostilities enthusiastically. In every country, ordinary folk believed that their nation was right to defend itself from foreign aggression. With the exception of a few extreme left-wingers, even socialists supported the war. Yet by mid-October generals and politicians had begun to realize that victory would require more than patriotism. Each combatant country experienced a desperate need for men and weapons. To keep the war machine from sputtering to a stop, national leaders aggressively intervened in society and the economy.

By the late nineteenth century the responsive national state had already shown an eagerness to manage the welfare of its citizens (see Chapter 24). Now the state intruded even further into people's daily lives. Each combatant state established new government ministries to mobilize soldiers and armaments and to provide care for war widows and wounded veterans. Censorship offices controlled news about the course of the war. Free-market capitalism was abandoned, at least for the duration. Instead, government planning boards set mandatory production goals, established rationing programs, and set limits on wages and prices. Based on tremendously productive industrial economies controlled from above, government management yielded an effective — and therefore immensely destructive — war effort on all sides.

Germany went furthest in developing a planned economy to wage total war. As soon as war began, Walter Rathenau, the talented Jewish industrialist in charge of Germany's largest electric company, convinced the government to set up the War Raw Materials Board to ration and distribute raw materials. Under Rathenau's direction, every useful material from foreign oil to barnyard manure was inventoried and rationed. Moreover, the board launched successful attempts to produce substitutes, such as synthetic rubber and synthetic nitrates, needed to make explosives and essential to the blockaded German war machine. Food was also rationed in accordance with physical need. At the same time, Germany failed to tax the war profits of private firms heavily enough. This failure contributed to massive deficit

German Ration Card The burdens of total war forced governments to control the distribution of the most basic goods, including food. This German ration card from 1915 has tear-away coupons for weekly allotments of potatoes. (Private Collection Newbury/The Art Archive)

financing, inflation, the growth of a black market, and the eventual re-emergence of class conflict.

Following the terrible Battles of Verdun and the Somme in 1916, German military leaders forced the Reichstag to accept the Auxiliary Service Law, which required all males between seventeen and sixty to work only at jobs considered critical to the war effort. Women also worked in war factories, mines, and steel mills, where they labored, like men, at heavy and dangerous jobs. With the passage of the law, many more women followed. People lived on little more than one thousand calories a day. War production increased while some Germans starved to death.

After 1917 Germany's leaders ruled by dictatorial decree. Generals Hindenburg and Ludendorff drove Chancellor Bethmann-Hollweg from office. With the support of the newly formed ultra-conservative and prowar Fatherland Party, the generals established a military dictatorship. Hindenburg called for the ultimate mobilization for total war. Germany could win, he said, only "if all the treasures of our soil that agriculture and industry can produce are used exclusively for the conduct of War. . . . All other considerations must come second."[7] Thus in Germany total war led to the establishment of history's first "totalitarian" society, a model for future national socialists.

Only Germany was directly ruled by a military government, yet leaders in all the belligerent nations took power from parliaments, suspended civil liberties, and ignored democratic procedures. After 1915 the British Ministry of Munitions organized private industry to produce for the war, allocated labor, set wage and price rates, and settled labor disputes. In France a weakened parliament met in secret, and the courts jailed pacifists who dared criticize the state. Once the United States entered the war, new federal agencies such as the War Labor Board and the War Industries Board regulated industry, labor relations, and agricultural production. The war may have been deadly for citizen armies, but it was certainly good for the growth of the bureaucratic nation-state.

The Social Impact

The social impact of total war was no less profound than the economic impact, though again there were important national variations. National conscription sent millions of men to the front, exposing many to foreign lands for the first time in their lives. The insatiable needs of the military created a tremendous demand for workers, and jobs were readily available. This situation—seldom, if ever, seen before 1914, when unemployment

> ❝ . . . if all the treasures of our soil that agriculture and industry can produce are used exclusively for the conduct of War. . . . All other considerations must come second. ❞
>
> —**GENERAL HINDENBURG**

and poverty had been facts of urban life—brought momentous changes.

The need for workers meant greater power and prestige for labor unions. Unions now cooperated with war governments on workplace rules, wages, and production schedules in return for real participation in important decisions. The entry of labor leaders and unions into policymaking councils paralleled the entry of socialist leaders into the war governments. Both reflected a new government openness to the needs of those at the bottom of society.

The role of women also changed dramatically. In every country, large numbers of women left home and domestic service to work in industry, transportation, and offices. The production of vast amounts of arms and ammunition required huge numbers of laborers, and women moved into skilled industrial jobs long

Women Factory Workers Building a Truck, London, 1917 Millions of men on all sides were drafted to fight in the war, creating a serious labor shortage. When women left home to fill jobs formerly reserved for men, they challenged traditional gender roles. (© Hulton-Deutsch Collection/Corbis)

considered men's work only. Some women believed that the war promised to permanently break down the barriers between men's and women's work. One French woman argued that

> Like you [men]—we [women] are ambitious. Give us the chance to learn the inner workings of the engineering trade, so that one day we may become overseers and forewomen. The prospect that one might rise through the ranks and so gain a better future is a powerful stimulant.[8]

Moreover, women became highly visible in public—not only as munitions workers but also as bank tellers and mail carriers, and even as police officers, firefighters, and farm laborers. Women also served as auxiliaries and nurses at the front. (See "Individuals in Society: Vera Brittain," at right.)

The war expanded the range of women's activities and helped change attitudes about gender, but the long-term results were mixed. Women across Europe gained experience in jobs previously reserved for men, and as a result of women's many-sided war effort, the United States, Britain, Germany, Poland, and other countries granted women the right to vote immediately after the war. At the war's end, however, millions of demobilized soldiers demanded their jobs back, and governments forced women out of the workplace. Their employment gains were mostly temporary, except in nursing and social work, already considered "women's work." The great dislocations of war loosened sexual morality, and some women bobbed their hair, shortened their skirts, and smoked in public. Yet supposedly "loose" women were often criticized for betraying their soldier-husbands away at the front. And women's rights movements faded in the 1920s and 1930s, in large part because feminist leaders found it difficult to regain momentum after the crisis of war.

To some extent, the war promoted greater social equality, blurring class distinctions and lessening the gap between rich and poor. This blurring was most apparent in Great Britain, where the bottom third of the population generally lived better than they ever had, for the poorest gained most from the severe shortage of labor. Elsewhere, greater equality was reflected in full employment, rationing according to physical needs, and a sharing of hardships. In general, European society became more uniform and egalitarian, in spite of some war profiteering.

Death itself had no respect for traditional social distinctions. It savagely decimated the young aristocratic officers who led the charge, and it fell heavily on the mass of drafted peasants and unskilled workers who followed, leading commentators to speak of a "lost generation." Yet death often spared highly skilled workers and foremen. Their lives were too valuable to squander at the front, for they were needed to train the newly recruited women and older unskilled men laboring valiantly in war plants at home.

Growing Political Tensions

During the first two years of war, many soldiers and civilians supported their governments. Belief in a just cause and patriotic nationalism united peoples behind their national leaders. Each government used rigorous censorship and crude propaganda to bolster popular support. German propaganda pictured black soldiers from France's African empire raping German women, while the French and British ceaselessly recounted and exaggerated German atrocities in Belgium and elsewhere. Patriotic posters and slogans, slanted news, and biased editorials inflamed national hatreds and helped control public opinion, encouraging soldiers to continue fighting.

Despite such efforts, by the spring of 1916 people were beginning to crack under the strain of total war. On May 1 that year, several thousand demonstrators in Berlin heard the radical socialist leader Karl Liebknecht (1871–1919) attack the costs of the war effort. Liebknecht was immediately arrested and imprisoned, but his daring action electrified Europe's far left. Strikes and protest marches over inadequate food flared up on every home front. In April 1916 Irish nationalists in Dublin took advantage of this situation and revolted against British rule in the great Easter Rebellion. A week of bitter fighting passed before the rebels were crushed and their leaders executed. In France, Georges Clemenceau (zhorzh kleh-muhn-SOH) (1841–1929) established a virtual dictatorship, pouncing on strikers and jailing without trial journalists and politicians who dared to suggest a compromise peace with Germany.

On all sides, soldiers' morale began to decline. Numerous French units refused to fight after the disastrous French offensive of May 1917. Only tough military justice for mutiny leaders and a tacit agreement with the troops that there would be no more grand offensives enabled the new general in chief, Henri-Philippe Pétain (pay-TAN), to restore order. Facing defeat, wretched conditions at the front, and growing hopelessness, Russian soldiers deserted in droves, providing fuel for the Russian Revolution of 1917. After the murderous Battle of Caporetto in northern Italy in 1917, the Italian army collapsed in despair. In the massive battles of 1916 and 1917, the British armies had been "bled dry." Only the promised arrival of fresh troops from the United States stiffened the resolve of the allies.

The strains were even worse for the Central Powers. In October 1916, a young socialist assassinated the chief minister of Austria. The following month, when the aging Emperor Francis Joseph died, a symbol of unity disappeared. In spite of absolute censorship, political dissatisfaction and conflicts among nationalities grew. Both Czech and Yugoslav leaders demanded independent states for their peoples. In April 1917 Austria's chief minister summed up the situation in the gloomiest possible terms. The country and army were

INDIVIDUALS IN SOCIETY

ALTHOUGH THE GREAT WAR UPENDED MILLIONS OF LIVES, it struck Europe's young people with the greatest force. For Vera Brittain (1893–1970), as for so many in her generation, the war became life's defining experience, which she captured forever in her famous autobiography, *Testament of Youth* (1933).

Brittain grew up in a wealthy business family in northern England, bristling at small-town conventions and discrimination against women. Very close to her brother Edward, two years her junior, Brittain read voraciously and dreamed of being a successful writer. Finishing boarding school and beating down her father's objections, she prepared for Oxford's rigorous entry exams and won a scholarship to its women's college. Brittain also fell in love with Roland Leighton, an equally brilliant student from a literary family and her brother's best friend. All three, along with two more close friends, Victor Richardson and Geoffrey Thurlow, confidently prepared to enter Oxford in late 1914.

When war suddenly loomed in July 1914, Brittain shared with millions of Europeans a thrilling surge of patriotic support for her government, a prowar enthusiasm she later played down in her published writings. She wrote in her diary that her "great fear" was that England would declare its neutrality and commit the "grossest treachery" toward France.* She supported Roland's decision to enlist, agreeing with his glamorous view of war as "very ennobling and very beautiful." Later, exchanging anxious letters with Roland in France in 1915, Brittain began to see the conflict in personal, human terms. She wondered if any victory or defeat could be worth Roland's life.

Struggling to quell her doubts, Brittain redoubled her commitment to England's cause and volunteered as an army nurse. For the next three years she served with distinction in military hospitals in London, Malta, and northern France, repeatedly torn between the vision of noble sacrifice and the reality of human tragedy. She lost her sexual inhibitions caring for mangled male bodies, and she longed to consummate her love with Roland. Awaiting his return on leave on Christmas Day in 1915, she was greeted instead with a telegram: Roland had been killed two days before.

Roland's death was the first of the devastating blows that eventually overwhelmed Brittain's idealistic patriotism. In 1917 first Geoffrey and then Victor died from gruesome wounds. In early 1918, as the last great German offensive covered the floors of her war-zone hospital with maimed and dying German prisoners, the bone-weary Vera felt a common humanity and saw only more victims. A few weeks later Edward—her last hope—died in action. When the war ended, she was, she said, a "complete automaton," with "my deepest emotions paralyzed if not dead."

Returning to Oxford and finishing her studies, Brittain gradually recovered. She formed a deep, restorative friendship with another talented woman writer, Winifred Holtby, published novels and articles, and became a leader in the feminist campaign for gender equality. She also married and had children. But her wartime memories were always with her. Finally, Brittain succeeded in coming to grips with them in *Testament of Youth*, her powerful antiwar autobiography. The unflinching narrative spoke to the experiences of an entire generation and became a runaway bestseller. Above all, Brittain captured the ambivalent, contradictory character of the war, when millions of young people found excitement, courage, and common purpose but succeeded only in destroying their lives with their superhuman efforts and futile sacrifices. Becoming ever more committed to pacifism, Brittain opposed England's entry into World War II.

QUESTIONS FOR ANALYSIS

1. What were Brittain's initial feelings toward the war? How and why did they change as the conflict continued?

2. Why did Brittain volunteer as a nurse, as many women did? How might wartime nursing have influenced women of her generation?

3. In portraying the ambivalent, contradictory character of World War I for Europe's youth, was Brittain describing the character of all modern warfare?

*Quoted in the excellent study by P. Berry and M. Bostridge, *Vera Brittain: A Life* (London: Virago Press, 2001), p. 59; additional quotations are from pp. 80 and 136.

Vera Brittain was marked forever by her wartime experiences. (Vera Brittain Archive, William Ready Division of Archives and Research Collections, McMaster University Library)

Picturing the Past

Wartime Propaganda Posters This famous French propaganda poster from 1918 (left) proclaims "They shall not pass" and expresses the French determination to hold back the German invaders at any cost. The American recruitment poster from 1917 (right) encourages "fighting men" to "join the Navy." (French poster: Archives Municipales Versailles/Gianni Dagli Orti/The Art Archive; American poster: Museum of the City of New York/The Art Archive)

ANALYZING THE IMAGE How would you describe the soldier and sailor pictured on these posters? What messages about the war do the posters convey?

CONNECTIONS The "They shall not pass" poster was created after France had been at war for four years, while the naval recruitment poster came out before American troops were actively engaged overseas. How might the country of origin and the date of publication have affected the messages conveyed?

To complete this activity online, go to the Online Study Guide at bedfordstmartins.com/mckaywest.

exhausted. Another winter of war would bring revolution and disintegration.

Germans on the home front likewise suffered immensely from the burdens of total war. The British naval blockade greatly limited food imports, and scarcity and poorly implemented rationing plans had horrific results: some 750,000 German civilians starved to death. For the rest, heavy rationing of basic goods such as matches, bread, cooking oil, and meat undermined morale. The national political unity of the first year of the war collapsed as the social conflicts of prewar Germany re-emerged. A growing minority of moderate so-

cialists in the Reichstag called for a compromise "peace without annexations or reparations."

Such a peace was unthinkable for the conservatives and military leaders in the Fatherland Party. So also was the surge in revolutionary agitation and strikes by war-weary workers that occurred in early 1917. When the bread ration was further reduced in April, more than 200,000 workers and women struck and demonstrated for a week in Berlin, returning to work only under the threat of prison and military discipline. That same month, radicals left the Social Democratic Party to form the Independent Social Democratic Party; in 1918 they would found the German Communist Party. Thus militaristic Germany, like its ally Austria-Hungary (and its enemy France), was beginning to crack in 1917. Yet it was Russia that collapsed first and saved the Central Powers—for a time.

The Russian Revolution

What led to the Russian Revolution, and what was its outcome? ■

The Russian Revolution of 1917 was one of modern history's most momentous events. Directly related to the growing tensions of World War I, it had significance far beyond the wartime agonies of a single European nation. For some, the revolution was Marx's socialist vision come true; for others, it was the triumph of dictatorship. To all, it presented a radically new prototype of state and society.

The Fall of Imperial Russia

Like its allies and its enemies, Russia had embraced war with patriotic enthusiasm in 1914. At the Winter Palace, while throngs of people knelt and sang "God save the tsar," Tsar Nicholas II (r. 1894–1917) repeated the oath Alexander I had sworn in 1812 during Napoleon's invasion of Russia (see Chapter 20), vowing never to make peace as long as the enemy stood on Russian soil. Russia's lower house of parliament, the Duma, voted to support the war. Conservatives anticipated expansion in the Balkans, while liberals and most socialists believed that alliance with Britain and France would bring democratic reforms. For a moment, Russia was united.

Enthusiasm for the war soon waned as better-equipped German armies inflicted terrible losses. By 1915 substantial numbers of Russian soldiers were sent to the front without rifles; they were told to find their arms among the dead. Russia's battered peasant army nonetheless continued to fight, and Russia moved toward full mobilization on the home front. The Duma and organs of local government set up special committees to coordinate defense, industry, transportation, and agriculture. These efforts improved the military situation, but overall Russia mobilized less effectively than the other combatants.

One problem was weak leadership. Under the constitution resulting from the revolution of 1905 (see Chapter 24), the tsar had retained complete control over the bureaucracy and the army. A kindly but narrow-minded aristocrat, Nicholas II failed to form a close partnership with his citizens. He distrusted the publicly elected Duma and resisted popular involvement in government, relying instead on the old bureaucratic apparatus. As a result, the Duma, the educated middle classes, and the masses became increasingly critical of the tsar's leadership. In September 1915 parties ranging from conservative to moderate socialist formed the Progressive bloc, which called for a completely new government responsible to the Duma instead of the tsar. In answer, Nicholas temporarily adjourned the Duma. The tsar then announced that he was traveling to the front in order to lead and rally Russia's armies, leaving the government in the hands of his wife, the strong-willed and autocratic Tsarina Alexandra.

His departure was a fatal turning point. In his absence, Tsarina Alexandra arbitrarily dismissed loyal political advisers and turned to her court favorite, the disreputable and unpopular Rasputin. Rasputin was an uneducated Siberian preacher whose influence with the tsarina rested on his purported healing powers. Alexis, who was Alexandra's only son and heir to the throne, suffered from the rare blood disease hemophilia. Rasputin claimed that only he could stop the bleeding, using his miraculous powers. In a desperate attempt to right the situation and end unfounded rumors that Rasputin was the empress's lover, three members of the high aristocracy murdered Rasputin in December 1916. The ensuing scandal further undermined support for the tsarist government.

Imperial Russia had entered a terminal crisis. Despite limited success against the Austrians in the summer of 1916, heavy casualties, bad food and equipment, and concern for those at home led to opposition in the ranks. Tens of thousands of soldiers deserted, swelling the number of the disaffected at home. By early winter 1917, the cities were wracked by food shortages, heating fuel was in short supply, and the economy was breaking down. In mid-March violent street demonstrations broke out in Petrograd (formerly St. Petersburg), spread to the factories, and then engulfed the city. From the front, the tsar ordered the army to open fire on the protesters, but the soldiers refused to shoot and joined the revolutionary crowd. The Duma declared a provisional government on March 12, 1917. Three days later, Nicholas abdicated.

The Provisional Government

This **February Revolution** that led to the establishment of the provisional government and the abdication of the tsar was the result of an unplanned uprising of hungry, angry people in the capital, but it was eagerly accepted throughout the country. (The name of the revolution matches the Russian calendar, which used to use a different dating system.)

February Revolution
Unplanned uprisings accompanied by violent street demonstrations begun in March 1917 (old calendar February) in Petrograd, Russia, that led to the abdication of the tsar and the establishment of a provisional government.

The patriotic upper and middle classes embraced the prospect of a more determined war effort, while workers anticipated better wages and more food. After generations of autocracy, the provisional government established equality before the law; freedom of religion, speech, and assembly; and the right of unions to organize and strike.

Petrograd Soviet A huge, fluctuating mass meeting of two to three thousand workers, soldiers, and socialist intellectuals modeled on the revolutionary soviets of 1905.

Yet both liberal and moderate socialist leaders of the provisional government rejected these broad political reforms. Though the Russian people were sick of fighting, the new leaders also refused to take Russia out of the war. A new government formed in May 1917 included the fiery agrarian socialist Alexander Kerensky, who became prime minister in July. He refused to confiscate large landholdings and give them to peasants, fearing that such drastic action would only complete the disintegration of Russia's peasant army. For the patriotic Kerensky, as for other moderate socialists, the continuation of war was still a national duty. Human suffering and war-

weariness grew, testing the limited strength of the provisional government.

From its first day, the provisional government had to share power with a formidable rival—the **Petrograd Soviet** (or council) of Workers' and Soldiers' Deputies. Modeled on the revolutionary soviets of 1905, the Petrograd Soviet comprised two to three thousand workers, soldiers, and socialist intellectuals. Seeing itself as a true grassroots product of revolutionary democracy, the Soviet acted as a parallel government. It issued its own radical orders, weakening the authority of the provisional government.

The most famous edict of the Petrograd Soviet was Army Order No. 1, issued in May 1917, which stripped officers of their authority and placed power in the hands of elected committees of common soldiers. Designed primarily to protect the revolution from resistance by the aristocratic officer corps, the order led to a collapse of army discipline.

In July 1917 the provisional government ordered a poorly considered summer offensive against the Germans. The campaign was a miserable failure, and peas-

The Radicalization of the Russian Army Russian soldiers inspired by the Bolshevik cause carry banners with Marxist slogans calling for revolution and democracy, around July 1917. One reads "All Power to the Proletariat," a telling response to the provisional government's failure to pull Russia out of the war. Sick of defeat and wretched conditions at the front, the tsar's troops welcomed Lenin's promises of "Bread, Land, and Peace" and were enthusiastic participants in the Russian Revolution. (Hulton/Getty Images)

ant soldiers began "voting with their feet." They deserted in droves, returning to their villages to help their families get a share of the land, which peasants were seizing as they settled old scores in a great agrarian upheaval. Russia was descending into anarchy in the summer of 1917. It was an unparalleled opportunity for the most radical and talented of Russia's many revolutionary leaders, Vladimir Ilyich Lenin (1870–1924).

Lenin and the Bolshevik Revolution

Lenin's life had been dedicated to the cause of revolution. Born into the middle class, he became an enemy of imperial Russia when his older brother was executed for plotting to kill the tsar in 1887. As a law student, Lenin eagerly studied Marxist socialism, which began to win converts among radical intellectuals as industrialization surged forward in Russia in the 1890s. A pragmatic and flexible thinker, Lenin updated Marx's revolutionary philosophy to address existing conditions in Russia.

Three interrelated concepts were central for Lenin. First, he stressed that only violent revolution could destroy capitalism. He tirelessly denounced all theories of a peaceful evolution to socialism as a betrayal of Marx's message of violent class conflict. Second, Lenin argued that under certain conditions a socialist revolution was possible even in a nonindustrialized agrarian country like Russia. The Russian industrial working class was admittedly tiny, but peasants, like workers, were numerous, poor, and exploited, and they could thus take the place of Marx's traditional working class in the coming conflict.

Third, Lenin believed that the possibility of revolution was determined more by human leadership than by vast historical laws. He called for a highly disciplined workers' party strictly controlled by a small, dedicated elite of intellectuals and professional revolutionaries like himself. Unlike ordinary workers and trade-union officials, this elite would never be seduced by short-term gains. It would not stop until revolution brought it to power. Lenin's version of Marxism had a major impact on events in Russia and ultimately changed the way future revolutionaries undertook radical revolt around the world.

Lenin's ideas did not go unchallenged by other Russian Marxists. At meetings of the Russian Social Democratic Labor Party in London in 1903, matters came to a head. Lenin demanded a small, disciplined, elitist party, while his opponents wanted a more democratic party with mass membership. The Russian Marxists

Key Events of the Russian Revolution

August 1914	Russia enters the war
1916–1917	Tsarist government in crisis
March 1917	February Revolution; establishment of provisional government; tsar abdicates
April 1917	Lenin returns from exile
July 1917	Bolshevik attempt to seize power fails
October 1917	Bolsheviks gain a majority in the Petrograd Soviet
November 7, 1917	Bolsheviks seize power; Lenin named head of new communist government
March 1918	Treaty of Brest-Litovsk; Trotsky becomes head of the Red Army
1918–1920	Civil war
1920	Civil war ends; Lenin and Bolshevik-Communists take control of Russia

promptly split into two rival factions. Lenin called his camp the **Bolsheviks**, or "majority group"; his opponents were Mensheviks, or "minority group." The Bolsheviks had only a tenuous majority of a single vote, but Lenin kept the name for propaganda reasons and developed the revolutionary party he wanted: tough, disciplined, and led from above.

Unlike most other socialists, Lenin had not rallied around the national flag in 1914. Observing

Bolsheviks Lenin's radical, revolutionary arm of the Russian party of Marxian socialism, which successfully installed a dictatorial socialist regime in Russia.

events from neutral Switzerland, where he lived in exile to avoid persecution by the tsar's police, Lenin viewed the war as a product of imperialist rivalries and a marvelous opportunity for socialist revolution. After the February Revolution of 1917, the German government provided the impatient Lenin, his wife, and about twenty trusted colleagues with safe passage across Germany and back into Russia. The Germans hoped that Lenin would undermine the sagging war effort of the provisional government. They were not disappointed. Arriving triumphantly at Petrograd's Finland Station on April 3, Lenin attacked at once. To the astonishment of the local Bolsheviks, he rejected all cooperation with what he called the "bourgeois" provisional government. His slogans were radical in the extreme: "All power to the soviets"; "All land to the peasants"; "Stop the war now." Lenin was a superb tactician. His promises of "Bread, Land, and Peace" spoke to the expectations of suffering workers, peasants, and soldiers alike, and earned the Bolsheviks substantial popular support. The moment for revolution was at hand.

Yet Lenin and the Bolsheviks almost lost the struggle for Russia. An attempt to seize power in July collapsed, and Lenin went into hiding. This temporary setback

Lenin Rallies Soldiers Lenin, known for his fiery speeches, addresses Red Army soldiers in Moscow in the midst of the Russian civil war, May 1920. Leon Trotsky, the leader of the Red Army, stands on the podium stairs to the right. (Mansell/Time Life Images/Getty Images)

made little difference in the long run. Intrigue between Kerensky, who became prime minister in July, and his commander in chief, General Lavr Kornilov, resulted in Kornilov's leading a feeble coup against the provisional government in September. In the face of this rightist counter-revolutionary threat, the Bolsheviks were re-armed and redeemed. Kornilov's forces disintegrated, but Kerensky lost all credit with the army, the only force that might have saved democratic government in Russia.

Trotsky and the Seizure of Power

Throughout the summer, the Bolsheviks greatly increased their popular support. Party membership soared from 50,000 to 240,000, and in October the Bolsheviks gained a fragile majority in the Petrograd Soviet. Now Lenin's supporter Leon Trotsky (1879–1940), a spell-binding revolutionary orator and radical Marxist, brilliantly executed the Bolshevik seizure of power.

Painting a vivid but untruthful picture of German and counter-revolutionary plots, Trotsky convinced the Petrograd Soviet to form a special military-revolutionary committee in October and make him its leader. Thus military power in the capital passed into Bolshevik hands. On the night of November 6, militants from Trotsky's committee joined with trusted Bolshevik soldiers to seize government buildings and pounce on members of the provisional government. Then they went on to the Congress of Soviets where a Bolshevik majority — roughly 390 of 650 excited delegates — declared that all power had passed to the soviets and named Lenin head of the new government. John Reed, a sympathetic American

journalist, described the enthusiasm that greeted one of Lenin's speeches at the congress:

> *Now Lenin, gripping the edge of the reading stand . . . stood there waiting, apparently oblivious to the long-rolling ovation, which lasted several minutes. When it finished, he said simply, "We shall now proceed to construct the Socialist order!" Again that overwhelming human roar.*[9]

The Bolsheviks came to power for three key reasons. First, by late 1917 democracy had given way to anarchy: power was there for those who would take it. Second, in Lenin and Trotsky the Bolsheviks had an utterly determined and superior leadership, which both the tsarist and the provisional governments lacked. Third, as Reed's comments suggest, the Bolsheviks appealed to soldiers and urban workers who were exhausted by war, weary of tsarist autocracy, and ready for radical changes. With time, many Russians would become bitterly disappointed with the Bolshevik regime, but for the moment they had good reason to hope for peace, better living conditions, and a more equitable society.

Dictatorship and Civil War

The truly monumental accomplishment of Lenin, Trotsky, and the rest of the Bolsheviks was not taking power, but keeping it. Over the next four years, the Bolsheviks conquered the chaos they had helped create and began to build a communist society. The conspirators became conquerors. How was this done?

Lenin had the genius to profit from developments over which he and the Bolsheviks had little control.

Since summer, a peasant revolution had swept across Russia, as impoverished peasants invaded and divided among themselves the estates of the landlords and the church. Thus when Lenin mandated land reform from above, he merely approved what peasants were already doing. Popular unrest had also spread to the cities. Urban workers established their own local soviets or committees and demanded direct control of individual factories. This, too, Lenin ratified with a decree in November 1917.

The Bolsheviks cleverly proclaimed their regime a "provisional workers' and peasants' government," promising that a freely elected Constituent Assembly would draw up a new constitution. But free elections in November produced a stunning setback: the Bolsheviks won only 23 percent of the elected delegates. The Socialist Revolutionary Party—the peasants' party—had a clear majority with about 40 percent of the vote. The Constituent Assembly met for only one day, on January 18, 1918. It was then permanently disbanded by Bolshevik soldiers acting under Lenin's orders. Thus just two months after the Bolshevik victory, Lenin began to form a one-party state.

Unlike many of his colleagues, Lenin acknowledged that Russia had effectively lost the war with Germany and that the only realistic goal was peace at any price. That price was very high. Germany demanded that the Soviet government give up all its western territories.

These areas were inhabited by Poles, Finns, Lithuanians, and other non-Russians—people who had been conquered by the tsars over three centuries and put into the "prisonhouse of nationalities," as Lenin had earlier called the Russian empire.

At first, Lenin's fellow Bolsheviks refused to accept such great territorial losses. But when German armies resumed their unopposed march into Russia in February 1918, Lenin had his way in a very close vote. A third of old Russia's population was sliced away by the **Treaty of Brest-Litovsk** (BREHST lih-TAWFSK), signed with Germany in March 1918. With peace, Lenin escaped the disaster of continued war and could pursue his goal of absolute political power for the Bolsheviks—now also called Communists—within Russia.

The war's end and the destruction of the democratically elected Constituent Assembly inspired armed opposition to the Bolshevik regime. People who had supported self-rule in November saw that once again they were getting dictatorship from the capital. The officers of the old army rejected the peace treaty and organized the so-called White opposition to the Bolsheviks in southern Russia, Ukraine, and Siberia and west of Petrograd. The Whites came from many social groups

> **Treaty of Brest-Litovsk**
> Peace treaty signed in March 1918 between the Central Powers and Russia that ceded Russian territories containing a third of the Russian empire's population to the Central Powers.

Spreading Communism Bolshevik supporters and propagandists worked diligently to enlist the backing of ordinary people across Russia. Standing in front of a portrait of Lenin, this bearded agitator explains the benefits of the Bolshevik program to a group of Russian peasants. (Bettmann/Corbis)

and were united only by their hatred of communism and the Bolsheviks—the Reds.

By the summer of 1918, Russia was in a full-fledged civil war. Fully eighteen self-proclaimed regional governments—several of which represented minority nationalities—were challenging Lenin's government in Moscow. By the end of the year, White armies were on the attack. In October 1919 they closed in on central Russia from three sides, and it appeared they might triumph. They did not.

Lenin and the Red Army beat back the counter-revolutionary White armies for several reasons. Most important, the Bolsheviks had quickly developed a better army. Once again, Trotsky's leadership was decisive. At first the Bolsheviks had preached democracy in the military and even elected officers in 1917. But beginning in March 1918, Trotsky became war commissar of the newly formed Red Army. He re-established strict discipline and the draft. Soldiers deserting or disobeying an order were summarily shot. Moreover, Trotsky made effective use of former tsarist army officers, who were actively recruited and given unprecedented powers over their troops. In short, Trotsky formed a disciplined and effective fighting force, which repeatedly defeated the Whites in the field.

war communism The application of centralized state control during the Russian civil war, in which the Bolsheviks seized grain from peasants, introduced rationing, nationalized all banks and industry, and required everyone to work.

Other conditions favored the Bolsheviks. Strategically, the Reds controlled central Russia and the crucial cities of Moscow and Petrograd. The Whites attacked from the fringes and lacked coordination. Moreover, the poorly defined political program of the Whites was a mishmash of liberal republicanism and monarchism, and it never united the Bolshevik's enemies under a progressive democratic banner. And while the Bolsheviks promised the ethnic minorities in Russian-controlled territories substantial autonomy, the nationalist Whites wished to preserve the tsarist empire.

The Bolsheviks mobilized the home front for the war effort by establishing a system of centralized controls called **war communism**. All banks and industries were nationalized, and private enterprise was outlawed. Bolshevik commissars introduced rationing, seized grain from peasants to feed the cities, and maintained strict workplace discipline. Although these measures contributed to a breakdown of normal economic activity, they maintained labor discipline and kept the Red Army supplied with men and material.

Revolutionary terror also contributed to the Communist victory. Lenin and the Bolsheviks set up a fearsome secret police known as the Cheka, dedicated to suppressing counter-revolutionaries of all types. During the civil war, the Cheka imprisoned and executed without trial tens of thousands of supposed class enemies. Victims included clergymen, aristocrats and wealthy Russian bourgeoisie, deserters from the Red Army, and political opponents of all kinds, including the tsar and his family, who were executed in July 1918. The so-called Red Terror of 1918–1920 helped establish the secret police as a central tool of the new communist government.

Foreign military intervention to support the White armies in the civil war also ironically helped the Bolsheviks. For a variety of reasons, but primarily to stop the spread of communism, the Western Allies (including the United States, Britain, France, and Japan) sent troops to support the Whites. Yet their efforts were limited and halfhearted. In 1919 Westerners were sick of war, and few politicians wanted to get involved in a new military crusade. Thus Allied intervention did not aid the Whites effectively, though it did permit the Bolsheviks to appeal to the patriotic nationalism of ethnic Russians, in particular former tsarist army officers who objected to foreign involvement in Russian affairs.

By the spring of 1920, the White armies were almost completely defeated, and the Bolsheviks had retaken much of the territory ceded to Germany under the Treaty of Brest-Litovsk. The Red Army reconquered Belarus and Ukraine, both of which had gained a brief moment of independence at the end of World War I. Building on this success, the Bolsheviks moved westward into Polish territory, but they were halted on the outskirts of Warsaw in August 1920 by troops under the leadership of the Polish field marshal and chief of state Jozef Pilsudski. The defeat halted Bolshevik attempts to spread communism into western Europe, though in 1921 the Red Army overran the independent nationalist governments of the Caucasus. The Russian civil war was over. Despite losses to Poland, the Bolsheviks had won an impressive victory.

The Peace Settlement

How did the Allies fashion a peace settlement, and why was it unsuccessful? ■

Even as civil war spread in Russia and chaos engulfed much of eastern Europe, the war in the west was coming to an end. In the spring of 1918, the German high command launched a desperate attack against France. This offensive failed, and the United States, Britain,

- Ceded after Treaty of Brest-Litovsk, 1918
- Bolshevik territory, 1919
- Occupied by Allies, 1919
- White Army forces
- Boundary of U.S.S.R., 1921

Barents Sea

NORWAY
SWEDEN
FINLAND
Archangel
Petrograd
Moscow
Warsaw
BELARUS RUSSIA
POLAND
UKRAINE
ROMANIA
BULGARIA Black Sea
Caspian Sea
TURKEY

The Russian Civil War, 1917–1922

"The Deceiving Brothers Have Fallen Upon Us!" This pro-Bolshevik propaganda poster from the Russian civil war is loaded with symbolism. It draws on the Greek myth of Hercules battling the hydra to depict the enemies of the revolution as a many-headed snake. Ugly caricatures of Germany, France, Tsar Nicholas, Britain, and the church bleed from the blows of a powerful Russian worker, who embodies the revolutionary working class. At the bottom of the page, a lengthy poem calls on the Russian people to stand together to defeat the "deceiving brothers," and in the background a booming industrial landscape represents the development that will follow Bolshevik victory. (The New York Public Library/Art Resource, NY)

and France defeated Germany. The guns of world war finally fell silent, and the victorious Western Allies came together in Paris to establish a lasting peace. Expectations were high; optimism was almost unlimited.

The Allies soon worked out terms for peace with Germany and for the creation of the peacekeeping League of Nations. Nevertheless, the hopes of peoples and politicians were disappointed, for the peace settlement of 1919 turned out to be a failure. Rather than lasting peace, the immediate postwar years brought economic crisis and violent political conflict.

The End of the War

In early 1918 the German leadership decided that the time was ripe for a last-ditch, all-out attack on France. The defeat of Russia had released men and materials for the western front. The looming arrival of fresh U.S. troops and the growth of dissent at home quickened German leaders' resolve, and General Ludendorff and company fell on France once more in the great spring offensive of 1918. German armies came within thirty-five miles of Paris, but Ludendorff's exhausted, overextended forces never broke through. They were stopped in July at the second Battle of the Marne, where 140,000 American soldiers saw action. The late but massive American intervention tipped the scales in favor of Allied victory.

By September British, French, and American armies were advancing steadily on all fronts, and a panicky General Ludendorff realized that Germany had lost the war. Not wanting to shoulder the blame, he insisted that moderate politicians should take responsibility for the defeat. On October 4 the German emperor formed a new, more liberal civilian government to sue for peace.

As negotiations over an armistice dragged on, the frustrated German people rose up in revolt. On November 3 sailors in Kiel mutinied, and throughout northern Germany soldiers and workers began to establish revolutionary councils on the Russian soviet model. The same day, Austria-Hungary surrendered to the Allies and began breaking apart. Revolution broke out in Germany, and masses of workers demonstrated for peace in Berlin. With army discipline collapsing, Emperor William II abdicated and fled to Holland. Socialist leaders in Berlin proclaimed a German republic on November 9 and agreed to tough Allied terms of surrender. The armistice went into effect on November 11, 1918. The war was over.

Revolution in Austria-Hungary and Germany

Military defeat brought turmoil and revolution to Austria-Hungary and Germany, as it had to Russia. Having started the war to preserve an imperial state, the Austro-Hungarian Empire perished in the attempt.

The independent states of Austria, Hungary, and Czechoslovakia, and a larger Romania, were carved out of its territory (Map 26.4). A greatly expanded Serbian monarchy gained control of the western Balkans and took the name Yugoslavia. For four months in 1919, until conservative nationalists seized power, Hungary became an independent Soviet republic. Austria-Hungary no longer existed.

In late 1918 Germany likewise experienced a dramatic revolution that resembled the Russian Revolution of March 1917. In both cases, a genuine popular uprising welled up from below, toppled an authoritarian monarchy, and created a liberal provisional republic. In both countries, liberals and moderate socialist politicians struggled with more radical workers' and soldiers' councils (or soviets) for political dominance. In Germany, however, moderates from the Social Democratic Party and their liberal allies held on to power and established the Weimar Republic—a democratic government that would lead Germany for the next fifteen years. Their success was a deep disappointment for the Russian Bolsheviks, who had hoped that a more radical revolution in Germany would help spread communism across the European continent.

There were several reasons for the German outcome. The great majority of the Marxist politicians in the Social Democratic Party were not revolutionaries and were really moderates, as they had been before the war. They wanted political democracy and civil liberties and favored the gradual elimination of capitalism. They were also German nationalists, appalled by the prospect of civil war and revolutionary terror. Of crucial importance was the fact that the moderate Social Democrats quickly came to terms with the army and big business, which helped prevent Germany from reaching total collapse.

Yet the triumph of the German Social Democrats brought violent chaos to Germany in 1918–1919. The new republic was attacked from both sides of the political spectrum. Radical communists led by Karl Liebknecht and Rosa Luxemburg and their supporters in the councils tried to seize control of the government in the Spartacist Uprising in Berlin in January 1919. The moderate Social Democrats called in nationalist Free Corps militias, bands of demobilized soldiers who had kept their weapons, to crush the uprising. Liebknecht and Luxemburg were arrested and then brutally murdered by Free Corps soldiers. In Bavaria, a short-lived Soviet-style republic was violently overthrown on government orders by the Free Corps. Nationwide strikes by leftist workers and a short-lived military takeover—the Kapp Putsch—were also repressed by the central government.

By the summer of 1920, the situation had calmed down, but the new republican government faced deep discontent. Communists and radical socialists blamed

North
Sea

Baltic Sea

ATLANTIC
OCEAN

Mediterranean Sea

Black
Sea

Mapping the Past

Map 26.4 Territorial Changes After World War I World War I brought tremendous changes to eastern Europe. New nations and new boundaries were established, and a dangerous power vacuum was created by the relatively weak states established between Germany and Soviet Russia.

ANALYZING THE MAP What territory did Germany lose, and to whom? Why was Austria referred to as a head without a body in the 1920s? What new independent states were formed from the old Russian empire?

CONNECTIONS How were the principles of national self-determination applied to the redrawing of Europe after the war, and why didn't this theory work in practice?

To complete this activity online, go to the Online Study Guide at **bedfordstmartins.com/mckaywest**.

the Social Democrats for the murders of Liebknecht and Luxemburg and the repression of the Bavarian Soviet. Right-wing nationalists, including the new Nazi Party, despised the government from the start. They spread the myth that the German army had never actually lost the war—instead, the nation was "stabbed in the back" by socialists and pacifists at home. In Germany, the end of the war brought only a fragile sense of political stability.

The Treaty of Versailles

In January 1919 over seventy delegates from twenty-seven nations met in Paris to hammer out a peace accord. The conference produced the **Treaty of Versailles**, which laid out the terms of the postwar settlement and was signed by the victorious Allies and the defeated Germany. The peace negotiations inspired great expectations.

Treaty of Versailles The 1919 peace settlement that ended war between Germany and the Allied powers.

841

> ❝ [The victors] were journeying to Paris . . . to found a new order in Europe. We were preparing not Peace only, but Eternal Peace. ❞

—**BRITISH DIPLOMAT**

A young British diplomat later wrote that the victors "were journeying to Paris . . . to found a new order in Europe. We were preparing not Peace only, but Eternal Peace."[10]

This idealism was greatly strengthened by U.S. President Wilson's January 1918 peace proposal, the **Fourteen Points**. The proposal called for open diplomacy, a reduction in armaments, freedom of commerce and trade, and the establishment of a **League of Nations**, an international body designed to provide a place for peaceful resolution of world problems. Perhaps most important, Wilson demanded that the peace be based on the notion of **national self-determination**, meaning that peoples should be able to choose their own national governments through democratic majority-rule elections, and live free from outside interference in territories with clearly defined permanent borders. Despite the general optimism inspired by these ideas, the conference and the treaty itself quickly generated disagreement.

The controlling powers at the conference were termed the "Big Three": the United States, Great Britain, and France. Germany, Austria-Hungary, and Russia were excluded from the conference, though their lands were placed on the negotiating table. Italy was included, but its role was quite limited. The conference included smaller nations as well, from the Middle East, Africa, and East Asia, but their concerns, for the most part, were simply ignored.

Almost immediately upon their arrival in Paris, the Big Three began to quarrel. President Wilson, who was wildly cheered by European crowds as the champion of democratic international cooperation, was almost obsessed with creating the League of Nations. Wilson insisted that this question come first, for he passionately believed that only a permanent international organization could avert future wars. Wilson had his way, although prime ministers Lloyd George of Great Britain and especially Georges Clemenceau of France were unenthusiastic. They were primarily concerned with punishing Germany.

The question of what to do with Germany in fact dominated discussions among the Big Three. Clemenceau wanted Germany to pay for its aggression. The war in the west had been fought on French soil, and like most French people, Clemenceau wanted revenge, economic retribution, and lasting security for France. This, he believed, required the creation of a buffer state between France and Germany, the permanent demilitarization of Germany, and vast German reparations. Lloyd George supported Clemenceau, but was less harsh. Wilson disagreed. Clemenceau's demands seemed vindictive, and they violated Wilson's sense of Christian morality and the principle of national self-determination. By April the countries attending the conference were deadlocked on the German question, and Wilson packed his bags to go home.

In the end, Clemenceau was convinced that France could not afford to face Germany alone in the future and agreed to a compromise. He gave up the French demand for a Rhineland buffer state in return for a formal defensive alliance with the United States and Great Britain. Under the terms of this alliance, both Wilson and Lloyd George promised that their countries would come to France's aid in the event of a German attack. The Allies moved quickly to finish the settlement, believing that further adjustments would be possible within the dual framework of a strong Western alliance and the League of Nations.

The Treaty of Versailles was the key to the settlement. Its terms redrew the map of Europe, and the war's losers paid the price. The new independent nations carved out of the Austro-Hungarian and Russian Empires included Poland, Czechoslovakia, Finland, the Baltic states, and Yugoslavia. The Ottoman Empire (which had fought on the German side) was split apart, its territories placed under the control of the victors. Germany's African and Asian colonies were given to France, Britain, and Japan as League of Nations mandates or administered territories, though Germany's losses within Europe were relatively minor, thanks to Wilson. Alsace-Lorraine was returned to France. Ethnic Polish territories seized by Prussia during the eighteenth-century partition of Poland (see Chapter 17) were returned to the new Polish state. Predominately German Danzig was also placed within the Polish border, but as a self-governing city under League of Nations protection. Germany had to limit its army to one

Fourteen Points Wilson's 1918 peace proposal calling for open diplomacy, a reduction in armaments, freedom of commerce and trade, the establishment of the League of Nations, and national self-determination.

League of Nations A permanent international organization, established during the 1919 Paris peace conference, designed to protect member states from aggression and avert future wars.

national self-determination The notion that people should be able to live free from outside interference in nations with clearly defined borders, and should be able to choose their own national governments through democratic majority-rule elections.

hundred thousand men and agree to build no military fortifications in the Rhineland.

More harshly, in Article 231, the famous **war guilt clause**, the Allies declared that Germany (with Austria) was solely responsible for the war. Germany therefore had to pay reparations equal to all civilian damages caused by the fighting. This unfortunate and much-criticized clause expressed French and to some extent British demands for revenge. For the Germans, reparations were a crippling financial burden. Moreover, the war guilt clause was a cutting insult to German national pride. Many Germans believed wartime propaganda that had repeatedly claimed that Germany was an innocent victim, forced into war by a circle of barbaric enemies.

When presented with the treaty, the new German government protested vigorously. But there was no alternative, especially since the people of Germany were still starving because the Allies had not yet lifted their naval blockade. On June 28, 1919, German representatives of the ruling moderate Social Democrats and the Catholic Party signed the treaty in Louis XIV's hall of mirrors at Versailles, where Bismarck's empire had been joyously proclaimed almost fifty years before (see Chapter 24).

The rapidly concluded Versailles treaty was far from perfect, but within the context of war-shattered Europe it was a beginning. Germany had been punished, but not dismembered. A new world organization complemented a traditional defensive alliance of satisfied powers: Britain, France, and the United States. The remaining serious problems, the Allies hoped, could be worked out in the future. Moreover, Allied leaders had seen speed as essential for another reason. They detested Lenin and feared that his Bolshevik Revolution might spread. They realized that their best answer to Lenin's unending calls for worldwide upheaval was peace and tranquillity for war-weary peoples.

Yet the great hopes of early 1919 had turned to ashes by the end of the year. The Western alliance had collapsed, and a grandiose plan for permanent peace had given way to a fragile European truce. There were several reasons for this turn of events. First, the U.S. Senate and, to a lesser extent, the American people rejected Wilson's handiwork. Republican senators led by Henry Cabot Lodge believed that the treaty gave away Congress's constitutional right to declare war and demanded changes in the articles. In failing health, Wilson, with narrow-minded self-righteousness, rejected all attempts at compromise. In doing so, he ensured that the treaty would never be ratified by the United States in any form and that the United States would never join the League of Nations. Moreover, the Senate refused to ratify Wilson's treaties forming a defensive alliance with France and Great Britain. America in effect had turned its back on

Europe. The Wilson-Lodge fiasco and the newly found gospel of isolationism represented a tragic renunciation of America's responsibility. Using U.S. actions as an excuse, Great Britain too refused to ratify its defensive alliance with France. Bitterly betrayed by its allies, France stood alone.

The principle of national self-determination, which had engendered such enthusiasm after the war, was good in theory but flawed in practice. Even in Europe, the borders of new states such as Poland, Czechoslovakia, and Yugoslavia cut through a jumble of ethnic and religious groups who often despised each other. The new central European nations would prove to be economically weak and politically unstable, the focus of conflict in the interwar years. In the colonies, desires for self-determination were simply ignored. The Great Powers happily received Germany's colonies but were hardly ready to give up their own. The problems with self-determination were particularly evident in the fate of the territories of the former Ottoman Empire, where the victorious Allies paid little attention to the desires of the native peoples of the Middle East.

> **war guilt clause** An article in the Treaty of Versailles that declared that Germany (with Austria) was solely responsible for the war and had to pay reparations equal to all civilian damages caused by the fighting.

The Peace Settlement in the Middle East

Although Allied leaders at Versailles focused mainly on European questions, they also imposed a political settlement on what had been the Ottoman Empire. This settlement brought radical and controversial changes to the Middle East. In short, the Ottoman Empire was broken up, Britain and France expanded their power and influence in the Middle East, and Arab nationalists felt cheated and betrayed.

The British government had encouraged the wartime Arab revolt against the Ottoman Turks (see page 826) and had even made vague promises of an independent Arab kingdom. However, when the fighting stopped, the British and the French chose instead to honor secret wartime agreements to divide and rule the Ottoman lands. Most important was the Sykes-Picot Agreement of 1916, named after British and French diplomats. In the secret accord, Britain and France basically agreed that France would receive modern-day Lebanon and Syria and much of southern Turkey, and that Britain would receive Palestine, Transjordan, and Iraq. Thus the Allies never truly intended to grant Arab self-determination after the war. When Britain and France set about implementing their secret plans after the armistice, Arab nationalists reacted with surprise and resentment.

British plans for the Ottoman province of Palestine also angered Arab nationalists. The **Balfour Declaration** of November 1917, written by British foreign secretary Arthur Balfour, had declared that Britain favored a "National Home for the Jewish People" in Palestine, but without prejudicing the civil and religious rights of the non-Jewish communities already living in Palestine. Some members of the British cabinet believed that the declaration would appeal to German, Austrian, and American Jews and thus help the British war effort. Others sincerely supported the Zionist vision of a Jewish homeland (see Chapter 24), which they hoped would also help Britain maintain control of the Suez Canal. In any event, Palestinian Arabs were dismayed.

In 1914 Jews accounted for about 11 percent of the population in the three Ottoman districts that would

> **Balfour Declaration** A 1917 British statement that declared British support of a National Home for the Jewish People in Palestine.

subsequently be lumped together by the British to form Palestine; the rest of the population was predominantly Arab. Yet both groups understood that the National Home for the Jewish People mentioned in the Balfour Declaration implied the establishment of some kind of Jewish state that would violate majority rule. Moreover, a state founded on religious and ethnic exclusivity was out of keeping with both Islamic and Ottoman tradition, which had historically been more tolerant of religious diversity and minorities than the Christian monarchs or nation-states in Europe.

Though Arab leaders attended the Versailles Peace Conference, efforts to secure autonomy in the Middle East came to nothing. Only the kingdom of Hejaz—today part of Saudi Arabia—was granted independence (Map 26.5). In response, Arab nationalists came together in Damascus as the General Syrian Congress in 1919 and unsuccessfully called again for political independence. (See "Listening to the Past: Resolution of the

Map 26.5 **The Partition of the Ottoman Empire, 1914–1923** By 1914 the Ottoman Turks had been pushed out of the Balkans, and their Arab provinces were on the edge of revolt. That revolt, in alliance with the British, erupted during the First World War and contributed greatly to the Ottoman defeat. Refusing to grant independence to the Arabs, the Allies established League of Nations mandates and replaced Ottoman rulers in Syria, Iraq, Transjordan, and Palestine.

General Syrian Congress at Damascus," page 846.) The Congress proclaimed Syria an independent kingdom, and a similar congress declared Iraqi independence.

The Western reaction was swift and decisive. A French army stationed in Lebanon attacked Syria, taking Damascus in July 1920. The Arab government fled, and the French took over. Meanwhile, the British put down an uprising in Iraq with bloody fighting and established effective control there. Brushing aside Arab opposition, the British mandate in Palestine furthermore formally incorporated the Balfour Declaration and its commitment to a Jewish national home. Western imperialism, in the form of League of Nations mandates, appeared to have replaced Ottoman rule in the Arab Middle East.

The Allies sought to impose even harsher terms on the defeated Turks than on the "liberated" Arabs. A treaty forced on the helpless Ottoman sultan dismembered the Turkish heartland. Great Britain and France occupied parts of modern-day Turkey, and Italy and Greece also claimed shares. There was a sizable Greek minority in western Turkey, and Greek nationalists wanted to build a modern Greek empire modeled on

long-dead Christian Byzantium. In 1919 Greek armies carried by British ships landed on the Turkish coast at Smyrna (SMUHR-nuh) and advanced unopposed into the interior, while French troops moved in from the south. Turkey seemed finished.

Yet Turkey survived the postwar invasions. Led by Mustafa Kemal (1881–1938), the Turks refused to acknowledge the Allied dismemberment of their country and gradually mounted a forceful resistance. Kemal had directed the successful Turkish defense at the Battle of Gallipoli with Britain, and despite staggering losses, the newly established Turkish army repulsed the invaders. The Greeks and their British allies sued for peace. In 1923, after long negotiations, the resulting Treaty of Lausanne (loh-ZAN) recognized the territorial integrity of a truly independent Turkey and solemnly abolished the hated Capitulations that the European powers had imposed over the centuries to give their citizens special privileges in the Ottoman Empire.

Kemal, a nationalist without religious faith, believed that Turkey should modernize and secularize along Western lines. He established a republic, had himself elected

Prince Faisal at the Versailles Peace Conference, 1919 Standing in front, Faisal is supported by his allies and black slave. Nur-as-Said, an officer in the Ottoman army who joined the Arab revolt, is second from the left, and the British officer T. E. Lawrence — popularly known as Lawrence of Arabia — is fourth from the left in back. Faisal failed to win political independence for the Arabs, as the British backed away from the vague promises they had made during the war. (Courtesy of the Trustees of the Imperial War Museum)

Resolution of the General Syrian Congress at Damascus

LISTENING TO THE PAST

President Wilson insisted at Versailles that the right of self-determination should be applied to the conquered Ottoman territories, and he sent an American commission of inquiry to Syria, even though the British and French refused to participate. The commission canvassed political views throughout greater Syria, and its long report with many documents reflected public opinion in the region in 1919.

To present their view to the Americans, Arab nationalists from present-day Syria, Lebanon, Israel, and Jordan came together in Damascus as the General Syrian Congress and passed the following resolution on July 2, 1919.

❝ We the undersigned members of the General Syrian Congress, meeting in Damascus on Wednesday, July 2nd, 1919, . . . provided with credentials and authorizations by the inhabitants of our various districts, Moslems, Christians, and Jews, have agreed upon the following statement of the desires of the people of the country who have elected us to present them to the American Section of the International Commission; the fifth article was passed by a very large majority; all the other articles were accepted unanimously.

1. We ask absolutely complete political independence for Syria within these boundaries. [Describes the area including the present-day states of Syria, Lebanon, Israel, and Jordan.]

2. We ask that the Government of this Syrian country should be a democratic civil constitutional Monarchy on broad decentralization principles, safeguarding the rights of minorities, and that the King be the Emir Faisal, who carried on a glorious struggle in the cause of our liberation and merited our full confidence and entire reliance.

3. Considering the fact that the Arabs inhabiting the Syrian area are not naturally less gifted than other more advanced races and that they are by no means less developed than the Bulgarians, Serbians, Greeks, and Roumanians at the beginning of their independence, we protest against Article 22 of the Covenant of the League of Nations, placing us among the nations in their middle stage of development which stand in need of a mandatory power.

4. In the event of the rejection by the Peace Conference of this just protest for certain considerations that we may not understand, we, relying on the declarations of President Wilson that his object in waging war was to put an end to the ambition of conquest and colonization, can only regard the mandate mentioned in the Covenant of the League of Nations as equivalent to the rendering of economical and technical assistance that does not prejudice our complete independence. And desiring that our country should not fall prey to colonization and believing that the American Nation is farthest from any thought of colonization and has no political ambition in our country, we will seek the technical and economical assistance from the United States of America, provided that such assistance does not exceed 20 years.

5. In the event of America not finding herself in a position to accept our desire for assistance, we will seek this assistance from Great Britain, also provided that such assistance does not infringe the complete independence and unity of our country and that the duration of such assistance does not exceed that mentioned in the previous article.

6. We do not acknowledge any right claimed by the French Government in any part whatever of our Syrian country and refuse that she should assist us or

Palestinian Arabs protest against large-scale Jewish migration into Palestine.
(Roger-Viollet/Getty Images)

have a hand in our country under any circumstances and in any place.

7. We oppose the pretensions of the Zionists to create a Jewish commonwealth in the southern part of Syria, known as Palestine, and oppose Zionist migration to any part of our country; for we do not acknowledge their title but consider them a grave peril to our people from the national, economical, and political points of view. Our Jewish compatriots shall enjoy our common rights and assume the common responsibilities.

8. We ask that there should be no separation of the southern part of Syria, known as Palestine, nor of the littoral western zone, which includes Lebanon, from the Syrian country. We desire that the unity of the country should be guaranteed against partition under whatever circumstances.

9. We ask complete independence for emancipated Mesopotamia [today's Iraq] and that there should be no economical barriers between the two countries....

The noble principles enunciated by President Wilson strengthen our confidence that our desires emanating from the depths of our hearts, shall be the decisive factor in determining our future; and that President Wilson and the free American people will be our supporters for the realization of our hopes, thereby proving their sincerity and noble sympathy with the aspiration of the weaker nations in general and our Arab people in particular.

We also have the fullest confidence that the Peace Conference will realize that we would not have risen against the Turks, with whom we had participated in all civil, political, and representative privileges, but for their violation of our national rights, and so will grant us our desires in full in order that our political rights may not be less after the war than they were before, since we have shed so much blood in the cause of our liberty and independence.

We request to be allowed to send a delegation to represent us at the Peace Conference to defend our rights and secure the realization of our aspirations. 〞

Source: "Resolution of the General Syrian Congress at Damascus, 2 July 1919," from the King-Crane Commission Report, in *Foreign Relations of the United States: Paris Peace Conference*, 1919, 12:780–781.

QUESTIONS FOR ANALYSIS

1. What kind of state did the delegates want?

2. Did the delegates view their "Jewish compatriots" and the Zionists in different ways? Why?

3. How did the delegates appeal to American sympathies?

president, and created a one-party system—partly inspired by the Bolshevik example—to transform his country. The most radical reforms pertained to religion and culture. For centuries, most of the intellectual and social activities of believers had been regulated by Islamic religious authorities. Profoundly influenced by the example of western Europe, Kemal set out to limit the place of religion and religious leaders in daily affairs. He decreed a revolutionary separation of church and state, promulgated law codes inspired by European models, and established a secular public school system. Women received rights that they never had before. By the time of his death in 1938, Kemal had implemented much of his revolutionary program. He had moved Turkey much closer to Europe, foretelling current efforts by Turkey to join the European Union as a full-fledged member.

The Human Costs

World War I broke empires, inspired revolutions, and changed national borders on a world scale. It also had immense human costs, and ordinary people in the combatant nations struggled to deal with its legacy in the years that followed. The raw numbers are astonishing: estimates vary, but total deaths on the battlefield numbered between 10 and 13 million soldiers. Germany had the highest number of military casualties, with about 2 million dead and 4 million wounded. France had the highest proportionate number of losses; about 1.2 million were killed, or one out of every ten adult males. The other belligerents paid a high price as well (Figure 26.1). Between 7 and 10 million civilians died because of the war and war-related hardships, and another 20 million people died in the worldwide influenza epidemic that followed the war in 1918.

The vast number of violent deaths and the scope of trench warfare made proper burials difficult, if not impossible. Soldiers were typically interred where they fell, and by 1918 there were thousands of ad hoc military cemeteries scattered across northern France and Flanders. When remains were gathered, the chaos and danger of the battlefield limited accurate identification. After the war, the bodies were moved to more formal cemeteries, but hundreds of thousands remained unidentified. British and German soldiers ultimately remained in foreign soil, in graveyards managed by national commissions. After some delay, the bodies of most of the French combatants were brought home to local cemeteries.

Millions of ordinary people grieved, turning to family, friends, neighbors, and the church for comfort. Towns and villages across Europe raised public memorials to honor the dead and held memorial ceremonies on important anniversaries: on November 11, the day the war ended; in Britain on July 1 to commemorate the Battle of the Somme. These were poignant and often tearful moments for participants. For the first time, each nation built a tomb of the unknown soldier as a national memorial site. Memorials were also built on the main battlefields of the war. All expressed the general need to recognize the great sorrow and suffering caused by so much death.

The victims of the First World War included millions of widows and orphans and huge numbers of disabled and emotionally scarred veterans. Some 10 million soldiers came home disfigured or mutilated. Governments tried to take care of the disabled and the survivor families, but there was never enough money to adequately fund pensions and job training programs. Artificial limbs were expensive, uncomfortable, and awkward, and employers rarely wanted disabled workers on the payroll. Crippled veterans were often forced to beg on the streets, a common sight for the next decade.

The German case is instructive. Nearly 10 percent of German civilians were direct victims of the war, and taking care of them was one of the most difficult problems faced by the new German government. Veterans groups organized to lobby for state support, and fully one-third of the federal budget of the Weimar Republic was tied up in war-related pensions and benefits. With the onset of the Great Depression in 1929, benefits were cut, leaving bitter veterans vulnerable to Nazi propagandists who paid homage to the sacrifices of the war even as they called for the overthrow of the republican government. The human cost of the war thus had another steep price: across Europe, newly formed radical right-wing parties, including the German National Socialists and the Italian Fascists, successfully manipulated popular feelings of loss and resentment to undermine fragile parliamentary governments.

Figure 26.1 Casualties of World War I The losses of World War I were the highest ever for a war in Europe. These numbers are approximate because of problems with record keeping caused by the destructive nature of total war.

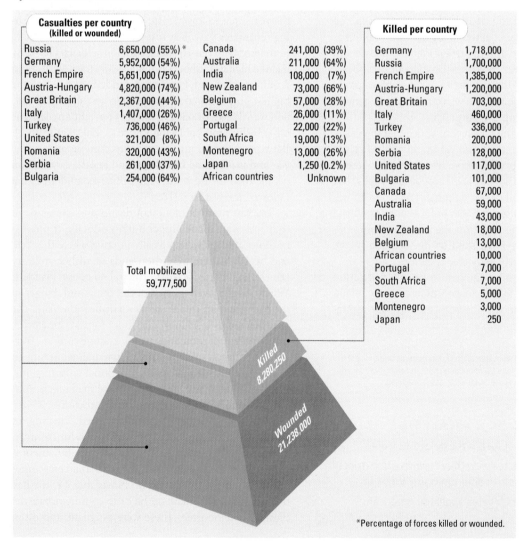

Casualties per country (killed or wounded)

Country	Casualties	Country	Casualties
Russia	6,650,000 (55%) *	Canada	241,000 (39%)
Germany	5,952,000 (54%)	Australia	211,000 (64%)
French Empire	5,651,000 (75%)	India	108,000 (7%)
Austria-Hungary	4,820,000 (74%)	New Zealand	73,000 (66%)
Great Britain	2,367,000 (44%)	Belgium	57,000 (28%)
Italy	1,407,000 (26%)	Greece	26,000 (11%)
Turkey	736,000 (46%)	Portugal	22,000 (22%)
United States	321,000 (8%)	South Africa	19,000 (13%)
Romania	320,000 (43%)	Montenegro	13,000 (26%)
Serbia	261,000 (37%)	Japan	1,250 (0.2%)
Bulgaria	254,000 (64%)	African countries	Unknown

Killed per country

Country	Killed
Germany	1,718,000
Russia	1,700,000
French Empire	1,385,000
Austria-Hungary	1,200,000
Great Britain	703,000
Italy	460,000
Turkey	336,000
Romania	200,000
Serbia	128,000
United States	117,000
Bulgaria	101,000
Canada	67,000
Australia	59,000
India	43,000
New Zealand	18,000
Belgium	13,000
African countries	10,000
Portugal	7,000
South Africa	7,000
Greece	5,000
Montenegro	3,000
Japan	250

Total mobilized 59,777,500

Killed 8,280,250

Wounded 21,238,000

*Percentage of forces killed or wounded.

Disabled French Veterans The war killed millions of soldiers and left many more permanently disabled, making the sight of men missing limbs or disfigured in other ways a common one in the 1920s. (Bettmann/Corbis)

 LOOKING BACK LOOKING AHEAD WHEN CHIEF OF THE GERMAN General Staff Count Helmuth von Moltke imagined the war of the future in a letter to his wife in 1905, his comments were surprisingly accurate. "It will become a war between peoples which will not be concluded with a single battle," the general wrote, "but which will be a long, weary struggle with a country that will not acknowledge defeat until the whole strength of its people is broken."[11] As von Moltke foresaw, World War I broke peoples and nations. The trials of total war increased the power of the centralized state and in the end brought down the Austro-Hungarian, Ottoman, and Russian Empires. The brutal violence shocked and horrified observers across the world; ordinary citizens were left to mourn their losses.

Despite high hopes for Wilson's Fourteen Points, the Treaty of Versailles hardly brought a lasting peace. The war's disruptions encouraged the radical political struggles of the 1920s and 1930s and the rise of totalitarian regimes across Europe, which led to the even more extreme violence of the Second World War. Indeed, some historians believe that the interwar years of 1914 to 1945 might mostly accurately be labeled a modern European Thirty Years' War, since the problems unleashed in August 1914 were only really resolved in the 1950s. This strong assertion contains a great amount of truth. For all of Europe, World War I was a revolutionary conflict of gigantic proportions with lasting traumatic effects.

CHAPTER REVIEW

■ What caused the First World War, and why did it have significant popular support? (page 816)

The immediate cause of the war was the assassination of the heir to the Austro-Hungarian throne by a Serbian nationalist who sought to unify all Serbs in one national state. Backed by Germany, Austria-Hungary reacted harshly, setting off a chain of diplomatic and political events that turned a potentially little war into a world war. The assassination set into play a number of other long-term conflicts, including the diplomatic problems created by Germany's rise to Great Power status after the Franco-Prussian War. By 1912 Europe was divided into two hostile alliances: the Triple Alliance (Germany, Austria, and Italy) on one side and the Dual Alliance (France and Russia) on the other. Diplomatic crises in the colonies and the Balkans, and an arms race between Germany and Britain, increased international tensions. The mood of 1914 was another important factor. Political leaders and ordinary people shared strong feelings of nationalism and believed that military action would be a honorable test of national strength. Europeans underestimated the effects of modern weapons, and leading statesmen willingly engaged in aggressive foreign policy to distract from social tensions at home. Thus the start of the war cannot be blamed on a single factor.

■ How did the First World War change the nature of modern warfare? (page 821)

The violence of a new type of "total war" helps explain why so many died and so many were crippled physically and psychologically. Total war required service by soldiers and civilians alike. New weapons such as the machine gun and poison gas made the war especially deadly. Generals adapted slowly to these new weapons, and men died by the millions. Trench warfare favored the defender, and both sides saw only minimal territorial gains despite enormous losses. On the eastern front, Russians made initial gains in Germany, only to be pushed back into Russia where millions were killed or starved to death. On both the eastern and western fronts, the war degenerated into a persistent stalemate. As it ground on, neutral countries were brought into the conflict, which eventually spread to the Middle East and into some parts of colonial East Asia and Africa.

■ What was the impact of total war on civilian populations? (page 828)

To meet the growing demand for men and weapons, governments began to control many aspects of economic and social life. The result of the need to mobilize entire societies and economies for total war was an administrative revolution that greatly increased the power of the central state.

The need for workers led to growing power and prestige of labor unions and to the entry of women into the workplace. Women received new rights and experimented with new roles, though the long-term results were mixed. As the war ground on, protests against it grew. In addition, countries such as Germany experienced strikes and protest marches over inadequate food supplies. Soldiers deserted in growing numbers, contributing to increasing political tensions at home. Overall, though, civilian populations achieved greater social equality through full employment and the sharing of hardships.

■ What led to the Russian Revolution, and what was its outcome? (page 833)

Severe losses in the war, an ineffective war effort, and poor leadership by Nicholas II created conditions that led to the February Revolution of 1917. After the tsar abdicated, a new provisional government was created. Returning from exile, Lenin and his Bolshevik Party built popular support for his brand of Marxist socialism among war-weary soldiers and the urban poor. Led by the brilliant tactician Trotsky, Lenin and the Bolsheviks took advantage of anarchy in the capital to seize power. The Bolsheviks established a radical regime, smashed existing capitalist institutions, and stayed in power with a new kind of authoritarian rule that posed a powerful ongoing revolutionary challenge to Europe and its colonial empires.

■ How did the Allies fashion a peace settlement, and why was it unsuccessful? (page 838)

The "war to end war" did not bring peace—only a fragile truce. The Big Three powers of the United States, Great Britain, and France had to compromise to reach a settlement. The resulting Treaty of Versailles redrew the map of Europe, dissolving the Austro-Hungarian and Ottoman Empires. But in the west, the Allies failed to maintain their wartime solidarity. Germany, angered by the war guilt clause, remained unrepentant, and the financial burden of war reparations sowed the seeds for World War II. Moreover, the victory of national self-determination in eastern Europe created small, weak states and thus a power vacuum between a still-powerful Germany and a potentially mighty communist Russia. Europeans refused to extend the rights of self-determination to colonized peoples in Africa, Asia, and the Arab Middle East. As in Europe, the borders of the new nation-states often ignored the diversity of peoples on the ground, and so left unresolved problems for the postwar world.

Suggested Reading

Audoin-Rouzeau, Stéphane. *Men at War, 1914–1918: National Sentiment and Trench Journalism in France During the First World War*. 1992. Reconstructs the everyday life of the ordinary French soldier on the western front.

Davis, Belinda J. *Home Fires Burning: Food, Politics, and Everyday Life in Berlin in World War I*. 2000. A moving account of women struggling to feed their families and their protests against the imperial German state.

Fitzpatrick, Sheila. *The Russian Revolution 1917–1932*. 1982. An important interpretation that considers the long-term effects of the revolution.

Fromkin, David. *A Peace to End All Peace*. 2001. A brilliant reconsideration of the collapse of the Ottoman Empire and its division by the Allies.

Gatrell, Peter. *Russia's First World War: A Social and Economic History*. 2005. An excellent resource for students and specialists.

Grayzel, Susan R. *Women and the First World War*. 2002. This useful introduction offers an overview of women's experience of war across Europe.

Horne, John N., and Larry Kramer. *German Atrocities 1914: A History of Denial*. 2001. An evenhanded and revealing account of the atrocities committed by the German army in occupied Belgium.

Hull, Isabel V. *Absolute Destruction: Military Culture and the Practices of War in Imperial Germany*. 2005. A controversial book about the military culture that dominated German society from the Franco-Prussian to the First World War.

Joll, James. *The Origins of the First World War*. 1992. A thorough review of the causes of the war that brings together military, diplomatic, economic, political, and cultural history.

Keegan, John. *The Face of Battle: A Study of Agincourt, Waterloo, and the Somme*. 1983. A famous study by a famous historian that compares the Battle of the Somme to other famous battles.

Liulevicius, Vejas Gabriel. *War Land on the Eastern Front: Culture, National Identity, and German Occupation in World War I*. 2000. An important and pathbreaking work on the eastern front.

Macmillan, Margaret. *Paris, 1919: Six Months That Changed the World*. 2001. A comprehensive, exciting account of all aspects of the peace conference.

Mosse, George. *Fallen Soldiers: Reshaping the Memory of the World Wars*. 1990. A pathbreaking yet accessible account of how Europeans remembered the world wars.

Neiberg, Michael S. *Fighting the Great War: A Global History*. 2006. A lively and up-to-date account.

Read, Christopher. *From Tsar to Soviets: The Russian People and Their Revolution, 1917–1921*. 1996. A fine narrative of the events of the Russian Revolution.

Remarque, Erich Maria. *All Quiet on the Western Front*. 1928. This novel remains one of the most moving fictional treatments of World War I.

Whalen, Richard. *Bitter Wounds: German Victims of the Great War*. 1984. An excellent treatment of the human costs of the war in Germany.

Winter, Jay. *Rites of Memory, Sites of Mourning: The Great War in European Cultural History*. 1998. A new interpretation of the way Europeans came to terms with the war, by a well-respected historian in the field.

Notes

1. Quoted in J. Remak, *The Origins of World War I* (New York: Holt, Rinehart & Winston, 1967), p. 84.
2. On the mood of 1914, see J. Joll, *The Origins of the First World War* (New York: Longman, 1992), pp. 199–233.
3. Quoted in George L. Mosse, *Fallen Soldiers: Reshaping the Memory of the World Wars* (New York: Oxford University Press, 1990), p. 64.
4. Quoted in Noel Malcolm, *Bosnia: A Short History* (New York: New York University Press, 1996), p. 153.
5. Quoted in S. Audoin-Rouzeau, *Men at War, 1914–1918: National Sentiment and Trench Journalism in France During the First World War* (Oxford, U.K.: Berg, 1992), p. 69.
6. V. G. Liulevicius, *War Land on the Eastern Front: Culture, National Identity, and German Occupation in World War I* (New York: Cambridge University Press, 2000), pp. 54–89; quotation on p. 71.
7. Quoted in F. P. Chambers, *The War Behind the War, 1914–1918* (London: Faber & Faber, 1939), p. 168.
8. Quoted in L. L. Downs, *Manufacturing Inequality: Gender Divisions in the French and British Metalworking Industries, 1914–1939* (Ithaca, N.Y.: Cornell University Press, 1995), p. 95.
9. John Reed, *Ten Days That Shook the World* (New York: International Publishers, 1967), p. 126.
10. Quoted in H. Nicolson, *Peacemaking 1919* (New York: Grosset & Dunlap Universal Library, 1965), pp. 8, 31–32.
11. Quoted in C. Barnett, *The Swordbearers: Supreme Command in the First World War* (New York: Morrow, 1964), p. 40.

Key Terms

Triple Alliance (p. 817)
Triple Entente (p. 817)
Schlieffen Plan (p. 821)
total war (p. 821)
trench warfare (p. 823)
February Revolution (p. 833)
Petrograd Soviet (p. 834)
Bolsheviks (p. 835)
Treaty of Brest-Litovsk (p. 837)
war communism (p. 838)
Treaty of Versailles (p. 841)
Fourteen Points (p. 842)
League of Nations (p. 842)
national self-determination (p. 842)
war guilt clause (p. 843)
Balfour Declaration (p. 844)

For practice quizzes and other study tools, visit the Online Study Guide at **bedfordstmartins.com/mckaywest**.

For primary sources from this period, see ***Sources of Western Society*, Second Edition**.

For Web sites, images, and documents related to topics in this chapter, visit Make History at **bedfordstmartins.com/mckaywest**.

27

The Age of Anxiety

1900–1940

(akg-images. © Estate of George Grosz/Licensed by VAGA, New York, NY)

When Allied diplomats met in Paris in early 1919 with their optimistic plans for building a lasting peace, most people looked forward to happier times. After the terrible trauma of total war, they hoped that life would return to normal and would make sense in the familiar prewar terms of peace, prosperity, and progress. Their hopes were in vain. The First World War and the Russian Revolution had mangled too many things beyond repair. Life would no longer fit neatly into the old molds.

Instead, great numbers of men and women felt themselves increasingly adrift in a strange, uncertain, and uncontrollable world. They saw themselves living in an age of anxiety and continual crisis. Radical developments in the arts and sciences challenged received wisdom of all kinds. Political stability remained elusive, and the Great Depression in 1929 shocked the status quo. Democratic liberalism was besieged by the rise of authoritarian and fascist governments, and another world conflict seemed imminent. In the early 1920s the French poet and critic Paul Valéry (va-lay-REE) (1871–1945) described the widespread "impression of darkness" in this age of anxiety, where "almost all the affairs of men remain in a terrible uncertainty. We think of what has disappeared, and we are almost destroyed by what has been destroyed; we do not know what will be born, and we fear the future, not without reason."[1] Valéry's words captured the sense of gloom and foreboding that dominated the decades between the world wars. ∎

Life in the Age of Anxiety. Dadaist George Grosz's *Inside and Outside* is a disturbing image of the class conflict wrought by the economic crises of the 1920s. Wealthy and bestial elites celebrate a luxurious New Year's Eve "inside," while "outside" a disabled veteran begs in vain for money from uncaring passersby.

CHAPTER PREVIEW

Uncertainty in Modern Thought
■ In what ways did new and sometimes radically experimental ideas in philosophy, religion, physics, psychology, and literature reflect the general crisis in Western thought?

Modernism in Architecture, Art, and Music
■ How did modernism revolutionize architecture, painting, and music?

An Emerging Consumer Society
■ How did the emerging consumer society and mass culture of the interwar years change the everyday lives of ordinary men and women?

The Search for Peace and Political Stability
■ How did the democratic leaders of the 1920s deal with deep-seated instability and try to establish real peace and prosperity?

The Great Depression, 1929–1939
■ What caused the Great Depression, and how did the Western democracies respond to this challenge?

Uncertainty in Modern Thought

In what ways did new and sometimes radically experimental ideas in philosophy, religion, physics, psychology, and literature reflect the general crisis in Western thought? ▪

The decades surrounding the First World War—from the 1880s to the 1930s—brought intense cultural and intellectual experimentation. Dramatic changes shook the fields of philosophy, science, and literature. After the war, these new ideas spread rapidly. Western society began to question and even abandon many of the cherished values and beliefs that had guided it since the eighteenth-century Enlightenment and the nineteenth-century triumph of industrial development and scientific advance. Ordinary people found many of these revolutionary ideas unsettling. In response, many turned to Christianity, which experienced a remarkable revival in this period.

Modern Philosophy

Before 1914 most people still believed in Enlightenment philosophies of progress, reason, and individual rights. At the turn of the century, supporters of these philosophies had some cause for optimism. Political rights were gradually spreading to women and workers, and the rising standard of living, the taming of the city, and the growth of state-supported social programs suggested that things were indeed improving. Such developments en-

couraged faith in the ability of a rational human mind to understand the universe through intellectual investigation. Just as there were laws of science, many thinkers felt that there were laws of society that rational human beings could discover and then wisely act on.

Nevertheless, as the nineteenth century drew to a close, a small group of serious thinkers and creative writers mounted a determined attack on these well-worn optimistic ideas. These critics rejected the general faith in progress and the rational human mind. The German philosopher Friedrich Nietzsche (NEE-chuh) (1844–1900) was particularly influential. Nietzsche worked as a professor of classical languages at the University of Basel until ill health forced him to retire at an early age. Never a systematic philosopher, he wrote as a prophet in a provocative and poetic style. In the first of his *Untimely Meditations* (1873), he argued that ever since classical Athens, the West had overemphasized rationality and stifled the authentic passions and animal instincts that drive human activity and true creativity.

Nietzsche went on to question the conventional values of Western society. He believed that reason, democracy, progress, and respectability were outworn social and psychological constructs whose influence was suffocating self-realization and excellence. Though he was the son of a Lutheran minister, Nietzsche famously rejected religion. In his 1877 book *On the Genealogy of Morals*, he claimed that Christianity embodied a "slave morality" that glorified weakness, envy, and mediocrity. In one of his most famous lines, a wise fool proclaims that "God is dead," metaphorically murdered by lackadaisical modern Christians who no longer really believed in him.

"Existence Precedes Essence" Slogans such as this one captured the basic meaning of the philosophy of existentialism by underscoring the meaninglessness of human life and helped turn French intellectual Jean-Paul Sartre into a public celebrity. Here Sartre gives a radio interview in 1948 as his intellectual partner Simone de Beauvoir looks on. (Bettmann/Corbis)

Nietzsche painted a dark world, perhaps foreshadowing his loss of sanity in 1889. The West was in decline; false values had triumphed. The death of God left people disoriented and depressed. According to Nietzsche, the only hope for the individual was to accept the meaninglessness of human existence and then make that very meaninglessness a source of self-defined personal integrity and hence liberation. In this way, at least a few superior individuals could free themselves from the humdrum thinking of the masses and become true heroes.

Little read during his active years, Nietzsche's works attracted growing attention in the early twentieth century. Artists and writers experimented with his ideas, which were fundamental to the rise of the philosophy of existentialism in the 1920s. Subsequent generations have remade Nietzsche to suit their own needs, and his influence remains enormous to this day.

The growing dissatisfaction with established ideas before 1914 was apparent in other important thinkers. In the 1890s French philosophy professor Henri Bergson (1859–1941) argued that immediate experience and intuition were as important as rational and scientific thinking for understanding reality. According to Bergson, a religious experience or a mystical poem was often more accessible to human comprehension than was a scientific law or a mathematical equation.

Another thinker who challenged the certainties of rational thinking was French socialist Georges Sorel (1847–1922). Sorel concluded that Marxian socialism was an inspiring but unprovable religion, rather than a scientific truth as Marx himself had argued. Socialism would shatter capitalist society, Sorel believed, through a great general strike of all working people inspired by a myth of revolution. Sorel rejected democracy and believed that the masses of the new socialist society would have to be tightly controlled by a small revolutionary elite.

The First World War accelerated the revolt against established certainties in philosophy, but that revolt went in two very different directions. In English-speaking countries, the main development was the acceptance of logical positivism in university circles. In the continental countries, the primary development in philosophy was existentialism.

Logical positivism was truly revolutionary. Adherents of this worldview argued that what we know about human life must be based on rational facts and direct observation. They concluded that theology and most of traditional philosophy was meaningless because even the most cherished ideas about God, eternal truth, and ethics were impossible to prove using logic. This outlook is often associated with the Austrian philosopher Ludwig Wittgenstein (VIT-guhn-shtighn) (1889–1951), who later immigrated to England, where he trained numerous disciples. Wittgenstein argued in his pugnacious *Tractatus Logico-Philosophicus* (Essay on Logical Philosophy) in 1922 that philosophy is only the logical clarification of thoughts, and that therefore it should concentrate on the study of language, which expresses thoughts. In his view, the great philosophical issues of the ages—God, freedom, morality, and so on—are quite literally senseless, a great waste of time, for neither scientific experiments nor the logic of mathematics could demonstrate their validity. Statements about such matters reflected only the personal preferences of a given individual. As Wittgenstein put it in the famous last sentence of his work, "Of what one cannot speak, of that one must keep silent." Logical positivism, which has remained dominant in England and the United States to this day, drastically reduced the scope of philosophical inquiry and offered little solace to ordinary people.

logical positivism A philosophy that sees meaning in only those beliefs that can be empirically proven, and that therefore rejects most of the concerns of traditional philosophy, from the existence of God to the meaning of happiness, as nonsense.

1919	Treaty of Versailles; Freudian psychology gains popularity; Keynes, *Economic Consequences of the Peace*; Rutherford splits the atom; Bauhaus school founded
1920s	Existentialism, Dadaism, and surrealism gain prominence
1922	Eliot, *The Waste Land*; Joyce, *Ulysses*; Woolf, *Jacob's Room*; Wittgenstein writes on logical empiricism
1923	French and Belgian armies occupy the Ruhr
1924	Dawes Plan
1925	Berg's opera *Wozzeck* first performed; Kafka, *The Trial*
1926	Germany joins the League of Nations
1927	Heisenberg's principle of uncertainty
1928	Kellogg-Briand Pact
1929	Faulkner, *The Sound and the Fury*
1929–1939	Great Depression
1933	The National Socialist Party takes power in Germany
1935	Riefenstahl's documentary film *The Triumph of the Will*
1936	Formation of Popular Front in France

On the continent, others looked for answers in **existentialism**. This new philosophy loosely united highly diverse and even contradictory thinkers in a search for usable moral values in a world of anxiety and uncertainty. Modern existentialism had many forerunners, including Nietzsche and the Danish religious philosopher Søren Kierkegaard (1813–1855). The philosophy gained recognition in Germany in the 1920s when philosophers Martin Heidegger and Karl Jaspers found a sympathetic audience among disillusioned postwar university students. These existentialist writers placed great emphasis on the loneliness and meaninglessness of human existence in a godless world and the individual's need to come to terms with the fear caused by this situation.

existentialism A philosophy that stresses the meaninglessness of existence and the importance of the individual in searching for moral values in an uncertain world.

Most existential thinkers in the twentieth century were atheists. Often inspired by Nietzsche, who had proclaimed the death of God, they did not believe that a supreme being had established humanity's fundamental nature and given life its meaning. In the words of the famous French existentialist Jean-Paul Sartre (ZHAWN-pawl SAHR-truh) (1905–1980), "existence precedes essence." By that, Sartre meant that there are no God-given, timeless truths outside or independent of individual existence. Only after they are born do people struggle to define their essence, entirely on their own. According to thinkers like Sartre, existence itself is absurd. Human beings are terribly alone, for there is no God to help them. They are left to confront the inevitable arrival of death and so are hounded by despair. The crisis of the existential thinker epitomized the modern intellectual crisis—the shattering of beliefs in God, reason, and progress.

Existentialists did recognize that human beings must act in the world. Indeed, in the words of Sartre, "man is condemned to be free." Because life is meaningless, existentialists believe that individuals are forced to create their own meaning and define themselves through their actions. Such radical freedom is frightening, and Sartre concluded that most people try to escape their unwanted freedom by structuring their lives around conventional social norms. According to Sartre, to escape is to live in "bad faith," to hide from the hard truths of existence. To live authentically, individuals must become "engaged" and choose their own actions in full awareness of their inescapable responsibility for their own behavior. Existentialism thus had a powerful ethical component. It placed great stress on individual responsibility and choice, on "being in the world" in the right way.

Existentialism came of age in France during and immediately after World War II. The terrible conditions of that war, discussed in the next chapter, reinforced the existential view of and approach to life. On the one hand, the armies of the German dictator Hitler had conquered most of Europe and unleashed a hideous reign of barbarism. On the other hand, men and women had more than ever to define themselves by their actions. Specifically, individuals had to choose whether to resist Hitler or accept and even abet tyranny. Joining the French resistance, as Sartre did, represented a clear choice between good and evil, and perhaps even life and death. After World War II, leading French existentialists such as Sartre and Albert Camus (1913–1960) became enormously influential. They offered powerful but unsettling answers to the profound moral issues and the crises of the first half of the twentieth century.

The Revival of Christianity

Though philosophers such as Nietzsche, Wittgenstein, and Sartre all argued that religion had little to teach people in a modern age, the decades after the First World War witnessed a tenacious revival of Christian thought. Christianity and religion in general had been on the defensive in intellectual circles since the Enlightenment. In the years before 1914, some theologians, especially Protestant ones, had felt the need to interpret Christian doctrine and the Bible so that they did not seem to contradict science, evolution, and common sense. In these circles, Christ was seen primarily as a great moral teacher, and the mysterious, spiritual aspects of his divinity were played down. Indeed, some modern theologians were embarrassed by the miraculous, unscientific aspects of Christianity and turned away from them.

Especially after World War I, a number of thinkers and theologians began to revitalize the fundamentals of Christianity. Sometimes described as Christian existentialists because they shared the loneliness and despair of atheistic existentialists, they stressed human beings' sinful nature, the need for faith, and the mystery of God's forgiveness. The revival of fundamental Christian belief after World War I was fed by the rediscovery of the work of the nineteenth-century Danish theologian Søren Kierkegaard (1813–1855), whose ideas became extremely influential. Kierkegaard (KIHR-kuh-gahrd) believed it was impossible for ordinary individuals to prove the existence of God, but he rejected the notion that Christianity was an empty practice. In his classic work *Sickness unto Death* (1849), Kierkegaard mastered his religious doubts by suggesting that people must take a "leap of faith" and accept the existence of an objectively unknowable but nonetheless awesome and majestic God.

In the 1920s the Swiss Protestant theologian Karl Barth (1886–1968) propounded similar ideas. In a series of brilliant and influential writings, Barth argued that human beings were imperfect, sinful creatures whose reason and will are hopelessly flawed. Religious truth is therefore made known to human beings only through God's grace, not through reason. People have to accept

God's word and the supernatural revelation of Jesus Christ with awe, trust, and obedience, not reason or logic.

Among Catholics, the leading existential Christian was Gabriel Marcel (1887–1973). Born into a cultivated French family, Marcel found in the Catholic Church an answer to what he called the postwar "broken world." Catholicism and religious belief provided the hope, humanity, honesty, and piety for which he hungered. Flexible and gentle, Marcel and his countryman Jacques Maritain (1882–1973) denounced anti-Semitism and supported closer ties with non-Catholics.

After 1914 religion became much more relevant and meaningful to thinking people than it had been before the war. In addition to Marcel and Maritain, many other illustrious intellectuals turned to religion between about 1920 and 1950. Poets T. S. Eliot and W. H. Auden, novelists Evelyn Waugh and Aldous Huxley, historian Arnold Toynbee, writer C. S. Lewis, psychoanalyst Karl Stern, physicist Max Planck, and philosopher Cyril Joad were all either converted to religion or attracted to it for the first time. Religion, often of a despairing, existential variety, was one meaningful answer to uncertainty and anxiety. In the words of a famous Roman Catholic convert, English novelist Graham Greene, "One began to believe in heaven because one believed in hell."[2]

The New Physics

Progressive minds believed that science, unlike religion and philosophical speculation, was based on hard facts and controlled experiments. Ever since the scientific revolution of the seventeenth century, scientific advances and their implications had greatly influenced the beliefs of thinking people. By the late nineteenth century, science was one of the main pillars supporting Western society's optimistic and rationalistic worldview. Unchanging natural laws seemed to determine physical processes and permit useful solutions to more and more problems. All this was comforting, especially to people who were no longer committed to traditional religious beliefs. And all this was challenged by the new physics.

An important first step toward the new physics was the discovery at the end of the nineteenth century that atoms were not like hard, permanent little billiard balls. They were actually composed of many far-smaller, fast-moving particles, such as electrons and protons. Polish-born physicist Marie Curie (1867–1934) and her French husband, Pierre, discovered that radium constantly emits subatomic particles and thus does not have a constant atomic weight. Building on this and other work in radiation, German physicist Max Planck (1858–1947) showed in 1900 that subatomic energy is emitted in uneven little spurts, which Planck called "quanta," and not in a steady stream, as previously believed. Planck's

The Christian Revival Swiss theologian Karl Barth helped rejuvenate Protestant thought in the 1920s by arguing for the awesome and unknowable nature of God. The liberal Barth, shown delivering a sermon in 1946, remained a powerful advocate of religious tolerance in the decades after World War II. (Ullstein Bild/akg-images)

discovery called into question the old sharp distinction between matter and energy: the implication was that matter and energy might be different forms of the same thing. The old view of atoms as the stable basic building blocks of nature, with a different kind of unbreakable atom for each of the ninety-two chemical elements, was badly shaken.

In 1905 the German-Jewish genius Albert Einstein (1879–1955) went further than the Curies and Planck in undermining Newtonian physics. His famous **theory of special relativity** postulated that time and space are relative to the viewpoint of the observer and that only the speed of light is constant for all frames of reference in the universe. In order to make his revolutionary and

theory of special relativity Albert Einstein's theory that time and space are relative to the observer and that only the speed of light remains constant.

En amerikansk tecknares bekymmer för framtiden.

Då professorn äntligen efter årslånga experiment lyckades sönderdela en atom.

Unlocking the Power of the Atom
Many of the fanciful visions of science fiction came true in the twentieth century, although not exactly as first imagined. This 1927 Swedish cartoon satirizes a professor who has split the atom and unwittingly destroyed his building and neighborhood in the process. In the Second World War professors harnessed the atom in bombs and decimated faraway cities and foreign civilians. (Mary Evans Picture Library/The Image Works)

paradoxical idea somewhat comprehensible to the non-mathematical layperson, Einstein used analogies involving moving trains. For example, if a woman in the middle of a moving car got up and walked forward to the door, she had gone, relative to the train, a half car length. But relative to an observer on the embankment, she had gone farther. In addition, Einstein's theory stated clearly that matter and energy are interchangeable and that even a particle of matter contains enormous levels of potential energy. Einstein's ideas unified an apparently infinite universe with the incredibly small, fast-moving subatomic world. In comparison, the closed framework of the Newtonian physics developed during the scientific revolution, exemplified by Newton's supposedly immutable laws of motion and mechanics, was quite limited (Chapter 17).

The 1920s opened the "heroic age of physics," in the apt words of Ernest Rutherford (1871–1937), one of its leading pioneers. Breakthrough followed breakthrough. In 1919 Rutherford showed that the atom could be split. By 1944 seven subatomic particles had been identified, the most important of which was the neutron. The neutron's capacity to pass through other atoms allowed for an even more intense bombardment of matter, leading to chain reactions of unbelievable force. This discovery was fundamental to the subsequent construction of the atomic bomb.

Although few nonscientists understood this revolution in physics, the implications of the new theories and discoveries, as presented by newspapers and popular writers, were disturbing to millions of men and women in the 1920s and 1930s. In 1927, for example,

German physicist Werner Heisenberg (VER-nuhr HIGH-zuhn-buhrg) (1901–1976) formulated the "uncertainty principle," which postulates that nature itself is ultimately unknowable and unpredictable. Heisenberg suggested that the universe lacked any absolute objective reality. Everything was "relative," that is, dependent on the observer's frame of reference. Such ideas caught on among ordinary people, who found the unstable, relativistic world described by the new physicists strange and troubling. Instead of Newton's dependable, rational laws, there seemed to be only tendencies and probabilities in an extraordinarily complex and uncertain universe. Like modern philosophy, physics no longer provided comforting truths about natural laws or optimistic answers about humanity's place in an understandable world.

Freudian Psychology

With physics presenting an uncertain universe so unrelated to ordinary human experience, questions regarding the power and potential of the human mind assumed special significance. The findings and speculations of Sigmund Freud (Chapter 23) were particularly influential, yet also deeply disturbing.

Before Freud, poets and mystics had probed the unconscious and irrational aspects of human behavior. But most professional scientific psychologists assumed that the conscious mind processed sense experiences in a rational and logical way. Human behavior in turn was the result of rational calculation — of "thinking." Freud developed a very different view of the human psyche beginning in the late 1880s. Basing his insights on the analysis of dreams and of hysteria, Freud concluded that human behavior was basically irrational, governed by the unconscious, a sort of mental reservoir that contained vital instinctual drives and powerful memories. The unconscious was unknowable to the conscious mind but it deeply influenced people's behavior, so that they were often unaware of the source or meaning of their actions.

Elaborating on these ideas, Freud described three structures of the self — the **id**, the **ego**, and the **superego** — that were basically at war with one another. The primitive, irrational id was entirely unconscious. The source of sexual, aggressive, and pleasure-seeking instincts, the id sought immediate fulfillment of all desires and was totally amoral. The id was kept in check by the superego, the conscience or internalized voice of parental or social control. For Freud, the superego was also irrational. It was overly strict and puritan, and it was constantly in conflict with the pleasure-seeking id. The third component of human psychology was the ego, the rational self that was mostly conscious and worked to negotiate between the demands of the id and the superego.

For Freud, the healthy individual possessed a strong ego that effectively balanced the id and superego. Neurosis, or mental illness, resulted when the three structures were somehow out of balance. Since the id's instinctual drives were extremely powerful, the ever-present danger for individuals and whole societies was that unacknowledged drives might overwhelm the control mechanisms of the ego in a violent, distorted way. Freud's famous "talking cure" — in which neurotic patients lay back on a couch and shared their innermost thoughts with the psychoanalyst — was an attempt to resolve such unconscious tensions and restore the rational ego to its predominant role.

Yet Freud, like Nietzsche, believed that the mechanisms of rational thinking and traditional moral values could be too strong. In his famous book *Civilization and Its Discontents* (1930), Freud argued that civilization was possible only when individuals renounced their irrational instincts in order to live peaceably in groups. Such renunciation made communal life possible, but it left basic instincts unfulfilled and so led to widespread unhappiness. Freud gloomily concluded that Western civilization was itself inescapably neurotic.

Freudian psychology and clinical psychiatry had become an international movement by 1910, but only after 1919 did they receive popular attention, especially in northern Europe and the United States. Many opponents and even some enthusiasts interpreted Freud as saying that the first requirement for mental health was an uninhibited sex life. Thus after the First World War, the popular interpretation of Freud reflected and encouraged growing sexual experimentation, particularly among middle-class women. For more serious students, the psychology of Freud and his followers drastically undermined the old easy optimism about the rational and progressive nature of the human mind.

Twentieth-Century Literature

Western literature was deeply influenced by the general intellectual climate of pessimism, relativism, and alienation. The great nineteenth-century novelists had typically written as all-knowing narrators, describing realistic characters and their relationships to an understandable, if sometimes harsh, society. Writers now developed new techniques to express new realities. In the twentieth century, many authors adopted the limited, often confused viewpoint of a single individual. Like Freud, these novelists focused their attention on the complexity and irrationality of the human mind, where feelings, memories, and desires are forever scrambled. The great French novelist Marcel Proust (1871–1922), in his semi-autobiographical

id, ego, and superego Freudian terms to describe the three parts of the self and the basis of human behavior, which Freud saw as basically irrational.

Freud's Couch As part of his "talking cure," Austrian neurologist Sigmund Freud invited neurotic patients to lie back on a couch and speak about their dreams and innermost thoughts. This famous photo shows Freud's couch in his office in Vienna. His theories about the unconscious and instinctual motivation of human behavior cast doubt on Enlightenment ideals of rationalism and progress. (© Edmund Engelman)

Remembrance of Things Past (1913–1927), recalled bittersweet memories of childhood and youthful love and tried to discover their innermost meaning. To do so, Proust lived like a hermit in a soundproof Paris apartment for ten years, withdrawing from the present to dwell on the past.

Serious novelists also used the **stream-of-consciousness technique** with its reliance on internal monologues to explore the psyche. In *Jacob's Room* (1922), Virginia Woolf (1882–1941) created a novel made up of a series of internal monologues in which she tried to capture the inner voice in prose. In this and other stories, Woolf portrayed characters whose ideas and emotions from different periods of time bubble up as randomly as from a patient on a psychoanalyst's couch. William Faulkner (1897–1962), one of America's greatest twentieth-century novelists, used the same technique in *The Sound and the Fury* (1929), much of

stream-of-consciousness technique A literary technique, found in works by Virginia Woolf, James Joyce, and others, that uses interior monologue—a character's thoughts and feelings as they occur—to explore the human psyche.

whose intense drama is confusedly seen through the eyes of a man who is mentally disabled.

The most famous stream-of-consciousness novel is *Ulysses*, published by Irish novelist James Joyce (1882–1941) in 1922. Into an account of a single day in the life of an ordinary man, Joyce weaves an extended ironic parallel between his hero's aimless wanderings through the streets and pubs of Dublin and the adventures of Homer's hero Ulysses on his way home from Troy. *Ulysses* was surely one of the most disturbing novels of its generation. Abandoning any sense of a conventional plot, breaking formal rules of grammar, and blending foreign words, puns, bits of knowledge, and scraps of memory together in bewildering confusion, the language of *Ulysses* is intended to mirror modern life itself: a gigantic riddle waiting to be unraveled. Joyce furthermore included frank descriptions of the main character's sexual thoughts and encounters. In Great Britain and the United States, the novel was considered obscene and was banned until the early 1930s.

As creative writers turned their attention from society to the individual and from realism to psychological relativity, they rejected the idea of progress. Some described "anti-utopias," nightmare visions of things to come. In 1918 an obscure German high school teacher named Oswald Spengler (1880–1936) published *The Decline of the West*, which quickly became an international sensation. According to Spengler, every culture experiences a life cycle of growth and decline. Western civilization, in Spengler's opinion, was in its old age and would soon be overtaken by the rise of East Asia. T. S. Eliot (1888–1965), in his famous poem *The Waste Land* (1922), likewise depicted a world of growing desolation:

> April is the cruelest month, breeding
> Lilacs out of the dead land, mixing
> Memory and desire, stirring
> Dull roots with spring rain. . . .
> What are the roots that clutch, what branches grow
> Out of this stony rubbish? Son of man,
> You cannot say, or guess, for you know only
> A heap of broken images, where the sun beats,
> And the dead tree gives no shelter, the cricket no relief,
> And the dry stone no sound of water.[3]

With its biblical references and its images of a ruined and wasted nature and general human incomprehension, Eliot's poem expressed the widespread despair that followed the First World War. Writer Franz Kafka (1883–1924) also portrayed an incomprehensible, alienated world. Kafka's novels *The Trial* (1925) and *The Castle* (1926), as well as his famous novella *The Metamorphosis* (1915)—in which the main character turns into a giant insect—portray helpless individuals crushed by inexplicably hostile forces. The German-Jewish Kafka died young, at forty-one, and so did not see the world of his nightmares materialize in the Nazi state. In these and many other works, authors between the wars used new literary techniques and dark imagery to portray the widespread unease of the age of anxiety.

Modernism in Architecture, Art, and Music

How did modernism revolutionize architecture, painting, and music? ■

Like the scientists and intellectuals who were part of the same modern culture, creative artists rejected old forms and old values. **Modernism** in architecture, art, and music meant constant experimentation and a search for new kinds of expression. Even today the modernism of the immediate prewar years and the 1920s still seems strikingly fresh and original. And though many people find the varied modern visions of the arts strange and disturbing, the first half of the twentieth century, so dismal in many respects, stands as one of Western civilization's great artistic eras.

Architecture and Design

Already in the late nineteenth century, architects inspired by modernism had begun to transform the physical framework of urban society. The United States, with its rapid urban growth and lack of rigid building traditions, pioneered in the new architecture. In the 1890s the Chicago school of architects, led by Louis H. Sullivan (1856–1924), used cheap steel, reinforced concrete, and electric elevators to build skyscrapers and office buildings lacking almost any exterior ornamentation. In the first decade of the twentieth century, Sullivan's student Frank Lloyd Wright (1869–1959) built a series of radically modern houses featuring low lines, open interiors, and mass-produced building materials. Europeans were inspired by these and other American examples of functional construction, like the massive, unadorned grain elevators of the Midwest.

Promoters of modern architecture argued that buildings and living spaces in general should be ordered according to a new principle: **functionalism**. Buildings, like industrial products, should be useful and "functional"—that is, they should serve, as well as possible, the purpose for which they were made. According to the Franco-Swiss architect Le Corbusier (luh cowr-booz-YAY) (1887–1965), one of the great champions of modernism, "a house is a machine for living in."[4]

Corbusier's polemical work *Towards a New Architecture*, published in 1923, laid out a series of guidelines meant to revolutionize building design. Corbusier argued that architects should adopt the latest technologies in their construction practices. They should no longer decorate their buildings with fancy ornamentation, but should rather find beauty in the clean straight lines of practical construction and efficient machinery. The resulting buildings, fashioned according to what was soon called the "international style," were typically symmetrical rectangles made of concrete, glass, and steel.

In Europe architectural leadership centered in German-speaking countries until Hitler took power in 1933. In 1911 twenty-eight-year-old Walter Gropius (1883–1969) broke sharply with the past in his design of the Fagus shoe factory at Alfeld, Germany—a clean, light, elegant building of glass and iron. In 1919 Gropius merged the schools of fine and applied arts at Weimar into a single interdisciplinary school, the **Bauhaus**. The Bauhaus brought together many leading modern architects, designers, and theatrical innovators. Working as an effective, inspired team, they combined the study of fine art, including painting and sculpture, with the study of applied art in the crafts of printing, weaving, and furniture making. Throughout the 1920s the Bauhaus,

modernism A label given to the artistic and cultural movements of the late nineteenth and early twentieth centuries, which were typified by radical experimentation that challenged traditional forms of artistic expression.

functionalism The principle that buildings, like industrial products, should serve as well as possible the purpose for which they were made.

Bauhaus A German interdisciplinary school of fine and applied arts that brought together many leading modern architects, designers, and theatrical innovators.

Modern Design for Everyday Use

LIVING IN THE PAST

EUROPEAN DESIGN MOVEMENTS OF THE EARLY TWENTIETH CENTURY had a lasting impact on everyday lifestyles. Many ordinary elements of living, from apartment buildings to interior furnishings, were transformed by modernist experimentation. The Bauhaus (or House of Building), an institute founded in Germany by architect Walter Gropius in 1919, exemplified modern design at its most original and influential. It attracted an international array of highly talented artists, designers, architects, and students, including the Russian painter Wassily Kandinsky, the Swiss artist Paul Klee, and the Hungarian-Jewish photographer and painter László Moholy-Nagy.

The instructors and students at the Bauhaus sought to revolutionize product design by unifying art, craft, and technology. They argued that everyday objects should openly reflect the highly rationalized, industrialized, and modern society in which — and for which — they were made.

Bauhaus adherents believed that form should follow function and that, as director Mies van der Rohe put it in a famous aphorism, "less is more." The result was streamlined, functional designs stripped of all ornamentation that were nonetheless works of great style and lasting beauty.

The angular, streamlined furnishings shown in the Bauhaus director's office (ca. 1923) exemplify the school's attempt to use modern materials and design to combine beautiful form and practical function in everyday goods, as do the chair designed by Marcel Breuer and the teapot by Marianne Brandt, the head of the Bauhaus metal workshop. (office: Courtesy, University of California, San Diego/ARTstor Slide Gallery. © 2010 Artists Rights Society [ARS], New York/VGBK, Bonn; chair: Digital Image © The Museum of Modern Art/Licensed by SCALA/Art Resource; teapot: Image © The Metropolitan Museum of Art/Art Resource, NY. © 2010 Artists Rights Society [ARS], New York/VG Bild-Kunst, Bonn)

The Bauhaus School in Dessau, Germany, designed by Walter Gropius in 1925–1926. (imagebroker/alamy)

Bauhaus designers created extensive public buildings as well as common household goods. Working-class housing projects, industrial factories, and private residences all were designed and built by Bauhaus architects. At home, no everyday item was too insignificant to be treated as an object of high design. The industrial ethos of the Bauhaus was brought to bear on textiles, typography, furniture, and even teapots and dishware. The famous steel tube and leather "Wassily chair," created by German designer Marcel Breuer, exemplified Bauhaus concepts and remains a classic icon of modernism. Such goods were mass-produced and marketed at affordable prices, bringing high-concept design into the lives of ordinary Europeans.

In 1933 Adolf Hitler and the Nazi Party, zealous opponents of modern art of all kinds, shut down the Bauhaus Institute. Many of the institute's prominent teachers and students fled Nazi persecution. Gropius, Breuer, Mies van der Rohe, and numerous others moved to the United States, where they helped spread Bauhaus ideas around the world after the end of the Second World War.

QUESTIONS FOR ANALYSIS

1. How do the Bauhaus designs shown here reflect the modern industrial society in which they were created?

2. Why did Bauhaus designers work in so many different fields? Why is their work still influential today?

with its stress on functionalism and good design for everyday life, attracted enthusiastic students from all over the world. It had a great and continuing impact. (See "Living in the Past: Modern Design for Everyday Use," at left.)

Another leading modern architect, Ludwig Mies van der Rohe (1886–1969), followed Gropius as director of the Bauhaus in 1930. Like many modernist intellectuals, he immigrated to the United States to escape the repressive Nazi regime. His classic steel-frame and glass-wall Lake Shore Apartments in Chicago, built between 1948 and 1951, epitomized the triumph of the modernist international style in the great building boom that followed the Second World War.

New Artistic Movements

In the decades surrounding the First World War, the visual arts, like other realms of culture, experienced radical change and experimentation. For the last several centuries, artists had tried to portray accurate representations of reality. Now a new artistic avant-garde emerged to challenge the assumptions of their elders. From Impressionism and Expressionism to Dadaism and surrealism, a sometimes bewildering array of artistic movements followed one after another. Modern painting and sculpture became increasingly abstract. Artists turned their backs on figurative representation and began to break down form into its constituent parts: lines, shapes, and colors.

Berlin, Munich, Moscow, Vienna, New York, and especially Paris became famous for their radical artistic undergrounds. Commercial art galleries and exhibition halls exhibited the new work, and schools and institutions, such as the Bauhaus, emerged to train a generation in modern techniques. Young artists flocked to these urban cultural centers to participate in the new movements, earn a living making art, and perhaps change the world with their revolutionary ideas.

One of the earliest and best-known modernist movements was Impressionism, which blossomed in Paris in the 1870s. French artists such as Claude Monet (1840–1926) and Edgar Degas (1834–1917) and the American Mary Cassatt (1844–1926), who settled in Paris in 1875, tried to portray their sensory "impressions" in their work. Impressionists looked to the world around them for subject matter, and they turned their backs on traditional themes such as battles, religious scenes, and wealthy elites. Monet's colorful and atmospheric paintings of farmland haystacks and Degas's many pastel drawings of ballerinas exemplify the way Impressionists moved toward abstraction. Capturing a fleeting moment of color and light, in often blurry and quickly painted images, was far more important than portraying a heavily detailed and precise rendering of an actual object.

By the 1890s new artistic movements had emerged alongside of Impressionism. Postimpressionists and Expressionists, such as Vincent van Gogh (1853–1890), built on Impressionist motifs of color and light but added a deep psychological element to their pictures, reflecting the attempt to search within the self and reveal (or express) deep inner feelings on the canvas. Some groups directly challenged the art world status quo. In Vienna, the Secessionists—so named because they broke with or seceded from traditional Viennese art institutions in 1897—created rich, colorful images that were highly decorative but also deeply expressive of inner feelings. *The Kiss*, a well-known painting by the Viennese painter Gustav Klimt (1862–1918), exemplifies the way Secessionists created abstract works rooted in the depths of emotion, in this case love and sensuality.

In Paris in 1907 the famous painter Pablo Picasso, along with other artists, established Cubism—a highly analytical approach to art concentrated on a complex

Dadaism An artistic movement of the 1920s and 1930s that attacked all accepted standards of art and behavior and delighted in outrageous conduct.

geometry of zigzagging lines and sharply angled overlapping planes. About three years later came the ultimate stage in the development of abstract, nonrepresentational art. Artists such as the Russian-born Wassily Kandinsky (VAS-uh-lee kan-DIHN-skee) (1866–1944) turned away from nature completely. "The observer," said Kandinsky, "must learn to look at [my] pictures . . . as form and color combinations . . . as a representation of mood and not as a representation of *objects*."[5]

The shock of World War I encouraged further radicalization. In 1916 a group of artists and intellectuals in exile in Zurich, Switzerland, championed a new movement they called **Dadaism**, which attacked all the familiar standards of art and delighted in outrageous behavior. The war had shown once and for all that life was meaningless, the Dadaists argued, so art should be meaningless as well. Dadaists tried to shock their audiences with what they called "anti-art," works and public performances that were entirely nonsensical. A famous example is a reproduction of Leonardo da Vinci's *Mona Lisa* in which the famous painting is ridiculed with a hand-drawn mustache and an obscene inscription. After the war, Dadaism became an international movement, spreading to Paris, New York, and particularly Berlin in the early 1920s.

After 1924 many Dadaists were attracted to surrealism. Surrealists such as Salvador Dali (1904–1989) were deeply influenced by Freudian psychology and portrayed images of the unconscious in their art. They painted fantastic worlds of wild dreams and uncomfortable symbols, where watches melted and giant metronomes beat time in precisely drawn but impossible alien landscapes.

Many modern artists sincerely believed that art had a radical mission. By calling attention to the supposed bankruptcy of mainstream society, art had the power to produce radical social change. Beyond producing art, groups such as the Dadaists and the surrealists wrote radical and sometimes nonsensical manifestos meant to spread their ideas and challenge conventional assumptions of all kinds. Dadaist Richard Huelsenbeck's *Collective Dada Manifesto* of 1920 captured the playfulness of Dada but also the movement's serious critical edge:

> *Art in its execution and direction is dependent on the time in which it lives, and artists are creatures of their epoch. The highest art will be that which in its conscious content presents the thousandfold problems of the day, the art which has been visibly shattered by the explosions of last week, which is forever trying to collect its limbs after yesterday's crash. . . . Dada is the international expression of our times, the great rebellion of artistic movements, the artistic reflex of all these offensives, peace congresses, riots in the vegetable market. . . . Blast the bloodless abstraction of expressionism! Blast the literary hollowheads and their theories for improving the world! . . . To be against this manifesto is to be a Dadaist!*[6]

The Shock of the Avant-Garde Dadaist Hugo Ball recites his nonsense poem "Karawane" at the notorious Cabaret Voltaire in Zurich, Switzerland, in 1916. Avant-garde artists such as Ball consciously used their work to overturn familiar artistic conventions and challenge the assumptions of the European middle classes. (Apic/Getty Images)

As such words suggest, by the 1920s art had become increasingly politicized. Many avant-garde artists sided with the far left; some became committed communists. Such artists and art movements had a difficult time surviving the political crises of the 1930s. Between 1933 and 1945, when the National Socialist (Nazi) Party came to power in Germany and brought a second world war to the European continent, hundreds of artists and intellectuals migrated to the United States to escape the war and the repressive Nazi state. After World War II, New York greatly benefited from this transfusion of talent and replaced Paris and Berlin as the capital of modern art.

Modern Music

Developments in modern music were strikingly parallel to those in painting. Composers, too, attempted to express emotional intensity in radically experimental forms. The ballet *The Rite of Spring* by composer Igor Stravinsky (1882–1971) practically caused a riot when it was first

❝ Dada is the international expression of our times, the great rebellion of artistic movements. . . . Blast the bloodless abstraction of expressionism! ❞

—**RICHARD HUELSENBECK**

performed in Paris in 1913 by a famous Russian dance company. The combination of pulsating, dissonant rhythms from the orchestra pit and the earthy representation of lovemaking by the strangely dressed dancers on the stage was a shocking, almost pornographic enactment of a primitive fertility rite.

After the First World War, when irrationality and violence had seemed to pervade human experience, modernism flourished in opera and ballet. One of the most famous and powerful examples was the opera *Wozzeck*, by Alban Berg (1885–1935), first performed

Salvador Dali, *Metamorphosis of Narcissus* Dali was a leader of the surrealist art movement, which emerged in the late 1920s. Surrealists were deeply influenced by the theories of Sigmund Freud and used strange and evocative symbols to capture the inner workings of dreams and the unconscious in their work. In this 1937 painting, Dali plays with the Greek myth of Narcissus, who fell in love with his own reflection and drowned in a pool. What mysterious significance, if any, lies behind this surreal reordering of everyday reality? (Tate, London/Art Resource, NY. © 2010 Salvador Dali, Gala-Salvador Dali Foundation/Artists Rights Society [ARS], New York)

Musical Modernism Dancers in Russian composer Igor Stravinsky's avant-garde opera *The Rite of Spring* perform at the Paris premiere. The dissonant music, wild sets and costumes, and unpredictable dance movements shocked and insulted the audience, which rioted on the opening night in May 1913. (Lebrecht/The Image Works)

in Berlin in 1925. Blending a half-sung, half-spoken kind of dialogue with harsh, atonal music, *Wozzeck* is a gruesome tale of a soldier driven by Kafka-like inner terrors and vague suspicions of unfaithfulness to murder his mistress.

Some composers turned their backs on long-established musical conventions. Just as abstract painters arranged lines and color but did not draw identifiable objects, so modern composers arranged sounds without creating recognizable harmonies. Led by Viennese composer Arnold Schönberg (SHUHN-buhrg) (1874–1951), they abandoned traditional harmony and tonality. The musical notes in a given piece were no longer united and organized by a key; instead they were independent and unrelated. Schönberg's twelve-tone music of the 1920s arranged all twelve notes of the scale in an abstract mathematical pattern, or "tone row." This pattern sounded like no pattern at all to the ordinary listener and could be detected only by a highly trained eye studying the musical score. Accustomed to the harmonies of classical and romantic music, audiences generally resisted modern atonal music. Only after the Second World War did it begin to win acceptance.

An Emerging Consumer Society

How did the emerging consumer society and mass culture of the interwar years change the everyday lives of ordinary men and women?

After the First World War, European society experienced fundamental changes in the basic consumption of goods and services. Modern business forms of credit, retail, and advertising helped sell increasing numbers of mass-produced goods — the products of a highly industrialized factory system — to ever-larger numbers of people. With the arrival of cinema and radio, the leisure time of ordinary people was increasingly dominated by commercial entertainment. These changes had roots in the prosperous decades before World War I and would not be fully consolidated until the consumer revolution of the 1950s and 1960s. Yet in the years between the end of World War I in 1918 and the start of World War II in 1939 the outlines of a modern consumer society emerged with startling clarity.

Mass Culture

The emerging consumer society of the 1920s is a good example of the way technological developments can lead to widespread social change. The arrival of a highly industrialized manufacturing system dedicated to mass-producing inexpensive goods, the establishment of efficient transportation systems that could bring these goods to national markets, and the rise of professional advertising experts and agencies to sell them were all part of a revolution in the way consumer goods were made, marketed, and used by ordinary people. Contemporaries viewed the new mass culture as a distinctly modern aspect of everyday life. It seemed that consumer goods themselves were modernizing society by changing so many ingrained habits. Some people embraced the new ways, while others worried that the changes wrought by an increasingly unavoidable consumer culture threatened familiar values and precious traditions.

Critics had good reason to worry. Mass-produced goods indeed had a profound impact on the lives of ordinary people. Housework and private life were increasingly organized around an array of modern appliances, from telephones and radios to electric ovens, washing machines, and refrigerators. The aggressive marketing of fashionable clothing and personal care products, such as shampoos, perfume, and makeup, encouraged a cult of youthful "sex appeal"; individual attractiveness was increasingly determined by the use of brand-name products. The mass production and marketing of automobiles and the rise of established tourist agencies opened roads to increased mobility and travel.

Commercialized mass entertainment likewise prospered and began to dominate the way people spent their leisure time. Movies and radio thrilled millions (see page 869). Professional sporting events drew throngs of fans. Thriving print media brought readers an astounding variety of newspapers, inexpensive books, and glossy illustrated magazines. Flashy restaurants, theatrical revues, and nightclubs competed for evening customers.

Department stores epitomized the emergence of consumer society. Already well established across Europe and the United States by the 1890s, by the 1920s they had become veritable cornucopias of commerce. The typical store had over forty departments that sold an enticing variety of goods, including clothing, magazines, housewares, food, and spirits. The larger stores included travel bureaus, movie theaters, and refreshment stands. Aggressive advertising campaigns, youthful and attractive salespeople, and easy credit and return policies attracted customers in droves.

> ❝ [The] woman of today refuses to be regarded as a physically weak being . . . and seeks to support herself through gainful employment. . . . Her task is to clear the way for equal rights for women in all areas of life. ❞
>
> —GERMAN FEMINIST

The emergence of modern consumer culture both undermined and reinforced existing social differences. On one hand, consumerism helped democratize Western society. Since everyone could purchase any good, if he or she had the means, mass culture helped break down old social barriers between class, region, and religion. Yet it also reinforced social differences. Manufacturers soon realized they could profit by marketing goods to specific groups. Catholics, for example, could purchase their own popular literature and inexpensive devotional items, and young people eagerly bought the latest fashions marketed directly to them. The expense of many items meant that only the wealthy could purchase them. Automobiles and, in the 1920s, even vacuum cleaners cost so much that ownership became a sign of status.

The changes in women's lives were particularly striking. The new household items transformed the way women performed housework. Advice literature of all kinds encouraged housewives to rush out and buy the latest appliances so they could "modernize" their domestic labor. In public, consumer culture brought growing visibility to women, especially the young. Girls and young women worked behind the counters and shopped in the aisles of department stores, and they went out on the street alone in ways unthinkable in the nineteenth century. Contemporaries spoke repeatedly about the arrival of the **"new woman,"** a surprisingly independent female who could vote and held a job, spent her salary on the latest fashions, applied makeup and smoked cigarettes, and used her sex appeal to charm any number of young men. "The woman of yesterday," wrote one German feminist in 1929, yearned for marriage and children and "honor[ed] the achievements of the 'good old days.'" The new "woman of today," she continued, "refuses to be regarded as a physically weak being . . . and seeks to support herself through gainful employment. . . . She is organically bound up with the economic and cultural developments of the last few decades. Her task is to clear the way for equal rights for women in all areas of life."[7] Despite such enthusiasm,

"new woman" Somewhat stereotypical image of the modern and independent working woman popular in the 1920s.

the new woman was in some ways a stereotype, a product of marketing campaigns dedicated to selling consumer goods to the masses. Few young women could afford to live up to the image promoted in the mass press, even if they had jobs. Yet the changes associated with the First World War (see Chapter 26) and the emergence of consumer society did loosen traditional limits on women's behavior.

The emerging consumer culture generated a chorus of complaint from cultural critics of all stripes. On the left, socialist writers worried that the appeal of mass culture was undermining working-class radicalism, creating passive consumers rather than active class-conscious revolutionaries. On the right, conservatives complained that money spent on poor-quality mass-produced goods sapped the livelihood of industrious artisans and undermined proud national traditions. Religious leaders believed that modern consumerism encouraged rampant individualism and that greedy materialism was replacing spirituality. Many others bemoaned the loose morals of

Picturing the Past

The New Woman: Image or Reality? A young woman enjoys a drink at the Romanesque Café in Berlin in 1924. The independence of this "new woman," wearing fashionable clothes with a revealing hemline and lacking an escort, transgressed familiar gender roles and shocked and fascinated contemporaries. Images of the new woman appeared in movies, illustrated magazines, and advertisements, such as this German poster selling "this winter's perfume." (café: Bildarchiv Preussischer Kulturbesitz/Art Resource, NY; advertisement: Lordprice Collection/Alamy)

ANALYZING THE IMAGE How do these portrayals of the new woman challenge conventional gender roles? Do you think the woman in the Berlin café was influenced by advertisements for consumer products such as perfume and clothing?

CONNECTIONS What role did the emergence of a modern consumer culture play in the way contemporaries understood the new woman? Did consumer goods marketed to women open doors for liberating behavior, or did they set new standards that limited women's options?

To complete this activity online, go to the Online Study Guide at bedfordstmartins.com/mckaywest.

the new woman and fretted over the decline of traditional family values.

Despite such criticism—which would continue after World War II—consumer society was here to stay. Ordinary people enjoyed the pleasures of mass consumption, and individual identities were tied ever more closely to modern mass-produced goods. Yet the Great Depression of 1929 (see page 874) would make actual participation in the new world of goods fleeting and elusive. The promise of prosperity would only truly be realized during the great economic boom that followed the Second World War.

The Appeal of Cinema

Nowhere was the influence of mass culture more evident than in the rapid growth of standardized commercial entertainment, especially cinema and radio. Both became major industries in the interwar years, and an eager public enthusiastically embraced the new media. Across Europe and the United States, many millions spent their hard-earned money and their leisure hours watching movies or listening to radio broadcasts. The arrival of the modern mass media overshadowed and began to replace the traditional arts and amusements of people in villages and small towns, changing familiar ways of life.

Cinema first emerged in the United States around 1880, driven in part by the inventions of Thomas Edison. By 1910 American directors and business people had set up "movie factories," at first in the New York area and then in Los Angeles. Europeans were quick to follow. By 1914 Great Britain, France, Germany, and Italy, among others, had established their own small production companies. World War I quickened the pace. National leaders realized that movies offered distraction to troops and citizens and were furthermore an effective means of spreading propaganda. Audiences lined up to see *The Battle of the Somme*, a British film released in August 1916 that was frankly intended to encourage popular support for the war. The effect of this early example of national propaganda was immediate and heart wrenching. "The tears in many people's eyes and the silence that prevailed when I saw the film showed that every heart was full of love and sympathy for our soldiers," wrote one viewer to the *London Times* that September.[8]

Cinema became a true mass medium in the 1920s, the golden age of silent film. The United States was again a world leader, but European nations also established important national studios. Germany's Universal Film Company (or UFA) was particularly renowned. In the massive Babelsberg Studios just outside Berlin, talented directors produced classic Expressionist films such as *Nosferatu* (1922), a creepy vampire story, and *Metropolis* (1927), about a future society in the midst of a working-class revolt. Such films used the latest production techniques, thrilling audiences with fast and slow motion, montage sequences, unsettling close-ups, and strange dissolves.

Film making was big business on an international scale. Studios competed to place their movies on foreign screens, and by 1926 U.S. money was drawing German directors and stars to Hollywood and consolidating America's international domination. European theater owners were sometimes forced to book whole blocks of American films to get the few pictures they really wanted; in response, European governments set quotas on the number of U.S. films they imported. This system put European producers at a disadvantage until "talkies" permitted a revival of national film industries in the 1930s, particularly in France.

Motion pictures would remain the central entertainment of the masses until after the Second World War. Growing numbers of ordinary people flocked to the gigantic movie palaces built across Europe in the mid-1920s, splendid theaters that could seat thousands. There they viewed the latest features, which were reviewed by critics in newspapers and flashy illustrated magazines. Cinema audiences grew rapidly in the 1930s. In Great Britain in the late 1930s, one in every four adults went to the movies twice a week, and two in five went at least once a week. Other countries had similar figures.

As these numbers suggest, motion pictures could be powerful tools of indoctrination, especially in countries with dictatorial regimes. Lenin encouraged the development of Soviet film making, believing that the new medium was essential to the social and ideological transformation of the country. Beginning in the mid-1920s, a series of epic films, the most famous of which were directed by Sergei Eisenstein (1898–1948), brilliantly dramatized the communist view of Russian history. In Nazi Germany a young and immensely talented woman film maker, Leni Riefenstahl (REE-fuhn-shtahl) (1902–2003) directed a masterpiece of documentary propaganda, *The Triumph of the Will*, based on the 1934 Nazi Party rally at Nuremberg. Riefenstahl combined stunning aerial photography with images of joyful crowds welcoming Hitler, the Nazi leader, and mass processions of young Nazi fanatics. Her film, released in 1935, was a brilliant and all-too-powerful documentary of Germany's Nazi rebirth.

The Arrival of Radio

Like film, radio became a full-blown mass medium in the 1920s. Experimental sets were available in the 1880s; the work of Italian inventor Guglielmo Marconi (1874–1937) around 1900 and the development of the vacuum tube in 1904 made possible primitive transmissions of speech and music. But the first major public broadcasts of special events in Great Britain and the United

States occurred only in 1920. Lord Northcliffe, who had pioneered in journalism with the inexpensive, mass-circulation *Daily Mail,* sponsored a broadcast of "only one artist . . . the world's very best, the soprano Nellie Melba."[9] Singing from London in English, Italian, and French, Melba was heard simultaneously all over Europe on June 16, 1920. This historic event captured the public's imagination and launched the meteoric career of radio.

Every major country quickly established national broadcasting networks. In the United States such networks were privately owned and were financed by advertising, but in Europe the typical pattern was direct control by the government. In Great Britain, for example, Parliament set up an independent public corporation, the British Broadcasting Corporation (BBC), supported by licensing fees. Whatever the institutional framework, radio became popular and influential. By the late 1930s

more than three out of every four households in both democratic Great Britain and dictatorial Germany had at least one cheap mass-produced radio.

Like the movies, radio was well suited for political propaganda. Dictators such as Mussolini and Hitler controlled the airwaves and could reach enormous national audiences with their frequent dramatic speeches. In democratic countries, politicians such as American president Franklin Roosevelt and British prime minister Stanley Baldwin effectively used informal "fireside

"The Greatest Cinema in the World" With 3,400 seats, the Gaumont Palace in Paris was the largest cinema in the world in its heyday. Crowds lined up to see films such as this 1931 family drama by the noted French writer and film director Marcel Pagnol. (photo: Maurice Branger/Roger-Viollet/The Image Works; poster: Paramount Pictures/Photofest © Paramount Pictures)

chats" to bolster their popularity. The new media of mass culture offered audiences pleasant distractions but were at the same time potentially dangerous instruments of political manipulation.

The Search for Peace and Political Stability

How did the democratic leaders of the 1920s deal with deep-seated instability and try to establish real peace and prosperity? ■

As established patterns of thought and culture were challenged and mangled by the ferocious impact of World War I, so too was the political fabric stretched and torn. The Versailles settlement had established a shaky truce, not a solid peace. Thus national leaders faced a gigantic task as they sought to create a stable international order within the general context of intellectual crisis and revolutionary cultural change.

The pursuit of real and lasting peace proved difficult for many reasons. Germany hated the Treaty of Versailles. France was fearful and isolated. Britain was undependable, and the United States had turned its back on European problems. Eastern Europe was in ferment, and no one could predict the future of communist Russia. Moreover, the international economic situation was poor and greatly complicated by war debts and disrupted patterns of trade. Yet from 1925 to late 1929, it appeared that peace and stability were within reach. When the economic collapse of the 1930s mocked these hopes and brought the rise of brutal dictators, the disillusionment of liberals in the democracies intensified.

Germany and the Western Powers

Germany was the key to lasting peace. Yet to Germans of all political parties, the Treaty of Versailles represented a harsh dictated peace, to be revised or repudiated as soon as possible. Germany still had the potential to become the strongest country in Europe and remained a source of instability. Moreover, with ominous implications for the future, France and Great Britain did not see eye to eye on Germany. By the end of 1919, France wanted to stress the harsh elements in the Treaty of Versailles. Most of the war in the west had been fought on French soil, and the expected costs of reconstruction, as well as of repaying war debts to the United States, were staggering. Thus French politicians believed that massive reparations from Germany were a vital economic necessity. And after having compromised with President Wilson only to be betrayed by America's failure to ratify the treaty, many French leaders saw strict implementation of all provisions of the Treaty of Versailles as France's

last best hope. Large reparation payments could hold Germany down indefinitely, and France would realize its goal of security.

The British soon felt differently. Prewar Germany had been Great Britain's second-best market in the entire world, and after the war a healthy, prosperous Germany appeared to be essential to the British economy. Many English people agreed with the analysis of the young English economist John Maynard Keynes (caynz) (1883–1946), who eloquently denounced the Treaty of Versailles in his famous *Economic Consequences of the Peace* (1919). According to Keynes's interpretation, astronomical reparations and harsh economic measures would impoverish Germany, encourage Bolshevism, and increase economic hardship in all countries. "There are no precedents of the indemnity imposed on Germany under the present treaty," he wrote. "The policy of reducing Germany to servitude for a generation, of degrading the lives of millions of human beings, and of depriving a whole nation of happiness should be abhorrent and detestable."[10] Only a complete revision of the foolish treaty could save Germany—and Europe. Keynes's attack engendered much public discussion and became very influential. It created sympathy for Germany in the English-speaking world, which often paralyzed English and American leaders in their relations with Germany between the First and Second World Wars.

❝ The policy of reducing Germany to servitude for a generation, of degrading the lives of millions of human beings, and of depriving a whole nation of happiness should be abhorrent and detestable. ❞

—John Maynard Keynes

The British were also suspicious of France's army—the largest in Europe, and authorized at Versailles to occupy the German Rhineland until 1935—and of France's foreign policy. Ever since 1890 France had looked to Russia as a powerful ally against Germany. But with Russia hostile and communist, and with Britain and the United States unwilling to make any firm commitments, France turned to the newly formed states of eastern Europe for diplomatic support. In 1921 France signed a mutual defense pact with Poland and associated itself closely with the so-called Little Entente, an alliance that joined Czechoslovakia, Romania, and Yugoslavia against defeated and bitter Hungary.

While French and British leaders drifted in different directions, the Allied reparations commission completed its work. In April 1921 it announced that Germany had to pay the enormous sum of 132 billion gold marks ($33 billion) in annual installments of 2.5 billion gold marks. Facing possible occupation of more of its territory, the young German republic—generally known as the Weimar Republic—made its first payment in 1921.

Then in 1922, wracked by rapid inflation and political assassinations and motivated by hostility and arrogance as well, the Weimar Republic announced its inability to pay more. It proposed a moratorium on reparations for three years, with the clear implication that thereafter reparations would be either drastically reduced or eliminated entirely.

The British were willing to accept a moratorium on reparations, but the French were not. Led by their tough-minded prime minister, Raymond Poincaré (1860–1934), they decided they had to either call Germany's bluff or see the entire peace settlement dissolve to France's great disadvantage. So, despite strong British protests, in early January 1923 armies of France and its ally Belgium moved out of the Rhineland and began to occupy the Ruhr district, the heartland of industrial Germany, creating the most serious international crisis of the 1920s. If forcible collection proved impossible, France would use occupation to paralyze Germany and force it to accept the Treaty of Versailles.

Strengthened by a wave of patriotism, the German government ordered the people of the Ruhr to stop working and passively resist the French occupation. The coal mines and steel mills of the Ruhr fell silent, leaving 10 percent of Germany's total population out of work. The French answer to passive resistance was to seal off the Ruhr and the entire Rhineland from the rest of Germany, letting in only enough food to prevent starvation. German opinion was in-

censed when the French sent over forty thousand colonial troops from North and West Africa to control the territory. German propagandists labeled the colonial occupying troops the "black shame," warning that the African soldiers were savages, eager to brutalize civilians and assault German women. Such accounts were entirely unfounded; they expressed the all-too-common racial prejudice of the time. This racial panic nonetheless intensified German-French tensions.

By the summer of 1923, France and Germany were engaged in a great test of wills. French armies could not collect reparations from striking workers at gunpoint. But French occupation was paralyzing Germany and its economy. Faced with the need to support the striking Ruhr workers and their employers, the German government began to print money to pay its bills, causing runaway inflation. Prices soared as German money rapidly lost all value. People went to the store with big bags of banknotes; they returned home with handfuls of groceries. The accumulated savings of many retired and middle-class people were wiped out. Catastrophic inflation cruelly mocked the old middle-class virtues of thrift, caution, and self-reliance. Many Germans felt betrayed. They hated and blamed the Western governments, their own government, big business, the Jews, the workers, and the communists for their misfortune. Right-wing nationalists including Adolf Hitler and the newly established Nazi Party eagerly capitalized on the widespread feelings of discontent.

French Occupation of the Ruhr, 1923–1925

"German Women Protest the Colored Occupation on the Rhine" In 1923 the French army occupied the industrial district of the Ruhr in Germany in an effort to force reparations payments. The occupying forces included colonial troops from West Africa, and Germans responded with a racist propaganda campaign that cast the West African troops as uncivilized savages. (Stiftung Deutsches Historiches Museum, Berlin, P62/1483.2)

In August 1923, as the mark lost value and political unrest grew throughout Germany, Gustav Stresemann (GOOS-tahf SHTRAY-zuh-mahn) (1878–1929) assumed leadership of the government. Stresemann adopted an attitude of compromise. He called off passive resistance in the Ruhr and in October agreed in principle to pay reparations, but asked for a re-examination of Germany's ability to pay. Poincaré accepted. His hard line was becoming increasingly unpopular with French citizens, and it was hated in Britain and the United States. (See "Individuals in Society: Gustav Stresemann," page 875.)

More generally, in both Germany and France, power was finally passing to more moderate leaders who realized that continued confrontation was a destructive, no-win situation. Thus, after five long years of hostility and tension, culminating in a kind of undeclared war in the Ruhr in 1923, Germany and France decided to give compromise and cooperation a try. The British, and even the Americans, were willing to help. The first step was a reasonable agreement on the reparations question.

Hope in Foreign Affairs

In 1924 an international committee of financial experts headed by American banker Charles G. Dawes met to re-examine reparations from a broad perspective. The resulting **Dawes Plan** (1924) was accepted by France, Germany, and Britain. Germany's yearly reparations were reduced and linked to the level of German economic prosperity. Germany would also receive large loans from the United States to promote economic recovery. In short, Germany would get private loans from the United States in order to pay reparations to France and Britain, thus enabling those countries to repay the large war debts they owed the United States.

This circular flow of international payments was complicated and risky, but for a while it worked. The German republic experienced a shaky economic recovery. With continual inflows of American capital, Germany paid about $1.3 billion in reparations in 1927 and 1928, enabling France and Britain to repay the United States. In this way the Americans belatedly played a part in the general economic settlement that, though far from ideal, facilitated the worldwide recovery of the late 1920s.

This economic settlement was matched by a political settlement. In 1925 the leaders of Europe signed a number of agreements at Locarno, Switzerland. Germany and France solemnly pledged to accept their common border, and both Britain and Italy agreed to fight either France or Germany if one invaded the other. Stresemann reluctantly agreed to settle boundary disputes with Poland and Czechoslovakia by peaceful means, but did not agree to permanent borders to Germany's east. In response, France promised those countries military aid if Germany attacked them. The refusal to settle Germany's eastern borders angered the Poles, and though the "spirit of Locarno" lent some hope to those seeking security and stability in international affairs, political tensions deepened in eastern Europe.

Other developments strengthened hopes for international peace. In 1926 Germany joined the League of Nations, and in 1928 fifteen countries signed the Kellogg-Briand Pact, initiated by French prime minister Aristide Briand and U.S. secretary of state Frank B. Kellogg. The signing states agreed to "renounce [war] as an instrument of international policy" and settle international disputes peacefully. The pact made no provisions for action in case war actually occurred and in fact did little to halt the arrival of the Second World War in 1939. It nonetheless fostered a cautious optimism in the late 1920s and encouraged the hope that the United States would accept its responsibilities as a great world power by contributing to European stability.

Hope in Democratic Government

Domestic politics also offered reason to hope. During the occupation of the Ruhr and the great inflation, republican government in Germany had appeared on the verge of collapse. In 1923 communists momentarily entered provincial governments, and in November an obscure politician named Adolf Hitler leaped onto a table in a beer hall in Munich and proclaimed a "national socialist revolution." But Hitler's plot to seize control of the government was easily crushed, and Hitler was sentenced to prison, where he outlined his theories and program in his book *Mein Kampf* (My Struggle). Throughout the 1920s, Hitler's National Socialist Party attracted support primarily from fanatical anti-Semites, ultranationalists, and disgruntled ex-servicemen. In 1928 his party had just twelve insignificant seats in the Reichstag. Indeed, after 1923 liberal democracy seemed to take root in Weimar Germany. A new currency was established, and the economy stabilized.

The moderate businessmen who tended to dominate the various German coalition governments were convinced that economic prosperity demanded good relations with the Western Powers, and they supported parliamentary government at home. Stresemann himself was a man of this class, and he was the key figure in every government until his death in 1929. Elections were held regularly, and republican democracy appeared to have growing support among a majority of Germans.

> **Dawes Plan** War reparations agreement that reduced Germany's yearly payments, made payment dependent on economic prosperity, and granted large U.S. loans to promote recovery.

There were, however, sharp political divisions in the country. Many unrepentant nationalists and monarchists populated the right and the army. Members of Germany's recently formed Communist Party were noisy and active on the left. The Communists, directed from Moscow, reserved their greatest hatred and sharpest barbs for their cousins the Social Democrats, whom they endlessly accused of betraying the revolution. The working classes were divided politically, but a majority supported the nonrevolutionary but socialist Social Democrats.

The situation in France was similar to that in Germany. Communists and Socialists battled for the support of the workers. After 1924 the democratically elected government rested mainly in the hands of coalitions of moderates, and business interests were well represented. France's great accomplishment was the rapid rebuilding of its war-torn northern region. The expense of this undertaking led, however, to a large deficit and substantial inflation. By early 1926, the franc had fallen to 10 percent of its prewar value, causing a severe crisis. Poincaré was recalled to office, while Briand remained minister for foreign affairs. The Poincaré government proceeded to slash spending and raise taxes, restoring confidence in the economy. The franc was stabilized at about one-fifth of its prewar value, and the economy remained fairly stable until 1930.

Great Depression

A worldwide economic depression from 1929 through 1939, unique in its severity and duration and with slow and uneven recovery.

Britain, too, faced challenges after 1920. The wartime trend toward greater social equality continued, however, helping maintain social harmony. The great problem was unemployment. In June 1921 almost 2.2 million people—23 percent of the labor force—were out of work, and throughout the 1920s unemployment hovered around 12 percent. Yet the state provided unemployment benefits to those without jobs and supplemented the payments with subsidized housing, medical aid, and increased old-age pensions. These and other measures kept living standards from seriously declining, defused class tensions, and pointed the way toward the welfare state Britain would establish after World War II.

Relative social harmony was accompanied by the rise of the Labour Party as a determined champion of the working classes and of greater social equality. Committed to the kind of moderate revisionist socialism that had emerged before World War I (see Chapter 24), the Labour Party replaced the Liberal Party as the main opposition to the Conservatives. The new prominence of the Labour Party reflected the decline of old liberal ideals of competitive capitalism, limited government control, and individual responsibility. In 1924 and 1929, the Labour Party under Ramsay MacDonald (1866–1937) governed the country with the support of the smaller Liberal Party. Yet Labour moved toward socialism gradually and democratically, so that the middle classes were not overly frightened as the working classes won new benefits.

The British Conservatives showed the same compromising spirit on social issues. In 1922 Britain granted southern, Catholic, Ireland full autonomy after a bitter guerrilla war, thereby removing a key source of prewar friction. Despite conflicts such as the 1926 strike by hard-pressed coal miners, which led to an unsuccessful general strike, social unrest in Britain was limited in the 1920s and 1930s. Thus developments in both international relations and the domestic politics of the leading democracies gave cause for optimism in the late 1920s.

The Great Depression, 1929–1939

What caused the Great Depression, and how did the Western democracies respond to this challenge? ■

This fragile optimism was short-lived. Beginning in 1929, a massive economic downturn struck the entire world with ever-greater intensity, and recovery was slow and uneven. Contemporaries labeled the economic crisis the **Great Depression**, to emphasize its severity and duration. Only with the Second World War did the depression disappear in much of the world.

The social and political consequences of the Great Depression were enormous. Mass unemployment and failing farms made insecurity and unemployment a reality for millions of ordinary people (Map 27.1). In Europe and the United States, governments instituted a variety of social welfare programs intended to manage the crisis. Yet the prolonged economic collapse shattered the fragile political stability of the mid-1920s and encouraged the growth of extremists on both ends of the political spectrum. Democratic government faltered, and authoritarian fascist parties gained power across Europe.

The Economic Crisis

Though economic activity was already declining moderately in many countries by early 1929, the crash of the stock market in the United States in October of that year initiated a worldwide crisis. The American economy had prospered in the late 1920s, but there were large inequalities in income and a serious imbalance between actual investment and stock market speculation. Thus net investment—in factories, farms, equipment, and the like—actually fell from $3.5 billion in 1925 to $3.2 billion in 1929. In the same years, as money flooded into stocks, the value of shares traded on the

INDIVIDUALS IN SOCIETY

THE GERMAN FOREIGN MINISTER GUSTAV STRESEMANN (1878–1929) is a controversial historical figure. Hailed by many as a hero of peace, he was denounced as a traitor by radical German nationalists and then by Hitler's Nazis. After World War II, revisionist historians stressed Stresemann's persistent nationalism and cast doubt on his peaceful intentions. Weimar Germany's most renowned leader is a fascinating example of the restless quest for convincing historical interpretation.

Stresemann's origins were modest. His parents were Berlin innkeepers and retailers of bottled beer, and of their five children only Gustav was able to attend high school. Attracted first to literature and history, Stresemann later turned to economics, earned a doctoral degree, and quickly reached the top as a manager and director of German trade associations. A highly intelligent extrovert with a knack for negotiation, Stresemann became a deputy in the German Reichstag (parliament) in 1907 as a business-oriented liberal and nationalist. When World War I erupted, he believed, like most Germans, that Germany had acted defensively and was not at fault. He emerged as a strident nationalist and urged German annexation of conquered foreign territories. Germany's collapse in defeat and revolution devastated Stresemann. He seemed a prime candidate for the hateful extremism of the far right.

Yet although Stresemann opposed the Treaty of Versailles as an unjust and unrealistic imposition, he turned back toward the center. He accepted the new Weimar Republic and played a growing role in the Reichstag as the leader of his own small pro-business party. His hour came in the Ruhr crisis, when French and Belgian troops occupied the district. Named chancellor in August 1923, he called off passive resistance and began talks with the French. His government also quelled communist uprisings; put down rebellions in Bavaria, including an attempted coup by Hitler; and ended runaway inflation with the introduction of a new currency. Stresemann fought to preserve German unity, and he succeeded.

Voted out as chancellor in November 1923, Stresemann remained as foreign minister in every German government until his death in 1929. Proclaiming a policy of peace and agreeing to pay reparations, he achieved his greatest triumph in the Locarno agreements of 1925 (see page 873). But the interlocking guarantees of existing French and German borders (and the related agreements to resolve peacefully all disputes with Poland and Czechoslovakia) did not lead the French to make any further concessions that might have disarmed Stresemann's extremist foes. He made little additional progress in achieving international reconciliation and sovereign equality for Germany. His premature death in office was a serious blow to German pragmatism that encouraged the turn to a more aggressive and nationalist foreign policy.

Stresemann was no fuzzy pacifist. Historians debunking his legend are right in seeing an enduring patriotism in his defense of German interests. But Stresemann, like his French counterpart Aristide Briand, was a statesman of goodwill who wanted peace through mutually advantageous compromise. A realist trained by business and politics in the art of the possible, Stresemann also reasoned that Germany had to be a satisfied and equal partner if peace was to be secure. His unwillingness to guarantee Germany's eastern borders (see Map 26.4 on page 841), which is often criticized as contributing to the coming of the Second World War, reflected his conviction that keeping some Germans under Polish and Czechoslovakian rule created a ticking time bomb in Europe.

Stresemann was no less convinced that war on Poland would almost certainly re-create the Allied coalition that had crushed Germany in 1918.* His insistence on the necessity of peace in the east as well as the west was prophetic. Hitler's 1939 invasion of Poland resulted in an even mightier coalition that almost annihilated Germany in 1945.

Foreign Minister Gustav Stresemann of Germany (right) leaves a meeting with Aristide Briand, his French counterpart. (Corbis)

QUESTIONS FOR ANALYSIS

1. What did Gustav Stresemann do to promote reconciliation in Europe? How did his policy toward France differ from that toward Poland and Czechoslovakia?
2. What is your interpretation of Stresemann? Does he arouse your sympathy or your suspicion and hostility? Why?

*Robert Grathwol, "Stresemann: Reflections on His Foreign Policy," *Journal of Modern History* 45 (March 1973): 52–70.

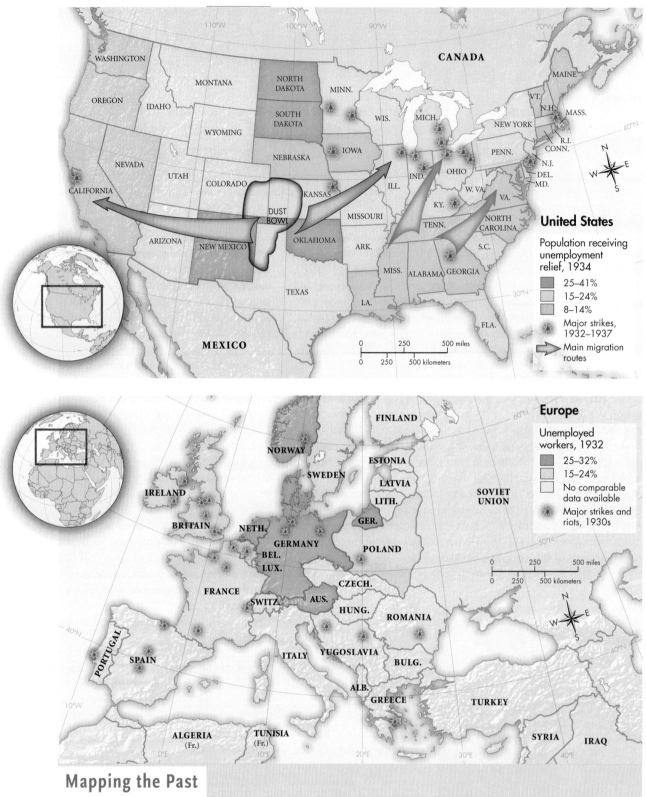

Mapping the Past

Map 27.1 The Great Depression in the United States and Europe, 1929–1939 These maps show that unemployment was high almost everywhere, but that national and regional differences were also substantial.

ANALYZING THE MAP Which European countries had the highest rate of unemployment? How do the rates of people on unemployment relief in the United States compare to the percentage of unemployed workers in Europe? In the United States, what were the main channels of migration for workers?

CONNECTIONS What tactics of reform and recovery did European nations use to combat the deprivations of the Great Depression?

To complete this activity online, go to the Online Study Guide at bedfordstmartins.com/mckaywest.

exchanges soared from $27 billion to $87 billion. Such inflated prices should have raised serious concerns about economic solvency, but even experts failed to predict the looming collapse.

The American stock market boom was built on borrowed money. Many wealthy investors, speculators, and people of modest means had bought stocks by paying only a small fraction of the total purchase price and borrowing the remainder from their stockbrokers. Such buying "on margin" was extremely dangerous. When prices started falling, the hard-pressed margin buyers either had to put up more money, which was often impossible, or sell their shares to pay off their brokers. Thousands of people started selling all at once. The result was a financial panic. Countless investors and speculators were wiped out in a matter of days or weeks.

The consequences were swift and severe. Stripped of wealth and confidence, battered investors and their fellow citizens started buying fewer goods. Prices fell, production began to slow down, and unemployment began to rise. Soon the entire American economy was caught in a spiraling decline.

The financial panic in the United States triggered an international financial crisis. Throughout the 1920s, American bankers and investors had lent large amounts of capital to many countries. Once the panic broke, New York bankers began recalling these short-term loans. Gold reserves began to flow rapidly out of European countries, particularly Germany and Austria, toward the United States. It became very hard for European business people to borrow money, and the panicky public began to withdraw its savings from the banks. These banking problems eventually led to the crash of the largest bank in Austria in 1931 and then to general financial chaos. The recall of private loans by American bankers also accelerated the collapse in world prices when businesses around the world dumped industrial goods and agricultural commodities in a frantic attempt to get cash to pay what they owed.

The financial crisis led to a general crisis of production: between 1929 and 1933, world output of goods fell by an estimated 38 percent. As this happened, each country turned inward and tried to manage the crisis alone. In 1931, for example, Britain went off the gold standard, refusing to convert banknotes into gold, and reduced the value of its money. Britain's goal was to make its goods cheaper and therefore more salable in the world market. But because more than twenty nations, including the United

States in 1934, also went off the gold standard, few countries gained a real advantage. Similarly, country after country followed the example of the United States when in 1930 it raised protective tariffs to their highest levels ever and tried to seal off shrinking national markets for American producers only. Such actions further limited international trade. Within this context of fragmented and destructive economic nationalism, a halting recovery only began in 1933.

Although opinions differ, two factors probably best explain the relentless slide to the bottom from 1929 to early 1933. First, the international economy lacked leadership able to maintain stability when the crisis came. Neither Britain nor the United States—the world's economic leaders at the time—successfully stabilized the international economic system in 1929. The United States, which had momentarily played a positive role after the occupation of the Ruhr, cut back its international lending and erected high tariffs.

The second factor was poor national economic policy in almost every country. Governments generally cut their budgets when they should have raised spending and run large deficits in order to stimulate their economies. After World War II, such a "counter-cyclical policy," advocated by John Maynard Keynes, became a well-established weapon against downturn and depression. But in the 1930s, Keynes's prescription was generally regarded with horror by orthodox economists.

Mass Unemployment

The lack of large-scale government spending contributed to the rise of mass unemployment. As the financial crisis led to cuts in production, workers lost their jobs and had little money to buy goods. In Britain, where unemployment had averaged 12 percent in the 1920s, it averaged more than 18 percent between 1930 and 1935. Far worse was the case of Germany, where in 1932 one in every three workers was jobless. In the United States, unemployment had averaged only 5 percent in the 1920s. In 1932 it soared to about 33 percent: 14 million people were out of work (see Map 27.1). Only by pumping new money into the economy could the government increase demand and break the vicious cycle of decline.

Mass unemployment created great social problems. Poverty increased dramatically, although in most countries unemployed workers generally received some kind of

British Unemployment, 1932

Insured workers unemployed
- More than 35%
- 25–35%
- 15–24%
- Less than 15%

LISTENING TO THE PAST

Periodic surges in unemployment were an old story in capitalist economies, but the long-term joblessness of millions in the Great Depression was something new and unexpected. In Britain especially, where the depression followed a weak postwar recovery, large numbers suffered involuntary idleness for years at a time. Whole families lived "on the dole," the weekly welfare benefits paid by the government.

One of the most insightful accounts of unemployed workers was written by the British journalist and novelist George Orwell (1903–1950), who studied the conditions in northern England and wrote The Road to Wigan Pier *(1937), an excerpt of which follows. An independent socialist who distrusted rigid Marxism, Orwell believed that socialism could triumph in Britain if it came to mean commonsense "justice and liberty" for a broad sector of the working classes. Orwell's disillusionment with authoritarian socialism and Soviet-style communism pervades his other famous works,* Animal Farm *(1945) and* 1984 *(1949).*

❝ When you see the unemployment figures quoted at two millions, it is fatally easy to take this as meaning that two million people are out of work and the rest of the population is comparatively comfortable.... [Adding in the destitute,] you might take the number of underfed people in England (for *everyone* on the dole or thereabouts is underfed) as being, at the very most, five millions.

This is an enormous under-estimate, because, in the first place, the only people shown on unemployment figures are those actually drawing the dole — that is, in general, heads of families. An unemployed man's dependants do not figure on the list unless they too are drawing a separate allowance.... In addition there are great numbers of people who are in work but who, from a financial point of view, might equally be unemployed, because they are not drawing anything that can be described as a living wage.

Allow for these and their dependants, throw in as before the old-age pensioners, the destitute and other nondescripts, and you get an *underfed* population of well over ten millions.... Take the figures for Wigan, which is typical enough of the industrial and mining districts.... The total population of Wigan is a little under 87,000; so that at any moment more than one person in three out of the whole population — not merely the registered workers — is either drawing or living on the dole....

Nevertheless, in spite of the frightful extent of unemployment, it is a fact that poverty — extreme poverty — is less in evidence in the industrial North than it is in London. Everything is poorer and shabbier, there are fewer motor-cars and fewer well-dressed people; but also there are fewer people who are obviously destitute.... In the industrial towns the old communal way of life has not yet broken up, tradition is still strong and almost everyone has a family — potentially, therefore, a home. In a town of 50,000 or 100,000 inhabitants there is no casual and as it were unaccounted-for population; nobody sleeping in the streets, for instance. Moreover, there is just this to be said for the unemployment regulations, that they do not discourage people from marrying. A man and wife on twenty-three shillings a week are not far from the starvation line, but they can make a home of sorts; they are vastly better off than a single man on fifteen shillings....

But there is no doubt about the deadening, debilitating effect of unemployment upon everybody, married or single, and upon men more than upon women.... Everyone who saw Greenwood's play *Love on the Dole* must remember that dreadful moment when the poor, good, stupid working man beats on the table and cries out, "O God, send me some work!" This was not dramatic exaggeration, it was a touch from life. That cry must have been uttered, in almost those words, in tens of thousands, perhaps hundreds of thousands of English homes, during the past fifteen years.

But, I think not again — or at least, not so often.... When people live on the dole for years at a time they grow used to it, and drawing the dole, though it remains unpleasant, ceases to be shameful. Thus the old, independent, workhouse-fearing tradition is undermined....

So you have whole populations settling down, as it were, to a lifetime of the P.A.C.... Take, for instance,

meager unemployment benefits or public aid that prevented starvation. (See "Listening to the Past: George Orwell on Life on the Dole," above.) Millions of people lost their spirit, condemned to an apparently hopeless search for work. Homes and ways of life were disrupted in millions of personal tragedies. Young people postponed marriages, and birthrates fell sharply. There was an increase in suicide and mental illness. Poverty or the threat of poverty became a grinding reality. In 1932 the workers of Manchester, England, appealed to their city officials — a typical plea echoed throughout the Western world:

Poster used in the British election campaign of 1931, when unemployment rose to a new record high. (Conservative Research Department/The Bridgeman Art Library)

of cheap smart clothes since the war. The youth who leaves school at fourteen and gets a blind-alley job is out of work at twenty, probably for life; but for two pounds ten on the hire-purchase system he can buy himself a suit which, for a little while and at a little distance, looks as though it had been tailored in Savile Row. The girl can look like a fashion plate at an even lower price.... You can stand on the street corner, indulging in a private daydream of yourself as Clark Gable or Greta Garbo, which compensates you for a great deal....

Trade since the war has had to adjust itself to meet the demands of underpaid, underfed people, with the result that a luxury is nowadays almost always cheaper than a necessity. One pair of plain solid shoes costs as much as two ultra-smart pairs.... And above all there is gambling, the cheapest of all luxuries. Even people on the verge of starvation can buy a few days' hope ("Something to live for," as they call it) by having a penny on a sweepstake.... Twenty million people are underfed but literally everyone in England has access to a radio. What we have lost in food we have gained in electricity. Whole sections of the working class who have been plundered of all they really need are being compensated, in part, by cheap luxuries which mitigate the surface of life.

Do you consider all this desirable? No, I don't. But it may be that the psychological adjustment which the working class are visibly making is the best they could make in the circumstances. They have neither turned revolutionary nor lost their self-respect; merely they have kept their tempers and settled down to make the best of things on a fish-and-chip standard. The alternative would be God knows what continued agonies of despair; or it might be attempted insurrections which, in a strongly governed country like England, could only lead to futile massacres and a régime of savage repression. **"**

Source: Excerpts from Chapter V in *The Road to Wigan Pier* by George Orwell. Copyright © 1958 and renewed 1986 by the Estate of Sonia B. Orwell. Reprinted by permission of Houghton Mifflin Harcourt Publishing Company, from *The Complete Works of George Orwell* by George Orwell. Copyright © George Orwell, 1986. Reproduced by permission of Bill Hamilton as the Literary Executor of the Estate of the Late Sonia Brownell Orwell and Seeker & Warburg Ltd.

the fact that the working class think nothing of getting married on the dole.... Life is still fairly normal, more normal than one really has the right to expect. Families are impoverished, but the family-system has not broken up. The people are in effect living a reduced version of their former lives.

Instead of raging against their destiny they have made things tolerable by lowering their standards. But they don't necessarily lower their standards by cutting out luxuries and concentrating on necessities; more often it is the other way about — the more natural way, if you come to think of it. Hence the fact that in a decade of unparalleled depression, the consumption of all cheap luxuries has increased. The two things that have probably made the greatest difference of all are the movies and the mass-production

QUESTIONS FOR ANALYSIS

1. According to Orwell, "extreme poverty" was less visible in the northern industrial towns than in London. How did family relations contribute to social stability in the face of growing poverty?

2. What were the consequences of long-term unemployment for English workers? How did joblessness change attitudes and behaviors?

3. Judging from Orwell's description, did radical revolution seem likely in England in the Great Depression? Why?

We tell you that thousands of people . . . are in desperate straits. We tell you that men, women, and children are going hungry. . . . We tell you that great numbers are being rendered distraught through the stress and worry of trying to exist without work. . . . If you do not do this — if you do not provide useful work for the unemployed — what, we ask, is your alternative? Do not imagine that this colossal tragedy of unemployment is going on endlessly without some fateful catastrophe. Hungry men are angry men.[11]

Only strong government action could deal with mass unemployment, a social powder keg preparing to explode.

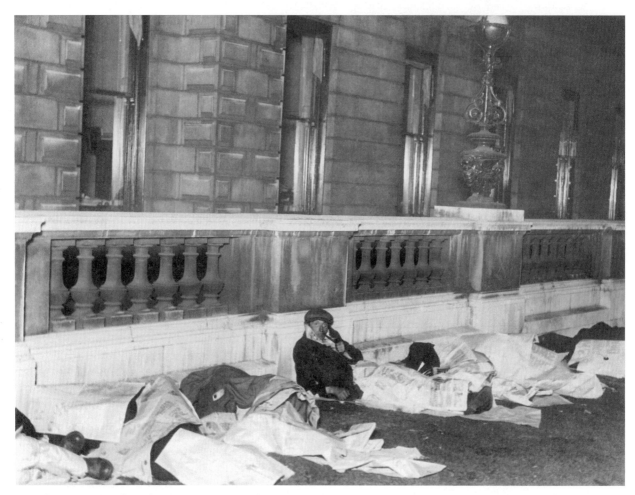

Homelessness in London The Great Depression of the 1930s disrupted the lives of millions across the United States and Europe. The frustration and agony of unemployment are evident in this common scene of unemployed and homeless Londoners wrapping themselves in newspaper against the cold. (Mary Evans Picture Library/The Image Works)

The New Deal in the United States

The Great Depression and the response to it marked a major turning point in American history. President Herbert Hoover (r. 1929–1933) and his administration initially reacted to the stock market crash and economic decline with dogged optimism but limited action. When the full force of the financial crisis struck Europe in the summer of 1931 and boomeranged back to the United States, people's worst fears became reality. Banks failed; unemployment soared. Between 1929 and 1932 industrial production fell by about 50 percent.

In these tragic circumstances, Franklin Delano Roosevelt (r. 1933–1945) won a landslide presidential victory in 1932 with grand but vague promises of a "New Deal for the forgotten man." Roosevelt's basic goal was to reform capitalism in order to preserve it. Though Roosevelt rejected socialism and government ownership of industry in 1933, he nonetheless advocated forceful government intervention in the economy

and instituted a broad range of government-supported social programs designed to stimulate the economy and provide jobs for ordinary people. Across Europe, governments engaged in similar actions in desperate attempts to relieve the economic crisis.

In the United States, innovative federal programs promoted agricultural recovery, a top priority. Almost half of the American population still lived in rural areas, and American farmers were hard hit by the depression. Roosevelt took the United States off the gold standard and devalued the dollar in an effort to raise American prices and rescue farmers. The Agricultural Adjustment Act of 1933 also aimed at raising prices and farm income by limiting agricultural production. These planning measures worked for a while, and in 1936 farmers repaid Roosevelt with overwhelming support.

The most ambitious attempt to control and plan the economy was the National Recovery Administration (NRA). Intended to reduce competition and fix prices and wages for everyone's benefit, the NRA broke with

❝ Do not imagine that this colossal tragedy of unemployment is going on endlessly without some fateful catastrophe. Hungry men are angry men. ❯❯

—WORKERS IN MANCHESTER, ENGLAND

the cherished American tradition of free competition and aroused conflicts among business people, consumers, and bureaucrats. It did not work well and was declared unconstitutional in 1935.

Roosevelt and his advisers then attacked the key problem of mass unemployment directly. The federal government accepted the responsibility of employing directly as many people as financially possible. New agencies were created to undertake a vast range of projects. The most famous of these was the Works Progress Administration (WPA), set up in 1935. One-fifth of the entire U.S. labor force worked for the WPA at some point in the 1930s, constructing public buildings, bridges, and highways. The WPA was enormously popular, and the hope of a government job helped check the threat of social revolution in the United States.

In 1935 the U.S. government also established a national social security system with old-age pensions and unemployment benefits. The National Labor Relations Act of 1935 gave union organizers the green light by declaring collective bargaining to be the policy of the United States. Union membership more than doubled from 4 million in 1935 to 9 million in 1940. In general, between 1935 and 1938 government rulings and social reforms chipped away at the privileges of the wealthy and tried to help ordinary people.

Relief programs like the WPA were part of the New Deal's fundamental commitment to use the federal government to provide for the welfare of all Americans. This commitment marked a profound shift from the traditional stress on family support and community responsibility. Embraced by a large majority in the 1930s, this shift in attitudes proved to be one of the New Deal's most enduring legacies.

Yet despite undeniable accomplishments in social reform, the New Deal was only partly successful as a response to the Great Depression. At the height of the recovery in May 1937, 7 million workers were still unemployed, in contrast to a high of 15 million in 1933. The economic situation then worsened seriously in the recession of 1937 and 1938, and unemployment had risen to a staggering 10 million when war broke out in Europe in September 1939. The New Deal never did pull the United States out of the depression; it took the Second World War to do that.

The Scandinavian Response to the Depression

Of all the Western democracies, the Scandinavian countries under Social Democratic leadership responded most successfully to the challenge of the Great Depression. Having grown steadily in the late nineteenth century, the Social Democrats became the largest political party in Sweden and then in Norway after the First World War. In the 1920s they passed important social reform legislation for both peasants and workers and developed a unique kind of socialism. Flexible and nonrevolutionary, Scandinavian socialism grew out of a strong tradition of cooperative community action. Even before 1900 Scandinavian agricultural cooperatives had shown how individual peasant families could join together for everyone's benefit. Labor leaders and capitalists were also inclined to work together.

When the economic crisis struck in 1929, socialist governments in Scandinavia built on this pattern of cooperative social action. Sweden in particular pioneered in the use of large-scale deficits to finance public works and thereby maintain production and employment. In ways that paralleled some aspects of Roosevelt's New Deal, Scandinavian governments also increased such social welfare benefits as old-age pensions, unemployment insurance, subsidized housing, and maternity allowances. All this spending required a large bureaucracy and high taxes, first on the rich and then on practically everyone. Yet both private and cooperative enterprise thrived, as did democracy. Some observers saw Scandinavia's welfare socialism as an appealing middle way between sick capitalism and cruel communism or fascism.

Recovery and Reform in Britain and France

In Britain MacDonald's Labour government and then, after 1931, the Conservative-dominated coalition government followed orthodox economic theory. The budget was balanced, but spending was tightly controlled and unemployed workers received barely enough welfare to live. Despite government lethargy, the economy recovered considerably after 1932. By 1937 total production was about 20 percent higher than in 1929. In fact, for Britain the years after 1932 were actually somewhat

Oslo Breakfast Scandinavian socialism championed cooperation and practical welfare measures, playing down strident rhetoric and theories of class conflict. The Oslo breakfast exemplified the Scandinavian approach. It provided every schoolchild in the Norwegian capital with a good breakfast free of charge. (Courtesy, Directorate for Health and Social Affairs, Oslo)

better than the 1920s had been, the opposite of the situation in the United States and France.

This good but by no means brilliant performance reflected the gradual reorientation of the British economy. After going off the gold standard in 1931 and establishing protective tariffs in 1932, Britain concentrated increasingly on the national, rather than the international, market. The old export industries of the Industrial Revolution, such as textiles and coal, continued to decline, but new industries, such as automobiles and electrical appliances, grew in response to British home demand. Moreover, low interest rates encouraged a housing boom. By the end of the decade, there were highly visible differences between the old, depressed industrial areas of the north and the new, growing areas of the south. These developments encouraged Britain to look inward and avoid unpleasant foreign entanglements.

Because France was relatively less industrialized and more isolated from the world economy, the Great Depression came late. But once the depression hit France, it stayed and stayed. Decline was steady until 1935, and a short-lived recovery never brought production or employment back up to predepression levels. Economic stagnation both reflected and heightened an ongoing political crisis. There was no stability in government. As before 1914, the French parliament was made up of many political parties that could never cooperate for long. In 1933, for example, five coalition cabinets formed and fell in rapid succession.

The French lost the underlying unity that had made government instability bearable before 1914. Fascist-type organizations agitated against parliamentary democracy and looked to Mussolini's Italy and Hitler's Germany for inspiration. In February 1934 French fascists rioted and threatened to take over the republic. At the same time, the Communist Party and many workers opposed to the existing system were looking to Stalin's Russia for guidance. The vital center of moderate republicanism was weakened by attacks from both sides.

Frightened by the growing strength of the fascists at home and abroad, the Communists, the Socialists, and the Radicals formed an alliance—the **Popular Front**—for the national elections of May 1936. Their clear victory reflected the trend toward polarization. The number of Communists in the parliament jumped dramatically

Popular Front A short-lived New Deal–inspired alliance in France led by Léon Blum that encouraged the union movement and launched a far-reaching program of social reform.

from 10 to 72, while the Socialists, led by Léon Blum, became the strongest party in France, with 146 seats. The really quite moderate Radicals slipped badly, and the conservatives lost ground to the far right.

In the next few months, Blum's Popular Front government made the first and only real attempt to deal with the social and economic problems of the 1930s in France. Inspired by Roosevelt's New Deal, the Popular Front encouraged the union movement and launched a far-reaching program of social reform, complete with paid vacations and a forty-hour workweek. Popular with workers and the lower middle class, these measures were quickly sabotaged by rapid inflation and cries of revolution from fascists and frightened conservatives. Wealthy people sneaked their money out of the country, labor

unrest grew, and France entered a severe financial crisis. Blum was forced to announce a "breathing spell" in social reform.

Political dissension in France was encouraged by the Spanish Civil War (1936–1939), during which authoritarian fascist rebels overthrew the democratically elected republican government. Communists demanded that France support the Spanish republicans, while many French conservatives would gladly have joined Hitler and Mussolini in aiding the Spanish fascists. Extremism grew, and France itself was within sight of civil war. Blum was forced to resign in June 1937, and the Popular Front quickly collapsed. An anxious and divided France drifted aimlessly once again, preoccupied by Hitler and German rearmament.

LOOKING BACK LOOKING AHEAD

THE DECADES BEFORE and especially after World War I brought intense intellectual and cultural innovation. The results were both richly productive and deeply troubling. From T. S. Eliot's poem "The Waste Land" to Einstein's theory of special relativity and the sleek glass and steel buildings of the Bauhaus, the intellectual products of the time stand among the highest achievement of Western arts and sciences. At the same time, mass culture, embodied in cinema, radio, and an emerging consumer culture, had transformative effects on everyday life. Yet the modern vision was often bleak and cold. The arrival of consumer society undermined traditional values, contributing to feelings of disorientation and pessimism. The situation was worsened by ongoing political and economic turmoil. The Treaty of Versailles had failed to create a lasting peace or resolve the question of Germany's role in postwar Europe. The Great Depression revealed the fragility of the world economic system and cast millions out of work. In the end, perhaps, the era's intellectual achievements and the overall sense of crisis and anxiety were closely related.

Writing in 1930, Sigmund Freud captured the general mood of gloom and foreboding. "Men have gained control over the forces of nature to such an extent that . . . they would have no difficulty in exterminating one another to the last man," wrote the famous psychologist. "They know this, and hence comes a large part of their current unrest, their unhappiness and their mood of anxiety."[12] Freud's dark words reflected the extraordinary human costs of World War I and the horrific power of modern weaponry. They also expressed his despair over the growing popularity of repressive dictatorial regimes. During the interwar years, many grand European nations—including Italy, Germany, Spain, Poland, Portugal, Austria, and Hungary—would fall one by one to authoritarian or fascist dictatorships, and so succumb to the temptations of totalitarianism. Liberal democracy was severely weakened. European stability was threatened by the radical programs of Soviet Communists on the left and fascists on the right, and Freud uncannily predicted the great conflict to come.

CHAPTER REVIEW

◼ **In what ways did new and sometimes radically experimental ideas in philosophy, religion, physics, psychology, and literature reflect the general crisis in Western thought? (p. 854)**

After the First World War, Western intellectual life underwent a general crisis marked by pessimism, uncertainty, and fascination with irrational forces. Philosophers, building on the prewar writings of Nietzsche, rejected the traditional philosophical questions, focusing instead on the rules of language or an existential morality. Christianity experienced a fundamentalist revival, albeit of an existentialist nature that stressed the sins of humanity and the unknowable mystery of God. Einstein's theories reordered the universe and overturned Newtonian physics, and Freudian psychology privileged the power of the irrational in human thought. Ceaseless experimentation and rejection of old forms characterized literature and reflected the unease of this period. In short, almost every field of Western thought experienced revolutionary change.

◼ **How did modernism revolutionize architecture, painting, and music? (p. 861)**

Modernism had a powerful impact on many cultural endeavors in the decades around World War I. Architects such as Walter Gropius, director of the Bauhaus, promoted stripped-down glass and steel buildings that emphasized function over form and that formed the basis of the international style after World War II. Modern schools of painting, from the Impressionists to the Dadaists and surrealists, broke with past traditions, producing images that were increasingly radical and abstract. Arnold Schönberg and other musicians wrote dissonant, atonal music that discarded familiar melodies and harmonies. Such disturbing works reflected the crises of the age of anxiety but also became classic examples of modern Western art and culture.

◼ **How did the emerging consumer society and mass culture of the interwar years change the everyday lives of ordinary men and women? (p. 866)**

Modern consumer society brought inexpensive mass-produced goods of all kinds to ordinary men and women, including household appliances, clothing, shampoos and makeup, and automobiles. The use of leisure time was likewise transformed by mass culture. Motion pictures and radio provided entertainment and relaxation for the masses, even as dictatorial governments used the new media for political propaganda. Consumer culture was enormously popular because it offered escape from the hard realities of everyday life. But new forms of consumerism also generated debate and controversy, particularly among those worried about the decline of traditional values and lifestyles, and the arrival of the Great Depression made the purchase of even basic consumer goods increasingly difficult.

◼ **How did the democratic leaders of the 1920s deal with deep-seated instability and try to establish real peace and prosperity? (p. 871)**

The Treaty of Versailles left defeated Germany and the victorious Allies bitterly divided. The question of German reparations soon led to political stalemate, French occupation of Germany's Ruhr district, runaway German inflation, and the prospect of a general European collapse. In 1923 courageous new leaders turned to compromise. Led by Stresemann in Germany and Briand in France and backed by Great Britain and the United States, the new leaders worked out a complicated financial and political settlement that led to economic recovery and fragile political stability. Germany recovered, France rebuilt its war-ravaged areas, and Britain's Labour Party expanded social services, but the stability such measures achieved was short-lived.

◼ **What caused the Great Depression, and how did the Western democracies respond to this challenge? (p. 874)**

The Great Depression grew out of the fragile international financial system and a speculative boom in the U.S. stock market in the 1920s. The stock market crash in 1929 shattered international banking and triggered a disastrous downward spiral in prices and production, bringing massive unemployment to millions of workers. Turning inward to cope with the economic crisis and the related social problems, the Western democracies responded with relief measures, extended unemployment benefits, labor reforms, and social concern. These measures eased distress and prevented revolutions in the leading nations, but with the significant exception of the Scandinavian countries, the Western democracies failed to restore prosperity, eliminate high unemployment, or prevent widespread disillusionment. The old liberal ideals of individual rights and responsibilities, elected government, and economic freedom declined and appeared outmoded to many citizens.

Suggested Reading

Berend, Ivan T. *Decades of Crisis: Central and Eastern Europe Before World War II*. 2001. An up-to-date study of this complex region.

Berghahn, Volker R. *Europe in the Era of Two World Wars: From Militarism and Genocide to Civil Society*. 2006. A short and stimulating account.

Bullock, Alan, ed. *The Twentieth Century: A Promethean Age*. 1971. Particularly noteworthy because it is a lavish visual feast combined with penetrating essays on major developments.

Burrow, J. W. *The Crisis of Reason: European Thought, 1848–1914*. 2002. A rewarding intellectual history.

Cawood, Ian. *Britain in the Twentieth Century*. 2003. A useful national survey.

Eksteins, Modris. *Rites of Spring: The Great War and the Birth of the Modern Age*. 1989. A penetrating analysis of the links between World War I and modern culture and politics.

Exra, Elizabeth. *European Cinema*. 2004. A concise history of European film and movie industries from their origins to the present.

Kertzer, David I., and Marzio Barbagli, eds. *The History of the European Family*, vol. 3: *Family Life in the Twentieth Century*. 2003. A distinguished collection of essays by experts.

Kracauer, Siegfried. *From Caligari to Hitler: A Psychological History of the German Film*. 1947. An early and critical look at the Weimar-era German film industry by a contemporary critic that remains a cultural studies classic.

McMillan, James F. *Twentieth-Century France: Politics and Society, 1898–1991*. 1992. A recommended national survey.

Paxton, Robert O. *Europe in the Twentieth Century*. 2004. An excellent account of contemporary history with a liberal viewpoint.

Roberts, Mary Louise. *Civilization Without Sexes: Reconstructing Gender in Postwar France, 1917–1927*. 1994. A fascinating interpretation of gender roles in France after the First World War.

Schwartz, Vanessa R. *Spectacular Realities: Early Mass Culture in Fin-de-Siècle Paris*. 1999. Explores the foundation of modern mass culture in late-nineteenth-century Paris.

Slater, Don. *Consumer Culture and Modernity*. 1997. An informative review of scholarly interpretations of consumer society.

Weitz, Eric. *Weimar Germany: Promise and Tragedy*. 2007. A thorough exploration of modern art, culture, and politics in interwar Germany.

Winders, James A. *European Culture Since 1848: From Modernism to Postmodern and Beyond*. 1998. A lively and accessible account.

Notes

1. P. Valéry, *Variety*, trans. M. Cowley (New York: Harcourt Brace, 1927), pp. 27–28.
2. G. Greene, *Another Mexico* (New York: Viking Press, 1939), p. 3.
3. T. S. Eliot, "The Waste Land," in *The Norton Anthology of Poetry Revised*, ed. A. W. Allison et al. (New York: Norton, 1975), p. 1034.
4. C. E. Jeanneret-Gris (Le Corbusier), *Towards a New Architecture* (London: J. Rodker, 1931), p. 15.
5. Quoted in A. H. Barr, Jr., *What Is Modern Painting?* 9th ed. (New York: Museum of Modern Art, 1966), p. 25.
6. R. Huelsenbeck, "Collective Dada Manifesto (1920)," in *The Dada Painters and Poets*, ed. Robert Motherwell and Jack D. Flam (Boston: G. K. Hall, 1981), pp. 242–246.
7. Elsa Herrmann, *This Is the New Woman* (1929), quoted in *The Weimar Republic Sourcebook*, ed. A. Kaes, M. Jay, and E. Dimendberg (Berkeley: University of California Press, 1994), pp. 206–208.
8. Quoted in R. Smither, ed., *The Battles of the Somme and Ancre* (London: Imperial War Museum, 1993), p. 67.
9. Quoted in A. Briggs, *The Birth of Broadcasting*, vol. 1 (London: Oxford University Press, 1961), p. 47.
10. J. M. Keynes, *The Economic Consequences of the Peace* (1919), quoted in M. A. Kishlansky, *Sources of the West: Readings in Western Civilization* (New York: Pearson Longman, 2008), p. 252.
11. Quoted in S. B. Clough et al., eds., *Economic History of Europe: Twentieth Century* (New York: Harper & Row, 1968), pp. 243–245.
12. S. Freud, *Civilization and Its Discontents* (New York: W. W. Norton, 1961), p. 112.

Key Terms

logical positivism (p. 855)
existentialism (p. 856)
theory of special relativity (p. 857)
id, ego, and superego (p. 859)
stream-of-consciousness technique (p. 860)
modernism (p. 861)
functionalism (p. 861)
Bauhaus (p. 861)
Dadaism (p. 864)
"new woman" (p. 867)
Dawes Plan (p. 873)
Great Depression (p. 874)
Popular Front (p. 882)

For practice quizzes and other study tools, visit the Online Study Guide at **bedfordstmartins.com/mckaywest**.

For primary sources from this period, see *Sources of Western Society*, **Second Edition**.

For Web sites, images, and documents related to topics in this chapter, visit Make History at **bedfordstmartins.com/mckaywest**.

28

Dictatorships and the Second World War

1919–1945

The intense wave of artistic and cultural innovation in the 1920s and 1930s, which shook the foundations of Western thought, was paralleled by radical developments in the realm of politics. In the age of anxiety, communist and fascist states undertook determined assaults on democratic government and individual rights across Europe. On the eve of the Second World War, popularly elected governments survived only in Great Britain, France, Czechoslovakia, the Low Countries, Scandinavia, and Switzerland.

Across the 1920s and 1930s, totalitarian regimes in the communist Soviet Union and fascist Italy and Germany practiced a ruthless and dynamic tyranny. Their attempts to revolutionize state and society went far beyond familiar forms of conservative authoritarianism. Communist and fascist states ruled with unprecedented severity. They promised to greatly improve the lives of ordinary citizens and intervened radically in those lives in pursuit of utopian schemes of social engineering. Their drive for territorial expansion threatened neighboring nations and put the democracies on the defensive. The human costs were appalling. Millions died as Stalin forced communism on the Soviet Union in the 1930s. Attempts to build a "racially pure" New Order in Europe by Hitler's Nazi Germany led to the deaths of millions more in World War II and the Holocaust.

Such brutalities may seem a thing of the distant past that "can't happen again." Yet horrible atrocities in Cambodia, Bosnia, and Rwanda show that they continue to plague the world in our time. It remains vital that we understand Europe's era of overwhelming violence in order to guard against the possibility of its recurrence in the future. ■

Life at Auschwitz. This rough painting by an anonymous inmate of the Auschwitz-Birkenau Nazi concentration camp is preserved on the ceiling of a camp barracks. Guarded by SS officers, prisoners labor on a drainage canal under the worst conditions, while two carry a dead worker off the field.

CHAPTER PREVIEW

Authoritarian States
■ How did radical totalitarian dictatorship differ from conservative authoritarianism, and in what ways were communism and fascism totalitarian systems?

Stalin's Soviet Union
■ How did Stalin and the Communist Party build a modern totalitarian state in the Soviet Union?

Mussolini and Fascism in Italy
■ How did Mussolini's dictatorship come to power and govern in Italy?

Hitler and Nazism in Germany
■ How did Hitler gain power, what policies did totalitarian Nazi Germany pursue, and why did they lead to World War II?

The Second World War
■ How did Germany and Japan create enormous empires, and how were they defeated by the Allies?

Authoritarian States

How did radical totalitarian dictatorship differ from conservative authoritarianism, and in what ways were communism and fascism totalitarian systems? ■

Both conservative and radical dictatorships swept through Europe in the 1920s and 1930s. Although these two types of dictatorship shared some characteristics and sometimes overlapped in practice, in essence they were quite different. Conservative authoritarian regimes were long established in Europe. Radical totalitarian dictatorships, based on the ideologies of Stalinist communism and fascism, were a new and frightening development aimed at the radical reconstruction of existing society.

Conservative Authoritarianism and Radical Totalitarian Dictatorships

The traditional form of antidemocratic government in European history was conservative authoritarianism. Like Catherine the Great in Russia and Metternich in Austria, the leaders of such governments relied on obedient bureaucracies in their efforts to control society. Liberals, democrats, and socialists were often jailed or exiled, but old-fashioned authoritarian governments were limited in their power and objectives. They had neither the ability nor the desire to control many aspects of their subjects' lives. These governments largely limited their demands to taxes, army recruits, and passive acceptance. As long as the people did not try to change the system, they often had considerable personal independence.

After the First World War, authoritarianism revived, especially in the less-developed eastern part of Europe. But new kinds of radical dictatorship that went much further than conservative authoritarianism emerged in the Soviet Union, Germany, and to some extent Italy and other countries. Communist dictatorship had ruled the Soviet Union since the Russian Revolution (see Chapter 26). Fascist dictators took over in Italy in 1922 and in Germany in 1933. By the start of World War II, fascist governments controlled Spain, Portugal, Austria, Hungary, and Romania. And both Communist and fascist political parties were well established in all major European nations, where they ran for parliamentary office even as they challenged the very basis of liberal democracy.

Some scholars use the term **totalitarianism** to describe these radical dictatorships, which made unprec-

totalitarianism A radical dictatorship that exercises "total claims" over the beliefs and behavior of its citizens by taking control of the economic, social, intellectual, and cultural aspects of society.

edented "total claims" on the beliefs and behavior of their citizens. The totalitarian model emphasizes the characteristics that fascist and communist dictatorships had in common, and the term gained prominence after World War II. Scholars showed that the one-party totalitarian state used violent political repression and intense propaganda to gain complete power. But it did not stop there. Increasingly, the state tried to dominate the economic, social, intellectual, and cultural aspects of people's lives. Deviation from the norm, even in art or family behavior, could become a crime.

Most historians agree that totalitarianism owed much to the experience of total war in 1914–1918 (see Chapter 26). World War I required state governments to limit individual liberties and intervene in the economy in order to achieve one supreme objective: victory. The brutality of the war eroded the ideal of individual rights; after so many casualties, the value of one life seemed far less important than the good of the entire nation. Totalitarian politicians were inspired by the example of the modern state at war. They showed a callous disregard for human life and greatly expanded the power of the state in pursuit of social control.

Communist and fascist dictatorships shared other characteristics. Both violently rejected parliamentary government and liberal values. Classical liberalism (see Chapter 22) sought to limit the power of the state and protect the rights of the individual. Totalitarians, on the other hand, believed that liberal individualism undermined equality and unity. They rejected democracy in favor of one-party political systems ruled from the top.

A charismatic leader typically dominated the totalitarian state—Stalin in the Soviet Union, Mussolini in Italy, Hitler in Germany. All three created political parties of a new kind, dedicated to promoting idealized visions of collective harmony. They used force and terror to intimidate and destroy political opponents and pursued policies of imperial expansion to exploit other lands. They censored the mass media and instituted propaganda campaigns meant to advance their goals. Finally, and perhaps most important, totalitarian governments engaged in massive projects of state-controlled social engineering dedicated to replacing individualism with a unified "people" capable of exercising the collective will.

Communism and Fascism

Communism and fascism clearly shared a desire to revolutionize state and society. Yet some scholars argue that the differences between the two systems are more important than the similarities, and so move beyond the totalitarian model. What were the main differences between these two systems? To answer this question, it is important to consider the way ideology, or a guiding political philosophy, was linked to the use of state-sponsored repression and violence.

Following Marx, Soviet Communists strove to create an international brotherhood of workers. In this idealized communist utopia, class differences would supposedly disappear, resulting in a society free of capitalist inequality (see Chapter 22). In pursuit of this social leveling, the Soviet government under Stalin aggressively intervened in all walks of life. Under Stalinism—the name given to the Communist system under Stalin—the state used force to destroy the upper and middle classes. The Stalinist state nationalized private property, pushed rapid industrialization, and collectivized agriculture (see pages 891–896). As the Stalinization of Soviet society proceeded in the late 1920s and the 1930s, millions lost their livelihoods and their lives.

The fascist vision of a new society was quite different. Leaders who embraced **fascism**, such as Mussolini and Hitler, claimed that they were striving to build a new community on a national—not an international—level. Extreme nationalists and often racists, fascists glorified war and the military and sought to destroy independent working-class movements. For them, the nation was the highest embodiment of the people, and the powerful leader was supposedly the materialization of the people's collective will.

Like communists, fascists promised to improve the lives of ordinary workers. Fascist governments intervened in the economy, but unlike communist regimes they did not try to level class differences and nationalize private property. Instead, they countered the vision of communist equality with the ideal of a community rooted in the bonds of nationalism. In the ideal fascist state, society would no longer be a battlefield of class versus class or individual self-interest. Instead, all strata and classes would work together to build a harmonious national community.

Communists and fascists differed in another crucial respect: the question of race. Where communists sought to build a new world around the destruction of class differences, fascists typically sought to build a new national community grounded in racial homogeneity. Fascists embraced the doctrine of **eugenics**, a pseudoscience that maintained that the selective breeding of human beings could improve the general characteristics of a national population. Eugenics was popular throughout the United States and Europe in the 1920s and 1930s, and many scientists, doctors, and government bureaucrats viewed it as a legitimate means of social

1921	New Economic Policy (NEP) in U.S.S.R.
1922	Mussolini seizes power in Italy
1924–1929	Buildup of Nazi Party in Germany
1927	Stalin comes to power in U.S.S.R.
1928	Stalin's first five-year plan
1929	Lateran Agreement; start of collectivization in Soviet Union
1929–1939	Great Depression
1931	Japan invades Manchuria
1932–1933	Famine in Ukraine
1933	Hitler appointed chancellor in Germany; Nazis begin control of state and society
1935	Mussolini invades Ethiopia
1936	Start of great purges under Stalin; Spanish civil war begins
1937	Japanese army attacks China
1939	Germany occupies Czech lands and invades western Poland; Britain and France declare war on Germany, starting World War II; Soviet Union occupies eastern Poland
1940	Germany defeats and occupies France
1940	Battle of Britain
1941	Germany invades U.S.S.R.; Japan attacks Pearl Harbor; United States enters war
1941–1945	The Holocaust
1942–1943	Battle of Stalingrad
1944	Allied invasion at Normandy
1945	Soviet and U.S. forces enter Germany; United States drops atomic bombs on Japan; World War II ends

planning and improvement. But fascists, especially the German National Socialists or Nazis, pushed these ideas to their limit.

Adopting ideologies of eugenics, the Nazis believed that the German nation had to be "purified" of outsider groups. Jews, Gypsies, homosexuals, the mentally and physically disabled, and others were deemed unable to contribute to the nation's "racial stock" and needed to be segregated or eliminated. Such ideas ultimately led to the Holocaust, the attempt to purge Germany and Europe of all Jews and other groups who were deemed

fascism A movement characterized by extreme, often expansionist nationalism, antisocialism, a dynamic and violent leader, and glorification of war and the military.

eugenics A pseudoscientific doctrine that maintains that the selective breeding of human beings can improve the general characteristics of a national population, which helped inspire Nazi ideas about "race and space" and ultimately contributed to the Holocaust.

889

Picturing the Past

The Appeal of Propaganda Totalitarian leaders used extensive propaganda campaigns to enlist the support of the masses. Italian dictator Benito Mussolini repeatedly linked his regime to the glory of ancient Rome. Here he has donned the costume of a legionnaire to lead a parade in front of the Roman Coliseum (top). The Soviet dictator Stalin presented himself as the friend of all humankind. In this propaganda poster (bottom), titled "The Great Stalin, the Banner of Friendship of the Peoples of the U.S.S.R.," he receives flowers from a diverse group of Soviet citizens, including ethnic Russians and East and Central Asians. This idealized testament to peaceful coexistence within the Soviet empire masked the tensions aroused by Russian domination. (Mussolini: Stefano Bianchetti/Corbis; Stalin: Bedford/St. Martin's)

ANALYZING THE IMAGE How do these images present the role of the dictatorial leader? How do they represent the relationship between the leader and the led?

CONNECTIONS How might these idealized portrayals have helped build support for their respective regimes? Was there any truth behind the propaganda?

To complete this activity online, go to the Online Study Guide at bedfordstmartins.com/mckaywest.

"undesirable" by mass killing during World War II (see page 912). Though the Soviets sometimes persecuted specific ethnic groups, they never attempted to destroy a group entirely. Communists, in fact, denounced eugenics and never sought to build a society based on race or biological engineering.

Perhaps because both championed the revolutionary overthrow of existing society, communists and fascists were sworn and deadly enemies. The result was a great clash of ideologies, which was in large part responsible for the horrific destruction and loss of life in the middle of the twentieth century. Explaining the nature of totalitarian dictatorships thus remains a crucial project for historians, even as they look more closely at the ideological differences between communism and fascism.

One important set of questions explores the way dictatorial regimes generate popular consensus. Neither Hitler nor Stalin ever achieved the total control each sought. Nor did they rule alone; modern dictators need the help of large state bureaucracies and large numbers of ordinary people. Which was more important for generating popular support: terror and coercion, or practical material rewards? Why did so many people seem to approve of dictatorial rule, even as it cost the lives of millions? When, why, and how did people resist the demands of tyranny? Seeking answers to such questions leads us toward what Holocaust survivor Primo Levi called the "gray zone" of moral compromise, which defined everyday life in totalitarian societies. (See "Individuals in Society: Primo Levi," page 915.)

Eugenics in Nazi Germany Nazi "race scientists" believed they could use the eugenic methods of social engineering to build a powerful Aryan race. In this photograph, published in a popular magazine in 1933, a clinician measures a man's nose. Such pseudoscientific methods were used to determine an individual's supposed "racial value." (Hulton-Deutsch Collection/Corbis)

Stalin's Soviet Union

How did Stalin and the Communist Party build a modern totalitarian state in the Soviet Union?

Lenin's harshest critics claim that he established the basic outlines of a modern totalitarian dictatorship after the Bolshevik Revolution and during the Russian civil war. If this is so, then Joseph Stalin (1879–1953) certainly finished the job. A master of political infighting, Stalin cautiously consolidated his power and eliminated his enemies in the mid-1920s. Then in 1928, as undisputed leader of the ruling Communist Party, Stalin launched the first **five-year plan** — the "revolution from above," as he so aptly termed it.

The 1928 five-year plan and those that followed were extremely ambitious. They marked the beginning of a radical attempt to transform Soviet society into a communist state. The ultimate goal was to generate new attitudes, new loyalties, and a new socialist humanity. The means chosen by Stalin and the small Communist Party elite in order to do so were constant propaganda, enormous sacrifice by the people, harsh repression that included purges and executions, and rewards for those

who followed the party line. Thus the Soviet Union in the 1930s became a dynamic modern totalitarian state.

From Lenin to Stalin

By spring 1921 Lenin and the Bolsheviks had won the civil war, but they ruled a shattered and devastated land. Many farms were in ruins, and food supplies were exhausted. In southern Russia drought combined with the ravages of war to produce the worst famine in generations. Industrial production had broken down completely. In the face of economic disintegration, riots by peasants and workers, and an open rebellion by previously pro-Bolshevik sailors at Kronstadt, the tough but ever-flexible Lenin changed course. He repressed the Kronstadt rebels, and in March 1921 he replaced war communism (see Chapter 26) with the **New Economic Policy (NEP)**, which re-established limited economic freedom in an attempt to rebuild agriculture

five-year plan A plan launched by Stalin in 1928, and termed the "revolution from above," aimed at modernizing the Soviet Union and creating a new communist society with new attitudes, new loyalties, and a new socialist humanity.

New Economic Policy (NEP) Lenin's 1921 policy to re-establish limited economic freedom in an attempt to rebuild agriculture and industry in the face of economic disintegration.

and industry. During the civil war, the Bolsheviks had simply seized grain without payment. Now peasant producers were permitted to sell their surpluses in free markets, and private traders and small handicraft manufacturers were allowed to reappear. Heavy industry, railroads, and banks, however, remained wholly nationalized.

The NEP was a political and economic success. Politically, it was a necessary but temporary compromise with the Soviet Union's overwhelming peasant majority. Realizing that his government was not strong enough to take land from the peasants and turn them into state workers, Lenin made a deal with the only force capable of overturning his government. The NEP brought rapid economic recovery, and by 1926 industrial output surpassed, and agricultural production was almost equal to, prewar levels.

As the economy recovered and the government partially relaxed its censorship and repression, an intense struggle for power began in the inner circles of the Communist Party, for Lenin had left no chosen successor when he died in 1924. The principal contenders were Stalin and Trotsky. The son of a shoemaker, Joseph Dzhugashvili (joo-guhsh-VEEL-yih) — later known as Stalin — had studied for the priesthood but was expelled from his seminary. By 1903 he was a Bolshevik revolutionary in southern Russia.

Stalin was a good organizer but a poor speaker and writer, and he had no experience outside of Russia. Trotsky, a great and inspiring leader who had planned the 1917 takeover and then created the victorious Red Army, appeared to have all the advantages in the struggle to take power. Yet Stalin won because he was more effective at gaining the all-important support of the party, the only genuine source of power in the one-party state. Rising to general secretary of the party's Central Committee in 1922, he used his office to win friends and allies with jobs and promises.

Stalin also won because he was better able to relate Marxian teaching to Soviet realities in the 1920s. Stalin developed a theory of "socialism in one country" that was more appealing to the majority of communists than was Trotsky's doctrine of "permanent revolution." Stalin argued that the Russian-dominated Soviet Union had the ability to build socialism on its own. Trotsky maintained that socialism in the Soviet Union could succeed only if a socialist revolution swept throughout Europe. To many Russian communists, Trotsky's views sold their country short and promised risky conflicts with capitalist countries. Stalin's willingness to break with the NEP and "build socialism" at home appealed to young militants in the party, who detested the capitalist-appearing NEP.

> ## " We are fifty or a hundred years behind the advanced countries. We must make good this distance in ten years. Either we do it, or we shall go under. "
>
> **—Joseph Stalin**

With cunning skill, Stalin gradually achieved supreme power between 1922 and 1927. First he allied with Trotsky's personal enemies to crush Trotsky, and then he moved against all who might challenge his ascendancy, including his former allies. Stalin's final triumph came at the party congress of December 1927, which condemned all "deviation from the general party line" formulated by Stalin. The dictator and his followers were then ready to launch the revolution from above, radically changing the lives of millions of ordinary Russians.

The Five-Year Plans

The party congress of 1927, which ratified Stalin's consolidation of power, marked the end of the NEP and the beginning of the era of socialist five-year plans. The first five-year plan had staggering economic objectives. In just five years, total industrial output was to increase by 250 percent. Heavy industry, the preferred sector, was to grow even faster. Agricultural production was slated to increase by 150 percent, and one-fifth of the peasants in the Soviet Union were scheduled to give up their private plots and join socialist collective farms. By 1930 economic and social change was sweeping the country.

Stalin unleashed his "second revolution" for a variety of interrelated reasons. There were, first of all, ideological considerations. Like Lenin, Stalin and his militant supporters were deeply committed to socialism as they understood it. They feared a gradual restoration of capitalism, wished to promote the working classes, and were eager to abolish the NEP's private traders, independent artisans, and property-owning peasants.

Economic motivations were also important. A fragile economic recovery stalled in 1927 and 1928, and a new socialist offensive seemed necessary to ensure industrial and agricultural growth. Economic development would allow the U.S.S.R. to catch up with the West and so overcome traditional Russian "backwardness." As Stalin said in 1931, pressing for ever-greater speed and sacrifice, "We are fifty or a hundred years behind the advanced countries. We must make good this distance in ten years. Either we do it, or we shall go under." (See "Listening to the Past: Stalin Justifies the Five-Year Plan," page 894.)

The independent peasantry remained a major problem. For centuries the peasants had wanted to own the land, and finally they had it. Sooner or later, the communists reasoned, the peasants would embrace conservative capitalism and pose a threat to the regime. At the same time, the mainly urban communists believed that the feared and despised "class enemy" in the villages could be squeezed to provide the enormous sums needed for all-out industrialization.

To resolve these issues, in 1929 Stalin ordered the **collectivization of agriculture**—the forced consolidation of individual peasant farms into large, state-controlled enterprises. Peasants all over the Soviet Union were compelled to move off their small plots onto large state-run farms, where their tools, livestock, and produce would be held in common and central planners could control their work.

The increasingly repressive measures instituted by the state focused on the **kulaks**, the class of well-off peasants who had benefited the most from the market policies of the NEP. The kulaks were actually a very small group, but they were held up as a great enemy of progress, and Stalin called for their "liquidation" and seizure of their land. Stripped of land and livestock, many starved or were deported to forced-labor camps for "re-education."

The forced collectivization of agriculture led to disaster. Peasant resistance caused chaos in the countryside, and large numbers of farmers slaughtered their animals and burned their crops rather than turn them over to state commissars. Between 1929 and 1933, the number of horses, cattle, sheep, and goats in the Soviet Union fell by at least half. Nor were the state-controlled collective farms more productive. The output of grain barely increased, and collectivized agriculture was unable to make any substantial financial contribution to Soviet industrial development in the first five-year plan.

In Ukraine the drive against peasants snowballed into an assault on Ukrainians in general, who had sought independence from Soviet rule after the First World War. In 1932, as collectivization and deportations continued, Stalin and his associates set levels of grain deliveries for the Ukrainian collective at excessively high levels, and they refused to relax those quotas or even allow

food relief when Ukrainian communist leaders reported that starvation was occurring. The result was a terrible man-made famine in Ukraine in 1932 and 1933, which probably claimed 6 million lives.

Collectivization was a cruel but real victory for Stalinist ideologues. Its human cost was staggering. Millions of people died as a direct result—more than the total number of deaths in World War I. Yet by the end of 1938, fully 93 percent of peasant families had been herded onto collective farms, effectively neutralizing them as a political threat. Yet the opposition of the peasantry had forced the supposedly all-powerful state to make modest concessions. Peasants secured the right to limit a family's labor on the state-run farms and to cultivate tiny family plots, which provided them with much of their food. In 1938 these family plots produced 22 percent of all Soviet agricultural produce on only 4 percent of all cultivated land.

The industrial side of the five-year plans was more successful—indeed, quite spectacular. A huge State Planning Commission, the "Gosplan," oversaw the program by setting production goals and controlling deliveries of raw and finished materials. This was a complex and difficult task, and production bottlenecks and slowdowns often resulted. In addition, Stalinist planning

collectivization of agriculture The forcible consolidation of individual peasant farms into large state-controlled enterprises in the Soviet Union under Stalin.

kulaks The better-off peasants who were stripped of land and livestock under Stalin and were generally not permitted to join collective farms; many of them starved or were deported to forced-labor camps for "re-education."

Day Shift at Magnitogorsk Beginning in 1928, Stalin's government issued a series of ambitious five-year plans designed to rapidly industrialize the Soviet Union. The plans focused primarily on boosting heavy industry and included the building of a gigantic steel complex at Magnitogorsk in the Ural Mountains. Here steelworkers review production goals at the Magnitogorsk foundry. (Sovfoto)

Stalin Justifies the Five-Year Plan

LISTENING TO THE PAST

On February 4, 1931, Joseph Stalin delivered the following address, entitled "No Slowdown in Tempo!" to the First Conference of Soviet Industrial Managers. Published the following day in Pravda, *the newspaper of the Communist Party, and widely publicized at home and abroad, Stalin's speech reaffirmed the leader's commitment to the breakneck pace of industrialization and collectivization set forth in the first five-year plan.*

Arguing that more sacrifices were necessary, Stalin sought to rally the people and generate support for the party's program. His address captures the spirit of Soviet public discourse in the early 1930s.

Stalin's concluding idea, that Bolsheviks needed to master technology and industrial management, reflected another major development. The Soviet Union was training a new class of communist engineers and technicians, who were beginning to replace foreign engineers and "bourgeois specialists," Russian engineers trained in tsarist times who were grudgingly tolerated after the revolution.

❝ It is sometimes asked whether it is not possible to slow down the tempo somewhat, to put a check on the movement. No, comrades, it is not possible! The tempo must not be reduced! On the contrary, we must increase it as much as is within our powers and possibilities. This is dictated to us by our obligations to the workers and peasants of the U.S.S.R. This is dictated to us by our obligations to the working class of the whole world.

To slacken the tempo would mean falling behind. And those who fall behind get beaten. But we do not want to be beaten. No, we refuse to be beaten! One feature of the history of old Russia was the continual beatings she suffered because of her backwardness. She was beaten by the Mongol khans, . . . the Turkish beys, . . . and the Japanese barons. All beat her—because of her backwardness, cultural backwardness, political backwardness, industrial backwardness, agricultural backwardness. They beat her because to do so was profitable and could be done with impunity. . . . Such is the law of the exploiters—to beat the backward and the weak. It is the jungle law of capitalism. You are backward, you are weak—therefore you are wrong; hence you can be beaten and enslaved. You are mighty—therefore you are right; hence we must be wary of you. That is why we must no longer lag behind.

In the past we had no fatherland, nor could we have had one. But now that we have overthrown capitalism and power is in our hands, in the hands of the people, we have a fatherland, and we will uphold its independence. Do you want our socialist fatherland to be beaten and to lose its independence?

"Our program is realistic," Stalin proclaims on this poster, "because it is you and me working together." (David King Collection)

generally favored heavy industry over the production of consumer goods, often leading to shortages of basic necessities. Despite such problems, Soviet industry produced about four times as much in 1937 as it had in 1928. No other major country had ever achieved such rapid industrial growth. Forced industrial growth went hand in hand with urban development: more than 25 million people migrated to cities during the 1930s, mostly peasants who left their villages to become laborers in Russia's growing industrial centers.

Steel was the idol of the Stalinist age. The Soviet state needed heavy machinery for rapid development, and an industrial labor force was created almost overnight as peasant men and women began working in the huge steel mills and plants built across the country. Between 1930 and 1932, independent trade unions lost most of their power. The government could assign workers to any job anywhere in the country, and an internal passport system ensured that individuals could not move without the permission of the police. When factory manag-

If you do not want this, you must put an end to its backwardness in the shortest possible time and develop a genuine Bolshevik tempo in building up its socialist economy. There is no other way. That is why Lenin said on the eve of the October Revolution: "Either perish, or overtake and outstrip the advanced capitalist countries."

We are fifty or a hundred years behind the advanced countries. We must make good this distance in ten years. Either we do it, or we shall go under. That is what our obligations to the workers and peasants of the U.S.S.R. dictate to us.

But we have yet other, more serious and more important, obligations. They are our obligations to the world proletariat. . . . We achieved victory not solely through the efforts of the working class of the U.S.S.R., but also thanks to the support of the working class of the world. Without this support we would have been torn to pieces long ago. . . .

Why does the international proletariat support us? How did we merit this support? By the fact that we were the first to hurl ourselves into the battle against capitalism, we were the first to establish working-class state power, we were the first to begin building socialism. By the fact that we are engaged on a cause which, if successful, will transform the whole world and free the entire working class. But what is needed for success? The elimination of our backwardness, the development of a high Bolshevik tempo of construction. We must march forward in such a way that the working class of the whole world, looking at us, may say:

There you have my advanced detachment, my shock brigade, my working-class state power, my fatherland; they are engaged on their cause, *our* cause, and they are working well; let us support them against the capitalists and promote the cause of the world revolution. Must we not justify the hopes of the world's working class, must we not fulfill our obligations to them? Yes, we must if we do not want to utterly disgrace ourselves.

Such are our obligations, internal and international.

As you see, they dictate to us a Bolshevik tempo of development.

I will not say that we have accomplished nothing in regard to management of production during these years. In fact, we have accomplished a good deal. . . . But we could have accomplished still more if we had tried during this period really to master production, the technique of production, the financial and economic side of it. In ten years at most we must make good the distance that separates us from the advanced capitalist countries. We have all the "objective" possibilities for this. The only thing lacking is the ability to make proper use of these possibilities.

And that depends on us. *Only* on us! . . . If you are a factory manager — interfere in all the affairs of the factory, look into everything, let nothing escape you, learn and learn again. Bolsheviks must master technique. It is time Bolsheviks themselves became experts. . . .

It is said that it is hard to master technique. That is not true! There are no fortresses that Bolsheviks cannot capture. We have solved a number of most difficult problems. We have overthrown capitalism. We have assumed power.

We have built up a huge socialist industry. We have transferred the middle peasants on the path of socialism. We have already accomplished what is most important from the point of view of construction. What remains to be done is not so much: to study technique, to master science. And when we have done that we shall develop a tempo of which we dare not even dream at present. And we shall do it if we really want to. »

Source: Joseph Stalin, "No Slowdown in Tempo!" *Pravda*, February 5, 1931, excerpted from "Reading No. 14" in *Soviet Economic Development: Operation Outstrip, 1921–1965*, by Anatole G. Mazour.

QUESTIONS FOR ANALYSIS

1. What reasons does Stalin give to justify an unrelenting "Bolshevik" tempo of industrial and social change? In the light of history, which reason seems most convincing? Why?

2. Imagine that the year is 1931 and you are a Soviet student reading Stalin's speech. Would Stalin's determination inspire you, frighten you, or leave you cold? Why?

3. Some historians argue that Soviet socialism was a kind of utopianism, where the economy, the society, and even human beings could be completely remade and perfected. What utopian elements do you see in Stalin's declaration?

ers needed more hands, they called on their counterparts on the collective farms, who sent them millions of "unneeded" peasants over the years.

Workers typically lived in deplorable conditions in hastily built industrial cities such as Magnitogorsk (Magnetic Mountain City) in the Ural mountains. Yet they also experienced some benefits of upward mobility. In a letter published in the Magnitogorsk newspaper, an ordinary electrician described the opportunities created by rapid industrialization:

In old tsarist Russia, we weren't even considered people. We couldn't dream about education, or getting a job in a state enterprise. And now I'm a citizen of the USSR. Like all citizens I have the right to a job, to education, to leisure. . . . In 1931, I came to Magnitogorsk. From a common laborer I have turned into a skilled worker. . . . I live in a country where one feels like living and learning. And if the enemy should attack this country, I will sacrifice my life in order to destroy the enemy and save my country.[1]

We should read such words with care, since they appeared in a state-censored publication. Yet the enthusiasm was at least partly authentic. The great industrialization drive, concentrated between 1928 and 1937, was an awe-inspiring achievement purchased at enormous sacrifice on the part of ordinary Soviet citizens.

Life and Culture in Soviet Society

The aim of Stalin's five-year plans was to create a new kind of society with a strong industrial economy and a powerful army. Stalin and his helpers were good Marxian economic determinists. Once everything was owned by the state, they believed, a socialist society composed of committed socialists would inevitably emerge. Their utopian vision of a new humanity floundered, but they did build a new society whose broad outlines existed into the mid-1980s. Life in this society had both good and bad aspects.

Because consumption was reduced to pay for investment, there was little improvement in the average standard of living in the years before World War II. Studies show that the average nonfarm wage purchased only about half as many goods in 1932 as it had in 1928. After 1932 real wages rose slowly, but by 1937 workers could still buy only about 60 percent of what they had bought in 1928 and less than in 1913. Collectivized peasants experienced greater hardships.

Daily life was difficult in Stalin's Soviet Union. Many people lived primarily on black bread and wore old, shabby clothing. There were constant shortages, although very heavily taxed vodka was always readily available. Housing was a particularly serious problem. Millions were moving into the cities, but the government built few new apartments. A relatively lucky family received one room for all its members and shared both a kitchen and a toilet with others on the floor.

Life was hard but by no means hopeless. Idealism and ideology had real appeal for many communists and ordinary citizens, who saw themselves heroically building the world's first socialist society while capitalism crumbled in a worldwide depression and degenerated into fascism in the West. This optimistic belief in the future of the Soviet Union also attracted many disillusioned Westerners to communism in the 1930s.

On a more practical level, Soviet workers did receive important social benefits, such as old-age pensions, free medical services, free education, and day-care centers for children. Unemployment was almost unknown. Finally, there was the possibility of personal advancement.

The keys to improving one's position were specialized skills and technical education. Rapid industrialization required massive numbers of trained experts, such as skilled workers, engineers, and plant managers. Thus the Stalinist state broke with the egalitarian policies of the 1920s and provided tremendous incentives to those who could serve its needs. It paid the mass of unskilled workers and collective farmers very low wages, but it dangled high salaries and special privileges before its growing technical and managerial elite. This elite joined with the political and artistic elites in a new upper class, whose members were rich and powerful.

The radical transformation of Soviet society had a profound impact on women's lives. Marxists had traditionally believed that both capitalism and middle-class husbands exploited women. The Russian Revolution of 1917 immediately proclaimed complete equality of rights for women. In the 1920s divorce and abortion were made easily available, and women were urged to work outside the home. After Stalin came to power, he reversed this trend. The government now revoked many laws supporting women's emancipation in order to strengthen the traditional family and build up the state's population.

The most lasting changes for women involved work and education. Peasant women continued to work on farms, and millions of women toiled in factories and in heavy construction, building dams, roads, and steel mills in summer heat and winter frost. The Soviets also opened higher education to women, who could now enter the ranks of the better-paid specialists in industry and science. Medicine practically became a woman's profession. By 1950, 75 percent of all doctors in the Soviet Union were women.

Alongside such advances, Soviet society demanded great sacrifices from women. The vast majority of women had to work outside the home. Wages were so low that it was almost impossible for a family or couple to live only on the husband's earnings. Men continued to dominate the very best jobs. Finally, rapid change and economic hardship led to many broken families, creating further physical and emotional strains for women. In any event, the massive mobilization of women was a striking characteristic of the Soviet state.

Culture was thoroughly politicized for propaganda and indoctrination purposes. Party activists lectured workers in factories and peasants on collective farms while newspapers, films, and radio broadcasts endlessly recounted socialist achievements and capitalist plots. Whereas the 1920s had seen considerable experimentation in modern art and theater, in the 1930s intellectuals were ordered by Stalin to become "engineers of human minds." They were instructed to exalt the lives of ordinary workers and glorify Russian nationalism. Russian history was rewritten so that early tsars such as Ivan the Terrible and Peter the Great became worthy forerunners of the greatest Russian leader of all—Stalin. Writers and artists who could effectively combine genuine creativity and political propaganda became the darlings of the regime.

Stalin seldom appeared in public, but his presence was everywhere—in portraits, statues, books, and quotations from his "sacred" writings. Although the government persecuted religion and turned churches into "museums of atheism," the state had both an earthly religion and a high priest—Marxism-Leninism and Joseph Stalin.

Stalinist Terror and the Great Purges

In the mid-1930s, the great offensive to build socialism and a new society culminated in ruthless police terror and a massive purging of the Communist Party. First used by the Bolsheviks in the civil war to maintain their power, terror as state policy was revived in the collectivization drive against the peasants. The top members of the party and government publicly supported Stalin's initiatives, but there was some grumbling. At a small gathering in November 1932, even Stalin's wife complained bitterly about the misery of the people and the horrible famine in Ukraine. Stalin showered her with insults, and she died that same night, apparently by her own hand. In late 1934 Stalin's number-two man, Sergei Kirov, was mysteriously murdered. Although Stalin himself probably ordered Kirov's murder, he blamed the assassination on what he called "fascist agents" within the Communist Party. Stalin used the incident to launch a reign of terror that purged the party of supposed traitors and solidified his own control.

Murderous state-sponsored repression picked up steam over the next two years. It culminated in the "great purge" of 1936–1938, a series of spectacular public show trials in which false evidence, often gathered using torture, was used to incriminate party administrators and Red Army leaders. In August 1936 sixteen "Old Bolsheviks"—prominent leaders who had been in the party since the Russian Revolution (see Chapter 26)—confessed to all manner of contrived plots against Stalin in Moscow; all were executed. Then in 1937 the secret police arrested a mass of lesser party officials and newer members, torturing them and extracting confessions for more show trials. In addition to the party faithful, union officials, managers, intellectuals, army officers, and countless ordinary citizens were accused of counterrevolutionary activities and struck down. At least 8 million people were arrested, and millions of these were executed or never returned from prisons and forced-labor camps.

Stalin and the remaining party leadership recruited 1.5 million new members to take the place of those purged. Thus more than half of all Communist Party members in 1941 had joined since the purges, and they experienced rapid social advance. Often the children of workers, they had usually studied in the new technical schools, and they soon proved capable of managing the government and large-scale production. Despite its human costs, the great purges brought substantial practical rewards to this new generation of committed communists. They would serve Stalin effectively until his death in 1953, and they would govern the Soviet Union until the early 1980s.

Stalin's mass purges remain baffling, for most historians believe that those purged posed no threat and were innocent of their supposed crimes. Certainly the highly publicized purges sent a warning to the people: no one was secure; everyone had to serve the party and its leader

Life in a Forced-Labor Camp Deported peasants and other political prisoners work under the most dehumanizing conditions to build the Stalin–White Sea Canal in far northern Russia, around 1933. In books and plays, Stalin's followers praised the project as a model for the regeneration of "reactionaries" and "kulak exploiters" through the joys of socialist work. (David King Collection)

with redoubled devotion. Some scholars have argued that the terror was part of a fully developed totalitarian state, which must always fight real or imaginary enemies.

The long-standing interpretation that puts the blame for the great purges on Stalin has nevertheless been challenged. Some historians argue that Stalin's fears about resistance to his rule were exaggerated but real. Moreover, many in the party and in the general population shared his fears. Bombarded with ideology and political slogans, the population responded energetically to Stalin's directives. Investigations and trials snowballed into mass hysteria, resulting in a modern witch-hunt that claimed millions of victims. In this view of the 1930s, a deluded Stalin found large numbers of willing collaborators for crime as well as for achievement.[2]

Mussolini and Fascism in Italy

How did Mussolini's dictatorship come to power and govern in Italy? ■

Mussolini's fascist movement and his seizure of power in 1922 were important steps in the rise of dictatorships in Europe between the two world wars. Mussolini began his political career as a revolutionary socialist, but after World War I he turned against the working class and successfully sought the support of conservatives. Mussolini and his supporters were the first to call themselves "fascists" — revolutionaries determined to create a new totalitarian state based on extreme nationalism and militarism. Few scholars today would argue that Mussolini succeeded. His dictatorship was brutal and theatrical, but it included elements of conservative authoritarianism as well as dynamic totalitarianism.

The Seizure of Power

In the early twentieth century, Italy was a liberal state with civil rights and a constitutional monarchy. On the eve of World War I, the parliamentary regime finally granted universal male suffrage, and Italy appeared to be moving toward democracy. But there were serious problems. Much of the Italian population was still poor, and many peasants were more attached to their villages and local interests than to the national state. Moreover, the papacy, many devout Catholics, conservatives, and landowners remained strongly opposed to liberal institutions and to the middle-class lawyers and politicians who ran the country largely for their own benefit. Relations between church and state were often tense. Class differences were also extreme, leading to the development of a powerful revolutionary socialist movement. Only in Italy among the main European countries did the radical left wing of the Socialist Party gain leadership as early as 1912, and only in Italy did the Socialist Party unanimously oppose World War I from the very beginning.

The war worsened the political situation. Having fought on the side of the Allies almost exclusively for purposes of territorial expansion, the parliamentary government bitterly disappointed Italian nationalists with Italy's modest gains at Versailles. Workers and peasants also felt cheated: to win their support during the war, the government had promised social and land reform, which it did not deliver after the war.

Instead, unemployment and inflation soared after the war ended, creating mass hardship. The Russian Revolution, which promised ordinary workers a way out, energized Italy's revolutionary socialist movement. The Italian Socialist Party followed the Bolshevik example, and radical workers and peasants began occupying factories and seizing land in 1920. These actions scared and mobilized the property-owning classes. Moreover, after the war the pope lifted his ban on participation by Catholics in Italian politics, and a strong Catholic party quickly emerged. Thus by 1921 revolutionary socialists, antiliberal conservatives, and anxious property owners were all opposed — though for different reasons — to the liberal parliamentary government.

Into these crosscurrents of unrest and fear stepped the blustering, bullying Benito Mussolini (1883–1945). Son of a village schoolteacher and a poor blacksmith, Mussolini began his political career as a Socialist Party leader and radical newspaper editor before World War I. In 1914, powerfully influenced by antidemocratic cults of violent action, the young Mussolini urged that Italy join the Allies, a stand for which he was expelled from the Italian Socialist Party. Later Mussolini fought at the front and was wounded in 1917. Returning home, he began organizing bitter war veterans like himself into a band of fascists — from the Italian word for "a union of forces."

At first Mussolini's program was a radical combination of nationalist and socialist demands, including territorial expansion, benefits for workers, and land reform for peasants. As such, it competed directly with the well-organized Socialist Party and failed to get off the ground. When Mussolini saw that his violent verbal assaults on rival Socialists won him growing support from conservatives and the frightened middle classes, he shifted gears in 1920 and became a sworn enemy of socialism.

Mussolini and his private militia of **Black Shirts** grew increasingly violent. Typically, a band of fascist toughs

Black Shirts Mussolini's private militia that destroyed socialist newspapers, union halls, and Socialist Party headquarters, eventually pushing Socialists out of the city governments of northern Italy.

would roar off in trucks at night and swoop down on a few isolated Socialist organizers, beating them up and force-feeding them almost deadly doses of castor oil. Few people were killed, but socialist newspapers, union halls, and local Socialist Party headquarters were destroyed, and the Black Shirts managed to push Socialists out of city governments in northern Italy.

Fascism soon became a mass movement. A skillful politician, Mussolini convinced his followers that they were not just opposing the "Reds" but also making a revolution of their own, forging a strong, dynamic movement that would help the little people against the established interests. As the government collapsed in 1922, largely because of the chaos created by his Black Shirt militias, Mussolini stepped forward as the savior of order and property. Striking a conservative note in his speeches and gaining the support of army leaders, Mussolini demanded the resignation of the existing government. In October 1922 a band of armed fascists marched on Rome to threaten the king and force him to appoint Mussolini prime minister of Italy. The threat worked. Victor Emmanuel III (r. 1900–1946), who had no love for the old liberal politicians, asked Mussolini to take over the government and form a new cabinet. Thus, af-

ter widespread violence and a threat of armed uprising, Mussolini seized power using the legal framework of the Italian constitution.

The Regime in Action

Mussolini became prime minister in 1922, yet his long-term political intentions were by no means clear until 1924. Some of his radical Black Shirt supporters wished to immediately construct a revolutionary fascist state. Mussolini's ministers, however, included old conservatives, moderates, and even Socialists, and he at first moved cautiously to establish control. He promised a "return to order" and consolidated his support among Italian elites. Fooled by Mussolini's apparent moderation, the Italian parliament passed a new electoral law that gave two-thirds of the representatives in the parliament to the party that won the most votes. This change allowed the Fascist Party and its allies to win an overwhelming majority in April 1924. Shortly thereafter, a group of fascist extremists kidnapped and murdered the Socialist politician Giacomo Matteotti (JAHK-oh-moh mat-tee-OH-tee). This outrage alarmed Mussolini's opponents, and a group of prominent

Fascist Youth on Parade Totalitarian governments in Italy and Nazi Germany established mass youth organizations to instill the values of national unity and train young soldiers for the state. These members of the Balila, Italy's fascist youth organization, raise their rifles in salute at a mass rally in 1939. (Hulton-Deutsch Collection/Corbis)

parliamentary leaders demanded that Mussolini's armed squads be dissolved and all violence be banned.

Mussolini may not have ordered Matteotti's murder, but he took advantage of the resulting political crisis. After first hesitating, he charged forward. Declaring his desire to "make the nation Fascist," he imposed a series of repressive measures. The government ruled by decree, abolished freedom of the press, and organized fixed elections. Mussolini arrested his political opponents, disbanded all independent labor unions, and put dedicated Fascists in control of Italy's schools. Mussolini trumpeted his goal in a famous slogan of 1926: "Everything in the state, nothing outside the state, nothing against the state." By the end of that year, Italy was a one-party dictatorship under Mussolini's unquestioned leadership.

Mussolini's Fascist Party drew support from broad sectors of the population, in large part because he was willing to compromise with the traditional elites that controlled the army, the economy, and the state. He never tried to purge these groups or even move very vigorously against them. He left big business to regulate itself, and there was no land reform. Mussolini also drew increasing support from the Catholic Church. In the **Lateran Agreement** of 1929, he recognized the Vatican as a tiny independent state, and he agreed to give the church significant financial support. The pope expressed his satisfaction and urged Italians to support Mussolini's government. Because he was forced to compromise with these conservative elites, Mussolini never established complete totalitarian control.

Mussolini's government nonetheless proceeded with attempts to bring fascism to Italy. The state engineered popular consent by staging massive rallies and sporting events, creating fascist youth and women's movements, and providing new welfare benefits. Newspapers, radio, and film promoted a "cult of the Duce" (leader), portraying Mussolini as a powerful strongman who embodied the highest qualities of the Italian people.

Like other fascist regimes, Mussolini's government was vehemently opposed to liberal feminism and promoted instead traditional gender roles. The "new fascist man" was supposed to be a virile, patriotic warrior; at the same time his wife was the guardian of the home who raised children to support the values of the fascist state. Some women found great satisfaction in their devo-

Lateran Agreement A 1929 agreement that recognized the Vatican as an independent state, with Mussolini agreeing to give the church heavy financial support in return for public support from the pope.

tion to family, national service, and the Italian "race":

> *Be it in the family, be it in the state, we Italian women are always ready to sacrifice petty personal vanity and outward appearances to collaborate effectively with work and advice toward spiritual unity, toward real uplift, with absolute dedication of our persons to the Chief [Mussolini] to whom we have vowed our faith and our love.*[3]

Mussolini also gained popularity by manipulating popular pride in the grand history of the ancient Roman Empire. "Fascism, in its entirety, is the resurrection of Roman-ness," wrote one enthusiast. Propagandists criticized liberalism and parliamentary government as foreign imports that violated "Roman" traditions.[4]

Italy's Ethiopian Campaign, 1935–1936

SUDAN (Gr. Br.)
ERITREA (It.)
FRENCH SOMALILAND
BRITISH SOMALILAND
Addis Ababa
ETHIOPIA
ITALIAN SOMALILAND
KENYA (Gr. Br.)
INDIAN OCEAN

→ Italian campaigns, 1935–1936

Mussolini matched his aggressive rhetoric with military action: Italian armies invaded the African nation of Ethiopia in October 1935. After surprising setbacks at the hands of the poorly armed Ethiopian army, the Italians won in 1936, and Mussolini could proudly declare that Rome again had its empire. The brutal colonial war shocked international opinion and cemented ties between Italy and Nazi Germany. After a visit to Berlin in the fall of 1937, the Italian dictator pledged support for Hitler and promised that Italy and Germany would "march together right to the end."[5]

Deeply influenced by Hitler's example (see below), Mussolini's government passed a series of anti-Jewish racial laws in 1938. The laws were unpopular, and the fascist government did not aggressively persecute Jews until late in World War II, when Italy was under Nazi control. Nor did Mussolini establish a truly ruthless police state. Only twenty-three political prisoners were condemned to death between 1926 and 1944. Mussolini's fascist Italy, though repressive and undemocratic, was never really totalitarian.

Hitler and Nazism in Germany

How did Hitler gain power, what policies did totalitarian Nazi Germany pursue, and why did they lead to World War II? ∎

The most frightening dictatorship developed in Nazi Germany. A product of Hitler's tactical genius as well as of Germany's social and political situation, National Socialism (or Nazism) shared some of the characteristics of Italian fascism. But Nazism was far more interventionist than its Italian counterpart. Under Hitler, the Nazi dictatorship smashed or took over most independent organizations, established firm control over the German state and society, and violently persecuted the Jewish population. Truly totalitarian in its aspirations, the dynamism of Nazi Germany, based on racial aggression and territorial expansion, led to history's most destructive war.

The Roots of National Socialism

National Socialism grew out of many complex developments, of which the most influential were extreme nationalism and racism. These two ideas captured the mind of the young Adolf Hitler (1889–1945), and he dominated Nazism until the end of World War II.

The son of a successful Austrian customs official, Hitler spent his childhood in small towns in Austria. He was a mediocre student who dropped out of high school at age fourteen. Hitler then moved to Vienna, where he was exposed to extreme Austro-German nationalists who believed Germans to be a superior people and the natural rulers of central Europe. They advocated union with Germany and violent expulsion of "inferior" peoples as the means of maintaining German domination of the Austro-Hungarian Empire.

In Vienna Hitler eagerly absorbed this virulent anti-Semitism and a deep hatred of Slavs. He developed an unshakable belief in the crudest distortions of Social Darwinism (see Chapter 25), the superiority of Germanic races, and the inevitability of racial conflict. The Jews, he claimed, directed an international conspiracy of finance capitalism and Marxian socialism against German culture, German unity, and the German people.

Hitler was not alone. Racist anti-Semitism became wildly popular on the far right wing of European politics in the decades surrounding the First World War. Such irrational beliefs, rooted in centuries of Christian anti-Semitism, were given pseudoscientific legitimacy by nineteenth-century developments in biology and eugenics. These ideas came to define Hitler's worldview and would play an immense role in the ideology and actions of National Socialism.

Hitler greeted the outbreak of the First World War as a salvation. The struggle and discipline of war gave life meaning, and Hitler served bravely as a dispatch carrier on the western front. When Germany was defeated

Events Leading to World War II

1919	Treaty of Versailles is signed
1920	Founding of National Socialist German Workers' Party (Nazis)
1922	Mussolini seizes power in Italy
1927	Stalin takes full control in the Soviet Union
1929–1939	Great Depression
1931	Japan invades Manchuria
January 1933	Hitler is appointed chancellor of Germany
March 1933	Reichstag passes the Enabling Act, granting Hitler absolute dictatorial power
October 1933	Germany withdraws from the League of Nations
1935	Nuremberg Laws deprive Jews of all rights of citizenship
March 1935	Hitler announces German rearmament
October 1935	Mussolini invades Ethiopia and receives Hitler's support
March 1936	German armies move unopposed into the demilitarized Rhineland
1936–1939	Civil war in Spain, culminating in taking of power by fascist regime under Franco
October 1936	Rome-Berlin Axis created
1937	Japan invades China
March 1938	Germany annexes Austria
September 1938	Munich Conference: Britain and France agree to German seizure of the Sudetenland from Czechoslovakia
March 1939	Germany occupies the rest of Czechoslovakia; appeasement ends in Britain
August 1939	Nazi-Soviet pact is signed
September 1, 1939	Germany invades Poland
September 3, 1939	Britain and France declare war on Germany

in 1918, Hitler's world was shattered. Convinced that Jews and Marxists had "stabbed Germany in the back," he vowed to fight on.

In late 1919 Hitler joined a tiny extremist group in Munich called the German Workers' Party. In addition to denouncing Jews, Marxists, and democrats, the German Workers' Party promised a uniquely German National Socialism that would abolish the injustices of capitalism and create a mighty "people's community." By 1921 Hitler had gained absolute control of this small but growing party, which had been renamed the National Socialist German Workers' Party, or Nazis, in 1920. Hitler became a master of mass propaganda and political showmanship. In wild, histrionic speeches, he worked his

National Socialism A movement born of extreme nationalism and racism, led by Adolf Hitler, that ruled Germany from 1933 to 1945 and forced Europe into the Second World War.

audience into a frenzy with demagogic attacks on the Versailles treaty, Jews, war profiteers, and Germany's Weimar Republic.

Party membership multiplied tenfold after early 1922. In late 1923 the Weimar Republic seemed on the verge of collapse, and Hitler, inspired by Mussolini's recent victory, organized an armed uprising in Munich—the so-called Beer Hall Putsch. Despite the failure of the poorly planned coup and Hitler's arrest, National Socialism had been born.

Hitler's Road to Power

At his trial, Hitler violently denounced the Weimar Republic, and he gained enormous publicity. From the failed revolt, Hitler concluded that he had to come to power through electoral competition rather than armed rebellion. He used his brief prison term to dictate his book *Mein Kampf* (My Struggle). Here Hitler laid out his basic ideas on "racial purification" and territorial expansion that would increasingly define National Socialism.

In *Mein Kampf* Hitler claimed that Germans were a "master race" that needed to defend its "pure blood" from groups he labeled "racial degenerates," including Jews, Slavs, and others. The German race was destined to triumph and grow, and, according to Hitler, it needed *Lebensraum* (living space). This space could be found to Germany's east, in central Europe, which Hitler claimed was inhabited by the "subhuman" Slavs and Jews. The future dictator portrayed a sweeping vision of war and conquest in which the German master race would colonize and ultimately replace these "subhumans" across east-central Europe. He championed the idea of the leader-dictator or *Führer* (FYOUR-uhr), whose unlimited power would embody the people's will and lead the German nation to victory. These ideas—a deadly combination of race and space—would ultimately propel Hitler's Germany into the Second World War.

Cover of Hitler's *Mein Kampf* Nazi dictator Adolf Hitler wrote *Mein Kampf* (My Struggle) in 1923 while serving a prison sentence for armed rebellion against the democratic German government. The book, which sold millions of copies during Hitler's rule, presents his detailed plans for the "racial purification" of Germany and the expansion of the German state. How does the cover photo convey the idea of powerful leadership? (Bildarchiv Preussischer Kulturbesitz/Art Resource, NY)

In the years of relative prosperity and stability between 1924 and 1929, Hitler built up the Nazi Party. By 1928 it had a hundred thousand members. To appeal to middle-class voters, Hitler de-emphasized the anti-capitalist elements of National Socialism and vowed to fight communism. The Nazis still remained a small splinter group in 1928, when they received only 2.6 percent of the vote in the general elections and twelve seats in the Reichstag, the German parliament. There the Nazi deputies pursued the legal strategy of using democracy to destroy democracy.

The Great Depression of 1929 brought the ascent of National Socialism. Now Hitler promised German voters economic as well as political salvation. His appeals for "national rebirth" appealed to a broad spectrum of voters, including middle- and lower-middle-class groups—small business owners, officeworkers, artisans, and peasants—as well as skilled workers striving for middle-class status. Seized by panic as bankruptcies increased, unemployment soared, and the communists made dramatic election gains, voters deserted the conservative and moderate parties for the Nazis. In the election of 1930 the Nazis won 6.5 million votes and 107 seats, and in July 1932 they gained 14.5 million votes—38 percent of the total. They were now the largest party in the Reichstag.

The breakdown of democratic government helped the Nazis seize power. Unable to gain the support of a majority in the Reichstag, in summer 1930 Chancellor Heinrich Brüning (BROU-nihng) dissolved the parliament. He convinced the president, the aging war hero General Hindenburg, to authorize rule by decree under Article 48 of the constitution, which allowed the central government to govern without the consent of the parliament. Brüning tried to overcome the economic crisis by cutting back government spending and ruthlessly forcing down prices and wages. His conservative policies intensified Germany's economic collapse and convinced many voters that the country's republican leaders were stupid and corrupt, adding to Hitler's appeal.

Division on the left also contributed to Nazi success. Even though the two left-wing parties together outnumbered the Nazis in the Reichstag, the Communists refused to cooperate with the Social Democrats. German communists had long competed with the socialists for the allegiance of the working classes. Now in the crisis of the early 1930s, they failed to resolve their differences and mount an effective opposition to the Nazi takeover.

Finally, Hitler excelled in the dirty backroom politics of the decaying Weimar Republic. In 1932 Hitler cleverly gained the support of conservative politicians and key leaders in the army and big business. These people thought they could use Hitler for their own advantage, to resolve the political crisis, but also to get increased military spending, fat contracts, and tough measures against workers. They accepted Hitler's demand to be appointed chancellor in a coalition government, reasoning that he could be used and controlled. On January 30, 1933, Adolf Hitler, leader of the largest party in Germany, was legally appointed chancellor by President Hindenburg.

State and Society in Nazi Germany

Hitler moved rapidly and skillfully to establish an unshakable dictatorship that would pursue the Nazi program of race and space. First, Hitler and the Nazi Party worked to consolidate their power. To maintain legal appearances, Hitler called for new elections. In February 1933, in the midst of a violent electoral campaign, the Reichstag building was partly destroyed by fire. Hitler blamed the Communist Party, and he convinced President Hindenburg to sign dictatorial emergency acts that abolished freedom of speech and assembly as well as most personal liberties.

The façade of democratic government was soon torn asunder. When the Nazis won only 44 percent of the vote in the elections, Hitler outlawed the Communist Party and arrested its parliamentary representatives. Then on March 23, 1933, the Nazis pushed through the Reichstag the so-called **Enabling Act**, which gave Hitler absolute dictatorial power for four years. Armed with the Enabling Act, the Nazis moved to smash or control all independent organizations. Their deceitful stress on legality, coupled with divide-and-conquer techniques, disarmed the opposition until it was too late for effective resistance.

Germany became a one-party Nazi state. Elections were farces. The new regime took over the government bureaucracy intact, installing Nazis in top positions. At the same time, they created a series of overlapping Nazi Party organizations responsible solely to Hitler. As research in recent years has shown, the resulting system of dual government was riddled with rivalries, contradictions, and inefficiencies. The Nazi state was often disorganized and lacked the all-encompassing unity that its propagandists claimed. Yet this fractured system suited Hitler and his purposes. The lack of unity encouraged competition among state personnel, who worked to outdo each other to fulfill Hitler's vaguely expressed goals. The Führer thus played the established bureaucracy against his personal party government and maintained dictatorial control.

Once the Nazis were firmly in command of the government, Hitler and the party turned their attention to constructing a National Socialist society defined by national unity and racial exclusion. First the Nazis attacked their political enemies. Communists, Social Democrats, and trade-union leaders were forced out of their jobs or arrested and taken to hastily built concentration camps. The Nazis outlawed strikes and abolished independent labor unions, which were replaced by the Nazi-controlled German Labor Front.

Hitler then purged the Nazi Party of its more extremist elements. The Nazi storm troopers (the SA), the quasi-military band of 3 million toughs in brown shirts who had fought communists and beaten up Jews before the Nazis took power, now expected top positions in the army. Some SA radicals even talked of a "second revolution" that would create equality among all Germans by sweeping away the capitalist system. Now that the Nazis were in power, however, Hitler was eager to win support of the traditional military and maintain social order. He decided that the leadership of the SA had to be eliminated. On the night of June 30, 1934, Hitler's elite personal guard—the SS—arrested and shot without trial roughly a thousand SA leaders and other political enemies. Afterward the SS grew rapidly. Under its methodical, ruthless leader Heinrich Himmler (1900–1945), the SS took over the political police and the concentration camp system.

The Nazi Party instituted a policy it called "coordination" that was meant to force society to conform to National Socialist ideology. Professional people—doctors and lawyers, teachers and engineers—saw their previously independent organizations swallowed up by Nazi associations. Publishing houses were put under Nazi control, and universities and writers were quickly brought into line. Democratic, socialist, and Jewish literature was put on ever-growing blacklists. Passionate students and pitiful professors burned forbidden books in public squares. Modern art and architecture—which the Nazis considered "degenerate"—were ruthlessly prohibited. Life became violently anti-intellectual. By 1934 a brutal dictatorship characterized by frightening dynamism and obedience to Hitler was largely in place.

Acting on its vision of racial purity, the party began a many-faceted campaign against those they deemed incapable of making a positive contribution to the "master race." The Nazis persecuted a number of

Enabling Act An act pushed through the Reichstag by the Nazis that gave Hitler absolute dictatorial power for four years.

supposedly undesirable groups based on their reputed racial characteristics. Jews headed the list, but Slavic peoples, Gypsies (Sinti and Roma), homosexuals, Jehovah's Witnesses, people considered handicapped, and a loosely defined group of so-called asocials were also targets of ostracism and brutal state-sponsored repression.

In what some historians term the Nazi "racial state," barbarism and race hatred were institutionalized with the force of science and law.[6] New university academies, such as the German Society for Racial Research, wrote studies that measured and defined racial differences; prejudice was thus presented in the guise of enlightened science, a means for creating a strong national race. The ethical breakdown was exemplified in a series of sterilization laws, which led to the forced sterilization of some four hundred thousand "undesirable" citizens.

From the beginning, German Jews were a special object of Nazi persecution. By the end of 1934, most Jewish lawyers, doctors, professors, civil servants, and musicians had been banned from their professions. In 1935 the infamous Nuremberg Laws classified as Jewish anyone having three or more Jewish grandparents. The Nuremberg Laws also outlawed marriage and sexual relations between Jews and those defined as German and deprived Jews of all rights of citizenship. Conversion to Christianity and abandonment of the Jewish faith made no difference. In their commentary on the Nuremberg Laws, two leading German lawyers made the close connections between "blood" and the legal definition of citizenship quite clear:

> *What is German, and what either benefits or harms the German people and the Reich, can only be known by those of German blood. . . . Only he who is a racial comrade can be a citizen. Only one who is of German blood, no matter what his religious faith, can be a racial comrade. Therefore no Jew can be a racial comrade.*[7]

For the vast majority of German citizens not targeted by such laws, the creation of a demonized outsider group may well have contributed to feelings of national unity and support for the Hitler regime.

In late 1938 the assault on the Jews accelerated. During a well-organized wave of violence known as Kristallnacht (the night of broken glass), Nazi gangs smashed windows, looted Jewish-owned shops, and destroyed homes and synagogues. German Jews were then rounded up and made to pay for the damage. Confronted with ever-increasing prejudice, by 1939 some 300,000 of Germany's 500,000 Jews had emigrated, sacrificing almost all their property in order to leave Germany. Some Germans privately opposed these outrages, but most went along or looked the other way. This lack of opposition reflected anti-Semitism to a degree still being debated by historians, but it certainly revealed the strong popular support enjoyed by Hitler's government.

Popular Support for National Socialism

Why did millions of ordinary Germans back a brutally repressive regime? A combination of coercion and reward enlisted popular support for the racial state. Using the secret police and the growing concentration camp system in a reign of ruthless terror, the regime persecuted its political and "racial" enemies. Yet for the large majority of ordinary German citizens who were not Jews, communists, or members of other outsider groups, Hitler's government brought new opportunities. The German "master race" clearly benefited from Nazi ideologies of race and space.

Hitler had promised the masses economic recovery—"work and bread"—and he delivered. The Nazi state launched a large public works program to help pull Germany out of the depression. Work began on superhighways, offices, gigantic sports stadiums, and public housing, which created jobs and instilled pride in national recovery. By 1938 unemployment had fallen to 2 percent, and there was a shortage of workers. Thus between 1932 and 1938, the standard of living for the average employed worker increased moderately. Business profits rose sharply.

The persecution of Jews brought substantial benefits to ordinary Germans. As Jews were forced out of their jobs and then their homes, Germans stepped in to take their place. In a process known as Aryanization (named after the "Aryan master race" prized by the Nazis for their supposedly pure German blood), many Jews were forced to sell their businesses to "racially pure" Germans at rock-bottom prices. For millions of so-called Aryans, a rising standard of living—at whatever ethical price—was tangible evidence that Nazi promises were more than show and propaganda.

Economic recovery was accompanied by a great wave of social and cultural innovation intended to construct what Nazi propagandists called the *Volksgemeinschaft*—a people's community for all racially pure Germans. The party organized mass organizations to spread Nazi ideology and enlist volunteers for the Nazi cause. Millions of Germans joined the Hitler Youth, the League of German Women, and the German Labor Front. The Nazi Winter Relief charity drives, with captains on almost every block, handed out donations to the needy. Mass rallies, such as annual May Day celebrations and Nazi Party conventions in Nuremberg, brought together thousands of participants. Reports on such events in the Nazi-controlled press brought the message home to millions more.

The Nazis made great attempts to control the private lives and leisure time of ordinary Germans. State-sponsored "Strength Through Joy" programs set up exercise classes, beautified workplaces, and took working-class Germans on free vacations. A series of newly invented holidays, from Hitler's birthday to "people's Christmas" encouraged Germans to celebrate the values of the racial state at home. The government promised prosperity and proudly touted a glittering array of inexpensive and enticing people's products. Items such as the Volkswagen (the people's car) were intended to link individual desires for consumer goods to the collective ideology of the people's community. (See "Living in the Past: Nazi Propaganda and Consumer Goods," page 906.) Though such programs faltered as the state turned its resources toward rearmament for the approaching war (see page 909), they suggested to all that the regime sincerely wished to improve German living standards.

Women played a special role in the Nazi state. Promising to "liberate women from women's liberation," Nazi ideologues championed a return to traditional family values. They outlawed abortion, discouraged women from holding jobs or obtaining higher education, and glorified domesticity and motherhood.

Women were cast as protectors of the hearth and home and were instructed to raise young boys and girls in accordance with Nazi ideals. In the later 1930s, facing labor shortages, the Nazis reluctantly reversed course and encouraged women to enter the labor force. At the same time, the millions of women enrolled in Nazi mass organizations, which organized charity drives and other social programs, experienced a new sense of community in public activities.

Few historians today believe that Hitler and the Nazis brought about a real social revolution, as an earlier generation of scholars often argued. Yet Hitler's rule corresponded to a time of economic growth, and Nazi propagandists continually triumphed the supposed accomplishments of the regime. The vision of the people's community, the national pride of German recovery, and the feelings of belonging created by acts of racial exclusion led many Germans to support the regime. Hitler himself remained popular with broad sections of the population well into the war.

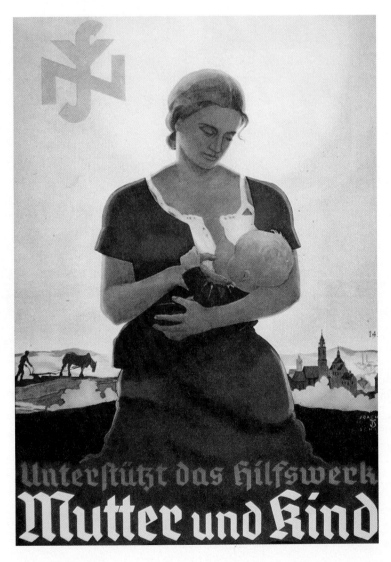

Unterstützt das Hilfswerk
Mutter und Kind

Mothers in the Fatherland Nazi ideologues promoted strictly defined gender roles for men and women, the Nazi state implemented a variety of social programs to encourage "racially correct" women to stay home and raise "Aryan" children. This colorful poster portrays the joy of motherhood and calls for donations to the Mother and Child division of the National Socialist People's Welfare office. A woman who had four children was awarded the bronze Cross of Honor for the German Mother (above). The medal came with a letter of appreciation signed by Hitler. (poster: akg-images; medal: Private Collection/Peter Newark Military Pictures/The Bridgeman Art Library)

LIVING IN THE PAST

IT IS EASY TO FORGET THAT THE VOLKSWAGENS that zip around America's streets today got their start in Hitler's Germany, introduced as part of a Nazi campaign to provide inexpensive but attractive consumer goods to the *Volk* (the People). Marketed to Aryans, but not to Jews and other "racial enemies," the Volkswagen (or People's Car) and other People's Products, including the People's Radio, the People's Refrigerator, and even the People's Single Family Home, symbolized a return to German prosperity. As these advertisements suggest, the appeal of material abundance was a central plank in Nazi propaganda.

Despite Hitler's promise of a "new, happier age" that would "make the German people rich,"* many of these consumer goods remained out of reach of ordinary Germans. The Volkswagen was a case in point. The car was sold by subscription, and a customer made weekly deposits into a savings account. When the balance was paid off, the customer would receive a car. By the end of the Nazi regime, some 340,000 Germans had opened such savings accounts. Yet because of problems with production, the car's relatively high price, and the concentration on armaments production in the late 1930s, not even one People's Car was delivered to a private customer.

In contrast, the People's Radio was a unique success. The modest VE-301 radio was much cheaper than standard models, and between 1934 and 1942, the number of Germans who owned radios doubled. Many people could now sit at home and listen to broadcasts ranging from popular and classical music to speeches from regime leaders like Minister of Propaganda Joseph Goebbels, whose tirades were so inescapable that Germans nicknamed the VE-301 the "Goebbels snout."

QUESTIONS FOR ANALYSIS

1. What do these images suggest about everyday life in Nazi Germany? What do they reveal about the aspirations of the German people for a good life in the 1930s?

2. Consider why both the government and the commercial manufacturers attached the prefix "Volk," or People, to products like the Volkswagen. What larger message did these two groups seek to convey through the use of this prefix?

3. How are these images similar to advertisements today? How are they different?

*Peter Fritzsche, *Life and Death in the Third Reich* (Cambridge, Mass.: Harvard University Press, 2008), p. 59.

This 1938 advertisement for the Volkswagen, produced by the Nazi Strength Through Joy organization, highlights the pleasures of a family vacation. (Deutsches Historisches Museum, Berlin/DHM Sebastian Ahlers/The Bridgeman Art Library)

"All Germany listens to the Führer on the People's Radio."
(poster: Bundesarchiv Koblenz Plak 003-022-025; radio: Victoria & Albert Museum/V&A Picture Library)

Not all Germans supported Hitler, however, and a number of German groups actively resisted him after 1933. But opponents of the Nazis were never unified, which helps account for their lack of success. In addition, the regime clamped down: tens of thousands of political enemies were imprisoned, and thousands were executed. In the first years of Hitler's rule, the principal resisters were communists and socialists in the trade unions, groups smashed by the expansion of the SS system. A second group of opponents arose in the Catholic and Protestant churches. However, their efforts were directed primarily at preserving religious life, not at overthrowing Hitler. In 1938 and again during the war, a few high-ranking army officers, who feared the consequences of Hitler's reckless aggression, plotted against him, but all were unsuccessful.

Aggression and Appeasement

The nazification of German society fulfilled only part of the larger Nazi agenda. Even as it built up the people's community, the regime aggressively pursued policies meant to achieve territorial expansion for the supposedly superior German race. At first, Hitler carefully camouflaged his expansionist foreign policy. Germany was still militarily weak, and the Nazi leader loudly proclaimed his peaceful intentions. Germany's withdrawal from the League of Nations in October 1933, however, indicated that Gustav Stresemann's policy of peaceful cooperation was dead (see Chapter 27). Then in March 1935 Hitler openly proclaimed that Germany would no longer abide by the disarmament clauses of the Treaty of Versailles. He established a military draft and began to build up the German army. France, Italy, and Great Britain protested strongly and warned against future aggressive actions.

Yet the emerging united front against Hitler quickly collapsed. Britain adopted a policy of **appeasement**, granting Hitler everything he could reasonably want (and more) in order to avoid war. British appeasement, which practically dictated French policy, was motivated in large part by the pacifism of a population still horrified by the memory of the First World War. As in Germany, many powerful conservatives in Britain underestimated Hitler. They believed that Soviet communism was the real danger and that Hitler could be used to stop it. Such strong anticommunist feelings made an alliance between the Western Powers and Stalin unlikely.

appeasement The British policy toward Germany prior to World War II that aimed at granting Hitler whatever he wanted, including western Czechoslovakia, in order to avoid war.

When Hitler suddenly marched his armies into the demilitarized Rhineland in March 1936, brazenly violating the Treaties of Versailles and Locarno (Map 28.1), Britain refused to act. France could do little without British support. Emboldened, Hitler moved ever more aggressively in international affairs. He enlisted powerful allies in the Nazi cause. Italy and Germany established the so-called Rome-Berlin Axis in 1936. Japan, also under the rule of a fascist dictatorship, joined the Axis alliance.

At the same time, Germany and Italy intervened in the Spanish civil war (1936–1939), where their military aid helped General Francisco Franco's revolutionary fascist movement defeat the democratically elected republican government. Republican Spain's only official aid in the fight against Franco came from the Soviet Union, for public opinion in Britain and especially in France was hopelessly divided on whether to intervene.

In late 1937 Hitler moved forward with plans to crush Austria and Czechoslovakia as the first step in his long-contemplated drive for living space in the east. By threatening Austria with invasion, Hitler forced the Austrian chancellor to put local Nazis in control of the government in March 1938. The next day, in the Austrian Anschluss (annexation), German armies moved in unopposed, and Austria became two more provinces of Greater Germany (see Map 28.1).

Simultaneously, Hitler demanded that territories inhabited mostly by ethnic Germans in western Czechoslovakia — the Sudetenland — be ceded to Nazi Germany. Though democratic Czechoslovakia was allied with France and the Soviet Union and prepared to defend itself, appeasement triumphed again. In September 1938 British prime minister Arthur Neville Chamberlain flew to Germany three times in fourteen days. In these negotiations, Chamberlain and the French agreed with Hitler that Germany should immediately take over the Sudetenland. Returning to London from the Munich Conference, Chamberlain told cheering crowds that he had secured "peace with honor . . . peace for our time." Sold out by the Western Powers, Czechoslovakia gave in.

Chamberlain's peace was short-lived. In March 1939 Hitler's armies invaded and occupied the rest of Czechoslovakia. The effect on Western public opinion was electrifying. This time, there was no possible rationale of self-determination for Nazi aggression, since Hitler was seizing ethnic Czechs and Slovaks as captive peoples.

Map 28.1 The Growth of Nazi Germany, 1933–1939 Until March 1939 Hitler's conquests brought ethnic Germans into the Nazi state; then he turned on the Slavic and Jewish peoples he had always hated. He stripped Czechoslovakia of its independence and prepared to attack Poland in September 1939.

"Peace in Our Time" British prime minister Neville Chamberlain speaks at the London airport on his return from a meeting with Adolf Hitler in Munich in September 1938. In return for acceptance of the German annexation of the Czech Sudetenland, Hitler promised to halt foreign aggression, and Chamberlain famously announced that he had negotiated "peace in our time" with the Nazi leader. Less than a year later, Germany invaded Poland and Europe was at war. (Hulton Archive/Getty Images)

When Hitler next used the question of German minorities in Danzig as a pretext to confront Poland, a suddenly militant Chamberlain declared that Britain and France would fight if Hitler attacked his eastern neighbor. Hitler did not take these warnings seriously and pressed on.

In August 1939, in an about-face that stunned the world, sworn enemies Hitler and Stalin signed a so-called nonaggression pact that in fact paved the road to war. Each dictator promised to remain neutral if the other became involved in open hostilities. An attached secret protocol ruthlessly divided Poland and east-central Europe into German and Soviet zones. Stalin agreed to the pact because he remained distrustful of Western intentions and Hitler offered immediate territorial gain.

For Hitler, everything was now set. On September 1, 1939, German armies and warplanes smashed into Poland from three sides. Two days later, Britain and France, finally true to their word, declared war on Germany. The Second World War had begun.

The Second World War

How did Germany and Japan create enormous empires, and how were they defeated by the Allies? ▪

Nazi Germany's unlimited ambition unleashed an apocalyptic cataclysm of world war. Hitler's armies quickly conquered much of western and eastern Europe, establishing a vast empire of death and destruction based on Nazi ideas of race and space. At the same time, Japa-

nese armies overran much of Southeast Asia and created their own racial empire. This reckless aggression brought together a coalition of unlikely but powerful allies determined to halt the advance of fascism: Britain, the United States, and the Soviet Union. After years of slaughter that decimated much of Europe and East Asia, this "Grand Alliance" decisively defeated the Axis powers.

German Victories in Europe

Using planes, tanks, and trucks in the first example of a blitzkrieg, or "lightning war," Hitler's armies crushed Poland in four weeks. While the Soviet Union quickly took its part of the booty—the eastern half of Poland and the independent Baltic states of Lithuania, Estonia, and Latvia—French and British armies prepared their defenses in the west.

In spring 1940 the Nazi lightning war struck again. After occupying Denmark, Norway, and Holland, German motorized columns broke into France through southern Belgium, split the Franco-British forces, and trapped the entire British army on the French beaches of Dunkirk. By heroic efforts, the British withdrew their troops but not their equipment, and France was taken by the Nazis. By July 1940 Hitler ruled practically all of western continental Europe. Italy was an ally; Romania, Hungary, and Bulgaria joined the Axis powers; and the Soviet Union, Spain, and Sweden were friendly neutrals. Only Britain, led by the uncompromising Winston Churchill (1874–1965), remained unconquered.

To prepare for an amphibious invasion of Britain, Germany sought to gain control of the air. In the Battle of Britain, which began in July 1940, up to a thousand

German Bombers over Warsaw Germany opened its September 1939 attack on Poland by subjecting the Polish capital to repeated bombardment. By the end of the war, both sides had engaged in massive air campaigns against civilian targets, taking the lives of millions of civilians and leading finally to the use of the atomic bomb against Japan in 1945. (INTERFOTO/Alamy)

German planes a day attacked British airfields and key factories, dueling with British defenders high in the skies. Losses were heavy on both sides. In September 1940 Hitler angrily turned from military objectives to indiscriminate bombing of British cities in an attempt to break British morale. British aircraft factories increased production, and the heavily bombed people of London defiantly dug in. By October Britain was beating Germany three to one in the air war, and the Battle of Britain was over. Unsuccessful in Britain, the Nazi war machine turned south and invaded and occupied Greece and the Balkans.

New Order Hitler's program based on racial imperialism, which gave preferential treatment to the Nordic peoples; the French, an "inferior" Latin people, occupied a middle position, and Slavs and Jews were treated harshly as "subhumans."

Hitler now allowed his lifetime obsession of creating a vast eastern European empire ruled by the master race to dictate policy. In June 1941 German armies attacked the Soviet Union along a vast front, breaking the Nazi-Soviet pact (Map 28.2). By October Leningrad was practically surrounded, most of Ukraine had been conquered, and Moscow was besieged. But the Soviets did not collapse, and when a severe winter struck German armies outfitted in summer uniforms, the invaders were stopped. Stalled in Russia, Hitler and his allies still ruled over a vast European empire stretching from the outskirts of Moscow to the English Channel. Hitler, the Nazi leadership, and the loyal German army were positioned to greatly accelerate construction of their New Order in Europe.

Europe Under Nazi Occupation

Hitler's **New Order** was based firmly on the guiding principle of National Socialism: racial imperialism. Occupied peoples were treated according to their place on the Nazi racial hierarchy. All were subject to harsh policies dedicated to ethnic cleansing and the plunder of resources for the Nazi war effort.

Within the New Order, the so-called Nordic peoples—the Dutch, Norwegians, and Danes—received preferential treatment, for the Germans believed they were racially related to the Aryan master race. Here the Nazis established puppet governments of various kinds; though most people hated the conquerors, the Nazis found collaborators willing to rule these states in accord with German needs. France was divided into two parts. The German army occupied the north, including Paris. The southeast remained nominally independent. There the aging Marshal Henri-Philippe Pétain formed a new French government—the so-called Vichy (VIH-shee) regime—that adopted many aspects of National Socialist ideology and willingly placed French Jews in the hands of the Nazis.

In all conquered territories, the Nazis used a variety of techniques to enrich Germans and support the war

Map legend:
- Axis powers and their allies
- Occupied by Germany and its allies
- Allied powers and their allies
- Neutral nations
- Boundary of Greater Germany
- Major battle

Siege of Leningrad,
Sept. 1941–Jan. 1944

Germans repulsed,
Dec. 1941

Moscow
Oct. 1941–Jan. 1942

SOVIET UNION

Russian front, spring 1944

Russian front, Nov. 1942

Siege of Stalingrad,
Aug. 21, 1942–
Jan. 31, 1943

Russian front, Dec. 1941

FINLAND
Helsinki
Leningrad

NORWAY
Oslo

SWEDEN
Stockholm

ESTONIA

Riga
LATVIA

LITHUANIA

BELARUS

Smolensk
Tula

Kursk
July–Aug. 1943

Dnieper
Aug.–Dec. 1943

Kiev

Stalingrad

DENMARK
Copenhagen

Germany
surrenders,
May 8, 1945

Siege, Sept. 1939
Uprising, Aug.–Sept. 1944

Baltic Sea

NORTHERN
IRELAND

North
Sea

IRELAND

GREAT
BRITAIN

Battle of Britain,
fall 1940

NETHERLANDS
London

Dunkirk

BELGIUM

Invasion of Normandy,
June 6, 1944

ATLANTIC
OCEAN

Paris

Battle of
the Bulge,
Dec. 1944

FRANCE

Vichy

SWITZERLAND

Axis troops occupy
Vichy France,
Nov. 10 and 11, 1942

VICHY
FRANCE

PORT.

Madrid
Lisbon

SPAIN

Berlin

Russian front, Feb. 1945

Posen

Warsaw

POLAND

Kraków

GERMANY

SLOVAKIA

Vienna

HUNGARY

Budapest

UKRAINE

Pinsk

Dnieper R.

Don R.

Volga R.

Yalta

Western front, Feb. 1945

Rhine R.

Danube R.

Po R.

Ebro R.

Bologna

Italian front
Feb. 1945

ITALY

Rome
(Liberated June 1944)

Monte Cassino,
May 1944

Corsica

Sardinia

Adriatic Sea

CROATIA

SERBIA

ROMANIA

Bucharest

Danube R.

Sofia

BULGARIA

ALBANIA

Black Sea

Ankara

TURKEY

SPANISH
MOROCCO

Casablanca
Nov. 1942

MOROCCO
(Fr.)

ALGERIA
(Vichy France)

GIBRALTAR
(Gr. Br.)

Axis troops
evacuated,
May 1943

Joined Allies,
Nov. 1942

TUNISIA
(Fr.)

Salerno,
Sept. 1943

Allies invade Sicily and
Italy, July–Sept. 1943

Sicily

Sicily,
July 1943

Malta
(Gr. Br.)

Battle for Crete
May 20–June 1,
1941

Crete (Gr.)

GREECE

Athens

Cyprus
(Gr. Br.)

SYRIA
(Fr. Mandate)

IRAQ
(Br.
Mandate)

LEBANON
(Fr. Mandate)

PALESTINE
(Br. Mandate)

TRANS-
JORDAN
(Br. Mandate)

SAUDI
ARABIA

El Alamein,
summer 1942

Suez
Canal

Nile R.

Cairo

Mediterranean Sea

LIBYA
(It.)

EGYPT

N
W   E
S

0   200   400 miles
0   200   400 kilometers

Mapping the Past

Map 28.2 World War II in Europe and Africa, 1939–1945 This map shows the extent of Hitler's empire before the Battle of Stalingrad in late 1942 and the subsequent advances of the Allies until Germany surrendered on May 7, 1945. Compare this map with Map 28.1 on page 908 to trace the rise and fall of the Nazi empire over time.

ANALYZING THE MAP What was the first country conquered by Hitler (see Map 28.1)? Locate Germany's advance and retreat on the Russian front in December 1941, November 1942, spring 1944, and February 1945. How does this compare to the position of British and American forces on the battlefield at similar points in time?

CONNECTIONS What implications might the battle lines on February 1945 have had for the postwar settlement in Europe?

To complete this activity online, go to the Online Study Guide at **bedfordstmartins.com/mckaywest**.

Vichy France, 1940

Boundary of Poland, 1938
Germany, 1938
Annexed by Germany, 1939
German civil administration, 1942
German military occupation, 1942
Boundary of Greater Germany, 1942

Nazi Occupation of Poland and East-Central Europe, 1939–1942

effort. Occupied nations were forced to pay for the costs of the war and for the occupation itself, and the price was high. Nazi administrators stole goods and money from local Jews, set currency exchanges at favorable rates, and forced occupied peoples to accept worthless wartime scrip. Soldiers were encouraged to steal but also to purchase goods at cheap exchange rates and send them home. A flood of plunder reached Germany, which helped maintain high living standards and preserved popular morale well into the war. Nazi victory furthermore placed national Jewish populations across Europe under German control, and so eased the planning and implementation of the mass murder of Europe's Jews.

In the occupied territories on the eastern front, German rule was ruthless and deadly. From the start, the Nazi leadership had cast the war in the east as a war of annihilation. They now set out to build a vast eastern colonial empire where Jews would be exterminated and Poles, Ukrainians, and Russians would be enslaved and forced to die out. According to the plans, ethnic German peasants would resettle the resulting abandoned lands. In pursuit of such goals, large parts of western Poland were incorporated into Germany. Another part of Poland was set up as the General Government and placed under the rule of a merciless civilian administration.

With the support of military commanders, German policemen, and bureaucrats in the occupied territories, Nazi administrators and Himmler's elite SS corps now implemented a program of destruction and annihilation to create a "mass settlement space" for racially pure Germans. Across the east, the Nazi armies destroyed cities and factories, stole crops and farm animals, and subjected conquered peoples to forced starvation and mass murder. The murderous sweep of Nazi occupation destroyed the lives of millions, as the example of

Belarus makes clear. There fewer than 7 million of the 9 million original inhabitants were still in the country when the Red Army liberated the territory in 1944. Of these, 3 million were homeless. In Belarus the Nazis killed some 700,000 Soviet prisoners of war, 550,000 Jews, 340,000 peasants and refugees, and 100,000 members of other groups. In addition more than 380,000 people were transported to Germany to work as forced laborers.[8]

In response to such atrocities, small but determined underground resistance groups fought back. They were hardly unified. Communists and socialists often disagreed with more centrist or nationalist groups on long-term goals and short-term tactics. In Yugoslavia, for example, communist and royalist military resistance groups attacked the Germans, but also each other. The resistance nonetheless presented a real challenge to the Nazi New Order. Poland, under German occupation longer than any other nation, had the most determined and well-organized resistance. The Nazis had closed all Polish universities and outlawed national newspapers, but the Poles organized secret classes and maintained a thriving underground press. Underground members of the Polish Home Army, led by the government in exile in London, passed intelligence about German operations to the Allies and committed sabotage; communist groups in Poland likewise attacked the Nazis. The famous French resistance undertook similar actions, as did groups in Italy, Greece, Russia, and the Netherlands.

The German response was swift and deadly. The Nazi army and the SS tortured captured resistance members and executed hostages in reprisal for attacks. Responding to actions undertaken by resistance groups, the German army murdered the male populations of Lidice (Czechoslovakia) and Oradour (France) and leveled the entire towns—brutal examples of Nazi barbarism in pursuit of a racial New Order in occupied Europe.

The Holocaust

The ultimate abomination of Nazi racism was the condemnation of all European Jews and other peoples considered racially inferior to extreme racial persecution and then annihilation in the **Holocaust**, a great spasm of racially inspired mass murder that took place during the Second World War.

Immediately after taking power, the Nazis began to use social, legal, and economic means to persecute Jews and other "undesirable" groups. Between 1938 and 1940, persecution turned deadly in the Nazi euthanasia (mercy killing) campaign, an important step toward genocide. Just as Germany began the war, some 70,000 people with physical and mental disabilities were forced into special hospitals, barracks, and camps. Deemed by Nazi administrators as "unworthy lives" who might "pollute" the German race, they were murdered in cold blood. The victims were mostly ethnic Germans, and the euthanasia campaign was stopped after church leaders and ordinary families spoke out. The staff involved took what they learned in this program with them to the extermination camps the Nazis would soon build in the east (Map 28.3).

The German victory over Poland in 1939 brought some 3 million Jews under Nazi control. Jews living in German-occupied territories were soon forced to move into centralized urban areas known as ghettos. In walled-off districts in cities large and small—two of the most important were in Warsaw and Lodz—hundreds of thousands of Polish Jews were forced to live in highly crowded and unsanitary conditions, without real work or adequate sustenance. Over 500,000 people died in the Nazi ghettos.

The racial violence reached new extremes when the German war of annihilation against the Soviet Union opened in 1941. Three military death squads known as Special Action Units (*Einsatzgruppen*) and other military groups followed the advancing German armies into central Europe. With systematic intent, they moved from town to town shooting Jews and other target populations. The victims of these mobile killing units were often forced to dig their own graves in local woods or country fields before they were shot down. In this way the German armed forces murdered some 2 million innocent civilians.

In late 1941 Hitler and the Nazi leadership, in some still-debated combination, ordered the SS to implement the mass murder of all Jews in Europe. What the Nazi leadership called the "final solution of the Jewish question" had begun. The Germans set up an industrialized killing machine that remains unparalleled. The SS established an extensive network of concentration camps, industrial complexes, and railroad transport lines to imprison and murder Jews and other so-called undesirables, and to exploit their labor before they died. In the occupied eastern territories, the surviving residents of the ghettos were loaded onto trains and taken to camps such as Auschwitz-Birkenau, the best known of the Nazi killing centers, where over 1 million people—the vast majority of them Jews—were murdered in gas chambers. Some few were put to work as expendable laborers. The Jews of Germany and then of occupied western and central Europe were likewise rounded up, put on trains, and sent to the camps. Even after it was quite clear that Germany would lose the war, the killing continued.

The murderous attack on European Jews was the ultimate monstrosity of Nazi racism and racial imperialism. By 1945 the Nazis had killed about 6 million Jews. (See "Individuals in Society: Primo Levi," page 915.) Who was responsible for this terrible crime? Historians continue to debate this critical question. Some lay the

The Holocaust The Nazi drive to establish a racial empire in east-central Europe led to the Holocaust, the mass murder of approximately 6 million Jews during World War II. The Nazis also persecuted and killed millions of Slavic peoples, Gypsies (Sinta and Roma), Soviet prisoners of war, communists, and other groups deemed undesirable by the Nazi state. In this horrifying photograph, German soldiers and members of the Reich Labor Service look on as a member of a Special Action Unit (*Einsatzgruppe*) executes a Ukrainian Jew who kneels at the edge of a mass grave. (Library of Congress, LC-USZ61-671)

guilt on Hitler and the Nazi leadership, arguing that ordinary Germans had little knowledge of the extermination camps or were forced to participate by Nazi terror and totalitarian control. Other scholars conclude that far more Germans knew about and were at best indifferent to the fate of "racial inferiors."

Yet the question remains: what inspired those who actually worked

Holocaust The systematic effort of the Nazi state to exterminate all European Jews and other groups deemed racially inferior during the Second World War.

Map 28.3 The Holocaust, 1941–1945 The leadership of Nazi Germany established an extensive network of ghettos and concentration and extermination camps to persecute their political opponents and those people deemed "racially undesirable" by the regime. The death camps, where the Nazi SS systematically murdered millions of European Jews, Soviet prisoners of war, and others, were located primarily in Nazi-occupied territories in eastern Europe, but the conditions in the concentration camps within Germany's borders were almost as brutal.

in the killing machine—the "desk murderers" in Berlin who sent trains to the east, the soldiers in the military units who shot Jews in the Polish forests, the guards at Auschwitz? Some historians believe that extremist and widely shared anti-Semitism led "ordinary Germans" to become Hitler's "willing executioners." Others argue that heightened peer pressure, the desire to advance in the ranks, and the need to prove one's strength under the most brutalizing wartime violence turned average Germans into reluctant killers. The conditioning of racist Nazi propaganda clearly played a role. Whatever the motivation, numerous Germans were somehow prepared to join the SS ideologues and perpetrate ever-greater crimes, from mistreatment to arrest to mass murder.[9]

Japanese Empire and the War in the Pacific

The racist war of annihilation in Europe was matched by racially inspired warfare in East Asia. In response to political divisions and economic crisis, a fascist government had taken control of Japan in the 1930s. As in Nazi Germany and fascist Italy, the Japanese system was highly nationalistic and militaristic and was deeply committed to imperial expansion. The Japanese shared extremist European ideas about racial hierarchy, but with a twist. According to Japanese theorists, the Asian races were far superior to western Aryans. In speeches, schools, and newspapers, ultranationalists eagerly voiced the extreme anti-Western views that had risen in the 1920s and 1930s. They glorified the warrior virtues of honor

INDIVIDUALS IN SOCIETY

MOST JEWS DEPORTED TO AUSCHWITZ WERE MURDERED as soon as they arrived, but the Nazis made some prisoners into slave laborers, and a few of them survived. Primo Levi (1919–1987), an Italian Jew who was one of these laborers, lived to become one of the most influential witnesses to the Holocaust and its death camps.

Like much of Italy's small Jewish community, Levi's family belonged to the urban professional classes. Primo graduated from the University of Turin with highest honors in chemistry in 1941. But starting in 1938, when Italy introduced racial laws, he had faced growing discrimination, and in 1943 he joined the antifascist resistance movement. Quickly captured, he was deported to Auschwitz with 650 Italian Jews in February 1944. Stone-faced SS men picked only 96 men, Levi among them, and 29 women from this transport to work in their respective labor camps; the rest were gassed upon arrival.

Levi and his fellow Jewish prisoners were kicked, punched, stripped, branded with tattoos, crammed into huts, and worked unmercifully. Hoping for some sign of prisoner solidarity in this terrible environment, Levi found only a desperate struggle of each against all and enormous status differences among prisoners. Many stunned and bewildered newcomers, beaten and demoralized by their bosses — the most privileged prisoners — simply collapsed and died. Others struggled to secure their own privileges, however small, because food rations and working conditions were so abominable that ordinary Jewish prisoners perished in two to three months.

Sensitive and noncombative, Levi found himself sinking into oblivion. But instead of joining the mass of the "drowned," he became one of the "saved" — a complicated surprise with moral implications that he would ponder all his life. As Levi explained in *Survival in Auschwitz* (1947), the usual road to salvation in the camps was some kind of collaboration with German power. Savage German criminals were released from prison to become brutal camp guards; non-Jewish political prisoners competed for jobs entitling them to better conditions; and, especially troubling for Levi, a small number of Jewish men plotted and struggled for the power of life and death over other Jewish prisoners.

Though not one of these Jewish bosses, Levi believed that he himself, like almost all survivors, had entered the "gray zone" of moral compromise. "Nobody can know for how long and under what trials his soul can resist before yielding or breaking," Levi wrote. "The harsher the oppression, the more widespread among the oppressed is the willingness, with all its infinite nuances and motivations, to collaborate."* According to Levi, there were no saints in the concentration camps: the Nazi system degraded its victims, forcing them to commit sometimes bestial acts against their fellow prisoners in order to survive.

For Levi, compromise and salvation came from his profession. Interviewed by a German technocrat for work in the camp's synthetic rubber program, Levi spoke fluent German, including scientific terminology, and so was chosen for this relatively easy labor. Work in the warm camp laboratory offered Levi opportunities to pilfer equipment that could then be traded to other prisoners for food and necessities. Levi also gained critical support from three prisoners who refused to do wicked and hateful acts. And he counted "luck" as essential for his survival: in the camp infirmary with scarlet fever in February 1945 as advancing Russian armies prepared to liberate the camp, Levi was not evacuated by the Nazis and shot to death like most Jewish prisoners.

After the war Primo Levi was haunted by the nightmare that the Holocaust would be ignored or forgotten. Ashamed that so many people whom he considered better than himself had perished, and wanting the world to understand the genocide in all its complexity so that never again would people tolerate such atrocities, he turned to writing about his experiences. He grappled tirelessly with his vision of individual choice and moral ambiguity in a hell designed to make the victims collaborate and persecute each other. Bearing witness to the Holocaust, Levi wrote and lectured tirelessly to preserve the memory of Jewish victims and guilty Nazis.

QUESTIONS FOR ANALYSIS

1. Describe Levi's experience at Auschwitz. How did camp prisoners treat each other? Why?

2. What does Levi mean by the "gray zone"?

3. Will a vivid historical memory of the Holocaust help to prevent future genocide?

Primo Levi, who never stopped thinking, writing, and speaking about the Holocaust. (Giansanti/Corbis Sygma)

*Primo Levi, *The Drowned and the Saved* (New York: Vintage, 1989), pp. 43, 60. See also Levi, *Survival in Auschwitz: The Nazi Assault on Humanity*, rev. ed. 1958 (London: Collier Books, 1961). These powerful testimonies are highly recommended.

and sacrifice and proclaimed that Japan would liberate East Asia from Western colonialists.

Japan soon acted on its racial-imperial ambitions. In 1931 Japanese armies invaded and occupied Manchuria, a vast territory bordering northeastern China. In 1937 Japan brutally invaded China itself. Seeking to cement ties with the fascist regimes of Europe, in 1940 the Japanese entered into a formal alliance with Italy and Germany, and in summer 1941 Japanese armies occupied southern portions of the French colony of Indochina (now Vietnam and Cambodia).

The goal was to establish what the Japanese called the Greater East Asia Co-Prosperity Sphere. Under the slogan "Asia for Asians," propagandists maintained that Japanese expansion was intended to liberate East Asian people from the hated Western colonialists. By promising to create a mutually advantageous union for long-term development, the Japanese tapped currents of nationalist sentiment, and most local populations were glad to see the Western Powers go.

But the Co-Prosperity Sphere was a sham. Real power remained in the hands of Japanese military commanders and their superiors in Tokyo, and the occupiers exploited local peoples for Japan's wartime needs. In addition, the Japanese often exhibited great cruelty toward civilian populations and prisoners of war, which aroused local populations against the invaders. Nonetheless, the ability of the Japanese to defeat the Western colonial powers set a powerful example for national liberation groups in East Asia in the years of decolonization that followed World War II.

Japanese expansion in the Pacific evoked a sharp response from the U.S. administration under President Roosevelt, and Japan's leaders came to believe that war with the United States was inevitable. After much debate they decided to launch a surprise attack on the U.S. fleet in Pearl Harbor in the Hawaiian Islands. On December 7, 1941, the Japanese sank or crippled every American battleship, but by chance all the American aircraft carriers were at sea and escaped unharmed. Pearl Harbor brought the Americans into the war in Europe and Asia in a spirit of anger and revenge.

As the Americans mobilized for war, Japanese armies overran more European and American colonies in Southeast Asia. By May 1942 Japan controlled a vast empire (Map 28.4) and was threatening Australia. The Americans pushed back and engaged the Japanese in a series of hard-fought naval battles. In July 1943 the Americans and their Australian allies opened a successful island-hopping campaign that slowly forced Japan out of its conquered territories. The war in the Pacific was extremely brutal—a "war without mercy," in the words of a leading American scholar—and atrocities were committed on both sides. A product of spiraling violence, mutual hatred, and dehumanizing racial stereotypes, the fighting intensified as the United States moved toward Japan.[10]

The "Hinge of Fate"

While the Nazis and the Japanese built their savage empires, Great Britain, the United States, and the Soviet Union joined together in a military pact Churchill termed the Grand Alliance. This was a matter of chance more than choice. Only the Japanese surprise attack had brought the isolationist United States into the war. Moreover, the British and Americans were determined opponents of Soviet communism, and disagreements between the Soviets and the capitalist powers sowed mutual distrust. Stalin repeatedly urged Britain and the United States to open a second front to relieve pressure on Soviet forces by attacking the Germans in western Europe, but Churchill and Roosevelt refused until the summer of 1944. Despite such tensions, the overriding goal of defeating the Axis powers brought together these reluctant allies.

To ease tensions, the Grand Alliance agreed on a policy of "Europe first." Only after Hitler was defeated would the Allies mount an all-out attack on Japan, the lesser threat. The Allies also agreed to concentrate on immediate military needs, postponing tough political questions about the eventual peace settlement that might have divided them. To further encourage mutual trust, the Allies adopted the principle of the unconditional surrender of Germany and Japan. This policy cemented the Grand Alliance because it denied Hitler any hope of dividing his foes. It also meant that Soviet and Anglo-American armies would almost certainly be forced to invade and occupy all of Germany, and that Japan would fight to the bitter end.

The military resources of the Grand Alliance were awesome. The United States harnessed its vast industrial base to wage global war and in 1943 outproduced not only Germany, Italy, and Japan, but all of the rest of the world combined. Great Britain became an impregnable floating fortress, a gigantic frontline staging area for the decisive blow to the heart of Germany. After a determined push, the Soviet Union's military strength was so great that it might well have defeated Germany without Western help. Stalin drew heavily on the heroic resolve of the Soviet people, especially those in the central Russian heartland. Broad-based Russian nationalism, as opposed to narrow communist ideology, became a powerful unifying force in what the Soviet people appropriately called the Great Patriotic War of the Fatherland.

The combined might of the Allies forced back the Nazi New Order on all fronts (see Map 28.2). In North Africa, heavy fighting between British and Axis forces had resulted in significant German advances. At the Battle of El Alamein (el al-uh-MAYN) in May 1942, British forces decisively defeated combined German and Italian armies and halted the Axis penetration of North Africa. Winston Churchill called the battle the "hinge of fate" that cemented Allied victory. Shortly

Map 28.4 World War II in the Pacific In 1942 Japanese forces overran an enormous amount of territory, which the Allies slowly recaptured in a long, bitter struggle. As this map shows, Japan still held a large Asian empire in August 1945 when the unprecedented devastation of atomic warfare suddenly forced it to surrender.

thereafter, an Anglo-American force landed in Morocco and Algeria. These French possessions, which were under the control of Pétain's Vichy government, went over to the Allies. Fearful of an Allied invasion across the Mediterranean, in November 1942 German forces occupied Vichy France, and the collaborationist French government effectively ceased to exist.

After driving the Axis powers out of North Africa, in spring 1943 U.S. and British forces invaded Sicily and then mainland Italy. Mussolini was overthrown by a coup d'état, and the new Italian government publicly accepted unconditional surrender. The Germans had anticipated such a move. Nazi armies invaded and seized control of northern and central Italy, and German paratroopers rescued Mussolini in a daring raid and put him at the head of a puppet government. Facing stiff German resistance, the Allies battled their way up the Italian peninsula. The Germans still held northern Italy, but they were clearly on the defensive.

The spring of 1943 brought crucial Allied victories at sea and in the air. In the first years of the war, Ger-

man submarines had successfully attacked North Atlantic shipping, severely hampering the British war effort. New antisubmarine technologies favored the Allies. Soon massive convoys of hundreds of ships were streaming across the Atlantic, bringing much-needed troops and supplies from the United States to Britain.

The German air force had never really recovered from its defeat in the Battle of Britain. With almost unchallenged air superiority, the United States and Britain now mounted massive bombing raids on German cities to maim industrial production and break civilian morale. By the war's end, hardly a German city of any size remained untouched, and many—including Dresden, Hamburg, Berlin, and Cologne—lay in ruins.

Great Britain and the United States had made critical advances in the western theater of operations, but the German forces suffered worse defeats at the hands of the Red Army on the eastern front. Although the Germans had almost captured the major cities of Moscow and Leningrad in early winter 1941, they were forced back by determined Soviet counterattacks. The Germans mounted a second and initially successful invasion of the Soviet Union in the summer of 1942, but the campaign turned into a disaster. The downfall came at the Battle of Stalingrad, when in November 1942 the Soviets surrounded and systematically destroyed the entire German Sixth Army of 300,000 men. In January 1943 only 123,000 soldiers were left to surrender. Hitler, who had refused to allow a retreat, suffered a catastrophic defeat. For the first time, German public opinion turned decisively against the war. In summer 1943 the larger, better-equipped Soviet armies took the offensive and began to push the Germans back along the entire eastern front (see Map 28.2).

Allied Victory

The balance of power was now clearly in Allied hands, yet bitter fighting continued in Europe for almost two years. Germany, less fully mobilized for war than Britain in 1941, stepped up its efforts. The German war industry, under the Nazi minister of armaments Albert Speer, put to work millions of prisoners of war and slave laborers from across occupied Europe. Between early 1942 and July 1944, German war production tripled despite heavy Anglo-American bombing.

German resistance against Hitler also failed to halt the fighting. An unsuccessful attempt by conservative army leaders to assassinate Hitler in July 1944 only brought increased repression by the fanatic Nazis who had taken over the government. Closely disciplined by the regime, frightened by the prospect of unconditional surrender, and terrorized by Nazi propaganda

that portrayed the advancing Russian armies as rapacious Slavic beasts, the Germans fought on with suicidal resolve.

On June 6, 1944, American and British forces under General Dwight Eisenhower landed on the beaches of Normandy, France, in history's greatest naval invasion. In a hundred dramatic days, more than 2 million men and almost half a million vehicles pushed inland and broke through the German lines. Rejecting proposals to strike straight at Berlin in a massive attack, Eisenhower moved forward cautiously on a broad front. Not until March 1945 did American troops cross the Rhine and enter Germany. By spring of 1945 the Allies had also pushed the Germans out of the Italian peninsula. That April, Mussolini was captured in northern Italy by antifascist communist partisans and executed, along with his mistress and other fascist leaders.

The Soviets, who had been advancing steadily since July 1943, reached the outskirts of Warsaw by August 1944. Anticipating German defeat, the Polish underground Home Army ordered an uprising, so that the Poles might take the city on their own and establish independence from the Soviets. The Warsaw Uprising was a tragic miscalculation. Citing military pressure, the Red Army refused to enter the city and allowed the Germans to destroy the Polish insurgents. Only after the Home Army surrendered did the Red Army continue its advance. Warsaw was decimated, and between 150,000 and 200,000 Poles—mostly civilians—lost their lives.

Over the next six months, the Soviets moved southward into Romania, Hungary, and Yugoslavia. In January 1945 the Red Army crossed Poland into Germany,

German Prisoners of War After the Battle of Stalingrad
Wrapped in coats and blankets to protect against the bitter Russian winter, these German prisoners of war were marched through the destroyed streets of Stalingrad after their defeat in February 1943. The battle was a major turning point that marked the start of the destruction of Nazi Germany. Hundreds of thousands of soldiers on both sides lost their lives, and of the approximately 100,000 German prisoners taken by the Red Army only about 5,000 returned home after the war. (Corbis)

Nuclear Wasteland at Hiroshima Only a handful of buildings remain standing in the ruins of Hiroshima in September 1945. Fearing the costs of a prolonged ground and naval campaign against the Japanese mainland, the United States dropped atomic bombs on Hiroshima and Nagasaki in August 1945. The bombings ended the war and opened the nuclear age. (AP Images)

and on April 26 met American forces on the Elbe River. The Allies had closed their vise on Nazi Germany and had overrun Europe. As Soviet forces fought their way into Berlin, Hitler committed suicide in his bunker, and on May 8 the remaining German commanders capitulated.

The war in the Pacific also drew to a close. In spite of repeated U.S. victories, Japanese troops had continued to fight with enormous courage and determination. American commanders believed the conquest of Japan might cost a million American casualties and claim 10 to 20 million Japanese lives. In fact, Japan was almost helpless, its industry and dense, fragile wooden cities largely destroyed by intense American bombing. Yet the Japanese seemed determined to fight on, ready to die for a hopeless cause.

On August 6 and 9, 1945, after much discussion at the upper levels of the U.S. government, American planes dropped atomic bombs on Hiroshima and Nagasaki in Japan. The mass bombing of cities and civilians, one of the terrible new practices of World War II, now ended in the final nightmare—unprecedented human destruction in a single blinding flash. On August 14, 1945, the Japanese announced their surrender. The Second World War, which had claimed the lives of more than 50 million soldiers and civilians, was over.

 LOOKING BACK LOOKING AHEAD THE FIRST HALF of the twentieth century brought almost unimaginable violence and destruction, leading historian Eric Hobsbawm to label the era the "age of catastrophe."[11] Shaken by the rapid cultural change and economic collapse that followed the tragedy of World War I, many Europeans embraced the radical politics of communism and fascism. For some, visions of a classless society or a racially pure national community offered a way out of the age of anxiety. Totalitarian dictators like Stalin and Hitler capitalized on the desire for social order, building dictatorial regimes that demanded total allegiance to an ideological vision. Even as these regimes rewarded supporters and promised ordinary people a new age, they ruthlessly repressed their enemies, real and imagined. The vision proved fatal: the great clash of ideologies that emerged in the 1920s and 1930s led to history's most deadly war, killing millions and devastating large swathes of Europe and East Asia.

Only the reluctant Grand Alliance of the liberal United States and Great Britain with the communist Soviet Union was able to defeat the Axis powers. After 1945, fascism was finished, discredited by total defeat and the postwar revelation of the Holocaust. To make sure, the Allies would occupy the lands of their former enemies. Rebuilding a devastated Europe proved a challenging but in the end manageable task: once recovery took off, the postwar decades brought an economic boom that led to levels of prosperity unimaginable in the interwar years. Maintaining an alliance between the capitalist West and the communist East was something else. Trust quickly broke down. Europe was divided into two hostile camps, and Cold War tensions between East and West would dominate European and world politics for the next fifty years.

CHAPTER REVIEW

▦ How did radical totalitarian dictatorship differ from conservative authoritarianism, and in what ways were communism and fascism totalitarian systems? (p. 888)

Conservative authoritarianism was a familiar form of government in Europe. Such states were concerned with preserving the status quo. They limited political participation but for the most part did not interfere in the lives of their citizens. Totalitarian dictatorships, such as Stalin's Soviet Union, Hitler's Germany, and to some extent Mussolini's Italy, were very different. Using censorship, propaganda, and harsh repression, communists and fascists tried to gain total control over their populations in order to construct radically new societies. Both types of totalitarian societies sought to remake state and society, but communists tried to build a classless international brotherhood of workers while fascists placed the nation above all. The Nazis, the most extreme fascists, tried to construct a state based on racial exclusion.

▦ How did Stalin and the Communist Party build a modern totalitarian state in the Soviet Union? (p. 891)

Stalin consolidated his power in the 1920s, and in 1928 he launched the five-year plans. In doing so, Stalin's Soviet Union asserted a total claim on the lives of its citizens. It posed ambitious goals in the form of rapid state-directed industrialization and savage collectivization of agriculture. And it found enthusiastic supporters who believed that Stalin and the Communist Party were building their kind of socialism and a new socialist personality at home. Relentless propaganda and the great purges reinforced the party's unlimited control of its citizens.

▦ How did Mussolini's dictatorship come to power and govern in Italy? (p. 898)

Mussolini began as a socialist, but he turned to the right when he received growing support from conservatives. His private militia of Black Shirts used intimidation and violence to take over the government. Coming to power "legally" with the king's help, Mussolini proclaimed the revolutionary totalitarian character of his one-party rule, implementing state control of the press and education, rigging elections, and disbanding all labor unions. Nevertheless, his fascist party received broad support, in part because he was willing to compromise with the army and business leaders. In this way, Mussolini's government retained many elements of conservative authoritarianism, such as compromising with the Catholic Church and keeping women in traditional roles.

▦ How did Hitler gain power, what policies did totalitarian Nazi Germany pursue, and why did they lead to World War II? (p. 900)

Failing to overthrow the government in an attempted coup in 1923, Hitler came to power legally in 1933 by promising voters national renewal and economic recovery from the Great Depression. His policies appeared to help the economy, and he quickly established a one-party totalitarian regime with ambitious goals and widespread popular support. Through legal manipulation, repression, and violence, the Nazis controlled all aspects of the German state and society. But whereas Stalin concentrated on building socialism at home, Hitler and the Nazi elite aimed at unlimited territorial and racial aggression on behalf of a master race against Jews and other peoples they deemed undesirable. He proceeded gradually at first, and Britain and France sought to appease him with various diplomatic concessions. Hitler's unprovoked attack on Poland in 1939 brought a military response from Britain and France and the beginning of World War II.

■ How did Germany and Japan create enormous empires, and how were they defeated by the Allies? (page 909)

Germany used force to implement a policy of territorial expansion based on race and space, first with the Western European democracies, then with its eastern neighbors in a quest to create living space for a German master race. Hitler's forces overran much of western and eastern Europe, plundered the occupied territories to enrich Germans and support the war effort, and annihilated millions of Jews and other "subhumans." Allied with Germany after Pearl Harbor, Japan too had racial-imperial ambitions and used its army to invade Manchuria, China, and other parts of Southeast Asia in order to create a Japanese empire under the pretense of "Asia for Asians." But unlimited aggression unwittingly forged a mighty coalition led by Britain, the Soviet Union, and the United States. This Grand Alliance held together to smash the racist Nazi empire in Europe and destroy Japan's vast, overextended empire in the Pacific.

Suggested Reading

Aly, Götz. *Hitler's Beneficiaries: Plunder, Racial War, and the Nazi Welfare State.* 2005. A controversial interpretation of popular support for the Hitler regime focused on the material benefits of wartime plunder.

Applebaum, Anne. *Gulag: A History.* 2004. An excellent study of Soviet police terror.

Bergen, Doris. *War and Genocide: A Concise History of the Holocaust,* 2d ed. 2009. A concise and accessible discussion of National Socialism and the murderous Nazi assault on European Jews and other groups.

Bosworth, R. J. B. *Mussolini's Italy: Life Under the Fascist Dictatorship, 1915–1945.* 2007. An outstanding study of Italy under Mussolini.

Browning, Christopher R. *Ordinary Men: Reserve Police Battalion 101 and the Final Solution in Poland,* 2d ed. 2001. A carefully researched, unnerving account of German atrocities in Poland during World War II.

Burleigh, Michael. *The Third Reich: A New History.* 2001. A splendid accomplishment that refurbishes the concept of totalitarianism.

Conquest, Robert. *The Great Terror: A Reassessment.* 1991. An excellent account of Stalin's purges of the 1930s.

Fitzpatrick, Sheila, and Michael Geyer, eds. *Beyond Totalitarianism: Stalinism and Nazism Compared.* 2009. A collection of essays that challenges the usefulness of the totalitarian model by comparing the two dictatorships.

Kaplan, Marion A. *Between Dignity and Despair: Jewish Life in Nazi Germany.* 1998. A deeply moving book about the Jewish response to the Holocaust, with a compelling focus on women's history.

Kotkin, Stephen. *Magnetic Mountain: Stalinism as Civilization.* 1995. An extraordinary account of Stalinism and forced industrialization in the 1930s.

Merridale, Catherine. *Ivan's War: Life and Death in the Red Army, 1939–1945.* 2007. A fascinating account of ordinary Soviet soldiers.

Ransel, David L. *Village Mothers: Three Generations of Change in Russia and Tataria.* 2005. A pathbreaking study based on oral histories made in the 1990s.

Roberts, David D. *The Totalitarian Experiment in Twentieth-Century Europe: Understanding the Poverty of Great Politics.* 2006. Makes a case for the totalitarian model by comparing Stalinism, Nazism, and Italian fascism.

Weinberg, Gerhard L. *World at Arms: A Global History of World War II,* new ed. 2005. A masterful military history of World War II that places Europe in global context.

Williamson, D. G. *The Age of the Dictators: A Study of the European Dictatorships, 1918–53.* 2007. An accessible overview.

Notes

1. Quoted in S. Kotkin, *Magnetic Mountain: Stalinism as a Civilization* (Berkeley: University of California Press, 1997), pp. 221–222.
2. R. Thurston, *Life and Terror in Stalin's Russia, 1934–1941* (New Haven, Conn.: Yale University Press, 1996), esp. pp. 16–106; also M. Malia, *The Soviet Tragedy: A History of Socialism in Russia, 1917–1991* (New York: Free Press, 1995), pp. 227–270.
3. Quoted in V. de Grazia, *How Fascism Ruled Women: Italy, 1922–1945* (Berkeley: University of California Press, 1992), p. 236.
4. Quoted in C. Duggan, *A Concise History of Italy* (New York: Cambridge University Press, 1994), p. 227.
5. Quoted in ibid, p. 234.
6. M. Burleigh and W. Wippermann, *The Racial State: Germany 1933–1945* (New York: Cambridge University Press, 1991).
7. W. Stuckart and H. Globke, "Commentary on the German Racial Law" (1936), quoted in G. Mosse, *Nazi Culture: A Documentary History* (New York: Schocken, 1981), p. 332.
8. On the German occupation of Belarus, see C. Gerlach, "German Economic Interests, Occupation Policy, and the Murder of the Jews in Belorussia, 1941–43," in U. Herbert, ed., *National Socialist Extermination Policies: Contemporary German Perspectives and Controversies* (New York: Berghan Books, 2000), pp. 210–239. See also M. Allen, *The Business of Genocide: The SS, Slave Labor, and the Concentration Camps* (Chapel Hill: University of North Carolina Press, 2002), pp. 270–285.
9. D. Goldhagen, *Hitler's Willing Executioners: Ordinary Germans and the Holocaust* (New York: Vintage Books, 1997); for an alternate explanation see C. Browning, *Ordinary Men: Reserve Police Battalion 101 and the Final Solution in Poland* (New York: Harper, 1992).
10. J. Dower, *War Without Mercy: Race and Power in the Pacific War* (New York: Pantheon, 1986).
11. E. Hobsbawm, *The Age of Extremes: A History of the World, 1914–1991* (New York: Vintage, 1996), p. 21.

Key Terms

totalitarianism (p. 888)
fascism (p. 889)
eugenics (p. 889)
five-year plan (p. 891)
New Economic Policy (NEP) (p. 891)
collectivization of agriculture (p. 893)
kulaks (p. 893)
Black Shirts (p. 898)
Lateran Agreement (p. 900)
National Socialism (p. 901)
Enabling Act (p. 903)
appeasement (p. 907)
New Order (p. 910)
Holocaust (p. 912)

For practice quizzes and other study tools, visit the Online Study Guide at **bedfordstmartins.com/mckaywest**.

For primary sources from this period, see *Sources of Western Society*, Second Edition.

For Web sites, images, and documents related to topics in this chapter, visit Make History at **bedfordstmartins.com/mckaywest**.

29
Cold War Conflict and Consensus

1945–1965

The defeat of the Nazis and their allies in 1945 left Europe in ruins, but also laid the basis for one of Western civilization's most remarkable recoveries. In the immediate postwar years, Europeans struggled to overcome the effects of rampant death and destruction, and the victorious Allies worked to shape an effective peace treaty. Disagreements between the Soviet Union and the Western allies emerged during the peace process and quickly led to an apparently endless Cold War between the two new superpowers — the United States and the Soviet Union.

Europe was divided into a Soviet-aligned Eastern bloc and a U.S.-aligned Western bloc, and Cold War rivalry spurred military, economic, and technological competition. Amid these overarching tensions, battered western Europe fashioned a great renaissance, building strong democratic institutions and vibrant economies. After a period of political repression, the Soviet Union and the East Bloc also saw some reforms, leading to stability there as well.

But the postwar period was by no means peaceful. Anti-Soviet uprisings across eastern Europe led to military intervention and tragedy for thousands. Colonial independence movements in the developing world sometimes erupted in violence, even after liberation was achieved. Cold War hostilities had an immense impact on the decolonization process, often to the detriment of formerly colonized peoples.

Global Cold War conflicts notwithstanding, the postwar decades witnessed the construction of a surprisingly durable consensus in both communist eastern Europe and liberal western Europe. At the same time, changing class structures, new roles for women and youths, and new migration patterns had a profound impact on European society, laying the groundwork for major transformations in the decades to come. ■

Georgios Makkas/Alamy

Life in Eastern Europe. This relief sculpture, a revealing example of socialist realism from 1952 that portrays a mail carrier, industrial workers, and peasants, adorns the wall of the central post office in Banská Bystrica, a regional capital in present-day Slovakia (the former Czechoslovakia). Citizens in the Soviet satellite nations of the East Bloc frequently saw similar works of public art, which idealized the dignity of ordinary laborers and the advantages of communism.

CHAPTER PREVIEW

Postwar Europe and the Origins of the Cold War
■ How did the events at the close of World War II contribute to the emergence of the Cold War, and how did the U.S.-Soviet rivalry affect life in Europe?

The Western Renaissance
■ Why did western Europe recover so successfully, and what were the sources of postwar stability?

Soviet Eastern Europe
■ What was the pattern of postwar rebuilding and development in the Soviet Union and communist eastern Europe?

The End of Empires
■ What circumstances led to the postwar colonial independence movements, and how did the Cold War influence the process?

Postwar Social Transformations
■ How did large-scale changes in social structures and relations contribute to European stability on both sides of the iron curtain?

Postwar Europe and the Origins of the Cold War

How did the events at the close of World War II contribute to the emergence of the Cold War, and how did the U.S.-Soviet rivalry affect life in Europe? ▪

In 1945 triumphant American and Soviet soldiers came together and embraced on the banks of the Elbe River in the heart of vanquished Germany. At home, in the United States and in the Soviet Union, the soldiers' loved ones erupted in joyous celebration. Yet millions had perished in the war, Europe was devastated, and countless refugees wandered through the rubble.

The victors now faced the momentous challenges of rebuilding the shattered European nations, dealing with Nazi criminals, and creating a lasting peace. Reconstruction began, and war crimes were punished, but the Allies failed to truly cooperate in peacemaking. Motivated by different goals and hounded by misunderstandings, the United States and the Soviet Union soon found themselves at loggerheads. By the end of 1947 Europe was rigidly divided into East and West Blocs allied with the Soviet Union and the United States, respectively. The resulting Cold War was waged around the world for the next forty years as the competing superpowers engaged in an all-out competition for political, military, and technological superiority.

The Legacies of the Second World War

In the summer of 1945 Europe lay in ruins. Across the continent, the fighting had destroyed cities and landscapes and had obliterated buildings, factories, farms, rail tracks, roads, and bridges. Many cities—including Leningrad, Warsaw, Vienna, Budapest, Rotterdam, and Coventry—were completely devastated. Surviving cities such as Prague and Paris were left relatively unscathed, mostly by chance. The Germans had engaged in bombing attacks against London and other cities, destroying vast swathes of property and killing tens of thousands of innocent civilians. Allied air assaults on civilian targets were even more destructive. British and American bombers had flattened Hamburg, Dresden, and other German cities large and small, with great loss of life. As opposing armies seesawed between Warsaw and Moscow, the scorched earth policy had left few buildings stand-

Displaced Persons in the Ruins of Berlin The end of the war in 1945 stopped the fighting, but not the suffering. For the next two years, millions of displaced persons wandered the streets of Europe searching for sustenance, lost family members, and a place to call home. (Fred Rampage/Getty Images)

ing. Postwar observers compared the remaining rubble piles to moonscapes.

The human costs of the Second World War are almost incalculable (Map 29.1). The death toll far exceeded the mortality figures for World War I. The war killed at least 20 million Soviets, including soldiers and civilians. Between 9 and 11 million noncombatants lost their lives in Nazi concentration camps, including 6 million Jews and over 220,000 Sinti and Roma Gypsies. One out of every five Poles died in the war, including 3 million of Poland's 3.25 million Jews. German deaths numbered 5 million, only 3 million of them soldiers. France and Britain both lost fewer soldiers than in World War I, but the British civilian population suffered 60,000 dead and 300,000 wounded. Over 400,000 U.S. soldiers died in the European and Pacific campaigns, and other nations across Europe and the globe also lost staggering numbers. The best estimates are that about 50 million human beings perished in the conflict.

The destruction of war furthermore left tens of millions homeless — 25 million in the Soviet Union and 20 million in Germany alone, joined by countless French, Czechs, Poles, Italians, and others. The wartime policies of Hitler and Stalin had forced some 30 million people from their homes in the hardest hit nations of east-central Europe. The end of the war and the start of the peace increased their numbers. Some 13 million ethnic Germans fled west before the advancing Soviet troops or were forced to leave the states of eastern Europe under the terms of the peace accords. Forced laborers from Poland, France, the Balkans, and other nations, brought to Germany by the Nazis, now sought to go home. A woman in Berlin described the flow of refugees passing through the city in spring 1945:

> The streets were filled with small, tired caravans of people. . . . Most were headed east. All the vehicles looked the same: pitiful handcarts piled high with sacks, crates, and trunks. Often I saw a woman or an older child in front, harnessed to a rope, pulling the cart forward, with the smaller children or a grandpa pushing from behind. There were people perched on top, too, usually very little children or elderly relatives. The old people look terrible amid all the junk, the men as well as the women — pale, dilapidated, apathetic. Half-dead sacks of bones.[1]

These **displaced persons** or DPs — their numbers increased by concentration camp survivors, released prisoners of war, and hundreds of thousands of orphaned children — searched for food and shelter. From 1945 to 1947 the newly established United Nations Relief and Rehabilitation Administration (UNRRA) opened over 760 DP camps and spent $10 billion to house, feed, clothe, and repatriate the refugees.

For DPs, going home was not always the best option. Soviet and Eastern European nationals who had spent time in the West were seen as politically unreliable by the new Stalinist regimes of the Soviet bloc. Many faced prison terms, exile to labor camps in the Siberian gulag, and even execution upon their return. Jewish DPs faced unique problems. Their communities had been destroyed, there was persistent anti-Semitism, and for the most part they were not welcome in their former homelands. Many stayed in special Jewish DP camps in Germany for years. After the creation of Israel in 1948 (see page 947), over 330,000 European Jews left the continent where they had experienced so much suffering and destruction for the new Jewish state. By 1957, when the last DP camp closed, the UNRRA had cared for and resettled many millions of refugees under the most difficult conditions.

Postwar authorities were also left to deal with the crimes committed by the Nazis. Across Europe and

displaced persons Postwar refugees, including 13 million Germans, former Nazi prisoners and forced laborers, and orphaned children.

Chronology

1945	Yalta Conference; end of World War II; Potsdam Conference; Nuremberg trials
1945–1960s	Decolonization of Asia and Africa
1945–1965	United States takes lead in Big Science
1947	Truman Doctrine; Marshall Plan
1948	Founding of Israel
1948–1949	Berlin airlift
1949	Creation of East and West Germany; formation of NATO; establishment of COMECON
1950–1953	Korean War
1953	Death of Stalin
1955–1964	Khrushchev rises to power; de-Stalinization of Soviet Union
1955	Warsaw Pact founded
1956	Pasternak, *Doctor Zhivago*; Suez crisis
1957	Formation of Common Market
1961	Building of Berlin Wall
1962	Cuban missile crisis; Solzhenitsyn, *One Day in the Life of Ivan Denisovich*
1964	Brezhnev replaces Khrushchev as Soviet leader

FINLAND
Helsinki
From Finland, 1940-1956
Leningrad

NORWAY
Oslo
SWEDEN
Stockholm

ESTONIA
to U.S.S.R. 1940

GREAT BRITAIN
IRELAND • Dublin

LATVIA
to U.S.S.R., 1940

Moscow

North Sea

DENMARK
Copenhagen

Baltic Sea

LITHUANIA
to U.S.S.R. 1940

Königsberg
Incorp. into U.S.S.R. 1945

SOVIET UNION

Coventry
London

Hamburg
U.S. Zone
Kiel
Soviet Zone
Bremen

Berlin

Warsaw
Brest

Amsterdam
NETHERLANDS
Rotterdam
British Zone
Brussels
BELGIUM
Cologne
Bonn
WEST GERMANY
Frankfurt
EAST GERMANY

Incorporated into Poland, 1945

from Poland, 1940-1947

Kiev

ATLANTIC OCEAN

Caen
Paris
LUX.
Würzburg
U.S. Zone

Dresden
Prague
Kraków

POLAND

UKRAINE

Dnieper R.

From Czechoslovakia, 1945-1947

From Romania, 1940-1947

FRANCE

French Zone
Bern
SWITZ.
Munich
French Zone

U.S. Zone
Soviet Zone
Vienna
British Zone

CZECHOSLOVAKIA

BESSARABIA

AUSTRIA
Milan

HUNGARY
Budapest

ROMANIA

Yalta

PORTUGAL
Lisbon
Madrid
SPAIN

Genoa
ITALY
Bologna

From Italy, 1945

Belgrade
YUGOSLAVIA

Danube R.

Ploești
Bucharest

Black Sea

Corsica

Rome

Adriatic Sea

BULGARIA
Sofia

From Romania, 1940

Balearic Is.

Sardinia

Tiranë
Naples
ALBANIA

Istanbul
Ankara

Refugee movements
Baltic →
Czech →
Finns →
Germans →
Poles →
Russians →
Peoples settled by International Refugee Organization →

Sicily

Malta

GREECE
Athens

TURKEY

City substantially destroyed
Allied occupation of Germany and Austria, 1945-1955
Territory lost by Germany
Territory gained by Soviet Union

0   100   200 miles
0 100 200 kilometers

Crete

Cyprus

Mediterranean Sea

Mapping the Past

Map 29.1 **The Aftermath of World War II in Europe, ca. 1945–1950** By 1945 millions of people displaced by war and territorial changes were on the move. The Soviet Union and Poland took land from Germany, which the Allies partitioned into occupation zones. Those zones subsequently formed the basis of the East and West German states. Austria was detached from Germany, but the Soviets subsequently permitted Austria to reunify as a neutral state.

ANALYZING THE MAP Which groups fled west? Who went east? How would you characterize the general direction of most of these movements?

CONNECTIONS What does the widespread movement of people at the end of the war suggest about the war? What does it suggest about the ensuing political climate?

To complete this activity online, go to the Online Study Guide at bedfordstmartins.com/mckaywest.

particularly in the east, almost 100,000 Germans and Austrians were convicted of wartime crimes. Many more were investigated or indicted. Collaborators, those non-Germans who had assisted the occupying forces, were also punished. In the days and months immediately after the war, spontaneous acts of retribution brought some collaborators to account. In both France and Italy, unofficial groups seeking revenge summarily executed some 25,000 persons. French women accused of "horizontal collaboration" — having sexual relations with men in the occupying German forces — were publicly humiliated by angry mobs. Newly established postwar governments quickly established authority over questions of guilt and punishment, and in trials across

Europe collaborators were sanctioned or sentenced to prison. A minority received the death sentence.

In Germany, Allied occupation governments set up denazification procedures meant to identify former Nazi Party members and punish those responsible for the worst crimes of the National Socialist state. At the Nuremberg trials (1945–1946), an international military tribunal organized by the four Allied powers—the Soviet Union, the United States, Britain, and France—tried and sentenced the highest-ranking Nazi military and civilian leaders who had survived the war. The twenty-two defendants were charged with war crimes and crimes against humanity. After chilling testimony from victims of the regime, which revealed the full systematic horror of Nazi atrocities, twelve were sentenced to death.

The Nuremberg trials marked the last time the four Allies worked together to punish former Nazis. As the Cold War developed and the Soviets and the Western allies drew increasingly apart, each carried out separate denazification programs in its own zone of occupation. In the West, U.S. military courts at first actively prosecuted leading Nazis. But the huge numbers implicated in Nazi crimes, West German opposition to the proceedings, and the need for stability in the looming Cold War made thorough denazification impractical. Except for the worst offenders, the West had quietly shelved denazification by 1948. The process was similar in the Soviet zone. At first, punishment was swift and harsh. About 45,000 former party officials, upper-class industrialists, and large landowners were identified as Nazis and sentenced to prison or death. As in the West, however, former Nazis who cooperated with the new regime could avoid prosecution, and many soon found leading positions in government and industry in both the Soviet and U.S. zones.

In the years immediately after the war, ordinary people across Europe came to terms with the war and slowly regained normal lives, working at steady civilian jobs, living in good housing, and raising families. Still, the revelation of Nazi barbarism, the destruction of so many lives, and the great disruptions of the postwar years had deeply shaken European confidence. As German philosopher Theodor Adorno wrote in 1951, "There can be no poetry after Auschwitz." Against this background of postwar ruin, despair, and slow recovery, the victorious Allies struggled to shape a reasonable and lasting peace.

The Peace Accords and Cold War Origins

The most powerful allies in the wartime coalition—the Soviet Union and the United States—began to quarrel almost as soon as the unifying threat of Nazi Germany disappeared. The hostility between the Eastern and Western superpowers was the sad but logical outgrowth of military developments, wartime agreements, and long-standing political and ideological differences that stretched back to the Russian Revolution (see Chapter 26).

In the early phases of the Second World War, the Americans and the British made military victory their highest priority. They avoided discussion of Stalin's war aims and the shape of the eventual peace settlement. Stalin received a military alliance only and no postwar commitments. Yet the United States and Britain did not try to take advantage of the Soviet Union's precarious position in 1942 because they feared that hard bargaining would encourage Stalin to consider making a separate peace with Hitler. They focused instead on the policy of unconditional surrender to solidify the alliance. By late 1943 discussion about the shape of the postwar world could no longer be postponed. The conference that the "Big Three"—Stalin, Roosevelt, and Churchill—held in the Iranian capital of Teheran in November 1943 thus proved of crucial importance in determining subsequent events.

At the Teheran Conference, the Big Three jovially reaffirmed their determination to crush Germany, discussed Poland's postwar borders, and crafted a strategy to win the war. Stalin, concerned that the Soviet Union was bearing the brunt of the fighting, asked his allies to relieve his armies by opening a second front in France. Churchill, fearful of the military dangers of a direct attack, argued that American and British forces should follow up their Italian campaign with an indirect attack on Germany through the Balkans. Roosevelt, however, agreed with Stalin that an American-British frontal assault through France would be better. This agreement was part of Roosevelt's general effort to meet Stalin's wartime demands whenever possible, and it had momentous political implications. It meant that the Soviet and the American-British armies would come together in defeated Germany along a north-south line and that only Soviet troops would liberate eastern Europe. Thus the basic shape of postwar Europe was emerging even as the fighting continued.

When the Big Three met again in February 1945 at Yalta on the Black Sea in southern Russia, advancing Soviet armies were within a hundred miles of Berlin. The Red Army had occupied Poland as well as Bulgaria, Romania, Hungary, part of Yugoslavia, and much of Czechoslovakia. The temporarily stalled American-British forces had yet to cross the Rhine into Germany. Moreover, the United States was far from defeating Japan. In short, the Soviet Union's position was strong and America's weak.

There was little the increasingly sick and apprehensive Roosevelt could do but double his bet on Stalin's peaceful intentions. The Allies agreed at the Yalta Conference that each of the victorious powers would occupy

The Big Three In 1945 a triumphant Winston Churchill, an ailing Franklin Roosevelt, and a determined Stalin met at Yalta in southern Russia to plan for peace. Cooperation soon gave way to bitter hostility, and the decisions made by these leaders transformed the map of Europe. (Franklin D. Roosevelt Presidential Library)

a separate zone of Germany, and that the Germans would pay heavy reparations to the Soviet Union. At American insistence, Stalin agreed to declare war on Japan after Germany was defeated. As for Poland, the Big Three agreed that the Soviet Union would permanently incorporate the eastern Polish territories its army had occupied at the start of the war, and that Poland would be compensated with German lands to the west. They also agreed in an ambiguous compromise that eastern European governments were to be freely elected but pro-Russian.

The Yalta compromise over elections in eastern Europe broke down almost immediately. Even before the conference, Bulgaria and Poland were under the control of communists who had arrived home from the eastern front with the Red Army. Elsewhere in eastern Europe, the advancing Soviets formed coalition governments that included Social Democrats and other leftist parties, but reserved key government posts for Moscow-trained communists. At the postwar Potsdam Conference of July 1945, the long-avoided differences over eastern Europe finally surged to the fore. The compromising Roosevelt had died and had been succeeded by the more determined President Harry Truman (r. 1945–1953), who demanded immediate free elections throughout eastern Europe. Stalin refused point-blank. "A freely elected government in any of these East European countries would be anti-Soviet," he admitted simply, "and that we cannot allow."[2]

Here, then, were the keys to the much-debated origins of the Cold War. When the Allies were fighting Germany, they could maintain an alliance of necessity. As

the war drew to a close, however, long-standing hostility between East and West reemerged. Mutual distrust, anxious security concerns, and antagonistic desires for economic and territorial control now destroyed the former partnership.

Stalin, who had lived through two enormously destructive German invasions, was determined to establish a defensive buffer zone of sympathetic states around the Soviet Union and at the same time expand the reach of communism and the Soviet state. Stalin believed that only communists could be truly dependable allies, and that free elections would result in independent and possibly hostile governments on his western border. With Soviet armies in central Europe, there was no way short of war for the United States to control the region's political future. War was out of the question, and Communist regimes would govern in east-central Europe for the next forty-five years. The United States, for its part, wished to maintain liberal democracy and free-market capitalism in western Europe. The Americans quickly showed that they were willing to use their vast political, economic, and military power to maintain predominance in their own sphere of influence.

West Versus East

The Cold War escalated over the next five years as both sides hardened their positions. In May 1945, as the fighting ended, Truman abruptly cut off all aid to the ailing Soviet Union. In October he declared that the United States would never recognize any government established by force against the free will of its people. In March

1946 former British prime minister Churchill ominously informed an American audience that an "iron curtain" had fallen across the continent, dividing Germany and all of Europe into two antagonistic camps (Map 29.2).

Stalin had indeed consolidated his hold on eastern Europe. Recognizing that communists could not take power in free elections, he purged the last remaining noncommunist elements from the coalition governments set up after the war and established Soviet-style one-party communist dictatorships. Stalin's seizure of power in Czechoslovakia in February 1948, after the Czech Communist Party had won significant electoral support, was particularly antidemocratic. It greatly strengthened Western fears of limitless communist expansion.

In the West, the large, well-organized Communist Parties of France and Italy returned to what they called the "struggle against capitalist imperialism." They criticized the growing role of the United States in western Europe and challenged their own governments with violent rhetoric and large strikes. At the same time, com-

munist revolutionaries were waging bitter civil wars in Greece and China (see below and page 947). By the spring of 1947 it appeared to many Americans that Stalin and the Soviet Union were determined to export communism by subversion throughout Europe and around the world.

The United States responded with the **Truman Doctrine**, aimed at "containing" communism to areas already occupied by the Red Army. The United States, President Truman promised, would use diplomatic, economic, and even military means to resist the expansion of communism anywhere on the globe. At first, Truman asked Congress for military aid to Greece and Turkey, countries that Britain, weakened by war and financially overextended, could no longer protect. With American support, both remained in the Western bloc. The U.S. government restructured its military to meet the Soviet threat, pouring money into defense spending and testing nuclear weapons. The

> **Truman Doctrine** America's policy geared to containing communism to those countries already under Soviet control.

Map 29.2 Cold War Europe in the 1950s The Cold War divided Europe into two hostile military alliances that formed to the east and west of an "iron curtain."

> ❝ Our policy [of aid] is not directed against any country or doctrine but against hunger, poverty, desperation, and chaos. ❞
>
> —U.S. SECRETARY OF STATE GEORGE C. MARSHALL

American determination to enforce containment hardened when the Soviets exploded their own atomic bomb in 1949. Emotional, moralistic denunciations of Stalin and communist Russia emerged as part of American public life. At home and abroad, the United States engaged in an anticommunist crusade.

The expansion of the U.S. military was only one aspect of Truman's policy of containment. In 1947 western Europe was still on the verge of economic collapse. Food was scarce across the continent, inflation was high, and black markets flourished. Recognizing that an economically and politically stable western Europe could be an effective block against the popular appeal of communism, U.S. Secretary of State George C. Marshall offered Europe economic aid — the **Marshall Plan** — to help it rebuild. As Marshall wrote in a State Department bulletin:

> *The truth of the matter is that Europe's requirements for the next three or four years of foreign food and other essential products — principally from America — are so much greater than her present ability to pay that she must have substantial additional help or face economic, social, and political deterioration of a very grave character. . . . Our policy [of aid] is not directed against any country or doctrine but against hunger, poverty, desperation, and chaos. Its purpose should be the revival of a working economy in the world so as to permit the emergence of political and social conditions in which free institutions can exist.[3]*

The Marshall Plan was one of the most successful foreign aid programs in history. When it ended in 1951, the United States had given about $13 billion in aid (equivalent to over $200 billion in today's dollars) to fifteen western European nations, and Europe's economy was on the way to recovery. Marshall Plan funding was initially offered to East Bloc countries as well, but fearing Western interference in the Soviet sphere, Stalin rejected the offer. In 1949 the Soviets established the **Council for Mutual Economic Assistance (COME-** CON), an economic organization of communist states intended to rebuild the East Bloc independently of the West. The generous aid of the Marshall Plan was limited to countries in the Western bloc, increasing Cold War tensions.

In the late 1940s Berlin, the capital city of Germany, was on the front line of the Cold War. Like the rest of Germany, Berlin had been divided among the victorious Allies into east and west zones. In June 1948 the Western allies replaced the currency in West Germany and West Berlin, a first move in plans to establish a separate West German state. This action violated the peace accords, and in response Stalin blocked all traffic through the Soviet zone of Germany to Berlin in an attempt to reunify the city under Soviet control. Acting firmly, the Western allies coordinated around-the-clock flights of hundreds of planes over the Soviet roadblocks, supplying provisions to West Berliners and thwarting Soviet efforts to swallow up the western half of the city. After 324 days, the Berlin airlift had proven successful, and the Soviets backed down.

The U.S. success in breaking the Berlin blockade had several lasting results. First, it paved the way for the creation of two separate German states in 1949: the Federal Republic of West Germany, aligned with the United States, and the German Democratic Republic (or East Germany), aligned with the Soviet Union. Germany would remain divided into two separate states for the next fifty years, a radical solution to the "German problem" that satisfied people fearful of the nation's possible military resurgence.

The Berlin crisis also seemed to show that containment worked, and thus strengthened U.S. resolve to maintain a military presence in western Europe. In 1949 the United States formed **NATO** (the North Atlantic Treaty Organization), an anti-Soviet military alliance of Western governments. As one British diplomat put it, NATO was designed "to keep the Russians out, the Americans in and the Germans down."[4] With U.S. backing, West Germany joined NATO in 1955 and was allowed to rebuild its military so as to defend western Europe against possible Soviet attack. West Germany was now firmly allied with the West. The Soviets countered in 1955 by organizing the **Warsaw Pact**, a military alliance among the satellite nations of eastern Europe. In both political and military terms, Europe was divided into two hostile blocs.

Marshall Plan American plan for providing economic aid to western Europe to help it rebuild.

Council for Mutual Economic Assistance (COMECON) An economic organization of communist states meant to help rebuild eastern Europe under Soviet auspices.

NATO The North Atlantic Treaty Organization, an anti-Soviet military alliance of Western governments.

Warsaw Pact Soviet-backed military alliance of eastern European nations.

The Berlin Airlift Standing in the rubble of their bombed-out city in 1948, a German crowd in the American section awaits the arrival of a U.S. transport plane flying in over the Soviet blockade. The crisis over Berlin was a dramatic indication of growing tensions among the former Allies, which resulted in the division of Europe into two hostile camps. (Time Life Pictures/Getty Images)

The superpower confrontation that emerged from the ruins of World War II took shape in central Europe and Germany, but it quickly spread around the globe. The Cold War turned hot in East Asia. When the Soviet-backed communist army of North Korea invaded South Korea in 1950, President Truman swiftly sent U.S. troops. In 1953 a fragile truce was negotiated, and the fighting stopped. The United States thus extended its policy of containment to Asia but drew back from an attack on communist China and possible nuclear war. In the end the Korean War was indecisive: Korea remained divided between the communist north and the liberal south. The war nonetheless showed that while the superpowers might maintain a fragile peace in Europe, they were perfectly willing to engage in open conflict in non-Western territories (see also page 944).

In the decade after World War II, the Soviet-American confrontation became institutionalized and formed the bedrock of the long Cold War era, which lasted until 1989, with intermittent periods of relaxation. For the next forty-five years, the superpowers would struggle to win political influence and territorial control, and also to achieve technological superiority. Cold War hostilities directly fostered a nuclear arms race, the U.S. and Soviet space programs, and the computer revolution,

all made possible by stunning achievements in science and technology.

Big Science and New Technologies

With the advent of the Second World War, pure theoretical science had already lost its impractical innocence when it was joined with practical technology (applied science) on a massive scale. Most leading university scientists went to work on top-secret projects to help their governments fight the war. The development by British scientists of radar to detect enemy aircraft was a particularly important outcome of this new kind of sharply focused research. The air war also greatly stimulated the development of rocketry and jet aircraft and spurred further work on electronic computers that calculated the complex mathematical relationships between fast-moving planes and anti-aircraft shells to increase the likelihood of a hit. The most spectacular and deadly result of directed scientific research during the war was the atomic bomb, which showed the world both the awesome power and the heavy moral responsibilities of modern science and its high priests.

The impressive results of directed research during World War II inspired a new model for science — Big

Science. By combining theoretical work with sophisticated engineering in a large organization, Big Science could tackle extremely difficult problems, from new and improved weapons for the military to better products for consumers. Big Science was extremely expensive, requiring large-scale financing from governments and large corporations. Highly specialized modern scientists and technologists typically worked as members of a team in a large bureaucratic organization, where the individual was very often a small cog in a great machine.

Throughout the Cold War, in both the capitalist United States and the socialist Soviet Union, the government stepped in to provide generous funding for scientific activity. Populous, victorious, and wealthy, the United States took the lead in Big Science after World War II. Between 1945 and 1965 government spending on scientific research and development in the United States grew five times as fast as the national income, and by 1965 such spending took 3 percent of all U.S. income. As the Soviet Union recovered, it too devoted heavy subsidies to scientific research.

One reason for the parallel between the two countries was that science was not demobilized in either country after the war. Scientists remained a critical part of every major military establishment, and a large portion of all postwar scientific research supported the growing Cold War arms race. New weapons such as missiles, nuclear submarines, and spy satellites demanded breakthroughs no less remarkable than those responsible for radar and the first atomic bomb. After 1945 roughly one-quarter of all men and women trained in science and engineering in the West — and perhaps more in the Soviet Union — were employed full-time in the production of weapons to kill other humans. By the 1960s both sides had enough

Picturing the Past

A Soviet View of the Arms Race This propaganda poster from the 1950s reads, "We are a peaceful people, but our armored train stands in ready reserve." The reference to the armored train recalls the Bolshevik use of trains in combat against the White armies during the Russian civil war of the early 1920s. (Sovfoto)

ANALYZING THE IMAGE What does the "armored train" of the 1950s look like? How does the artist portray the Soviet people, and how does this supposedly peaceful image express Cold War hostility?

CONNECTIONS Why might the Soviet citizens again need protection, and why would the artist reference the Russian civil war? How did the emergence of Big Science contribute to the global confrontation between the superpowers?

To complete this activity online, go to the Online Study Guide at **bedfordstmartins.com/mckaywest.**

nuclear firepower to destroy each other and the rest of the world many times over.

Sophisticated science, lavish government spending, and military needs all came together in the space race of the 1960s. In 1957 the Soviets used long-range rockets developed in their nuclear weapons program to put a satellite in orbit. In 1961 they sent the world's first cosmonaut circling the globe. Embarrassed by Soviet triumphs, the United States made an all-out commitment to catch up with the Soviets and landed a crewed spacecraft on the moon in 1969. Four more moon landings followed by 1972.

Advanced nuclear weapons and the space race would have been impossible without the concurrent revolution in computer technology. The search for better weaponry in World War II had boosted the development of sophisticated data-processing machines, including the electronic Colossus computer used by the British to break German military codes. The massive mainframe ENIAC (Electronic Numerical Integrator and Computer), built for the U.S. Army at the University of Pennsylvania, went into operation in 1945. The invention of the transistor in 1947 further hastened the spread of computers. From the mid-1950s on, bulky vacuum tubes were increasingly replaced by this small, efficient electronic switching device. By the 1960s sophisticated computers were indispensable tools for a variety of military, commercial, and scientific uses, foreshadowing the rise of personal computers in the decades to come.

Big Science also had more humane and tangible results for ordinary people. During the postwar green revolution, directed research into agriculture greatly increased the world's food supplies. Farming was industrialized and became more and more productive per acre, and far fewer people worked in rural areas. The application of scientific techniques to industrial processes also made consumer goods less expensive and more readily available to larger numbers of people. The transistor, for example, was applied to computers but was also used in portable radios and kitchen appliances, and in any number of other electronic consumer products. In sum, in both the East and the West Blocs, epoch-making inventions and new technologies created new sources of material well-being and entertainment as well as destruction.

The Western Renaissance

Why did western Europe recover so successfully, and what were the sources of postwar stability? ■

As the Cold War divided Europe into two blocs, the future appeared bleak. Economic conditions were the worst in generations, and Europe was weak and divided, a battleground for Cold War ambitions. Yet Europe recovered, with the nations of western Europe in the vanguard.

In less than a generation, western Europeans constructed democratic political institutions that paved the way for unprecedented economic growth. A true consumer revolution brought improved living standards and a sense of prosperity to ever-larger numbers of people. Western European countries also entered collective economic agreements and established the European Economic Community, the first steps toward broad European unity. It was an amazing rebirth—a true renaissance.

The Search for Political and Social Consensus

After the war, economic conditions in western Europe were terrible. Infrastructure of all kinds barely functioned, and runaway inflation and a thriving black market testified to severe shortages and hardships. In 1948, as Marshall Plan dollars poured in, however, the battered economies of western Europe began to improve. The outbreak of the Korean War in 1950 further stimulated economic activity, and Europe entered a period of rapid economic progress that lasted into the late 1960s. Never before had the European economy grown so fast.

There were many reasons for this stunning economic performance. American aid got the process off to a fast start. Moreover, economic growth became a basic objective of all western European governments, for leaders and voters alike were determined to avoid a return to the dangerous and demoralizing stagnation of the 1930s.

The postwar governments in western Europe thus embraced new political and economic policies that led to a remarkably lasting social consensus. They turned to liberal democracy and generally adopted Keynesian economics (see Chapter 28) in successful attempts to stimulate their economies. In addition, whether they leaned to the left or to the right, national leaders applied an imaginative mixture of government planning and free-market capitalism to promote economic growth. They relied on limited regulation of the economy and established generous welfare provisions for both workers and the middle classes. This consensual framework for good government lasted until the middle of the 1970s, when Western governments responded to a stubborn economic crisis by cutting state spending and turning to the right.

In politics, the Nazi occupation and the war had discredited old ideas and old leaders, and a new team of European politicians emerged to guide national recovery. Across the West, newly formed Christian Democratic parties became important power brokers. Rooted in the Catholic parties of the prewar decades (see Chapters 24 and 28), the **Christian Democrats** offered voters tired of radical politics a center-right vision

> **Christian Democrats**
> Center-right political parties that rose to power in western Europe after the Second World War.

of reconciliation and recovery. The socialists and the communists, active in the resistance against Hitler, also increased their power and prestige, especially in France and Italy. They, too, provided fresh leadership and pushed for social change and economic reform.

Across much of continental Europe, the Christian Democrats defeated their left-wing competition. In Italy the Christian Democrats were the leading party in the first postwar elections in 1946, and in early 1948 they won an absolute majority in the parliament in a landslide victory. In France the Popular Republican Movement, a Christian Democratic party, provided some of the best postwar leaders after General Charles de Gaulle (duh-GOHL) resigned from the office of prime minister in January 1946. West Germans, too, chose a Christian Democratic government that governed West Germany from 1949 until 1966.

As they provided effective leadership for their respective countries, the Christian Democrats drew inspiration from a common Christian and European heritage. They steadfastly rejected authoritarianism and narrow nationalism and placed their faith in democracy and liberalism. They were steadfast cold warriors, and their anticommunist rhetoric was harsh and unrelenting. Rejecting the class politics of the left, they championed a return to traditional family values, a vision with great appeal after a war that left many broken families and destitute households; the Christian Democrats often received a majority of women's votes.

Following their U.S. allies, the Christian Democrats advocated free-market economics and promised voters prosperity and ample consumer goods. At the same time, they instituted welfare measures such as education subsidies, family and housing allowances, public transportation, and public health insurance throughout continental Europe. When necessary, Christian Democratic leaders accepted the need for limited government planning. In France the government established modernization commissions for key industries, and state-controlled banks funneled money into industrial development. In postwar West Germany, the Christian Democrats broke decisively with the straitjacketed Nazi economy and promoted a "social-market economy" based on a combination of free-market liberalism, some state intervention, and an extensive social welfare network.

By contrast, in Great Britain the social-democratic Labour Party took power after the war and ambitiously tried to establish a "cradle-to-grave" welfare state. Although the Labour Party suffered defeats throughout much of the 1950s and early 1960s, its Conservative opponents maintained much of the welfare state when they came to power. Many British industries were nationalized, or placed under state control, including banks, iron and steel industries, utilities and public transportation networks, and even the famous travel agency Thomas Cook and Sons. The British government gave

its citizens free medical services and hospital care, generous retirement pensions, and unemployment benefits, all subsidized by progressive taxation. Even though wartime austerity and rationing programs were in place until the mid-1950s, Britain offered the most comprehensive coverage outside the extensive welfare systems set up in the Scandinavian countries. In eastern and western Europe alike, state-sponsored welfare measures meant that, by the early 1960s, Europeans had more food, better homes, and longer lives than ever before.

Western Europe's recovery was spectacular in the generation after 1945. By the late 1950s, contemporaries were talking about a widespread "economic miracle" that had brought robust growth to most western European countries. The booming economy complemented political transformation and social reform, creating solid foundations for a new European stability.

Toward European Unity

The political and social consensus that emerged in the postwar decade was accompanied by the first tentative steps on the long road toward a more unified Europe. Christian Democrats were particularly committed to cultural and economic cooperation, and other groups shared their dedication. Many Europeans believed that only a new "European nation" could effectively rebuild the war-torn continent and reassert the continent's influence in world affairs.

A number of new financial arrangements and institutions encouraged slow but steady moves toward European unity, as did cooperation with the United States. The Bretton Woods agreement of 1944 had already linked Western currencies to the U.S. dollar and established the International Monetary Fund and the World Bank to facilitate free markets and world trade. To receive Marshall Plan aid, the European states were required by the Americans to cooperate with one another, leading to the creation of the Organization for European Economic Cooperation (OEEC) and the Council of Europe in 1948, both of which promoted commerce and international cooperation among European nations.

European federalists hoped that the Council of Europe would quickly evolve into a European parliament with sovereign rights, but this did not happen. Britain, with its vast empire and its close relationship with the United States, consistently opposed conceding real political power—sovereignty—to the council. Many continental nationalists and communists agreed with the British. Frustrated in the direct political approach, European federalists turned to economics as a way of working toward genuine unity. In 1950 two far-seeing French statesmen, the planner Jean Monnet and Foreign Minister Robert Schuman, called for a special international organization to control and integrate all European steel and coal production. Christian Democratic governments in West Germany, Italy, Belgium, the Netherlands, and Luxembourg accepted the French idea and founded the European Coal and Steel Community in 1951 (the British steadfastly refused to join). The immediate economic goal—a single continental steel and coal market without national tariffs or quotas—was rapidly realized. The more far-reaching political goal was to bind the six member nations so closely together economically that war among them would eventually become unthinkable and virtually impossible.

In 1957 the six nations of the Coal and Steel Community signed the Treaty of Rome, which created the European Economic Community, generally known as the **Common Market**. The first goal of the treaty was a gradual reduction of all tariffs among the six in order to create a single market almost as large as that of the United States. Other goals included the free movement of capital and labor and common economic policies and institutions. The Common Market created a solid foundation for economic growth; it encouraged trade among European states, promoted global exports, and helped build shared resources for the modernization of national industries. The movement toward European unity thus brought increased transnational cooperation, and at the same time bolstered national self-interest.

The development of the Common Market fired imaginations and encouraged hopes of rapid progress toward political as well as economic union. In the 1960s, however, these hopes were frustrated by a resurgence of more traditional nationalism. France again took the lead. French president Charles de Gaulle, elected to office in 1959, was at heart a romantic nationalist. De Gaulle viewed the United States as the main threat to genuine French (and European) independence. He withdrew all French military forces from what he called an "American-controlled" NATO, developed France's own nuclear weapons, and vetoed the scheduled advent of majority rule within the Common Market. Thus the 1950s and 1960s established a lasting pattern: Europeans would establish ever-closer economic ties, but the Common Market remained a union of independent sovereign states.

Common Market The European Economic Community, created by six western European nations in 1957 as part of a larger search for European unity.

The Consumer Revolution

In the late 1950s western Europe's rapidly expanding economy led to a rising standard of living and remark-

Life and Leisure in the Consumer Revolution By the late 1950s a rapidly expanding economy was making more consumer goods available to more people on both sides of the iron curtain, transforming the way they spent their leisure time. British teens listened to the latest rock 'n' roll hits on long-playing record albums. The *Six-Five Special* album pictured here featured recordings from the successful BBC television series of the same name. Consumer goods were not as readily available in the East, and the state controlled what goods were produced. Citizens of communist Czechoslovakia could tune into state-censored television broadcasts on this Czech-made ten-inch tabletop receiver. (television: Martin Hajek/Visual Connection Archive; album: Science Museum/Science & Society Picture Library)

able growth in the number and availability of standard-ized consumer goods. Modern consumer society had precedents in the decades before the Second World War (see Chapter 28), but these years saw the arrival of a veritable consumer revolution: as the percentage of income spent on necessities such as housing and food declined dramatically, near full employment and high wages meant that more Europeans could buy more things than ever before. Shaken by war and eager to rebuild their homes and families, western Europeans eagerly embraced the new products of consumer society. Like Americans, they filled their houses and apartments with modern appliances such as washing machines, and they eagerly purchased the latest entertainment devices of the day: radio sets, record players, and televisions.

The purchase of consumer goods was greatly facili-tated by the increased use of installment purchasing, which allowed people to buy on credit. With the expan-sion of social security safeguards reducing the need to accumulate savings for hard times and old age, ordinary people were increasingly willing to take on debt, and new banks and credit unions offered loans for consumer pur-chases on easy terms. Free-market economics and gov-ernment promotion of the consumer sector were thus quite successful. For example, the European automobile industry expanded phenomenally after lagging far be-hind that of the United States since the 1920s. In 1948 there were only 5 million cars in western Europe; by 1965 there were 44 million. Car ownership was democ-ratized and became possible for better-paid workers.

The consumer revolution included a vast array of small, everyday goods that changed both lifestyles and attitudes, as a young woman growing up in 1950s Wales remembered:

We began to acquire material possessions. A car (but no television), a hoover (but no fridge). Presents became more lavish. By the end of the decade I was the proud owner of a transistor radio, an alarm clock . . . a hula hoop, and even a few new clothes (my first pair of jeans was purchased, against fierce opposition, out of saved-up pocket money). It is difficult to be sure to what extent this was the result of our own rise in the world and how much a product of the general surge in consumerism. However, it certainly left me with the feeling I was lucky. I was constantly being reminded by my eldest sister that "when I was your age, we never had. . . ."[5]

The consumer revolution had powerful ramifica-tions in an era of Cold War competition. Politicians in both the East and the West claimed that their respec-tive systems could best provide citizens with ample consumer goods. (See "Listening to the Past: The Nixon-Khrushchev 'Kitchen Debate,'" page 942.) In the com-petition over consumption, Western free markets clearly surpassed Eastern planned economies in the produc-tion and distribution of inexpensive products. Western leaders championed the arrival of prosperity and prom-ised new forms of social equality based on equal access to consumer goods rather than forced class leveling—as in the hated East Bloc. As the West German minister

Rebellion in East Germany
In June 1953 disgruntled construction workers in East Berlin walked off the job to protest low pay and high work quotas, setting off a nation-wide rebellion against the Communist regime. The protesters could do little against the Soviet tanks and troops who entered the country to put down the revolt. (Bildarchiv Preussischer Kulturbesitz/Art Resource, NY)

of economics claimed in a 1957 speech, only liberal capitalism—not communist planning—would "lead the German people out of misery and despair to a happier future, prosperity, and social security."[6] The race to provide ordinary people with higher living standards would be a central if often overlooked aspect of the Cold War, as Soviet eastern Europe struggled to catch up to Western standards of prosperity.

Soviet Eastern Europe

What was the pattern of postwar rebuilding and development in the Soviet Union and communist eastern Europe? ■

While western Europe surged ahead economically after the Second World War and increased its independent political power as American influence gradually waned, eastern Europe followed a different path. The Soviet Union first tightened its grip on the "liberated" nations of eastern Europe under Stalin and then refused to let go. Though limited reforms after Stalin's death led to some economic improvement and limited gains in freedoms, postwar recovery in eastern Europe proceeded along Soviet lines, and political and social developments there were strongly influenced by changes in the Soviet Union.

Postwar Life Under Stalin

The "Great Patriotic War of the Fatherland" had fostered Russian nationalism and a relaxation of dictatorial terror. It also had produced a rare but real unity between Soviet rulers and most Russian people. Having made a heroic war effort, the vast majority of the Soviet people hoped in 1945 that a grateful party and government would grant greater freedom and democracy. Such hopes were soon disappointed.

Even before the war ended, Stalin was moving the Soviet Union back toward rigid dictatorship. As early as 1944 the leading members of the Communist Party were given a new motivating slogan: "The war on Fascism ends, the war on capitalism begins."[7] By early 1946 Stalin was arguing that war was inevitable as long as capitalism existed. Working to extend communist influence across the globe, the Soviets established the Cominform, or Communist Information Bureau, an international organization dedicated to maintaining Russian control over Communist parties abroad, in western as well as eastern Europe. Stalin's new foreign foe in the West served as an excuse for re-establishing a harsh dictatorship in the Soviet Union itself. Stalin reasserted the Communist Party's complete control of the government and his absolute mastery of the party. Rigid ideological indoctrination, attacks on religion, and the absence of civil liberties were soon facts of life for citizens of the Soviet empire. Millions of supposed political enemies were sent to prison, exile, or forced-labor camps.

The new satellite states in Soviet-controlled east-central Europe, including Poland, Hungary, Czechoslovakia, Romania, Albania, Bulgaria, and East Germany, were remade on the Soviet model. Though there were significant differences in what was soon known as the East Bloc, developments followed a similar pattern. Popular Communist leaders who had led the resistance against Germany were ousted as Stalin sought to create obedient instruments of domination in eastern Europe. With Soviet backing, national Communist Parties established one-party dictatorships subservient to the Communist Party in Moscow. Dissenters were arrested, imprisoned, and sometimes executed. Show trials of supposedly disloyal Communist Party leaders in Romania and Czechoslovakia in the early 1950s testified to the unrestrained influence of the Soviet Communists and Stalin's urge to establish complete control—as well as his increasing paranoia.

Only Josip Broz Tito (TEE-toh) (1892–1980), the resistance leader and Communist chief of Yugoslavia, was able to proclaim independence and successfully resist Soviet domination. Tito stood up to Stalin in 1948, and because there was no Russian army in Yugoslavia, he got away with it. Yugoslavia became communist but remained outside of the Soviet-dominated East Bloc. The country prospered as a multiethnic state until it began to break apart in the 1980s.

Within the East Bloc, the newly installed communist governments moved quickly to restructure national economies along Soviet lines. East Germany, Hungary, and Romania—countries that had fought against Russia in World War II—were forced to pay substantial war reparations to the Soviet Union. In East Germany, the Russians seized factories and equipment, even tearing up railroad tracks and sending the rails to the Soviet Union. At the same time, Communist authorities introduced Soviet-style five-year plans (see Chapter 28) to cope with the enormous task of economic reconstruction. Most industries and businesses across the East Bloc were nationalized (turned over to state ownership). Such efforts recast economic life in the Stalinist mold and created great disruptions in everyday life, even as they laid the groundwork for industrial development later in the decade. (See "Living in the Past: A Model Socialist Steel Town," page 938.)

Communist planners gave top priority to heavy industry and the military, and neglected consumer goods and housing. In addition, East Bloc leaders were suspicious of Western-style consumer culture. An overabundance of consumer goods, they believed, created waste and encouraged rampant individualism and social inequality. Thus, for practical and ideological reasons, the provision of consumer goods clearly lagged in the East

A Model Socialist Steel Town

LIVING IN THE PAST

STEEL WAS KING IN THE POSTWAR SOVIET BLOC. On both sides of the iron curtain, economic recovery required the development of heavy industry, but socialist planners were especially eager to promote large-scale industrial production centered on coal, iron, and steel. Following Soviet examples, East Bloc countries built model socialist cities, including Nowa Huta (NOH-vuh HOO-tuh; New Foundry), a steel town erected in the early 1950s on the outskirts of Kraków, Poland.

Nowa Huta was one of the grandest construction projects of the Stalinist era. An entire city surrounded the massive Lenin steelworks, both built with Soviet assistance. By the mid-1960s Polish leaders bragged that Nowa Huta produced more steel per day than any foundry in Europe.

The monumental Central Square, complete with an imposing statue of Lenin, was the center of the planned city. Streets radiated out into blocks of workers' apartment buildings designed by socialist architects. In theory, Nowa Huta brought together working and living space and included everything a working family might need: green space, department and grocery stores, recreation facilities, kindergartens and schools,

cultural centers, and an extensive streetcar system. And indeed, Nowa Huta created real opportunities for Polish workers. Many moved from the farm to the city, where they enjoyed relatively good housing and good wages. Yet workers labored under party oversight and strict workplace discipline, including demanding production quotas, and the pollution from the foundry fouled the air and damaged Kraków's historic architecture.

By 1957 over one hundred thousand people lived in Nowa Huta, most of them employed at the steelworks. At mass rallies and workplace meetings—attendance was mandatory—workers and their families

The main square of Nowa Huta with the Lenin Works foundry in the background. (Sovfoto)

met colleagues and friends and listened to lengthy speeches about the honor of simple labor and the superiority of socialism. Despite protests from workers, who were mostly Catholic, the Communist authorities sought to repress religious belief and refused to build a church until 1966.

According to propagandists, cities like Nowa Huta proved that the East could surpass the West in terms of industrial output while creating humane and equitable living spaces. But the grand experiment reveals one of the weaknesses of the East Bloc economy. By the mid-1970s the steel produced by the "tiger nations" of East Asia was better and less expensive than that made at Nowa Huta, and the foundry could no longer compete in global markets. The Communist Party clung to its vision of the workers' state, and continued government subsidies helped bankrupt the Polish state. Today, much of the plant is closed, but visitors can still explore an important example of socialist planning and ponder everyday life in a model industrial suburb.

QUESTIONS FOR ANALYSIS

1. How did planned cities like Nowa Huta reflect and promote socialist values?

2. Why would Polish leaders continue to support Nowa Huta when its products were no longer competitive?

3. Imagine yourself a worker in Nowa Huta. What would you find appealing about the living conditions? What would you find objectionable?

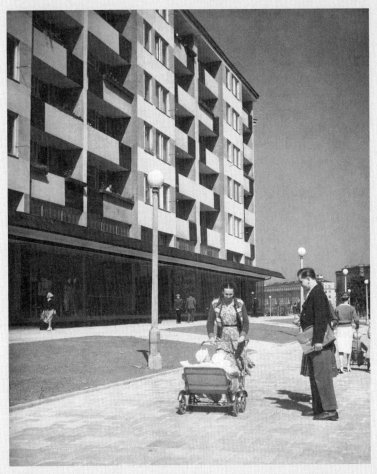

According to socialist planners, the newly built workers' apartments at Nowa Huta had everything a growing family could want, but the happiness depicted in this staged photo stands in contrast to the difficult working conditions and the state repression of Catholicism that led to popular unrest. (Sovfoto)

This photo from a 1951 May Day parade in Nowa Huta depicts marchers carrying posters of (from left to right) Marx, a Polish Communist leader, Lenin, and Engels. (Wiktor Pental/visavis.pl)

Bloc, leading to popular complaints and disillusionment with the constantly deferred promise of socialism.

Communist regimes also moved aggressively to collectivize agriculture, as they had in the Soviet Union in the 1930s (see Chapter 28). By the early 1950s independent farmers had virtually disappeared in most of the East Bloc. Poland was the exception: there the Stalinist regime tolerated the existence of private agriculture, hoping to maintain stability in the large and potentially rebellious country.

For ordinary eastern Europeans, everyday life was hard throughout the 1950s. Socialist planned economies often led to production problems and persistent shortages of basic household items. Party leaders encouraged workers to perform almost superhuman labor to "build socialism," often for low pay and under poor conditions. In East Germany, popular discontent with this situation led to open revolt in June 1953. A strike by Berlin construction workers protesting poor wages and increased work quotas led to nationwide demonstrations that were put down with Soviet troops and tanks. Over 350 protesters were killed and thousands jailed, though when the revolt was over the East German government instituted reforms designed to meet the most pressing demands of the demonstrators.

Communist censors purged culture and art in aggressive campaigns that reimposed rigid anti-Western ideological conformity. The regime required artists and writers to conform to the dictates of socialist realism, which idealized the working classes and the Soviet Union. Artists who strayed from the party line were denounced, and many talented writers, composers, and film directors were forced to produce works that conformed to the state's political goals. In short, the postwar East Bloc resembled the U.S.S.R. in the 1930s, although police terror was less intense (see Chapter 28).

Reform and De-Stalinization

In 1953 the aging Stalin finally died, and the dictatorship that he had built began to change. Even as Stalin's heirs struggled for power, they realized that reforms were necessary because of the widespread fear and hatred of Stalin's political terrorism. The power of the secret police was curbed, and many forced-labor camps were gradually closed. Change was also necessary to spur economic growth, which had sputtered under Stalin's five-year plans. Moreover, Stalin's belligerent foreign policy had led directly to a strong Western alliance, which isolated the Soviet Union.

The Soviet Communist leadership was badly split on the question of just how much change should be permitted in order to preserve the system. Conservatives

de-Stalinization The liberalization of the post-Stalin Soviet Union led by reformer Nikita Khrushchev.

wanted to make as few changes as possible. Reformers, who were led by Nikita Khrushchev (1894–1971), argued for major innovations. Khrushchev (kroush-CHAWF), who had joined the party as an uneducated coal miner in 1918 and had risen to a high-level position in the 1930s, emerged as the new Soviet premier in 1955.

To strengthen his position and that of his fellow reformers within the party, Khrushchev launched a surprising attack on Stalin and his crimes at a closed session of the Twentieth Party Congress in 1956. In his famous "secret speech," Khrushchev described to the startled Communist delegates how Stalin had "supported the glorification of his own person with all conceivable methods" to build a propagandistic "cult of personality." The delegates applauded when Khrushchev went on to report that Stalin had tortured and murdered thousands of loyal Communists and bungled the country's defense in World War II:

> [Stalin] discarded the Leninist method of convincing and educating . . . for that of administrative violence, mass repressions, and terror. . . . Mass arrests and deportations of many thousands of people, execution without trial and without normal investigation created conditions of insecurity, fear, and even desperation. . . . And what was the result of [Stalin's failed leadership at the Battle for Kharkov]? The Germans surrounded our army concentrations and consequently we lost hundreds of thousands of our soldiers. . . . Not Stalin, but the party as a whole, the Soviet Government, our heroic army . . . the whole Soviet nation—these are the ones who assured victory in the Great Patriotic War. (Tempestuous and prolonged applause.)[8]

The liberalization—or **de-Stalinization**, as it was called in the West—of the Soviet Union was genuine. Khrushchev's secret speech was read at Communist Party meetings held throughout the country, and it strengthened the reform movement. The Communist Party jealously maintained its monopoly on political power, but Khrushchev shook up the party and brought in new members. Some resources were shifted from heavy industry and the military toward consumer goods and agriculture, and Stalinist controls over workers were relaxed. The Soviet Union's low standard of living finally began to improve and continued to rise substantially throughout the booming 1960s.

De-Stalinization also created great ferment among writers and intellectuals who sought cultural freedom, such as the poet Boris Pasternak (1890–1960), who finished his great novel *Doctor Zhivago* in 1956. Published in the West but not in Russia, *Doctor Zhivago* is both a literary masterpiece and a powerful challenge to communism. It tells the story of a prerevolutionary intellectual who rejects the violence and brutality of the revolution of 1917 and the Stalinist years. Pasternak was denounced—

but under Khrushchev he was not shot. Other talented writers followed Pasternak's lead, and courageous editors let the sparks fly. The writer Aleksandr Solzhenitsyn (sohl-zhuh-NEET-suhn) (1918–2008) created a sensation when his *One Day in the Life of Ivan Denisovich* was published in the Soviet Union in 1962. Solzhenitsyn's novel portrays in grim detail life in a Stalinist concentration camp—a life to which Solzhenitsyn himself had been unjustly condemned—and is a damning indictment of the Stalinist past.

Khrushchev was proud of Soviet achievements and liked to boast that East Bloc living standards and access to consumer goods would soon surpass the West. (See "Listening to the Past: The Nixon-Khrushchev 'Kitchen Debate,'" page 942.) Socialist citizens in fact experienced a limited consumer revolution. Their options were more modest than those in the West, but eastern Europeans purchased automobiles, televisions, and other consumer goods in ever-increasing numbers in the 1960s.

Foreign Policy and Domestic Rebellion

Khrushchev also de-Stalinized Soviet foreign policy. "Peaceful coexistence" with capitalism was possible, he argued, and great wars were not inevitable. Khrushchev even made concessions, agreeing in 1955 to real independence for a neutral Austria after ten long years of Allied occupation. Thus there was considerable relaxation of Cold War tensions between 1955 and 1957. At the same time, Khrushchev began wooing the new nations of Asia and Africa—even those that were not communist—with promises and aid.

In the eastern European satellites, de-Stalinization stimulated rebelliousness. Having suffered in silence under Stalin, communist reformers and the masses were quickly emboldened to seek much greater liberty and national independence. Poland took the lead in 1956, when extensive rioting brought a new government to power. The new first secretary of the Polish Communist Party argued that there were "many roads to socialism" and managed to win greater autonomy from Soviet control. The new leadership maintained Communist control even as it tolerated a free peasantry and an independent Catholic Church.

Hungary experienced a real and tragic revolution the same year. Led by students and workers—the classic urban revolutionaries— the people of Budapest installed Imre Nagy, a liberal communist reformer, as their new prime minister in October 1956. Nagy forced Soviet troops to leave the country, but the victory was short-

> **66** Mass arrests and deportations of many thousands of people, execution without trial and without normal investigation created conditions of insecurity, fear, and even desperation. **99**
>
> —**NIKITA KHRUSHCHEV**

lived. After the new government promised free elections and renounced Hungary's military alliance with Moscow, the Russian leaders ordered an invasion and crushed the national and democratic revolution. Around 2,700 Hungarians died in the revolt. Fighting was bitter until the end, for the Hungarians hoped that the United States would come to their aid. When this did not occur, most people in eastern Europe concluded that their only hope was to strive for small domestic gains while following Russia obediently in foreign affairs. The re-established Communist regime executed the revolt's leaders and sent another 22,000 to prison.

The outcome of the Hungarian uprising weakened support for Soviet-style communism in western Europe; for those who still believed in socialist equality, the brutal repression was deeply discouraging. Across western Europe, tens of thousands of Communist Party members resigned in disgust. At the same time, Western leaders saw that the Soviets would use military force to defend their control over the Communist bloc, and that only open war between East and West had the potential to overturn authoritarian Communist rule. This price was too high, and it seemed that Communist domination of east-central Europe was here to stay.

The Limits of Reform

By late 1962 opposition to Khrushchev's reformist policies had gained momentum in party circles. Khrushchev's Communist colleagues began to see de-Stalinization as a dangerous threat to the dictatorial authority of the party. Moreover, Khrushchev's policy toward the West was erratic and ultimately unsuccessful. In 1958, in a failed attempt to close the open border between East and West Berlin, he ordered the Western allies to evacuate the city within six months. In response, the allies reaffirmed their unity in West Berlin, and Khrushchev backed down. Then in 1961 Khrushchev ordered the East Germans to build a wall between East and West Berlin, thereby sealing off West Berlin in clear violation of existing access agreements between the Great Powers. The recently elected U.S. president, John F. Kennedy (r. 1961–1963), insisted publicly that the United States would never abandon Berlin. Hoping that the Berlin

The Nixon-Khrushchev "Kitchen Debate"

LISTENING TO THE PAST

During the Cold War, the United States and the Soviet Union waged political battles in Europe and wars of influence in the former colonies. But the two superpowers also sparred over which system — communism or capitalism — provided the best lifestyle for its citizens.

In a late-1950s effort to relieve Cold War tensions, the Americans and Soviets allowed one another to set up public displays in each other's

territory. The American National Exhibition in Moscow in 1959 included a model U.S. suburban home, complete with modern kitchen appliances, a television and stereo console, and a Cadillac sedan, all meant to demonstrate the superiority of capitalism to local visitors.

Against this backdrop, U.S. vice president Richard Nixon and Soviet premier Nikita Khrushchev engaged in an impromptu and sometimes ham-fisted argument over the merits of their respective political systems. As this exchange from the famous "kitchen debate" suggests, dishwashers were also on the front line of the Cold War.

❝ KHRUSHCHEV: We want to live in peace and friendship with Americans because we are the two most powerful countries and if we live in friendship then other countries will also live in friendship. But if there is a country that is too war-minded we could pull its ears a little and say: Don't you dare; fighting is not allowed now; this is a period of atomic armament; some foolish one could start a war and then even a wise one couldn't finish the war. Therefore, we are governed by this idea in our policy—internal and foreign. How long has America existed? Three hundred years?

NIXON: One hundred and fifty years.

KHRUSHCHEV: One hundred and fifty years? Well then we will say America has been in existence for 150 years and this is the level she has reached. We have existed not quite 42 years and in another seven years we will be on the same level as America. When we catch you up, in passing you by, we will wave to you. Then if you wish we can stop and say: Please follow up. Plainly speaking, if you want capitalism you can live that way. That is your own affair and doesn't concern us. We can still feel sorry for you but since you don't understand us — live as you do understand. . . . [Wrapping his arms about a Soviet workman.] Does this man look like a slave laborer? [Waving at others.] With men with such spirit how can we lose?

NIXON: [Pointing to American workmen.] With men like that we are strong. But these men, Soviet and American, work together well for peace, even as they have worked together in building this exhibition. This is the way it should be. Your remarks are in the tradition of what we have come to expect — sweeping and extemporaneous. Later on we will both have an opportunity to speak and consequently I will not comment on the various points that you raised, except to say this — this color television is one of the most advanced developments in communication that we have. I can only say that if this competition in which you plan to outstrip us is to do the best for both of our peoples and for peoples everywhere, there must be a free exchange of ideas. After all, you don't know everything.

KHRUSHCHEV: If I don't know everything you don't know anything about communism except fear of it.

NIXON: There are some instances where you may be ahead of us, for example in the development of the thrust of your rockets for the investigation of outer space; there may be some instances in which we are ahead of you — in color television, for instance.

KHRUSHCHEV: No, we are up with you on this, too. We have bested you in one technique and also in the other.

NIXON: You see, you never concede anything.

KHRUSHCHEV: I do not give up.

NIXON: Wait till you see the picture. Let's have far more communication and exchange in this very area that we speak of. We should hear you more on our televisions. You should hear us more on yours.

KHRUSHCHEV: That's a good idea. Let's do it like this. You appear before our people. We will appear before your people. People will see and appreciate this. . . .

NIXON: [Halting Khrushchev at the model kitchen in the model house.] You had a very nice house in your exhibition in New York. My wife and I saw and enjoyed it very much. I want to show you this kitchen. It is like those of our houses in California.

KHRUSHCHEV: [After Nixon calls attention to a built-in panel-controlled washing machine.] We have such things.

NIXON: This is the newest model. This is the kind which is built in thousands of units for direct installation in the houses. [He adds that Americans are interested in making life easier for their women.] ❞

Mr. Khrushchev remarked that in the Soviet Union, they did not have "the capitalist attitude toward women."

❝ NIXON: I think that this attitude toward women is universal. What we want to do is make easier the life of our housewives. ❞

Khrushchev and Nixon discuss the merits of the American way during the famous kitchen debate. (AP Images)

Nixon explained that the house could be built for $14,000 and that most veterans had bought houses for between $10,000 and $15,000.

❝ NIXON: Let me give you an example you can appreciate. Our steelworkers, as you know, are on strike. But any steelworker could buy this house. They earn $3 an hour. This house costs about $100 a month to buy on a contract running 25 to 30 years.

KHRUSHCHEV: We have steelworkers and we have peasants who also can afford to spend $14,000 for a house. . . .

KHRUSHCHEV: Don't you have a machine that puts food into the mouth and pushes it down? Many things you've shown us are interesting but they are not needed in life. They have no useful purpose. They are merely gadgets. We have a saying, if you have bedbugs you have to catch one and pour boiling water into the ear.

NIXON: We have another saying. This is that the way to kill a fly is to make it drink whisky. But we have a better use for whisky. [Aside] I like to have this battle of wits with the Chairman. He knows his business. . . .

KHRUSHCHEV: The Americans have created their own image of the Soviet man and think he is as you want him to be. But he is not as you think. You think the Russian people will be dumbfounded to see these things, but the fact is that newly built Russian houses have all this equipment right now. Moreover, all you have to do to get a house is to be born in the Soviet Union.

You are entitled to housing. I was born in the Soviet Union. So I have a right to a house. In America, if you don't have a dollar — you have the right to choose between sleeping in a house or on the pavement. Yet you say that we are slaves of communism. . . .

NIXON: We do not claim to astonish the Russian people. We hope to show our diversity and our right to choose. We do not wish to have decisions made at the top by government officials who say that all homes should be built in the same way. Would it not be better to compete in the relative merits of washing machines than in the strength of rockets. Is this the kind of competition you want?

KHRUSHCHEV: Yes that's the kind of competition we want. But your generals say: "Let's compete in rockets. We are strong and we can beat you." But in this respect we can also show you something.

NIXON: To me you are strong and we are strong. In some ways, you are stronger. In others, we are stronger. We are both strong not only from the standpoint of weapons but from the standpoint of will and spirit. ❞

Source: Transcript of the "Kitchen Debate" at the opening of the American National Exhibition at Sokolniki Park in Moscow, July 24, 1959.

QUESTIONS FOR ANALYSIS

1. Why do Nixon and Khrushchev spend so much time talking about the lives of workers in the United States and the Soviet Union?

2. Why were consumer goods, such as washing machines and television sets, such important symbols of modernity and progress for both Nixon and Khrushchev?

3. What does the kitchen debate reveal about the different ways in which communist and capitalist leaders viewed women's role in society?

Wall would lessen Cold War tensions, Kennedy nonetheless allowed its construction.

Emboldened and seeing a chance to change the balance of military power decisively, Premier Khrushchev next ordered missiles with nuclear warheads installed in Fidel Castro's communist Cuba in 1962. President Kennedy countered with a naval blockade of Cuba. After a tense diplomatic crisis, Khrushchev agreed to remove the Soviet missiles in return for American pledges not to disturb Castro's regime. In a secret agreement, Kennedy also promised to remove U.S. nuclear missiles from Turkey.

Khrushchev's influence, already slipping, declined rapidly after the Cuban missile crisis. In 1964 the reformist premier was displaced in a bloodless coup, and he spent the rest of his life under house arrest. Under his successor, Leonid Brezhnev (1906–1982), the Soviet Union began a period of stagnation and limited re-Stalinization. Almost immediately, Brezhnev (BREHZH-nehf) and his supporters started talking quietly of Stalin's "good points" and ignoring his crimes. This change informed Soviet citizens that further liberalization could not be expected at home. Soviet leaders, determined never to suffer Khrushchev's humiliation in the face of American nuclear superiority, also launched a massive arms buildup. Yet Brezhnev and company proceeded cautiously in the mid-1960s and avoided direct confrontation with the U.S.

Despite popular protests and changes in leadership, the Soviet Union and its satellite countries had achieved some stability by the late 1950s. Communist regimes addressed dissent and uprisings with an effective combination of military force, political repression, and limited economic reform. East and West traded propaganda threats, but both sides basically accepted the division of Europe into spheres of influence. More violent conflicts now took place in the developing world, where decolonization was opening new paths for Cold War confrontation.

decolonization The postwar reversal of Europe's overseas expansion caused by the rising demand of the colonized peoples themselves, the declining power of European nations, and the freedoms promised by U.S. and Soviet ideals.

The End of Empires

What circumstances led to the postwar colonial independence movements, and how did the Cold War influence the process? ■

In the postwar era, in one of world history's great turning points, Europe's long-standing overseas expansion was dramatically reversed. The retreat from imperial control—what Europeans called **decolonization**—remade the world map. Some one hundred new nations in Africa, Asia, and the Middle East joined the global community (Map 29.3).

In some cases, decolonization proceeded relatively smoothly, with an orderly transition and little violence. In others, the European powers were determined to preserve colonial rule—long a source of profit and national pride—and colonized peoples won independence only after long and bloody struggles.

The Cold War had a profound impact on decolonization. Anticolonial independence movements often had to choose sides in the struggle between the superpowers, and after independence was won, both the United States and the Soviet Union struggled to exert influence in the former colonies. Liberation from colonial domination was a proud achievement that brought fundamental gains in political freedom, but also left lasting problems for the former colonized and colonizers alike.

Decolonization and the Cold War

The most basic cause of imperial collapse was the rising demand of non-Western peoples for national self-determination, racial equality, and personal dignity. This demand spread from intellectuals to the masses in nearly every colonial territory after the First World War. By 1939 colonial empires had already been shaken, and the Second World War prepared the way for the eventual triumph of independence movements.

European empires had been based on an enormous power differential between the rulers and the ruled, a difference that had greatly declined by 1945. Western Europe was economically devastated and militarily weak immediately after the war. Moreover, the Japanese had driven imperial rulers from large parts of East Asia during the war in the Pacific, shattering the myth of European superiority and invincibility. In East Asia, European imperialists confronted strong anticolonial nationalist movements that had developed under the Japanese occupation.

To some degree, the Great Powers also regarded their empires very differently after 1945 than before 1914, or even before 1939. Empire had rested on self-confidence and self-righteousness; Europeans had believed their superiority to be not only technical and military but also spiritual and moral. The horrors of the Second World War destroyed such complacent arrogance and gave opponents of imperialism much greater influence in Europe. Increasing pressure from the United States, which had long presented itself as an enemy of empire, further encouraged Europeans to let go of their former colonies. Economically weakened, and with their political power and moral authority in tatters, the imperial powers could hardly afford to engage in bloody colonial wars and wanted instead to concentrate on rebuilding at home.

Map 29.3 Decolonization in Africa and Asia, 1947 to the Present Divided primarily along religious lines into two states, British India led the way to political independence in 1947. Most African territories achieved statehood by the mid-1960s as European empires passed away, unlamented.

Around the globe, the Cold War had an inescapable impact on decolonization. Liberation from colonial rule had long been a communist goal, a key component of world revolution. The Soviets and Red Chinese advocated rebellion in the developing world and promised native peoples an end to colonial exploitation followed by freedom and equality in a socialist state. They supported communist independence movements with economic and military aid, and the insurgent guerrilla, armed with a Soviet-produced AK-47 machine gun, became the new symbol of Marxist revolution.

Western Europe and particularly the United States offered a competing vision of independence based on free-market economics and liberal democracy. Like the Soviet Union, the United States extended aid and arms to decolonizing nations. The Americans promoted cautious moves toward self-determination in the context of containment, attempting to limit the influence of communism in newly liberated states.

After they had won independence, the leaders of the new nations often found themselves trapped between the superpowers, compelled to voice support for one bloc or the other. Many new leaders followed a policy of **nonalignment**, remaining neutral in the Cold War and playing both sides for what they could get.

nonalignment Policy of postcolonial governments to remain neutral in the Cold War and play both the United States and the Soviet Union for what they could get.

The Struggle for Power in Asia

The first major fight for independence that followed World War II, between the Dutch and anticolonial insurgents in the Dutch East Indies (today's Indonesia), in many ways exemplified decolonization in the Cold War world. The Dutch had been involved in Indonesia since the early seventeenth century (see Chapter 15), and in the crisis that followed the Second World War they hoped to use Indonesia's raw materials, particularly rubber, to support economic recovery. During the war, however, the Japanese had overrun the archipelago and encouraged hopes for independence from Western control. When the Dutch returned in 1945, they faced a determined group of rebels inspired by a powerful combination of nationalism, Marxism, and Islam. Four years of deadly guerrilla war followed, and in 1949 the Netherlands reluctantly accepted Indonesian independence. The new Indonesian president became an effective advocate of nonalignment. He relied on the support of the Indonesian Communist Party but received foreign aid from both the United States and the Soviet Union.

A similar combination of communism and anticolonialism inspired the independence movement in French Indochina (now Vietnam, Cambodia, and Laos). France desperately wished to maintain control over these prized colonies and tried its best to re-establish colonial rule after the Japanese occupation collapsed at the end of World War II. Despite substantial American aid, the French army was defeated in 1954 by forces under the guerrilla leader Ho Chi Minh (hoh chee mihn) (1890–1969), who was supported by the Soviet Union and China. Indochina was divided: a shaky truce established the states of North and South Vietnam, which led to civil war and subsequent intervention by the United States.

India, Britain's oldest, largest, and most lucrative imperial possession, played a key role in decolonization. Nationalist opposition to British rule coalesced after the First World War under the leadership of British-educated lawyer Mohandas (Mahatma) Gandhi (1869–1948), one of the twentieth century's most significant

and influential figures. In the 1920s and 1930s Gandhi (GAHN-dee) built a mass movement preaching non-violent "noncooperation" with the British. In 1935 Gandhi wrested from the frustrated and unnerved British a new, liberal constitution that was practically a blueprint for independence. The Second World War interrupted progress toward Indian self-rule, but when the Labour Party came to power in Great Britain in 1945, it was ready to relinquish sovereignty. British socialists had always been critical of imperialism, and the heavy cost of governing India had become a large financial burden.

Britain withdrew peacefully, but conflict between India's Hindu and Muslim populations posed a lasting dilemma for the South Asian subcontinent. As independence neared, the Muslim minority grew increasingly anxious about their status in an India dominated by the Hindu majority. Muslim leaders called for partition — the division of India into separate Hindu and Muslim states — and the British agreed. When independence was made official on August 15, 1947, predominantly Muslim territories on India's eastern and western borders became East Pakistan (today Bangladesh) and West Pakistan. A wave of massive migration and violence accompanied the partition of India. Seeking relief from ethnic conflict, some 10 million Muslim and Hindu refugees fled across the new borders, and an estimated five hundred thousand lost their lives in the riots that ensued. Gandhi was assassinated in January 1948 by a radical Hindu nationalist who opposed partition, and Jawaharlal Nehru became Indian prime minister.

As the Cold War heated up in the following decade, Pakistan, an Islamic republic, developed close ties with the United States. Under the leadership of Nehru, India successfully established a liberal, if socialist-friendly, democratic state and maintained a policy of nonalignment, dealing with both the United States and the Soviet Union. Pakistan and India both joined the British Common-

Gandhi Arrives in Delhi, October 1939
From the 1920s until his death in 1948, the Indian anticolonial leader Mahatma Gandhi led a determined and ultimately successful campaign against British imperialism. His advocacy of nonviolent resistance inspired the Indian masses, nurtured Indian national identity, and left a lasting model for later protest movements. Here Gandhi arrives for negotiations with the British viceroy after the outbreak of World War II. (Corbis)

wealth, a voluntary and cooperative association of former British colonies that already included Canada, Australia, and New Zealand.

If Indian nationalism drew on Western parliamentary liberalism, Chinese nationalism developed and triumphed in the framework of Marxist-Leninist ideology. After the withdrawal of the occupying Japanese army in 1945, China erupted in open civil war between Jiang Jieshi (traditionally called Chiang Kai-shek; 1887–1975), the leader of the conservative Guomindang (Kuomintang, National People's Party), and the Chinese communists, headed by Mao Zedong (MAOU dzuh-DOUNG). Stalin gave Mao aid, and the Americans gave Jiang much more. Winning the support of the peasantry by promising to expropriate the holdings of the big landowners, the tougher, better-organized communists forced the Guomindang to withdraw to the island of Taiwan in 1949. Mao and the communists united China's 550 million inhabitants in a strong centralized state. The Chinese communists expelled foreigners and began building a new society that adapted Marxism to Chinese conditions and brought Stalinist-style repression—mass arrests, forced-labor camps, and ceaseless propaganda campaigns—to the Chinese people. The new government also promoted land reform and extended education and health-care programs to the peasantry, and it introduced five-year plans that successfully boosted industrial production.

Independence and Conflict in the Middle East

In some areas of the Middle East, the movement toward political independence went relatively smoothly. The French League of Nations mandates in Syria and Lebanon had collapsed during the Second World War, and Saudi Arabia and Transjordan had already achieved independence from Britain. But events in the British mandate of Palestine and in Egypt showed that decolonization in the Middle East could be a dangerous and difficult process.

As part of the peace accords that followed the First World War, the British government had advocated a Jewish homeland alongside the Arab population (see Chapter 26). This tenuous compromise unraveled after World War II. Neither Jews nor Arabs were happy with British rule, and violence and terrorism mounted on both sides. In 1947 the frustrated British decided to leave

Israel, 1948

Palestine, and the United Nations voted in a nonbinding resolution to divide the territory into two states—one Arab and one Jewish. The Jews accepted the plan and founded the state of Israel in 1948. The Palestinians and the surrounding Arab nations viewed Jewish independence as a betrayal of their own interests, and they attacked the Jewish state as soon as it was proclaimed. The Israelis drove off the invaders and conquered more territory. Roughly nine hundred thousand Arab Palestinians fled or were expelled from their homes, creating a persistent refugee problem. Holocaust survivors from Europe streamed into Israel, as Theodor Herzl's Zionist dream came true (see Chapter 24). The next fifty years saw four more wars between the Israelis and the Arab states and innumerable clashes between Israelis and Palestinians.

The Arab defeat in 1948 triggered a powerful nationalist revolution in Egypt in 1952, led by the young army officer Gamal Abdel Nasser (1918–1970). The revolutionaries drove out the pro-Western king, and in 1954 Nasser became president of an independent Egyptian republic. A crafty politician, Nasser advocated nonalignment and expertly played the superpowers against each other, securing loans from the United States and purchasing Soviet arms.

In July 1956 Nasser abruptly nationalized the foreign-owned Suez Canal Company, the last symbol and substance of Western power in the Middle East. Infuriated, the British and the French, along with the Israelis, secretly planned a military invasion. The resulting Suez crisis marked a watershed in the history of European imperialism. The Israeli army invaded the Sinai Peninsula bordering the canal, and British and French bombers attacked Egyptian airfields. This was, however, the dying gasp of traditional imperial power. World opinion was outraged, and the United States feared that such a blatant show of imperialism would propel the Arab states

The Suez Crisis, 1956

Nationalizing the Suez Canal Egyptian president Nasser greets cheering crowds in Cairo after the surprise takeover of the Suez Canal. Jubilation throughout Egypt and the Arab world quickly turned to humiliation as invading forces from Israel, Britain, and France crushed the Egyptian army, and a shell-shocked Nasser offered to resign. But the Egyptian masses demanded that he stay, and the charismatic Nasser emerged triumphant after the Americans and Soviets forced Israel, Britain, and France to back down. (Hulton-Deutsch Collection/Corbis)

into the Soviet bloc. The Americans joined with the Soviets to force the British, French, and Israelis to back down. Egyptian nationalism triumphed: Nasser got his canal, and Israel left the Sinai in 1957. The Suez crisis showed that the European powers could no longer maintain their global empires, and it demonstrated the power and appeal of nonalignment.

The African Awakening

In less than a decade, most African states won independence from European imperialism, a remarkable event of world historical importance. In much of the continent south of the Sahara, decolonization proceeded relatively smoothly. Yet the new African states were quickly caught up in the struggles between the Cold War superpowers, and decolonization all too often left a lasting legacy of economic decline and political instability (see Map 29.3).

Starting in 1957 most of Britain's African colonies achieved independence with little or no bloodshed and then entered a very loose association with Britain as members of the British Commonwealth. Ghana, Nigeria, Tanzania, and other nations gained independence in this way, but there were exceptions to this smooth transfer of power. In Kenya in the early 1950s, British forces brutally crushed the Mau Mau rebellion, but nonetheless had to grant Kenyan independence in 1963. In the former British colony of South Africa, white settlers left the Commonwealth in 1961 and declared an independent republic in order to preserve the unequal advantages

of apartheid—an exploitative system of racial segregation enforced by law.

The decolonization of the Belgian Congo was one of the great tragedies of the Cold War. Belgian leaders, profiting from the colony's wealth of natural resources and proud of their small nation's imperial status, maintained a system of apartheid and dragged their feet in granting independence. These conditions sparked an anticolonial movement that grew increasingly aggressive in the late 1950s under the able leadership of the charismatic Patrice Lumumba. In January 1960 the Belgians gave in, hastily announcing that the Congo would be independent six months later, a schedule that was irresponsibly fast. Lumumba was chosen prime minister in democratic elections, but when the Belgians pulled out on schedule, the new government was entirely unprepared. Chaos broke out when the Congolese army rioted against the Belgian military officers who remained in the country.

With substantial financial investments in the Congo, the United States and western Europe worried that the new nation might fall into Soviet hands. U.S. leaders cast Lumumba as a Soviet proxy, an oversimplification of his nonalignment policies, and American anxiety increased when Lumumba turned to the Soviet Union for aid and protection. A cable from the CIA chief in the Congo revealed the way Cold War anxieties framed the situation:

Embassy and station believe Congo experiencing classic Communist takeover government. . . . Whether or not Lumumba actually Commie or just playing Commie game to assist solidifying his power, anti-West forces rapidly increasing power [in] Congo and there may be little time left in which to take action to avoid another Cuba.[9]

In a troubling example of containment in action, the CIA helped implement a military coup against Lumumba, who was assassinated in captivity in January 1961. The Congolese military set up a U.S.-backed dictatorship under the corrupt general Joseph Mobutu. Mobutu ruled until 1997 and became one of the world's wealthiest men, while the Congo remains one of the poorest and most politically troubled nations in the world.

French colonies in Africa followed several roads to independence. Like the British, the French offered most of their African colonies the choice of a total break with France or independence within a kind of French commonwealth. All but one of the new states chose association with France, largely because they identified with French culture and wanted aid from their former colonizer. The French were eager to help — provided their former colonies would accept close ties with France on French terms. As in the past, the French and their Common Market partners, who helped foot the bill, saw themselves as continuing their civilizing mission in sub-Saharan Africa (see Chapter 25). More important, they saw in Africa untapped markets for their industrial goods, raw materials for their factories, outlets for profitable investment, and good temporary jobs for their engineers and teachers.

Things were more difficult in the French colony of Algeria, a large Muslim state on the Mediterranean Sea, where some 500,000 French and Europeans had taken up permanent residency by the 1950s. Nicknamed *pied noirs* (people with black feet), many of these Europeans had raised families in Algeria for three or four generations, and they enforced a two-tiered system of citizenship, maintaining complete control of politics and the economy. When Muslim rebels, inspired by Islamic fundamentalism and communist ideals, established the National Liberation Front (FLN) and revolted against French colonialism in the early 1950s, the presence of the pied noirs complicated matters. Worried about their position in the colony, the pied noirs pressured the French government to help them. In response, the French army sent some 400,000 troops to crush the FLN and put down the revolt.

The resulting Algerian war — long, bloody, and dirty, with numerous atrocities on both sides — lasted from 1954 to 1962. The excesses of the French army included systematic torture, the so-called resettlement or forced relocation of the Muslim population, and attacks on civilians who supported the insurgents. News reports turned French public opinion and indeed the government against the war, but efforts to open peace talks instigated a revolt by the Algerian French and threats of a

French Checkpoint in Algeria, 1962 French soldiers search a civilian in Algiers, the capital of Algeria. Inspired by a potent mix of communism and Islamic radicalism, the Algerian National Liberation Front fought a lengthy and bloody struggle against the French colonial government that finally led to Algerian independence in 1962. (Agence France Presse/Hulton Archive/Getty Images)

coup d'état by the French army. In 1958 the immensely popular General Charles de Gaulle was reinstated as French prime minister as part of the movement to keep Algeria French, and his appointment calmed the army, the pied noirs, and the French public. Yet de Gaulle pragmatically accepted the principle of Algerian self-determination, and in 1962 he ended the conflict. After more than a century of French rule, Algeria became independent, and its European population quickly fled to France.

By the mid-1960s most African states had won independence, some through bloody insurrections. There were exceptions: South African blacks still longed for liberation from apartheid, and the tiny nation of Portugal waged war against independence movements in its colonies of Angola and Mozambique until the 1970s. Even in liberated nations, the colonial legacy had long-term negative effects. African leaders may have expressed support for socialist or democratic principles in order to win aid from the superpowers. In practice, however, corrupt and authoritarian African leaders like Mobutu in the Congo often established lasting authoritarian dictatorships and enriched themselves at the expense of their populations.

Even after decolonization, western European countries managed to increase their economic and cultural ties with their former African colonies in the 1960s and 1970s. Above all, they used the lure of special trading privileges, and provided heavy investment in French- and English-language education to enhance a powerful Western presence in the new African states. This situation led a variety of leaders and scholars to charge that western Europe (and the United States) had imposed a system of neocolonialism on the former colonies. According to this view, neocolonialism was a system designed to perpetuate Western economic domination and undermine the promise of political independence, thereby extending to Africa (and much of Asia) the economic subordination that the United States had established in Latin America in the nineteenth century. Such economic ties were clearly better than open political domination, but, according to critics, they still worked to the former colony's disadvantage.

Postwar Social Transformations

How did large-scale changes in social structures and relations contribute to European stability on both sides of the iron curtain? ■

While Europe staged its astonishing political and economic recovery from the Nazi nightmare, the basic structures of Western society were changing no less rapidly and remarkably. New forms of European migration, a changing class structure, and new roles for women and youths had dramatic impacts on everyday life in postwar Europe. These large-scale changes were experienced differently in communist eastern and democratic western Europe. Nonetheless, such large-scale changes had transformative effects on both sides of the iron curtain. Thus social and cultural trends joined political and economic recovery to build stability in the postwar decades.

Changing Class Structures

Rapid economic growth went a long way toward creating a new society in Europe after the Second World War. European society became more mobile. Old class barriers relaxed, and class distinctions became fuzzier.

Changes in the structure of the middle class were particularly influential in the general drift toward a less rigid class structure. In the nineteenth and early twentieth centuries, the model for the middle class had been the independent, self-employed individual who owned a business or practiced a liberal profession such as law or medicine. Ownership of property—very often inherited property—and strong family ties had often been the keys to wealth and standing within the middle class. After 1945 this pattern declined drastically in western Europe. A new breed of managers and experts—so-called white-collar workers—replaced traditional property owners as the leaders of the middle class. Ability to serve the needs of a big organization largely replaced inherited property and family connections in determining an individual's social position in the middle and upper-middle classes. At the same time, the middle class grew massively and became harder to define.

There were several reasons for these developments. Rapid industrial and technological expansion created a powerful demand for technologists and managers in large corporations and government agencies. Moreover, the old propertied middle class lost control of many family-owned businesses, and many small businesses (including family farms) simply passed out of existence as their former owners joined the ranks of salaried employees.

Similar processes were at work in the communist states of the East Bloc, where class leveling was an avowed goal of the authoritarian socialist state. The forced nationalization of industry, the expropriation of property, and aggressive attempts to open employment opportunities to workers and equalize wage structures effectively reduced class differences. Party members typically received better jobs and more pay, but the income differentials between the top and bottom strata of East Bloc societies were far smaller than those in the West.

In both East and West, managers and civil servants represented the model for a new middle class of salaried specialists. Well-paid and highly trained, often with backgrounds in engineering or accounting, these pragmatic experts were primarily concerned with efficiency and with practical solutions to concrete problems.

The structure of the lower classes also became more flexible and open. There was a mass exodus from farms and the countryside; the population of one of the most traditional and least mobile groups in European society—farmers—drastically declined. Meanwhile, the number of industrial workers in western Europe also began to decline, as new jobs for white-collar and service employees grew rapidly. This change marked a significant transition in the world of labor. In general, European workers were better educated and more specialized than before, and the new workforce bore a greater resemblance to the growing middle class of salaried specialists than to traditional industrial workers. The welfare benefits extended by postwar governments also worked to promote greater social equality by raising lower-class living standards and by being paid for in part by higher taxes on the wealthy.

Patterns of Postwar Migration

Changing patterns of migration also had a significant impact on European society. From the 1850s to the 1930s, countless European immigrants had left the continent for colonies or foreign states, seeking economic opportunity or freedom from political or religious persecution (see Chapter 26). In the 1950s and 1960s the trend reversed. Europeans now saw an influx of migrants into their lands, particularly in the prosperous northwest, where the demand for labor encouraged mass immigration.

Some migration took place within national borders. Declining job prospects in Europe's rural areas encouraged many peasants and small farmers to seek better prospects in the cities. In the poorer nations in southern Europe such as Spain, Portugal, and Italy, millions moved to more developed regions of their own countries. The process was similar in the Soviet bloc, where the forced collectivization of agriculture and state subsidies for heavy industry opened opportunities in urban areas. Before the erection of the Berlin Wall in 1961,

some 3.5 million East Germans also crossed the open border into the Federal Republic of Germany, seeking higher pay and a better life.

Many other Europeans moved across national borders seeking work. The general pattern was from south to north. Workers from less-developed countries like Italy, Spain, and socialist Yugoslavia moved to the industrialized nations of the north, and particularly to war-ravaged Germany, which had lost 5 million people during the Second World War and was in desperate need of able-bodied workers. In the 1950s and 1960s West Germany and other prosperous countries implemented a series of **guest worker programs** that were designed to recruit much-needed labor for the booming economy. West Germany signed labor agreements with Italy, Greece, Spain, Portugal, Yugoslavia, Turkey, and the North African countries of Tunisia and Morocco. By the early 1970s there were 2.8 million foreign workers in Germany and 2.3 million in France, where they made up 11 percent of the French workforce.

guest worker programs
Government-run programs in western Europe designed to recruit labor for the booming postwar economy.

Most guest workers were young, unskilled single men who labored for low wages in entry-level jobs and sent much of their pay to their families at home. (See "Individuals in Society: Armando Rodrigues, West Germany's

The *Empire Windrush* Docks in London On June 22, 1948, almost five hundred Jamaicans seeking to emigrate to Great Britain arrived in London on the former troopship *Empire Windrush*. The event symbolized the changing patterns of postwar migration that would bring cultural and ethnic diversity to western Europe. (Keystone/Getty Images)

Armando Rodrigues, West Germany's "One-Millionth Guest Worker"

INDIVIDUALS IN SOCIETY

POPPING FLASHBULBS GREETED PORTUGUESE WORKER ARMANDO RODRIGUES when he stepped off a train in Cologne in September 1964. Celebrated in the national media as West Germany's one-millionth guest worker, Rodrigues was met by government and business leaders — including the minister of labor — who presented him with a motorcycle and a bouquet of carnations. A famous photograph of the event shows a modestly dressed Rodrigues mounted on his bike and surrounded by clapping dignitaries.

In most respects, Rodrigues was hardly different from the many foreign workers recruited to work in West Germany and other northern European countries. Yet given his moment of fame, he is an apt symbol of a troubled labor program that helped turn Germany into a multiethnic society.

By the late 1950s the new Federal Republic desperately needed able-bodied men to fill the low-paying jobs created by rapid economic expansion. West Germany had signed its first bilateral labor agreement with Italy in 1955, and treaties with other Mediterranean countries soon followed.

Rodrigues and hundreds of thousands of other young men signed up for the employment program and then submitted to an arduous application process. Rodrigues traveled from his village to the regional Federal Labor Office, where he filled out forms and took written and medical exams. Months later, after he had received an initial one-year contract from a German employer, Rodrigues and twelve hundred other Portuguese and Spanish men boarded a special train reserved for foreign workers and embarked for the Federal Republic.

For labor migrants, life was hard in West Germany. In the first years of the guest worker program, most recruits were young men between the ages of twenty and forty who were either single or willing to leave their families at home. They typically filled low-level jobs in construction, mines, and factories, and they lived in segregated barracks close to their workplaces, with six to eight workers in a room.

According to official plans, the so-called guest workers were supposed to return home after a specified period of time. Rodrigues went back to Portugal in the late 1970s, but despite government pressure, millions of temporary "guests" raised families and became permanent West German residents, building substantial ethnic minorities in the Federal Republic. Because of strict naturalization laws, however, they could not become West German citizens.

West Germans gave Rodrigues and his fellow migrants a mixed reception. Though they were a welcome source of inexpensive labor, the men who

Armando Rodrigues received a standing ovation and a motorcycle when he got off the train in Cologne in 1964. (DPA/Landov)

emigrated from what West Germans called "the southern lands" faced discrimination and prejudice. "Order, cleanliness, and punctuality seem like the natural qualities of a respectable person to us," wrote one official in 1966. "In the south, one does not learn or know this, so it is difficult [for a person from the south] to adjust here."*

Despite such hostility, foreign workers established a lasting and powerful presence in West Germany, and they were a significant factor in the country's swift economic recovery. Over time, West Germans came to terms with the tensions surrounding cultural integration and ethnic pluralism. Some forty-five years after Rodrigues arrived in Cologne, his motorcycle is on permanent display in the House of History Museum in Bonn. The exhibit is a remarkable testament both to the contribution of migrant labor to West German economic growth and to the benefits of multiculturalism in a democratic German society.

QUESTIONS FOR ANALYSIS

1. How did Rodrigues's welcome at his 1964 reception differ from the general attitude toward guest workers in Germany at the time?

2. What were the long-term costs and benefits of West Germany's labor recruitment policies?

*Quoted in Rita Chin, *The Guest Worker Question in Postwar Germany* (New York: Cambridge University Press, 2007), p. 43.

'One-Millionth Guest Worker,'" at left.) According to government plans, guest workers were supposed to return to their home countries after a specified period. In time, however, they built new lives, and to the dismay of the authorities many chose to live permanently in their adoptive countries. The number of Turkish foreign residents in West Germany soon surpassed the number of members of other ethnic groups, creating a large Turkish Muslim minority in the Federal Republic.

Europe was also changed by **postcolonial migration**, the movement of people from the former colonies (see pages 944–950) and the developing world into the prosperous states of Europe. In contrast to guest workers, who migrated as a result of formal recruitment programs, postcolonial migrants, who could often claim citizenship rights from their former colonizers, moved spontaneously to the former imperial powers. Immigrants from the Caribbean, India, Africa, and Asia moved to Britain; North Africans and especially Algerians moved to France; and Indonesians from the former Dutch East Indies migrated to the Netherlands. Postcolonial migrants also moved to eastern Europe, though in fewer numbers.

> **postcolonial migration**
> The postwar movement of people from former colonies and the developing world into Europe.

These new migration patterns had dramatic results. Immigrant labor fueled economic recovery. Growing ethnic diversity changed the face of Europe and enriched the cultural life of the continent. The new residents were not always welcome, however. Adaptation to European lifestyles could be difficult, and migrants often held on to their own languages and lived in separate communities. They faced employment and housing discrimination, and they were targeted by the anti-immigration policies of xenophobic politicians. Some Europeans worried that Muslim migrants from North Africa and Turkey would fail to properly adapt to European values and customs. In the twenty-first century Europeans continue to deal with the challenges of a multiethnic society.

New Roles for Women

The postwar culmination of a one-hundred-year-long trend toward early marriage, early childbearing, and small family size in wealthy urban societies (see Chapter 23) had revolutionary implications for women. Above all, pregnancy and child care occupied a much smaller portion of a woman's life than in earlier times. The postwar baby boom did make for larger families and fairly rapid population growth of 1 to 1.5 percent per year in many European countries, but the long-term decline in birthrates resumed by the 1960s. By the early 1970s about half of Western women were having their last baby by the age of twenty-six or twenty-seven. When the youngest child trooped off to kindergarten, the average mother had more than forty years of life in front of her.

This was a momentous transition. Throughout history male-dominated society insisted on defining most women as mothers or potential mothers, and motherhood was very demanding. In the postwar years, however, motherhood no longer absorbed the energies of a lifetime, and more and more married women looked for new roles in the world of work outside the family.

Women's roles in the workforce also changed after World War II. The ever-greater complexity of the modern economy meant that many women had to go outside the home to find cash income. Three major forces helped women searching for jobs. First, the economy boomed from about 1950 to 1973 and created strong demand for labor. Second, the economy continued its gradual shift away from the old male-dominated heavy industries, such as coal, steel, and shipbuilding, to the more dynamic white-collar service industries in which some women had always worked, such as government, education, trade, and health care. Third, young Western women shared fully in the postwar education revolution (see page 955) and could take advantage of the growing need for officeworkers and well-trained professionals. Thus more and more married women became full-time and part-time wage earners.

In the East Bloc, communist leaders asserted that they had opened up numerous jobs to women, and in large part they were correct. In eastern Europe, women accounted for almost half of all employed persons, and many women made their way into previously male professions, such as medicine and engineering. In western Europe and North America, there was a good deal of variation, with the percentage of married women in the workforce rising from a range of roughly 20 to 25 percent in 1950 to a range of 30 to 60 percent in the 1970s.

All was not easy for women entering paid employment. Married women entering (or re-entering) the labor force faced widespread and long-established discrimination in pay, advancement, and occupational choice in comparison to men. Moreover, many women could find only part-time work. As the divorce rate rose in the 1960s, part-time work, with its low pay and scanty benefits, often meant poverty for many women with teenage children. Finally, in the best of circumstances, married working women still carried most of the child-rearing and housekeeping responsibilities. Trying to live up to society's seemingly contradictory ideals was one reason for

many women to accept part-time employment; women working full-time typically faced an exhausting "double day"—on the job and at home.

The injustices that married women encountered as wage earners contributed greatly to the subsequent movement for women's equality and emancipation. Sexism and discrimination in the workplace—and in the home—grew loathsome and evoked the sense of injustice that drives revolutions and reforms. When in the 1960s a powerful feminist movement arose in the United States and western Europe to challenge the system, it found widespread support among working women.

Youth Culture and the Generation Gap

Postwar Europe also witnessed remarkable changes in youth roles and lifestyles, as the bulging cohort of so-called baby boomers born after World War II created a distinctive and very international youth culture. In the 1950s young people across western Europe and the United States created unique subcultures rooted in fashion and musical taste that set them off from their elders

British Teddy Boys, 1953 These young men are dressed in the "Teddy boy" style with velvet collars, narrow ties, and peg trousers that combine British Edwardian and American fashion. Like other subcultures in the 1950s, the Teds used their appearance to express their youthful rebelliousness. Teddy Boys quickly earned a reputation for street fighting, low-level criminal activity, and attacks on Britain's growing West Indian community. (© Henry Grant Collection/Museum of London)

and fueled anxious comments about a growing "generation gap."

Youth styles in the United States often provided inspiration for movements in Europe. Groups like the British Teddy Boys, the West German *Halbstarken* (half-strongs), and the French *blouson noirs* (black jackets) modeled their rebellious clothing and cynical attitudes on the bad-boy characters played by U.S. film stars such as James Dean and Marlon Brando. American jazz and rock 'n' roll spread rapidly in western Europe, aided by the invention of the long-playing record album (or LP) and the 45 rpm "single" in the late 1940s, and the growth of the corporate music industry. American musicians such as Elvis Presley, Bill Haley and the Comets, and Gene Vincent thrilled youths and worried parents, teachers, and politicians.

Youths played a key role in the consumer revolution. Postwar prosperity gave young people more purchasing power than ever before, and marketing experts and manufacturers quickly recognized that the young people they now called "teenagers" had money to spend. An array of advertisements and products now consciously targeted the youth market. In France, for example, magazine advertising aimed at adolescents grew by 400 percent between 1959 and 1962. As the baby boomers entered their late teens, they eagerly purchased trendy clothing and the latest pop music hits, as well as record players, transistor radios, magazines, hairstyles, and makeup, all marketed for the "young generation."

The new youth culture became an inescapable part of European society. One clear sign of this new presence was the rapid growth in the number of universities—and college students. In contrast to the United States, university education in Europe had been limited for centuries to a small elite. In 1950 only 3 to 4 percent of western European youths went on to higher education. Then, as government subsidies made education more affordable to the masses, enrollments skyrocketed. By 1960 at least three times more students attended some kind of university than they had before World War II, and the number continued to rise sharply until the 1970s.

The rapid expansion of higher education opened new opportunities for the middle and lower classes, but it also meant that classrooms were badly overcrowded. Many students felt that they were not getting the kind of education they needed for jobs in the modern world. At the same time, some reflective students feared that universities would soon do nothing but turn out docile technocrats both to stock and to serve "the establishment." Thus it was no coincidence that students became leaders in a counterculture that attacked the ideals of the affluent society and shocked the West in the late 1960s.

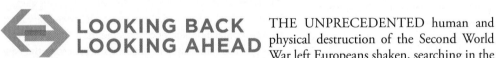

LOOKING BACK
LOOKING AHEAD

THE UNPRECEDENTED human and physical destruction of the Second World War left Europeans shaken, searching in the ruins for new livelihoods and a workable political order. A tension-filled peace settlement left the continent divided into two hostile political-military blocs, and the resulting Cold War, complete with the possibility of atomic annihilation, threatened to explode into open confrontation. Albert Einstein voiced a common anxiety when he said, "I do not know with what weapons World War III will be fought, but World War IV will be fought with sticks and stones."

Despite such fears, the division of Europe led to the emergence of a remarkably enduring world system. In the West, liberal democracy and the Western alliance brought social and political consensus. In the East, a combination of political repression and partial reform likewise limited dissent and encouraged stability. During the height of the Cold War, Europe's former colonies won liberation in a process that was often flawed, but that nonetheless resulted in political independence for millions of people. And large-scale transformations, including the rise of Big Science and rapid economic growth, opened new opportunities for women and immigrants and contributed to stability on both sides of the iron curtain.

By the early 1960s Europeans had entered a remarkable age of affluence that almost eliminated real poverty on most of the continent. Superpower confrontations had led not to European war but to peaceful coexistence. The following decades, however, would see substantial challenges to this postwar consensus. Youth revolts and a determined feminist movement, an oil crisis and a deep economic recession, and political dissent and revolution in the socialist bloc would shake and remake the foundations of Western society.

CHAPTER REVIEW

■ **How did the events at the close of World War II contribute to the emergence of the Cold War, and how did the U.S.-Soviet rivalry affect life in Europe? (p. 924)**

The Cold War grew out of the way World War II was fought in Europe and out of deep tensions between the victorious superpowers. Near the end of World War II, American and British forces met Stalin's armies in the middle of Germany and central Europe, so that the war-torn continent was already divided militarily in 1945. In the postwar political settlement, the division became official, and a divided Germany became the epicenter of an East-West Cold War. Stalin gradually established dependent communist dictatorships in eastern Europe to ensure the security of the Soviet Union, and the United States instituted a policy of containment aimed at stopping the spread of communism into western Europe and around the world. Western European nations joined U.S.-backed NATO to protect against Soviet attack, and the Soviet-aligned states formed their own Warsaw Pact in retaliation. As the Cold War matchup in Europe was institutionalized, competition between the two superpowers for military, economic, and technological superiority led to a surge in scientific innovation.

■ **Why did western Europe recover so successfully, and what were the sources of postwar stability? (p. 933)**

Western Europe's success was due to a combination of political recovery and unprecedented economic expansion. Political recovery included the emergence of the Christian Democrats and the movement toward European unity. The center-right Christian Democrats won sweeping victories across continental Europe, ushering in a new era of politics that catered to family values and the rejection of communism. They also promoted a free-market economy but advocated government assistance in such areas as finance and health care. In the mid-1950s economic growth took off for a generation, fueled by Marshall Plan aid and the liberal trade policies of the new Common Market. The resulting consumer revolution brought increasing prosperity to increasing numbers of people.

■ **What was the pattern of postwar rebuilding and development in the Soviet Union and communist eastern Europe? (p. 937)**

Immediately following World War II, Stalin imposed harsh one-party rule in the lands occupied by the Soviet armies, and he reimposed rigid central planning in both the Soviet Union and its eastern European satellite countries. Nationalized industry led to a scarcity of consumer goods, and

ordinary citizens faced difficult lives. In the mid-1950s Khrushchev instituted a policy of de-Stalinization that eased government controls, led to more cultural freedoms, and relaxed Cold War tensions. A modest consumer revolution and a rising standard of living improved everyday life in the Soviet Union in the late 1950s and the 1960s.

■ **What circumstances led to the postwar colonial independence movements, and how did the Cold War influence the process? (p. 944)**

Several causes led to the struggle for postwar independence in the European colonies. First, intellectuals had been calling for colonized peoples to move toward self-determination and racial equality since the early decades of the twentieth century, and their ideas were finally gaining momentum. In addition, World War II had drained Europe of much of the military and economic strength necessary to maintain a hold on its colonies, and Europeans began questioning their own moral authority to undertake a "civilizing mission," given the destruction they had caused in their own nations. In some cases, colonized peoples gained independence through peaceful negotiation with the imperial powers. In others, independence was won only after fierce revolts or all-out wars. Meanwhile, the two postwar superpowers jockeyed for position among the former colonies, their competing ideologies each offering its own version of freedom. As former colonial nations such as France, Belgium, and Great Britain relaxed their hold on their imperial territories, the United States and the Soviet Union struggled for influence. Both provided economic aid and military arms to anticolonial independence movements, leading to proxy wars and the establishment of client states among the new nations in Asia, Africa, and the Middle East.

■ **How did large-scale changes in social structures and relations contribute to European stability on both sides of the iron curtain? (p. 950)**

In the years after 1945 economic expansion led to a more fluid, less antagonistic class structure in western Europe. In eastern Europe, communist policies attacked class distinctions and promised equality for all. Economic growth and social welfare programs drew new workers to European countries, and internal migration, guest worker programs, and postcolonial migration opened Europe to new peoples and cultures. Married women also entered the labor force in growing numbers. The growing prosperity of the postwar era gave young people more money and educational opportunities, spurring the development of a distinct youth culture in the 1960s.

Suggested Reading

Bernstein, Serge. *The Republic of de Gaulle, 1958–1969*. 2006. An outstanding work on France.

Bessel, Richard. *Germany 1945: From War to Peace*. 2009. Examines the extensive destruction of Germany after the war and its transition into the postwar period.

Chamberlain, M. E. *Decolonization: The Fall of European Empires*, 2d ed. 1999. A clear, up-to-date account.

Chin, Rita. *The Guest Worker Question in Postwar Germany*. 2007. An engaging interpretation of postwar migration patterns in the Federal Republic.

Deak, Istav, Jan Tomasz Gross, and Tony Judt, eds. *The Politics of Retribution in Europe: World War II and Its Aftermath*. 2000. A collection of essays on postwar attempts to punish those responsible for Nazi crimes.

de Grazia, Victoria. *Irresistible Empire: America's Advance Through Twentieth-Century Europe*. 2005. Lively, provocative account of the Americanization of Europe from 1900 to the 1950s.

de Senarclens, Pierre. *From Yalta to the Iron Curtain: The Great Powers and the Origins of the Cold War*. 1995. A valuable work on the Cold War.

Eksteins, Modris. *Walking Since Daybreak: A Story of Eastern Europe, World War II, and the Heart of Our Century*. 2000. A powerful, partly autobiographical account that is highly recommended.

Hitchcock, William I. *The Struggle for Europe: The Turbulent History of a Divided Continent, 1945 to the Present*. 2004. A valuable general study with extensive bibliographies.

Jaraush, Konrad. *After Hitler: Recivilizing Germans, 1945–1995*. 2006. A stimulating survey by a distinguished historian.

Judt, Tony. *Postwar: A History of Europe Since 1945*. 2005. A masterful reconsideration, especially strong on smaller countries.

Tipton, Frank B., and Robert Aldrich. *An Economic and Social History of Europe from 1939 to the Present*. 1987. An interesting wide-ranging account.

Westad, Odd Arne. *The Global Cold War: Third World Interventions and the Making of Our Times*. 2007. Up-to-date study of the Cold War's global impact.

Notes

1. Anonymous, *A Woman in Berlin: Eight Weeks in the Conquered City: A Diary* (New York: Metropolitan Books, 2005), pp. 239–240.
2. Quoted in N. Graebner, *Cold War Diplomacy, 1945–1960* (Princeton, N.J.: Van Nostrand, 1962), p. 17.
3. From a speech delivered by George Marshall at Harvard University on June 5, 1947, reprinted in *Department of State Bulletin* (June 15, 1947), pp. 1159–1160.
4. Quoted in T. Judt, *Postwar: A History of Europe Since 1945* (New York: Penguin, 2005), p. 150.
5. Liz Heron, ed., *Truth, Dare or Promise*, quoted in M. H. Hunt, *The World Transformed, 1945 to the Present: A Documentary Reader* (Boston: Bedford/St. Martin's, 2004), pp. 192–193.
6. L. Erhard, *The Economics of Success* (Princeton, N.J.: D. Van Nostrand, 1963), p. 207.
7. Quoted in D. Treadgold, *Twentieth Century Russia*, 5th ed. (Boston: Houghton Mifflin, 1981), p. 442.
8. Nikita Khrushchev, "On the Cult of Personality and Its Consequences" (1956), quoted in J. M. Brophy et al., *Perspectives from the Past* (New York: Norton, 2009), pp. 804–805.
9. Quoted in M. Huband, *The Skull Beneath the Skin: Africa After the Cold War* (Boulder: Westview Press, 2001), p. 9.

Key Terms

displaced persons (p. 925)
Truman Doctrine (p. 929)
Marshall Plan (p. 930)
Council for Mutual Economic Assistance (COMECON) (p. 930)
NATO (p. 930)
Warsaw Pact (p. 930)
Christian Democrats (p. 933)
Common Market (p. 935)
de-Stalinization (p. 940)
decolonization (p. 944)
nonalignment (p. 945)
guest worker programs (p. 951)
postcolonial migration (p. 953)

For practice quizzes and other study tools, visit the Online Study Guide at **bedfordstmartins.com/mckaywest**.

For primary sources from this period, see ***Sources of Western Society***, **Second Edition**.

For Web sites, images, and documents related to topics in this chapter, visit Make History at **bedfordstmartins.com/mckaywest**.

30

Challenging the Postwar Order

1960–1991

As Europe entered the 1960s, the consensus established in the postwar era appeared stable and secure. Centrist politicians in western Europe agreed that abundant jobs and extensive state spending on welfare benefits would continue to improve living standards at all levels of society. In the Soviet Union and the East Bloc, although conditions varied country by country, modest economic growth and limited reforms amid continued political repression likewise contributed to a sense of stability. Cold War tensions relaxed, and it seemed that a remarkable age of affluence would ease political differences and lead to social harmony.

In the late 1960s, however, this hard-won consensus began to unravel. In 1968 counterculture protesters across the globe challenged dominant certainties. In the early 1970s the astonishing postwar economic advance ground to a halt, with serious social consequences. In western Europe, a new generation of more conservative political leaders drastically cut welfare benefits to deal with economic decline and growing global competition. New political groups — including feminists and environmentalists, national separatists and new-right populists — criticized centrist politics from across the political spectrum.

In the East Bloc, postwar leaders continued to vacillate between reform and repression, leading to frustrating stagnation. In the 1980s a broad movement to transform the communist system took root in Poland, and efforts to reform and revitalize the communist system in the Soviet Union snowballed out of control. In 1989 revolutions swept away communist rule throughout the entire Soviet bloc as the Cold War reached a dramatic conclusion. ■

© Berlin Wall Art 1999–2009

Life in a Divided Europe. Watchtowers, armed guards, and minefields controlled the communist eastern side of the Berlin Wall, the primary symbol of Cold War division in Europe. In the liberal West, to the contrary, ordinary folk turned the easily accessible wall into an ad hoc art gallery — this whimsical graffiti art appeared in the late 1980s.

CHAPTER PREVIEW

Reform and Protest in the 1960s
■ How did social and political changes in the 1960s contribute to growing criticism of the postwar consensus that had emerged in the 1950s?

Changing Consensus in Western Europe
■ How did economic decline in the 1970s contribute to fundamental social and political change in the 1980s in western Europe and North America?

The Decline of "Really Existing Socialism"
■ What internal and external factors weakened communist power in the East Bloc, and how did Soviet leader Mikhail Gorbachev try to reform the system from above?

The Revolutions of 1989
■ Why did anticommunist revolutions sweep through eastern Europe in 1989, and what were the immediate consequences?

Reform and Protest in the 1960s

How did social and political changes in the 1960s contribute to growing criticism of the postwar consensus that had emerged in the 1950s? ■

Looking at the wealth and prosperity of the early 1960s, commentators asserted that western Europe had entered an age of affluence. Compared to the previous fifty years, things looked good. After fifteen years of steady economic expansion, western Europeans began to enjoy the benefits of a well-established modern consumer society, and politics decidedly shifted to the left. Newly elected Social Democratic governments moved to normalize relations with the East Bloc and increased their countries' spending on welfare provisions. In the East, tensions lessened, eased by modest economic growth and forced underground by political repression. On both sides of the iron curtain, it seemed that the stability hammered out in the postwar decades was here to stay.

Challenges to the postwar consensus emerged in the mid-1960s, first in the form of a student counterculture that confronted the values of mainstream society with radical politics and lifestyle rebellions. Discontent spread to the East Bloc as well, particularly in Czechoslovakia, where in 1968 a rapid push toward liberalization was crushed by Soviet military force.

détente The progressive relaxation of Cold War tensions.

Cold War Tensions Thaw

The first decades of postwar reconstruction had been overseen by the center-right Christian Democrats, who successfully shaped the postwar consensus around Cold War politics, free-market economics with limited state intervention, and welfare provisions (see Chapter 29). Now, buoyed by the rapidly expanding economy, the politics shifted to the left. In Britain, the Labour Party returned to power in 1964, after thirteen years in opposition. In the Scandinavian countries of Denmark, Norway, and Sweden, Social Democratic parties maintained a leading role throughout the period. In West Germany, the aging postwar chancellor Konrad Adenauer (1876–1967) retired in 1963, and in 1969 Willy Brandt (1913–1992) became the first Social Democratic West German chancellor; his party would govern Germany until 1982. Even the tough-minded, independent French president Charles de Gaulle resigned in 1969.

One result of the victory of Social Democrats was the policy of **détente** (day-TAHNT), the progressive relaxation of Cold War tensions. While the Cold War continued to rage outside Europe and generally defined relations between the Soviet Union and the United States, western Europe took major steps toward genuine peace along the iron curtain. West German chancel-

A West German Leader Apologizes for the Holocaust In 1970 West German chancellor Willy Brandt knelt before the Jewish Heroes' Monument in Warsaw, Poland, to ask forgiveness for the German mass murder of European Jews and other groups during the Second World War. Brandt's action, captured in photo and film by the onlooking press, symbolized the chancellor's policy of Ostpolitik, the normalization of relations between the East and West Blocs. (AP Images)

lor Willy Brandt took the lead. In December 1970 he flew to Poland for the signing of a historic treaty of reconciliation. In a dramatic moment rich in symbolism, Brandt laid a wreath at the tomb of the Polish unknown soldier and another at the monument commemorating the armed uprising of Warsaw's Jewish ghetto against occupying Nazi armies. Standing before the ghetto memorial, a somber Brandt fell to his knees as if in prayer. "I wanted," Brandt said later, "to ask pardon in the name of our people for a million-fold crime which was committed in the misused name of the Germans."[1]

Brandt's gesture at the Warsaw Ghetto memorial and the treaty with Poland were part of his policy of reconciliation with eastern Europe, termed *Ostpolitik* (German for eastern policy). Brandt aimed at nothing less than a comprehensive peace settlement for central Europe and the two German states established after 1945. The Federal Republic of Germany (West Germany) had from its founding refused to recognize the communist German Democratic Republic (East Germany). West Germany also refused to accept the loss of German territory ceded to Poland and the Soviet Union after 1945.

According to Brandt, the building of the Berlin Wall in 1961 revealed the limitations of West Germany's official hard line toward communist eastern Europe. A new foreign policy was needed. Brandt negotiated treaties with the Soviet Union, Poland, and Czechoslovakia that formally accepted existing state boundaries in return for a mutual renunciation of force or the threat of force. Using the imaginative formula of "two German states within one German nation," Brandt's government also broke decisively with the past and entered into direct relations with East Germany. Brandt aimed for modest practical improvements rather than reunification, which at that point was completely impractical.

The policy of détente reached its high point when the United States, Canada, the Soviet Union, and all European nations (except isolationist Albania and tiny Andorra) signed the Final Act of the Helsinki Conference in 1975. The thirty-five participating nations agreed that Europe's existing political frontiers could not be changed by force. They also solemnly accepted numerous provisions guaranteeing the human rights and political freedoms of their citizens. Although the East did continue to curtail certain domestic freedoms and violate human rights guarantees (see pages 980–982), the

Chronology

1961	Building of Berlin Wall suggests permanence of the East Bloc
1962–1965	Second Vatican Council
1963	Wolf, *Divided Heaven*; Friedan, *The Feminine Mystique*
1964	Civil Rights Act in the United States
1964–1973	U.S. involvement in Vietnam War
1966	Formation of National Organization for Women (NOW)
1968	Soviet invasion of Czechoslovakia; "May events" protests in France
1971	Founding of Greenpeace
1973	OPEC oil embargo
1975	Final Act of the Helsinki Conference
1979	Margaret Thatcher becomes British prime minister; founding of West German Green Party; Soviet invasion of Afghanistan
1985	Mikhail Gorbachev named Soviet premier
1987	United States and Soviet Union sign arms reduction treaty
1989	Soviet withdrawal from Afghanistan
1989–1991	Fall of communism in eastern Europe
December 1991	Dissolution of the Soviet Union

agreement was generally effective in maintaining international peace.

Newly empowered Social Democrats also engaged in reform at home. Building on the welfare systems established in the 1950s, politicians increased state spending on public services even further. Society under western European social democracy was not "socialist," as it was in the Soviet bloc, where economic planning, government ownership, and one-party dictatorships ensured overwhelming state control. To the contrary, Social Democrats maintained a firm commitment to capitalist free markets and democratic electoral politics. At the same time, they viewed welfare provisions as a way to ameliorate the inevitable inequalities of a competitive market economy. As a result, western European democracies spent more and more state funds on health care, education, old-age insurance, and public housing.

By the early 1970s state spending on such programs hovered around 40 percent of the gross domestic product in France, West Germany, and Great Britain. Scandinavia and the Netherlands spent even more, all paid for with very high tax rates. Despite doctrinal differences, the center-right Christian Democrats also supported spending on public benefits and entitlements—as long as the economy prospered. With the economic slowdown of the mid-1970s, growing inflation and unemployment strained state budgets and undermined support for the welfare state consensus (see pages 972–974).

The Affluent Society

The political shift to the left in the 1960s was accompanied by rapid social change across western Europe. High wages meant that more and more people could afford the goods and gadgets provided by the consumer revolution that began in the 1950s (see Chapter 29), and the arrival of a full-blown consumer society had a profound impact on daily life. Labor-saving devices in family homes—vacuum cleaners, refrigerators, washing machines, and many others—transformed women's housework. Later studies showed that these new goods caused women to spend even more time cleaning and cooking to new exacting standards, but at the time electric appliances were considered indispensable to what contemporaries called a "modern lifestyle." The establishment of U.S.-style self-service supermarkets across Europe changed the way food was produced, purchased, and prepared, and threatened to force independent bakers, butchers, and neighborhood grocers out of business. (See "Living in the Past: The Supermarket Revolution," page 964.)

Europeans at all levels of society had more money to spend on leisure time and recreational pursuits. One of the most astonishing leisure-time developments was the blossoming of mass travel and tourism. With month-long paid vacations required by law in most western European countries and with widespread automobile ownership, travel to beaches and ski resorts came within the reach of the middle class and much of the working class. By the late 1960s packaged tours with cheap group airfares and bargain hotel accommodations had made even distant lands easily accessible. At home, more and more Europeans oriented their leisure time around television, watching news and entertainment and the latest American imports in the evenings.

Intellectuals and cultural critics greeted the age of affluence with a chorus of criticism. Some worried that rampant consumerism created a bland conformity that wiped out regional and national traditions and undermined intellectual activity. The great majority of ordinary people, they concluded, now ate the same foods, wore the same clothes, and watched the same programs on television, sapping creativity and individualism. Other critics complained bitterly that these changes threatened to Americanize European culture, but they could do little to stop the spread of consumer culture.

Worries about the Americanization of Europe were overstated—European nations preserved distinctive national cultures even during the consumer revolution—but social change was nonetheless unavoidable. The

moral authority of religious doctrine lost ground before the growing individualism of consumer society. Church membership declined, and fewer Europeans attended regular Sunday services. Even in traditionally Catholic countries, such as Italy, Ireland, and France, outward signs of popular belief seemed to falter. At the Second Vatican Council, convened from 1962 to 1965, Catholic leaders agreed on a number of reforms meant to democratize and renew the church and broaden its appeal. They called for new openness in Catholic theology, and masses would henceforth be said in local languages rather than in Latin, which few could understand. Their resolutions did little to halt the slide toward secularization. In Protestant lands—Great Britain, Scandinavia, the Netherlands, and most of West Germany—the decline in church membership was even greater.

Family ties also weakened in the age of affluence, and the number of adults living alone grew remarkably. Men

Braniff Airways Hostesses, ca. 1968 Sporting the latest "mod" styles, hostesses for Braniff International Airways wear uniforms made by world-renowned Italian fashion designer Emilio Pucci. The 1960s counterculture helped popularize the use of kaleidoscopic fluorescent colors and wild shapes in fashion, the fine arts, and advertising. (Braniff Archives)

and women married later, the nuclear family became smaller and more mobile, and divorce rates rose rapidly. By the 1970s the baby boom of the postwar decades was over, and population growth leveled out and even began to decline in the prosperous nations of northwest Europe.

The Growing Counterculture Movement

One of the dramatic results of economic prosperity and a more tolerant society was the emergence of a youthful counterculture that came of age in the mid-1960s to challenge the assumptions of the affluent society. What accounts for the emergence of the counterculture in the mid-1960s? Simple demographics played an important role. Young soldiers returning home after World War II in 1945 eagerly established families, and the next two decades brought a dramatic increase in the number of births per year in Europe and the United States. The children born during this baby boom grew up in an era of political liberalism and unprecedented material affluence. They learned about the horrors of totalitarian government during World War II, watched as colonial peoples forged new paths to freedom during the decades of decolonization, and worried about the growing conformity that seemed to be an inherent part of consumer society. Impressed by the U.S. civil rights movement and dismayed by ongoing Western imperialism and war, the baby boomers had the education—and perhaps most important the freedom from material want—to act on their concerns about inequality and social justice.

Counterculture movements in both Europe and the United States drew much inspiration from the American civil rights movement. In the late 1950s and early 1960s African Americans effectively challenged institutionalized inequality using legal means, as well as through public demonstrations, sit-ins, and bus boycotts, and threw off a deeply entrenched system of segregation and repression. The landmark Civil Rights Act of 1964, which prohibited discrimination in public services and on the job, and the Voting Rights Act of 1965, which guaranteed all African Americans the right to vote, were the crowning achievements of the long struggle against racism.

If dedicated African Americans and their white supporters could successfully reform entrenched power structures, student leaders reasoned, so could they. At the University of California–Berkeley in 1964 and 1965, students consciously adapted the tactics of the civil rights movement, including demonstrations and sit-ins, to challenge limits on free speech and academic freedom at the university. Their efforts were contagious. Soon students across the United States and in western Europe, where rigid rules controlled student activities at overcrowded new universities, were engaged in active protests. The youth movement had come of age, and it mounted a determined challenge to the Western consensus.

Dreaming of complete freedom and simpler, purer societies, many student activists in western Europe and the United States embraced an updated, romanticized version of Marxism, creating a movement that came to be known as the **New Left**. Adherents of the New Left argued that Marxism in the Soviet Union had been perverted to serve the needs of a repressive totalitarian state. Western capitalism, with its cold disregard for social equality, was little better. What was needed was a more humanitarian style of socialism, a rather vaguely defined Marxist program that could avoid the worst excesses of both capitalism and Soviet-style communism. New Left critics also attacked what they saw as the conformity of consumer society. The so-called culture industry, they argued, fulfilled only false needs and so contributed to the alienation of Western society.

New Left A movement of students in the West who advocated simpler, purer societies based on an updated, romanticized version of Marxism.

Such rarefied ideas fascinated student intellectuals, but much counterculture activity revolved around a lifestyle rebellion that apparently had broader appeal. Politics and lifestyles merged, a process captured in the popular 1960s slogan "the personal is the political." Nowhere was this more obvious than in the so-called sexual revolution. The 1960s brought frank discussion about sexuality in general, a new willingness to engage in premarital sex, and a growing acceptance of homosexuality. Sexual experimentation was facilitated by the development of the birth-control pill, which could eliminate the risk of unwanted pregnancy and went on the market in most western European countries in the 1960s. By 1970 "the pill" was being taken daily by millions of women across the Western world. Much of the new openness about sex crossed generational lines, but for the young the idea of sexual emancipation was closely linked to radical politics. Sexual openness and "free love," the sixties generation argued, not only moved people beyond traditional norms, but might also form the foundation of a more humane society.

The revolutionary aspects of the sexual revolution are easily exaggerated. According to a poll of German college students taken in 1968, the overwhelming majority wished to establish permanent families on traditional middle-class models. Yet the sexual behavior of young people did change in the 1960s and 1970s. More young people engaged in premarital sexual intercourse, and they did so at an earlier age than ever before. A 1973 study reported that only 4.5 percent of West German youths born in 1945 and 1946 had experienced sexual relations before their seventeenth birthday, but that 32 percent of those born in 1953 and 1954 had done so.[2] Such trends continued in the following decades.

The Supermarket Revolution

LIVING IN THE PAST

IN FEBRUARY 1961 SUPERMARKET ITALIANI OPENED its first supermarket-style grocery store in Florence, Italy, an ancient city famous for its Renaissance art and culture. The opening was an apparent triumph: some fifteen thousand customers mobbed the store, and police were called in to control the crowd. Owned by a multinational U.S.-based corporation, Supermarket Italiani proudly advertised "self

service" — in English — the slogan expressing a new cachet for all things American. Yet all was not well in Florence. Small grocers greeted the supermarket with strikes. Demonstrators called for boycotts. Angry letters to local newspapers complained that Italian traditions were in decay.

No wonder. The supermarket brought dramatic changes. For centuries residents of Florence — like most Europeans — had bought their food from local butchers, bakers, and fruit and vegetable dealers. In these tiny neighborhood stores, a shopkeeper and family greeted customers, discussed quality and price, and gossiped about neighborhood events. Customers could not handle the merchandise, which was sold fresh and in bulk. In a typical exchange, the shopkeeper took an order, calculated the price, weighed and wrapped the goods, and often provided home delivery.

Shopping in a well-lit American-style supermarket changed all that. Consumers entered a much larger store, picked up a cart, and strolled through long aisles stocked with pre-packaged and pre-priced goods. Frozen meat and canned vegetables meant that seasonal items were now available all year round. Competing brands introduced many versions of the same product, and advertising campaigns and cut-rate pricing enticed customers, who paid for all of their food selections in one place: at the checkout counter, where anonymous clerks tallied bills and made change using modern cash registers.

The bright lights and colorful packaging masked changes in both production and consumption. New farming methods, distribution networks, and packaging and advertising industries emerged to meet the demands of supermarket retailing. Supermarketing encouraged the rise of huge international chains such as Aldi, which started as a small chain in postwar

For decades before the supermarket revolution of the 1950s, Europeans shopped in small stores featuring specialty selections, such as this Italian shop selling meats, cheese, and preserved goods. Shoppers asked for items that were displayed behind the counter and were typically served by the store owner or members of the family. (From "50 anni di supermercati," Gallerie fotographiche, larepubblica.it)

In the new supermarkets, customers enjoyed self-service from a vastly expanded array of mass-produced goods, colorfully packaged and displayed on open shelves in long, impersonal aisles. Shoppers in this British supermarket in the 1960s carried their selections in baskets or carts to checkout counters at the front of the store. (Mary Evans Picture Library/ The Image Works)

Germany and now owns over eight thousand stores around the world. At home, the supermarket changed recipes and meal plans as well as household budgets and shopping styles. Supermarkets also transformed city space. Large stores on busy roads meant more traffic, and automobiles and parking lots threatened the very existence of neighborhood corner stores.

This was all new when Supermarket Italiani opened in Florence in 1961. By 1971, however, there were 538 supermarkets in Italy, 1,833 in France, and over 2,000 in West Germany. Though they never entirely displaced small grocers—and never totally dominated the food retail sector, as in the United States—by the 1980s supermarkets were a normal part of everyday life, vivid evidence of how the consumer revolution transformed the way Europeans shopped for, ate, and thought about food.

QUESTIONS FOR ANALYSIS

1. Why did Italians greet the arrival of supermarket shopping with both protest and enthusiasm?

2. In what ways does the supermarket exemplify the consumer revolution that swept through Europe in the late 1950s and the 1960s? What were its implications for family life?

Advertisement for the opening of a new supermarket in France. (From "50 anni di supermercati," Gallerie fotographiche, larepubblica.it)

Swinging London Pop-art decorations on Carnaby Street, the center of swinging London, herald the coming Christmas season in December 1967. (Bettmann/Corbis)

Along with sexual openness, drug use and rock music were at the center of the lifestyle revolt. For "the 68ers"—as the sixties generation in Europe came to be called—using drugs was a way to break free from conventional morals, to "turn on, tune in, and drop out," in the words of the American cult figure Timothy Leary. The popular music of the 1960s championed countercultural lifestyles. Rock bands like the Beatles, the Rolling Stones, and many others sang songs about drugs and casual sex. Counterculture "scenes" developed in cities such as San Francisco, Paris, and West Berlin. Carnaby Street, the center of "swinging London" in the 1960s, was world famous for its clothing boutiques and record stores, underscoring the close connections between generational revolt and consumer culture.

The United States and Vietnam

The growth of the counterculture movement was closely linked to the course of the Vietnam War. Although many student radicals at the time believed that imperialism was the main cause, American involvement in Vietnam was more clearly a product of the Cold War and the policy of containment (see Chapter 29). From the late 1940s on, most Americans and their leaders viewed the world in terms of a constant struggle to stop the spread of communism. As western Europe began to revive and China established a communist government in 1949, efforts to contain communism shifted to Asia. The bloody Korean War (1950–1953) ended in stalemate, but the United States did succeed in preventing a communist victory in South Korea.

After Vietnam won independence from France in 1954, U.S. president Dwight D. Eisenhower (r. 1953–1961) refused to sign the Geneva Accords that temporarily divided the country into two zones—a socialist north and an anticommunist south. When the South Vietnamese government declined to hold free elections that would unify the north and south zones, Eisenhower provided the south with military aid. President John F. Kennedy (r. 1961–1963) later increased the number of American "military advisers" to sixteen thousand, and in 1964 President Lyndon B. Johnson (r. 1963–1969) greatly expanded America's role in the Vietnam conflict, providing South Vietnam with massive military aid and a half million American troops. Though the United States bombed North Vietnam with ever-greater intensity, it did not invade the north or set up a naval blockade. In the end, the American strategy of limited warfare backfired. It was the American people who grew weary and the American leadership that cracked.

The undeclared war in Vietnam, fought nightly on American television, eventually divided the nation. Initial support was strong. The politicians, the media, and the population as a whole saw the war as part of a legitimate defense against communist totalitarianism in all poor countries. But an antiwar movement quickly emerged on college campuses, where the prospect of being drafted to fight savage battles in Asian jungles made male stomachs churn. In October 1965 student protesters joined forces with old-line socialists, New Left intellectuals, and pacifists in antiwar demonstrations in fifty American cities. The protests spread to western Europe. By 1967 a growing number of critics in the United States and Europe denounced the American presence in Vietnam as a criminal intrusion into a complex and distant civil war.

Criticism reached a crescendo after the Vietcong Tet Offensive in January 1968. The communists' first comprehensive attack on major South Vietnamese cities failed militarily, with the Vietcong suffering heavy losses, but the Tet Offensive signaled that the war was not close to ending, as Washington had claimed. America's leaders lost heart, and within months President Johnson announced that he would not stand for re-election and called for negotiations with North Vietnam.

President Richard M. Nixon (r. 1969–1974) sought to gradually disengage America from Vietnam beginning in 1968. Intensifying the continuous bombardment of the enemy while simultaneously pursuing peace talks with the North Vietnamese, Nixon suspended the draft, so hated on college campuses, and cut American forces in Vietnam from 550,000 to 24,000 in four years. In 1973 Nixon finally reached a peace agreement with North Vietnam that allowed remaining American forces to complete their withdrawal, and gave the United States the right to resume bombing if the accords were broken. Fighting declined markedly in South Vietnam, where the South Vietnamese army appeared to hold its own against the Vietcong.

Although the storm of criticism in the United States seemed to have passed, America's disillusionment with the war had far-reaching repercussions. In early 1974, when North Vietnam launched a general invasion against South Vietnamese armies, the U.S. Congress refused to permit any American military response. After more than thirty-five years of battle, the South Vietnamese were forced in 1975 to accept a unified country under a communist dictatorship.

Student Revolts and 1968

The intensification of the Vietnam War in the late 1960s was accompanied by worldwide opposition. Many politically active students believed that the United States was fighting an immoral and imperialistic war against a small and heroic people, and the counterculture became increasingly radical. In European and American cities, students and sympathetic followers organized massive demonstrations against the war, and then extended their protests to support colonial independence movements, to demand an end to the nuclear arms race, and to call for world peace and liberation from social conventions of all kinds.

Youth activism erupted in 1968 in a series of protests and riots that circled the globe. African Americans rioted across the United States after the assassination of civil rights leader Martin Luther King, Jr. Antiwar demonstrators battled police at the Democratic National Convention in Chicago. Police in Mexico City shot and killed several hundred protesters calling for political reform (the exact number of deaths is still unknown), and students in Tokyo demonstrated against the war in Vietnam. Clashes between protesters and police occurred across western Europe and in the East Bloc as well. Students in Warsaw marched to protest government censorship, and youths in Prague were in the forefront of

Student Rebellion in Paris These rock-throwing students in the Latin Quarter of Paris are trying to force education reforms and even topple de Gaulle's government. In May 1968, in a famous example of the protest movements that swept the world in the late 1960s, Parisian rioters clashed repeatedly with France's tough riot police in bloody street fighting. De Gaulle remained in power, but a major reform of French education did follow. (Bruno Barbey/Magnum Photos)

the attempt to radically reform communism from within (see pages 982–983).

One of the most famous and perhaps far-reaching of these revolts occurred in France in May 1968, when angry students and striking workers brought the French economy to a standstill. A group of students inspired by New Left ideals initially occupied buildings and took over the University of Paris. Violent clashes with police followed. When police tried to clear the area around the university on the night of May 10, a pitched street battle took place. At the end of the night, 460 arrests had been made, 367 people were wounded, and protesters had burned about 200 cars. The slogans that appeared on posters put up overnight on the walls in Paris expressed the spirit of the New Left: "Power to the imagination"; "Be realistic, demand the impossible"; "Beneath the paving stones, the beach." The critique of the dehumanization of modern society captured in these slogans reflects both the imagination and also the vagueness of the demands of the counterculture.

The so-called May events might have been a typically short-lived student protest against American involvement in Vietnam and the abuses of capitalism, but the demonstrations triggered a national revolt. By May 18 some 10 million workers were out on strike, and protesters occupied factories across France. For a brief moment, it seemed as if counterculture dreams of a revolution from below would come to pass. The French Fifth Republic was on the verge of collapse, and a shaken President de Gaulle surrounded Paris with troops.

In the end, however, the idealistic goals of the radical students did not really correspond to the bread-and-butter demands of the striking workers. When the government promised workplace reforms, including immediate pay raises, the strikers returned to work. President de Gaulle dissolved the French parliament and called for new elections. His conservative party won almost 75 percent of the seats, showing that the majority of the French people supported neither general strikes nor student-led revolutions. The universities shut down for the summer, and the movement had dissipated by the time fall semester began. The May events marked the high point of counterculture protest in Europe; in the early 1970s the movement declined.

As the political enthusiasm of the counterculture waned, committed activists were divided among themselves about the best way to continue to fight for social change. Some followed what German student leader Rudi Dutschke called "the long march through the institutions" and began to work for change from within the system. They entered national politics and joined emerging feminist, antinuclear, and environmental groups that would play an important role in the coming decades (see pages 974–979).

Other groups, however, followed a more radical path. Across Europe, but particularly in Italy and West Germany, fringe New Left groups tried to bring radical change by turning to violence and terrorism. The Italian Red Brigades and the West German Red Army Faction robbed banks, bombed public buildings, and kidnapped and killed politicians and business leaders. After spasms of violence in the late 1970s—in Italy, for example, the Red Brigades murdered former prime minister Aldo Moro—security forces succeeded in incarcerating most of the terrorist leaders, and the movement fizzled out.

Counterculture protests generated a great deal of excitement and trained a generation of activists, but New Left ideologies focused on alienation and dehumanization captured in slogans like "Power to the imagination" resulted in little practical political change. Lifestyle rebellions involving sex, drugs, and rock music transformed individual behavior, but they hardly led to revolution.

The 1960s in the East Bloc

The building of the Berlin Wall in 1961 suggested that communism was here to stay, and the failure of NATO to intervene showed that the United States and western Europe basically accepted the premise. It also encouraged socialist regimes to experiment with some economic and cultural liberalization. East Bloc economies clearly lagged behind those of the West, exposing the weaknesses of heavy-handed central planning. To address these problems, socialist leaders now implemented cautious forms of decentralization and limited market policies. The results were mixed. Hungary's so-called New Economic Mechanism, which broke up state monopolies, allowed some private retail stores, and encouraged private agriculture, was perhaps most successful. East Germany's New Economic System, inaugurated in 1963, brought limited privatization and also showed moderate success, though it was reversed when the government returned to centralization in the late 1960s. In other East Bloc countries, however, economic growth flagged.

Recognizing that the emphasis on heavy industry could lead to popular discontent, Communist planning commissions redirected resources to the consumer sector. Again, the results varied across the East Bloc. By 1970, for example, ownership of televisions in the more developed nations of East Germany, Czechoslovakia, and Hungary approached that of the West, and other consumer goods were also more available. In Poland, however, the economy stagnated in the 1960s. In the more conservative Albania and Romania, where leaders held fast to Stalinist practices, provision of consumer goods faltered. In general, ordinary people in the East Bloc grew increasingly tired of the shortage of consumer goods that seemed an endemic part of socialist society.

In the 1960s Communist regimes also granted cautious cultural freedoms. In the Soviet Union, the cul-

The East German Trabi This small East German passenger car, produced between 1963 and 1990, was one of the best-known symbols of everyday life in East Germany. Though the cars were notorious for their poor engineering, the growing number of Trabis on East German streets nonetheless testified to the increased availability of consumer goods in the East Bloc in the 1960s and 1970s. (Visual Connection Archive)

tural thaw allowed dissidents like Aleksandr Solzhenitsyn and Boris Pasternak to publish critical works of fiction (see Chapter 29), and this relative tolerance spread to eastern European countries as well. In East Germany, for example, during the Bitterfeld Movement—named after a conference of writers, officials, and workers in Bitterfeld, an industrial city south of Berlin—the regime encouraged intellectuals to take a more critical view of life in the East Bloc, so long as they did not directly oppose communism itself. Author Christa Wolf's novel *Divided Heaven* (1963) is a classic example of the genre. Though her boyfriend immigrates to West Germany in search of better work conditions, the leading character remains committed to building socialism, despite the very real problems she sees in a small-town factory.

Despite some cultural openness, the most outspoken dissidents were harassed and often forced to emigrate to the West, and an underground *samizdat* (SAH-meez-daht) literature critical of communism emerged in the Soviet Union and the East Bloc. The label *samizdat*, a Russian term meaning "self-published," referred to books, periodicals, newspapers, and pamphlets that directly criticized communism and thus went far beyond the limits of criticism accepted by the state. Written and published secretly to avoid regime censors, and then passed hand to hand by dissident readers, samizdat literature emerged in Russia, Poland, and other countries in the mid-1950s and blossomed in the 1960s. These unofficial networks of communication kept critical thought alive and built contacts among dissidents, building the foundation for the protest movements of the 1970s and 1980s.

Modest prosperity and limited cultural tolerance only went so far. The citizens of East Bloc countries sought political liberty as well, and the limits on reform were sharply revealed in Czechoslovakia during the 1968

"Prague spring" (named for the country's capital city). In January 1968 reform elements in the Czechoslovak Communist Party gained a majority and voted out the long-time Stalinist leader in favor of Alexander Dubček (1921–1992), whose new government launched dramatic reforms. Educated in Moscow, Dubček (DOOB-chehk) was a dedicated communist, but he and his allies believed that they could reconcile genuine socialism with personal freedom and internal party democracy. They called for "socialism with a human face" and relaxed state censorship and replaced rigid bureaucratic planning with local decision making by trade unions, managers, and consumers. The reform program proved enormously popular.

Although Dubček remembered the lesson of the Hungarian revolution (see Chapter 29) and constantly proclaimed his loyalty to the Soviet Union and the Warsaw Pact, the determination of the Czechoslovak reformers to build a more liberal and democratic socialism frightened hard-line Communists. These fears were particularly strong in Poland and East Germany, where leaders knew full well that they lacked popular support. Moreover, the Soviet Union feared that a liberalized Czechoslovakia would eventually be drawn to neutrality or even to the democratic West. Thus the East Bloc leadership launched a concerted campaign of intimidation against the Czechoslovak reformers, and five hundred thousand Russian and allied eastern European troops suddenly occupied Czechoslovakia in August 1968. The Czechoslovaks made no attempt to resist militarily, and the arrested leaders surrendered to Soviet demands. The reform program was abandoned, and the Czechoslovak experiment in humanizing communism came to an end.

Shortly after the invasion of Czechoslovakia, Soviet premier Leonid Brezhnev (1906–1982) declared the

The Invasion of Czechoslovakia Armed with Czechoslovakian flags, courageous Czechs in downtown Prague try to stop a Soviet tank and repel the invasion and occupation of their country by the Soviet Union and its eastern European allies. This dramatic confrontation was ultimately unsuccessful. Realizing that military resistance would be suicidal, the Czechs capitulated to Soviet control. (AP Images)

so-called **Brezhnev Doctrine**, according to which the Soviet Union and its allies had the right to intervene in any socialist country whenever they saw the need. The 1968 invasion of Czechoslovakia was the crucial event of the Brezhnev era: it showed that only the threat of the Soviet military was holding the East Bloc together. At the same time, it demonstrated the determination of the ruling elite to maintain the status quo throughout the Soviet bloc, which would last for the next twenty years.

Brezhnev Doctrine
Doctrine created by Leonid Brezhnev that held that the Soviet Union had the right to intervene in any socialist country whenever it saw the need.

Changing Consensus in Western Europe

How did economic decline in the 1970s contribute to fundamental social and political change in the 1980s in western Europe and North America? ■

The great postwar economic boom came to a close in the early 1970s, opening a long period of economic stagnation, widespread unemployment, and social dislocation. Western European leaders drifted to the right, cutting taxes and state spending and selling off state-owned companies. A number of new political groups entered national politics, including feminists and environmentalists on the left and neo-nationalist political parties on the right. By the end of the 1980s the postwar stability based on economic prosperity, generous welfare provisions, and consensus politics had been deeply shaken, and the West had restructured its economy and entered the information age.

Economic Crisis and Hardship

Starting in the early 1970s the West entered into a long period of economic decline. One of the early causes of the downturn was the collapse of the international monetary system, which since 1945 had been based on the American dollar, valued in gold at $35 an ounce. In the postwar decades, the United States spent billions of dollars on foreign aid and foreign wars, weakening the value of American currency. In 1971 President Nixon attempted to reverse this trend by abruptly stopping the exchange of U.S. currency for gold. The value of the dollar fell sharply, and inflation accelerated worldwide. Fixed rates of exchange were abandoned, and great uncertainty replaced postwar predictability in international trade and finance.

Even more damaging to the global economy was the dramatic reversal in the price and availability of energy. The great postwar boom had been fueled in part by cheap oil from the Middle East, which permitted Big Science and other energy-intensive industries—automobiles, chemicals, and electric power—to expand rapidly and lead other sectors of the economy forward (see Chapter 29). The fate of the developed world was thus increasingly linked to this turbulent region, and strains began to show in the late 1960s. In 1967, in the Six-Day War between Israel and its Arab neighbors, Israel quickly defeated Egypt, Jordan, and Syria and expanded its territory in the former territories of Palestine, angering Arab leaders. The conflict exacerbated anti-Western feeling in the Arab states. By 1971 **OPEC**, the Arab-led Organization of Petroleum Exporting Countries, had watched the price of crude oil decline consistently compared with the rising price of Western manufactured goods. OPEC decided to reverse that trend by presenting a united front against Western oil companies.

The stage was set for a revolution in energy prices when Egypt and Syria launched a surprise attack on Israel in October 1973, setting off the fourth Arab-Israeli war. With the help of U.S. military arms, Israel again achieved a quick victory. OPEC then declared an embargo on oil shipments to the United States, Israel's ally, and within a year crude oil prices quadrupled. Western nations realized that the rapid price increase was economically destructive, but together they did nothing. Thus governments, industry, and individuals had no choice other than to deal piecemeal with the so-called oil shock—a "shock" that turned out to be an earthquake.

Coming on the heels of upheaval in the international monetary system, the revolution in energy prices plunged the world into its worst economic decline since the 1930s. The energy-intensive industries that had driven the economy up in the 1950s and 1960s now dragged it down. Unemployment rose, productivity and living standards declined, and inflation soared. By 1976 a modest recovery was in progress, but when a fundamentalist Islamic revolution struck Iran and oil production collapsed in that country in 1979, the price of crude oil doubled, and the world economy succumbed to its second oil shock. Unemployment and inflation rose dramatically before another uneven recovery began in 1982. Economists coined a new term—**stagflation**—to describe the combination of low growth and high inflation that led to a worldwide recession.

Anxious observers, recalling the disastrous consequences of the Great Depression, worried that the Common Market would disintegrate in the face of severe economic dislocation and that economic nationalism would halt steps toward European unity. Yet the Common Market—now officially known as the European Economic Community—continued to attract new members. In 1973 Denmark and Iceland, in addition to Britain, finally joined. Greece joined in 1981, and Portugal and Spain entered in 1986. The nations of the European Economic Community cooperated more closely in international undertakings, and the movement toward unity for western Europe stayed alive.

The developing world was hit hard by slowed growth, and the global economic downturn widened the gap between rich and poor countries. Governments across South America, sub-Saharan Africa, and South Asia borrowed heavily from the United States and western Europe in attempts to restructure their economies, setting the stage for a serious international debt crisis. At the same time, the East Asian countries of Japan and then Singapore, South Korea, and Taiwan started exporting high-tech consumer goods to the West. Competition from these East Asian "tiger economies," whose labor costs were comparatively low, shifted manufacturing jobs away from the highly industrialized countries of northern Europe.

Even as the world economy slowly began recovering in the 1980s, it could no longer create enough jobs to replace those that were lost. By the end of the 1970s, the foundations of economic growth had begun shifting to high-tech information industries, such as computing and biotechnology, and to services, including medicine, banking, and finance. Scholars spoke of the shift as the arrival of "the information age" or **postindustrial society**. Technological advances streamlined the production of many goods, making many industrial jobs superfluous. In western Europe, heavy industry, such as steel, mining, automobile manufacture, and shipbuilding, lost ground. Factories closed, leading to the emergence of "rust belts"—formerly industrialized areas that were now ghost lands, with vacant lots, rusting machinery, and empty inner cities where prosperous workers once lived. The highly industrialized Ruhr district in northwest West Germany and the factory belts around Detroit, Michigan, were classic examples.

One telling measure of the troubled economy was the misery index, which combined rates of inflation and unemployment in a single, powerfully emotional number. Misery increased on both sides of the Atlantic, but the increase was substantially greater in western Europe, where the hard times were often referred to simply as "the crisis" and unemployment numbers rose dramatically. By 1985 the unemployment rate in western Europe had risen to its highest level since the Great Depression. Nineteen million people were without work.

Ordinary people were hard hit by the crisis, and there were heartbreaking human tragedies—lost jobs, bankruptcies, homelessness, and mental breakdowns. Punk rock songs of the late 1970s captured the mood of

OPEC The Arab-led Organization of Petroleum Exporting Countries.

stagflation Term coined in the early 1980s to describe the combination of low growth and high inflation that led to a worldwide recession.

postindustrial society Society that relies on high-tech and service-oriented jobs for economic growth rather than on heavy industry and manufacturing jobs.

hostility and cynicism among young people. Yet on the whole, the welfare system fashioned in the postwar era prevented mass suffering and degradation. The responsive, socially concerned national state undoubtedly contributed to the preservation of political stability and democracy in the face of economic difficulties that might have brought revolution and dictatorship in earlier times.

The energetic response of governments to support social needs helps explain why total government spending in most European countries continued to rise sharply during the 1970s and early 1980s. In 1982 western European governments spent an average of more than 50 percent of all national income on social programs, as compared to only 37 percent fifteen years earlier. In all countries, people were willing to see their governments increase spending, but they resisted higher taxes. This imbalance contributed to the rapid growth of budget deficits, national debts, and inflation. By the late 1970s a powerful reaction against government's ever-increasing role had set in.

The Conservative Backlash

The transition to a postindustrial society was led by a new generation of conservative political leaders who were willing to make the difficult reforms necessary to restructure the economy, even though this typically led to social dislocation and growing inequality. During the thirty years following World War II, both Social Democrats and the more conservative Christian Democrats had agreed that economic growth and social stability were best achieved through full employment and high wages, some government regulation, and generous welfare provisions. In the late 1970s, however, with a weakened economy and increased global competition, this consensus began to unravel. Whether politics turned to the right, as in Great Britain, the United States, and West Germany, or to the left, as in France and Spain, leaders moved to cut government spending and regulation in attempts to improve economic performance.

The new conservatives of the 1980s followed a philosophy that came to be known as **neoliberalism** because of its distant roots in the laissez-faire policies favored by nineteenth-century liberals such as Adam Smith (see Chapter 22). Neoliberal theorists like U.S. economist Milton Friedman argued that government should cut support of social services such as housing, education, and health insurance; limit business subsidies; and retreat from regulation of all kinds. (Neoliberalism should thus be distinguished from modern American liberalism, which supports welfare programs and some state regulation of the

neoliberalism Philosophy of 1980s conservatives who argued for decreased government spending on social services and privatization of state-run industries.

economy.) Neoliberals also called for privatization — the sale of state-managed industries to private owners. Placing government-owned industries such as transportation and communication networks in private hands, they argued, would both tighten government spending and lead to greater workplace efficiency. The main goal was to increase private profits, which neoliberals believed were the real engine of economic growth.

The effects of neoliberal policies are best illustrated by events in Great Britain. The broad shift toward greater conservatism, coupled with growing voter dissatisfaction with high taxes and runaway state budgets, helped elect Margaret Thatcher (b. 1925) prime minister in 1979. A member of the Conservative Party and a convinced neoliberal, Thatcher was determined to scale back the role of government, and in the 1980s — the "Thatcher years" — she pushed through a series of controversial free-market policies that transformed postwar Britain. Thatcher's Conservative Party government cut spending on health care, education, and public housing. The Conservatives reduced taxes and privatized or sold off government-run enterprises. In one of the most popular actions, Thatcher encouraged low- and moderate-income renters in state-owned housing projects to buy their apartments at rock-bottom prices. This initiative, part of Thatcher's broader privatization campaign, created a whole new class of property owners, thereby eroding the electoral base of Britain's socialist Labour Party. (See "Individuals in Society: Margaret Thatcher," page 973.)

Though she never eliminated all social programs, Thatcher's policies helped replace the interventionist ethos of the welfare state with a greater reliance on private enterprise and the free market. There were significant human costs involved in this transition. In the first three years of her first term, heavy industries such as steel, coal mining, and textiles shut down, and unemployment rates in Britain doubled to over 12 percent. The gap between rich and poor widened, and increasing poverty led to discontent and crime. Working-class strikes and protests sometimes led to violent riots. Street violence often had unfortunate racial overtones: immigrants from former British colonies in Africa, India, and the Caribbean, dismayed with poor jobs and racial prejudice, clashed repeatedly with police. For a while, the "iron lady" successfully rallied support around British victory over Argentina in the brief Falklands War (1982), but over time her position weakened. By 1990 Thatcher's popularity had fallen to record lows, and she was replaced by Conservative Party leader John Major.

In the United States, two-term president Ronald Reagan (r. 1981–1989) followed a similar path, though his success in cutting government was more limited. A leader of the U.S. neoconservative movement, Reagan's campaign slogan — "government is not the solution to

INDIVIDUALS IN SOCIETY

MARGARET THATCHER, THE FIRST WOMAN ELECTED TO LEAD a major European state, was one of the late twentieth century's most significant leaders. The controversial "iron lady" attacked socialism, promoted capitalism, and changed the face of modern Britain.

Raised in a lower-middle-class family in a small city in southeastern England, Thatcher entered Oxford in 1943 to study chemistry. She soon dis-

covered a passion for politics. Elected president of student Conservatives, she ran for Parliament in 1950 in a solidly Labour district to gain experience. Articulate and attractive, she gained the attention of Denis Thatcher, a wealthy businessman who drove her to campaign appearances in his Jaguar. Married a year later, the new Mrs. Thatcher abandoned chemistry, went to law school, gave birth to twins, and became a tax attorney. In 1959 she returned to politics and won a seat in the Conservative triumph.

For the next fifteen years Thatcher served in Parliament and held various ministerial posts when the Conservatives governed. In 1974, as the economy soured and the Conservatives lost two close elections, a rebellious Margaret Thatcher adroitly ran for the leadership position of the Conservative Party and won. In the 1979 election, as the Labour government faced rampant inflation and crippling strikes, Thatcher promised to reduce union power, lower taxes, and promote free markets. Attracting swing votes from skilled workers, she was elected prime minister.

A self-described "conviction politician," Thatcher rejected postwar Keynesian efforts to manage the economy, arguing that governments had created inflation by printing too much money. Thus her government reduced the supply of money and credit, and it refused to retreat as interest rates and unemployment soared. Her popularity plummeted. But Thatcher maintained her position, in part through an aggressive pursuit of foreign policy. In 1982 the generals ruling Argentina suddenly seized the Falkland Islands off the Argentine coast, the home of 1,800 British citizens. Ever a staunch nationalist, Thatcher detached a naval armada that recaptured the Falklands without a hitch. Britain admired Thatcher's determination and patriotism, and she was re-elected in 1983.

Thatcher's second term was the high point of her influence. Her whole-hearted commitment to privatization transformed British industry. More than fifty state-owned companies, ranging from the state telephone monopoly to the nationalized steel trust, were sold to private investors. Small investors were offered shares at bargain prices to promote "people's capitalism." Thatcher also curbed the power of British labor unions with various laws and actions. Most spectacularly, when in 1984 the once-mighty coal miners rejected more mine closings and doggedly struck for a year, Thatcher stood firm and beat them. This outcome had a profound psychological impact on the public, who blamed her for growing unemployment. Thatcher was also accused of mishandling a series of protest hunger strikes undertaken by the Irish Republican Army—in 1981 ten IRA members starved themselves to death in British prisons—but she held her ground, refusing to compromise with those she labeled criminals. As a result, the revolt in Northern Ireland entered one of its bloodiest phases.

Margaret Thatcher as prime minister. (AP Images/ Staff-Caulkin)

Elected to a third term in 1987, Thatcher became increasingly stubborn, overconfident, and uncaring. Working with her neoliberal ideological soul mate, U.S. president Ronald Reagan, she opposed greater political and economic unity within the European Community. This, coupled with rising inflation, stubborn unemployment, and an unpopular effort to assert financial control over city governments, proved her undoing. In 1990, as in 1974, party stalwarts suddenly revolted and elected a new Conservative leader. The transformational changes of the Thatcher years nonetheless endured, consolidated by her Conservative successor and largely accepted by the New Labour prime minister, the moderate Tony Blair.

QUESTIONS FOR ANALYSIS

1. Why did Margaret Thatcher want to change Britain, and how did she do it?
2. How do Thatcher's policies reflect the conservative backlash of the 1970s and 1980s?

our problem, government is the problem"—summed up the movement's neoliberal philosophy. With widespread popular support and the agreement of most congressional Democrats as well as Republicans, Reagan in 1981 pushed through major across-the-board cuts in income taxes. But Reagan and Congress failed to limit government spending, which increased as a percentage of national income in the course of his presidency. A massive military buildup was partly responsible, but spending on social programs also grew rapidly. The harsh recession of the early 1980s required the government to spend more on unemployment benefits, welfare benefits, and medical treatment for the poor. Moreover, Reagan's antiwelfare rhetoric mobilized the liberal opposition and eventually turned many moderates against him. The budget deficit soared, and the U.S. government debt tripled in a decade.

The Social Consequences of Thatcherism As police watch in the background, picketers outside the largest coal mine in Britain hold up a poster reading "Save the Pits" during the miners' strike of 1984–1985. Prime Minister Margaret Thatcher broke the strike, weakening the power of Britain's trade unions and easing the turn to free-market economic reforms. Thatcher's neoliberal policies revived economic growth but cut state subsidies for welfare benefits and heavy industries, leading to lower living standards for many working-class Britons and, as this image attests, to popular protest.
(Bride Lane Library/Pepperfoto/Getty Images)

West Germany also turned to the right. After more than a decade in power, the Social Democrats were foundering, and in 1982 Christian Democrat Helmut Kohl (b. 1930) became the new chancellor. Like Thatcher, Kohl cut taxes and government spending. His policies led to increasing unemployment in heavy industry but also to solid economic growth. By the mid-1980s West Germany was one of the most prosperous countries in the world. In foreign policy, Kohl drew close to President Reagan. The chancellor agreed to deploy U.S. Pershing II and cruise missiles on West German territory, and so contributed to renewed superpower tensions. In power for sixteen years, Kohl and the Christian Democrats presided over the dismantling of the Berlin Wall in 1989, the reunification of East and West Germany in 1990, and the end of the Cold War (see pages 988–989).

The most striking temporary exception to the general drift to the right in European politics was François Mitterrand (1916–1996) of France. After his election as president in 1981, Mitterrand and his Socialist Party led France on a lurch to the left. This marked a significant change in French politics, which had been dominated by center-right parties for some twenty-five years. Working at first in a coalition that included the French Communist Party, Mitterrand launched a vast program of nationalization and public investment designed to spend the country out of economic stagnation. By 1983 this attempt had clearly failed, and Mitterrand's Socialist government made a dramatic about-face. The Socialists were compelled to reprivatize industries nationalized during the first term. They imposed a wide variety of austerity measures and maintained those policies for the rest of the decade.

Despite persistent economic crises and high social costs, by 1990 the developed nations of western Europe and North America were far more productive than they had been in the early 1970s. Western Europe was at the center of the emerging global economy, and its citizens were far richer than those in Soviet bloc countries (see pages 962–963). Yet the collapse of the postwar consensus and the remaking of Europe in the transitional decades of the 1970s and 1980s generated new forms of protest and dissent across the political spectrum.

Challenges and Victories for Women

The 1970s marked the arrival of a broad-based feminist movement devoted to securing genuine gender equality and promoting the general interests of women. Three basic reasons accounted for this major development. First, ongoing changes in underlying patterns of motherhood and paid work created novel conditions and new demands (see Chapter 29). Second, a vanguard of feminist intellectuals articulated a powerful critique of gender relations, which stimulated many women to rethink

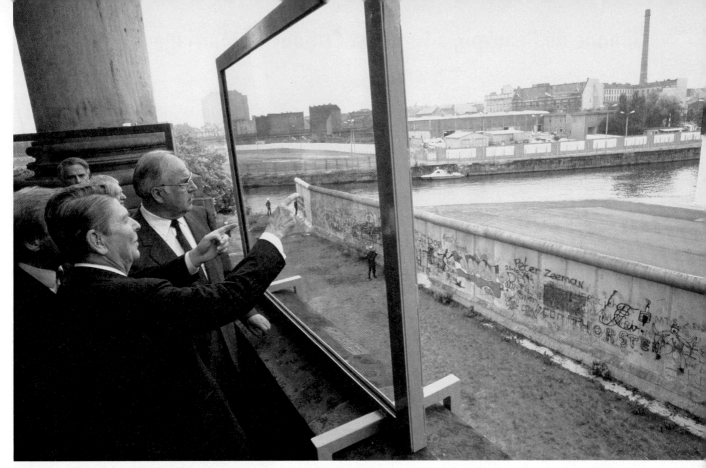

Kohl and Reagan View the Berlin Wall Protected by a sheet of bulletproof glass, West German chancellor Helmut Kohl (right) and U.S. president Ronald Reagan look over the Berlin Wall into East Germany from the balcony of the West German Parliament building during Reagan's state visit in June 1987. In a famous speech made during the trip, Reagan challenged Soviet leader Mikhail Gorbachev to "tear down this wall!" and liberalize the East Bloc. (Dick Halstead/Time Life Pictures/Getty Images)

their assumptions and challenge the status quo. Third, taking a lesson from the civil rights movement in the United States and worldwide student protest against the Vietnam War, dissatisfied women recognized that they had to band together if they were to influence politics and secure fundamental reforms.

Feminists could draw on a long heritage of protest, stretching back to the French Revolution and the women's movements of the late nineteenth century (see Chapters 20 and 23). They were also inspired by more recent works, such as the foundational book *The Second Sex* (1949) by the French writer and philosopher Simone de Beauvoir (1908–1986). Beauvoir, who worked closely with the existentialist philosopher Jean-Paul Sartre (see Chapter 28), analyzed the position of women within the framework of existential thought. Drawing on history, philosophy, psychology, biology, and literature, Beauvoir argued that women had almost always been trapped by particularly inflexible and limiting conditions. Only through courageous action and self-assertive creativity could a woman become a completely free person and escape the role of the inferior "other" that men had constructed for her gender. (See "Listening to the Past: Simone de Beauvoir, a Feminist Critique of Marriage," page 976.)

The Second Sex inspired a generation of women intellectuals, and by the late 1960s and the 1970s a broad-based feminist movement had spread through the United States and Europe. In the United States, American writer and organizer Betty Friedan's (1921–2006) pathbreaking study *The Feminine Mystique* (1963) pointed the way. Friedan called attention to the stifling aspects of women's domestic life, devoted to the service of husbands and children. Housewives lived in a "gilded cage," she concluded, because they were usually not allowed to hold professional jobs or become mature adults and genuine human beings. In 1966 Friedan helped found the National Organization for Women (NOW) to press for women's rights. NOW flourished, growing from seven hundred members in 1967 to forty thousand in 1974.

Many other women's organizations rose to follow NOW in Europe and the United States. The new feminists attacked patriarchy, the domination of society by men, and sexism, the inequalities faced by women simply because they were female. Throughout the 1970s a proliferation of publications, conferences, and institutions devoted to women's issues reinforced the emerging international movement. Advocates of women's rights pushed for new statutes in the workplace: laws against discrimination, equal pay for equal work, and

Simone de Beauvoir, a Feminist Critique of Marriage

Having grown up in Paris in a middle-class family and become a teacher, novelist, and intellectual, Simone de Beauvoir (1908–1986) turned increasingly to feminist concerns after World War II. Her most influential work was The Second Sex *(1949), a massive declaration of independence for contemporary women.*

As an existentialist, Beauvoir believed that all individuals must accept responsibility for their lives and strive to overcome the tragic dilemmas they face. Studying the experience of women since antiquity, Beauvoir argued that men had generally used education and social conditioning to create a dependent "other," a negative nonman who was not permitted to grow and strive for freedom. Marriage — on men's terms — was part of this unjust and undesirable process. Beauvoir's conclusion that some couples could establish free and equal unions was based in part on her experience with philosopher Jean-Paul Sartre, Beauvoir's encouraging companion and sometime lover.

Simone de Beauvoir as a teacher in 1947, when she was writing *The Second Sex*. (Hulton-Deutsch Collection/Corbis)

❝ All human existence is transcendence and immanence at the same time; to go beyond itself, it must maintain itself; to thrust itself toward the future, it must integrate the past into itself; and while relating to others, it must confirm itself in itself. These two moments are implied in every living movement: for *man*, marriage provides the perfect synthesis of them; in his work and political life, he finds change and progress, he experiences his dispersion through time and the universe; and when he tires of this wandering, he establishes a home, he settles down, he anchors himself in the world; in the evening he restores himself in the house, where his wife cares for the furniture and children and safeguards the past she keeps in store. But the wife has no other task save the one of maintaining and caring for life in its pure and identical generality; she perpetuates the immutable species, she ensures the even rhythm of the days and the permanence of the home she guards with locked doors; she is given no direct grasp on the future, nor on the universe; she goes beyond herself toward the group only through her husband as mouthpiece.

Marriage today still retains this traditional form. . . . The male's vocation is action; he needs to produce, fight, create, progress, go beyond himself toward the totality of the universe and the infinity of the future; but traditional marriage does not invite woman to transcend herself with him; it confines her in immanence. She has no choice but to build a stable life where the present, prolonging the past, escapes the threats of tomorrow, that is, precisely to create a happiness. . . .

It is through housework that the wife comes to make her "nest" her own; this is why, even if she has "help," she insists on doing things herself; at least by watching over, controlling, and criticizing, she endeavors to make her servants' results her own. By administrating her home, she achieves her social justification; her job is also to oversee the food, clothing, and care of the familial society in general. Thus she too realizes herself as an activity. But, as we will see, it is an activity that brings her no escape from her immanence and allows her no individual affirmation of herself. . . .

Few tasks are more similar to the torment of Sisyphus than those of the housewife; day after day, one must wash dishes, dust furniture, mend clothes that will be dirty, dusty, and torn again. The housewife wears herself out running on the spot; she does nothing; she only perpetuates the present; she never gains the sense that she is conquering a positive Good, but struggles indefinitely against Evil. . . .

Washing, ironing, sweeping, routing out tufts of dust in the dark places behind the wardrobe, this is holding away death but also refusing life: for in one movement time is created and destroyed; the housewife only grasps the negative aspect of it. . . .

So the wife's work within the home does not grant her autonomy; it is not directly useful to the group, it does not open onto the future, it does not produce anything. It becomes meaningful and dignified only if it is integrated into existences that go beyond themselves, toward the society in production or action: far from enfranchising the matron, it makes her dependent on her husband and children; she justifies her existence through them: she is no more than an inessential mediation in their lives. . . .

The drama of marriage is not that it does not guarantee the wife the promised happiness — there is no guarantee of happiness — it is that it mutilates her; it dooms her to repetition and routine. The first twenty years of a woman's life are extraordinarily rich; she experiences menstruation, sexuality, marriage, and motherhood; she discovers the world and her destiny. She is mistress of a home at twenty, linked from then on to one man, a child in her arms, now her life is finished forever. Real activity, real work, are the privilege of man: her only occupations are sometimes exhausting but never fulfill her. . . .

Marriage must combine two autonomous existences, not be a withdrawal, an annexation, an escape, a remedy. . . . The couple should not consider itself a community, a closed cell: instead, the individual as individual has to be integrated into a society in which he can thrive without assistance; he will then be able to create links in pure generosity with another individual equally adapted to the group, links founded on the recognition of two freedoms.

This balanced couple is not a utopia; such couples exist sometimes even within marriage, more often outside of it; some are united by a great sexual love that leaves them free in their friendships and occupations; others are linked by a friendship that does not hamper their sexual freedom; more rarely there are still others who are both lovers and friends but without seeking in each other their exclusive reason for living. Many nuances are possible in the relations of a man and a woman: in companionship, pleasure, confidence, tenderness, complicity, and love, they can be for each other the most fruitful source of joy, richness, and strength offered to a human being. **"**

Source: Simone de Beauvoir, *The Second Sex*, trans. Constance Borde and Sheila Malovany-Chevallier. Used by permission of Alfred A. Knopf, a division of Random House, Inc. Originally published in French as *Le deuxième sexe*. Copyright © 1949 by Éditions Gallimard. Reprinted by permission of Georges Borchardt, Inc., for Éditions Gallimard.

QUESTIONS FOR ANALYSIS

1. How did Beauvoir analyze marriage and marriage partners in terms of existential philosophy?

2. To what extent does a married woman benefit from a "traditional" marriage, according to Beauvoir? Why?

3. What was Beauvoir's solution to the situation she described? Was her solution desirable? Realistic?

4. What have you learned about the history of women that supports or challenges Beauvoir's analysis? Include developments since World War II and your own reflections.

measures such as maternal leave and affordable day care designed to help women combine careers and family responsibilities.

The movement further concentrated on gender and family questions, including the right to divorce (in some Catholic countries), legalized abortion, the needs of single mothers, and protection from rape and physical violence. In almost every country, the effort to decriminalize abortion served as a catalyst in mobilizing an effective, self-conscious women's movement (and in creating opposition to it, as in the United States).

In countries that had long placed women in a subordinate position, the legal changes were little less than revolutionary. In Italy, for example, new laws abolished restrictions on divorce and abortion, which had been strengthened by Mussolini and defended energetically by the Catholic Church in the postwar era. By 1988 divorce and abortion were common in Italy, which had the lowest birthrate in Europe. More generally, the sharply focused women's movement of the 1970s won new rights for women. Subsequently, the movement became more diffuse, a victim of both its successes and the resurgence of an antifeminist opposition.

In addition to the feminist movement, many newly empowered women were active in the antinuclear peace movement, which had its roots in the anti-Vietnam

Italian Feminists These women demonstrate in Rome in 1977 for the passage of legislation legalizing abortion, which the pope and the Catholic Church have steadfastly opposed. The demonstrators raise their hands in a feminist salute during the peaceful march. (Bettmann/Corbis)

protests of the 1960s and took on new life as the Cold War heated up in the late 1970s. Appalled by the Soviet invasion of Afghanistan in 1979, the United States and NATO took a number of countermeasures, including an agreement to station limited-range nuclear missiles in Britain, West Germany, Italy, Belgium, and the Netherlands (see pages 983–984). Concerned citizens quickly realized that if a low-level tactical nuclear war broke out between the superpowers, western Europe and particularly West Germany would suffer the consequences. In 1981 hundreds of thousands of demonstrators marched in protest in major cities across western Europe, carrying signs that read "We are not America's guinea pigs" and "Reagan's peace is our death."[3] Western European leaders went ahead with the missile deployment, but determined citizens' groups continued to call attention to the brutal costs of modern war.

The Rise of the Environmental Movement

Like feminist activists and peace advocates, newly formed environmental groups had roots in the 1960s counterculture. Early environmentalists drew inspiration from writers like biologist Rachel Carson, whose book *Silent Spring*, published in the United States in 1962, was quickly translated into twelve European languages. Carson's chilling title referred to a future spring when people in developed society would wake up and hear no birds singing because the birds had all been killed by the rampant overuse of pesticides. The book had a striking impact on the growth of environmental movements in Europe.

By the 1970s the destructive environmental costs of industrial development were everywhere apparent.

Picturing the Past

Green Party Representatives Enter Parliament In 1983 members of the environmentally conscious West German Green Party won enough votes to send several representatives to the parliament for the first time, an important victory for the protest movements that emerged in the 1970s and 1980s. (Bildarchiv Preussischer Kulturbesitz/Art Resource, NY)

ANALYZING THE IMAGE How do the Green Party representatives (center) use visual presentation and symbolism to portray their political beliefs? How would you describe the reaction of the more traditionally dressed members of parliament?

CONNECTIONS What does the Green Party victory in 1983 tell us about political debate in a postindustrial society? Are there continuities with the social activism of the 1960s counterculture, or is this something new?

To complete this activity online, go to the Online Study Guide at bedfordstmartins.com/mckaywest.

The mighty Rhine River, which flows from Switzerland, past France, and through Germany and the Netherlands, was an industrial sewer. The forests of southwestern Germany were dying from acid rain, a result of smokestack effluents. The pristine coasts of Brittany, in northwest France, were fouled by oil spills from massive tanker ships. Nuclear power plants across western Europe were generating toxic waste that would last for centuries (Map 30.1). These are just some examples of the environmental degradation that inspired a growing ecology movement to challenge government and industry to clean up their acts.

The new ecologists had two main agendas. First, they worked to lessen the effects of unbridled industrial development on the natural environment. Second, they linked local environmental issues to poverty, inequality, and violence on a global scale. Environmental groups pursued these goals in many ways. Some used the mass media to reach potential supporters; some worked closely with politicians and public officials to change state policies. Others took a more activist stance. In Denmark in March 1969, in a dramatic example, student protesters at the University of Copenhagen took over a scientific conference on natural history. They locked the conference hall doors, sprayed the professors in attendance with polluted lake water, and held up an oil-doused duck, shouting, "Come and save it . . . you talk about pollution, why don't you do anything about it!"[4]

Environmental protest also took on institutional forms. In 1971 Canadian activists established Greenpeace, a nongovernmental organization dedicated to environmental conservation and protection. Greenpeace quickly grew into an international organization, with strong support in Europe and the United States. In West Germany in 1979 environmentalists founded the Green Party, a political party intended to fight for environmental causes. The West German Greens met with astounding success when they elected members to parliament in the 1983 elections, the first time in sixty years that a new political party had been seated in Germany. Their success was a model for like-minded activists across Europe and the United States, and Green Party members have been elected to parliaments in Belgium, Italy, and Sweden.

Separatism and Right-Wing Extremism

The 1970s also saw the rise of determined separatist movements across Europe. In Ireland, Spain, Belgium, and Switzerland—and in Yugoslavia and Czechoslovakia in the East Bloc—regional ethnic groups struggled for special rights, political autonomy, and even national independence from ruling governments. This new separatist nationalism was most violent in Spain and Northern Ireland, where well-established insurgent groups used

Map 30.1 Pollution in Europe, ca. 1990
Despite attempts to remedy the negative consequences of the human impact on the environment, pollution remains a significant challenge for Europeans in the twenty-first century.

terrorist attacks to win government concessions. In the ethnic Basque region of northern Spain, the ETA (short for Basque Homeland and Freedom) tried to use bombings and assassinations to force the government to grant territorial independence. After the death in 1975 of the Spanish fascist dictator Francisco Franco, who had ruled Spain for almost forty years, a new constitution granted the Basque region special autonomy, but it was not enough. The ETA stepped up its terrorist campaigns, killing over four hundred people in the 1980s.

The Provisional Irish Republican Army (IRA), a paramilitary organization in Northern Ireland, used similar tactics. Though Ireland had won autonomy in 1922, Great Britain retained control of six primarily Protestant counties in the north of the country (see Chapter 27). In the late 1960s violence re-emerged as the IRA attacked British security forces its members saw as occupying the district. On Bloody Sunday in January 1972, British soldiers shot and killed thirteen demonstrators, who had been protesting anti-Catholic discrimination, in the town of Derry, and the violence escalated. For the next thirty years the IRA attacked soldiers and civilians in Northern Ireland and in Britain itself. Over two thousand British soldiers, civilians, and IRA members were killed during "the Troubles" before negotiations between the IRA and the British government opened in the late 1990s.

Mainstream European politicians also faced challenges from new political forces on the far right. New right groups such as the National Front in France, the Northern League in Italy, the Austrian Freedom Party, and the National Democratic Party in West Germany were founded or gained popularity in the 1970s and 1980s. Populist leaders like Jean-Marie Le Pen, the founder of the French National Front, opposed European integration and promised a return to traditional national customs, often at the expense of the non-European immigrants who were a growing proportion of the continent's working-class population (see Chapter 29). New right politicians promoted themselves as the champions of ordinary (white) workers, complaining that immigrants swelled welfare rolls and stole jobs from native-born Europeans. Though their programs at times veered close to open racism, they began to win seats in national parliaments in the 1980s.

really existing socialism
A term used by Communist leaders to describe the socialist accomplishments of their societies, such as nationalized industry and collective agriculture.

The Decline of "Really Existing Socialism"

What internal and external factors weakened communist power in the East Bloc, and how did Soviet leader Mikhail Gorbachev try to reform the system from above?   ■

In the postwar decades, the communist states of the East Bloc had achieved a shaky social consensus based on a rising standard of living, an extensive welfare system, and the inevitable political repression. When the Marxist utopia still had not arrived in the 1970s, propagandists told citizens that their totally egalitarian society would be realized sometime in the future. In the meantime, they would have to accept the system as it was; in the long run, leaders claimed, socialism would prove that it was better than capitalism. Such claims were an attempt to paper over serious tensions in socialist society. Everyday life could be difficult; limits on personal and political freedoms encouraged the growth of determined reform movements; and a revival of Cold War tensions accompanied the turn to the right in the United States and western Europe in the 1980s.

When Mikhail Gorbachev burst on the scene in 1985, the new Soviet leader opened an era of reform that was as sweeping as it was unexpected. Although many believed that Gorbachev would soon fall from power, his reforms rapidly transformed Soviet culture and politics, and drastically reduced Cold War tensions. But communism, which Gorbachev wanted so desperately to revitalize, continued to decline.

State and Society in the East Bloc

By the 1970s many of the professed goals of communism had been achieved. Communist leaders in eastern Europe and the Soviet Union adopted the term **really existing socialism** to describe the accomplishments of their societies. Agriculture had been successfully collectivized, and though Poland was an exception, 80 to 90 percent of Soviet and East Bloc farmers worked on huge collective farms. Industry and business had been nationalized, and only a small percentage of the economy remained in private hands in most East Bloc countries. The state had also gone some way to level class differences. Though some people—particularly party members—clearly had greater access to better opportunities and resources, the gap between rich and poor was far smaller than in the West. An extensive system of government-supported welfare benefits included free medical care, guaranteed employment, inexpensive public transportation, and large subsidies for rent and food.

Everyday life under really existing socialism was defined by an uneasy mixture of outward conformity and private disengagement—or apathy. The Communist Party dominated public life. Mass organizations for youth, women, workers, and sports groups instituted huge rallies, colorful festivals, and new holidays that exposed citizens to the values of the socialist state. East Bloc citizens might grudgingly participate in party-sponsored public events, but at home, and in private, they grumbled about and often sidestepped Communist authority.

East Bloc living standards were well above those in the developing world, but well below living standards in the West. Centralized economic planning continued to lead to shortages of the most basic goods, and people complained about poor quality and lack of choice. Family ties were especially valuable in the bureaucratic one-party state. Informal networks of family and friends helped people find hard-to-get goods and offered support beyond party organizations. Though the secret police persecuted those who openly challenged the system and generated mountains of files on ordinary people, those who put up and shut up had little to fear.

Women in particular experienced the contradictions of the socialist system. On the one hand, the state advocated equal rights for women and encouraged them to join the workforce in positions formerly reserved for men, such as medicine, in numbers greater than those in the West. In addition, an extensive system of state-supported child care freed women to take outside employment and eased the work of parenting. On the other

Crossing the Border Between East and West Berlin During the Christmas season of 1965, West Berliners were given special permission to visit relatives in the walled-off eastern part of the city. The limits on travel in the East Bloc were one of the most hated aspects of life under Communist rule. (Bundesarchiv, Berlin)

hand, women rarely made it into the upper ranks of business or politics. And East Bloc women faced the same double burden as those in the West—on top of their full-time jobs, they were expected to do the shopping, the cooking, and the cleaning at home.

The countries of eastern Europe—like those in the West—were hit hard by the energy crisis and stagflation of the 1970s. For a time, access to inexpensive oil from the Soviet Union, which had huge resources, provided a buffer, but this cushion began to fall apart in the 1980s. For a number of reasons, East Bloc leaders refused to make the economic reforms that might have made the socialist system more effective.

First, the transformation to Western-style postindustrial societies would have required fundamental changes in the Communist system. As in the West, it would have hurt the already tenuous living standard of industrial workers. But the workers' states of the East Bloc were dedicated to the working class: coal miners, shipbuilders, factory and construction workers. To pursue the sorts of reforms required to develop a postindustrial economy would have undermined the livelihoods and support of these basic constituencies, which were already showing signs of wear.

East Bloc regimes also refused to cut spending on the welfare state, which was, after all, one of the proudest achievements of socialism. In addition, socialist governments continued to provide subsidies to heavy industries such as steel and mining. High-tech industries failed to take off in eastern Europe, in part because the West maintained embargos on technology exports. The industrial goods produced in the East Bloc became increasingly uncompetitive in the new global system. To stave off total collapse, governments borrowed massive amounts of hard currency from Western banks and governments, helping to convince ordinary people that communism was bankrupt, and setting up a cycle of indebtedness that helped bring down the East Bloc in 1989.

Economic decline was not the only reason people increasingly questioned the socialist system. The best career and educational opportunities were reserved for party members or handed out as political favors, leaving many talented people underemployed and resentful. Tight controls on travel continually called attention to the burdens of daily life in a repressive society. The one-party state had repeatedly quashed popular reform movements and retreated from economic liberalization, even when presented in a nonthreatening way. The liberal freedoms and consumer prosperity of the West were evident for all to see in the television broadcasts that streamed across the iron curtain every evening. Many East Bloc citizens came to doubt the legitimacy of communism altogether:

the dream of distributing goods "from each according to his means, to each according to his needs" (as Marx had once put it) hardly made up for the great weaknesses of really existing socialism.

Reform Movements in Czechoslovakia and Poland

Economic and social stagnation in the East Bloc encouraged small numbers of dedicated people to try to change society from within. Developments in Czechoslovakia and Poland were the most striking and significant, and determined reform movements emerged in both countries in the mid-1970s. Remembering a history of violent repression and Soviet invasion, reformists carefully avoided direct challenges to government leaders. Nor did they try to reform the Communist Party itself, as Dubček and his followers had attempted in the Prague spring of 1968. Instead, they worked to build a civil society from below—to create a realm of freedom beyond formal politics where civil liberties and human rights could be exercised within the Communist system.

Solidarity Outlawed Polish trade union that worked for workers' rights and political reform throughout the 1980s.

In Czechoslovakia in 1977 a small group of citizens, including future Czechoslovak president Václav Havel (see page 988), signed a manifesto that came to be known as Charter 77. The group criticized the government for ignoring the human rights provision of the Helsinki Accords and called on Communist leaders to respect civil and human rights. They also criticized censorship and argued for improved environmental policies. Despite government retaliation, Czech leaders challenged passive acceptance of Communist authority and contributed to growing public dissatisfaction with really existing socialism.

In Poland, which had been an unruly satellite from the beginning, the Communists had failed to monopolize society. Most agricultural land remained in private hands, and the Catholic Church thrived. The Communists also failed to manage the economy effectively. The 1960s saw little economic improvement, and in 1970 Poland's working class rose again in angry protest. A new Communist leader came to power, and he wagered that massive inflows of Western capital and technology, especially from rich and now-friendly West Germany, could produce a Polish economic miracle. Instead, bureaucratic incompetence and the first oil shock in 1973 put the economy into a nosedive. Workers, intellectuals, and the church became increasingly restive. Then the real Polish miracle occurred: Cardinal Karol Wojtyla (KAH-rohl voy-TIH-lah), archbishop of Kraków, was elected pope in 1978 as John Paul II. In June 1979 he returned to Poland from Rome, preaching love of Christ and

country and the "inalienable rights of man." The pope drew enormous crowds and electrified the Polish nation.

In August 1980 the sixteen thousand workers at the gigantic Lenin Shipyards in Gdansk (formerly known as Danzig) laid down their tools and occupied the plant. As other workers joined "in solidarity," the strikers advanced the ideals of civil society, including the right to form free-trade unions, freedom of speech, release of political prisoners, and economic reforms. After eighteen days of shipyard occupation, the government gave in and accepted the workers' demands in the Gdansk Agreement. In a state in which the Communist Party claimed to rule on behalf of the proletariat, a working-class revolt had won an unprecedented, even revolutionary, victory.

Led by feisty Lenin Shipyards electrician and devout Catholic Lech Walesa (lehk vah-LEHN-suh) (b. 1943), the workers proceeded to organize a free and democratic trade union called **Solidarity**. As had been the case in Czechoslovakia, Solidarity worked cautiously to shape an active civil society. Joined by intellectuals and supported by the Catholic Church, it became a national union with a full-time staff of 40,000 linking 9.5 million union members. Cultural and intellectual freedom blossomed in Poland, and Solidarity enjoyed tremendous public support. But Solidarity's leaders insisted that they were asking for a self-limiting revolution, meant only to defend the cultural and trade-union freedoms won in the Gdansk Agreement. Solidarity thus practiced moderation, refusing to challenge directly the Communist monopoly on political power. Yet the ever-present threat of calling a nationwide strike gave them real power in ongoing negotiations with the Communist bosses.

Solidarity's combination of strength and moderation postponed a showdown, as the Soviet Union played a waiting game of threats and pressure. After a confrontation in March 1981 Walesa settled for minor government concessions, and Solidarity dropped plans for a massive general strike. Criticism of Walesa's moderate leadership gradually grew, and Solidarity lost its cohesiveness. The worsening economic crisis also encouraged radical actions among disgruntled Solidarity members, and the Polish Communist leadership shrewdly denounced Solidarity for promoting economic collapse and provoking a possible Soviet invasion. In December 1981 Communist leader General Wojciech Jaruzelski (VOY-chek yahr-oo-ZEL-skee) suddenly proclaimed martial law and arrested Solidarity's leaders.

Outlawed and driven underground, Solidarity survived in part because of the government's unwillingness (and probably its inability) to impose full-scale terror. Moreover, millions of Poles decided to continue acting as if they were free—the hallmark of civil society—even though they were not. Cultural and intellectual life remained extremely vigorous as the faltering Polish economy continued to deteriorate. Thus popular sup-

Lech Walesa and Solidarity
An inspiration for fellow workers at the Lenin Shipyards in the dramatic and successful strike against the Communist bosses in August 1980, Walesa played a key role in Solidarity before and after it was outlawed. Speaking here to old comrades at the Lenin Shipyards after Solidarity was again legalized in 1988, Walesa personified an enduring opposition to Communist rule in eastern Europe. (Georges Merillon/Gamma)

port for outlawed Solidarity remained strong under martial law in the 1980s, preparing the way for the union's political rebirth toward the end of the decade.

The rise and survival of Solidarity showed the desire of millions of eastern Europeans for greater political liberty and the enduring appeal of cultural freedom, trade-union rights, patriotic nationalism, and religious feeling. Not least, Solidarity's challenge encouraged fresh thinking in the Soviet Union, ever the key to lasting change in the Eastern bloc.

From Détente Back to Cold War

The Soviets and the leaders of the Soviet satellite states also faced challenges from abroad as optimistic hopes for détente in international relations gradually faded in the late 1970s. Brezhnev's Soviet Union ignored the human rights provisions of the Helsinki agreement, and East-West political competition remained very much alive outside Europe. Many Americans became convinced that the Soviet Union was taking advantage of détente, steadily building up its military might and pushing for political gains and revolutions in Africa, Asia, and Latin America. The Soviet invasion of Afghanistan in December 1979, which was designed to save an increasingly unpopular Marxist regime, was especially alarming to the West. Many Americans feared that the oil-rich states of the Persian Gulf would be next, and once again they looked to the NATO alliance and military might to thwart communist expansion.

President Jimmy Carter (r. 1977–1981) tried to lead NATO beyond verbal condemnation and urged economic sanctions against the Soviet Union, but only Great Britain among the European allies supported the American initiative. The alliance showed the same lack of concerted action when the Solidarity movement rose in Poland. Some observers concluded that NATO had lost the will to act decisively in dealing with the Soviet bloc.

The Atlantic alliance endured, however, and the U.S. military buildup launched by Carter in his last years in office was greatly accelerated by President Reagan, who was swept into office in 1980 by a wave of patriotism and economic discontent. The new American leadership acted as if the military balance had tipped in favor of the Soviet Union, which Reagan anathematized as the "evil empire." Increasing defense spending enormously, the Reagan administration deployed short-range nuclear missiles in western Europe and built up the navy to preserve American power in

The Soviet War in Afghanistan, 1979–1989

☐ Afghanistan
☐ Soviet Union
→ Soviet invasion
☐ Controlled by Soviet forces

UZBEKISTAN   KIRGHIZIA
Dushanbe   TAJIKISTAN
Amu Darya
TURKMENISTAN
Mary
Mazar-e Sharif
Kabul ✸ →   Peshawar
Herat
Kandahar   Indus R.
IRAN   PAKISTAN
INDIA

the post-Vietnam age. The broad shift toward greater conservatism in the 1980s gave Reagan invaluable allies in western Europe. Margaret Thatcher worked well with Reagan and was a forceful advocate for a revitalized Atlantic alliance, and under Helmut Kohl West Germany and the United States once again coordinated military and political policy toward the Soviet bloc.

Gorbachev's Reforms in the Soviet Union

Cold War tensions aside, the Soviet Union's Communist Party elite seemed secure in the early 1980s as far as any challenge from below was concerned. The long-established system of administrative controls continued to stretch downward from the central ministries and state committees to provincial cities, and from there to factories, neighborhoods, and villages. At each level of this massive state bureaucracy, the overlapping hierarchy of the 17.5-million-member Communist Party continued to watch over all decisions and manipulate every aspect of national life. Organized opposition was impossible, and average people left politics to the bosses.

Although the massive state and party bureaucracy safeguarded the elite, it promoted apathy in the masses. When the ailing Brezhnev finally died in 1982, his successor, the long-time chief of the secret police, Yuri Andropov (1914–1984), tried to invigorate the system. Relatively little came of his efforts, but they combined with a sharply worsening economic situation to set the stage for the emergence in 1985 of Mikhail Gorbachev (b. 1931), the most vigorous Soviet leader in a generation.

Trained as a lawyer and having worked his way up as a Communist Party official in the northern Caucasus, Gorbachev was smart, charming, and tough. Gorbachev believed in communism, but he realized it was failing to keep up with Western capitalism and technological developments, and that the Soviet Union's status as a superpower was eroding. Thus Gorbachev (and his intelligent, influential wife, Raisa, a dedicated professor of Marxist-Leninist thought) wanted to save the Soviet system by revitalizing it with fundamental reforms. Gorbachev was also an idealist who wanted to improve conditions for ordinary citizens. Understanding that the endless waste and expense of the Cold War arms race had had a disastrous impact on living conditions in the Soviet Union, he realized that improvement at home required better relations with the West.

In his first year in office, Gorbachev attacked corruption and incompetence in the bureaucracy, and he consolidated his power. He condemned alcoholism and drunkenness, which were deadly scourges of Soviet society, and elaborated his ambitious reform program.

perestroika Economic restructuring and reform implemented by Soviet premier Gorbachev in 1985.

glasnost Soviet premier Gorbachev's popular campaign for openness in government and the media.

Mikhail Gorbachev In his acceptance speech before the Supreme Soviet (the U.S.S.R.'s parliament), newly elected president Mikhail Gorbachev vowed to assume "all responsibility" for the success or failure of perestroika. Previous Soviet parliaments were little more than tools of the Communist Party, but this one actively debated and even opposed government programs. (Boris Yurchenko/AP Images)

The first set of reform policies was designed to transform and restructure the economy in order to provide for the real needs of the Soviet population. To accomplish this economic restructuring, or **perestroika** (pehr-uh-STROY-kuh), Gorbachev and his supporters permitted an easing of government price controls on some goods, more independence for state enterprises, and the setting up of profit-seeking private cooperatives to provide personal services for consumers. These timid economic reforms initially produced a few improvements, but shortages grew as the economy stalled at an intermediate point between central planning and free-market mechanisms. By late 1988 widespread consumer dissatisfaction posed a serious threat to Gorbachev's leadership and the entire reform program.

Gorbachev's bold and far-reaching campaign "to tell it like it is" was much more successful. Very popular in a country where censorship, dull uniformity, and outright lies had long characterized public discourse, the newfound openness, or **glasnost** (GLAZ-nohst), of the government and the media marked an astonishing break with the past. Long-banned and -vilified émigré writers sold millions of copies of their works in new editions, while denunciations of Stalin and his terror became standard fare in plays and movies. Thus initial openness in government pronouncements quickly went much further than Gorbachev intended and led to something approaching free speech and free expression, a veritable cultural revolution.

Democratization was the third element of reform. Beginning as an attack on corruption in the Communist Party, it led to the first free elections in the Soviet Union since 1917. Gorbachev and the party remained in control, but a minority of critical independents was elected in April 1989 to a revitalized Congress of People's Deputies. Millions of Soviets then watched the new congress for hours on television as Gorbachev and his ministers saw their proposals debated and even rejected. Thus millions of Soviet citizens took practical lessons in open discussion, critical thinking, and representative government. An active civil society was emerging—a new political culture at odds with the Communist Party's monopoly of power and control. Democratization ignited demands for greater autonomy and even for national independence by non-Russian minorities, especially in the Baltic region and in the Caucasus.

Finally, Gorbachev brought new political thinking to the field of foreign affairs and acted on it. He withdrew Soviet troops from Afghanistan in February 1989 and sought to reduce East-West tensions. Of enormous importance, the Soviet leader sought to halt the arms race with the United States and convinced President Reagan of his sincerity. In a Washington summit in December 1987, the two leaders agreed to eliminate all land-based intermediate-range missiles in Europe, setting the stage for more arms reductions. Gorbachev also encouraged reform movements in Poland and Hungary and pledged to respect the political choices of the peoples of eastern Europe, repudiating the Brezhnev Doctrine. By early 1989 it seemed that if Gorbachev held to his word, the tragic Soviet occupation of eastern Europe might wither away, taking the long Cold War with it once and for all.

The Collapse of Communism

1977	Charter 77 reform movement founded in Czechoslovakia
1980	Polish Solidarity movement formed
1981	Solidarity outlawed by communist leaders
1982	Soviet premier Leonid Brezhnev dies
1985	Mikhail Gorbachev becomes Soviet premier and institutes perestroika and glasnost reforms
1988	Polish workers strike throughout country
■ 1989	
April	Solidarity legalized in Poland
August	Noncommunist prime minister elected in Poland
November	Berlin Wall opened
November–December	Velvet Revolution ends communism in Czechoslovakia
December	Communist dictator of Romania executed
■ 1990	
February	Communist Party defeated in Soviet elections
March	Free elections in Hungary
May	Boris Yeltsin elected leader of Russian Soviet Republic
October	Reunification of Germany
November	Paris Accord arms reductions across Europe
December	Lech Walesa elected president of Poland
■ 1991	
July–August	Communist hardliners kidnap Gorbachev and try to overthrow Soviet government
December	Soviet Union dissolved

culture after having been conquered and brutalized by Nazis and communists for almost sixty years. Second, West Germany quickly absorbed its East German rival and emerged as the most influential country in Europe. Third, Gorbachev's reforms boomeranged, and a complicated anticommunist revolution swept through the Soviet Union as the multinational empire broke into a large Russia and fourteen other independent states. The long Cold War came to an abrupt end, and the United States suddenly stood as the world's only superpower.

The Revolutions of 1989

Why did anticommunist revolutions sweep through eastern Europe in 1989, and what were the immediate consequences? ■

In 1989 Gorbachev's plan to reform communism in order to save it snowballed out of control. A series of largely peaceful revolutions swept across eastern Europe (Map 30.2), overturning existing communist regimes. The revolutions of 1989 had momentous consequences. First, the peoples of eastern Europe joyfully re-entered the mainstream of contemporary European life and

The Collapse of Communism in Eastern Europe

Solidarity and the Polish people led the way to revolution in eastern Europe. In 1988 widespread labor unrest and strikes, raging inflation, and the outlawed Solidarity's refusal to cooperate with the military government had brought Poland to the brink of economic collapse. Thus Solidarity skillfully pressured Poland's frustrated Communist leaders into another round of negotiations that might work out a sharing of power to resolve the political stalemate and the economic crisis. The subsequent agreement in early 1989 legalized Solidarity and declared

Mapping the Past

Map 30.2 Democratic Movements in Eastern Europe, 1989 Countries that had been satellites in the orbit of the Soviet Union began to set themselves free in 1989.

ANALYZING THE MAP Which countries experienced the largest number of demonstrations? Which countries and/or states within the Soviet Union experienced the fewest?

CONNECTIONS How did Gorbachev's reforms in the Soviet Union contribute to the spread of democratic movements in eastern Europe, and which specific action of his hastened the end of the Cold War?

To complete this activity online, go to the Online Study Guide at bedfordstmartins.com/mckaywest.

that a large minority of representatives to the Polish parliament would be chosen by free elections that June. Still guaranteed a parliamentary majority and expecting to win many of the contested seats, the Communists believed that their rule was guaranteed for four years and that Solidarity would keep the workers in line.

Lacking access to the state-run media, Solidarity succeeded nonetheless in mobilizing the country and winning most of the contested seats in an overwhelming victory. Moreover, many angry voters crossed off the names of unopposed party candidates, so that the Com-

munist Party failed to win the majority its leaders had anticipated. Solidarity members jubilantly entered the Polish parliament, and a dangerous stalemate quickly developed. But Solidarity leader Lech Walesa, a gifted politician who always repudiated violence, adroitly obtained a majority by securing the allegiance of two minor pro-communist parties that had been part of the coalition government after World War II. In August 1989 Tadeusz Mazowiecki (b. 1927), the editor of Solidarity's weekly newspaper, was sworn in as Poland's new noncommunist prime minister.

The Fall of the Berlin Wall The sudden and unanticipated opening of the Berlin Wall in 1989 dramatized the spectacular fall of communism throughout east-central Europe. Built on the orders of the Soviet leader Nikita Khrushchev in 1961, the hated barrier had stopped the flow of refugees from East Germany to West Germany. Over the twenty-eight years of its existence, the Wall came to symbolize the limits on personal freedom enforced by Communist dictatorships. (Patrick Piel/Gamma)

In its first year and a half, the new Solidarity government cautiously introduced revolutionary political changes. It eliminated the hated secret police, the Communist ministers in the government, and finally Communist Party leader Jaruzelski himself, but it did so step-by-step in order to avoid confrontation with the army or the Soviet Union. However, in economic affairs, the Solidarity-led government was radical from the beginning. It applied economic **shock therapy**, an intense dose of neoliberal policy designed to make a clean break with state planning and move quickly to market mechanisms and private property. Thus the Solidarity government abolished controls on many prices on January 1, 1990, and reformed the monetary system with a big bang.

Hungary followed Poland. Hungary's Communist Party boss János Kádár (KAH-dahr) had permitted liberalization of the rigid planned economy after the 1956 uprising in exchange for political obedience and continued Communist control. In May 1988, in an effort to retain power by granting modest political concessions, the party replaced Kádár with a reform communist. But opposition groups rejected piecemeal progress, and in the summer of 1989 the Hungarian Communist Party agreed to hold free elections in March 1990. Welcoming Western investment and moving rapidly toward multiparty democracy, Hungary's Communists now enjoyed considerable popular support, and they believed, quite mistakenly it turned out, that they could defeat the opposition in the upcoming elections.

In an effort to strengthen their support at home and also put pressure on East Germany's hard-line Communist regime, the Hungarians opened their border to East Germans and tore down the barbed-wire iron curtain with Austria. Then tens of thousands of dissatisfied East German "vacationers" poured into Hungary, crossed into Austria as refugees, and continued on to immediate resettlement in thriving West Germany. The flight of East Germans led to the rapid growth of a homegrown protest movement in

shock therapy The Solidarity-led government's radical take on economic affairs that abruptly ended state planning and moved to market mechanisms and private property.

Demonstrators During the Velvet Revolution Hundreds of thousands of Czechoslovakian citizens flooded the streets of Prague daily in peaceful protests after the police savagely beat student demonstrators in mid-November 1989. On the night of November 24 three hundred thousand people roared "Dubček-Havel" when Alexander Dubček, the aging reformer ousted in 1968 by the Soviets, stood on a balcony with Václav Havel, the leading opponent of communism. That night the Communists agreed to share power, and a few days later they resigned from the government. (Corbis)

East Germany. Intellectuals, environmentalists, and Protestant ministers took the lead, organizing huge candlelight demonstrations and arguing that a democratic but still socialist East Germany was both possible and desirable. These "stayers" failed to convince the "leavers," however, who continued to flee the country en masse. In a desperate but ad hoc attempt to stabilize the situation, the East German government opened the Berlin Wall in November 1989, and people danced for joy atop that grim symbol of the prison state. East Germany's aging Communist leaders were swept aside, and a reform government took power and scheduled free elections.

In Czechoslovakia, communism died quickly in November–December 1989 in an almost good-humored ousting of Communist bosses. This so-called Velvet Revolution grew out of popular demonstrations led by students, intellectuals, and a dissident playwright-turned-moral-revolutionary named Václav Havel (VAH-slahf HAH-vuhl) (b. 1936). The protesters practically took control of the streets and forced the Communists into a power-sharing arrangement, which quickly resulted in the resignation of the Communist government. As 1989 ended, the Czechoslovakian assembly elected Havel president.

Only in Romania was revolution violent and bloody. There ironfisted Communist dictator Nicolae Ceauşescu (chow-SHES-kou) (1918–1989) had long combined Stalinist brutality with stubborn independence from Moscow. Faced with mass protests in December 1989, Ceauşescu, alone among eastern European bosses, ordered his ruthless security forces to slaughter thousands, thereby sparking a classic armed uprising. After Ceauşescu's forces were defeated, the tyrant and his wife were captured and executed by a military court. A coalition government emerged from the fighting, although the legacy of Ceauşescu's oppression left a very troubled country.

German Unification and the End of the Cold War

The sudden death of communism in East Germany in 1989 reopened the "German question" and raised the threat of renewed Cold War conflict over Germany. Taking power in October 1989, East German reform communists, enthusiastically supported by leading East German intellectuals and former dissidents, wanted to preserve socialism by making it genuinely democratic and responsive to the needs of the people. They argued for a "third way" that would go beyond the failed Stalinism they had experienced and the ruthless capitalism they saw in the West. These reformers supported closer ties with West Germany, but they feared unification and wanted to preserve a distinct East German identity.

Their efforts failed, and over the next year, East Germany was absorbed into an enlarged West Germany, much like a faltering company is merged into a stronger rival and ceases to exist. Three factors were particularly important in this sudden absorption. First, in the first week after the Berlin Wall was opened, almost 9 million East Germans — roughly half of the total population — poured across the border into West Germany. Almost all returned to their homes in the East, but the joy of warm welcomes from long-lost friends and loved ones and the exhilarating experience of shopping in the well-stocked stores of the much wealthier West aroused long-dormant hopes of unity among ordinary citizens.

Second, West German chancellor Helmut Kohl and his closest advisers skillfully exploited the historic opportunity on their doorstep. Sure of support from the United States, whose leadership he had steadfastly followed, in November 1989 Kohl presented a ten-point plan for a step-by-step unification in cooperation with both East Germany and the international community. Kohl then promised the struggling citizens of East Germany an immediate economic bonanza — a one-for-one exchange of all East German marks in savings accounts and pensions into much more valuable West German marks. This generous offer helped a well-financed conservative-liberal Alliance for Germany, which was set up in East Germany and was closely tied to Kohl's West German Christian Democrats, to overwhelm those who argued for the preservation of some kind of independent socialist society in East Germany. In March 1990 the Alliance outdistanced the Socialist Party and won almost 50 percent of the votes in an East German parliamentary election. (The Communists ignominiously fell to fringe-party status.) The Alliance for Germany quickly negotiated an economic union on favorable terms with Chancellor Kohl.

Finally, in the summer of 1990 the crucial international aspect of German unification was successfully resolved. Unification would once again make Germany the strongest state in central Europe and would directly affect the security of the Soviet Union. But Gorbachev swallowed hard — Western cartoonists showed Stalin turning over in his grave — and negotiated the best deal he could. In a historic agreement signed by Gorbachev and Kohl in July 1990, a uniting Germany solemnly affirmed its peaceful intentions and pledged never to develop nuclear, biological, or chemical weapons. Germany also sweetened the deal by promising to make enormous loans to the hard-pressed Soviet Union. In October 1990 East Germany merged into West Germany, forming henceforth a single nation under the West German laws and constitution.

The peaceful reunification of Germany accelerated the pace of agreements to liquidate the Cold War. In November 1990 delegates from twenty-two European countries joined those from the United States and the Soviet Union in Paris and agreed to a scaling down of all their armed forces. The delegates also solemnly affirmed that all existing borders in Europe — from unified Germany to the newly independent Baltic republics — were legal and valid. The Paris Accord was for all practical purposes a general peace treaty, bringing an end to World War II and the Cold War that followed.

Peace in Europe encouraged the United States and the Soviet Union to scrap a significant portion of their nuclear weapons in a series of agreements. In September 1991 a confident President George H. W. Bush canceled the around-the-clock alert status for American bombers outfitted with atomic bombs, and a floundering Gorbachev quickly followed suit. For the first time in four decades, Soviet and American nuclear weapons were not standing ready to destroy capitalism, communism, and life itself.

The Reunification of Germany, 1990

DENMARK

Hamburg

NETH.

Berlin

GERMANY

Cologne   Leipzig
Bonn   Dresden
                                Elbe R.

LUX.   Rhine R.   Frankfurt

FRANCE   CZECH.

Munich

AUSTRIA

— Former boundary between East and West Germany

The Disintegration of the Soviet Union

As 1990 began, revolutionary changes had triumphed in all but two eastern European states — tiny Albania and the vast Soviet Union. The great question now became whether the Soviet Union would follow its former satellites and whether reform communism would give way to a popular anticommunist revolution.

In February 1990, as competing Russian politicians noisily presented their programs and nationalists in the non-Russian republics demanded autonomy or independence from the Soviet Union, the Communist Party suffered a stunning defeat in local elections throughout the country. As in the eastern European satellites, democrats and anticommunists won clear majorities in the leading cities of the Russian Soviet Republic (SFSR), the largest republic in the Soviet Union. Moreover, in Lithuania the people elected an uncompromising nationalist as president, and the newly chosen parliament declared Lithuania an independent state.

Gorbachev responded by placing an economic embargo on Lithuania, but he refused to use the army to crush the separatist government. The result was a tense political stalemate that undermined popular support for Gorbachev. Separating himself further from Communist hardliners, Gorbachev asked Soviet citizens to ratify a new constitution that formally abolished the Communist Party's monopoly of political power and expanded the power of the Congress of People's Deputies. Retaining his post as party secretary, Gorbachev convinced a majority of deputies to elect him president of the Soviet Union.

Gorbachev's eroding power and his unwillingness to risk a universal suffrage election for the presidency strengthened his great rival, Boris Yeltsin (1931–2007). A radical reform communist who had been purged by party conservatives in 1987, Yeltsin embraced the democratic movement, and in May 1990 he was elected parliamentary leader of the Russian Soviet Republic. He boldly announced that Russia

itself would put its interests first, and declare its independence from the Soviet Union, thereby broadening the base of the anticommunist movement as he joined the patriotism of ordinary Russians with the democratic aspirations of big-city intellectuals. Gorbachev tried to save the Soviet Union with a new treaty that would link the member republics in a looser, freely accepted confederation, but six of the fifteen Soviet republics rejected Gorbachev's pleas.

Opposed by democrats and nationalists, Gorbachev was also challenged again by the Communist old guard. After Gorbachev was defeated at the Communist Party congress in July 1990, a gang of hardliners kidnapped him and his family in the Caucasus and tried to seize the Soviet government in August 1991. The attempted coup collapsed in the face of massive popular resistance that rallied around Yeltsin, who had recently been elected president of the Russian Soviet Republic by universal

Yeltsin Resists a Coup by Russian Communist Hardliners Standing atop a tank in Moscow in August 1991, the president of the Russian Soviet Republic, Boris Yeltsin (left), reads a statement denouncing the conspirators who were attempting to halt Gorbachev's reforms and hold the Soviet empire together. Yeltsin's brave public demonstration helped foil the coup and paved the way for the dissolution of the Soviet Union. (AP Images)

suffrage. As the spellbound world watched on television, Yeltsin defiantly denounced the rebels from atop a stalled tank in central Moscow and declared the "rebirth of Russia." The army supported Yeltsin, and Gorbachev was rescued and returned to power as head of the Soviet Union.

The leaders of the coup wanted to preserve Communist power, state ownership, and the multinational Soviet Union, but they succeeded only in destroying all three. An anticommunist revolution swept the Russian Soviet Republic as Yeltsin and his supporters outlawed the Communist Party and confiscated its property. Locked in a personal and political duel with Gorbachev, Yeltsin and his democratic allies declared Russia independent, withdrew from the Soviet Union, and renamed the Russian Soviet Republic the Russian Federation. All the other Soviet republics also left. The Soviet Union—and Gorbachev's job—ceased to exist on December 25, 1991. The independent republics of the old Soviet Union then established a loose confederation, the Commonwealth of Independent States, which played only a minor role in the 1990s.

LOOKING BACK LOOKING AHEAD

THE UNEXPECTED AND RAPID collapse of communism in Europe capped three decades of turbulent historical change. In the 1960s powerful challenges to the status quo steered western Europe to the left and attempted (but failed) to wrest power from the communists in the East. In the 1970s a global recession had devastating effects for everyday people in the West and East Blocs alike. And in the 1980s conservative Western leaders made the hard choices necessary to face economic decline and new global competition.

With the world economy on the road to recovery and new free-market systems in place across the former East Bloc, all of Europe would now have the opportunity to enter the information age. After forty years of Cold War division, the continent regained an underlying unity as faith in democratic government and market economics became the common European creed. In 1991 hopes for peaceful democratic progress were almost universal. According to philosopher Francis Fukuyama, the world had reached "the end of history" in that the end of the Cold War would lead to peaceful development based on growing tolerance, free-market economics, and liberal democracy.

The post–Cold War years saw the realization of some of these hopes, but the new era brought its own problems and tragedies. New ethnic and nationalist tensions flared, leading to a disastrous civil war in the former Yugoslavia. The struggle to rebuild the shattered societies of the former East Bloc countries was far more difficult than observers had hoped. Poor economic growth continued to complicate attempts to deal with the wide-open global economy. New conflicts with Islamic nations in the Middle East involved some European nations in open war. The European Union expanded, but political disagreements, environmental issues, increased anxiety about non-Western immigrants, and a host of other problems undermined moves toward true European unity. History was far from over: the realities of a post–Cold War world continued to produce difficult challenges as Europe entered the twenty-first century.

CHAPTER REVIEW

■ **How did social and political changes in the 1960s contribute to growing criticism of the postwar consensus that had emerged in the 1950s? (p. 960)**

In the early 1960s the prosperous western European society remained relatively stable, and East Bloc governments, bolstered by modest economic growth and committed to generous welfare benefits for their citizens, also generally maintained stability. As the 1960s progressed, however, politics in the West began shifting noticeably to the left, and Social Democratic governments promoted policies of détente designed to normalize East-West relations. Amid this more liberalized society, a youthful counterculture emerged among the children of affluence to critique the status quo. In the East, Khrushchev's limited reforms also inspired rebellions. Activists around the world rose in protest against the perceived inequalities of both capitalism and socialism, leading to dramatic events in 1968, exemplified in Paris and Prague. The actual political results of 1960s-era protests were mixed, but they did create more tolerance for a broad range of lifestyle activities.

■ **How did economic decline in the 1970s contribute to fundamental social and political change in the 1980s in western Europe and North America? (p. 970)**

In the early 1970s economic crises in Europe and North America shook the hard-won consensus of the postwar decades. The oil shocks of the 1970s created economic turmoil and brought real hardship to millions of people. Governments struggled to maintain welfare programs for their citizens as the global recession slowed growth and the boom years came to an end. By the late 1970s a post-industrial society had begun to emerge, causing even higher rates of unemployment in industrial sectors, but leading to growth in new high-tech and service industries. Even so, frustration with the policies and the perceived ineptitudes of governments set in, ushering in a new era of conservative politics. Leaders like Margaret Thatcher in Great Britain, Helmut Kohl in West Germany, and Ronald Reagan in the United States embraced neoliberal economic philosophies, championing private initiative, lowering taxes, and cutting government spending. At the same time, liberal groups such as feminists and environmentalists gained momentum and promoted their own interests to offset conservative rhetoric and government cutbacks. At the opposite end of the political spectrum, emboldened separatists and right-wing extremists sought political victories with sometimes violent tactics.

■ **What internal and external factors weakened communist power in the East Bloc, and how did Soviet leader Mikhail Gorbachev try to reform the system from above? (p. 980)**

Though the East Bloc achieved modest economic growth and some social stability during the 1960s, a number of factors weakened Communist rule. Failure to engage in significant internal reforms led to political and economic stagnation, and the global recession further hampered economic growth. Ordinary people chafed under party favoritism and limits on political and social freedom, and they complained about the relative lack of consumer prosperity. Reformists and dissident groups, such as Charter 77 in Czechoslovakia and Solidarity in Poland, worked to establish an active civil society that would expand civil rights within the system, and the revival of Cold War pressures under conservative Western governments further challenged East Bloc leaders. Gorbachev's attempts to use economic restructuring (perestroika) and civil openness (glasnost) to reform the system addressed some of these problems, but they were too little and too late to prevent communism's collapse.

■ **Why did anticommunist revolutions sweep through eastern Europe in 1989, and what were the immediate consequences? (p. 985)**

By the 1980s the socialist governments of the East Bloc lacked any true popular legitimacy. Moreover, the economies of eastern European countries, already strained by the global crisis, were being pushed to the brink of disaster by striking workers and other protesters, most notably the Solidarity movement in Poland. In 1988 the Polish government finally agreed to negotiate with the leaders of the outlawed Solidarity movement in order to prevent economic collapse. Solidarity's political demands led to a new non-communist government, which proceeded cautiously in order to avoid Soviet military intervention. Soon all the East Bloc countries followed suit, with anticommunist groups demanding — and finally winning — a voice in their government, and Communist leaders were largely ousted. In part because the reformist Soviet leader Mikhail Gorbachev refused to use force, the revolutions of 1989 were almost all nonviolent, celebratory occasions. In a dramatic finale, the two Germanys joined in a single democratic state, and the democratic movement triumphed in the Soviet Union. The Soviet empire fell apart, the Cold War ended, and the United States remained the only superpower.

Suggested Reading

Ash, Timothy Garten. *The Magic Lantern: The Revolution of '89 Witnessed in Warsaw, Budapest, Berlin, and Prague.* 1993. An exciting firsthand narrative of the collapse of the East Bloc in 1989 and 1990.

Bell, Daniel. *The Coming of Post-Industrial Society.* 1976. An early and prophetic forecast of the way the arrival of the information age would transform Western society.

Bernstein, Serge. *The Republic of de Gaulle, 1958–1969.* 2006. An outstanding work on France.

Caute, David. *The Year of the Barricades: A Journey Through 1968.* 1990. A high-energy examination that brings the upheavals of 1968 to life.

Cioc, Mark. *The Rhine: An Eco-Biography, 1815–2000.* 2002. A pace-setting environmental history of one of Europe's great rivers.

de Grazia, Victoria. *Irresistible Empire: America's Advance Through Twentieth-Century Europe.* 2005. Lively, provocative account of Europe's Americanization.

Guha, Ramachandra. *Environmentalism: A Global History.* 2000. A powerful and readable overview of environmentalism that puts Europe in world context.

Kurlansky, Mark. *1968: The Year That Rocked the World.* 2003. Popular history at its best, a gripping account of the 1960s generation and 1968 across the globe.

McLeod, Hugh. *The Religious Crisis of the 1960s.* 2007. A comparative study of Western religion in decline.

Port, Andrew I. *Conflict and Stability in the German Democratic Republic.* 2007. A penetrating analysis of popular support for communism in this major East Bloc country.

Reitan, Earl. *Tory Radicalism: Margaret Thatcher, John Major, and the Transformation of Modern Britain, 1979–1997.* 1997. Clear, concise, and very useful.

Ross, Kirsten. *May 1968 and Its Afterlives.* 2004. An important book on the way contested memories continue to shape our understanding of France's May events.

Rothschild, Joseph, and Nancy M. Wingfield. *Return to Diversity: A Political History of East Central Europe Since World War II.* 1999. A general overview of politics in the Soviet Bloc.

Scott, Joan W. *Only Paradoxes to Offer: French Feminists and the Rights of Man.* 1997. An important study of French feminism.

Slater, Don. *Consumer Culture and Modernity.* 1997. An overview of consumer society that includes an in-depth look at the consumer revolution of the 1960s.

Smith, Bonnie G. *Global Feminisms Since 1945.* 2000. A broadly cast and accessible overview of feminism after World War II that puts European and American movements in global context.

Stokes, Gale. *The Walls Came Tumbling Down: The Collapse of Communism in Eastern Europe.* 1993. A concise overview of the struggle for liberation from communist domination in the East Bloc.

Notes

1. Quoted in Kessing's Research Report, *Germany and East Europe Since 1945: From the Potsdam Agreement to Chancellor Brandt's "Ostpolitik"* (New York: Charles Scribner's Sons, 1973), pp. 284–285.
2. M. Mitterauer, *The History of Youth* (Oxford: Basil Blackwell, 1992), p. 40.
3. Quoted in F. Gilbert and D. C. Large, *The End of the European Era: 1890 to the Present* (New York: Norton, 2009), p. 498.
4. See R. Guha, *Environmentalism: A Global History* (New York: Longman, 2000), p. 79.

Key Terms

détente (p. 960)
New Left (p. 963)
Brezhnev Doctrine (p. 970)
OPEC (p. 971)
stagflation (p. 971)
postindustrial society (p. 971)
neoliberalism (p. 972)
really existing socialism (p. 980)
Solidarity (p. 982)
perestroika (p. 984)
glasnost (p. 984)
shock therapy (p. 987)

For practice quizzes and other study tools, visit the Online Study Guide at **bedfordstmartins.com/mckaywest**.

For primary sources from this period, see ***Sources of Western Society*, Second Edition**.

For Web sites, images, and documents related to topics in this chapter, visit Make History at **bedfordstmartins.com/mckaywest**.

31

Europe in an Age of Globalization

1990 to the Present

On November 9, 2009, the twentieth anniversary of the fall of the Berlin Wall, jubilant crowds filled the streets around the Brandenburg Gate at the former border between East and West Berlin. International leaders and tens of thousands of onlookers applauded as former Polish president Lech Walesa pushed over a line of one thousand eight-foot-tall foam dominos, symbolizing communism's collapse.

The crowd had reason to celebrate. The end of the Cold War had opened a new chapter in European and world history. Capitalism spread across the former East Bloc and the Soviet Union (now the Russian Federation), bringing potential for democratic reform. Some of these hopes were realized, but the new era also brought its own problems and tragedies. In eastern Europe, the process of rebuilding shattered societies was more difficult than optimists had envisioned in 1991. Across the West and around the world, individuals experienced the benefits and disadvantages of globalization and the digital revolution. The ongoing influx of immigrants into western Europe brought ethnic diversity to formerly homogeneous societies, which sometimes led to fear and conflict.

As Europe faced serious tensions and complex changes at the turn of the century, it also came together to form a strong new European Union that would prove a formidable economic competitor to the United States. Though old ties between Europe and the United States began to loosen, the nations of the West — and the world — could not ignore the common challenges they now faced. Finding solutions to ever-present problems regarding security, energy, the environment, and human rights would require not only innovation, but also cooperation. ∎

AFP/Getty Images

994

Life in an Age of Globalization. Established in 1895, the Venice Biennale is a major international contemporary art exhibition held every other year in Venice, Italy. Housed at a park where art is displayed at thirty permanent national pavilions, the show draws visitors from around the world and suggests the effect of globalization on the arts. Here a woman takes in a work by the Italian artist Gian Marco Montesano commissioned for the Italian pavilion at the 53rd Biennale in 2009.

CHAPTER PREVIEW

Rebuilding Russia and Eastern Europe
■ How did Russia and the former East Bloc countries meet the challenges of postcommunist reconstruction and political and economic reform?

The New Global System
■ What are the defining features of globalization, and how did changing international structures transform European societies?

Toward a Multicultural Continent
■ How did population decline and large-scale immigration lead to demographic changes in contemporary Europe, and what were the main results of growing ethnic diversity?

Confronting Twenty-First-Century Challenges
■ What key problems faced European societies in the twenty-first century, and how did European states and peoples deal with these critical issues?

Rebuilding Russia and Eastern Europe

How did Russia and the former East Bloc countries meet the challenges of postcommunist reconstruction and political and economic reform? ■

Establishing liberal democratic governments in the former East Bloc countries and the Soviet Union, now renamed Russia, would not prove an easy task. While Russia initially moved toward economic reform and political openness, the nation returned to its authoritarian traditions in the early 2000s.

The transition to democracy in the former communist countries of East-Central Europe was also difficult. After a period of tense reform, some countries, such as Poland, the Czech Republic, Hungary, and the Baltic states, established relatively prosperous democracies and joined NATO and then the European Union. Others, such as Romania and Bulgaria, lagged behind. In multiethnic Yugoslavia, the collapse of communism led to a disastrous civil war and the violent dissolution of the country. Russia and eastern Europe struggled to catch up to and integrate with the West, with mixed results.

Economic Shock Therapy in Russia

Politics and economics were closely intertwined in Russia after the attempted communist coup in 1991 and the dissolution of the Soviet Union (see Chapter 30). President Boris Yeltsin, his democratic supporters, and his economic ministers wanted to create conditions that would prevent a return to communism and would also right the faltering economy. Following the example of some postcommunist governments in eastern Europe, and agreeing with neoliberal Western advisers who argued that a quick turn to free markets and private economies would speed economic growth, the Russian reformers opted for breakneck liberalization in January 1992. Applying the type of economic shock therapy used by Poland (see Chapter 30), the Russians moved quickly to privatize the market, freeing prices on 90 percent of all Russian goods, with the exception of bread, vodka, oil, and public transportation. The government also launched a rapid privatization of industry and

Rich and Poor in Today's Russia A woman sells knitted scarves in front of a department store window in Moscow in September 2005. The collapse of the Soviet Union and the use of shock therapy to reform the Russian economy created new poverty as well as new wealth. (TASS/Sovfoto)

turned thousands of factories and mines over to new private companies. Each citizen received a voucher worth 10,000 rubles (about $22) to buy stock in private companies, but ownership of the privatized companies usually remained in the hands of the old bosses, the managers and government officials from the communist era.

President Yeltsin and his economic reformers believed that shock therapy would revive production and bring widespread prosperity after a brief period of hardship. The results of the reforms were in fact quite different. Prices increased 250 percent on the very first day, and they kept on soaring, increasing twenty-six times in the course of 1992. At the same time, Russian production fell a staggering 20 percent. Nor did the situation stabilize quickly. After 1995, rapid but gradually slowing inflation raged, and output continued to fall. According to most estimates, in 1996 the Russian economy produced at least one-third and possibly as much as one-half less than in 1991. The Russian economy crashed again in 1998 in the wake of Asia's financial crisis.

Rapid economic liberalization worked poorly in Russia for several reasons. Soviet industry had been highly monopolized and strongly tilted toward military goods. Production of many items had been concentrated in one or two gigantic factories or in interconnected combines that supplied the entire economy. With privatization these powerful state monopolies became powerful private monopolies that cut production and raised prices in order to maximize their financial returns. Moreover, powerful corporate managers and bureaucrats forced Yeltsin's government to hand out enormous subsidies to reinforce the positions of big firms and to avoid bankruptcies. New corporate leaders included criminals who intimidated would-be rivals in attempts to prevent the formation of new businesses. In the end, as enterprise directors and politicians converted large portions of previously state-owned industry into their own private property, they undermined the ideal goal of worker ownership.

Runaway inflation and poorly executed privatization brought a profound social revolution to Russia. The new capitalist elite acquired great wealth and power, while large numbers of people fell into abject poverty, and the majority struggled to make ends meet. Managers, former Communist officials, and financiers who came out

Chronology

1980s–1990s	Emergence of globalization
1990s–2000s	New waves of legal and illegal immigration to Europe
1990–1991	Persian Gulf War
1991	Maastricht Treaty
1991–2001	Civil war in Yugoslavia
1992–1997	Decline of Russian economy
1993	Creation of the European Union
1997–1998	Global economic downturn
1999	Protests against World Trade Organization in Seattle
2000–2008	Resurgence of Russian economy under Putin
2001	September 11 terrorist attack on the United States; war in Afghanistan begins
2002	Euro introduced in European Union
2003	Iraq War begins
2004	Train bombings in Madrid by Islamic extremists
2005	Young Muslims riot in France; subway bombing in London by Islamic extremists
2006	Sectarian conflict in Iraq increases
2008	Worldwide financial crisis
2009	Ratification of Treaty of Lisbon; young Muslims riot in France; Copenhagen summit on climate change

of the privatization process with large shares of the old state monopolies stood at the top of the reorganized society. The richest plums were found in Russia's huge oil and natural resources industries, where unscrupulous enterprise directors pocketed enormous dishonest gains.

The new elite was more highly concentrated than ever before, and maintained control with corrupt business practices and rampant cronyism. By 1996 Moscow, with 5 percent of Russia's population, controlled 80 percent of its capital resources. At the other extreme, the vast majority of people saw their savings become practically worthless. Pensions lost much of their value, and whole markets were devoted to people selling off their personal goods to survive. Perhaps the most telling statistic, which reflected the hardship caused by the collapse of the Soviet welfare state and growing poverty, was the catastrophic decline in the life expectancy of the average Russian male from sixty-nine years in 1991 to only fifty-eight years in 1996. Under these conditions, effective representative government failed to develop, and many Russians came to equate democracy with the corruption, poverty, and national decline they experienced throughout the 1990s.

Russian Revival Under Vladimir Putin

The widespread disillusionment in the first decade of postcommunist Russia set the stage for the "managed democracy" of Vladimir Putin (VLAH-duh-mihr POO-tihn) (b. 1952). First elected president as Yeltsin's chosen successor in 2000, Putin won in a landslide in March 2004. An officer in the secret police in the Communist era, Putin and his United Russia Party maintained relatively free markets in the economic sphere but re-established semi-authoritarian political rule. Proponents of liberal democracy were in retreat, while conservative Russian intellectuals were on the offensive, arguing that free markets and capitalism required strong political rule to control corruption and prevent chaos.

The combination of Putin's autocratic politics and the turn to market economics — aided greatly by high prices for oil and natural gas, Russia's most important exports — led to a decade of strong economic growth. Russia became one of western Europe's main energy sup-

Vladimir Putin on Vacation in 2009 After serving two terms as Russian president (2000–2008), Putin was appointed prime minister and continues to be a powerful Russian leader. Putin's high approval ratings were due in part to his carefully crafted image of strength and manliness. (AFP/Getty Images)

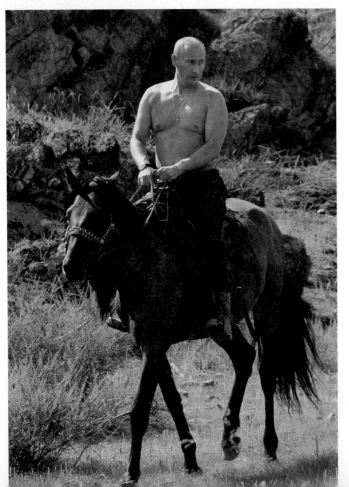

pliers. In 2008 the Russian economy had been expanding for over nine years, encouraging the growth of a new middle class. That same year, the global financial crisis and a rapid drop in the price of oil reversed these trends. Economic growth ground to a halt. The Russian stock market collapsed; although the government initiated a $200 billion rescue plan, the economy continued to falter in 2010.

During his term as president, Putin championed a return to an assertive anti-Western Russian nationalism. He took a forceful stand against the expansion of NATO in the former East Bloc and increasingly challenged the United States in world affairs. Putin expressed pride in the accomplishments of the Soviet Union and downplayed the abuses of the Stalinist system. In addition, the Russian president centralized power in the Kremlin, increased military spending, and expanded the secret police. Putin's carefully crafted manly image and his forceful interaction in international diplomacy soothed the country's injured pride and symbolized its national revival.

Putin's government moved decisively to limit political opposition. The arrest and imprisonment for tax evasion of the corrupt billionaire oil tycoon Mikhail Khodorkovsky, who had openly supported opposition parties, showed that Putin and the United Russia Party would use state powers to stifle dissent. Though freedom of the press is guaranteed by the constitution, the Russian government also cracked down on the independent media. Using a variety of tactics, officials and pro-government businessmen worked to influence news reports and intimidate critical journalists. The suspicious murder in 2006 of journalist Anna Politkovskaya, a prominent critic of Russian human rights abuses and Russia's war in Chechnya, reinforced Western worries that the country was returning to Soviet-style press censorship.

Putin also took an aggressive and at times interventionist stance toward the Commonwealth of Independent States, a loose confederation of the newly independent states on the borders of the former Soviet Union, including Ukraine, Georgia, and the Republic of Belarus (Map 31.1). Conflict has been particularly intense in the oil-rich Caucasus region to the south, where an unstable combination of nationalist separatism and ethnic and religious tensions challenges Russian dominance. Since the breakup of the Soviet Union, Russian troops have repeatedly invaded Chechnya (CHECH-nyuh), a tiny republic of 1 million Muslims on Russia's southern border that in 1991 had declared its independence from the Russian Federation.

Despite nominal Russian control over Chechnya, the cost of the conflict has been high. Thousands on both sides have lost their lives, and both sides have committed serious human rights abuses. Russian security forces have tortured and summarily executed insur-

Map 31.1 Russia and the Successor States, 1991–2010 After the failure of an attempt in August 1991 to depose Gorbachev, an anticommunist revolution swept the Soviet Union. Led by Russia and Boris Yeltsin, the republics that formed the Soviet Union declared their sovereignty and independence. Eleven of the fifteen republics then formed a loose confederation called the Commonwealth of Independent States, but the integrated economy of the Soviet Union dissolved into separate national economies, each with its own goals and policies. Conflict continues to simmer over these goals and policies, as evidenced by the ongoing civil war in Chechnya and the recent conflict between Russia and Georgia over South Ossetia.

gents they had captured. Chechen terrorists, for their part, occupied a crowded theater in Moscow in 2002 and took some twelve hundred hostages in a Russian school in 2004. In both cases government efforts to free the hostages killed not only the terrorists but also hundreds of innocent Russian civilians.

Moscow declared an end to military operations in Chechnya in April 2009, but Chechen insurgents, inspired by separatist nationalism and Islamic radicalism, continued their violent struggle for national independence. The ongoing civil war in Chechnya also contributed to an ongoing crisis in the independent state of Georgia, which won independence from Russia in 1991. Russian troops invaded Georgia in 2008 to sup-

port a separatist movement in South Ossetia (ah-SEE-shuh), which eventually established a breakaway independent republic recognized by Russia, but not by much of the West.

Despite his turn to illiberal domestic politics and heavy-handed foreign intervention, Putin stepped down when his term limits expired in 2008. His handpicked successor, Dimitri Medvedev (mehd-VEHD-yehf) (b. 1965), easily won the Russian presidential elections that year and then appointed Putin prime minister, leading observers to conclude that the former president was still the dominant leader. Medvedev cast himself as a relative liberal compared to the former president, and Russian citizens enjoyed a relatively open cultural life in

❝ What we want is for our life to be as easy as it was in the Soviet Union, with the guarantee of a good, stable future and low prices — and at the same time this freedom that did not exist before. **❞**

—Russian pensioner

cafés and cultural institutions and on the Internet. Yet by 2010 it seemed clear that Russia had slowed attempts to establish a Western-style democracy and instead re-instituted a system of authoritarian presidential control. Tensions between political centralization and liberal openness continued to define Russia's difficult road away from communism.

Coping with Change in Eastern Europe

Developments in eastern Europe were similar to those in Russia in important ways. The postcommunist former satellites worked to replace state planning and socialism with market mechanisms and private property. Western-style electoral politics also took hold; as in Russia, this politics was marked by intense battles between presidents and parliaments and by weak political parties.

Economic growth in the former communist countries was varied, but most observers agreed that Poland, the Czech Republic, and Hungary were the most successful. Each met the critical challenge of economic reconstruction more successfully than did Russia, and each could claim to be the economic leader in eastern Europe, depending on the criteria selected. The reasons for these successes included considerable experience with limited market reforms before 1989, flexibility and lack of dogmatism in government policy, and an enthusiastic embrace of capitalism by a new entrepreneurial class. In the first five years of reform, Poland created twice as many new businesses as did Russia, with a total population only one-fourth as large.

Ostalgie German term referring to nostalgia for the lifestyles and culture of the vanished East Bloc.

Poland, the Czech Republic, and Hungary also did far better than Russia in creating new civic institutions, legal systems, and independent media outlets that reinforced political freedom and national revival. Lech Walesa in Poland and Václav Havel in Czechoslovakia were elected presidents of their countries and proved as remarkable in power as in opposition (see Chapter 30). After Czechoslovakia's Velvet Revolution in 1989, Havel and the Czech parliament accepted a "velvet divorce" in 1993 when Slovakian nationalists wanted to break

off and form their own state. Above all, and in sharp contrast to Russia, the popular goal of adopting the liberal democratic values of western Europe reinforced political moderation and compromise. In 1997 Poland, Hungary, and the Czech Republic were accepted into the NATO alliance, and in 2004 these countries plus Slovakia gained admission to the European Union (EU) (see page 1005).

Romania and Bulgaria were the eastern European laggards in the postcommunist transition. Western traditions were much weaker there, and both countries were much poorer than their neighbors to the north. Romania and Bulgaria did make progress after 2000, however, and joined NATO in 2004 and the EU in 2007.

The social consequences of reconstruction in the former East Bloc were similar to those in Russia. Ordinary citizens and the elderly were once again the big losers, while the young and former Communists were the big winners. Inequalities between richer and poorer regions also increased. Capital cities such as Warsaw, Prague, and Budapest concentrated wealth, power, and opportunity as never before, while provincial centers stagnated and old industrial areas declined. Crime and gangsterism increased in both the streets and the executive suites.

Though few former East Bloc residents wanted to return to communism, they nonetheless expressed some longings for the stability of the old system. Some missed the guaranteed jobs and generous social benefits provided by the Communist state, and they found the individualism and competitiveness of capitalist democracy cold and difficult. One Russian woman living on a pension of $448 a month in 2003 summed up the dilemma: "What we want is for our life to be as easy as it was in the Soviet Union, with the guarantee of a good, stable future and low prices—and at the same time this freedom that did not exist before."[1] Even the shoddy consumer goods so bemoaned during the communist years became objects of affection. Germans coined the term **Ostalgie**—a combination of the German words for "East" and "nostalgia"—to label this fondness for the lifestyles and culture of the vanished East Bloc.

At the same time, many East Bloc citizens had never fully accepted communism, primarily because they equated it with Russian imperialism and the loss of national independence. The joyous crowds that toppled communist regimes in 1989 believed that they were liberating the nation as well as the individual. Thus, when communism died, nationalism was reborn. Reflecting this new sense of popular nationalism, conservative politicians in the mold of Russia's president Putin found success in Poland, the Czech Republic, and other former East Bloc countries.

The question of whether or how to punish former Communist leaders who had committed political crimes or abused human rights emerged as a pressing question in the former East Bloc. Germany tried major offenders and opened the records of the East German secret police (the Stasi) to the public, and by 1996 more than a million former residents had asked to see their files.[2] Other countries designed various means to deal with former elites who might have committed crimes, with conservative leaders generally taking a more punitive stand against the old Communist bosses. Finding fair solutions proceeded slowly and with much controversy, an ongoing reminder of the troubling legacies of communism and the Cold War.

Tragedy in Yugoslavia

The great postcommunist tragedy was Yugoslavia, which under Josip Tito had been a federation of republics and regions under centralized Communist rule (see Chapter 29). After Tito's death in 1980, power passed increasingly to the sister republics, which encouraged a revival of regional and ethnic conflicts that were exacerbated by charges of ethnically inspired massacres during World War II and a dramatic economic decline in the mid-1980s.

The revolutions of 1989 accelerated the breakup of Yugoslavia. Serbian president Slobodan Milosevic (SLOH-buh-dayn muh-LOH-suh-vihch) (1941–2006), a former Communist bureaucrat, intended to grab land from other republics and unite all Serbs, regardless of where they lived, in a "greater Serbia." In 1989 Milosevic arbitrarily abolished self-rule in the Serbian province of Kosovo, where Albanian-speaking, primarily Islamic peoples constituted the overwhelming majority. Milosevic's moves strengthened the cause of national separatism in the Serbian-controlled federation, and in June 1991 relatively wealthy Slovenia and Croatia declared their independence from Yugoslavia. Milosevic's armies invaded to reassert Serbian control. The Serbs were quickly repulsed in Slovenia, but managed to take about 30 percent of Croatia.

In 1992 the civil war spread to Bosnia-Herzegovina, which had also declared its independence. Serbs—about 30 percent of that region's population—refused to live under the more numerous Bosnian Muslims (Map 31.2). Yugoslavia had once been a tolerant and largely successful multiethnic state with different groups living side by side and often intermarrying. The new goal of both sides in the Bosnian civil war was **ethnic cleansing**: the attempt to establish

ethnic cleansing The attempt to establish ethnically homogeneous territories by intimidation, forced deportation, and killing.

Map 31.2 The Breakup of Yugoslavia, 1991–2006 Yugoslavia had the most ethnically diverse population in eastern Europe. The republic of Croatia had substantial Serbian and Muslim minorities. Bosnia-Herzegovina had large Muslim, Serbian, and Croatian populations, none of which had a majority. In June 1991 Serbia's brutal effort to seize territory and unite all Serbs in a single state brought a tragic civil war.

ethnically homogeneous territories by intimidation, forced deportation, and killing. Serbian armies and irregular militias attempted to "cleanse" the territory of its non-Serb residents, unleashing ruthless brutality, with murder, rape, destruction, and the herding of refugees into concentration camps. Before the fighting in Bosnia ended, some three hundred thousand people were dead, and millions had been forced to flee their homes.

While appalling scenes of horror shocked the world, the Western nations had difficulty formulating an effective and unified response. The turning point came in July 1995 when Bosnian Serbs overran Srebrenica—a Muslim city previously declared a United Nations safe area. Pursuing their violent ethnic cleansing campaign, Serb forces killed 7,400 of the city's Muslim civilians, primarily men and boys. Europe had not seen such atrocities since the horrors of the Nazi Holocaust in World War II (see Chapter 28). Public outrage prompted NATO to bomb Bosnian Serb military targets intensively, and the Croatian army drove all the Serbs from Croatia. In November 1995 President Bill Clinton helped the warring sides hammer out a complicated accord that gave the Bosnian Serbs about 49 percent of Bosnia and the Muslim-Croatian peoples the rest. Troops from NATO countries patrolled Bosnia to try to keep the peace.

The Albanian Muslims of Kosovo had been hoping for a restoration of self-rule, but they gained nothing from the Bosnian agreement. In early 1998 frustrated Kosovar militants formed the **Kosovo Liberation Army (KLA)** and began to fight for independence. Serbian repression of the Kosovars

Kosovo Liberation Army (KLA) Military organization formed in 1998 by Kosovar militants who sought independence from Serbia.

increased, and in 1998 Serbian forces attacked both KLA guerrillas and unarmed villagers, displacing 250,000 people within Kosovo.

By January 1999 the Western Powers, led by the United States, were threatening Milosevic with heavy air raids if he did not withdraw Serbian armies from Kosovo and accept self-government (but not independence) for Kosovo. Milosevic refused, and in March 1999 NATO began bombing Yugoslavia. Serbian paramilitary forces responded by driving about 865,000 Albanian Kosovars into exile. NATO redoubled its highly destructive bombing campaign, which eventually forced Milosevic to withdraw and allowed the Kosovars to regain their homeland. A UN–NATO peacekeeping force occupied the territory, bringing the ten-year cycle of Yugoslavian civil wars to a close. Although U.S.-led NATO intervention finally brought an end to the conflict, the failure to take a stronger stand in the early years led to widespread and unnecessary suffering in the former Yugoslavia.

The war-weary and impoverished Serbs eventually voted the still-defiant Milosevic out of office, and in July 2001 a new pro-Western Serbian government turned him over to the war crimes tribunal in the Netherlands to stand trial for crimes against humanity. After blustering his way through the initial stages of his trial, Milosevic died in 2006 before the proceedings were complete. In 2008, after eight years of administration by the United Nations and NATO peacekeeping forces, the Republic of Kosovo declared its total independence from Serbia. The United States and many western European nations recognized the declaration. Serbia and Russia did not, and the long-term status of this troubled emerging state remained uncertain.

Escape from Srebrenica
A Bosnian Muslim refugee arrives at the United Nations base in Tuzla and with anguished screams tells the world of the Serbian atrocities. Several thousand civilians were murdered at Srebrenica, and Western public opinion finally demanded decisive action. Efforts continue to arrest the Serbs believed responsible and to try them for crimes against humanity. (J. Jones/Corbis)

The New Global System

What are the defining features of globalization, and how did changing international structures transform European societies? ▪

Contemporary observers often assert that the world has entered a new era of **globalization**. Though the term is difficult to define, such assertions do not mean that there were never international connections before. Europe has long had close—sometimes productive, sometimes destructive—ties to other parts of the world. Yet new global relationships did emerge in the last decades of the twentieth century.

First, the expansion and ready availability of highly efficient computer and media technologies led to ever-faster exchanges of information and entertainment around the world. Second, the growth of multinational corporations restructured national economies on a global scale. Third, an array of international governing bodies, such as the European Union, the United Nations, the World Bank, and the World Trade Organization, increasingly set policies that challenged the authority of traditional nation-states. Taken together, these global transformations had a remarkable impact—both positive and negative—on many aspects of Western society.

The Digital Age and the Changing Economy

The development of sophisticated personal computer technologies and the Internet at the end of the twentieth century, coupled with the deregulation of national and international financial systems, had a revolutionary impact on international trade. The ability to rapidly exchange information and capital meant that economic activity was no longer centered on national banks or stock exchanges, but rather flowed quickly across international borders. Large cities like London, Moscow, New York, and Hong Kong became global centers of banking, trade, and financial services. The influence of stock markets and insurance companies, as well as of communications conglomerates and energy and legal firms headquartered in these new global cities, extended far beyond the borders of the traditional nation-state.

Multinational corporations flourished in the new global climate. Conglomerates such as Siemens and Vivendi exemplified the new business model. Siemens, with international headquarters in Berlin and Munich and offices around the globe, is one of the world's largest engineering companies, with vast holdings in energy, construction, health care, financial services, and industrial production. Vivendi, an extensive media and tele-communications company headquartered in Paris, controls a vast international network of products, including music and film, publishing, television broadcasting, pay-TV, Internet services, and video games.

The growing global reach of multinational corporations and the development of sophisticated information technologies have had astonishing effects on everyday life. Cable television, DVDs, and online video streaming greatly diversified home entertainment. Europe's once stodgy public broadcasting systems now competed with a variety of commercial private providers. Compact discs and downloadable audio files replaced vinyl records and cassettes, and digital cameras eliminated the need for film. E-mail and text messaging changed the way friends and families exchanged news, and letter writing with pen and paper became a quaint relic of the past. Many people now relied on the Internet to access consumer goods, entertainment, and information from around the globe. The smart phone, with its multimedia telecommunications features, combined all these activities and more in one small hand-held device.

globalization The emergence of a freer, more technologically connected global economy, accompanied by a worldwide exchange of cultural, political, and religious ideas.

Though globalization in some ways fueled the booming economy and helped create a flashy new world of instant entertainment and communication, the close connections between national economies also made the entire world vulnerable to economic panics and downturns. In 1997 a banking crisis in Thailand spread to Indonesia, South Korea, and Japan, and then echoed around the world. The resulting decline in prices for raw materials such as petroleum and natural gas hit Russia especially hard, leading to high inflation, bank failures, and the collapse of the Russian stock market. The crisis then spread to Latin America, where most countries entered a severe economic downturn in 1998.

A decade later, in 2008, the global recession, triggered by a crisis in the U.S. housing market and financial system, created the worst worldwide economic crisis since the Great Depression of the 1930s. The U.S. government spent massive sums in attempts to recharge the economy. Banks, insurance agencies, auto companies, and financial service conglomerates received billions of federal dollars, but unemployment, a weak housing market, and stagnant production continued.

The recession quickly swept through Europe. One of the worst hit was Iceland, where in October 2008 the currency and banking system collapsed outright. Other countries across Europe were also rocked by the crisis. Ireland and Latvia were forced to make deep and painful cuts in government spending to balance national budgets. By 2010 Britain was deeply in debt, and Spain, Portugal, and especially Greece were close to bankruptcy. In May 2010 Greece promised to raise consumption taxes and drastically reduce spending on public pensions and other popular social benefits in order to accept a 110 billion euro bailout package from the

Financial Meltdown in Iceland These protesters are on their way to the parliament in Reykjavik, the capital of Iceland, in March 2010 to protest the government's proposed debt repayment policies after the collapse of the Icelandic banking system. One protester carries a sign reading "Stop the Financial Casino." Iceland's financial meltdown, sparked by a major recession in the United States, underscored the close links between national economies in the new era of globalization. (S. Olads/EPA/Corbis)

International Monetary Fund and the European Union. National governments used a variety of initiatives to recharge their flagging economies, even as experts worried about the long-term effects of the recession on European stability and demonstrators took to the streets to protest against cuts in popular social programs.

The Human Side of Globalization

In addition to the financial vulnerabilities inherent in a global economy, the varied forces of globalization encouraged far-reaching social change tied closely to the technological advances of the postindustrial society (see Chapter 30). Low labor costs in the industrializing world—including the former East Bloc, South America, and East Asia—encouraged corporations to outsource labor-intensive manufacturing jobs to these regions. Neoliberal free-trade policies and lowered tariffs made it less expensive to manufacture goods such as steel, automotive parts, computer components, and all manner of consumer goods in developing countries, and then import them for sale in the West. In these new conditions, a car made by Volkswagen could still be sold as a product of high-quality German engineering, but be assembled in Volkswagen's new plant in Chattanooga, Tennessee, with steel imported from South Korea and computer chips made in Taiwan.

Globalization dramatically changed the nature of work in western Europe. In France in 1973, for example, some 40 percent of the employed population worked in industry—in mining, construction, manufacturing, and utilities. About 49 percent worked in services, including retail, the hotel and restaurant trades, transpor-

tation, communications, financial and business services, and social and personal services. In 2004 only 24 percent of the French worked in industry, and a whopping 72 percent worked in services. The numbers varied country by country, yet across Europe the trend was clear: by 2005 only about one in three workers was still employed in the once-booming manufacturing sector.[3]

The deindustrialization of Europe established a multitiered society with real winners and losers. In the top tier was a small, affluent group of highly paid experts, executives, and professionals—about one-quarter of the total population—who managed the new information industries. In the second, larger tier, a struggling middle class experienced stagnating incomes and a declining standard of living. Workers from the formerly well-paid industrial sector faced stubborn unemployment and cuts in both welfare and workplace benefits. Many were forced to take low-paying jobs in the retail service sector.

In the bottom tier—in some areas as much as a quarter of the population—a poorly paid underclass performed the unskilled jobs of a postindustrial economy. In Europe and the United States inclusion in this lowest segment of society was often predicated on race and ethnicity. Recently arrived immigrants had trouble finding jobs and often lived in unpleasant, hastily built suburban apartment blocks, where they teetered on the edge of poverty. In London, unemployment rates among young black men soared above those of their white compatriots, and the connections between race and poverty were similar in other urban areas.

Geographic contrasts further revealed the unequal aspects of globalization. Regions in Europe that had successfully made the move to a postindustrial economy, such as northern Italy and southern Germany and Austria, were centers of affluence and prosperity. Regions that had depended on heavy industry or were historically underdeveloped, including the former East Bloc countries, the factory districts north of London, and the largely rural areas of southern Italy and Spain, lagged behind. In addition, a global north-south divide increasingly separated the relatively affluent countries of Europe and North America from the industrializing nations of Africa and South America. Though India, China, and other East Asian nations experienced solid growth, other industrializing nations struggled to overcome decades of underdevelopment.

The New European Union

Global economic pressures encouraged the expansion and consolidation of the European Community (EC), which in 1993 proudly rechristened itself the **European Union (EU)** (Map 31.3). With its roots in Europe's Common Market (see Chapter 29), the EU worked to add the free movement of European labor, capital, and services to the existing free trade in goods. In addition, member states sought to create a monetary union in which all EU countries would share a single currency. Membership in the monetary union required states to meet the strict financial criteria defined in the 1991 **Maastricht Treaty**, which also set legal standards and anticipated the development of common policies on defense and foreign affairs.

Western European elites and opinion makers generally supported the decisive step toward economic integration embodied in the Maastricht Treaty. They felt that membership requirements, which imposed financial discipline on national governments, would combat Europe's ongoing economic problems, and they viewed the establishment of a single European currency as an irreversible historic step toward basic political unity. This unity would allow western Europe as a whole to regain its place in world politics and to deal with the United States as an equal.

Support for the Maastricht Treaty was not universal. Ordinary people, leftist political parties, and populist nationalists expressed widespread skepticism and considerable opposition to the new rules. Many people resented the EU's ever-growing bureaucracy in Brussels, which sought to impose common standards on everything from cheese to day care and undermined national practices and local traditions. Moreover, increased unity meant yielding still more power to distant "Eurocrats" and political insiders, thereby undermining popular sovereignty and democratic control.

Above all, many ordinary citizens feared that the new Europe was being created at their expense. Joining the monetary union required national governments to meet stringent fiscal standards, impose budget cuts, and contribute to the EU operating budget. The resulting reductions in health care and social benefits hit ordinary citizens and did little to reduce western Europe's high unemployment rate. When put to the public for a vote, ratification of the Maastricht Treaty was usually very close. In France, for example, the treaty passed with just 50.1 percent of the vote.

Even after the Maastricht Treaty was ratified, battles over budgets and high unemployment throughout the EU in the 1990s raised profound questions about the meaning of European unity and identity. Would the EU expand as promised to include the postcommunist nations of eastern Europe, and if it did, how could Muslim Turkey's long-standing application be ignored? How could a European Union of twenty-five to thirty countries have any real cohesion and common identity? Conversely, would a large, cohesive Europe remain closely linked with the United States in the NATO alliance? Would—or could—the EU develop an independent military defense policy? In the face of these questions, western Europeans proceeded cautiously in considering new requests for EU membership, even though former communist states pressed for admission.

> **European Union (EU)**
> The economic, cultural, and political alliance of twenty-seven European nations.
>
> **Maastricht Treaty** The basis for the formation of the European Union, which set financial and cultural standards for potential member states and defined criteria for membership in the monetary union.

Turkey's Struggle for EU Membership Turkey's leaders and the general population seek to join the European Union, but the road to membership is proving difficult. The EU has required Turkey to make many constitutional reforms and to give greater autonomy to Turkish Kurds. Yet even as the other nations standing in line gain admission, the Turks face ever more demands, leading to accusations that the real roadblock is Europe's anti-Muslim feeling. (CartoonStock Limited)

The European Union
- Original members, 1951
- New members, 1973
- New members, 1981
- New members, 1986
- German reunification, 1990
- New members, 1995
- New members, 2004
- New members, 2007
- Candidate countries, 2010
- € Euro Zone countries, 2010

Mapping the Past

Map 31.3 The European Union, 2010 No longer divided by ideological competition and the Cold War, much of today's Europe has banded together in a European Union that facilitates the open movement of people, jobs, and currency across borders.

ANALYZING THE MAP Trace the expansion of membership from its initial founding as the European Economic Union to today. How would you characterize the members who joined during 2004–2007? Whose membership is still pending?

CONNECTIONS Which countries are and are not part of the Euro Zone, and what does this suggest about how successful the European Union has been in adopting the euro?

To complete this activity online, go to the Online Study Guide at bedfordstmartins.com/mckaywest.

Then on January 1, 2002, brand-new euros finally replaced the national currencies of all Euro Zone residents. (See "Living in the Past: The Euro," page 1008). The establishment of the European monetary union built confidence and increased willingness to accept new members. On May 1, 2004, the European Union finally began admitting its former East Bloc neighbors, and by 2007 the EU was home to 493 million citizens in twenty-seven different countries. It included most of the former East Bloc and, with the Baltic republics, several territories that had once been inside the Soviet Union.

This rapid expansion underscored the need to reform the EU's unwieldy governing structure. In June 2004 a special commission presented a new EU constitution that created a president, a foreign minister, and a voting system weighted to reflect the populations of the different states. The proposed constitution moved toward a more centralized federal system, but each state retained veto power over taxation, social policy, foreign affairs, and other sensitive areas. After many noisy and contentious referendum campaigns across the continent, the constitution failed to win the unanimous support that it needed to take effect. Ultimately, nationalist fears about losing sovereignty and cultural identity outweighed the perceived benefits of a more unified Europe. Fears that an unwieldy European Union would grow to include Ukraine, Georgia, and Muslim Turkey—countries with cultures and histories that were very different from those of western Europe—were particularly telling.

Though the constitution would not go into effect as written, the long postwar march toward greater European unity did not stop. In 2007 the rejected constitution was replaced with the Treaty of Lisbon. The new treaty kept many sections of the constitution, but further streamlined the EU bureaucracy and reformed its political structure. By November 2009 it had been ratified by all the EU states. When the Treaty of Lisbon went into effect on December 1, 2009, it capped a remarkable fifty-year effort to unify what had been a deeply divided and war-torn continent.

Supranational Organizations

Beyond the European Union, the trend toward globalization empowered a variety of other supranational organizations whose interests and activities crossed the borders of the world's nation-states. National governments still played the leading role in defining and implementing policy, but they increasingly had to take the interests of institutions such as the United Nations and the World Trade Organization into consideration.

The United Nations (UN), established in 1945 after World War II, remains one of the most important players on the world stage. Representatives from all independent countries meet in the UN General Assembly in New York City to manage international agreements and crises. The UN's many offices deal with issues such as world hunger and poverty, and the International Court of Justice in The Hague, Netherlands, hears cases that violate international law. The UN also sends troops to police crisis situations in attempts to preserve peace between warring parties—as in Yugoslavia in the 1990s.

The UN's governing Security Council, which includes the United States, Russia, France, Great Britain, and China, has the power to veto resolutions passed by the General Assembly. The predominance of the United States and western European powers on the Security Council has led some critics to accuse the UN of being a forum for the expression of neocolonial interests (see Chapter 29). Others argue that UN policies should never take precedent over national needs, and UN resolutions are at times ignored or downplayed. The organization nonetheless retains enormous international prestige.

A number of nonprofit international financial institutions, including the World Bank, the International Monetary Fund (IMF), and the **World Trade Organization (WTO)** have also gained power in a globalizing

world. Like the United Nations, the World Bank and the IMF were established in the years following World War II. Initially founded to help rebuild war-torn Europe, the IMF and the World Bank now provide loans to the developing world. Their funding comes primarily from donations from the United States and western Europe, and they often extend loans on the condition that recipient countries adopt free trade, deregulation, and other neoliberal economic policies. After the 1990s the World Bank and the IMF played active roles in shaping economic and social policy in the former East Bloc.

With headquarters in Geneva, Switzerland, the WTO is one of the most powerful supranational financial institutions. It sets trade and tariff agreements for over 150 member countries and so helps manage a large percentage of the world's import-export policies. Like the IMF and the World Bank, the WTO promotes neoliberal policies around the world.

The rise of these institutions, which typically represent the interests of combined national governments in international forums, was paralleled by the emergence of

World Trade Organization (WTO) A powerful supranational financial institution that sets trade and tariff agreements for over 150 member countries and so helps manage a large percentage of the world's import-export policies. Like the IMF and the World Bank, the WTO promotes neoliberal policies around the world.

Antiglobalization Activism French protesters carry the figure of Ronald McDonald through the streets to protest the trial of José Bové, a prominent leader in campaigns against the human and environmental costs associated with globalization. Bové was accused of demolishing a McDonald's franchise in a small town in southern France. With its worldwide fast-food restaurants that pay little attention to local traditions, McDonald's has often been the target of antiglobalization protests. (Witt/Haley/Sipa)

LIVING IN THE PAST

ON JANUARY 1, 2002, THE RESIDENTS OF MANY EUROPEAN UNION COUNTRIES exchanged their familiar national currencies for the euro, the newly approved coins and banknotes that signaled the arrival of the EU monetary union. The German deutschmark, the French franc, the Italian lira, and many others were now part of history, collectibles, perhaps, but on the way out as legal tender.

The move to the euro was one of the most controversial aspects of the Maastricht Treaty of 1991 that reshaped the EU and laid out a timetable for monetary union. While some countries signed up, Britain, Denmark, and Sweden accepted the main terms of the treaty but refused to join the currency union (or Euro Zone, the group of countries that used the new money). Citizens there rejected the euro, fearing its economic impact and its effects on national autonomy.

To join the Euro Zone, a country was required to maintain stringent economic conditions — low inflation, tight budgets, and small deficits. In 2010 only sixteen of the EU's twenty-seven member states used the euro as their official currency. The former East Bloc nations, such as Poland and Hungary, that joined the EU in 2004 and 2007 were excluded from the Euro Zone, and so remained something of second-class members.

The euro raised basic questions about a common European identity. What images could be portrayed on the new coins and bills that would do justice to both membership in a larger European community and the variety of national states that made up what was in fact a very diverse continent? The solution was ingenious. The front of the coins would show the denomination and a map of Europe, but the reverse would portray national images chosen by individual EU members. Thus the two-euro coin minted in Ireland features a traditional Celtic harp, while that made in France portrays the liberty tree. Banknotes, by contrast, would feature generic architectural images on both sides that looked real but were not, in order to prevent any national prejudice. Thus the arches on the five-euro note resemble a Roman viaduct; the bridge on the ten-euro note resembles a Renaissance bridge; and the glass and steel façade on the five-hundred-euro note resembles a modern urban office building. All are imaginary structures that look "European" but do not actually exist.

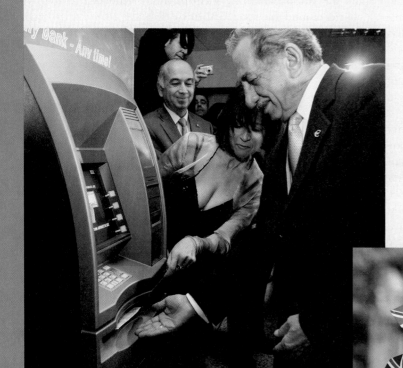

The president of Cyprus withdraws the country's first euros on January 1, 2008, after the country formally adopted the euro as its official currency. (Petros Karadjilas/AP Images)

A colorfully dressed anti-euro protester stands outside the British Houses of Parliament in June 2003. (Scott Barbour/Getty Images)

Five-euro, ten-euro, and twenty-euro bills (above). The back of the French (top) and Greek (below) euro coins. (bills: Thinkstock Images/Getty Images; coins: Courtesy, Eurocoins.co.uk)

QUESTIONS FOR ANALYSIS

1. Why did the leaders of the European Union push for a common currency?

2. How do the images portrayed on euro coins and banknotes reflect the dilemmas of establishing a workable European identity?

a variety of so-called **nongovernmental organizations (NGOs)**. Some NGOs act as lobbyists for specific issues; others conduct international programs and activities. Exemplary NGOs include Doctors Without Borders, a charitable organization of physicians headquartered in France; Greenpeace, an international environmental group; and Oxfam, a British-based group dedicated to alleviating famine, disease, and poverty in the developing world. Though NGOs generally rely on donations from governments and private citizens for financial support, their annual budgets can total hundreds of millions of dollars and their work can be quite extensive. Oxfam, for example, in 2008 employed about six thousand staff members across the globe, had over twenty thousand volunteers and thousands of other contributors, and managed an annual budget of about £300 million (about $500 million U.S.).[4]

nongovernmental organizations (NGOs) Independent organizations with specific agendas, such as humanitarian aid or environmental protection, that conduct international programs and activities.

The rise of globalization has also encouraged the growth of new forms of global protest, often aimed at the leaders and economic structures of globalization itself. Such protest is typically aimed at global corporations and financial groups, which have done little to resolve the world's serious inequalities and problems, such as environmental pollution, unfair labor practices, and poor health and human rights policies. The Slow Food movement that began in Italy, for example, criticized American-style fast-food chains that proliferated in Europe and the world in the 1990s. Cooking with local products and traditional methods, followers argued, was healthier and kept jobs and profits in local neighborhoods. The fast-food giant McDonald's was often targeted as an example of the ills of corporate globalization. José Bové, a French farmer and antiglobalization activist, made world headlines when he drove his truck through the windows of a McDonald's in a small French village to protest the use of hormone-fed beef and genetically modified foods, and the reach of corporate capital.

The general tone of antiglobalization protest was captured in 1999 at the meeting of the World Trade Organization in Seattle, Washington. Tens of thousands of grassroots protesters from around the world, including environmentalists, consumer and antipoverty activists, and labor-rights groups, marched in the streets and disrupted the meeting. As one activist put it, "The WTO seems to be on a crusade to increase private profit at the expense of all other considerations, including the well-being and quality of life of the mass of the world's people. . . . It seems to have a relentless drive to extend its power."[5] Similar protests took place at later meetings of the WTO, the World Bank, and other supranational groups, as activists struggled with powerful public officials to influence the course of world development.

Toward a Multicultural Continent

How did population decline and large-scale immigration lead to demographic changes in contemporary Europe, and what were the main results of growing ethnic diversity?   ■

As the twenty-first century opened and globalization began to affect European society and politics, Europeans also saw changes in the ethnic makeup of their nations. On the one hand, Europe experienced a remarkable decline in birthrates that seemed to predict a shrinking and aging population in the future. On the other hand, the peaceful, wealthy European Union attracted rapidly growing numbers of refugees and legal and illegal immigrants from the former Soviet Union, the Middle East, Africa, and Asia. The unexpected arrival of so many newcomers raised perplexing questions about ethnic diversity and the costs and benefits of multiculturalism.

The Prospect of Population Decline

Population is still growing rapidly in many poor countries, but not in the world's industrialized nations. In 2000, families in developed countries had only 1.6 children on average; only in the United States did families have, almost exactly, the 2.1 children necessary to maintain a stable population. In European countries, where birthrates had been falling since the 1950s, national fertility rates ranged from 1.2 to 1.8 children per woman of childbearing age. Italy, once renowned for large Catholic families, had achieved the world's lowest birthrate—a mere 1.2 babies per woman. By 2006 the average European fertility rate was about 1.4 children per woman.

If the current baby bust continues, the long-term consequences could be dramatic, though hardly predictable. At the least, Europe's population would decline and age. Projections for Germany are illustrative. Total German population, barring much greater immigration, would gradually decline from 82 million in 2001 to only 62 million around 2050. The number of people of working age would drop by a third, and almost half of the population would be over sixty. Social security taxes paid by the shrinking labor force would need to soar to meet the skyrocketing costs of pensions and health care for seniors—a recipe for generational tension and conflict. As the premier of Bavaria, Germany's biggest state, has warned, the prospect of demographic decline is a "ticking time bomb under our social welfare system and entire economy."[6]

Why, in times of peace, were Europeans failing to reproduce? The uneven, uninspiring European economic conditions of the 1980s and much of the 1990s played a role. High unemployment fell heavily on young people and often frustrated their plans to settle down and have children. Some observers have also argued that a partial rejection of motherhood and parenting was critical, noting that many Europeans chose to have no children or only one child.

The ongoing impact of careers for married women and the related drive for gender equality were decisive factors in the long-term decline of postwar birthrates. After World War II, Western women married early, had their children early, and then turned increasingly to full-time employment, where they suffered from the discrimination that drove the women's movement. As the twenty-first century opened, women had attained many (but not all) of their objectives. They did as well as or better than men in school, and educated young women earned almost as much as their male counterparts.

Research has shown that European women and men in their twenties, thirties, and early forties still wanted two or even three children—about the same number as their parents had wanted. But unlike their parents, young couples did not realize their ideal family size. Many women postponed the birth of their first child into their thirties in order to finish their education and establish themselves in their careers. Then, finding that balancing a child and a career was more difficult and time-consuming than anticipated, new mothers tended to postpone and eventually forgo the second child. The better educated and the more economically successful a woman was, the more likely she was to stop with a single child or to have no children at all.

By 2005 some population experts believed that European women were no longer postponing having children. At the least, birthrates appeared to have stabilized. Moreover, the frightening implications of dramatic population decline had emerged as a major public issue. Opinion leaders, politicians, and the media started to press for more babies and more support for families with children. Europeans may yet respond with enough vigor to limit the extent of their population decline and avoid societal disaster.

Changing Immigration Flows

As European demographic vitality waned in the 1990s, a surge of migrants from Africa, Asia, and eastern Europe headed for western Europe. Some migrants entered the European Union legally, but increasing numbers were smuggled in past beefed-up border patrols. Large-scale immigration, both legal and illegal, emerged as a critical and controversial issue.

Historically a source rather than a destination of immigrants, booming western Europe drew heavily on North Africa and Turkey for manual laborers from about 1960 until about 1973, when unemployment started to rise and governments abruptly stopped the inflow. Many foreign workers stayed on, however, eventually bringing

Illegal Immigrants from Eritrea Italian police have just rescued these young immigrants from an overloaded boat off the coast of Italy. Fleeing civil war and desperate for work, the immigrants are weary because of the long and dangerous voyage from Libya. Every year, thousands of illegal immigrants try to reach Italy and Spain from North Africa. Many are found dead on the shoreline. (Mimi Mollica/Corbis)

their families and establishing permanent immigrant communities. The postcolonial immigration that began in the 1950s also continued apace (see Chapter 29).

A new and different surge of migration into western Europe began in the 1990s. The collapse of communism in the east and savage civil wars in Yugoslavia sent hundreds of thousands of refugees fleeing westward. Equally brutal conflicts in Afghanistan, Iraq, Somalia, and Rwanda—to name only four countries—brought thousands more from Central Asia and Africa. Illegal immigration into the European Union also exploded, rising from an estimated 50,000 people in 1993 to perhaps 500,000 a decade later, far exceeding the estimated 300,000 unauthorized foreigners entering the United States each year. In 1998 the European Union abolished all border controls between member states, meaning that illegal entrance into one country allowed for unimpeded travel in almost any direction.

Though many migrants in the early twenty-first century continued to apply for political asylum and refugee status, most were eventually rejected and classified as illegal job seekers. Economic opportunity undoubtedly was a major attraction for illegal immigrants. Germans, for example, earned on average five times more than neighboring Poles, who in turn earned much more than people farther east and in North Africa.

Illegal immigration was aided by powerful criminal gangs that turned to people smuggling for big, low-risk profits. Gangs also contributed to the large number of young female illegal immigrants from eastern Europe, especially Russia and Ukraine. Often lured by criminals promising jobs as maids or waitresses, and sometimes simply kidnapped and sold from hand to hand for a few thousand dollars, these women were smuggled into the most prosperous parts of Europe and forced into prostitution.

Ethnic Diversity in Contemporary Europe

By 2010 immigration to Europe had worked profound changes on the ethnic makeup of the continent, though the effects were unevenly distributed. In 2005 immigrants composed about 10 percent of most western European nations, while the former East Bloc nations had far fewer foreign residents. One way to measure the effect of these new immigrants is to consider the rapid rise of their numbers. Since the 1960s the foreign population of western European nations has grown by five to ten times. In the Netherlands in 1960 only 1 percent of the population was foreign born. In 2006 the foreign-born made up 10 percent. Over the same time period the proportion of immigrants grew from 1.2 to 12.3 percent in Germany and from 4.7 to almost 11 percent in France.[7] For centuries the number of foreign residents living in Europe had been relatively small. Now, permanently displaced ethnic groups or **diasporas** brought ethnic diversity to the continent.

The new immigrants were divided into two main groups. A small percentage of the recent arrivals were highly trained specialists who could find work in the upper ranks of education, business, and the high-tech industry. Engineers from English-speaking India, for example, took positions in international computer companies. Many immigrants, however, did not have access to high-quality education or language training, which limited their employment

> **diasporas** Enclaves of ethnic groups settled outside of their homelands.

opportunities and made integration more difficult. They often lived in separate city districts marked by poor housing and crowded conditions, which set them apart from more established residents. In large German cities like Berlin and Hamburg, migrants from Turkey built vast communities with Turkish grocery stores, restaurants, civic organizations, and mosques. Parts of London were home to tens of thousands of immigrants from the former colonies, and in Paris North Africans dominated some working-class *banlieues* (suburbs).

A variety of new cultural forms, ranging from sports and cuisine to music, the fine arts, and film, brought together native and foreign traditions and transformed European lifestyles. The makeup of the teams who play European football (soccer), the continent's favorite sport, clearly reflected the new diversity. In the 1950s and 1960s regional football teams were made almost entirely of local players. By 2005 a single football club in North London included players from across Europe as well as from the Ivory Coast, Brazil, and the United States.[8]

Food is another important case in point. Recipes and cooks from former colonies in North Africa enlivened French cooking, while the döner kebab — the Turkish version of a gyros

multiculturalism The mixing of ethnic styles in daily life and in cultural works such as film, music, art, and literature.

sandwich — became Germany's "native" fast food. Indian restaurants proliferated across Britain, and controversy raged when the British foreign minister announced in 2001 that chicken tikka masala — a spicy Indian stew — was Great Britain's new national dish. In fact, tikka masala is a hybrid, a remarkable example of the way that peoples, recipes, and ingredients from Central Asia, Persia, and Europe had interacted for over four centuries, changing eating habits in Europe and on the Indian subcontinent alike.[9]

The new ethnic diversity associated with globalization has inspired numerous works in literature and the fine arts. The string of bestselling short stories and novels by Jhumpa Lahiri, an ethnic Bengali born in London, includes *Interpreter of Maladies* (1999) and *The Namesake* (2003), which explore the clash between immigrant and host cultures and the conflict between first- and second-generation immigrants. The bestselling novel *White Teeth* (2000), by British author Zadie Smith, likewise uses family settings to describe the at times painful contact between Bangladeshi Muslims and British Jews and Christians. Museums and annual art exhibitions regularly feature the works of non-Western artists who further explore the conflicts and new forms generated by cultural interaction.

This **multiculturalism** has also had a profound affect on popular music and film. Rai, a folk music that

The Changing Face of London's Arsenal Football Club Growing ethnic diversity is transforming many aspects of everyday life in contemporary Europe, including the ethnic makeup of European football (soccer) teams. In 1950 the Arsenal Football Club of northern London was composed entirely of white ethnic Britons (right). Today, its diverse roster includes players from around the globe (above). (1950 team: J. A. Hampton/Hulton Archive/ Getty Images; 2010 team: Stuart MacFarlane/Arsenal Football Club)

originated in the Bedouin culture of North Africa, exemplifies the new forms that emerge from cultural mixing. In the 1920s rai traveled with Algerian immigrants to France. In its current form, it blends Arab and North African folk music, U.S. rap, and French and Spanish pop styles. Lyrics range from sentimental love stories to blunt and sometimes bawdy descriptions of daily life. The Algerian Cheb Khaled, the unofficial "king of rai," has become an international superstar. Lyrics of his song "To Flee, but Where?" capture Khaled's dismay with collapsing Islamic traditions in Algeria and the burdens of life in the Algerian diaspora in France:

> *Where has youth gone?*
> *Where are the brave ones?*
> *The rich gorge themselves,*
> *The poor work themselves to death,*
> *The Islamic charlatans show their true face . . .*
> *You can always cry or complain*
> *Or escape . . . but where?*[10]

Feature films have also been an important venue for dramatizing the experience of cross-cultural contact, and they reach large audiences. Older movies typically pictured Europeans and non-Europeans as distinct social groups with radically different social customs. Now the emphasis is on cultural mixing and the surprising new combinations that emerge in a globalized society. In *Bend It Like Beckham* (2002), by Indian-Anglo direc-

tor Gurinder Chada, a teenage girl from Pakistan becomes an accomplished high school soccer player and falls in love with her Irish coach, challenging the traditional values of her family, first-generation Punjabi-Sikhs from northern India. The French film *The Class* (2008), set in a high school in a working-class banlieue in Paris, portrays a bold teacher's attempts to understand and inspire his students, who come from France, North and sub-Saharan Africa, and East Asia. These films and many others reflect both the new openness of cinematic production companies to non-Western directors and stories, and a growing public interest in cross-cultural interaction.

The growth of immigration and ethnic diversity has created rich hybrid social and cultural interactions, but it has also generated intense controversy and conflict in western Europe. Under the citizenship policies of most EU nations, immigrants can become citizens with full rights if they meet certain legal qualifications, even though they might not adopt the culture of the host country. This legal process has raised questions about who, exactly, could or should be European, and about the way these new citizens might change European society. Some commentators have accused the newcomers of taking jobs from the unemployed and undermining national unity. The idea that cultural and ethnic diversity could be a force for vitality and creativity has run counter to deep-seated beliefs about national homogeneity.

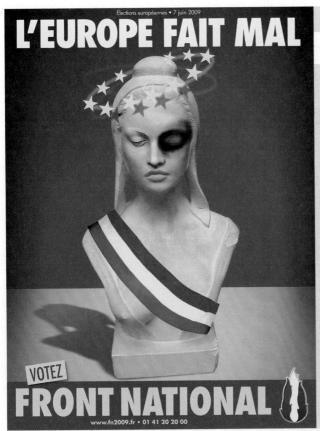

Picturing the Past

National Front Campaign Poster This 2009 campaign poster calls on viewers to vote for the far-right French National Front in elections to the European Parliament. It portrays the familiar French image of Lady Liberty (see the image on page 629) with European Union stars circling her head. (Handout/Reuters)

ANALYZING THE IMAGE How is Lady Liberty depicted? What type of mood is the creator trying to elicit in voters via this image?

CONNECTIONS According to the National Front, which issue facing Europe today is a key contributor to Lady Liberty's distress? How effective do you think emotional appeals like this one are in garnering support for far-right parties across Europe?

To complete this activity online, go to the Online Study Guide at bedfordstmartins.com/mckaywest.

Government welfare programs intended to support struggling immigrants have been seen as a misuse of money, especially in times of economic downturn.

Immigration is a highly charged political issue. By the 1990s in France, some 70 percent of the population believed that there were "too many Arabs," and 30 percent supported right-wing politician Jean Marie Le Pen's calls to rid France of its immigrants altogether. Even then-future president Jacques Chirac could claim in 1991 that he understood that good French workers could be driven "understandably crazy" by the "noise and smell" of foreigners in the country.[11] Le Pen's National Front and other far-right political parties, such as the Danish People's Party and Austria's Freedom Party, successfully exploited popular prejudice about what they called "foreign rabble" to make impressive gains in national elections.

Europe and Its Muslim Citizens

General concerns with migration have often fused with fears of Muslim migrants and Muslim residents who have grown up in Europe. Islam is now the largest minority religion in Europe. The EU's 15 to 20 million Muslims outnumber Catholics in Europe's mainly Protestant north, and they outnumber Protestants in Europe's Catholic south. Major cities have substantial Muslim minorities. Muslim residents make up about 25 percent of the population in Marseilles and Rotterdam, 15 percent in Brussels, and about 10 percent in Paris, Copenhagen, and London.[12]

The worries increased after the September 11, 2001, al-Qaeda attack on New York's World Trade Center (see page 1017) and the subsequent war in Iraq. Terrorist attacks in Europe organized by Islamic extremists heightened anxieties. On a morning in March 2004 radical Moroccan Muslims living in Spain exploded bombs planted on trains bound for Madrid, killing 191 commuters and wounding 1,800 more. A year later an attack on the London transit system carried out by British citizens of Pakistani descent killed over 50 innocent people.

The vast majority of Europe's Muslims clearly support democracy and reject radical extremism, but these spectacular attacks and lesser actions by Islamic militants nonetheless sharpened the European debate on immigration. A shrill chorus warned that, in addition to the security danger, Europe's rapidly growing Muslim population posed a dire threat to the West's entire Enlightenment tradition, which embraced freedom of thought, representative government, toleration, separation of church and state, and, more recently, equal rights for women and gays. Conservative critics proclaimed that Islamic extremists and radical clerics settled in Europe rejected these fundamental Western values and preached the supremacy of Islamic laws for Muslims living in Europe.

Some secular Europeans have had a hard time understanding Muslim spirituality. As busy mosques came to outnumber dying churches in parts of some European cities, nationalist-minded politicians tried to exploit widespread doubts that immigrant populations

Terrorist Attack in Madrid   In March 2004 radical Islamic terrorists set bombs on commuter trains in Madrid, killing almost two hundred people. The motivation of the perpetrators remains unclear, but the bombings were probably a response to Spanish involvement in the Iraq War. A similar bombing occurred in London the next year, exacerbating anti-Muslim feeling in Europe. (Pablo Torres/Guerrero/El Pais/Reuters)

from Muslim countries would ever assimilate to the different national cultures. A Danish-Muslim imam (spiritual leader) captured the dilemma: "The Danish shelves for faith and spirituality are empty," he said. "They fill them instead with fear of the 'strong foreigner.'"[13] Moreover, conservative critics claimed, many so-called moderate Islamic teachers were really anti-Western radicals playing for time. (See "Individuals in Society: Tariq Ramadan," page 1016.) Time was on the side of Euro-Islam, the critics warned. Europe's Muslim population, estimated at some 20 million in 2010, appeared likely to grow to 30 million by 2025 and to increase rapidly thereafter.

Admitting that Islamic extremism could pose a serious challenge, more mainstream observers have focused instead on the problem of integration. Whereas the first generation of Muslim migrants—predominately Turks in Germany, Algerians in France, Pakistanis in Britain, and Moroccans in the Netherlands—had found jobs as unskilled workers in Europe's great postwar boom, they and their children had been hard hit after 1973 by the general economic downturn. Immigrants also suffered from the ongoing decline of European manufacturing due to globalization. Provided for modestly by the welfare state and housed minimally in dilapidated housing projects, many Muslims of the second and third generations were finding themselves outcasts in their adopted countries. In short, observers suggested, economics, inadequate job training, and discrimination had more influence on immigrant attitudes about their host communities than did religion and extremist teachings.

This argument was strengthened by widespread rioting in France in 2005 and again in 2009 that saw hundreds of young second- and third-generation Muslim immigrants go on a rampage. Almost always French by birth, language, and education, marauding groups labeled "Arabs" in press reports torched hundreds of automobiles night after night in Paris suburbs and large cities. (See "Listening to the Past: William Pfaff, Will the French Riots Change Anything?" page 1018.) The rioters complained bitterly of very high unemployment, systematic discrimination, and exclusion, and studies sparked by the rioting showed that religious ideology had almost no effect on their thinking.

An articulate minority used such arguments to challenge anti-migrant, anti-Muslim discrimination and its racist overtones. They argued that Europe badly needed newcomers—preferably talented newcomers—to limit the impending population decline and provide valuable technical skills. Some scholars conclude that Europe must recognize that Islam is now a European religion and a vital part of European life. This recognition might open the way to eventual political and cultural acceptance of European Muslims and head off the resentment that can drive Europe's Muslim believers to separatism and acts of terror.

Confronting Twenty-First-Century Challenges

What key problems faced European societies in the twenty-first century, and how did European states and peoples deal with these critical issues? ◼

As the first decade of the twenty-first century drew to a close, European societies were faced with a number of critical challenges. Growing distance between the United States and Europe revealed differences in international policies and values. Though they had security issues of their own, Washington's traditional western European allies criticized the U.S.-led war on terror. Climate change and water pollution revealed the dangers of heavy dependence on fossil fuels for energy consumption. At the same time, the relative wealth of European societies prompted serious thinking about European identity, Europe's humanitarian mission, and Europe's place in the larger community of nations. These problems underscored Europe's close ties to the rest of the world, and leaders sought global as well as national solutions.

Growing Strains in U.S.-European Relations

In the fifty years after World War II, the United States and western Europe generally maintained close diplomatic relations. Though they were never in total agreement, they usually worked together to promote international consensus under U.S. guidance, as represented by the NATO alliance. For example, a U.S.-led coalition attacked Iraqi forces in Kuwait in the 1990–1991 Persian Gulf War, freeing the small nation from attempted annexation by Iraqi dictator Saddam Hussein. The need for allied force was rare in the post–Cold War world, however. Over time, the growing power of the European Union and the new unilateral thrust of Washington's foreign policy created strains in familiar transatlantic relations.

There were many reasons for the growing gap between the United States and Europe. For one, the European Union was now the world's largest trading block, challenging the predominance of the United States. Prosperous European businesses invested heavily in the United States, reversing a decades-long economic relationship in which investment dollars had flowed the other way. For another, under President George W. Bush (r. 2001–2009), the United States was often willing to ignore international opinion in pursuit of its own interests. Citing the economic impact, Washington refused to ratify the Kyoto Treaty of 1997, which was intended to limit global warming. Nor did the United States join

Tariq Ramadan

INDIVIDUALS IN SOCIETY

RELIGIOUS TEACHER, ACTIVIST PROFESSOR, AND MEDIA STAR, Tariq Ramadan (b. 1962) is Europe's most famous Muslim intellectual. He is also a controversial figure, praised by many as a moderate bridge-builder and denounced by others as an Islamic militant in clever disguise. Born in Switzerland of Egyptian ancestry, Ramadan is the grandson of Hassan al-Banna, the charismatic founder of the powerful Muslim Brother-hood. Al-Banna, who was assassinated in 1949, fought to reshape Arab nationalism within a framework of Islamic religious orthodoxy and anti-British terrorism. Tariq grew up in Geneva, where his father had sought refuge in 1954 after Nasser's anti-Islamic crackdown in Egypt. He attended mainstream public schools, played soccer, and absorbed a wide-ranging Islamic heritage. For example, growing up fluent in French and Arabic, he learned English mainly from listening to Pakistani Muslims discuss issues with his father, who represented the Muslim Brotherhood and its ideology in Europe.

Ramadan studied philosophy and French literature as an undergraduate at the University of Geneva, and then earned a doctorate in Arabic and Islamic studies. Marrying a Swiss woman who converted to Islam, Ramadan moved his family to Cairo in 1991 to study Islamic law and philosophy. It proved to be a pivotal experience. Eagerly anticipating the return to his Muslim roots, Ramadan gradually realized that only in Europe did he feel truly at home. In this personal experience he found the message that Western Muslims should participate fully as active citizens and feel "at home" in their adopted countries. In developing this message, Ramadan left the classroom and became a publicly prominent intellectual, writing nonscholarly books and making audio cassettes that sell in the tens of thousands.

Slim and elegant in well-tailored suits and open collars, Ramadan is a brilliant speaker. His public lectures in French and English draw hundreds of Muslims and curious non-Muslims. Ramadan argues that Western Muslims basically live in security, have fundamental legal rights, and can freely practice their religion. He notes that Muslims in the West are often more secure than are believers in the Muslim world, where governments are frequently repressive and arbitrary. According to Ramadan, Islamic teaching requires Western Muslims to obey Western laws, although in rare cases they may need to plead conscientious objection and disobey on religious grounds. Becoming full citizens and refusing to live in parallel as the foreign Other, Muslims should work with non-Muslims on matters of common concern, such as mutual respect, better schools, and economic justice.*

Ramadan is most effective with second- and third-generation college graduates. He urges them to think for themselves and to distinguish the sacred revelation of Islam from the nonessential cultural aspects that their parents brought from African and Asian villages.

With growing fame has come growing controversy. In 2004, preparing to take up a professorship in the United States, he was denied an entry visa on the grounds that he had contributed to a Palestinian charity with ties to terrorists. Defenders disputed the facts and charged

Tariq Ramadan. (Salvatore Di Nolfi/Keystone)

that his criticism of Israeli policies and the invasion of Iraq were the real reasons for the denial. Ramadan's critics also claim that he says different things to different groups: hard-edged criticism of the West found on tapes for Muslims belies the reasoned moderation of his books. Some critics also argue that his recent condemnation of Western capitalism and globalization is an opportunistic attempt to win favor with European leftists and does not reflect his self-proclaimed Islamic passion for justice. Yet in 2010 the U.S. State Department lifted the ban that prevented Ramadan from entering the United States, and the scholar's reputation remains intact.† An innovative bridge-builder, he symbolizes the growing importance of Europe's Muslim citizens.

QUESTIONS FOR ANALYSIS

1. What is Ramadan's message to Western Muslims? How did he reach his conclusions?

2. Do you think Ramadan's ideas are realistic? Why?

*See, especially, Tariq Ramadan, *Western Muslims and the Future of Islam* (Oxford: Oxford University Press, 2004).

†See Ian Buruma, "Tariq Ramadan Has an Identity Issue," *The New York Times Magazine*, February 4, 2007.

the International Criminal Court, a global tribunal meant to prosecute individuals accused of crimes against humanity. These unilateral positions troubled EU leaders, as did unflagging U.S. support for Israel in the ongoing Arab-Israeli crisis.

Hard-nosed geopolitical issues relating to NATO widened the gap further. The dissolution of the communist Warsaw Pact left NATO without its traditional Cold War adversaries. Yet NATO continued to expand, primarily in the territories in the former East Bloc. In 1999 Poland, Hungary, and the Czech Republic joined the alliance. By 2010 France had returned to full membership, and the addition of new countries from eastern Europe and the Balkans, including the Baltic republics, Romania, Croatia, and Albania, had swelled the total number of member states to twenty-eight.

With so many members, it could prove difficult for NATO to win unanimous support for its actions. France, for example, did not support NATO's engagement in Bosnia in 1995 (see page 1002) because the alliance failed to get UN approval for the action. NATO allies only reluctantly supported U.S. president Barack Obama's 2010 push for increased troop levels in Afghanistan (see page 1020). As the EU expanded, some argued that Europe should establish its own independent military and defense policy. Meanwhile, Russian leaders were angered by NATO's expansion into former East Bloc countries adjacent to Russia—the defensive belt between the West and the Soviet Union established after World War II—particularly when President Bush moved to deploy missile defense systems in Poland and the Czech Republic in 2008.

The Iraq War, which began in 2003 (see page 1020), likewise placed heavy strains on U.S.-European relations. Some of America's traditional allies, including France and Germany, bitterly opposed the war. The only substantial support for the war came from Great Britain, under Prime Minister Tony Blair. Even there, the majority of the population was opposed, and Blair's popular approval eroded rapidly. The French foreign minister openly questioned the need for war, and in Germany in 2004 Chancellor Gerhard Schröder eked out a paper-thin re-election victory by refusing to support the United States. Hostility increased when U.S. Secretary of Defense Donald Rumsfeld suggested that France and Germany now represented "old Europe," in contrast to the "new" European countries, including Poland, Spain, and Italy, which supported U.S. actions. By 2006 even these supporters had withdrawn their small troop contingents from Iraq.

There was also a values gap. Ever more secular Europeans had a hard time understanding the religiosity of many Americans and of the openly Christian President Bush. Relatively lax gun control laws and the frequent execution of criminals in the United States were viewed with dismay; most European countries had outlawed the private use of handguns and had abolished the death penalty. U.S. reluctance to reform its health-care system shocked Europeans, who took their extensive state-financed medical benefits for granted. Though many Europeans continued to enjoy American films and popular music, critics nonetheless expressed disdain for what they saw as the overcommercialization of U.S. society. Public opinion polls showed that the depth of anti-American sentiment among ordinary European citizens was worse in 2008 than it had been during the war in Vietnam.

The election of Barack Obama, America's first African American president, in 2008 brought some improvement to U.S.-European relations. Though Obama's policies proved divisive at home, the new president was wildly popular among ordinary Europeans. When Obama visited Germany during his 2008 presidential campaign, over two hundred thousand Berliners cheered as he called for a new approach to diplomatic relations and international justice and, in an implicit critique of Bush administration policies, for a renewal of the U.S.-European alliance:

> The walls between old allies on either side of the Atlantic cannot stand. The walls between the countries with the most and those with the least cannot stand. The walls between races and tribes, natives and immigrants, Christian and Muslim and Jew cannot stand. These now are the walls we must tear down.[14]

After his election, Obama made a number of changes in foreign policy that set his administration apart from that of George W. Bush. His attempts to open diplomatic negotiations with countries hostile to U.S. interests, such as North Korea and Iran, and his willingness to advocate climate change control measures won support in European capitals. Obama announced that he would not deploy missiles in central Europe and agreed to reductions in nuclear arms, easing tensions with Russia. When Obama traveled to Oslo, Norway, in December 2009 to accept the Nobel Peace Prize, Europeans hoped that this symbolic recognition, rarely bestowed upon sitting heads of state, would encourage the president to bring a more cooperative face to U.S. foreign policy. Despite these changes, President Obama and the United States continued to fight two unpopular wars in the Middle East, making it difficult to resolve divisions in U.S.-European interests.

The War on Terror and European Security

On the morning of September 11, 2001, two hijacked passenger planes from Boston crashed into and destroyed the World Trade Center towers in New York City. Shortly thereafter a third plane crashed into the Pentagon, and a fourth, believed to be headed for the White House or

William Pfaff, Will the French Riots Change Anything?

LISTENING TO THE PAST

In late November 2005 young Muslim males rioted for several nights in the suburbs of Paris and other French cities. Receiving saturation coverage from the media, their explosion of car-burning and arson ignited controversy and debate throughout France and across Europe. Similar outbreaks occurred in 2007 and 2009. What caused the riots, and why did they persist? Anti-immigrant conservatives interpret the events as

an example of the inevitable conflict between Christians and Muslims. More liberal observers have argued that dismal living conditions and failures of assimilation were to blame.

One penetrating commentary, written after the unrest in 2005 and aimed at an American audience, came from William Pfaff, a noted author and political columnist with many years of European experience. As you read Pfaff's analysis, note in particular the portrait he draws of daily life in France's immigrant ghettos and the role of religion in French Muslim society.

❝ The rioting in France's ghetto suburbs is a phenomenon of futility — but a revelation nonetheless. It has no ideology and no purpose other than to make a statement of distress and anger. It is beyond politics. It broke out spontaneously and spread in the same way, communicated by televised example, ratified by the huge attention it won from the press and television and the politicians, none of whom had any idea what to do.

It has been an immensely pathetic spectacle, whose primary meaning has been that it happened. It has been the most important popular social phenomenon in France since the student uprisings of 1968. But those uprisings . . . had consequences for power. The new riots have nothing to do with power.

They started with the accidental electrocutions of two boys hiding from the police, who they thought were after them. The police say there was no pursuit and they had no interest in the boys. However, under the policies of the minister of interior — the presidential candidate Nicolas Sarkozy — there had been a general police crackdown in these ugly suburban clusters of deteriorating high-rise apartments built years ago to house immigrant workers. They were meant to be machines for living. The police attention meant random identity checks, police suspicion, and harassment of young men hanging about — maybe dealing in drugs, maybe simply doing nothing because there is nothing for them to do. (In the past, they at least had to do national military service, which was a strong integrative force, but now France has a professional army.)

Their grandfathers came to France, mostly from North Africa, to do the hard labor in France's industrial reconstruction after the Second World War. Their fathers saw the work gradually dry up as Europe's economies slowed, following the first oil shock in the early 1970s. After that came unemployment. The unemployment rate in the zones where there has been the most violence is nearly 40 percent and among young people it is higher. Many of the young men in these places have never been offered a job. When they applied, their names often excluded them.

Their grandfathers were hard-working men. Their fathers saw their manhood undermined by unemployment. These young men are doomed to be boys. They often take their frustration out on their sisters and girlfriends, who are more likely to have done well in school and found jobs — and frequently a new life — outside the ghetto. . . .

The Muslim mothers and wives of the French ghetto are often confined in the home. Drugs are big business in the American ghetto; they are not that big in France. The crimes of the French ghetto are robbery and shoplifting, stealing mobile phones, stealing cars for joyrides, burning them afterward to eliminate fingerprints, or burning cars just for the hell of it, as well as robbing middle-class students in the city and making trouble on suburban trains, looking for excitement.

Religion is important . . . in the French ghetto, it provides the carapace that protects against the France that excludes Muslims. To the European Muslim, it seems that all of the powerful in the world are in collusion to exclude Muslims — or are at war with them. The war in Iraq, on television, is the constant backdrop to Muslim life in Europe. There are itinerant imams

---

war on terror American policy under President Bush to fight global terrorism in all its forms.

the U.S. Capitol, crashed into a field in rural Pennsylvania. These terrorist attacks, perpetrated by the radical Islamic group al-Qaeda, took the lives of more than three thousand people from many countries and put the personal safety of ordinary citizens at the top of the West's agenda.

At first, the terrorist attacks seemed to bridge the growing gap between the United States and its European allies. Stunned and horrified, the peoples and governments of Europe and the world joined Americans in heartfelt solidarity. Over time, however, tensions between Europe and the United States re-emerged and deepened markedly, particularly after President Bush declared a unilatwho can put the young ghetto Muslim on the road to danger and adventure in Afghanistan, Pakistan, Iraq — or elsewhere. There are plenty more who preach a still deeper ghettoization: a retreat inside Islamic fundamentalism, totally shutting out a diabolized secular world.

One would think there would be a revolutionary potential in these ghettos, vulnerability to a mobilizing ideology. This seems not to be so. We may be living in a religious age, but it is not one of political ideology. In any case, it is difficult to imagine how the marginalized, thirteen- to twenty-three-year-old children of the Muslim immigration could change France other than by what they are doing, which is to demonstrate that the French model of assimilating immigrants as citizens, and not as members of religious or ethnic groups, has failed for them. It has failed because it has not seriously been tried.

The ghettoization of immigrant youth in France is the consequence of negligence. It has been as bad as the ghettoization through political correctness of Muslims in Britain and the Netherlands, where many people who thought of themselves as enlightened said that assimilation efforts were acts of cultural aggression. The immigrant in France is told that he or she is a citizen just like everyone else, with all the rights and privileges of citizenship — including the right to be unemployed.

Nicolas Sarkozy's zero tolerance of crime and of the petty mafias in the ghetto contributed to touching off these riots, but until recently he was the only French politician to say there has to be affirmative action to get an immigrant elite out of the ghettos and into important roles in French life, where they can pull their communities after them. Some affirmative action has been attempted in recruiting candidates for the elite *grandes écoles* [state schools] that train the French administrative and political class, where the cultural hurdles are immense for candidates. Virtually no children of the Muslim immigration are prominent in mainstream electoral politics; the political parties have yet to make a serious effort to include them. The present government has one junior minister of Algerian origin. I am not aware of any Muslims of immigrant origin in French diplomacy or the top ranks of police and military.

President Jacques Chirac has announced a civilian national service agency to give training and employ-

Angry youths set vehicles on fire in October 2005 as riots erupt on the streets around Clichy-Sous-Bois, a Paris suburb in which foreign-born residents make up over 35 percent of the population. The riots began after two teenage boys were electrocuted and died while hiding from police in a local power substation. (Jean-Michel Turpin/Corbis)

ment to 50,000 young people from the troubled zones by 2007. The age of apprenticeship has been lowered to fourteen, with a corresponding drop in the age of compulsory academic schooling and new measures to support apprenticeships. There will be more money for schools, local associations, and housing construction and renovation. This is change. Whether it is enough, and in time, is another matter. »

Source: William Pfaff, "The French Riots: Will They Change Anything?" *The New York Review of Books*, vol. 52, no. 20, December 15, 2005, pp. 88–89. Reprinted with permission from The New York Review of Books. Copyright © 2005 NYREV, Inc.

QUESTIONS FOR ANALYSIS

1. Describe the situation of young Muslims in France. What elements of their situation strike you most forcefully? How might these contribute to ongoing outbreaks of civic unrest?
2. France has maintained that, since all citizens are equal, they should all be treated the same way. Why has this policy failed for French Muslims? What alternatives would you suggest? Why?

eral U.S. **war on terror** — a determined effort to fight terrorism in all its forms, around the world.

Shortly after the September 11 attacks, the United States announced it would invade Afghanistan to destroy the perpetrators of the crime — Saudi-born millionaire Osama bin Laden's al-Qaeda network of terrorists and Afghanistan's reactionary Muslim government, the Tali-

ban. Drawing on the world's sympathy and building a broad international coalition that included western Europe, Russia, and Pakistan, the United States joined its tremendous air power with local anti-Taliban resistance fighters. In mid-November the Taliban government collapsed. The war in Afghanistan, however, was not over. U.S. and European NATO troops failed to find bin

Dutch Troops in Afghanistan
The commander of a Dutch army platoon serving with NATO forces in the war in Afghanistan speaks with an Afghan village elder during a routine patrol in January 2010. Sending European troops to support U.S. and NATO efforts to end the Taliban insurgency in this central Asian country was unpopular with ordinary Europeans and contributed to growing strains in U.S.-European foreign relations. (Deshakalyan Chowdhury/AFP/ Getty Images)

Laden, and the Taliban insurgents retreated into the mountainous southern regions of the country, where they continued to engage in determined guerrilla warfare. By 2010, as President Obama deployed thirty thousand additional U.S. troops to quell the insurgency, Germany, Italy, the Netherlands, and other NATO contributors were facing growing popular discontent with the war.

Although fighting continued in Afghanistan, in late 2001 the Bush administration turned its attention to Saddam Hussein's Iraq, arguing that it was necessary to expand the war on terror to other hostile regimes in the Middle East. Many in the administration believed that the United States could create a democratic, pro-American Iraq. A remade Iraq, they believed, would transform the Middle East, make peace with Israel, provide easy access to the world's second largest oil reserves, and show small countries the folly of opposing the United States. The most effective prowar argument, however, played on American fears of renewed terrorism and charged that Saddam Hussein was still developing weapons of mass destruction in flagrant disregard of his 1991 promise to end all such programs.

Many Americans shared the widespread doubts held by Europeans about the legality—and wisdom—of an American attack on Iraq. Protesters and some politicians in the United States and Europe argued for a peaceful settlement of the Iraqi crisis, especially after UN inspectors found no weapons of mass destruction in the country. Though the UN failed to approve an invasion, in March 2003 the United States and Britain, with token support from a handful of other European states, invaded Iraq from bases in Kuwait. They quickly overwhelmed the Iraqi army, and Saddam's dictatorship collapsed.

America's subsequent efforts to establish a stable pro-American Iraq proved difficult, if not impossible. Poor postwar planning and management by President Bush and his top aides was one factor, but there were others. Modern Iraq, a creation of Western imperialism after World War I (see Chapter 26), is a fragile state with three distinct groups: non-Arab Kurds, Arab Sunni Muslims, and Arab Shi'ite Muslims. The two groups of Muslims had been divided by a great schism in the seventh century. Ethnic and religious tensions among these groups directly contributed to instability in occupied Iraq, and by 2006 a deadly sectarian conflict had taken hold in Baghdad. American soldiers, continuing loyally to do their duty, were increasingly caught in the crossfire between Sunni and Shi'ite militias.

The fighting had reached a high point in 2006–2007, when President Bush announced that he would initiate new counterinsurgency policies and send additional troops to bolster U.S. forces. By the time President Obama took office in 2009, this troop surge had successfully reduced violence across the country. Though insurgents continued to mount attacks, the number of casualties had declined dramatically, and the Obama administration moved forward with agreements negotiated by President Bush to withdraw all U.S. troops by the end of 2011. The Iraqi government continued to struggle with ethnic divisiveness and security concerns.

Iraq, ca. 2010

TURKEY

Areas that are predominantly
■ Sunni
□ Shi'ite
▨ Mixed
— Kurdish

SYRIA

Fallujah
Baghdad
IRAN

IRAQ

SAUDI ARABIA
Basra

KUWAIT

Finding the best way to share power among Iraq's main ethnic groups and divide the country's rich oil resources, particularly with Kurdish groups in the north, proved particularly difficult.

The U.S. invasion of Iraq caused some European leaders, notably in France and Germany, to question Washington's general rationale for the war on terror. Europeans shared U.S. worries about stability in the Middle East, and they faced their own problems with Islamic terrorism, especially after the Madrid and London subway bombings of 2004 and 2005. But European leaders worried that the tactics used in the war, exemplified by Washington's readiness to use its military without international agreements or UN backing, violated international law. Moreover, the U.S.-led war raised serious human rights concerns. The revelation of the harsh interrogation techniques used on prisoners held by American forces in the Iraqi prison Abu Ghraib shocked European public opinion. U.S. willingness to engage in "extraordinary rendition"—secretly moving terrorism suspects to countries that allow coercive interrogation techniques—further disturbed European observers.

Indeed, some leaders in Europe questioned the very idea of a war on terror. Because terrorism is a stateless phenomenon, European security experts asked whether war was the best approach. Terrorism, they maintained, was better fought through police and intelligence measures than through military action. Military victory in a single state, they argued, would hardly end terrorism. Rather, militant groups would simply move to other areas. European states preferred a more controlled but nonetheless determined approach to terrorism. Their security services focused on tighter EU borders, stepped-up airport security, increased public surveillance, and additional support for antiterrorist police investigations. Acknowledging their common goal of preventing future attacks, security forces in Europe also coordinated counterterrorism efforts with experts in the United States to investigate international terrorist cells.

The Dependence on Fossil Fuels

One of the most significant challenges facing Europe and indeed the world in the twenty-first century is the search for adequate energy resources. Maintaining standards of living in industrialized countries requires extremely high levels of energy, and current supplies are heavily dependent on fossil fuels, including oil, coal, and natural gas.

Global conflicts over access to limited energy resources have become an increasingly familiar aspect of life in the twenty-first century. In 2008 Europe and Russia combined had 12 percent of the world's population but consumed about 40 percent of the world's annual natural gas production, 25 percent of the world's oil, and 16 percent of the world's coal. Scholars argue that such high levels of usage are unsustainable over the long run, that fossil fuel supplies will run out, especially when the nations of the developing world increase their own rates of consumption.[15]

Struggles to control and profit from these shrinking resources often cut across ethnic, religious, and national lines, leading to intractable conflicts and tense new geopolitical arrangements. The need to preserve access to oil has led to a great transformation in military power in the post–Cold War world. Between 1945 and 1990 the largest areas of military buildup were in central Europe, along the iron curtain that separated western Europe from the East Bloc, and in East Asia, where U.S. forces formed a bulwark against the spread of communism. Today military power is increasingly concentrated in oil-producing areas such as the Middle East, which holds about 65 percent of the world's oil reserves. According to some scholars, the Persian Gulf War and the ongoing Iraq War were "resource wars" fought, in large part, to preserve the West's access to the region's oil.[16]

Russian territory has massive quantities of oil and natural gas, and the global struggle for ample energy has placed Russia in a powerful but strained position. The Russian invasions of Chechnya and Georgia were attempts to maintain political influence in these formerly Soviet borderlands, and also to preserve control of the region's rich energy resources.

Beyond military invasions, Russian leaders readily use their control over energy to assert political influence. The Russian corporation Gazprom, one of the world's largest producers of natural gas, sells Europe 28 percent of its natural gas, and the EU treads softly in order to maintain this supply. Russia is willing to play hardball: there have been over fifty politically motivated disruptions of natural gas supply in the former Soviet republics, including one in January 2009 when Russia shut off supplies to Ukraine for three weeks, closing factories and leaving hundreds of thousands without heat. "Yesterday tanks, today oil," a Polish politician remarked about Russia's willingness to use energy to exert influence in central Europe.[17]

Environmental Problems and Progress

Even if the supply of fossil fuels were not of concern, the use of these energy sources has led to serious environmental problems. Burning oil and coal releases

— Oil pipeline
— Gas pipeline
— Supplied by Russia

Primary Oil and Gas Pipelines to Europe, ca. 2005

global warming The increase of average temperatures around the world, caused primarily by carbon dioxide emissions from the burning of fossil fuels.

massive amounts of carbon dioxide (CO_2), the leading cause of **global warming**, into the atmosphere. Thus, fossil fuel usage directly contributes to climate change and the degradation of the world's oceans. While the future effects of climate change are difficult to predict, climatologists meeting in March 2009 in Copenhagen concluded that climate change was proceeding dramatically faster than previously predicted and that some climatic disruption is now unavoidable. Rising average temperatures were melting glaciers and leading to the retreat of glacial ice packs, resulting in the drying up of freshwater sources across the world. Moreover, in the next fifty years rising sea levels will threaten low-lying coastal areas with flooding and inundation.

Since the 1990s the EU has spearheaded efforts to control energy consumption and contain climate change. EU leaders have imposed tight restrictions on emissions, and Germany, the Netherlands, and Denmark have become world leaders in harnessing alternate energy sources such as solar and wind power. Some countries have also taken preemptive measures in an effort to combat the future effects of global warming. The Dutch government, for example, has spent billions of dollars on the construction of new dykes, levees, and floodgates in an attempt to manage the potential crisis.

In addition to the problems presented by climate change, the world's oceans and freshwater lakes, which once seemed to be inexhaustible sources of food and drinking water, have been threatened by overuse and pollution. Usable water resources have been jeopardized by a number of toxins, including chemicals and heavy metals dumped by industry, oil spills, acid rain, and the disposal of nonbiodegradable solid waste, such as plastic packaging, which threatens marine life. Runoff of nitrate-based fertilizers, necessary to feed the growing world population, encourages rapid algae growth that leads to dead zones where marine life cannot survive. The environmental disaster that resulted when an offshore oil rig exploded in the Gulf of Mexico in April 2010, spewing millions of gallons of oil into the gulf waters, underscored the close connections between energy needs and water pollution.

In a revealing example of the international reach of the new global institutions, the EU has issued stringent policies in an effort to limit the human impact on water resources. In 2003, after an extensive review of existing agreements, the EU implemented a new Common Fisheries Policy. The new regulations were designed to halt the dumping of hazardous pollutants into rivers and oceans and preserve noncommercial species such as whales, birds, and sea turtles from harm during fishing. They also addressed public health issues by requiring the strict labeling of seafood for poisonous contaminants

such as PCBs and dioxins. To maintain stocks of commercially valuable fish, the EU placed caps on total allowable catch, limited the number of fishing boats in specific regions, and regulated fishing technology.

Though EU efforts to regulate energy use and control pollution showed some success, the overall effort to control energy consumption has been an uphill battle, underscoring the interconnectedness of the contemporary world. Developing nations such as India have had a difficult time balancing environmental concerns and economic growth. China, however, which surpassed the United States as the largest emitter of CO_2 in 2008, began encouraging "green" energy and moving away from coal. In December 2009 the representatives of 192 nations met in Copenhagen, Denmark, and agreed to reduce CO_2 emissions responsibly and extend financial support to developing countries to help them deal with the effects of global warming. Whether leaders have the political will to carry out this and other plans to limit the human impact on the environment, however, remains uncertain.

Promoting Human Rights

Though regional differences persisted in the twenty-seven EU member states, European residents entering the twenty-first century enjoyed some of the highest living standards in the world, the sweet fruit of more than fifty years of peace, security, and overall economic growth. The agonies of barbarism and war in the former Yugoslavia vividly recalled the horrors of World War II and cast in bold relief the ever-present reality of collective violence in today's world. For some Europeans, the realization of this contrast—that they had so much and so many others had so little—kindled a desire to help. As a result, European intellectuals and opinion makers began to envision a new historic mission for Europe: the promotion of domestic peace and human rights in lands plagued by instability, violence, and oppression.

European leaders and humanitarians believed that more global agreements and new international institutions were needed to set moral standards and to regulate countries, political leaders, armies, corporations, and individuals. In practice, this meant more curbs on the sovereign rights of the world's states, just as the states of the European Union had imposed increasingly strict standards of behavior on themselves in order to secure the rights and welfare of EU citizens. As one EU official concluded, the European Union has a "historical responsibility" to make morality "a basis of policy," because "human rights are more important than states' rights."[18]

In practical terms, western Europe's evolving human rights mission would require, first of all, military intervention to stop civil wars and to prevent tyrannical governments from slaughtering their own people. Thus the

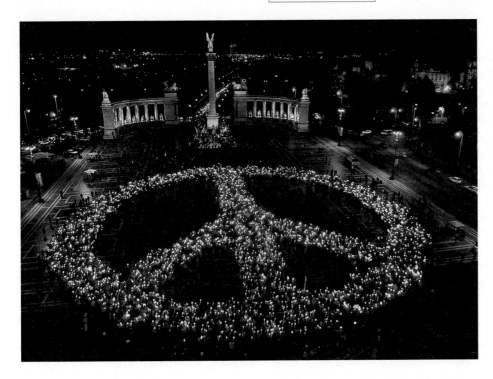

Demonstrating for Peace
Holding torches, some 3,500 people form the peace sign in Heroes Square in central Budapest, the capital of Hungary, in 2006. The rally marked the third anniversary of the U.S.-led invasion of Iraq. Millions long for peace, but history and current events suggest that bloody conflicts will continue. Yet Europeans have cause for cautious optimism: despite episodes of intense violence and suffering, since 1945 wars have been localized, cataclysmic catastrophes like World Wars I and II have been averted, and Europe has become a world leader in the push for global human rights. (Peter Kollanyi/epa/Corbis)

European Union joined with the United States to intervene militarily to stop the killing in Bosnia, Croatia, and Kosovo and to protect the rights of embattled minorities. The states of the EU also vigorously supported UN initiatives to verify the compliance of anti–germ warfare conventions, outlaw the use of land mines, and establish a new international court to prosecute war criminals.

Europeans also pushed for broader definitions of individual rights. Abolishing the death penalty in the European Union, for example, they condemned its continued use in China, the United States, Saudi Arabia, and some other countries as inhumane and uncivilized. Rights for Europeans in their personal relations also continued to expand. In the pacesetting Netherlands, for example, a growing network of laws gave pensions and full worker's rights to prostitutes (legally recognized income-earners since 1917) and legalized gay and lesbian marriages, the smoking of marijuana in licensed coffee shops, and assisted suicide (euthanasia) for the terminally ill.

As the first decade of the twenty-first century drew to a close, western Europeans also pushed to extend their broad-based concept of social and economic rights to the world's poor countries. These efforts were often related to sharp criticism of globalization and unrestrained neoliberal capitalism. Quite typically, Europe's moderate Social Democrats joined human rights campaigners in 2001 to secure drastic price cuts from international pharmaceutical corporations selling drugs to combat Africa's AIDS crisis. Strong advocates of greater social equality and state-funded health care, European socialists embraced morality as a basis for action and the global expansion of human rights as a primary goal.

LOOKING BACK LOOKING AHEAD

THE TWENTY-FIRST CENTURY opened with changes and new challenges for the Western world. The collapse of the East Bloc brought democracy to central and eastern Europe, but left millions struggling to adapt to a radically different way of life. High-tech information systems that quickened the pace of communications and the global reach of new supranational institutions made the world a smaller place, but globalization left some struggling to maintain their livelihoods. New contacts between peoples, made possible by increased migration, revitalized European society, but raised concerns about cultural difference and sometimes led to violent confrontations.

One thing is sure: despite the success of European democracy and liberalism, and despite the high living standards enjoyed by most of those on the European subcontinent, the challenges won't go away. The search for solutions to environmental degradation and conflicts between ethnic and religious groups and the promotion of human rights across the globe will clearly occupy European and world leaders for some time to come.

However these issues play out, the study of the past puts the present and the future in perspective. Others before us have trodden the paths of uncertainty and crisis, and the historian's ability to analyze and explain the choices they made helps us understand our current situation and helps save us from exaggerated self-pity in the face of our own predicaments. Perhaps our Western heritage may rightly inspire us with measured pride and self-confidence. We stand, momentarily, at the head of the long procession of Western civilization. Sometimes the procession has wandered, or backtracked, or done terrible things. But it has also carried the efforts and sacrifices of generations of toiling, struggling ancestors. Through no effort of our own, we are the beneficiaries of those sacrifices and achievements. Now that it is our turn to carry the torch onward, we may remember these ties with our forebears.

To change the metaphor, we in the West are like card players who have been dealt many good cards. Some of them are obvious, such as our technical and scientific heritage, our environmental resources, and our commitment to human rights and individual freedoms. Others are not so obvious, sometimes half-forgotten or even hidden up the sleeve. Think, for example, of the almost miraculous victory of peaceful revolution in eastern Europe in 1989—in what Czech playwright-turned-president Václav Havel called "the power of the powerless." Here we again see the regenerative strength of the Western ideals of individual rights and representative government in the European homeland. We hold a good hand.

Our study of history, of mighty struggles and fearsome challenges, of shining achievements and tragic failures, gives a sense of the essence of life itself: the process of change over time. Again and again we have seen how peoples and societies evolve, influenced by ideas, human passions, and material conditions. This process of change will continue as the future becomes the present and then the past. Students of history are better prepared to make sense of this unfolding process because they have already observed it. They understand that change is rooted in existing historical forces, and they have tools to explore the intricate web of change that propels life forward. Students of history are prepared for the new and unexpected in human development, for they have already seen great breakthroughs and revolutions. They have an understanding of how things really happen.

CHAPTER REVIEW

■ **How did Russia and the former East Bloc countries meet the challenges of postcommunist reconstruction and political and economic reform? (p. 996)**

Russia and the former East Bloc countries had mixed success as they worked to remake their political, economic, and social systems after forty-five years of communism. In part, economic problems limited the speed of reform. Russia's experimentation with shock therapy and rapid privatization under President Yeltsin led to runaway inflation, corruption, and a host of social problems. Later, President Putin returned the country to a more managed democracy with some success, but his hard-line anti-Western approach meant fewer freedoms for ordinary people, more human rights abuses, and violent confrontations with Russian provinces and neighboring countries. The newly independent countries of eastern Europe, especially Poland, Hungary, and the Czech Republic, fared somewhat better than Russia, though they generally followed a similar pattern. The former Yugoslavia,

tragically destroyed by resurgent ethnic nationalism and civil war, was a glaring exception to the relative success in the former Soviet bloc.

■ **What are the defining features of globalization, and how did changing international structures transform European societies? (p. 1003)**

Under globalization, neoliberal economic policies, along with the computer and communications revolutions, transformed economic, business, and personal relations around the world. Multinational corporations expanded with great success, but the vulnerabilities of a global economy were revealed in 1997 and 2008 when national crises triggered worldwide recessions. Moreover, globalization, coupled with the effects of the postindustrial society, left many people without the skills to compete and widened the gap between rich and poor. Meanwhile, the European Union, along with other supranational organizations such as the United Nations and the World Trade Organization, grew more powerful under globalization, challenging the traditional prerogatives of the nation-state. Thus, although some corporations, nations, and entities prospered under globalization and many individuals enjoyed the conveniences of new technologies, globalization also had a negative impact on a sizable number of people, not to mention on worldwide financial stability.

■ How did population decline and large-scale immigration lead to demographic changes in contemporary Europe, and what were the main results of growing ethnic diversity? (p. 1010)

After 1990 birthrates across Europe continued to decline, even as ever-larger numbers of legal and illegal immigrants moved to the continent in search of economic opportunity and political asylum. These demographic changes helped make formerly homogeneous societies more ethnically diverse, and by 2010 foreign-born residents made up between 10 and 15 percent of the total population in most western European countries. Growing ethnic diversity had profound effects on European art, culture, and lifestyles, all of which revealed the benefits and challenges of multiculturalism. The social impact of the new immigrants was controversial. Right-wing politicians used anti-immigrant sentiment to make gains in national elections. The growing number of Muslims living in Europe generated intense debate, particularly after the terrorist attacks of September 11, 2001, in the United States and the subway bombings in London and Madrid. War in the Middle East encouraged shrill cries about an ominous Muslim threat from immigrants living in western Europe, but thoughtful consideration by more tolerant observers suggested that these fears were greatly exaggerated.

■ What key problems faced European societies in the twenty-first century, and how did European states and peoples deal with these critical issues? (p. 1015)

As the twenty-first century began, European societies faced a number of different problems, many of which underscored the challenges of an increasingly interconnected world. While the European Union expanded and gained power, the United States increasingly pursued a unilateral foreign policy. Over time, different international interests undermined the close transatlantic ties that the United States and Europe had established after World War II. Though European states had supported U.S. efforts to deal with international terrorism immediately following September 11, 2001, many disagreed with the American war on terror, which led to further distance between Europe and the United States. The West's dependence on a dwindling supply of fossil fuels led to political crises and grave environmental problems, including climate change and the degradation of water supplies. The European Union led global efforts to

address important energy and environmental concerns, and by 2010 it had made some progress. The relatively wealthy European countries also played leading roles in promoting human rights around the world, agreeing to intervene in civil wars, promoting international courts of justice, and offering support to poor countries struggling in the face of neoliberal globalization.

Suggested Reading

Caldwell, Christopher. *Reflections on the Revolution in Europe: Immigration, Islam, and the West.* 2009. A controversial and thought-provoking book that emphasizes the problems associated with growing numbers of Muslim immigrants in Europe.

Gillingham, John. *European Integration, 1950–2003: Superstate or New Market Economy?* 2003. A brilliant interpretive history.

Johnson, Lonnie R. *Central Europe: Enemies, Neighbors, Friends.* 2001. A book that ably interprets developments in eastern Europe before and after the revolutions of 1989.

Jordan, Andrew. *Environmental Policy in the European Union: Actors, Institutions and Processes.* 2005. A critical look at the European Union's response to major environmental problems.

Klausen, Jyette. *The Islamic Challenge: Politics and Religion in Western Europe.* 2006. Reviews the goals of Europe's Islamic leaders and takes a positive view of future Muslim integration in western Europe.

Koopmans, Ruud, et al. *Contested Citizenship: Immigration and Cultural Diversity in Europe.* 2005. Explores issues of ethnic diversity, cultural identity, and citizenship in five European countries.

Lampe, John R. *Yugoslavia as History: Twice There Was a Country,* 2d ed. 2003. An excellent, judicious work on the tragedy in Yugoslavia.

Lucassen, Leo. *The Immigrant Threat: The Integration of Old and New Immigrants in Western Europe Since 1850.* 2005. Argues effectively that Muslims are assimilating as rapidly as previous immigrants.

Pinder, John, and Simon Usherwood. *The European Union: A Very Short Introduction.* 2008. Readable overview of the history, institutions, and policies of the European Union.

Reid, T. R. *The United States of Europe: The New Superpower and the End of American Supremacy.* 2005. A lively, informative examination by a perceptive American.

Sakwa, Richard. *Putin: Russia's Choice.* 2003. Puts the Russian leader in social and historical context.

Stiglitz, Joseph E. *Making Globalization Work.* 2006. An excellent overview of the successes and failures of globalization by a distinguished economist.

Key Terms

Ostalgie (p. 1000)
ethnic cleansing (p. 1001)
Kosovo Liberation Army (KLA) (p. 1002)
globalization (p. 1003)
European Union (EU) (p. 1005)
Maastricht Treaty (p. 1005)
World Trade Organization (WTO) (p. 1007)
nongovernmental organizations (NGOs) (p. 1009)
diasporas (p. 1011)
multiculturalism (p. 1012)
war on terror (p. 1019)
global warming (p. 1022)

Suny, Ronald Grigor. *The Soviet Experiment: Russia, the USSR, and the Successor States*. 1998. An outstanding history of Russia in the 1990s.

Tarrow, Sidney. *The New Transnational Activism*. 2005. A sympathetic account of the transnational activism opposed to corporate globalization.

Notes

1. Quoted in T. Judt, *Postwar: A History of Europe Since 1945* (New York: Penguin, 2005), p. 691.
2. Ibid., pp. 698–699.
3. *Quarterly Labor Force Statistics, Volume 2004/4* (Paris: OECD Publications, 2004), p. 64.
4. Oxfam, *Annual Report and Accounts 07/08* (Oxford, U.K.: Oxfam House, 2008), pp. 17, 43.
5. Quoted in Geoffrey Lean, "Trade Wars — The Hidden Tentacles of the World's Most Secret Body," *The Independent*, July 18, 1999.
6. Quoted in *The Economist*, January 6, 2001, p. 6.
7. Mark Mazower, *Dark Continent: Europe's Twentieth Century* (New York: Vintage, 2000), p. 415; *United Nations International Migration Report 2006* (UN Department of Economic and Social Affairs), http://www.un.org/esa/populationpublications/2006_MigrationRep/report.htm.
8. Judt, *Postwar*, p. 783.
9. L. Collingham, *Curry: A Tale of Cooks and Conquerors* (London: Oxford University Press, 2006), pp. 2, 9.
10. J. Gross, D. McMurray, and T. Swedenborg, "Rai, Rap, and Ramadan Nights: Franco-Maghribi Cultural Identities," in *Political Islam: Essays from Middle East Report*, ed. Joel Beinin and Joe Stork (London: I. B. Tauris, 1997), p. 265.
11. Ibid., p. 258.
12. J. Klausen, *The Islamic Challenge: Politics and Religion in Western Europe* (New York: Oxford University Press, 2006), p. 16; Malise Ruthven, "The Big Muslim Problem!" *New York Review*, December 17, 2009, p. 62.
13. Quoted in Klausen, *The Islamic Challenge*, p. 16.
14. J. Zeleny and N. Kulish, "Obama, in Berlin, Calls for Renewal of Ties with Allies," *New York Times*, July 25, 2008, p. 1.
15. Statistics in *BP Statistical Review of World Energy June 2009*, www.bp.com/statisticalreview.
16. M. T. Klare, *Resource Wars: The New Landscape of Global Conflict* (New York: Henry Holt, 2001), pp. 25–40.
17. A. E. Kramer, "Eastern Europe Fears New Era of Russian Sway," *New York Times*, October 13, 2009, p. A1.
18. Quoted in Flora Lewis, *International Herald Tribune*, June 15, 2001, p. 6.

Document-Based Question (DBQ) Essay Topics Correlated by Chapter

Writing the Document-Based Question (DBQ) Essay

This section is designed to be used in conjunction with the chapters of *A History of Western Society* and to provide you with opportunities to practice writing the DBQ, an essential part of the AP* European History exam. The Document-Based Question (DBQ) essay tests your ability to analyze historical documents and think critically like a historian. It is *not* an assessment of your historical recall, but rather an assessment of your ability to analyze and think critically about documented history.

The DBQ question looks like a standard free-response essay question. Following the question is a series of documents, usually ten to twelve. The documents may be written sources, pictures, artwork, maps, graphs, tables, or charts. Your task is to read and interpret the documents and then to use them as evidence to answer the question in essay format. Your essay should include the elements of a regular essay (introduction, thesis statement, supporting paragraphs, and conclusion). The information, or evidence, that you use to support your thesis must come from the documents provided.

Your essay will be assessed on the following criteria:

1. Thesis statement: must be original and specific, not simply a rewording of the question
2. Use of the documents: must use a majority of the documents to support the thesis; documents must be used *individually* and *specifically*
3. Accuracy of interpretation of documents
4. Analysis of bias and point of view in several documents
5. Organization of documents into groups

It is essential that you directly answer the essay question/prompt. While this may seem obvious, many students struggle to understand the terms of the question. The College Board uses the task words listed below in crafting essay questions. Often the task words may be combined, making the question more complex—for example, *identify AND analyze*, *explain to what extent*, and so on.

Task Words & Their Meanings[†]

1. **ANALYZE**: determine the component parts; examine the nature and relationship

2. **ASSESS/EVALUATE**: judge the value or character of something; appraise; evaluate the positive points and the negative ones; give an opinion regarding the value of; discuss the advantages and disadvantages of
3. **COMPARE**: examine for the purpose of noting similarities and differences
4. **CONTRAST**: examine in order to show dissimilarities or points of difference
5. **DESCRIBE**: give an account of; tell about; give a word picture of
6. **DISCUSS**: talk over; write about; consider or examine by argument or from various points of view; debate; present the different sides of
7. **EXPLAIN**: make clear or plain; make clear the causes or reasons for; make known in detail; tell the meaning of
8. **IDENTIFY**: cite specific events and phenomena, and show a connection
9. **TO WHAT EXTENT**: the range over which something extends; scope; the point, degree, or limit to which something extends; magnitude

Before writing your essay you need to devote some time to planning and developing your answer. The following guidelines outline the steps you should follow in answering each DBQ.

Before You Begin to Write the essay you will be afforded a fifteen-minute reading and planning period. Use this time to read the documents and begin to categorize or group them. As you read, make notes in the margins, or underline important information. Interrogate the document by asking the following questions:[†]

1. What is the document? (newspaper article, diary entry, public speech, and so on)
2. Who wrote the document? Consider the writer's education and social class.
3. When and where was the document written? Link this to a historical era or event.
4. Why was the document written? What was the motivation of the author?
5. Who was the intended audience for the document? Is this document public or private?
6. What does the document mean?
7. How does the document help you answer the essay question?
8. How can you categorize or group the document?

Group the Documents according to the terms of the question. You want to create specific groupings, such as by gender, similar opinion, social class, or time period. You may also group documents that appear to counter each other; this practice is called juxtaposition. If applicable, you may want to use broad categories such as political, economic, religious, social, intellectual, or artistic views. Students who create specific groups according to the terms of the question usually write more sophisticated essays. Remember that it takes at least *two* documents used properly as evidence to make one group.

Formulate a Thesis that addresses the terms of the question. You are expected to create an original and specific thesis, not simply reword the question. The thesis should serve as a road map for your essay, and it should demonstrate to the reader how you plan to answer the question. Include a strong introduction that previews the body paragraphs of your essay by articulating the way you intend to group the documents and organize the essay.

While Writing the Essay it is important to create strong topic sentences that introduce the groupings for each of your body paragraphs. Your analysis of the documents as they relate to the terms of the question should be used as evidence to support your thesis. Also, it is essential to refer to the documents *individually* and *specifically* and to properly *attribute* the documents you cite. Use the source information provided with each source when referring to the document—for example, *According to Protestant reformer Martin Luther,* or *A Catholic priest from Paris stated.*

Analyze the Point of View of the documents at least three times throughout your essay. This is very important because it demonstrates that you can think critically about the docu-ments and their context as it relates to history. To demonstrate analysis of bias or point of view of the document you must explain WHY a particular source expresses the stated view in the following ways:*

1. Relating authorial *point of view* to the author's place in society—for example, motive, position, status
2. Evaluating the *credibility* of the source
3. Recognizing that different *types of documents* serve different purposes
4. Analyzing the *tone* of the language used in the document

Here is an example of proper analysis of point of view as well as proper attribution of the document:

> In a picture taken at the Royal Palace in Berlin, August 1914 (Doc. 2), German unity is clearly demonstrated. The photograph shows a large mass of people with similar hats and clothing. They are seen cheering in honor of Germany. This photograph, however, may contain bias, having been taken at the Royal Palace by a government news agency. The photo shows only those who support German unity, a cause that the government wants to portray positively as Germany prepares for war.

Use the steps and techniques discussed here when answering the following sample DBQs. These questions will help you practice and prepare for the test. Each of the DBQ topics is correlated to one of the chapters in your text.

---

*Adapted from *AP European History Course Description.* Copyright © 2010 The College Board. Reproduced with permission. http://apcentral.collegeboard.com.

DBQ 1
Long-Distance Trade in Late Medieval Europe

Analyze the extent and effects of long-distance trade in late medieval Europe, ca. 1250–1450.

<u>Historical Background</u>: Advances in ship design and navigation enabled year-round long-distance trade, expanding medieval trade networks. While it became easier to exchange food and other highly valued goods among countries, ships moved between ports bearing more sinister passengers as well—rats carrying the plague. International trade gave rise to complex political dynamics between countries and provided the impetus for the discovery of new trade routes and distant lands with untapped resources.

Document 1

Source: Adapted from Colin McEvedy, *The New Penguin Atlas of Medieval History*, Penguin, 1992.

Cities with estimated populations between 50,000 and 125,000, ca. 1000–1483

1000	1212	1346	1483
Baghdad	Baghdad	Cairo	Cairo
Constantinople	Cairo	Constantinople	Florence
	Constantinople	Florence	Genoa
		Genoa	Istanbul
		Ghent	Milan
		Milan	Naples
		Paris	Paris
		Tabriz	Tabriz
		Venice	Venice

Population data adapted from pages 57, 75, 89, and 103 in *The New Penguin Atlas of Medieval History*, maps devised by Colin McEvedy and drawn by David Woodroffe (Penguin Books, 1992). Copyright © Colin McEvedy, 1961–1992.

Document 2

Source: An English money-changer, 1226.

Concerning the denarii of Venice: a pound was under weight only by one penny. The same for the money of Genoa. Likewise those of Montpellier of Spain. The legal money of Cologne: a pound lacked six pence. The false money of Cologne: whence a pound failed by three shillings. The Brussels pound is commonly short three shillings. The Marseilles pound lacks six pence. But in these things the money-changer is watchful so that he may buy a pound of whatever silver he pleases according to what returns a better profit to himself rather than to what will redound to the profit of the king.

Document 3

Source: Bills of Sale for a Saracen (North African) slave girl, England, 1248.

Bill of Sale for Purchase of one "Aissa," May 19, 1248

May the nineteenth, in year of the Lord 1248. We, William Alegnan and Bernard Mute, of Cannet, have sold jointly in good faith and without guile to you, John Aleman, son of Peter Aleman, a certain Saracen maid of ours, commonly called Aissa, for a price of nine pounds and fifteen solidi in the mixed money now current in Marseilles. Witnesses, etc.

Bill of Sale for Purchase of one "Aissa," July 2, 1248

July the second. I, John Aleman, citizen of Marseilles, in good faith and without guile, sell and transfer to you, Peter Bertoumieu, son of the late Raymond Bertoumieu, a certain Saracen maid of ours, commonly called Aissa, for a price of ten pounds in the mixed money now current in Marseilles, which I confess to have had and to have received from you, renouncing the benefit of all laws, etc. And if the said Saracen maid is worth more at any time in the future I grant it all with the price, or I give all that extra worth to you and yours, etc. Witnesses, etc.

Document 4

Source: Humbert de Romans, French Master General of the Dominican Order, *On Fairs and Markets*, ca. 1270.

Though markets and fairs are terms often used indiscriminately, there is a difference between them, for fairs deal with larger things and only once in the year, or at least rarely in the same place, and to them come men from afar. But markets are for lesser things, the daily necessaries of life; they are held weekly and only people from near at hand come. Hence markets are usually morally worse than fairs.

Document 5

Source: Norwegian king Magnus's grant of privilege to Hanseatic (German) merchants in Norway, 1278.

We have therefore upon the request and prayer of the Councilors and citizens of many German ports, but especially upon the humble request of our friends, the Burgomaster, Councilors and citizens of the city of Lübeck, presented to us by the wise and honorable Councilor Herrik Skenken and Alexander, graciously deemed it proper and to the honor of God and of service to them to grant certain privileges to such merchants of German speech as come, either as guests or travelers, to our kingdom with their wares.

Document 6

Source: Detail from the French manuscript *Vigiles de Charles VII*, depiction of the siege of Orléans (1428–1429) during the Hundred Years' War, ca. 1483.

Bibliothèque nationale de France/Art Resource, NY.

Document 7

Source: *Chronicle* of Matteo Villani, Florence, ca. 1350.

In the year of Christ's Incarnation for our salvation, 1346, . . . there arose . . . in the parts of the Orient that lie closest to Cathay [China] and northern India, and in the ports and other provinces surrounding the coastal ones a pestilence [that struck] men of all conditions and ages and both sexes. . . . This pestilence came intermittently, and passing from one nation to the next, before the end of one year, it had struck all of that third part of the world that is called Asia. Toward the end of this time, it reached the nations of the Great Sea [the Mediterranean], the shore of the Tyrrhenian Sea, Syria, and Turkey down into Egypt and to the shores of the Red Sea and, to the North, to Russia and Greece, Armenia, and other nearby countries. . . . Next, the ports of Africa and its eastern provinces. . . . By 1349 it had extended all the way west to the shores of the Oceanic Sea of Europe, Africa, Ireland, the island of England and Scotland.

Document 8

Source: Jean Froissart, report of peasant uprisings (*jacqueries*) in France, 1358.

For certain people of the common villages, without any head or ruler, assembled together in Beauvoisin. In the beginning they passed not a hundred in number they said how the noblemen of the realm of France, knights and squires, shamed the realm, and that it should be a great wealth to destroy them all: and each of them said it was true, and said all with one voice: "Shame have he that cloth not his power to destroy all the gentlemen of the realm!"

Document 9

Source: Chinese declaration of ascension of the Ming emperor to the Byzantine emperor, 1372.

We have established peace in the Empire, and restored the old boundaries of [China]. We were selected by Our people to occupy the Imperial throne of [China] under the dynastic title of "the Great Ming," commencing with Our reign styled Hung-wu, of which we now are in the fourth year. We have sent officers to all the foreign kingdoms with this Manifesto except to you, [Byzantium], who, being separated from us by the western sea, have not as yet received the announcement. We now send a native of your country, Nieh-ku-lun [Friar Nicolaus de Bentra, Archbishop of Peking], to hand you this Manifesto. Although We are not equal in wisdom to our ancient rulers whose virtue was recognized all over the universe, We cannot but let the world know Our intention to maintain peace within the four seas. It is on this ground alone that We have issued this Manifesto.

Document 10

Source: Jewish cartographers Abraham and Jehuda Cresques, Catalan (modern northeast Spain) map of the Mediterranean world, 1375.

Bibliothèque nationale de France/The Bridgeman Art Library.

Document 11

Sources: Details depicting Portuguese *caravela* (below) and *carrack* (opposite), from the view of Lisbon in the *Civitates Orbis Terrarum*, ca. 1600, and a manuscript atlas of Sebastião Lopes, ca. 1565. Commentary by Roger Smith of the Institute of Nautical Archaeology, 1985.

Although the first documented use of the word *caravela* appears in a Portuguese manuscript of 1255 describing coastal fishing vessels, heavily planked *barchas* and *barinels* initially propelled Portuguese mariners down African shores in the fifteenth century. Headwinds and currents in the Gulf of Guinea, however, slowed the progress of exploration under square sail and oar. A slightly longer, larger and lighter vessel, with finer lines and partial decking, emerged to ride over heavy seas and to venture up equatorial river mouths. Greater sailing distances prompted a need for increased crews, provisions and trading truck, but also swifter and more maneuverable craft in which to return home to Lisbon.

(cont.)

The exact origin of the *carrack* is unknown, but almost certainly was a product of the fusion between Baltic and Mediterranean shipbuilding in the fifteenth century. Developed for their generous cargo capacity, [carracks] could undertake long voyages outside of the Mediterranean Sea in the wake of European exploration and discovery. The broad-bellied hull of the *carrack* contained the largest cargo hold of her day; the narrow but towering bulwarks and castles protected against enemy fire, and provided defense from assault by boarding.

Both photos from the Hermon Dunlap Smith Center for the History of Cartography. The Newberry Library.

Document 12

Source: 1481 travel journal of Rabbi Meshullam Ben R. Menahem of Florence, first published in Vienna, 1882.

Alexandria (Egypt) is as big as Florence. . . . I saw four large *fondaks* [warehouses], one for the Franks and another for the Genoese and their Consul and two for the Venetians and their Consul.

Document 13

Source: Jared Diamond, Professor of Geography and Physiology at UCLA,
Guns, Germs, and Steel: The Fates of Human Societies, 1997.

The expertise at distillation that medieval Islamic alchemists developed to produce alcohols and perfumes also let them distill petroleum into fractions, some of which proved to be even more powerful incendiaries. Delivered in grenades, rockets, and torpedoes, those incendiaries played a key role in Islam's eventual defeat of the Crusaders. By then, the Chinese had observed that a particular mixture of sulfur, charcoal, and saltpeter, which became known as gunpowder, was especially explosive. An Islamic chemical treatise about A.D. 1100 describes seven gunpowder recipes, while a treatise from A.D. 1280 gives more than 70 recipes that proved suitable for diverse purposes (one for rockets, another for cannons).

DBQ 2
Perspectives of Renaissance Writers

Identify and analyze various perspectives of Renaissance writers.

<u>Historical Background</u>: The Renaissance was characterized by self-conscious awareness among fourteenth- and fifteenth-century Italians that they were living in a new era. The realization that something new and unique was happening first came to men of letters. The Renaissance also manifested itself in a new attitude toward men, women, and the world.

Document 1

Source: Italian humanist Petrarch, in letters to fellow Italian humanist, Boccaccio, 1364.

O inglorious age! that scorns antiquity, its mother, to whom it owes every noble art, that dares to declare itself not only equal but superior to the glorious past. I say nothing of the vulgar, the dregs of mankind, whose sayings and opinions may raise a laugh but hardly merit serious censure.

Document 2

Source: Peter Paul Vergerio (1370–1444), in a letter to Ubertinus, ruler of Carrara, Italy.

For the education of children is a matter of more than private interest; it concerns the State, which indeed regards the right training of the young as, in certain aspects, within its proper sphere. . . . Tutors and comrades alike should be chosen from amongst those likely to bring out the best qualities to attract by good example, and to repress the first signs of evil. . . . Above all, respect for Divine ordinances is of the deepest importance; it should be inculcated from the earliest years. Reverence towards elders and parents is an obligation closely akin. We call those studies liberal which are worthy of a free man; those studies by which we attain and practice virtue and wisdom.

Document 3

Source: Leonardo Bruni, Italian humanist from Arezzo, *On Learning and Literature*, 1472.

But we must not forget that true distinction is to be gained by a wide and varied range of such studies as conduce to the profitable enjoyment of life, in which, however we must observe due proportion in the attention and time we devote to them. First amongst such studies I place History: a subject which must not on any account be neglected by one who aspires to true cultivation. For it is our duty to understand the origins of our own history and its development; and the achievements of Peoples and of Kings.

Document 4

Source: Pico della Mirandola, Italian Renaissance philosopher, *Oration on the Dignity of Man*, 1486.

For why should we not admire more the angels themselves and the blessed choirs of heaven? At last it seems to me I have come to understand why man is the most fortunate of creatures and consequently worthy of all admiration and what precisely is that rank which is his lot in the universal chain of Being—a rank to be envied not only by brutes but even by the stars and by minds beyond this world. . . . For it is on this very account that man is rightly called and judged a great miracle and wonderful creature indeed.

Document 5

Source: Laura Cereta, Italian humanist, *Letter to Bibulus Sempronius*, 1488.

You brashly and publicly not merely wonder but indeed lament that I am said to possess as fine a mind as nature ever bestowed upon the most learned man. You seem to think so learned a woman has scarcely before been seen in the world. You are wrong. . . . The explanation is clear: women have been able by nature to be exceptional, but have chosen lesser goals. For some women are concerned with parting their hair correctly, adorning themselves with lovely dresses . . . or standing at mirrors to smear their lovely faces. But those in whom a deeper integrity yearns for virtue, restrain from the start their youthful souls, reflect on higher things, harden the body with sobriety and trials, and curb their tongues, open their ears, compose their thoughts in wakeful hours, their minds in contemplation to letters bonded to righteousness. For knowledge is not given as a gift, but [is gained] with diligence. Nature has generously lavished its gifts upon all people, opening to all the doors of choice through which reason sends envoys to the will.

Document 6

Source: Lorenzo de' Medici, Italian statesman, in a letter to his son Giovanni after his son became a cardinal at the age of fourteen, ca. 1491.

Converse on general topics with all. . . . A handsome house and a well-ordered family will be preferable to a great retinue and a splendid residence. . . . Silk and jewels are not suitable for persons in your station. Your taste will be better shown in the acquisition of a few elegant remains of antiquity, or in the collecting of handsome books, and by your attendants being learned and well-bred rather than numerous. Invite others to your house oftener than you receive invitations. . . . Let your own food be plain. . . . The station of a cardinal is not less secure than elevated; on which account those who arrive at it too frequently become negligent; conceiving their object is attained and that they can preserve it with little trouble. . . . Be attentive, therefore, to your conduct, and confide in others too little rather than too much.

Document 7

Source: Erasmus, Dutch humanist, *The Praise of Folly*, 1509.

As for the theologians, perhaps it would be better to pass them over in silence, "not stirring up the hornets' nest" and "not laying a finger on the stinkweed," since this race of man is incredibly arrogant and touchy. For they might rise up en masse and march in ranks against me with six hundred conclusions and force me to recant. And if I should refuse, they would immediately shout "heretic." For this is the thunderbolt they always keep ready at a moment's notice to terrify anyone to whom they are not very favorably inclined.

Document 8

Source: Juan Luis Vives, Spanish humanist, from *The Education of a Christian Woman*, addressed to Catherine of Aragon, Queen of England, and dedicated to her daughter, Princess Mary, published 1524.

In addition, she will learn the art of cooking. . . . I have seen wives hated by their husbands, daughters-in-law by their fathers-in-law, and daughters by their fathers because they said they had no skill in preparing meals. And I have come to the conclusion that the principal reason why men here in Belgium spend so much time in inns and taverns is the negligence and laziness of their women in cooking meals, which forces men to avoid their own homes and seek elsewhere what they do not find there. . . . With regard to chastity in women, we must consider the chaste woman is beautiful, charming, gifted, noble, fertile, and possessed of every best and outstanding quality, while the unchaste woman is a sea and storehouse of all evils.

Document 9

Source: Niccolò Machiavelli, Italian philosopher and writer, *The History of Florence*, 1525.

In peaceful times he [Lorenzo de' Medici] often entertained the people with various festivities, such as jousts, feats of arms, and representations of triumphs of olden times. He aimed to maintain abundance in the city, to keep the people united and the nobility honoured. He had the greatest love and admiration for all who excelled in any art, and was a great patron of learning and of literary men. . . . Lorenzo took the greatest delight in architecture, music and poetry; and many of his own poetic compositions, enriched with commentaries, appeared in print. And for the purpose of enabling the Florentine youths to devote themselves to the study of letters, he established a university in the city of Pisa, where he employed the most eminent men of all Italy as professors. . . . And thus, beloved of God and fortune, all his enterprises were crowned with success, whilst those of his enemies had the opposite fate.

Document 10

Source: Francois Rabelais, French writer, *Celebration of the Worldly Life*, 1532.

In their rules there was only one clause: DO WHAT YOU WILL because people who are free, well-born, well-bred, and easy in honest company have a natural spur and instinct which drives them to virtuous deeds and deflects them from vice; and this they called honour.

DBQ 3
Reform and Renewal in the Christian Church

Discuss the extent to which the religious schism during the sixteenth century was symptomatic of political, social, and economic problems.

<u>Historical Background</u>: At the beginning of the sixteenth century there was just one type of Christian church in western Europe, but by the end of the century there were many. The dramatic shift in the religious landscape of Europe was tumultuous, with many factions—political and religious leaders, radical thinkers, and humanists, to name a few—in ever-changing states of conflict. The rapid spread of the Reformation was fueled in part by the decentralization of the Holy Roman Empire. As reformers encouraged laypeople to seek a more direct relationship with God, the church and state developed new ways to gain funds and power, leading to riots, civil wars, and international conflicts.

Document 1

Source: Albrecht of Brandenburg, *Instructions for Selling Indulgences*, 1517.

Respecting now the contribution to the chest [church funds], for the rebuilding of the said church of the chief of the apostles, the penitentiaries and confessors, after they have explained to those making confession the full remission and privileges, shall ask of them, for how much money or other temporal goods they would conscientiously go without, the most complete remission and privileges; and this shall be done in order that hereafter they may be brought the more easily to contribute.

Document 2

Source: Albrecht Dürer, *Four Horsemen of the Apocalypse*, German, ca. 1497–1498.

British Museum/Art Resource, NY.

Document 3

Source: Martin Luther, German Protestant theologian, *Against the Murderous, Thieving Hordes of Peasants*, ca. 1525.

Let everyone who can smite, slay, and stab [the peasants], secretly and openly, remembering that nothing can be more poisonous, hurtful, or devilish than a rebel.

Document 4

Source: Martin Luther, German Protestant theologian, *Address to the Christian Nobility of the German Nation Concerning the Reform of the Christian Estate*, 1520.

Therefore, when necessity demands it, and the pope is an offense to Christendom, the first man who is able should, as a true member of the whole body, do what he can to bring about a truly free council. No one can do this so well as the temporal authorities, especially since they are also fellow-Christians, fellow-priests, fellow-members of the spiritual estate, fellow-lords over all things. Whenever it is necessary or profitable, they ought to exercise the office and work they have received from God over everyone.

Document 5

Source: Michael Eisenhart, *The Peasant's War Engulfs Rothenburg*, Holy Roman Empire, 1525.

. . . through certain citizens here who adhere to the heresy of Luther, it has come about that bad, false teaching has greatly got the upper hand, owing also to the dissimulation and concessions of some of the town authorities. . . .

On March 21, a Tuesday, thirty or forty peasants got together in a mob in Rothenburg, bought a kettled rum, and marched about the town. . . . They got together again on Thursday and on Friday, as many as four hundred. The working classes in the town now begin to revolt. They cease to obey the authorities and form a committee of thirty-six to manage affairs.

Document 6

Source: The Act of Supremacy, English Parliament, 1534.

[B]e it enacted, by the authority of this present Parliament, that the king, our sovereign lord, his heirs and successors, kings of this realm, shall be taken, accepted and reputed the only supreme head in earth of the Church of England, called *Anglicans Ecclesia*; and shall have and enjoy . . . all honors, dignities, preeminences, jurisdictions, privileges, authorities, immunities, profits and commodities to the said dignity of the supreme head of the same Church belonging and appertaining.

Document 7

Source: Ignatius Loyola, Spanish priest, *Rules for Thinking with the Church*, 1540.

In order to have the proper attitude of mind in the Church Militant [all active, living Christians] we should observe the following rules: . . .

7. Putting aside all private judgment, we should keep our minds prepared and ready to obey promptly and in all things the true spouse of Christ our Lord, our Holy Mother, the hierarchical Church.

Document 8

Source: *The Religious Peace of Augsburg*, by Imperial Diet, 1555.

In order that . . . peace, which is especially necessary in view of the divided religions . . . , and is demanded by the sad necessity of the Holy Roman Empire of the German nation, may be the better established and made secure and enduring between his Roman Imperial Majesty and us, on the one hand, and the electors, princes, and estates of the Holy Empire of the German nation on the other, therefore his Imperial Majesty, and we, and the electors, princes, and estates of the Holy Empire, will not make war on any estate of the empire on account of the Augsburg Confession and the doctrine, religion, and faith of the same.

Document 9

Source: John Calvin's regulations for the villages around Geneva, 1561.

He who blasphemes, swearing by the body or blood of our Lord, or in like manner, shall kiss the earth for the first offense, pay five sous [form of currency] for the second and ten for the third. He who contradicts the word of God shall be sent before consistory for reproof, or before the council for punishment, as the case may require. If any one sings indecent, licentious songs, or dances . . . he shall be kept in prison three days and then sent to council. [There are similar provisions for drunkenness, gambling, quarreling, taking more than five percent interest, and so on.]

Document 10

Source: *Canons and Decrees of the Council of Trent*, 1563.

Canon 6: If anyone says that in the Catholic Church there is not instituted a hierarchy by divine ordinance, which consists of bishops, priests and ministers, let him be anathema [excommunicated].

DBQ 4
Attitudes and Responses to European Exploration and Conquest

Identify and analyze motives, attitudes, and consequences of the European age of exploration and conquest.

<u>Historical Background</u>: Overseas expansion broadened the geographical horizons of Europeans and brought them into confrontations with ancient civilizations in Africa, Asia, and the Americas. These confrontations led first to conquest, then to exploitation, and finally to profound social changes in both Europe and the conquered territories.

Document 1

Source: King Ferdinand and Queen Isabella of Spain, "Privileges and Prerogatives Granted by Their Catholic Majesties," missive to Christopher Columbus, 1492.

For as much of you, *Christopher Columbus*, are going by our command, with some of our vessels and men, to discover and subdue some Islands and Continent in the ocean, and it is hoped that by God's assistance, some of the said Islands and Continent in the ocean will be discovered and conquered by your means and conduct, therefore it is but just and reasonable, that since you expose yourself to such danger to serve us, you should be rewarded for it. And we being willing to honour and favour You for the reasons aforesaid: Our will is, That you, *Christopher Columbus*, after discovering and conquering the said Islands and Continent in the said ocean, or any of them, shall be our Admiral of the said Islands and Continent you shall so discover and conquer; and that you be our Admiral, Vice-Roy, and Governour in them.

Document 2

Source: Christopher Columbus, letter to Lord Sanchez, written in Lisbon shortly after returning from his first voyage across the Atlantic, March 14, 1493.

Thus they bartered, like idiots, cotton and gold for fragments of bows, glasses, bottles, and jars; which I forbad as being unjust, and myself gave them many beautiful and acceptable articles which I had brought with me taking nothing from them in return; I did this in order that I might the more easily conciliate them, that they might be led to become Christians, and be inclined to entertain a regard for the King and Queen, our Princes and all Spaniards, and that I might induce them to take an interest in seeking out and collecting, and delivering to us such things as they possessed in abundance, but which we greatly needed. They practice no kind of idolatry, but have a firm belief that all strength and power, and indeed all good things, are in heaven, and that I had descended from thence with these ships and sailors and under this impression was I received after they had thrown aside their fears.

Document 3

Source: Fra Soncino, letter to Ludovico Sforza, Duke of Milan, regarding John Cabot's first voyage, 1497.

And in the spring he says that his Majesty will arm some ships, and will give him all the criminals, so that he may go to this country and plant a colony there. And in this way he hopes to make London a greater place for spices than Alexandria. And the principals of the business are citizens of Bristol, great mariners that now know where to go. They say that the voyage will not take more than fifteen days, if fortune favors them after leaving Ireland. I have talked with a Burgundian, a companion of Messer Joanne, who affirms the same, and who is willing to go, since the Admiral, as Messer Joanne is already styled, has given him an island, and has also given another to his barber, a Genoese, and they regard the two as Counts, and my lord, the Admiral, the chief. And I believe that some poor Italian friars will go on the voyage, who have the promise of being bishops. And I, being a friend of the admiral, if I wished to go, could have an archbishopric.

Document 4

Source: Queen Isabella of Spain, letter to her husband, Ferdinand of Aragon, and her daughter Joanna, heiress to the Kingdom of Castile, written shortly before her death in November 1504.

Our principal intention, in soliciting from Pope Alexander VI the concession of the lands discovered and to be discovered, was to convert their peoples to our holy Catholic faith. . . . I beg the King my lord very affectionately, I order and command the Princess my daughter and the Prince my son, to execute and accomplish this intention.

Document 5

Source: Sixteenth-century drawing of Aztecs suffering from smallpox during the Cortes invasion, from *A History of the People of New Spain* by Spanish Catholic missionary Fray Bernardino de Sahagun, ca. 1575–1580.

Biblioteca Medicea Laurenziana.

Document 6

Source: Antonio Pigafetta, Venetian scholar and traveler, *Magellan's Voyage Around the World*, November 28, 1520.

When we reached land, [the enemy natives] formed in three divisions to the number of more than one thousand five hundred persons. When they saw us, they charged down upon us with exceeding loud cries. . . . So many of them charged down upon us that they shot the captain through the right leg with a poisoned arrow. On that account he ordered us to retire [retreat] slowly, but the men took to flight, except six or eight of us who remained with the captain. . . . One of them wounded him on the left leg with a large cutlass. . . . That caused the captain to fall face downward, when immediately they rushed upon him with iron and bamboo spears . . . until they killed our mirror, our light, our comfort, and our true guide.

Document 7

Source: Pope Paul III, *Sublimus Dei*, May 29, 1537.

We, who, though unworthy, exercise on earth the power of our Lord and seek with all our might to bring those sheep of His flock who are outside into the fold committed to our charge, consider, however, that the Indians are truly men and that they are not only capable of understanding the Catholic Faith but, according to our information, they desire exceedingly to receive it. Desiring to provide ample remedy for these evils, We define and declare by these Our letters, or by any translation thereof signed by any notary public and sealed with the seal of any ecclesiastical dignitary, to which the same credit shall be given as to the originals, that, notwithstanding whatever may have been or may be said to the contrary, the said Indians and all other people who may later be discovered by Christians, are by no means to be deprived of their liberty or the possession of their property, even though they be outside the faith of Jesus Christ; and that they may and should, freely and legitimately, enjoy their liberty and the possession of their property; nor should they be in any way enslaved; should the contrary happen, it shall be null and have no effect.

Document 8

Source: Bartolome de Las Casas, Spanish priest and missionary, *Historia de las Indias*, ca. 1524–1561.

The reason the Christians have murdered on such a vast scale and killed anyone and everyone in their way is purely and simply greed. . . . Their insatiable greed and overweening ambition know no bounds; the land is fertile and rich, the inhabitants simple, forbearing and submissive. The Spaniards have shown not the slightest consideration for these people, treating them (and I speak from first-hand experience, having been there from the outset) not as brute animals—indeed, I would to God they had done and had shown them the consideration they afford their animals—so much as piles of dung in the middle of the road. They have had as little concern for their souls as for their bodies, all the millions that perished having gone to their deaths with no knowledge of God and without the benefit of the Sacraments.

Document 9

Source: Pope Paul III, *Ipsa Veritas*, a papal bull (proclamation) written in response to a complaint from the Bishop of Tlascala in Mexico concerning the enslavement of natives, 1537.

Wishing to correct this . . . we declare that the Indians . . . even if they are outside the Christian faith cannot and must not be deprived of their liberty, or their property, and must by no means be reduced to servitude.

Document 10

Source: Coconut cup with silver mounts and an Old Testament engraving, Dutch, ca. 1590.

DBQ 5
Absolutism

Analyze the extent to which rulers and their subjects viewed the proper role of an absolute monarch differently.

<u>Historical Background</u>: Absolutist governments were viewed by some as a solution to the upheaval of the Reformation and the subsequent rapid growth and change in seventeenth-century Europe. Absolute monarchs ruled over centralized bureaucracies that oversaw armies, trade, and agriculture, and they negotiated with other rulers to help maintain peace in the "age of crisis." This new political system was adopted by governments in France, Spain, Prussia, Austria, and Russia. They were viewed by their subjects as the literal embodiment of a government that used suppression and the claim of God-given authority to carry out its abuses.

Document 1

Source: Jean-Baptiste Colbert, French Minister of Finance, letter to Louis XIV, 1664.

Having summarized the condition of domestic and foreign trade, it will perhaps not be inappropriate to say a few words about the advantages of trade.

I believe everyone will easily agree to this principle, that only the abundance of money in a State makes the difference in its greatness and power.

Aside from the advantages that the entry of a greater quantity of cash into the kingdom will produce, it is certain that, thanks to the manufactures, a million people who now languish in idleness will be able to earn a living. An equally considerable number will earn their living by navigation and in the seaports.

The almost infinite increase in the number of [French] ships will multiply to the same degree the greatness and power of the State.

These, in my opinion, are the goals that should be the aim of the King's efforts and of his goodness and love for his people.

Document 2

Source: Frontispiece for *Leviathan or The Matter, Forme and Power of a Common Wealth Ecclesiasticall and Civil*, etching by Abraham Bosse, with input from author Thomas Hobbes, 1651.

Private Collection/The Bridgeman Art Library.

Document 3

Source: *The Twelve Articles*, manifesto of German peasants in Swabia, 1524.

It has been the custom hitherto for men to hold us as their own property, which is pitiable enough, considering that Christ has delivered and redeemed us all, without exception, by the shedding of his precious blood, the lowly as well as the great. Accordingly, it is consistent with Scripture that we should be free and should wish to be so. . . . We are aggrieved by the appropriation by individuals of meadows and fields which at one time belonged to the community. These we will take again into our own hands.

Document 4

Source: King James VI of Scotland, *True Law of Free Monarchies*, 1598.

And according to these fundamental laws already alleged, we daily see that in the Parliament (which is nothing else but the head court of the King and his vassals) the laws are but craved by his subjects, and only made by him at their rogation and with their advice. For albeit the King made daily statutes and ordinances, enjoining such pains thereto as he thinks meet, without any advice of Parliament or Estates, yet it lies in the power of no Parliament to make any kind of law or statute without his sceptre be to it for giving it the force of a law. . . . And as ye see it manifest that the King is overlord of the whole land, so is he master over every person that inhabiteth the same, having power over the life and death of every one of them. For although a just prince will not take the life of any of his subjects without a clear law, yet the same laws whereby he taketh them are made by himself or his predecessors, and so the power flows always from himself; as by daily experience we see good and just princes will from time to time make new laws and statutes, adjoining the penalties to the breakers thereof, which before the law was made had been no crime to the Subject to have committed.

Document 5

Source: Arthur Young, English agricultural scientist, *Travels [in France] During the Years 1787, 1788 and 1789*.

The abuses attending the levy of taxes were heavy and universal. . . . Such an enormous power, constantly acting and from which no man was free, must in the nature of things, degenerate in many cases into absolute tyranny. . . . What must have been the state of the poor people paying heavy taxes from which the nobility and clergy were exempted? A cruel aggravation of their misery to see those who could best afford to pay, exempted. . . . The *Capitaineries* [lords' exclusive hunting rights] were a dreadful scourge on all the occupiers of the land. . . . Such were the exertions of arbitrary power which the lower orders felt directly from the royal authority.

Document 6

Source: Adam Olearius, German diplomat to Moscow, *Travels in Moscovy*, ca. 1630.

Although the Russians, especially the common populace living as slaves under a harsh yoke, can bear and endure a great deal out of love for their masters, yet if the pressure is beyond measure . . . a dangerous indignation results, turned not so much against their sovereign as against the lower authorities, especially if the people have been much oppressed by them . . . and have not been protected by the higher authorities.

Document 7

Source: French bishop Jacques Bossuet, *Politics Drawn from the Very Words of Holy Scripture*, 1708.

There are four qualities essential to royal authority. First, the royal authority is sacred; second, it is paternal [fatherly]; third, it is absolute; fourth, it is submitted to reason. . . . Even when princes do not do their duty, we must respect their office and ministry. . . . However, because their power comes from above, princes must not think that they are free to use it at their pleasure; rather must they use it with fear and discretion, as a thing which comes to them from God, and of which God will demand a strict account.

Document 8

Source: Catherine the Great, empress of Russia, Instruction (*Nakaz*) to the Legislative Commission of 1767.

9. The Sovereign is absolute. . . .
10. The Extent of the Dominion [of Russia] requires an absolute Power to be vested in that Person who rules over it. . . .
13. What is the true End of Monarchy? Not to deprive people of their natural Liberty; but to correct their Actions, in order to obtain the *supreme Good.* . . .
36. General or political Liberty does not consist in that licentious Notion, *That a Man may do whatever he pleases.*

Document 9

Source: Louis XIV, king of France, letter to his heir from *Mémoires for the Instruction of the Dauphin*, ca. 1670.

Kings are absolute seigneurs, and from their nature have full and free disposal of all property both secular and ecclesiastical, to use it as wise dispensers, that is to say, in accordance with the requirements of their State.

Document 10

Source: Hyacinthe Rigaud, *Louis XIV, King of France and Navarre*, 1701.

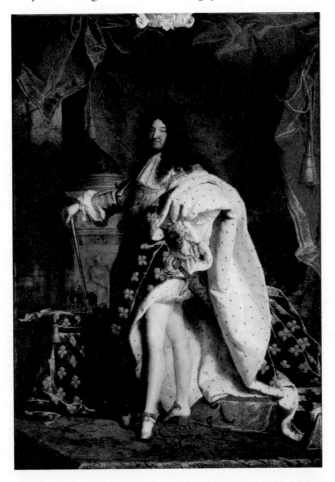

Document 11

Source: Siegfried Isaacsohn, *History of the Prussian Civil Service*, ca. 1874–1884.

The absolute subordination of the Civil Service from the highest to the lowest, their unquestioning obedience to the King, together with their absolute responsibility not only for their own actions, but also for those of their colleagues and their inferiors, created among them an extremely strong sense of professional honour, solidarity, and of professional pride. . . . The service of the King required undivided attention.

The King's uniform, which every Civil Servant had to wear when on duty, kept the feeling alive among them that they were the King's servants and had to represent the King's interests.

DBQ 6
Toward a New Worldview

Describe and analyze how the new worldviews of the seventeenth and eighteenth centuries affected the way enlightened Europeans thought about society and human relations.

<u>Historical Background</u>: As the study of nature supplanted religious precedence in certain philosophical circles, the discoveries of the seventeenth-century scientific revolution fueled the Enlightenment movement of the eighteenth century, greatly advancing debates about concepts of human capacity, innate human rights, and the value of each individual. The spread of new ideas was facilitated by an explosive growth in book consumption, but the new natural philosophy had its own dark side. In their attempts to reconcile current social dilemmas through scientific inquiry, some wielded this new science to explain their own superiority and to rationalize attitudes such as racism and male chauvinism.

Document 1

Source: René Descartes, French philosopher, *Discourse on Method*, 1637.

[I]n my travels I had found that those who held opinions contrary to ours were neither barbarians nor savages, but that any of them were at least as reasonable as ourselves.

Document 2

Source: John Locke, Scottish philosopher, *Some Thoughts Concerning Education*, 1693.

I think I may say that of all the men we meet with, nine parts of ten are what they are, good or evil, useful or not, by their education. 'Tis that which makes the great difference in Mankind.

Document 3

Source: Catherine the Great of Russia, Decree on Serfs, 1767.

[A]ccording to the laws that have been enacted from time immemorial by the autocratic forefathers of Her Imperial Majesty and which have not been repealed . . . all persons who dare to incite serfs and peasants to disobey their landlords shall be arrested and taken to the nearest government office, there to be punished forthwith as disturbers of the public tranquility, according to the laws and without leniency.

Document 4

Source: Mary Wollstonecraft, British writer and philosopher, *A Vindication of the Rights of Woman*, 1792.

[W]omen, in particular, are rendered weak and wretched by a variety of concurring causes, originating from one hasty conclusion. The conduct and manners of women, in fact, evidently proof that their minds are not in a healthy state; for, like the flowers which are planted in too rich a soil, strength and usefulness are sacrificed to beauty; and the flaunting leaves, after having pleased a fastidious eye, fade, disregarded on the stalk, long before the season when they ought to have arrived at maturity. One cause of this barren blooming I attribute to a false system of education, gathered from the books written on this subject by men who, considering females rather as women than human creatures, have been more anxious to make them alluring mistresses than affectionate wives and rational mothers; and the understanding of the sex has been so bubbled by this specious homage, that the civilized women of the present century, with a few exceptions, are only anxious to inspire love, when they ought to cherish a nobler ambition, and by their abilities and virtues exact respect.

Document 5

Source: Voltaire, French philosopher, *A Plea for Tolerance and Reason*, 1763.

It does not require any great art or studies elocution to prove that Christians ought to tolerate one another. I will go even further and say that we ought to look upon all men as our brothers. What! Call a Turk, a Jew, and a Siamese, my brother? Yes, of course; for are we not all children of the same father, and the creatures of the same God?

Document 6

Source: French-German atheist Baron d'Holbach, *Good Sense*, 1772.

How could the human mind make any considerable progress, while tormented with frightful phantoms, and guided by men, interested in perpetuating its ignorance and fears? Man has been forced to vegetate in his primitive stupidity: he has been taught nothing but stories about invisible powers upon whom his happiness was supposed to depend. Occupied solely by his fears, and by unintelligible reveries, he has always been at the mercy of his priests, who have reserved to themselves the right of thinking for him, and directing his actions.

Document 7

Source: Denis Diderot, French philosopher, *Encyclopedia*, excerpt concerning the role of government, 1772.

Government . . . The good of the people must be the great purpose of the government. The governors are appointed to fulfill it; and the civil constitution that invests them with this power is bound therein by the laws of nature and by the law of reason, which has determined that purpose in any form of government as the cause of its welfare. The greatest good of the people is its liberty. Liberty is to the body of the state what health is to each individual; without health man cannot enjoy pleasure; without liberty the state of welfare is excluded from nations.

Document 8

Source: Tomb of Sir Isaac Newton, English physicist, Westminster Abbey, London, 1727.

Werner Forman/Corbis.

Document 9

Source: Italian economist and criminologist Caesare Beccaria, *On Crimes and Punishments*, 1764.

Is the death penalty really useful and necessary for the security and good order of society? Are torture and torments just, and do they attain the end for which laws are instituted? What is the best way to prevent crimes? Are the same punishments equally effective for all times? What influence have they on customary behavior? These problems deserve to be analyzed with that geometric precision which the mist of sophisms, seductive eloquence, and timorous doubt cannot withstand.

Document 10

Source: Marquis Nicolas de Condorcet, French thinker, *The Evils of Slavery*, 1788.

Reducing a man to slavery, buying him, selling him, keeping him in servitude: these are truly crimes, and crimes worse than theft. In effect, they take from the slave, not only all forms of property but also the ability to acquire it, the control over his time, his strength, of everything that nature has given him to maintain his life and his needs. To this wrong they add that of taking from the slave the right to dispose of his own person.

DBQ 7
European Expansion and the Changing Life of the People

Examine the extent to which fundamental changes in the European economy during the eighteenth and early nineteenth centuries affected the standards of living of both the urban and rural working classes.

<u>Historical Background</u>: While the innovations of the Agricultural and Industrial Revolutions improved and dramatically sped the production of food and goods, they upended the economic system that had been in place since the Middle Ages and changed the face of home and work for many. People moved away from their families to find employment, learned new skills, and struggled to reshape the social structures of their communities. The positive economic growth was measurable in many ways; less easily quantifiable was the cost paid in workers' mental and physical well-being.

Document 1

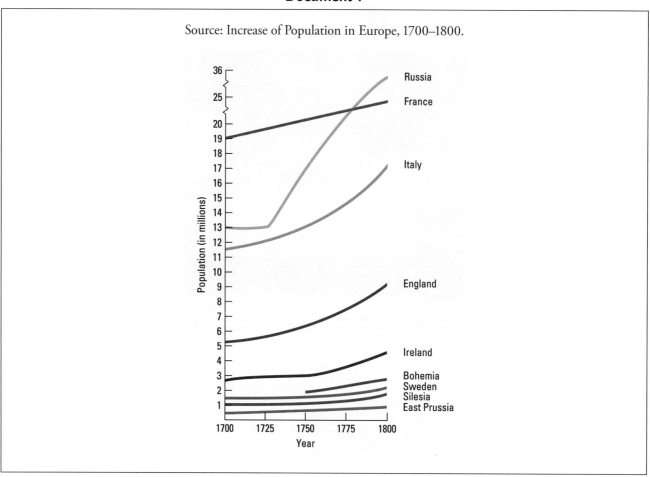

Source: Increase of Population in Europe, 1700–1800.

Document 2

Source: Adam Smith, Scottish philosopher, *An Inquiry into the Nature and Causes of the Wealth of Nations*, 1776.

[Every individual generally] neither intends to promote the public interest, nor knows how much he is promoting it. . . . He is in this case, as in many cases, led by an invisible hand to promote an end which was no part of his intention. Nor is it always worse for the society that it was not part of it. I have never known much good done by those who affected to trade for the public good.

Document 3

Source: Inquiry of English Parliament, from *Parliamentary Papers*, 1842.

West Riding of Yorkshire: Southern Part—In many of the collieries [coal mines] in this district, as far as relates to the underground employment, there is no distinction of sex, but the labour is distributed indifferently among both sexes, except that it is comparatively rare for the women to hew or get the coals, although there are numerous instances in which they regularly perform even this work. In great numbers of the coalpits in this district the men work in a state of perfect nakedness and are in this state assisted in the labour by females of all ages, from girls of six years old to women of twenty-one, these females being themselves quite naked down to the waist.

Document 4

Source: Anonymous, *Observations . . . on the Loss of Woollen Spinning*, 1794.

But from the establishment of the Spinning Machines in many countries where I was last Summer, no Hand Work could be had, the consequence of which is the whole maintenance of the family devolves on the father, and instead of six or seven shillings a week, which a wife and four children could add by their [spinning] wheels, *his* weekly pay is *all* they have to depend. . . . Shut up from morning till night, except when they are sent home for their meals, these girls [of 14 or so] are ignorant of, and unhandy at every domestic employment, whereas if at her wheel in her mother's cottage, the girl assists in every occupation of the family.

Document 5

Source: Testimony Before the Sadler Commission, British Parliament, 1832.

Elizabeth Bentley—a doffer (child whose job it was to clean the machines used in textile manufacturing)

Q: *What time did you begin to work at a factory?*
A: When I was six years old.

Q: *What were your hours of labor in that mill?*
A: From 5 in the morning till 9 at night, when they were thronged [busy].

Q: *Do you consider doffing a laborious employment?*
A: Yes.

Q: *Explain what you had to do.*
A: When the frames are full, they have to stop the frames, and take the flyers off, and take the full bobbins off, and carry them to the roller; and then put empty ones on, and set the frames on again.

Q: *Were they in the habit of strapping [beating with a strap] those who are last in doffing? Constantly? Girls as well as boys? Severely?*
A: Yes [to all].

Q: *Were you generally there on time?*
A: Yes, my mother has been up at 4 o'clock in the morning and at 2 o'clock in the morning. . . . I have sometimes been at Huslet Car at 2 o'clock in the morning, when it was streaming down with rain, and we had to stay till the mill was open.

Document 6

Source: "The Clothier's Delight," or "The Rich Men's Joy and the Poor Men's Sorrow," English popular song, ca. 1700.

We heapeth up riches and treasure great store
Which we get by griping and grinding the poor.
And this is a way for to fill up our purse
Although we do get it with many a curse.

Document 7

Source: Citizen John Aikin's observations concerning the growth of Manchester, England, 1795.

The prodigious extension of the several branches of the Manchester manufactures has likewise greatly increased the business of several trades and manufactures connected with or dependent upon them. The making of paper at mills in the vicinity has been brought to great perfection, and now includes all kinds. . . . Within the last twenty or thirty years the vast increase of foreign trade has caused many of the Manchester manufactures to travel abroad, and agents or partners to be fixed for a considerable time on the continent, as well as foreigners to reside at Manchester. And the town has now in every respect assumed the style and manners of one of the commercial capitals of Europe.

Document 8

Source: Robert Malthus, political economist, *Essay on the Principle of Population*, 1798.

Assuming, then, my postulate as granted, I say, the power of population is indefinitely greater than the power in the earth to produce subsistence for man. Population, when unchecked, increases in a geometrical ratio. Subsistence only increases in an arithmetical ratio. A slight acquaintance with numbers will show the immensity of the first power in comparison of the second. By that law of our nature which makes food necessary to the life of man, the effects of these two unequal powers must be kept equal. This implies a strong and constantly operating check on population from the difficulty of subsistence. This difficulty must fall somewhere; and must necessarily be severely felt by a large portion of mankind.

Document 9

Source: Robert Owen, English cotton manufacturer and social reformer,
Observations on the Effect of the Manufacturing System, 1815.

The employer regards the employed as mere instruments of gain, while these acquire a gross ferocity of character, which, legislative measures shall not be judiciously devised to prevent its increase, and ameliorate [improve] the condition of this class, will sooner or later plunge the country into a formidable and perhaps inextricable state of danger.

Document 10

Source: Richard Cobden, British member of Parliament, *A Denunciation of the Corn Laws*, 1838.

With all sincerity I declare that I am for the total repeal of those taxes which affect the price of bread and provisions of every description, and I will not allow it to be said without denying it that the three millions of people who have petitioned the House for the total repeal of those taxes are not sincere in their prayer. What are those taxes upon food? They are taxes levied on the great body of the people, and the honorable gentlemen opposite, who show such sympathy for the working classes after they have made them paupers, cannot deny my right to claim on their behalf that those taxes should be a primary consideration.

DBQ 8
Eighteenth-Century Medical Practices

Identify and analyze various practices used in the eighteenth century to care for the sick.

<u>Historical Background</u>: Although sickness, pain, and disease—intractable challenges built into the human condition—permeated the European experience in the eighteenth century, medical science played a very small part in improving the health of most people. Yet the Enlightenment's growing focus on discovering the laws of nature and on human problems did give rise to a great deal of research and experimentation.

Document 1

Source: Nicholas Culpeper, English "gentleman student in Physick and Astrology," *A Directory for Midwives*, 1716.

What insufferable injury it is that men and women should be trained up in such ignorance, that when they are sick and have herbs in their gardens conducing to their cure, they are so hoodwinked, that they know not their virtues. Is not this to uphold a company of lazy doctors, most of whose covetousness outweighs their wits as much as a millstone outweighs a feather? How they will answer for it another day, God knows, I pity their conditions.

Document 2

Source: Hendrik van Deventer, *The Art of Midwifery Improved*, English translation published 1716.

If you make safe of them [the rules of midwifery] you will find your work easy, and you need not call for the help of a *man midwife*, which is a disparagement not only to yourself but also to your profession. And let me tell you this (and I'll tell you but the truth) to your knowledge care and skill committed both the being and well-being of women in labour.

Document 3

Source: Lady Wortley Montagu, English writer, in a letter sent from Constantinople, April 1, 1717.

The smallpox, so fatal and so general amongst us [British], is here [made] entirely harmless by the invention of ingrafting. . . . Every year thousands undergo this operation. . . . There is no example of anyone that had died of it. You may believe that I am very well satisfied of the safety of the experiment, since I intend to try it on my dear little son.

Document 4

Source: John Wesley, founder of the Methodist Church, describes a mystical emotional conversion in his journal, 1738.

In the evening I went to a [Christian] society in Aldersgate Street where one was reading Luther's preface to the Epistle to the Romans. About a quarter before nine, while he was describing the change which God works in the heart through faith in Christ, I felt my heart strangely warmed. I felt I did trust in Christ, Christ alone for salvation; and an assurance was given me that he had taken away my sins, even mine, and saved me from the law of sin and death.

Document 5

Source: John Atkins, English surgeon, *The Navy Surgeon; or, a Practical System of Surgery*, 1742.

As medicine has increased with vice and navigation, so together with gun-powder, ambition, and bad politics, men are helped to more broken bones than formerly, and enlarged the surgeons' practice; a branch that has the preference of others, either in respect to antiquity, reputation, or usefulness.

Document 6

Source: Académie Royale de Chirurgie, *Memoirs of the Royal Academy of Surgery, at Paris*, 1750.

The Ancients [Greeks and Romans] were of the opinion, that the choice of particular parts of bleeding was not an indifferent matter. According to their notions, the opening of certain veins and arteries in those parts which lay near each other, and, what is still more surprising, even in the same parts, was dignified with the title of *Specific Remedies* for very difficult diseases. These absurd prejudices were notwithstanding founded upon observations; and a course of two thousand years was not sufficient to make the closest observers change their opinions in this respect; so that the diseased gave up their blood and their lives to the caprice of physicians and surgeons, upon the credit of the most unequivocal observations.

Document 7

Source: William Buchan, Edinburgh physician, *Domestic Medicine*, 1769.

Should all other means of comfort fail, the Christian religion affords an inexhaustible source of consolation. It teaches us, that the sufferings of this life are designed to prepare us for a future state of happiness; and that all who pursue the paths of virtue shall at last arrive at complete felicity [happiness].

Document 8

Source: Denis Diderot, French philosopher, *Encyclopedia*, excerpt concerning the French hospital Hôtel-Dieu, Paris, 1770.

Imagine a long series of communicating wards filled with sufferers of every kind of disease who are sometimes packed three, four, five or even six into a bed, the living alongside the dead and dying, the air polluted by this mass of unhealthy bodies, passing pestilential germs of their afflictions from one to the other, and the spectacle of suffering and agony on every hand. That is the Hôtel-Dieu.

Document 9

Source: Edward Jenner, English physician, *An Inquiry into the Causes and Effects of the Variolae Vaccinae*, 1798.

Case III.—John Phillips, a tradesman of this town, had the cowpox at so early a period as nine years of age. At the age of sixty-two I inoculated him, and was very careful in selecting matter in its most active state. It was taken from the arm of a boy just before the commencement of the eruptive fever, and instantly inserted. It very speedily produced a sting-like feel in the part. An efflorescence appeared, which on the fourth day was rather extensive, and some degree of pain and stiffness were felt about the shoulder: but on the fifth day these symptoms began to disappear, and in a day or two after went entirely off, without producing any effect on the system.

Document 10

Source: Eighteenth-century French illustration of "trepanation," a form of surgery in which a hole is drilled into the skull in order to treat intracranial diseases.

The Wellcome Trust Medical Photographic Library.

DBQ 9
The French Revolution

Describe and analyze how the ideas and objectives of the men and women who participated in the French Revolution changed over time.

<u>Historical Background</u>: In 1789 the National Assembly formed during Louis XVI's Estates General and spurred to action the aggrieved third estate of Paris, who literally stormed the Bastille and rose in revolution against a king floundering in debt. The Assembly abolished the French nobility, shook up the guild system, overhauled political boundaries, and established a national church. The revolution rippled outward geographically and socially, extending to the French peasantry and the women of Paris, with both positive and negative results, and inspired multiple revolts abroad.

Document 1

Source: Petition from the Women of the Third Estate, January 1789.

We ask to be enlightened, to have work, not in order to usurp men's authority, but in order to be better esteemed by them, so that we might have the means of living out of the way of misfortune. . . .

We implore you, Sire, to set up free schools where we could learn our language. . . .

We ask to be able to come out of the state of ignorance, to be able to give our children a sound and reasonable education so as to make of them subjects worthy of serving you.

Document 2

Source: M. Dufourny de Villiers, French revolutionary pamphlet: "Cahier of the Fourth Order [Estate] of the poor, the infirm, the indigent, etc., the Sacred Order of the Unfortunates: . . . To make up for the right to directly elect [representatives to] the Estates which appertains to all of France, but which this Order does not enjoy," Paris, April 1789.

Reason dictates that, contrary to the [current] configuration of the Orders [Estates] . . . the true Orders should be these: the poor; those who have only the necessities; the well-off; the rich; the opulent; the bloated. Now, according to this classification, the poor, far from paying, will have the right to receive assistance; those who have only necessities will neither pay nor receive, because only indigents will receive and because only those with excess will pay and those with real needs don't come close to having excess; if the well-off must pay a twentieth, the rich must pay two and half times [more than the twentieth], the opulent six [times that], the bloated ten [times that].

Document 3

Source: Preamble to the *Declaration of the Rights of Man*, August 1789.

The representatives of the French people, organized as a National Assembly, believing that the ignorance, neglect, or contempt of the rights of man are the sole causes of public calamities and of the corruption of governments, have determined to set forth in a solemn declaration the natural, inalienable, and sacred rights of man, . . . in order that the grievances of the citizens, based hereafter upon simple and incontestable principles, shall tend to the maintenance of the constitution and redound to the happiness of all.

Document 4

Source: Olympe de Gouges, *Declaration of the Rights of Woman and the Female Citizen*, September 1791.

Mothers, daughters, sisters, [and] representatives of the nation demand to be constituted into a national assembly. Believing that ignorance, omission, or scorn for the rights of woman are the only causes of public misfortunes and of the corruption of governments, [the women] have resolved to set forth in a solemn declaration the natural, inalienable, and sacred rights of woman, . . . in order that citizens' demands, henceforth based on simple and incontestable principles, will always support the constitution, good morals, and the happiness of all.

Document 5

Source: National Convention, Presiding Session of 9 Brumaire, November 1793.

Several . . . self-proclaimed Revolutionary Women may have been led astray by an excess of patriotism, but others, doubtless, were motivated only by malevolence. . . .

The Section of Marches . . . requests . . . that popular societies of women be strictly prohibited, at least during the revolution. . . .

To govern is to rule the commonwealth by laws, the preparation of which demands extensive knowledge, unlimited attention and devotion, a strict immovability, and self-abnegation. . . . Are women capable of these cares and of the qualities they call for? In general, we can answer, no. . . .

We believe, therefore, that a woman should not leave her family to meddle in affairs of government. . . .

[I]t is not possible for women to exercise political rights.

Document 6

Source: Pierre Antoine Le Sueur, *The Planting of a Liberty Tree*, 1792.

Document 7

Source: Proclamation of the National Convention to the French People
following the execution of King Louis XVI, January 1793.

Now, above all, we need peace in the interior of the French Republic, and the most active surveillance of the domestic enemies of liberty. Never did circumstances more urgently require of all citizens the sacrifice of their passions and their personal opinions concerning the act of national justice which has just been effected. Today the French people can have no other passion than that for liberty.

Document 8

Source: Speech by revolutionary Maximilien Robespierre, February 1794.

The French are the first people in the world who have established true democracy by calling all men to equality and to full enjoyment of the rights of citizenship. . . . Since virtue [good citizenship] and equality are the soul of the republic . . . it follows that the first rule of your political conduct must be to relate all of your measures to the maintenance of equality and to the development of virtue. . . . That which is immoral is impolitic, and that which tends to corrupt is counter-revolutionary. Weakness, vices, and prejudices are the road to monarchy. . . . It is necessary to annihilate both the internal and external enemies of the republic or perish with its fall.

Document 9

Source: Durand de Maillane, politician, description of the execution of Robespierre, July 1794.

Robespierre's turn had come at last. . . . He dictated decrees and directed the administration. Nothing was done except by his orders or with his approval. His caprices were flattered, and his very manias were praised. . . . His power seemed too terrible to his accomplices as it did to his victims. A number had been sacrificed already and others feared the same fate. They banded together to pull down the idol they themselves had set up.

Document 10

Source: Excerpts from Napoleon Bonaparte's speech to his troops, April 1796.

Soldiers of liberty, only republican phalanxes [infantry troops] could have endured what you have endured. . . . The grateful Patrie [nation] will owe its prosperity to you. . . . All of you are consumed with a desire to extend the glory of the French people; all of you long to humiliate those arrogant kings who dare to contemplate placing us in fetters; all of you desire to dictate a glorious peace, one which will indemnify [compensate] the Patrie for the immense sacrifices it has made; all of you wish to be able to say with pride as you turn to your villages: "I was with the victorious army of Italy!"

Document 11

Source: Napoleon Bonaparte describes the coup d'état of Brumaire, in which he seized power in France, November 1799.

On my return to Paris [from Egypt] I found division among all authorities, and agreement upon only one point, namely, that the Constitution was half destroyed and was unable to save liberty.

All parties came to me, confided to me their designs, disclosed their secrets, and requested my support; I refused to be the man of a party.

A plan of general restoration had been devised by men whom the nation has been accustomed to regard as the defenders of liberty, equality, and property; this plan required an examination, calm, free, exempt from all influence and all fear.

I presented myself at the Council of Five Hundred, alone, unarmed, my head uncovered, just as the Elders had received and applauded me; I came to remind the majority of its wishes, and to assure it of its power.

DBQ 10
Women in the Industrial Revolution

Discuss how the profound social changes introduced by the Industrial Revolution affected women working in the factories. To what extent did women's experiences reflect continuities with traditional working-class ways of life?

Historical Background: The Industrial Revolution began in Great Britain in the 1780s and created a rapid domino effect that forever changed the face of industry, from agricultural production, to textile manufacture, to the ever-faster methods by which goods and people were able to be moved. The resulting changes in the nature of work had a direct impact on families, and on women in particular. As industrialized nations became wealthier, women's roles in the family and the workforce were increasingly stratified.

Document 1

Source: Land register in the Silesian Village of Zedlitz, 1790.

The eighteen households . . . are obliged to send as workers every day two people, that is the husband and also the wife . . . to do whatever work is necessary. . . . The fieldworkers begin harvest at sunrise, stop from 6:30 to 7 for a half-hour breakfast, work again until 10, when they eat for an hour in the fields, and then work from 11 until 2. They eat an evening meal from 2 to 3, then they work again without stopping until sunset. The wives of the fieldworkers begin work once they have taken care of the herds, work with the men and maids until 6:30, and then go from the fields back to the house to prepare the meal, which they bring to the men and maids in the fields at 10:00. They eat until 11, and then stay working in the fields until evening, although they do the same things between 2 and 3 with the evening meal.

Document 2

Source: Mrs. Britton of Wiltshire, England, agricultural worker's wife and former factory worker, from her testimony to the British Parliament, ca. 1833.

I went to school till I was eight years old. . . . At ten years old I went to work at a factory, where I was till I was 26. . . . I have seven children, all boys. . . . I have worked in the fields, and when I went out I left the children in the care of the eldest boy, and frequently carried the baby with me as I could not go home to nurse it. I have worked at hay-making and at harvest, and at other times in weeding and keeping the ground clean. I generally work from half-past seven till five, or half past. When at work in the spring, I have received 10*d.* [pence] a day, that is higher than the wages of women in general; . . . I never felt that my health was hurt by the work. Hay-making is hard work, very fatiguing, but it never hurt me. Working in the fields is not such hard work as working in the factory. I am always better when I can get out to work in the fields.

Document 3

Source: Testimony of Matthew Crabtree, a worker in a blanket mill, from the Sadler Commission, British Parliament, *Report on Child Labor*, 1832.

Q: *Do you find that the children, the females especially, are very early demoralized in them [the mills]?*
A: They are.

Q: *Is their language indecent?*
A: Very indecent, and both sexes take great familiarities with each other in the mills, without at all being ashamed of their conduct.

Q: *Do you connect their immorality of language and conduct with their excessive labor?*
A: It may be somewhat connected with it, for it is to be observed that most of that goes on towards night, when they begin to be drowsy, it is a kind of stimulus which they use to keep them awake; they say some pert thing or other to keep themselves from drowsiness, and it generally happens to be some obscene language.

Q: *Have not a considerable number of the females employed in mills illegitimate children very early in life?*
A: I believe there are; I have known some of them have illegitimate children when they were between 16 and 17 years of age.

Q: *How many of [the grown-up] females had illegitimate children?*
A: A great many of them. . . .

Q: *Did they generally marry the men by whom they had the children?*
A: No, it sometimes happens that young women have children by married men.

Document 4

Source: 1833 engraving of women operating power looms in a large English cotton mill.

Time Life Pictures/Getty Images.

Document 5

Source: Friedrich Engels, German communist, *The Conditions of the Working Class in England in 1844*.

The employment of women at once breaks up the family; for when the wife spends twelve or thirteen hours every day in the mill, and the husband works the same length of time there or elsewhere, what becomes of the children? Women often return to the mill three or four days after confinement [for childbirth], leaving the baby, of course; in the dinner hour they must hurry home to feed the child and eat something.

Document 6

Source: Testimony of Patience Kershaw, age seventeen, gathered by Ashley's Mines Commission, *Parliamentary Papers*, 1842.

I never went to day-school; I go to Sunday-school, but I cannot read or write; I go to pit at five o'clock in the morning and come out at five in the evening; I get my breakfast of porridge and milk first; I take my dinner with me, a cake, and eat it as I go; I do not stop or rest any time for the purpose; I get nothing else until I get home, and then have potatoes and meat, not every day meat. I hurry in the clothes I have now got on, trousers and ragged jacket; the bald place upon my head is made by thrusting the corves [wagons used to transport coal]; my legs have never swelled, but sisters' did when they went to mill; I hurry the corves a mile and more under ground and back; . . . I hurry 11 a-day; I wear a belt and chain at the workings, to get the corves out; sometimes [the coal-getters] beat me, if I am not quick enough, with their hands; they strike me upon my back.

Document 7

Source: Benjamin Disraeli, British novelist and Tory politician, from the novel *Sybil, or the Two Nations*, 1845.

They come forth: the mine delivers its gang and the pit its bondsmen; the forge is silent and the engine is still. The plain is covered with the swarming multitude: bands of stalwart men, . . . troops of youth, alas! Of both sexes, though neither their raiment [clothing] nor their language indicates the difference; all are clad in male attire. . . . Yet these are to be, some are, the mothers of England!

Document 8

Source: Jean-Francois Millet, *The Gleaners*, 1857.

Réunion des Musées Nationaux/Art Resource, NY.

Document 9

Source: Annie Besant, "White Slavery in London," article describing women working in a match factory, 1888.

The hour for commencing work is 6:30 in summer and 8 in winter, work concludes at 6 P.M. . . . the long day of work is performed by young girls, who have to stand the whole of the time. A typical case is that of a girl of 16, a piece-worker who earns 4s. [shillings] a week and lives with her sister, employed by the same firm, who "earns good money, as much as 8s. or 9s. per week."

Out of the earnings 2s. is paid for the rent of one room; the child lives on only bread-and-butter and tea, alike for breakfast and dinner. . . . The splendid salary of 4s. is subject to deductions in the shape of fines; if the feet are dirty, or the ground under the bench is left untidy, a fine of 3d. [pence] is inflicted; for putting "burnts"—matches that have caught fire during the work—on the bench 1s. has been forfeited. . . . Day work is a little better aid than piecework, and is done chiefly by married women, who earn as much sometimes as 10s. a week. . . . Such is a bald account of one form of white slavery as it exists in London. With chattel slaves, Mr. Bryant could not have made his huge fortune, for he could not have fed, clothed, and housed them for 4s. a week each.

Document 10

Source: Journalist's report on the working conditions of female textile workers in Germany in the 1880s and 1890s.

[T]he dust is breathed in by the girls, since they are not allowed to open the windows. To this has to be added the terrible nerve-racking noise of the rattling machines so that no one can hear himself speak. . . . In consequence all the girls have screeching, irritating voices even when the shop has gone quiet. . . .

Many girls work happily, particularly those weaving small carpets or curtains woven as one piece who can observe the building up of the pattern. They love their machines like loving a faithful dog; they polish them, and tie colored ribbons. . . .

The girls work hard, very hard. . . . I could not have stood this for long. No one would dream of stopping work and taking a rest even when suffering from violent headache or toothache, not even a quarter of an hour of being late was tolerated without a substantial fine. . . .

The work of the carpet weavers should not be underrated, it is anything but monotonous or repetitive. . . .

She [the weaver] has to think and coordinate, calculate and pay attention and concentrate all her thought.

DBQ 11
The Romantic Movement

Analyze the characteristics of the romantic movement.

<u>Historical Background</u>: Romanticism swept the literary and artistic scenes of Europe starting around 1750. Considered a response, both conscious and subliminal, to the Enlightenment emphasis on rationality, order, and restraint, the romantic movement encompassed the works of famously emotive and individualistic poets, artists, and musicians.

Document 1

Source: Friedrich Schiller, German author and philosopher (1759–1805), quotations from his letters and the play *Wilhelm Tell*, concerning a Swiss folk hero.

Nothing leads to good that is not natural.

It does not prove a thing to be right because the majority say it is so.

[The character Wilhelm Tell]: The strong man still is strongest, when *alone*.

Document 2

Source: Johann von Herder, German philosopher, *Materials for the Philosophy of the History of Mankind*, 1784.

No greater injury can be inflicted on a nation than to be robbed of her national character, the peculiarity of her spirit and her language. Reflect on this and you will perceive our irreparable loss. Look about you in Germany for the character of the nation, for their own particular cast of thought, for their own peculiar vein of speech; where are they? Read Tacitus; there you will find their character: "The tribes of Germany, who never degrade themselves by mingling with others, form a peculiar, unadulterated, original nation, which is its own archetype. Even their physical development is universally uniform, despite the large numbers of the people," and so forth. Now look about you and say: "The tribes of Germany have been degraded by mingling with others; they have sacrificed their natural disposition in protracted intellectual servitude; and, since they have, in contrast to others, imitated a tyrannical prototype for a long time, they are, among all the nations of Europe, the least true to themselves."

Document 3

Source: Edmund Burke, English statesman, *Reflections on the French Revolution*, 1790.

Instead of destroying the old state the French should have built on the foundation their ancestors had left them. . . .

You [the French] would have had a free constitution, a potent monarchy, a disciplined army, a reformed and venerated clergy, a mitigated but spirited nobility to lead your virtue, not to overlay it; you would have had a liberal order of commons to emulate and to recruit that nobility; you would have had a protected, satisfied, laborious, and obedient people, taught to seek and to recognize the happiness that is to be found by virtue in all conditions; in which consists the true moral equality of mankind, and not in that monstrous fiction which, by inspiring false ideas and vain expectations into men destined to travel in the obscure walk of laborious life, serves only to aggravate and embitter that real inequality which it never can remove, and which the order of civil life establishes as much for the benefit of those whom it must leave in a humble state as those whom it is able to exalt to a condition more splendid, but not more happy.

Document 4

Source: Francisco de Goya, etching, *The Sleep of Reason Produces Monsters*, 1799.

Bibliothèque nationale de France/The Bridgeman Art Library.

Document 5

Source: On Beethoven's *Eroica (Heroic) Symphony* of 1803, from *Biographische Notizen über Beethoven (Biographical Notes about Beethoven)*, Franz Gerhard Wegeler and Ferdinand Ries, 1838.

In 1803 Beethoven composed his third symphony (now known as the *Sinfonia Eroica*) in Heiligenstadt, a village about one and a half hours from Vienna. . . . In writing this symphony Beethoven had been thinking of Bonaparte, but Bonaparte while he was First Consul. At that time Beethoven had the highest esteem for him and compared him to the greatest consuls of ancient Rome. Not only I, but many of Beethoven's closer friends, saw this symphony on his table, beautifully copied in manuscript, with the word "Bonaparte" inscribed at the very top of the title-page and "Luigi van Beethoven" at the very bottom. Whether or how the intervening gap was to be filled out I do not know. I was the first to tell him the news that Bonaparte had declared himself Emperor, whereupon he broke into a rage and exclaimed, "So he is no more than a common mortal! Now, he too will tread under foot all the rights of man, indulge only his ambition; now he will think himself superior to all men, become a tyrant!" Beethoven went to the table, seized the top of the title-page, tore it in half and threw it on the floor. The page was later re-copied and it was only now that the symphony received the title "Sinfonia *Eroica*."

Document 6

Source: Johann Wolfgang von Goethe, German writer, monologue from the play *Faust*, 1808.

> *Faust:* I've studied now Philosophy
> And Jurisprudence, Medicine,
> And even, alas! Theology
> All through and through with ardour keen!
> Here now I stand, poor fool, and see
> I'm just as wise as formerly.
> Am called a Master, even Doctor too,
> And now I've nearly ten years through
> Pulled my students by their noses to and fro
> And up and down, across, about,
> And see there's nothing we can know!
> That all but burns my heart right out.

Document 7

Source: William Wordsworth, English romantic poet, *Lines Composed a Few Miles Above Tintern Abbey*, 1816.

> Therefore am I still
> A lover of the meadows and the woods,
> And mountains; and of all that we behold
> From this green earth; of all the mighty world
> Of eye, and ear,—both what they half create,
> And what perceive; well pleased to recognise
> In nature and the language of the sense
> The anchor of my purest thoughts, the nurse,
> The guide, the guardian of my heart, and soul
> Of all my moral being.

Document 8

Source: Mary Wollstonecraft Shelley, British writer, on her conception of her novel *Frankenstein*, 1817.

I saw [dreamed] the pale student of unhallowed arts kneeling beside the thing he had put together. I saw the hideous phantasm of a man stretched out, and then, on the working of some powerful engine, show signs of life, and stir with an uneasy, half vital motion. Frightful must it be; for supremely frightful would be the effect of any human endeavour to mock the stupendous mechanism of the Creator of the world.

Document 9

Source: Caspar David Friedrich, *Cloister Cemetery in the Snow*, 1817–1819.

Bildarchiv Preussischer Kulturbesitz/Art Resource, NY.

Document 10

Source: J. M. W. Turner, *Rain, Steam and Speed — The Great Western Railway*, 1844.

National Gallery, London/The Bridgeman Art Library.

Document 11

Source: Charles Baudelaire, French author, "What Is Romanticism?," 1846.

Romanticism is precisely situated neither in choice of subjects nor in exact truth, but in a mode of feeling. . . . For me, Romanticism is the most recent, the latest expression of the beautiful. . . . To say the word Romanticism is to say modern art—that is, intimacy, spirituality, colour, aspiration towards the infinite, expressed by every means available to the arts.

DBQ 12
Science and Philosophy in the Nineteenth Century

To what extent did major changes in science and thought reflect the new urban society of the nineteenth century?

Historical Background: Inspired by the incredible technical advances of the Industrial Revolution, nineteenth-century scientists sought new scientific explanations and technologies, often in the name of social reform. Charles Lyell and Charles Darwin presented astonishing theories in geology and biology, respectively, just two of the many scientists who did ground-breaking work in this period; the new field of social science sprang forth from the increased availability of statistics. Each field of inquiry informed the others and had far-reaching applications in the new urban society of the nineteenth century.

Document 1

Source: Charles Lyell, British geologist, *Principles of Geology*, 1830.

A close comparison of the recent and fossil species, and the inferences drawn in regard to their habits, accustomed the geologist to contemplate the earth as having been at successive periods the dwelling place of animals and plants of different races, some of which were discovered to have been terrestrial and others aquatic—some fitted to live in seas, others in the waters of lakes and rivers. . . . Whether our investigation of the earth's history and structure will eventually be productive of as great practical benefits to mankind, as a knowledge of the distant heavens, must remain for the decision of posterity.

Document 2

Source: Karl Marx and Friedrich Engels, German philosophers and social scientists, *The Communist Manifesto*, 1848.

The history of all hitherto existing society is the history of class struggles. Freeman and slave, patrician and plebeian, lord and serf, guildmaster and journeyman, in a word, oppressor and oppressed, stood in constant opposition to one another, carried on an uninterrupted, now hidden, now open fight, a fight that each time ended, either in a revolution-ary reconstitution of society at large, or in the common ruin of the contending classes.

Document 3

Source: Professor Michael Faraday, "Observations on the Filth of the Thames," letter to the editor of *The Times* of London, July 7, 1855.

I traversed this day by steam-boat the space between London and Hangerford Bridges between half-past one and two o'clock; it was low water, and I think the tide must have been near the turn. The appearance and the smell of the water forced themselves at once on my attention. The whole of the river was an opaque pale brown fluid. In order to test the degree of opacity, I tore up some white cards into pieces, moistened them so as to make them sink easily below the surface, and then dropped some of these pieces into the water at every pier the boat came to; before they had sunk an inch below the surface they were indistinguishable, though the sun shone brightly at the time; and when the pieces fell edgeways the lower part was hidden from sight before the upper part was under water. . . . I have thought it a duty to record these facts, that they may be brought to the attention of those who exercise power or have responsibility in relation to the condition of our river; there is nothing figurative in the words I have employed, or any approach to exaggeration; they are the simple truth. If there be sufficient authority to remove a putrescent pond from the neighbourhood of a few simple dwellings, surely the river which flows for so many miles through London ought not to be allowed to become a fermenting sewer.

Document 4

Source: John Snow, M.D., *On the Mode of Communication of Cholera*, London, 1855.

Nothing has been found to favour the extension of cholera more than want of personal cleanliness, whether arising from habit or scarcity of water, although the circumstance till lately remained unexplained. The bed linen nearly always becomes wetted by the cholera evacuations, and as these are devoid of the usual colour and odour, the hands of persons waiting on the patient become soiled without their knowing it; and unless these persons are scrupulously cleanly in their habits, and wash their hands before taking food, they must accidentally swallow some of the excretion, and leave some on the food they handle or prepare, which has to be eaten by the rest of the family, who, amongst the working classes, often have to take their meals in the sick room: hence the thousands of instances in which, amongst this class of the population, a case of cholera in one member of the family is followed by other cases; whilst medical men and others, who merely visit the patients, generally escape.

Document 5

Source: Charles Darwin, English naturalist, *On the Origin of Species*, 1859.

As natural selection acts solely by accumulating slight, successive, favorable variations, it can produce no great or sudden modifications; it can act only by short and slow steps. . . . As natural selection acts by competition, it adapts and improves the inhabitants of each country only in relation to their co-inhabitants; so that we need feel no surprise at the species of any one country, although on the ordinary view supposed to have been created and specially adapted for that country, being beaten and supplanted by the naturalized productions from another land.

Document 6

Source: A biography of Joseph Lister, English surgeon (1827–1912), from *Encyclopedia of World Biography*, 1997.

Lister's research centered on the microscopic changes in tissue that result in inflammation. When he read Pasteur's work on germs in 1864, Lister immediately applied Pasteur's thinking to the problem he was investigating. He concluded that inflammation was the result of germs entering and developing in the wound. Since Pasteur's solution of killing germs with heat could not be applied to the living body, Lister decided to try a chemical to destroy the germs.

That same year Lister read in the newspaper that the treatment of sewage (liquid waste matter from sewers) with a chemical called carbolic acid had led to a reduction of diseases among the people of Carlisle, England, and among the cattle grazing on sewage-treated fields. In 1865 he developed a successful method of applying carbolic acid to wounds.

Document 7

Source: German socialist labor leaders of the Gotha Program, at a meeting of a labor congress in Gotha, Germany, 1875.

Labor is the source of all wealth, and of all civilization; and since it is only through society that generally productive labor is possible, the whole product of labor, where there is a general obligation to work, belongs to society,—that is, to all its members, by equal right, to each according to his reasonable needs.

The emancipation of labor requires the conversion of the means of production into the common property of society and the social regulation of all labor and its application for the general good, together with the just distribution of the product of labor. . . .

2. Proceeding from these principles, the socialist labor party of Germany endeavors by every lawful means to bring about a free state and a socialistic society, to effect the destruction of the iron law of wages by doing away with the system of wage labor, to abolish exploitation of every kind, and to extinguish all social and political inequality.

Document 8

Source: Artist unknown, etching of *The Clearing of Saint Germain Boulevard in Paris During Haussmann's Work in 1887.*

Apic/Hulton Archive/Getty Images.

Document 9

Source: Dmitri Ivanovich Mendeleev, Russian chemist, "The Periodic Law of the Chemical Elements," lecture before the Fellows of the Chemical Society in the Theatre of the Royal Institution, England, 1889.

The periodic law of the elements is only 20 years old: it is not surprising therefore that, knowing nothing about the causes of gravitation and mass, or about the nature of the elements, we do not comprehend the *rationale* of the periodic law. It is only by collecting established laws, that is by working at the acquirement of truth, that we can hope gradually to lift the veil which conceals from us the causes of the mysteries of Nature and to discover their mutual dependency. Like the telescope and the microscope, laws founded on the basis of experiment are the instruments and means of enlarging our mental horizon.

Document 10

Source: Pope Leo XIII, encyclical (letter to bishops) on capital and labor, issued May 15, 1891.

There is general agreement, that some opportune remedy must be found quickly for the misery and wretchedness pressing so unjustly on the majority of the working class. . . . [T]he hiring of labor and the conduct of trade are concentrated in the hands of comparatively few; so that a small number of very rich men have been able to lay upon the teeming masses of the laboring poor a yoke little better than that of slavery itself. To remedy these wrongs the socialists, working on the poor man's envy of the rich, are striving to do away with private property, and contend that individual possessions should become the common property of all, to be administered by the State or by municipal bodies. They hold that by thus transferring property from private individuals to the community, the present mischievous state of things will be set to rights, inasmuch as each citizen will then get his fair share of whatever there is to enjoy. But their contentions are so clearly powerless to end the controversy that were they carried into effect the working man himself would be among the first to suffer. They are, moreover, emphatically unjust, for they would rob the lawful possessor, distort the functions of the State, and create utter confusion in the community.

Document 11

Source: Continental Industrialization, ca. 1850.

DBQ 13
The Growth of Nationalism

Analyze the growth of nationalism in Europe from 1850 to 1914.

Historical Background: A powerful force since the French Revolution, the concept of nationalism made few inroads politically, failing most spectacularly during the nationalistic revolutions of 1848 in France, Austria, and Prussia. But after 1850 European society became increasingly nationalistic, and by 1914 nationalism had become the dominant faith in Europe and the United States. By translating cultural unity into a political identity, nationalists empowered citizens with a greater sense of belonging, whereas before they had been fragmented by social strata, war, and other internal divisions.

Document 1

Source: Proclamation of the Second French Republic, 1848.

Citizens: royalty, under whatever form, is abolished; no more legitimism, no more Bonapartism, no regency. The provisional government has taken all the measures necessary to render impossible the return of the former dynasty or the advent of a new dynasty. The republic is proclaimed. The people are united. . . . Let us show that this symbol of equality, of liberty, and of fraternity is at the same time the symbol of order—of order the more real, the more durable, since justice is its foundation and the whole people its instrument. . . . Let this example be imitated everywhere.

Document 2

Source: Artist unknown, *Märzrevolution* painting depicting a Berlin uprising, March 1848.

akg-images.

Document 3

Source: Italian patriot Giuseppe Mazzini on nationality, from his essay "Europe: Its Condition and Prospects," 1852.

The nationality . . . founded upon the following principle: — *Whichever people, by its superiority of strength, and by its geographical position, can do us an injury, is our natural enemy; whichever cannot do us an injury, but can by the amount of its force and by its position injure our enemy, is our natural ally,* — is the princely nationality of aristocracies or royal races. The nationality of the peoples has not these dangers; it can only be founded by a common effort and a common movement; sympathy and alliance will be its result. In principle, as in the ideas formerly laid down by the men influencing every national party, nationality ought only to be to humanity that which the division of labour is in a workshop — the recognised symbol of association; the assertion of the individuality of a human group called by its geographical position, its traditions, and its language, to fulfil a special function in the European work of civilisation.

Document 4

Source: Louis Kossuth, Hungarian politician and revolutionary hero, speech delivered at a dinner given in his honor by the U.S. Congress, 1852.

This is my confident hope. Then will at once subside the fluctuations of Germany's fate. It will become the heart of Europe; not by melting North Germany into a Southern frame, or the South into a Northern; not by absorbing historical peculiarities by centralized omnipotence; not by mixing in one State, but by federating several sovereign States into a Union like yours. Upon a similar basis will take place the national regeneration of the Slavonic States, and not upon the sacrilegious idea of Panslavism, equivalent to the omnipotence of the Czar. [Applause.] Upon a similar basis will we see fair Italy independent and free. Not unity, but union will and must become the watchword of national bodies, severed into desecrated limbs to provincial rivalries, out of which a flock of despots and common servitude arose. To be sure, it will be a noble joy to this your great Republic, to feel that the moral influence of your glorious example has operated this happy development in mankind's destiny, and I have not the slightest doubt of the efficacy of your example's influence.

Document 5

Source: Charles Darwin, English naturalist, *On the Origin of Species*, 1859.

Although much remains obscure, and will long remain obscure, I can entertain no doubt . . . that the view which most naturalists until recently entertained . . . namely, that each species has been independently created — is erroneous. I am fully convinced that species are not immutable; but that those belonging to what are called the same genera are lineal descendents of some other and generally extinct species. . . . Furthermore, I am convinced that Natural Selection has been the most important, but not the exclusive, means of modification.

Document 6

Source: Austrian Constitution, 1867.

Article 1. For all natives of the various kingdoms and countries represented in the Reichsrat there exists a common right of Austrian citizenship. The law shall determine under what conditions Austrian citizenship is gained, exercised, and lost.

Article 2. All citizens are equal before the law.

Article 3. Public offices shall be equally open to all citizens. The admission of foreigners to public office is dependent upon their acquisition of Austrian citizenship. . . .

Article 19. All the races of the state shall have equal rights, and each race shall have the inviolable right of maintaining and cultivating its nationality and language.

The state recognizes the equality of the various languages in the schools, public offices, and in public life. In the countries populated by several races, the institutions of public instruction shall be so organized that each race may receive the necessary instruction in its own language, without being obliged to learn a second language.

Document 7

Source: Robert Gascoyne-Cecil, British statesman, advocating that Europe reject the Treaty of San Stefano imposed by Russia on the Ottomans, from *The Salisbury Circular*, 1878.

The most important consequences to which the treaty practically leads are those which result from its action as a whole upon the nations of Southeastern Europe. By the articles erecting the new Bulgaria, a strong Slav state will be created under the auspices and control of Russia, possessing important harbours upon the shores of the Black Sea and the Archipelago, and conferring upon that Power a preponderating influence over both political and commercial relations in those seas. It will be so constituted as to merge in the dominant Slav majority a considerable mass of population which is Greek in race and sympathy, and which views with alarm the prospect of absorption in a community alien to it not only in nationality but in political tendency and in religious allegiance.

Document 8

Source: Jules Ferry, French statesman, "France Must Be a Great Country!," 1883.

I repeat that superior races have a right, because they have a duty. They have the duty to civilize inferior races. . . . [I]n Europe as it is today, in this competition of so many rivals which we see growing around us some by perfecting their military or maritime forces, others by the prodigious development of an ever growing population; in a Europe, or rather in a universe of this sort, a policy of peaceful seclusion or abstention is simply the highway to decadence! Nations are great in our times only by means of the activities which they develop; it is not simply by the peaceful shining forth of institutions *(Interruptions and laughter on the left and right)* that they are great at this hour.

Document 9

Source: Otto von Bismarck, German chancellor, "War and Armaments in Europe," address to the German Reichstag, 1888.

When I say that we must strive continually to be ready for all emergencies, I advance the proposition that, on account of our geographical position, we must make greater efforts than other powers would be obliged to make in view of the same ends. We lie in the middle of Europe. We have at least three fronts on which we can be attacked. France has only an eastern boundary; Russia only its western, exposed to assault. We are, moreover, more exposed than any other people to the danger of hostile coalition because of our geographical position, and because, perhaps, of the feeble power of cohesion which, until now, the German people has exhibited when compared with others.

Document 10

Source: Prince Ukhtomskii, "Russia's Imperial Destiny," 1891.

It is this sacred conviction which has given birth to the steadfast belief both of our rulers and of the ruled, that Russia is the source and center of an invincible might, which is but increased by the attacks of her foes. The East believes no less than we do, and exactly as we do, in the preternatural qualities of the Russian national spirit, but values and understands them just in the same measure as we treasure the most precious of our national traditions—autocracy. Without it, Asia would be incapable of sincere liking for Russia and of painless identification with her. Without it, Europe would find it mere child's-play to dismember and overpower us as thoroughly as she has overpowered and dismembered the Slavs of the West, now suffering a bitter fate. The question is: In whose name and by whose single will shall the heritage of Russia be ruled in the future?

Document 11

Source: Kaiser Wilhelm II, "Germany's Place in the Sun," 1901.

It will now be my task to see to it that this place in the sun shall remain our indisputed possession, in order that the sun's rays may fall fruitfully on our activity and trade in foreign ports, that our industry and agriculture may develop within the state and our sailing ports upon the water for our future lies upon the water. . . . For when the German has once learned to direct his glance upon what is distant and great, the pettiness which surrounds him in daily life on all sides will disappear.

DBQ 14
The West and the World

Identify and analyze the variety of responses that the colonized peoples advocated toward the European colonizers in the late nineteenth and early twentieth centuries.

Historical Background: Driven by the pressures of population, the trade economy, and a nationalistic quest for empire, Europeans set their sights on the natural resources of their neighboring continents. The colonized peoples of Asia and Africa responded to the often hostile invasions of their home countries with arguments ranging from cautious optimism to violent outrage.

Document 1

Source: Chinese imperial official Lin Zexu, in a letter to Queen Victoria, 1839.

They [British merchants] may not intend to harm others on purpose, but the fact remains that they are so obsessed with material gain that they have no concern whatever for the harm they can cause to others. Have they no conscience? I have heard you strictly prohibit opium in your own country, an indication unmistakably that you know how harmful opium is. You do not wish opium to harm your own country, but you choose to bring that harm to other countries such as China. Why? . . . Since a foreigner who goes to England to trade has to obey the English law, how can an Englishman not obey the Chinese law when he is physically present within China? The present law calls for the imposition of the death sentence on any Chinese who had peddled or smoked opium.

Document 2

Source: Statement from the people of Canton, China, 1842.

Behold that vile English nation! Its ruler is at one time a woman, then a man, and then perhaps a woman again; its people are at one time like vultures, and then they are like wild beasts, with dispositions more fierce and furious than the tiger or wolf, and natures more greedy than anacondas or swine. These people having long steadily devoured all the western barbarians, and like demons of the night, they now suddenly exalt themselves here.

Verily, the English barbarians murder all of us that they can. They are dogs, whose desires can never be satisfied. Therefore we need not inquire whether the peace they have now may be real or pretended. Let us all rise, arm, unite, and go against them.

We do here bind ourselves to vengeance, and express these, our sincere intentions in order to exhibit our high principles and patriotism. The gods from on high now look down upon us; let us not lose our just and firm resolution.

Document 3

Source: Dadabhai Naoroji, Indian politician, "The Benefits of British Rule," 1871.

The Benefits of British Rule for India: . . .

In the Cause of Civilization: Education, both male and female. . . . Resuscitation of India's own noble literature, modified and refined by the enlightenment of the West.

Politically: Peace and order. Freedom of speech and liberty of the press. Higher political knowledge and aspirations. . . . Security of life and property. . . .

Materially: Loans for railways and irrigation. Development of a few valuable products, such as indigo, tea, coffee, silk, etc. Increase of exports. Telegraphs.

Generally: A slowly growing desire of late to treat India equitably, and as a country held in trust. Good intentions. No nation on the face of the earth has ever had the opportunity of achieving such a glorious work as this. . . .

Our great misfortune is that you [the British] do not know our wants. When you will know our real wishes, I have not the least doubt that you would do justice. The genius and spirit of the British people is fair play and justice.

Document 4

Source: Requests of the Fanti people of Ghana to the British authorities, 1872.

1. [The Fanti Confederation] must have the recognition, . . . support, and hearty co-operation of Her Majesty's Government, and its friendly aid and advice. We do not for one single moment pretend to be able to carry on a Government in the interior without such recognition and assistance. . . .

4. That the courts of the Confederation be recognized as the courts of first instance in matters or disputes between its subjects. . . .

7. . . . [O]n considering the vast improvements to be made in the country, and the great extent of the Confederation . . . the vast efforts to be made to open up the country for traffic and other purposes, the want of good and substantial roads, the backwardness of education, and the immense efforts which will have to be made to spread civilization, and diffuse knowledge over the country inland, we find that the Confederation must have a revenue of some . . . 20,000 [British pounds].

Document 5

Source: Memorandum from the chiefs of Brass, a city-state on the Niger Delta, to the British Royal Niger Company, June 1895.

The Niger Company are cleverer than we are. We humbly submit that we have a right, confirmed by our Treaty, to go and trade freely in the places we have traded at for all these generations. We are ready to pay to do so, but let us pay a fair duty, and conform to fair Regulations.

Document 6

Source: Bal Gangadhar Tilak, leader in the Indian independence movement, address to the Indian National Congress, 1907.

We are not armed, and there is no necessity for arms either. We have a stronger weapon, a political weapon, in boycott. We have perceived one fact, that the whole of this administration, which is carried on by a handful of Englishmen, is carried on with our assistance. We are all in subordinate service. This whole government is carried on with our assistance and they try to keep us in ignorance of our power of cooperation between ourselves by which that which is in our own hands at present can be claimed by us and administered by us. The point is to have the entire control in our hands. I want to have the key of my house, and not merely one stranger turned out of it. Self-government is our goal; we want a control over our administrative machinery. We don't want to become clerks and remain [clerks]. . . . We shall not give them assistance to collect revenue and keep peace. We shall not assist them in fighting beyond the frontiers or outside India with Indian blood and money. We shall not assist them in carrying on the administration of justice. We shall have our own courts, and when time comes we shall not pay taxes.

Document 7

Source: Mohandas K. Gandhi (1869–1948), *Hind Swaraj*, or *Indian Home Rule*, 1908.

Many examples can be given in which acts of majorities will be found to have been wrong and those of minorities to have been right. All reforms owe their origins to the initiation of minorities in opposition to majorities. . . . So long as the superstition that men should obey unjust laws exists, so long will their slavery exist. . . .

Passive resistance is a method of securing rights by personal suffering; it is the reverse of resistance by arms. When I refuse to do a thing that is repugnant to my conscience, I use soul-force [*satyagraha*]. For instance, the government of the day has passed a law which is applicable to me: I do not like it; if, by using violence, I force the government to repeal the law I am employing what may be termed body-force. If I do not obey the law and accept the penalty for its breach, I use soul-force. It involves sacrifice of self.

Document 8

Source: "Leopold, King of the Congo," English cartoon, 1908.

H. M. Leopold, King of the Congo,
in his national dress.

Document 9

Source: "Announcement to the Arabs," manifesto of Arab nationalists printed in Arabic in Cairo, Egypt, 1914.

O sons of Quahtan [south Arabs]! Oh descendants of Adnan [north Arabs]! . . . When will you realize the truth? When will you know that your country has been sold to foreigners? See how your natural resources have been alienated from you and have come into the possession of England, France, and Germany. Have you no right to these resources? You have become humiliated slaves in the hands of the usurping tyrants; the foreigner unjustly dispossesses you of the fruit of your work and labor and leaves you to suffer the pangs of hunger. How long will it be before you understand that you have become the plaything in the hand of him who has no religion but to kill the Arabs and forcibly to seize their possessions?

Document 10

Source: A missionary school with portraits of Emperor Wilhelm II and his wife in Dar es Salaam, German East Africa, early twentieth century before 1914.

Ullstein Bilderdienst/The Granger Collection, New York.

World War I and the Home Front

Describe and analyze the effects of the Great War on the European home fronts during the course of the war.

Historical Background: The four years of "total war" that constituted World War I (1914–1918) changed the lives not only of those men who fought as soldiers, but of the people who remained at home. Women and other noncombatants tried to maintain structure within their everyday lives while grappling to understand their countries' positions and enduring their own mental and physical challenges. Stretching food and materials to provide both for the people at home and for the troops, citizens on the home front witnessed the devastation of war from a wholly unique perspective.

Document 1

Source: Employment of women in wartime British industry, 1914–1918. From *Report of the War Cabinet Committee on Women in British Industry*, London, 1919.

Trades	Est. Number Females Employed in July 1914	Est. Number Females Employed in July 1918	Difference Between Numbers of Females Employed in July 1914 and July 1918	Percentage of Females to Total Number People Employed — July 1914	Percentage of Females to Total Number People Employed — July 1918	Est. Number Females Directly Replacing Males in Jan. 1918
Metal	170,000	594,000	+424,000	9	25	195,000
Chemical	40,000	104,000	+64,000	20	39	35,000
Textile	863,000	827,000	–36,000	58	67	64,000
Clothing	612,000	568,000	–44,000	68	76	43,000
Food, drink, and tobacco	196,000	235,000	+39,000	35	49	60,000
Paper and printing	147,500	141,500	–6,000	36	48	21,000
Wood	44,000	79,000	+35,000	15	32	23,000
China and earthenware	32,000 }					
Leather	23,100 }	197,100	+93,000	4	10	62,000
Other	49,000 }					
Government establishments	2,000	225,000	+223,000	3	47	197,000
Total	2,178,600	2,970,600	+792,000	26	37	704,000

Document 2

Source: Stefan Zweig, Austrian writer, describing the reaction to the outbreak of the war in Vienna, from his 1941 autobiography.

There were parades in the street, flags, ribbons, and music burst forth everywhere, young recruits were marching triumphantly, their faces lighting up at the cheering. . . .

As never before, thousands and hundreds of thousands felt what they should have felt in peace time, that they belonged together. . . . All differences of class, rank, and language were flooded over at that moment by the rushing feeling of fraternity. Strangers spoke to one another on the streets, people who had avoided each other for years shook hands, everywhere one saw excited faces.

Document 3

Source: Bertrand Russell, British philosopher, *The Autobiography of Bertrand Russell, 1914–1944.*

The day war was declared . . . I spent the evening walking around the streets . . . noticing cheering crowds. . . . I discovered to my amazement that average men and women were delighted at the prospect of war.

Document 4

Source: Naomi Loughnan, British woman describing her work in a munitions plant during World War I, 1918.

Though we munition workers sacrifice our ease we gain a life worth living. Our long days are filled with interest, and with the zest of doing work for our country in the grand cause of Freedom. . . .

The day is long, the atmosphere is breathed and rebreathed, and the oil smells. Our hands are black with warm, thick oozings from the machines, which coat the work and, incidentally, the workers. We regard our horrible, begrimed members [limbs] with disgust and secret pride.

Document 5

Source: Minutes from a meeting of the Russian tsar's Council of Ministers, 1915.

The Council of Ministers knows that there were disturbances in Moscow which ended in bloodshed. . . . There were even more serious disorders at Ivanovo-Voznesensk when it was necessary to fire on the crowd with the result that sixteen were killed and thirty wounded.

You cannot quiet the whole of Russia by the police alone, especially now when the ranks of the police are being thinned out . . . hourly and the population is growing daily more excited by the speeches in the Duma, by newspaper stories, by continuous defeats, and rumors of disorder in the rear.

Document 6

Source: Anna Eisenmenger, *Blockade: Diary of an Austrian Middle-Class Woman, 1914–24*, 1932.

We housewives have during the last four years grown accustomed to standing in queues; we have also grown accustomed to being obliged to go home with empty hands and still emptier stomachs. Only very rarely do those who are sent away disappointed give cause for police intervention. On the other hand, it happens more and more frequently that one of the pale, tired women who have been waiting for hours collapses from exhaustion.

Document 7

Source: Rosa Luxemburg, German socialist, "The War and the Workers," 1916.

The scene has changed fundamentally. . . . Gone is the euphoria. Gone the patriotic noise in the streets, . . . the swaying crowds in the coffee shops with ear-deafening patriotic songs surging ever higher. . . .

The spectacle is over. . . . The trains full of reservists are no longer accompanied by virgins fainting from pure jubilation. They no longer greet the people from the windows of the train with joyous smiles. . . .

Business thrives in the ruins. Cities become piles of ruins; villages become cemeteries; countries [become] deserts; populations are beggared; churches [become] horse stalls. International law, treaties and alliances, the most sacred words and the highest authority have been torn in shreds. . . . There are food riots in Venice, in Lisbon, Moscow, Singapore. There is plague in Russia, and misery and despair everywhere.

Document 8

Source: Vladimir Ilyich Lenin, Russian revolutionary and communist leader, "The Call to Power," October 24, 1917.

It would be an infinite crime on the part of the revolutionaries were they to let the chance slip by, knowing that the *salvation of the revolution*, the offer of peace, the salvation of Petrograd, salvation from famine, the transfer of the land to the peasants depend on them.

The government is tottering. It must be *given the death-blow* at all costs.

To delay action is fatal.

Document 9

Source: Letter from the prefect (governor) of the department of Isère to France's minister of the interior, June 17, 1917.

I have the honour to reply herewithin to the questions contained in your confidential telegram circulated on 10 June: . . .

[The farmers] work, but they do not hide the fact that "it's been going on too long"; they are tired of their continuous over-exertion in the fields, of the lack of hands and of the very heavy burden of the requisitions. . . . In the towns . . . the workers, the ordinary people—are upset about the duration of the struggle, impatient with the increasing cost of living, irritated by the considerable profits being made out of the war by the big industrialists in their neighborhood, and increasingly taken in by the propagandists of the united Socialist Party and their internationalist ideas.

Document 10

Source: Food Production Department poster, London, ca. 1918.

DBQ 16
Age of Anxiety

Discuss how European culture after World War I challenged the assumptions of the prewar, nineteenth-century European culture.

Historical Background: The disillusionment that many felt in the wake of World War I manifested itself in new philosophies that emphasized the unconscious mind and the existentialist nature of the individual, and new artistic and literary styles that experimented with structure and chaos. These trends in intellectual thought were accompanied by equally unsettling advances in physics that postulated that the universe was infinite and composed of a subatomic world. While some sought understanding in the new sciences or a shared experience through art, others turned back to religion and faith for reassurance.

Document 1

Source: Oswald (Otto) Spengler, German historian and philosopher, from *The Decline of the West*, 1922.

The last century [the nineteenth] was the winter of the West, the victory of materialism and scepticism, of socialism, parliamentarianism, and money. But in this century [the twentieth] blood and instinct will regain their rights against the power of money and intellect. The era of individualism, liberalism and democracy, of humanitarianism and freedom, is nearing its end. The masses will accept with resignation the victory of the *Caesars*, the strong men, and will obey them. Life will descend to a level of general uniformity, a new kind of primitivism, and the world will be better for it. . . .

Document 2

Source: Pablo Picasso, Spanish artist, *Three Musicians*, 1921.

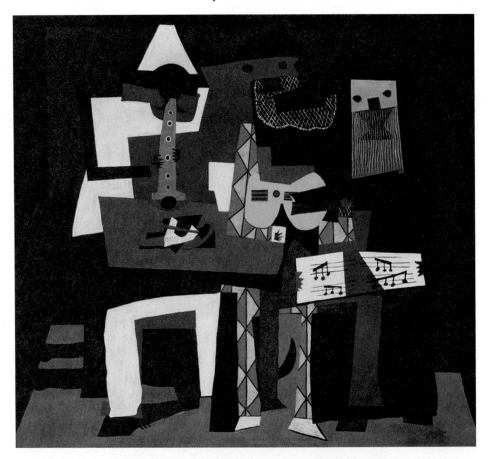

Document 3

Source: Sigmund Freud, Austrian neurologist and developer of psychoanalysis, *Civilization and Its Discontents*, 1930.

The element of truth behind all this, which people are so ready to disavow, is that men are not gentle creatures who want to be loved, and who at most can defend themselves if they are attacked; they are, on the contrary, creatures among whose instinctual endowments is to be reckoned a powerful share of aggressiveness. . . . In consequence of this primary mutual hostility of human beings, civilized society is perpetually threatened with disintegration. The interest of work in common would not hold it together; instinctual passions are stronger than reasonable interests.

Document 4

Source: William Butler Yeats, Irish poet, lines from "The Second Coming," composed 1919, published 1920.

> Turning and turning in the widening gyre [spiral]
> The falcon cannot hear the falconer;
> Things fall apart; the center cannot hold;
> Mere anarchy is loosed upon the world,
> The blood-dimmed tide is loosed, and everywhere
> The ceremony of innocence is drowned;
> The best lack all conviction, while the worst
> Are full of passionate intensity.

Document 5

Source: Erich Maria Remarque, German author, *All Quiet on the Western Front*, 1929.

What would our fathers do if we suddenly stood up and came before them and proffered our accounts? . . . Through the years our business has been killing;—it was our first calling in life. Our knowledge of life is limited to death. What will happen afterwards? And what shall come out of us?

Document 6

Source: Benito Mussolini, Italian dictator, "The Political and Social Doctrine of Fascism," 1932.

For if the nineteenth century was a century of individualism (Liberalism always signifying individualism) it may be expected that this will be the century of collectivism, and hence the century of the State.

Document 7

Source: Helena Swanwick, English journalist and pacifist, "The War in Its Effect upon Women," 1916.

The course and conduct of the war, throwing upon women greater and greater responsibilities, bringing home to them how intimately their own lives and all they hold dear and sacred are affected by the government of the country, will tend greatly to strengthen and enlarge their claim for a share in the government.

Document 8

Source: Sir Arthur S. Eddington, British physicist and philosopher, referencing *The Nature of the Physical World*, Ernest Rutherford's work on the structure of the atom, 1928.

When we compare the universe as it is now supposed to be with the universe as we had ordinarily preconceived it, the most arresting change is not the rearrangement of space and time by Einstein but the dissolution of all that we regard as most solid into tiny specks floating in void.

Document 9

Source: Chorus girls posing as a New Year's Eve jazz band, Budapest, 1927.

Ulstein Bilderdienst/The Granger Collection, New York.

DBQ 17
Dictatorships and the Second World War

Identify the key concepts that motivated authoritarian governments and rulers in the interwar years (1919–1939), and explain why those concepts were so appealing.

Historical Background: Taking stock of the collateral damage of the First World War, many citizens believed that their prewar enthusiasm for a government for the people and by the people had propelled them on a disastrous path. Additionally, during the "total war" people became accustomed to having their individual rights suppressed for a greater good. No longer trusting the democratic collective to make wise decisions, they hoped that alternative models of government such as communism and fascism would provide salvation and direction. Out of these conditions grew widespread acceptance of radical totalitarian dictatorships, with the most brutal regimes flourishing in Hitler's Germany, Mussolini's Italy, and Stalin's Soviet Union.

Document 1

Source: Klara Zetkin, Rosa Luxemburg, Karl Liebknecht, and Franz Mehring, German revolutionaries, *Spartacist Manifesto*, November–December 1918, as it appeared in the *New York Times*, January 24, 1919.

Europe has been ruined through the infamous international murder. Twelve million bodies cover the grewsome [*sic*] scenes of the imperialistic crime. The flower of youth and the best man power [*sic*] of the peoples have been mowed down. Uncounted productive forces have been annihilated. . . . The great criminals of this fearful anarchy, of this chaos let loose—the ruling classes—are not able to control their own creation. The beast of capital that conjured up the hell of the world war is not capable of banishing it again, of restoring real order, of insuring bread and work, peace and civilization, justice and liberty, to tortured humanity.

Document 2

Source: Paul Valéry, French philosopher, speech at the University of Zurich, November 1922.

One can say that all the fundamentals of the world have been affected by the war, or more exactly, by the circumstances of the war; something deeper has been worn away than the renewable parts of the machine. You know how greatly the general economic situation has been disturbed, and the polity of states, and the very life of the individual; you are familiar with the universal discomfort, hesitation, apprehension. *But among all these injured things is the Mind.* The Mind has indeed been cruelly wounded; its complaint is heard in the hearts of intellectual man; it passes a mournful judgment on itself. It doubts itself profoundly.

Document 3

Source: German Nazi Party poster, "The String-Puller. White Collar and Manual Laborers: Vote for the Volkischen Block," 1924.

Courtesy, Langewiesche-Brandt KG Verlag, Ebenhausen, Germany.

Document 4

Source: José Ortega y Gasset, Spanish philosopher, *Revolt of the Masses*, 1930.

Under . . . Fascism there appears for the first time in Europe a type of man who does not want to give reasons or to be right, but simply shows himself resolved to impose his opinions. This is the new thing: the right not to be reasonable, the "reason of unreason." Here I see the most palpable manifestation of the new mentality of the masses, due to their having decided to rule society without the capacity for doing so. . . . The average man . . . wishes to have opinions, but is unwilling to accept the conditions and presuppositions that underlie all opinion. Hence his ideas are in effect nothing more than appetites in words.

Document 5

Source: Joseph Stalin, leader of the Soviet Union, "Address to Industrial Managers," 1931.

Do you want our socialist fatherland to be beaten and to lose its independence? If you do not want this you must put an end to its backwardness in the shortest possible time and develop genuine Bolshevik tempo in building up its socialist system of economy. There is no other way. That is why Lenin said during the October Revolution: "Either perish, or overtake and outstrip the advanced capitalist countries." We are fifty or a hundred years behind the advanced countries. We must make good this distance in ten years. Either we do it or they crush us.

Document 6

Source: Benito Mussolini, Italian dictator, "Fascist Doctrines," from the *Enciclopedia Italiana*, 1932.

Given that the nineteenth century was the century of Socialism, of Liberalism, and of Democracy, it does not necessarily follow that the twentieth century must also be the century of Socialism, Liberalism, and Democracy: political doctrines pass, but humanity remains; and it may rather be expected that this will be a century of authority, . . . a century of Fascism. For if the nineteenth century was a century of individualism (Liberalism always signifying individualism) it may be expected that this will be the century of collectivism and hence the century of the State.

Document 7

Source: The Great Depression in Europe, 1932.

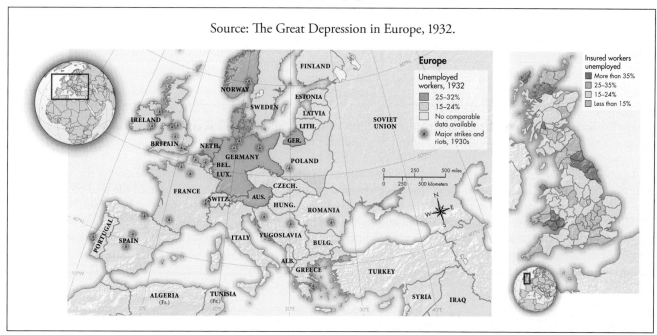

Document 8

Source: Jakob Graf, excerpt from *Hereditary and Racial Biology for Students*, a German textbook, 1935.

How We Can Learn to Recognize a Person's Race

Assignments

1. Summarize the spiritual characteristics of the individual races. . . .
3. What are the expressions, gestures, and movements which allow us to make conclusions as to the attitude of the racial soul?
4. Determine also the physical features which go hand in hand with the specific racial soul characteristics of the individual figures. . . .
9. Observe people whose special racial features have drawn your attention, also with respect to their bearing when moving or speaking. Observe their expressions and gestures.
10. Observe the Jew: his way of walking, his bearing, gestures, and movements when walking.

Document 9

Source: Nicolas Berdyaev, exiled Russian philosopher, *The Fate of Man in the Modern World*, 1935.

The new world which is taking form is moved by other values than the value of man or of human personality, or the value of truth: it is moved by such values as power, technics, race-purity, nationality, the state, the class, the collective. The will to justice is overcome by the will to power. . . . The results of the Christian-humanistic process of unifying humanity seem to be disappearing. We are witnessing the paganization of Christian society. Nationalism is polytheism: it is incompatible with monotheism.

Document 10

Source: Arthur Koestler, Hungarian-born British writer and journalist, "I Was Ripe to Be Converted," from *The God That Failed*, 1949.

A considerable portion of the middle classes in central Europe was, like ourselves, ruined by the inflation of the 'twenties. It was the beginning of Europe's decline. This disintegration of the middle strata of society started the fatal process of polarization which continues to this day. The pauperized bourgeois became rebels of the Right or Left; Schickelgruber [Hitler] and Djugashwili [Stalin] shared about equally the benefits of social migration. Those who . . . clung to the empty shell of gentility, joined the Nazis blaming their fate on Versailles and the Jews. . . . The other half turned Left, thus confirming the prophecy of the Communist Manifesto.

DBQ 18
Views Regarding Decolonization

Identify and analyze the various views regarding the decolonization of Algeria from France in the middle of the twentieth century.

<u>Historical Background</u>: On the eve of World War II, France controlled a colonial empire second in size only to that of Britain. The empire was more than twenty times as large as the home country, and it contained one and a half times as many inhabitants. By 1962 only scattered remnants were left. The French had fought to prevent the loss of their colonies, and the process of decolonization in the French empire, especially in Algeria, was violent and brutal. Algeria, invaded by the French in 1830, was the jewel of France's empire. By 1954 Algeria's population included over a million settlers of European origin.* The Algerians fought a war for independence against France from 1954 to 1962; they gained their independence on March 19, 1962, with the signing of the Evian Accords.

Document 1

Source: 1954 French trade in billions of francs. From *Annuarre statistique de la France,* government-released statistics of France, 1954.

	Export	Import	Balance
Algeria (French colony)	172.38	115.76	+56.62
Morocco (French colony)	77.63	51.30	+26.33
Tunisia (French colony)	42.02	28.75	+13.27
W. Germany	123.13	119.69	+3.44
U.S.A.	54.07	133.31	-79.24
Iraq	1.29	77.70	-76.41

Document 2

Source: "The Incompetent Governance of the IVth Republic," manifesto published by the right-wing French Poujadist movement, 1956.

The collapse of our Empire due to the venality [susceptibility to bribery or corruption] and the cowardice of our governments who take their orders from foreigners and international financiers, French Indo-China lost after a war that could have been avoided, the territories in India conceded without discussion. . . . As from now Tunisia and Morocco are no longer under our influence. . . . NOUS VOMISSONS LA POLITIQUE! [We vomit on the politicians!]

Document 3

Source: Conservative manifesto of Haute-Loire, a French department, 1958.

We all know the price we have paid for our blindness towards Hitler and the policies he proclaimed in *Mein Kampf.* Today Abdul Nasser [president of Egypt] reminds us that Lenin envisaged the encirclement of Europe by way of the Mediterranean. Let us beware. We must keep Algeria for many reasons but the most important one is the need to prevent the communist victory on the continent of Europe just as we should have kept the frontier on the Rhine to avoid the slaughters of 1939–45.

---

*Christopher Harrison, "French Attitudes to Empire and the Algerian War," *African Affairs* 82 (1983): 75–95.

Document 4

Source: Socialist manifesto concerning attitudes to colonies in general and Algeria in particular, published by Charente-Maritime, a French department, 1956.

France has accomplished a truly civilizing task in her overseas territories and this has resulted in the formation of recognizable local elites. The misconceptions of the reactionary ministers, partners in crime with the colonialists who exploit the native populations, and their refusal to grant these people the rights for which they yearn have triggered off some serious incidents and in the Aures [region of east Algeria] and the Rif [mountainous region of northern Morocco] there is a veritable war being fought which is immobilizing our youth, exposing them to danger and wasting France's credit digging us deeply into a worrying debt. The Socialist Party, faithful to its doctrine of the emancipation of native peoples, proposes to grant them the freedom of self-government.

Document 5

Source: Statement by French president Charles de Gaulle to Pierre Laffont, editor of the *Echo d'Alger*, April 29, 1959.

Yet those who are now calling most loudly for "integration" [the bringing together of France and Algeria] are the very voices who were once loudest against the measure. What they want is for someone to give them back the "Algeria of Daddy's day," but the Algeria of Daddy's day is dead, and if we fail to understand that, we shall die with it.

Document 6

Source: "Declaration on the Granting of Independence to Colonial Countries and Peoples," resolution adopted by the United Nations General Assembly, December 14, 1960.

Recognizing that the peoples of the world ardently desire the end of colonialism in all its manifestations,

Convinced that the continued existence of colonialism prevents the development of international economic co-operation, impedes the social, cultural and economic development of dependent peoples and militates against the United Nations ideal of universal peace, . . .

Believing that the process of liberation is irresistible and irreversible and that, in order to avoid serious crises, an end must be put to colonialism and all practices of segregation and discrimination associated therewith, . . .

Solemnly proclaims the necessity of bringing to a speedy and unconditional end colonialism in all its forms and manifestations.

Document 7

Source: Statement by Ferhat Abbas, leader of the Algerian National Liberation Front, to the press in Montreux, Switzerland, 1957.

For 125 years, we have served as guinea pigs for French schemes. We will settle for nothing short of independence.

Document 8

Source: Statement by Jacques Chaban-Delmas, mayor of Bordeaux, printed in the Conservative Party newspaper, *France Independante*, 1956.

If we were chased from Africa it would mean calamity for the Africans and the unemployment queue [line] for one out of every three French workers. [An] Increase in public expenditure and a worsening of the National Debt which already stands at 1,000 milliards [billion]. [And] Inflation ruining our currency, causing widespread poverty and leading to the triumph of Communism.

Document 9

Source: Jean-Paul Sartre, French existentialist and philosopher, "The System of Colonialism,"
published in *Les Temps Modernes*, 1956.

[If one wants to institute reforms] it is impossible to begin by economic transformations because the misery and the despair of the Algerians are the direct and necessary effect of colonialism and these will never be surpassed so long as colonialism endures.

Document 10

Source: Statement by Cardinal Lienart of Lille, France, concerning methods of torture used during the war for independence, from *Documents Action Catholique Ouvrière*, April 1959.

The war is a fact. And whatever the horror in our hearts against the war, we must recognize that it exists. But when war exists, we have no right as Christians or even as men (for this is a question of natural law) to use any measures at all, on the pretext that they are effective. The Cardinals and Archbishops have already reminded us on two occasions that it is not permissible to use "methods" which are intrinsically bad. You know the objection to this; it can be heard from both sides: "If such methods are not used, the war cannot be won." The answer is clear: "Then, it is better to lose the war!"

Document 11

Source: Statement by French archbishop Guerry made during the Franco-Algerian agreements, March 1962.

Think of all those European families who have lived during the past seven years in fear, anguish, daily insecurity, and uncertainty for the future with its dangers of death. So many of them lost members of their families, massacred, butchered by the troops. Think of those who worked and toiled for generations, desiring to serve France and to make Algeria a great country by cultivating, equipping it, and opening it to modern civilization. Now they are forced to leave their native soil, the land of their ancestors. They wished to remain French and, though minorities will have rights, they will be forced to give up their French nationality in three years if they remain in Algeria.

Document 12

Source: French tanks are surrounded by protesters during French president Charles de Gaulle's visit to Algiers, December 10, 1960.

Dalmas/Sipa Press.

DBQ 19
Communism and Eastern Europe

To what extent did criticisms of communism by citizens of the eastern European socialist states change over time?

Historical Background: Between the 1961 erection of the Berlin Wall and the 1989 revolutions that abolished Communist rule throughout the Soviet Union, the relationship between citizens of states in the Eastern bloc and their Communist governments underwent a radical shift. Short-lived economic upswings were supplanted by greater underlying trade and industry problems, and "really existing socialism" in the East Bloc became unsustainable, oppressive, and unfair. Small working-class groups in Czechoslovakia and Poland gained tremendous popular support for their calls to reform the government.

Document 1

Source: Andor Heller, account of the Hungarian Revolution of 1956, *No More Comrades*, 1957.

The walls of Budapest are plastered with leaflets put up by the students during the night. They list the fourteen demands adopted at the storm meetings held at the universities:

  1. Withdrawal of all Soviet troops from Hungary
  2. Complete economic and political equality with the Soviet Union, with no interference in Hungary's internal affairs . . .
  8. A secret general multi-party election
  9. The organization of Hungary's economy on the basis of her actual resources
  10. Revision of the workers' output quotas and recognition of the right to strike
  11. Revisions of the system of compulsory agricultural quotas
  12. Equal rights for individual farms and cooperative members . . .

Someone grabs a Hungarian flag and cuts out the hated hammer and sickle that the Communists had placed at its center. One after another of the purified Hungarian flags appear. Suddenly someone remembers to put the old Kossuth [the leader of the Hungarian uprising of 1848–1849] coat-of-arms on the flag. . . . We have created a new flag of freedom!

Document 2

Source: Milovan Djilas, Yugoslavian Communist politician, *The New Class*, 1957.

In contrast to earlier revolutions, the Communist revolution, conducted in the name of doing away with classes, has resulted in the most complete authority of any single new class. Everything else is a sham and an illusion. . . . This new class, the bureaucracy . . . may be said to be made up of those who have special privileges and economic preference because of the administrative monopoly they hold. . . . The Communist Party is the backbone of the entire political, economic and ideological activity. . . . The exclusive, if unwritten, law that only party members can become policemen, officers, diplomats, and only they can exercise actual authority, creates a special privileged group of bureaucrats. . . . The so-called "dictatorship of the proletariat" which is the beginning of and under the best circumstances becomes the authority of the party, inevitably evolves into the dictatorship of the leaders.

Document 3

Source: Ludvik Vaculik, Czech writer and journalist, "2,000 Words to Workers, Farmers, Scientists, Artists, and Everyone," published in the literary journal *Literární listy* in Prague, Czechoslovakia, spring 1968.

The communist party betrayed the great trust the people put in it after the war [World War II]. It preferred the glories of office, until it had those and nothing more. The disappointment was great among communists as well as non-communists. . . . There was no criticism of the state and economic organizations. Parliament forgot how to deliberate, the government forgot how to rule and managers how to manage. Elections had no significance and the laws lost their value. . . . Personal and collective honor deteriorated. . . . No organization was run by its members, not even the communist party. . . . Honesty led nowhere, and it was useless to speak of rewards according to ability. As a result, most citizens lost interest in public affairs.

Document 4

Source: "Workers of All Countries Unite—Or I'll Shoot," cartoon published in a Czech journal, August 28, 1968.

Document 5

Source: "Charter 77," published by the group Charter 77, an informal organization in Czechoslovakia composed of intellectuals, including founding member Václav Havel, 1977.

Freedom of public expression is repressed by the centralized control of all the communications media and of publishing and cultural institutions. No philosophical, political, or scientific view or artistic expression that departs ever so slightly from the narrow bounds of official ideology or aesthetics is allowed to be published. Further civil rights are seriously vitiated by the various forms of interference in the private life of citizens exercised by the Ministry of the Interior, for example, by bugging telephones and houses, opening mail, following personal movements, searching homes, setting up networks of neighborhood informers.

Document 6

Source: "Twenty-one Demands: A Call for Workers' Rights and Freedom in a Socialist State," issued by the Solidarity trade union in Poland, 1980.

1. Acceptance of Free Trade Unions independent of both the Party and employers, in accordance with the International Labor Organization's Convention number 87 on the freedom to form unions, which was ratified by the Polish government.
2. A guarantee of the right to strike and guarantees of security for strikers and their supporters.
3. Compliance with the freedoms of press and publishing guaranteed in the Polish constitution. A halt to repression of independent publications and access to the mass media for representatives of all faiths.
4. (a) Reinstatement to their former positions for: people fired for defending workers' rights, in particular those participating in the strikes of 1970 and 1976; students dismissed from school for their convictions. (b) The release of all political prisoners. . . . (c) A halt to repression for one's convictions. . . .
6. The undertaking of real measures to get the country out of its present crisis by: (a) providing comprehensive, public information about the socio-economic situation; (b) making it possible for people from every social class and stratum of society to participate in open discussions concerning the reform program. . . .
11. The rationing of meat and meat products through food coupons (until the market is stabilized).
12. Abolition of "commercial prices" and hard currency sales in so-called "internal export" shops.
13. A system of merit selection for management positions on the basis of qualifications rather than Party membership. . . .
19. Reduce the waiting time for apartments.

Document 7

Source: "What's this? You have your own opinion?," cartoon published during the Brezhnev years in the magazine *The Crocodile*, U.S.S.R., ca. early 1980s.

"What's this? You have your own opinion?"

—А У ВАС ЧТО, СВОЕ МНЕНИЕ?

Vneshtorgizdat, Moscow.

Document 8

Source: Mikhail Gorbachev, Soviet leader, *Perestroika*, 1987.

The presentation of a "problem-free" reality backfired: a breach had formed between word and deed, which bred public passivity and disbelief in the slogans being proclaimed. . . . Decay began in public morals; . . . and the penetration of stereotypes of mass culture alien to us, which bred vulgarity and low tastes and brought about ideological barrenness, increased.

One specific feature of socialism . . . [is] the high degree of social protection in our society. On the one hand, it is, doubtless, a benefit and a major achievement of ours. On the other hand, it makes some people spongers. There is virtually no unemployment. . . . Health care is free, and so is education. People are protected from the vicissitudes of life, and we are proud of this. But we also see that dishonest people try to exploit these advantages of socialism: they know only their rights, but they do not want to know their duties: they work poorly, shirk, and drink hard.

Document 9

Source: Václav Havel, president of Czechoslovakia, "The Failure of Communism," New Year's Day address, 1990.

Our country is not flourishing. The great creative and spiritual potential of our nation is not being applied meaningfully. Entire branches of industry are producing things for which there is no demand while we are short of things we need.

The state, which calls itself a state of workers, is humiliating and exploiting them instead. Our outmoded economy wastes energy, which we have in short supply. The country, which could once be proud of the education of its people, is spending so little on education that today, in that respect, we rank 72nd in the world. We have spoiled our land, rivers, and forests, inherited from our ancestors, and have, today, the worst environment in the whole of Europe. Adults die here earlier than in the majority of European countries. . . .

The worst of it is that we live in a spoiled moral environment. . . . The previous regime, armed with a proud and intolerant ideology, reduced people into the means of production, and nature in its tools. So it attacked their very essence, and their mutual relations. . . . None of us are only its victims; we are all also responsible for it.

Document 10

Source: Olga Havlová, wife of Václav Havel, letter to the editor, *New York Review of Books*, June 14, 1990.

The handicapped in our country have been forced into isolation, removed from sight into homes and institutions. There are a million of them in Czechoslovakia, in a population of only fifteen million. This did not trouble us. The state said they were being looked after, so we chose to believe it.

This was our habit of inhumanity. It would have been inhuman even if the state had been looking after these people well. But it turns out that it has been looking after them badly. There is practically no equipment, no nursing, sometimes not even the most basic conditions for living in dignity.

We are now changing the state. But we also need to change our habits.

Document 11

Source: Slavenka Drakulić, Croatian columnist, "A Letter from the United States: The Critical Theory Approach," from *How We Survived Communism and Even Laughed*, 1991.

Every mother in Bulgaria can point to where communism failed, from the failure of the planned economy [and the consequent lack of food and milk], to the lack of apartments, child-care facilities, clothes, disposable diapers, or toilet paper. The banality of everyday life is where it has really failed, rather than on the level of ideology.

Document 12

Source: Boris Yeltsin (bottom left), president of the Russian Federation, resists a coup by Russian communist hardliners in Moscow, August 1991.

AP Images.

DBQ 20
Western Europeans' Relations with Muslims and the Islamic World

Analyze the relations between western Europeans and Muslims in the late twentieth and early twenty-first centuries.

Historical Background: The plight of eastern European Muslims was brought to world attention during the 1991–2001 civil war in Yugoslavia, where they were victims of ethnic cleansing. The European response was initially slow, but NATO ultimately intervened and brought peace to the region. Though Islam has grown to be the largest minority religion in Europe, religious extremism, lack of cultural understanding, and the economic fears associated with a rapidly growing immigrant population have all contributed to a complex and hard-to-navigate relationship between western Europeans and Muslims. Tensions between these groups grew after the al-Qaeda attacks in New York and Washington, D.C., on September 11, 2001, and subsequent terrorist attacks in England and Spain. Cultural and religious differences continue to raise questions about what it means to be European in today's globalized world.

Document 1

Source: Lionel Jospin, French minister of education and member of the Socialist Party, interview in *Le Nouvel Observateur* (French newspaper), September 18, 1989.

Reporter: Mr. Minister of National Education, Yes or no? Is it necessary to let young Muslim women wear a headscarf in secondary schools?

Mr. Jospin: The secular school is a place of confessional neutrality. Thus, religious symbols must not be worn there. . . .

Reporter: To establish secular education, it was necessary to fight against the Catholic church. To maintain it, is it not necessary to battle against Islam?

Mr. Jospin: In France, secularism was founded, at the beginning of the twentieth-century, against the Catholic church, which itself was opposed to the Republic. The separation of the church and state was one of the foundational elements of the modern Republic. Today, it is a completely different question. . . .

Reporter: The secular school, free and obligatory for everyone, rests on the equality of men and women. . . . To the contrary, in Islam the wearing of a headscarf, veil, or chador sanctions inequality between people. Will you have to accept this promotion of a retrograde status for women in academic establishments?

Mr. Jospin: Obviously, I support equality between men and women, and the school must contribute to its promotion. . . . It would be a serious mistake, in adopting a rigid attitude, to overgeneralize. . . . I worry about the abusive generalization that descends upon Islam. It is not by provoking disobedience, in practicing exclusion, that we will promote the evolution of Islam in the Western world.

Document 2

Source: "European Union," from *Turkey: A Country Study*, part of the Country Studies/Area Handbook Series, Federal Research Division of the Library of Congress, sponsored by the U.S. Department of the Army, 1995.

The principal economic objections to Turkish membership [in the EU] center on the relative underdevelopment of Turkey's economy compared to the economies of EC/EU members and Turkey's high rate of population growth. The latter issue is perceived as a potentially serious problem because of free labor movement among EU members and the fact that Turkey's already large population is expected to surpass that of Germany—the most populous EU member—by 2010. Closely related to the concern about there being too many Turkish workers for too few jobs is the social problem of integrating those workers into European culture. Throughout Western Europe, the early 1990s witnessed a rise in anti-immigrant feeling directed primarily against Muslim workers from North Africa and Turkey. For the most part, EU governments have not developed policies to combat this resurgence of prejudice.

Document 3

Source: "The Freedom Party of Austria," from *Austria: A Country Study*, part of the Country Studies/Area Handbook Series, Federal Research Division of the Library of Congress, sponsored by the U.S. Department of the Army, 1994.

A major element in [Jorg] Haider's [right-wing politician] prescriptions for Austria is his desire to cut down drastically on the number of foreigners allowed to live in the country. Haider consistently argues that immigration is excessive and is causing serious problems for Austrian citizens in the areas of jobs and housing. Haider's campaign against foreigners was a major reason for the passage of a 1991 law that decreed that foreign workers could not make up more than 10 percent of the work force. In 1993 this ceiling was reduced to 9 percent when a new law, the Resident Alien Law, went into effect. Early in the same year, Haider sponsored a referendum to further tighten the control over the number of foreigners in Austria. Although he got only half of the 800,000 signatures he sought, the language Haider used in his campaign was extreme enough to cause large counter-demonstrations.

Document 4

Source: The Breakup of Yugoslavia, 1991–2006, map showing the ethnic composition of Yugoslavia in 1991 and the division of the country as a result of civil war.

Document 5

Source: Joachim Krautz, German journalist, "Violence and Xenophobia in Germany," 1993.

Of all the immigrant nationalities the Turks have a culture the most foreign to German sensibilities. And yet it is not only their Muslim religion and their extremely patriarchal family structure but their sheer number—with 1.8 million the Turks represent the largest minority in Germany—which has kindled a subliminal anxiety within many Germans. The foreign loses its exotic fascination if it becomes common and usual.

Document 6

Source: Martin Woollacott, "Living in the Age of Terror," *Guardian* (British newspaper), August 22, 1995.

The global village can be a violent place. Its curse is that new combination of intimacy and aggression, with societies so penetrated by each other physically and culturally that awful damage can be wreaked at close quarters in a way that was not possible in the past.

Document 7

Source: Philippe de Schoutheete, Belgium's representative to the European Union, *The Case for Europe: Unity, Diversity, and Democracy in the European Union*, 2000.

Taking the reasoning a step further, one might say that the aim of the joint venture pursued in Western Europe for almost a half a century has been to develop a model of society. The sense of a shared destiny, based on one same vision of mankind, represents both the cause and the condition of common policy and common legislation. . . .

Diversity is clearly one of the keys to European society. It is already very prominent, and sometimes a source of conflict inside many of the member states. Within the Union it is structural, and it gives the Union its singular nature. The bonds created by history and the upholding of shared values coexist with cultural diversity and national identities.

Document 8

Source: Terrorist attack on the World Trade Center, September 11, 2001.

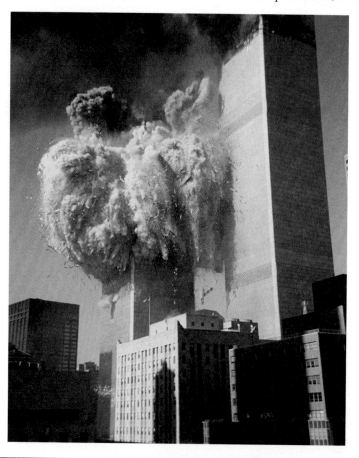

Document 9

Source: "Austria: A Country of Immigration?" by Michael Jandl and Albert Kraler, International Centre for Migration Policy Development, 2003.

According to the 2001 census, of Austria's roughly eight million inhabitants, more than 730,000 (or 9.1 percent) were foreign residents, with 62.8 percent of them coming from the successor states of the former Yugoslavia and from Turkey. Between 1985 and 2001, over 254,000 foreigners were naturalized. Austria's proportion of foreign-born residents in 2001 was even higher than that of the United States, reaching a level of 12.5 percent.

Document 10

Source: Indictment and charges against Slobodan Milosevic for his actions in Bosnia and Herzegovina, by the United Nations International Criminal Tribunal for the former Yugoslavia, November 22, 2001.

It was alleged that, from on or about 1 March 1992 until 31 December 1995, Slobodan Milosevic [former president of Serbia and the Federal Republic of Yugoslavia], acting alone or in concert with other members of the JCE [joint criminal enterprise], planned, instigated, ordered, committed or otherwise aided and abetted the planning, preparation and execution of the widespread killing of thousands of Bosnian Muslims during and after the take-over of territories within Bosnia and Herzegovina and the detention of thousands of Bosnian Muslims in detention facilities within Bosnia and Herzegovina, under conditions of life calculated to bring about the partial physical destruction of those groups. During their confinement in detention facilities, thousands of Bosnian Muslims were killed or caused serious bodily and mental harm. . . . The charges also include numbers of acts of intentional and wanton destruction . . . of cultural and religious institutions, historical monuments and other sacred sites and the appropriation and plunder of property belonging to Bosnian Muslim, Bosnian Croat and other non-Serb civilians.

Document 11

Source: Refugee Populations and Asylum Seekers data from 2005, adapted from *Pocket World in Figures*, 2008 published by *The Economist* magazine, 2007.

Western industrialized countries with the largest refugee populations, 2005

World Ranking	Country	Refugees per 100,000 Citizens
#3	Germany	700
#5	United States	379
#7	United Kingdom	293
#19	France	137

Asylum applications in Western industrialized countries, 2005

World Ranking	Country	Applications per 100,000 Citizens
#1	France	49.7
#2	United States	48.8
#3	United Kingdom	30.8
#4	Germany	28.9
#5	Sweden	23.2
#6	Austria	22.5
#7	Canada	19.7
#8	Belgium	16.0
#9	Switzerland	14.3
#10	Netherlands	12.4
#11	Italy	9.6
#12	Greece	9.1
#13	Cyprus	7.8
#14	Poland	6.9
#15	Norway	5.4
#16	Spain	5.3
#17	Ireland	4.3
#18	Czech Republic	4.2

Glossary

Afrikaners Descendants of the Dutch settlers in the Cape Colony in southern Africa. (p. 795)

Agincourt The location near Arras in Flanders where an English victory in 1415 led to the reconquest of Normandy. (p. 350)

agricultural revolution The period in Europe from the mid-seventeenth through the mid-nineteenth centuries during which great agricultural progress was made and the fallow, or idling of a field to replenish nutrients, was gradually eliminated. (p. 555)

anticlericalism Opposition to the clergy. (p. 408)

appeasement The British policy toward Germany prior to World War II that aimed at granting Hitler whatever he wanted, including western Czechoslovakia, in order to avoid war. (p. 907)

Atlantic slave trade The forced migration of Africans across the Atlantic for slave labor on plantations and in other industries; the trade reached its peak in the eighteenth century and ultimately involved more than twelve million Africans. (p. 573)

Babylonian Captivity Period from 587 to 538 B.C.E. during which the survivors of a Babylonian attack on the southern kingdom of Judah were exiled in Babylonia. The term was later used to refer to the period from 1309 to 1376 when the popes resided in Avignon rather than in Rome. (p. 355)

Balfour Declaration A 1917 British statement that declared British support of a National Home for the Jewish People in Palestine. (p. 844)

Battle of Peterloo A protest that took place at Saint Peter's Fields in Manchester in reaction to the revision of the Corn Laws in 1819; it was broken up by armed cavalry. (p. 702)

Bauhaus A German interdisciplinary school of fine and applied arts that brought together many leading modern architects, designers, and theatrical innovators. (p. 861)

Berlin conference A meeting of European leaders held in 1884 and 1885 in order to lay down some basic rules for imperialist competition in sub-Saharan Africa. (p. 797)

Black Death Plague that first struck Europe in 1347 and killed perhaps one-third of the population. (p. 341)

Black Shirts Mussolini's private militia that destroyed socialist newspapers, union halls, and Socialist Party headquarters, eventually pushing Socialists out of the city governments of northern Italy. (p. 898)

blood sports Popular with the eighteenth-century European masses, events such as bull-baiting and cockfighting that involved inflicting violence and bloodshed on animals. (p. 597)

Bloody Sunday A massacre of peaceful protesters at the Winter Palace in St. Petersburg in 1905 that triggered a revolution that overturned absolute tsarist rule and made Russia into a conservative constitutional monarchy. (p. 761)

Bolsheviks Lenin's radical, revolutionary arm of the Russian party of Marxian socialism, which successfully installed a dictatorial socialist regime in Russia. (p. 835)

bourgeoisie The middle-class minority who owned the means of production and, according to Marx, exploited the working-class proletariat. (p. 696)

boyars The highest-ranking members of the Russian nobility. (p. 498)

Brezhnev Doctrine Doctrine created by Leonid Brezhnev that held that the Soviet Union had the right to intervene in any socialist country whenever it saw the need. (p. 970)

cameralism View that monarchy was the best form of government, that all elements of society should serve the monarch, and that, in turn, the state should use its resources and authority to increase the public good. (p. 544)

caravel A small, maneuverable, three-mast sailing ship developed by the Portuguese in the fifteenth century that gave the Portuguese a distinct advantage in exploration and trade. (p. 450)

Carlsbad Decrees Issued in 1819, these decrees were designed to uphold Metternich's conservatism, requiring the German states to root out subversive ideas and squelch any liberal organizations. (p. 689)

carnival The few days of revelry in Catholic countries that preceded Lent and that included drinking, masquerading, dancing, and rowdy spectacles that turned the established order upside down. (p. 597)

Cartesian dualism Descartes's view that all of reality could ultimately be reduced to mind and matter. (p. 527)

Christian Democrats Center-right political parties that rose to power in western Europe after the Second World War. (p. 933)

Christian humanists Northern humanists who interpreted Italian ideas about and attitudes toward classical antiquity and humanism in terms of their own religious traditions. (p. 384)

class-consciousness An individual's sense of class differentiation. (p. 672)

collectivization of agriculture The forcible consolidation of individual peasant farms into large state-controlled enterprises in the Soviet Union under Stalin. (p. 893)

Columbian exchange The exchange of animals, plants, and diseases between the Old and the New Worlds. (p. 463)

Combination Acts English laws passed in 1799 that outlawed unions and strikes, favoring capitalist business people over skilled artisans. Bitterly resented and widely disregarded by many craft guilds, the acts were repealed by Parliament in 1824. (p. 680)

Common Market The European Economic Community, created by six western European nations in 1957 as part of a larger search for European unity. (p. 935)

communes Sworn associations of free men in Italian cities led by merchant guilds that sought political and economic independence from local nobles. (p. 375)

community controls A pattern of cooperation and common action in a traditional village that sought to uphold the economic, social, and moral stability of the closely knit community. (p. 588)

conciliarists People who believed that the authority in the Roman church should rest in a general council composed of clergy, theologians, and laypeople, rather than in the pope alone. (p. 356)

confraternities Voluntary lay groups organized by occupation, devotional preference, neighborhood, or charitable activity. (p. 357)

Congress of Vienna A meeting of the Quadruple Alliance—Russia, Prussia, Austria, and Great Britain—and restoration France to fashion a general peace settlement that began after the defeat of Napoleon's France in 1814. (p. 686)

conquistador Spanish for "conqueror"; Spanish soldier-explorers, such as Hernando Cortés and Francisco Pizarro, who sought to conquer the New World for the Spanish crown. (p. 449)

constitutionalism A form of government in which power is limited by law and balanced between the authority and power of the government on the one hand and the rights and liberties of the subject or citizen on the other hand; could include constitutional monarchies or republics. (p. 506)

constitutional monarchy A form of government in which the king retains his position as head of state, while the authority to tax and make new laws resides in an elected body. (p. 630)

consumer revolution The wide-ranging growth in consumption and new attitudes toward consumer goods that emerged in the cities of northwestern Europe in the second half of the eighteenth century. (p. 601)

Continental System A blockade imposed by Napoleon to halt all trade between continental Europe and Britain, thereby weakening the British economy and military. (p. 649)

Copernican hypothesis The idea that the sun, not the earth, was the center of the universe. (p. 522)

Corn Laws British laws, revised in 1815, that prohibited the importation of foreign grain unless the price at home rose to improbable levels, thus benefiting the aristocracy but making food prices high for working people. (p. 702)

Cossacks Free groups and outlaw armies originally comprising runaway peasants living on the borders of Russian territory from the fourteenth century onward. By the end of the sixteenth century they had formed an alliance with the Russian state. (p. 498)

cottage industry A stage of industrial development in which rural workers used hand tools in their homes to manufacture goods on a large scale for sale in a market. (p. 560)

Council for Mutual Economic Assistance (COMECON) An economic organization of communist states meant to help rebuild eastern Europe under Soviet auspices. (p. 930)

courts Magnificent households and palaces where the signori and the most powerful merchant oligarchs required political business to be conducted. (p. 376)

Crystal Palace The location of the Great Exhibition in 1851 in London, an architectural masterpiece made entirely of glass and iron. (p. 664)

Dadaism An artistic movement of the 1920s and 1930s that attacked all accepted standards of art and behavior and delighted in outrageous conduct. (p. 864)

Dawes Plan War reparations agreement that reduced Germany's yearly payments, made payment dependent on economic prosperity, and granted large U.S. loans to promote recovery. (p. 873)

debate about women Debate among writers and thinkers in the Renaissance about women's qualities and proper role in society. (p. 396)

debt peonage A form of serfdom that allowed a planter or rancher to keep his workers or slaves in perpetual debt bondage by periodically advancing food, shelter, and a little money. (p. 572)

dechristianization Campaign to eliminate Christian faith and practice in France undertaken by the revolutionary government. (p. 638)

decolonization The postwar reversal of Europe's overseas expansion caused by the rising demand of the colonized peoples themselves, the declining power of European nations, and the freedoms promised by U.S. and Soviet ideals. (p. 944)

de-Stalinization The liberalization of the post-Stalin Soviet Union led by reformer Nikita Khrushchev. (p. 940)

détente The progressive relaxation of Cold War tensions. (p. 960)

diasporas Enclaves of ethnic groups settled outside of their homelands. (p. 1011)

displaced persons Postwar refugees, including 13 million Germans, former Nazi prisoners and forced laborers, and orphaned children. (p. 925)

Dreyfus affair A divisive case in which Alfred Dreyfus, a Jewish captain in the French army, was falsely accused and convicted of treason in 1894. The Catholic Church sided with the anti-Semites against Dreyfus; after Dreyfus was declared innocent, the French government severed all ties between the state and the church. (p. 769)

dual revolution A term that historian Eric Hobsbawm used for the economic and political changes that tended to fuse and reinforce each other after 1815. (p. 687)

Duma The Russian parliament that opened in 1906, elected indirectly by universal male suffrage but controlled after 1907 by the tsar and the conservative classes. (p. 764)

economic liberalism A belief in free trade and competition based on Adam Smith's argument that the invisible hand of free competition would benefit all individuals, rich and poor. (p. 568)

economic nationalism Policies aimed at protecting and developing a country's economy. (p. 672)

Edict of Nantes A document issued by Henry IV of France in 1598, granting liberty of conscience and of public worship to Calvinists, which helped restore peace in France. (p. 434)

empiricism A theory of inductive reasoning that calls for acquiring evidence through observation and experimentation rather than reason and speculation. (p. 526)

Enabling Act An act pushed through the Reichstag by the Nazis that gave Hitler absolute dictatorial power for four years. (p. 903)

enclosure The movement to fence in fields in order to farm more effectively, at the expense of poor peasants who relied on common fields for farming and pasture. (p. 556)

encomienda system A system whereby the Spanish crown granted the conquerors the right to forcibly employ groups of Indians; it was a disguised form of slavery. (p. 461)

English Peasants' Revolt Revolt by English peasants in 1381 in response to changing economic conditions. (p. 360)

enlightened absolutism Term coined by historians to describe the rule of eighteenth-century monarchs who, without renouncing their own absolute authority, adopted Enlightenment ideals of rationalism, progress, and tolerance. (p. 543)

Enlightenment The influential intellectual and cultural movement of the late seventeenth and eighteenth centuries that introduced a new worldview based on the use of reason, the scientific method, and progress. (p. 530)

estates The three legal categories, or orders, of France's inhabitants: the clergy, the nobility, and everyone else. (p. 620)

Estates General A legislative body in prerevolutionary France made up of representatives of each of the three classes, or estates; it was called into session in 1789 for the first time since 1614. (p. 625)

ethnic cleansing The attempt to establish ethnically homogeneous territories by intimidation, forced deportation, and killing. (p. 1001)

eugenics A pseudoscientific doctrine that maintains that the selective breeding of human beings can improve the general characteristics of a national population, which helped inspire Nazi ideas about "race and space" and ultimately contributed to the Holocaust. (p. 889)

European Union (EU) The economic, cultural, and political alliance of twenty-seven European nations. (p. 1005)

evolution The idea, applied by thinkers in many fields, that stresses gradual change and continuous adjustment. (p. 744)

existentialism A philosophy that stresses the meaninglessness of existence and the importance of the individual in searching for moral values in an uncertain world. (p. 856)

experimental method The approach, pioneered by Galileo, that the proper way to explore the workings of the universe was through repeatable experiments rather than speculation. (p. 524)

Factory Act of 1833 English law that led to a sharp decline in the employment of children by limiting the hours that children over age nine could work and requiring younger children to attend factory-run elementary schools. (p. 678)

fascism A movement characterized by extreme, often expansionist nationalism, antisocialism, a dynamic and violent leader, and glorification of war and the military. (p. 889)

February Revolution Unplanned uprisings accompanied by violent street demonstrations begun in March 1917 (old calendar February) in Petrograd, Russia, and that led to the abdication of the tsar and the establishment of a provisional government. (p. 833)

five-year plan A plan launched by Stalin in 1928, and termed the "revolution from above," aimed at modernizing the Soviet Union and creating a new communist society with new attitudes, new loyalties, and a new socialist humanity. (p. 891)

flagellants People who believed that the plague was God's punishment for sin and sought to do penance by flagellating (whipping) themselves. (p. 347)

Fourteen Points Wilson's 1918 peace proposal calling for open diplomacy, a reduction in armaments, freedom of commerce and trade, the establishment of the League of Nations, and national self-determination. (p. 842)

Fronde A series of violent uprisings during the early reign of Louis XIV triggered by growing royal control and oppressive taxation. (p. 487)

functionalism The principle that buildings, like industrial products, should serve as well as possible the purpose for which they were made. (p. 861)

germ theory The idea that disease was caused by the spread of living organisms that could be controlled. (p. 721)

Girondists A moderate group that fought for control of the French National Convention in 1793. (p. 635)

glasnost Soviet premier Gorbachev's popular campaign for openness in government and the media. (p. 984)

globalization The emergence of a freer, more technologically connected global economy, accompanied by a worldwide exchange of cultural, political, and religious ideas. (p. 1003)

global warming The increase of average temperatures around the world, caused primarily by carbon dioxide emissions from the burning of fossil fuels. (p. 1022)

Grand Empire The empire over which Napoleon and his allies ruled, encompassing virtually all of Europe except Great Britain and Russia. (p. 649)

Great Depression A worldwide economic depression from 1929 through 1939, unique in its severity and duration and with slow and uneven recovery. (p. 874)

Great Famine A terrible famine in 1315–1322 that hit much of Europe after a period of climate change, and the name of the mid-nineteenth-century famine that was the result of four years of potato crop failure in Ireland, a country that had grown dependent on potatoes as a dietary staple. (pp. 340, 705)

Great Fear The fear of noble reprisals against peasant uprisings that seized the French countryside and led to further revolt. (p. 629)

great migration The mass movement of people from Europe in the nineteenth century; one reason that the West's impact on the world was so powerful and many-sided. (p. 788)

Great Rebellion The 1857 and 1858 insurrection by Muslim and Hindu mercenaries in the British army that spread throughout northern and central India before finally being crushed. (p. 804)

Great Schism The division, or split, in church leadership from 1378 to 1417 when there were two, then three, popes. (p. 355)

great white walls Laws designed by Americans and Australians in the 1880s to keep Asians from settling in their countries. (p. 794)

guest worker programs Government-run programs in western Europe designed to recruit labor for the booming postwar economy. (p. 951)

guild system The organization of artisanal production into trade-based associations, or guilds, each of which received a monopoly over its trade and the right to train apprentices and hire workers. (p. 566)

gunboat diplomacy The use or threat of military force to coerce a government into economic or political agreements. (p. 786)

Haskalah The Jewish Enlightenment of the second half of the eighteenth century, led by the Prussian philosopher Moses Mendelssohn. (p. 549)

Holocaust The systematic effort of the Nazi state to exterminate all European Jews and other groups deemed racially inferior during the Second World War. (p. 912)

Holy Alliance An alliance formed by the conservative rulers of Austria, Russia, and Prussia in September 1815 that became a symbol of the repression of liberal and revolutionary movements all over Europe. (p. 687)

Holy Office The official Roman Catholic agency founded in 1542 to combat international doctrinal heresy. (p. 430)

Homestead Act A result of the American Civil War that gave western land to settlers, reinforcing the concept of free labor in a market economy. (p. 758)

Huguenots French Calvinists. (p. 433)

humanism A program of study designed by Italians that emphasized the critical study of Latin and Greek literature with the goal of understanding human nature. (p. 378)

hundred days of reform A series of Western-style reforms launched in 1898 by the Chinese government in an attempt to meet the foreign challenge. (p. 807)

id, ego, and superego Freudian terms to describe the three parts of the self and the basis of human behavior, which Freud saw as basically irrational. (p. 859)

illegitimacy explosion The sharp increase in out-of-wedlock births that occurred in Europe between 1750 and 1850, caused by low wages and the breakdown of community controls. (p. 589)

Inca Empire The vast and sophisticated Peruvian empire centered at the capital city of Cuzco that was at its peak from 1438 until 1532. (p. 459)

indulgence A document issued by the Catholic Church lessening penance or time in purgatory, widely believed to bring forgiveness of all sins. (p. 409)

Industrial Revolution A term first coined in the 1830s to describe the burst of major inventions and economic expansion that took place in certain industries, such as cotton textiles and iron. (p. 656)

industrious revolution The shift that occurred as families in northwestern Europe focused on earning wages instead of producing goods for household consumption; this reduced their economic self-sufficiency but increased their ability to purchase consumer goods. (p. 566)

Institutes of the Christian Religion, The Calvin's formulation of Christian doctrine, which became a systematic theology for Protestantism. (p. 425)

iron law of wages Theory proposed by English economist David Ricardo suggesting that the pressure of population growth prevents wages from rising above the subsistence level. (p. 665)

Jacobin club A political club in revolutionary France whose members were well-educated radical republicans. (p. 634)

Jacquerie A massive uprising by French peasants in 1358 protesting heavy taxation. (p. 358)

janissary corps The core of the sultan's army, composed of slave conscripts from non-Muslim parts of the empire; after 1683 it became a volunteer force. (p. 504)

Jansenism A sect of Catholicism originating with Cornelius Jansen that emphasized the heavy weight of original sin and accepted the doctrine of predestination; it was outlawed as heresy by the pope. (p. 608)

Jesuits Members of the Society of Jesus, founded by Ignatius Loyola, whose goal was the spread of the Roman Catholic faith. (p. 431)

Junkers The nobility of Brandenburg and Prussia, they were reluctant allies of Frederick William in his consolidation of the Prussian state. (p. 495)

just price The idea that prices should be fair, protecting both consumers and producers, and that they should be imposed by government decree if necessary. (p. 599)

Kosovo Liberation Army (KLA) Military organization formed in 1998 by Kosovar militants who sought independence from Serbia. (p. 1002)

kulaks The better-off peasants who were stripped of land and livestock under Stalin and were generally not permitted to join collective farms; many of them starved or were deported to forced-labor camps for "re-education." (p. 893)

Kulturkampf Bismarck's attack on the Catholic Church within Germany from 1870 to 1878, resulting from Pius IX's declaration of papal infallibility. (p. 767)

labor aristocracy The highly skilled workers, such as factory foremen and construction bosses, who made up about 15 percent of the working classes from about 1850 to 1914. (p. 727)

laissez faire A doctrine of economic liberalism that believes in unrestricted private enterprise and no government interference in the economy. (p. 691)

Lateran Agreement A 1929 agreement that recognized the Vatican as an independent state, with Mussolini agreeing to give the church heavy financial support in return for public support from the pope. (p. 900)

law of inertia A law formulated by Galileo that states that motion, not rest, is the natural state of an object, that an object continues in motion forever unless stopped by some external force. (p. 524)

law of universal gravitation Newton's law that all objects are attracted to one another and that the force of attraction is proportional to the object's quantity of matter and inversely proportional to the square of the distance between them. (p. 526)

League of Nations A permanent international organization, established during the 1919 Paris peace conference, designed to protect member states from aggression and avert future wars. (p. 842)

liberalism The principal ideas of this movement were equality and liberty; liberals demanded representative government and equality before the law as well as individual freedoms such as freedom of the press, freedom of speech, freedom of assembly, and freedom from arbitrary arrest. (p. 691)

logical positivism A philosophy that sees meaning in only those beliefs that can be empirically proven, and that therefore rejects most of the concerns of traditional philosophy, from the existence of God to the meaning of happiness, as nonsense. (p. 855)

Luddites Group of handicraft workers who attacked whole factories in northern England in 1812 and after, smashing the new machines that they believed were putting them out of work. (p. 674)

Maastricht Treaty The basis for the formation of the European Union, which set financial and cultural standards for potential member states and defined criteria for membership in the monetary union. (p. 1005)

Marshall Plan American plan for providing economic aid to western Europe to help it rebuild after WWII. (p. 930)

Meiji Restoration The restoration of the Japanese emperor to power in 1867, leading to the subsequent modernization of Japan. (p. 806)

mercantilism A system of economic regulations aimed at increasing the power of the state based on the belief that a nation's international power was based on its wealth, specifically its supply of gold and silver. (p. 489)

Methodists Members of a Protestant revival movement started by John Wesley, so called because they were so methodical in their devotion. (p. 607)

Mexica Empire Also known as the Aztec Empire, a large and complex Native American civilization in modern Mexico and Central America that possessed advanced mathematical, astronomical, and engineering technology. (p. 457)

millet system A system used by the Ottomans whereby subjects were divided into religious communities with each millet (nation) enjoying autonomous self-government under its religious leaders. (p. 505)

Mines Act of 1842 English law prohibiting underground work for all women and girls as well as for boys under ten. (p. 680)

modernism A label given to the artistic and cultural movements of the late nineteenth and early twentieth centuries, which were typified by radical experimentation that challenged traditional forms of artistic expression. (p. 861)

modernization The changes that enable a country to compete effectively with the leading countries at a given time. (p. 759)

Mountain, the Led by Robespierre, the French National Convention's radical faction, which seized legislative power in 1793. (p. 635)

multiculturalism The mixing of ethnic styles in daily life and in cultural works such as film, music, art, and literature. (p. 1012)

Napoleonic Code French civil code promulgated in 1804 that reasserted the 1789 principles of the equality of all male citizens before the law and the absolute security of wealth and private property as well as restricting rights accorded to women by previous revolutionary laws. (p. 644)

National Assembly The first French revolutionary legislature, made up primarily of representatives of the third estate and a few from the nobility and clergy, in session from 1789 to 1791. (p. 627)

nationalism The idea that each people had its own genius and its own specific unity, which manifested itself especially in a common language and history, and often led to the desire for an independent political state. (p. 691)

national self-determination The notion that people should be able to live free from outside interference in nations with clearly defined borders, and should be able to choose their own national governments through democratic majority-rule elections. (p. 842)

National Socialism A movement born of extreme nationalism and racism, led by Adolf Hitler, that ruled Germany from 1933 to 1945 and forced Europe into the Second World War. (p. 901)

NATO The North Atlantic Treaty Organization, an anti-Soviet military alliance of Western governments. (p. 930)

natural philosophy An early modern term for the study of the nature of the universe, its purpose, and how it functioned; it encompassed what we would call "science" today. (p. 520)

Navigation Acts A series of English laws that controlled the import of goods to Britain and British colonies. (p. 569)

neoliberalism Philosophy of 1980s conservatives who argued for decreased government spending on social services and privatization of state-run industries. (p. 972)

New Christians A fourteenth-century term for Jews and Muslims who accepted Christianity; in many cases they included Christians whose families had converted centuries earlier. (p. 401)

New Economic Policy (NEP) Lenin's 1921 policy to re-establish limited economic freedom in an attempt to rebuild agriculture and industry in the face of economic disintegration. (p. 891)

new imperialism The late-nineteenth-century drive by European countries to create vast political empires abroad. (p. 794)

New Left A movement of students in the West who advocated simpler, purer societies based on an updated, romanticized version of Marxism. (p. 963)

New Order Hitler's program based on racial imperialism, which gave preferential treatment to the Nordic peoples; the French, an "inferior" Latin people, occupied a middle position, and Slavs and Jews were treated harshly as "sub-humans." (p. 910)

"new woman" Somewhat stereotypical image of the modern and independent working woman popular in the 1920s. (p. 867)

nonalignment Policy of postcolonial governments to remain neutral in the Cold War and play both the United States and the Soviet Union for what they could get. (p. 945)

nongovernmental organizations (NGOs) Independent organizations with specific agendas, such as humanitarian aid or environmental protection, that conduct international programs and activities. (p. 1009)

October Manifesto The result of a great general strike in October 1905, it granted full civil rights and promised a popularly elected Duma (parliament) with real legislative power. (p. 764)

OPEC The Arab-led Organization of Petroleum Exporting Countries. (p. 971)

opium trade The sale of opium—grown legally in British-occupied India—by British merchants in China, where the drug was illegal; it became a destructive and ensnaring vice of the Chinese. (p. 785)

Ostalgie German term referring to nostalgia for the lifestyles and culture of the vanished East Bloc. (p. 1000)

patronage Financial support of writers and artists by cities, groups, and individuals, often to produce specific works or works in specific styles. (p. 374)

Peace of Utrecht A series of treaties, from 1713 to 1715, that ended the War of the Spanish Succession, ended French expansion in Europe, and marked the rise of the British Empire. (p. 492)

Peace of Westphalia The name of a series of treaties that concluded the Thirty Years' War in 1648 and marked the end of large-scale religious violence in Europe. (p. 483)

People's Budget A bill proposed after the Liberal Party came to power in England in 1906, it was designed to increase spending on social welfare services, but was initially vetoed in the House of Lords. (p. 769)

perestroika Economic restructuring and reform implemented by Soviet premier Gorbachev in 1985. (p. 984)

Petrograd Soviet A huge, fluctuating mass meeting of two to three thousand workers, soldiers, and socialist intellectuals modeled on the revolutionary soviets of 1905. (p. 834)

philosophes A group of French intellectuals who proclaimed that they were bringing the light of knowledge to their fellow creatures in the Age of Enlightenment. (p. 531)

Pietism A Protestant revival movement in early-eighteenth-century Germany and Scandinavia that emphasized a warm and emotional religion, the priesthood of all believers, and the power of Christian rebirth in everyday affairs. (p. 607)

pluralism The clerical practice of holding more than one church benefice (or office) at the same time and enjoying the income from each. (p. 408)

politiques Catholic and Protestant moderates who held that only a strong monarchy could save France from total collapse. (p. 434)

popolo Disenfranchised common people in Italian cities who resented their exclusion from power. (p. 375)

Popular Front A short-lived New Deal–inspired alliance in France led by Léon Blum that encouraged the union movement and launched a far-reaching program of social reform. (p. 882)

postcolonial migration The postwar movement of people from former colonies and the developing world into Europe. (p. 953)

postindustrial society Society that relies on high-tech and service-oriented jobs for economic growth rather than on heavy industry and manufacturing jobs. (p. 971)

predestination The teaching that God has determined the salvation or damnation of individuals based on his will and purpose, not on their merit or works. (p. 426)

proletarianization The transformation of large numbers of small peasant farmers into landless rural wage earners. (p. 558)

proletariat The industrial working class who, according to Marx, were unfairly exploited by the profit-seeking bourgeoisie. (p. 696)

Protectorate The English military dictatorship (1653–1658) established by Oliver Cromwell following the execution of Charles I. (p. 508)

Protestant The name originally given to Lutherans, which came to mean all non-Catholic Western Christian groups. (p. 412)

Ptolemy's *Geography* A second-century-c.e. work that synthesized the classical knowledge of geography and introduced the concepts of longitude and latitude. Reintroduced to Europeans in 1410 by Arab scholars, its ideas allowed cartographers to create more accurate maps. (p. 450)

public sphere An idealized intellectual space that emerged in Europe during the Enlightenment, where the public came together to discuss important issues relating to society, economics, and politics. (p. 537)

Puritans Members of a sixteenth- and seventeenth-century reform movement within the Church of England that advocated purifying it of Roman Catholic elements, such as bishops, elaborate ceremonials, and wedding rings. (p. 507)

putting-out system The eighteenth-century system of rural industry in which a merchant loaned raw materials to cottage workers, who processed them and returned the finished products to the merchant. (p. 561)

rationalism A secular, critical way of thinking in which nothing was to be accepted on faith, and everything was to be submitted to reason. (p. 530)

reading revolution The transition in Europe from a society where literacy consisted of patriarchal and communal reading of religious texts to a society where literacy was commonplace and reading material was broad and diverse. (p. 535)

realism A literary movement that stressed the depiction of life as it actually was. (p. 744)

really existing socialism A term used by Communist leaders to describe the socialist accomplishments of their societies, such as nationalized industry and collective agriculture. (p. 980)

Red Shirts The guerrilla army of Giuseppe Garibaldi, who invaded Sicily in 1860 in an attempt to liberate it, winning the hearts of the Sicilian peasantry. (p. 754)

Reform Bill of 1832 A major British political reform that increased the number of male voters by about 50 percent and gave political representation to new industrial areas. (p. 702)

Reichstag The popularly elected lower house of government of the new German Empire after 1871. (p. 767)

Reign of Terror The period from 1793 to 1794 during which Robespierre's Committee of Public Safety tried and executed thousands suspected of treason and a new revolutionary culture was imposed. (p. 637)

Renaissance A French word meaning "rebirth," first used by art historian and critic Giorgio Vasari to refer to the rebirth of the culture of classical antiquity. (p. 374)

representative assemblies Deliberative meetings of lords and wealthy urban residents that flourished in many European countries between 1250 and 1450 and were the precursors to the English parliament, German diets, and Spanish cortes. (p. 354)

republicanism A form of government in which there is no monarch and power rests in the hands of the people as exercised through elected representatives. (p. 506)

revisionism An effort by moderate socialists to update Marxian doctrines to reflect the realities of the twentieth century. (p. 775)

Rocket The name given to George Stephenson's effective locomotive that was first tested in 1830 on the Liverpool and Manchester Railway at 16 miles per hour. (p. 663)

rococo A popular style in Europe in the eighteenth century, known for its soft pastels, ornate interiors, sentimental portraits, and starry-eyed lovers protected by hovering cupids. (p. 537)

romanticism A movement at its height from about 1790 to the 1840s that was in part a revolt against classicism and the Enlightenment, characterized by a belief in emotional exuberance, unrestrained imagination, and spontaneity in both art and personal life. (p. 697)

salons Regular social gatherings held by talented and rich Parisian women in their homes, where philosophes and their followers met to discuss literature, science, and philosophy. (p. 536)

sans-culottes The laboring poor of Paris, so called because the men wore trousers instead of the knee breeches of the aristocracy and middle class; the word came to refer to the militant radicals of the city. (p. 636)

Schlieffen Plan Failed German plan calling for a lightning attack through neutral Belgium and a quick defeat of France before turning on Russia. (p. 821)

second industrial revolution The burst of industrial creativity and technological innovation that promoted strong economic growth toward the end of the nineteenth century. (p. 741)

second revolution From 1792 to 1795, the second phase of the French Revolution, during which the fall of the French monarchy introduced a rapid radicalization of politics. (p. 635)

separate spheres A gender division of labor with the wife at home as mother and homemaker and the husband as wage earner. (p. 679)

shock therapy The Solidarity-led government's radical take on economic affairs that abruptly ended state planning and moved to market mechanisms and private property. (p. 987)

signori Government by one-man rule in Italian cities such as Milan. (p. 376)

Social Darwinists A group of thinkers who applied the theory of biological evolution to human affairs and saw the human race as driven by an unending economic struggle that would determine the survival of the fittest. (p. 744)

socialism A backlash against the emergence of individualism and the fragmentation of society, and a move toward cooperation and a sense of community; the key ideas were economic planning, greater economic equality, and state regulation of property. (p. 693)

Solidarity Outlawed Polish trade union that worked for workers' rights and political reform throughout the 1980s. (p. 982)

Spanish Armada The fleet sent by Philip II of Spain in 1588 against England as a religious crusade against Protestantism. Weather and the English fleet defeated it. (p. 425)

spinning jenny A simple, inexpensive, hand-powered spinning machine created by James Hargreaves in 1765. (p. 657)

stadholder The executive officer in each of the United Provinces of the Netherlands, a position often held by the princes of Orange. (p. 513)

stagflation Term coined in the early 1980s to describe the combination of low growth and high inflation that led to a worldwide recession. (p. 971)

Statute of Kilkenny Laws issued in 1366 that discriminated against the Irish, forbidding marriage between the English and the Irish, requiring the use of the English language, and denying the Irish access to ecclesiastical offices. (p. 367)

steam engines A breakthrough invention by Thomas Savery in 1698 and Thomas Newcomen in 1705 that burned coal to produce steam, which was then used to operate a pump; the early models were superseded by James Watt's more efficient steam engine, patented in 1769. (p. 660)

stream-of-consciousness technique A literary technique, found in works by Virginia Woolf, James Joyce, and others, that uses interior monologue—a character's thoughts and feelings as they occur—to explore the human psyche. (p. 860)

sultan The ruler of the Ottoman Empire; he owned all the agricultural land of the empire and was served by an army and bureaucracy composed of highly trained slaves. (p. 504)

sweated industries Poorly paid handicraft production, often by married women paid by the piece and working at home. (p. 730)

Tanzimat A set of reforms designed to remake the Ottoman Empire on a western European model. (p. 764)

tariff protection A government's way of supporting and aiding its own economy by laying high taxes on imported goods from other countries, as when the French responded to cheaper British goods flooding their country by imposing high tariffs on some imported products. (p. 670)

Test Act Legislation passed by the English parliament in 1673 to secure the position of the Anglican Church by stripping Puritans, Catholics, and other dissenters of the right to vote, preach, assemble, hold public office, and attend or teach at the universities. (p. 510)

theory of special relativity Albert Einstein's theory that time and space are relative to the observer, and that only the speed of light remains constant. (p. 857)

Thermidorian reaction A reaction to the violence of the Reign of Terror in 1794, resulting in the execution of Robespierre and the loosening of economic controls. (p. 643)

thermodynamics A branch of physics built on Newton's laws of mechanics that investigated the relationship between heat and mechanical energy. (p. 741)

Third World A term that refers to the nonindustrialized nations of Africa, Asia, and Latin America as a single unit. (p. 782)

totalitarianism A radical dictatorship that exercises "total claims" over the beliefs and behavior of its citizens by taking control of the economic, social, intellectual, and cultural aspects of society. (p. 888)

total war A war in which distinctions between the soldiers on the battlefield and civilians at home are blurred, and where the government plans and controls economic social life in order to supply the armies at the front with supplies and weapons. (p. 821)

Treaty of Brest-Litovsk Peace treaty signed in March 1918 between the Central Powers and Russia that ceded Russian territories containing a third of the Russian empire's population to the Central Powers. (p. 837)

Treaty of Paris The treaty that ended the Seven Years' War in Europe and the colonies in 1763 and ratified British victory on all colonial fronts. (p. 571)

Treaty of Tordesillas The 1494 agreement giving Spain everything to the west of an imaginary line drawn down the Atlantic and giving Portugal everything to the east. (p. 456)

Treaty of Versailles The 1919 peace settlement that ended war between Germany and the Allied powers. (p. 841)

trench warfare A type of fighting behind rows of trenches, mines, and barbed wire used in WWI; the cost in lives was staggering and the gains in territory minimal. (p. 823)

Triple Alliance The alliance of Austria, Germany, and Italy. Italy left the alliance when war broke out in 1914 on the grounds that Austria had launched a war of aggression. (p. 817)

Triple Entente The alliance of Great Britain, France, and Russia in the First World War. (p. 817)

Truman Doctrine America's policy geared to containing communism to those countries already under Soviet control. (p. 929)

Union of Utrecht The alliance of seven northern provinces (led by Holland) that declared its independence from Spain and formed the United Provinces of the Netherlands. (p. 435)

utilitarianism The idea of Jeremy Bentham that social policies should promote the "greatest good for the greatest number." (p. 719)

viceroyalties The name for the four administrative units of Spanish possessions in the Americas: New Spain, Peru, New Granada, and La Plata. (p. 461)

virtù The quality of being able to shape the world according to one's own will. (p. 379)

war communism The application of centralized state control during the Russian civil war, in which the Bolsheviks seized grain from peasants, introduced rationing, nationalized all banks and industry, and required everyone to work. (p. 838)

war guilt clause An article in the Treaty of Versailles that declared that Germany (with Austria) was solely responsible for the war and had to pay reparations equal to all civilian damages caused by the fighting. (p. 843)

war on terror American policy under President Bush to fight global terrorism in all its forms. (p. 1019)

Warsaw Pact Soviet-backed military alliance of eastern European nations. (p. 930)

water frame A spinning machine created by Richard Arkwright that had a capacity of several hundred spindles and used waterpower; it therefore required a larger and more specialized mill—a factory. (p. 657)

wet-nursing A widespread and flourishing business in the eighteenth century in which women were paid to breast-feed other women's babies. (p. 591)

white man's burden The idea that Europeans could and should civilize more primitive nonwhite peoples and that imperialism would eventually provide nonwhites with modern achievements and higher standards of living. (p. 802)

World Trade Organization (WTO) A powerful supranational financial institution that sets trade and tariff agreements for over 150 member countries and so helps manage a large percentage of the world's import-export policies. Like the IMF and the World Bank, the WTO promotes neoliberal policies around the world. (p. 1007)

Young Turks Fervent patriots who seized power in the revolution of 1908 in the Ottoman Empire, forcing the conservative sultan to implement reforms. (p. 765)

Zionism A movement toward Jewish political nationhood started by Theodor Herzl. (p. 771)

▪ Index

end of, 919, 924–925
in Europe, 909–912, 911(m), 912(m), 916,
   917–919
Great Depression and, 881
Holocaust during, 912–914, 914(m)
Normandy invasion in, 918
opening of, 909–910
origins of, 875(b), 907–909
in Pacific Ocean region, 914–916, 917(m),
   919
recovery after, 920, 922, 924
resistance during, 912, 915(b)
results in Europe, 924–928, 926(m),
   933–937
science, technology, and, 931–933
society after, 950–955
Secret police
in East Bloc, 980
in East Germany, 1001
in Nazi Germany, 904
in Poland, 987
in Russia, 998
in Soviet Union, 838, 897
Secularism
Ottoman, 765
in society, 962
in Turkey, 845–847
in 21st century, 1014, 1017
Security Council (United Nations), 1007
Sedan, battle at, 757, 768
Segregation
of American natives from Europeans, 463
apartheid as, 798(b)
in British India, 804
in U.S., 963
Self-determination, 803, 843, 846(b), 908
decolonization and, 945, 949
Metternich on, 689
after Second World War, 935, 944
Treaty of Versailles and, 842
Self-government
nationalism and, 692
in Ottoman Empire, 505
Semiskilled workers, 727, 730
Senegal, 797
Senses
Hume and, 535
Locke and, 531
Separate spheres, 679, 733, 736(i)
Separation of church and state, in France, 353
Separation of powers, 533
Separatist movements
Chechen, 999
in former Yugoslavia, 1001
in Ireland, 979–980
in Spain, 979
September 11, 2001 terrorist attacks, 1014,
   1017–1019
September Massacres (France), 635
Serbia, 1001(m)
ethnic cleansing and, 1002
First World War and, 820–821, 840
local autonomy for, 764
Milosevic and, 1001
Serbian people, 709, 820, 1001, 1001(m), 1002
Serfs and serfdom. See also Peasant(s)
in Austria, 495, 547, 709, 712

in eastern Europe, 482, 482(i), 555
in England, 361
in France, 649
in Prussia, 544
in Russia, 500–501(b), 500(i), 503, 545,
   760, 761, 762–763(b), 762(i), 763(i)
Servants
black, 394
domestic, 680, 730
in 18th century, 586(i), 587
of middle class, 726
women as, 730
Servetus, Michael, 426
Service employees, 950
Service nobility, in Russia, 498, 503
Services, globalization and, 1004
Settlement(s), in Americas, 455, 461–470
Seven Years' War, 460
European North American claims before
   and after, 572(m)
France and, 622
Prussia and, 543–544
Seville, 394
Sewage systems, 720, 722
Sewing machine, 730
Sex and sexuality. See also Homosexuality;
   Prostitutes and prostitution
in 18th century, 589–591
First World War and, 830, 859
Freud and, 740, 859
gender segregation of jobs and, 679–680
in marriage, 738
master-slave relations and, 463
middle-class youth and, 734–735(b)
in 19th century, 732–733
premarital sex and, 588, 732, 963
Protestantism and, 413(i), 419
servant girls and, 730
sexual behavior of children and, 740
in urban areas, 361–365
women and, 734(b)
in youth counterculture, 963
Zweig, Stephan, on, 734–735(b)
Sexism, 954, 975
Sextant, 523(i)
Sexual division of labor. See Gender
Sexual harassment, of women in service,
   587–588
Sexual revolution, 963
Seymour, Jane, 423
Sforza family, 377
Ludovico, 391(b)
Shakespeare, William, 472, 473–475
Sharif, 826
Shelley, Percy Bysshe, 698
Shi'ite (Shi'a) Muslims, 446, 1020
"Ship money," 508
Ships and shipping, 659, 817. See also Navy;
   Seaborne trade
Black Death and, 341
British dominance of, 782(i)
British Navigation Acts and, 569
Portuguese, 450, 451(i)
in Second World War, 917
in slave trade, 574
steam power in, 783–784
technological innovations and, 450

Shock therapy
in Polish economy, 987
in Russian economy, 996–997
Shogun, 806
Show trials, 897, 937
Shrines, 408
Siberia, 499, 788, 837, 925
Sicily, 752, 754, 917. See also Kingdom of the
   Two Sicilies
riots in, 486
Sickness unto Death (Kierkegaard), 856
Siderus Nuncius (Galileo), 525
Siemens, 1003
Siena, 375, 377
Sieyès, Emmanuel Joseph, 625, 626–627(b),
   626(i), 644
Sigismund (Germany), 357
Sigismund I (Poland), 427
Signorelli, Luca, 398(i)
Signori (rulers), 376
Silent Spring (Carson), 978
Silesia, 483, 543, 570–571
Silk mill, 659(i)
Silk trade, 470
Silver
from Americas, 461, 468–470, 471(i)
China as buyer of, 470
Spain and, 468–470, 572–573
Sin, Luther on, 409
Sinai region, 947, 948
Sino-Japanese War, 807
Sinti Gypsies, 904, 913(i), 925
Sister Carrie (Dreiser), 745
Sistine Chapel, Michelangelo and, 387, 388(i),
   390
Six Acts (England), 702
Six-Day War, 971
Sixtus IV (Pope), 401–402
68ers, the (1960s generation), 966
Skepticism, 530, 534, 607
Skilled workers, 670, 672, 681, 727, 727(i),
   830
Skin color
categorizing people by, 394, 540
inferiority of darkness and, 472–473
in Saint-Domingue, 633, 642, 647
Skyscrapers, 861
Slave labor. See also Forced labor
for Nazi Germany, 915(b)
Slaves and slavery. See also Africans; Race and
   racism; Serfs and serfdom; Slave labor;
   Slave trade
in Balkans, 448
Christian conversions and, 578
costs of colonial goods and, 601
in France and French colonies, 707
freedom and, 469(b)
master-slave sexual relations and, 463
in Ottoman Empire, 504
Portugal and, 452, 465
reconquista and, 469(b)
in Renaissance, 394–395, 394(i)
in Saint Domingue, 632–633, 632(i)
sugar plantations and, 464–468, 464(i),
   576(i)
in United States, 758–759, 759(m)
whites as slaves, 464–465

	Government	Society and Economy
3000 B.C.E.	Emergence of first cities in Mesopotamia, ca. 3000 Unification of Egypt; Archaic Period, ca. 3100–2600 Old Kingdom of Egypt, ca. 2660–2180 Dominance of Akkadian empire in Mesopotamia, ca. 2331–2200 Middle Kingdom in Egypt, ca. 2080–1640	Neolithic peoples rely on settled agriculture, while others pursue nomadic life, ca. 7000–3000 Expansion of Mesopotamian trade and culture into the modern Middle East and Turkey, ca. 2600
2000 B.C.E.	Babylonian empire, ca. 2000–1595 Code of Hammurabi, ca. 1790 Hyksos invade Egypt, ca. 1640–1570 Hittite Empire, ca. 1600–1200 New Kingdom in Egypt, ca. 1570–1075	First wave of Indo-European migrants, by ca. 2000 Extended commerce in Egypt, by ca. 2000 Horses introduced into western Asia, by ca. 2000
1500 B.C.E.	Third Intermediate Period in Egypt, ca. 1100–653 Unified Hebrew kingdom under Saul, David, and Solomon, ca. 1025–925	Use of iron increases in western Asia, by ca. 1300–1100 Second wave of Indo-European migrants, by ca. 1200 "Dark Age" in Greece, ca. 1100–800
1000 B.C.E.	Hebrew kingdom divided into Israel and Judah, 925 Assyrian Empire, ca. 900–612 Phoenicians found Carthage, 813 Kingdom of Kush conquers and reunifies Egypt, ca. 800–700 Roman monarchy, ca. 753–509 Medes conquers Persia, 710 Babylon wins independence from Assyria, 626 Dracon issues law code at Athens, 621 Solon's reforms at Athens, ca. 594 Cyrus the Great conquers Medes, founds Persian Empire, 550 Persians complete conquest of ancient Near East, 521–464 Reforms of Cleisthenes in Athens, 508	Phoenician seafaring and trading in the Mediterranean, ca. 900–550 First Olympic games, 776 Concentration of landed wealth in Greece, ca. 750–600 Greek overseas expansion, ca. 750–550 Beginning of coinage in western Asia, ca. 640
500 B.C.E.	Persian wars, 499–479 Struggle of the Orders in Rome, ca. 494–287 Growth of the Athenian Empire, 478–431 Peloponnesian War, 431–404 Rome captures Veii, 396 Gauls sack Rome, 390 Roman expansion in Italy, 390–290 Phillip II of Macedonia conquers Greece, 338 Conquests of Alexander the Great, 334–323 Punic Wars, 264–133 Reforms of the Gracchi, 133–121	Growth of Hellenistic trade and cities, ca. 330–100 Beginning of Roman silver coinage, 269 Growth of slavery, decline of small farmers in Rome, ca. 250–100 Agrarian reforms of the Gracchi, 133–121

Religion and Philosophy	Science and Technology	Arts and Letters
Growth of anthropomorphic religion in Mesopotamia, ca. 3000–2000	Development of wheeled transport in Mesopotamia, by ca. 3000	Egyptian hieroglyphic writing, ca. 3100
Emergence of Egyptian polytheism and belief in personal immortality, ca. 2660	Use of widespread irrigation in Mesopotamia and Egypt, ca. 3000	Sumerian cuneiform writing, ca. 3000
Spread of Mesopotamian and Egyptian religious ideas as far north as modern Turkey and as far south as central Africa, ca. 2600	Construction of Stonehenge monument in England, ca. 3000–1600	
	Construction of first pyramid in Egypt, ca. 2600	
Emergence of Hebrew monotheism, ca. 1700	Construction of first ziggurats in Mesopotamia, ca. 2000	*Epic of Gilgamesh*, ca. 1900
Mixture of Hittite and Near Eastern religious beliefs, ca. 1595	Widespread use of bronze in ancient Near East, ca. 1900	
	Babylonian mathematical advances, ca. 1800	
Exodus of the Hebrews from Egypt into Palestine, ca. 1300–1200	Hittites introduce iron technology, ca. 1400	Phoenicians develop alphabet, ca. 1400
Akhenaten imposes monotheism in Egypt, 1367–1350		Naturalistic art in Egypt under Akhenaten, 1367–1350
		Egyptian *Book of the Dead*, ca. 1300
Era of the prophets in Israel, ca. 1100–500	Babylonian astronomical advances, ca. 750–400	Homer, traditional author of *Iliad* and *Odyssey*, ca. 800
Beginning of the Hebrew Bible, ca. 950–800	Construction of Parthenon in Athens begins, 447	Hesiod, author of *Theogony* and *Works and Days*, ca. 800
Intermixture of Etruscan and Roman religious cults, ca. 753–509		Aeschylus, first significant Athenian tragedian, ca. 525–456
Growing popularity of local Greek religious cults, ca. 700 B.C.E.–337 C.E.		
Introduction of Zoroastrianism, ca. 600		
Babylonian Captivity of the Hebrews, 587–538		
Pre-Socratic philosophers, ca. 500–400	Hippocrates, formal founder of medicine, ca. 430	Sophocles, tragedian whose plays explore moral and political problems, ca. 496–406
Socrates executed, 399	Building of the Via Appia begins, 312	Herodotus, "father of history," ca. 485–425
Plato, student of Socrates, 427–347	Aristarchos of Samos, advances in astronomy, ca. 310–230	Euripides, most personal of the Athenian tragedians, ca. 480–406
Diogenes, leading proponent of cynicism, ca. 412–323	Euclid codifies geometry, ca. 300	Thucydides, historian of Peloponnesian War, ca. 460–440
Aristotle, student of Plato, 384–322	Herophilus, discoveries in medicine, ca. 300–250	Aristophanes, greatest Athenian comic playwright, ca. 445–386
Epicurus, founder of Epicurean philosophy, 340–270	Archimedes, works on physics and hydrologics, ca. 287–212	
Zeno, founder of Stoic philosophy, 335–262		
Emergence of Mithraism, ca. 300		
Greek cults brought to Rome, ca. 200		
Spread of Hellenistic mystery religions, ca. 200–100		

	Government	Society and Economy
100 B.C.E.	Dictatorship of Sulla, 88–79 B.C.E. Civil war in Rome, 88–31 B.C.E. Dictatorship of Caesar, 45–44 B.C.E. Principate of Augustus, 31 B.C.E.–14 C.E. "Five Good Emperors" of Rome, 96–180 C.E. "Barracks Emperors'" civil war, 235–284 C.E.	Reform of the Roman calendar, 46 B.C.E. "Golden age" of Roman prosperity and vast increase in trade, 96–180 C.E. Growth of serfdom in Roman Empire, ca. 200–500 C.E. Economic contraction in Roman Empire, ca. 235–284 C.E.
300 C.E.	Constantine removes capital of Roman Empire to Constantinople, ca. 315 Visigoths defeat Roman army at Adrianople, 378 Bishop Ambrose asserts church's independence from the state, 380 Odoacer deposes last Roman emperor in the West, 476 Clovis issues Salic law of the Franks, ca. 490	Barbarian migrations throughout western and northern Europe, ca. 378–600
500	Law code of Justinian, 529 Spread of Islam across Arabia, the Mediterranean region, Spain, North Africa, and Asia as far as India, ca. 630–733	Gallo-Roman aristocracy intermarries with Germanic chieftains, ca. 500–700 Decline of towns and trade in the West; agrarian economy predominates, ca. 500–1800
700	Charles Martel defeats Muslims at Tours, 732 Pippin III anointed king of the Franks, 754 Charlemagne secures Frankish crown, r. 768–814	Height of Muslim commercial activity with western Europe, ca. 700–1300
800	Imperial coronation of Charlemagne, Christmas 800 Treaty of Verdun divides Carolingian kingdom, 843 Viking, Magyar, and Muslim invasions, ca. 850–1000 Establishment of Kievan Rus, ca. 900	Invasions and unstable conditions lead to increase of serfdom in western Europe, ca. 800–900 Height of Byzantine commerce and industry, ca. 800–1000
1000	Seljuk Turks conquer Muslim Baghdad, 1055 Norman conquest of England, 1066 Penance of Henry IV at Canossa, 1077	Decline of Byzantine free peasantry, ca. 1025–1100 Growth of towns and trade in the West, ca. 1050–1300 *Domesday Book* in England, 1086
1100	Henry I of England, r. 1100–1135 Louis VI of France, r. 1108–1137 Frederick I of Germany, r. 1152–1190 Henry II of England, r. 1154–1189	Henry I of England establishes the Exchequer, 1130 Beginnings of the Hanseatic League, 1159

Religion and Philosophy	Science and Technology	Arts and Letters
Mithraism spreads to Rome, 27 B.C.E.–270 C.E.	Engineering advances in Rome, ca. 100 B.C.E.–180 C.E.	Flowering of Latin literature: Virgil, 70–19 B.C.E.; Livy, ca. 59 B.C.E.–17 C.E.; Ovid, 43 B.C.E.–17 C.E.
Life of Jesus, ca. 3 B.C.E.–29 C.E.		
Constantine legalizes Christianity, 312	Construction of Arch of Constantine, ca. 315	St. Jerome publishes Latin *Vulgate*, late 4th c.
Theodosius declares Christianity the official state religion, 380		Byzantines preserve Greco-Roman culture, ca. 400–1000
Donatist heretical movement at its height, ca. 400		
St. Augustine, *Confessions*, ca. 390; *The City of God*, ca. 425		
Clovis adopts Roman Christianity, 496		
Rule of St. Benedict, 529	Using watermills, Benedictine monks exploit energy of fast-flowing rivers and streams, by 600	Boethius, *The Consolation of Philosophy*, ca. 520
Life of the Prophet Muhammad, ca. 571–632		Justinian constructs church of Santa Sophia, 532–537
Pope Gregory the Great publishes *Dialogues*, *Pastoral Care*, *Moralia*, 590–604	Heavy plow and improved harness facilitate use of multiple-ox teams; harrow widely used in northern Europe, by 600	
Monasteries established in Anglo-Saxon England, ca. 600–700	Byzantines successfully use "Greek fire" in naval combat against Arab fleets attacking Constantinople, 673, 717	
Publication of the Qur'an, 651		
Synod of Whitby, 664		
Bede, *Ecclesiastical History of the English Nation*, ca. 700		Lindisfarne Gospel Book, ca. 700
Missionary work of St. Boniface in Germany, ca. 710–750		*Beowulf*, ca. 700
Iconoclastic controversy in Byzantine Empire, 726–843		Carolingian Renaissance, ca. 780–850
Pippin III donates Papal States to the papacy, 756		
Foundation of abbey of Cluny, 909	Stirrup and nailed horseshoes become widespread in combat, 900–1000	Byzantines develop Cyrillic script, late 10th c.
Byzantine conversion of Russia, late 10th c.	Paper (invented in China, ca. 150) enters Europe through Muslim Spain, ca. 900–1000	
Schism between Roman and Greek Orthodox churches, 1054	Arab conquests bring new irrigation methods, cotton cultivation, and manufacture to Spain, Sicily, southern Italy, by 1000	Muslim musicians introduce lute, rebec (stringed instruments, ancestors of violin), ca. 1000
Lateran Council restricts election of pope to College of Cardinals, 1059	Avicenna, Arab scientist, d. 1037	Romanesque style in architecture and art, ca. 1000–1200
Pope Gregory VII, 1073–1085		*Song of Roland*, ca. 1095
Theologian Peter Abelard, 1079–1142		
First Crusade, 1095–1099		
Founding of Cistercian order, 1098		
Universities begin, ca. 1100–1300	Europeans, copying Muslim and Byzantine models, construct castles with rounded towers and crenellated walls, by 1100	Troubadour poetry, especially of Chrétien de Troyes, circulates widely, ca. 1100–1200
Concordat of Worms ends investiture controversy, 1122		*Rubaiyat of Umar Khayyam*, ca. 1120
Height of Cistercian monasticism, 1125–1175		Dedication of abbey church of Saint-Denis launches Gothic style, 1144

Government	Society and Economy

1100 (cont.)

Thomas Becket, archbishop of Canterbury, murdered 1170

Philip Augustus of France, r. 1180–1223

1200

Spanish victory over Muslims at Las Navas de Tolosa, 1212

Frederick II of Germany and Sicily, r. 1212–1250

Magna Carta, charter of English political and civil liberties, 1215

Louis IX of France, r. 1226–1270

Mongols end Abbasid caliphate, 1258

Edward I of England, r. 1272–1307

Philip IV (the Fair) of France, r. 1285–1314

European revival, growth of towns; agricultural expansion leads to population growth, ca. 1200–1300

Crusaders capture Constantinople (Fourth Crusade) and spur Venetian economy, 1204

1300

Philip IV orders arrest of Pope Boniface at Anagni, 1303

Hundred Years' War between England and France, 1337–1453

Political disorder in Germany, ca. 1350–1450

Merchant oligarchies or despots rule Italian city-states, ca. 1350–1550

"Little ice age," European economic depression, ca. 1300–1450

Black Death appears ca. 1347; returns intermittently until ca. 1720

Height of the Hanseatic League, 1350–1450

Peasant and working-class revolts: Flanders, 1328; France, 1358; Florence, 1378; England, 1381

1400

Joan of Arc rallies French monarchy, 1429–1431

Medici domination of Florence begins, 1434

Princes in Germany consolidate power, ca. 1450–1500

Ottoman Turks under Mahomet II capture Constantinople, May 1453

War of the Roses in England, 1455–1471

Establishment of the Inquisition in Spain, 1478

Ferdinand and Isabella complete reconquista in Spain, 1492

French invasion of Italy, 1494

Population decline, peasants' revolts, high labor costs contribute to decline of serfdom in western Europe, ca. 1400–1650

Flow of Balkan slaves into eastern Mediterranean, of African slaves into Iberia and Italy, ca. 1400–1500

Christopher Columbus reaches the Americas, 1492

Portuguese gain control of East Indian spice trade, 1498–1511

1500

Charles V, Holy Roman emperor, 1519–1556

Habsburg-Valois Wars, 1521–1559

Philip II of Spain, r. 1556–1598

Revolt of the Netherlands, 1566–1598

St. Bartholomew's Day massacre in France, 1572

English defeat of the Spanish Armada, 1588

Henry IV of France issues Edict of Nantes, 1598

Consolidation of serfdom in eastern Europe, ca. 1500–1650

Balboa discovers the Pacific, 1513

Magellan's crew circumnavigates the earth, 1519–1522

Spain and Portugal gain control of regions of Central and South America, ca. 1520–1550

Peasants' Revolt in Germany, 1524–1525

"Time of Troubles" in Russia, 1598–1613

Religion and Philosophy	Science and Technology	Arts and Letters
Aristotle's works translated into Latin, ca. 1140–1260 Third Crusade, 1189–1192 Pope Innocent III, height of the medieval papacy, 1198–1216	Underground pipes with running water and indoor latrines installed in some monasteries, such as Clairvaux and Canterbury Cathedral Priory, by 1100; elsewhere rare until 1800 Windmill invented, ca. 1180	
Founding of the Franciscan order, 1210 Fourth Lateran Council accepts seven sacraments, 1215 Founding of Dominican order, 1216 Thomas Aquinas, height of scholasticism, 1225–1274	*Notebooks* of architect Villard de Honnecourt, a major source for Gothic engineering, ca. 1250 Development of double-entry bookkeeping in Florence and Genoa, ca. 1250–1340 Venetians purchase secrets of glass manufacture from Syria, 1277 Mechanical clock invented, ca. 1290	*Parzifal, Roman de la rose, King Arthur and the Round Table* celebrate virtues of knighthood and chivalry, ca. 1200–1300 Height of Gothic style, ca. 1225–1300
Pope Boniface VIII declares all Christians subject to the pope in *Unam Sanctam*, 1302 Babylonian Captivity of the papacy, 1309–1376 Theologian John Wyclif, ca. 1330–1384 Great Schism in the papacy, 1378–1417	Edward III of England uses cannon in siege of Calais, 1346 Clocks in general use throughout Europe, by 1400	Paintings of Giotto mark emergence of Renaissance movement in the arts, ca. 1305–1337 Dante, *Divine Comedy*, ca. 1310 Petrarch develops ideas of humanism, ca. 1350 Boccaccio, *The Decameron*, ca. 1350 Jan van Eyck, Flemish painter, 1366–1441 Brunelleschi, Florentine architect, 1377–1446 Chaucer, *Canterbury Tales*, ca. 1387–1400
Council of Constance ends the schism in the papacy, 1414–1418 Pragmatic Sanction of Bourges affirms special rights of French crown over French church, 1438 Expulsion of Jews from Spain, 1492	Water-powered blast furnaces operative in Sweden, Austria, the Rhine Valley, Liège, ca. 1400 Leonardo Fibonacci's *Liber Abaci* popularizes use of Hindu-Arabic numerals, important in rise of Western science, 1402 Paris and largest Italian cities pave streets, making street cleaning possible, ca. 1450 European printing and movable type, ca. 1450	Height of Renaissance movement: Masaccio, 1401–1428; Botticelli, 1444–1510; Leonardo da Vinci, 1452–1519; Albrecht Dürer, 1471–1528; Michelangelo, 1475–1564; Raphael, 1483–1520
Machiavelli, *The Prince*, 1513 More, *Utopia*, 1516 Luther, *Ninety-five Theses*, 1517 Henry VIII of England breaks with Rome, 1532–1534 Merici establishes Ursuline order for education of women, 1535 Loyola establishes Society of Jesus, 1540 Calvin establishes theocracy in Geneva, 1541 Council of Trent shapes essential character of Catholicism until the 1960s, 1545–1563 Peace of Augsburg, official recognition of Lutheranism, 1555	Scientific revolution in western Europe, ca. 1540–1690: Copernicus, *On the Revolutions of the Heavenly Bodies*, 1543; Galileo, 1564–1642; Kepler, 1571–1630; Harvey, 1578–1657	Erasmus, *The Praise of Folly*, 1509 Castiglione, *The Courtier*, 1528 Baroque movement in arts, ca. 1550–1725: Rubens, 1577–1640; Velasquez, 1599–1660 Shakespeare, West's most enduring and influential playwright, 1564–1616 Montaigne, *Essays*, 1598

Government	Society and Economy
1600	
Thirty Years' War begins, 1618	Chartering of British East India Company, 1600
Richelieu dominates French government, 1624–1643	English Poor Law, 1601
Frederick William, Elector of Brandenburg, r. 1640–1688	Chartering of Dutch East India Company, 1602
English Civil War, 1642–1649	Height of Dutch commercial activity, ca. 1630–1665
Louis XIV, r. 1643–1715	
Peace of Westphalia ends the Thirty Years' War, 1648	
The Fronde in France, 1648–1660	
1650	
Anglo-Dutch wars, 1652–1674	Height of mercantilism in Europe, ca. 1650–1750
Protectorate in England, 1653–1658	Agricultural revolution in Europe, ca. 1650–1850
Leopold I, Habsburg emperor, r. 1658–1705	Principle of peasants' hereditary subjugation to their lords affirmed in Prussia, 1653
English monarchy restored, 1660	Colbert's economic reforms in France, ca. 1663–1683
Ottoman siege of Vienna, 1683	Cossack revolt in Russia, 1670–1671
Glorious Revolution in England, 1688–1689	
Peter the Great of Russia, r. 1689–1725	
1700	
War of the Spanish Succession, 1701–1713	Foundation of St. Petersburg, 1701
Peace of Utrecht redraws political boundaries of Europe, 1713	Last appearance of bubonic plague in western Europe, ca. 1720
Frederick William I of Prussia, r. 1713–1740	Growth of European population, ca. 1720–1789
Louis XV of France, r. 1715–1774	Enclosure movement in England, ca. 1730–1830
Maria Theresa of Austria, r. 1740–1780	
Frederick the Great of Prussia, r. 1740–1786	
1750	
Seven Years' War, 1756–1763	Growth of illegitimate births in Europe, ca. 1750–1850
Catherine the Great of Russia, r. 1762–1796	Industrial Revolution in western Europe, ca. 1780–1850
Partition of Poland, 1772–1795	Serfdom abolished in France, 1789
Louis XVI of France, r. 1774–1792	
American Revolution, 1775–1783	
French Revolution, 1789–1799	
Slave insurrection in Saint-Domingue, 1791	
1800	
Napoleonic era, 1799–1815	British takeover of India complete, 1805
Haitian republic declares independence, 1804	British slave trade abolished, 1807
Congress of Vienna re-establishes political power after defeat of Napoleon, 1814–1815	German Zollverein founded, 1834
Greece wins independence from Ottoman Empire, 1830	European capitalists begin large-scale foreign investment, 1840s
French conquest of Algeria, 1830	Great Famine in Ireland, 1845–1851
Revolution in France, 1830	First public health law in Britain, 1848
Great Britain: Reform Bill of 1832; Poor Law reform, 1834; Chartists, repeal of Corn Laws, 1838–1848	
Revolutions in Europe, 1848	

Religion and Philosophy	Science and Technology	Arts and Letters
Huguenot revolt in France, 1625	Further development of scientific method: Bacon, *The Advancement of Learning*, 1605; Descartes, *Discourse on Method*, 1637	Cervantes, *Don Quixote*, 1605, 1615 Flourishing of French theater: Molière, 1622–1673; Racine, 1639–1699 Golden age of Dutch culture, ca. 1625–1675: Rembrandt van Rijn, 1606–1669; Vermeer, 1632–1675
Social contract theory: Hobbes, *Leviathan*, 1651; Locke, *Second Treatise on Civil Government*, 1690 Patriarch Nikon's reforms split Russian Orthodox Church, 1652 Test Act in England excludes Roman Catholics from public office, 1673 Revocation of Edict of Nantes, 1685 James II tries to restore Catholicism as state religion, 1685–1688	Tull (1674–1741) encourages innovation in English agriculture Newton, *Principia Mathematica*, 1687	Construction of baroque palaces and remodeling of capital cities, central and eastern Europe, ca. 1650–1725 Bach, great late baroque German composer, 1685–1750 Enlightenment begins, ca. 1690: Fontenelle, *Conversations on the Plurality of Worlds*, 1686; Voltaire, French philosopher and writer whose work epitomizes Enlightenment, 1694–1778 Pierre Bayle, *Historical and Critical Dictionary*, 1697
Wesley, founder of Methodism, 1703–1791 Montesquieu, *The Spirit of Laws*, 1748	Newcomen develops steam engine, 1705 Charles Townsend introduces four-year crop rotation, 1730	
Hume, *The Natural History of Religion*, 1755 Rousseau, *The Social Contract* and *Emile*, 1762 Fourier, French utopian socialist, 1772–1837 Papacy dissolves Jesuits, 1773 Smith, *The Wealth of Nations*, 1776 Church reforms of Joseph II in Austria, 1780s Kant, *What Is Enlightenment?*, 1784 Reorganization of church in France, 1790s Wollstonecraft, *A Vindication of the Rights of Women*, 1792 Malthus, *Essay on the Principle of Population*, 1798	Hargreaves's spinning jenny, ca. 1765 Arkwright's water frame, ca. 1765 Watt's steam engine promotes industrial breakthroughs, 1780s Jenner's smallpox vaccine, 1796	*Encyclopedia*, edited by Diderot and d'Alembert, published 1751–1765 Classical style in music, ca. 1770–1830: Mozart, 1756–1791; Beethoven, 1770–1827 Wordsworth, English romantic poet, 1770–1850 Romanticism in art and literature, ca. 1790–1850
Napoleon signs Concordat with Pope Pius VII regulating Catholic Church in France, 1801 Spencer, Social Darwinist, 1820–1903 Comte, *System of Positive Philosophy*, 1830–1842 Height of French utopian socialism, 1830s–1840s List, *National System of Political Economy*, 1841 Nietzsche, radical and highly influential German philosopher, 1844–1900 Marx, *Communist Manifesto*, 1848	First railroad, Great Britain, 1825 Faraday studies electromagnetism, 1830–1840s	Staël, *On Germany*, 1810 Balzac, *The Human Comedy*, 1829–1841 Delacroix, *Liberty Leading the People*, 1830 Hugo, *The Hunchback of Notre Dame*, 1831

Government	Society and Economy
1850	
Second Empire in France, 1852–1870	Crédit Mobilier founded in France, 1852
Crimean War, 1853–1856	Japan opened to European influence, 1853
Britain crushes Great Rebellion in India, 1857–1858	Russian serfs emancipated, 1861
Unification of Italy, 1859–1870	First Socialist International, 1864–1871
U.S. Civil War, 1861–1865	
Bismarck leads Germany, 1862–1890	
Unification of Germany, 1864–1871	
Britain's Second Reform Bill, 1867	
Third Republic in France, 1870–1940	
1875	
Congress of Berlin, 1878	Full property rights for women in Great Britain, 1882
European "scramble for Africa," 1880–1900	Second Industrial Revolution; birthrate steadily declines in Europe, ca. 1880–1913
Britain's Third Reform Bill, 1884	Social welfare legislation, Germany, 1883–1889
Dreyfus affair in France, 1894–1899	Second Socialist International, 1889–1914
Spanish-American War, 1898	Witte directs modernization of Russian economy, 1892–1899
South African War, 1899–1902	
1900	
Russo-Japanese War, 1904–1905	Women's suffrage movement, England, ca. 1900–1914
Revolution in Russia, 1905	Social welfare legislation, France, 1904, 1910; Great Britain, 1906–1914
Balkan wars, 1912–1913	Agrarian reforms in Russia, 1907–1912
1914	
World War I, 1914–1918	Planned economics in Europe, 1914
Armenian genocide, 1915	Auxiliary Service Law in Germany, 1916
Easter Rebellion, 1916	Bread riots in Russia, March 1917
U.S. declares war on Germany, 1917	
Bolshevik Revolution, 1917–1918	
Treaty of Versailles, World War I peace settlement, 1919	
1920	
Mussolini seizes power in Italy, 1922	New Economic Policy in U.S.S.R., 1921
Stalin comes to power in U.S.S.R., 1927	Dawes Plan for reparations and recovery, 1924
Hitler gains power in Germany, 1933	Great Depression, 1929–1939
Rome-Berlin Axis, 1936	Rapid industrialization in U.S.S.R., 1930s
Nazi-Soviet Non-Aggression Pact, 1939	Start of Roosevelt's New Deal in U.S., 1933
World War II, 1939–1945	
1940	
United Nations founded, 1945	Holocaust, 1941–1945
Decolonization of Asia and Africa, 1945–1960s	Marshall Plan enacted, 1947
Cold War begins, 1947	European economic progress, ca. 1950–1970
Founding of Israel, 1948	European Coal and Steel Community founded, 1952
Communist government in China, 1949	European Economic Community founded, 1957
Korean War, 1950–1953	
De-Stalinization of Soviet Union under Khrushchev, 1953–1964	
1960	
Building of Berlin Wall, 1961	Civil rights movement in U.S., 1960s
U.S. involvement in Vietnam War, 1964–1973	Stagflation, 1970s
Student rebellion in France, 1968	Feminist movement, 1970s

Religion and Philosophy	Science and Technology	Arts and Letters
Decline in church attendance among working classes, ca. 1850–1914 Mill, *On Liberty*, 1859 Pope Pius IX, *Syllabus of Errors*, denounces modern thoughts, 1864 Marx, *Das Capital*, 1867 Doctrine of papal infallibility, 1870	Modernization of Paris, ca. 1850–1870 Great Exhibition in London, 1851 Freud, founder of psychoanalysis, 1856–1939 Darwin, *On the Origin of Species*, 1859 Pasteur develops germ theory of disease, 1860s Suez Canal opened, 1869 Mendeleev develops periodic table, 1869	Realism in art and literature, ca. 1850–1870 Flaubert, *Madame Bovary*, 1857 Tolstoy, *War and Peace*, 1869 Impressionism in art, ca. 1870–1900 Eliot (Mary Ann Evans), *Middlemarch*, 1872
Growth of public education in France, ca. 1880–1900 Growth of mission schools in Africa, 1890–1914	Emergence of modern immunology, ca. 1875–1900 Electrical industry: lighting and streetcars, ca. 1880–1900 Trans-Siberian Railroad, 1890s Marie Curie, discovery of radium, 1898	Zola, *Germinal*, 1885 Kipling, "The White Man's Burden," 1899
Separation of church and state in France, 1901–1905 Hobson, *Imperialism*, 1902 Schweitzer, *Quest of the Historical Jesus*, 1906	Planck develops quantum theory, ca. 1900 First airplane flight, 1903 Einstein develops theory of special relativity, 1905–1910	Modernism in art and literature, ca. 1900–1929 Conrad, *Heart of Darkness*, 1902 Cubism in art, ca. 1905–1930 Proust, *Remembrance of Things Past*, 1913–1927
Keynes, *Economic Consequences of the Peace*, 1919	Submarine warfare introduced, 1915 Ernest Rutherford splits atom, 1919	Spengler, *The Decline of the West*, 1918
Emergence of modern existentialism, 1920s Revival of Christianity, 1920s–1930s Wittgenstein, *Essay on Logical Philosophy*, 1922 Heisenberg's principle of uncertainty, 1927	"Heroic age of physics," 1920s First major public radio broadcasts in Great Britain and U.S., 1920 First talking movies, 1930 Radar system in England, 1939	Gropius, Bauhaus, 1920s Dadaism and surrealism, 1920s Woolf, *Jacob's Room*, 1922 Joyce, *Ulysses*, 1922 Eliot, *The Waste Land*, 1922 Remarque, *All Quiet on the Western Front*, 1929 Picasso, *Guernica*, 1937
De Beauvoir, *The Second Sex*, 1949 Communists fail to break Catholic Church in Poland, 1950s	U.S. drops atomic bombs on Japan, 1945 Big Science in U.S., ca. 1945–1965 Watson and Crick discover structure of DNA molecule, 1953 Russian satellite in orbit, 1957	Cultural purge in Soviet Union, 1946–1952 Van der Rohe, Lake Shore Apartments, 1948–1951 Orwell, *1984*, 1949 Pasternak, *Doctor Zhivago*, 1956 "Beat" movement in U.S., late 1950s
Second Vatican Council announces sweeping Catholic reforms, 1962–1965 Pope John II, 1978–2005	European Council for Nuclear Research founded, 1960 Space race, 1960s	The Beatles, 1960s Solzhenitsyn, *One Day in the Life of Ivan Denisovich*, 1962

	Government	Society and Economy
1960 (cont.)	Soviet tanks end Prague Spring, 1968	Collapse of postwar monetary system, 1971
	Détente between U.S. and U.S.S.R., 1970s	OPEC oil price increases, 1973, 1979
	Soviet occupation of Afghanistan, 1979–1989	
1980	U.S. military buildup, 1980s	Growth of debt in the West, 1980s
	Solidarity in Poland, 1980	Economic crisis in Poland, 1988
	Unification of Germany, 1989	Maastricht Treaty proposes monetary union, 1990
	Revolutions in eastern Germany, 1989–1990	European Community becomes European Union, 1993
	Persian Gulf War, 1990–1991	Migration to western Europe increases, 1990s
	Dissolution of Soviet Union, 1991	
	Civil war in Yugoslavia, 1991–2001	
	Separatist war breaks out in Chechnya, 1991	
2000	Terrorist attacks on U.S., Sept. 11, 2001	Euro enters circulation, 2002
	War in Afghanistan begins, 2001	Voters reject new European Union constitution, 2005
	War in Iraq begins, 2003	Immigrant riots in France, 2005, 2009
		Worldwide financial crisis begins, 2008

Religion and Philosophy	Science and Technology	Arts and Letters
	Russian cosmonaut first to orbit globe, 1961 American astronaut first person on moon, 1969	Carson, *Silent Spring*, 1962 Friedan, *The Feminine Mystique*, 1963 Servan-Schreiber, *The American Challenge*, 1967
Revival of religion in Soviet Union, 1985– Growth of Islam in Europe, 1990s Fukuyama proclaims "end of history," 1991	Reduced spending on Big Science, 1980s Computer revolution continues, 1980s–1990s U.S. Genome Project begins, 1990 First World Wide Web server and browser, 1991 Pentium processor invented, 1993 First genetically cloned sheep, 1996	Solzhenitsyn returns to Russia, 1994; dies 2008 Author Salman Rushdie exiled from Iran, 1989 Gehry, Guggenheim Museum, Bilbao, 1997
Ramadan, *Western Muslims and the Future of Islam*, 2004 Conservative elected as Pope Benedict XVI, 2005	Growing concern about global warming, 2000s First hybrid car, 2003 Copenhagen Summit on climate change, 2009	Movies and books exploring clash between immigrants and host cultures popular: *Bend It Like Beckham*, 2002; *The Namesake*, 2003; *White Teeth*, 2003; *The Class*, 2008

THE CONTEMPORARY WORLD

Greenland
(Den.)

ICELAND

UNITED
KINGDOM

IRELAND

FRANCE

SPAIN

PORTUGAL

MOROCCO

Azores
(Port.)

Canary Is.
(Sp.)

Western Sahara
(Mor.)

MAURITANIA

Alaska
(U.S.)

CANADA

UNITED STATES

ATLANTIC
OCEAN

Bermuda (U.K.)

Hawaii (U.S.)

MEXICO

BAHAMAS
DOMINICAN
REPUBLIC
HAITI
Puerto Rico (U.S.)
CUBA
ST. KITTS AND NEVIS
JAMAICA
ANTIGUA AND BARBUDA
BELIZE
Guadeloupe (Fr.)
DOMINICA
GUATEMALA
Martinique (Fr.)
ST. VINCENT AND THE GRENADINES
HONDURAS
ST. LUCIA
BARBADOS
EL SALVADOR
NICARAGUA
GRENADA
TRINIDAD AND TOBAGO
COSTA RICA
VENEZUELA
GUYANA
PANAMA
SURINAME
COLOMBIA
French Guiana (Fr.)

CAPE
VERDE

SENEGAL
GAMBIA
GUINEA-BISSAU
GUINEA
BURKINA FASO
SIERRA LEONE
LIBERIA
CÔTE D'IVOIRE

MALI

GHANA

PACIFIC OCEAN

Galápagos Is.
(Ec.)

ECUADOR

Equator

PERU

BRAZIL

SAMOA

BOLIVIA

TONGA

PARAGUAY

Easter I.
(Chile)

CHILE

URUGUAY

ARGENTINA

ATLANTIC
OCEAN

Falkland Is.
(U.K.)

N
W   E
S

0   1,500   3,000 miles
0   1,500   3,000 kilometers

80°N

60°N

40°N

20°N

0°

20°S

40°S

60°S

80°S

160°W   140°W   120°W   100°W   80°W   60°W   40°W   20°W

ARCTIC OCEAN

NORWAY
SWEDEN
FINLAND
ESTONIA
LATVIA
LITHUANIA
EN.
TH.
BELARUS
RMANY POLAND
EL.
UX.
CZ. SLK. UKRAINE
TZ. AUS. HUNG. MOLDOVA
SLN. CR. SE. ROMANIA
ITALY B.H. BULGARIA
MO. KO. MAC.
ALB. GREECE
TUNISIA MALTA
CYPRUS LEBANON
ISRAEL
Gaza Strip
West Bank
JORDAN

RUSSIAN FEDERATION

KAZAKHSTAN

MONGOLIA

UZBEKISTAN KYRGYZSTAN
TURKMENISTAN TAJIKISTAN

GEORGIA
ARMENIA
AZERBAIJAN
TURKEY
SYRIA
IRAQ
IRAN
AFGHANISTAN

N. KOREA
S. KOREA

JAPAN

CHINA

PACIFIC OCEAN

LIBYA
EGYPT
KUWAIT
BAHRAIN
SAUDI ARABIA
QATAR
UNITED ARAB
EMIRATES
OMAN

PAKISTAN
BHUTAN
NEPAL
BANGLADESH
INDIA
MYANMAR
(BURMA)
LAOS
VIETNAM
THAILAND
CAMBODIA

Taiwan

Mariana Is.
(U.S.)

Guam
(U.S.)

MARSHALL
IS.

RIA
NIGER
CHAD
SUDAN
YEMEN
ERITREA
DJIBOUTI
ETHIOPIA

PHILIPPINES

GERIA
O
IN
CAMEROON
CENTRAL
AFRICAN REP.
A
GABON
ÃO
OMÉ
NCIPE
CONGO

MALDIVES

SRI
LANKA

SOMALIA
UGANDA
RWANDA
KENYA
DEM. REP. OF
THE CONGO
BURUNDI TANZANIA

BRUNEI

PALAU

FEDERATED STATES
OF MICRONESIA

MALAYSIA

NAURU

KIRIBATI

SINGAPORE

INDONESIA

PAPUA
NEW
GUINEA

TUVALU

SOLOMON
IS.

COMOROS
SEYCHELLES

INDIAN OCEAN

TIMOR
LESTE

VANUATU

FIJI

ANGOLA
ZAMBIA MALAWI
ZIMBABWE
MADAGASCAR
NAMIBIA
BOTSWANA

MAURITIUS

New Caledonia
(Fr.)

AUSTRALIA

SOUTH
AFRICA
MOZAMBIQUE
SWAZILAND
LESOTHO

NEW
ZEALAND

Tasmania
(Aust.)

ANTARCTICA

ABBREVIATIONS	
ALB.	ALBANIA
AUS.	AUSTRIA
BEL.	BELGIUM
B.H.	BOSNIA AND HERZEGOVINA
CR.	CROATIA
CZ.	CZECH REPUBLIC
DEN.	DENMARK
HUNG.	HUNGARY
KO.	KOSOVO
LUX.	LUXEMBOURG
MAC.	MACEDONIA
MO.	MONTENEGRO
NETH.	NETHERLANDS
SE.	SERBIA
SLK.	SLOVAKIA
SLN.	SLOVENIA
SWITZ.	SWITZERLAND

CONTEMPORARY EUROPE

20°W
10°W
0°
10°E
60°N

ATLANTIC OCEAN

N
W · E
S

North Sea

• Bergen

NORWAY ⊛ Oslo
SWEDEN
• Stockholm

• Göteborg

DENMARK
Aarhus •
⊛ Copenhagen

Baltic Sea

RUS
Kaliningrad ⊛

Gdańsk •

SCOTLAND
• Edinburgh
• Glasgow

NORTHERN IRELAND
Belfast •

IRELAND
⊛ Dublin

UNITED KINGDOM
• Liverpool

WALES
• Birmingham
ENGLAND
Thames R.
⊛ London

50°N

English Channel

NETHERLANDS
Amsterdam ⊛
• Rotterdam

Berlin ⊛

POLAND

Kraków ⊛

• Cork

Antwerp •
Brussels ⊛
BELGIUM

Rhine R.
GERMANY

• Frankfurt

Elbe R.

Oder R.

Vistula R.

Wa

Prague ⊛
CZECH REP.

Brno •

SLOVAK

Mi

• Paris
Seine R.

Luxembourg ⊛
LUXEMBOURG

FRANCE

Loire R.

LIECHTENSTEIN

Zürich •
Bern ⊛
SWITZERLAND
Vaduz •

A L P S

• Munich
Danube R.

Vienna ⊛
• Innsbruck
AUSTRIA
Graz •

Bratislava ⊛

Budapest ⊛

HUNGARY

SLOVENIA
Ljubljana ⊛

• Lyons
Rhône R.

• Milan
Po R.

CROATIA
Zagreb ⊛

Belgr

Bay of Biscay

San Marino •
SAN MARINO

BOSNIA AND HERZEGOVINA
Sarajevo •

SER

40°N

Oporto •

PORTUGAL

ANDORRA
Andorra la Vella ⊛

• Marseilles

MONACO

Corsica

APENNINES
Rome ⊛
ITALY

Adriatic Sea

Split •

Podgorica ⊛
MONTENEGRO

Tiranë •
ALBAN

PYRENEES

Ebro R.

• Madrid

• Barcelona

SPAIN

• Lisbon

• Seville

Gibraltar (Gr. Br.) •

Balearic Is.

• Naples

Sardinia

Tyrrhenian Sea

Ionian Sea

Algiers ⊛

Tunis •

• Palermo

Sicily

• Valletta
MALTA

• Rabat

MOROCCO

ALGERIA

TUNISIA

Mediterranean

Tripoli •

LIBYA

Elevation

Feet	Meters
Over 13,120	Over 4,001
6,561–13,120	2,001–4,000
1,641–6,560	501–2,000
661–1,640	201–500
0–660	0–200
Below sea level	Below sea level

⊛ National capital
• Major city

0 — 150 — 300 miles
0 — 150 — 300 kilometers

About the Authors

John P. McKay (Ph.D., University of California, Berkeley) is professor emeritus at the University of Illinois. He has written or edited numerous works, including the Herbert Baxter Adams Prize–winning book *Pioneers for Profit: Foreign Entrepreneurship and Russian Industrialization, 1885–1913* (1970) and *Tramways and Trolleys: The Rise of Urban Mass Transport in Europe* (1976). He most recently contributed to *Imagining the Twentieth Century* (1997).

Bennett D. Hill (Ph.D., Princeton University), late of the University of Illinois, was the history department chair from 1978 to 1981. He published *English Cistercian Monasteries and Their Patrons in the Twelfth Century* (1968), *Church and State in the Middle Ages* (1970), and numerous articles and reviews, and was one of the contributing editors to *The Encyclopedia of World History* (2001). A Benedictine monk of St. Anselm's Abbey in Washington, D.C., he was also a visiting professor at Georgetown University.

John Buckler (Ph.D., Harvard University) taught history at the University of Illinois. Published books include *Theban Hegemony, 371–362 B.C.* (1980), *Philip II and the Sacred War* (1989), and *Aegean Greece in the Fourth Century B.C.* (2003). With Hans Beck, he most recently published *Central Greece and the Politics of Power in the Fourth Century* (2007).

Clare Haru Crowston (Ph.D., Cornell University) teaches at the University of Illinois, where she is currently associate professor of history. She is the author of *Fabricating Women: The Seamstresses of Old Regime France, 1675–1791* (2001), which won the Berkshire and Hagley Prizes. She edited two special issues of the *Journal of Women's History* (vol. 18, nos. 3 and 4), has published numerous journal articles and reviews, and is a past president of the Society for French Historical Studies and a former chair of the Pinkney Prize Committee.

Merry E. Wiesner-Hanks (Ph.D., University of Wisconsin–Madison) taught first at Augustana College in Illinois, and since 1985 at the University of Wisconsin–Milwaukee, where she is currently UWM Distinguished Professor in the department of history. She is the coeditor of the *Sixteenth Century Journal* and the author or editor of more than twenty books, most recently *The Marvelous Hairy Girls: The Gonzales Sisters and Their Worlds* (2009) and *Gender in History* (2nd ed., 2010). She currently serves as the Chief Reader for Advanced Placement World History.

Joe Perry (Ph.D., University of Illinois at Urbana-Champaign) is associate professor of modern German and European history at Georgia State University. He has published numerous articles and is author of the recently published book *Christmas in Germany: A Cultural History* (2010). His current research interests include issues of consumption, gender, and television in East and West Germany after World War II.